THE YEARBOOK OF EUROPEAN ENVIRONMENTAL LAW

Volume 8

THE YEARBOOK OF

European Environmental Law

Volume 8

T.F.M. ETTY

Researcher at the Institute for Environmental Studies (IVM), and Faculty of Law, Vrije Universiteit Amsterdam

H. SOMSEN

Professor at Tilburg Institute for Law, Technology, and Society (TILT), Tilburg University

(EDITORS-IN-CHIEF)

V. HEYVAERT

Lecturer at the Department of Law London School of Economics

CURRENT SURVEY EDITOR

T.F.M. ETTY

Researcher at the Institute for Environmental Studies (IVM), and Faculty of Law, Vrije Universiteit Amsterdam

BOOK REVIEWS EDITOR

P. GALIZZI

Visiting Professor at the Leitner Center for International Law & Justice, Fordham University School of Law

DOCUMENTS EDITOR

OXFORD
UNIVERSITY PRESS

OXFORD
UNIVERSITY PRESS

Great Clarendon Street, Oxford OX2 6DP

Oxford University Press is a department of the University of Oxford.
It furthers the University's objective of excellence in research, scholarship,
and education by publishing worldwide in

Oxford New York

Auckland Cape Town Dar es Salaam Hong Kong Karachi
Kuala Lumpur Madrid Melbourne Mexico City Nairobi
New Delhi Shanghai Taipei Toronto

With offices in

Argentina Austria Brazil Chile Czech Republic France Greece
Guatemala Hungary Italy Japan Poland Portugal Singapore
South Korea Switzerland Thailand Turkey Ukraine Vietnam

Oxford is a registered trade mark of Oxford University Press
in the UK and in certain other countries

Published in the United States
by Oxford University Press Inc., New York

First published 2008

British Library Cataloguing in Publication Data
Data available

Library of Congress Cataloging in Publication Data
Data available

Typeset by Newgen Imaging Systems (P) Ltd., Chennai, India
Printed in Great Britain
on acid-free paper by
CPI Antony Rowe, Chippenham, Wiltshire

ISBN 978–0–19–954526–1

1 3 5 7 9 10 8 6 4 2

Editorial Advisory Committee

Editorial Advisory Committee

[illegible]

[illegible]

[illegible]

[illegible]

[illegible]

[illegible]

[illegible]

Editors' Preface

Nearly ten years have passed since the plans for this *Yearbook of European Environmental Law* were first launched by Ludwig Krämer. In the eight volumes that have been published since 2000, many thousands of pages have been devoted to the scholarly pursuit of environmental law, as the fruit of many nocturnal hours of painstaking research and writing by the dozens of environmental law scholars that have contributed to this *Yearbook* throughout the years. Much more important than the sense of accomplishment upon publication of each individual volume, is the opportunity that the totality of the scholarship offers to assess the development of European environmental law over the past decade. In this preface, we will therefore attempt to articulate some general impressions on the basis of the eight *Yearbook* volumes that have been published to date, and try to connect these with the articles featured in the present volume.

Many contributions have concerned what we would term 'classical issues' of environmental regulation, i.e. those issues that have always been important, and that will surely continue to occupy the minds of environmental scholars and regulators in the future. Four such 'classical issues' in particular emerge from the literature:

Firstly, *the effectiveness of the Community's institutional apparatus to respond decisively to environmental threats.*

The article in the present volume by *Lee and Stokes* falls into this category. It offers suggestions for how the European Community (EC) may overcome its age-old but tenacious problem to articulate a workable conception of waste that is informed by the protective aims of EC waste law; suggestions the authors in this case derive from a recent United Kingdom (UK) Court of Appeal judgment in *OSS Group* v. *Environment Agency*.[1] EC lawyers that have been trained instinctively to reach for the doctrine of supremacy to finish off any such budding national innovations that depart from EC wisdom would do well first to consider if, actually, these do not offer a way out to an impasse that has marred EC waste law since its conception more than 30 years ago.

Secondly, *the most appropriate mix of regulatory tools to channel behaviour impacting on the environment.*

Initially, and in its simplest form, this discussion focused on the respective virtues of directives and regulations as the two instruments that were most widely used for EC environmental law-making. Later national developments in the sphere of self-regulation, pioneered in particular in the Netherlands, eventually

[1] *The Queen (On the Application of OSS Group Limited)* v. *Environment Agency and Others (DEFRA, Intervening)* (2007) 3 *Common Market Law Reports* 30.

seemed to reach the Commission, which culminated in the adoption of a series of self-regulatory instruments to curb atmospheric pollution caused by cars. This development went hand-in-hand with a greater appreciation of economic and fiscal instruments although, absent sufficient competences and national enthusiasm to support Community recourse to such instruments, their use at the EC-level remains disappointing.

Gehring and Price take this discussion one step further in their article, by conceiving of the international export credit regime itself as a possible regulatory tool to achieve environmental and sustainable development goals, after which they go through a full range of regulatory and institutional options that might allow that regime to play such a role in practice.

Thirdly, *the friction between striving for internal market uniformity, and the recognition of the very different needs of Europe's heterogeneous environment.*

The analysis in this volume by *Doherty*, of the so-called 'environmental guarantee'[2] contained in Article 95(4)–(6) EC, to some extent is a sequel to one of the first articles published in this *Yearbook*, nearly a decade ago.[3] Whereas the original article was dubious about the extent to which Member States could rely on those provisions to justify the maintenance or introduction of national regulations that differ from harmonized EC rules, the present update makes for even more sobering reading.

Fourthly, *concerns about implementation and enforcement deficits.*

Issues concerning implementation of EC environmental law, but more still its enforcement, will always remain of primary importance. For example, in this volume *Caddell* focuses on the implementation of the conservation objectives in the Bonn Convention[4] as well as the Birds[5] and Habitats[6] Directives, arguing for closer convergence between both regimes.

These classical issues at times may almost seem to have disappeared, but invariably they resurface. Their reappearance occurs, for instance, after each new EU enlargement wave, when mass implementation of the environmental *acquis* takes place in new Member States. In such cases, the Community and new Member States alike have the advantage of recourse to invaluable past experience that may avoid and, where necessary, effectively address implementation gaps.

[2] Note, however, that Doherty explains why this terminology is both inadequate and inappropriate to describe the actuality of these provisions, and why the European courts' terminology of 'safeguard clause' appears more fitting.

[3] H. Sevenster, 'The Environmental Guarantee after Amsterdam: Does the Emperor Have New Clothes?' (2000) 1 *Yearbook of European Environmental Law,* 291–310.

[4] Convention on the Conservation of Migratory Species of Wild Animals 1979 (Bonn Convention/CMS), Bonn (Germany), 23 June 1979 (entered into force 1 Nov. 1983), (1980) 19 *International Legal Materials* 11, 15.

[5] Dir. 79/409/EEC on the Conservation of Wild Birds [1979] OJ L103/1.

[6] Dir. 92/43/EEC on the Conservation of Natural Habitats and of Wild Fauna and Flora [1992] OJ L206/7.

Another more unpredictable reason for dormant environmental law to resurrect is the reintroduction of technologies that, for various reasons, were shelved previously. A prime example is nuclear energy, which is experiencing a remarkable revival in the wake of the mounting global political attention for the environmental threat posed by climate change. An increasing number of policy-makers and countries around the world are beginning to reconsider nuclear energy, as the only conceivable way to comply with even the existing (relatively forgiving) carbon dioxide (CO_2) emission reduction targets, let alone with undoubtedly more stringent future regimes. Consequently, in many countries, largely forgotten and outdated national regulatory regimes pertaining to nuclear safety are now being frantically reassessed and redrafted. *Barnes* is the first author since the conception of the *Yearbook* who considers the EURATOM Treaty[7] at length. She argues that, even though it is outdated and biased towards the nuclear industry, we may be better off reviving it than discarding it.

To be sure, past experience with European environmental law will not merely continue to assist present and future new Member States. Rather, with the accelerated emergence of new industrial powers, classical EC environmental law will also be keenly analysed in other regions and continents. News about the unveiling in New Dehli (India) of the TATA Nano (the world's cheapest car at little over €1,500), which amounts to something of a pre-announcement of imminent environmental problems in India's overpopulated cities that Europe itself is not even close to tackling, provides a fine example. Distinctly aware of Greenpeace's protests outside the auditorium while he spoke, Mr Tata was keen to emphasize that his little car complied with 'Euro IV' emission standards.[8]

Secondly, next to these classical areas of EC environmental law, there are contributions that show that some of the more recent principles of EC environmental law have matured to the extent that their value now exceeds that of mere symbolic sources of inspiration or propaganda. *Scotford's* excellent chapter regarding the roles played by Article 174(2) EC provides an analytical framework to begin to disentangle the various roles that such principles play at present. The single most important such principle is undoubtedly the precautionary principle, which was subject to serious institutional debate for the first time in 2000, following the publication of the Commission Communication on the Precautionary Principle.[9] The development of literature on the precautionary principle has since evolved from exploring its origins, aim, and meaning within the EC legal and institutional orders, to its possible role in the global trade arena, and in this volume of the *Yearbook* to its application in concrete cases involving scientific uncertainty

[7] Treaty establishing the European Atomic Energy Community (EURATOM), Rome (Italy), 9 Mar. 1957.

[8] See, e.g., 'The Environmental Impact of India's Nano Car', *New Scientist*, 11 Jan. 2008; 'Facts about Tata's Nano, the World's Cheapest Car', *Agence France Presse*, 10 Jan. 2008; 'The cheapest car in the world unveiled', *Malta Star*, 10 Jan. 2008.

[9] COM(2000)1, 2 Feb. 2000.

about ecological impacts of human activity in the Member States. Thus, *Fleurke* transcends the doctrinal focus that has kept the academic debate concerning precaution in its grip for far too long. On the basis of a relatively straightforward analytical framework, two case studies in which the principle played a prominent role provide concrete suggestions under what circumstances precaution might best serve its intended purpose. Such lessons may be partly incompatible with the inflexible approach the European Court of Justice (ECJ) has pursued in its case law, in particular in the *Waddenzee* case.[10]

Once again, however, the impact of European environmental law extends well beyond the EU's external borders, and this certainly applies to precaution. If the precautionary principle—as a distinctly European regulatory innovation—is proving its worth within the EU, then other countries and organizations should follow, including most notably the World Trade Organization (WTO). In this vein, *Thayyil* in this volume constructs precaution in such a way as to enable it to become instrumental in overcoming the science/policy divide that acts to exclude 'other legitimate considerations' besides positivistic conceptions of science, including regulatory diversity and the value of deliberative democracy, from being accommodated in risk analyses in WTO cases, such as most notably and recently *EC–Biotech Products*.[11]

It is encouraging that, increasingly, *Yearbook* contributions situate issues of EC environmental law in their wider world context. We regard this as another promising sign that EC environmental law is maturing from a perhaps rather introspective exercise occupying the minds of a handful of specialists, to a much more cosmopolitan discipline in which scholars from different geographical and disciplinary backgrounds exchange ideas and perspectives from which more effective and equitable European and global environmental regulation may arise. In this volume, the article by *Claessens* exemplifies this development, as it marries the traditionally isolated world of global patent law with (national) environmental law concerns about the misappropriation of genetic resources. As precaution is undergoing a transformation from a symbolic acknowledgement that the human capacity to change the environment outstrips its understanding of the consequences of such changes, the Community's established but largely unfulfilled claim to global environmental stewardship likewise may be beginning to take more concrete shape.

While these are unmistakable signs of progress, there remain curious gaps even in the thousands of pages that we have published in this *Yearbook* over the past years. Many of these gaps correspond to those articulated by *Ludwig Krämer*

[10] Case C-127/02 *Landelijke Vereniging tot Behoud van de Waddenzee and Nederlandse Vereniging tot Bescherming van Vogels* v. *Staatssecretaris van Landbouw, Natuurbeheer en Visserij* [2004] ECR I-7405 (*Waddenzee*).

[11] *EC–Measures Affecting the Approval and Marketing of Biotech Products* (*EC–Biotech Products*), WT/DS291 (US), WT/DS292 (Canada), and WT/DS291 (Argentina).

in his annual commentaries on official EU publications, but it is useful briefly to name just three of these unexplored areas by way of illustration.

Firstly, few authors have attempted to construe a public duty to gather data pertaining to the state of the environment. And yet, a minimal precondition for sound environmental regulation is the availability of reliable environmental data. Data is necessary for the development of new regulatory initiatives, as well as for the appraisal of existing efforts. True, great progress has been made concerning *access* to environmental information, first as a result of the 1990 Directive on Access to Environmental Information,[12] and more recently following implementation[13] of the Aarhus Convention.[14] Yet, even though citizens have won the right to access to environmental information, this is still far removed from granting them a right per se to environmental information. An implied public duty constantly to gather environmental data arises on an ad hoc basis in all cases where public authorities invoke precaution to ban or restrict some activity. Such precautionary restrictions are temporary (i.e. for as long as the scientific uncertainty that triggered precautionary regulation prevails), and public authorities should actively strive to end that uncertainty by gathering relevant data.

Secondly, although somewhat similar to the previous point, academic environmental lawyers often appear to care surprisingly little about the actual performance of their brainchildren, even though this is an indispensable prerequisite for the growth of regulatory theory. How many academics that cheered on the Commission in its efforts to enter into gentlemen's agreements with the European, Korean, and Japanese car industries have held their theoretical arguments in favour of self-regulation at the time against the light of the results that we now know have actually been achieved?[15] Similarly, important lessons could have been learned by now from, for example, the 'Brent Spar saga' by simply comparing the actual ecological impact of its decommissioning in Norway with opposing claims about the best available environmental option at the time by Greenpeace and the oil companies respectively. Insofar as we are aware, however, such post mortems have rarely been undertaken in legal academic literature, which again is a lost opportunity to learn.

[12] Dir. 90/313/EEC on Freedom of Access to Information on the Environment [1990] OJ L158/56.

[13] Dir. 2003/4/EC on Public Access to Environmental Information and Repealing Directive 90/313/EEC [2003] OJ L41/26; Reg. (EC) No. 1367/2006/EC on the Application of the Provisions of the Aarhus Convention on Access to Information, Public Participation in Decision-Making and Access to Justice in Environmental Matters to Community Institutions and Bodies [2006] OJ L264/13.

[14] Aarhus (Denmark), 25 June 1998 (entered into force 30 Oct. 2001), (1999) 38 *International Legal Materials* 3, 517; published on the Internet at: http://www.unece.org/env/pp.

[15] See Commission Rec. 1999/125/EC, 2000/303/EC, and 2000/304/EC on the Reduction of CO_2 Emissions from Passenger Cars (ACEA, KAMA, and JAMA, respectively) [1999] OJ L40/49, [2000] OJ L100/55, and [2000] OJ L100/57.

Thirdly and finally, environmental regulation has gone through a number of distinct phases, from command-and-control in the 1970s and 1980s, to self-regulation in the 1980s and 1990s, to reflexive and 'smart' forms of (co)regulation more recently. In fact, of the four modalities of regulation associated with Lessig (hierarchy, society, market, and code),[16] environmental scholars and regulators have enthusiastically explored the first three with varying degrees of success, but appear to shy away wholeheartedly from proposing technology itself as a regulatory instrument. Some of these normative technologies are in use (such as so-called 'pingers' to avoid by-catches of whales and dolphins, explored by *Caddell*), but this has never been preceded by a thorough analysis of the moral and practical implications of the widespread use of technologies that remove the human capacity to choose to cause environmental harm. Devices that automatically enforce speed controls or disable cars when smog alarms apply, cut off domestic fresh water supplies at times of scarcity, or shut down installations that exceed limit values: these are all possibilities that could and perhaps should be explored.

It is hoped that the scholarship contained in this and earlier volumes of this *Yearbook* will continue to inspire academics and regulators in their common goal to protect and preserve the global environment.

THIJS ETTY
HAN SOMSEN
(*Editors-in-Chief*)

[16] L. Lessig, *Code and Other Laws of Cyberspace* (New York: Basic Books, 1999).

Acknowledgements

Each volume of the *Yearbook* is the fruit of extensive academic collaboration of a great number of individuals and institutions, to whom we owe gratitude and recognition.

First and foremost, we must extend a very warm and special thanks to the 'founding father' of this *Yearbook*, Ludwig Krämer, without whom this series would never have seen the light of day. Throughout the last decade, even after his retirement from the European Commission, Ludwig has played an invaluable and stimulating role in the editorship of the *Yearbook*, well beyond his formal responsibilities as Documents editor. We are delighted to be ensured of his continued affiliation with the *Yearbook* as a member of the Editorial Advisory Committee, now that he has decided to pass on his hands-on editorial responsibilities to a younger generation of EC environmental law scholars. We are also pleased that Paolo Galizzi has agreed to take on this challenging task of succeeding Ludwig Krämer as Documents editor, starting with this eighth volume.

Our gratitude also extends to Maria Lee, who after having served as co-editor of Book Reviews for several years, will now lend her support to the editors as a member of our Editorial Advisory Committee.

It is to Veerle Heyvaert that we owe a tremendous thanks for her continued excellent editorship of the voluminous Current Survey section.

We are also indebted to a number of other individuals who have offered their assistance at various stages of the preparation of this volume, in particular Kyla Tienhaara, Marjan Oomens, and Rissa Philip.

The Institute for Environmental Studies at the Vrije Universiteit Amsterdam, in particular the Department of Environmental Policy Analysis, have provided support for the editorial assistance that has been necessary to produce this volume. In addition, as in previous years, we are grateful for the personal support of Professor Michael Faure of the Faculty of Law at Maastricht University and Ius Commune Research School, and for the financial assistance provided by the Institute for Transnational Legal Research (METRO) at Maastricht University. The editorial team at Oxford University Press is highly appreciated for once again having diligently guided this manuscript through to publication.

As always, we are deeply indebted to the many referees who have provided expert advise and criticism in our double-blind peer review process, to assist the contributors and editors in their ambition to produce articles of the highest academic quality.

Last but far from least, we are indebted to all the contributors of articles, current survey entries, and book reviews, for continuing to entrust their work to the *Yearbook of European Environmental Law*.

THIJS ETTY
HAN SOMSEN
(*Editors-in-Chief*)

Contents

Editors' Preface	vii
Acknowledgements	xiii
List of Contributors	xxi
Table of Cases	xxv
Table of Legislation	xxxvii

ARTICLES

Mapping the Article 174(2) EC Case Law: A First Step to Analysing Community Environmental Law Principles 1
Eloise Scotford

The Application of Article 95(4)–(6) of the EC Treaty: Is the Emperor Still Unclothed? 48
Michael G. Doherty

Innovation through Precaution: The Case of the Dutch Wadden Sea 80
Floor M. Fleurke

Deliberative Turning from a Law-Science Cul-de-Sac: Speculations regarding Community Transgenic Regulation 133
Naveen Thayyil

Rehabilitating the Definition of Waste: Is it Fully Recovered? 162
Robert G. Lee and Elen Stokes

The Resurrection of the EURATOM Treaty: Contributing to the Legal and Constitutional Framework for Secure, Competitive, and Sustainable Energy in the European Union 182
Pamela M. Barnes

Biodiversity Loss and the Prospects for International Cooperation: EU Law and the Conservation of Migratory Species of Wild Animals 218
Richard Caddell

The Disclosure of Origin Requirement: Europe Moving Towards Pro-CBD Implementation 265
Fleur Claessens

Export Credits for Sustainable Development? 294
Markus W. Gehring and Kristin Price

CURRENT SURVEY

I. Atmospheric Pollution 327
Alexandra González-Calatayud

II. Energy 340
Michael Rodi and Michael Mehling

III. Biotechnology 364
Thijs Etty

IV. Chemicals 403
Candido Garcia Molyneux

V. Nature Conservation 442
Agustín García-Ureta

VI. Waste 489
Geert van Calster and Wim Vandenberghe

VII. Water 510
Mark Stallworthy

VIII. Horizontal Instruments and Miscellaneous Issues 524
Diane Ryland

IX. Case Law of the European Court of Justice 562
Nicola Notaro

REVIEWS OF BOOKS

I. Introduction 579
Thijs Etty

II. Review Articles:
A. A Positive Agenda for Public International Law of the Sea Scholarship 579
Katrina M. Wyman

[Review of Freestone, Barnes, and Ong (eds.), *The Law of the Sea: Progress and Prospects*; and Strati, Gavouneli, and Skourtos (eds.), *Unresolved Issues and New Challenges to the Law of the Sea: Time Before and Time After*]

B. Taking Sustainable Development Seriously: Compliance Synergies in International Environmental and Economic Law 589
Marie-Claire Cordonier Segger and Ravi Shankar Kuar Singh

[Review of Richardson and Wood (eds.), *Environmental Law for Sustainability*; Zaelke, Kaniaru, and Kruzikova (eds.), *Making Law Work: Environmental Compliance & Sustainable Development*; Kirton and Hajnal (eds.), *Sustainability, Civil Society and International Governance: Local, North American and Global Contributions*; and Sampson, *The WTO and Sustainable Development*]

III. Book Reviews

Hedemann-Robinson, *Enforcement of European Union Environmental Law: Legal Issues and Challenges* *(Peter Davies)* 599

Fisher, Jones, and von Schomberg (eds.), *Implementing the Precautionary Principle: Perspectives and Prospects* *(Peter H. Sand)* 602

Trouwborst, *Precautionary Rights and Duties of States* *(Jaye Ellis)* 607

Peeters & Deketelaere (eds.), *EU Climate Change Policy: The Challenge of New Regulatory Initiatives* *(Roda Verheyen)* 611

Oberthür & Gehring (eds.), *Institutional Interaction in Global Environmental Governance: Synergy and Conflict among International and EU Policies* *(Camilla Adelle)* 616

Breitmeier, Young, and Zürn, *Analyzing International Environmental Regimes: From Case Study to Database* *(Philipp Pattberg)* 618

Plaza Martín, *Derecho ambiental de la Union Europea* *(Ludwig Krämer)* 621

IV. Highlights of Recent Publications in Environmental Law and Policy 624

A. Atmospheric Pollution, Climate Change, and Energy 624
B. Biotechnology and Food Safety 626
C. Chemicals 628
D. Nature Conservation 629
E. Waste 629
F. Water and Fisheries 629
G. Horizontal Instruments and Aarhus Convention Rights 630

H. Trade and Environment, World Trade Organization 631
I. Agriculture 632
J. Risk, Precaution, Science, and Technology in Law and Policy 633
K. Sustainable Development 634
L. Environmental Economics, Management, and Accounting 635
M. Environmental Sociology, Philosophy, Ethics, Environmental Justice, and Human Rights 636
N. General European (Environmental) Law, Policy, and Governance, and EU Member States' Environmental Law 638
O. General International and Comparative (Environmental) Law, Policy, and Governance; and Non-EU National Environmental Law 640
P. Yearbooks 644
Q. Journals 644

DOCUMENTS

Paolo Galizzi

I. Introduction 645

II. Summaries of Communications, Green Papers, and White Papers 646

A. Commission Communication: Halting the Loss of Biodiversity by 2010—and Beyond—Sustaining Ecosystem Services for Human Well-Being 646
B. Commission Communication on an EU Forest Action Plan 648
C. Commission Communication: Thematic Strategy for Soil Protection 650
D. Commission Communication: An EU Strategy for Biofuels 652
E. Commission Communication—Action Plan for Energy Efficiency: Realizing the Potential 654
F. Commission Communication: An Energy Policy for Europe 655
G. Commission Communication—Limiting Global Climate Change to 2 Degrees Celsius: The Way Ahead for 2020 and Beyond 660
H. Commission Communication—Mobilizing Public and Private Finance Towards Global Access to Climate-Friendly, Affordable and Secure Energy Services: The Global Energy Efficiency and Renewable Energy Fund 661

I. Commission Communication—Establishing an Environment Strategy for the Mediterranean 663

III. Summaries of Reports 666

A. Commission Communication: Progress Report on the Sustainable Development Strategy 2007 667

Index 673

List of Contributors

Pamela M. Barnes is holder of a Jean Monnet Chair *'ad personam'* in European Political Integration at the University of Lincoln (United Kingdom), where she is a principal lecturer in the School of Law. She has co-authored several books including: P. M. Barnes and I. G. Barnes, *Environmental Policy in the EU* (Cheltenham: Edward Elgar, 2000). She is the author of articles and book chapters on enlargement and EU environmental policy, EU environmental management and audit legislation, the environmental impact of CAP reforms, development of EU's nuclear energy strategy, EU citizenship, EU institutional developments and the decision-making process. Her most recent publications include: 'The Nuclear Industry: A Particular Challenge to Democracy in Europe' (2006) 48 *Managerial Law* 4, 400–29; 'Europeanization of Environmental Policy' in A. Massey and F. Carr (eds.), *Public Policy and the New European Agenda* (Cheltenham: Edward Elgar, 2006), 277–96; and 'The Future of EURATOM' in N. Neuwahl and S. Haack (eds.), *Unresolved Issues in the European Constitution: Rethinking the Crisis* (Montreal: Les Editions Themis, 2007).

Richard Caddell is Lecturer in Law at Swansea University (United Kingdom), where he specializes in international law, with a particular emphasis on the law of the sea, biodiversity conservation, and international and EC environmental governance. He read law at Cardiff University (United Kingdom), gaining an LLM with distinction, where he is also currently finalizing a PhD thesis on the conservation of cetaceans under international law.

His recent publications include: 'International Law and the Protection of Migratory Wildlife: An Appraisal of Twenty-Five Years of the Bonn Convention' (2005) 16 *Colorado Journal of International Environmental Law and Policy* 1, 101–44; 'By-Catch Mitigation and the Protection of Cetaceans: Recent Developments in EC Law' (2005) 8 *Journal of International Wildlife Law and Policy* 3, 241–59; and 'The Prohibition on Driftnet Fishing in European Community Waters: Problems, Progress and Prospects' (2006) 13 *Journal of International Maritime Law* 4, 265–89.

He is the Regional Seas correspondent for the *Yearbook of International Environmental Law* and has contributed a series of essays to the forthcoming *Max Planck Encyclopaedia of Public International Law*. He has also recently acted as a legal consultant to the World Wildlife Fund (WWF) and also to the Advisory Committee of the Agreement on Conservation of Small Cetaceans of the Baltic and North Seas (ASCOBANS) on dolphin conservation law and policy.

Fleur Claessens is a programme officer on Intellectual Property at the International Centre for Trade and Sustainable Development (ICTSD) and a PhD candidate at the University of Maastricht.

Michael G. Doherty is Principal Lecturer at Lancashire Law School, University of Central Lancashire (United Kingdom). He teaches Environmental Law and Public Law and leads the postgraduate Masters programme. A former Chair of the UK Association of Law Teachers, he takes an interest in pedagogy and, in particular, the development of e-learning in environmental law. He publishes on European human rights law, but his main research interests are in the judicial use of environmental principles and flexibility in environmental law, with publications including 'Challenging a Commission Refusal to Allow the Introduction of More Stringent National Measures' (2004) 6 *Environmental Law Review* 2, 120–6, and 'Hard Cases and Environmental Principles: An Aid to Interpretation?' (2002) 3 *Yearbook of European Environmental Law*, 155–74.

Floor M. Fleurke is a PhD student at the Centre for Environmental Law of the University of Amsterdam (The Netherlands), finalizing her thesis on the application of the precautionary principle in environmental law and policy. She published 'The Impact of the EU Air Quality Standards on the Planning and Authorisation of Large Scale Infrastructure Projects in the Netherlands' (2005) 2 *Journal of European Environmental & Planning Law* 5, 375–84 (with Niels Koeman).

Markus W. Gehring is Lecturer in International and European Law at the Centre of International Studies, University of Cambridge and Fellow in Law at Robinson College (United Kingdom). He holds an LLM from the Yale Law School (United States) where he was Walter W. Oberreit Scholar, and a Dr.jur. from the University of Hamburg (Germany). He has lectured in several universities around the world and is a visiting Professor at the University of Ottawa, Faculty of Law, Civil Law Section (Canada). He also serves as Lead Counsel for Sustainable International Trade, Investment and Competition Law with the Centre of International Sustainable Development Law (CISDL), based at the Faculty of Law of McGill University, in Montreal (Canada).

Dr Gehring is a member of the Frankfurt/Main Bar (Germany), and a former member of the Brussels Bar (Belgium). He serves on the International Law Association (ILA) Committee on International Law on Sustainable Development. Prior to joining Robinson College, he practised European Competition and International Trade law at Cleary Gottlieb in their Brussels office (Belgium). He was also at Oxford University (United Kingdom), as a Tutor in Public International Law at the Faculty of Law and other Colleges, and as a legal researcher with Prof. Vaughan Lowe at All Souls College. He has taught at the Faculty of Law of the University of Hamburg (Germany), and was legal fellow at the International Centre for Trade and Sustainable Development (ICTSD) in Geneva, where he edited the *BRIDGES* Journal legal column.

Dr Gehring has published on various aspects of sustainable development, trade, European, and climate change law. His recent books include M. W. Gehring and M.-C. Cordonier Segger (eds.), *Sustainable Development in World Trade Law* (The Hague: Kluwer Law International, 2005); M. C. Gehring, J. Hepburn, and M.-C. Cordonier Segger (eds.), *World Trade Law in Practice* (London: Globe Publishing, 2006); and M. W. Gehring, *Nachhaltigkeit durch Verfahren im Welthandelsrecht* (Berlin: Duncker & Humblot, 2007).

Robert G. Lee is Professor of Law at Cardiff Law School. He was head of the school from 1996 to 1999, and is currently a Co-Director of the ESRC Centre on Business Relationships, Accountability, Sustainability and Society (BRASS), which works on issues of business and sustainability/social responsibility. He is a professional development consultant with the Environment Products and Regulation Group of Freshfields Bruckhaus Deringer. Bob is Editor of *Environmental Law Monthly*, Series Editor for the *International Library of Environmental Law & Policy*, and the Environmental Editor for the *Journal of Business Law*. He is a trustee of the Environmental Law Foundation and an adviser to UN bodies such as UNEP and UNDP. He is a Fellow of the Royal College of Medicine and has a book on the regulation of biomedicine and a further book on food regulation due out later this year.

Kristin Price is an Associate Fellow at the Center for International Sustainable Development Law (CISDL), based at McGill University Faculty of Law in Montreal (Canada), and works specifically in the Trade, Investment and Competition Law for Sustainable Development Research Programme. She is currently an intern at the United Nations Institute for Training and Research (UNITAR) Environmental Law Programme in Geneva (Switzerland). Previously, she obtained her MPhil in International Relations from Cambridge University (United Kingdom) and her BA in Political Science at Brown University (United States). Her recent publications include 'UK and Canadian Approaches to Kyoto Protocol Implementation' (with Markus Gehring), in C. P. M. Waters (ed.), *British and Canadian Perspectives on International Law* (Leiden: Martinus Nijhoff, 2006).

Eloise Scotford is the Career Development Fellow in Environmental Law at Corpus Christi College, Oxford (United Kingdom). In 2006, as a Clarendon and James Fairfax Scholar, she graduated from the University of Oxford with distinction in the BCL, and went on to defend successfully her MPhil thesis in late 2007. Prior to moving to Oxford, she studied as a law and science undergraduate at the University of Sydney (Australia), and obtained the University Medal in Law. She has worked as Associate to the Chief Justice of Australia, and as a Lecturer in law at the Universities of Sydney and New South Wales (Australia).

Her current doctoral project extends the work of her MPhil thesis in environmental law and concerns judicial implementation of environmental principles.

Her most recent publication is 'Trash or Treasure: Policy Tensions in EC Waste Regulation' (2007) 19 *Journal of Environmental Law* 3, 367–88.

Elen Stokes currently holds a Leverhulme Trust Early Career Fellowship at Manchester University Law School (United Kingdom), where she is conducting research into the precautionary principle in practice. Her project focuses specifically on the regulation of new technologies, and she recently co-authored a report for the former UK Department of Trade and Industry (DTI) entitled An Overview of the Framework of Current Regulation Affecting the Development and Marketing of Nanomaterials. Elen has also published work on risk regulation and the precautionary principle, including 'Liberalising the Threshold of Precaution: Cockle Fishing, the Habitats Directive, and Evidence of a New Understanding of "Scientific Uncertainty"' (2005) 7 *Environmental Law Review* 3, 206–14; and 'The Contribution of Recent Developments in United Kingdom Environmental Law to the Legal Principles of Sustainable Development' (2006) 10 *Revue Européenne de Droit de l'Environnement* 1, 57–69 (with Ben Pontin); and 'Ecological Modernisation and the Precautionary Principle' (with Robert Lee), in J. Gunning, and S. Holm (eds.), *Ethics, Law and Society:* Volume One (Aldershot: Ashgate, 2005), 103–15.

Her other research interests include the tension between trade liberalization and environmental protection, and the role of the European courts in overcoming definitional ambiguities in environmental law.

Naveen Thayyil obtained his LLM degree from the University of London (United Kingdom), and is currently doing a PhD on GMO regulation in the European Community. An alumnus of the National Law School of India, Bangalore, he previously practised public law with a particular emphasis on human rights and environment, as an Advocate in the Supreme Court of India at New Delhi. He has also been a consultant for a host of civil society organizations including the Centre for International Environmental Law, Washington DC, Action Aid India, New Delhi, and the Lawyers Collective, New Delhi.

Table of Cases

Australia

BGP Properties Pty Ltd v. *Lake Macquarie City Council* (2004) 1

Canada

Canada Ltee 114957 (Spraytech, Societe d'arrosage) v. *Hudson (Town)* 2001. 1

European Union

ALPHABETICAL

Abfall Service AG (ASA) v. *Bundesminster fur Umwelt, Jugend und Familie* (Case C-6/00) [2002] ECR I-1961 507
ABNA Ltd v. *Secretary of State for Health* (Joined Cases C-11/04, C-12/04, C-194/04, and C-453/03) [2005] ECR I-10423 35
Affish (Case C-183/95) [1997] ECR I-4315. 88
Agrarproduktion Staebelow Gmbh v. *Landrat Des Landkreises Bad Doberan* (Case C-504/04) [2006] ECR I-679 39–40
Ahokainen & Leppik v. *Virallinen Syyttäjä* (Case C-434/04) [2006] ECR I-9171 29
Alliance for Natural Health and Othersv. Secretary of State for Health (Joined Cases C-154/04 and C-155/04) [2005] ECR I-6451 39–40
Alpharma v. *Council* (*Alpharma*) (Case T-70/99) [2002] ECR II-3495 . . . . 31–5, 38, 42, 146
Andrea Francovich and Danila Bonifaci and Others v. *Italy* (Joined cases C-6/90 and C-9/90) (*Francovich*) [1991] ECR I-5357 . . . . 600, 613
Andreas Rodenbröker v. *Commission* (Case T-117/05R) [2005] OJ C229/24 472
ARCO Chemie Ltd. Nederland v. *Minister van Volkshuisvesting, Ruimtelijke Ordening en Milieubeheer* (C-418/97) *and Vereniging Dorpsbelang Hees, Stichting Werkgroep Weurt and Vereniging Stedelijk Leefmilieu Nijmegen* v. *Directeur van de Dienst Milieu en Water van de Provincie Gelderland* (C-419/97) (Joined cases C-418/97 and C-419/97) (*ARCO*) [2000] ECR I-4475 . . . . 21–3, 163, 168–79
Arizona Chemical Bv and Others v. *Commission* (Case T-369/03), Order of the CFI of 14 Dec. 2005 4
Artegodan Gmbh and Others v. *Commission* (Joined Cases T-74/00, T-76/00, T-83/00, T-84/00, T-85/00, T-132/00, T-137/00, and T-141/00) [2002] ECR II-4945 (*Artegodan*) 4, 8–9, 23, 30–1, 36–41, 73, 84
Association Greenpeace France and Others v. *Ministère de l' agriculture et de la pêche and Others* (Case C-6/99) (*Greenpeace*) [2000] ECR I-1651 . . . . 14, 17, 144
Association pour la protection des animaux sauvages et Préfet de Maine-et-Loire et Préfet de la Loire-Atlantique (Case C-435/92) [1994] ECR I-67. 137
Associazione Italiana per il WWF and Others v. *Regione Veneto* (Case C-118/94) [1996] ECR I-1223 237
Austria v. Council (C-445/00) [2003] ECR I-8549. 14
AvestaPolarit Chrome Oy, formerly Outokumpu Chrome Oy (Case C-114/01) [2003] ECR I-8725 22
Barker v. *London Borough of Bromley* (Case C-290/03) [2006] ECR I-3949 577–8

Basses Corbières. See *Commission* v. *France* (Case C-374/98)
Bavendam and Others v. *Commission* (Case T-80/05) [2005] OJ C143/36 472
Beer Purity Law. See *Commission* v. *Germany* (Case 178/84)
Benkö and Others v. *Commission* (Case T-122/05) [2006] OJ C249/49. 472
BSE. See *United Kingdom* v. *Commission* (Case C-180/96)
Bund Naturschutz in Bayern eV, Johann Märkl and Others, Angelika Graubner-Riedelsheimer and Others, Friederike Nischwitz and Others, v. *Freistaat Bayern* (Case C-244/05) [2006] ECR I-8445 . . . . 469–72, 570–1
Cassis de Dijon. See *Rewe Zentral AG* v. *Bundesmonopolverwaltung für Branntwein* (*Rewe Zentral / Cassis de Dijon*) (Case 120/78)
Codacons. See *Ministero della Salute* v. *Coordinamento delle Associazioni per la Difesa dell'Ambiente e dei Diritti Degli Utenti e dei Consumatori, Federconsumatori, and Others* (Case C-132/03)
Commission v. *Austria* (Case C-320/03) [2004] ECR I-3593 28
Commission v. *Austria* (Case C-78/04), [2005] OJ C6/18. 557
Commission v. *Austria* (Case C-209/04) [2006] ECR I-2755 449–53
Commission v. *Belgium* (Case C-247/85) [1987] ECR I-3029. . . . . 237, 454
Commission v. *Belgium* (Case C-2/90) (*Walloon Waste*) [1992] ECR I-4431 . . . . 28, 41
Commission v. *Belgium* (Case C-221/03) [2005] ECR I-8307. 515
Commission v. *Belgium* (Case C-33/05) [2006] OJ C48/9 514
Commission v. *Council* (*AETR*) (Case C-22/70) [1971] ECR 263. 565–7
Commission v. *Council* (*Titanium Dioxide*) (Case C-300/89) [1991] ECR I-2867. 25
Commission v. *Council* (Case C-155/91) (*Waste Directive*) [1993] ECR I-939. 25
Commission v. *Council* (Case C-29/99) [2002] ECR I-11221 206
Commission v. *Council* (Case C-338/01) [2004] ECR I-4829 570
Commission v. *Council* (Case C-94/03) [2006] ECR-1 567
Commission v. *Council* (Case C-176/03) [2005] ECR-7879 601
Commission v. *Denmark* (Case C-192/01) [2003] ECR I-9693. . . . . 41–3, 84
Commission v. *EP and Council* (Case C-178/03) [2006] ECR I-107. 567–8
Commission v. *Finland* (Case C-344/03) [2006] OJ C48/3. 454
Commission v. *Finland* (Case C-107/05) [2006] ECR I-10. 350
Commission v. *France* (Case 42/82) [1983] ECR 1013 466
Commission v. *France* (Case C-252/86) [1988] ECR 2243 232–6
Commission v. *France* (Case C-252/85) [1988] ECR I-2243. 454
Commission v. *France* (Case C-166/97) (*Seine Estuary*) [1999] ECR I-1719 234
Commission v. *France* (Case C-374/98) (*Basses Corbières*) [2000] ECR I-10799 236
Commission v. *France* (Case C-38/99) [2000] ECR I-4007. . . . . 237, 463
Commission v. *France* (Case C-24/00) [2004] ECR I-1277. 41–3
Commission v. *France* (Case C-429/01) [2004] OJ C21/4. 376
Commission v. *France* (Case C-280/02) [2004] ECR I-8573. . . . . 21, 515–6
Commission v. *France* (Case C-239/03) [2004] ECR I-9325. 564
Commission v. *France* (Case C-419/03) [2004] OJ C228/15. 375–6
Commission v. *France* (Case C-191/04) [2005] OJ C193/7. 515
Commission v. *France* (Case C-121/07) [2007] OJ C95/31. 375–6
Commission v. *Germany* (Case 178/84) (*Beer Purity Law*) [1987] ECR 1227 42
Commission v. *Germany* (Case C-131/88) [1991] ECR 825 462
Commission v. *Germany* (Case C-57/89) (*Leybucht Dykes*) [1991] ECR I-883. . . . . 235, 256
Commission v. *Germany* (Case C-422/92) [1995] ECR I-1097 169
Commission v. *Germany* (Case C-431/92) [1995] ECR I-2189 453
Commission v. *Germany* (Case C-71/93) [2001] ECR I-5811 474
Commission v. *Germany* (Case C-98/03) [2006] ECR I-53 . . . . 22, 457–65, 570
Commission v. *Germany* (Case C-67/05) [2006] OJ C36/17. 514

Commission v. *Greece* (Case C–103/00) [2002] ECR I–1147 .... 239, 467, 475
Commission v. *Greece* (Case C-119/02) [2004] ECR I-1433 .... 21, 516
Commission v. *Greece* (Case C-140/03) [2005] ECR I-3177 350
Commission v. *Greece* (Case C-163/03) [2005] OJ C143/8........................... 517
Commission v. *Greece* (Case C–518/04) [2006] ECR I–42 469
Commission v. *Greece* (Case C-390/05) [2005] ECR I-135 333
Commission v. *Ireland* (Case C-117/00) [2002] ECR I-883 93
Commission v. *Ireland* (Case C-494/01) [2005] ECR-3331............................. 14
Commission v. *Ireland* (Case C-459/03) [2006] ECR I-4635 563–6
Commission v. *Ireland* (Case C-216/05) [2006] ECR I-10787 577
Commission v. *Italy* (Case C-262/85) [1987] ECR I-3073 237
Commission v. *Italy* (Case C-113/86) [1988] ECR 607................................ 466
Commission v. *Italy* (Case C-157/89) [1991] ECR I-57 455
Commission v. *Italy* (Case C-362/90) [1992] ECR I-2353 474
Commission v. *Italy* (Case C-228/91) [1993] ECR I-2701 42
Commission v. *Italy* (Case C-207/00) [2001] ECR I-4571 332
Commission v. *Italy* (Case C-396/00) [2002]ECR I-3949 516
Commission v. *Italy* (Case C-323/01) [2002] ECR I-4711 350
Commission v. *Italy* (Case C-270/03) [2005] ECR I-5233 22
Commission v. *Italy* (Case C-139/04) [2006] ECR I-5 331–2
Commission v. *Italy* (Case C-486/04) [2006] ECR I-11025 174
Commission v. *Italy* (Case C-122/05) [2006] OJ C 115/1............................. 350
Commission v. *Italy* (Case C-179/06) [2006] OJ C143/26 474
Commission v. *Italy* (Case C-503/06R) [2006] ECR I-141 457
Commission v. *Luxembourg* (Case C-32/05) [2006] ECR I-11323 .... 515, 574–5
Commission v. *Luxembourg* (Case C-198/06) [2006] ECR I-137......................... 333
Commission v. *Netherlands* (Case C-339/87) [1990] ECR I-851 455
Commission v. *Netherlands* (Case C-3/96) [1998] ECR I-3031 .... 235–6, 450–2
Commission v. *Netherlands* (Case C-41/02) [2005] ECR I-11375 41–3
Commission v. *Portugal* (Case C-239/04) [2006] ECR I-10183................... 467–9, 570
Commission v. *Portugal* (Case C-191/05) [2006] ECR I-6853........................ 456–7
Commission v. *Spain* (Case C-355/90) (*Santoña Marshes*) 235
Commission v. *Spain* (Case C-214/96) [1998] ECR I-7661 517
Commission v. *Spain* (Joined cases C-416/02 and C-121/03) [2005] ECR I-7487 ...... 174, 517
Commission v. *Spain* (Case C-79/03) [2004] ECR I-11619......................... 237, 454
Commission v. *Spain* (Case C-121/03) [2005] ECR I-7569......................... 174, 517
Commission v. *Spain* (Case C-26/04) [2005] ECR I-11059 517
Commission v. *Spain* (Case C-135/04) [2005] ECR I-5261............................. 237
Commission v. *Spain* (Case C-221/04) [2006] ECR I-4515.......................... 465–7
Commission v. *Spain* (Case C-332/04) [2006] ECR I-40............................... 575
Commission v. *Spain* (Case C-186/06) [2006] OJ C154/10 473
Commission v. *United Kingdom* (Case C-421/02) [2004] OJ C201/5 555
Commission v. *United Kingdom* (Case C-508/03) [2006] ECR I-3969 .... 554, 575–7
Commission v. *United Kingdom* (Case C-6/04) (*Conformity*) [2005] ECR I-9017 22
Commission v. *United Kingdom* (Case C-37/05) [2006] ECR I 6 575
Commission v. *United Kingdom* (Case C-138/06) [2006] ECR I-136 332
Compagnie d'enterprises CFE SA (Brussels, Belgium) v. *Commission* (Case T-100/05) [2005]
OJ C106/1.. 472
Conformity. See *Commission* v. *United Kingdom* (Case C-6/04)
Criminal Proceedings against Antonio Saetti and Andrea Frediani (Case C-235/02) (*Saetti*) [2004]
ECR I-1005 22

Criminal Proceedings against E. Zanetti and Others (Case C-359/88) (*Zanetti*) [1990] ECR I-1509 169
Criminal Proceedings against Godefridus van der Feesten (Case C-202/94) (*Godefridus van der Feesten*) [1996] ECR I-355 232–3
Criminal Proceedings against Gourmetterie Van den Burg (Case C-169/89) [1990] ECR I-2143 232
Criminal Proceedings against Greenham and Abel (Case C-95/01) (*Greenham and Abel*) [2004] ECR I-1333 41–3
Criminal Proceedings against Gustave Keck and Daniel Mithouard (*Keck*) (Joined Cases C-267/91 and C-268/91) [1993] ECR I-6097 50
Criminal Proceedings against Leendert Van Bennekom (Case 227/82) [1983] ECR 3883 42
Criminal Proceedings against Lirussi and Bizzaro (Joined Cases C-175/98 and C-177/98) (*Lirussi & Bizzaro*) [1999] ECR I-6881 22
Criminal Proceedings against Matteo Peralta (Case C-379/92) (*Peralta*) [1994] ECR I-3453 . . . . 14–6, 45
Criminal Proceedings against Niselli (Case C-457/02) (*Nilessi*) [2004] ECR I-10853 . . . . 22, 177
Criminal Proceedings against Sandoz BV (Case 174/82) [1983] ECR 2445 42–3
Criminal Proceedings against Tombesi (Joined Cases C-304/94, 330/94, 342/94, and 224/95) (*Tombesi*) [1997] ECR I-3561 168–72
Criminal Proceedings against Tullio Ratti (Case C-148/78) (*Ratti*) [1979] ECR I-1629 70
Criminal Proceedings against Vessoso and Zanetti (Joined Cases C-206/88 and C-207/88) [1990] ECR-I 1461 172
Danish Foods/Nutrients. See *Denmark* v. *Commission* (Case C-3/00)
Denmark v. *Commission* (Case C-3/00) (*Danish Food/Nutrients*) [2003] ECR I-2643 . . . . 14, 53–4
Deponiezweckverband Eiterköpfe v. *Land Rheinland-Pfalz* (Case C-6/03) [2005] ECR I-2753 14–5
EP v. *Council* (Case C-187/93) (*Waste Regulation*) [1994] ECR I-2857 25
EP v. *Council* (Joined cases C-164/97 and C-165/97) [1999] ECR I-1139 570
EREF v. *Commission* (Case T-94/07) [2007] OJ C117/31 312
European Environmental Bureau (EEB), Pesticides Action Network Europe, International Union of Food, Agricultural, Hotel, Restaurant, Catering, Tobacco and Allied Worker's Associations (IUF), European Federation of Trade Unions in the Food, Agricultural and Tourism sectors and allied branches (EFFAT), Stichting Natuur en Milieu and Sevenska Naturskyddföreningen v. *Commission* (Case T-94/04) [2005] ECR II-4919 552–3
European Environmental Bureau (EEB) and Stichting Natuur en Milieu v. *Commission* (Joined cases T-236/04 and T-241/04) [2005] ECR II-4945 552–3
EU-Wood-Trading GmbH (Case C-277/02) [2004] ECR I-11957 507
France v. *Commission* (Case C-41/93) [1994] ECR I-1829 . . . . 67, 146
Francovich. See *Andrea Francovich and Danila Bonifaci and Others* v. *Italy* (Joined cases C-6/90 and C-9/90)
Freiherr von Cramer-Klett and Rechtlerverband Pfronten v. *Commission* (Case T-136/04) [2004] OJ C190/17 472
Gedeputeerde Staten van Noord-Holland (Case C-81/96) [1998] ECR I-3923 453
Germany v. *Commission* (Case C-240/90) [1992] ECR I-5383 553
Germany v. *Commission* (Case C-512/99) [2003] ECR I-845 58
Godefridus van der Feesten. See *Criminal Proceedings against Godefridus van der Feesten* (Case C-202/94)
Gourmetterie Van den Burg. See *Criminal Proceedings against Gourmetterie Van den Burg* (Case C-169/89)
Greenham and Abel. See *Criminal Proceedings against Greenham and Abel* (Case C-95/01)
Greenpeace. See *Association Greenpeace France and Others* v. *Ministère De L'agriculture et de la Pêche and Others* (Case C-6/99)

Industrias Químicas del Vallés v. *Commission* (Case T-158/03) (*IQV*) [2005] ECR II-2425 . . . . 31, 39–40
Inter-Environnement Wallonie ASBL v. *Région Wallone* (*Inter-Environnement Wallonie*) (Case C-129/96) [1997] ECR I-7411 168–9
Jose Maria Sison v. *Council* (Joined Cases T-110/03, T-150/03, and T-405/03) [2005] ECR II-1429 398
Keck. See *Criminal Proceedings against Gustave Keck and Daniel Mithouard* (Joined Cases C-267/91 and C-268/91)
Kemikalieinspektionen v. *Toolex Alpha AB* (Case C-473/98) (*Toolex*) [2000] ECR I-5681 . . . . 62, 70, 88
Kvz Retec Gmbh v. *Republik Österreich* (Case C-176/05) [2007] ECR I-1721 22
Land Oberösterreich and Austria v. *Commission* (Joined Cases T-366/03 and T-235/04) (*Land Oberösterreich*) [2005] ECR II-4005. . . . . 5, 14, 20, 56–64, 72–3, 77, 146
Land Oberöstereich (Joined Cases C-439/05P and C-454/05P) [2007] ECR I-0000. 14
Landelijke Vereniging tot Behoud van de Waddenzee and Nederlandse Vereniging tot Bescherming van Vogels v. *Staatssecretaris van Landbouw, Natuurbeheer en Visserij* (*Waddenzee*) (Case C-127/02) [2004] ECR I-7405 . . . . x, 14, 23–4, 80–132, 468
Les Laboratoires Servier v. *Commission* (Case T-147/00) [2003] ECR II-85 38
Leybucht Dykes. See *Commission* v. *Germany* (Case C-57/89)
Ligue pour la protection des oiseaux and Others v. *Premier Ministre et Ministre de l'Aménagement du territoire et de l'environnement* (Case C-182/02) [2003] ECR I-12105 . . . . 237, 455
Lirussi & Bizzaro. See *Criminal Proceedings against Lirussi and Bizzaro* (Joined cases C-175/98 and C-177/98)
Marius Pedersen A/S v. *Miljostyrelsen* (Case C-215/04) [2006] ECR I-1465. . . . . 506, 572
Ministero della Salute v. *Coordinamento delle Associazioni per la Difesa dell'Ambiente e dei Diritti Degli Utenti e dei Consumatori, Federconsumatori, and Others* (Case C-132/03) (*Codacons*) [2005] ECR I-4167 . . . . 14–9, 45
Monsanto Agricoltura Italia SpA and Others v. *Presidenza del Consiglio dei Ministri and Others* (*Monsanto Italia*) (Case C-236/01) [2003] ECR I-8105 . . . . 1, 4, 14–25, 30, 37, 45, 84, 144
Netherlands v. *Commission* (Case T-182/06) [2007] ECR-0000 . . . . 49, 58–61, 76
NFU. See *The Queen* v. *Ministry of Agriculture, Fisheries and Food, Commissioners of Customs & Excise, ex parte National Farmers' Union and Others* (Case C-157/96)
Niselli. See *Criminal Proceedings against Niselli* (Case C-457/02)
Palin Granit Oy v. *Vehmassalon Kansanterveystyön Kuntayhtymän Hallitus* (*Palin Granit*) (Case C–9/00) [2002] ECR I–3533. . . . . 22, 163, 166, 172–7, 497
Peralta. See *Criminal Proceedings against Matteo Peralta* (Case C-379/92)
Pfizer Animal Health v. *Council* (*Pfizer*) (Case T-13/99) [2002] ECR II-3305. . . . . 1, 18, 31–45, 84, 88, 146
Pretore di Torino (Case C-187/94) [1985] OJ C270/4 72
The Queen v. *Secretary of State for the Environment, Transport and the Regions ex parte First Corporate Shipping Ltd., Interveners: World Wide Fund for Nature UK (WWF) and Avon Wildlife Trust* (Case C-371/98) [2000] ECR I-9235 . . . . 451, 470–1
The Queen v. *Ministry of Agriculture, Fisheries and Food, Commissioners of Customs & Excise*, Ex Parte *National Farmers' Union and Others* (Case C-157/96) (*NFU*) [1998] ECR I-2265. . . 30
The Queen v. *Minister of Agriculture, Fisheries and Food and Secretary of State for Health*, Ex Parte *Fedesa and Others* (Case C-331/88) [1990] ECR I-4023. 29
The Queen v. *Secretary of State for the Environment and Ministry of Agriculture, Fisheries and Food, ex parte H.A. Standley and Others and D.G.D. Metson and Others (Standley)* (Case C-293/97) [1999] ECR I-2603 . . . . 14, 17–9
The Queen v. *Secretary of State for the Environment and Ministry of Agriculture, Fisheries and Food, ex parte Royal Society for the Protection of Birds* (Case C-44/95) [1996] ECR I-3805 . . . . 232, 451, 457

Case C-214/96, *Commission* v. *Spain* [1998] ECR I-7661 517
Case C-127/97, *Willi Burstein,*v. *Freistaat Bayern* [1998] ECR I-6005 69
Joined Cases C-164/97 and C-165/97, *EP* v. *Council* [1999] ECR I-1139. 570
Case C-166/97, *Commission* v. *France (Seine Estuary)* [1999] ECR I-1719 234
Case C-293/97, *The Queen Case* v. *Secretary of State for the Environment and Ministry of Agriculture, Fisheries and Food, ex parte H.A. Standley and Others and D.G.D. Metson and Others* [1999] ECR I-2603 . . . . 14, 17–9
Joined Cases C-418/97 and C-419/97, *ARCO Chemie Ltd. Nederland* v. *Minister van Volkshuisvesting,Ruimtelijke Ordening en Milieubeheer* (C-418/97) *and Vereniging Dorpsbelang Hees, Stichting Werkgroep Weurt and Vereniging Stedelijk Leefmilieu Nijmegen* v. *Directeur van de Dienst Milieu en Water van de Provincie Gelderland* (C-419/97) (*ARCO*) [2000] ECR I-4475 . . . . 21–3, 163, 168–79
Joined Cases C-175/98 and C-177/98, *Criminal Proceedings against Lirussi and Bizzaro* [1999] ECR I-6881 (*Lirussi & Bizzaro*) 22
Case C-209/98, *Sydhavnens Sten & Grus Aps* [2000] ECR I-3743 28
Case C-371/98, *The Queen* v. *Secretary of State for the Environment, Transport and the Regions ex parte First Corporate Shipping Ltd., Interveners: World Wide Fund for Nature UK (WWF) and Avon Wildlife Trust* [2000] ECR I-9235 . . . . 451, 470–1
Case C-374/98, *Commission* v. *France* (*Basses Corbières*) [2000] ECR I-10799 236
Case C-473/98, *Kemikalieinspektionen* v. *Toolex Alpha AB* (*Toolex*) [2000] ECR I-5681 . . . . 62, 70, 88
Case C-6/99, *Association Greenpeace France and Others* v. *Ministère de l'agriculture et de la pêche and Others* (*Greenpeace*) [2000] ECR I-1651 . . . . 14, 17, 144
Case T-13/99, *Pfizer Animal Health* v. *Council* (*Pfizer*) [2002] ECR II-3305. . . . . 1, 18, 31–45, 84, 88, 146
Case C-29/99, *Commission* v. *Council* [2002] ECR I-11221. 206
Case C-38/99, *Commission* v. *France* [2000] ECR I-4007. . . . . 237, 463
Case T-70/99, *Alpharma* v. *Council* (*Alpharma*) [2002] ECR II-3495. . . . . 31–5, 38, 42, 146
Case C-512/99, *Germany* v. *Commission* [2003] ECR I-845. 58
Case C-3/00, *Denmark* v. *Commission* (*Danish Food/Nutrients*) [2003] ECR I-2643. . . . . 14, 53–4
Case C-6/00, *Abfall Service AG (ASA)* v. *Bundesminster fur Umwelt, Jugend und Familie* [2002] ECR I-1961 507
Case C–9/00, *Palin Granit Oy* v. *Vehmassalon Kansanterveystyön Kuntayhtymän Hallitus* (*Palin Granit*) [2002] ECR I–3533 . . . . 22, 163, 166, 172–7, 497
Case C-24/00, *Commission* v. *France* [2004] ECR I-1277. 41–3
Joined Cases T-74/00, T-76/00, T-83/00, T-84/00, T-85/00, T-132/00, T-137/00, and T-141/00, *Artegodan Gmbh and Others* v. *Commission* (*Artegodan*) [2002] ECR II-4945. . . . . 4, 8–9, 23, 30–1, 36–41, 73, 84
Case C–103/00, *Commission* v. *Greece* [2002] ECR I–1147 . . . . 239, 467, 475
Case C-117/00, *Commission* v. *Ireland* [2002] ECR I-883 93
Case T-147/00, *Les Laboratoires Servier* v. *Commission* [2003] ECR II-85. 38
Case C-207/00, *Commission* v. *Italy* [2001] ECR I-4571 332
Case C-396/00, *Commission* v. *Italy* [2002]ECR I-3949 516
Case C-445/00, *Austria v. Council* [2003] ECR I-8549 14
Case C-95/01, *Criminal Proceedings against Greenham and Abel* (*Greenham and Abel*) [2004] ECR I-1333 41–3
Case C-114/01, *AvestaPolarit Chrome Oy, formerly Outokumpu Chrome Oy* [2003] ECR I-8725 22
Case C-192/01, *Commission* v. *Denmark* [2003] ECR I-9693 . . . . 41–3, 84
Case C-236/01, *Monsanto Agricoltura Italia SpA and Others* v. *Presidenza del Consiglio dei Ministri and Others* (*Monsanto Italia*) [2003] ECR I-8105. . . . . 1, 4, 14–25, 30, 37, 45, 84, 144

Case C-323/01, *Commission* v. *Italy* [2002] ECR I-4711 350
Case C-338/01, *Commission* v. *Council* [2004] ECR I-4829. 570
Case C-429/01, *Commission* v. *France* [2004] OJ C21/4 376
Case C-494/01, *Commission* v. *Ireland* [2005] ECR-3331 14
Case C-41/02, *Commission* v. *Netherlands* [2005] ECR I-11375. 41–3
Case T-92/02, *Stadtwerke Schwabisch Hall GmbH et al* v. *Commission* [2006] ECR II-11 203
Case C-119/02, *Commission* v. *Greece* [2004] ECR I-1433. . . . . 21, 516
Case C-127/02, *Landelijke Vereniging tot Behoud van de Waddenzee and Nederlandse Vereniging tot Bescherming van Vogels* v. *Staatssecretaris van Landbouw, Natuurbeheer en Visserij* (*Waddenzee*) [2004] ECR I-7405 . . . . x, 14, 23–4, 80–132, 468
Case C-182/02, *Ligue pour la protection des oiseaux and Others* v. *Premier Ministre et Ministre de l'Aménagement du territoire et de l'environnement* [2003] ECR I-12105. . . . . 237, 455
Case C-235/02, *Criminal Proceedings against Antonio Saetti and Andrea Frediani* (*Saetti*) [2004] ECR I-1005 22
Case C-277/02, *EU-Wood-Trading GmbH* [2004] ECR I-11957 507
Case C-280/02, *Commission* v. *France* [2004] ECR I-8573. . . . . 21, 515–6
Case T-392/02, *Solvay Pharmaceuticals BV* v. *Council* [2003] ECR II-4555 36–43
Joined Cases C-416/02 and C-121/03, *Commission* v. *Spain* [2005] ECR I-7487. . . . . . . 174, 517
Case C-421/02, *Commission* v. *United Kingdom* [2004] OJ C201/5 555
Case C-457/02, *Criminal Proceedings against Niselli* (*Niselli*) [2004] ECR I-10853. . . . . . . 22, 177
Case C-1/03, *Criminal Proceedings* v. *Paul Van de Walle, Daniel Laurent, Thierry Mersch and Texaco Belgium SA* (*Van de Walle*) [2004] ECR I-0000 22
Case C-6/03, *Deponiezweckverband Eiterköpfe* v. *Land Rheinland-Pfalz (Deponiezweckverband Eiterköpfe)* [2005] ECR I-2753. 14–5
Case C-79/03, *Commission* v. *Spain* [2004] ECR I-11619 . . . . 237, 454
Case C-94/03, *Commission* v. *Council* [2006] ECR-1 567
Case C-98/03, *Commission* v. *Germany* [2006] ECR I-53. . . . . 22, 457–65, 570
Joined Cases T-110/03, T-150/03, and T-405/03, *Jose Maria Sison* v. *Council* [2005] ECR II-1429 398
Case C-117/03, *Società Italiana Dragaggi SpA and Others* v. *Ministero delle Infrastrutture e dei Trasporti and Regione Autonoma Friuli Venezia Giulia* [2005] ECR I-167 470
Case C-121/03, *Commission* v. *Spain* [2005] ECR I-7569 . . . . 174, 517
Case C-132/03, *Ministero della Salute* v. *Coordinamento delle Associazioni per la Difesa dell'Ambiente e dei Diritti Degli Utenti e dei Consumatori, Federconsumatori, and Others (Codacons)* [2005] ECR I-4167 . . . . 14–9, 45
Case C-140/03, *Commission* v. *Greece* [2005] ECR I-3177. 350
Case T-158/03, *Industrias Químicas del Vallés* v. *Commission* (*IQV*) [2005] ECR II-2425. . . . . 31, 39–40
Case C-163/03, *Commission* v. *Greece* [2005] OJ C143/8 517
Case C-176/03, *Commission* v. *Council* [2005] ECR-7879. 601
Case C-178/03, *Commission* v. *EP and Council* [2006] ECR I-107. 567–8
Case C-221/03, *Commission* v. *Belgium* [2005] ECR I-8307 515
Case C-239/03, *Commission* v. *France* [2004] ECR I-9325. 564
Case C-270/03, *Commission* v. *Italy* [2005] ECR I-5233 22
Case C-290/03, *Barker* v. *London Borough of Bromley* [2006] ECR I-3949 577–8
Case C-320/03, *Commission* v. *Austria* [2004] ECR I-3593 28
Case C-344/03, *Commission* v. *Finland* [2006] OJ C48/3 454
Joined Cases T-366/03 and T-235/04, *Land Oberösterreich and Austria* v. *Commission* (*Land Oberösterreich*) [2005] ECR II-4005. . . . . 5, 14, 20, 56–64, 72–3, 77, 146
Case T-369/03, *Arizona Chemical Bv and Others* v. *Commission*, Order of the CFI of 14 Dec. 2005. 4

Case C-419/03, *Commission* v. *France* [2004] OJ C228/15 375–6
Case C-459/03, *Commission* v. *Ireland* [2006] ECR I-4635 563–6
Case C-508/03, *Commission* v. *United Kingdom* [2006] ECR I-3969 . . . . 554, 575–7
Case C-6/04, *Commission* v. *United Kingdom* (*Conformity*) [2005] ECR I-9017 22
Joined Cases C-11/04, C-12/04, C-194/04, and C-453/03, *ABNA Ltd* v. *Secretary of State for Health* [2005] ECR I-10423. 35
Case C-26/04, *Commission* v. *Spain* [2005] ECR I-11059 517
Case C-78/04, *Commission* v. *Austria* [2005] OJ C6/18 557
Case T-94/04, *European Environmental Bureau (EEB), Pesticides Action Network Europe, International Union of Food, Agricultural, Hotel, Restaurant, Catering, Tobacco and Allied Worker's Associations (IUF), European Federation of Trade Unions in the Food, Agricultural and Tourism sectors and allied branches (EFFAT), Stichting Natuur en Milieu and Sevenska Naturskyddföreningen* v. *Commission* [2005] ECR II-4919 552–3
Case C-135/04, *Commission* v. *Spain* [2005] ECR I-5261 237
Case T-136/04, *Freiherr von Cramer-Klett and Rechtlerverband Pfronten* v. *Commission* [2004] OJ C190/17 472
Case C-139/04, *Commission* v. *Italy* [2006] ECR I-5 331–2
Joined Cases C-154/04 and C-155/04, *Alliance for Natural Health and Others* v. *Secretary of State for Health* (*Alliance Health*) [2005] ECR I-6451. 39–40
Case C-191/04, *Commission* v. *France* [2005] OJ C193/7 515
Case C-209/04, *Commission* v. *Austria* [2006] ECR I-2755 449–53
Case C-215/04, *Marius Pedersen A/S* v. *Miljostyrelsen* [2006] ECR I-1465 . . . . 506, 572
Case C-221/04, *Commission* v. *Spain* [2006] ECR I-4515 465–7
Joined Cases T-236/04 and T-241/04, *European Environmental Bureau (EEB) and Stichting Natuur en Milieu* v. *Commission* [2005] ECR II-4945 552–3
Case C-239/04, *Commission* v. *Portugal* [2006] ECR I-10183 . . . . 467–9, 570
Case C-316/04, *Stichting Zuid-Hollandse Milieufederatie* v. *College voor de Toelating van Bestrijdingsmiddelen* [2005] ECR I-9759 436
Case C-332/04, *Commission* v. *Spain* [2006] ECR I-40 575
Case C-434/04, *Ahokainen & Leppik* v. *Virallinen Syyttäjä* [2006] ECR I-9171 29
Case C-486/04, *Commission* v. *Italy* [2006] ECR I-11025 174
Case C-504/04, *Agrarproduktion Staebelow Gmbh* v. *Landrat Des Landkreises Bad Doberan* (*Agrarproduktion*) [2006] ECR I-679 39–40
Case C–518/04, *Commission* v. *Greece* [2006] ECR I–42 469
Case C-32/05, *Commission* v. *Luxembourg* [2006] ECR I-11323 . . . . 515, 574–5
Case C-33/05, *Commission* v. *Belgium* [2006] OJ C48/9 514
Case C-37/05, *Commission* v. *United Kingdom* [2006] ECR I-6 575
Case C-60/05, *WWF Italia and Others* v. *Regione Lombardia* [2006] ECR I-5083 . . . . 454–6, 571–2
Case C-67/05, *Commission* v. *Germany* [2006] OJ C36/17 514
Case T-80/05, *Bavendam and Others* v. *Commission* [2005] OJ C143/36 472
Case T-100/05, *Compagnie d'enterprises CFE SA (Brussels, Belgium)* v. *Commission* [2005] OJ C106/1. 472
Case C-107/05, *Commission* v. *Finland* [2006] ECR I-10. 350
Case T-117/05R, *Andreas Rodenbröker* v. *Commission* [2005] OJ C229/24. 472
Case C-122/05, *Commission* v. *Italy* [2006] OJ C 115/1. 350
Case T-122/05, *Benkö and Others* v. *Commission* [2006] OJ C249/49 472
Case C-138/05, *Stichting Zuid-Hollandse Milieufederatie* v. *Minister van Landbouw, Natuur en Voedselkwaliteit* [2006] ECR I-8339. 437
Case C-174/05, *Stichting Zuid-Hollandse Milieufederatie and Stichting Natuur en Milieu* v. *College voor de Toelating van Bestrijdingsmiddelen* [2006] ECR I-2443 436

Case C-176/05, *Kvz Retec Gmbh* v. *Republik Österreich* [2007] ECR I-1721 22
Case C-191/05, *Commission* v. *Portugal* [2006] ECR I-6853 456–7
Case C-216/05, *Commission* v. *Ireland* [2006] ECR I-10787 577
Case C-244/05, *Bund Naturschutz in Bayern eV, Johann Märkl and Others, Angelika Graubner-Riedelsheimer and Others, Friederike Nischwitz and Others,* v. *Freistaat Bayern* [2006] ECR I-8445 . . . . 469–72, 570–1
Case C-390/05, *Commission* v. *Greece* [2005] ECR I-135 333
Joined Cases C-439/05P and C-454/05P, *Land Oberöstereich* [2007] ECR I-0000 14
Case C-138/06, *Commission* v. *United Kingdom* [2006] ECR I-136 332
Case C-179/06, *Commission* v. *Italy* [2006] OJ C143/26 474
Case T-182/06, *Netherlands* v. *Commission* [2007] ECR-0000 . . . . 49, 58–61, 76
Case C-186/06, *Commission* v. *Spain* [2006] OJ C154/10 473
Case C-198/06, *Commission* v. *Luxembourg* [2006] ECR I-137 333
Case C-503/06R, *Commission* v. *Italy* [2006] ECR I-141 457
Case T-94/07, *EREF* v. *Commission* [2007] OJ C117/31 312
Case C-121/07, *Commission* v. *France* [2007] OJ C95/31 375–6

ECJ OPINIONS

Opinion 2/2000, on the Cartagena Protocol on Biosafety [2001] ECR I-9713 564

France

Superphénix (Council of State – *Conseil d'Etat,* 1997) 601

Germany

Kalkar (Federal Constitutional Court, 1978) 605

India

AP Pollution Control Board v. *Prof. M.V. Nayudu* 1999 1

International

WORLD TRADE ORGANIZATION (WTO)

Apples, (Japan). See *Japan—Measures Affecting the Importation of Apples*
Australia—Measures Affecting Importation of Salmon, WT/DS18/AB/R, AB-1998–5 154
Beef Hormones. See *EC—Measures concerning Meat and Meat Products (Hormones)*
Biotech Products, (EC). See *EC—Measures Affecting the Approval and Marketing of Biotech Products (US, Canada, and Argentina)*
EC—Measures Affecting the Approval and Marketing of Biotech Products, WT/DS291 (US), WT/DS292 (Canada), and WT/DS291 (Argentina) . . . . x, 133–6, 149, 153–6, 366, 395–401, 608
EC—Measures concerning Meat and Meat Products (Hormones), WT/DS26/AB/R; WT/DS48/AB/R; AB-1997–4 . . . . 5–6, 36, 137, 154–6, 397
Hormones, (EC). See *EC—Measures concerning Meat and Meat Products (Hormones)*
Japan—Measures Affecting Agricultural Products, WT/DS76/AB/R, AB-1998–8 154
Japan—Measures Affecting the Importation of Apples, WT/DS245/AB/R; AB-2003–4 154
Salmon. See *Australia—Measures Affecting Importation of Salmon*
Shrimp-Turtles. See *US—Import Prohibition of Certain Shrimp and Shrimp Products*
US—Import Prohibition of Certain Shrimp and Shrimp Products, WT/DS58/AB/R; WT/DS58/AB/RW 155

Netherlands

Administrative Law Division of the Council of State (*ABRvS*), 25 May 1982, No. 1625 120
Administrative Law Division of the Council of State (*ABRvS*), 10 Feb. 2000. 117
Administrative Law Division of the Council of State (*ABRvS*), 10 Feb. 2000, No. E01.98.0406 117
Administrative Law Division of the Council of State (*ABRvS*), 22 Feb. 2001, No. . 200001521/1 117
Administrative Law Division of the Council of State (*ABRvS*), 27 June 2001, No. 200003667/1/R3. 117
Administrative Law Division of the Council of State (*ABRvS*), 12 Dec. 2001, No. 200001861/1. 117
Administrative Law Division of the Council of State (*ABRvS*), 17 Dec. 2003 117
Administrative Law Division of the Council of State (*ABRvS*), 3 Dec. 2004, No. 200409107/2.. 118
Administrative Law Division of the Council of State (*ABRvS*), 24 Dec. 2004, No. 200000690/I-A and 200101670/I. 118
Administrative Law Division of the Council of State (*ABRvS*), 9 Feb. 2005, No. 200202184/I and 200305972.. 118
Administrative Law Division of the Council of State (*ABRvS*), 1 June 2005, No. 200409107/2. 118
Administrative Law Division of the Council of State (*ABRvS*), 29 Aug. 2007, No. 20060602811 126
Administrative Law Division of the Council of State (*ABRvS*), 27 Feb. 2008, No. 200607555/1. 118
District Court of Amsterdam, 4 Oct. 2004, No. AWB 04/4114. 117
District Court of Leeuwarden, 17 July 1998. 124
District Court Leeuwarden, 31 Dec. 2003 117
President of the District Court of Leeuwarden, 21 Oct. 1997 123

Pakistan

Zia v. *WAPDA* 1994. 1

United Kingdom

Arscott v. *The Coal Authority* (2005) 514
Castle Cement v. *Environment Agency* (2001). 171–2
Joined cases *Solvent Resource Management* v. *Environment Agency*, and *OSS Group* v. *Environment Agency* (2007) 170, 175–81
Mayer Parry Recycling v. *Environment Agency* (1999) 169–70
The Queen v. *Environment Agency ex parte Mayer Parry (No 2)* (2001). 177
The Queen (On the Application of OSS Group Limited) v. *Environment Agency and Others (DEFRA, Intervening)* (2007) . . . . . vii, 162–81
The Queen (On the Application of Diane Barker) v. *London Borough of Bromley* (2006) 553–4
Scottish Power Generation Ltd. v. *Scottish Environment Protection Agency* (2005) 176–8
Solvent Resource Management v. *Environment Agency* (2007) 170, 175–81
OSS Group v. *Environment Agency* (2007). 170, 175–81

Table of Legislation

Australia

Environmental Protection and Biodiversity Conservation Act 1999 1
  s. 391 1
Intergovernmental Agreement on the Environment 1992 (IGAE) between the Commonwealth and the Australian States and Territories 604

Austria

Law on Federal Roads of 1971 452

Brazil

Constitution. 1
  Art. 225 1

Canada

Access to Information Act 318
Financial Administration Act 317

European Union

TREATIES

EC Treaty. *See* Treaty Establishing the European Community
Euratom Treaty. *See* Treaty Establishing the European Atomic Energy Community
EU Treaty. *See* Treaty on the European Union
Amsterdam Treaty. *See* Treaty of Amsterdam
Maastricht Treaty. *See* Treaty on the European Union
Rome Treaty. *See* Treaty Establishing the European Community
Treaty of Amsterdam 1997 (ToA). 48, 184
Treaty Establishing the European Atomic Energy Community 1957 (Euratom) . . . . ix, 182–217, 495–6
  Preamble 185–8
  Art. 1 188
  Art. 2 185
  Art. 2b 206
  Art. 2h 189
  Art. 7 211
  Art. 30 206
  Art. 31 206
  Art. 32 206
  Art. 35 188
  Art. 37 188
  Art. 40 656
  Art. 101 193
Treaty Establishing the European Community (EC Treaty/Treaty of Rome 1957, as amended) 1–47

Art. 2 5
Art. 3 . . . . . 5, 8
Art. 6 . . . . . 30, 84, 623
Art. 10 . . . . . 563–7, 601
Art. 14 165
Art. 28 . . . . . 13, 26–9, 40–4, 70, 573, 621
Art. 29 . . . . . 70, 573, 621
Art. 30 . . . . . 27, 41–4, 50–1, 63–7, 70, 573, 621
Art. 81 536
Art. 82 536
Art. 86 536
Art. 87 . . . . . 312, 536
Art. 89 312–3
Art. 92 312–3
Art. 93 312
Art. 95 (ex 100a) . . . . . viii, 5, 14, 19–20, 26–7, 45, 48–79, 146, 335, 377, 401, 439–40, 621
Art. 132 312
Art. 133 . . . . . 312, 567–9, 621
Art. 152 . . . . . 5, 8
Art. 153 . . . . . 5, 8, 18
Art. 172 88
Art. 174 (ex 130r) . . . . . ix, 28, 1–47, 60, 63, 84, 545, 564–5, 621
Art. 175 (ex 130s) 21, 24–5, 542, 545, 567–9, 621
Art. 176 . . . . . 15–6, 564, 569, 621
Art. 220 . . . . . 3, 27, 566
Art. 226 . . . . . 20, 27–8, 42, 351, 458, 466, 474, 514–5, 532, 536, 554–5, 576, 599–600
Art. 228 . . . . . 515–7, 536, 555, 599–600
Art. 230 . . . . . 27–8, 302, 417–8, 553, 600
Art. 232 (ex. Art. 177) 15–6
Art. 234 . . . . . 20, 26–7, 553
Art. 249 437–8
Art. 250 346
Art. 280 536
Art. 292 . . . . . 563, 566
Art. 300 568
Treaty on the European Union 1992 (TEU/Treaty of Maastricht) 159, 192, 600

DECISIONS

Council Framework Decision 2003/80/JHA on the Protection of the Environment through Criminal Law [2003] OJ L29/55 [Annulled] 601
EP and Council Dec. No. 2119/98/EC setting up a Network for the Epidemiological Surveillance and Control of Communicable Diseases in the Community [1998] OJ L268/1 534
EP and Council Dec. No. 2455/2001/EC establishing the List of Priority Substances in the Field of Water Policy and Amending Directive 2000/60/EC [2001] OJ L331/1 513
EP and Council Dec. No. 1786/2002/EC adopting a Programme of Community Action in the Field of Public Health [2002] OJ L271/1 534
EP and Council Dec. 1600/2002/EC laying down the Sixth Community Environment Action Programme [2002] OJ L242/1 . . . . . 173, 438, 447, 499, 534, 645
EP and Council Dec. 280/2004/EC concerning a Mechanism for Monitoring Community Greenhouse Gas Emissions and for Implementing the Kyoto Protocol [2004] OJ L49/1 351

EP and Council Dec. No. 1982/2006/EC concerning the Seventh Framework Programme of the European Community for Research, Technological Development and Demonstration Activities (2007–2013) [2006] OJ L412/1 658
Commission Dec. of 3 May 2000 Replacing Decision 94/3/EC Establishing a List of Wastes pursuant to Article 1(a) of Council Directive 75/442/EEC on Waste and Council Decision 94/904/EC establishing a List of Hazardous Waste pursuant to Article 1(4) of Council Directive 91/689/EEC on Hazardous Waste [2000] OJ L226/3 181
Commission Dec. of 7 Mar. 2007 repealing Decision 2005/317/EC on Emergency Measures regarding the Non-authorised Genetically Modified Organism Bt10 in Maize Products, COM(2007)674 402
Dec. 82/72/EEC concerning the Conclusion of the Convention on the Conservation of European Wildlife and Natural Habitats [1982] OJ L210/10 230
Commission Dec. 94/783/EC concerning the Prohibition of Pentachlorophenol (PCP) notified by the Federal Republic of Germany (*Germany PCP-II*) [1994] OJ L316/43 . . . . 53, 56, 59, 65–6, 69–70
Dec. 96/191/EC concerning the Conclusion of the Convention on the Protection of the Alps (Alpine Convention) [1996] OJ L61/31 446
Commission Dec. 96/211/EC concerning the Prohibition of Pentachlorophenol (PCP) notified by Denmark (*Denmark PCP*) [1996] OJ L68/32 . . . . 53, 56, 59, 70
Dec. 97/265/EC on the Recognition of the International Standard ISO 14001:1966 and the European Standard EN ISO 14001:1996 [1997] OJ L104/37 540–1
Dec. 97/266/EC concerning a Site Information Format for Proposed Natura 2000 Sites [1997] OJ L107/1 451
Dec. 98/294/EC concerning the Placing on the Market of Genetically Modified Maize (*Zea Mays L.* Line Mon 810), pursuant to Council Directive 90/220/EEC [1998] OJ L131/33 373
Commission Dec. 1999/391/EC concerning the Questionnaire relating to Council Directive 96/61/EC concerning Integrated Pollution Prevention and Control (IPPC) (implementation of Council Directive 91/692/EEC) [1999] OJ L148/39 541
Dec. 98/414/EC on the Ratification by the European Community of the Agreement for the Implementing of the Provisions of the United Nations Convention on the Law of the Sea of 10 December 1982 relating to the Conservation and Management of Straddling Stocks and Highly Migratory Fish Stocks [1998] OJ L189/14 565
Dec. 1999/468/EC Laying Down the Procedures for the Exercise of Implementing Powers Conferred on the Commission (Comitology Dec.) [1999] OJ L184/23 . . . . 143, 374–5, 415
Art. 5a 374
Commission Dec. 99/831/EC concerning the National Provisions notified by the Kingdom of the Netherlands concerning the Limitations of the Marketing and Use of Pentachlorophenol (PCP) (*Netherlands PCP*) [1999] OJ L329/15 . . . . 53–4, 56, 59, 70
Commission Dec. 1999/833/EC on the National Provisions notified by the Federal Republic of Germany concerning the Limitations of the Marketing and Use of Creosote (*Germany Creosote*) [1999] OJ L329/43 . . . . 57–62, 66
Dec. 2000/479/EC on the Implementation of a European Pollutant Emission Register (EPER) according to Article 15 [2000] OJ L192/36 526
Dec. 2001/76/EC Replacing the Decision of 4 April 1978 on the Application of Certain Guidelines in the Field of Officially Supported Export Credits [2001] OJ L32/1 312
Commission Dec. 2001/570/EC on Draft National Provisions notified by the Federal Republic of Germany on Limitations on the Marketing and Use of Organostannic Compounds (*Germany Organostannics*) [2001] OJ L202/37 . . . . 55–60, 64–6
Commission Dec. 2001/720/EC granting Portugal a Derogation regarding Urban Waste-Water Treatment for the Agglomeration of the Estoril Coast [2001] OJ L269/14 516
Dec. 2001/792/EC/Euratom establishing a Community Mechanism to Facilitate Reinforced Cooperation in Civil Protection Assistance Interventions [2001] OJ L297/7 542

Dec. 2001/839/EC laying down a Questionnaire to be used for Annual Reporting on Ambient Air Quality Assessment under Council Directives 96/62/EC and 1999/30/EC [2001] OJ L319/45 331–2
Art. 1 331–2
Commission Dec. 2002/59/EC concerning Draft National Provisions Notified by the Kingdom of the Netherlands under Article 95(5) of the EC Treaty on Limitations on the Marketing and Use of Creosote-Treated Wood (*Netherlands Creosote II*) [2002] OJ L23/37 . . . . . 50 -2, 55–63, 68
Dec. 2002/358/EC concerning the Approval, on Behalf of the European Community, of the Kyoto Protocol to the United Nations Framework Convention on Climate Change and the Joint Fulfilment of Commitments Thereunder [2002] OJ L130/1 341
Commission Dec. 2002/366/EC on the National Provisions Notified by the Republic of Austria under Article 95(4) of the EC Treaty concerning the Maximum Admissible Content of Cadmium in Fertilizers (*Austria Cadmium*) [2002] OJ L132/65 54–68
Commission Dec. 2002/399/EC on the National Provisions notified by the Kingdom of Sweden under Article 95(4) of the EC Treaty concerning the Maximum Admissible Content of Cadmium in Fertilizers (*Sweden Cadmium*) [2002] OJ L138/24 54–68
Commission Dec. 2003/1/EC relating to National Provisions on Limiting the Importation and Placement on the Market of Certain NK Fertilizers of High Nitrogen Content and Containing Chlorine notified by France pursuant to Article 95(5) of the EC Treaty (*France NK Fertilizers*) [2003] OJ L1/72 64
Dec. 2003/199/EC on the Non-inclusion of Aldicard in Annex I to Council Directive 91/414 [2003] OJ L76/21 436–7
Commission Dec. 2003/829/EC concerning National Provisions on the Use of Azodyes notified by Germany under Article 95(4) of the EC Treaty (*Germany Azodyes*) [2003] OJ L311/46 . . . . . 66–9, 72
Commission Dec. 2003/653/EC relating to National Provisions on Banning the Use of Genetically Modified Organisms in the Region of Upper Austria Notified by the Republic of Austria pursuant to Article 95(5) of the EC Treaty [2003] OJ L230/34 56
Commission Dec. 2005/317/EC on Emergency Measures Regarding the Non-Authorised Genetically Modified Organism *Bt*10 in Maize Products (*Bt*10 Emergency Measure Dec.) [2005] OJ L101/14 402
Dec. 2005/370/EC on the Conclusion on Behalf of the European Community of the Convention on Access to Information, Public Participation in the Decision-Making Process and Access to Justice in Environmental Matters [2005] OJ L124/1 524
Commission Dec. 2005/608/EC concerning the Placing on the Market, in Accordance with Directive 2001/18/EC, of a Maize Product (Zea Mays L., Line MON 863) Genetically Modified for Resistance to Corn Rootworm [2005] OJ L207/17 373
Commission Dec. 2006/10/EC concerning the Provisional Prohibition in Greece of the Marketing of Seeds of Maize Hybrids with the Genetic Modification MON 810 Inscribed in the Common Catalogue of Varieties of Agricultural Plant Species, Pursuant to Directive 2002/53/EC [2006] OJ L7/27 400–1
Dec. 2006/39/EC on the National Provisions notified by the Czech Republic under Article 95(4) of the EC Treaty concerning the Maximum Admissible Content of Cadmium in Fertilizers [2006] OJ L150/15 439–40
Commission Dec. 2006/47/EC concerning the Placing on the Market, in Accordance with Directive 2001/18/EC, of a Maize Product (Zea Mays L., Hybrid MON 863 × MON 810) Genetically Modified for Resistance to Corn Rootworm and Certain Lepidopteran Pests of Maize [2006] OJ L26/17 372–3
Dec. 2006/61/EC on the Conclusion, on behalf of the EC, of the UN/ECE Protocol on Pollutant Release and Transfer Registers [2006] OJ L32/54 525

Commission Dec. 2006/68/EC Authorising the Placing on the Market of Foods and Food Ingredients Derived from Genetically Modified Maize Line MON 863 as Novel Foods or Novel Food Ingredients under Regulation (EC) No. 258/97 [2006] OJ L34/26. 372–3
Commission Dec. 2006/69/EC Authorising the Placing on the Market of Foods and Food Ingredients Produced from Genetically Modified Roundup Ready Maize Line GA21 as Novel Foods or Novel Food Ingredients under Regulation (EC) No. 258/97 [2006] OJ L34/29. 372–3
Commission Dec. 2006/86/EC concerning Certain Interim Protection Measures in relation to Suspected Cases of Highly Pathogenic Avian Influenza in Wild Birds in Greece [2006] OJ L40/26 445–6
Commission Dec. 2006/115/EC concerning Certain Protection Measures in relation to Highly Pathogenic Avian Influenza in Wild Birds in the Community and repealing Decisions 2006/86/EC, 2006/90/EC, 2006/91/EC, 2006/94/EC, 2006/104/EC and 2006/105/EC [2006] OJ L48/28 445–6
Commission Dec. 2006/193/EC on the Use of the EMAS Logo on Tertiary Packaging [2006] OJ L70/63 541
Commission Dec. 2006/194/EC establishing a Questionnaire relating to Council Directive 96/61/EC concerning Integrated Pollution Prevention and Control (IPPC) [2006] OJ L70/65. 541
Annex 541
Commission Dec. 2006/197/EC Authorising the Placing on the Market of Food containing, consisting of, or produced from Genetically Modified Maize Line 1507 (DAS-O15O7–1) pursuant to Regulation (EC) No. 1829/2003 [2006] OJ L70/82 . . . . 373, 379
Dec. 2006/235/EC on the Conclusion, on behalf of the European Community, of the Agreement between the European Community and the Swiss Confederation concerning the latter's participation in the European Environment Agency and the European Environment Information and Observation Network [2006] OJ L90/36. 541
Commission Dec. 2006/255/EC concerning National Provisions Imposing on Supermarkets an Obligation to Place Genetically Modified Foods on Separate Shelves from Non-Genetically Modified Foods, Notified by Cyprus Pursuant to Article 95(5) of the EC Treaty [2006] OJ L92/12 401
Commission Dec. 2006/310/EC amending, for the purposes of Adapting to the Technical Progress, the Annex to Directive 2002/95/EC of the European Parliament and of the Council as regards Exemptions for Applications of Lead [2006] OJ L115/38. 503
Commission Dec. 2006/335/EC Authorising the Republic of Poland to Prohibit on Its Territory the Use of 16 Genetically Modified Varieties of Maize with the Genetic Modification MON 810 Listed in the Common Catalogue of Varieties of Agricultural Plant Species, Pursuant to Council Directive 2002/53/EC [2006] OJ L24/26. 400
Commission Dec. 2006/348/EC on the National Provisions notified by the Republic of Finland under Article 95(4) of the EC Treaty concerning the Maximum Admissible Content of Cadmium in Fertilizers (*Finland Cadmium II*) [2006] OJ L129/25 62–8
Commission Dec. 2006/348/EC on the National Provisions notified by the Republic of Finland under Article 95(4) of the EC Treaty concerning Maximum Admissible Content of Cadmium in Fertilizers [2006] OJ L129/25. 439–40
Commission Dec. 2006/349/EC on the National Provisions notified by the Republic of Austria under Article 95(4) of the EC Treaty concerning the Maximum Content of Cadmium in Fertilizers [2006] OJ L129/31 439–40
Dec. 2006/350/EC determining the Quantities of Methyl Bromide permitted to be used for Critical Uses in the Community from 1 January to 31 December 2006 pursuant to Regulation (EC) No. 2037/2000 of the European Parliament and of the Council on Substances that Deplete the Ozone Layer (2006/350/EC) [2006] OJ L130/29 327

Dec. 2006/372/EC concerning Draft National Provisions notified by the Kingdom of the Netherlands under Article 95(5) of the EC Treaty laying down Limits on the Emissions of Particulate Matter by Diesel Powered Vehicles [2006] OJ L142/16 335
Commission Dec. 2006/374/EC on the National Provisions notified by the Kingdom of Sweden under Article 95(4) of the EC Treaty concerning the Maximum Admissible Content of Cadmium in Fertilizers [2006] OJ L129/19. 439–40
Dec. 2006/402/EC establishing the Community Eco-label Working Plan [2006] OJ L162/78. 537–8
Art. 1 537
Art. 2. 537
Commission Dec. 2006/512/EC amending Decision 1999/468/EC laying down the Procedures for the Exercise of Implementing Powers Conferred on the Commission (New Comitology Dec.) [2006] OJ L200/11 . . . . 374–5, 415
Art. 1. 374
Commission Dec. 2006/578/EC on Emergency Measures Regarding the Non-Authorised Genetically Modified Organism LL RICE 601 in Rice Products (Provisional LL 601 Rice Emergency Measure Dec.) [2006] OJ L230/8 368–70
Commission Dec. 2006/601/EC on Emergency Measures Regarding the Non-Authorised Genetically Modified Organism LL RICE 601 in Rice Products (LL 601 Rice Emergency Measure Dec.) [2006] OJ L244/27 370–1
Art. 1. 370–1
Dec. 2006/613/EC adopting, pursuant to Directive 92/43/EEC, the List of Sites of Community Importance for the Mediterranean biogeographical region [2006] OJ L259/1 442–4
Preamble 443
Dec. 2006/655/EC on the Approval, on behalf of the European Community, of the Protocol on the Implementation of the 1991 Alpine Convention in the Field of Mountain Farming [2006] OJ L271/61 446
Commission Dec. 2006/690/EC amending, for the Purposes of Adapting to Technical Progress, the Annex to Directive 2002/95/EC as regards Exemptions for Applications of Lead in Crystal Glass [2006] OJ L283/47. 503
Commission Dec. 2006/691/EC amending, for the Purposes of Adapting to Technical Progress, the Annex to Directive 2002/95/EC as regards Exemptions for Applications of Lead and Cadmium [2006] OJ L283/48. 503
Commission Dec. 2006/692/EC amending, for the Purposes of Adapting to Technical Progress, the Annex to Directive 2002/95/EC as regards Exemptions for Applications of Hexavalent Chromium [2006] OJ L283/50 503
Dec. 2006/730/EC on the Conclusion, on behalf of the European Community, of the Rotterdam Convention on the Prior Informed Consent Procedure for certain Hazardous Chemicals and Pesticides in International Trade [2006] OJ L299/23 569
Commission Dec. 2006/754/EC Amending Decision 2006/601/EC on Emergency Measures Regarding the Non-Authorised Genetically Modified Organism 'LL RICE 601' in Rice Products [2006] OJ L306/17 370–1
Commission Dec. 2006/780/EC on Avoiding Double Counting of Greenhouse Gas Emission Reductions under the Community Emissions Trading Scheme for Project Activities under the Kyoto Protocol pursuant to Directive 2003/87/EC [2006] OJ L316/12. 346–7
Preamble 346
Art. 3. 347
Art. 4. 347
Annexes. 347
Dec. 2006/871/EC on the Conclusion on behalf of the European Community of the Agreement on the Conservation of African-Eurasian Migratory Waterbirds [2006] OJ

L345/25 . . . . 254–6, 442–3
Art. 3 256
Art. 4 256
Decision 2006/957/EC on the Conclusion, on Behalf of the European Community, of an Amendment to the Convention on Access to Information, Public Participation in Decision-making and Access to Justice in Environmental Matters [2006] OJ L386/46 . . . . 368, 387
Dec. 2006/1009/EC concerning the Non-inclusion of Dimethanamid in Annex I to Council Directive 91/414/ECC and the Withdrawal of the Authorizations for Plant Protection Products containing that Substance [2006] OJ L379/125 426
Dec. 2006/1010 concerning the Non-inclusion of Phosalone in Annex I to Council Directive 91/414/EEC and the Withdrawal of Authorizations for Plant Protection Products containing that Substance [2006] OJ L379/127 426

DIRECTIVES

Dir. 65/65/EEC relating to Proprietary Medicinal Products [1965] OJ L22/369 38–9
Art. 11 38
Dir. 67/548/EEC relating to the Classification, Packaging, and Labelling of Dangerous Substances (Dangerous Substances Packaging Dir.) [1967] OJ L196/1 . . . . 70, 409–13, 428–31
Annex I 428–30
Dir. 70/220/EEC relating to Measures to be taken against Air Pollution by Gases from Positive-ignition Engines of Motor Vehicles [1970] OJ L76/1 335
Dir. 75/439/EEC on the Disposal of Waste Oils (Waste Oils Dir.) [1975] OJ L194/23 509
Dir. 75/442/EEC on Waste (Waste Framework Dir.) [1975] OJ L194/38; amended by Dir. 91/156/EEC [1991] OJ L78/32; and by Dir. 2006/12/EC [2006] OJ L114/9 . . . . 21–2, 25–6, 162–81, 489–90, 497, 504–9, 526
Art. 1 . . . . 162, 165
Art. 4 . . . . 22, 507
Art. 8 22
Art. 15 25
Annex IIA 22, 167–71, 526
Annex IIB 22, 167–71
Dir. 76/160/EEC concerning the Quality of Bathing Water (Bathing Water Dir.) [1976] OJ L31/1 . . . . 510–1, 521–2
Dir. 76/464/EEC on Pollution Caused by certain Dangerous Substances Discharged into the Aquatic Environment (Dangerous Substances Discharge Dir.) [1976] OJ L129/23 517
Annex 513
Dir. 76/768/EC on Cosmetic Products (Cosmetics Dir.) [1976] OJ L262/169 406–8
Art. 2 407–8
Dir. 76/769/EEC on Restrictions on the Marketing and Use of Certain Dangerous Substances and Preparations (Marketing and Use Restrictions Dir.) [1976] OJ L262/201 . . . 70, 419–24
Annex I 70, 419, 423
Annex XVIII 419
Dir. 79/409/EEC on the Conservation of Wild Birds (Birds Dir.) [1979] OJ L103/1 . . . . viii, 92–4, 97, 109–10, 114–7, 127, 131, 218–9, 230–45, 255–6, 261–3,442–3, 447–57, 468, 472–7, 489, 571–2, 666, 669
Preamble 231–2, 455
Art. 1 233
Art. 2 . . . . 233, 472–3
Art. 3 . . . . 93, 233, 472–3

Art. 4 . . . . . 93, 233–8, 449–52, 456–7, 472–3
Art. 5 . . . . . 233, 453, 476
Art. 6 . . . . . 449, 452–3, 457
Art. 7 . . . . . 236–7, 453
Art. 8 . . . . . 453, 477
Art. 9 . . . . . 237–8, 453–7, 477, 571
Art. 10 477
Art. 12 475–6
Art. 16 454
Annex I 93, 234–6, 450–1, 456–7, 468
Annex II 93, 236, 457
Dir. 79/923/EEC on the Quality Required of Shellfish Waters (Shellfish Water Dir.) [1979] OJ L281/47 517
Dir. 80/68/EEC on the Protection of Groundwater against Pollution Caused by Certain Dangerous Substances (Groundwater Dir.) [1980] OJ L20/43 511–2
Dir. 82/176/EEC on Limit Values and Quality Objectives for Mercury Discharges from the Chlor-alkali Electrolysis Industry [1982] OJ L81/29 513
Dir. 85/203/EEC on Air Quality Standards for Nitrogen Dioxide [1985] OJ L87/1 69
Art. 5 69
Dir. 83/513/EEC on Limit Values and Quality Objectives for Cadmium Discharges [1983] OJ L291/1 513
Dir. 84/156/EEC on Limit Values and Quality Objectives for Mercury Discharges by Sectors other than the Chlor-alkali Electrolysis Industry [1984] OJ L74/49 513
Dir. 84/491/EEC on Limit Values and Quality Objectives for Discharges of Hexachlorocyclohexane [1984] OJ L274/11 513
Dir. 85/337/EEC on the Assessment of the Effects of certain Public and Private Projects on the Environment (EIA Dir./Environmental Impact Assessment Dir.) [1985] OJ L175/40; amended by Dir. 97/11/EC [1997] OJ L73/5 . . . . . 21, 453, 459–60, 553–5, 575–8
Art. 1 . . . . . 460, 553–4, 577
Art. 2 . . . . . 21, 554, 576
Art. 4 . . . . . 554, 576
Art. 5 . . . . . 69, 576
Art. 6 577–8
Art. 8 576–8
Annex II 576
Dir. 86/280/EEC on Limit Values and Quality Objectives for Discharges of Certain Dangerous Substances included in List 1 of the Annex to Directive 76/464/EEC [1986] OJ L221/51 513
Dir. 86/278/EEC on the Protection of the Environment, and in particular of the Soil, when Sewage Sludge is Used in Agriculture (Sewage Sludge Dir.) [1986] OJ L181/6 509
Dir. 90/219/EEC on the Contained Use of Genetically Modified Micro-Organisms (Contained Use Dir.) [1990] OJ L117/1 375–6
Dir. 90/220/EEC on the Deliberate Release into the Environment of Genetically Modified Organisms ((Former) Deliberate Release Dir.) [1990] OJ L117/15 . . . . . 142, 375–6
Dir. 90/313/EEC on Freedom of Access to Information on the Environment ((former) Access to Information Dir.) [1990] OJ L158/56; repealed by Dir. 2003/4/EC [2003] OJ L41/26 . . . . . xi, 578, 600
Dir. 91/156/EEC amending Directive 75/442/EEC ((Revised) Waste Framework Dir.) [1991] OJ L78/32, amended by Dir. 2006/12/EC 21–2, 25–6, 162–81, 489–90, 497, 504–9
Art. 1 21
Art. 4 . . . . . 22, 507
Art. 8 22

Annex IIA 22, 167–71
Annex IIB 22, 167–71
Dir. 91/157/EEC on Batteries and Accumulators Containing Certain Dangerous Substances ((Former) Batteries Dir.) [1991] OJ L78/38 499–500
Dir. 91/271/EEC concerning Urban Waste-Water Treatment (Urban Waste-Water Dir.) [1991] OJ L135/40 . . . . . 21, 511, 515–6
Dir. 91/414/EEC concerning the Placing of Plant Protection Products on the Market (Pesticides Dir.) [1997] OJ L353/26. . . . . 424–7, 431–9, 542–3, 550, 669
Art. 4 438
Art. 8 436–8
Annex I 426, 436–8
Annex II 432
Dir. 91/676/EEC concerning the Protection of Waters against Pollution Caused by Nitrates from Agricultural Sources (Nitrates Dir.) [1991] OJ L375/1. . . . . 19, 511, 515–7
Dir. 91/689/EEC on Hazardous Waste (Hazardous Waste Dir.) [1991] OJ L377/20 . . . . . 509, 525–6
Art. 8 526
Dir. 92/3/Euratom on the Supervision and Control of Shipments of Radioactive Waste between Member States and into and out of the Community [1992] OJ L35/24, amended by Dir. 2006/117/Euratom [2006] OJ L337/28. 495–6
Art. 3 495
Art. 5 495
Art. 6 496
Art. 9 496
Art. 12 496
Art. 15 496
Dir. 92/32/EEC Amending for the Seventh Time Dir. 67/548/EEC on the Classification, Packaging and Labelling of Dangerous Substances [1992] OJ L154/1 410
Dir. 92/40/EEC introducing Community Measures for the Control of Avian Influenza [1992] OJ L167/1 445–6
Dir. 92/43/EEC on the Conservation of Natural Habitats and of Wild Fauna and Flora (Habitats Dir.) [1992] OJ L206/7 . . . . . viii, 21, 23, 92–5, 97, 109–10, 114–9, 123, 127, 131–2, 218–9, 230, 238–63, 442–3, 447–53, 457–75, 481, 488–9, 570–2, 669
Preamble 115, 463
Art. 2 115
Art. 3 . . . . . 238, 470–1
Art. 4 . . . . . 93, 238, 470–1
Art. 6 . . . . . 23, 93–5, 114–9, 123, 131–2, 240, 449, 452, 457–62, 468–9, 470–2, 489
Art. 7 . . . . . 93, 240
Art. 10 239
Art. 12 . . . . . 239, 259, 457, 462–9, 472
Art. 13 . . . . . 457, 463–4
Art. 15 466
Art. 16 . . . . . 457, 462–6, 472
Art. 23 . . . . . 6, 465
Annex I 238, 450–1, 481
Annex II 238, 481
Annex III . . . . . 471, , 481, 570–1
Annex IV 239, 246, 259, 464–6, 469, 481
Annex V 466, 481
Annex VI 465–6, 481

Dir. 92/75/EEC on the Indication by Labelling and Standard Product Information of the Consumption of Energy and other Resources by Household Appliances [1992] OJ L297/16 359
Dir. 94/62/EC on Packaging and Packaging Waste (Packaging and Packaging Waste Dir.) [1994] OJ L365/10 . . . . . 509, 666
Dir. 95/2/EC on Food Additives other than Colours and Sweeteners (Food Additives Dir.) [1995] OJ L61/1 66
Dir. 96/29/Euratom laying down Basic Safety Standards for the Protection of the Health of Workers and the General Public against the Dangers arising from Ionising Radiation [1996] OJ L314/20 495
Dir. 96/61/EC concerning Integrated Pollution Prevention and Control (IPPC Dir.) [1996] OJ L257/26 . . . . . 346–7, 493, 525–6, 529, 541, 555–9, 613–4
Art. 9 558
Art. 15 526
Art. 16 . . . . . 541, 557
Dir. 96/62/EC On Ambient Air Quality and Management (Air Quality Framework Dir.) [1996] OJ L296/55 . . . . . 328–32, 669
Art. 3 332
Art. 4 331–2
Art. 11 331–2
Dir. 97/11/EC amending Dir. 85/337/EEC on the Assessment of the Effects of certain Public and Private Projects on the Environment ((New) EIA Dir./(New) Environmental Impact Assessment Dir.) [1997] OJ L73/5 553–4
Dir. 98/8/EC concerning the Placing of Biocidal Products on the Market (Biocides Dir.) [1998] OJ L123/1 . . . . . 423–5, 436–9, 550
Art. 16 . . . . . 423–5, 437
Annex I 424–5
Annex IA 424
Annex IVA 424–5
Annex IVB 424–5
Dir. 98/29/EC on Harmonisation of the Main Provisions Concerning Export Credit Insurance for Transactions with Medium and Long Term Cover (Credit Insurance Dir.) [1998] OJ L148/22 312
Dir. 98/34/EC laying down a Procedure for the Provision of Information in the Field of Technical Standards and Regulations [1998] OJ L204/37 376–7
Dir. 98/44/EC on the Legal Protection of Biotechnological Inventions (Biotechnology Patent Dir./Biotech Dir.) [1998] OJ L213/13 282–4
Preamble 283–4
Dir. 98/70/EC relating to the Quality of Petrol and Diesel Fuels and Amending Directive 93/12/EEC (Fuel Quality Dir.) [1998] OJ L350/58 336
Art. 8 336
Dir. 98/83/EC on the Quality of Water Intended for Human Consumption (Drinking Water Dir.) [2006] OJ L330/21 517
Dir. 1999/22/EC relating to the Keeping of Wild Animals in Zoos (Zoos Dir.) [1999] OJ L94/24 475
Art. 4 475
Art. 13 40
Dir. 1999/30/EC relating to Limit Values for Sulphur Dioxide, Nitrogen Dioxide and Oxides of Nitrogen, Particulate Matter, and Lead in Ambient Air (First Air Quality Daughter Dir.) [1999] OJ L163/41 331–2
Art. 3 332

Art. 5 . . . 332
Art. 9 . . . 332
Annex I . . . 331–2
Annex II . . . 332
Annex III . . . 332
Annex IV . . . 332
Annex V . . . 332
Dir. 1999/31/EC on the Landfill of Waste (Waste Landfill Dir.) [1999] OJ L182/1 . . . 15, 497, 509
Dir. 1999/33/EC amending Council Dir. 67/548/EEC as Regards the Labelling of Certain Dangerous Substances in Austria and Sweden [1999] OJ L1999/57 . . . 70
Dir. 1999/45/EC on the Classification, Packaging, and Labelling of Dangerous Preparations (Dangerous Preparations Dir.) [1999] OJ L200/1 . . . 408, 413–5, 427–31
Annex II . . . 427
Annex III . . . 427–8
Annex V . . . 428
Annex VI . . . 427
Dir. 1999/94/EC relating to the Availability of Consumer Information on Fuel Economy and CO2 Emissions in Respect of the Marketing of New Passenger Cars (CO_2 Labelling Dir.) [1999] OJ L12/16 . . . 333
Art. 9 . . . 333
Dir. 2000/53/EC on End-of-Life Vehicles (ELV Dir.) [2000] OJ L269/34 . . . 500–1, 666
Dir. 2000/60/EC establishing a Framework for Community Action in the Field of Water Policy (Water Framework Dir.) [2000] OJ L327/1 . . . 70, 106, 439, 448–9, 460, 498, 510–23, 574–5, 666, 669
Preamble . . . 512
Art. 1 . . . 515
Art. 3 . . . 513
Art. 16 . . . 512
Dir. 2001/18/EC on the Deliberate Release into the Environment of Genetically Modified Organisms and Repealing Dir. 90/220/EEC ((Revised) Deliberate Release Dir.) [2001] OJ L106/1 . . . 1, 14–5, 20, 135, 142–7, 160–1, 371–6, 399–400, 424, 541–2, 666
Preamble . . . 1
Art. 4 . . . 143
Art. 13 . . . 143
Art. 14 . . . 143
Art. 15 . . . 143
Art. 23 . . . 146, 399
Annex 26a . . . 147
Art. 30 . . . 146
Annex II . . . 143
Dir. 2001/42/EC on the Assessment of the Effects of certain Plans and Programmes on the Environment (SEA Dir./Strategic Environmental Impact Assessment Dir.) [2001] OJ L197/30 . . . 525, 559–61
Art. 2 . . . 560
Art. 3 . . . 560
Art. 11 . . . 561
Art. 12 . . . 559–60
Dir. 2001/59/EC adapting to technical progress for the 28th time Council Directive 67/548/EEC on the Classification, Packaging and Labelling of Dangerous Substances [2001] OJ L225/1 . . . 428

Dir. 2001/77/EC on the Promotion of Electricity Produced from Renewable Energy Sources in the Internal Electricity Market (RES Dir.) [2001] OJ L283/33 .... 197, 351–2
Art. 3 352
Art. 10 352
Dir. 2001/83/EC on the Community Code relating to Medicinal Products for Human Use (Medicines Dir.) [2001] OJ L311/67 406
Dir. 2002/49/EC relating to the Assessment and Management of Environmental Noise [2002] OJ L189/12 332
Art. 14 332–3
Dir. 2002/53/EC on the Common Catalogue of Agricultural Plant Species (Common Catalogue Dir.) [2002] OJ L193/1 399–400
Art. 16 399
Art. 18 399–400
Art. 23 399
Dir. 2002/91/EC on the Energy Performance of Buildings [2003] OJ L1/65 358
Dir. 2002/95/EC on the Restriction of the Use of Certain Hazardous Substances in Electrical and Electronic Equipment (RoHS Dir.) [2003] OJ L37/19 .... 441, 500, 503–4
Art. 4 503
Art. 5 503
Annex 503
Dir. 2002/96/EC on Waste Electrical and Electronic Equipment (WEEE Dir.) [2003] OJ L37/24 .... 499–502, 509–10
Dir. 2003/4/EC on Public Access to Environmental Information and Repealing Dir. 90/313/EEC ((New) Access to Information Dir.) [2003] OJ L41/26 .... xi, 158–9, 528–9, 534, 555, 578, 600
Art. 4 528
Art. 6 529
Dir. 2003/30/EC on the Promotion of the Use of Biofuels and other Renewable Fuels for Transport (Biofuels Dir.) [2003] OJ L123/1 .... 352, 360, 653
Art. 3 352
Art. 4 352
Dir. 2003/35/EC Providing for Public Participation in respect of the Drawing up of certain Plans and Programmes relating to the Environment and Amending with regard to Public Participation and Access to Justice Council Dirs. 85/337/EEC and 96/61/EC (Public Participation in Plans and Programmes Dir.) [2003] OJ L156/17 .... 431–2, 554–5
Dir. 2003/87/EC establishing a Scheme for Greenhouse Gas Emission Allowance Trading within the Community and Amending Dir. 96/61/EC (Emissions Trading Dir.) [2003] OJ L275/32 .... 346–51, 354–7, 613–4, 666
Art. 9 .... 348, 351
Art. 10 348
Art. 11 347
Art. 14 614
Art. 16 614
Art. 30 .... 347, 350, 355, 666
Annexes 613
Annex III 348, 354
Dir. 2003/112/EC amending Dir. 91/414/EEC to include Paraquat as an Active Substance [2003] OJ L321/32 553
Dir. 2003/122/Euratom on the Control of High-activity Sealed Radioactive Sources and Orphan Sources [2003] OJ L346/57 495

Dir. 2004/35/EC on Environmental Liability with regard to the Prevention and Remedying of Environmental Damage (Environmental Liability Dir.) [2004] OJ L143/56 . . . . . . 147, 497, 543–5, 601, 650–2
Art. 18 147
Dir. 2004/101/EC amending Dir. 2003/87/EC establishing a Scheme for Greenhouse Gas Emission Allowance Trading within the Community, in respect of the Kyoto Protocol's Project Mechanisms (Linking Dir.) [2004] OJ L338/18 614
Dir. 2005/32/EC Establishing a Framework for the Setting of Eco-design Requirements for Energy-using Products and Amending Directives 92/42/EEC, 96/57/EC and 2000/55/EC (Eco-Design Dir./Energy Using Products Dir.) [2005] OJ L191/29 668
Dir. 2005/33/EC Amending Directive 1999/32/EC as regards the Sulphur Content of Marine Fuels (Sulphur-free Shipping Fuel Dir.) [2005] OJ L191/59 333–4
Dir. 2006/7/EC concerning the Management of Bathing Water Quality and repealing Directive 76/160/EEC [2006] OJ L64/37 (Revised/New Bathing Water Dir.) 510–1, 521–2
Dir. 2006/8/EC amending, for the purposes of their adaptation to technical progress, Annex II, III and VI to Directive 1999/45/EC on the Classification, Packaging and Labelling of Dangerous Preparations ((Revised) Dangerous Preparations Dir.) [2006] OJ L19/12 427–8
Dir. 2006/12/EC on Waste Framework ((Revised) Waste Framework Dir./WFD) [2006] OJ L114/9 . . . . . . 162–81, 405, 489–90, 493, 497, 504–9
Preamble 162–4
Art. 1 . . . . . . 162, 165–73, 504–5
Art. 2 166
Art. 3 . . . . . . 180, 493
Art. 4 493
Art. 7 493
Art. 10 493
Art. 19 505
Art. 29 505
Annex I 162, 165–9
Annex IIA 167–72
Annex IIB 167–72
Dir. 2006/21/EC on the Management of Waste from Extractive Industries and Amending Directive 2004/35/EC (Mining Waste Dir.) [2006] OJ L102/15 497–9
Preamble 498
Art. 2 497
Art. 5 498
Art. 6 498–9
Art. 7 497
Art. 10 498
Art. 12 499
Art. 13 498
Art. 14 497
Art. 22 497
Art. 24 497
Art. 25 497
Art. 26 497
Annex II 498
Annex III 501
Dir. 2006/32/EC on Energy End-use Efficiency and Energy Services and Repealing Council Directive 93/76/EEC [2006] OJ L114/64 (Energy Services Dir.) 344–6

Art. 1 . . . 345
Art. 3 . . . 345
Art. 4 . . . 345
Art. 5 . . . 345
Art. 6 . . . 345
Art. 7 . . . 345
Art. 13 . . . 345
Art. 18 . . . 346
Art. 19 . . . 3462
Annexes . . . 345
Dir. 2006/39/EC amending Council Directive 91/414/EEC to include Clodainfop, Pirimicarb, Risufuron, Tolclofos-methyl and Triticonazole as Active Substances [2006] OJ L104/30 . . . 426
Dir. 2006/44/EC on the Quality of Fresh Waters Needing Protection or Improvement in order to Support Fish Life [2006] OJ L264/20 . . . 510–1
Art. 3 . . . 511
Art. 5 . . . 511
Annex I . . . 511
Dir. 2006/50/EC amending Annexes IVA and IVB to Directive 98/8/EC on the Placing on the Market of Biocidal Products [2006] OJ L142/6 . . . 424
Dir. 2006/66/EC on Batteries and Accumulators and Waste Batteries and Accumulators and repealing Directive 91/157/EEC (Revised/New Batteries Dir.) [2006] OJ L266/1 . . . 499–503
Art. 2 . . . 500
Art. 3 . . . 500–1
Art. 4 . . . 500
Art. 8 . . . 500
Art. 9 . . . 501
Art. 10 . . . 501
Art. 11 . . . 502
Art. 12 . . . 501
Art. 13 . . . 501
Art. 14 . . . 501
Art. 16 . . . 501–2
Art. 17 . . . 502
Art. 18 . . . 502
Art. 20 . . . 501–2
Art. 21 . . . 502
Art. 27 . . . 503
Annex III . . . 501
Dir. 2006/131/EC amending Council Directive 91/414/EEC to include Methamidophos as an Active Substance [2006] OJ L349/17 . . . 426
Dir. 2006/132/EC amending Council Directive 91/414/EEC to include Procymidone as an Active Substance [2006] OJ L349/22 . . . 426
Dir. 2006/133/EC amending Council Directive 91/414/EEC to include Flusilazole as an Active Substance [2006] OJ L349/27 . . . 426
Dir. 2006/134/EEC amending Council Directive 91/414/EEC to include Fenarimol as an Active Substance [2006] OJ L349/32 . . . 426
Dir. 2006/135/EC amending Council Directive 91/414/EEC to include Carbendazim as an Active Substance [2006] OJ L149/37 . . . 426
Dir. 2006/136/EC amending Council Directive 91/414/EEC to include Dinocap as an Active Substance [2006] OJ L149/42 . . . 426

Dir. 2006/139/EC amending Council Directive 76/769/EEC as regards Restrictions on the Marketing and Use of Arsenic Compounds for the purpose of adapting its Annex I to Technical Progress [2006] OJ L384/94. 423
Dir. 2006/140/EC amending Directive 98/8/EC to Include Sulfuryl Fluoride as an Active Substance in Annex I Thereto [2006] OJ L414/78 425
Dir. 2007/76/EC on the Incineration of Waste (WID /Waste Incineration Dir.) [2007] OJ L332/91 175–7
Art. 3 177
Dir. 2006/117/Euratom on the Supervision and Control of Shipments of Radioactive Waste and Spent Fuel [2006] OJ L337/28 495–6
Art. 3 495
Art. 5 495
Art. 6 496
Art. 8 496
Art. 9 496
Art. 12 496
Art. 17 496
Art. 20 496

REGULATIONS

Reg. (EEC) No. 3600/92 on detailed rules for the Implementation of the First Stage of the Programme of Work of Council Directive 91/414/EEC [1992] OJ L366/10 426
Reg. (EEC) No. 259/93 on the Supervision and Control of Shipments of Waste within, into and out of the European Community (Waste Shipments Reg.) [1993] OJ L30/1 . . . . 490–9, 504–8, 572–4, 666–7
Art. 2 572–3
Art. 4 493
Art. 6 572–4
Art. 7 . . . . 493, 572–4
Reg. (EEC) No. 793/93 on the Evaluation and Control of the Risks of Existing Substances (Existing Substances Reg.) [1993] OJ L84/1 409
Reg. (EC) No. 1164/94 establishing a Cohesion Fund [1994] OJ L130/1 555
Reg. (EC) No. 258/97 concerning Novel Foods and Novel Food Ingredients (Novel Foods Reg.) [1997] OJ L43/1 . . . . 18–9, 24–5, 142, 372
Art. 3 18
Art. 5 18
Art. 12 . . . . 18–9, 24–5
Reg. (EC) No. 338/97 on the Protection of Species of Wild Fauna and Flora by Regulating Trade Therein (CITES Reg.) [1997] OJ L61/1; amended by Reg. (EC) No. 1332/2005 [2005] OJ L215/1 . . . . 443–5, 488
Art. 8 445
Annex A 443–5
Annex B 443–5
Reg. (EC) No. 1139/98 concerning the Compulsory Indication of the Labelling of Certain Foodstuffs Produced from Genetically Modified Organisms of Particulars other Than Those Provided for in Directive 79/112/EEC (Former GM Food Labelling Reg.) [1998] OJ L159/4; amended by Commission Reg. (EC) No. 49/2000 [2000] OJ L6/13. 17
Art. 2 17
Reg. (EC) No. 2821/98 Amending, as regards Withdrawal of the Authorisation of Certain Antibiotics, Directive 70/224/EEC concerning Additives in Feeding Stuff s [1998] OJ L351/4 32–40

Preamble 32, 40
Reg. (EC) No. 1257/1999 on Support for Rural Development from the European Agricultural Guidance and Guarantee Fund (EAGGF) and amending and repealing certain Regulations [1999] OJ L160/80 559–60
Art. 49 560
Reg. (EC) No. 1260/1999 laying down General Provisions on the Structural Funds (Structural Funds Reg.)) [1999] OJ L161/1 559–61
Art. 2 560
Reg. (EC) No. 999/2001 laying down Rules for the Prevention, Control and Eradication of Certain Transmissible Spongiform Encephalopathies [2001] OJ L147/1 40
Preamble 40
Art. 13 40
Reg. (EC) No. 1980/2000 on a Revised Community Eco-Label Award Scheme ((Revised) Eco-Label Reg.) [2000] OJ L237/1 . . . . 70, 537–40
Reg. (EC) No. 2037/2000 on Substances that Deplete the Ozone Layer (Ozone Reg.) [2000] OJ L244/1 . . . . 327, 333
Art. 16 333
Art. 17 333
Reg. (EC) No. 761/2001 Allowing Voluntary Participation by Organisations in a Community Eco–Management and Audit Scheme ((Revised) EMAS Reg.) [2001] OJ L114/1 540–1
Annex I 540–1
Reg. (EC) No. 1049/2001 Regarding Public Access to European Parliament, Council and Commission Documents (Public Access to Documents Reg.) [2001] OJ L145/43 . . . . 158, 398–9, 529
Preamble 532–3
Art. 2 532–6
Art. 4 . . . . 398–9, 533–4
Art. 5 533
Art. 6 . . . . 529, 533
Art. 7 . . . . 529, 534
Art. 8 . . . . 529, 534
Art. 9 535–6
Art. 10 536–7
Art. 11 . . . . 532, 537
Art. 12 . . . . 532, 537
Art. 13 . . . . 532, 537
Reg. (EC) No. 1808/2001 laying down Detailed Rules concerning the Implementation of Council Regulation (EC) No. 338/97 on the Protection of Species of Wild Fauna and Flora by Regulating Trade Therein [2001] OJ L250/1 445
Reg. (EC) No. 178/2002 Laying Down the General Principles and Requirements of Food Law, Establishing the European Food Safety Authority and Laying Down Procedures in Matters of Food Safety (General Food Law Reg./Food Safety Reg.) [2002] OJ L31/1 . . . . 84, 145, 368–70, 407
Art. 53 368–9
Reg. (EC) No. 2371/2002 on the Conservation and Sustainable Exploitation of Fisheries Resources under the Common Fisheries Policy [2002] OJ L358/59 246
Art. 2 246
Reg. (EC) No. 304/2003 concerning the Export and Import of Dangerous Chemicals (Chemicals Export and Import Reg.) [2003] OJ L63/1 . . . . 435, 567–9, 666
Reg. (EC) No. 1829/2003 on Genetically Modified Food and Feed (GM Food and Feed Reg.) [2003] OJ L268/1 . . . . 143–7, 366–8, 373–5, 379–80, 541–2

Art. 2 144
Art. 4 143
Art. 5 143
Art. 6 143–5
Art. 7 . . . . . 143, 147
Art. 12 380
Art. 13 144
Art. 16 143
Art. 17 143
Art. 18 143
Art. 19 . . . . . 143, 147
Art. 24 144
Art. 25 144
Art. 28 143
Art. 32 366–7
Art. 34 146
Art. 43 147
Art. 46 379
Art. 48 379
Annex 367
Reg. (EC) No. 1830/2003 concerning the Traceability and Labelling of Genetically Modified Organisms and the Traceability of Food and Feed Products Produced from Genetically Modified Organisms and Amending Dir. 2001/18/EC (GM Traceability and Labelling Reg.) [2003] OJ L268/24 . . . . . 144, 367, 380–1, 666
Art. 4 144
Art. 5 144
Art. 6 144
Art. 12 381
Reg. (EC) No. 2003/2003 on Fertilizers [2005] OJ L304/1 439–40
Reg. (EC) No. 2032/2003 on the Second Phase of the Ten-Year Work Program Referred to in Art. 16(2) of Dir. 98/8/EC (Second Review Reg.) [2003] OJ L307/1 423
Art. 4 424
Art. 4b 424
Art. 11 424
Reg. (EC) No. 2152/2003 concerning Monitoring of Forests and Environmental Interactions in the Community [2003] OJ L324/1 445
Reg. (EC) No. 641/2004 on Detailed Rules for the Implementation of Regulation (EC) No. 1829/2003 as Regards the Application for the Authorization of New Genetically Modified Food and Feed, the Notification of Existing Products and Adventitious or Technically Unavoidable Presence of Genetically Modified Material which has Benefited from a Favourable Risk Evaluation [2004] OJ L102/14 379
Reg. (EC) No. 648/2004 on Detergents [2004] OJ L104/1 427
Annex III 427
Annex VII 427
Reg. (EC) No. 726/2004 laying down Community Procedures for the Authorization and Supervision of Medicinal Products for Human and Veterinary Use and Establishing a European Medicines Agency (Medicines/Pharmaceuticals Reg.) [2004] OJ L136/1 406
Reg. (EC) No. 812/2004 concerning Incidental Catches of Cetaceans in Fisheries and amending Regulation (EC) No. 88/98 (Incidental Catches Reg.) [2004] OJ L150/12 . . . 246–7, 252–3
Reg. (EC) No. 396/2005 on Maximum Residue Levels of Pesticides in Food and Feed [2005] OJ L70/1 . . . . . 438, 550

Commission Reg. (EC) No. 1332/2005 Amending Regulation (EC) No. 338/97 on the Protection of Species of Wild Fauna and Flora by Regulating Trade Therein [2005] OJ L215/1 445
Reg. (EC) No. 1698/2005 on Support for Rural Development by the European Agricultural Fund for Rural Development (EAFRD) (Rural Development Fund Reg.) [2005] OJ L277/1 . . . . 478, 560–1
Art. 84 561
Reg. (EC) No. 2173/2005 on the Establishment of a FLEGT Licensing Scheme for Imports of Timber into the European Community [2005] OJ L374/1 . . . . 482–3, 669
Reg. (EC) No. 166/2006 concerning the Establishment of a European Pollutant Release and Transfer Register and Amending Council Directives 91/689/EEC and 96/61/EC [2006] OJ L33/1 525–9
Preamble 526
Art. 1 526
Art. 2 526–8
Art. 3 527
Art. 4 527
Art. 5 526–7
Art. 6 526
Art. 7 527
Art. 8 527–8
Art. 9 528
Art. 10 528
Art. 11 528
Art. 12 529
Art. 13 529
Art. 14 529
Art. 15 529
Art. 16 529
Art. 20 529
Annex I 526–7, 529
Annex II 526
Annex III 527
Reg. (EC) No. 196/2006 amending Annex 1 to Regulation (EC) No. 761/2001 to take Account of the European Standard EN ISO 14001:2004, and repealing Decision 97/265/EC [2006] OJ L32/4 540–1
Preamble 540
Art. 1 540
Art. 2 540–1
Annex I 540
Commission Reg. (EC) No. 605/2006 amending Regulation (EC) No. 349/2003 Suspending the Introduction into the Community of Specimens of certain Species of Wild Fauna and Flora [2006] OJ L107/3 443–4
Commission Reg. (EC) No. 865/2006 laying down Detailed Rules concerning the Implementation of the CITES Regulation [2006] OJ L166/1 445
Commission Reg. (EC) No. 907/2006 amending Regulation (EC) No. 648/2004 on Detergents [2006] OJ L168/5 427
Reg. (EC) No. 1013/2006 on Shipments of Waste (Revised Waste Shipments Reg.) [2006] OJ L190/1 . . . . 490–9, 504–8
Art. 2 490
Art. 5 491
Art. 6 . . . . 496–9, 507–8

Art. 7 . . . 492, 507–8
Art. 9 . . . 496
Art. 10 . . . 498
Art. 11 . . . 493
Art. 12 . . . 493, 496, 499
Art. 13 . . . 492, 498
Art. 14 . . . 492
Art. 15 . . . 492, 496
Art. 17 . . . 496
Art. 20 . . . 496
Art. 22 . . . 494
Art. 23 . . . 494
Art. 24 . . . 494
Art. 25 . . . 494
Art. 49 . . . 494
Annex III . . . 491
Annex IV . . . 491
Annex V . . . 491
Annex VIII . . . 494
Reg. (EC) No. 1083/2006 laying down general provisions on the European Regional Development Fund, the European Social Fund and the Cohesion Fund and repealing Regulation (EC) No. 1260/1999 [2006] OJ L239/248 . . . 560–1
Art. 47 . . . 560
Reg. (EC) No. 1198/2006 on the European Fisheries Fund (EFF) [2006] OJ L223/1 560–1, 669
Reg. (EC) No. 1367/2006 on the Application of the Provisions of the Aarhus Convention on Access to Information, Public Participation in Decision-Making and Access to Justice in Environmental Matters to Community Institutions and Bodies (Community Institutions and Bodies Reg.) [2006] OJ L264/13 . . . xi, 404–5, 524–5, 529–37, 553–4, 600–1
Preamble . . . 530–3
Art. 1 . . . 530
Art. 2 . . . 530–6
Art. 4 . . . 531–3
Art. 5 . . . 533
Art. 6 . . . 533
Art. 7 . . . 534
Art. 8 . . . 534
Art. 9 . . . 536
Art. 10 . . . 536–7
Art. 11 . . . 531, 537
Art. 12 . . . 531, 537, 553
Art. 13 . . . 531, 537
Commission Reg. (EC) No. 1737/2006 laying down Detailed Rules for the Implementation of Regulation (EC) No. 2152/2003 concerning Monitoring of Forests and Environmental Interactions in the Community [2006] OJ L334/1 . . . 445
Commission Reg. (EC) No. 1849/2006 amending Regulation (EC) No. 2032/2003 (Second Review Regulation) [2006] OJ L355/63 . . . 423–4
Art. 4 . . . 424
Art. 4b . . . 424
Art. 11 . . . 424

Reg. (EC) No. 1907/2006 on the Registration, Evaluation, Authorisation and Restriction of Chemicals (REACH) and establishing a European Chemicals Agency (REACH Reg.) [2007] OJ L136/3 . . . . 403–22, 428–31, 440–1
Preamble 408
Art. 1 441
Art. 2 405–8
Art. 3 . . . . 405–6, 409–10, 413
Art. 5 408
Art. 6 409
Art. 7 420–2
Art. 8 . . . . 408, 413
Art. 11 412
Art. 12 411
Art. 13 411
Art. 14 . . . . 407, 410
Art. 17 409
Art. 18 409
Art. 23 410
Art. 24 410
Art. 26 413
Art. 27 413
Art. 28 410
Art. 30 412–3
Art. 31 413
Art. 32 406
Art. 33 422
Art. 40 415
Art. 41 415
Art. 52 417
Art. 56 . . . . 407, 416
Art. 57 416
Art. 58 417
Art. 59 417
Art. 60 418
Art. 61 418
Art. 62 417
Art. 64 418
Art. 67 . . . . 407, 419
Art. 68 422
Art. 69 422
Art. 113 430–1
Art. 128 419
Art. 138 409
Art. 139 419
Annex III 411
Annex IV 409
Annex V 409
Annex VI 429
Annex VII 411, 415
Annex VIII 411, 415–6
Annex IX 411, 414–5
Annex X 411, 414–5

Annex XI . . . 411
Annex XIII . . . 416
Annex XIV . . . 416–7
Annex XVII . . . 419
Annex XVIII . . . 419
Reg. (EC) No. 1981/2006 on Detailed Rules for the Implementation of Article 32 of Regulation (EC) No. 1829/2003 as Regards the Community Reference Laboratory for Genetically Modified Organisms (CRL Regulation) [2006] OJ L368/99 . . . 366–8
Art. 3 . . . 367
Art. 4 . . . 367
Art. 5 . . . 367
Art. 6 . . . 367–8
Annex I . . . 367–8
Annex II . . . 367–8
Annex III . . . 368

France

Charte de l'Environnement 2004 . . . 603
Art. 5 . . . 603
Loi Barnier . . . 603

Germany

Federal Law on Protection against Pollution . . . 460–1
Federal Law on Soil Protection . . . 460
Para. 17 . . . 460
Federal Law on Water Use . . . 460–1
Federal Nature Protection Law of 1998 . . . 458
Federal Nature Protection Law 2002 . . . 458–65
Para. 5 . . . 459
Para. 10 . . . 458–62
Para. 17 . . . 459
Para. 18 . . . 459–61
Para. 39 . . . 464–5
Federal Plant Protection Law 1998 . . . 463
Para. 6 . . . 463

India

Biodiversity Act 2002 . . . 282

International

Agreement on the Conservation of African-Eurasian Migratory Waterbirds (AEWA). *See* Convention on the Conservation of Migratory Species of Wild Animals
Aarhus Convention. *See* UN/ECE Convention on Access to Information, Public Participation in Decision–Making, and Access to Justice in Environmental Matters
African-Eurasian Waterbird Agreement 1995 (AEWA). *See* Convention on the Conservation of Migratory Species of Wild Animals
Agreement on the Conservation of Bats in Europe (EUROBATS). *See* Convention on the Conservation of Migratory Species of Wild Animals
Agreement on the Conservation of Small Cetaceans of the Baltic and North Seas (ASCOBANS). *See* Convention on the Conservation of Migratory Species of Wild Animals

Agreement on the Conservation of Cetaceans of the Black Sea, Mediterranean Sea, and Contiguous Atlantic Area (ACCOBAMS). *See* Convention on the Conservation of Migratory Species of Wild Animals
Alpine Convention. *See* Convention on the Protection of the Alps
Barcelona Convention. *See* Convention concerning Cooperation in Preventing Pollution from Ships and in Combating Pollution of the Mediterranean Sea by Oil and Hazardous and Noxious Substances in Cases of Emergency
Basel Convention. *See* Convention on the Control of Transboundary Movements of Hazardous Wastes and their Disposal
Bonn Convention. *See* Convention on the Conservation of Migratory Species of Wild Animals
BSP. *See* UN Convention on Biological Diversity (Cartagena Protocol on Biosafety)
Cartagena Biosafety Protocol. *See* UN Convention on Biological Diversity (Cartagena Protocol on Biosafety)
CBD. *See* UN Convention on Biological Diversity
CITES Convention. *See* Convention on International Trade in Endangered Species of Fauna and Flora
CMS. *See* Convention on the Conservation of Migratory Species of Wild Animals
Convention on Biological Diversity (CBD). *See* UN Convention on Biological Diversity
Convention on the Conservation of Migratory Species of Wild Animals 1979 (CMS/Bonn Convention) . . . . viii, 218–64, 443, 445
Preamble 223
Art. I 224–6
Art. II 224
Art. III. 225–6
Art. IV. 226–8, 244, 250, 254, 257, 442
Art. V 226–7
Appendix I. 224–6, 445
Appendix II 224–8, 443
Agreement on the Conservation of African-Eurasian Migratory Waterbirds 1995 (AEWA). 244, 254–6, 442–3
Preamble 254
Art. I 254
Art. II 255
Art. III. 255
Art. IV. 255
Art. VI. 255
Art. IX. 255
Art. X. 443
Annex 2. . . . . 254, 443
Annex 3. . . . . 255, 443
Agreement on the Conservation of Bats in Europe (EUROBATS) 244–5, 257–9
Preamble 258–9
Art. I 258
Art. III. 258
Art. IV. 258
Art. V 258
Art. VI. 258
Art. VIII 258
Annex 1. 258–9
Agreement on the Conservation of Small Cetaceans of the Baltic and North Seas (ASCOBANS) 245–63

Art. 2 248
Agreement on the Conservation of Cetaceans of the Black Sea, Mediterranean Sea, and Contiguous Atlantic Area (ACCOBAMS) 245–53, 261–3
Art. I 250
Art. II 251
Convention on the Control of Transboundary Movements of Hazardous Wastes and their Disposal 1989 (Basel Convention) 339, 487, 493–4
Art. 4 493
Convention concerning Cooperation in Preventing Pollution from Ships and in Combating Pollution of the Mediterranean Sea by Oil and Hazardous and Noxious Substances in Cases of Emergency 1976 (Barcelona Convention) 664
Convention on International Trade in Endangered Species of Fauna and Flora 1973 (CITES Convention) 222–4, 260, 443–5, 617
Art. VII 445
Appendix I 224
Appendix II 224
Convention on the Law of Treaties. *See* Vienna Convention on the Law of Treaties 1969 (VCLT)
Convention for the Prevention of Marine Pollution from Ships. *See* International Maritime Organization (IMO) Convention for the Prevention of Marine Pollution from Ships
Convention on the Protection of the Alps 1991 (Alpine Convention) 446, 652
Protocol on the Implementation in the Field of Mountain Farming 446
Convention on the Protection of the Environment through Criminal Law. *See* Council of Europe (CoE) European Convention on the Protection of the Environment through Criminal Law
Convention for the Protection of the Marine Environment of the North–East Atlantic 1992 (OSPAR Convention) 106, 241
Convention on Wetlands of International Importance Especially as Waterfowl Habitat 1971 (Ramsar Convention) 91–2
Council of Europe (CoE) European Convention on the Protection of the Environment through Criminal Law 1998 148
EUROBATS. *See* Agreement on the Conservation of Bats in Europe
European Patent Convention 284
GATT. *See* Global Agreement on Tariffs and Trade
Geneva Convention relating to the Simplification of Customs Formalities 1923 266
Global Agreement on Tariffs and Trade 1994 (GATT) 136, 152, 268, 615
Helsinki Water Convention. *See* UN/ECE Convention on the Protection and Use of Transboundary Watercourses and International Lakes
International Atomic Energy Agency (IAEA) Joint Convention on the Safety of Spent Fuel Management and on the Safety of Radioactive Waste Management 495–6
Art. 27 496
International Convention on Nuclear Safety 210
International Convention for the Regulation of Whaling 1946 222
International Maritime Organization (IMO) Convention for the Prevention of Marine Pollution from Ships 1973 (MARPOL Convention) 16
Protocol of 1978 (MARPOL 73/78) 16
International Plant Protection Convention (IPP). *See* UN/FAO International Plant Protection Convention
International Treaty on Plant Genetic Resources for Food and Agriculture (ITPGRFA/International Treaty) 277, 281, 284
Art. 12 284
Annex I 284
International Tropical Timber Agreement 1994 487–8

Art. 46 488
International Tropical Timber Agreement 2006 488
IPP Convention. *See* UN/FAO International Plant Protection Convention
Joint Convention on the Safety of Spent Fuel Management and on the Safety of Radioactive Waste Management. *See* International Atomic Energy Agency (IAEA)
Kyoto Protocol. *See* UN Framework Convention on Climate Change
LRTAP Convention. *See* UN/ECE Convention on Long–Range Transboundary Air Pollution
MARPOL Convention. *See* International Maritime Organization (IMO) Convention for the Prevention of Marine Pollution from Ships
Montreal Protocol. *See* UNEP Vienna Convention for the Protection of the Ozone Layer
Multilateral Agreement on Investment (MAI) 299–300
Nuclear Non-Proliferation Treaty 1968 (NPT) 190, 210
OSPAR Convention. *See* Convention for the Protection of the Marine Environment of the North–East Atlantic
PIC Convention. *See* Rotterdam Convention on the Prior Informed Consent Procedure for certain Hazardous Chemicals and Pesticides in International Trade
POPs Convention. *See* UNEP Stockholm Convention on Persistent Organic Pollutants
Ramsar Convention (Convention on Wetlands of International Importance Especially as Waterfowl Habitat)
Rio Declaration on Environment and Development 1992 (Rio Declaration) . . . 83, 298, 602, 608
Principle 15 . . . . 83, 602, 608
Rotterdam Convention on the Prior Informed Consent Procedure for certain Hazardous Chemicals and Pesticides in International Trade 1998 (Rotterdam Convention/PIC Convention) 339, 567–9
Preamble 568
SPS Agreement. *See* WTO Agreement on Sanitary and Phytosanitary Measures
Stockholm POPs Convention. *See* UNEP Stockholm Convention on Persistent Organic Pollutants
Subsidies Agreement. *See* WTO Agreement on Subsidies and Countervailing Measures
TBT Agreement. *See* WTO Agreement on Technical Barriers to Trade
United Nations (UN) Agreement on Straddling Fish Stocks and Highly Migratory Fish Stocks 92
United Nations (UN) Declaration on the Rights of Indigenous Peoples 273
UNCLOS. *See* UN Convention on the Law of the Sea
UN Convention on Biological Diversity 1992 (CBD) 83, 155, 218, 222, 243, 260, 265–94, 366–85, 391–4, 485–7, 617, 646–7, 652
Art. 1 267
Art. 8 . . . . 267, 272, 285, 393–6
Art. 15 . . . . 267, 272, 284
Art. 16 . . . . 269, 272, 276, 289–90
Art. 22 288
Dec. V/5-III, Genetic Use Restriction Technologies (GURTs) 392–4
Dec. VIII/19, Forest Biological Diversity 391
Dec. VIII/23(C), Agricultural Biodiversity 394
Cartagena Protocol on Biosafety 2000 (BSP/Cartagena Biosafety Protocol) 1, 155, 241, 366, 381–6, 391, 396–7, 485–7, 568–9
Art. 10 1
Art. 18 382–5
Art. 27 385–6
Art. 34 386
Dec. BS-I/6, Handling, Transport, Packaging and Identification of Living Modified Organisms (Article 18) 384

Dec. BS-I/8, Establishment of an Open-ended Ad Hoc Working Group of Legal and Technical Experts on Liability and Redress in the Context of the Protocol 385–6
Dec. BS-III/8, Handling, Transport, Packaging and Identification of Living Modified Organisms 382–4
Dec. BS-III/12, Liability and Redress under the Biosafety Protocol 386
UN Convention to Combat Desertification (UNCCD) 652
UN Convention on the Law of the Sea 1982 (UNCLOS) . . 92, 222, 486–7, 524, 563–7, 579–89
Annex VII 563
UNCCD. *See* UN Convention to Combat Desertification
UNFCCC. *See* UN Framework Convention on Climate Change
UN Framework Convention on Climate Change 1992 (UNF CCC) 1, 340–1, 346–7, 361–2, 391, 612–3, 617, 649
Art. 3 1
Kyoto Protocol 1997 . . . . 341–51, 355, 361–2, 391–2, 612–5, 649, 652–3, 660–2, 667
Dec. 19/CP.9 on Modalities and Procedures for Afforestation and Reforestation Projects under the Clean Development Mechanism in the First Commitment Period of the Kyoto Protocol 391–2
UN/ECE Convention on Access to Information, Public Participation in Decision–Making, and Access to Justice in Environmental Matters 1998 (Aarhus Convention) . . . . xi, 158–9, 253, 368, 386–7, 404–5, 480–1, 524–5, 529–34, 541–2, 553,600–1, 606, 612
Preamble 159
Art. 6 606
Art. 6*bis* 606
Art. 9 530–1
Dec. II/1 on Genetically Modified Organisms 368, 386–7, 606
Protocol on Pollutant Release and Transfer Registers 2003 (PRTR Protocol) 525–7
UN/ECE Convention on Long–Range Transboundary Air Pollution 1979 (LRTAP Convention) 620
UN/ECE Convention on the Protection and Use of Transboundary Watercourses and International Lakes 1992 (Helsinki Water Convention) 1
Art. 2 1
UNEP Stockholm Convention on Persistent Organic Pollutants 2001 (POPs Convention/ Stockholm POPs Convention) 338–40
UNEP Vienna Convention for the Protection of the Ozone Layer 1985 (Ozone Convention) 337–8
Montreal Protocol on Substances that Deplete the Ozone Layer 1987 (Montreal Protocol) 241, 327, 337–8
Art. 5 337–8
UN/FAO International Plant Protection Convention 1997 (IPP Convention) 284
Art. 12 284
Annex 1 284
VCLT. *See* Vienna Convention on the Law of Treaties 1969
Vienna Convention on the Law of Treaties 1969 (VCLT) 156, 397, 569
Art. 31 . . . . 156, 397
Art. 46 569
Water Convention. *See* UN/ECE Convention on the Protection and Use of Transboundary Watercourses and International Lakes 1992
Whaling Convention. *See* International Convention for the Regulation of Whaling
World Intellectual Property Organization (WIPO) Patent Co-operation Treaty (PCT) 266, 271, 276–86

World Intellectual Property Organization (WIPO) Substantive Patent Law Treaty (SPLT) 266, 271, 277–84
Art. 6 279
World Trade Organization (WTO) Agreement 1994 . . . . . 152–3 , 617
Art. 4 . . . . . 152, 299
WTO Agreement on Government Procurement. 299
WTO Agreement on Sanitary and Phytosanitary Measures (SPS Agreement). 5–6, 136, 152–61, 396, 607–8
Preamble 153
Art. 1 153
Art. 2 153
Art. 3 153
Art. 5 . . . . . 6, 153–5, 396
Art. 8 396
Art. 11 152
Annex A.1 153
Annex A.3 153
Annex C 396
WTO Agreement on Technical Barriers to Trade (TBT Agreement). 136, 152–6, 310, 604
Art. II 153
Art. II 604
Art. XX 152
WTO Agreement on Trade Related Aspects of Intellectual Property (TRIPS) 241, 266–80, 286–93, 310
Art. 6 269
Art. 7 269–70
Art. 8 269–70
Art. 27 . . . . . 269–70, 280
Art. 29 . . . . . 278–80, 286
Art. 29*bis* 275–7, 286–7, 292
Art. 32 287
Art. 62 280
Art. 66 269
Art. 71 269–70
WTO Agreement on Subsidies and Countervailing Measures (1994) 300–3
Agreement on Trade-Related Investment Measures (TRIMS) 615
WTO General Agreement on Trade in Services (GATS) 309–10, 615
WTO-GATT. *See* Global Agreement on Tariffs and Trade

Italy

Decree of the Ministry of the Environment of 18 Jan. 2006. 475
Energy Law 2004 197

Netherlands

Dredging Rule 1934. 94
Fishery Act 1963 94
Law on Spatial Planning. 95
Mining Act. 94, 124
Mining Law 2002 (*Mijnwet*) 119
Art. 5 119
Nature Conservation Act 1968. 94–5

Art. 19d 94–5
Art. 19f 95
Nature Conservation Act 1998 119
Art. 43 119
Nature Conservation Act 2005 94–5
Art. 19d 94–5
Art. 19f 95
Nature Protection Law 95, 110–1, 119–20

Norway

General Civil Penal Code 276
Para. 166 276
Patent Act 275–6
Para. 8 275
Para. 33 276

Portugal

Decree-Law of 1999 (SPA designation) 456
Decree-Law of 2002 (SPA designation) 456–8

Sweden

Environmental Protection Act 1969 603

Switzerland

Federal Paten Law/Act (Draft) 281–3
Art. 49a 281
Art. 81a 283

United Kingdom

STATUTES

Environmental Protection Act 1990 166
s. 75 166
Finance Act 1996 165
S. 39 165

STATUTORY INSTRUMENTS

Waste Management Licensing Regulations 1994 166–7
Reg. 1(3) 166
Schedule 4 167

United States of America

FEDERAL STATUTES

Fishery Conservation and Management Reauthorization Act 2006 587
National Environmental Policy Act (NEPA) 320–1
Sustainable Fisheries Act 1996 587

Mapping the Article 174(2) EC Case Law: A First Step to Analysing Community Environmental Law Principles

*Eloise Scotford**

I. Introduction

'Environmental principles' appear extensively in international, supranational, and national legal and policy contexts.[1] This article considers the nature of 'environmental principles' in European Community (EC) law. More particularly, it considers the roles of the four environmental principles in Article 174(2) of the EC Treaty[2]—the preventive principle, the precautionary principle, the polluter pays principle, and the principle of rectification at source—in the case law of the

* Career Development Fellow in Environmental Law, Corpus Christi College, Oxford (UK). This article is an edited version of a thesis submitted for the MPhil (Law) at the University of Oxford. My thanks go to Dr Liz Fisher and William Heath for their generous and timely help and comments in the development of this article and its thesis progenitor.

[1] For example, the 'precautionary principle' appears in various international treaties, e.g. Art. 2(5)(a) of the UN/ECE Convention on the Protection and Use of Transboundary Watercourses and International Lakes (Helsinki Water Convention), Helsinki (Finland), 17 Mar. 1992 (entered into force 6 Oct. 1996), (1992) 31 *International Legal Materials* 6, 1312; Art. 3(3) of the UN Framework Convention on Climate Change (UNFCCC), New York, NY (US), 9 May 1992 (entered into force 21 Mar. 1994), (1992) 31 *International Legal Materials* 4, 849; Art. 10(2) of the Cartagena Protocol on Biosafety (BSP), Montreal (Canada), 29 Jan. 2000 (entered into force 11 Sept. 2003), (2000) 39 *International Legal Materials* 5, 1027. Its presence in domestic legislation includes, e.g. s. 391 of the Australian Environmental Protection and Biodiversity Conservation Act 1999 (Cth); Art. 225 of the Brazilian Constitution. National cases involving the principle include, e.g. *Zia* v. *WAPDA* PLD 1994 SC 693 (Pakistan); *BGP Properties Pty Ltd* v. *Lake Macquarie City Council* (2004) 138 LGERA 237 (Australia); *AP Pollution Control Board* v. *Prof. M.V. Nayudu*, AIR 1999 SC 812 (India); *114957 Canada Ltee (Spraytech, Société d'arrosage)* v. *Hudson (Town)* [2001] 2 SCR 241 (Canada). In the European context, references include the EC Treaty (Art. 174(2) EC), policy documents (Commission Communication on the Precautionary Principle COM(2000)1, 2 Feb. 2000); the preambles of various EC legislation (e.g. recital 8 of Dir. 2001/18/EC on the Deliberate Release of Genetically Modified Organisms into the Environment and Repealing Directive 90/220/EEC [2001] OJ L106/1), and many decisions of the Community courts (e.g. Case T-13/99 *Pfizer Animal Health SA* v. *Council* [2002] ECR II-3305 (*Pfizer*); and Case C-236/01 *Monsanto Agricoltura Italia SpA and Others* v. *Presidenza del Consiglio dei Ministri and Others* [2003] ECR I-8105 (*Monsanto*).

[2] Treaty Establishing the European Community, as amended [2002] OJ C325/33 (hereafter 'EC' or 'Treaty').

Community courts. This article shows that in order to understand the roles of the four environmental principles in Article 174(2) EC in Community case law, one must analyse their treatment by the Community courts, and, for this, one must appreciate their ambiguous nature as instruments of both law and policy.

These four environmental principles appear in a large but disparate body of case law of the European Court of Justice (ECJ) and the Court of First Instance (CFI). This case law is intriguing because it engages these four principles, which are laid down as prescriptions of Community policy in the EC Treaty, in apparently legal roles. This article maps the Article 174(2) case law, charting the *treatment* or *use* of the Article 174(2) principles by the Community courts, with a view to unpacking this ambiguous legal/policy identity, and thereby to explaining the role of these principles in the EC case law. By charting the judicial treatment and roles of these principles in a manner that is sensitive to their Community law context, this article re-orients discussion and debate about the preventive principle, the polluter pays principle, the precautionary principle, and the principle of rectification at source in EC environmental law. At the outset, it is important to note that there is no clear and settled doctrine concerning what an 'Article 174(2) environmental principle' *is* and *does*.[3] Accordingly, the mapping exercise undertaken in this article begins to build an analysed jurisprudence of the Article 174(2) environmental principles.

Section II introduces the Article 174(2) principles and their unique Treaty context. A brief survey of how the literature approaches this unique context is then undertaken. Section II also proposes an analytical framework for analysing the Article 174(2) case law that is inspired by that context. Section III goes on to map the Article 174(2) cases. Two caveats should be made at this stage. Firstly, the mapping exercise here undertaken and its frame of analysis together constitute a first-step exercise in understanding the role of the Article 174(2) principles in Community case law. Further steps in identifying the nature the Article 174(2) principles and how they are (or should be) applied in EC law, and of environmental principles in Community law more generally, should be founded on the analytical platform here set out. Some such further steps are suggested in the concluding Section IV. Secondly, only the decisions of the ECJ and CFI will be considered (as well as any relevant Opinions of Advocates General) in mapping the Article 174(2) case law. Thus, references to 'Community courts' in this article are to courts constituted under Section 4 of the EC Treaty (the ECJ and CFI, for present purposes), and not to Member State courts in any sense. Similarly, 'Community (or EC) case law' refers to the case law of the Community courts. It is the Community courts that have the authoritative role in interpreting and

[3] Cf. J. Scott, 'The Precautionary Principle before the European Courts' in R. Macrory, I. Havercroft, and R. Purdy (eds.), *Principles of European Environmental Law* (Groningen: Europa Law Publishing, 2004), 51–72, at 54. See also T. Tridimas, *The General Principles of EU Law. 2nd Edn.* (Oxford: Oxford University Press, 2006), 25–35.

applying the EC Treaty,[4] thus their treatment of the Article 174(2) principles is the focus of this article.

II. Article 174(2) EC Principles: Legal and Policy Principles

A. Article 174(2) Principles: Relevance of Definition and Unique Treaty Context

Article 174(2) EC introduces four principles which must found EC environmental policy:

> *Community policy on the environment* shall aim at a high level of protection taking into account the diversity of situations in the various regions of the Community. It *shall be based* on the **precautionary principle** and on the **principles that preventive action should be taken, that environmental damage should as a priority be rectified at source and that the polluter should pay.**[5]

Unhelpfully, these Article 174(2) principles are undefined in the EC Treaty. Their substantive meaning has been the subject of considerable academic discussion, mostly concluding that they are incapable of clear definition.[6] This article aims to avoid the difficulties associated with fixing a *definition* of the principles by focusing instead on their *treatment* or *use* by courts. It is only in understanding how the principles are treated in the particular context of the Community jurisprudence regarding 174(2) EC that an appreciation of their definition becomes helpful, or even possible. As will be seen, apparent conflicts of judicial definition are the result of the principles being used for different purposes in different cases. To the extent that the principles are defined judicially, this will be understood as an aspect of their treatment by the Community courts. However, having some introductory and general ideas about the ideas underlying these four environmental principles is helpful, even if they are not definitive.

Broadly speaking, the ideas underlying the four environmental principles listed in Article 174(2) EC can be understood as follows. The *preventive principle* refers to the idea of preventing environmental pollution and nuisances, rather

[4] Art. 220 EC.

[5] Art. 174(2) EC, emphasis added.

[6] See, e.g., N. de Sadeleer, *Environmental Principles: From Political Slogans to Legal Rules* (Oxford: Oxford University Press, 2002), 2, 37–44, 60, 72–9, 92; L. Krämer, 'The Genesis of EC Environmental Principles' in Macrory et al., n. 3 above, 31–47, at 47; L. Krämer, *EC Environmental Law. 6th Edn.* (London: Sweet and Maxwell, 2007), 25–7; M. Lee, *EU Environmental Law: Challenges, Change and Decision-Making* (Oxford: Hart Publishing, 2005), 97–8; Scott, n. 3 above, 53; S. Tromans, 'High Talk and Low Cunning: Putting Environmental Principles into Practice' (1995) 22 *Journal of Planning and Environmental Law*, 779 and 790; and generally, cf. A. Epiney, 'Environmental Principles' in R. Macrory (ed.), *Reflections on 30 Years of EU Environmental Law* (Groningen: Europa Law Publishing, 2006), 19–39, at 30–1.

than trying to undo their damaging effects. It reflects a preventive rather than curative solution to environmental problems. The *principle of rectification at source* is related, and essentially refines the preventive principle. It embraces the idea that environmental damage should be rectified by targeting its original cause, by requiring preventive action at source rather than at any other point on the continuum of activity that results in environmental harm. The *polluter pays principle* posits that polluters pay for environmental harm that they generate. Identifying the relevant polluter and the appropriate measure of liability are matters on which the principle gives no guidance.[7] The *precautionary principle* is the most difficult to explain simply. Generally, whereas the preventive principle is concerned with *known* environmental risks, the precautionary principle concerns *unknown* environmental risks; that is, cases of scientific uncertainty.[8] Fisher paraphrases what she finds to be the most common version of the precautionary principle, which has been developed in the international law context:

> [W]here there is a threat to human health or environmental protection a lack of full scientific certainty should not be used as a reason to postpone measures that would prevent or minimise such a threat.[9]

It has been observed, however, that the principle is 'deeply ambivalent and apparently infinitely malleable'.[10]

Particularly in the EC context, the substantive versions of the precautionary principle vary greatly,[11] and it is distinct from the other environmental principles in Article 174(2) EC in three significant respects.[12] Firstly, it has been extended (or also applied), in EC policy and in case law, to fields other than the environment, in particular to policy domains concerned with the protection of human, animal, and plant health. In this extended case law, the courts rely on Article 174(2) EC as the source of the precautionary principle, and so its cases come within the scope of the mapping exercise in this article, however questionably logical might this translation be of the principle when Article 174(2) EC concerns 'environmental' policy. The reasons offered by the Commission and the courts[13] for this extension centre

[7] De Sadeleer, ibid., 37–44.

[8] Cf. Krämer (2007), n. 6 above, 25.

[9] E. Fisher, *Risk Regulation and Administrative Constitutionalism* (Oxford: Hart Publishing, 2007), 40.

[10] J. Scott and E. Vos, 'The Juridification of Uncertainty: Observations on the Ambivalence of the Precautionary Principle within the EU and the WTO' in C. Joerges and R. Dehousse (eds.) *Good Governance in Europe's Integrated Market* (Oxford: Oxford University Press, 2002), 253–86, at 253.

[11] See, e.g., Case C-180–96 *United Kingdom* v. *Commission* [1998] ECR I-3906 (*BSE*), para. 99; Joined Cases T-74/00, T-76/00, T-83/00, T-84/00, T-85/00, T-132/00, T-137/00, and T-141/00 *Artegodan Gmbh and Others* v. *Commission* [2002] ECR II-4945 (*Artegodan*), para. 184; and Case T-369/03 *Arizona Chemical Bv and Others* v. *Commission*, Order of the CFI of 14 Dec. 2005, para. 85.

[12] Cf. Scott, n. 3 above, 51.

[13] Communication, n. 1 above, 3; *Artegodan*, ibid., paras 183–4; *Monsanto*, n. 1 above, Opinion of AG Alber, para. 134.

around the idea that the precautionary principle, concerning as it does situations of scientific uncertainty, logically extends to all policy issues involving the management of risk, in light of the often substantive connections between these policy domains,[14] and the 'high level of protection' required by the Treaty in different Community policy areas.[15]

Secondly, the precautionary principle is distinct from the other three environmental principles in that it has also been comprehensively addressed by a Commission policy document, the Commission Communication on the Precautionary Principle of February 2000 (Communication).[16] The Communication goes to great lengths to give guidelines on how the precautionary principle should be applied by the Commission, 'when faced with taking decisions relating to the containment of risk'.[17] The Communication identifies the precautionary principle as a 'key tenet of its policy' in the areas of the environment, human, animal, and plant health,[18] and focuses primarily on locating the application of the principle within a tripartite risk decision-making process that embraces risk assessment, risk management, and risk communication. While the Communication purports to identify the 'constituent parts' of the precautionary principle,[19] its concern is primarily to set out a decision-making process, centred on scientific evaluation, within which political decisions based on the precautionary principle should be made. The Communication's central concern is that maximal scientific objectivity supports precautionary decisions, so as to minimize the arbitrariness of decisions made in the face of uncertain risk. The Communication can be seen as reflecting the Commission's concern to legitimize its own decision-making,[20] and, for now, its basis as a *policy document*, guiding institutional decision-making and supporting the legally binding policy prescription in Article 174(2) EC, is highlighted.

Thirdly, it should also be noted that the Commission's policy statement on the precautionary principle in the Communication is reminiscent of the position taken by the World Trade Organization (WTO) Appellate Body (AB) in the *Hormones* decision.[21] That decision concerned a dispute, under the WTO Agreement on Sanitary and Phytosanitary Measures (SPS Agreement),[22] between the United Kingdom (UK) and the United States (US) over an EC ban on hormones in beef

[14] Art. 174(1) EC provides that one of the goals of EC environment policy shall be 'protecting human health'. Some cases might be viewed as relating to both environmental and public health protection: e.g. Joined Cases T-366/03 and T-235/04 *Land Oberösterreich and Austria* v. *Commission* [2005] ECR II-4005. See also de Sadeleer, n. 6 above, 7.

[15] Arts. 2, 3(p), 95(3), 152(1), 153(1), and 174(2) EC.

[16] Communication, n. 1 above.

[17] Ibid., 9.

[18] Ibid., 3.

[19] Ibid., 13.

[20] Fisher, n. 9 above, 224–5.

[21] *EC–Measures Concerning Meat and Meat Products (Hormones)*, 16 Jan. 1998 (WT/DS26/AB/R), published on the Internet at: http://docsonline.wto.org.

[22] The SPS Agreement is contained in Annex 1 to the WTO Agreement.

imports. In that case, the WTO AB was particularly concerned that protective measures taken by contracting States under the SPS Agreement should be based on assessable, not theoretical, risk.[23] It also discussed at length the need for adequate risk assessment in adopting such measures.[24] These concerns did not relate to the precautionary principle explicitly (in fact the AB avoided basing its decision on the precautionary principle), rather they reflected the particular risk assessment requirements of the SPS Agreement relevant to the dispute,[25] since the AB was interpreting the provisions of that Agreement in *Hormones*. Despite this difference in context, it might be surmised, from the language and approach of the Communication,[26] that WTO law has influenced the discourse relating to the precautionary principle in EC policy. This influence can be seen as a further feature that distinguishes the precautionary principle from the other Article 174(2) principles.

Turning to consider the Treaty context of Article 174(2) EC more closely, that Treaty provision establishes an ambiguity in the principles that is central to understanding their Community legal role. Inherent in the provision is an ambiguity between policy and law that characterizes the four environmental principles in this particular context: the Treaty-based law of the EC. The principles appear ambiguously in Article 174(2) EC as they are set out as instruments of both law *and* policy—according to the article's precise terms, they are *policy* prescriptions expressed in a *legally binding form*. This split policy/law identity gives rise to ambiguity when considering their legal role, and thus to a unique identity for these particular environmental principles in the EC context. The Communication adds another layer to this ambiguity in the case of the precautionary principle. The Communication is a policy document designed to guide Commission decision-making. However, as will be seen in Section III, it has had a huge influence on the legal tests applied by the Community courts in reviewing Community (and Member State) action taken on the basis of the precautionary principle. Here is a policy document, of no directly binding legal effect, applicable only to the procedures of the Commission, which is used judicially as the basis for determining issues of Community law involving risk regulation by institutions across the Community and Member States. The heavy reliance by the Community courts on this policy guidance highlights the policy-based nature of the precautionary principle in its legal guise. It is a central contention of this article that this conflation of law and policy characterizes the role of the Article

[23] *Hormones*, n. 21 above, para. 186.

[24] Ibid., Section XI generally.

[25] In particular, Art. 5.1 SPS requires that sanitary and phytosanitary measures are to be based on risk assessments, 'as appropriate to the circumstances'.

[26] The Communication, n. 1 above, at 13, states that '[f]ollowing the example set by the other members of the WTO, the Commission considers that the Community is entitled to prescribe the level of protection... that it considers appropriate [under the precautionary principle]', then going on to adopt several of the ideas in the *Hormones* decision concerning risk assessment in setting out justifiable recourse to the precautionary principle.

174(2) principles in legal contexts, which will be revealed from the mapping exercise in Section III.

Before moving on to analyse the Article 174(2) case law in detail, it is worth noting that the policy/law ambiguity of the Article 174(2) principles is reflected in, but not directly addressed by, the literature in this area. Of that academic work that has considered the Article 174(2) principles within its scope, two extreme positions with respect to the principles can be identified, tracking the split policy and legal nature of the principles. Krämer has consistently argued that the Article 174(2) principles are instruments of *policy*, 'leitmotifs' to guide political and legislative decisions, not 'binding rules of law which apply to each individual Community measure'.[27] Krämer does acknowledge that the policy guiding role of the principles gives rise to 'indirect' legal effects—informing legal issues of subsidiarity, legal basis, and Community legislative interpretation—however he engages in no comprehensive analysis of the nature or extent of these indirect legal effects.[28] Other commentators, by contrast, are concerned with the binding *legal* nature and *legal* consequences of the Article 174(2) principles.[29] Doherty, for example, has extensively examined the 'presumed' legal effect of the principles[30] and the extent to which the principles do and *should* play a role in the adjudicative functions of the ECJ, particularly in enabling the Community courts 'to respond to distinct environmental concerns within cases'.[31]

Both of these approaches in the literature are deficient; with respect to the Article 174(2) principles and their place in Community law, there is something more complex going on that stretches between the two understandings of the principles as instruments of policy and instruments of law. None of the literature has so far analysed the principles by focusing squarely and currently on their unique EC Treaty identity and their simultaneously legal and policy nature.[32] Thus existing academic

[27] Krämer (2007), n. 6 above, 15.

[28] Ibid.

[29] See, in particular, M. Doherty, 'The Status of the Principles of EC Environmental Law: Gianni Bettati against Safety High Tech' (1999) 11 *Journal of Environmental Law* 2, 354–86; M. G. Doherty, 'The Judicial Use of the Principles of EC Environmental Policy' (2000) 2 *Environmental Law Review* 4, 251–63; M. Doherty, 'Hard Cases and Environmental Principles: An Aid to Interpretation?' (2002) 3 *Yearbook of European Environmental Law*, 57–78; A. Doyle and T. Carney, 'Precaution and Prevention: Giving Effect to Article 130r without Direct Effect' (1999) 8 *European Environmental Law Review* 2, 44–7; Epiney, n. 6 above; V. Heyvaert, 'Facing the Consequences of the Precautionary Principle in European Community Law' (2006) 31 *European Law Review* 2, 185–206; Scott, n. 3 above, 53–4; G. Winter, 'The Legal Nature of Environmental Principles in International, EC and German Law' in R. Macrory et al., n. 3 above, 11–27.

[30] Doherty (1999), ibid., text accompanying n. 87.

[31] Doherty (2000), ibid., text accompanying n. 10. See also Doherty (2002), ibid., 57–8.

[32] The work of de Sadeleer comes closest to analysing the Art. 174(2) principles in terms of their simultaneously legal and policy nature. He identifies 'directing' environmental principles, which include the preventive principle, precautionary principle, and polluter pays principle, as normatively autonomous and typical of 'post-modern law', which is characterized by an increase in discretion, competing norms, and openness to extra-legal spheres, including economic, ethical, and policy spheres. He identifies these environmental principles with governance by goal-oriented public policy programmes that are grand in scope, the application of which may affect the workings of the legal

analyses of the Article 174(2) principles do not greatly assist the enterprise of this article. The judicial treatment of the Article 174(2) principles, as the mapping of case law will show, reveals an approach to the principles that is somewhere in between the conceptions of the principles as instruments of policy and instruments of law.[33] A more sophisticated theory of Article 174(2) EC is needed to understand this treatment than is currently offered in the literature. Rather than developing such a theory, however, this article now takes a modest step and proposes some analytical tools that will be used to tease out the legal/policy ambiguity of the Article 174(2) principles, inherent in the wording of the EC Treaty, in the mapping exercise that follows in Section III. This step, while modest, is by no means trivial. Discerning what precisely is going on in the diverse body of Community case law that considers the Article 174(2) principles is a complex exercise, and a necessary one in order to determine the nature of those principles in EC law.

B. Analytical Tools

In one of the seminal cases involving the precautionary principle, *Artegodan*, an ambiguity between policy and law, reflecting that inherent in Article 174(2) EC, is strongly evident. In that case, the CFI described the precautionary principle as an autonomous 'general principle of Community law'.[34] This description might suggest that the precautionary principle is akin to other 'general principles of Community law' devised by the Community judicature in its case law, including the principles of equality, proportionality, direct effect, and subsidiarity.[35] However, if one reads the reasoning of the CFI in *Artegodan* closely, one sees that the Court's focus is on the *generality* of the principle. The CFI identifies a principle that, while articulated only in Article 174(2) EC, is reflected in a range of EC Treaty provisions requiring a 'high level of protection',[36] and so it mandates policy objectives across the domains of public health, consumer safety, and the environment.[37] The Court is identifying a *common policy position*, and its

order (de Sadeleer, n. 6 above, 248–50). This overarching thesis of environmental principles taps into the policy/law ambiguity inherent in Art. 174(2) EC. However, de Sadeleer's focus is much wider than the principles of Art. 174(2) EC, so that—while he selectively considers (albeit important) decisions of the Community courts to build his thesis—the ambition of his work limits its usefulness in identifying the precise roles that the Art. 174(2) principles play in the law of the Community courts. In any case, as with the other academic work in this area, de Sadeleer's survey of the EC case law, as well as not being comprehensive, is not up to date. Cf., in the international law context, U. Beyerlin, 'Different Types of Norms in International Environmental Law: Policies, Principles and Rules' in D. Bodansky, J. Brunnée, and E. Hey (eds.), *The Oxford Handbook of International Environmental Law* (Oxford: Oxford University Press, 2007), 425–48.

33 See Section C generally.

34 *Artegodan*, n. 11 above, para. 184.

35 Scott, n. 3 above, 53–6; cf. de Sadeleer, n. 6 above, 36–43, and 258–60; and Tridimas, n. 3 above, 1–5.

36 In particular, Arts. 3(p), 152(1), 153(1)-(2), and 174(2) EC.

37 *Artegodan*, n. 11 above, paras. 182–3.

assertion that this is one of 'law' reflects its mandatory nature, as dictated by the Treaty. *Artegodan* is thus a curious case in which the precautionary principle looks like a legal principle, but in which there is something more complicated going on. To assist in identifying what is in fact going on in cases like *Artegodan*, an analytical framework is now developed for making sense of the Article 174(2) case law that teases out the ambiguity between policy and law that infuses the cases.

In this way, and for the purpose of analysing the Article 174(2) Community case law, a set of analytical tools is proposed, provoked by their ambiguous policy/legal nature in Article 174(2) EC. In order to identify the nature of the Article 174(2) principles as they appear in Community judgments, we adopt two possibilities: they might appear as 'legal principles' or as 'policy principles'. The importance of this distinction stems from its contextual focus on Article 174(2) EC, thereby shifting away from the 'rule'/'principle' distinction seen in the literature concerning 'environmental principles', which derives from theoretical discussion in other contexts.[38] The utility of this distinction between policy principles and legal principles will be demonstrated in the analysis of the Article 174(2) Community case law that follows in Section III.

Legal principles, for the purposes of this article, are identified as those that are employed by the courts *legally to influence, but not necessarily to determine, the outcome of a case*.[39] A 'legal principle' that legally influences the outcome of a case is one that is used as a basis for the reasoning in a particular case. The principle might be a reason itself, or the supporting rationale for a reason, or it might inform or generate a legal test applied by the courts. In all these senses, a principle is a general concept applied by judges to influence their reasoning and so it is identified as 'legal'. The idea of this tool is that it should isolate those cases in which the Article 174(2) principles are *legally* relevant in EC law (as understood through the lens of its judicial application), and in some way influential of legal outcomes in Community cases.

[38] Much academic literature that considers 'environmental principles', including those in Art. 174(2) EC, and their role in judicial reasoning draws on the jurisprudential ideas of Dworkin and Alexy, both of whom focus heavily on the distinction between legal principles and rules in judicial reasoning. See R. Dworkin, *Taking Rights Seriously (2nd Edn.)* (London: Duckworth, 1978), ch. 2; R. Alexy, *A Theory of Constitutional Rights* (Oxford: Oxford University Press, 2002), 44–110. This body of jurisprudence provides an inadequate theoretical framework for analysing the Art. 174(2) case law since, not only is it contested (cf. N. MacCormick, *Legal Reasoning and Legal Theory* (Oxford: Clarendon Press, 1994); J. Raz, 'Legal Principles and the Limits of the Law' (1972) 81 *Yale Law Journal*, 823–54; L. M. Soriano, 'A Modest Notion of Coherence in Legal Reasoning: A Model for the European Court of Justice' (2003) 16 *Ratio Juris* 3, 296–323), but it was formulated in other legal contexts (in particular, common law adjudication of civil disputes and German constitutional law), which do not take into account the jurisprudential framework of the EC legal order, including the unique articulation of the principles in Art. 174(2) EC. See, e.g., Doherty (2002), n. 29 above, 68–71; E. Fisher, 'Precaution, Precaution Everywhere: Developing a "Common Understanding" of the Precautionary Principle in the European Community' (2002) 9 *Maastricht Journal of European and Comparative Law* 1, 7–28, at 7 and 15–17; R. Macrory, 'Principles into Practice' in Macrory et al., n. 29 above, 3–8; and Winter, n. 29 above, 14–18.

[39] Cf. Dworkin, ibid., 24–6.

On the other hand, *policy principles* are those that:

1. *represent policy positions* on particular issues;[40] and
2. appear in judicial reasoning *by way of observation of, or deference to, relevant political positions/developments*.

The principles expressed in Article 174(2) EC represent Community policy positions with respect to the environment, meeting the first element of this definition. Whether they also meet the second element will become clear from Section III's analysis of the cases. This understanding of a 'policy principle' stands in contradistinction to that of a 'legal principle'. Policy principles perform a different function from legal principles: they are acknowledged by Community courts as representing policy positions, rather than influencing the determination of legal issues. It is the courts' *acknowledgment* of them as policy positions, rather than any judicial definition of that policy, that is important here. The focus of this article on the judicial roles and treatment of the Article 174(2) principles, as opposed to the definition of the principles, can be seen in both these basic analytical tools adopted.

The concepts of legal and policy principles here defined are not mutually exclusive. For example, a policy principle might conceivably support the judicial development of a legal test (thereby acting also as a legal principle), so that both types of principle are relevant to the reasoning of a case. Equally, courts might rely on a policy as a reason in their judgments, thereby justifying a decision as 'one which will tend to secure a desirable [and, in the case of the Article 174(2) principles, politically prescribed] state of affairs',[41] thereby both observing a political position in their reasoning (policy principle) and using the policy legally to influence the outcome of the case (legal principle). Whether it is possible to draw a distinction between legal and policy principles in the case of the Article 174(2) principles, as they are treated by the Community courts, is a question that the mapping exercise that follows will explore.

It should also be noted that these definitions of legal and policy principles are not incontestable or intended to be jurisprudentially rigorous.[42] Rather they are guiding posts for ascertaining how the Community courts apply the Article 174(2) principles. Discerning when these principles are used as instruments of law and are used as instruments of policy is an important way of understanding

[40] For the purposes of this definition, 'policy positions' will be defined as 'courses of action adopted to secure or tend to secure a state of affairs which are conceived to be desirable': Soriano, n. 38 above, 308–9, following MacCormick, n. 38 above, 261.

[41] Ibid.

[42] An important step here is to move away from jurisprudential ideas about principles devised in other legal contexts, to identify how the Art. 174(2) principles are in fact used by courts in the Community context.

and assessing the Community judicial treatment of the Article 174(2) principles, particularly in drawing out the inherent law/policy ambiguity in their Treaty formulation. As will be seen in Section III, the case law veers between treating the Article 174(2) principles purely as policy principles and appearing to engage with them as legal principles, resulting in a confused judicial picture of the principles. The analytical 'principle' tools here defined will help to unpack the case law by identifying when and how this policy/law manoeuvring takes place, which will in turn assist in determining the judicial function of the Article 174(2) principles in Community law.

III. Mapping the Article 174(2) EC Case Law

As already suggested, the Community judicial role played by the Article 174(2) principles is characterized by fluidity between ideas of law and policy. This will now be confirmed by analysing the Article 174(2) case law in detail; the principles will often be identified in the cases acting as both policy and legal principles. To cater for this fluidity, a policy/law spectrum is a useful device for tracking the policy and legal elements at play in the Community courts' treatment of the Article 174(2) principles: cases can be plotted along an axis running between principles operating as policy principles and legal principles (Figure 1).

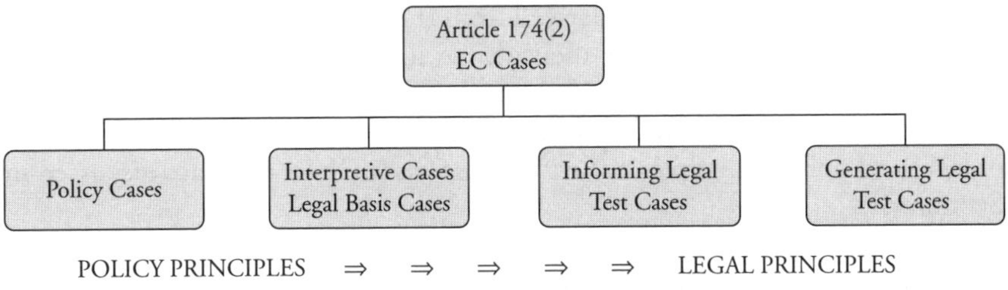

Figure 1. Article 174(2) Community Case Law Mapping Categories on a Policy/Law Spectrum

With this policy/law spectrum and fluidity in mind, concrete mapping analysis begins by categorizing the Article 174(2) case law according to the Community courts' treatment of the principles. The treatment categories adopted for this purpose will now be explored.

A. Mapping Concepts

The Community case law in which the Article 174(2) principles are mentioned can be categorized according to the judicial techniques associated with their appearance: the judicial treatment, or legal use made (or not made), of the principles. This section identifies five such judicial techniques, reflected in discrete treatment categories; these are set out in Figure 1, plotted along the policy/law spectrum.

The first treatment category, *policy cases*, consists of cases in which the Community courts do not use the Article 174(2) principles in resolving the legal issue before them, either as reasons or in informing or generating legal tests. Rather, they treat the principles as policy ideas that *are* to be applied in institutional legislative or decision-making processes, or that *have been* applied in such processes. In both cases, it is not the business of the courts to interfere, and they avoid arguments that encourage them to do so. Also in this category of cases are those in which the principles are mentioned as part of the policy background to the case. In all policy cases, the Article 174(2) principles appear as 'policy principles'. Cases falling in this category are examined in Section III.B.

The second treatment category, *interpretive cases*, comprises those cases in which the Community courts use Article 174(2) principles purposively to interpret Community legislation. The judicial technique adopted with respect to the principles in these cases is teleological interpretation that engages the principles as purposes. On one view, the principles look like legal principles in these cases, in that they are used as a basis for interpreting ambiguous rules and so appear as reasons that influence the outcome of the case. However, in representing the substantive policy (derived from the EC Treaty) behind the legislation under consideration and so identified as its purpose, the principles appear in the courts' reasoning by way of observation of that identified policy; in this way, they also operate as policy principles. Confluence between the concepts of legal and policy principles occurs in these cases. These cases are discussed in Section III.C.

The third treatment category is the group of *legal basis cases*. In these cases, the Article 174(2) principles are drawn on by the courts to assist in resolving disputes between the Community institutions over the correct legal bases of Community measures. In this category, the principles take on a particular legal role, assisting the courts in identifying the (policy) provision of the EC Treaty that founds a contested Community measure. As in the interpretive cases, the courts are looking for the purpose underlying the challenged legislation, finding it in the Article 174(2) policy principles that the measure is intended to implement; it is the policy nature of the principles that determines their legal role. It might be said that the principles in these cases are legal principles, acting as reasons that influence legal outcomes. However, their role as reasons derives from their judicial observation as policies implemented by Community legislation, highlighting their character as policy principles.

The final two, most voluminous and complex, treatment categories, *informing* and *generating legal test cases*, are considered together in Section III.E. 'Informing legal test cases' are those in which the Article 174(2) principles, as mandated policy ideas, are used to inform Community legal tests applied by the courts, in particular those of proportionality and manifest error of assessment. In these cases, the policy nature of the principles is apparent, but they also serve to influence the outcome of the cases, and as such they act as legal principles. 'Generating legal test cases' are those in which the principles are used, notably the precautionary principle (and even more notably in light of the Commission Communication on the Precautionary Principle),[43] to generate legal tests applied by the Community courts. Here the precautionary principle looks most like a legal principle, but its derived policy basis also stands out. The reason for considering together these informing and generating legal test cases is that, while they involve courts doing two different things with the principles, the courts often do both together in the cases, to the extent the subcategories collapse into each other as the case law progresses. The cases in this treatment category are predominantly Article 230 EC Community review actions or Article 28 EC infringement actions brought against Member States. In these cases, compared with those in the other treatment categories, the fluidity between the Article 174(2) principles acting as policy principles and legal principles is most apparent. The irony of these cases is that, the more legal becomes the treatment of the principles by the courts, the more the courts rely on policy to guide that legal treatment (using the Article 174(2) principles as policy principles and the Communication to inform and generate the legal tests applied). How this happens will be considered in detail in Section III.E, and will be understood in the light of the task undertaken by the courts in these cases—legal review of policy discretion.

B. Policy Cases

These are cases in which the Community courts find that there is no room to consider legal arguments based on the Article 174(2) principles. The courts acknowledge that the principles are valid as policy ideas but find them *legally* irrelevant. The Article 174(2) principles articulate policy positions to be adopted at the discretion of the Community and Member State institutions, and the exercise of that discretion is either not at issue in the cases or it is challenged in a manner that is found to be not justiciable by the courts. In these cases, the Article 174(2) principles are

[43] N. 1 above.

marked out as 'policy principles', appearing in judgments but having no effect on the outcome of the cases. Four kinds of policy cases are identifiable:

1. those in which the principles are observed as part of the policy background to the case;[44]
2. those in which the policy discretion conferred by the Article 174(2) principles has yet to be exercised in an unharmonized area of environmental policy, and which exercise is no business of the courts to compel;[45]
3. those in which the policy discretion of the Community legislative institutions has been exercised to harmonize or otherwise legislate in an area of public health or environmental policy, exhausting any role of the Article 174(2) principles;[46] and
4. those cases in which the relevant legal inquiries, prescribed by Article 95(4) and (5) EC concerning Member State derogation from harmonizing measures, leave no room for any consideration of the precautionary principle, which should be considered in political fora.[47]

Cases in all four groups are linked by the common theme that, while the Article 174(2) principles provide a basis for the environmental policy (and health policy) of the Community, they are not principles that are directly engaged or relevant in resolving the legal issues before the courts. Rather, the principles are part of institutional decision-making processes (legislative or otherwise) relevant to these cases, whether in the background or built into the legislative structure under consideration, but not legally at issue or not justiciable. Advocate General (AG) Sharpston, in the recent appeal in *Land Oberösterreich*,[48] observes why Community courts are often reluctant to engage with, in this instance, the precautionary principle to resolve particular legal issues. In this case, the Austrian government had defended its national ban on genetically modified plants and animals, which contravened Directive 2001/18/EC on the Deliberate Release of Genetically Modified Organisms into the Environment and Repealing Directive

[44] Case C-6/03 *Deponiezweckverband Eiterköpfe* v. *Land Rheinland-Pfalz* [2005] ECR I-2753 (*Deponiezweckverband Eiterköpfe*); Case C-494/01 *Commission* v. *Ireland* [2005] ECR I-3331.

[45] Case C-379/92 *Criminal Proceedings against Matteo Peralta* [1994] ECR I-3453 (*Peralta*); Case C-445/00 *Austria* v. *Council* [2003] ECR I-8549.

[46] Case C-293/97 *The Queen* v. *Secretary of State for the Environment and Ministry of Agriculture, Fisheries and Food, ex parte H.A. Standley and Others and D.G.D. Metson and Others* [1999] ECR I-2603 (*Standley*); Case C-6/99 *Association Greenpeace France and Others* v. *Ministère de l' agriculture et de la Pêche and Others* [2000] ECR I-1651 (*Greenpeace*); *Monsanto*, n. 1 above; Case C-127/02 *Landelijke Vereniging tot Behoud van de Waddenzee and Nederlandse Vereniging tot Bescherming van Vogels* v. *Staatssecretaris van Landbouw, Natuurbeheer en Visserij* [2004] ECR I-7405 (*Waddenzee*); Case C-132/03 *Ministero della Salute* v. *Coordinamento delle Associazioni per la Difesa dell'Ambiente e dei Diritti Degli Utenti e dei Consumatori, Federconsumatori, and Others* [2005] ECR I-4167 (*Codacons*).

[47] Case C-3/00 *Denmark* v. *Commission* [2003] ECR I-2643; *Land Oberösterreich*, n. 14 above.

[48] Joined Cases C-439/05P and C-454/05P *Land Oberösterreich and Austria* v. *Commission* [2007] ECR I-0000; appeal of the CFI judgment in Joined Cases T-366/03 and T-235/04 *Land Oberösterreich* v. *Commission* [2005] ECR II-4005.

90/220/EEC (Deliberate Release Directive),[49] arguing that the Commission's refusal to approve the ban did not adequately take into account the precautionary principle. Reflecting the view of the CFI at first instance, AG Sharpston observed that:

> ... the concerns [raised by the Austrian government in argument] are *policy concerns* which must be dealt with in political fora. It is not for this or any other court to determine proper national or Community environmental policy. And the concerns in question are *not in themselves directly relevant to the legal issues* raised in this case ...[50]

This idea of separation between legal issues and policy concerns filters through the cases in this treatment category.

i. *Principles as Policy Background*

In this first subcategory of environmental policy cases, the references to the Article 174(2) principles are passing ones. The Community courts observe the principles as part of the contextual policy background to the case, but they play no direct role in the reasoning of the particular decisions. One such case is *Deponiezweckverband Eiterköpfe*,[51] in which the interpretation of Directive 1999/31/EC on the Landfill of Waste (Landfill Directive) and Article 176 EC were at issue.[52] The ECJ found that German national landfill measures, which were more stringently protective than those set out in the Directive, were compatible with the Community law, primarily because the Community rules did not harmonize this area of waste regulation. In finding that the Landfill Directive permitted this shared regulation of German landfill waste, the ECJ set out the policy background informing the adoption of the Directive, including the four principles in Article 174(2).[53]

ii. *Principles of Community Environmental Policy—Unexercised Discretion*

In this second subcategory of policy cases, the Community courts reject arguments based on the Article 174(2) principles, finding them legally irrelevant since the principles are limited to defining the policy discretion of the Community and do not empower the courts to compel its exercise. *Peralta* is the central case in this subcategory.[54] This is a case in which the ECJ finds that it has no business compelling the exercise of Community environmental policy discretion. This case

[49] [2001] OJ L106/1.

[50] N. 48 above, Opinion of AG Sharpston of 15 May 2007, para. 145, emphasis added. In its decision, the ECJ upheld the decision of the CFI, but did not comment on Austria's precautionary principle argument specifically. This result impliedly rejects the argument that infringement of the precautionary principle could be a legal ground for reviewing the Commission's decision in this case.

[51] *Deponiezweckverband Eiterköpfe*, n. 44 above.

[52] [1999] OJ L182/1.

[53] *Deponiezweckverband Eiterköpfe*, n. 44 above, para. 28.

[54] *Peralta*, n. 45 above. See also *Austria* v. *Council*, n. 45 above.

involved an Article 234 EC (ex-Article 177 EEC) reference to the ECJ from an Italian court asking, inter alia, whether an Italian law that prohibited national vessels from discharging certain harmful substances into the seas, in contravention of internationally accepted practice, was precluded by the preventive principle.[55] The ECJ found that the preventive principle did not preclude the national legislation because Article 174 EC is 'confined to defining the general [environmental] objectives of the Community'.[56] Moreover, it is the responsibility of the Council to determine what action is to be taken in this policy field, and Article 176 EC allows Member States to adopt more stringent environmental protective measures in any case, so long as they are compatible with the Treaty. This reasoning can be read in one of two ways. Firstly, the appeal to the preventive principle was unsuccessful since Article 174(2) EC extends only to *Community* policy on the environment, and does not affect Member State actions;[57] however the ECJ does not explicitly say this. It refers instead to the general nature of Article 174 EC, to the responsibility of the Council to adopt Community environmental policy, and to the latitude afforded to Member States to adopt complementary and more protective measures. A second way to read this case is that the preventive principle argument was unsuccessful because the ECJ was being asked to adopt and compel a policy position, which it feels it is not its job to do. While Member State action was at issue, Community environmental policy and Member State environmental policy (covering common territory) overlap (as acknowledged by Article 176 EC) and, while the Community could take action in this unharmonized area if it wanted to, whether it does so is not an issue for the Community courts. The preventive principle did not have legal force beyond its general policy prescription role.

iii. Principles of Community Public Health and Environmental Policy—Unchallenged Discretion

In this third subcategory of policy cases, the Article 174(2) principles were unsuccessfully relied on in argument either to challenge, or to interpret, Community legislative schemes. The courts found that, with respect to the Community legislative schemes examined in each case, the principles were relevant only to the discretion accorded to Community or Member State institutions in exercising decision-making power under, or in implementing, these schemes. The exercise

[55] This argument may seem counter-intuitive; the argument put to the Italian court was that the level of environmental protection required by the preventive principle in the EC Treaty should match that set out in the MARPOL Convention (International Maritime Organization (IMO) Convention for the Prevention of Marine Pollution from Ships 1973, as modified by the Protocol of 1978 relating thereto (MARPOL 73/78), London (UK), 17 Feb. 1978 (entered into force on 2 Oct. 1983). Published on the Internet at: http://www.imo.org), the relevant provisions of which were not as stringent as those in Italian national law.

[56] *Peralta*, n. 45 above, para. 57.

[57] N. de Sadeleer, 'The Precautionary Principle in EC Health and Environmental Law' (2006) 12 *European Law Journal* 2, 139–72, at 143.

of such discretion was not at issue in the cases. The Article 174(2) principles were identified by the ECJ as guiding the following types of policy discretion:

1. Commission decision-making processes supporting the relevant scheme;[58]
2. Member State discretion in opting out of the scheme through a safeguard clause;[59] and
3. Member State discretion in implementing the relevant scheme.[60]

Those decision-making processes or discretions were not subject to scrutiny in these cases, and can be seen as reflecting the policy-making elements of the schemes under consideration by the courts. Beyond influencing that policy-making discretion (as policy principles), the Article 174(2) principles were found to have no role to play in testing the legality of, or interpreting, the measures at issue (that is, no role as legal principles).

Most of the cases in this subsection are public health cases that involve harmonizing Community legislation relating to genetically modified organisms (GMOs). The exercise of policy discretion by the Community institutions engaged in decision-making in relation to the relevant harmonized area (and that of Member States under safeguard clauses) exhausts any possible role for the precautionary principle. Thus, the ECJ finds that the precautionary principle acts as a policy principle.

A good example is *Codacons*.[61] This was a preliminary reference from an Italian court concerning the interpretation of Article 2(2)(b) of Regulation (EC) No. 1139/98 concerning the Compulsory Indication of the Labelling of Certain Foodstuffs Produced from Genetically Modified Organisms of Particulars other Than Those Provided for in Directive 79/112/EEC.[62] Article 2(2)(b) provided an exception from the Regulation's labelling requirements in the case of foodstuffs where the concentration of GM food was less than 1 per cent and such presence was 'adventitious'. The issue for the ECJ was whether that exception applied to infant food, and the Court found that it did, since there was no indication from the wording, the context, or the purpose of Article 2(2)(b) that it should not so apply, and the Community measures adopted with respect to the labelling of infant food had not been extended to derogate from this provision.[63] There was no room for calling into question this interpretation 'on the basis of the precautionary principle', which was found to be applicable only as part of the decision-making process involved in putting the relevant GM foods on the market in the first place, which is intended to ensure that the GMOs are safe for

[58] *Monsanto*, n. 1 above; *Codacons*, n. 46 above.
[59] *Greenpeace*, n. 46 above; *Monsanto*, n. 1 above.
[60] *Standley*, n. 46 above.
[61] *Codacons*, n. 46 above.
[62] [1998] OJ L159/4, as amended.
[63] *Codacons*, n. 46 above, paras. 54–5.

the consumer.[64] Once such a decision had been made, there was no longer any relevant 'uncertainty as to the existence or extent of risks to human health', a 'presupposition' of the precautionary principle.[65] The Court made no attempt to explore this decision-making process, since it was not challenged in argument (or because the referred question did not extend that far).[66] In any case, the precautionary principle, whatever it involves, in this case was confined to a role of influencing the policy decision-making of the Commission and not the legal issue of interpretation before the Court. In observing this role of the precautionary principle, the Court treats it as a policy principle and not as a legal principle.

Monsanto is another GM food case in which the precautionary principle is raised in argument, largely unsuccessfully.[67] *Monsanto* developed out of the Italian government's abiding concern over the risks involved in releasing GMOs and putting GM products on the market. At issue in the case was the 'simplified procedure' for authorizing the introduction of novel GM foods on to the European market, under Articles 3(4) and 5 of Regulation (EC) No. 258/97 concerning Novel Foods and Novel Food Ingredients (Novel Foods Reg.).[68] This procedure could be employed when a novel food was produced from, but no longer contained any, GMOs, *and* when it was 'substantially equivalent' to an existing food. This procedure required mere notification to the Commission once substantial equivalence was established (by existing science or in the opinion of a relevant national food authority), and no detailed risk assessment by the Commission as required by the formal (non-simplified) novel food authorization process. The Italian government, relying on the safeguard procedure in Article 12 of the Regulation, passed a decree temporarily banning novel foods produced from particular strands of GM maize which still contained small amounts of transgenic protein. This decree was challenged in the Italian national courts by the producers of the GM maize (Monsanto and others). The Italian court referred several questions to the ECJ, the two most relevant (as understood by the ECJ) concerning: (a) the interpretation of the safeguard clause in Article 12, particularly in relation to the ability of Member States to take action on the basis of the precautionary principle; and (b) the legality of the 'simplified procedure', in particular whether it breached Articles 153 and 174 EC and the precautionary and proportionality principles.

Arguments on the basis of the precautionary principle were made on both issues, suggesting that the principle might have a legal role which overlaid the scheme of the Regulation, and which could be relied on by the Member States. To an extent a legal role was given to the precautionary principle as an aid in interpreting

64 Ibid., paras. 56 and 63.

65 Ibid., para. 61.

66 Cf. *Pfizer*, n. 1 above.

67 *Monsanto*, n. 1 above. This case falls into two of the mapping categories: see text accompanying nn. 95–8 below.

68 [1997] OJ L43/1.

Article 12, which will be discussed in Section III.C below.[69] However, it was not a legal role independent of the scheme of the Regulation, since the Court found that a Member State could only take action on the basis of the precautionary principle in accordance with Article 12 of the Regulation, which gives legislative expression to the principle. When it came to the legality challenge, the ECJ gave short shrift to the precautionary principle-based argument, finding that the precautionary principle was already relevantly taken into account in the authorization and safeguard decision-making procedures set up by the Novel Foods Regulation.[70] The precautionary principle was not a legal ground for reviewing the legality of the simplified authorization procedure; rather, as in *Codacons*, it was treated as a policy principle, to be taken into account in the decision-making processes involved in the normal authorization and safeguard procedures of the Regulation.

An interesting environmental case also falls into this subsection. *Standley* involved a challenge to the legality of provisions of Directive 91/676/EEC concerning the Protection of Waters against Pollution Caused by Nitrates from Agricultural Sources (Nitrates Directive),[71] on the basis, inter alia, of infringement of the principle of rectification at source and the polluter pays principle.[72] In this case, the principles were found not to be exhausted by the provisions of the Directive, rather they were consistent with, and capable of being observed by, them. The Directive's scheme was sufficiently flexible for the Member States to implement its measures in accordance with the principle of rectification at source and polluter pays principle.[73] The result of the case is that, until the Directive is interpreted and applied by the Member States in a manner that is incompatible with those principles, they remain policy principles which are incorporated into the provisions of the Directive and guide the discretion of Member States in overseeing their implementation into national law.

iv. Principles of Community Public Health Policy—Member State Derogation under Article 95(4) and (5) EC

This final subcategory of policy cases comprises cases in which the ECJ rejects arguments of Member States defending derogation from harmonizing Community GMO measures under Article 95 EC on the basis of the precautionary principle. In these cases, the arguments based on the precautionary principle are rejected since they are not relevant to the legal inquiries required by Article 95(4) and (5) EC, which sets out in its wording the precise circumstances in which Member States are permitted to derogate from harmonizing measures, giving rise to simple legal tests to be applied by the courts and leaving no room

69 Below, text accompanying nn. 95–8
70 *Monsanto*, n. 1 above, para. 133.
71 [1991] OJ L375/1.
72 *Standley*, n. 46 above.
73 Ibid., paras. 51–3.

for consideration of the precautionary principle. Arguments based on the precautionary principle are dismissed as considerations that should be addressed in national and Community political arenas.

In *Land Oberösterreich*, mentioned above,[74] the Austrian government had sought to derogate from the Deliberate Release Directive[75] (a harmonizing measure) by imposing, in a particular farming area, a general ban on the cultivation of genetically modified plants or seed, and on the breeding and release of transgenic animals. The Commission had refused to allow this derogation, and the CFI and the ECJ supported the Commission's position, since Austria had failed to fulfil the conditions in Article 95(5) EC that permit derogation (in particular, in failing to present 'new scientific evidence' and to identify 'a problem specific to that Member State').[76] Arguments that the Commission had failed adequately to consider the precautionary principle in assessing the submissions of the Austrian government, in this case where the risks associated with releasing and propagating GMOs were highly contestable, failed. In this case, arguments based on the precautionary principle added nothing to the legal conditions imposed by the Treaty. The precautionary principle was found to be a policy principle, belonging in the harmonized policy domain of the Community, and having no legally instrumental role in the tests (mandated by the Treaty conditions in Article 95(4) and (5) EC) applied by the courts to decide these cases.

In all these policy cases, there is a consistent theme: the Article 174(2) principles appear in the reasoning of these cases without playing any role in influencing their legal outcomes. They appear either by way of policy background, or in arguments put to the Community courts that are rejected as inappropriate or irrelevant to the applicable legal tests. The principles are treated in these cases as policy principles and not legal principles.

C. Interpretive Cases

This second treatment category comprises cases in which the Community courts are called upon to interpret secondary Community legislation.[77] In these cases, the Article 174(2) principles are relied on by the ECJ to elucidate the meaning of ambiguous Community legislative provisions. Unlike the Article 95(4) and (5) cases considered in the previous section, the legal tools to be used by the courts in these interpretive cases are not articulated by the EC Treaty, and the role of the Article 174(2) principles is not dismissed as legally irrelevant in these cases. The ECJ adopts a judicial technique of teleological interpretation in these cases, relying on the principles to inform the purposive inquiry thereby undertaken,

[74] N. 48 above, and accompanying text.

[75] N. 49 above.

[76] Joined Cases T-366/03 and T-235/04 *Land Oberösterreich* v. *Commission* [2005] ECR II-4005.

[77] These are primarily referred by Member State courts under Art. 234 EC, but also Art. 226 EC infringement proceedings in which issues of interpretation arise.

which introduces a legal role for the principles. In each case in this section, the ECJ identifies one (or more) of the principles as indicating the purpose or aim of the legislation in question, then using it (them) to guide the interpretive outcome. In this role, the Article 174(2) principles look most like 'legal principles' as understood in other jurisprudential contexts;[78] however, those contexts do not lend much analytical assistance to principles that ambiguously prescribe policy in a legal form.[79] For present purposes, the Article 174(2) principles, in interpretive cases, are better understood as 'legal principles' as defined in this article; they are employed by the Community courts as the basis for reasoning in interpretive cases, influencing their legal outcomes. However, in these purposive exercises of interpretation, the ECJ is looking to the legislative intent, or policy, behind measures to identify their purposes. Thus, in construing environmental directives based on Article 175 EC, the policy purposes in Article 174(2) EC are observed by the Court as the purposes underlying the relevant legislation.[80] Principles identified in this way to assist interpretation are also policy principles. The mixed policy and legal nature of the Article 174(2) principles is hereby apparent.

The interpretive cases are mainly environmental ones concerning the construction of three Community directives: Directive 91/156/EEC amending Directive 75/442/EEC (Waste Framework Directive),[81] Directive 92/43/EEC on the Conservation of Natural Habitats and of Wild Fauna and Flora (Habitats Directive),[82] and Directive 91/271/EEC concerning Urban Waste-Water Treatment (Urban Waste-Water Directive).[83] Rather than speculating on why these particular directives, as opposed to other environmental directives with ambiguous provisions that have come before the courts for interpretation,[84] have been interpreted in light of the Article 174(2) principles, the point here is to focus on the fact of their having been so interpreted.

A large body of the interpretive case law concerns the definition of 'waste' in the Waste Framework Directive.[85] There has been much litigation about the definition of waste, since it is unhelpfully undefined in the Directive and it is the central concept that triggers regulatory consequences that follow under the Directive. In *ARCO*,[86] the ECJ concluded from the fact that Community policy on the environment, under Article 174(2) EC, 'is to aim at a high level of

[78] In this guise, the principles also resemble 'legal principles' as understood in other jurisprudential contexts: Tridimas, n. 3 above, 2; Dworkin, n. 38 above, 26; and Winter, n. 29 above, 16.

[79] See n. 38 above.

[80] Cf. *Monsanto*, text accompanying nn. 95–8.

[81] [1991] OJ L78/32.

[82] [1992] OJ L206/7.

[83] [1991] OJ L135/40. See Case C-280/02 *Commission* v. *France* [2004] ECR I-8573; cf. Case C-119/02 *Commission* v. *Greece* [2004] ECR I-1433.

[84] Cf. Art. 2(1) of Dir. 85/337/EEC on the Assessment of the Effects of certain Public and Private Projects on the Environment (EIA Dir.) [1985] OJ L175/40; as amended.

[85] N. 81 above, Art. 1(a).

[86] Joined Cases C-418/97 and C-419/97 *ARCO Chemie Ltd. Nederland* v. *Minister van Volkshuisvesting, Ruimtelijke Ordening en Milieubeheer* (C-418/97) *and Vereniging Dorpsbelang Hees,*

protection and is to be based, in particular, on the precautionary principle and the principle that preventive action should be taken', that the definition of 'waste' in the Directive should not be interpreted restrictively.[87] In reaching this interpretive conclusion, the ECJ relied explicitly on a policy position derived from the preventive and precautionary principles. The Article 174(2) principles, in these waste cases, act as legal principles in directing the outcome of the cases, but they operate also as policy principles, informing the policy background of the legislation at issue. In a line of cases following *ARCO*, the ECJ has repeatedly adopted this same interpretive reasoning.[88]

In *Lirussi & Bizzaro*,[89] the ECJ again uses the preventive and precautionary principles as interpretive aids. This case also involved the interpretation of the Waste Framework Directive, in respect of the obligations it imposes on temporarily stored waste. In this case, the interpretive leap from the preventive and precautionary principles is explained in more detail. Those principles are found to give rise to obligations on the part of the Community and Member States 'to prevent, reduce and, in so far as is possible, eliminate from the outset, the sources of pollution or nuisance by adopting measures of a nature such as to eliminate recognised risks'.[90] From that interpretive step, the ECJ concluded that the obligations under Articles 4 and 8 of the Directive,[91] which were intended to implement the principles of precaution and preventive action, applied to temporarily stored waste. In this case, a minimum content of the principles is ascertained by the Court and used to resolve the identified issue for interpretation. In this way, the Article 174(2) principles, with an identified content in this context, operate as both policy principles and legal principles in the reasoning of the ECJ. While this mapping exercise is concerned with identifying the legal techniques adopted by

Stichting Werkgroep Weurt and Vereniging Stedelijk Leefmilieu Nijmegen v. *Directeur van de Dienst Milieu en Water van de Provincie Gelderland* (C-419/97) [2000] ECR I-4475 (*ARCO*).

[87] Ibid., paras. 36–40.

[88] Case C-9/00 *Palin Granit Oy* v. *Vehmassalon Kansanterveystyön Kuntayhtymän Hallitus* [2002] ECR I–3533 (*Palin Granit*); Case C-114/01 *AvestaPolarit Chrome Oy, formerly Outokumpu Chrome Oy* [2003] ECR I-8725; Case C-457/02 *Criminal Proceedings against Niselli* [2004] ECR I-10853; Case C-235/02 *Criminal Proceedings against Saetti and Frediani* [2004] ECR I-1005; Case C-1/03 *Criminal Proceedings against Van De Walle* [2004] ECR I-7613; Case C-176/05 *Kvz Retec Gmbh* v. Republik *Österreich* [2007] ECR I-1721. Cf. Case C-270/03 *Commission* v. *Italy* [2005] ECR I-5233, in which the reference to the Art. 174(2) principles is not directly connected to the interpretive conclusion reached by the ECJ; rather they are mentioned as policy principles, setting out the policy background to the issue, relevant generally to the particular reasons put forward by the Court (at para. 24).

[89] Joined Cases C-175/98 and C-177/98 *Criminal Proceedings against Lirussi and Bizzaro* [1999] ECR I-6881 (*Lirussi & Bizzaro*).

[90] Ibid., para. 51.

[91] Art. 4 requires that Member States prohibit the abandonment, dumping, and uncontrolled disposal of waste, while Art. 8 requires that they ensure that any holder of waste has it handled by a private or public waste collector, or by an undertaking which carries out the operations listed in Annex II A or B, or recovers or disposes of it himself in accordance with the provisions of the Waste Framework Directive.

the Community courts with respect to the Article 174(2) principles, and not with defining the principles, it can be seen that defining the content of the principles is an aspect of their judicial treatment in these interpretive cases.[92]

In a similar fashion, in a line of cases concerning the interpretation of Article 6(3) of the Habitats Directive, the ECJ has had to resort to the precautionary principle as an interpretive aid, revealing some precision about its content in this particular EC interpretive context.[93] The Court finds that, with respect to uncertain environmental risks, the precautionary principle dictates that the protective measures of the Directive should apply where environmental risks cannot be excluded. Simply put, the precautionary principle advocates erring on the side of caution, and the regulatory scheme of the Directive allows for such an idea to be called on to resolve its ambiguities. In these cases, the precise issue for the ECJ is when a plan or project is 'likely to have a significant effect' on a special area of conservation, thereby triggering the requirement for an 'appropriate assessment' to be carried out. The Court concludes:

> In the light... of the precautionary principle, which is one of the foundations of the high level of protection pursued by Community policy on the environment [under] Article 174(2) EC, and by reference to which the Habitats Directive must be interpreted, such a risk [i.e. likelihood] exists if it cannot be excluded on the basis of objective information that the plan or project will have significant effects on the site concerned.[94]

In this way, the precautionary principle, with its content in this EC environmental context clarified, operates as a legal principle, influencing the issue of interpretation referred to the ECJ.

These environmental interpretive cases demonstrate a trend in purposive reasoning, involving the principles as legal principles. At the same time, these cases, where the preventive and precautionary principles are used to interpret ambiguous Community legislation, can generally be construed as cases in which the ECJ is appealing to a policy position to resolve the interpretive issue before it. The policy principle nature of the Article 174(2) principles stands out as an abiding and consistent one.

[92] Although not of all the interpretive cases: consider *ARCO*, n. 86 above, and accompanying text.

[93] *Waddenzee*, n. 46 above; Case C-6/04 *Commission* v. *United Kingdom* (*Conformity*) [2005] ECR I-9017; Case C-98/03 *Commission* v. *Germany* [2006] ECR I-53. Note that the Community courts do not identify a consistent content of the precautionary principle across all EC legal contexts: cf., e.g., *BSE*, n. 11 above, para. 99; *Artegodan*, n. 11 above, para. 184. The precautionary principle does not even have a consistent content across the interpretive cases: cf. *Monsanto*, nn. 97–8 below.

[94] *Waddenzee*, n. 46 above, para. 44. Cf. the second part of the construction exercise undertaken by the ECJ with respect to Art. 6(3) of the Habitats Directive, which the Court resolved by a close reading of the Directive itself. For this, resort to the precautionary principle was found to be unnecessary; there was no ambiguity that needed purposive resolution. In this case, the precautionary principle acted as a policy principle; it was enshrined in the legislation and played no operative role in the reasoning of the ECJ (at para. 59); see Opinion of AG Kokott in *Waddenzee*, n. 46 above, para. 101.

An interpretive role for the precautionary principle does not feature in public health cases in the way that the Article 174(2) principles do in environmental cases. Public health cases do not involve Community legislation that is based on Article 175 EC, so it is not surprising that the Community courts do not isolate the environmental principles as neatly informing the interpretive questions put to it in public health cases. However, there is one case in which the precautionary principle, extended into the public health domain, operates as a legal principle, informing an interpretive issue addressed by the ECJ. In *Monsanto*,[95] discussed above, the ECJ deflected most of the arguments based on the precautionary principle, but observed that the precautionary principle was given expression in the safeguard clause (Article 12) of the Novel Food Regulation. Thus, the Court finds, 'the conditions for the application of that clause must be interpreted having due regard to [the precautionary] principle'.[96] Relying on previous case law, the ECJ asserts that it follows from the precautionary principle that 'where there is uncertainty as to the existence or extent of risks to human health, protective measures *may* be taken without having to wait until the reality and seriousness of those risks become fully apparent'.[97] Thus, a Member State may take protective measures under Article 12 even if a full risk assessment cannot be carried out because of inadequate available scientific data. The ECJ has identified the relevant content of the precautionary principle, and used it to influence an interpretive outcome; the precautionary principle is thus acting as a legal principle.

The Court goes on to expand on the content of the precautionary principle, asserting that, despite inadequate scientific data, there must be:

> specific evidence which... makes it possible reasonably to conclude on the basis of the most reliable scientific evidence available... that the implementation of those measures is necessary in order to avoid... potential risks...[98]

The requirement of reliable scientific evidence in cases of scientific uncertainty will for now be noted as further informing the content of the principle here identified by the ECJ,[99] giving it an apparently different identity from that isolated in *Waddenzee*. This difference, or conflict, can be explained by appreciating that the courts are defining the principles with respect to different legal questions in these cases so that,[100] in giving marginal content to the principles in each case, the

[95] *Monsanto*, n. 1 above.
[96] Ibid., para. 110.
[97] Ibid., para. 111.
[98] Ibid., para. 113.
[99] This theme of adequate scientific information will be addressed further in Section III.D below.
[100] In *Waddenzee*, n. 46 above, the ECJ's interpretation focused on the precautionary principle's *requiring* protective measures in the face of uncertain environmental risks. Arguably, the difference lies in the nature of the issue before the Court; in those environmental cases, the Court needed to determine when environmental protective measures should apply (i.e. when they are *required* to apply), whereas, in this case, the concern is when a Member State is allowed to rely on the safeguard clause (i.e. when it *may* do so). Thus the legal context of the case determines the relevant content of the precautionary principle.

resulting definitional picture thus appears confused. The focus of this article on the treatment or use of the principles allows us to step away from this confusion and understand it contextually. What can be surmised from the courts' need to define the principles in these interpretive cases is that, as the Article 174(2) principles take on roles as legal principles, the courts need to substantiate them to some extent. We will see this trend develop, as we consider increasingly legal treatment of the principles by the courts.

As for the precautionary principle operating as a policy principle in *Monsanto*, the policy nature of the precautionary principle is not as clear, since the ECJ does not explicitly appeal to policy laid down in the EC Treaty to assist in its interpretive inquiry. However, the precautionary principle does also act as a policy principle in this case, since, as in the environmental interpretive cases, the ECJ looks to the precautionary principle as the policy behind Article 12 in order to guide its purposive interpretation.

In the above interpretive cases, it can be seen that the Article 174(2) principles are treated by the Community courts as aids to interpret ambiguous Community legislative provisions. In that role, they are legal principles in that they act as reasons that influence the outcomes of legal issues of interpretation, purposively guiding interpretation, and they are also policy principles in that the courts observe them as the policy underlying the legislation in question.

D. Legal Basis Cases

There are only a couple of cases in this treatment category, in which the Article 174(2) principles are relied on by the ECJ to determine the correct legal basis for contested Community measures. These cases are similar to the interpretive cases in that the Article 174(2) principles act as both legal and policy principles. As legal principles, they look different, since they are influencing a different type of legal question. However, as policy principles they look very similar, since the ECJ is engaged in a purposive exercise which draws out the principles as policies behind the legislative measure at issue. *Commission* v. *Council (Waste Directive)*[101] is the best example. In this case, the ECJ considered whether the Waste Framework Directive was properly adopted on the basis of Article 175 EC (ex-Article 130s EEC).[102] In finding that it was properly adopted on that basis, the ECJ looked to the aim and content of the measure,[103] finding that its aim was to implement the principle of rectification at source,[104] and that its content included, inter alia, a 'confirmation' of the polluter pays principle in Article 15. In this way, the Article

101 Case C-155/91 *Commission* v. *Council* (*Waste Directive*) [1993] ECR I-939.

102 See also Case C-187/93 *EP* v. *Council* (*Waste Regulation*) [1994] ECR I-2857, para. 20, which relies on the outcome in *Commission* v. *Council* (*Waste Directive*). Cf. Case C-300/89 *Commission* v. *Council (Titanium Dioxide)* [1991] ECR 2867.

103 N. 101 above, para. 7.

104 Ibid., paras. 13–14.

174(2) principles were observed as the legislative policy underlying the contested Directive, thus acting as policy principles. The principles also took on a legal role, acting as reasons influencing the outcome of the case, through the ECJ's purposive inquiry, and so can be seen as legal principles. That legal role, however, is very much infused with consideration of policy, since the task of the Court in this case is to determine which policy basis in the EC Treaty is being engaged by the Community legislature in promulgating this Directive. It is the policy nature of the principles that determines their legal role.

E. Informing and Generating Legal Test Cases

So far, we have seen three treatment categories in which the Article 174(2) principles variously act as legal and policy principles. This Section considers the final two treatment categories, in which the principles take on their strongest roles as legal principles: the informing and generating legal test cases. These are cases in which the Article 174(2) principles are relied on either:

1. to inform legal tests of Community or Member State review; or
2. to generate such tests.

In these cases, there is a progression from early cases in which the principles are employed by the Community courts to inform legal tests of review (rule of reason, proportionality), to cases in which the principles are discussed in more detail by the courts and used also to generate legal tests (adequate scientific evidence) as well as to inform legal review tests (manifest error, proportionality). The latter development occurred, in particular, with respect to the precautionary principle in public health cases, largely inspired by the policy guidance in the Commission Communication on the Precautionary Principle.[105] In those cases where the principles inform legal tests, it is the policy position represented by the principles that informs the relevant review test, so that they operate as both policy and legal principles. In the cases where the precautionary principle generates a legal test of review, the precautionary principle looks most like a legal principle; however, again, the influence of the precautionary principle as a policy principle is also strongly present.

The cases in this treatment category are generally Article 230 EC Community review actions, or Article 226 EC (Article EC 28 infringement) actions in which challenged Member State measures are reviewed by the courts for compatibility with Community law.[106] The legal issues to be addressed, and legal tests to be applied, by the Community courts are not easily isolated in these cases, due to minimal Treaty guidance.[107] With respect to Community review, the EC

[105] Communication, n. 1 above.
[106] Other cases are Art. 234 EC actions, which raise the same issues indirectly.
[107] Cf. Art. 95(4) and (5) EC policy cases: text accompanying nn. 73–6 above.

Treaty does not set out precise tests; Article 230 EC gives broad guidance as to the grounds of review that can found actions but sets no precise standards of review.[108] These the Community courts have had to develop independently. Equally, Article 30 EC gives a general description of market disruptive measures (infringing Article 28 EC) that Member States are entitled to take in the name of public health (and to an extent environmental) protection, but gives no clues as to the particular nature of or limits to that idea.[109] Where there is less guidance from the Treaty concerning how Community actions should be resolved, it will be seen that, in these cases, the reasoning involving the Article 174(2) principles is more involved and arguments based on them less readily dismissed.

All cases in this treatment category involve substantive review of policy decisions, in the form of Community or Member State legislative measures, which rely on the Article 174(2) principles. In determining the legally permissible limits of the (Community and Member State) policy discretion under review, the courts are faced with identifying the substantive scope of that discretion. The Article 174(2) policy principles prescribe that scope, and so it follows that they inform the tests applied by the courts in determining whether the Community and Member State institutions have overstepped bounds of their policy authority. The nature of the legal inquiry is complicated since the courts have a duty to police the legality of exercises of discretion,[110] but they also need to allow decisions to be made. The delicacy of this exercise translates into an inevitable messiness in the treatment of the Article 174(2) principles, since they form the basis for the exercise of policy discretion, but also for legally testing its bounds. And so the courts use the principles to inform or generate the legal tests applied to review discretion in these cases (legal principles), but also as the basis for deferring to the policy decisions of the Community institutions (and of the Member States in unharmonized domains) within the scope of permissible policy identified by the courts (policy principles). This dual role of the principles, as directing legal outcomes but preserving policy discretion, highlights ambiguous legal/policy nature of the Article 174(2) principles.

[108] Art. 230(2) EC admits Community review actions on the grounds of 'lack of competence, infringement of an essential procedural requirement, infringement of this Treaty or of any rule of law relating to its application, or misuse of powers', but the Treaty is silent on further elaborating these open-textured heads of review. See P. Craig, *EU Administrative Law* (Oxford: Oxford University Press, 2006), 265–83.

[109] The open-ended nature of the legal inquiries provoked by Arts. 28 and 30 EC are highlighted in academic analyses of Art. 28 EC cases, which find the legal approach of the ECJ complex to interpret. See generally, M. P. Maduro, *We the Court: The European Court of Justice and the European Economic Constitution—A Critical Reading of Article 30 of the EC Treaty* (Oxford: Hart Publishing, 1998), Chs. 2 and 3. In addition, the Treaty gives no guidance on the tests to be applied in determining whether a measure that offends Art. 28 EC is justified by the 'rule of reason', as established by the ECJ in Case 120/78 *Rewe Zentral* v. *Bundesmonopolverwaltung für Branntweinn* [1979] ECR 649 (*Cassis De Dijon*).

[110] Arts. 220 and 230 EC.

i. Informing Legal Test Cases

In the informing legal test cases, the Community courts use the Article 174(2) principles to inform legal tests of review applied to review Community and Member State discretion exercised in the environmental and public health policy domains. In this way, the principles act as legal principles, influencing legal outcomes. However, in using the principles to inform the legal tests applied, the courts also defer to policy decisions made within the permissible scope of discretion so identified, and so the principles act as policy principles as well. The policy/law nature of the Article 174(2) principles in these cases can be understood not only as a result of their inherently ambiguous nature, but also as a result of the nature of the actions involved in these cases, which concern legal review of policy discretion.

Walloon Waste presents a good starting point for analysing how the Community courts use the Article 174(2) principles to inform legal test of review.[111] This case concerned infringement by Belgium of Article 28 EC in preventing the import of waste from other Member States. The issue was whether this infringement was justified by 'imperative requirements relating to environmental protection' (the rule of reason), which could only be relied on if the Belgian measures were indistinctly applicable to waste from Belgium and from other Member States. The ECJ found that the infringement was justified, and that the rule of reason applied. The Court referred to the principle of rectification at source, relied on in argument by Belgium, in resolving the legal question before it thus:

> In assessing whether or not the barrier in question is discriminatory, account must be taken of the particular nature of waste. The principle that environmental damage should as a matter of priority be remedied at source, laid down by Article 130r(2) of the Treaty as a basis for action by the Community relating to the environment, entails that it is for each region, municipality or other local authority to take appropriate steps to ensure that its own waste is collected, treated and disposed of; it must accordingly be disposed of as close as possible to the place where it is produced, in order to limit as far as possible the transport of waste... It follows that having regard to the differences between waste produced in different places and to the connection of the waste with its place of production, the contested measures cannot be regarded as discriminatory.[112]

The principle of rectification at source is here operating at two levels. Formally and particularly, it informs the test of discrimination applied to trigger the 'imperative requirements' defence.[113] However, it can also be seen that the principle informs the rule of reason more generally. The principle of rectification at source informs the 'imperative requirement' of environment protection since it is prescribed in the

[111] Case C-2/90 *Commission* v. *Belgium* [1992] ECR I-4431 (*Walloon Waste*). Cf. Case C-209/98 *Sydhavnens Sten & Grus Aps* [2000] ECR I-3743; Case C-320/03 *Commission* v. *Austria* [2005] ECR I-9871.

[112] *Walloon Waste*, ibid., paras. 34–6.

[113] Cf. Doherty (2002), n. 29 above, 60–2; and S. Weatherill, 'Publication Review: "Free Movement of Goods in the European Community" (Peter Oliver)' (2003) 28 *European Law Review* 5, 756–8.

Treaty as founding Community environmental policy, and this seems to motivate the resolution of the discrimination question. In this way, Community environmental policy particularizes the Member State policy that may be adopted to derogate from the Article 28 EC free movement guarantee in the name of environmental protection ('Community environment policy' here broadly understood). Viewed either way, the principle of rectification at source is engaged somewhat crudely by the ECJ in relation to the rule of reason in order to support a Member State measure that is consistent with the principle. This crudeness can arguably be explained by the nature of the principle of rectification at source as a policy principle: the ECJ recognizes the implementation of a policy that conforms to that prescribed in Article 174(2) EC and adjusts its legal reasoning to fit. The ECJ is engaged in reviewing the limits of policy discretion afforded to Member States, relying on legal tests to do so, which in turn are informed by substantive policy prescriptions laid down in the EC Treaty. From this early case, the Article 174(2) principles have come to inform both Community and Member State review tests, and, while they do so in different ways, they perform one constant function: identifying the limits of the policy discretion afforded to Community and Member State institutions in environmental and public health matters.

The next early and fundamental informing legal test case, *BSE*,[114] involved the proportionality principle. Proportionality, described by the ECJ as a 'general principle of Community law',[115] is a principle, comprised of discrete legal tests, that limits the discretionary power of both Community and Member State institutions as they legislate and make decisions within the scope of Community law. The precise tests comprising, and manner of application of, the proportionality principle differ slightly from case to case, and particularly between review of Community and Member State measures.[116] However, for present purposes, it is sufficiently helpful to set out the basic three-pronged test of proportionality, which appears relatively consistently across contexts, and which is informed in various ways by the Article 174(2) principles in the case law. The proportionality principle requires that:

1. measures adopted by Community institutions do not exceed the limits of what is *appropriate and necessary* in order to attain the *objectives legitimately pursued* by the legislation in question ('necessity' or 'suitability' test);
2. when there is a choice between *several appropriate measures* recourse must be had to the least onerous;
3. the disadvantages caused must not be *disproportionate* to the aims pursued.[117]

[114] *BSE*, n. 11 above.

[115] Ibid., para. 96.

[116] Opinion of AG Maduro in Case C-434/04 *Ahokainen & Leppik* v. *Virallinen Syyttäjä* [2006] ECR I-9171, paras. 23–31.

[117] Case C-331–88 *The Queen* v. *Minister of Agriculture, Fisheries and Food and Secretary of State for Health, ex parte Fedesa and Others* [1990] ECR I-4023, para. 13.

These discrete limbs of the proportionality principle are informed differently by the Article 174(2) principles,[118] and they will be referred to individually in the cases that follow.

BSE, and its accompanying case *NFU*,[119] was a public health case,[120] which involved challenges to an emergency Commission decision banning the export of British beef. The 'precautionary principle', as recognized in later cases and the Commission Communication,[121] was first articulated (although not mentioned by name) in the following way by the ECJ in these cases:

> Where there is uncertainty as to the existence or extent of risks to human health, the institutions may take protective measures without having to wait until the reality and seriousness of those risks become fully apparent.[122]

This principle represents a policy position that is permissible for the Community legislative institutions to adopt. It was derived from Article 174 EC (ex-Article 130r EEC), which the ECJ found to be applicable in the public health domain since one of the objectives of Community environmental policy is the protection of human health.[123] Having acknowledged this policy principle, the ECJ then goes on to use it to inform the proportionality applied to review the legality of the contested Commission decision. In particular, it uses the precautionary principle to inform the first 'suitability' limb of proportionality, as set out above.[124] The ECJ finds that, in the context of EC agricultural policy, the Community institutions in that domain have considerable discretion; the legality of a measure taken can only be adjudged relevantly unsuitable if 'manifestly inappropriate' in relation to the objective pursued.[125] Narrowing down the particular context of this case further, the ECJ finds that, in cases of agricultural policy decision-making where the risks to human health are uncertain, as in this case, it is not manifestly inappropriate for the institutions to adopt protective measures before

[118] On environmental principles informing the constituent elements of proportionality, see also de Sadeleer (2002), n. 6 above, 291–391. Cf. Scott, n. 3 above, who points out that the CFI's assertion of the 'autonomous' nature of the precautionary principle in *Artegodan* released it from its former identity of being 'conflated' with proportionality (at 54).

[119] Case C-157/96 *The Queen* v. *Ministry of Agriculture, Fisheries and Food, Commissioners of Customs & Excise, ex parte National Farmers' Union and Others* [1998] ECR I-2265 (*NFU*). References will be to *BSE* only, since *NFU* is identical in all respects relevant to this article.

[120] It is in public health cases that extensive treatment of the precautionary principle in review cases has developed.

[121] E.g. *Monsanto*, n. 1 above, para. 111; Communication, n. 1 above, 24.

[122] *BSE*, n. 11 above, para. 99.

[123] The Court also relied on the 'integration principle' to find the precautionary principle relevant to the public health domain. The principle 'that environmental protection requirements must be integrated into the definition and implementation of other Community policies' used to be also located in Art. 130r(2) EEC, but now exists as a stand-alone principle in Art. 6 EC: *BSE*, n. 11 above, para. 100.

[124] See text accompanying n. 117 above.

[125] *BSE*, n. 11 above, para. 97.

the reality of risks become apparent.[126] In this way, the precautionary principle, as a policy principle that marks out the permissible area of Community discretion to which the courts defer, informs part of the legal review test applied by the ECJ,[127] thereby also acting as a legal principle. This judicial treatment of the precautionary principle, as informing the proportionality inquiry in review cases, is a trend that extends throughout the Community and Member State review cases. It should be noted that, in this case, the precautionary principle informed the question of what are measures 'appropriate and necessary' under the suitability test. In later informing legal test cases that involve proportionality, the principles are also used to inform other parts of the three-part test set out above.[128]

In these early informing legal test cases, the Article 174(2) principles are used to mark out an area of permissible institutional policy discretion to which the courts defer (acting as policy principles), which then informs the legal tests applied by the Community courts in reviewing exercises of such discretion (acting as legal principles). A similarity with the interpretive cases is here noted: in these cases, where again the principles take on legal roles, the courts define them marginally, substantiating them to the extent required to resolve the relevant legal issue.[129]

ii. Pfizer

The judicial role of the precautionary principle in the Community case law does not stop at informing legal tests for reviewing policy discretion. Its judicial treatment was considerably expanded and complicated in two seminal decisions of the CFI reviewing the public health discretion of the Community legislature, *Pfizer*[130] and *Alpharma*.[131] These cases mark a shift in the case law,[132] with the precautionary principle being used to generate as well as inform legal tests of review in these cases. That shift was precipitated by the Communication, which elaborated the Commission's view on applying the precautionary principle in its decision-making, and the ideas and language of which resonate through *Pfizer* and later cases. Heavily influenced by the contents of this policy document, the CFI gives the precautionary principle much more attention and importance as a legal principle, highlighting the policy/law ambiguity of the principle. In *Pfizer* and *Alpharma*, the precautionary principle is used both to generate a test of 'adequate scientific cogency and objectivity' (a procedural guarantee) and to inform the legal tests of manifest error of assessment and proportionality.

[126] Ibid., paras. 99 and 103.

[127] In *Artegodan*, the CFI acknowledged that the precautionary principle was 'implicitly applied in the review of proportionality [in *BSE*]': *Artegodan*, n. 11 above, para. 185.

[128] See, e.g., *Pfizer*, n. 1 above, paras. 441–4 (duty to take less onerous measures), and paras. 456 and 471 (disproportionality). See also Case T-158/03 *Industrias Químicas Del Vallés* v. *Commission* [2005] ECR II-2425 (*IQV*), paras. 133 and 137 (identification of objectives legitimately pursued).

[129] See text accompanying n. 100 above.

[130] N. 1 above.

[131] Case T-70/99R *Alpharma* v. *Council* [2002] ECR II-3495 (*Alpharma*).

[132] Fisher, n. 9 above, 229.

Unpacking the treatment of the precautionary principle in these cases is necessary to understand this dual role. This will now be done.[133]

Pfizer involved a challenge to Regulation (EC) No. 2821/98,[134] which withdrew Community authorization for an antibiotic, virginiamycin, used as a growth promoter in animals reared for human consumption.[135] The Regulation was explicitly adopted on the basis of the precautionary principle,[136] in the light of the risk that use of virginiamycin as an animal growth promoter would promote antibiotic resistance in humans through animal consumption. Pfizer challenged the Regulation on eight different grounds, including manifest errors of assessment, breach of the principle of proportionality, and breach of the precautionary principle.[137] Argued in this fashion, the precautionary principle looks like a ground for challenging the review of Community measures that is legally equivalent to the judicial review tests of manifest error or proportionality. However, this is not the case. The precautionary principle is not a 'test' of judicial review in the way that manifest error or proportionality are, rather it sets out a remit of substantive policy exercisable by the Community institutions. To a large extent, in the CFI's reasoning, the limits of this remit are policed by the other two review tests, but they are also policed by a procedural guarantee of scientific risk assessment and objectivity that derives from the Commission's Communication (which requires that the precautionary principle be applied within a process of decision-making founded on scientific risk assessment and evaluation)[138] and which is repeatedly stressed by the CFI throughout the judgment.

The reasoning of the decision is very lengthy and difficult to follow; in particular, there are layers of reasoning in involving the precautionary principle. While there is a particular section devoted to the application of the precautionary principle,[139] this is not a discrete section responding to the challenge to the Regulation on this ground. Rather this section needs to be seen in view of the overall approach taken by the CFI in responding to the eight grounds of review argued; the main part of the Court's response to these grounds is undertaken through the Court's understanding of risk-based decision-making, which is influenced by the structure of such decision-making set out in the Communication. The Court does not address each of the grounds in turn; rather, it finds that six

[133] *Pfizer* will be addressed in detail, and *Alpharma* only where relevantly different.

[134] Reg. (EC) No. 2821/98 Amending, as regards Withdrawal of the Authorisation of Certain Antibiotics, Directive 70/224/EEC concerning Additives in Feeding Stuffs [1998] OJ L351/4.

[135] *Alpharma* involved a similar challenge to Reg. (EC) No. 2821/98, ibid., which also banned the use of antibiotic bacitracin zinc as a fattening agent in animal feed.

[136] N. 134 above, recital 29.

[137] Note that the other grounds included breach of the principle of legitimate expectations, breach of the obligation to state reasons, misuse of powers, infringement of the right to property: *Pfizer*, n. 1 above, para. 107. These are not here considered since the CFI's discussion of these grounds did not engage the precautionary principle directly.

[138] See text accompanying nn. 16–19 above.

[139] *Pfizer*, n. 1 above, paras. 129–73.

of the grounds, including the three particularly relevant here (manifest error, and breach of proportionality and the precautionary principle), all 'in essence' concern alleged misapplication of the precautionary principle, and so are considered by analysing the application of that principle, understood as a two-step process of risk assessment and risk management.[140] In this way, the CFI addresses alleged errors in risk assessment and risk management in turn, applying the various grounds of review that are legal tests (manifest error and proportionality) within this structure. With the reasoning so structured around the approach to the precautionary principle laid down in the Communication, it is difficult to understand precisely what legal tests the CFI is applying and, more significantly for this article, how it treats the precautionary principle. How the CFI treats the precautionary principle, and how the principle can be seen to inform and generate the legal tests applied in this complicated reasoning, is best understood in four steps.

Firstly, the CFI finds that, in cases of scientifically uncertain risk to human health, the precautionary principle permits the Community institutions to take preventive measures without waiting for the reality or seriousness of those risks to become fully apparent.[141] As in *BSE*, the Court relies on Article 174(2) EC (ex-Article 130r(2) EEC) as the basis for this policy principle.[142]

Secondly, and unlike in *BSE*, the CFI examines closely the circumstances in which it can be said that there exists such scientifically uncertain risk.[143] At this stage, the CFI begins its process of generating a new legal test: a scientific risk assessment must be carried out before any preventive measures can be taken in the name of the precautionary principle to ensure that no arbitrary measures are adopted.[144] While a full scientific risk assessment cannot be carried out, since by definition we are in the territory of imperfect scientific information, another dimension to the procedural guarantee is introduced to shape the test of adequate scientific evidence developed by the CFI here:[145] 'as thorough a scientific risk assessment as possible', founded on the principles of 'excellence, transparency and independence', must be carried out to give the institutions 'sufficiently reliable and

[140] Ibid., para. 108.

[141] Ibid., paras. 140–1, and 385–6.

[142] Ibid., paras. 114 and 140.

[143] The extensive exercise that follows is in response to Pfizer's argument that the Community institutions did not correctly assess the scientific risk in this case, and adopted the Regulation 'for reasons of political expediency without a proper scientific basis': ibid., para. 127. Considering the width of discretion accorded to the Community institutions by the subsequent reasoning of the CFI (reflected in the ultimate result that the Regulation was lawfully adopted), and the acknowledgment that 'restoration of consumer confidence' may be an objective that the institutions might legitimately pursue (ibid., para. 462), it is arguable that the extensive scientific inquiry of the CFI was of limited value, and that the allegation of 'political expediency' concerned an area of substantive political decision-making that the CFI felt it was not its place to question.

[144] Ibid., paras. 155 and 162.

[145] This is a procedural guarantee conferred by the Community legal order in administrative proceedings, derived from the 'duty of the competent institution to examine carefully and impartially all the relevant aspects of the individual case': ibid., para. 171.

cogent information' on which to base their policy decision.[146] This procedural guarantee relating to a risk assessment requirement reflects Community policy, as set out in the Communication and other Commission policy documents;[147] the Communication clearly influences the reasoning of the Court. The CFI is here adopting a legal approach, generating a legal test, based on Community policy.

Thirdly, the CFI identifies two aspects of this risk assessment exercise, firstly, the determination of the level of risk to human health deemed unacceptable for society, and secondly, conducting a scientific assessment of the risks.[148] With respect to the former, which involves the definition of political objectives, the Community institutions enjoy a broad discretion, and the substance of any decision taken can only be vitiated by judicial review on the grounds of manifest error, misuse of powers, or clear excess of bounds of discretion.[149] Unhelpfully, the CFI does not elaborate on these tests, but the result of the case helps to illuminate them, since no such vitiation was found on the facts. With respect to the second aspect of risk assessment, which the Court spends much more time examining on the facts, the CFI finds that the same limited tests are applicable in judicially reviewing the scientific risk assessment undertaken by the institutions. In this case, since the Community institutions are required to 'evaluate highly complex scientific and technical facts', their discretion is broad and it is not the place of the CFI to substitute its assessment of the facts.[150] Again, the result of the case demonstrates the breadth of the institutions' discretion in drawing conclusions from the scientific material that they have access to. Even when the CFI comes close to suggesting that inadequate (scientific) reasons were given by the Community institutions for taking a certain position with respect to the scientific evidence, concerning their refusal to adopt the conclusions drawn by the Scientific Committee on Animal Nutrition (an advisory Community scientific body) that no immediate risk was posed by virginiamycin to human health, the Court defers to the institutions, finding that the institutions adequately explained their divergent opinion by relying on the precautionary principle![151] No manifest error was committed, since the institutions have the political responsibility and entitlement to adopt measures in the interests of human health protection, notwithstanding scientific uncertainty. In essence, and after much analysis, the CFI finds that sufficiently reliable and cogent scientific evidence (including international scientific reports and a Danish study on live rats) existed for the institutions to conclude that a risk to human health was posed, albeit an uncertain one, by the use of virginiamycin in animal feed.[152] The failure of that evidence to

[146] Ibid., paras. 162 and 172.
[147] Ibid., para. 158.
[148] Ibid., para. 149.
[149] Ibid., para. 166.
[150] Ibid., paras. 169 and 323.
[151] Ibid., paras. 204–5, and 208.
[152] Note that, in *Alpharma*, the CFI similarly held that the Community institutions had sufficiently objective and cogent scientific evidence on which to adopt preventive measures, despite their failure to obtain a SCAN opinion or to wait for a relevant forthcoming scientific report. It was in keeping with the precautionary principle, 'in the context of their broad discretion and their

confirm a conclusive risk did not undermine that conclusion and no manifest error was committed; a contrary view would render the precautionary principle devoid of purpose.[153] In the midst of this line of reasoning, verging on circularity, the precautionary principle, operating on multiple levels, both generates a procedural review test (of scientific adequacy/cogency of the risk assessment carried out by the Community institutions) and informs the manifest error standard applied to meet that test.

Fourthly, in the second section of its reasoning that engages the precautionary principle, the CFI is concerned with the *risk management* decisions made by the Community institutions. It examines whether the decision to impose a total ban on the use of virginiamycin in animal feed, as a response to the identified uncertain risk, was vitiated by manifest error, again in light of the broad discretion of the institutions in adopting such a political decision. At this point the manifest error and proportionality judicial review tests collide in the Court's reasoning, with the CFI applying a four-pronged proportionality test to determine whether any manifest error was committed by the institutions.[154] The precautionary principle is relied on by the Court to inform all four aspects of the proportionality inquiry, expanding its role as identified in *BSE* and reinforcing the treatment of the precautionary principle as a substantive policy idea that fills the gaps in legal review tests.[155] As in *BSE*, the suitability test was met since the ban was a preventive measure appropriately adopted on the basis of the precautionary principle (in the light of the entitlement of the institutions to conclude that a risk to human health existed).[156] In determining that a less onerous measure need not have been adopted, applying the second limb of proportionality,[157] the CFI finds that the ban was consonant with the precautionary principle, which can 'require' a public authority to act before any adverse effects have become apparent.[158] Another dimension to the precautionary principle was offered by the court in considering whether the ban was 'disproportionate', under the third limb of proportionality

responsibility for defining the public health policy', not to await more detailed scientific research: *Alpharma*, n. 131 above, paras. 317–18.

[153] *Pfizer*, n. 1 above, para. 386.

[154] The same three tests of proportionality as identified above (see text accompanying n. 117 above) are applied, along with an additional test of whether the disadvantages caused by Reg. (EC) No. 2821/98 are disproportionate to the advantages if no action were taken (on a cost benefit analysis): *Pfizer*, n. 1 above, para. 413. Note that this collision of the tests of manifest error and proportionality does not occur consistently in the case law, e.g. in *Alpharma*, the CFI undertakes a proportionality inquiry separately to its inquiry into manifest errors of assessment (the latter in the context of its examination of the risk assessment undertaken): *Alpharma*, n. 131 above, paras. 320–69.

[155] *Pfizer*, n. 1 above, paras. 419, 444, 456, and 471.

[156] Ibid., paras. 417 and 419.

[157] See text accompanying n. 117 above.

[158] *Pfizer*, n. 1 above, para. 444. Cf. Joined Cases C-11/04, C-12/04, C-194/04, and C-453/03 *ABNA Ltd* v. *Secretary of State for Health* [2005] ECR I-10423.

identified earlier (here considered in two parts).[159] The CFI concluded that 'the protection of public health... must take precedence over economic considerations'.[160] This policy assertion by the CFI does not necessarily follow from the elaboration of the precautionary principle so far (in this case or in *BSE*), however it is an aspect of the principle that is adopted in some later case law.[161]

A major shift comes in this judicial treatment of the precautionary principle in *Pfizer*, with the CFI's new focus on scrutinizing the scientific and procedural aspects of risk assessment, which it deems essential to the legislative application of the precautionary principle.[162] As noted, the CFI's splitting of its reasoning into issues of risk assessment and risk management reflects the position adopted in the Commission Communication, and its reasoning, particularly in generating a test of adequate scientific objectivity and cogency, is clearly inspired by the Communication.[163] While the Court points out that the Communication is not directly relevant to the case (since it was produced after the contested Regulation was adopted),[164] it refers to it as a 'codification of the law' in this area.[165] How a policy document can reflect and then generate the law is unclear, but this development demonstrates the confusing overlap of ideas of law and policy in this judicial review context (i.e. of legally reviewing exercises of policy discretion). This reliance on the Communication highlights the irony, pointed out above,[166] that, as the precautionary principle is treated as more of a legal principle in these cases (generating a legal test), the CFI increasingly relies on policy to inform that legal treatment, highlighting the role of the precautionary principle as a policy principle. It should also be noted that the CFI uses the policy document of the Communication not simply to define the precautionary principle in this case, but as the basis for structuring its entire (long and convoluted) legal reasoning. Thus the trend observed in previous cases of the courts defining the Article 174(2) principles as their judicial treatment becomes more legal is surpassed in this case, with the Communication's detailed policy approach (which involves more than simple definition of the precautionary principle) founding the legal treatment

[159] See text accompanying n. 117 above.

[160] *Pfizer*, n. 1 above, paras. 456 and 471.

[161] *Artegodan*, n. 11 above, para. 184; Case T-392/02 *Solvay Pharmaceuticals Bv* v. *Council* [2004] ECR II-4555, para. 121.

[162] Fisher, n. 9 above, 231–4.

[163] Note that it can also be said that the reasoning in *Pfizer* is inspired by WTO law. Not only does the Communication echo the WTO AB's decision in *Hormones* (n. 21 above, and text accompanying nn. 21–5), but the CFI explicitly refers to WTO law in elucidating the precautionary principle: *Pfizer*, n. 1 above, para. 150. This article is not, however, concerned with indirect effect of WTO law in EC law (cf. Scott, n. 3 above, 67–72), but with the role of the precautionary principle in EC case law. The influence of the Communication is of more relevance here (than WTO law) since it highlights the place of EC policy in understanding that role.

[164] *Pfizer*, n. 1 above, para. 122.

[165] Ibid. paras. 123 and 149.

[166] See text following n. 43 above.

adopted by the CFI. Again, focusing on definition is not a helpful way of determining the role of the Article 174(2) principles in the case law.

In summary, from *Pfizer*, we can conclude that the discretionary latitude afforded to the Community institutions by the precautionary principle is triggered by 'adequate' scientific assessment, but gives the institutions a broad discretion to take preventive measures. The former trigger is a legal test of adequate scientific objectivity and cogency in the identification of (uncertain) risk, which is *generated* by the precautionary principle. The latter discretion, also an aspect of the principle, *informs* the judicial review tests of manifest error and proportionality that are applied (here together) to monitor the limits of policy decisions taken by the Community institutions. When 'breach of the precautionary principle' is pleaded in argument, the legal plea is interpreted by the Community courts as raising some combination of these tests. The precautionary principle is a policy principle prompting deference by the courts to discretion exercised by the Community institutions, and it is also engaged with as a legal principle (generating and informing legal tests) to the extent that the courts are charged with reviewing the limits of its application by the Community institutions. The review cases that follow pick up on these different identified judicial treatments of the precautionary principle in reviewing Community and Member State action taken on the basis of the principle. While the reasoning in these cases is often conflated, as in *Pfizer*, these trends can be discerned.

iii. Generating Legal Tests Cases—Precautionary Principle Generating a Test of Adequate Scientific Evidence

Following *Pfizer*, other cases have treated the precautionary principle as a legal principle that generates a legal test of adequate scientific evidence. As in *Pfizer*, this role is conflated with its role in informing other legal review tests applied. The increased scrutiny of institutional discretion that comes with these layers of tests reduces the space in which the precautionary principle acts as a policy principle, but this role is still observed when the courts acknowledge the discretion of the Community institutions in applying the precautionary principle within the reviewed limits.[167]

Artegodan, discussed above,[168] is a decision in which the CFI found that there was inadequate objective scientific evidence to justify, on the basis of the precautionary principle, the challenged exercise of Commission discretion. The Commission was found to have failed the test of adequate scientific evidence generated by the precautionary principle. In this case, various pharmaceutical manufacturers challenged Commission decisions withdrawing marketing authorization for medicinal products containing particular amphetamines,

[167] Cf. *Monsanto*, n. 1 above, para. 113.

[168] See text accompanying nn. 34–7 above.

where those products were used in the treatment of obesity.[169] The legal grounds adduced to challenge the decisions were, as in *Pfizer*, numerous and overlapping, and notably they did not include 'infringement of the precautionary principle'. The CFI introduced the precautionary principle in its reasoning to inform the permissible scope of the Commission's discretion in making decisions to withdraw marketing authorizations under Article 11 of Directive 65/65/EEC on Proprietary Medicinal Products.[170] The logic of its approach was different from that in *Pfizer*, in particular, it identified the precautionary principle as 'corollary' of the principle that the requirements of the protection of public health are to prevail over economic interests,[171] in accordance with which the provisions of Directive 65/65/EEC must be interpreted, and so found that the precautionary principle 'requires' (rather than allows) Community institutions to take measures to prevent specific potential risks to public health, safety, and the environment.[172] In this way, the CFI identifies the substance of the policy discretion conferred by the precautionary principle slightly differently in this case.[173]

As in *Pfizer*, however, the precautionary principle was identified as a policy principle, deriving from Article 174(2) EC, which applied generally in the public health domain to guide the discretion of the Commission,[174] and on which the Commission implicitly based its decisions in this case.[175] Further, as in *Pfizer*, the Court finds that the precautionary principle generates a test of adequate scientific evidence: the Commission can only rely on the precautionary principle in exercising its discretion to withdraw authorization if 'a new potential risk or the lack of efficacy is substantiated by new, objective, scientific [evidence]'.[176] On the facts, the CFI found that there was no such new, objective evidence and the Commission decisions were thereby vitiated. As in *Pfizer*, the CFI set out the manifest error test in framing its inquiry into the Commission decisions, so that it might be said that the procedural guarantee of adequate scientific evidence generated by the precautionary principle in turn informs the manifest error test more broadly

[169] *Artegodan*, n. 11 above; Case T-147/00 *Les Laboratoires Servier* v. *Commission* [2003] ECR II-85, raised the same issues of fact and law and its reasoning is relevantly identical to that in *Artegodan*.

[170] [1965] OJ 22/369, as amended. Art. 11 provided that authorization for a product could be withdrawn where it is found that it is harmful in its normal use, lacking in therapeutic efficacy, or misleading as to its qualitative and quantitative composition.

[171] *Artegodan*, n. 11 above, para. 174. Cf. *Pfizer*, n. 1 above.

[172] *Artegodan*, n. 11 above, para. 184. For a similar approach to the discretion conferred by the precautionary principle, see *Solvay*, n. 161 above, para. 121. Cf. *BSE*, n. 11 above.

[173] Note that *Artegodan* was decided by a different chamber of the CFI shortly after *Pfizer* and *Alpharma* were handed down.

[174] As a 'general principle of Community law': *Artegodan*, n. 11 above, para. 184; see also text accompanying nn. 34–7 above.

[175] *Artegodan*, n. 11 above, para. 174.

[176] Ibid., para. 194. Although such evidence does not need to '[resolve] the scientific uncertainty' (ibid., para. 192).

applied (however the Court does not put it so nicely). So viewed, the precautionary principle both generates and informs legal tests of review in this case.

Unlike in *Pfizer*, however, the CFI does not defer (on the basis of the precautionary principle) to the assessment of complex scientific material made by the Commission, perhaps because the Commission in this case relied on the advice of the scientific body that it was bound to consult under Directive 65/65: the Committee for Proprietary Medicinal Products (CPMP). Instead, the Court strictly applies its test of adequate scientific evidence to the CPMP Opinion to find it an unsatisfactory basis for the Commission's exercise of discretion based on the precautionary principle, since it disclosed no new scientific evidence, merely a change in clinical practice with respect to the contested medicines. The intensity of the scientific review applied in this case is arguably undermined by two factors: (i) the CFI's reasoning based on the precautionary principle was superfluous since the Court had already found that the Commission was not competent to adopt the contested decisions on other grounds;[177] and (ii) no case that has followed *Artegodan* has submitted Community measures to such intense scrutiny, rather they have deferred to the institutions' application of precautionary principle and identified the scope of its policy discretion broadly.

In *Solvay*,[178] the CFI similarly applied a test of adequate scientific evidence, generated by the precautionary principle, to inform the manifest error of assessment review test.[179] As in *Artegodan*, the precautionary principle acts as a legal principle, generating a test of adequacy of scientific evidence that, although slightly differently formulated in each case, heavily influences the legal outcome. The result of this generated test is then used to inform the manifest error inquiry, again in slightly different ways, but again demonstrating the conflation of the roles in which the precautionary principle acts as a legal principle. As in all these review cases, the policy principle nature of the precautionary principle is also apparent, since the CFI treats the precautionary principle as representing a policy position which the Community institutions are entitled to adopt within limits. In deferring to the discretion so granted, the CFI treats the precautionary principle as a policy principle. In using the precautionary principle to generate and inform the legal tests applied, thereby influencing the legal outcome of the case, the CFI treats the principle as a legal principle as well.

iv. More Informing Legal Test Cases: Post-Pfizer

The 'informing legal test cases' that follow *Pfizer*, which all involve the precautionary principle, are best interpreted in light of the shift in the case law that it generated, and so are considered here. In these cases involving the review of Community discretion,[180] the courts have treated the precautionary principle

[177] Ibid., para. 155. [178] N. 161 above. [179] Ibid., para. 164.

[180] *IQV*, n. 128 above; Joined Cases C-154/04 and C-155/04 *Alliance for Natural Health and Others* v. *Secretary of State for Health* [2005] ECR I-6451 (*Alliance Health*); Case C-504/04 *Agrarproduktion Staebelow Gmbh* v. *Landrat des Landkreises Bad Doberan* [2006] ECR I-679 (*Agrarproduktion*).

as a policy principle that informs the proportionality inquiry—it operates as both a legal and policy principle in the same manner as in the informing legal test cases considered in subsection E.*i* above.[181] It should be noted that, in these cases, the grounds of review pleaded in argument (or framed in the preliminary reference) focus on the issue of proportionality, and do not directly raise the questions of manifest error or 'infringement' of the precautionary principle; this might explain the more focused treatment of the precautionary principle by the courts.[182] *Agrarproduktion* is a good example of these informing legal test cases.[183] In that case, the ECJ found that Article 13(1)(c) of Regulation (EC) No. 999/2001 laying down Rules for the Prevention, Control and Eradication of Certain Transmissible Spongiform Encephalopathies,[184] which required animals at risk of contracting identified BSE to be slaughtered, was not invalid in light of the proportionality principle. In resolving the proportionality inquiry, the ECJ used the precautionary principle to resolve the first limb 'appropriateness' test, as in *BSE*. The measures adopted by the Community legislature were found to be appropriate to the objective of the protection of human health, in light of the policy discretion afforded to Community institutions to take preventive measures in cases of scientific uncertainty.[185]

In contrast to *Pfizer* and *Artegodan*, the Court in *Agrarproduktion* does not test the scientific uncertainty in this case so as to determine whether the precautionary principle was justifiably exercised by the Community institutions; rather it accepts the identification of that uncertainty in the recitals to the Regulation.[186] It might be thus concluded that the ECJ has adopted a separate jurisprudence from that of the CFI with respect to the precautionary principle, a jurisprudence that is more deferential to the discretion involving its exercise by the Community institutions, by treating it as more of a policy principle that informs review tests rather than a legal principle that generates them. However, this is arguably due to the nature of the arguments/reference put to the courts,[187] and, as will be seen from the Article 28 EC infringement cases discussed in the following subsection,

[181] See Section III.E. above.

[182] In *Agrarproduktion*, n. 180 above, the only question referred to the ECJ was whether the contested provision infringed the principle of proportionality. In *Alliance Health*, a number of grounds, other than proportionality, contesting the validity of particular Community provisions were also referred (including absence of legal basis, infringement of the principles of subsidiarity and equal treatment, and failure to give reasons), although these were unlikely to raise issues relating to the precautionary principle; there was no pleaded ground of 'infringement of the precautionary principle'. Again, in *IQV*, n. 128 above, an action for annulment of a Community measure was brought on three grounds, only one of which, proportionality, gave rise to reasoning based on the precautionary principle.

[183] *Agrarproduktion*, n. 180 above.

[184] [2001] OJ L147/1.

[185] *Agrarproduktion*, n. 180 above, paras. 38–43.

[186] Ibid., paras. 41–2.

[187] N. 182 above, and accompanying text.

the ECJ does not shy away from treating the precautionary principle as a principle that generates legal tests in all cases.[188]

v. More Conflation of Generating and Informing Legal Review Test Cases—Reviewing Member State Discretion under Article 30 EC

The conflation of the roles of the precautionary principle, in generating and informing legal review tests, identified in *Pfizer, Artegodan*, and *Solvay* above, is also seen in another set of cases, this time involving review of Member State discretion in the public health domain. In these Article 28 EC infringement cases, the judicial techniques involving the precautionary principle in informing and generating legal tests again collapse into one another. The ECJ, in these cases, uses the test of adequate scientific evidence, again inspired by the Commission's Communication on the Precautionary Principle, to inform the legal review test of proportionality (not manifest error as in the Community review cases above). These cases involve review of Member State discretion that relies on the precautionary principle, similar to the review of Member State discretion (relying on the principle of rectification at source) analysed in *Walloon Waste*.[189] The difference is that these Article 28 EC cases do not involve the 'rule of reason' justification for infringing Article 28 EC, but the public health justification in Article 30 EC. In these public health cases, the ECJ is also more focused on interpreting the Article 30 EC exception strictly, thereby focusing on the proportionality inquiry that accompanies the Article 30 EC issue, and requiring that a current and detailed scientific assessment of the risk alleged by the Member State must demonstrate the 'necessity' of the contested measure.[190] The precautionary principle, which generates this test of adequate scientific evidence (in the form of an adequate risk assessment), is thus treated as informing the first limb of the proportionality inquiry in these cases. Only by satisfying the review tests so generated and informed can Member State discretion, relying on the precautionary principle, be compatible with Article 30 EC. In these cases, the precautionary principle appears as a policy principle, in that it expresses permissible Member State policy discretion within the legally prescribed policy framework of the Treaty, and also as a legal principle, in informing and generating the legal tests applied by the ECJ to monitor the limits of that discretion.

Commission v. *Denmark* is the seminal Article 28 EC case that involves this conflated treatment of the precautionary principle,[191] since its reasoning is followed by later Article 30 EC cases involving the precautionary principle.[192]

[188] See Section III.E. *v* below.

[189] N. 111 above; see text accompanying nn. 111–13 above.

[190] Case C-192/01 *Commission* v. *Denmark* [2003] ECR I-9693, paras. 45–6.

[191] Ibid.

[192] Case C-24/00 *Commission* v. *France* [2004] ECR I-1277; Case C-95/01 *Criminal Proceedings against Greenham and Abel* [2004] ECR I-1333 (*Greenham and Abel*); Case C-41/02 *Commission* v. *Netherlands* [2005] ECR I-11375.

These later cases involve reasoning largely carbon-copied from *Commission* v. *Denmark*, which makes sense to the extent that they similarly involve review of the legality of Member State measures and practices, restrictive of Community trade, concerning the banning of food additives. In this Article 226 EC infringement action brought by the Commission, the Danish government argued that its administrative practice of banning nutrient-enriched foods lawfully marketed or produced in other Member States unless they met a need in the Danish population, which infringed Article 28 EC, was justified on public health grounds. In particular, this practice was justified since the risks of overexposure to vitamins and minerals were uncertain and so danger to human health could not be excluded.[193] The ECJ had previously dealt with similar cases, in which products lawfully marketed in some Member States were refused marketing authorization in others ostensibly on public health grounds, in the light of uncertain risks to health. In those cases, the ECJ had consistently held that Member States, while scientific uncertainties persisted, and in the absence of Community harmonization, had discretion to limit the marketing of such products, so long as they demonstrated that their marketing constituted a serious risk to human health.[194] In *Commission* v. *Denmark*, the ECJ explicitly adopted reasoning, albeit similar, on the basis of the precautionary principle. Denmark had raised the precautionary principle in argument, asserting that its measures complied with the principle, as laid down in the Commission Communication.[195] The ECJ responded by finding that the scope of discretion accorded to Member States in these cases reflected the precautionary principle (as a policy principle),[196] and went on to consider what constituted a 'proper application of the precautionary principle' for the purposes of testing the limits of Denmark's discretion in this case.[197] Relying on similar reasoning to that in *Pfizer*, the ECJ then finds that applying the precautionary principle presupposes a detailed scientific risk assessment that shows real likelihood of harm, that is, it generates a test of adequate scientific evidence. While this test was present in some form in the Article 28 EC cases prior to *Commission* v. *Denmark*, it takes on a more comprehensive form in this case, which draws on both the judicial treatment of the precautionary principle from

[193] *Commission* v. *Denmark*, n. 190 above, para. 29.

[194] Case 174/82 *Criminal Proceedings against Sandoz BV* [1983] ECR 2445, para. 22; Case 227/82 *Criminal Proceedings against Leendert Van Bennekom* [1983] ECR 3883, para. 40; Case 178/84 *Commission* v. *Germany* [1987] ECR 1227 (*Beer Purity Law*), para. 46; Case C-228/91 *Commission* v. *Italy* [1993] ECR I-2701, para. 27.

[195] Opinion of AG Mischo in *Commission* v. *Denmark*, n. 190 above, para. 16. AG Mischo similarly relied on the risk assessment/risk management approach to applying the precautionary principle, which he discerns from the Communication and *Pfizer* and *Alpharma,* to emphasize the importance of scientific risk analysis in its application (at paras. 89–100).

[196] *Commission* v. *Denmark*, n. 190 above, para. 49.

[197] Ibid., n. 190, para. 51.

other Community case law, particularly *Pfizer*,[198] and the inspiration for that Community judicial treatment in the form of the Communication.

The result of this transfer of jurisprudence from Community to Member State review cases is that more comprehensive scientific inquiry is engaged in by the ECJ in *Commission* v. *Denmark*, and in the Article 28 EC cases that follow it.[199] It should be noted that, in these cases, there is less deference to the scientific assessments undertaken by the Member States than in the cases where Community measures are under review.[200] In the majority of cases, the ECJ finds that the scientific risk assessments relied on by the Member States to justify their infringing measures are inadequate.[201] This inadequacy then informs the test of proportionality applied. Thus, in *Commission* v. *Denmark,* the Court found that the contested practice was disproportionate, since it systematically prohibited the marketing of all enriched foods, without distinguishing them according to the particular vitamins and minerals added or according to the level of public risk that their addition might pose.[202] The Danish practice failed the test of adequate scientific evidence generated by the precautionary principle, since no adequate risk assessment was carried out, and this failure meant that the proportionality inquiry vitiated the reliance on Article 30 EC, since it could be said that the practice was 'necessary' for the purpose of protecting public health.

In the cases in this section, the Community courts review the discretion exercised by Community and Member State institutions in applying the Article 174(2) principles. As the courts are involved in substantively reviewing such policy discretion, it is no surprise that the lines between legal tests of review (law) and application of policy principles (policy) blur, and that the Article 174(2) principles, which embody a combination of ideas of law and policy, are heavily implicated in these cases where law and policy overlap. It has been observed that the courts apply distinct legal tests in reviewing these 'applications' of the principles. It is these tests that the courts are applying, not the principles themselves; the application of the latter is a task for the Community institutions. In this way, the legal tests applied by the courts monitor the limits of discretion granted by the principles, and defer to the exercise of that discretion within those limits. 'Breach of the precautionary principle', as argued in *Pfizer*,[203] are thus misleading descriptions of what the courts are examining in these cases.[204] Rather, the

[198] Opinion of AG Mischo, ibid., para. 96.

[199] *Commission* v. *France*, n. 192 above; *Commission* v. *Netherlands*, n. 192 above. Cf. *Greenham and Abel*, n. 192 above, in which the ECJ did not analyse the detail of the scientific assessment relied on, leaving the issue to be resolved by the French referring court.

[200] Opinion of AG Maduro in *Commission* v. *Netherlands*, n. 192 above, para. 30: different consequences flow from 'recourse to the precautionary principle' depending on whether it is invoked by Community institutions or the Member States.

[201] Exceptions are the findings in *Sandoz*, n. 194 above, and with respect to one of the contested measures in *Commission* v. *France*, n. 192 above.

[202] *Commission* v. *Denmark*, n. 190 above, para. 55.

[203] *Pfizer*, n. 1 above, para. 107.

[204] *Solvay*, n. 161 above, para. 120.

courts examine the decision-making processes adopted by political institutions when applying the principles through a variety of tests (that rely in various ways on the principles). The Article 174(2) principles thus exist as policy principles informing and generating legal tests for review, blurring the lines between the legal and policy principle concepts. This result makes sense when one appreciates the policy/law ambiguity inherent in the Article 174(2) principles, and the nature of the task of reviewing exercises of policy discretion with which the Community courts are engaged in these cases.

IV. Conclusion

This article has mapped the judicial treatment of the Article 174(2) principles to identify the roles played by the principles in the Community case law. Two analytical tools, legal and policy principles, were used to assist with this mapping exercise, reflecting the policy/law ambiguity in Article 174(2) EC. These tools helped to draw out the confusion between ideas of law and policy that infuses the case law, by identifying those cases in which the principles legally influence the outcome of a case (legal principles) and those in which they appear by way of observation, or deference to, policy positions on particular issues (policy principles). The case law becomes particularly complex when the principles perform both roles at the same time. To arrange this complexity, the cases were organized according to the judicial techniques used with respect to the principles, so that the particular roles played by the Article 174(2) principles in Community case law could be isolated.

In mapping the Article 174(2) case law in this way, five treatment categories were identified: policy cases, interpretive cases, legal basis cases, informing legal test cases, and generating legal test cases. The judicial treatment of the Article 174(2) principles in each of these categories varies, roughly along a spectrum from treatment as policy principles to legal principles. This spectrum is not meant to be definitive, but to demonstrate that the principles both: (i) represent Community policy positions on the environment and public health; and (ii) influence legal outcomes in the cases, and that they perform both functions in different measures in the five treatment categories. In the policy cases, it can be seen that the Article 174(2) principles have no role in influencing the legal outcome of the cases, and so they are identified purely as policy principles. In the other treatment categories, the principles have some legal role that identifies them as legal principles. For the purposes of this article, it has been accepted that the courts' treatment of the precautionary principle in informing review tests and particularly in generating the review test of scientific evidential adequacy is more 'legal' than their treatment of the Article 174(2) principles as interpretive aids and legal basis indicators, since the former more fundamentally influence the outcome of the legal questions at issue in the cases (particularly by establishing the very tests applied by the courts).

However, this point is debatable and it detracts from the important conclusions of this mapping exercise, which are fourfold.

Firstly, the Article 174(2) principles take on different roles (are treated differently by the courts) in the cases.

Secondly, those different roles reflect the extent to which the legal question at issue invites investigation into the exercise of (Community environmental and public health) policy discretion by the courts. In those cases where the legal tests to be applied by the Community courts are clearly laid down in the Treaty (Article 95(4) and (5) EC cases) or where the exercise of discretion in applying the principles is not called directly into question (*Monsanto*, *Codacons*), the courts have no need to give the principles a legal role. Equally, in cases where the courts find that an inquiry into the policy discretion exercised by the Community institutions is inappropriate (*Peralta*), the courts decline to give the principles a legal role. However, where the policy discretion exercised by the institutions in applying the principles is legally called into question, the principles are given legal roles, acting as legal principles. In the interpretive cases, the policy discretion exercised by the Community institutions is at issue to the extent that its manifestation (in legislation) is ambiguous. In the legal basis cases, a similar legal situation prevails, except that the (alleged) ambiguity derives not from the meaning of legislation but from its connection to its policy basis. In the informing and generating legal test cases, the exercise of policy discretion in applying the principles is directly at issue, and the principles are engaged legally to inform and partly to generate the tests applied by the courts to police the limits of the discretion embodied in the principles.

Thirdly, and flowing from this second conclusion, the principles act as policy principles in all the cases, but as legal principles in only some of them. In all cases, the principles are observed as representing a permissible Community (or Member State) policy position, with this observed position variously relevant to the legal outcome of the cases; in some, it is relevant only by way of background or not at all relevant to the legal question at issue, in others it informs the legal purposive inquiry or ambit of discretion under review (in the latter case, also prompting deference to policy decisions made within the legally identified ambit of discretion). This consistent policy principle nature of the Article 174(2) principles says something not only about the nature of the cases in which the principles are engaged, as seen through the various treatment categories and their varying concern with review institution discretion, but also about the nature of the principles themselves—they are fundamentally principles of Community policy.

Fourthly, judicial *definition* of the Article 174(2) principles arises as an aspect of their treatment by the courts in cases where they are treated as legal principles. However, extrapolating consistent definitions from the cases is not possible. This is because they are given only marginal definitions sufficient to dispose of the immediate legal question in the cases. In addition, in *Pfizer*, the precautionary principle is cast as a guide to exercising policy discretion that embodies not only substantive policy ideas but also procedures of decision-making, thus it is not capable of simple definition and the connection between acting as legal principles and principle definition breaks down. This mapping exercise demonstrated that definition of the principles may arise in the cases as a consequence of their particular legal treatment, with that particularity meaning that resulting definitions can look different, but that the trend observed between legal principles and definition is a loose one. Thus treatment of the principles, rather than their definition, is the starting point for thinking about the roles of Article 174(2) principles in EC law.

The mapping exercise here undertaken aimed to demonstrate the different ways in which the Article 174(2) principles are treated judicially, so as to determine their role and nature in Community law. The policy and legal principle concepts were devices to assist in charting the mass of Article 174(2) cases across treatment categories. They are not definitive of the nature of the principles. The conclusion reached, at the end of this mapping exercise, that the Article 174(2) principles, fundamentally, are principles of policy reveals something important about the nature of these environmental law principles in the EC context: they are principles that embody a political discretion to be exercised, and which are relevant legally to the extent that that discretion is justiciable/at issue in a case.

In conclusion, this article demonstrates that, in order to understand the roles played by the Article 174(2) principles in Community case law, the policy/law ambiguity fuelling their nature must be appreciated and focused on. It thus reorients discussion and debate about the preventive principle, the polluter pays principle, the precautionary principle, and the principle of rectification at source in the Community context by focusing on what is actually going on in the case law. It charts the judicial treatment and roles of the Article 174(2) principles in a manner that is sensitive to their Community context, embracing rather than furthering the ambiguity of their split policy/legal identity. It is hoped that future scholarship relating to environmental principles in the EC context will build on this contextual learning and exploit the analytical potential of the map drawn in this article. In particular, questions for future study that might do this, and which follow naturally from the mapping analysis in this article, include:

- to what extent, in light of the conclusions drawn in this article about the relationship between the Article 174(2) principles and review of institutional discretion, these principles should be seen in administrative law rather than environmental law terms in Community law;[205]
- to what extent the peculiar judicial treatment that has developed with respect to the precautionary principle is relevant to the other Article 174(2) principles;[206]

[205] Formulating the role of the Art. 174(2) principles in terms of review of institutional discretion is not something that has been done in the literature to date (cf. de Sadeleer (2002), n. 6 above, 270–2), and it ties in with an emerging jurisprudence and literature on EU administrative law (see, e.g., Craig, n. 108 above).

[206] Cf. de Sadeleer (2006), n. 55, 172 and generally.

- to what extent the treatment of environmental principles is shaped by the nature of the discretion (Community or Member State) under review, and how this is informed by considerations of subsidiarity;
- whether the Community courts' treatment of the principles is coherent and logical (measured according to some determined standard);
- what role the Article 174(2) principles *should* play in Community law, particularly in the developing jurisprudence of the Community courts.

Only by fully appreciating the role of the Article 174(2) principles in their EC Treaty and judicial context will academic work move debates of this nature forward. For now, the analytical approach set out in this paper provides a starting-point for considering these issues in a manner that comprehensively and accurately reflects the current state of Community law, and it goes a considerable way in identifying what that law, with respect to the environmental principles in Article 174(2) EC, in fact is.

The Application of Article 95(4)–(6) of the EC Treaty: Is the Emperor Still Unclothed?

*Michael G. Doherty**

I. Introduction

In the first volume of this *Yearbook*, Professor Sevenster assessed the potential for Member States to maintain or introduce national measures more stringent than those in a European Community (EC) harmonization measure under Article 95(4)–(6) EC shortly after the entry into force of the Treaty of Amsterdam, and questioned whether it represented an example of the 'Emperor's New Clothes'.[1] This article revisits the provisions some seven years later and through focusing on their interpretation and application in the intervening period aims to assess the reality of the protections provided.

It briefly outlines the genesis of the Treaty provisions in the Single European Act (SEA)[2] and their major reform in the Treaty of Amsterdam (ToA).[3] It explores the interpretation and application of Article 95(4)–(6) EC, and details the response to specific interpretive issues on, for example, the requirement for new scientific evidence justifying derogation and the need for a problem to be specific to the notifying State. It goes on to explore more general themes of interpretation and application in relation to, for example, the impact of environmental principles such as precaution, and the procedural framework.

The main argument presented here is that when the Community institutions have been presented with differing interpretative possibilities they have consistently taken options that restrict the operation of Article 95(4)–(6) EC. While there is some support for this in general interpretive practice, it is argued that the restrictive approach has gone too far, and that other, equally valid, interpretive principles have been ignored or under-utilized.

* Principal Lecturer, Lancashire Law School, University of Central Lancashire (UK). My thanks to the editor, Thijs Etty, and the referees of the *Yearbook*.

[1] H. Sevenster, 'The Environmental Guarantee after Amsterdam: Does the Emperor Have New Clothes?' (2000) 1 *Yearbook of European Environmental Law*, 291–310.

[2] Luxembourg (Luxembourg), 17 Feb. 1986 [1987] OJ L169/1.

[3] Amsterdam (The Netherlands), 2 Oct. 1997 [1997] OJ C340/1.

II. The Genesis of Article 95(4)–(6) EC

The term 'environmental guarantee' has been used by many writers[4] to describe the derogation provisions in Article 95(4)–(6) EC. This terminology is not adopted here, for the following reasons. Firstly, the Treaty provisions do not apply solely to environmental measures and have been invoked in relation to food safety, public health, and consumer protection. Secondly, the term 'guarantee' is an uncomfortable fit with the actuality of Article 95(4)–(6) EC. Whatever the intention of the drafters of the derogation procedure, the scope for unilateral action is very limited and is dependent on a wide discretion of the Community institutions to approve or reject the national measures. It is the breadth of this discretion that renders the term 'guarantee' unsuitable, and the Community courts have recently described it as a 'safeguard clause'.[5]

The derogation procedure first appeared in EC law through the SEA,[6] with the adoption of Article 100a(4) EEC. Up to that point, with the requirement for unanimity in the Council of Ministers, any single Member State could block the adoption of a proposed measure. It was common for specific derogations or a general safeguard clause allowing for more stringent national measures to be written into the terms of the directive itself, so as to facilitate agreement.

The introduction of qualified majority voting for market harmonization measures brought with it the possibility of a Member State being outvoted and forced to reduce its national level of protection to comply with the EC measure. Article 100a(4) EEC was adopted at the insistence of those Member States with progressive national environmental policies to preserve their prerogatives on this issue.[7] The ToA[8] significantly amended the derogation procedure introducing a distinction between *maintaining* and *introducing* more stringent national measures and clarifying that new national provisions could be introduced, subject to meeting onerous conditions.

III. The Treaty Provisions

This section will briefly outline the main aspects of the Article 95 EC derogation procedure.

[4] See, e.g., Sevenster, n. 1 above; R. Verheyen, 'The Environmental Guarantee in Practice: A Critique' (2000) 9 *Review of European Community and International Environmental Law* 2, 178–87; J. Zander, 'The "Green Guarantee" in the EC Treaty: Two Recent Cases' (2004) 16 *Journal of Environmental Law* 1, 65–85

[5] Case T-182/06 *Netherlands* v. *Commission* [2007] ECR-0000, para. 60.

[6] N. 2 above.

[7] In particular, Denmark; See, C. Gulman, 'The Single European Act—Some Remarks From a Danish Perspective' (1987) 24 *Common Market Law Review*, 31–9.

[8] N. 3 above.

Article 95(4) EC deals with Member States *maintaining* existing national laws after the adoption of an EC harmonization measure, and states that:

> If after the adoption by the Council or by the Commission of a harmonisation measure, a Member State deems it necessary to maintain national provisions on grounds of major needs referred to in Article 30, or relating to the protection of the environment or the working environment, it shall notify the Commission of these provisions as well as the grounds for maintaining them.

The most relevant grounds in Article 30 EC are the protection of the health and life of humans, animals, or plants. Following such a notification by a Member State the Commission has six months to approve or reject the national provisions, under Article 95(6) EC.[9] It must verify that the provisions are not a means of arbitrary discrimination, a disguised restriction on trade, or an obstacle to the functioning of the internal market.

The terms 'arbitrary discrimination' and 'disguised restriction on trade' are well known but far from self-evident concepts in EC law. They have given rise to much discussion and an exploration of their complexities is beyond the scope of this paper.[10] In any case, whilst their meaning is highly contested in general EC trade law, they have not caused many difficulties under Article 95(4)–(6) EC and their meanings can be summarized as, respectively, that no different treatment should be applied to similar situations (or similar treatment to different situations) and that measures must not in reality 'constitute economic measures introduced to impede the import of products from other Member States in order to protect indirectly national production'.[11] The further condition that the measures must not be an obstacle to the functioning of the internal market has been interpreted as a proportionality test and will be considered in Section IV.F below.

Article 95(5) EC deals with Member States *introducing* national provisions after the adoption of an EC harmonization measure, and states that:

> ...if after the adoption by the Council or by the Commission of a harmonisation measure, a Member State deems that it is necessary to introduce national provisions based

[9] This can be extended by six months where justified by the complexity of the matter and in the absence of a threat to human health.

[10] For a general discussion of these concepts see, e.g., Case C-267/91 *Criminal Proceedings against Bernard Keck and Daniel Mithouard* [1993] ECR I-6097 (*Keck*); F. Ortino, *Basic Legal Instruments for Globalisation of Trade: A Comparative Analysis of EC and WTO Law* (Oxford: Hart Publishing, 2004); N. Shuibne, 'The Free Movement of Goods and Article 28 EC: An Evolving Framework' (2002) 27 *European Law Review* 4, 408–25. In relation to consumer and environmental protection see, e.g., A. Ziegler, *Trade and Environmental Law in the European Community* (Oxford: Clarendon Press, 1996); D. Geradin, *Trade and the Environment: A Comparative Study of EC and US Law* (Cambridge: Cambridge University Press, 1997); G. van Calster, 'Export Restrictions: A Watershed for Article 30' (2000) 25 *European Law Review* 4, 335–52; D. Chalmers, 'Risk Anxiety and the European Mediation of the Politics of Life' (2005) 30 *European Law Review* 6, 649–74.

[11] Commission Dec. 2002/59/EC concerning Draft National Provisions Notified by the Kingdom of the Netherlands under Article 95(5) of the EC Treaty on Limitations on the Marketing and Use of Creosote-Treated Wood [2002] OJ L23/37 (*Netherlands Creosote II*), at 90.

on new scientific evidence relating to the protection of the environment or the working environment on grounds of a problem specific to that Member State arising after the adoption of the harmonisation measure, it shall notify the Commission of the envisaged provisions as well as the grounds for introducing them.

The Commission must deal with the notification in the manner outlined above, according to Article 95(6) EC. To approve a notification of new national measures, the Commission must be satisfied that derogation is necessary: (i) for the protection of the environment or working environment (*not* the Article 30 EC grounds); (ii) on the basis of new scientific evidence; (iii) to address a problem specific to the applicant Member State; (iv) where that problem has arisen after harmonization; and (v) that the national measure does not constitute arbitrary discrimination, a disguised restriction of trade, or an obstacle to the functioning of the internal market. These conditions are cumulative, so the Commission can dismiss an application on the basis of failure to satisfy any condition.

IV. Specific Interpretive Questions of Article 95(4)–(6) EC

Guidance on the interpretation and application of Article 95 EC comes from a number of sources. This section will discuss the Commission Communication on Article 95(4)–(6) EC, of 2002; Commission decisions on Member State notifications; a small number of cases challenging the rejection of a notification before the European Court of Justice (ECJ); and academic commentary.

Some scholars, reading the ToA amendments as strongly pro-environmental,[12] anticipated that Commission guidance would reflect this.[13] The guidance, when it arrived, was much more restrictive. It indicated that national measures would be allowed only where they were 'justified and without jeopardizing the unity of the internal market' and that requests for derogation 'must be interpreted in a restrictive manner, in line with the purpose of the provision in question'.[14]

There have been 23 derogation applications to the Commission decided under Article 95 EC,[15] of which 13 have been approved, with only one successful notification involving the introduction of new national measures. This seems like a high success rate, particularly for an exception to the general rule, but the

[12] There is general agreement on this; see, e.g., N. de Sadeleer, 'Procedures for Derogations from the Principle of Approximation of Laws under Article 95 EC' (2003) 40 *Common Market Law Review* 4, 889–915, who argues that the ToA 'places non-commercial values on a firmer footing within the context of the construction of the internal market', at 890.

[13] I. Tornero, 'Opinion' (1999) 1 *Environmental Law Review,* 235–6, notes 'in contrast to previous versions [Commission guidance is] expected to reinforce a presumption in favour of environmental protection over preservation of the internal market', at 235.

[14] Commission Communication concerning Article 95 (paras 4, 5, and 6) of the Treaty Establishing the European Community COM(2002)760, 23 Dec. 2002, para. 10.

[15] Many early notifications were submitted under Art. 100a(4) EEC but decided under Art. 95 EC.

successful applications have been clustered around three issues: regulation of PCP, creosote, and cadmium in fertilizers, where existing EC law was acknowledged as being inadequate. The reasoning of the Commission, as outlined in these decisions, shows that in practice the derogation procedure has been applied in a very strict manner. There have been four cases before the EC courts involving Article 95(4)–(6) EC disputes and some earlier cases under Article 100a(4) EEC continue to be of some relevance. Whilst the ECJ has been willing to find against aspects of the decision-making process on occasion, its general stance on the restrictive interpretation and limited availability of derogations has been broadly consistent with that of the Commission.

Perhaps as a result of these factors, Article 95(4)–(6) EC has been considered more by environmental scholars than by writers on the internal market. The introduction of the procedure in the SEA was accompanied by warnings as to the potential implications for the unity of Community law,[16] yet the application in practice of Article 95(4)–(6) EC and the way it has—sometimes controversially—thwarted proposals for higher environmental protection more than it has interfered with the functioning of the internal market, has fuelled this environmental interest.[17] The interpretation and application of Article 95(4)–(6) EC, based on these sources, will be explored through the questions below.

A. To What Extent are 'New Scientific Evidence' and Specificity Relevant to an Application to Maintain More Stringent National Measures?

Article 95(4) EC does not, on its face, require a notifying Member State wishing to maintain existing national laws to demonstrate a problem specific to its territory or that its derogation is based on new scientific evidence. Comparing paragraphs 4 and 5 of Article 95 EC, and interpreting them *a contrario*, reinforces the view that these criteria are not required to maintain existing measures.[18] Moreover, in relation to new scientific evidence, a further supporting factor is that the Member State will have to make the notification very shortly after the harmonization measure is adopted.[19]

Arguments in favour of their applicability to Article 95(4) EC were put forward in *Denmark* v. *Commission*, the only case so far on the interpretation of the

[16] The usual source that is cited (e.g. by Zander, n. 4 above) is P. Pescatore, 'Some Critical Remarks on "The Single European Act"' (1987) 24 *Common Market Law Review*, 9–18, but he says nothing specific about the environmental derogation provisions.

[17] Van Calster, n. 10 above, describes the rejection of Denmark's foodstuffs derogation as being 'received with outright hostility', at 339.

[18] See, Sevenster, n. 1 above, at 302.

[19] P. Wennerås, 'Fog and Acid Rain Drifting From Luxembourg over Article 95(4) EC' (2003) 12 *European Environmental Law Review* 6, 169–78, argues that it is likely that any evidence used to justify the national measures in the first place will be known to the Community legislature and because of the timeframe this requirement would become 'an almost impossible task', at 174.

fourth paragraph. The Commission argued that there was a requirement for a problem specific to the notifying State or new scientific evidence showing that the harmonized level did not provide a high level of protection.[20] Its submission was essentially that these are *alternative* conditions for a successful notification, rather than *cumulative* as under Article 95(5) EC.[21]

The Commission had raised the need for specificity, in most cases, in applications to maintain national measures under Article 100a(4) EEC where the requirement was similarly absent from the wording of the Treaty provision.[22] It could be argued that the requirement survived the ToA amendments and applies to Article 95(4) EC, and some writers have seen a specificity requirement as a logical consequence of harmonization. The Member State will have to show its *specific* need to depart from the agreed Community-wide standard.[23] This view though suggests that the harmonization level represents the requisite 'high level' of environmental protection and that Member State autonomy in deciding for itself the most appropriate level of protection is extinguished by harmonization.[24] There are two problems with this. First, to presume that the harmonized level is sufficient would be quite a presumption. The level of protection is likely to have been decided as part of a whole range of compromises, some internal (in relation to the volume of investment needed, current national levels of protection, etc.) and some external (support for this proposal traded for support for other proposals).[25] As Pescatore puts it: '[i]n international negotiations, they say, you must always make mutual concessions'.[26] This is the reality of EC law-making and to present it as a rational neutral process of risk management (if such a thing were possible) would be misleading. Second, the original intention behind the derogation provisions was that the Member States would decide what was sufficient for protection of their environments. Only if this was below the Community level, or disproportionate, would they be forced to amend their standards. This is addressed in more detail in Section V.C below.

20 As required by Art. 95(3) EC.

21 Case C-3/00 *Denmark* v. *Commission* [2003] ECR I-2543.

22 Commission Dec. 94/783/EC concerning the Prohibition of Pentachlorophenol (PCP) notified by the Federal Republic of Germany [1994] OJ L316/43 (*Germany PCP-II*); Commission Dec. 96/211/EC concerning the Prohibition of Pentachlorophenol (PCP) notified by Denmark [1996] OJ L68/32 (*Denmark PCP*), though not in Commission Dec. 99/831/EC concerning the National Provisions notified by the Kingdom of the Netherlands concerning the Limitations of the Marketing and Use of Pentachlorophenol (PCP) [1999] OJ L329/15 (*Netherlands PCP*).

23 Sevenster, n. 1 above, at 302.

24 J. Jans, *European Environmental Law (2nd Edn.)* (Groningen: Europa Law Publishing, 2000), argues that 'if national environmental legislation has been harmonized, the presumption must be that the level of protection resulting from harmonization is adequate', at 59.

25 See R. Schutze, 'Cooperative Federalism Constitutionalised: The Emergence of Complementary Competences in the EC Legal Order' (2006) 31 *European Law Review* 2, 167–84. See also C. Kimber, 'A Comparison of Environmental Federalism in the United States and the European Union' (1995) 54 *Maryland Law Review*, 1658–90, noting that members 'may reach agreement through a process of reciprocal concessions at a political level over a period of time', at 1663.

26 Pescatore, n. 16 above, at 9.

As regards the need for new scientific evidence, the Commission argues that a Member State cannot substitute its own assessment of the risks addressed by the harmonization measure. That is, if the Community legislature has looked at scientific evidence, theirs is the only admissible assessment of that evidence. The applicant, therefore, needs to show new scientific evidence, or at least, 'facts which should have been taken into account and which show that the Community legislation does not ensure sufficient protection'.[27]

The ECJ, in *Denmark* v. *Commission*, described the purpose of Article 95(4) EC as 'to assess the specific needs of a Member State', but went on to find that neither specificity nor new scientific evidence were conditions for approval of derogation under Article 95(4) EC. On examining the decision, though, the ECJ concluded that these had not, in practice, been treated as conditions, but as 'highly relevant in guiding the Commission'.[28] While this is to be welcomed as rejecting an unnecessary gloss on the Treaty provision, if the Commission in practice will not approve a notification to maintain national measures unless it provides new scientific evidence or a country specific problem then these are de facto conditions, regardless of the *de jure* position outlined by the Court. Wennerås argues that the Court's endorsement of a Commission decision that did appear to attach considerable importance to specificity means that we can question whether there is much difference between a highly relevant factor and a requirement.[29]

The structure of subsequent decisions, for example *Austria Cadmium*,[30] indicates that it would be de facto impossible for a Member State to convince the Commission that the measure was necessary for the protection of the environment without new scientific evidence or specificity. Even in decisions where there is probative new scientific evidence using Commission-mandated research methods demonstrating the general inadequacy of existing EC legislative protection, the Commission have raised the issue of the specificity of the evidence and the specific conditions of the applicant.[31] In *Sweden Cadmium*, for example, the Commission noted that the evidence referred to: 'the specific situation of the Swedish soil as well as the climatic conditions prevailing in Sweden'.[32] This is an unusually broad approach to the issue of specificity which should not be seen as an indicator of a generally liberal approach, but as a means to keep specificity visible as a concern even in Article 95(4) EC notifications.

[27] Case C-3/00, n. 21 above, para. 55.

[28] Ibid., para. 60.

[29] Wennerås, n. 19 above, 171.

[30] Commission Dec. 2002/366/EC on the National Provisions Notified by the Republic of Austria under Article 95(4) of the EC Treaty concerning the Maximum Admissible Content of Cadmium in Fertilizers [2002] OJ L132/65 (*Austria Cadmium*).

[31] E.g. *Netherlands PCP*, n. 22 above, where the derogation was approved on the basis that the Community harmonization level was being raised to the equivalent of the Dutch approach in less than three months of the Art. 95(6) EC decision.

[32] Commission Dec. 2002/399/EC on the National Provisions notified by the Kingdom of Sweden under Article 95(4) of the EC Treaty concerning the Maximum Admissible Content of Cadmium in Fertilizers [2002] OJ L138/24 (*Sweden Cadmium*), at 43.

A further question is, can the specificity criterion only be taken into account for the benefit of the Member State where country-specific data and problems are present (as in *Sweden Cadmium*) or can its absence count against the State?[33] The ECJ only talks of the relevance of the criterion 'when' a specific problem exists, but this is in the context of the Commission's power to 'approve or reject' a notification. Wennerås concludes that the absence of specificity can be used negatively against a Member State,[34] which is supported by the approach of the Commission in *Denmark* v. *Commission* and in later decisions.[35]

In practice, Member States will have to show specificity or new scientific evidence and therefore the main difference between Article 95(4) and (5) EC is that they are alternative, rather than cumulative, requirements.[36] This article argues below that this is a wrong turn and a frustration of the original rationale for the derogation provisions. For the moment, we can note that it represents a highly restrictive interpretation of the conditions for applying Article 95(4) EC.

B. How has the Requirement for New Scientific Evidence been Interpreted and Applied?

One constraint on an application to *introduce* national measures is that the Member State must justify its need for more stringent standards by reference to new scientific evidence. Early commentaries on Article 95(5) EC argued against a restrictive interpretation of this condition.[37] In itself, this highlights that there are a number of interpretive possibilities here. A very restrictive interpretation would recognize only data that was measured after the harmonization measure and which demonstrates the existence either of a wholly new environmental problem or that environmental risks are of an entirely different order to those previously perceived. A liberal interpretation could recognize any material that is relevant to the assessment of risks where the material, regardless of when it was published, was not explicitly taken into account in the decision-making process that led to harmonization.

Faced with the differing interpretive possibilities, the EC institutions have consistently adopted restrictive interpretations. The requirement of being 'new' has a temporal aspect and a quality aspect. Successful applications, e.g. *Netherlands Creosote II*, have relied on evidence clearly gathered and published after the harmonization measure.[38] In *Germany Organostannics,* though, the Commission

[33] Wennerås, n. 19 above, 171.

[34] Ibid.

[35] See, e.g., Commission Dec. 2001/570/EC on Draft National Provisions Notified by the Federal Republic of Germany on Limitations on the Marketing and Use of Organostannic Compounds [2001] OJ L202/37 (*Germany Organostannics*).

[36] Wennerås, n. 19 above, 174.

[37] Sevenster, n. 1 above, argues that this condition must not be interpreted to exclude 'scientific knowledge in progress', at 304. Jans, n. 24 above, argues that: '[w]atertight proof should not be necessary, as this clause must be interpreted in the light of the precautionary principle', at 124.

[38] N. 11 above, at 50.

noted that an element of Germany's evidence, a Greenpeace report, was published after the adoption of the Directive but that the report did not indicate when the data was measured. Whilst it concluded that the data was most likely measured after the harmonization,[39] to raise the issue as potentially relevant is troubling. One reading of this is that evidence is only regarded as 'new' if it is based on data collected after the harmonization rather than just published after that time.[40]

The Commission has been equally restrictive on whether material that is 'new' in time actually shows anything 'new'. In *Germany Organostannics*, new research had found pollution results markedly higher than from any existing tests.[41] This was described by the Commission as 'of a kind already known'. On an interpretive level, this seems to indicate that the Commission is indeed looking for evidence of new problems or at the very least 'different order' risks. On the question of application, it is difficult to see how this evidence did not reveal levels of contamination of a different order from those previously measured. The scientific evidence in *Land Oberösterreich* was also rejected as showing no new information.[42]

It should be noted that in most successful applications, for example the *PCP* decisions and the *cadmium* decisions, the Commission (or a Community scientific committee) had already, that is before the derogation notification by the Member State, reached the conclusion that there was new scientific evidence indicating that the Community standard was insufficient to protect the environment. In *Austria Cadmium*, for example, this evidence had been the basis for the proposed extension of the accession derogations to Austria, Finland, and Sweden.[43]

The approach proposed here is that 'new scientific evidence' should not necessarily be limited to material that was produced or published after the adoption of the harmonization measure, but should include all relevant material that was not looked at by the Community legislature in arriving at the harmonized standard.[44] The fact that data may have been 'for a large part available prior to the adoption' of the harmonization measure, as per *Austria GMOs*,[45] does not mean that it has been properly evaluated by the legislators.

[39] N. 35 above, at 71. Germany applied to maintain more stringent national measures on, inter alia, anti-fouling paints used on ships.

[40] A different reading of the decision could find that it refers to the issue of the problem having to arise after harmonization. This is unclear from the wording of the Decision and would be a rare engagement with this criterion.

[41] N. 35 above, at 57. Results showed pollution levels of 1,000–5,000 µg/kg in a number of German sites, with contamination in excess of 100,000 µg/kg at one site. The Commission compared it to worldwide studies showing pollution levels of 10–2,100 µg/kg.

[42] Joined Cases T-366/03 and T-235/04 *Land Oberösterreich and Republic of Austria* v. *Commission* [2005] ECR II-4005, para. 65.

[43] N. 30 above, 45.

[44] Related arguments are put forward by de Sadeleer, n. 12 above, arguing for the admissibility of scientific evidence 'already existing at the time of the adoption of the EC harmonization norm, but not entirely validated at that point in time', at 901.

[45] Commission Dec. 2003/653/EC relating to National Provisions on Banning the Use of Genetically Modified Organisms in the Region of Upper Austria notified by the Republic of Austria pursuant to Article 95(5) of the EC Treaty [2003] OJ L230/34 (Austria GMOs), at 65.

This is consistent with the ECJ's rationale for interpreting the conditions for *introducing* national measures as being more restrictive than those to *maintain* national measures; that the Community legislature had the opportunity to be guided by existing standards when it chose the harmonized level.[46] By analogy, it could not be guided by scientific evidence that it had not looked at and the material is 'new' in the sense of being new to the standard-setting process.[47] The authors of the Treaty could have excluded this analysis easily enough by using terms such as 'scientific evidence published after the adoption of the harmonization measure', but they did not. This approach is also reinforced by Article 95(3) EC: the requirement to base proposals on a high level of protection 'taking account in particular of any new development based on scientific facts'. If the Community legislature has omitted to consider relevant evidence at that stage,[48] the Commission ought to be estopped from rejecting its relevance to derogation decisions.

There may be counter-arguments based on the practicality of this approach: there is no central record of the evidence considered in a legislative process. Nonetheless, this is quite close to the approach to what is 'new' outlined by the Court in *Denmark* v. *Commission* ('facts which should have been taken into account and which show that the Community legislation does not ensure sufficient protection').[49] In any case, the questions will be resolvable as questions of fact and any concerns are outweighed by the need to base standards on all relevant evidence. By 'relevant', I simply mean that the material makes it more or less probable that a risk exists or as to the extent of that risk. This would be subject to de minimis, but the exclusionary approach of the Commission in *Germany Organostannics* ought not to be followed.

There has been limited discussion of the need for the new material to qualify as 'scientific evidence'. This requires some supervision by the Commission (in practice, the relevant Community scientific committee) to ensure that the material reaches some threshold level of sound science. There was a suggestion in *Netherlands Creosote II* that a national risk assessment would only be admissible if it was consistent with the standard European approach.[50] There was a strong emphasis on this in the cadmium decisions. In *Austria Cadmium*, for example, the fact that the methodology used by Austria to produce scientific data was

[46] N. 21 above.

[47] M. Doherty, 'Challenging a Commission Refusal to Allow the Introduction of "More Stringent National Measures"', (2004) 6 *Environmental Law Review* 2, 111–26, at 121.

[48] In *Denmark* v. *Commission*, n. 21 above, it appeared that the Commission had noted but misunderstood the full implications of a pre-harmonization SCF opinion.

[49] Ibid. There is also an ambiguous indication of this approach in Commission Dec. 1999/833/EC on the National Provisions Notified by the Federal Republic of Germany concerning the Limitations of the Marketing and Use of Creosote [1999] OJ L329/43 (*Germany Creosote*), 80: 'new data (i.e. data unknown during the deliberations preparing [Dir.] 94/60/EC)' and one study is discounted because it 'received due consideration before the adoption' of the Directive.

[50] N. 11 above, 71.

established at the Community level was given great prominence.[51] It is understandable that the Commission should give less intense scrutiny to data produced from Community-mandated methodologies but the danger is that this becomes another aspect of Commission control of Article 95(4)–(6) EC, reducing Member State autonomy. Beyond rejecting material that does not qualify as scientific,[52] or is so methodologically flawed as to invalidate any results, the Commission ought not to be too prescriptive. The terminology of 'scientific evidence' rather than 'data' means that projects, such as consolidation studies, that do not necessarily publish new raw data but can produce significant findings should be admissible. This could also apply (subject to relevance and threshold tests for 'sound science') to the interpretation of data, placing it within different hypotheses, or it linking to other bodies of knowledge. From the latest decisions, particularly *Austria GMOs* (where the Müller Report was described as a 'broad compilation'),[53] it seems that the Commission is not currently amenable to this line of argument.

C. How Has the Requirement for the Problem to be Specific to One Country Been Interpreted and Applied?

There are, again, a range of interpretive possibilities for this condition. It could be read as requiring that the problem is unique: that it exclusively threatens a particular aspect of public health or the environment within one country. The difficulty of imagining such a set of circumstances shows the implausibility of this stance and it was quickly dismissed by the Commission and Court,[54] as recently confirmed in *Netherlands* v. *Commission*.[55] Any other approach is an 'extent' argument:[56] that the problem is not unique but that it impacts on the notifying Member State to a greater or different extent than it does in other Member States. This covers a wide range of possibilities from just short of exclusivity to acknowledging factors, such as consumption levels, that mean the risk is materially different.[57]

In the early cases under Article 100a(4) EEC the Commission accepted 'extent' arguments with considerable latitude and it appeared 'not strictly necessary for

[51] N. 30 above.

[52] Using the broad criteria of repetition through testing and falsifiability, see K. Popper, *The Logic of Scientific Discovery* (London: Routledge, 2002).

[53] N. 45 above, 32.

[54] Case C-512/99 *Germany* v. *Commission* [2003] ECR I-845. Alternatively, if the impact of the environmental risk on the particular conditions of the Member State can be taken into account, as it seems they can, then every State is in a unique position. This is not going to be accepted by the Commission, but it does show the very 'open texture' of this condition.

[55] *Netherlands* v. *Commission*, n. 5 above, para. 65: 'it is not necessary that it is the result of an environmental danger within that State alone'.

[56] Doherty, n. 47 above, 123–4.

[57] De Sadeleer, n. 12 above, favours this liberal approach: 'particular demographic, geographic or epidemiological circumstances should render the problem particular to' the notifying State, at 900.

the problem to arise exclusively' in the applicant Member State.[58] The *PCP* cases show that both Germany and Denmark 'had a specific problem, albeit each for its own "local" reasons'.[59] The effective operation of this line of reasoning though, only works if the Commission is willing to take a broad view of extent arguments. Practice has been variable but generally restrictive on this question. As Sevenster pointed out, too strict an interpretation would lead to an 'absurd result' that the more widespread a problem the less chance of individual counter-measures.[60]

In *Netherlands Creosote II*, the applicant had included a comparative study as part of its submission. This was clearly very useful in persuading the Commission of the specificity of the Dutch position, but it was still based on extent arguments: that the geographical conditions in the Netherlands led to a significantly higher usage of creosote-treated wood in aquatic environments. This usage was not unique to the Netherlands but the extent of that use was greater and different in nature from other Member States. The Scientific Committee for Toxicity, Ecotoxicity and the Environment (CSTEE) stated that the specificity of the Dutch problem 'depends upon the extent to which exposure scenarios in the Netherlands differ from those in other Member States'.[61] The Commission wanted to check whether the Dutch concerns were of 'particular significance' to them, and found that compared to other Member States, the Netherlands was 'particularly vulnerable'.[62] On the whole, the specificity criterion seems to be subject to much lighter scrutiny when there is compelling evidence that the environmental risks are not being sufficiently addressed by current standards.[63]

The application of extent arguments will obviously be a question of fact in each decision, but it has not been clear what the comparative standard is. Is it based on a Community average, on the conditions in the majority of other States, or the position in *any* State other than the applicant Member State? The Commission's own guidance template requests scientific data on the specific situation of the Member State, 'e.g. for the Member State compared with data for other Member States or a Community average'.[64] This seems to invite either form of comparison as providing valid data on specificity and promotes extent arguments. On this reading the concentration of, for example, small farms and organic production in an area compared to the Community average *could*, as

[58] Sevenster, n. 1 above, 302.

[59] Ibid. In *Germany* PCP-II, n. 22 above, it said that: 'PCPs pose problems to health and the environment specific to Germany due to its high population density, degree of industrialisation, and local climatological factors'. In *Denmark* PCP, n. 22 above, the measure was specific because groundwater was the main source of drinking water in Denmark, and because PCPs are not readily absorbed by alkaline soils and they break down slowly because of low temperatures. Jans, n. 24 above, agreed that specific does not mean exclusive, the same problem can apply elsewhere.

[60] Sevenster, n. 1 above, 303.

[61] N. 11 above, at 76.

[62] Ibid., at 77.

[63] E.g. *Austria Cadmium*, n. 30 above, at 42.

[64] Commission, n. 14 above, Annex II.

was argued in *Land Oberösterreich,* be relevant to specificity.[65] Further, taking into account social and geographic conditions and issues like levels of consumption, population density, and historic record of pollution,[66] would accord with the Community's rhetoric on subsidiarity and integration of the environmental principles into all policy areas.[67]

The Commission, though, has sometimes been at pains to reject extent arguments. In *Germany Organostannics*, Germany referred to the increased danger of organostannic paints in sediments and mudflats and the impact on particularly important and vulnerable mudflats in the vicinity of German sea lanes and shipyards likely to use the polluting materials. The Commission noted that this problem is 'specific for all countries having mudflats that warrant protection'.[68] Germany pointed to new evidence on contamination from German dry-docks, with the Commission responding that this was 'applicable to any port *in the world* where dry-dock work involving anti-fouling painting is carried out'.[69] This approach that a problem will not be specific if it is in some way shared with any part of the Earth does not seem entirely consistent with the Commission request for Europe-wide comparative data.

The recent case of *Netherlands* v. *Commission* clarifies some aspects of the specificity requirement. The test put forward by the Court of First Instance (CFI) was that the Netherlands had the burden of showing that their pollution problems 'were so acute as to distinguish them significantly from those observed in other Member States'.[70] The CFI then framed this test as being essentially about the allocation of regulatory competence. Article 95(5) EC excluded the possibility that national derogations could be granted to deal with 'a general environmental danger in the Community'; a general danger being one that arose 'in terms which are on the whole comparable throughout the Member States'. Only if it is not 'apt' to deal with a localized problem by amendment to Community harmonized rules will a national derogation be appropriate.[71]

The clearest element of the judgment is that the comparative standard to be used in assessing specificity is with other Member States rather than the whole world. The Commission's approach of identifying a number of other Member States that had equivalent or worse pollution or traffic problems, was endorsed by the CFI, but the possibility of using a Community average as the comparative standard remains open.

[65] N. 45 above, 71, though it seems that Austria failed to provide sufficient information to press this argument strongly.

[66] De Sadeleer, n. 12 above, at 900.

[67] Art. 174 EC: EC environmental policy should aim to improve the quality of the environment and 'take into account the diversity of situations in the various regions of the Community'.

[68] N. 35 above, at 72.

[69] Ibid, at 73; emphasis added.

[70] N. 5 above, para. 61.

[71] Ibid.

It has been stated that a Member State's desire for a strong national environmental policy is not a specificity justification.[72] This should be carefully limited to Article 95(5) EC rather than Article 95(4) EC and there should be a distinction between the national policy and its effects. Where there is a strong environmental policy on, for example, domestic insulation and this has practical impacts on the levels of usage of particular materials then the comparative level of usage is a relevant consideration.[73] It is not the Member State's policy preference that is being recognized but the desire to address a concrete health or environment problem, regardless of the cause.

The alternative de facto requirement of specificity under Article 95(4) EC was criticized above, but this paper wants to go further by challenging its necessity as a formal cumulative condition for *introducing* more stringent measures. The argument is that the rationale for allowing the *maintenance* of national measures ought largely to derive from Member State environmental autonomy in a diverse Community, with all other criteria as secondary considerations. In relation to *introducing* national measures the focus ought to be on new scientific evidence: that the position has changed since harmonization. That change could be focused on conditions specific to the applicant Member State or could apply more generally. The counter to this, expressed by the CFI in *Netherlands* v. *Commission*, is that if there is a non-specific problem then Community-wide action is the appropriate response. Indeed, this is provided for in Article 95(7) EC, but it is not necessarily the exclusive response. A Member State that wants to protect its citizens or environment from an evidence-based threat in advance of the Community amending its harmonized level of protection ought to be able to do so. This ability would be subject to Community control through the proportionality test (which would need to recognize that any disruption to the internal market would be time-limited). The CFI in *Netherlands* v. *Commission* said that derogation could occur when 'it is appropriate to apply a remedy at the outset at the national level, without waiting for an amendment to the Community legislation', whilst maintaining that this can only occur in relation to purely local problems or problems that exhibit themselves in a particular way locally. Yet, arguably, the appropriateness of proceeding with an immediate derogation could come about through the nature of the threat revealed by the new scientific evidence or the likelihood of a timely Community-wide response. Supporting this view is the amount of time it can take to agree Community-wide measures.[74] In relation to cadmium in fertilizers for example, the accession countries raised

[72] Jans, n. 24 above.

[73] This was the issue that was raised but not addressed in *Germany* v. *Commission*, n. 54 above.

[74] This is a factor that was recognized by the Court in *Netherlands* v. *Commission,* n. 5 above. In a different context but following a similar theme, Bodansky argues that: 'often effective multilateral action is impossible, so the choice is not between unilateralism and multilateralism, but between unilateralism and inaction', D. Bodansky, 'What's So Bad about Unilateral Action to Protect the Environment?' (2000) 11 *European Journal of International Law* 2, 339–56, at 340.

their concerns with the Community prior to agreement of the Act of Accession in 1994.[75] The cadmium derogations were initially approved and then extended on three occasions in anticipation of an EC standard. At the time of writing, work is still in progress on preparing a draft law on this issue.[76]

D. How Has the Requirement for the Problem to Have Arisen After the Harmonization Measure under Article 95(5) EC Been Interpreted and Applied?

Environmental problems are notorious for only revealing themselves gradually and the leading philosophies of science emphasize that scientific knowledge usually proceeds incrementally.[77] Sevenster called for a 'common sense (i.e. not too narrow) interpretation' of this condition, so as not to undermine the *effet utile* of the Article as a whole.[78] Any strict interpretation of the condition could produce incongruous results. If the Netherlands, for example, had built embankments with creosote-treated wood before a harmonization measure and Denmark built them after the measure, a literal reading would only allow Denmark to introduce national measures to address this, even if the more longstanding practice in the Netherlands was resulting in more severe problems.

The small number of Article 95(5) EC applications have usually been rejected on other grounds, so there is very limited jurisprudence on this question, though it seems that the issue arising after harmonization cannot be simply a change of policy.[79] The Commission template for notifications does not even request specific information to show that the problem arose after the harmonization measure,[80] and in *Netherlands Creosote II* the issue is barely mentioned. The risk of pollution from creosote was known before the harmonization measure, which was why it was included in that measure. Creosote-treated wood was being used

[75] Documents concerning the Accession of the Republic of Austria, the Kingdom of Sweden, the Republic of Finland and the Kingdom of Norway to the European Union [1994] OJ C241/1.

[76] The Commission notes that the work 'has been subject to some delays', Commission Dec. 2006/348/EC on the National Provisions Notified by the Republic of Finland under Article 95(4) of the EC Treaty concerning the Maximum Admissible Content of Cadmium in Fertilizers [2006] OJ L129/25 (*Finland Cadmium II*), at 36.

[77] Popper, n. 52 above, required potential falsifiability through testing before knowledge could be called 'scientific', and even Kuhn's social psychology approach with its emphasis on paradigm shifts acknowledges that 'normal science' provides an accretion of new knowledge between those shifts: T. Kuhn, *The Structure of Scientific Revolutions* (Chicago: University of Chicago Press, 1996).

[78] Sevenster, n. 1 above, 303. In assessing the proportionality of the Swedish exemption scheme in Case C-473/98 *Kemikalieinspektion* v. *Toolex Alpha AB* [2000] ECR I-5681 (*Toolex*), AG Mischo in para. 96 of his Opinion condemned a particularly onerous requirement (to draw up a plan indicating when the chemical will be discontinued). As technical and scientific progress were difficult to predict, this meant that the 'granting of an exemption was virtually impossible in many cases'. Moreover the criterion was superfluous; it added nothing to the achievement of the desired objectives. The same line of reasoning can be employed here.

[79] Doherty, n. 47 above, 124.

[80] Commission, n. 14 above, Annex II.

in embankments long before the harmonization measure and must have been causing environment risks before then, though awareness of this only arose after new evidence demonstrated the extent of the problem. That evidence did not indicate when the problem first arose and the issue of when the problem arose is, in effect therefore, being conflated with the requirement for new scientific evidence. This is confirmed by the *Austria GMOs* decision, where the fact that the bulk of sources for the Müller Study were pre-harmonization, undermined the claim that it addressed specific problems arising after harmonization.[81]

Even if this is regarded as a separate condition it cannot be limited to the recognition of wholly new environmental problems. It must mean, therefore, a new perception arising after the harmonization, of the extent, nature, or effect of an environmental problem.[82] A highly restrictive interpretation of this condition would have been, and still is, possible. It could have been used to reject the Dutch creosote notification. This may illustrate that the Commission's application of Article 95(4)–(6) EC has not been quite as restrictive as is being generally portrayed here, or that a highly restrictive interpretation of the provisions is not a necessary consequence of its status as an exception to the general rule.

E. What is the Relevance of the Absence of the Grounds of Article 30 EC in Article 95(5) EC?

The structure of Article 95(4)–(6) EC is strange on this point. The terms 'environment and working environment' are normally seen as broader than the ground of 'the health and life of humans, animals and plants' in Article 30 EC. If the intention was to be more restrictive in relation to introducing national measures then the traditionally broader terms must mean something narrower,[83] and Bär and Kraemer thought this may be a drafting error.[84] Jans agreed that the distinction ought not to have any consequence, particularly in the light of the principles of Article 174 EC, but concluded that it probably did have a restrictive effect,[85] and the Commission's guidance paper does emphasize that the grounds in Article 30 EC are not available for Article 95(5) EC applications.[86]

There was some ambiguity in *Germany* v. *Commission* as to whether the ECJ would apply the distinction. In *Denmark* v. *Commission*, and as recently confirmed in *Land Oberösterreich*, it clarified that the grounds in Article 30 EC are not to be

[81] N. 45 above, at 65.

[82] De Sadeleer, n. 12 above, 'does not preclude the possibility of the risk already being present at the moment of drafting... of the EC harmonization measure, and only later manifesting itself', at 901.

[83] Sevenster, n. 1 above, at 301.

[84] S. Bär and A. Kraemer, 'European Environmental Policy after Amsterdam' (1998) 10 *Journal of Environmental Law* 2, 315–30; as did Verheyen, n. 4 above, at 180.

[85] Jans, n. 24 above, at 72.

[86] Commission, n. 14 above, paras. 21–2.

taken into account for Article 95(5) EC; they are a distinguishing feature.[87] This case also featured a typically restrictive reading of the requirements. Austria's concerns about the dangers of recombinant genes harming organic crop production were classified by the Commission as socio-economic rather than environmental, and therefore outside of the criteria for Article 95(5) EC.[88] Similarly, in *France NK Fertilizers*, having found that there was a clear and immediate danger from the transport and storage of these substances, the Commission noted that this did not demonstrate a link to the working environment;[89] which must be disappointing to transport and warehouse workers.

Sevenster considers the distinction to be regrettable and comments that '[i]t is curious that human (public) health is not a ground justifying new measures after harmonization, as it implies that there is no room for national initiatives to counter a threat to human (public) health once harmonization has taken place'.[90] This curious effect was confirmed by *Germany Organostannics*, where Germany said that its measures were necessary and justified partly on the basis of Article 30 EC, even though this was an Article 95(5) EC application.[91] The claim was that organostannics could contaminate fish caught for human consumption, i.e. a consumer public health issue. The Commission found that as this evidence did not relate to protection of the environment or working environment it was irrelevant to the claim. The notion that if a public health danger did not simultaneously involve a danger to the environment, then new measures could not be adopted, has been criticized.[92] The *Germany Organostannics* decision, though, goes further than this. Where the pollution danger raises environmental *and* public health issues then the evidence in relation to the public health effects of the environmental contamination will be divided out from the Member State's justification and deemed irrelevant to the Article 95(6) EC decision.[93]

The ECJ has stated that the rationale for the Treaty restricting the grounds for derogation under Article 95(5) EC is that existing national measures can be considered by and guide the Community legislature when it is deciding the appropriate level for harmonization, whereas later national measures cannot.[94] Even

[87] N. 21 above, para 58. Confirmed in *Land Oberösterreich*, n. 42 above, para. 62.

[88] N. 45 above, 67.

[89] Commission Dec. 2003/1/EC relating to National Provisions on Limiting the Importation and Placement on the Market of Certain NK Fertilizers of High Nitrogen Content and Containing Chlorine Notified by France pursuant to Article 95(5) of the EC Treaty [2003] OJ L1/72 (*France NK Fertilizers*), at 79.

[90] Sevenster, n. 1 above, at 300.

[91] N. 35 above, at 48.

[92] Sevenster, n. 1 above, at 301.

[93] This reading of the issue was particularly unfortunate in *Germany Organostannics* as the evidence on human consumption of contaminated fish was the most clearly 'new' element of the scientific evidence.

[94] Doherty, n. 47 above, at 121. Opinion of AG Tizzano, of 30 May 2002, in *Denmark* v. *Commission*, n. 21 above, who sought to align the two branches of Art. 95 EC. See Wennerås, n. 19 above, at 170.

if we accept that this means that it ought to be harder to get derogation under Article 95(5) EC, the significant issue that is excluded from national control by this distinction is public health. The logic of this remains elusive. In the absence of Treaty amendment the Commission ought not to take a blue-pencil approach to evidence that raises a combination of environmental and public health issues.

F. How is the Proportionality Principle Applied to the Decision-Making Processes of the Commission and Community Courts?

Under Article 95(6) EC, the Commission must verify that the national measures do not constitute an obstacle to the functioning of the internal market. The Commission has recognized that any notified measure will have this effect to some extent and 'to preserve the useful character of the procedure', it interprets this as a proportionality test.[95] In this sense it does not add anything to the previous practice, where the Commission assessed the justification of the measures in relation to their objectives.[96] The main issues in application of the test have been the range of factors to be taken into account, and the possibility of imposing conditions in a successful notification.

There have been some mixed messages on the range of factors to be taken into account in assessing proportionality. In *Denmark* v. *Commission*, the ECJ criticized the wording of the Commission decision on the grounds that it seemed to limit the range of factors considered (specifically the technological need for the food additive), though it found that, in substance, the issue was actually considered.[97] In the cadmium decisions, the Commission decided that the absence of information, viz. a CSTEE conclusion on the dangers of cadmium in fertilizers, meant that it could not find that the Member States were acting disproportionately.[98] This emphasizes the need to include all relevant factors in assessing the necessity of the national measures.

On the other hand, in *Denmark* v. *Commission* the ECJ excluded other public health factors from consideration, even though this was an Article 95(4) EC application. Denmark had argued that, by itself, moderate wine consumption could put an individual on the threshold of the recommended acceptable daily intake (ADI) for sulphites. As wines were regulated under other EC regulations

[95] N. 35 above, at 93.

[96] *Germany PCP II*, n. 22 above; P. Slot, 'Harmonization' (1996) 21 *European Law Review* 5, 378–87, at 386. Wennerås, n. 19 above, argues that what is described as proportionality actually has three distinct elements: suitability, necessity, and proportionality *stricto sensu*: '[t]he national measures must be suitable to achieve the desired end, there must be no other less restrictive means of achieving this aim and the restriction it causes intra-Community trade cannot be out of proportion to the intended objective or the result achieved', at 176.

[97] N. 21 above, paras. 82–3.

[98] N. 30 above, at 52.

that permitted no derogation, Denmark wanted to reduce as far as possible the intake of sulphites from other foodstuffs. The ECJ held that this was not relevant data. If a Member State wants to derogate in relation to certain foodstuffs 'it has the task of justifying those national provisions in relation to those foodstuffs and not in relation to other products'.[99] This must, with respect, be rejected. The public health issue had been recognized by the Scientific Committee for Food (SCF) with the creation of an ADI for sulphites. As Denmark could not derogate in relation to wine the only room for legislative manoeuvre to address the public health issue for its citizens was through derogation from Directive 95/2/EC on Food Additives other than Colours and Sweeteners (Food Additives Directive),[100] and the wider legislative framework was highly relevant for assessing the necessity of the national measures.

One obviously critical factor in applying proportionality *stricto sensu* is some indication of the damage to intra-Community trade that the national measure would entail. This seemed to have been an important factor in the early but not the more recent decisions. In *Germany PCP II*, for example, there were in-depth inquiries as to the actual effects of a product ban on intra-Community trade (which were found to be negligible).[101] In *Germany Organostannics*, the applicant argued, with much more limited data, that its measures would not hamper the operation of the internal market, but the Commission decided the application on other grounds and did not address this submission.[102] The Commission's template for notifications asks for socio-economic data on, for example, likely trends and evaluation of socio-economic impact, and projected effects of the Community measure.[103] Yet the focus should be on the projected effects of the national measures, the extent to which they will hinder trade and what the concomitant environmental benefits will be. The body with the status and expertise to mandate the sorts of studies necessary to obtain this crucial information is the Commission, which no longer seems willing to undertake them, and the regression in the quality of the decision-making process that this represents can be seen as a casualty of the six-month time limit imposed by the ToA.[104]

A further important factor is the existence of the Community harmonization measure. The Advocate General in *France* v. *Commission* pointed out that this made the proportionality test under Article 95(4)–(6) EC more onerous than the general test under Article 30 EC, because of the need to take account of

[99] N. 21 above, para. 88.

[100] [1995] OJ L61/1. See similarly, Wennerås, n. 19 above, at 173.

[101] *Germany PCP II*, n. 22 above. See *Germany Creosote*, n. 49 above, at 105–15.

[102] N. 35 above, at 60–2.

[103] Commission, n. 14 above, Annex II.

[104] N. 3 above. See the similar absence of 'trade' data in, e.g., Commission Dec. 2003/829/EC concerning National Provisions on the Use of Azodyes notified by Germany under Article 95(4) of the EC Treaty [2003] OJ L311/46 (*Germany Azodyes*), at 48.

the protection already being provided by the harmonization measure.[105] This is clearly correct, but the danger is that by focusing on the harmonization measure the Commission will assess *its suitability*. If it reaches a positive conclusion on that suitability then the Member State measures can be regarded as logically unnecessary, whilst the sufficiency of the harmonization measure seems to be taken for granted in some Commission decisions, for example, *Germany Azodyes*.[106]

In the context of an 'unharmonized' position in environment/market disputes, Notaro argues that the necessity and proportionality tests should be replaced with a single necessity test. This is because Member States have the right to choose the level of protection that they deem necessary.[107] This reasoning is still applicable, against the backdrop of the EC measure, after harmonization because that is what Article 95 EC allows. Its language is that notification is made where a 'Member State deems it necessary...'. This is not a subjective test (and is subject to the range of other conditions) but its starting point is the Member State's assessment of what is necessary. This is explored further in Section V.C. The single necessity test, proposed by Notaro, would leave Member States 'free in their choice of the desired level of protection, provided that the measures they take are necessary (causal link) and no less restrictive alternative is possible'.[108]

A further question here is whether the Commission can approve a notification with conditions, which is relevant because restricting the scope of national measures may help to address any shortcomings in the proportionality of their effect, and allow conditional acceptance of measures that would otherwise have to be rejected. Proportionality also invokes the sort of nuanced balancing of interests that can rarely be answered in a 'yes/no' fashion. Sevenster considered whether conditions on geographical restrictions or time limits could be approved, and proposed that '[t]he explicit authority of the Commission to reject a Member State application seems to imply such a power to attach conditions'.[109] The wording of the Commission's power though, to 'approve or reject', is starkly binary. Despite this the Commission did impose conditions on the derogation approvals in the cadmium decisions. There was an acknowledged deficit in the Community standard and those recently acceded States who wished to preserve their controls on the level of cadmium in fertilizers were authorized to do so. The Community was moving towards a new standard on this issue and the derogations were therefore made subject to the condition of a time limit.[110]

[105] Opinion of AG Tesauro, of 26 Jan. 1993, in Case C-41/93 *France* v. *Commission* [1994] ECR I-1829.

[106] N. 104 above: 'given that the harmonization measure already adopted...has itself taken as its base a high level of protection in accordance with Article 95(3) and pursues this objective in a proportionate way', at 32.

[107] N. Notaro, 'The New Generation Case Law on Trade and Environment' (2000) 25 *European Law Review* 5, 467–91, at 467.

[108] Ibid., 483.

[109] Sevenster, n. 1 above, 305.

[110] N. 32 above, 58.

An interpretation of Article 95(6) EC that allows the imposition of conditions is generally positive, for example, as in *Netherlands Creosote II* to allow flexible national legislation to be applied only in a manner which is consistent with the need for more stringent measures.[111] We should note, though, that in the cadmium decisions the conditions were imposed to avoid difficulties if the Community decided to harmonize at a lower level of protection than the strictest existing national measures, and therefore to preserve institutional privileges rather than allowing unilateral measures to be a motor for environmental improvement.

The general emphasis on a restrictive approach, even in the context of time-limit conditions has led the Commission into some difficulties. The cadmium derogations were limited to the end of 2005. When the harmonization measure was not forthcoming Austria, Finland, and Sweden had to go through the whole notification process again. The successful notifications were subject to a further condition that the derogations stayed in force until the harmonization measure took effect, whenever that might be.[112]

The overall conclusion on these specific interpretative questions is that the approach of the Commission and the Community Courts has significantly narrowed the availability of derogations to Member States. When alternative viable interpretations have been presented, the Commission and the Courts have consistently chosen internal market rather than environmental conclusions and emphasized the strictness of the conditions for successful derogation.

V. General Themes in the Interpretation and Application of Article 95(4)–(6) EC

This section explores some of the broader issues which have structured the interpretive approach of the EC institutions and considerations which, it is argued, should have a stronger influence on the way in which derogation applications are assessed.

A. The Non-absolute Nature of Harmonization and the Internal Market

References to the unity of the internal market and the uniform application of EC law are consistently made to justify the stringency with which Article 95(4)–(6) EC has been applied.[113] Commission decisions now contain a 'standard clause' outlining the centrality of the unity of the market to the decision-making

[111] N. 11 above. [112] N. 75 above. [113] N. 103 above, at 29.

process[114] (there is no equivalent clause restating the Community's Treaty commitments to improving the quality of the environment). Flexibility and differentiation, though, are provided by most aspects of EC environmental law. This scope for flexibility is often present even where the measure pursues the joint aims of environmental protection and promotion of the internal market,[115] demonstrating that the unity of the internal market is not an absolute value, and that additional principles and factors ought to condition the interpretive process.

As Slot points out, harmonization under Article 95 EC 'does not simply mean unification. The objective is the achievement of a common market rather than a single legal system.'[116] As Article 95 harmonization is not, by its nature, absolute, it carries within itself the scope for flexibility.[117] It needs to be appreciated that harmonization is not an end in itself, but rather a tool to promote the internal market and, if the effects on the internal market are minimal then the presumption of stringency in holding to the harmonized level ought to be reduced.

Differentiation can be perceived as largely negative, that is, as 'a reflection of fragmentation and the dissolution of solidarity in the EU and of special pleading by particular Members'.[118] Alternatively, flexibility allows for 'a more sensitive response to legitimate and genuine regional and local diversity and autonomy'.[119] This flexibility can take many forms, for example, derogations in directives can be specific in giving particular Member States longer implementation periods, whilst more general safeguard clauses are possible, such as 'Member States may, at any time, fix values more stringent than those laid down in this Directive'.[120] The continued use of these safeguard clauses is authorized by Article 95(10) EC, though they have become less common since the introduction of the derogation procedure. Where derogation is authorized by a provision within a directive there is no need to invoke Article 95 EC.

Differentiation is also facilitated by partial harmonization, that is, where there are limitations of the scope of a directive. In *Burstein*,[121] for example, after the Community had harmonized the conditions for the marketing of PCP, Germany continued to have strict rules on the marketing of products treated with PCP.

[114] See, e.g., *Germany Azodyes*, n. 104 above, 29.

[115] See, J. Scott, 'International Trade and Environmental Governance: Relating Rules (and Standards) in the EU and WTO' (2004) 15 *European Journal of International Law* 2, 307–53, at 309.

[116] Slot, n. 96 above, 379. Watt similarly argues that legal pluralism does not necessarily fragment the internal market; see H. Watt 'Experiences from Europe: Legal Diversity and the Internal Market' (2004) 39 *Texas International Law Journal*, 429–60, at 431.

[117] Scott, n. 115 above, argues that the term 'harmonization' is a misleading term for this process as it combines market integration with regulatory diversity, at 321.

[118] G. de Búrca, 'Legal Principles as an Instrument of Differentiation? The Principles of Proportionality and Subsidiarity', in B. de Witte, D. Hanf, and E. Vos (eds.), *The Many Faces of Differentiation in the EU* (Antwerp: Intersentia, 2001), 131–44, at 133.

[119] Ibid.

[120] Art. 5, Dir. 85/203/EEC on Air Quality Standards for Nitrogen Dioxide [1985] OJ L87/1.

[121] Case C-127/97 *Willi Burstein* v. *Freistaat Bayern* [1998] ECR I-6005.

The ECJ held that Germany remained free, in principle, to regulate products not specifically covered in the Annex to Directive 76/769/EEC on Restrictions on the Marketing and Use of Certain Dangerous Substances and Preparations (Marketing and Use Restrictions Directive).[122] Differences, even in relation to product standards, are tolerated subject to the control of Articles 28–30 EC.

Accession treaties can allow differentiation, though for limited periods of time. In *Toolex*, for example, the ECJ noted that the Accession Treaty with Austria, Finland, and Sweden laid down a transitional period of four years from accession,[123] which was extended by a further two years by Directive.[124] The transitional arrangements allowed Sweden to maintain its existing more stringent classification of one of the substances at issue in the case. Framework directives,[125] voluntary schemes,[126] and non-statutory agreements with industrial sectors[127] all provide further ways in which flexibility becomes a feature of environmental regulation.

In *Ratti*, the main rationale for saying that harmonization pre-empts more stringent national measures[128] was that allowing Member States to set up parallel regulatory structures would hinder the free movement of goods.[129] Article 95 EC, which allows the possibility of such parallel regulatory structures, is itself a move away from the *Ratti* position, but the general principle holds true. The extent of the hindrance, though, will vary widely and the decision-maker ought to look at the figures, context, and values involved as part of a proportionate balancing of interests. Indeed, the Commission did initially do this for some derogation applications, and found in the *PCP* applications, for example, that:

> [a]ccording to the undertakings, imports of PCP into the Community as a whole do not exceed 1,200 tonnes annually, a modest amount. PCP is a very cheap product, and its effect on the market is therefore negligible. Since there is no market for the product in Germany, nor indeed in any of the Scandinavian countries or Austria, the effects on intra-Community trade are practically non-existent.[130]

122 [1976] OJ L262/201, as amended.

123 *Toolex*, n. 78 above, para. 6. Art. 112, Accession Treaty with Austria, Finland, and Sweden [1994] OJ C241/21.

124 Dir. 1999/33/EC amending Council Dir. 67/548/EEC as Regards the Labelling of Certain Dangerous Substances in Austria and Sweden [1999] OJ L1999/57.

125 See, e.g., Dir. 2000/60/EC establishing a Framework for Action in the Field of Water Policy [2000] OJ L327/1 (Water Framework Directive).

126 See, e.g., Reg. (EC) No. 1980/2000 on a Revised Community Eco-label Award Scheme [2000] OJ L293/31.

127 See, e.g., the agreement with the European Automobile Manufacturers Association, Commission Rec. 1999/125/EC on the Reduction of CO_2 Emissions from Passenger Cars [1999] OJ L40/49.

128 Case C-148/78 *Criminal Proceedings against Tullio Ratti* [1979] ECR I-1629 (*Ratti*): 'A Member State may not introduce into its national legislation conditions which are more restrictive than those laid down in the Directive in question', at para. 27.

129 T. Joseph, 'Preaching Heresy: Permitting Member States to Enforce Stricter Environmental Laws than the European Community' (1995) 20 *Yale Journal of International Law,* 227–71.

130 N. 22 above, 9.

A second rationale is that permitting national standards contributes to legal uncertainty. Mollers describes derogation clauses, such as Article 95(4)–(6) EC, as 'highly problematic'; with the main disadvantage being the uncertainty and cost of double-checking what the applicable law is.[131] This is relevant, but ought to be only one factor affecting the interpretive approach. Third, derogation may be thought to undermine the division of powers by subverting the authority of Community institutions. I have argued elsewhere that the Commission's interest in guarding the exclusivity of its formal monopoly on setting the legislative agenda may be the most persuasive account of its narrow interpretation of Article 95(4)–(6) EC.[132] The fact that a successful notification will normally trigger the need for further Community measures may be thought to impinge on the privileges of Community institutions yet this process is provided for in the Treaty, and concerns on institutional balance need to be read in the context of that constitutional provision for derogation.

A counterbalance to these market concerns can be found in the work of Kimber. She concedes that some intervention is needed where there are multi-jurisdictional problems and where 'non-uniform regulation of products in different regions may lead states or countries with high environmental standards to exclude products which do not conform to those standards'.[133] On the other hand, in a large region there are often 'vast differences in geographical, ecological and industrial conditions' and because of their knowledge of the local environment regions may be better placed 'to assess local environmental needs, local environmental consequences of certain levels of pollution, and locally appropriate remedies'.[134] The regions may also be more aware of the particular problems and needs of the locality than a central authority. They will be quicker to discover and more concerned with abatement of a particular risk and ignoring these important differences in preferences can cause regional resentment.[135]

Further, the aim of protecting the environment should be seen as fluid and deliberative rather than capable of being met through a singular (harmonization) event. Overall, it is argued that harmonization ought not to be seen as exhausting the possibilities for divergent, more stringent, national approaches and that the permissibility of these ought to be assessed in the context of the principles outlined below.

131 T. Mollers, 'The Role of Law in European Integration' (2000) 48 *American Journal of Comparative Law*, 679–710, at 686.

132 Writing more generally, Majone goes further by arguing that there is 'an imperialistic tendency built into the Community method', G. Majone, 'Legitimacy and Effectiveness: A Response to Professor Michael Dougan's Review Article on Dilemmas of European Integration' (2007) 32 *European Law Review* 1, 70–82, at 79.

133 Kimber, n. 25 above, at 1661.

134 Ibid.

135 Ibid., at 1662.

B. The General Interpretive Approach

The conservative approach to the derogation procedure *is* supported by general principles of interpretation that exceptions to general rules ought to be read restrictively. The *Pretore di Torino* judgment requiring strict interpretation of safeguard clauses in environmental directives can be applied by analogy,[136] and the need for a strict reading of the derogation procedure has been stated from the outset.[137] This general principle of legal interpretation clearly applies and with some weight, as evidenced by the Commission's 'standard clause' mentioned in the section above which states that:

> [a]s Article 95 is precisely the expression of such a derogation [from fundamental Community rules], it must be interpreted strictly and only be applied under strict conditions with regard to the justification required.[138]

There has been little or no recourse to other principles that can apply to the interpretation of Article 95(4)–(6) EC with equal force.

Notaro argues that the important profile given to the environmental principles in the Treaty 'is indeed a new phenomenon and can have a remarkable influence on the trade and environment debate and on the Court's decisions in this area'.[139] De Sadeleer emphasizes that even non-Treaty general principles, such as the principle of substitution, are relevant and that their applicability through the integration principle points away from a restrictive interpretation.[140]

The role of principles in interpretation is that they can point, with more or less force, towards a particular conclusion.[141] It is possible to conceive of the Commission or ECJ invoking, for example, the requirement for a high level of environmental protection in considering the impact of new scientific evidence, or subsidiarity in assessing whether a localized solution to an environmental problem that has a minimal impact on intra-Community trade ought to be permitted.

Member States have attempted to invoke the precautionary principle to support the necessity of their national measures to protect the environment. These efforts have been largely rebuffed by the Commission, and the Community Courts in *Land Oberösterreich* declined to consider the precautionary arguments

[136] Case C-187/94 *Pretore di Torino* ([1985] OJ C270/4). Slot, n. 96 above, at 391.

[137] Opinion of AG Tesauro in *France* v. *Commission*, n. 105 above, para. 4: '[s]ince Article 100a(4) creates an exception to the principles of uniform application of EC law and unity of the market, it must, like all provisions which allow derogations, be strictly interpreted, so as to ensure that it is not extended to cases other than those strictly provided for in it'.

[138] *Germany Azodyes*, n. 104 above, 29.

[139] Notaro, n. 107 above, 468.

[140] De Sadeleer, n. 12 above, 895–7.

[141] See, G. Winter, 'The Legal Nature of Environmental Principles in International, EC and German Law', in R. Macrory (ed.) *Principles of European Environmental Law* (Groningen: Europa Law Publishing, 2004), 11–28: 'Principles stand in the background of rules and influence their interpretation and application. They enhance the normative power of rules, advise how to interpret them, help to fill regulatory gaps, guide discretionary powers and inform about necessary exceptions to a rule', at 16.

at all.[142] Sevenster argues that the shift from 'proof' to 'evidence' in the drafts of Article 95(5) EC during the ToA negotiations indicates that requiring proof would be incompatible with the precautionary principle.[143] The Commission, though, has generally supported a narrow interpretation of the precautionary principle,[144] and in *Germany* v. *Commission* argued that in the context of Article 95 EC, national measures could only be accepted if 'it is scientifically proven that they are necessary'.[145]

Uncertainty in assessing public health risks was also identified in *Denmark* v. *Commission,*[146] yet the ECJ went on to declare that a Member State 'cannot unilaterally invoke the precautionary principle in order to maintain derogating national provisions. In an area where Member State legislation has been harmonized, it is for the Community legislature to apply the precautionary principle.'[147] Scott though points out that the CFI has embraced the precautionary principle as a general principle of EC law.[148] As a general principle it binds not only the Community institutions, but also the Member States when they are acting within the scope of Community law.[149] The ECJ's finding in *Denmark* v. *Commission* is wholly inconsistent with this position.

In relation to notifications to maintain existing national measures it will be divergent interpretations of the same, incomplete, and uncertain, body of evidence that are at issue. In conditions of scientific uncertainty different interpretations of risk are scientifically legitimate and different stances on the management of risks whose extent and nature are unclear are politically legitimate. There is a tension between this scope for differentiation and the monolithic tendencies of harmonization but this should not exclude the interpretive impact of a key Treaty principle from an EC decision-making process.

The Commission has, on the whole, taken a softer tone on the possibility of precautionary action than the Court. It invoked precaution in the creosote decisions, where the SCTEE had found that there was a cancer risk but could not estimate the magnitude of the risk. The Commission authorized the notification, in part on the basis of the precautionary principle, but Verheyen notes that whilst there may have been uncertainty as to the full extent of some risks, there was no

[142] N. 42 above, paras. 70–2.

[143] Sevenster, n. 1 above, at 303; ToA, n. 3 above.

[144] Commission Communication on the Precautionary Principle COM(2000)1, 2 Feb. 2000.

[145] N. 54, Opinion of AG Tizzano, para. 88.

[146] N. 17 above, para. 64. J. McMahon, 'Learning From Experience? The SPS Agreement and European Community Law' (2004) 10 *International Trade Law & Regulation* 2, at 11–17.

[147] N. 21 above, para. 103.

[148] J. Scott, 'The Precautionary Principle Before the European Courts', in Macrory, n. 141 above, 51–72, citing Case T-74/00 *Artegodan GMbH* v. *Commission* [2002] II-ECR 4945, the principle 'is intended to be applied in order to ensure a high level of protection of health, consumer safety and the environment in all the Community's spheres of activity', at para. 183.

[149] Scott, ibid., at 54.

uncertainty as to the inadequacy of the Community measure.[150] She concludes that the reference to the precautionary principle was 'misleading'.[151]

More recent decisions have continued to hold open the possibility that if the Commission deems there to be a sufficiently strong evidence base, precautionary measures may be approved.[152] It is still keen to stress that precautionary regulation can only take place where a risk is adequately backed up by scientific data so as to exclude mere conjecture, and even this more open approach talks of keeping the burden of proof on the applicant with a standard of proof to produce new data that amounts to 'serious and conclusive' evidence to justify the national measures.[153]

In the context of the procedures under the EC Directives on genetically modified organisms (GMOs), Lee argues that:

> [n]o obvious space is provided by the precautionary principle, as interpreted by EC law, for the incorporation of ignorance or indeterminacy into the risk management process, let alone ethical or socio-economic concerns.[154]

Similar criticisms may be made of the Article 95(4)–(6) EC procedure, though the context is different in that the Community legislature is presumed to have weighed up the range of known scientific, technical, socio-economic, and political factors during harmonization. For introducing new measures, though, there is a requirement for new evidence on which the precautionary principle can affix. To say that this evidence must 'prove' the necessity of national measures or be 'conclusive' misconceives the role of precaution in decision-making and the ability of environmental sciences to provide that level of certainty. In relation to both new and existing measures, to separate the scientific justification to be presented by the Member State from a precautionary evaluation to be carried out only by the Commission is equally misconceived. The justification for national measures intrinsically calls for the Member State's assessment of the data, the risks involved and the areas of ignorance or indeterminacy.

In an earlier volume of this *Yearbook*, I argued that:

> [t]here is always likely to be some gap between the environmental rhetoric of the Community, and its achievements in practice. Interpretive application of the principles, however, takes part of that rhetoric and puts it to practical use, with the aim that contested terms are given an interpretation that coheres with the general objectives.[155]

[150] Verheyen, n. 4 above, 182.

[151] Ibid.

[152] See, e.g., *Austria GMOs*, n. 45 above, 72.

[153] N. 89 above, 82.

[154] M. Lee, *EU Environmental Law: Challenges, Change and Decision-making* (Oxford: Hart Publishing, 2005), 252.

[155] M. Doherty, 'Hard Cases and Environmental Principles: An Aid to Interpretation?' (2003) 3 *Yearbook of European Environmental Law*, 57–78, at 77.

It is argued here that the environmental principles have a role in the interpretation of Article 95(4)–(6) EC at least as legitimate as any other interpretive principle.

C. The Original Rationale for Derogation

The original intent theory of interpretation is one method of approaching difficult interpretive tasks.[156] It is a controversial element in US constitutional interpretation debates and its use here is more modest, as a counterweight to the equally valid interpretive notion that derogations ought to be applied restrictively. In particular it attaches to the principle of interpretation that exceptions to general schemes should not be extended beyond cases expressly foreseen,[157] and argues that a much greater level of Member State autonomy *was* expressly foreseen on the introduction of the derogation provisions.

The internal deliberations of the EC Treaty authors are confidential, but active participants did give their views (in a private capacity) at the time of the introduction of the SEA, in 1986.[158] It was said that the original intention of adopting the derogation provisions in the Treaty was to 'ensure that Member States which had found progressive answers to environmental problems were not obliged, by virtue of subsequent Community legislation, to reduce the degree of environmental protection which they had achieved on the national level'.[159] In relation to maintaining more stringent national provisions, there was no strong presumption against approving derogation. Further, the primary *locus* of the decision on whether to maintain higher national standards or to lower them to the EC level was the Member State. This was not a subjective process and it was subject to control by the Commission, but it would 'allow a Member State a real possibility of protecting the environment to the level which *in its opinion* was necessary' (emphasis added).[160]

Of those commentators writing at the time of the SEA, Gulman argued for a very liberal approach to derogation, but even those like Ehlermann, who favoured a more conservative approach, thought that derogation could take place where the Member State 'feels' that the harmonized level is too low.[161] When he talks about the need to interpret the derogation restrictively this is in the context of

156 F. Bennion, *Statutory Interpretation (4th Edn.)* (London: Butterworths, 2002).

157 N. 104 above, 29.

158 N. 2 above.

159 L. Krämer 'Differentiation in EU Environmental Policy', in de Witte, Hanf, and Vos, n. 118 above, at 83–100, at 84.

160 Gulman, n. 7 above, wrote that during the debate on the environmental derogation provisions surrounding the Danish SEA referendum, 'it was alleged by sceptics that the ECJ would limit its meaning to such an extent that it would not allow a Member State a real possibility of protecting the environment to the level which in its opinion was necessary. The Government pointed out that the jurisprudence of the Court of Justice did not give any basis for such a fear', at 33.

161 C. Ehlermann, 'The Internal Market Following the Single European Act' (1987) 24 *Common Market Law Review*, 361–410, at 388.

whether it is available against Commission, as well as Council, measures and not whether the Member State can set its level of protection.

Sevenster comments that:

> [n]ot only do environmental conditions within the European Union differ widely, necessitating discrimination between national environmental laws, the same must be presumed to apply to the relative importance which individual Member States attach to environmental objective *vis-à-vis*, in particular, economic goals.[162]

Yet, unless a Member State, which can be outvoted, can persuade its fellow Council members to allow derogation as part of the Directive itself, this 'relative importance' argument seems irrelevant to Article 95(4)–(6) EC. Interpretive approaches could legitimately re-connect with the original intention of the Treaty authors which seemed to allow for 'relative importance' to be a key factor.[163]

D. The Procedural Framework of Applying for Derogation

The interpretation and application of the procedure as well as the substance of the derogation provisions have been problematic. In response to what was seen as excessive delay in the decision-making process, a six-month time limit was introduced by the ToA. This was regarded by most commentators as a reform benefiting the Member States.[164] In practice, this has not generally been the case. It has turned a derogation application from an (albeit flawed) deliberative process into a quasi-judicial one where the applicant has to make their case at the outset, with the decision-maker returning a verdict of proven or not proven, without the safeguards of a judicial process such as the right to know and to comment on the other evidence.

Most of the discussion has centred on the right to be heard. The ECJ found in *Denmark* v. *Commission* that this right was not required under Article 95(4) EC.[165] The key for the ECJ was that, unlike other cases where it had insisted on the right, under Article 95(4) EC it is the *Member State* who initiates the procedure. The time limit for the Commission decision is equally important. The ECJ concluded that the intention of the Treaty authors (the original intent approach appears to be relevant here) was that:

> in the interests of both the applicant Member State and the proper functioning of the internal market, the procedure laid down by that Article should be speedily concluded.

[162] Sevenster, n. 1 above, 291.

[163] There is an allusive acknowledgment of joint responsibility in *Netherlands* v. *Commission*, n. 5 above, para. 58: Arts. 95(4)–(7) EC 'confer on the Member States and on the Commission the power to derogate . . . ', but the judgment keeps the decision on when it is suitable to introduce stricter pollution controls on particulates in the air firmly in the hands of the Community institutions.

[164] Sevenster, n. 1 above, 305.

[165] N. 21 above, para.42. The approach holds for Art. 95(5) EC applications; see n. 54, para. 42.

That objective would be difficult to reconcile with a requirement for prolonged exchanges of information and observations.[166]

The Commission in this case pointed out that Denmark already had opportunities to air its views during the legislative process and as part of the notification itself; if Denmark was given a right to a hearing that would be a third opportunity to state its case.[167] As a general proposition this must be questioned. Negotiations as part of the legislative process are a flux of competing concerns (economic, social, environmental, strategic). It is not appropriate to regard them as a formal opportunity to state why a certain level of national protection above the harmonized level ought to be allowed. Additionally, in most cases the Member State is not asking for the opportunity to re-present its case an additional time. It is asking for the right to comment on subsequent inputs into the decision-making process from other Member States or scientific committees. Wennerås prefers to call this 'the right of contradiction'. He argues that the right to be heard is already recognized in the procedure through the Member State's initial notification and justification. The opportunity to contradict other evidence is an essential element of that right to be heard.[168]

The ECJ in *Land Oberösterreich* returned to its explanation for the introduction of the time limit by the Treaty authors; so that the applicant is certain of the applicable rules and the proper functioning of the internal market.[169] Yet, as the ECJ points out, the national measures cannot come into effect until the Commission has decided to approve them. There is therefore no impact on the proper functioning of the internal market and the Member State *is* certain of the applicable rules, whilst the Member State has indicated that its interests lie in engaging with the decision-making process rather than in its speed.[170]

Even if it accepted that the time period is too constrained to have a formal legally enforceable right to be heard then the Community as a whole, including the Commission and Member States, still have an interest in ensuring that the decision-making process is of the highest possible quality. If a Member State feels that reports from other Member States or from scientific committees are misconceived or simply to clarify the nature of their justification in the context of the new inputs, then this ought to be pursued as an element of good governance.[171]

[166] Ibid., para. 47.

[167] Ibid., para. 36.

[168] Wennerås, n. 19 above, 175.

[169] N. 42, para. 43.

[170] Wennerås, n. 19 above: '[s]urely Denmark should be the better judge of whether it is in the interests of its citizens to have a comprehensive procedure', at 175.

[171] Wennerås points out that if Denmark had been allowed to comment on the interpretation of the SCF opinion, the Commission may have approved the national provisions avoiding three and half years of legal uncertainty and the exposure of Danish citizens to dangerously high levels of nitrites and nitrates; ibid.

The door appears to be firmly shut on this argument with the ECJ deeming the particular circumstances of the procedure irrelevant.[172] So where does this leave the notifying Member State? It must in its initial application outline the decision it wants (i.e. approval) and the evidence base and justification for its measures. It must also try to predict what evidence, views, and other information a scientific committee may look at and rebut data and arguments that it does not yet know.[173] This applies equally to any other inputs to the process that are made after the notification, e.g. consultations with other Member States. On procedural questions, then, Article 95(4)–(6) EC has been subject to narrow interpretations. The rationale for taking this strict approach is unconvincing and principles such as good governance point towards alternative procedural practices.

VI. Conclusion

Sevenster concluded her survey of Article 95(4)–(6) EC by stating that:

> with the prospect of an ever increasing number of Member States with environmental protection relatively low on their political agenda adopting legislation by a qualified majority, . . . the case for Member State autonomy in choosing to apply or introduce more stringent environmental (product) standards after harmonization appears more compelling than ever before.[174]

In a significantly enlarged Union, this is even more true today than it was then,[175] and it is clear that the 'green' interpretation of the derogation provisions that she called for has not happened.

This article has argued that the interpretation and application of Article 95(4)–(6) EC by the Commission and the Community Courts has unduly privileged uniformity and the internal market. It proposes that reference to a wider range of interpretive influences than are currently utilized, would go towards remedying that imbalance. It specifically proposes that a rebalanced approach to interpreting the provision would mean that:

(a) 'new scientific evidence' and specificity should not be treated as de facto alternative conditions under Article 95(4) EC;

[172] See, e.g,, n. 42 above, para. 45.

[173] A position that Wennerås, n. 19 above, describes as illogical, at 175.

[174] Sevenster, n. 1 above, at 292. See also van Calster, n. 6 above, 'almost by definition, the environmental standard reached in harmonizing legislation does not meet with the expectations of the "greenest" Member States', at 338.

[175] Majone, n. 26 above, 'National policy preferences in the enlarged Union are increasingly diverse', at 70, and the 'cost of uniformity in the provision of public goods . . . will tend to increase significantly', at 81.

(b) 'new scientific evidence' should include all material that was not considered in the harmonization process and should not be limited to new empirical data;

(c) the overall justification for a condition of specificity is doubtful, but if it is to be retained it should be interpreted flexibly to allow a Member State to show relevant differences compared to other Member States or to the Community average;

(d) that the problem arising after harmonization should be treated as an aspect of 'new scientific evidence' and should extend to a new perception of the extent, nature, or effect of an environmental risk;

(e) that public health should be a valid ground for action under Article 95(5) EC; and

(f) that there should be a return, as much as the time limits allow, to actual assessment of potential damage to intra-Community trade rather than an assumption of a monolithic and context-less weight to the internal market consideration.

In Hans Christian Anderson's tale, the *Emperor's New Clothes* represents a collective commitment to share in ignorance of the bare facts. The reality of the very narrow interpretation of Article 95(4)–(6) EC is much more apparent today than at any time since its introduction, but if it is still regarded as offering a 'guarantee' that environmentally progressive Member States can retain their high levels of protection after harmonization, or that it provides a procedure for Member States unilaterally to decide that current levels are inadequate to protect their citizens or environment, then it does need to be said 'But he has nothing on at all'.[176]

[176] H. C. Anderson, *Fairy Tales, Told For Children* (London: Random House, 1999).

Innovation through Precaution: The Case of the Dutch Wadden Sea

*Floor M. Fleurke**

I. Introduction and Background to the Case Study

The precautionary principle is designed to provide guidance in environmental cases where societal stakes are high and scientific claims are uncertain or complex. The principle hence serves to reconcile two seemingly opposite arenas, those of science and policy. It does this by lowering the burden of proof of harm, and by involving a wider range of interests in decision-making processes. This chapter endeavours to provide insights into the difficult relationship between science and decision-making by focusing on the practical application of the precautionary principle in policy-making regarding the Wadden Sea, which represents a particularly suitable case study for our purposes.

The constantly and regularly flooded areas of the Wadden Sea are home to about 2000 groups of organisms. The Wadden Sea is a shallow sea at the rim of the north-western European continent, and consists of tidal flats, salt marshes, and barrier islands. It is recognized as a wetland of international importance, and is listed as one of the 200 most important nature reserves in the world and is one of the last areas of remaining original nature in the Netherlands. The Wadden Sea has a high level of primary production and functions as a nursery for many fish species. Many animal species can be found in this area, and it is an important wintering and resting place for migratory birds.

For some 15 years, the question whether intensified mechanical fishing of especially cockles (*Cerastoderma Edule*) and mussels (*Edulis*) explained the rapid decline of shellfish-eating birds in the area has been hotly debated. Whereas cockles do not feature on the average Dutch menu, the Netherlands has long been Europe's biggest exporter of cockles, mainly to Spain where they enrich popular paella dishes.

* Ph.D candidate, University of Amsterdam, Centre for Environmental Law. The author wishes to thank the editor, Han Somsen, and the referees of the *Yearbook* for their constructive comments.

Between 1998 and 2004, a government sponsored research project *Evaluatie II* (EVA II) was therefore carried out. It focused on the ecological effects of mechanical shellfish fishery in the Dutch part of the Wadden Sea and several related questions. This resulted in 22 scientific reports and ten technical background papers, totalling 2,850 pages.

The research was conducted by a consortium of four Dutch ecological research institutes. The conclusion of these reports was that there are several factors that have contributed to the decline in the number of shellfish-eating birds, some of which are beyond immediate human control (such as climate change). However, mass mortality in the early 1990s was probably due to over fishing, albeit in combination with severe winter storms that delayed recovery.

However, even this huge research effort did not remove all controversies and scientific uncertainties. Moreover, the project gave rise to new questions. After this risk assessment was completed, the Dutch government proceeded to risk management. In preparation, it invited different advice groups to issue opinions aimed at the sustainable development and use of the Wadden Sea. Public consultations were organized with the aim of securing broad public acceptance of the new policy. On 28 June 2004, that advice culminated in a decision of the Minister of Agriculture, Nature Management and Fisheries to ban mechanical cockle fishing from the Wadden Sea altogether.

Simultaneously, an earlier debate on the ecological effects of gas drilling in the Wadden Sea was revived. In 1998, a ten-year moratorium on gas drilling, which had been justified by scientific uncertainties, had come to an end and new policy on the issue was needed. A connection was made with cockle fishery: it was proposed that gas revenues be used to create a fund for long-term investments in the Wadden Sea ecology, including buying out the most harmful activity, i.e. the mechanical cockle industry. New research concerning the effects of gas drilling to the ecology of the Wadden Sea started, and meetings were held with interested parties. The government eventually decided to proceed with gas extraction, claiming ecological risks were minimal. A licence conditioned by the so-called 'hand-to-tap principle' was granted to the Dutch mining company *Nederlandse Aardolie Maatschappij* (NAM). That principle implied independent monitoring of the limit values contained in the licence, with extensive enforcement powers for the competent authorities in case of breaches of those conditions. A commission that explored buying-out the cockle sector operating in the Wadden Sea was installed in September 2004.

This chapter focuses on decision-making processes giving rise to the ban on mechanical cockle fishery and NAM's permit to drill for gas in the Wadden Sea. In both cases scientific research played a pivotal role, as scientific uncertainty concerning the ecological effects of the activities prevailed. The stakes were high in both cases, leading to intense public debate in which societal and scientific arguments became intertwined: the ecological research itself became part of the controversy. When public engagement is modest, science is autonomous and *curiosity-driven*, but in this case scientific findings were used in an applied context.[1] Under these circumstances, as will be seen, scientific uncertainties are mobilized as a strategic element in the political debate. Science then becomes *issue-driven*, and scientific claims are interpreted and understood from economic, legal, ethical, and political perspectives.[2]

Section II provides a brief synopsis of key constitutive elements of the precautionary principle. It is not my intention exhaustively to discuss the doctrinal debate surrounding the principle. Rather, the analysis is designed to expose the core of precaution, for the purpose of ascertaining whether the decision-making processes under scrutiny indeed were 'precautionary' at a later point.

Sections III and IV outline the factual and legal backgrounds of the case study, and explain the positions of relevant stakeholders with regard to the notion 'risk'. The first part of the risk analysis, the risk assessment (EVA II), is discussed in Section V. When science is issue-driven, the precautionary principle often becomes operational in risk assessment.[3] In such cases, it becomes crucial *who* (i.e. policy-makers, non governmental organizations (NGOs), other interested parties) participates in the risk assessment, and thereby shapes its outcome.

It is equally crucial *how* scientists phrase their results; if uncertainties are openly addressed, risk managers will be better positioned to take into account other interests. Risk assessment then may bridge the science/society divide. Uncertainties may be concealed, however, especially by couching them into probabilities and certainties. In such cases, risk managers are left little scope for taking other societal interests into account.

Section VI then moves on to the risk management phase of the risk analysis, starting with an examination of reports from different advice groups. I will attempt to clarify how scientific results (including scientific uncertainties) have been translated into policy advice, and the role played by the precautionary principle.

In the literature it is often taken for granted that public participation addresses some of the legitimacy problems inherent to the regulation of issues surrounded by scientific uncertainty, and enhances the quality of decision-making. I will also enquire if the public consultation rounds can indeed be said to have increased the quality of the final decision, or that they have exclusively served the legitimacy of the decision-making process.

[1] J. A. A. Swart and J. van Andel, 'Rethinking the Interface Between Ecology and Society: the Case of Cockle Controversy in the Dutch Wadden Sea' (2007) *Journal of Applied Ecology Online Early Articles* (Oct.), 7.

[2] M. Gibbons, C. Limoges, H. Nowotny, S. Schwartzman, P. Scott and M. Throw, *The New Production of Knowledge: The Dynamics of Science and Research in Contemporary Societies* (Sage: London, 1994).

[3] T. O'Riordan, J. Cameron, and A. Jordan, *Reinterpreting the Precautionary Principle* (London: Cameron May, 2001), P. van Zwanenberg and A. Stirling, 'Risk and Precaution in the US and Europe: A Response to Vogel' (2003) 3 *Yearbook for European Environmental Law*, 41–51.

In Section VII, finally, I will assess how the constitutive elements of the precautionary principle, articulated in Section II, have impacted on decision-making regarding mechanical cockle fisheries and gas drilling in the Wadden Sea.

II. Rationale for Precaution

A. Key Concepts of the Precautionary Principle

The relationship between science, law, and policy-making is complex and controversial. This is especially so in the realm of environment and human health protection, where law in many ways relies on science for its legitimacy. Scientific and technical knowledge underpin decisions relating to, for example, the establishment of limit values for pollutants. The relationship becomes problematic when, due to scientific uncertainty, science by necessity cannot be the sole basis for decisions. At its most elementary, the precautionary principle allows decision-makers, in cases where there are threats of irreversible environmental harm to health or the environment, to take protective measures even when there is no scientific certainty about such harm. The most common formulation of the precautionary principle is found in Principle 15 of the Rio Declaration, which dictates *not* to use 'lack of full scientific certainty' as a reason for *not* taking measures to prevent irreversible harm.[4] It is somewhat perplexing and unfortunate that the most common manifestation of the principle employs a double negative.[5] This being as it may, the rationale for precaution has been usefully summarized by Somsen, who cites three reasons why the precautionary principle is a sensible tool in environmental law and policy:

First, there exists a worrisome imbalance between what we can *do* and what at present we can *understand*. Environmental precaution is a principle appropriate for a civilization in which technological and economic capabilities are out of synk with its scientific grasp of the ecological impacts of those activities. Crucial amongst the known unknowns that justify environmental precaution is the nature of ecological thresholds that trigger sudden global environmental catastrophes, e.g. the increasingly rapid disappearance of polar ice that in turn may reverse the gulf stream, etc. Second, we must acknowledge the disequilibria between those having a legal interest and voice in pursuing some industrial activity, and the environment, which does not possess legal personality and is not easily represented in the law, even if the law provides for access to justice for environmental Non Governmental Organizations (NGOs). Third, there are obvious conflicts

[4] Principle 15 Rio Declaration on Environment and Development 1992, Convention on Biological Diversity (Rio de Janeiro (Brazil), 5 June 1992 (entered into force 29 Dec. 1993), (1992) 31 *International Legal Materials* 4, 818).

[5] An exception is the definition of the principle formulated at the Wingspread Conference on the Precautionary Principle: 'When an activity raises threats of harm to human health or the environment, precautionary measures should be taken even if some cause and effect relationships are not fully established scientifically', published on the Internet at: http://www.gdrc.org/u-gov/precaution-3.html.

of interest between present and future generations. The costs of irreversible harm to the environment by definition are borne by future generations who are not represented in political and legal process. Precaution gives future generations a voice in legal and political processes.[6]

Over the past two decades, the precautionary principle has become an established feature of environmental, public health, and other risk regulation regimes in many different jurisdictions, including the European Union (EU).[7] In some cases, the precautionary principle has been included in concrete regulatory schemes, but in most cases it is formulated as a broad guiding principle. Scholars have followed this development closely, which has resulted in a bulk of literature regarding almost every conceivable aspect of the principle. Curiously, however, the crucial question if and how the principle *actually* works in the political-administrative arena has received little or no academic attention. Before shifting our attention precisely to this most important of questions, a brief explanation of the terminology that will be used is warranted.

Risk is a function of the probability of an adverse environmental or public health effect and the severity of that effect consequential to a hazard.[8] *Scientific uncertainty* implies that there is no objective basis to define meaningful probability distributions. Uncertainty thus is a condition under which possible outcomes are clear (such as specific degrees of harm or benefit), but where it is difficult to quantify probabilities.[9] A condition of *ambiguity* exists when a problem lies not with probabilities, but in agreeing the appropriate question to ask, values to adopt, priorities to assign, or limits to impose in the definition of the possible outcomes themselves.[10] *Ignorance* exists where neither probabilities nor outcomes may be fully confidentially characterized ('we don't know what we don't know').[11]

The precautionary principle hence deals with hypotheses related to possible hazards or threats.[12] Compared with the prevention principle, designed to address known hazards of which probabilities of their occurrences are also known, the

[6] H. Somsen, 'Cloning Trojan Horses: precautionary regulation of reproductive technologies' *Tilburg University Legal Studies Working Paper No.005/2007* published on the Internet at: http://papers.ssrn.com/sol3/papers.cfm?abstract_id=1053981.

[7] Art. 174(2) EC states that Community policy shall be 'based on' the precautionary principle. The integration principle contained in Art. 6 EC implies that the principle now applies to all EC policies. Case T-47/00 *Artegodan GmbH* v. *Commission* [2002] ECR II-4965.

[8] This definition is used by the Commission in drafting for example Reg. (EC) No. 178/2002 laying down the General Principles and Requirements of Food Law, Establishing the European Food Safety Authority and Laying Down Procedures in Matters of Food Safety [2002] OJ L31/1.

[9] S. O. Functowicz, and J. R. Ravetz, 'Science for the post-normal age' (1993) 25 *Futures*, 739–56.

[10] Van Zwanenburg and Stirling, n. 3 above, 46.

[11] Ibid.

[12] Ignorance is often not explicitly taken into account in precautionary decision-making since precautionary measures against 'hypothetical' risks are not accepted by the European Courts. See, e.g., Case T-13/99 *Pfizer Animal Health* v. *Council* [2002] ECR II-3305, para. 143; Case C-236/01 *Monsanto* [2003] ECR I-08105, para. 106; Case C-192/01 *Commission* v. *Denmark* [2003] ECR I-9693, para. 49.

main contribution of the precautionary principle to risk management is to make it possible to act under conditions of scientific uncertainty.[13] Although references to 'the precautionary principle', 'precaution', and 'precautionary approach' are sometimes believed to have different meanings, in this chapter I will use them interchangeably. Not only do I wish to avoid futile doctrinal discussions that inevitably arise when such subtle distinctions are employed, my focus in this chapter is also more on the versatile nature of precaution in decision-making processes than on its enforceability in a strictly judicial setting.

Risk assessment is defined as a 'science-based' process, using quantitative techniques to characterize hazards, model dose-response relationships, and measure exposures where possible. *Risk management* is generally conceived as distinct from risk assessment, in that it involves the process of decision-making itself, introducing non-scientific considerations beyond risk assessment, such as the level of protection, selection of instruments, alternative policies and the associate wider benefits, costs and evaluation of different parties.[14] *Risk communication* involves the interactive exchange of information, both within and beyond risk analysis as a whole, with an emphasis on 'the explanation of risk assessment findings and the basis of risk management decisions'.[15]

In order to expose the practical workings of the precautionary principle, a simple framework has to be established that enables us to establish if and how the principle has been used in the particular context of the Wadden Sea. The framework should provide a means to identify which were the relevant elements of precaution in dealing with the potential problem of biodiversity loss in the Dutch Wadden Sea. At the same time, the framework could prove significant for the purpose of understanding better which of the constitutive elements of the precautionary principle work, and which do not. The framework is informed by the literature on the precautionary principle, as well as the case law of the European courts.[16]

[13] O. Godard, 'The Precautionary principle and Catastrophism on Tenterhooks: lessons from a constitutional reform in France' in E. Fisher, J. Jones, and R. von Schomberg (eds.), *Implementing the Precautionary Principle* (Edward Elgar: Cheltenham UK, 2006), 65.

[14] A. Stirling , O. Renn, and P. van Zwanenberg, 'A framework for the Precautionary Governance of Food Safety: Intergrating Science and Participation in the Social Appraisal of Risk', in Fisher, Jones, and von Schomberg (eds.), see n. 13 above, at 286.

[15] Codex Alimentarius Commission (2001), *Procedural Manual,* 12th edn., Rome: UN Food and Agriculture Organization, Rome. Published on the Internet at: http://www.fao.org/documents/show_cdr.asp?url_=/DOCREP/005/Y2200E/y2200e07.htm.

[16] See, e.g., the framework developed by A. Deville and R. Harding in *Applying the Precautionary Principle* (Sydney: Federation Press, 1997), A. Stirling, *On Precautionary and Science Based Approaches to Risk Assessment and Environmental Appraisal: Field Study* (Sevilla: Institute for Prospective Technological Studies, 2001), at 3, or the framework developed by the European Commission in its *Communication on the Precautionary Principle* COM(2000)1, 2 Feb. 2000. For a comprehensive review of EC case law on the application of the precautionary principle see N. de Sadeleer, 'The Precautionary Principle in EC Health and Environmental Law' (2006) 12 *European Law Journal,* 139–72.

B. Theoretical Framework

i. Recognition of 'Serious or Irreversible Harm'

In order to trigger precautionary regulation, it first needs to be established whether there are threats of serious and irreversible damage. This requires consideration of the magnitude, longevity, spatial aspects, and manageability of harm, as well as consideration of public concerns and other socio-economic interests. This ultimately is a political assessment pertaining to the level of protection for the relevant environmental issues.

ii. Acknowledging Uncertainties

The second question concerns the degree of certainty with which it can be predicted that environmental damage will occur. It is scientific *uncertainty* that triggers precaution, which therefore has to be acknowledged. Decision-makers need to address the sufficiency of evidence, and the level and nature of uncertainty. Apart from uncertainty, ignorance and indeterminacy also need to be taken into account.[17] Decision-makers must therefore carefully describe and characterize the problem they are addressing. The European Commission in its Communication on the Precautionary Principle stresses that, notwithstanding existing uncertainties, a 'complete comprehensive assessment of risk' needs to be conducted.[18] Risk assessment is defined in strictly procedural terms, consisting of hazard identification, hazard characterization, appraisal of exposure, and risk characterization. The Communication does not indicate how uncertainty is to be identified in the risk assessment. The precautionary principle acknowledges that value debates influence scientific debates and vice versa, which would appear to imply that the precautionary principle is of relevance not only to the management but also the assessment of risk.[19]

iii. Shifting the Burden of Proof

The precautionary principle substantially lowers the threshold for State action, but does not shift the burden of proof completely to the applicant of any given activity. In practice, the burden to prove the safety or harm of an activity, product, or technology does not rest with a single party, but is shared depending on competence and knowledge. Likewise, the European Commission refused to adopt a position regarding the burden of proof, and instead proposed a pragmatic approach that depended on the particular authorization procedure at issue.

[17] Stirling, Renn, and van Zwanenberg, n. 14 above, at Ch. 14.

[18] N. 16 above, summary, at para. 5.1.2.

[19] Contrary to this view, the European Commission is of the opinion that the precautionary principle is mainly of relevance in the risk management phase, n. 16 above, summary, at para. 4.

iv. Consideration of Relevant Information and Views of Interested Parties

Science-based environmental risk assessment is difficult when both probability and impact of potential damage are highly uncertain. Many scholars sympathetic to precaution in such circumstances therefore advocate public participation. In this view, risk assessment and management must be conducted in a fashion that is in agreement with the principle of participation—engaging all interested parties not only in risk management, but also in risk assessment.[20] Participation in such cases involves interdisciplinary deliberation in the process of decision-making itself, amongst specialists from humanities, social, and natural sciences, and the wider public.[21] The aim of this kind of deliberation is ultimately to forge consensus. The deliberative process is consensual but also adversarial, since actors not only try to solve the problem, but also challenge the assessment of the problem.[22] This type of participatory process allows non-experts to bring to bear valuable local knowledge and represent certain social and political values. Most importantly, it endows decisions based on uncertain knowledge with the necessary additional legitimacy.[23]

The aim of participation can be substantively to contribute to a deliberative problem-solving process, or procedurally to aid legitimacy of the decision-making process. Von Schomberg is an exponent of the latter perspective, i.e. that legitimacy of reliance on the precautionary principle depends on the way it is accommodated in decision-making processes. In contrast, Fisher and Harding instrumentally value deliberation as a problem-solving device, and thus argue that deliberation needs to be thought of in administrative terms.[24]

v. Consideration of Alternative Options

Once decision-makers have established that the precautionary principle is applicable, they have to decide what measures to take. For this, they must identify a wide range of options and examine the available evidence about exposures, uncertainties, and costs associated with each alternative to address risks.[25] They must consider the ends and means of a policy proposal, and assess whether the end can be achieved in a manner most consistent with sustainability, taking into account the principle of proportionality and conducting a broad cost-benefit analysis.

[20] Stirling, Renn, and van Zwanenberg, n. 14 above, at 304.

[21] Ibid.

[22] E. Fisher, 'Drowning by numbers: Standard Setting in Risk Regulation and the Pursuit of Accountable Public Administration', (2000) 20 *Oxford Journal of Legal Studies*, 109–30.

[23] D. J. Fiorno, 'Citizen participation and environmental risk: A survey of institutional mechanism' 15 (1990) *Science, Technology & Human Value* 2, at 226.

[24] E. Fisher and R. Harding in Fisher, Jones, and von Schomberg (eds.), n. 13 above, at 123.

[25] J. A. Tickner, 'Precautionary Assessment: A Framework for Integrating Science, Uncertainty and Preventive Public Policy' in J. A. Tickner (ed.), *Precaution: Environmental Science and Preventive Public Policy* (Washington: Island Press, 2003), at 269.

vi. Principle of Proportionality

The yardstick for assessing the appropriateness of precautionary measures is the concept of proportionality. The precautionary principle is thus framed by the principle of proportionality. When scientific support for hypotheses in relation to any given risk is weak, measures should be less restrictive (all things being equal regarding the order of magnitude of seriousness of potential damage).[26] The proportionality requirement hence relates to the normative implications of possible alternatives, but does not eliminate the justification of taking measures based on the precautionary principle as such.[27] Proportionality dictates that measures should not exceed the limits of what is appropriate and necessary in order to attain the legitimate objectives pursued. The European Court of Justice (ECJ) views cost-benefit analyses as expressions of the proportionality principle.[28]

The most alarming criticism of the precautionary principle is probably that forfeited benefits of technological development are systematically disregarded. Cass Sunstein, likewise, argues that the precautionary principle shies away from cost-benefit analyses which, he argues, are essential for rational and consistent decision-making.[29] Cost-benefit also features as a requirement for environmental policy in the EC Treaty.[30] In examining cost-benefit in a European context, environmental and human health issues take precedence over economic ones.[31] Moreover, the guidelines of the European Commission state that this should not be reduced to a purely economic weighting process.[32] Many policy issues that underlie environmental risk management involve a risk against risk trade-off, rather than a classical cost-benefit analysis. This is especially so when risks are hypothetical, and potential and model calculations of costs and benefits are impossible.

vii. Precautionary Measures are Provisional

Precautionary measures are by definition provisional since they are taken under conditions of uncertainty, and therefore need to be regularly reviewed in light of pertinent scientific knowledge. Science is a discursive process, and standards have to be adapted when scientific knowledge advances.[33] In reality, however, this is

[26] Godard, n. 13 above, at 68.

[27] Von Schomberg, in Fisher, Jones, and von Schomberg, n. 13 above, at 27.

[28] Case T-13/99 *Pfizer Animal Health* v. *Council*, n. 11 above, at para. 410.

[29] C. Sunstein, *Laws of Fear: Beyond the Precautionary Principle* (Cambridge: Cambridge University Press, 2005).

[30] Art. 172 EC.

[31] In several cases, the European Court of Justice (ECJ) has confirmed that economic considerations do not have precedence over non-economic concerns, and in particular health concerns: Case C-180/96 P *UK* v. *Commission* [1996] ECR I-3903, at para. 93; Case C-183/95 *Affish* [1997] ECR I-4315, at para. 43; Case C-473/98 *Kemikale Inspektionen* v. *Toolex* [2000] ECR I-5681, at para. 45.

[32] N. 16 above, summary, at para. 6.

[33] Von Schomberg, in Fisher, Jones, and. von Schomberg, n. 13 above, at 34.

easier said than done: continuously to inform risk management and society at large about scientific progress amounts to a challenge of Herculean proportions.

viii. Monitoring, Evaluation, and Communication

Structural critical reflection on processes, methods, and action is a necessary component of a precautionary approach, because continuous data collection and monitoring are indispensable if scientific uncertainties are to be reduced.[34] Precaution therefore requires risk managers to be adaptive and flexible. It has been suggested that a forum for continuous reflexive deliberation, which evaluates and re-evaluates options in light of different perspectives and new evidence, would best serve this purpose.[35]

ix. Judicial Review

The precautionary principle lacks robust thresholds for its application, including the required degrees of seriousness and uncertainty, which obviously invites its arbitrary use. To counter this danger, it is imperative that recourse to the principle can be judicially reviewed. In fact, it is through the case law of the European Courts as well as the dispute settlement panels (DSP) and the Appellate Body (AB) of the WTO that the principle has evolved to its present form.

III. Object of Research

A. Wadden Sea

The Wadden Sea is a transboundary maritime coastal area with many inertial and subtidal flats on Dutch, German, and Danish territory, and an important habitat for many bird species. An estimated 10 million birds live in the Wadden Sea temporarily or permanently, of which 700,000 live in the Dutch section. The birds include oystercatchers, common eiders, knots, common scoters, and herring gulls, many of which depend on cockles for their food supply. The importance of the Wadden Sea is valued differently according to perspective: for conservationists it is the last Dutch wilderness, for fishermen it represents their traditional fishing grounds.

B. Cockles

In June, the cockle digs itself into the sandy bottom of the wetlands, just a few centimetres deep. The following year, in September, they may already be large enough to be fished. Under unfavourable conditions, they grow more slowly,

[34] Van Zwanenberg and Stirling, n. 3 above, at 53.
[35] J. A. Tickner, n. 25 above, at 14.

and a year or more may be needed before they reach fishing size. A cockle can grow up to five centimetres, and rarely lives longer than six years. The spat fall of cockles is irregular.[36] About once every five years there is a good spat fall, creating many new 'cockle beds'. A cockle bed exists when the density exceeds 50 per square metre.

Since the 1980s, mechanical methods have been used for fishing cockles, which involves dragging metal cages over the seabed. The upper four to five centimetres of the surface are scraped into a cage by a metal plate that is one metre wide. A pipe, from which a powerful water jet emerges, is attached directly in front of the sharp edge. This pulverizes the surface, so that a mixture of water, sand, cockles, and other organisms enter the trawl. The sieved content of the trawl is then sucked on board hydraulically. A hydraulic suction dredge mechanically 'sucks' off the top layer of the bottom of the mudflats. Once on the ship, the cockles are separated, and the remainder is dumped overboard. Modern ships have become so efficient that on average they catch 60 tonnes of cockles per day. At the same time, the number of ships increased from five in 1961 to 32 in 1981. Roughly during the same period of intensifying shell fishing, mass mortality of shellfish eating birds was observed. For instance, the number of wintering oystercatchers declined from 260,000 to 175,000. Numbers of common eiders also fell significantly. These mass mortalities among birds that largely depend on cockles and mussels gave rise to intense scientific and public debate.

Since 1975, in order to avoid over fishing, cockle fishing in the Wadden Sea has been subject to authorization. Initially, national law on nature conservation only required an exemption to which no further conditions were attached. Fishermen who possessed the licences required could fish as many seed mussels and cockles as they pleased. For the European flat oyster (*Ostrea edulis*) this resulted in a textbook example of the theory of the 'tragedy of the commons', and the oyster duly disappeared from the Wadden Sea during the first half of the twentieth century.[37] Other factors, such as hydrographical changes caused by the closure of the southern Zuiderzee in 1932, may also have played a role.[38] However, it is well known that stocks that are seriously depleted become more vulnerable to environmental variation.[39] In retrospect, this clearly is a case where precautionary

[36] Spat fall is the settlement of shellfish larvae from the water on the sea bed.

[37] G. Hardin, 'The Tragedy of the Commons' (1968) 162 *Science*, 1243–8.

[38] R. Dijkema, 'Molluscan Fisheries and Culture in the Netherlands', *US Dep. Commer., NOAA Tech. Report* 129 (NMFS: 1997). There are some examples of oysters being intensively fished, or even over fished, without going extinct. Fishing of European flat oysters has a long tradition in the Dutch Delta. Why some oyster populations are more susceptible to over fishing than others is not known, but may be related to the substrate. According to Vlas, wild European flat Oysters depended in the Wadden Sea on banks of dead shells, Alterra-rapport 1011; RIVO-rapport C056/04; RIKZ-rapport RKZ/2004.031, *Final Report on the Second Phase of the Scientific Evaluation of the Dutch Shellfish Fishery Policy (EVAII) 'The Effects of Shellfish Fishery on the ecosystem of the Dutch Wadden Sea and Oosterschelde'* (Final report EVAII) (Wageningen: Alterra, 2004), at 17.

[39] D. Pauly et al., 'Towards Sustainability in World Fisheries' (2002) 418 *Nature*, 689–95.

regulation could have prevented the European flat oyster from disappearing from the Dutch Wadden Sea.

Increasingly, awareness grew that the ecosystems of the Wadden Sea needed to be protected, and that negative impacts should be avoided. In 1990, an attempt by the Dutch government to ban cockle fishery in large parts of the Wadden Sea was blocked by the president of the Council of State, because Dutch legislation only provided for fishery conservation measures, and was silent on nature conservation measures.[40] In 1991, the law was changed to allow conservation values being taken into account. In 1993, the Policy Agreement on Coastal Fishery marked a new era in which the sector was subject to tighter regulation, such as closure of fishing grounds and reserved food stocks for birds. This policy document set the direction for national fisheries policy until 2003, when policy was evaluated. The 1993 policy aimed at integrating fishing activities and conserving natural values, where possible, and a separation of these two activities where necessary. The policy applied to the Wadden Sea and Oosterschelde estuary rests on three pillars: closed areas, food reservation, and co-management. On the basis of an interim report in 1998, and new observations in 1999 and 2000, it was decided to take additional measures in order to enhance the restoration of mussel beds in the Wadden Sea, and to improve food availability for eider ducks in the Wadden Sea and for oystercatchers in the Oosterschelde estuary.[41] Additional closure of 5 per cent of the inner tidal Wadden Sea area for cockle fishery aimed at the development of mussel beds, because restoration was slow. High mortality of eider ducks in the winter of 1999/2000 provoked a new discussion and further analysis of food availability and other possible causes. On the basis of a review of mortality factors and an evaluation of the policy of food restoration new measures were taken in order to prevent food shortage.

IV. Legal Framework for the Wadden Sea

The legal framework within which shellfish fishery has to be appreciated is very complex. Many international treaties have been signed and ratified, such as the Convention on Wetlands of International Importance especially as Waterfowl Habitat (Ramsar Convention),[42] and the African Eurasian Waterbird Agreement (AEWA).[43] There also exists a trilateral network consisting of Denmark, Germany, and the Netherlands, which organizes Trilateral Governmental Conferences on

[40] Final Report EVA II, n. 38 above, at 18.
[41] Parliamentary Documents II, 2001–2002 No. 27 400 XIV, 11:1–4.
[42] Ramsar (Iran), 2 Feb. 1971 (entered into force 21 Dec. 1975), (1972) 11 *International Legal Materials* 5, 963. The Ramsar Convention protects 'wetlands'. In practice the areas protected under this regime are also protected under designated areas of Natura 2000, and therefore we will not elaborate on this Treaty here.
[43] Published on the Internet at: http://www.cms.int/species/aewa/aew_text.htm.

the Wadden Sea, aiming to achieve a natural and sustainable ecosystem for the area with undisturbed natural processes. Also worth mentioning are the Code of Conduct for Responsible Fisheries, published by the Food and Agriculture Organization of the United Nations (FAO),[44] and the UN Agreement on Straddling Fish Stocks and Highly Migratory Fish Stocks.[45] The FAO code applies a 'precautionary approach' to fisheries.[46] Precaution in the Code covers uncertainties relating to individual stocks, other affected species, and environmental and socio-economic conditions. Account has to be taken of uncertainties in stock assessment models, namely to determine 'stock-specific target reference points and at the same time, the action to be taken if they are exceeded' and 'limit reference points' (the negative goal to the lowest acceptable stock size), and also the action taken if they are exceeded, meaning when a limit reference point is approached measures should be taken to ensure that it will not be exceeded. The explicit references to targets, limits, and predetermination were novel developments at that time. The UN Agreement prescribes that 'the fishing mortality rate that generates maximum sustainable yield (MSY) should be regarded as a minimum standard for limit reference points'. It continues: 'for stocks which are not overfished, fisheries management strategies shall ensure that fishing mortality does not exceed that which correspond to maximum sustainable yield, and that the biomass does not fall below a predefined threshold'. For over fished stocks, 'the biomass which would produce a maximum sustainable yield can serve as a rebuilding target'. Thus, both the UN Agreements and the FAO Code emphasize the level of maximizing long-term yields, which can be interpreted as an acknowledgement of the precautionary principle. Directive 92/43/EEC on the Conservation of Natural Habitats and of Wild Fauna and Flora (Habitats Directive),[47] and Directive 79/409/EEC on the Conservation of Wild Birds (Birds Directive)[48] are the most ambitious legal instruments to protect the ecological values of the Wadden Sea.[49] It may therefore be presumed that compliance with the provisions of these EU Directives will meet the requirements of (other) international and, as we will see, national instruments. For this reason I will not elaborate on the international context of fishing policy.

[44] Marine Fisheries and the Law of the Sea: A Decade of Change. Special Chapter (revised) on the State of Food and Agriculture (1992) Fisheries Circular No. 853, Food and Agriculture Organization of the United Nations, Rome (Italy), at 66.

[45] Agreement for the Implementation of the Provisions of the United Nations Convention on the Law of the Sea of 10 Dec. 1982 relating to the Conservation and Management of Straddling Fish Stocks and Highly Migratory Fish Stocks (dated 8 Sep. 1995), published on the Internet at: http://www.un.org/Depts/los/fish_stocks_conference/fish_stocks_conference.htm.

[46] The adoption of this phrase arose when the fishing industry started to get nervous that the precautionary principle would be captured by environmental NGOs so as to substantially reduce or even halt fishing.

[47] [1992] OJ L206/7.

[48] [1979] OJ L103/1.

[49] Agreement for the Implementation of the Provisions of the United Nations Convention on the Law of the Sea of 10 Dec. 1982 relating to the Conservation and Management of Straddling Fish Stocks and Highly Migratory Fish Stocks, published on the Internet at: http://www.un.org/Depts/los/fish_stocks_conference/fish_stocks_conference.htm.

A. The Birds and Habitats Directives

Areas that fall under the Birds Directive are referred to as Special Protection Areas (SPAs). Under the Habitats Directive these areas are termed Special Areas of Conservation (SACs). The Birds Directive requires that Member States pay particular attention to the protection of wetlands and particularly to wetlands of international importance.[50] To protect no less than 29 species, the Dutch government has designated the entire Dutch Wadden Sea as a SPA within the meaning of the Birds Directive.[51] In December 2004, the same area was also put on the list of Sites of Community Interest (SCI) by the European Commission, because it qualifies for nine habitat types listed in Annex I (one of which is a priority habitat type) and five species listed in Annex II.[52] The eider duck and oystercatcher are among those protected species, which for a significant part are dependent on cockles for their food supply.

Article 6 of the Habitats Directive provides for the protection of these areas. This provision is not only applicable to SACs designated under the Habitats Directive, but also applies to protected areas (SPAs) that fall under the Birds Directive.[53] In general, Member States have to make sure that the quality of natural habitats and habitats of species in SACs does not deteriorate, and there should be no disturbing factors for the species for which the SPA was designated. Human usage is allowed, but should not have significant deleterious impacts on the species and habitats. Article 6(1) contains a general obligation for Member States to take the necessary conservation measures to maintain the ecological requirements of the natural habitats types in Annex I and the species in Annex II present on the site. Article 6(2) constitutes another general obligation that Member States have to take appropriate steps to avoid the deterioration of natural habitats and the habitats of species, as well as the disturbance of species for which the areas have been designated, insofar as such disturbance could be significant in relation to the objective of this Directive.[54] Article 6(3) and (4) is more specific, and provide for the appraisal or assessment of plans and projects which are, either individually or in combination with other plans or projects, likely to have a significant effect on the site. According to Article 6(3), such a plan or project must be subject to an appropriate assessment of its implications for the site in view of its conservation objectives. The ECJ has established that Article 6(3) has direct

[50] Art. 3(2), Birds Dir.

[51] Art. 4(2), Birds Dir. Species from Annex I or regulatory occurring migratory species not listed in Annex I.

[52] Art. 4(2), Habitats Dir.

[53] Art. 7, Habitats Dir.

[54] If deterioration has taken place, even when the project or activity was permitted, the competent authority has the obligation to restore the damage that has been done. See Case C-117/00 *Commission* v. *Ireland* [2002] ECR I 883, at para. 37.

effect.[55] The 'appropriate assessment' has to take cumulative effects into account. A project can be harmless in isolation, but in conjunction with other projects may turn out to be harmful after all. It is not clear whether this requirement is only concerned with impacts of future projects, or that effects of existing projects also count. Verschuuren claims that effects of autonomous developments, such as climate change or invasive species, have to be taken into consideration as well.[56] Competent authorities can only agree with a plan or project after having ascertained that it will not adversely affect the integrity of the site concerned and, if appropriate, having obtained the opinion of the general public. Article 6(4) expresses an exception to this rule for imperative reasons of an overriding public interest, including those of a social or economic nature; in that case the Member State must take all compensatory measures necessary to ensure that the overall coherence of Natura 2000 is protected.

B. National Protection Regimes for the Wadden Sea

As observed, the national legal regime for the protection of the Wadden Sea as a nature conservation site has been of fairly recent origin. Initially, the area was therefore dominated by commercial businesses that exploited the resources of the area with no or few legislative constraints. The Mining Act, the Dredging Rule (1934), and the Fishery Act (1963) provided sectoral rules with no particular concern for ecological values. At one point, the Wadden Sea had even been designated for future land reclamation. This plan met with fierce local opposition led by the NGO 'De Waddenvereniging', and was abandoned in 1965.[57]

C. Nature Conservation Act

The Nature Conservation Act 1968 was aimed at the preservation of the Wadden Sea. Until 2005, there existed no proper Dutch regime that faithfully implemented Article 6 of the Habitats Directive, so that Article 6 had to apply directly. If an SPA was also a designated national protected nature monument (which is the case for large parts of the Wadden Sea), the Nature Conservation Act applied, and a licence based on this law had to be obtained. If the area did not enjoy that status, the habitats test had to be carried out by the body that granted permission for the activity. Shellfish fishery usually fell under the Fishery Act. In both cases, the minister of Agriculture, Nature Conservation and Fisheries was the competent authority. In 2005, the revision of the Nature Conservation Act took effect, which meant that finally implementation of Article 6 of the Habitats Directive

[55] Case C- 127/02 *Landelijke Vereniging tot Behoud van de Waddenzee en de Nederlandse Vereniging tot Bescherming van Vogels* v. *Staatssecretaris van Landbouw, Natuurbeheer en Visserij,* (n.y.r.), para. 66.

[56] J. M. Verschuuren, 'Shellfish for Fisherman or for Birds? Article 6 Habitats Directive and the Precautionary Principle' (2005) 17 *Journal of Environmental Law*, at 281.

[57] T. Verbeeten, *Wijs met de Waddenzee?* (Amsterdam: Thela Thesis, 1999), at 139.

was a fact. Since, all activities that can significantly impact on an SPA fall under Article 19d of this law, which provides for a permit system. Thus, mechanical fishing activities required an annually renewable authorization based on Article 19d of the Nature Conservation Act. Substantively, the permit system laid down in Article 19f–h is an almost *verbatim* copy of the regime covered by the Habitats Directive in Article 6. In 1999 and 2000, on the basis of this law and subject to certain conditions, the Minister for Agriculture, Nature Conservation and Fisheries granted an authorization for mechanical fishing of cockles in the Wadden Sea to the Cooperative Producers Organization for Dutch Cockle Fisheries. Each licence obtained by fishermen, stating the amount of shellfish they are allowed to catch in the current season (approximately from September until December), was challenged before the competent administrative court.

D. Key Planning Decision

In 1974, the government decided to design a *Planologische Kernbeslissing* (Key Planning Decision: KPD) for the area, which elevated the protection of the Wadden Sea to a key political goal.[58] It is the first attempt at integrated Wadden Sea Management, and the most important policy document on the planning of the Wadden Sea. A KPD is a tool for central government to coordinate all the intended goals and activities in several policy areas in the context of spatial planning for a period of ten years. It is a national framework of rules and decisions for specific areas like Schiphol Airport or the port of Rotterdam, or a framework for the planning of specific sectors like water reservoirs, traffic traces, etc. The KPD is indicative for provincial and local governments' spatial planning. Guidelines adopted in the KPD can be binding, for instance when Parliament wants to reserve an area for a specific purpose. Departures from 'decisions of fundamental significance' require revision of the KPD. There is an explicit possibility for public participation in the process of drawing up the KPD or the revision of it.

The KPD was partially revised in 1985, and the integral revision took place in 1993. This second version emphasized the goal of 'sustainable protection and development' of the nature reserve, and provided a more elaborate and detailed framework.[59] According to the explanatory memorandum, the procedures of the Nature Conservation Act create an adequate framework for controlling activities which might harm the main objectives of the KPD, namely, sustainable protection and development of that sea as a natural site and, in particular, the feeding, nesting, and resting areas for birds frequenting that site.

[58] Parliamentary Documents II, 1975–1976 No. 13 933, 6–7, entered into force in 1980.

[59] Parliamentary Documents II, 1992–1993, 22 605, No. 34. Interesting to note is that two governmental advice councils, the Council for the Wadden and the Public Administration Council issued a report in 2006 arguing for a Wadden Sea Management which should fall under Nature Protection Act, instead of the Law on spatial planning.

The section in the KPD devoted to coastal fisheries management is implemented in the government decision of 21 January 1993, i.e. the Structure Document on Marine and Inshore Fisheries 'Fishing for equilibrium'. This establishes the policy for shellfish fishing, inter alia in the Wadden Sea, for the years 1993 to 2003 and includes a number of restrictions as regards cockle fishing. Certain areas of the national natural site are permanently closed to cockle fishing and in years in which food is scarce, 60 per cent of the average food requirement of birds in the form of cockles and mussels is reserved for them.

In the KPD the precautionary principle is taken to mean that the benefit of the doubt will favour conservation of the Wadden Sea where:

> on the basis of the best available information, there appears to be obvious doubt as to the absence of a possible significant adverse effect on the ecosystem.[60]

The order for reference shows that most of the available scientific studies consulted do not unequivocally indicate the existence of significant adverse effects on the ecosystem of the Wadden Sea linked to mechanical cockle fishing. The third KPD resulted from a difficult and painful delivery. It was finally adopted on 19 December 2006, and remains valid for ten years.

V. The Case of Mechanical Cockle Fishery: Risk Assessment

From the start, the new shellfish policy has been informed by research intended to provide clarity about the nature and scale of the impact of shellfish fishing on the ecological values of the Wadden Sea and the Oosterschelde.

EVA (Evaluation) II is the follow up of EVA I, which was carried out in 1998 to evaluate the first measures taken in 1993 to protect wildlife in the Wadden. The results of the EVA I risk assessment provided direction to suggested adjustments of the Sea and Coastal Fisheries Policy, but many questions remained unanswered. Reservation policy has been pursued since 1993 for shellfish-eating birds, such as oystercatchers and eider ducks, for the purpose of which certain areas of the Wadden Sea were permanently closed to shellfish fishing as part of the new Sea and Coastal Fisheries Policy. EVA II examined whether the closed areas fulfilled their original goals of: (i) undisturbed development; (ii) monitoring and research; and (iii) protection and restoration of important habitats. Despite these measures, numbers of large shellfish-eating birds continued to decline. Some restoration of sea grass beds occurred, but fell behind expectations. The area of littoral mussel beds in the Wadden Sea increased to more than 2,000 hectares, after having disappeared completely in 1990. The risk assessment had to produce sufficient knowledge to support decision-making on new fishery policy.

60 PKB Tweede Nota Waddenzee, Deel 4, Ministerie van VROM, 1994, para. 3.2.

For the period 1999 to 2004, a monitoring programme was used to detect possible negative effects of shellfish fishery. Four policy questions were at the heart of the project:

1. What are the ecological impacts of shellfish fishery?
2. Did the policies implemented in 1993 achieve their objectives?
3. Is current shellfish fishery in line with the requirements of the Birds and Habitats Directives? and
4. What possibilities for improvement exist?

These policy questions translated into research questions concerning risk assessment.[61] In risk assessment, technical evidence is inseparable from assumptions about nature and society. This feature has been conceptualized in terms of the 'framing' of risk assessments. Put simply, this refers to the inevitable reality that in seeking and organizing facts about risk, socio-political choices about what potential harms to prevent and what opportunities to forego are made.[62] Aware of the importance of framing, and in pursuit of legitimacy, the Ministry of Agriculture, Nature and Food Quality (LNV) therefore wanted to involve different interested parties during the decision-making process in the risk assessment phase. Apart from the Ministry of LNV, this also involved the Ministry of Transport, Public Works and Water Management (VROM), as well as the main nature conservation and fisheries organizations. The EVA II risk assessment began in 1999 and ran until 2004. It is interesting that attention was afforded not only to the objectives and measures of the Structure Document[63] and the impact of shellfish fishing, but also to the development of the carrying capacity[64] of the Wadden Sea and the Oosterschelde for shellfish and shellfish-eating birds, a subject that technically lies outside the scope of the risk assessment on the effects of shellfish fishery on the ecosystem of the Dutch Wadden Sea and Oosterschelde. In this sense, the risk assessment went beyond the aim of a strict evaluation. The research programme provided a broad outline of individual risk assessment projects. Individual risk assessment proposals were submitted to the steering committee of EVA II for comments and prioritization. This resulted in 22 scientific reports and ten technical background papers.

Scientific quality was guaranteed in two ways. An audit-commission of experts was installed to ensure that the research questions formulated would provide the

[61] B. J. R. Lanters and A Smaal, *Onderzoeksplan EVA II* (RIKZ : Den Burg/DenHaag/Yerseke, 2000).

[62] S. Jasanoff, 'Bridging the Two Cultures of Risk Analysis' Vol. 13 (1993) *Risk Analysis* 2, at 129.

[63] Ministry of Agriculture, Nature and Food Quality (LNV), *Vissen naar Evenwicht. Regeringsbeslissing Structuurnota Zee- en Kustvisserij (Fishing for Balance, Governmental Decision Structure Report on Sea and Coastal Fishery)* (Den Haag, 1993).

[64] Carrying capacity is the maximum biomass which a particular species on a particular surface area can achieve in the given circumstances.

necessary information to inform new policy decisions, to evaluate the research framework in light of the research questions, and to exercise research results on their scientific quality. In addition, scientific quality was safeguarded by a system of external peer-review, as EVA II scientists published their results in acknowledged scientific journals.

A. Ecological Impacts of Cockle Fishery in the Wadden Sea

EVA II first addressed the question of whether mechanical fishing for cockles had led to large-scale long-term changes of the Wadden Sea ecosystem. The research focused on different categories of wildlife: the cockle population itself, miscellaneous benthic organisms, and bird populations. The results of EVA II are now briefly summarized below.[65]

i. Development of Cockle Stocks and Catches

The volume of cockle stocks varies significantly from year to year, and is strongly related to a good spat fall.[66] The annual average for the period 1990 to 2002 contained approximately 44 million cockles. In view of fluctuations, however, an annual average is not very useful. The average catch between 1990 and 2002 amounted to 4 million cockles per year. In the period 1999 to 2002, on average 11 per cent of the total cockle stock was fished.[67]

EVA II research observed differences regarding the development and distribution of the cockle stock in the open and closed areas. The number of cockles is significantly higher in closed areas than in open areas of the Wadden Sea. After closing off some parts in 1999, the density and biomass of two-year-old cockles increased. Nevertheless, scientists considered:

> The increase of biomass appears to be the effect of the successful spat fall of 1997, and not the effect of the closing.[68]

The total cockle stock was higher in closed areas in 1993 than in open areas in 1994 and from 2000 onwards. This is caused by better accretion of cockles in closed areas as well as fishing in the open areas. In general, survival rates of cockles are better in closed areas. The difference was significant in all waters. These results indicate favourable circumstances for cockle population in closed areas. This can possibly be explained by 'differences in habitats of the closed and open areas respectively, which already existed when the closing of areas was

[65] Final Report EVA II, n. 38 above, at 87.

[66] This can vary from 145 million kg in 1998 to only 3.8 million kg in other years. Dutch Institute for Fisheries Research (RIVO), *Cockle Habitat maps for the Wadden Sea and the Eastern and Western Scheldt*, Report C060/03.2003 (Yerseke, 2003).

[67] Ibid.

[68] Deelrapport H4, EVA II (2003), at 5.

executed'.[69] The quote reflects that differences between closed and open areas are now established. Simultaneously, it cannot be excluded that these differences are explained by other variables. One of those variables could be the long-term development in natural processes:

An analysis of the spreading of cockle stocks in the Wadden Sea in the period 1980–2002 shows that around 1990 a turning point took place in the scattering of cockle stocks. From then on, a bigger surface of cockle stocks was encountered in closed areas in comparison with the open areas. This turning point cannot be directly ascribed to mechanic cockle fishery, since the development could already be observed in areas that were closed long before they were closed for fishing, or in areas that were closed for a very long time. It appears that a long-term development in natural processes takes place.[70]

The EVA II report concludes that mechanical cockle dredging does lead to a decrease in cockle stocks in the years to follow.

ii. Effects of Mechanical Cockle Fishery on Sediment and Benthic Life

Successful recruitment of cockles in the low lying and sandy parts of the Wadden Sea occurs less than in the past, especially in areas open to fishery. These are mud-rich areas, whereas they formerly would lie in lower sandier areas. Consequently, conditions for their growth and development have deteriorated:

This moving up is credited to a change in the spreading of young cockles and for a smaller part to the selective fishing of cockles present on low mud-poor Wad. In the last two decades Cockle Fishery has shoved up to higher and mud-rich Wad, so that fishing now takes place in the most food en rich areas.[71]

The research into the impacts of mechanical cockle fishery on mud quality in the Wadden Sea is exemplary of risk assessments where many different variables are at play, making it almost impossible to draw reliable conclusions. Against this background, the audit-commission decided to rephrase the conclusion with regard to effects on mud quality:

Mechanical cockle fishery causes a deterioration of the mud quality at the bottom of the Wadden Sea at the short, mid-long and long term. Yet, the effect is disguised due to the fact that during the last decade fishing has taken place in areas that have become muddier than before. Statistical analysis is incapable of an accuracy that exceeds 95 per cent.[72]

There are indications of reduced silt contents on tidal flats that had been open to cockle fishery during longer periods. This can be explained by the low cockle

[69] Final Report EVA II, n. 38 above, at 125.
[70] Ibid.
[71] Ibid.
[72] Appendix 1 to the Final Report EVA II, Audit Commissie EVA II, *Beoordeling van het wetenschappelijk eindrapport*, n. 38 above, at 199.

stocks and consequently a reduced production of *faeces* and *pseudo faeces* in the open areas. There are other large-scale changes in the silt, which cannot be attributed to fisheries. Following closure, a higher proportion of the biomass of adult cockles was found in areas closed to shellfish fishing. Less cockle spat developed in the open areas than in the closed areas until 2000. The difference has steadily decreased, and spat fall is now slightly higher in the open areas. The number of benthic organisms on fished cockle beds decreased, with the exception of the worm *Nemis diversocolor*, which increased after fishery.

It is not clear, though, what the long-term effects are, or how long it takes before harm is repaired. Mechanical cockle fishing depletes the silt in the sediment of the mud flat immediately after fishing. Recovery may take more than a year. At a public consultation, one of the researchers indicated that mortality among the benthic fauna runs into dozens of per cents, and is not limited to the lane where dredging took place, but stretches to the whole area. It was asserted that restoration would occur after one or two years, but this claim has been widely contested.[73]

iii. Effects on Birds

The effects on bird populations featured most prominently in the risk assessment and risk management debate. An estimated 10 million birds live in the Wadden Sea, of which 700,000 live in the Dutch section. Four species of birds were identified as shellfish eaters: common eiders, oystercatchers, herring gulls, and knots. Numbers of all these species have declined in recent years, although the onset of the decline varies between species. Only two of the bird species mentioned feed on the large shellfish that are also targeted by fishermen: the oystercatcher (*Haematopus ostralegus*) and the common eider (*Somateria mollissima).* Over the past ten years, numbers of worm eating birds have increased more sharply in open areas than in closed areas. Around 1990, after the disappearance of the inner tidal mussel beds, oystercatchers started to decline in numbers slowly. A sudden reduction in numbers occurred during the severe winter of 1996/1997. No redistribution occurred, i.e. oystercatchers did not become more numerous in the areas that were closed for cockle fishery. These patterns in bird numbers may be partly explained by the presence of mussel beds, which initially returned to open areas. The oystercatchers caught in closed areas were in better condition than those caught in open areas, which may be related to high cockle stocks in closed areas. Cockle fishery reduces the food stock for oystercatchers.[74] On the basis of model calculations, it is estimated that this direct effect of cockle fishery amounts to a decrease of the carrying capacity of the Wadden Sea and Oosterschelde for

[73] Deelrapport C1, EVA II (2003), at 3.

[74] Final Report EVA II, n. 38 above, 159. See Verhulst et al., 'Shellfish Fishery Severly Reduces Conditions and Survival of Oystercatchers Despite Creation of Large Marine Protected Areas' 9 (2004) 17 *Ecology & Society*, published on the internet at: http://www.ecologyandsociety.org/vol19/iss1/art17/.

oystercatchers with a number in the order of 15,000 and 3,300 birds, respectively, during the evaluation period. These model calculations do not take cumulative effects of cockle fishery on stock sizes, recruitment, and age distribution of cockles into account. Moreover, the EVA II risk assessment claims that the disappearance of mussel beds is the primary reason for the decline of oystercatchers. It is stated that 'the decrease in the number of oystercatchers wintering in the Dutch Wadden Sea is primarily due to the disappearance and subsequent slow recovery of inner tidal mussel beds, and to a lesser extent due to the continuing cockle fishery'.[75]

At present, there is no evidence that cockle fishery has had a significant negative impact on common eiders, as their thick shells made them in any event less suitable for feeding. Cockle fishery may influence the food supply of knots through its influence on stocks of small shellfish. There are some indications that the quality of cockles in fished areas has suffered. It is possible that cockles favour some worm species that are an important food source for birds feeding on worms.

Reading the results of EVA II with regard to the ecological impacts of cockle fishery in the Wadden Sea, it can be concluded that without resolving all uncertainties, which are to some extent inherent to the science of a ecosystem such as the Wadden Sea, the immediate effects of cockle fishery are undisputed and consist of extraction of marketable cockles, mortality of non-benthic fauna, and washing out of fine sediments. The important question is how quickly the sediment and biota recover from this disturbance.[76] In other words: do the effects of mechanical cockle fishing amount to irreversible harm? In general, inner tidal dredging shows itself to be one of the more detrimental fishing activities, and recovery time is estimated at several years. However, major gaps in knowledge were also identified, and scientists are divided on this issue.[77]

B. Evaluating the Policy of Food Reservation

To counter the decline in numbers of shellfish-eating birds, a food reservation policy has been pursued since 1993 for shellfish-eating birds such as oystercatchers and eider ducks. This can be seen as an early attempt to adopt precautionary measures, particularly since EVA I did not produce all the information concerning the effects of cockle fishery needed for a classical risk management policy. The question dealt with by EVA II was whether these precautionary measures were sufficient to safeguard the ecological qualities of the Wadden Sea. Food reservation means that sufficient shellfish must remain for these birds after fishing. Policy must aim at protecting birds from suffering extra food shortages because of shellfish fishing, particularly in lean years. Analysis of the declining numbers requires an evaluation of the availability of shellfish compared to the reference

[75] Final Report EVA II, n. 38 above, at 160. [76] Ibid., at 83 [77] Ibid.

period, because the policy is based on reservation of shellfish as foods for birds.[78] The basis for the food reservation policy was the number of shellfish-eating birds in the Wadden Sea from 1980 until 1990, combined with the food requirement per bird. Overall, the food reservation policy of 1993 was unable to prevent a food shortage for reference numbers of shellfish eating birds caused by fishery.[79] EVA II research shows that the actual quantity was overestimated by an average of 38 per cent.[80] The most significant overestimates were made in cockle-rich years, since no account was taken of poorer growth in some areas during those years. In lean years, the estimates were nearer to the mark. Since 2003, the original estimates have been corrected.[81] It is calculated that cockles were by far the most important prey of oystercatchers during the period 1990 to 2001.[82] Before the inner tidal mussel beds disappeared in 1990, it was estimated that over half of the oystercatchers in the Wadden Sea fed on mussels.[83] The EVA II researchers therefore consider the disappearance of the inner tidal mussel beds as the primary reason for the decline of the number of oystercatchers.[84]

i. Oystercatchers

For oystercatchers, food reservation policy in 1993 had been largely based on their physiological food requirements. This is the amount of flesh an oystercatcher needs to consume in the course of winter in order to stay in good condition: around 65 kg of flesh per winter. This approach assumes that every bird will succeed in catching the full 100 per cent of the available quantity of shellfish flesh. In reality, if the shellfish density is too low, birds are unable to harvest them. Even at high densities,

[78] The model calculations used in the EVA II research evaluating the policy of food reservation applied to a single winter season. However, cockle fishing reduces cockle stocks in subsequent years. This even applies to years in which there were still sufficient stocks after fishing for oystercatchers, eider ducks, and other shellfish-eaters like gulls. Therefore, a more extensive model calculation is required for the overall cumulative impact of fishery, as is noted by the researchers themselves, Final Report EVA II, n. 37, at 117.

[79] The effect of food shortage only becomes apparent when the strong effects of severe winter weather are corrected for. In the mud flats freeze, the birds cannot reach the food they contain. See C. Camphuysem et al., 'Mass Mortality of Common Eiders (*Somateria Mollisima)* in the Dutch Wadden Sea 1999/2000: Starvation in a Commercially Exploited Wetland of International Importance' (2002) 106 *Biological Conservation*, 303–17.

[80] J. Kamermans et al., EVA II Deelproject H2: Evaluatie van de geschatte omvang en ligging van kokkelbestanden in de Waddenzee, Ooster-en Westerschelde, RIVO Rapport C054/03 (Yerseke:2003).

[81] Final Report EVA II, n. 38 above, at 111.

[82] Ibid., 112: most years cockles make up 40 to 70 per cent of the diet.

[83] C. J. Smit et al., 'Birds, Mussles, Cockles and Shellfish Fishery in the Dutch Wadden Sea: How to Deal with Low Food Stocks For Eiders and Oystercatchers?' (1998) 29 *Senckenbergiana Maritima*, 141–53. Mussel beds represent a much more stable source of food for oystercatchers than cockles, which are the next best alternative. The quantity of successful mussel recruitment in the Wadden Sea is very unpredictable due the high fluctuation of cockle stocks. See Final Report EVA II, n. 38 above, at para. 4.3.

[84] Final Report EVA II, n. 38 above, at Section 3.8.

harvesting is limited since at some point they will get in each other's way. Some of the shellfish are also too small to count as food. Furthermore, estimates of the total quantity of flesh weight are made in September, whereas shellfish actually lose weight in the course of winter. Some die off before the birds can eat them. For all these reasons, EVA II concludes that the ecological food requirement should be taken as the basis for the food reservation policy to prevent a food shortage for the birds. The ecological food requirement is defined as the quantity of food which must be available within the ecosystem per bird at the start of the winter, so that the bird can provide for its physiological need for food.[85]

The model indication of EVA II shows that, in the absence of mussel beds, 200 kg of cockle flesh would have to be available per oystercatcher in September. That is 3.1 times the physiological food requirement of the birds from September to March inclusive. The researchers note, in addition, that the error of this estimate of the ecological food requirement is difficult to determine accurately, but could amount to some dozens of kilograms.[86] A possible source of error in the derivation of the ecological food supply is that the decline in the oystercatcher population, manifested in the low return rate in some years, is not due to the poor supply in winter, but to a deterioration of conditions of the breeding grounds.

Although these findings surely may be difficult to be fully appreciated by environmental lawyers, they are in fact of fundamental importance for a study on the use of the precautionary principle, which in this particular case features strongly in the risk assessment phase. Whereas the 1993 policy was clearly based on a traditional science-based model, EVA II adopts a more open, precautionary approach by applying the ecological need requirement of birds as the decisive reference point for food reservation policy.

The EVA II report concludes that if the target figure of 260,000 oystercatchers remains the same, around 52 million kg of cockles would have to be available in the absence of mussel beds. These 52 million kg rarely occurred in the Wadden Sea during the research period. Continuation of the 1993 food reservation policy might lead to a further decline in numbers of oystercatchers, assuming that cockle stocks and the absence of inner tidal mussel beds in the 1990s are representative for the future.[87] The report points out that in order to assess options for achieving the reference numbers for birds, it is important to estimate how carrying capacity will develop. An estimate of a carrying capacity with a large margin of error indicates that the number of 17,000 could fall to around 13,000 if there are no mussel beds. Without restoration of inner tidal mussel beds in the Wadden

[85] Ibid., 113.

[86] Ibid., at 115. For more details on the derivation of the ecological food supply and the associated margin of error from the model calculations, see C. Rappoldt et al., 'Scholeksters en hun voedsel in de Waddenzee, Rapport voor deelproject B1 van EVA II, de tweede fase van het evaluatieonderzoek naar de effecten van schelpdiervisserij op natuurwaarden in de Waddenzee en Oosterschelde 1999–003' *Alterra Rapport 883* (Wageningen: Alterra, 2003).

[87] Final Report EVA II, n. 38 above, at 116.

Sea the target figure for oystercatchers will not be realized. Without cockle fishing, the estimated carrying capacity for oystercatchers would be in the order of 15,000 higher.[88]

ii. Eider Ducks

For eider ducks no food reservation policy was implemented in 1993. It was assumed that the cultivation of mussels and associated seed fishing would not entail great changes for eider ducks. Following high mortality in 1999 and a subsequent evaluation of the policy of food reservation, 8.6 million kg of flesh have been reserved in the sublittoral areas of the Wadden Sea and the North Sea coastal zone.[89] Again, this quantity is based on physiological rather than ecological food requirements. Even after the introduction of this new policy, the mass mortality among eider ducks continued in 2000 and 2001. In decreasing order of preference, after mussels, eider ducks will feed on the following shellfish: littoral cockles, sublittoral cockles, and *Spisula*.[90] Common eiders do not suffer from severe winters like oystercatchers do. The ecological food requirement can therefore be derived from a relationship between food supply and mortality.[91] The current reference number for eider ducks at the time of the research was 130,000. To prevent increased risk of mortality at this population level, around 60 million kg of half-grown and mature sublittoral mussels would need to be available at the start of the year. Estimates show that such stocks were generally available between 1970 and 1990, but in the last decade these levels have only been reached five times. The researchers of EVA II admit that the estimate of the ecological food requirements contain several arbitrary choices.[92] They observe:

> Instead of looking when the probability of a mass mortality starts to increase, one could decide which risk of a mass mortality is acceptable. Even more important is the fact that what one considers mass mortality is arbitrary. When more eider ducks must die before we speak of a mass mortality, it is clear that the food stocks at which this mortality will occur will be lower. Finally it is clear that the relationship between mortality and fish stocks, although significant, is not very tight. Thus, other factors also play an important role in the mortality of the common eiders.[93]

It therefore appears that the research team of EVA II was well aware of the fuzzy divide between risk assessment and risk management. They also acknowledge that there is insufficient knowledge to infer the population consequences of a particular mortality level. Another important knowledge gap concerns the relationship

[88] C. Rappoldt et al., n. 86 above.

[89] Parliamentary Documents II, 2000–2001, No. 27 400 XIV, 11:1–4.

[90] B. J. Ens and R. K. H. Kats, 'Evaluatie van voedselreservering Eidereenden in de Waddenzee—rapportage in het kader van EVA II deelproject B2', *Alterra rapport 931* (Wageningen: Alterra, 2004).

[91] Final Report EVA II, n. 38 above, at 119.

[92] Final Report EVA II, n. 38 above, at 120.

[93] Ibid.

between mussel culture and food stocks for common eiders. According to the report, it is relevant to consider what effect the cultivation of mussels may have had on the food supply of the eider ducks since the start of the 1950s. For the current case study, which is limited to effects of cockle fishing, it is sufficient merely to signal these existing scientific uncertainties.

In conclusion, the food reservation policy has been unable to prevent food shortages for the reference numbers of shellfish-eating birds in years with fishery-induced food shortage. The numbers of oystercatchers wintering in the Wadden Sea have fallen from 260,000 to 175,000. The numbers of eider ducks which winter in and around the Wadden Sea have also fallen, due to food shortage particularly of sublittoral mussels. This leads to the obvious conclusion that application of the precautionary principle has failed to address the risk of the effects of shellfish fishery on the ecosystem of the Wadden Sea sufficiently in the sea and coastal fishery policy of 1993. The main reason identified by EVA II is that this food reservation policy of 1993 was based on physiological food requirements. Interestingly, the scientific basis for the targets and reference values with regard to fishery in the Wadden Sea was not specified in the policy document itself or in later policy documents. The calculations underlying the policy of food reservation are found in an unpublished document of the Ministry.[94] EVA II researchers claim the policy should have been based on the ecological food requirement, which is around three times higher. There is a margin of error in this ecological food requirement, which is difficult to determine accurately, but which could amount to a dozens of kilograms per bird. The EVA II research thus takes a more precautionary approach: scientific uncertainties and ignorance are made explicit, and the assessment clearly errs on the side of caution by taking the ecological food requirement as a basis for future food reservation policy.

C. Long-term Ecosystem Changes and Future Developments

EVA II also examined long-term changes and future developments in the Wadden Sea that are not ascribed to fishing activities, such as carrying capacity for shellfish and eutrophication, climate change, tides, and oysters. These research results would turn out to be most controversial in the discussion on the future of mechanical cockle fishing in the subsequent risk management phase.

Carrying capacity is the maximum biomass which a particular species can achieve on particular surface areas in any given circumstances. Eutrophication is the enrichment of water with nutrients, particularly by the addition of phosphates and nitrates (P and N) to the ecosystem. Before 1980, increasing eutrophication of Dutch coastal waters and the Wadden Sea has been repeatedly reported. In other reports, it was observed that increased concentrations of P and N led to

[94] Ministerie van LNV, 'De Voedselbehoefte van vogels in de Waddenzee en Oosterschelde' Ambtelijke notitie LNV 17 June 1993 (LNV: Den Haag, 1993).

increasing algae biomass and increased primary production. This stirred a discussion in the policy-making arena on source, cause and effects of eutrophication of the Wadden Sea. From all publications, mainly based on monitoring data collected by governmental agencies, it becomes clear that concentrations of P and N have increased manifold compared to natural background concentrations. From the mid-1980s onwards, phosphorus loads and to a lesser extent also nitrogen loads began to decrease. In 2003, the Oslo and Paris Convention Commission for the Protection of the Marine Environment of the North-East Atlantic (OSPAR Commission) reported a reduction of N discharges from the Netherlands alone by 30 per cent for the period 1985 to 2000, almost completely due to industrial reduction and better treatment of household discharges.[95] According to the same Commission, a 70 per cent reduction of P discharges was achieved in that same period. Measurements in the Dutch coastal zone show an approximate 50 to 60 per cent reduction in total P, and 15 per cent of total N concentrations.[96] Since the increase of nutrient loads in the period prior to 1980 was generally considered a cause of the increasing algae content and primary production, one might expect that decreasing nutrient loads are followed by a decreasing primary production and algae biomass. The extent depends, among other things, on how crucial phosphate and nitrate are for algae growth. Simply put, the model calculations for the western Wadden Sea used in the EVA II research showed that maximal shellfish populations were lower in the 1990s compared to the 1980s as a result of lowered nutrient loads. According to nutrient policies, the nutrient loads are expected to decline further, which will lead to a further decline in maximal shellfish stocks.

The model results are strictly determined by the mathematical description of key processes and the parametric values chosen. The researchers acknowledge the limitations of their model, as it does not compute 'real' biomass values, but theoretical maximum possible biomass values.[97] Although the model thus produces some uncertainties, it yields relevant results.

Nevertheless, the conclusion regarding maximum shellfish biomass and algae contents has been criticized because field observations were said not to support results. For example, the observed concentrations from the monitoring data are sufficiently high to contradict a nutrient limitation of primary production. On the basis of these data, Colijn and Cadée concluded that primary production was limited by light, not by nutrients.[98]

[95] OSPAR Commission, 'Nutrients in the Convention Area' in OSPAR *Eutrophication and Nutrients Series*, published on the internet at: http://www.ospar.org/eng/html/welcome.html.

[96] In future, a further reduction of P and even more N needs to be achieved, according to Directive 2000/60/EC establishing a Framework for Community Action in the Field of Water Policy (Water Framework Directive), [2000] OJ L327/1.

[97] Final Report EVA II, n. 38 above, at 135.

[98] F. Colijn and G. C. Cadée, 'Is Phytoplankton Growth in the Wadden Sea Light or Nitrogen Limited?' (2003) 49 *Netherlands Journal of Sea Research*, 83–93. See for a further discussion of the state of the art research on this topic supporting the conclusions of the EVA-II research, Final Report EVA II, n. 38 above, at 136.

With regard to other factors that have an impact on the Wadden Sea ecosystem, EVA II establishes that in many years actual shellfish stocks were below maximal stocks as a result of recruitment dynamics and losses due to storms, ice winters, predation, and fishery. Mussel stocks, and to a lesser extent cockle stocks, can compensate in part for the declining carrying capacity because they accumulate organic matter. This gives rise to additional local mineralization, which stimulates the productivity of the area. In addition, climate change might reduce the likelihood of large spat falls of cockles and mussels, and increase of the Pacific oyster might go at the expense of other shellfish stocks.

D. Concluding Remarks: EVA II and Precaution

Impacts of mechanical cockle fishing qualify as 'possible significant effects', as becomes clear from EVA II, which clearly shows a number of negative effects, including a decrease in sediment up to a year after fishing took place, a significant decrease in cockle populations, death of other soil animals, and a decline in the number of oystercatchers. Although EVA II points to the disappearance of the sublittoral mussel beds as the primary cause for the decline of birds, cockle fishery thus reduces the food stock for oystercatchers.[99]

The model calculations do not take into account cumulative effects of cockle fishery on stock sizes, recruitment, and age distribution of cockles, and at present there is no evidence that cockle fishery has had a negative impact on common eiders. Several other factors also contributed to the decline in the number of shellfish-eating birds, some of which are beyond immediate human control (such as climate change and severe winter storms that delayed recovery).

However, even this extensive research left many questions unanswered. Ignorance, ambiguity and scientific uncertainty continue to pertain to the carrying capacity theory. The report itself acknowledges that further research is needed to end this state of affairs.[100] Risk managers should be aware that precautionary action with regard to a particular uncertain environmental harm may act as a catalyst for exposure of other uncertain environmental harms. When, in the initial appraisal process of a particular risk, distinct forms and degrees of incertitude are recognized, the precautionary principle becomes of relevance, not only to the management of risk, but also to its assessment, and carries a number of crucial implications.

EVA II did indeed adopt a precautionary approach in its assessment. This is evidenced, firstly, by deliberation with scientists, policy-makers, and stakeholders on the translation of policy questions into research questions, including use of lay knowledge of fishermen. Secondly, 'blind spots' were not swept under the carpet: uncertainties, ignorance, and ambiguities were made explicit by the EVA II

[99] Final Report EVA II, n. 38 above, at 159.

[100] *Recommendations*, Final Report EVA II, n. 38 above, at 165.

research team in their summary report. Thirdly, the research took an ecosystem-approach, rather than focusing on single stock management, thus accounting for 'real world' conditions.[101] Full account of the advantages and drawbacks of any one approach was taken. A good example is choosing the ecological food requirement as a basis for food reservation policy, instead of the more traditional physiological requirement used in 1993. Also consistent with precaution is the attempt to incorporate error, and the acknowledgement of the importance of value judgements. Although precaution is not an explicit goal in EVA II, it is clear that by imposing deliberatively conservative restrictions on catches with the intention of rebuilding, the burden of proof is now on the fishery industry to take account of uncertainties.

Despite this thorough precautionary approach, the summary report stirred up discussion about the scientific credibility of the research. Before EVA II was officially published, Wageningen University announced in a press bulletin that: 'declining numbers of wading birds are due to lower carrying capacity of the wetlands and shell fishing'.[102] According to this research, the size of the cockle population depended in large part on the nutrition values of water, the so-called carrying capacity. The fact that less and less waste products are drained into rivers meant a reduction of nutrients for benthic organisms in the tidal waters. Waste products like phosphates and nitrates are necessary for algae, which in turn is the basic food for cockles. Various wading birds fit in the same food pyramid, explaining the correlation between carrying capacity and bird populations. Taking these insights into account, the Minister of LNV concluded that EVA II would not supply a ground for removing fishermen from the tidal waters. This carrying capacity theory, contained in the public EVA II version and presented as the primary reason for the decline of cockles, was rejected by other scientists. As soon as EVA II was officially published in January 2004, the Royal Netherlands Institute for Sea Research (NIOZ) immediately criticized the carrying capacity theory. Although it has an excellent and global reputation in fundamental marine research, NIOZ was not involved in EVA II research.

Different interpretations of the research results started to circulate, which were picked up in several media reports. Fishermen, for example, felt that EVA II substantiated their opinion that the dramatic decrease in bird populations in the early 1990s had been caused by winter storms and other natural causes. They pointed to remaining uncertainties despite EVA II, and carried out their own research concerning, for example, the question whether species populations fluctuate as a function of food fluctuations. Environmental NGOs, on the other hand, viewed research results as confirmation of mechanical cockle fishing as a cause of damage to the Wadden Sea ecology.

[101] Scenario studies were also part of the EVA-II research.

[102] B. Ens, 'Reaction to the letter of J. van Andel' (2004) 14 *Bionieuws*, at 13.

In an attempt to settle the dispute, a conference was organized where experts could voice their opinions and debate the research results. One major criticism was that the carrying capacity was a model-based theory, and that it was therefore never tested if the decline in shellfish was caused by cleaner sea-water. It was argued that this theory should not have been applied to explain the decline in bird numbers. The research director of EVA II who presented the public version of EVA II a month earlier, Bruno Ens, now partly agreed with this argument. More advanced and novel insights brought this theory to the bottom of the list of nine reasons explaining the decline in shellfish populations, and thus birds. In the meeting, mechanical cockle fishery became the primary cause. NIOZ researcher Piersma presented new research results claiming the recovery period from mechanical cockle fishery for sediment and benthic life is much longer than previously assumed.[103] According to his research, it takes between 20 and 40 years before biodiversity is fully recovered. NIOZ researchers pointed out that the size of shellfish stocks in the Wadden Sea is primarily determined by recruitment success in preceding years, and that recruitment in turn appears to be primarily governed by climate-related predation by shrimp on early benthic stages of bivalves. This explanation differs strongly from declining nutrient levels as a key underlying process in the decline of shellfish stocks.[104]

VI. The Mechanical Cockle Fishery Case: Risk Management

EVA II was established to evaluate previous fishery policy and provide scientific footing for new policy. On 11 December 2003, the Minister of Agriculture, Nature and Food Quality offered the public version of the voluminous reports to Parliament.[105] In the accompanying letter the Minister first summarized the main conclusions. He then considered that:

> The abovementioned insights and conclusions imply that it has to be reconsidered which measures can prevent irreversible damage for nature values caused by shellfish-fisheries, while maintaining a vital fishing sector. The report does not immediately lead to the conclusion that mechanical cockle fishery in the coastal waters is not possible anymore. However, the fishing industry has to continue to make the sector more sustainable. This

[103] T. Piersma, A. Koolhaas, A Dekinga, J. J. Beukema, R. Dekker, and K. Essink, 'Long-term indirect effects of mechanical cockle-dredging on inter tidal bivalve stocks in the Wadden Sea' (2001) 38 *Journal of Applied Ecology*, 976–90.

[104] J. J. Beukema and R. Dekker, 'Decline of Recruitment Success in Cockles and Other Bivalves in the Wadden Sea: Possible Role of Climate Change, Predation on Postlarvae and Fisheries' (2005) 287 *Marine Ecology Progress Series*, 149–67.

[105] Parliamentary Documents II, 11-12-2003, Viss. 2003/7113. The scientific version was published in spring 2004.

means that shellfish fishing has to operate within the framework of the Bird- and Habitat Directive in order to prevent significant harm[106]

He explained how to proceed: the results of EVA II were to be shared with a wide audience. The Minister underlined that the Wadden Sea is an issue that remains hotly debated from many contrasting perspectives. Four public as well as administrative consultation sessions were planned. In addition, advisory bodies were asked to formulate opinions on the translation of EVA II results into concrete policy proposals. Ultimately, the Cabinet would adopt new policy based on the results of EVA II, public consultations, and the recommendations of the advisory bodies.[107] Advice was asked from: the *Raad voor de Wadden* (Wadden Sea Council), *Beleidsadviesgroep EVA II* (Policy Advice Group EVA II (BAG)), and *Adviesgroep Waddenzeebeleid* (Policy Advice Group Wadden Sea). None of the advice discussed in this section is binding.

A. Advice

The Wadden Sea Council is a permanent statutory independent expert advice organ. Its mandate is to provide the government with advice concerning different policy issues regarding the Wadden Sea. In its report on shellfish fishery, the Wadden Sea Council adopted the requirements of the Habitats Directive as the legal framework for its advice.[108] The scientific results of EVA II were confronted with levels of protection required by the Habitats Directive.[109] The Wadden Sea Council considered that suspected or unknown effects call for application of the precautionary principle. It sums up the cumulative effects of fishing and other environmental factors on shellfish population, such as decreasing nutrients and climate change, 'whereby absolute volume and pace of the changes are difficult or even impossible to estimate'.[110] It is settled that in the future, without quantification, the size of the cockle population will only decrease. The Wadden Sea Council states that from all causes, only measures aimed at the fishing industry have a positive effect on cockle stocks.[111]

The Wadden Sea Council therefore concluded that cockle fishery in its present form had to be ended, and that no new permits based on the Nature Protection

[106] Ibid., at 3.

[107] Ibid., at 4.

[108] Raad voor de Wadden, *Duurzaam duurt het langst—II: naar een nieuw schelpdiervisserijbeleid voor de Wadden* (Leeuwarden, 2004), No. 2004/01, published on the Internet at: http://www.raadvoordewadden.nl.

[109] Ibid., at 9.

[110] Ibid., at 19.

[111] Other measures such as climate policy will at best delay the development.

Law should be granted.[112] In substantiating its advice, the Council explicitly relied upon the precautionary principle in areas where effects are uncertain.[113]

To explore future policy choices on shellfish fishery, BAG was installed with the aim to enhance legitimacy by involving parties interested in the deliberative process.[114] Members of NGOs and the fishery branch took part in BAG. The idea was that representatives of different interests would debate the scientific results of EVA II, and try to reach a consensus. Although well-intended, BAG was a failure as it proved impossible to reconcile the opposite perspectives of the interested parties present. Fishermen maintained that the sector needed time and space for the development of a more sustainable fishing method. Environmentalists thought that this was prima facie impossible, and argued for an immediate ban on mechanical cockle fishery in all coastal waters. As the chair reports in a letter to the minister:[115]

> The results of the EVA II research did not or hardly come up for discussion after the representatives of environmental NGOs took position against mechanical cockle Fisheries, and the representatives of the Fishing industry felt cornered by this.[116]

The chair conceded that it had regretfully also been impossible to reach consensus on a new food reservation policy, so that the discussion remained limited to a new policy for mussel fishery. In the period January to February 2004, four public meetings took place. Interested parties and the general public were given the opportunity to voice their opinion on the subject of shellfish fishery. The aim of the meetings was to start a dialogue between the people present, to inform about the results of EVA II and new policy objectives, and to generate new ideas and possibilities that could contribute to a new policy. These meetings mainly served to generate information about the scientific results of EVA II to the public. No substantial reference was made to these consultations in the policy decision.[117]

The Policy Advice Group Wadden Sea was specifically installed by ministerial Decree with the task of exploring fishery and the drilling for gas in the Wadden Sea, and delivering advice regarding future integrated policy on the sustainable protection and development of the Wadden as an area of nature conservation.[118] The explanatory note of the Decree cites 'the great uncertainties (rise of the level

[112] N. 108 above, at 28.

[113] Ibid., 27, such as non-specified shellfish eating birds, worm-eating birds, biotopes at benthic level, estuarial, and littoral benthic life.

[114] The Policy Advice Group was set up by Minister Veerman of Agriculture, Nature and Food Quality (LNV) in June 2003.

[115] Siepie de Jong, former Secretary of State and former chair of the Wadden Sea Council.

[116] Niet-dossierstuk 2003–2004 lnv0400330 TK, *Brief van de Beleidsadviesgroep EVA II over het advies 'Duurzaam en Dynamisch'* (Den Haag: June 2004).

[117] See on the disappointing substantial contributions of public deliberation to decision-making processes C. Sunstein, *Infotopia* (Cambridge: Cambridge University Press, 2006).

[118] The Advice Group consisted of three independent members, in that they had no (former) affiliation with Wadden Sea policy issues. They were members of different political parties, and represented on account of their political status.

of the sea, biodiversity, shellfish fishery, etc.), that can be eliminated if timely investments are made' as the primary justification for this initiative.[119] The Policy Advice Group Wadden Sea, also known as Commission Meijer after its chair, presented its report 'Space for the Wadden' on 1 April 2004.[120] Starting point of the advice is 'the sustainable protection and development of the Wadden Sea and preservation of the unique open landscape'.[121] The Commission proposed an integrated policy framework that guarantees the protection of ecological values. Economic activities were to be subject to strict and similar limit values. Activities had to be appraised in totality, so that account could be taken of cumulative effects. By contrast, previous policy had articulated different requirements for different activities. Also, the advice stressed that it should be clear in advance what level of uncertainty is deemed acceptable. Another important aspect of the advice is the instrument of monitoring: activities had to be subject to intensive monitoring so that activities can be influenced or even completely abandoned when limit values are exceeded. Limit values were to protect the sediment and benthic life in the Wadden Sea, as well as bird populations. The Commission emphasized that the policy as well as its implementation had to be based on the latest knowledge, and that for this purpose a 'Wadden Academy' had to be established. Subject to a transitional period, all activities eventually would be subject to the regime: setting limit values, monitoring, implementation and enforcement, and adjustment of activities. Nevertheless, the Commission conceded that current scientific knowledge concerning the functioning of the complex ecosystem of the Wadden Sea is insufficient to fix precise limit values.

For individual activities surrounded by scientific uncertainty, recourse can be sought to the precautionary principle. In this interpretation, the precautionary principle should only apply if there exist *substantial* uncertainty regarding an activity. The Commission was of the opinion that, concerning both mechanical cockle fishing and the drilling for gas, the precautionary principle did not have to be employed, since the research undertaken and the ecological values fixed, in combination with the required monitoring, offered sufficient certainty that no harm woud be caused to the Wadden Sea.[122]

With regard to shellfish fisheries policy, on the basis of the research results of EVA II, the Commission draws a distinction between effects of shellfish-fishery that are 'certain' to occur, and effects that are 'likely' to happen.[123] No guidance is given as to what qualifies as 'certain' or 'likely' effects and, interestingly, no

[119] Niet-dossier stuk 2003–2004 vra2003–2004vrom—TK, *Brief ministers van VROM, EZ en LNV over de instelling van Beleidsadviesgroep Waddenzee* (Den Haag: Oct. 2003).

[120] Policy Advice Group Wadden Sea, *Ruimte voor de Wadden* (Space for the Wadden) (Den Haag: 2004). In preparing its advice, it organized two scientific expert meetings: one to discuss the results of EVA II and one concerning the effects of gas drillings. Parliamentary Documents II, 2003–2004, No. 26 431, at 63.

[121] Ibid., at 29.

[122] Ibid., 35–7, at 48.

[123] Ibid., at 35.

'uncertainties' are discussed. It concludes that, although none of the observed effects have a negative influence on the ecosystem of the Wadden Sea individually, their combined effects do. The Commission observed:

> Due to the repetitive character of mechanical cockle fishery, it is likely that a cumulative effect will appear from year to year. Moreover, this harm arises in relatively rich areas of the Wadden Sea, since that is where the fishing takes place.[124]

The Commission considered, on the basis of available scientific knowledge, that mechanical cockle fishery does imply precedence of economic interests over environmental concerns. It weighed various activities in and around the Wadden Sea according to their estimated actual and potential deleterious impacts. Mechanical cockle fishery topped the chart, while drilling for gas featured in the lower regions of the list. The government was therefore advised to set a timetable of seven years in which the cockle industry could develop more sustainable fishing techniques. If sustainability would not be realized in the given period, however, cockle fishery in the Wadden Sea had to come to an end.[125] During the transitional period, a monitoring commission was to be established to enforce limit values and ecological values, and to ensure correct interpretation of these values. In addition, a new food reservation policy had to be developed based on ecological food requirements and permanent closure of additional areas.

How this period was calculated is unclear, and biologists therefore voiced doubts whether this proposal would lead to sustainable practices. According to fishery organizations, in contrast, seven years was insufficient to transfer to sustainable harvesting methods. In response to the report, over 100 biologists signed a public letter to the Minister for Agriculture, Nature and Food Quality, expressing their concern that decisions with respect to the harmful effects of cockle fishing had not been based on scientific insights.[126]

The Wadden Sea Council and the the Meijer Commission both explicitly invoked the precautionary principle. Yet, their interpretation and application of the principle differ significantly. The Wadden Sea Council invoked the principle to propose a total ban on mechanical cockle fishery. The Meijer Commission presented its own interpretation of the precautionary principle: the principle only applied in cases of *substantial* uncertainty, and since in respect of mechanical cockle fishery scientific certainty prevailed, there was no need to apply the precautionary principle.

In reply to the advice of the Meijer Commission, the government stated that it would be possible to make the cockle industry more sustainable within a period of approximately 10 to 15 years.[127] However, it simultaneously observed that, based

[124] Ibid., at 36.
[125] Ibid., at 6.
[126] Brandbrief over schade kokkelvisserij (Urgent letter concerning the damage caused by cockle fishing) *Daily Newspaper Trouw,* 11 June 2004.
[127] Parliamentary Documents II, No. 29 684, 1:6.

on information furnished by the sector itself, execution of these plans would become extremely difficult taking into consideration mandatory food reservation and the planned expansion of closed areas.[128] It concluded that there were insufficient possibilities for the development of a sustainable mechanical cockle industry.[129] Thus, no more licences would be granted as of 1 January 2005. At the same time, a plan for the cessation of mechanical cockle fishery in the Wadden Sea had to be elaborated at short notice in anticipation of a pending ECJ decision concerning the annual granting of permits for mechanical cockle fishery.

B. Judicial Review

A few months after the government response had been sent to Parliament, the ECJ ruled in *Waddenzee*.[130] In a groundbreaking preliminary ruling for the interpretation of the precautionary principle, the ECJ clarified a number of issues concerning the effect of the Habitats Directive. At issue was the granting of authorization for the mechanical fishing of cockles in the Dutch part of the Wadden Sea, which as we have already seen is a SPA.

Two NGOs challenged the authorizations granted for 1999 and 2000.[131] They argued that (mechanical) cockle fishing is likely to affect the Wadden Sea as a habitat. In examining the case before it, the Council of State concluded that, on the basis of the information and studies, the defendant could have granted the authorization. In doing so, the Minister had rightly appraised and taken account of the available scientific knowledge in accordance with the requirements of Dutch national law. According to the judicial bench of the Council of State the defendant had, despite a lack of complete certainty regarding the consequences of cockle fishing activities, taken sufficient account of the precautionary principle by placing restrictions on fishing, in particular by closing large sections of the Wadden Sea to cockle fishing and laying down a fishing quota having regard to the food requirement of birds.

However, with regard to the requirements of the Birds and Habitats Directives, the Council of State entertained some doubts, and therefore referred questions to the ECJ regarding the interpretation of Article 6(3) of the Habitats Directive.

A crucial question the ECJ had to address was when a plan or project within the meaning of Article 6(3), either individually or in combination with other plans or projects, is likely to have a significant effect on a conservation site. This

[128] According to the results of EVA II, these expansions are necessary, also in light of the requirements set out in the Birds and Habitat Directives. See the letter of 8 Sept. 2004, Parliamentary Documents II, No.29 200 XIV, at 94.

[129] Parliamentary Documents II, 2003–2004, No. 29 684, 1: 7.

[130] Case C-127/02 *Landelijke Vereniging tot Behoud van de Waddenzee en de Nederlandse Vereniging tot Bescherming van Vogels* v. *Staatssecretaris van Landbouw, Natuurbeheer en Visserij* (n.y.r.).

[131] The 'Landelijke Vereniging tot Behoud van de Waddenzee' and the 'Nederlandse Vereniging tot Bescherming van Vogels'.

is fundamental, since the requirement for an appropriate assessment of the implications of a plan or project is conditional on it being likely to have a significant effect on the site. The ECJ first referred to the guidelines for interpreting Article 6 drawn up by the Commission, entitled 'Managing Natura 2000 Sites: The provisions of Article 6 of the "Habitats" Directive (92/43/EEC)'. It observed that triggering the environmental protection mechanism provided for in Article 6(3) of the Habitats Directive does not presume that the plan or project has significant effects on the site concerned, but follows from the mere probability that such an effect attaches to that plan or project. The ECJ continued by concluding that:

> It follows that the first sentence of Article 6(3) of the Habitats Directive subordinates the requirement for an appropriate assessment of the implications of a plan or project to the condition that there be *a probability or a risk* that the latter will have significant effects on the site concerned[132]

and:

> In the light, in particular, of the precautionary principle, which is one of the foundations of the high level of protection pursued by Community policy on the environment, in accordance with the first subparagraph of Article 174(2) EC, and by reference to which the Habitats Directive must be interpreted, *such a risk exists if it cannot be excluded on the basis of objective information that the plan or project will have significant effects on the site concerned* (see, by analogy, inter alia Case C-180/96 *United Kingdom* v *Commission* [1998] ECR I-2265, paragraphs 50, 105 and 107). Such an interpretation of the condition to which the assessment of the implications of a plan or project for a specific site is subject, *which implies that in case of doubt as to the absence of significant effects such an assessment must be carried out*, makes it possible to ensure effectively that plans or projects which adversely affect the integrity of the site concerned are not authorised, and thereby contributes to achieving, in accordance with the third recital in the preamble to the Habitats Directive and Article 2(1) thereof, its main aim, namely, ensuring biodiversity through the conservation of natural habitats and of wild fauna and flora.[133]

The ECJ thus first explained the meaning of the term 'likely' as *a probability or a risk* that there will be significant effects on the site concerned.[134] The ECJ went further, however: such a risk exists, with reference to the precautionary principle of Article 174(2), *if it cannot be excluded* on the basis of objective information that the plan or project will have significant effects on the site concerned. The ECJ explained that this implies that in case of doubt *as to the absence of significant effects* such an assessment must be carried out. The implication of this interpretation of the first sentence of Article 6(3) is that only if *a* risk of significant effects has been excluded no assessment needs to be carried out.

The practical consequence would appear to be that an assessment virtually always has to be carried out. After all, some doubts and uncertainty regarding

[132] Case C127/02, n. 130 above, at para. 43 (emphasis added).
[133] Ibid., at para. 44, (emphasis added).
[134] The Oxford dictionary meaning of 'likely' is: 'to be reasonable expected'.

long-term significant effects of an activity on a habitat or species almost invariably exist. The ECJ points to the site's conservation objectives as the critical point at which impacts become significant: if a plan or project is likely to undermine such conservation objectives, the project must be considered to have a 'significant effect'. The assessment of that risk must be made in light of, inter alia, the characteristics and specific environmental conditions of the site affected by such a plan or project.[135] Advocate General Kokott is clear on this point and states:

> if adverse effects resulting from plans and projects were accepted on the grounds that they merely rendered the attainment of these objectives difficult but not impossible or unlikely, the species numbers and habitat areas covered by Natura 2000 would be eroded by them. It would not even be possible to foresee the extent of this erosion with any degree of accuracy because no appropriate assessment would be carried out. These losses would not be offset because Article 6(4) of the habitats Directive would not apply. Thus in principle any adverse effect on the conservation objectives must be regarded as a significant adverse effect on the integrity of the site concerned.[136]

This makes sense. Long-term policy is necessary to protect the designated areas, and therefore the possibility of harmful effects is sufficient to require an appropriate assessment. This reading of the term 'significant' is consistent with the concept of significant effects as it is employed in biology, where an effect is 'significant' when the probability that an observed effect is accidental is smaller than 1 to 5 per cent.[137] The ECJ's interpretation of the term 'significant' hence mirrors its interpretation of the precautionary principle.

The assessment must show that it is certain that a project will not adversely affect the integrity of a site. No particular method for carrying out such an assessment is defined, although it must take into account cumulative effects which result from other plans or projects.[138]

All in all, this means that when doubts remain as to the absence of adverse effects on the integrity of the site linked to a plan or project, the competent authority must refuse authorization.[139] The ECJ then pointed out that the authorization criterion contained in the second sentence of Article 6(3) of the Habitats Directive integrates the precautionary principle as a means effectively to prevent adverse effects on the integrity of protected sites as the result of plans or projects.[140] This version of the precautionary principle is much more stringent than its common conception. Thus, in most definitions, the principle does not dictate that in case of uncertainties *no* activity is possible at all. Rather, common conceptions merely

[135] Case C-127/02, n. 130 above, at para. 49.

[136] Opinion of AG Kokott in Case C-127/02, n. 130 above, at paras. 84–5.

[137] J. M.Verschuuren, *Juridische Risicoanalyse 'Beleidsbesluit Schelpdiervisserij 2005–2020'Met het Oog op Toetsing aan de Vogel-en Habitatrichtlijn* (Tilburg: 2004) Appendix to Parliamentary Document Kamerstuk 29 675, 7.

[138] Case C-127/02, n. 130 above, paras. 52–3.

[139] Ibid., at para. 57.

[140] Ibid., at para. 58.

reflect that scientific uncertainty cannot be a reason to postpone cost-effective measures. It should be noted that Article 6(4) provides for an exemption, as far as the conditions in that provision are met. However, with regard to Article 6(4) the ECJ held that authorization could only be granted when:

> scientifically speaking there exist no reasonable doubt that there are harmful consequences [for the natural characteristics of the area].[141]

The only room for discretion resides in the term 'reasonable'. According to the Commission, there is no such thing as full certainty, so that it is impossible to reduce a risk to zero.[142] The Commission has observed that the seriousness of potential damage should be decisive for the proportionality of the measure, whereby when ecosystems are at stake the long-term consequences should be thoroughly appraised.[143] In this connection, it should be appreciated that the ECJ requires such a strict norm:

> With a less strict regime [than Article 6(3) thus interpreted] it would be impossible to guarantee the realization of the protection of the site's conservation objectives.[144]

It is evident that this ruling will influence decision-making pursuant to the Birds and Habitats Directives throughout the EU in the coming years, and it has already left its footprints in national courts. In the Netherlands, courts in the past have argued that a negative effect is significant when as a result the area could no longer qualify as a SPA.[145] In other decisions, courts considered any damage to the conservation objectives sufficient reason to force competent authorities to apply Article 6(3).[146] In cases concerning mechanical cockle fishery, the Administrative Jurisdiction Division of the Council of State took the approach that an appropriate assessment is only necessary after significant effects had been determined.[147]

This reasoning cannot be upheld in a future court case concerning application of Article 6(3): an appropriate assessment is necessary as soon as there exists a *possibility* of significant effects. The ECJ judgment in *Wadden Sea* was indeed followed by a Dutch court: on 4 October 2004 the District Court of Amsterdam, referring to the ECJ judgment, annulled a licence for mechanical fishing in the SPA Voordelta, which forms part of the North Sea coastal zone.[148] This national

141 Ibid., at para. 61.

142 Communication of the European Commission on the Precautionary Principle, COM(2000)1, 2 Feb. 2000, at 18.

143 Ibid.

144 Case C-127/02, n. 130 above, at para. 58.

145 Administrative Law Division of the Council of State 17 Dec. 2003, 31 *Milieu & Recht* 3 (2004) at 29. See Verschuuren, n. 56 above, at 280.

146 Ibid, See, e.g., District Court Leeuwarden 31 Dec. 2003, 31 *Milieu & Recht* 3 (2004), at 28.

147 ABRvS 10 Feb. 2000, No. E01.98.0406, ABRvS 22 Feb. 2001 No. 200001521/1, ABRvS 27 June 2001, No. 200003667/1/R3, ABRvS 12 Dec. 2001, No. 200001861/1.

148 District Court of Amsterdam 4 Oct. 2004, No. AWB 04/4114 WET, available on the Internet at: http://www.rechtspraak.nl (in Dutch).

case provides judicial confirmation that the door for mechanical cockle fishery in the Dutch Wadden Sea is closed.

Recently this line of case law was reaffirmed in a case on the legality of a permit for the fishing of mussel seeds. The Council of State again ruled that competent authorities could not have granted the permit since there existed scientific uncertainty of adverse effects for the ecosystem.[149]

C. Policy Decision Shellfish Fishery 2005 to 2020

As a result of this ECJ judgment a number of decisions by the minister of LNV have been annulled by the highest Dutch administrative court.[150] Hence, no permit could have been legally granted for at least the last couple of years preceding the ECJ case. The Minister considered on 15 July 2004 that mechanical cockle fishing was not in compliance with the nature conservation goal of the Wadden Sea, and this will not change in the foreseeable future. The Minister supports his judgment by referring to EVA II, the European nature conservation Directives, and the aim of an 'ecologically sustainable economic development of the Wadden Sea'.[151]

In October 2004, the Minister of Agriculture, Nature and Food Quality published the new national policy for shellfish fishing in a Policy Decision.[152] The Policy Decision is applicable to all shellfish fishing in all coastal water areas.[153] The government decided to ban mechanical cockle fishery in the Wadden Sea, and to grant fishermen a total compensation of approximately €92 million. In other SPAs mechanical cockle fisheries will also be gradually abolished in favour of sustainable methods. This applies to all shellfish fishing, e.g. mussel fishery of which the effects are still uncertain. If scientific uncertainty about possible significant effects is not resolved, however, no permit can be granted. The Policy Decision provides for permanent monitoring of shellfish stocks and the population of birds in light of a site's conservation objectives.[154] This means that monitoring must be designed so as to identify effects on habitats in such a way that competent authorities can act immediately when a deterioration is detected,

[149] ABRvS 27 Feb. 2008, No. 200607555/1.

[150] Administrative Law Division of the Council of State December 24 2004, No. 200000690/I-A and 200101670/I, Administrative Law Division of the Council of State 9 Feb. 2005, No. 200202184/I and 200305972 and Administrative Law Division of the Council of State 1 June 2005, No. 200409107/2. See also Vz. ABRvS Dec. 3 2004, No. 200409107/2.

[151] Parliamentary Documents II, No. 29684, 1:1.

[152] Parliamentary Documents II, 2004–005, No. 29 673, 3, *Ruimte voor een zilte oogst: naar een omslag in de Nederlandse schelpdiervisserij 2005–2020* (Room for a Brackish Harvest: Towards a Transition in Dutch Shellfish Fishing 2005–2020) (The Hague: 2004).

[153] Dec. No. J9115397, Stcrt. 1991, 220, at 12.

[154] N. 151 above, at para. 6.1.

which is in line with the requirements of Article 6(2).[155] An evaluation of the system of granting licences is also included in the Decision.[156]

VII. The Case of Wadden Gas

Mechanical cockle fishing and drilling for gas in the Wadden Sea were always dealt with as distinctly separate activities, although both sectors extracted their resources from the same wetlands. The Meijer Commission adopted a distinctly different approach: policy on the Wadden Sea should be integrated, and activities concerning use of the wetlands were to be considered in totality. The Commission believed that the debate around gas until that point had been determined by cultural and social perceptions without any supporting scientific evidence.[157]

The Wadden Sea hides several gas fields. In 1959, one of the largest gas fields in the world was discovered in the province of Groningen, bordering the Wadden Sea. Wadden gas is a high quality gas, because it is highly caloric and therefore very suitable for export. Compared to oil and coal, a major advantage of gas is that it is a relatively clean energy source.

The Dutch Mining Company (NAM)[158] acquired ownership quite easily in the 1960s.[159] The concession stated that pollution of water and soil had to be prevented, but failed to articulate further conditions. In 2002, total production value of gas was approximately €12,225 billion. The State receives 70 per cent of this output, which in 2002 amounted to €5,350 billion. Until 2004, gas revenues have earned the State an estimated €159 billion. In 2000, 11,000 people were employed in the business. According to conservative estimates, gas reserves in the Wadden total 40 billion m^3, 25 to 35 billion has already been extracted, which of course means that the necessary infrastructure is already in place. NAM has invested €300 million in gas infrastructure in the Wadden Sea, based on agreements with the government. The bulk of futures is estimated at between 30 and 130 billion m^3. On the basis of the Mining Law 2002, for gas extraction, the minister of Economic Affairs must grant approval to a so-called site-decision (*locatiebesluit*) in which nature and landscape interests must be taken into account. A separate permit is required by the Nature Protection Law (if it

155 Art. 43 of the Dutch Nature Conservation Law 1998 states that a licence can be withdrawn or changed.

156 N. 151 above, at para. 6.4.

157 Eindrapport Advies Group Waddenzeebeleid, *Ruimte voor de Wadden* (Den Haag: March 2004), at 6.

158 NAM is a joint venture between Shell and Esso.

159 For extraction of gas Art. 5 of the Mijnwet (Mining Law) requires a concession. The mining companies NAM-Mobil and Elf Petroland also acquired 'eternal concessions', of which 40 per cent is owned by the State. Stcrt., 1963, 126, no. 39; Stcr. 1969, 47, no. 32.

concerns an area protected as nature reservation), in which general interests must be weighed against the private interests of the proponent of the activity.[160]

A. Early Precaution

Although NAM has been active in the Wadden Sea since the early 1970s, from the 1980s onwards it encountered increasing opposition to its activities in these wetlands. Moreover, as the Wadden Sea had become a nationally and internationally acclaimed nature reserve, gas extraction became subject to a restrictive legal framework of rules and regulations.[161] The central question was whether the drilling for gas causes damage to the ecosystem of the Wadden Sea. In 1974, the NGO 'De Waddenvereniging' collected 22,338 signatures against a plan (*bestemmingsplan*) granting new concessions for the areas Zuidwal and Ameland, both in the Wadden Sea.[162] *Gedeputeerde Staten* (County Aldermen) of the province of Friesland gave in to this pressure, and declined to consent to the new plan for gas extraction on the island of Ameland. The Minister of Economic Affairs and the concession holders appealed this decision. The Crown sustained the appeal and NAM and Mobil Elf hence could continue their business.[163] The Cabinet subsequently decided in favour of a political compromise: since experimental drillings had been allowed at Ameland, the concession for Zuidwal was denied.[164]

Three governmental agencies (Rijksgeologische Dienst, Staatstoezicht op de Mijnen, and Mijnraad) advised in favour of the permit, and the province of Friesland would only approve subject to conditions. The research institute RIN (later renamed Alterra, Wageningen University) drew attention to certain ecological effects.

The denial of the permit for the Zuidwal was successfully appealed at the Administrative Law Division of the Council of State, on the ground that the activities were crucial for the survival of the mining company Elf Petroland.[165] Faced with this defeat, the government now found it necessary to protect the parts of the Wadden Sea that had not yet covered by a concession in line with the newly adopted KPD of 1980. The eastern part of the Wadden Sea was largely covered by concessions, so it was decided to keep the western Wadden Sea free of any mining activities, except for the small area of the Zuidwal.[166]

[160] In addition, a number of provincial and local permits are necessary.

[161] In 1980, the first KPD Waddenzee was adopted, establishing the Wadden Sea primarily as a nature conservation area.

[162] T. Verbeeten, *Wijs met de Waddenzee?* (Amsterdam: Thela Thesis, 1999), at 145.

[163] Ibid. The permit was granted under strict conditions, which were directed at the protection of nature values.

[164] Ministry of Economic Affairs, *Afwijzing van de aanvrage om concessie voor de ontginning van het 'Zuidwal' Aardgasvoorkomen—Nota van Toelichting* (Den Haag: 1981), at 14.

[165] Administrative Law Division of the Council of State, 25 May 1982 (1982) nr. 1625, at 12–13.

[166] Parliamentary Documents II, 1982–1983, No. 17 990, at 1.

In addition to protecting the western Wadden Sea against impacts of gas extraction, the government also partially revised the KPD in 1984. In this revised version, encouragement of gas extraction in the Wadden Sea was now substituted for 'the nature prevention principle', which may be viewed as an early manifestation of the precautionary principle.[167] To put this policy into practice, the government and NAM concluded a gentlemen's agreement to the effect that from 1984 to 1994 a moratorium on gas extraction in the Wadden Sea would apply.[168] No drilling or production activities would occur in the areas that fell within the ambit of the KPD. This severe precautionary measure represents an acknowledgement of the lack of knowledge about the ecological risks associated with gas extraction.

At the sixth trilateral conference on the protection of the Wadden Sea in 1991, Member States agreed to prevent construction of new installations for gas extraction.[169] Preparations for a new KPD followed in 1992, two years before the end of the moratorium. At the time, a majority in Parliament seemed against further gas extraction in the Wadden Sea.[170] In the parliamentary debate the Christian Democrats, which formed part of the coalition government, suddenly adopted a different position, and declared the party willing to allow gas extraction under strict conditions.[171] The Democrats argued that the Zuidwal experiences had shown no ecological effects since 1988. This political turnaround implied the loss of the parliamentary majority against extraction of Wadden gas. The Minister of Economic Affairs subsequently formed a Management Group 'Mining Activities in the Wadden Sea', whose mandate was to investigate gas extraction in a broad perspective.[172] Under consideration were the proposed activities, ecological effects, possible soil subsidence, visual effects, employment, and international obligations. The Management Group consisted of representatives of the mining companies (Mobil, Elf Petroland, and NAM) and the Ministries (EZ, VROM, V&W, and LNV). Opponents of gas extraction in the Wadden Sea were not represented. The Management Group issued its report in October 1993, and advised 11 experimental drillings for the period 1995 to 2000.[173] Arguments in favour of gas extraction concerned its social and economic relevance and the minor ecological effects associated with the Zuidwal and Ameland. According to the

[167] Parliamentary Documents II, 1984–1985, No. 18 220, at 12–13.

[168] Ministry of Economic Affairs, *Rapport Stuurgroep Mijnbouactiviteiten in de Waddenzee* (Den Haag: 1993).

[169] Ministerial Declaration, Sixth Trilateral Governmental Conference on the Protection of the Wadden Sea, 13 Nov. 1991, Esjberg. Published on the Internet at: http://cwss.www.de/tgc/MD-Esbjerg.html.

[170] Ministry of Housing, Spatial Planning and the Environment, *Nota Waddenzee—Deel 1: ontwerp planologische kernbeslissing* (Den Haag: 1992).

[171] Parliamentary Documents, 1992–1993, No. 19–26.

[172] Ministry of Economic Affairs, *Rapport Stuurgroep Mijnbouwactiviteiten in de Waddenzee* (The Hague: 1993), at 1–2.

[173] Ibid., Parliamentary Documents II, 1993–1994, No. 23 546, 1, at 2.

Ministry of Economic Affairs, ecological effects could be minimized by careful planning, and by taking into account the ecological circumstances.[174] In addition, it was stated that although soil subsidence can be expected, due to coastal erosion the latter could be compensated by sand suppletion.[175]

Environmentalists did not agree that the ecological risks could be minimized, and formulated four counter arguments.[176] Firstly, they argued that gas extraction causes negative ecological effects such as landscape erosion, noise pollution, and light pollution. Secondly, attention was focused on risks intrinsically associated with the drilling for gas, such as blow-outs. Thirdly, scientific uncertainties existed about effects such as soil subsidence. Fourthly, criteria of the KPD were referred to.

On the basis of these objections, the NGOs came to the conclusion that the precautionary principle should be applied. The Nature Protection Council that was asked to advise on the matter came to a similar conclusion, and advised against any activity involving gas extraction in the Wadden Sea.[177] The Wadden Sea Council considered that there was insufficient (quantitative) data to arrive at a robust decision.[178] Since gas extraction was not necessary to satisfy energy needs at the time, the Wadden Sea Council argued that the decision should be postponed until more scientific information was available.

In response, in September 1993 a public workshop on soil subsidence was organized by the research institute NIOZ to question the magnitude of the ecological effects associated with gas extraction in the Wadden Sea. It was predicted that soil subsidence of between zero and two centimetres could be expected.[179] In addition, it was argued that soil subsidence would only be a temporary phenomenon, as the holes would be filled again through natural processes.[180] Coastal erosion will also occur, but it was argued that there are methods to minimize these effects through sand suppletion.

The government now started to negotiate conditions for drilling with the mining companies. The Ministries of V&W, LNV, and after some hesitation also VROM, decided to allow five offshore exploration drillings under strict conditions.[181] One

[174] Ministry of Economic Affairs, *Rapport Stuurgroep .Mijnbouwactiviteiten in de Waddenzee* (Den Haag: 1993), 28. Estimated income for the state is about €4 billion.

[175] Ibid., at 37.

[176] Landelijke Vereniging tot Behoud van de Waddenzee, *Wat in het Wad zit verzuurt niet* (1993), 8–10, at 22. Local and provincial government expressed their dismay as well and advocated an extension of the moratorium.

[177] Natuurbeschermingsraad, *Advies naar aanleiding van het Stuurgroep-rapport 'Mijnbouwactiviteiten in de Waddenzee'* (Den Haag: 1993).

[178] Waddenadviesraad, *Advies over het rapport 'Mijnbouwactiviteiten in de Waddenzee'* (Leeuwarden: 1993), at 14.

[179] H. J. Gussinklo, 'Bodemdaling in de waddenzee door gaswinning' in H. J. Lindenboom, *Openbare Discussiedag 'Bodemdaling Waddenzee'* 14 (NIOZ: 1993) 23.

[180] A. P. Oost and K. S. Dijkema, *Effecten van bodemdaling door gaswinning in de Waddenzee* (IBN: 1993), at 15.

[181] T. Verbeeten, *Wijs met de Waddenzee?* (Amsterdam: Thela Thesis, 1999), at 154.

of the conditions was that drilling could only take place onshore and slantwise. These were experimental drillings, and no ecological damage was expected. This agreement to allow explorative drilling was also laid down in the KPD of 1994.[182] After a stormy debate in Parliament, it was decided to allow six experimental drillings in the Wadden Sea.[183]

In order for NAM to carry out these drillings, an Environmental Impact Assessment (EIA) was needed. According to the EIA procedure, developers are required to describe the proposed activities and their environmental effects, with reference to alternatives, including autonomous developments. Having examined the EIA report, the competent authority then decides in respect of the permit application.

The EIA Commission was not satisfied with the EIA Report 'Exploration drillings for natural gas in the Wadden Sea'[184] carried out by NAM, stating the report lacked scientific support.[185] Also, during public consultations the NGO 'De Waddenvereniging' and the Wadden Sea Council emphasized the uncertainties and sheer certainties, knowledge gaps, and insufficient insights in the collected data informing the report.[186] NAM needed to undertake a fresh EIA.

This second report did not fully satisfy the EIA Commission either.[187] The Commission advised to allow five of the six drillings, and demanded further research for the sixth application.[188] 'De Waddenvereniging' responded by appealing against the decision allowing the experimental drillings at Ameland at the Leeuwarden court, arguing that the requirement of Article 6(4) of the Habitats Directive had not been fulfilled, as urgent societal needs had not been considered.[189] The president of the court found a breach of Article 6(4) of the Habitats Directive. Moreover, it could not be excluded that the decision did not comply with the precautionary principle as defined in the KPD Wadden Sea.[190] On appeal, the court reaffirmed the judgment of the president, although merely on formal grounds: societal needs had been sufficiently established according to

[182] Parliamentary Documents II, 1993–1994, No. 22 605, 34:8.

[183] Parliamentary Documents II, 1993–1994, No. 23 546, 11:1.

[184] Waterloopkundig Laboratorium, Delft. Haskoning, Nederlandse Aardoliemaatschappij, *Proefboringen naar aardgas in de Waddenzee- Samenvatting Milieu-effectrapportage* (1995).

[185] Commissie voor de Milieu-effectrapportage, *Brief aan de Minister van Economische Zaken inzake aanvulling op het MER proefboringen Waddenzee* (11 June 1996).

[186] Waddenvereniging, *Reactie MER Proefboringen Waddenzee* (1996) 20; Wadden Sea Council, *Advies over het milieu-effectrapport 'Proefboringen naar aardgas in de Waddenzee' en bijbehorende vergunningaanvragen* (Leeuwarden, 1996), at 7.

[187] More information is requested about the prediction of ecological effects for the location Simonszand, information about noise and visual pollution and possible compensatory measures. Commissie voor de Milieu-effectrapportage, *Brief aan de Minister van Economische Zaken inzake Tweede aanvullend rapport behorend bij het MER proefboringen Waddenzee* (21 Oct. 1996).

[188] Commissie voor Milieueffect-rapportage, *Toetsingsadvies over het milieu-effectrapport en de aanvullingen op het MER proefboringen Waddenzee* (1996), at 7.

[189] Dir. 92/43/EEC, n. 47 above.

[190] President of the District Court of Leeuwarden, 21 Oct. 1997 (1997) 11 *Tijdschrift voor Milieu en Recht*, at 248.

the court. However, insofar as ecological effects were concerned, the court stated that certainty about only minor pollution existed, thereby applying the opposite of the precautionary principle.[191]

A year later, in 1999, a large majority in Parliament decided against Wadden gas, when a motion about uncertain ecological risks, long-term effects, and absence of social necessity was adopted.[192] In 2001, the government reiterated its position not to allow new drillings in the Wadden Sea 'for as long as there remain uncertainties about long-term effects on the Wadden Sea'.[193] The next couple of years were spent researching these remaining uncertainties.

B. Resolving Uncertainties

On 21 June 2005, NAM arranged a workshop with regard to Wadden Sea gas extraction. The aim of the meeting was to exchange knowledge and to discuss the scientific and legal aspects of the extraction activities proposed, in fulfilment of the requirements of a new EIA report. The workshop did not only serve to consult and inform scientists and public servants, it was also a means of keeping all relevant stakeholders on board. The discussion was set up broadly, giving space to all interested parties present to voice their arguments, concerns, and positions. The debate concentrated on how the administration could safeguard ecological values, while allowing gas extraction. NAM urged for monitoring ('hand on the tap') and assigning this task to a commission, following the example of Ameland, where soil subsidence was monitored.[194]

The research results that were generated in the preceding decade were clarifying. The research institute Alterra boldly stated 'there is hardly an issue concerning the Wadden Sea conceivable that is surrounded by more certainty'.[195] The Rijksinstituut voor Kust en Zee (Research Institute RIKZ) issued a report in June 2004 entitled 'Soil Subsidence Study Wadden Sea 2004: questions and uncertainties reconsidered'.[196] The Meijer Commission observed that scientific knowledge was out of step with public perception. Public and political perception was that gas extraction constituted one of the gravest dangers for the ecosystem of the Wadden Sea. This perception had been falsified by various research projects, but

[191] District Court of Leeuwarden, 17 July 1998 (1998) 7 *Tijdschrift voor Milieu en Recht* 8, 122–3.

[192] T. Witteveen-Hevinga, *Gas: winnen of verliezen—Een aanzet tot een herbezinning op het aardgasbeleid in het licht van de volgende eeuw* (1998).

[193] Ministry of VROM, *Derde Nota Waddenzee—deel 3:Kabinetsstandpunt planologische kernbeslissing* (Den Haag: 2001).

[194] The system of the Mining Act was recently changed, so that it is now possible to require a gas extraction and a monitoring plan.

[195] Alterra (University Wageningen), *Alterra Visie: Bodemdaling door gaswinning onder de Waddenzee*, (Wageningen: 2001).

[196] RIKZ, *Bodemdalingsstudie Waddenzee 2004: Vragen en onzekerheden opnieuw beschouwd*. This research was carried out in cooperation with other independent research institutes.

was repeated in a meeting of experts in soil subsidence and its effects organized by the Meijer Commission. The Commission now concluded that, since 1999, existing uncertainties had been removed by research on soil subsidence, geomorphology and infrastructure, wetlands and birds to such an extent that there was no need to uphold the moratorium on gas extraction in the Wadden Sea.[197]

The most important effect of gas extraction in the Wadden Sea is soil subsidence. Drilling causes the soil to subside, and consequently wetlands and flats can drop in relation to the sea surface, which can have negative effects on the ecosystem since wetlands are habitats for a rich variety of wildlife. Extraction thus causes so-called sand hunger. However, monitoring shows that the system is capable of self recovery by supplying extra sediment. This process proceeds relatively quickly, so that even extreme forms of soil subsidence can be compensated for. On flats the same process occurs, although at a somewhat slower pace. An important result of the research is that the need for sediment does not exceed its natural supply. If this was not structurally the case, wetlands and flats would not be able to catch up with the surface of the sea and eventually submerge. Model calculations are possible to predict the level of soil subsidence. This theory has been validated by monitoring gas extraction at Ameland. The research of this 'worst-case field experiment gas extraction Ameland' showed no significant negative effects for the ecosystem, and minor effects that were found could easily be compensated.[198] It has been suggested that in case of an accelerated rise of the sea surface, the Wadden Sea could give a non-linear response to a disturbance of morphology, like soil subsidence caused by gas extraction. Experts are of the opinion that the chances of this occurring are very remote, based on past responses of the Wadden Sea to large infrastructural projects (such as the construction of the dyke closing off the huge Ijselmeer), which had much bigger impacts than gas extraction. In short, ecological changes caused by gas extraction are minor, and uncertainties about the effects are almost theoretical.

The new EIA was published on 18 January 2006.[199] The EIA provided relevant scientific information that could predict effects of gas extraction in the Wadden Sea, and remove remaining uncertainties. In addition, NAM explicitly proposed to operationalize the process of gas extraction by taking the precautionary principle into account.[200] To implement this, NAM worked out the 'hand-to-tap' approach developed by the Meijer Commission to safeguard the ecological value of the Wadden Sea. Monitoring is at the core of this principle,

[197] It refers to the EIA produced by NAM: Nederlandse Aardgasoliemaatschappij, *Integrale Bodemdalingsstudie, hoofdrapport en bijbehorende deelrapporten inzake geomorfologie en infrastructuur, kwelders and vogels* (Groningen: 1998).

[198] Cliff formation, for example, can be compensated by placing rice-wooden dams.

[199] NAM, *MER Aardgaswinning Waddenzeegebied vanaf locatie Moddergat, Lauwersoog en Vierhuizen* (Groningen: 2006), published on the Internet at: http://www.nam.nl.

[200] Press release NAM, 1 Feb. 2006, available on the Internet at: http://www.nam.nl. The precautionary principle was not defined by NAM.

allowing enforcement of the limit values agreed. When breaches of limit values are detected, competent authorities can intervene. Prior to drilling, the critical speed is fixed at which sediment formation can still compensate for subsidence. Provided that the critical speed is observed, drilling should normally have no significant effects on wetlands and flats.

On the basis of scientific knowledge, an independent monitoring commission determines if limit values and other conditions are complied with. These and other (limit) values are of a conservative nature, i.e. reflect a precautionary paradigm. During the extraction period, soil subsidence is monitored in order to establish if there is indeed sufficient sediment, or if any other ecologically significant effects occur. In case soil subsidence occurs faster than expected, or if there are other significant ecological effects that can be ascribed to gas extraction, drilling is scaled down or even halted altogether.

Satisfied with the scientific data informing the EIA as well as the precautionary approach taken by NAM, the competent authorities decided to grant 30 permits. NAM planned to start gas extraction in 2007 at the Moddergat site. In 2008, the Vierhuizen and Lauwersoog sites will follow, all in accordance with the hand-to-tap principle. On 29 August 2007, the Administrative Jurisdiction Division of the Council of State rejected a final appeal lodged by environmental NGOs.[201]

VIII. Conclusion

The aim of these case studies was to provide insights into the nature of guidance provided by the precautionary principle in the development of scientifically complex and controversial environmental policy in practice. Dutch and ECJ decision-making processes concerning shellfish fishery policy on gas extraction in the Dutch part of the Wadden Sea provided us with two very different but instructive examples for this purpose.

The Wadden Sea has been subject to extensive research over the years, but due to the complexity of the ecosystem many scientific questions have remained unanswered, thus providing ample scope for the precautionary principle to impact on decision-making. Indeed, both cases show that science then becomes just one of the parameters that matter in conservation policy. In particular, under circumstances of scientific uncertainty, social perspectives and concerns become more influential in both risk assessment and risk management. This is not surprising, since from the outset the science mobilized to inform policy was issue-driven, i.e. was conducted specifically to provide answers to both conservational and political questions.

The preliminary question that must be addressed here is whether decision-makers actually applied the precautionary principle in deciding on mechanical

[201] Administrative Law Division of the Council of State, 29 Aug. 2007, No. 20060602811.

cockle fishery and gas extraction. Since it has become obvious that the answer to some extent is most certainly in the affirmative, we should focus on the individual elements of the precautionary principle as set out in Section II. To what extent were these discrete elements reflected in the decision-making process leading up to the decision to ban mechanical cockle fishery, and to allow gas extraction in the Wadden Sea?

With respect to each of the essential elements that support the precautionary principle articulated in Section II, the following can be observed.

Firstly, the chosen levels of protection for both cases reflect the requirements set out in the Habitat and Birds Directives. Therefore, the threshold for applying the precautionary principle is not serious or irreversible harm, but *likelihood of significant effects* on the integrity of the protected sites concerned.

Secondly, *uncertainties* were acknowledged in the risk assessment of both EVA II and the soil subsidence research. Scientific uncertainties concerning the Wadden Sea are an example of uncertainty where cause-effect relationships are problematic to establish, while at the same time the adverse effects are known. Researchers were frank about gaps in knowledge and deficiencies in understanding.

For cockle fishing, EVA I was methodologically insufficient to justify a purely science-based policy. It was therefore necessary to conduct EVA II, which was set up much more broadly: the research project ran from 1999 until 2003, producing 22 scientific reports and ten technical background papers. The EVA II risk assessment was conducted in a way that prepared the stage for the precautionary principle. For example, interested parties and policy-makers were involved in the framing of the risk assessment. Due to the highly complex and dynamic nature of the ecosystem of the Wadden Sea, initial attempts to establish scientific certainty soon proved in vain. Crucial for triggering precaution, these scientific uncertainties and ambiguities, and at times this scientific ignorance, were explicitly exposed in the reports. The precautionary principle subsequently functioned as a safety net, but was not explicitly relied upon. Researchers tried to validate the hypothesis that mechanical cockle fishery had negative long-term effects on the Wadden Sea ecosystem, and in particular for birds stocks who have their habitat in the Wadden Sea. However, when evidence appeared inconclusive (in view of several competing possible causes), the research in any case premised that risks due to mechanical cockle fishery are significant. Counter expertise of the fishing industry at best served to undermine claims of scientific certainty that informed the conclusions of EVA II, but could not negate the probability of irreversible damage to the environment. The precautionary principle had this particular effect, and as such was a powerful weapon for opponents of mechanical cockle fishing and policy-makers seeking to legitimize policy choices.

For the case of gas extraction, it was clear from the outset that there existed scientific uncertainty about the effects of gas extraction for the ecology of the Wadden Sea. This uncertainty particularly concerned soil subsidence and its effects. In 1989 it was therefore decided to exercise precaution in the form of a ten-year moratorium on gas extraction in the Wadden Sea. In this period NAM conducted a further risk assessment concerning the effects of gas extraction. That risk assessment finally did end existing uncertainties: it was established that gas extraction causes a certain degree of soil subsidence, but that this is usually compensated by natural processes. Risks therefore were found to be acceptable.

Thirdly, regarding *the burden of proof,* no real shift took place in the cockle fishery case. It was up to government to prove harmful effects were caused by the cockle fishing industry. In fact, the burden of proof was not lowered either when the EVA I risk assessment showed evidence of possible harm to the ecosystem of the Wadden Sea caused by mechanical cockle fishing. Although some precautionary measures were taken in the form of food reservation policy and the permanent closing of certain vulnerable areas, EVA II had to quantify these reasonable suspicions first before a final ban was installed on the activity. In case of gas extraction, the status quo was the moratorium. NAM, rather than the government, took the initiative, and perceived the moratorium as an opportunity to carry out research concerning ecological effects of gas extraction, taking experimental gas drilling at Ameland and Zuiderland as their object of study. NAM had to convince decision-making authorities of the safety of their proposed activities. Hence, although the burden of proof was not assigned formally to NAM, they took it upon themselves to prove minimal risks were associated with gas extraction. This is logical: those who generate risks are assumed to be those who know those risks best, and should be charged with producing the scientific information needed.

Fourthly, in line with the essence of the precautionary principle—which infers from scientific uncertainty a duty to revaluate other sources of knowledge—in the case of mechanical cockle fishery *relevant information and views of interested parties were actively gathered.* For the risk assessment in the mechanical cockle case it is important to note that a steering committee guiding the research was established in which interested parties participated, and an independent audit commission acted as peer review commission to provide oversight of scientific outcomes. The scientific findings regarding the effects of mechanical cockle fishery were published in peer-reviewed journals. In the risk management phase, in the context of which four public hearings were organized, several advice groups were asked to formulate advice based on their specific knowledge. Similarly, a public symposium with many delegates from outside the scientific community was organized by the Dutch scientific community of ecologists. In the case of gas extraction, no interested parties or stakeholders were involved in the risk assessment phase, as this was conducted exclusively by scientists commissioned by NAM. The only opportunity to take on board a wider array of perspectives was during the EIA procedure. For this purpose, NAM organized a workshop about risks and benefits of gas extraction in the Wadden Sea. The debate concentrated on how the administration could safeguard ecological values while allowing gas extraction.

The difference between the two cases resides in the structure of participation chosen. In the first case, participation concerned the decision to ban or to allow cockle fishing. This only reinforced initial positions. In the second case, it was not the decision itself that was at stake, but the conditions under which the decision had to be implemented. This resulted in a constructive debate leading to support of monitored gas extraction.

Fifthly, *alternatives* were considered in both cases. The search for alternatives was part of the pursuit of proportionality, the sixth element of the theoretical framework. The mechanical cockle industry wanted time to transform to more sustainable methods of fishing. It was proposed by the Commission Meijer to allow the sector a period of seven years to develop these sustainable methods. Scientists deemed this unfeasible. After a thorough analysis of the cost and benefits of a ban, it was decided that no realistic alternatives were available, while the profits of the industry were not of fundamental importance for the Dutch economy. The decision to ban mechanical cockle fishing was therefore considered proportional. For gas extraction, alternative techniques were examined that were the least onerous for the ecosystem of the Wadden Sea. Slantwise onshore drilling was considered to cause minimal effects on the soil of the Wadden Sea. This alternative drilling technique considerably helped to convince opponents of the minimal costs for the environment and the profound public and private benefits of gas extraction.

Sixthly, the decision to ban cockle fishing from the Dutch Wadden Sea was not a *provisional measure*; consensus was reached on significant effects of mechanical cockle fishery on wildlife of the Wadden Sea and the sector was bought out. The decision to allow gas extraction in the Wadden Sea has a more provisional character: The breakthrough came in the form of a regulatory innovation that came to be known as the 'hand-to-tap' principle. It compensated for any remaining existing and future uncertainties: even if the risk assessment would turn out to have been too optimistic, the risk was kept under permanent surveillance which could trigger a suitable regulatory response if limit values would be exceeded.

Seventhly, possible ecological effects were constantly *monitored* and knowledge was updated. In the mechanical cockle fishery case, monitoring was just a minor part of EVA II risk assessment. Most of the research carried out as part of EVA II consisted of analysing and combining data series collected for other purposes. Comparison of areas open and closed for fishing served as *quasi* experimental. The Policy Decision on shellfish fishery in 2005 to 2020 provides for permanent monitoring of shellfish stocks and the population of birds in light of a site's conservation objectives. Monitoring also forms an essential part of the decision to allow gas drillings in the Wadden Sea. An independent monitoring commission was set up in order immediately to detect deterioration caused by drillings, so that swift action can be taken. For the cockle fishery case a 'risk communication plan' was adopted to keep the public informed.

Finally, *judicial review* was conducted at both the national and the European levels. In both cases, NGOs basically argued against every permit decision in national courts. Before *Waddenzee*, national courts ruled that an appropriate assessment is only necessary after significant effects had been determined. After this landmark case by the ECJ, however, national courts followed the ECJ, thus requiring an appropriate assessment as soon as there exists a *possibility* of significant effects.

On the basis of this assessment, it can be concluded that both decision-making processes adopted precautionary procedures in arriving at policy decisions. And yet, 'precautionary principle', 'precaution', or even 'precautionary approach' are terms that have hardly even been mentioned in the decision-making processes. The precautionary card was mostly played by stakeholders (NGOs, but strikingly also NAM) as a strategy to pursue their interests.

Similarly, government documents advanced the precautionary principle as one of the guiding principles, but never explicitly invoked it to legitimize policy. Moreover, in formulating government policy decisions, scientific certainties were systematically emphasized and uncertainties played down. Does this mean that the decision-making processes at issue are simply examples of more traditional cost-benefit analyses, rather than instances of precautionary environmental regulation? Or, alternatively, has the logic of precaution trickled down into bureaucratic practices and processes, even though it is not explicitly invoked. There is some support for this latter view. In 1994, O'Riordan and Cameron already predicted that 'precaution will not explode onto the environmental stage' but will 'seep through the pores of decision-making institutions and the political consciousness of humanity by stealth'.[202] Tickner claims that precaution in its broadest most progressive construction is a means of stimulating innovation and social sustainability. Its aim is to foster democratic engagement, so that society may seek the safest alternative that would meet their needs.[203]

In a similar vein, the policy decisions discussed here cannot be disregarded as merely examples of cost-benefit analyses: the logic of precaution has been applied in both cases, finding expression in discrete approaches to both complex ecological and societal problems.

In 1993, the first precautionary measures were adopted for cockle fishery (food reservation and closing areas) as a result of strong indications that mechanical fishing was responsible for significant adverse ecological impacts in the Wadden Sea. While more research on the effects of mechanical fishery was carried out, the initial measures with hindsight turned out to be insufficiently precautionary. The measures were based on 'false negatives' as it was presumed that this form of fishery was not particularly harmful to Wadden Sea wildlife. From 1993, when first evidence of harmful effects surfaced, it took another 11 years before sufficient evidence would finally lead to a total ban on mechanical cockle fishery. Although

[202] T. O'Riordan and J. Cameron, 'The History and Contemporary Significance of the Precautionary Principle' in T. O'Riordan and J. Cameron (eds.) *Interpreting the Precautionary Principle* (London: Cameron May, 1994), at 26.

[203] J. A. Tickner, n. 25 above, at 56.

all constitutive elements of the precautionary principle to a greater or lesser extent played a role in this policy process, it can hardly be said to amount to a fully fledged 'precautionary approach'.

For gas extraction the picture is different. The moratorium was imposed in 1989, when the precautionary principle was not yet fully developed, and the government hence referred to a 'prevention for nature' principle. It can be assumed that the precautionary principle would have been invoked if it had been part of the regulatory toolbox. The moratorium was in response to insufficient knowledge, and a suspicion of significant irreversible effects of gas extraction. Clearly therefore, the moratorium was a precautionary measure *avant la lettre*. Monitoring later revealed no deleterious effects, and drillings could therefore be conducted in a relatively safe manner, taking precautionary conditions into consideration. The moratorium was a response to a 'false positive': action was taken on the basis of a precautionary approach that later turned out to be unnecessary.

This being as it may, the decision-making process on gas extraction is an excellent example of how precaution can guide decision-making in situations of uncertainty.

It has to be pointed out here that there is one decision-maker that does not shy away from explicitly relying on the precautionary principle: the ECJ. In *Waddenzee*, concerning the application of Article 6 of the Habitats Directive, the ECJ explicitly draws upon the precautionary principle. According to the ECJ, the precautionary principle implies that any scientific uncertainty about possible adverse effects on a site will not merely oblige precautionary regulatory action, but will trigger a ban on all activities.

It is to be expected that this decision will influence decision-making in environmental law, in any case in the context of the Birds and Habitats Directives throughout the EU in years to come. Although the fact that the protection of European species and habitats is taken seriously by the ECJ is to be applauded, the question arises if this rigid approach to application of the precautionary principle accords with its logics, i.e. the flexible character of the principle in decision-making, as evidenced in the gas extraction case, in which the principle can claim its most telling success. As a procedural principle, the principle requires decision-makers to reflect on how they justify their decisions, what factors are relevant to a decision, how that decision should be made, and who should be involved in the decision-making process. That means that the particular outcome of the application of the precautionary principle in a different setting than the Dutch Wadden Sea (for example concerning the German or Danish part) can be different. Particular environmental risks will create discrete and unique challenges for the implementation of the precautionary principle. This is not only so because scientific uncertainties differ in each case, but also because the socio-economic contexts of problems vary. Precaution thus understood leaves decision-makers discretion to foster innovation and environmentally friendly alternatives in ways best suited to the particular context of the case at hand. The ECJ, on the other hand, limits this discretion of Member States severely by requiring an appropriate assessment of virtually any risk in the context of the Habitats Directive. In so deciding, it went beyond the words of Article 6(3). It has to be said that an escape is offered by Article 6(4), stating that where there are no alternative options, a plan or project has to be carried out for imperative reasons of overriding public interest, including those of a social economic nature. In that case, compensatory measures have to be taken, and the Commission has to be informed. This escape, however, does not compensate for national authorities' loss of the possibility to mobilize societal and economic actors that, the case studies have shown, may act as drivers of ecological innovation.

Deliberative Turning from a Law-Science Cul-de-Sac: Speculations regarding Community Transgenic Regulation

*Naveen Thayyil**

I. Introduction

Lawyers and scientists have at least this much in common: Both harbor the intellectual conceit that a well defined problem is not only a necessary, but almost a sufficient, condition for a successful solution.[1]

GMO regulation in the European Community (EC) has often been charecterized as illustrative of the difficult and vexed relationship between law, politics, and science.[2] Effective regulation of transgenic agriculture, food, and feed is sought in furtherance of a plethora of objectives including Community harmonization in pursuit of the internal market,[3] the non-discrimination principle in international trade law,[4]

* Ph.D Researcher, Tilburg Institute for Law, Technology and Society (TILT), Tilburg University. This chapter forms part of a NWO (Dutch Research Council) funded Pioneer research project 'Regulating Biotechnology'. The author wishes to express his gratitude to the referees of the *Yearbook*.

[1] J. L. Mashaw, 'Law and Engineering: In search of the law-science problem' (2003) 66 *Law and Contemporary Problems* 4, 135–9, at 136.

[2] See for instance Z. K. Forsman, 'Community regulation of Genetically Modified Organisms: a difficult relationship between Law and Science' (2004) 19 *European Law Journal* 5, 580–94; T. Spanggaard, 'The marketing of GMOs: A supra-national battle over science and Precaution' (2003) 3 *The Yearbook of European Environmental Law*, 79–124, and T. Christoforou, 'The Regulation of Genetically Modified Organisms in the European Union: The interplay of science, law and politics' (2004) 41 *Common Market Law Review* 3, 637–709.

[3] See E. Brosset, 'The Prior Authorization Procedure adopted for the Deliberate Release into the Environment of Genetically Modified Organisms: the Complexities of Balancing Community and National Competences' (2004) 10 *European Law Journal* 5, 555–79 for an examination of the interplay between community and national competences in the realm of GMO regulation.

[4] The EC Biotech decision of the WTO Panel, was predicted as a development that will have a determinative impact on the community regulatory framework. Such predictions continued even subsequent to the release of the report—the US Trade representative Susan Schwab had stated that 'the WTO has ruled in favour of science based policy making over the unjustified, anti-biotech policies adopted in the EU, and... affirms what the world's farmers have known for many years... biotechnology crops not only are helping to meet the world's food needs, they also are having a positive environmental impact on our soil and natural resources', and Friends of the Earth Europe claimed that the panel has bluntly ruled that European safeguards should be sacrificed to benefit biotech corporations. Panel Reports, *European Communities—Measures Affecting and Marketing of Biotech*

investment in new technologies,[5] public opinion, and of course protection of health and the environment, howsoever variegated its constructions may be. These interests would often appear to tug in different tangents vis-à-vis the objective of effective and efficient regulation of GMOs in Europe. Which interest ought to dominate, or in what manner these interests ought to be harmonized is, at one level, intricately connected to the issue of the role scientific constructions and evidences play in regulation. At a more fundamental level, such harmonization is influenced by political values, choices, and practices that underpin governance in different societies.

Effective regulation of the introduction of transgenics into agriculture raises fundamental questions for democratic governance in modern societies. Even way after a decade of commercial introduction of the first transgenic tomato, only 22 countries have facilitated commercial release of transgenics in agricultural crops and food,[6] demonstrative of the apprehension and public concern prevalent in various parts of the globe.[7] GM crops evoke troubling doubts regarding toxicity, allergenicity, effects on non-target organisms, horizontal gene transfer, as well as grave and irreversible effects on biodiversity.[8] Simultaneously, GM crops are claimed to substantially increase agricultural yield, innovatively add nutritive nature and value in crops,[9] and also drastically decrease the use of pesticide, herbicide, and/or insecticide. Each set of claims of harm and beneficence is deeply contested, and the argument of 'absence of evidence is not evidence of absence' is tossed around in different manners.

Products, WT/DS292/R, WT/DS292/R, WT/DS293/R. See also D. Prévost, 'Opening Pandora's Box: The panel's findings in the EC-Biotech Products Dispute' (2007) 34 *Legal Issues of Economic Integration* 1, 67–101, at 68.

[5] This is underlined, for instance, in the European Council's quest for balance in its 2002 Presidency conclusion in Barcelona: encouraging 'measures and a timetable which enable Community businesses to exploit the potential of biotechnology while taking due account of the precautionary principle and meeting ethical and social standards', Barcelona European Council, *Presidency Conclusions* (SN 100/1/02/REV 1, 15 Mar. 2002), at 20.

[6] According to industry statistics, 10.3 million farmers in 22 countries cultivated transgenic crops on 102 million hectares in 2006: 'Biotech industry comments on French President Sarkozy's statements on the cultivation of biotech crops in France', 26 Oct. 2007, published on the Internet at: http://www.foodnavigator.com (accessed on 14 Dec. 2007).

[7] On the other hand, the global area of GM crops grew from 1.7 million hectares to 102 million hectares between 1996 and 2006. See C. James, 'Global review of commercialized transgenic crops: 2001', International Service for the Acquisition of Agri-biotech Acquisitions, ISAAA Brief # 24, 2002 and 'Global status of commercialized Biotech/ GM crops: 2006', International Service for the Acquisition of Agri-biotech Acquisitions, ISAAA Brief # 35, 2006.

The EC moratorium is estimated to have resulted in a loss of nearly $1 billion in sales of US soya and corn sales itself, indicative of the high stakes involved in the debate. See S. Zarilli, 'International Trade in Genetically Modified Organisms and Multilateral Negotiations: A new dilemma for Developing Countries', UNCTAD/DITC/TNCD/1 (Geneva: UNCTAD, 5 July 2000), 6–7.

[8] See, for instance, M. Ho, *Genetic Engineering Dream or Nightmare? The Brave New World of Bad Science and Big Business* (Bath: Gateway Books, 1998); J. Rifkin, *The Biotech Century* (New York: Putnum, 1998), J. Rissler and M. Mellon, *The Ecological Risks of Engineered Crops* (Cambridge: MIT Press, 1996); M. Lappe and B. Bailey, *Against The Grain: The Genetic Transformation of Global Agriculture* (London: Earthscan, 1999).

[9] See, for instance, Q. Schiermeier, 'Designer Rice to Combat Diet Deficiencies makes its Debut' (2001) 409 *Nature* 6820, at 551.

The issue of regulation of transgenics is rightly characterized as the most challenging task yet to be faced by environmental law regimes, in particular. It is Herculean even by the general standards of modern regulatory frameworks—having in its wake claims of revolutionary beneficence, irreversible risk, the need for precaution, scientific uncertainty, as well as issues of disguised protectionism, multi-lateral regulatory creep, democratic control of technology, and seed sovereignty.

The enactment of Directive 2001/18/EC on the Deliberate Release of Genetically Modified Organisms into the Environment and Repealing Directive 90/220/EEC (Deliberate Release Directive),[10] and the subsequent introduction of the two new regulations in July 2003 completed a new stage in Community harmonization of GM regulation,[11] a stage that arose from the neccessity to end the de facto moratorium. This stage sought to tackle the social and environmental issues emanating out of the release of GMOs, in a manner acceptable to concerns of international and internal credibility. However, the regulatory impasse has continued in reality, in the ensuing period, requiting a fresh examination of the regulatory structure.[12] Section III of this paper seeks to understand the current Community regulatory framework, with a special emphasis on the impact and hold of positivist science on risk regulation and release.

Section II seeks to identify various important problems that accompany the use of science and scientific evidence in legal and regulatory processes like risk and introduction of new technologies. These enumerated concerns have often been raised by various scholars who share fundamental sceptical concerns about the claims of scientific rationale and scientific methodology. The intent of identifying these problematiques of science is not necessarily to further an anti-science position. Much to the contrary, such an identification and appropriate characterization of the limits of use of science in regulation may help us in a more effective regulatory architecture. Understanding the problematizations of claims of objectivity, neautrality, and universality attributed to science has great utility in the conceptualization of effective regulatory incorporation of science. Further, ecological and other environmental approaches appear to require far more specificity than scientific methods can deliver. Especially, applied technologies like

[10] [2001] OJ L106.

[11] See the statements of the Environment Commissioner Margot Wallström and the Health and Consumer Protection Commissioner David Byrne, on the occasion of the adoption of the Food and Feed as well as traceability and labelling regulations. 'it will reinforce our international credibility and will certainly help in building public confidence in new technologies... we address the most critical concerns of the public regarding the environmental and health effects of GMOs and enable the consumers to choose... European consumers can now have confidence that any GM food or feed marketed in Europe has been subject to the most rigorous pre-marketing assessment in the world', Commission Press release, 'European Legislative Framework for GMOs in Place' (IP/03/1056, 22 July 2003). See Section III below for more on the Regulations.

[12] Amply demonstrated by the drastic fall in release applications and approvals. Germany has reportedly proposed a science based regulatory framework to break the current 'impasse', published on the Internet at: http://www.foodnavigator.com (accessed on 14 Dec. 2007).

biotechnology need to be differentiated from the legitimacy commanded by 'pure' scientific methods, since they are pragmatic in terms of integrating context specific information for commercial application.

However relevant and legitimate these various sociological and other scholarly gazes of science and its processes are,[13] given the reality of the normative and everyday presence science enjoys in modern societies, law still has to grapple with the difficult question of how these critical insights can be incorporated within the legal landscape during the employment of scientific findings in regulatory frameworks. For an effective regulation of GMOs, identification and appreciation of these limitations of science are important not so as to debunk it, rather to use the fruits of the technical/scientific enquiry in a manner that gives it neither too much nor too less importance. Section II seeks to lay the ground for such an endeavour.

Section IV examines the presence of science and science-based norms in the framework of the World Trade Organization (WTO). After differentiating the requirements in the Global Agreement on Tariffs and Trade (GATT), the WTO Agreement on Technical Barriers to Trade (TBT Agreement), and the WTO Agreement on Sanitary and Phytosanitary Measures (SPS agreement), the section examines a particular effect of the *EC-Biotech* decision of the WTO Panel. It concentrates on the continuing judicial expansion of science based norms in the SPS Agreement into the ambit of global trade frameworks, and also into other international frameworks like multilateral environmental agreements (MEAs) as an issue of concern for appropriate use of science in regulation. The section also examines the relevant jurisprudence of the WTO adjudicatory body towards identifying potential spaces for successful incorporation of other legitimate factors into the regulatory matrix. It further explores an appropriate manner towards such an endeavour. Notwithstanding platitudes, an examination of the final findings demonstrates that incorporation of other legitimate factors outside scientific risk assessment exercises are effectively frowned upon in such judicial review. Given this context, for various enumerated reasons, the section concludes that genuine attempts at deliberative public participation (notwithstanding legitimate concerns that such measures in their implementation may lead to placation, tokenism, and manipulation that will merely engineer legitimacy for unpopular decisions) during the stage of initial framing of the 'scientific' risk assessments would be the best way forward to incorporate these factors. The final section, Section V, further examines the merits of such a course of action.

[13] See P. Street, 'Constructing risks: GMOs, biosafety and environmental decision making', in H. Somsen (ed.), *The Regulatory Challenge of Biotechnology, Human Genetics, Food and Patents* (Cheltenham: Edward Elgar, 2007), 95–117.

II. Problematics of Science and its Appropriate Regulatory Incorporation

Transgenic crop regulation becomes important to understand and deal with in a wider matrix of introduction of new technologies, due to the existence of highly contradictory evidentiary claims that the law has to deal with. Contradictory claims of high benefits and serious hazards uneasily coexist, which is symptomatic of legal experiences with the introduction of many new technologies. The point at which the precautionary principle is sought to be employed, the manner of its employment within regulatory structures, and the ascertainment of the factum of scientific uncertainty within the legal and regulatory matrix are problem areas which require far more clarity than what is currently available.

There is a paradox in the manner in which precautionary principle has been sought to be employed in the regulation of new technologies. While the basis of the principle is a fundamental doubt about the efficacy of reliance on science, various *avatars* of the principle use science itself to decide the factum and manner of the invocation of the principle. This is illustrative of one of the many difficult facets of the *law-science* relationship in this realm. How does law examine contemporaneous assertions of the potential of revolutionary benefits to the public at large, with predictions of grave threats to health and environment; where claims of multiple revolutionary beneficience and serious and irreversible damage to health and environment are both uncertain. Thus, when such constructions of benign benificience uneasily coexist with grave and irreversible threats to human and animal health or the environment, what is the manner in which various *avatars* of precaution be employed? And what role can science meaningfully play when the principle sought to be employed bases itself on a premise of scientific uncertainty, and the identification of the limits of science. Whereby, science itself becomes a site of contestation to prove its own possibilities of certainty and uncertainty.

There are various problems that have been identified in the successful incorporation of science in environmental and health regulation. Despite assertions to the contrary, environmental law often demands far more specificity from science than it is able to deliver, since the nature of process and practice of applied sciences and technologies makes uncertainty unavoidable.

On the continuum between a merely speculative risk and a conclusively demonstrated one lies a vast strech of undemonstrated, unquantified, but scientifically plausible risks. Within that zone, the risk of harm is real so long as safety is unproven. The proving of safety itself, and proof of absence of risk and harm is done through the selection of specific frames, where deteminations of *safety* are not purely scientific, but are based on assumptions made pursuant to science policies.[14]

[14] See V. R. Walker, 'Keeping the WTO from Becoming the World Trans-science Organization: Scientific Uncertainty, Science Policy, and Fact-finding in the Growth Hormones Dispute' (1998) 31 *Cornell International Law Journal*, 251–320, at 325.

Though uncertainty may be overcome in some cases through better and more research, often regulatory frameworks can only benefit from the wisdom of hindsight.

The use of science in environmental regulation has fundamental difficulties, aptly demonstrated in this characterization:

> a prevailing [scientific] paradigm extends over time, informing and being informed by the experiments in which it is involved and by new knowledge learned. Sometimes the paradigm grows and flourishes and sometimes it is replaced by something revolutionary. But it is expected that there will be an extension through time as knowledge informs and modifies. The legal system, on the other hand, imposes brief windows of time defined by the rules of evidence applicable to a particular matter needing resolution such as a rule-making or litigation. In this sense, scientific knowledge is like an endless movie in which one is never sure where one has entered the theatre. The legal system, however, takes a single or discrete window of frames and tries to discern the entire plot.[15]

Given laws' aspirational fixation for certainty, any prudential acknowledgement of the inevitability of uncertainty in such processes would appear to be difficult for legal systems.[16] How, then, can attempts to incorporate various aspects of uncertainty into decision-making processes be made? It is imperative to identify the methodological, ontological, and teleological problems that science raises to its own successful incorporation in regulatory decision-making processes. This acceptance of uncertainty needs to be undertaken not necessarily as a calumnous brief for virulent anti-science positions. On the contrary, such identification of the assumptions in this law-science interaction, understanding the latent difficulties, and speculating on different and appropriate courses of actions is imperative for an effective regulation of the introduction of new technologies.

The normative claim to legitimacy that science asserts is based on assumptions of its certainty, accuracy, and objectiveness. These assumptions have their roots in the image of the scientific method, as an altruistic endeavour in pursuit of discovering functional relationships in basic science. An endeavour to make precise, objective, and accurate predictions of functional relationships in nature that are universal and independent of context and perspective. This identification of functional relationships is sought to be legitimated and accepted by the scientific

[15] M. J. Brennan et al., 'Square Pegs and Round Holes: Application of the "Best Scientific Data Available" Standard in the Endangered Species Act' (2003) 16 *Tulane Environmental Law Journal* 2, 387–444.

[16] I.e. where law processes science. A good illustration would be in the realm of species conservation law, for understanding the manner in which law uses science to build frames and choose regulatory measures. See M. H. Ruckesshaus et al., 'The Pacific Salmon Wars: What Science Brings to the Challenge of Recovering Species' (2003) 33 *Annual Review of Environmental Systems*, 665–732, at 693, 'uncertainty, lack of basic ecological understanding, and tremendous environmental variability make predicting species population dynamics precisely and accurately fruitless. But we can identify management actions that are likely to yield marked improvements in population status under a wide variety of scenarios'.

community through an important process of peer review, repeated testing, and intense scrutiny, so as to check for substantive methodological flaws.

These central assumptions of universality, certainty, and objectivity that legitimize science, of course, have been put through a consistent and powerful challenge by various scholarships, with varying success: including the post-structuralists, sociologists of science, and feminist scholars.[17] The assertion is that the particularity of scientific assumptions and findings, even inter se different scientific disciplines, becomes stark upon only careful examinations—a quantum physicist may note phenomena that a Newtonian physicist may miss and so on.[18] This leads us to the truism of how science is socially and culturally constructed, and that science can be variegated and conflicting depending upon its source and location.[19]

Further, employment of the normative claim of scientific method to validate applied sciences in general, and understanding the hazards to the environment in particular, encounters a fundamental critique that nature is replete with multiple known and unknown confounding variables, interacting with each other in unknown and unknowable ways; and exact circumstances like habitats, community dynamics, climate conditions, and ecosystem functions are impossible to recreate or replicate.[20] Applied sciences, like biotechnology, must be pragmatic as opposed to the attributes of methodology of scientific enquiry. This is since general scientific knowledge gained through the scientific method has to be integrated with context specific information that is currently available. The existence of considerable data gaps and uncertainties is possible, which makes the claims of accuracy and universality difficult to sustain.

Such integration through personal judgements is also naturally hit by subtle biases, shaped by personal perspectives, prior experiences, and culture—leading to scientific experts employed by different interest groups bringing different models to the table, each of which might point to a radically different solution to the

[17] Sociologists of science including Science and Technology scholars have produced a plethora of work that problematizes our monolithic understanding of science—see, for instance, D. J. Hess, *Science Studies: An Advanced Introduction* (New York: New York University Press, 1997) and S. Jasanoff, *Science at the Bar* (Cambridge: Harvard University Press, 1995). Feminist theory has mounted a devastating intellectual challenge to the nature and normative claims of scientific methods, viz., its neutrality, reliability, and accuracy. See, for instance, S. Harding, *Is Science Multicultural?: Post Colonialisms, Feminisms and Epistemologies* (Bloomington: Indiana University Press, 1998), and *Whose science? Whose Knowledge?: Thinking from Women's Lives* (Ithaca: Cornell University Press, 1991) as well as H. Crowley and S. Himmelweit (eds.), *Knowing Women: Feminism and Knowledge* (Milton Keynes: The Open University Press, 1992).

[18] See, for instance, D. Bloor, *Knowledge and Social Imagery (2nd edn.)* (London: University of Chicago Press, 1991).

[19] P. L. Berger and T. Luckman, *The Social Construction of Reality—A Treatise in the Sociology of Knowledge* (New York: Doubleday, 1966).

[20] Again the instance of ecosystem management is an apposite field for us to understand the nature of the problem, see R. D. Brunner and T. W. Clark, 'A Practice-Based Approach to Ecosystem Management' (1997) 11 *Conservation Biology* 1, 48–58, at 54.

problem at hand.[21] Such biases, thus, also affect which problems scientists decide are worth researching in the first place; and also leads to a bias in valuing certain scientific methods and applied scientific processes. Thus, the assertion is that much like legal methods, scientific training provides certain problem-solving skills, which involve conversion or redefinition of problems into those which science may 'solve'.[22] It hence becomes imperative to remember the centrality of the act of framing in scientific processes of hazard identification and risk assessment.

Finally, contrary to the claims of science being a neutral and foolproof yardstick against mercantilist protectionism, overreliance on science can also exacerbate profound imbalances on democratization in the context of international relationships in general, and international trade disputes in particular.

> Sociologists of science describe science in a variety of ways: as a community, as a dialogue and as a consensus... there is however a geography of science; scientific opinion, whatever that might mean, is concentrated in centers chiefly located in the United States, Europe and Japan. These centers of scientific authority correspond, not accidently, to the major players in the world trading system... science is a much challenged notion in contemporary thinking; as such, it promises little hope as a source for neutral principles to resolve economic disputes among nations. Science is a product of what questions are asked of it: a system that requires scientific bases for self-interested positions is likely to find them. Science then becomes hardly as universal as one might first imagine. The history of trade disputes already has demonstrated the possibility of rival scientific positions urging contrary regulatory stances. Scientific consensus is geographically distributed and flows from centers of influence.[23]

[21] For instance, science answers a question of risk, in relation to the question that is framed and posed to it. P. van Zwanenberg and A. Stirling, 'Risk and Precaution in Europe: A Response to Vogel' (2003) 3 *Yearbook of European Environmental Law*, 41–56, 52: 'While examining the BSE controversy over differing risk assesments of various national bodies remarked: "yet the divergent decisions over BSE differed not because one was evidently more reasonable than the other, but rather because of competing social framings of the issue and competing social views about the acceptability of residual uncertainties". Neither... claimed that UK beef was pathogen free. Rather the SSC assessed the risks relative to those posed by continental beef, where the AFSSA... assessed absolute risks'.

[22] See. K. Carden, 'Bridging the Divide: The role of science in species conservation law' (2006) 30 *Harvard Environmental Law Review*, 165–259, at 173, 180 and 181.

[23] See J. Atik, 'Science and International regulatory convergence' (1996–97) 17 *Northwestern Journal of International Law & Business*, 736–58 for an exploration of variegations of science in law. He postulates the existence of geography of science, where 'science if measured by factors such as research expenditures, published papers or number or doctorates, is largely centered in Europe, the United States and Japan. India has an important presence in certain fields as well. Analyzing specific scientific disciplines reveals more geographic texture; the Italians, for example, are prominent vulcanologists... Physicians and epidemiologists trained in the United States are likely to share a similar vision even when exercising their profession in other country—indeed they may speak with more authority in foreign countries on account of their U.S. scientific training than they would in the United States... Even regional differences arise in response to training a recent study has shown that radically different approaches in recommended treatment are taken by East Coast-trained cardiologists than by their West-trained colleagues', at 749, 754, and 758. See for more regarding the latter point G. Langley et al., 'Use of Written Cases to Study Factors Associated with Regional Variations in Referral Rates' (1991) 44 *Journal of Clinical Epidemiology* 4/5, 391–402.

While intellectually a pure science-based approach cannot seem to stand the scrutiny of critique from various sides, in reality the hold of positivist conceptualizations of science among legal regimes is significant. Science has become a touchstone of sorts for various regulatory actions, particularly pertaining to health and the environment. Regulatory decisions lacking scientific attire are often ridiculed, and are sitting ducks for judicial invalidation in various jurisdictions in the world. Often, regulatory decisions are dressed in scientific garb, as a way to preclude challenge from principles and processes of international economic law be it the WTO, North Amercian Free Trade Association (NAFTA), or EC frameworks. The image of universality and neutrality, grounded in the scientific method of observation and revelation, notwithstanding the intellectual challenges to the same notions, appear to make the claim to scientific rationale almost an impeccable one.

However, over-reliance on science can be myopic and an easy way out for politicians and technocrats who have to deal with difficult questions of regulation, since 'decisions attributed to science gain instant legitimacy through the image of science as a pure pursuit above the concerns of a partisan world'.[24] In Europe, however, consequent to various controversies including BSE, this legitimacy is substantially eroded, whereby public trust in organized science has drastically dwindled.[25]

Notwithstanding the underlying problematiques,[26] since science continues to be an important source of reason in modern societies, the obvious challenge for legal systems is to understand and bring into its own wake the fruits of scientific enquiries in a specific endeavour; to find appropriate ways to maximize protection of health and the environment, optimize public confidence and legitimacy, democratize governance processes and ensure safe technological innovation for wider societal welfare. The advent of the precationary principle is often characterized as a legal development that acknowledges the methodological problems of incorporating science, as well as one that furthers democratic control over technology.

[24] See W. Wagner, for instance, for an elaboration of this point: 'The Science Charade in Toxic Risk regulation' (1995) 95 *Columbia Law Review* 7, 1613–723.

[25] See for instance Eurobaromètre 55.2, *European Science and Technology*, Dec. 2001 and Eurobaromètre 58.0, *European Science and Technology (2nd edn.)*, Mar. 2003. 'Although the European public has often been characterized as technophobic, emotional or susceptible to NGO and media propaganda over GMOs, there is nothing irrational about disagreeing with a scientific estimate of risk. People may not know the technical details, but they have developed awareness of the broad issues involved and ways of forming their own judgments. Their previous experience, such as the BSE crisis, found concerns regarding the (un)reliability of scientific reassurances of safety and the authorities tendency to conceal information when powerful economic interests are at stake. It is suggested that transparency and access to adequate information, especially regarding uncertainties and gaps in knowledge, are of vital importance in order to have a comprehensive and structured public dialogue on the issue.' E. Tsioumani, 'Genetically Modified Organisms in the EU: Public Attitudes and Regulatory Developments' (2004) 3 *Review of European Community and International Environmental Law* 13, 279–88, at 281.

[26] If one were to skirt the philosophical enquiries of the anti-science position, which in any case is not appropriate at this juncture.

The precautionary principle empowers regulators to pursue high levels of protection despite absence of certainty of scientific evidence of harm.[27]

Ironically, employment of the principle has recently had a peculiar relationship with science due to the requirement of the scientific establishment of scientific uncertainty in some realms. This has led to fundamental problems in the case of GMOs, as often in the introduction of new technologies it is usually the very same institutional arenas which generate and fine tune these technologies that also provide the information, data, and expertise upon which these scientific judgements regarding uncertainty can be made. Such convergence of interests in institutional arenas makes application of the precautionary principle problematic, where concrete and legitimate exceptions sought to be made to use of such scientific expertise becomes tightly held by science itself. The European experience with the regulation of GMOs is an excellent aid to understanding the problems abound in this law-science relationship, and an opportunity to speculate on an appropriate way to overcome it, not merely for an effective, efficient, legitimate, and democratic way of using of transgenic crops, but also to look towards the introduction of future new technologies.

III. Bifurcation and Scientific Control in Community Risk Regulation

The EC regime for the regulation of GM food, feed, and and other related products attempts to engage with scientific processes and evidence in a salient manner. Broadly, the attempt has been to regulate transgenic agriculture through the twin tropes of risk and consumer awareness/preference. Following the end of the de facto moratorium,[28] an event which in itself demonstrated the disparities of regulatory concerns within Member States, EU multi-level governance has achieved high levels of harmonization in the realm of regulation of GMOs through the introduction of a new regulatory regime. Salient features in the

[27] The variegated constructions and usage of Precautionary Principle is beyond the scope of this paper. But see J. S. Applegate, 'The taming of the Precautionary Principle' (2002) 27 *William and Mary Environmental Law & Policy Review* 1, 13–78, for an account of the progressive emasculation of the principle. See also J. Peel, 'Precaution—A matter of Principle, Approach or Process?' (2004) 5 *Melbourne Journal of International Law* 2, 483–501, for a persuasive argument on the need for disentangling the principle from the divisive debate in the contemporary international arena.

[28] The moratorium had effectively replaced the first generation of GM regulation, of which Dir. 90/220/EEC and Reg. (EC) No. 258/97 were the most important texts. This regulatory framework was based on achieving a 'high level of protection of human health and the environment' through establishing procedure for a case-by-case assessment before authorizing the deliberate release of GMOs into the environment, and extending to the marketing of GMOs. The latter legislation established an approval process for *novel* foods, including those containing GMOs, and inter alia streamlined the procedure applied to GM foods and food ingredients that were 'substantially equivalent' to existing foods.

Deliberate Release Directive,[29] which forms the backbone of the current regulatory framework, include:

- elaboration of a detailed set of principles[30] required to be considered in environmental risk assessments;[31]
- a requirement that the aspiring marketer of the GMO performs its own risk assessment prior to submitting an application for approval;
- broadening of the relevant matters to be considered in assessing applications to include ethical concerns and the cumulative long-term effects of GMOs on human health and the environment;[32]
- a provision for public consultation regarding applications; and post-market surveillence requirements.

This new regime sought to ensure a single market through a regulation based on realms of risk evalution and consumer information, where once a transgenic food/feed is authorized by the Commission as safe for its intended use,[33] and

[29] See n. 10 above.

[30] Art. 4 (1) and (3) of the Deliberate Release Directive is key in identifying this set of principles. The former requires the Member States to ensure that all appropriate measures, in accordance with the precautionary principle, are undertaken to avoid adverse effects that might arise from the deliberate release of GMOs on human health and the environment. The latter obligates Member States and in appropriate cases the Commission, to accurately assess the potential adverse effects on human health and the environment, that may occur directly or indirectly through gene transfer from GMOs, on a case-by-case basis, taking into account the environmental impact according to the nature of the organism introduced and the receiving environment. Art. 13(2a) also requires, in this case, the applicant for the release to provide relevant information which shall inter alia take into account the diversity of sites of use of the GMO.

[31] Art. 4(2), Deliberate Release Dir., n. 10 above, specifies that the environmental risk assessment envisaged by the regulatory framework includes the evaluation of risks to human health and the environment that may be posed by the deliberate release or market placement of GMOs—be it direct or indirect, immediate or delayed.

[32] Annex II, Deliberate Release Dir., ibid.

[33] An application for deliberate release/market placement is initiated by the submission of a notification dossier to the Competent Authority of the Member State (Art. 13, Deliberate Release Dir, ibid.), who in turn is required to carry out a risk assessment of the product, of which an important part is to examine the environment risk assessment undertaken by the applicant that mandatorily accompanies the application. The resultant risk assessment of the Competent Authority needs to specify whether the product represents a risk to human health or the environment, and recommendations for safe use and handling of the product (Art. 13(1), (2), Deliberate Release Dir, ibid.). In case the relevant Member State exercises its regulatory discretion to arrive at a favourable opinion regarding the potential release, it must forward the dossier including the application, and the assessment report to the Commission (Art. 14(2), (3), Deliberate Release Dir., ibid.), who in turn must notify the *competent authorities* of other Member States by forwarding the relevant dossier (Art. 15(1), Deliberate Release Dir., ibid.). A decision on the release/market placement, in the event of objections by specific Member States (highly likely in the realm of the release of GMOs) is subject to the standard comitology procedure Council Dec. 1999/468/EC [1999] OJ L184/23, repealing Council Dec. 87/373/EEC, where a qualified majority is necessary for the approval of the release. See further, Arts. 4–7, 16–19 and 28 of Reg. (EC) No. 1829/2003 on Genetically Modified Food and Feed (GM Food and Feed Reg.) [2003] OJ L268/1.

appropriately labelled through requisite procedure,[34] the same can be grown, sold, or consumed in any individual Member State. Once authorization is considered by all Member States and the Commission, and consent has been granted for a GMO to be placed on the market, Member States must, as a matter of course, allow its free circulation, subject to certain provided exceptions (dealt with later). This harmonization of the release mechanism has arisen despite high sensitivities in the relationship between community and Member States' responsibilities in GMO authorization, sensitivities highlighted by the first clearance under the new regime itself, of Novartis Bt-11, in 2004.[35] This provides us with a window of opportunity to better understand the putative relationships between law and science during the introduction of new (controversial) technologies.

The high level of distrust among Member States about the different national risk assessment mechanisms is sought to be tackled through a certain degree of centralization of risk assessment, coupled with risk management under a comitology procedure that purports to be more reflective of multi-level decision-making than the earlier comitology procedure.[36] The European Food Safety Authority (EFSA),[37] the authority responsible for the Community risk assessment, plays a key centralizing role in GM food regulation.[38] However, EFSA is mandated to consult all national competent bodies to carry out food safety and environmental assessments in certain cases viz., the Deliberate Release Directive and Regulation (EC) No. 1829/2003 on Genetically Modified Food and Feed (GM Food and Feed Regulation)[39] overlap. Also while in the process of authorization of seeds or similar material, the EFSA must consult a national competent body to carry out an environmental risk assessment. Though the impact of such

[34] See Arts. 2, 13, 24, and 25 of the GM Food and Feed Reg., ibid., and Arts. 4–6 of Reg. (EC) No. 1830/2003 [2003] OJ L354 (Labelling Reg.).

[35] COM(2004)10. The appropriateness and adequacy of the scientific evidences related to risk, and of bases for labelling have been highly contentious in various *sectors*. Various authorizations starting from 2004 were marked by a deep division in the policy positions of Member States, a resultant inability to reach a qualified majority to proposals for commercial release, and subsequently the Commission's willingness to assume political responsibility and approve the placing of a transgenic product in the market. Such policy divisions have various underlying reasons including the capacity of agro-biotech industries, the influence of civil and political society actors like environmental and consumer NGOs and green parties, public attitude towards food, technology, and risk as well as differentiated degrees of public involvement in the various Member States, Tsioumani, n. 25 above, 280–4.

[36] Amply demonstrated by the facts of Case C-6/99 *Association Greenpeace France and Others* v. *Ministère de l'Agriculture et de la Pêche and Others* [2000] ECR I-1651. See, T. F. M. Etty and H. Somsen, 'ECJ: Case Report on Case C-236/01 *Monsanto Agricoltura Italia SpA and Others v. Presidenza Del Consiglio dei Ministeri and Others*' (2004) 13 *European Environmental Law Review* 1, 3–18, for a detailed commentary on the case.

[37] [2002] OJ L31/1.

[38] See S. Krapohl, 'Credible commitment in non-independent regulatory agencies: A comparative analysis of the European agencies for Pharmaceuticals and Foodstuffs' (2004) 10 *European Law Journal* 5, 518–38.

[39] N. 33 above.

consultation processes on the ultimate decision-making is unclear, transparency of the decision-making process at this stage makes GM regulation healthier.[40]

Moreover, the change of prescription for rejection of a Commission proposal in the comitology process from unanimity to a qualified majority seeks to amplify Member States concerns during harmonization processes. However, as already mentioned, the Novartis Bt-11 controversy highlights the continuing inadequacies, where the Commission is required to act positively, despite deep opposition that may not be strong enough for a qualified majority. Further, this process has also involved an increasing dependence on, and dominance over, a certain positivist conceptualization of science in the regulatory process.[41] This is ironic since GM regulation is plagued by significant differences in risk perceptions among Member States. These differences coupled with the existence of public alarm[42] underline the need for better incorporation of not only sociological understandings of risk but also the aforementioned critiques of use of science in regulation. Finally, the effectiveness of this harmonized system is moot, and reasons for the drastic fall in the applications for deliberate release under the new regime need deeper investigation.[43]

However, it is important to remember that European harmonization in the realm of release and use of GMOs does not merely pertain to the aspiration and movement towards a single unified market, but has an important environmental justification. Given the small territorial limits between various Member States, the risk of most releases in individual Member States in any case would be transboundary in essence, and thus there is an environmental issue at stake for other members of the Community in individual decisions of Member States.[44]

Notwithstanding this high level of harmonization, there exist a number of areas where Member States have room to channel the regulatory climate vis-à-vis the agricultural biotech industry. The first among these is the combination of internal market law and the safeguard clause, seen in all product-based harmonizing measures. The Deliberate Release Directive capacitates individual Member States to take action, subsequent to harmonization, with detailed 'scientific' grounds to demonstrate risk to human health and the environment, 'in the event

[40] A joint reading of Art. 6(6), GM Food and Feed Reg., n. 33 above and Reg. (EC) 178/2002, n. 37 above.

[41] See for a sensitive treatment of these complexities M. Lee, *EU Environmental Law: Challenges, Change and Decision-making* (Oxford: Hart Publishing, 2005), 239–48.

[42] See Tsioumani, n. 25 above.

[43] 'Commission Report on the Experience of Member States with GMOs placed on the Market under Directive 2001/18/EC', COM(2004)575; the document seeks to inform the public of the experience of Member States with GMOs placed on the markets since the start of the application of the Deliberate Release Directive, and covers a period until 30 Apr. 2004. See also L. Krämer, 'Summary of the Commission Report' (2006) 6 *Yearbook of European Environmental Law*, 484–85, for an insightful comment on the report.

[44] See A. A. Ostrovsky, 'Up Against a Wall: Europe's Options for Regulating Biotechnology through Regulatory Anarchy' (2007) 13 *European Law Journal* 1, 110–34, at 111, for the use of a similar idea.

of new or additional information' or 're-assessment of existing information on the basis of new or additional scientific knowldege'.[45] The safeguard clause under the GM Food and Feed Regulation provides for emergency measures of suspension and/or termination of commercial release in the event of a severe risk.[46] However, it is important to remember that these safeguards are expected to be provisional in nature, and a centralized review process of the emergency/other safeguard measures, that is tightly controlled by claims of scientific basis, ensues within the stipulated time.[47] Thus the safeguard clause, effectually, also harmonizes and centralizes long-term responses to even certain exceptional situations through the prism of science.

Secondly, environmental guarentee measures, under Article 95 EC, empower a Member State to undertake new measures in harmonized fields, based on availability of new scientific evidence related to the protection of the environment,[48] and/or grounds of public morality, public policy, or public security; protection of health and life of humans, animals or plants. However, there are considerable limitations to the operation of these principles, clearly spelt out in the judgment of the Court of First Instance (CFI) in *Austria* v. *Commission*.[49] The Commission has to approve these measures to avoid prejudice of the binding nature and uniform application of EC law, lest the establishment and functioning of the internal market be rendered ineffective by Member States retaining the unilateral right to apply derogatory national rules. Further, the *milieu* of this case duly testifies to the centrality of a 'science'-based assessment on the applicability of Article 95(4) EC, since the Member State is expected to demonstrate that the notified measure was justified in the light of new scientific evidence concerning protection of the environment, and also was a problem specific to the Member State.[50]

Thirdly, measures to ensure coexistence between GM, conventional, and organic crops are theoretically autonomous at present.[51] The Commission's recommendation sets out a subsidiarity based strategy to regulate coexistence at the national level.[52] Member States are empowered to introduce appropriate measures

[45] Art. 23, Deliberate Release Dir., n. 10 above.

[46] Art 34. Food and Feed Reg., n. 33 above.

[47] Arts. 23(2) and 30(2), Deliberate Release Dir., n. 10 above.

[48] Upon which the procedure established under Art. 95(6), (7), (8), and (9) EC shall be applicable.

[49] Judgment of the Court of First Instance (Fourth Chamber), 5 Oct. 2005 in Joined Cases T-366/03 and T-235/04 *Austria* v. *Commission* [2005] ECR II-4005, at para. 44 of the judgment in particular. This is analogous with procedure under Art. 100a(4) EC. See Case C-41/93 *France* v. *Commission* [1994] ECR I-1829, at paras. 29–30.

[50] See Case T-13/99 *Pfizer Animal Health SA* v. *Council* [2002] ECR II-3305 and Case T-70/99 *Alpharma Inc.* v. *Council* [2002] ECR II-3495.

[51] See T. F. M. Etty, 'Substantive European Community Law: Biotechnology' (2005) 5 *Yearbook of European Environmental Law*, 293–5 as a good starting point.

[52] Commission Rec. 2003/556/EC on 'Guidelines for the Development of National Strategies and Best Practices to Ensure the Coexistence of Genetically Modified Crops with Conventional and Organic Farming' [2003] OJ L189/36.

to avoid unintended presence of GMOs in other products.[53] However, the concerns of environmental hazards and risk due to genetic contamination and breach of coexistence norms is sought to be negated by the Commission guideline that coexistence measures are to be merely economic in nature.[54]

Finally, the crucial aspect of an appropriate liability regime for potential GMO damage is largely left to Member State regulation. Civil liability regimes are doubly important due to the widespread public concern about, what the Commission has termed as, negative effects of GMOs on 'our health' and the environment. The Commission White Paper recommended a Framework Directive providing for strict liability for damage caused by EC regulated dangerous activities, with defences, covering both traditional and environmental damage, and fault-based liability for damage to biodiversity caused by non-dangerous activities as the most appropriate option.[55] Importantly, the GM Food and Feed Regulation clarifies for the sake of abundant caution, that 'the granting of authorization shall not lessen the general civil and criminal liability' of any food/feed operator in respect of the respective food/feed concerned.[56] However, Directive 2004/35/EC on Environmental Liability with regard to the Prevention and Remedying of Environmental Damage (Environmental Liability Directive)[57] has left the issue of damage caused by modern biotechnology out of its purview, except for the impact on Community designated nature conservation sites or protected species.[58] Although there is a slim chance that the Commission would include damage caused by GMOs in the application of the Directive, through administrative provisions in 2014,[59] as of now civil and criminal liability is within the purview of Member State regulation.

Liability is an indirect but significant policy tool to encourage/discourage biotech investment. Presently, Member States can put in place strict liability regimes, and even criminal liability mechanisms, commensurate to national levels of risk perception. For instance, classification of biotech activities as dangerous or non-dangerous would be an important feature that is left to Member States. Further, moves towards criminal liability regimes, falling outside the

[53] Art. 26a, Deliberate Release Dir., n. 10 above inserted by Art. 43, Food and Feed Reg., n. 33 above. A significant number of Member States including Denmark, Germany, and the UK are putting in place national coexistence regimes.

[54] See Etty, n. 51, above.

[55] 'Commission White Paper on Environmental Liability', COM(2000)66. See G. Betlem and E. H. P. Brans, 'The future role of civil liability for environmental damage in the EU' (2002) 2 *Yearbook of European Environmental Law*, 183–222, for a useful discussion on the White Paper.

[56] See Arts. 7(7) and 19(7). See, for an early articulation of concerns about liability arising from contamination, R. Burrell and M. Lee, 'Liability for the Escape of GM seeds: Pursuing the Victim?'(2002) 65 *Modern Law Review* 4, 517–37.

[57] [2004] OJ L143/56.

[58] See further T. F. M. Etty, 'Substantive European Community Law: Biotechnology' (2006) 6 *Yearbook of European Environmental Law*, 252–3.

[59] Arts. 18(2) and 3(b), Environmental Liability Dir., n. 57 above.

traditional harmonization focus of the EU,[60] can potentially put biotech industry investment into a deep freeze in specific Member States.

Thus, one can see that despite high levels of harmonization of GMO regulation in the EU system of multi-level governance, Member States have limited opportunities to influence risk assessment processes. Some of these opportunities are, firstly, going through the enumerated mandatory/discretionary consultation mechanisms of national competent bodies, notwithstanding processes of centralization through the institution of EFSA. Further, especially in the post-enlargement context, there is a marginal increase in individual Member State influence in risk management processes in the new process of comitology, following which a qualified majority suffices for rejection of a Commission proposal. Safeguard clauses and environmental guarantee provisions, in paper, offer very limited opportunities for Member State deviation, since these measures need to be legitimated by new scientific evidence/specificities of any given Member State, and also have to be *post facto* accepted by the Commission. Coexistence measures, though tempered by labelling norms and Commission recommendations, provide more space for autonomous Member State action. However, it is in the realm of liability regimes, both civil and criminal, that maximum room for independent Member State action currently exists. It would be interesting to watch how the compatibility of such spaces with the principle of non-discrimination in the WTO framework would be judicially construed.

Notwithstanding these limited subsidiary spaces that can influence specific Member State policies, the role of positivist science continues to dominate risk assessment, and to a lesser extent risk management processes, for a variety of reasons.[61] An extremely important feature of the authorization related to environmental release and market placing is the bifurcation of release decisions into the two stages of risk assessment and risk management. In this two stage procedure, risk assessment exercises are conceived of as *scientific* determinations of the relationship between causes and effects of environmental harm that is to be undertaken at the beginning of the regulatory process. Risk assessment usually

[60] But see the Convention of the Council of Europe on the Protection of the Environment through Criminal Law (1998) 38 *International Legal Materials* 2, at 259. Importantly, the Convention takes into account the difference in legal cultures, wherein some States embrace the basic principle that corporations cannot commit criminal offences. See also, F. Comte, 'European Environmental Criminal Law—Recent developments' (2005) 4 *Yearbook of European Environmental Law*, 209–45.

[61] Christoforou, for instance, while examining the precautionary principle in the context of its effect of democratizing expertise, asserts that 'science has always been the basis of risk regulation in the EC' so as to 'establish the internal market and to resist national protection', and re-emphasizes the point that even disparate national standards to effectuate protection of health and the environment can be based only on new scientific evidence' T. Christoforou, 'The Precautionary Principle and democratising expertise: A European legal perspective' (2003) 30 *Science and Public Policy* 3, 205–11.

involves processes of hazard identification, hazard characterization,[62] exposure assessment, and finally risk characterization.[63]

Risk management is the supposed political stage of the regulatory phase where various factors including the results of the risk assessment, potentially scientific information about costs, benefits, and causal consequences of management choices and value judgements, like acceptable level of risk in a society, the identification of the principle upon which this selected level of risk is adhered to, and so on, are taken into consideration by the regulators. In the artificial, albeit often useful, division of risk assessment and risk management, the question as to what role science ought to play is heavily contested.[64] The bifurcation rightly assumes that technical competence including *scientific* competence is an important factor in the regulatory process. However, the assumption that scientific questions can be isolated and addressed in an objective manner right at the beginning of the regulatory process, upon which political choices and decisions can be later made is based upon a peculiar reading of the connection between law and science. This assumption is oblivious to the necessary inferences, choices, and assumptions of scientific identification of hazards and assessment of risks that are to be made at the first stage. The uncertainties which are present in most environmental assessments make quantifying risks impossible without making value laden simplifying assumptions.[65] Often called science-policy, it is wrong to assume that these crucial aspects can be democratically controlled at the latter stage of risk management.[66]

This institutional separation seeks to identify and divide regulation in such a manner as to make democratic control more pronounced. However, to take the

[62] Evaluation of quantitative aspects of the causal relationship between the identified hazard and incidence/severity of adverse effects to the environment. In frames that are relatively broader this evaluation of causal relationship could also be qualitative.

[63] An estimation of the total risk of adverse effects on the environment.

[64] See for a detailed critique of the risk assessment/risk management bifurcation D. G. Mayo and R. D. Hollander (eds.) *Acceptable Evidence: Science and Values in Risk Assessment* (Oxford: Oxford University Press, 1991) and also E. Silbergeld, 'The Uses and Abuses of Scientific Uncertainty in Risk Assessment' (1986) 2 *Natural Resources and Environment* 2, 17–20.

[65] See for an elaboration of this point J. P. Dwyer, 'Limits of Environmental Risk Assessment' (1990) 116 *Journal of Energy Engineering*, 231–9. The authors of one of the three amicus briefs in the *EC-Biotech* case take the view, inter alia for the same point, that risk assessment involving public deliberation is particularly appropriate in GM regulation. Page 15 of the amicus brief submitted on 1 June 2004 by the Center for International Environmental Law, Friends of the Earth—United States, Defenders of Wildlife, Institute of Agriculture and Trade Policy and the Organic Consumer Association.

[66] For instance, report of the National Research Council of the US Federal Government, examining the environmental and health and safety regulation of the 1980s had an interesting rejection of calls for institutional separation of risk assessment and risk management. Often called the *Red Book* the report has remained an influential guide in US regulatory circles. It, however, emphasized the importance of keeping the two functions of assessment and management of risk analytically separate. An important contribution of the report was the recognition of science policy—the role and judgment of regulators—in bridging the gaps in scientific understanding. See R. Merril, 'Foreword' (2003) 66 *Law and Contemporary Problems* 4, 1–5, at 2.

positivist assumption that technical competence is devoid of policy issues seriously, and further give it a certain primacy by putting it in a prior phase in a *quasi* determinative manner is erroneous. The assumptions and choices made become a preserve of the scientific community, which is not always desirable. For instance, in the case of an inquiry into a nuclear processing plant, whether to treat the plant in isolation or whether key issues like the safe transporation and storage of waste, and the issues of the nuclear industry as a whole should be included in the risk assessment becomes key to the ultimate findings of the assessment exercise.[67] Moreover, placing the scientific/technical assessment exercise in such a vantage position right at the beginning of the regulatory process ensures that the construction and definition of risk is hugely determined by it in a manner which borders on technocratic determinism. It would then appear that divisive voting at the political stage would naturally flow from this technocratic exercise. Thus, the current manner in which bifurcation is carried out negates democratic control over the crucial phase of framing, and later in proper articulation and assessment of risk perceptions.

To a certain extent, in the case of GMOs, legislative injunctions of precautionary policy could have had an impact on how such assumptions are made and frames chosen. However, as it stands today, precaution is situated at the risk management stage.[68] As noted earlier, legal systems have been encountering consistent problems with the stage and manner of ascertaining scientific uncertainty, a legal process that is intricately related to the frames chosen. Even for these two reasons, i.e. that precaution ought to be equally employed in the risk assessment stage, as well as the basic principle that it might not be desirable or prudent for science to exclusively decide scientific uncertainty,[69] the bifurcation of risk regulation in the current manner has undesirable effects on regulation of GM releases into the environment.

This assertion is further supported by the record of deeply divided political voting at the risk management stage.[70] It shows that framing needs to take place in a way so as to make assessment of risk more inclusive of various concerns that emanate from certain Member States. There exists a serious problem when scientific establishments repeatedly come up with positive risk assessments, which are

[67] B. Wynne, 'Rationality and Ritual: The Windscale inquiry and nuclear decisions in Britain', *British Society for the History of Science* (Chalfont St. Giles: The British Society for the History of Science, 1982), 278, see also L. Levidow, S. Carr, D. Wield and R. von Schomberg, 'European Biotechnology Regulation: Framing the Risk Assessment of a Herbicide-tolerant Crop' (1997) 22 *Science, Technology & Human Values* 4, 472–505.

[68] 'Communication from the Commission on the precautionary principle', COM(2000)1, at para. 5.1.1.

[69] For the various reasons enumerated in the second section.

[70] Apart from the deeply divided voting vis-à-vis releases this division is also visible in other areas. For instance, the bloc voting in the Environmental Council with respect to the Commission proposal to lift Austria's safeguard measure ban of two GM maize varieties (MON810 and T25) repeatedly four times in June 2005, Dec. 2006, Feb. 2007, and Oct. 2007.

then subsequently accompanied by deep divisions at the risk management phase. This leads to a stubborn scenario where risk assessment is framed and undertaken in a fairly technical manner, devoid of wider concerns, which consequently are brought to the fore in a divisive manner at the voting stage. One can envisage two ways of bridging this gap of scientific and technical ascertainment of risks, and wider concerns. It could be undertaken either through institutional incorporation of other legitimate factors at the risk management stage, or alternatively through wider framing at the risk assessment stage itself. Both options recognize the limitations of a *purely* scientific assessment and the problems with it. In the latter option there is a spectrum of options available to make framing wider, including framing of risks and science policy constructions being made into a multidisciplinary technical exercise, where multi-level consultations are had before the assesment, to more fundamental interventions like moving towards deliberative public participation at this stage. Such a deliberative process can potentially occur where the technical and the *scientific* coalesce with wider public participation.

Either of these options, or a combination of both, could be a bridgehead for the current impasse in EU GMO regulation. Political voting at the management stage will surely continue to be driven by home constituency concerns. But precisely by taking such concerns into consideration during the framing of risk assessments, moves towards consensus could become viable. What makes such fine-tuning of risk assessment and management mechanisms difficult are concerns that these may be judicially construed as contradictory to requirements of global economic integration within the WTO framework. For instance, there exists deep ambivalence in the manner in which the precautionary principle is sought to be employed in the Community regulatory regime pertaining to GMOs. As already mentioned, the precautionary principle itself is an acknowledgement of the inadequacy of science in at least certain situations of scientific uncertainty.[71] However, the Commission requires that the identification and analysis of scientific data relating to risk be prior to the invocation of the precautionary principle; and specifically that this preliminary evaluation of the existence and degree of uncertainty has to be scientific.[72] This ambivalence is at least partly because of the exigencies of the WTO framework,[73] which requires a science-based regulatory framework.[74] Hence, it is important to understand the contours of this WTO framework to speculate on the possibilities and manners of employing legitimate factors other than *science* within the regulatory matrix. Further, this is important to understand how science itself can be employed appropriately within the regulatory matrix.

[71] N. 68 above, at para. 5.

[72] Ibid., at paras. 6.1 and 5.1.1.

[73] See Forsman, n. 2 above, at 591 for a similar observation. She also notes the similarity with the approach of *Codex Alimentarius* Commission in this aspect.

[74] See Section IV below for an elaboration.

IV. WTO Regime and Subsisting Spaces for Extra Science Reasons

Whether science or other sources of 'reason' can or should be the central basis for national and regional regulation will intellectually continue to be an open question, especially in the cases of regulation of health and the environmental impacts of new technologies. Wider framing of risk assessment can be a possible bridgehead, to take on board fundamental problems of science as evidence; the movement away from such a pure 'science' based reasoning in the new European GM release regime is a recognition of these concerns. However, in reality the hold of positivist science on framing and determining regulatory frameworks is fairly strong—arguably leading to the current impasse. Moreover, the presence of a global free trade regime, basing itself on the principle of non-discrimination in a specific manner, would appear to create hurdles for *experiments* with explicit extra-science reasoning in national regulation. This section seeks to understand these aspects better, and make certain specific speculations about the permissible ambits of the global trade framework.

The obligations of members appear in GATT as well as in the two consequent WTO side agreements viz., the TBT Agreement and the SPS Agreement. The framework of non-discrimination sought to be set up by GATT allows barriers that are 'neccessary to protect human, animal or plant life or health, that are justifiable and non-arbitrary'.[75] The two latter agreements arose out of the concern that measures that appear to be made for the purpose of protection of human health, safety, and environment were, in reality, disguised protectionist measures, taken in the name of the protection of the environment etc., and hence there is a neccessity to create a regime to deal with this issue.[76]

The Dispute Settlement Body of the WTO, set up by the Dispute Settlement Understanding,[77] is the arbiter of the legality of the fine balance between sovereign rights of members to take measures to protect human and animal health as well as other technical matters in their respective jurisdictions, and their compliance

[75] Prior to the Uruguay Round, the 1979 TBT agreement had limited effects, wherein as long as a 'health regulation was necessary and was not a means of arbitrary or unjustifiable discrimination or pose a disguised restriction on international trade' such a measure was legitimate. Art. XX ,1979 TBT agreement was extended during the Uruguay Round, and the current SPS stipulations for WTO members regarding permissible protection of health concerns of human, animal, and plant health put in place. See (1979) 18 *International Legal Materials* 4, 1079–111. This agreement was replaced by the TBT Agreement of 1994 in the General Agreement on Trade and Tariffs, (1994) 33 *International Legal Materials* 5, 1140–97.

[76] See G. Marceau and J. Trachtman, 'The technical barriers to trade agreement, the sanitary and phytosanitary measures agreement, and the general agreement on tariffs and trade' (2002) 36 *Journal of World Trade* 5, 811–81.

[77] See Uruguay Round Understanding on Rules and Procedure Governing the Settlement of Disputes (1994) 33 *International Legal Materials* 1226, Arts. 1.1, 23, App. 1; Art. 4.3, WTO agreement and Art. 11.1, SPS Agreement.

with SPS and TBT provisions in particular reference to arbitrary discriminatory measures that restrict global free trade.

The current SPS regime of the WTO[78] sets forth rights and obligations of members with respect to any measure taken by a member to protect the health or life of humans, animals, or plants that may, directly or indirectly, affect international trade.[79] The letter and scheme of the SPS Agreement has science, *scientific* principles, process, and evidence as the yardstick for such a judicial review to ascertain the legality of national regulatory measures.[80] The agreement also embodies an ideal to promote global harmonization of these regulatory measures, through establishment of scientific standards, guidelines, and recommendations by certain international institutions.[81]

The TBT Agreement is similar in its scheme to achieve a balance between regulatory measures and 'protectionist' discrimination in the realm of technical regulations; albeit with far less emphasis on scientific justification.[82] The balancing between national regulatory autonomy and checks against protectionism is configured in a different manner in the TBT Agreement, whereby technical regulations that are restrictive of trade are permitted as long as it is necessary to fulfil a legitimate objective such as protection of human health or safety, animal and plant life, or health or protection of the environment.[83] It thus contrasts itself with the SPS framework through the absence of a formal and strict requirement of risk assessment and a scientific basis.

[78] The Agreement on the Application of Sanitary and Phytosanitary Measures, 15 Apr. 1994, Annex 1A-4 to Final Act Embodying the results of the Uruguay Round of the Multi-lateral trade negotiations.

[79] SPS Agreement, preamble, Art. 1.1, Annex A.1.

[80] The SPS Agreement requires that any sanitary measure is based on scientific 'principles', is not maintained without sufficient scientific evidence, and that a risk assessment procedure is undertaken that took into account the existing available information on toxicity and exposure. See Arts. 2.2, 3, and 5. Art. 5 provides for situations of insufficiency in scientific evidence, where the members can choose to adopt provisional measures on the basis of available pertinent information. However, members in the wake of such provisional measures are enjoined to conduct a new risk assessment to review its provisional measures within a reasonable 'period of time'. Such a precautionary provision is generally considered to be weaker than the principle of precaution found in international environmental law. See Applegate, n. 27 above, 51–5. See also Walker, n. 14 above, 253–4. The interpretation of the Panel in *Japan—Measures Affecting the Importation of Apples (Japan Apples),* WTO Doc WT/DS245/AB/R, AB-2003–4 (2003) (Report of the Appellate Body), that this provision is primarily intended to deal with new risks where little or no reliable evidence is available on the subject matter, and that the insufficiency condition is not fulfilled if 'the body of available scientific evidence does not allow, in quantitative or qualitative terms, the performance of an adequate assessment of risks as required under Art. 5.1, SPS para. 179', is important in this context.

[81] Preamble, Art. 3, Annex A.3. See Walker, n. 14 above, 272–7 for an elaboration of this point.

[82] The TBT Agreement, however, focuses less on scientific justification than the SPS Agreement. See A. Thomison, 'A new and controversial mandate for the SPS Agreement: The WTO Panel's Interim report in the E.C.-Biotech Dispute' (2007) 32 *Columbia Journal of Environmental Law* 2, 287–307, 291–2.

[83] Art. 2.2, TBT Agreement. Here, necessity is evaluated in judicial review as a measure which is least restrictive of trade to achieve the chosen objective. See Marceau and Trachtman, n. 76 above, 825.

A Dispute Resolution panel is not expected to engage in a *de novo* assessment of the matter, but exigencies of judicial review usually go beyond the matter of veracity of formal procedures and the evalution of the existence of manifest error. The panel often examines questions as to whether the studies or reports cited by a member amount to a 'risk assessment' for the purposes of the SPS Agreement, whether 'available scientific evidence' is taken into account during the course of the assessment, and whether the measures are supported by sufficient scientific evidence.[84] Various commentators have correctly pointed out that the institutional and other kinds of rigours vis-à-vis environmental and health regimes the world over will be tightened due to the widening ambit of the SPS Agreement.[85] Though there were a limited number of decisions[86] which preceded the *EC-Biotech* dispute, it is in this decision that the expansion of SPS architecture into national regulatory geographies, over and above the other trade principles, clearly manifests itself.[87] Such expansion in the *EC-Biotech* dispute, elaborated later, makes environmental regulations with wider framing potentially prone to attacks at the WTO level.

Earlier, speculative anticipation of the *EC-Biotech* decision provided a wide plethora of literature, which also brought more attention to the putative relationships between the SPS and other trade regimes inter se, as well as between trade regimes and protection of the environment and health.[88] The reshaping of

[84] For an examination of whether the requirement of risk assessment is procedural or substantive under the SPS process, with particular reference to *EC Hormones*, see J. Peel, 'Risk regulation under the WTO SPS Agreement: Science as an International Normative Yardstick?', Jean Monnet Working Paper 02/04, published on the Internet at: http://www.jeanmonnetprogram.org/papers/04.

[85] See, for instance, C. Joerges and J. Neyer, 'Politics, Risk Management, World Trade Organization Governance and the Limits of Legalisation' (2003) 30 *Science and Public Policy* 3, 219–25, and J. Scott, 'On Kith and Kine (and Crustaceans): Trade and Environment in the EU and WTO', in J. H. H. Weiler (ed.), *The EU, the WTO, and the NAFTA: Towards a common law of International Trade?* (Oxford: Oxford University Press, 2000), 125–43.

[86] The four relevant decisions previous to the *EC-Biotech* decision are *Beef Hormones,* WTO Doc. WT/DS26/AB/R, WT/DS48/AB/R, AB-1997–4 (1998); *Australia–Measure Affecting Importation of Salmon,* WTO Doc. WT/ DS18/ AB/ R, AB-1998–5 (1998) (Report of the Appellate Body); *Japan–Measures Affecting Agricultural Products,* WTO Doc. WT/DS76/AB/R, AB-1998–8 (1999) (Report of the Appellate Body); and *Japan–Measures Affecting the Importation of Apples,* WTO Doc. WT/DS245/AB/R, AB-2003–4 (2003) (Report of the Appellate Body). All the decisions appear to have involved various degrees of substantial examination of the regulatory measures. See J. Pauwelyn, 'The WTO Agreement on Sanitary and Phytosanitary (S.P.S.) measures as applied in the First three S.P.S. Disputes EC–Hormones, Australia–Salmon and Japan Apples' (1999) 2 *Journal of International Economic Law* 4, 641–65, at 644.

[87] See for an apt elaboration of this point J. Peel, 'A GMO by any other name... Might be an SPS Risk!: Implications of Expanding the Scope of the WTO Sanitary and Phytosanitary measures Agreement' (2007) 17 *The European Journal of International Law* 5, 1009–31. Also see Thomison, n. 82 above, 307, 'with its demanding requirements for SPS measures and now a broadened mandate, the SPS agreement appears increasingly likely to surface on the WTO scene as the premier instrument for attacking disputed health and environmental protection measures in the global trade arena'.

[88] See, for instance, G. Winham, 'International Regime Conflict in Trade and Environment: The Bio-safety Protocol and the WTO' (2003) 2 *World Trade Review* 2, 131–55, J. Scott, 'European Regulation of GMOs and the WTO' (2003) 9 *Columbia Journal of European Law* 2, 213–40, G. Isaac and W. Kerr, 'Genetically Modified Organisms and Trade Rules: Identifying Important Challenges

national regulatory architecture around science as the sole legimitizing factor was predicted even before the institution of the *EC-Biotech* case though.[89] However it would appear, despite initial alarmist commentary on the Panels findings, it has been correctly noted as 'one which will not alter the system or framework within which the EU takes decisions on GMOs'[90].

Notwithstanding the caution the panel in *EC-Biotech* case appeared to employ by stressing that it has not determined 'whether biotech products in general are safe or not', the framing of the ambit of SPS framework in such an expanded way has far reaching and potentially debilitating effects on regulation of environmental risks.[91] What is of particular importance is the manner in which the Panel sought to read the trade rules under the WTO framework in isolation of other rules of international law, in particular the precautionary principle as expressed in the Convention on Biological Diversity (CBD)[92] and the Cartagena Protocol on Biosafety, 2000.[93] After taking notice of the Appellate Body ruling in the US-Shrimp dispute that 'WTO law cannot be read in clinical isolation from public international law', it held that such a drawing from other rules of international law was not an obligation but was merely a discretionary aid to inform and interpret SPS provisions.[94]

for the WTO (2003) 26 *World Economy* 1, 29–42, R. A. Neff, 'The Cartagena Protocol and the WTO: Will the EU Biotech products case leave room for the Protocol' (2005) 16 *Fordham Environmental Law Review* 2, 261–88, M. Bridgers, 'Genetically Modified Organisms and the Precautionary Principle: How the GMO Dispute before the World Trade Organization could decide the fate of international GMO Regulation', 22 (2004) *Temple Environmental Law and Technology Journal* 2, 171–93, and G. Goh, 'GM Food labelling and the WTO Agreements' (2004) 13 *RECIEL* 3, 306–19.

[89] See, for instance, D. Victor, 'The Sanitary and Phytosanitary Agreement of the World Trade Organization: An assessment after five years' (2000) 32 *New York University Journal of International Law and Politics* 4, 865–938.

[90] See, for an excellent treatment of this point, and also for a very good commentary on the decision, Prévost, n. 4 above. The complainants in any case shied away from substantially challenging the EC GMO regulatory regime per se, but concentrated on the delays which the regime generated. Canada even argued that the EC would not have erred in any manner if it had adhered to its own assessment and approval procedure. I am of course not dealing with all the important issues emanating from the report—for instance the ambit and trigger of Art. 5.7, and its connection to the safeguard measures—that the insufficiency of scientific evidence rather than the provisional nature of the measures can trigger Art. 5.7.

[91] Peele, n. 87 above, identifies the logic used by the Panel to expand the ambit of SPS Agreement beyond the conventional understanding of the realm of the SPS Agreement into the realm of not only the TBT Agreement, but also of multi-lateral environmental agreements. She convincingly argues how the textualist reading of the SPS provisions is not only patently incorrect, but also that it has undesirable implications for the development of national and international environmental regulatory regimes. For an argument regarding the lack of institutional capacity of a WTO process to consider non-market values in general, and specifically how *EC-Biotech* fails to consider cultural factors see L. Zurek, 'The European Communities Biotech Dispute: How the WTO fails to consider cultural factors in the GM food debate' (2006/7) 42 *Texas International Law Journal* 2, 345–68.

[92] Rio de Janeiro (Brazil), 5 June 1992 (entered into force 29 Dec. 1993), (1992) 31 *International Legal Materials* 818.

[93] Montreal, 29 Jan. 2000 (entered into force 11 Sept. 2003), (2000) 39 *International Legal Materials* 5, 1027.

[94] *EC-Biotech* Products Report, n. 4 above, para. 7.94.

Interestingly, while the panel acknowledged that if the precautionary principle has become *jus cogens* or a general principle of international law it must be taken into account in the interpretation,[95] it felt that it was unneccessary to give a finding on the legal status of the principle itself.[96] However, the second reasoning used to exclude precautionary approaches—that such an agreement can only be considered as relevant if all the WTO members have signed and ratified the specific environmental agreement, poses greater concerns due to its debilitating effects on the application of multilateral environmental agreements.[97] The United Nations International Law Comission has expressedly criticized this stand of the Panel, and has sought to address this important issue of fragmentation of international law.[98] Thus it would appear that the science-based requirements that an SPS framework textually demands is sought to be judicially extended not only to other trade realms like the TBT Agreement, but also to the environmental realm.

The Appellate Body in *Beef Hormones* appears to entertain possibilities of legality of concerns that are outside the strict sense of science considerations in risk assessment. It held that 'not only risk ascertainable in a science laboratory operating under strictly controlled conditions, but also risk in human socieities as they usually exist, in other words, the actual potential for adverse effects on human health in the real world where people live and work and die... to bear in mind that responsible, representative governments commonly act from perspectives of prudence and precaution where risks of irreversible e.g., life terminating, damage to human health are concerned'.[99] Further, the panel attempted to show an awareness of the factor of uncertainty in such processes by accepting that minority or divergent scientific opinion could legitimate SPS measures.[100] The Appellate Body also merely required a rational relationship between the SPS

[95] *Qua* Art. 31.3(c) of the Vienna Convention on the Law of Treaties, (1969) 8 *International Legal Materials* 4, 679–735.

[96] *EC-Biotech* Products Report, n.4 above, para. 7.89. This was putatively in line with the Appellate Body's finding in *EC Hormones*, that the status of the precautionary principle is an ongoing debate, despite its incorporation in a number of international treaties, and it would be imprudent for it to take a position on the same. See *EC Hormones* report, n. 86 above.

[97] See Prévost, n. 4 above, at 86–93.

[98] International Law Commission, 58th Session, *Fragmentation of International Law: Difficulties Arising from the Diversification and Expansion of International Law,* Report of the Study Group of the International Law Commission, A/CN.4/L.682, 13 Apr. 2006. 'Bearing in mind the unlikeliness of a precise congruence in the membership of most important multilateral conventions, it would become unlikely that any use of conventional international law could be made in the interpretation of such conventions. This would have the ironic effect that the more the membership of a multilateral treaty such as the WTO covered agreements expanded, the more those treaties would be cut off from the rest of international law. In practice, the result would be the isolation of multilateral agreements as "islands" permitting no references inter se in their application', para. 471.

[99] *EC Hormones*, Panel Report, n. 86 above, para. 187.

[100] Ibid., para. 194. However, despite this the Appellate Body found fault with studies relied on by the defendants because 'they dealt only with the general association between exposure to increased hormone levels and the development of cancer, rather than the specific situation of cancer risk posed by consuming hormone residues in beef'.

measure and the risk assessment, which would appear to suggest that it is only a procedural obligation. However, these remarks are contrary to the reality of the final findings of the Appellate Body, which finds fault with the specific minority opinion for the perceived lack of specificity, the mere suggestivity, and the lack of direct relationship to the risk.[101] Thus it would appear that there is little flexibility in the judicial approach towards members' discretion to deviate from a scientific assessment of risk, through the incorporation of other legitimate factors in the risk management stage.

Given this scenario of increasing ambit of science based SPS framework, and the aforementioned textualism in requiring a strict *scientific* assessment processes, what is a more appropriate manner of incorporating extra-science legitimate factors as well as responding to criticisms of use of science? There are legitimate critiques, identified in the previous two sections, that the existing framework can systemically exclude other legitimate factors. Inclusion of such factors could be through its identification and incorporation over and above the current bifurcated regulation. It could also be undertaken, as it is done now, at the risk management stage; the systemic deficiencies of which we have already examined. The judicial acceptability of possible incorporation of science critiques, as well as extra-science factors through these two routes, as we have seen, is in serious doubt. Realistically, I assert, that to attempt broader framing of risk assessment through deliberative public participation in science policy would be least likely to invite judicial invalidation from the WTO. Such an approach has various positives, dealt with in the next section. Notwithstanding the Herculean nature of operationalizing such a suggestion, given its political and normative superiority,[102] the possibility of public participation transforming narrow risk assessment exercises into broader frames at the stage of framing of risks, stands far less chance of outright WTO censure.

V. A Case for Deliberative Public Participation in Framing of Risk Assessment

If scientists think lawyers can present one sided cases, they may wish to rediscover themselves . . . the same can be said of the members of the public.[103]

[101] Scott's comment that the Appellate Body's bite was more muted than its bark is apposite, especially since there was a finding that the specific measure could not have been based on a risk assessment, n. 85 above, at 139.

[102] Especially since this can be constructed as trade-offs which 'are made explicitly, transparently and in a manner consistent with conception of democratic rationality' R. Howse, 'Democracy, Science and Free trade: Risk Regulation on Trial at the World Trade Organization' (2000) 98 *Michigan Law Review* 7, 2329–57, at 2337.

[103] R. Nader, 'Obligation of Scientists to Respond to Society's Needs', in W. A. Thomas (ed.) *Scientists in the Legal System: tolerated meddlers or essential contributors?* (Ann Arbor: Michigan, 1974).

The case for national regulatory autonomy and the important value of legal pluralism is underpinned by the legitimate need to respond to local conceptions of risks, health, and the environment. Such a need demands that risk assessment is open, transparent, participative, and inter-disciplinary; a process that is not purely based on the 'opinion' of scientific experts, so that a range of value judgements can inform and shape assessment of risk. This is important not only because all health, environmental, and other policy goals are seldom shared by all countries, but also because within each state there are various groups which might have legitimate divergences of perceptions regarding risk and harm. If respecting regulatory diversity is an acceptable value for the WTO mechanism, accepting deliberative public participation towards framing risk assessment procedures might be a way out of the cul-de-sac. It is clear that value judgements influence science policy at the stage of risk assessment, in particular data selection and assessment methods, including hazard identification and characterization, leading to differential risk identification, estimation, and evaluation. This can in turn lead to substantial divergence in regulatory approaches, for instance due to considerable variance of local ecological neccessities and approaches.

The spirit of the Aarhus Convention[104] requites a radical rethinking of regulatory processes towards open and democratic public participation; a spirit that ought not be shelved in an insignificant corner through platitudinal provisions of its implementing Directive and Regulations.[105] An effective way to make the conceptualization of risk more democratic and less positivist is to make the risk assessment stage more participatory. A deep involvement of the public in the risk assessment stage not only makes assessment more open and accessible, but also makes controversial decisions like GM regulation help gain more confidence and legitimacy with that public.[106] Such an approach provides a limited but important way forward to realize the ideals of deliberation and real democratic engagement in EC regulation. This is especially so in the face of stubbornly continuing but legitimate concerns of democratic deficit[107] within European governance,

[104] The Convention on Access to Information, Public Participation in Decision-Making, and Access to Justice in Environmental Matters, 1998 (1999) 38 *International Legal Materials* 3, 517. See also Dir. 2003/04/EC on Public Access to Environmental Information [2003] OJ L41/26 and Reg. 1049/2001/EC Regarding Public Access to European Parliament, Council and Commission Documents, [2001] OJ L145/43.

[105] See the Sixth Environmental Action Programme Environment 2010: 'Our Future, Our Choice', Proposal for a Decision of the European Parliament and of the Council Laying down the Community Environmental Action Programme 2001–2010 (Action Programme Proposal), COM(2001)31.

[106] Though deliberation and public participation are usually associated with legitimacy, assertions of deliberation enhancing the quality of problem solving on questions of environmental risk also exist. See J. Steele, 'Participation and Deliberation in Environmental Law: Exploring a Problem-Solving Approach' (2001) 21 *Oxford Journal of Legal Studies* 3, 415–42. For an excellent case study involving constructive use of precaution in risk assessment, see F. M. Fleurke, 'Innovation through Precaution: the Case of the Dutch Wadden Sea', also published in this volume.

[107] C. Lord, 'Assessing Democracy in a Contested Polity' (2001) 39 *Journal of Common Market Studies* 4, 641–61, at 646.

which neither the Maastrict Treaty nor the Aarhus Convention process could fructify, despite their generation of high hopes.[108]

A turn for proceduralization of participation was sought as an answer to concerns of democratic deficit in the Aarhus Convention,[109] the Directive implementing the Aarhus Convention[110] and the European Governance White Paper[111]. It underlined the desirability of 'opening up policy making process' in European policy-making and regulation. This has considerable potential to develop flesh and sinew, in a specific sector, through this endeavour of public participation in risk assessment.

The intricate complexities in GM regulation[112] makes the framing of risk assessment uni-dimensional if it is singularly left to scientific institutions. Especially since all necessary knowledge cannot possibly be located in a single centralized institution or discipline, genuine public participation spurs wider and more appopropriate framing. This is particularly important as scientific organizations and risk assessment procesess per se would appear to have very little direct or indirect democratic control. What constitutes scientific uncertainty is a question which is not only vexed in practice but also to a large extent in principle, and public participation is essential in risk assessment to address this in a more appropriate and acceptable manner.

How can precaution be effectively employed at the later stage of risk management, if political managers are not informed about the proper extent and nature of uncertainty? In other words, can the precautionary principle merely reside in its application on the risk management stage? Surely, it is relevant in the risk management stage to ascertain and fix the level of risk which is politically acceptable.[113] But this is only part of the picture. For an effective appreciation of variegated pictures of risk, precaution needs to be employed at the risk assessment stage itself. This is also important for a better ascertainment of scientific uncertainty. In such a scenario, prudence suggests that the precautionary

[108] See G. de Bùrca, 'The quest for legitimacy in EU' (1996) 59 *Modern Law Review* 3, 349–76 and J. H. H. Weiler, *The Constitution of Europe* (Cambridge: Cambridge University, 1999), 323–55. See further, M. Lee, 'Public Participation in EC Environmental Law' (2004) 3 *Yearbook of European Environmental Law*, 193–226 for an excellent critique of the confusing and competing notions of participation that occur in the Aarhus Convention.

[109] The Convention also, in its recitals, specifically recognizes the concern of the public about the deliberate release of genetically modified organisms into the environment and the need for increased transparency and greater public participation in decision-making in this field.

[110] Dir. 2003/04/EC, n. 104 above.

[111] European Commission, *A White Paper on European Governance White paper*, COM(2001)428. See also 'Commission Work Programme, White Paper on European Governance: Enhancing Democracy in the European Union', SEC(2000)1547, 11 Oct. 2000. The White Paper had identified the five principles of openness, participation, accountability, effectiveness, and coherence as fundamental to good governance, each of which will be enhanced by better public engagement in the risk assessment phase.

[112] See nn. 2, 3 above.

[113] In any case, the level of acceptable risk and the necessity for precaution in the case of GM regulation is already statutorily ascertained.

principle needs also to impact on risk assessment mechanisms, and genuine public participation at the stage of construction of risk is an apt and imperative way of ensuring this. There exist genuine concerns that measures taken in the name of public participation may often lead to placation, tokenism, and manipulation towards engineering legitamacy for possibly unpopular decisions. While these are valid concerns in themselves, they ought to be used as sign posts that make implementaion of the objectives of public participation more optimal.

Such participation also helps better incorporation of variegated conceptualizations of risk,[114] prevalent among various sections of society, brought to the regulatory table in a more inclusive, transparent, and accountable manner. In this endeavour public participation helps in wider hazard identification. For instance, various occasions have been identified where wider engagement has putatively lead to better risk assessment and regulatory decisions, including in a 2000 scientific review of BSE risks in the UK.[115] Thus, public participation has the potential to bring into account a wide range of perspectives and interdisciplinary possibilities, wider than the currently available limited spaces. Such a measure would thus help make risk assessment not merely more transparent and democratic, but more rigorous in scientific terms and put through a wider and more meaningful peer review.[116] For instance, the choice of a baseline from which to assess risks is crucial to any risk assessment exercise, which for instance is a policy decision that cannot be merely left to the realm of scientific or technical expertise.[117]

While the deep divisions regarding GM use has been the main justification for centralization of regulation at the Community level, it is this very concern that makes a compelling case for greater European public participation in an institutionalized and fundamentally meaningful manner. Of course, this participation needs to go beyond participation by large NGOs, and should include smaller groups and organizations from various sectors and geographical regions, and dealing with different issues so as to broaden the base of participation and framing.

Finally, the Deliberate Release Directive also recognizes the legitimacy of concerns and data of general relevance, which through conservative construction has

[114] Beck and Giddens' theory of risk society is ubiquitously quoted in anthropologies of science, as well as law, science, and technology scholarship. Without dwelling on the details of theorization around 'risk society', it is important to recognize that risks are distributed in varying ways among different groups in modern society; and that democratizing processes needs to take into account these variegations. See U. Beck, *Risk Society: Towards a New Modernity* (London: Sage Publications, 1992) and A. Giddens, L. Scot, and U. Beck, *Reflexive modernization: politics, tradition and aesthetics in the modern social order* (Cambridge: Polity Press, 1994).

[115] Van Zwanenberg and Stirling, n. 21 above, at n. 18. See also, *Review of BSE Controls* (London: Food Standards Agency, 2000) and P. Harremöes, D. Gee, M. MacGarvin, A. Stirling, J. Keys, B. Wynne, and S. Guedes-Vaz (eds.), *Late lessons from Early Warnings: The Precautionary Principle 1896–2000,* Environmental Issue Report No. 22 (Office for Official Publications of the European Communities, 2001).

[116] For a similar opinion on the possibilities of careful validation of socio-economic context as associated with date in scientific ascertainment Van Zwanenberg and Stirling, ibid., at 50.

[117] Ibid.

been regarded as non-technical, i.e. unrelated to strict conceptualizations of environment or health. An absence of any meaningful mechanism by the Directive to incorporate concerns of this kind (say questions like the societal value of GM technology itself), is a lacuna which can be filled by this measure.

To conclude, making the act of framing more transparent and democratic by attempting institutionalized deliberation and public participation, can help us deviate from the contemporary route of the overwhelmingly scientific and technological approach to risk assessment. The current political impasse, partly due to this technocratic approach, and partly due to public anxiety, has the potential to be resolved through making the release measures more responsive to political and public opinion. Putatively, widening of framing of risk assessment through institutionalized public participation is a way which is not necessarily at odds with the pull of global economic integration asserted through a certain textualist interpretation of the SPS framework. Such a move will also help us move towards a more democratic Europe, especially in the context of conceptualizations of contemporary societies being risk societies. Equally importantly, this could help Europe find a way out of the current deadlock and gain a toehold towards a more effective and efficient regulation of GMOs in Europe. There is an uneasy and difficult relationship between law, science, and democratic decision-making, which comes to the fore when new technologies that have the potential to cause irreversible damage to the environment or public health are introduced. Perhaps this suggested sophistication, if attempted, could also help us gain fresher insights that serve to improve regulatory introduction of new technologies.

Rehabilitating the Definition of Waste: Is it Fully Recovered?

Robert G. Lee and Elen Stokes***

I. Introduction

In the words of Stephen Tromans, 'waste policy should be simple'.[1] Yet, questions surrounding the scope and implementation of the European Community (EC) waste regime rarely have straightforward answers. This is particularly evident in the interpretation of Directive 2006/12/EC on Waste Framework (Waste Framework Directive).[2] The principal aim of the Waste Framework Directive in its original format in 1975[3] was to establish coherence amongst approaches to waste control across Member States. The need to achieve consistency continues to underpin waste policy, and the amendment and consolidation of the Directive has only confirmed the importance of securing uniform understandings of 'waste' and waste management. Indeed, another of the key objectives of the Directive is to establish a common terminology and to fix the meaning of 'waste'.[4] In Article 1, 'waste' is defined as 'any substance or object in the categories set out in Annex I which the holder discards or intends to discard'. The definition of waste is critical to the functioning of the Directive because it determines which materials fall within its remit and are to be subject to control. In many instances it will be clear what constitutes waste and what does not. However, there are a number of grey areas; particularly where a waste material is *re-used* for another purpose. The task of ascertaining the point at which waste ceases to be waste has proved extremely difficult. The boundary between waste and a secondary material of functional quality is poorly marked out.

Inevitably, this draws attention to the judicial interpretation of waste. This article considers a judgment recently handed down by the United Kingdom (UK)

* Professor of Law, Cardiff Law School, and Co-Director of the ESRC-funded Centre for Business Relationships, Accountability, Sustainability & Society (BRASS), at Cardiff University (UK).

** Leverhulme Trust Early Career Research Fellow, Manchester Law School (UK).

1 S. Tromans, 'EC Waste Law—A Complete Mess?' (2001) 13 *Journal of Environmental Law* 2, 133–56, at 134.

2 [2006] OJ L114/9.

3 Dir. 75/442/EEC on Waste [1975] OJ L194/39.

4 N. 2 above, recital 3.

Court of Appeal, *OSS Group* v. *Environment Agency*,[5] which reviews interpretations of waste deriving predominantly from EC case law. In so doing it draws attention to the definitional problems under the Directive, exemplified by inconsistencies in the approach taken by the European Court of Justice (ECJ) to the meaning of 'waste'. This article argues that the judgment in *OSS Group* v. *Environment Agency* makes progress towards overcoming some of the practical difficulties embroiled in ECJ jurisprudence, particularly on the 'end-of-waste' question. A review of this case allows a consideration of when waste ceases to be waste and becomes a material so readily capable of re-use or other use that it should no longer be subject to waste controls. The argument is structured as follows.

Following this Introduction, Section II sets out the legal framework. Section III offers an exposition of case law dealing with definitional problems under the Waste Framework Directive. There is already an extensive body of case law in which the ECJ has ruled on when a material constitutes waste, and when it does not. Equally, the UK courts have on a number of occasions considered the meaning of 'waste' and, as one might expect, such cases broadly align with the EC judgments. This pattern of convergence only serves to emphasize the significance of the UK Court of Appeal's recent departure in *OSS Group* v. *Environment Agency* from the ECJ's interpretation.

Cases brought before the ECJ have been unequivocal in their finding that the courts, in interpreting the notion of 'waste', are to have regard for the basic aims of the Waste Framework Directive and ensure that its effectiveness is not undermined.[6] In practice, this has had two, not unrelated, consequences. First, it has placed a premium on the protection of health and the environment, and as a consequence, there have been repeated calls from the ECJ to construe 'waste' in a broad rather than restrictive manner.[7] Second, the ECJ has given wide meaning, and in turn central status, to the notion of 'discarding' which is pivotal in the categorization of materials as waste.

Adopting a highly inclusive definition of waste ensures that potentially hazardous materials remain tightly controlled throughout their life cycle, which in turn reflects the protective aims of the Directive. This broad brush approach, however, simultaneously serves to undermine the Directive's auxiliary aim of encouraging the re-use and recycling of waste. Reincorporating waste into the economic cycle is recognized as an important element in resource management, and one

[5] *The Queen (On the Application of OSS Group Limited)* v. *Environment Agency and Others (DEFRA, Intervening)* (2007) 3 *Common Market Law Reports* 30.

[6] E.g. Joined Cases C-418/97 and C-419/97 *ARCO Chemie Ltd. Nederland* v. *Minister van Volkshuisvesting, Ruimtelijke Ordening en Milieubeheer* (C-418/97) *and Vereniging Dorpsbelang Hees, Stichting Werkgroep Weurt and Vereniging Stedelijk Leefmilieu Nijmegen* v. *Directeur van de Dienst Milieu en Water van de Provincie Gelderland* (C-419/97) [2000] ECR I-4475 (*ARCO*), paras. 73, 88, and 97; Case C-9/00 *Palin Granit Oy* v. *Vehmassalon Kansanterveystyön Kuntayhtymän Hallitus* [2002] ECR I–3533 (*Palin Granit*), para. 24.

[7] E.g. *ARCO*, n. 6 above.

which is consistent with the letter and spirit of the Directive.[8] Nonetheless, given the obligation to interpret the concept of waste widely, the courts have shown little inclination to interpret the re-use of waste as a point at which the material so used has *ceased* to be 'waste' for the purposes of the Directive. The economic costs of compliance with the Directive's requirements, together with the negative image created by the labelling of material as 'waste', weaken prospects of a competitive market in secondary materials.[9]

The decision in *OSS Group* v. *Environment Agency*, however, brings into sharp focus the limitations to the ECJ's approach. This is explored in Section IV. It highlights how strict adherence to broad interpretations of 'waste' can lead to the inappropriate application of the Directive to waste materials that are clearly destined for re-use. Recognizing that the Directive might be applied in a manner which subverts the objectives of recovering, re-using, and recycling waste materials, the Court of Appeal suggests a move towards defining waste in a manner which is more in line with these aims. This article is largely sympathetic to the Court of Appeal's handling of European jurisprudence in this area and the inconsistencies that arise therefrom. Whilst it does not entirely overcome the ambiguity embedded in the definition of 'waste', *OSS Group* v. *Environment Agency* nonetheless advances objectives of re-using and recycling waste previously undervalued by case law.

II. Legal Framework

The *principal* aims of the Waste Framework Directive, which originally came into force in 1975,[10] and whose successive amendments were consolidated in 2006,[11] are twofold. Firstly, its essential objective is to protect human health and the environment against harmful effects of the collection, transport, treatment, storage, and tipping of waste.[12] Secondly, and more importantly for the purposes of this article, it seeks to establish a common terminology and definition of waste in order to improve the efficiency of waste management in the Community.[13] More recently, discussion has turned to other goals ostensibly served by the Directive, such as promoting the re-use and recycling of waste materials.[14] As this article illustrates, the re-use of waste begs questions about the definitional territory occupied by notions of 'waste' and 'non-waste'.

[8] Communication from the Commission Towards a Thematic Strategy on the Prevention and Recycling of Waste COM(2003)301, 27 May 2003, 6.

[9] Ibid., 22.

[10] N. 3 above.

[11] N. 2 above.

[12] Ibid., recital 2.

[13] Ibid., recital 3.

[14] See, e.g., E. Scotford, 'Trash or Treasure: Policy Tensions in EC Waste Regulation' (2007) 19 *Journal of Environmental Law* 3, 1–22.

The distinction between 'waste' and 'non-waste' has proved difficult to ascertain and to apply.[15] The central definition of 'waste' that governs the EC waste regime is by no means clear cut. As the EC Commission noted in 1996:

> The discussion on the distinction between waste and goods has been going for almost twenty years now. No satisfactory definition has yet been found to determine when a material becomes waste and when waste becomes a good again.[16]

This sentiment was reiterated in 2005, when the Commission observed that the definition of waste fails to set clear boundaries to determine when waste has been adequately treated and should be regarded a product.[17] Yet, waste definitions are crucial. The classification of a material as 'waste' renders it subject to intense regulatory control. For example, it is taxed on disposal to landfill.[18] Conversely, it makes no sense to levy tax, to control movement, or to seek to govern contractual relationships in the passage of goods, or non-wastes. Indeed, in keeping with the principles of the European Single Market,[19] the safeguarding of the free and unrestricted movement of goods is imperative. The distinction upheld by the Council[20] and Commission[21] between 'goods' and waste' might reasonably be criticized for being too crude. In spite of the fact that it may be less optimal to categorize materials as 'wastes', wastes are still, broadly speaking, 'goods'. In light of their uncertain market value, however, wastes are *marginal* goods at best, for which effective markets may not develop. The possibility of market failure together with the social costs that might then result from the abandonment of these marginal goods makes the case for regulation.

The definition of waste, therefore, straddles two key EC Treaty objectives: environmental protection and the functioning of the internal market.[22] It follows that in one direction lies considerable freedom of operation and in the other tight control. Regulatory costs attach to this control and materials carrying the label 'waste' are likely to be perceived as having little or no value. It ought to come as no surprise, therefore, that the interpretation of waste is heavily contested, and its scope and meaning are frequently the focal points of litigation.

Article 1 of the Waste Framework Directive characterizes 'waste' as 'any substance or object in the categories set out in Annex I which the holder discards or intends to discard'. There are two components to Article 1 that must be satisfied before a material can be deemed to be waste. Firstly, the substance or object has

[15] Commission Communication on the Interpretive Communication on Waste and By-Products COM(2007)59, 21 Feb. 2007, 3.
[16] Draft Council Resolution on Waste Policy COM(96)399, 30 July 1996, para. 13.
[17] Commission Communication on Taking Sustainable Use of Resources Forward—A Thematic Strategy on the Prevention and Recycling of Waste COM(2005)666, 21 Dec. 2005, 13.
[18] S. 39, Finance Act 1996.
[19] Art. 14 EC.
[20] N. 16 above.
[21] N. 17 above.
[22] N. 16 above, 14.

to fall within the categories of waste in Annex I. These include, for example, production or consumption residues, residues of industrial processes, and products for which the holder has no further use. The last of the Annex's categories is especially broad, extending to *any* materials, substances, or products which are not contained in the abovementioned categories.

Secondly, the substance or object must be *discarded*. Given the span of individual categories referred to in Annex I (most notably the last category), the definition of waste turns on the notion of 'discarding'. A holder must discard, or intend to, or be required to discard the substance or object in question. In the ordinary sense of the word, to 'discard' is to 'throw away, as not needed or not allowed'.[23] Its precise meaning under Article 1, however, is renowned for being difficult to isolate. The Directive alone does not provide any decisive criteria for determining whether discarding has taken place.[24]

This concern over definitional ambiguity is apparent in the UK. In English law, the definition of 'waste' is contained in Section 75 of the Environmental Protection Act 1990. This definition was amended by the Waste Management Licensing Regulations 1994 which transposed the requirements of the Directive. 'Waste' under the Regulations reflects the definition in the Directive, meaning:

> any substance or object in the categories set out in Part II of Schedule 4 which the producer or the person in possession of it discards or intends to discard but with the exception of anything excluded from the scope of the Directive by Article 2 of the Directive. 'Discard' has the same meaning as in the Directive.[25]

This apparently quick and simply incorporation of EC law was accompanied by 16 pages of detailed guidance from (what was then) the Department of the Environment in Circular 11/94.[26] Recognizing the difficulties associated with definitional ambivalence, it seeks to answer the following questions: *what is waste*; *when is a substance or object discarded*; and *can waste cease to be waste?*[27] Since the Circular pre-dates much of the case law on these issues, its role as a guide to the interpretation of obligations arising from the Directive and the 1994 Regulations is somewhat limited.[28] However, the Circular is a useful starting point not only because it provides a benchmark against which subsequent cases can be measured, but also because some of the most recent judgments analysing waste begin to resemble the Circular's appraisal.

[23] *Chambers English Dictionary* (Edinburgh: Chambers Publishers, 1990).

[24] *Palin Granit*, n. 6 above, para. 25.

[25] Reg. 1(3).

[26] Department of the Environment, *Environmental Protection Act 1990: Part II Waste Management Licensing, The Framework Directive* (London: Her Majesty's Stationery Office, 1994), Annex 2.

[27] Ibid., paras. 2.53–2.59.

[28] Precedence must be given to ECJ rulings on the matter. See I. Cheyne and M. Purdue, 'Fitting Definition to Purpose: The Search for a Satisfactory Definition of Waste' (1995) 7 *Journal of Environmental Law* 2, 149–68, at 160.

Circular 11/94 explains that the purpose of the Directive is 'to supervise the collection, transport, storage, recovery and disposal of those substances or objects which fall out of the commercial cycle or out of the chain of utility'.[29] This is intended as an aid to decision-making with regard to licensing activity. Throughout the Circular, references are made to the Directive and its implications, though notions of 'the commercial cycle' or 'chain of utility' do not emanate from the Directive at all. Moreover, no explanation of the meaning of either concept is offered. Nonetheless, the test for determining whether waste exists under the Directive and the ensuing Waste Management Licensing Regulations is said to work in the following way. A material is 'waste' if it meets the following cumulative conditions, that is, if:

(a) it falls into one of the categories set out in Part II of Schedule 4 to the Regulations (which essentially reiterates Annex I of the Directive); *and*
(b) it is discarded (or intended or required to be discarded) by the holder; *and*
(c) on account of its being so discarded, it no longer forms part of the normal commercial cycle or chain of utility.[30]

The first two tests above accord with the provisions of the Directive. The third test, however, finds no textual basis in the Directive. Rather, it is an invention of the Department of the Environment. On the face of it, it looks to be suggesting that a substance or object falls out of the commercial cycle or chain of utility as soon as it is consigned to disposal or recovery under Annexes IIA and IIB, respectively, of the Directive. The Circular qualifies this slightly by introducing the notion of a 'specialised recovery operation'.[31] Again, this does not appear in the Directive, although the Department of the Environment claims that it is useful in determining whether a substance or object has indeed been discarded. It posits the following question in order to ascertain whether the act of discarding has taken place: 'Can the substance or object be used in its present form (albeit after repair) or in the same way as any other raw material *without* being subject to a specialised recovery operation?'[32] Accordingly, if this question can be answered in the affirmative (i.e. in that the substance or object is likely to be so used) then it is said to be a 'reasonable indication' that the substance or object has *not* been discarded and does *not* constitute waste. Equally, if the substance or object requires a specialized recovery operation, then this should present a reasonable indication that it *has* been discarded as waste.[33]

By retaining notions that waste may be evaluated according to whether the material in question remains in the commercial cycle or the chain of utility, the Circular appears to suggest that materials capable of immediate re-use do not constitute waste. However, the Circular should not be regarded as an

[29] N. 26 above, para. 2.14.
[30] Ibid., paras. 2.53–2.56.
[31] Ibid., paras. 2.27–2.31.
[32] Ibid., para. 2.28.
[33] Ibid., para. 2.47.

authoritative commentary on the Directive, particularly because it is an elaboration of the Directive rather than a strict interpretation. Precise meaning must be gleaned from the Directive and over time from decisions of the ECJ. As the following section illustrates, uncertainties pertaining to the definition of waste have played out through detailed judicial analyses of the term 'discard'. At the level of the ECJ these have tended to depart from the approach of the Circular.

One of the greatest difficulties facing the courts has been to differentiate between materials that have been discarded which happen to be re-used at some later stage, and materials that are re-used rather than discarded.[34] Whereas the ECJ has rigorously adhered to the notion of waste being 'discarded', it has failed to pay equivalent attention to when it might be fruitfully re-utilized. Though the ECJ has attempted to fix criteria indicating exactly when a substance or object has been discarded, its efforts have been compounded by its simultaneous findings that the meaning of waste is to be 'determined in the light of all circumstances'[35] and on a 'case-by-case basis'.[36] Armed with these insights, it is not altogether surprising that the courts have been unsuccessful in generating a coherent definition.

III. Exposition of Case Law

A. The ECJ Jurisprudence

In two cases in 1997, *Tombesi*[37] and *Inter-Environnement Wallonie*,[38] the ECJ was asked to giving preliminary rulings on issues relating to the meaning of 'waste' in Article 1 of the Waste Framework Directive. The Court was charged with determining whether a material could constitute waste *notwithstanding* the fact that it still had commercial value and formed part of industrial production process.[39] In spite of the fact that such circumstances could not easily be reconciled with the concept of 'discarding' in its ordinary sense,[40] the ECJ held that neither their value, nor their use in the commercial cycle, precluded the materials in question

[34] Scotford, n. 14 above, 10.

[35] *ARCO*, n. 6 above, paras. 73, 88, and 97.

[36] Opinion of AG Alber of 8 June 1999 in *ARCO*, n. 6 above, para. 109.

[37] Joined Cases C-304/94, 330/94, 342/94, and 224/95 *Criminal Proceedings against Tombesi* [1997] ECR I-3561 (*Tombesi*).

[38] Case C-129/96 *Inter-Environnement Wallonie ASBL* v. *Région Wallone* [1997] ECR I-7411 (*Inter-Environnement Wallonie*).

[39] Ibid., para 25.

[40] I. Cheyne, 'The Definition of Waste in EC Law' (2002) 14 *Journal of Environmental Law* 1, 61–73, at 65.

from falling within the definition of 'waste'. 'Waste' does not exclude substances or objects that are capable of economic re-utilization.[41]

Advocate General (AG) Jacobs, however, was more radical in his approach. Sitting on both cases, he suggested that the term 'discard' ought to be understood by reference to notions of disposal and recovery under Articles IIA and IIB.[42] As such, the act of 'discarding' ought to be inferred from disposal or recovery operations in Annex II. On the facts of *Tombesi*, the AG held that materials transferred from one person to another for immediate re-use in their present state did *not* constitute waste on the basis that they underwent neither disposal nor recovery operations.[43] This approach came to be known as the 'Tombesi by-pass'.[44] In effect, it was an attempt to circumvent elements of the definition of waste (notably the 'discarding' requirement) by reducing the critical factor in determining 'waste' to whether or not the substance or object fell within the remit of Annex II.[45]

This downplaying of the notion of 'discarding' was also evident before the UK courts in *Mayer Parry Recycling*.[46] Mayer Parry Recycling claimed before the High Court that various types of scrap metal that it had handled might fall outside the definition of waste because it had not been discarded. Carnwath J in giving judgment in the case accepted that offcuts of metal or other scrap not requiring any recovery operation need not be treated as waste.[47] However, where some element of recovery in line with Annex IIB was required, the metals would remain waste until the operation had been fully carried out.[48] This certainly emulates aspects of the guidance contained in Circular 11/94. Carnwath J's judgment goes close to saying that for a material (falling under Annex I) to be deemed to be waste it must have undergone an Annex II process. In the words of the judge:

> materials which are to be re-used but which do not require any recovery operation before being put to their new use are not treated as waste. Similarly, materials which are made ready for re-use by a recovery operation, cease to be waste when the recovery operation is complete.[49]

This contrasts sharply with more recent attempts by the ECJ to refine the notion of 'discard'. In fleshing out the definition of waste, the Court's judgment

[41] *Inter-Environnement Wallonie*, n. 38 above, para. 31 (upholding Case C-359/88) *Criminal Proceedings against E. Zanetti and Others* [1990] ECR I-1509, paras. 12–13; Case C-422/92 *Commission* v. *Germany* [1995] ECR I-1097, paras. 22–3; and *Tombesi*, n. 37 above, paras. 47–8.

[42] Opinion of AG Jacobs of 24 Oct. 1996 in *Tombesi*, n. 37 above, para. 50.

[43] Ibid., para. 52.

[44] G. Van Calster, 'The EC Definition of Waste: The Euro Tombesi Bypass and Basel Relief Routes' (1997) 8 *European Business Law Review* 5/6, 137–43.

[45] Though as Tromans notes this approach might circumvent the question of when a material is discarded, it simply shifts the issue to the meaning of 'recovery', Tromans, n. 1 above, 142.

[46] *Mayer Parry Recycling* v. *Environment Agency* (1999) 1 *Common Market Law Reports* 963.

[47] Ibid., para. 56.

[48] Ibid., para. 51.

[49] Ibid., para. 46.

in *ARCO*[50] turned the 'Tombesi by-pass' on its head. In a reference for a preliminary ruling, the ECJ considered two separate actions brought by different companies—ARCO and Epon. Both companies re-used waste materials as fuel. ARCO was a chemical manufacturer that re-used 'LUWA bottoms' to produce fuel for cement kilns. LUWA bottoms are a by-product of a manufacturing process producing molybdenum, a metallic element used as a hardening agent in various alloys. Epon was an electricity generating company. It bought wood residues (in the form of wood chips) from the construction and demolition sectors to be transformed into wood powder and used as fuel to generate electricity. The ECJ in these joined cases had to determine whether materials destined for combustion remained waste following their transformation into materials suitable for burning. The question facing the Court was essentially this: when does waste cease to be waste? Underpinning this inquiry by the ECJ was the meaning of 'discard'. Were the materials in question discarded at their point of transformation, or some time before? Or, could they only have been discarded once burnt?

In his Opinion, AG Alber offered these insights:

> If a waste material is recovered or reprocessed so that a substance is obtained that no longer poses a danger typical of waste and, when used in a normal manufacturing process, does not pollute the environment any more than, but at most in the same way as, a raw material, that substance probably is no longer to be regarded as waste in the sense of being subject to control or authorisation for its further use.[51]

Broadly speaking, therefore, a complete recovery operation will result in a substance ceasing to be waste. This reflects the judgment in *Mayer Parry Recycling*. Further, it closely resembles the test proposed by Circular 11/94. There are two strands to AG Alber's understanding of the distinction between waste and non-waste. The first of the 'Alber tests'[52] is the 'danger typical of waste' test. The second is the 'no more polluting' test. Provided a material does *not* pose a danger typical of waste such that supervision of the waste does *not* appear necessary, *and* that material poses no greater danger than a comparable raw material, it falls outside the definition of waste.[53]

The ECJ did not endorse AG Alber's analysis. In fact, the Alber tests have since been criticized for being 'wholly unworkable' and likely to 'undermine and be inimical to the European waste regime, and the very careful control, particularly of incineration of waste, which governs this area'.[54] Whilst the ECJ in *ARCO* accepted that waste *ceases* to be waste when it has been subject to a complete recovery operation,[55] it went on to note that:

[50] N. 6 above.

[51] Opinion of AG Alber of 8 June 1999 in *ARCO*, n. 6 above, para. 109.

[52] So called by Burton J in joined cases *Solvent Resource Management* v. *Environment Agency*, and *OSS Group* v. *Environment Agency* (2007) *Environmental Law Reports* 19, paras. 63–72.

[53] AG Opinion in *ARCO*, n. 6 above, para. 110.

[54] N. 52 above, para. 65.

[55] N. 6 above, para. 93.

even where waste has undergone a complete recovery operation which has the consequence that the substance in question has acquired the same properties and characteristics as a raw material, that substance may nonetheless be regarded as waste if, in accordance with the definition in Article 1(a) of the Directive, its holder discards it or intends or is required to discard it.[56]

Immediately, this gives the notion of 'discard' critical status in determining whether a substance remains waste. It could not be inferred simply from the performance of a recovery process under Article IIB that a material constituted waste. The act of discarding would remain the dominant factor. In its rejection of approaches that narrowed the definition of waste to presumptions based on Annex II, the ECJ essentially closed the *Tombesi* by-pass in order to give 'waste' a broader meaning.

As stated earlier much of the UK case law has followed the lead of the ECJ and a similar line of reasoning was adopted by the English courts in *Castle Cement* v. *Environment Agency*.[57] The issue here was whether waste solvents, which had been blended for use as fuel to fire cement kilns, were no longer waste but fuel. Stanley Burnton J held that the solvents continued to constitute waste, maintaining that the carrying out of a recovery operation did not necessarily result in the substance in question ceasing to be waste.[58] In his judgment, Stanley Burnton J was careful to draw a distinction between different recovery operations listed in Annex IIB. According to Stanley Burnton J, recovery operation R1, which deals principally with uses as fuel or other means of energy generation, ought to be regarded as referring to an 'end use' of waste. Recovery operations R2–R9, on the other hand, allude to operations conducted so as to *enable* waste to be used. Recovery operation R1 reflects the Article 3 objective to use waste as a source of energy. Recovery operations R2–R9 are directed towards achieving an alternative objective, which is also set out in Article 3, to recover waste by means of recycling, re-use, or reclamation or any other means *with a view to extracting secondary raw materials*. In the judge's opinion, the categories in Annex IIB do not overlap, so it must be said that solvent wastes are not recovered under R1 until used as a fuel.[59] Other recovery processes (R2–R9) are intended to lead to some form of re-use and not simply incineration.

This follows the line toed by the ECJ in *ARCO*; that is to say, the scope of the definition of waste depends on more than the simple question of whether a material is analogous with a material in its raw form. Even if a material, deemed to be waste, is found to be identical to a raw material, it might still amount to waste under the Directive. The definition requires that there is also be a consideration of whether the material has in fact been *discarded*. Emphasis on the notion

[56] N. 6 above, para. 94.
[57] *Castle Cement* v. *Environment Agency* (2001) 2 *Common Market Law Reports* 19.
[58] Ibid., para. 45.
[59] Ibid., para. 34.

of 'discarding' is significant, and contrasts starkly with earlier cases in which simple conformity with Annex IIB to the Directive sufficed. In *ARCO* (and indeed in *Castle Cement* v. *Environment Agency*) the Court found that the fact that a substance is the result of a recovery process under Annex IIB is only *one* of the factors to be taken into account for the purposes of establishing whether that substance still constitutes waste.[60] It has become progressively evident in case law in the EC and the UK that the scope of the definition of 'waste' turns on the meaning of the term 'discard'. The ECJ has stipulated that the classification of a substance or object as waste is 'primarily to be inferred from the holder's actions, which depend on whether or not he intends to discard the substances in question'.[61] Two principal criticisms can be directed at this jurisprudential trend. The first is that factors indicating that material has indeed been discarded are eminently uncertain. This is well recognized in existing literature on the topic.[62] The second is that the centrality of 'discard' begins to make less sense in situations where waste materials are re-used. This second point is explored further below.

B. Implications for Secondary Material Resources

In an extremely thoughtful paper on the connotations of the ECJ's understanding of 'waste' and 'discard', Eloise Scotford argues that the courts have developed something of 'an unhealthy obsession with interpreting the concept of waste widely and upholding the regulatory "effectiveness" of the Directive'.[63] Moreover, the definition provided by the ECJ in *ARCO* 'fails to give sufficient flexibility to the concept of waste so that actions of industry in finding productive uses for by-products can be appropriately exempted'.[64] The problem is that the Court's insistence that decisions concerning the waste status of materials are made on a case-by-case basis is at odds with its continuing attempt to lay down principles that shape the interpretation of the Directive. Undoubtedly, the ECJ's yielding, albeit implicitly, to the Directive's overarching aim of definitional consistency has led to the formulation of a set of criteria underpinning the Court's decision-making. For example, the ECJ has held that: the mere fact that a substance or object can have a positive value does not mean that it has not been discarded;[65] 'waste' can include substances discarded by their owners even if they have a commercial value and are collected on a commercial basis for recycling, reclamation, or re-use;[66] 'waste' can also include substances that can be used in an environmentally

[60] *ARCO*, n. 6 above, para. 97.

[61] *Palin Granit*, n. 6 above, para. 22.

[62] See, e.g., J. Fluck 'The Term "Waste" in EU Law' (1994) 3 *European Environmental Law Review* 3, 79–84; Cheyne, n. 40 above.

[63] Scotford, n. 14 above, 19–20.

[64] Ibid., 16.

[65] Joined Cases C-206/88 and C-207/88 *Criminal Proceedings against Vessoso and Zanetti* [1990] ECR-I 1461; see also *Palin Granit*, n. 6 above, para. 25.

[66] *Tombesi*, n. 37 above, para. 52.

responsible manner;[67] and furthermore, the harmlessness of the substance in question is not a decisive criterion for determining whether it constitutes waste.[68] What is clear is that, where materials are part of a 'commercial cycle' (i.e. where there is a lack of explicit evidence of discarding), the Court continues to rely solely on factors that might indicate that the holder's *intention* was indeed to discard. This speculative process is fraught with difficulty.[69] Consequently, the ECJ has tended to err on the side of caution by interpreting 'waste' and 'discard' as broadly as possible.

When the courts are faced with determining whether a material has *become* waste under Article 1, a wide definition of 'waste' helps to ensure that any harmful effects are minimized through the Directive's regulatory regime. When, however, they seek to determine whether a material has *ceased* to be waste, the protective aims of the Directive become more convoluted. In this instance, a wide definition of 'waste' extends the reach of the Directive, bringing within its remit of control materials that could otherwise be put to beneficial uses as *products*. Inevitably, there is a danger that increasing the scope of the Directive, and thereby extending the sphere in which a 'regulatory burden'[70] is imposed, will have the effect of discouraging the re-use of waste substances or objects. In other words, adopting a highly inclusive definition of waste 'can reduce the attractiveness of materials that would otherwise be returned into the economy'.[71]

If this is considered in the light of Article 3 of the Waste Framework Directive, a tension arises.[72] As well as stipulating that Member States shall take appropriate measures to prevent or reduce waste production and its harmfulness, it requires that they encourage 'the recovery of waste by means of recycling, re-use or reclamation or any other processes with a view to extracting secondary raw materials'. Furthermore, if the ECJ's approach is placed in the context of EC waste policy generally, it is immediately apparent that initiatives to encourage the re-use and recycling of waste materials are of central importance.[73] The Sixth Environmental Action Programme,[74] for example, specifically earmarks this objective as a thematic strategy in itself.

The ECJ, in the aftermath of the *ARCO* decision, has placed some restriction on the meaning of 'waste'.[75] For example, the Court in *Palin Granit*[76] introduced the notion of 'secondary product' or 'by-product'. The ECJ explained that, according

[67] *ARCO*, n. 6 above, para. 73.
[68] *Palin Granit*, n. 6 above, paras. 50–1.
[69] See *OSS Group* v. *Environment Agency*, n. 5 above, para. 59.
[70] Van Calster, n. 44 above.
[71] COM(2007)59, n. 15 above, 5.
[72] Scotford, n. 14 above, 12.
[73] COM(2003)301, n. 8 above; EP and Council Dec. 1600/2002/EC laying down the Sixth Community Environment Action Programme [2002] OJ L242/1.
[74] EP and Council Dec. 1600/2002/EC, ibid.
[75] Scotford, n. 14 above, 16.
[76] *Palin Granit*, n. 6 above, para. 32.

to its ordinary meaning, waste is 'what falls away when one processes a material or an object and is not the end-product which the manufacturing process directly seeks to produce'.[77] However, it went on to note that materials generated during the manufacturing of an end-product will not *always* constitute waste. There are circumstances in which those additional materials might amount to genuine products, rather than waste. The Court drew a distinction between a 'production residue', and a 'secondary product' or 'by-product'. A production residue is a product which is not in itself sought for its subsequent use. It is therefore tantamount to waste. A secondary product, or by-product, is intended to be exploited or marketed in a subsequent process and does not constitute waste. Its subsequent re-use, however, must be a certainty, not merely a possibility.[78] This position was upheld by the ECJ in *Commission* v. *Spain*,[79] where the Court observed that:

> There is ... no reason to hold that the provisions of that directive ... apply to goods, materials or raw materials which have an economic value as products regardless of any form of processing ... provided that such reuse is not a mere possibility but a certainty, without any further processing prior to reuse, and as part of the continuing process of production.[80]

There are two points worth noting here. The first is that the ECJ's reference to the 'continuing process of production' bears something of a resemblance to the concepts of 'commercial cycle' and 'chain of utility' contained in the Department of the Environment's Circular 11/94. The second is that, in spite of the indications in the *Palin Granit* judgment that the definition of 'waste' is not as wide as previous cases might have suggested, the concept of 'secondary product' is still only a relatively narrow exception—imposing requirements that there is *certainty* of re-use within an *ongoing* production process. Arguably, this requirement that the re-use of goods forms an integral part of the production process carries an assumption that the process of production is carried out by one person, failing to adequately address situations in which waste materials are intended to be transferred to *third parties* for recovery and re-use.[81] *Palin Granit* therefore still reflects the position consistently adopted by the ECJ that 'waste' cannot be interpreted restrictively,[82] and that the scope of the Directive ultimately rests on an intention to discard.[83] More recently, AG Colomer, commenting on the distinction between 'recovery' and 'disposal', has highlighted the difficulties with strict adherence to tests to discern an intention to discard where waste is recovered and re-used.[84] Whereas

[77] Ibid.
[78] Ibid. para. 36.
[79] Joined Cases C-416/02 and C-121/03 *Commission* v. *Spain* [2005] ECR I-07487.
[80] Ibid., para. 58.
[81] Scotford, n. 14 above, 16–17.
[82] *Palin Granit*, n. 6 above, para. 23; Scotford, n. 14 above, 21.
[83] *Palin Granit*, n. 6 above, para. 22.
[84] Opinion of AG Colomer of 30 May 2006 in Case C-486/04 *Commission* v. *Italy* [2006] ECR I-11025, para. 53.

'disposal' indeed 'evoked the idea of "dispensing" with or "discarding" something in an orderly manner with no view to reclaiming it', the notion of 'recovery' is much more difficult to grapple with under the basic waste test which rests on an intention to discard. Recognizing these difficulties, the UK Court of Appeal recently put ECJ case law in this area under the spotlight. Not only did the Court of Appeal question the ECJ's approach to interpreting the Directive, but it harnessed an understanding of 'waste' which attempts to circumvent some of the problems encountered in defining the notion of 'discarding'.

IV. The Court of Appeal's Approach: *OSS Group* v. *Environment Agency*

The case at first instance involved not only OSS Group but also Solvent Resources Management (SRM) which recovers and recycles industrial waste materials, particularly waste solvent materials.[85] Essentially, SRM 'launder' solvents.[86] They collect used solvents from their customers, and are either recovered and refined to their customers' specification and returned, or are recovered and refined into product grade distillates and sold on the open market. Alongside SRM appeared OSS Group, 75 per cent of whose turnover, and a substantially greater proportion of their profits, comes from selling a substance called 'recycled fuel oil'. This recycled fuel oil derives largely from waste lubricating oils, including used engine and gear/transmission oils, collected from some 15,000 waste oil producer locations, such as garages and workshops. OSS Group sells recycled fuel oil to their customers to be burnt as fuel.

The passage of Directive 2007/76/EC on the Incineration of Waste (WID)[87] had repercussions for this commercial enterprise. The WID now applies to all existing waste incineration installations (with effect from 28 December 2005). The Environment Agency, under the WID regime, issues Pollution Prevention and Control (PPC) permits where waste is incinerated. Both SRM and OSS Group faced a situation in which their waste derived fuels would be treated as 'waste' falling subject to the WID requirements. OSS Group was concerned that if its recycled fuel oil was to be treated as waste, so that their customers would be required to be WID-compliant, they would lose substantial business to the natural oils industry which fell outside the scope of the WID. Anticipating the effects of the WID, OSS Group had spent £3 million allowing them to generate higher quality fuel oil, conforming to the British Standard for clean fuel oil.

[85] Joined Cases *Solvent Resource Management* v. *Environment Agency*; *OSS Group* v. *Environment Agency*, n. 52 above.

[86] Ibid., para. 7.

[87] [2000] OJ L332/91.

SRM and OSS Group challenged the scope of the 'waste' interpretation because it triggered the operation of the WID. The Environment Agency argued before the High Court that a product, which was waste or derived from waste, may cease to be waste following certain successful processes allowing it to be sold or used for other purposes. Where it is to be burnt as fuel, however, it will not ordinarily cease to be waste until it is burnt and its energy is recovered. The Agency did allow one exception to this rule. Where the material was originally a fuel, or was used or available for the common (though not necessarily the only) purpose of being used as fuel, it can be considered as recovered as a fuel by an appropriate process and would cease to be waste *if* it is chemically and physically identical to the original material and requires no further processing.

The High Court upheld the Agency's position. SRM were in a position to at least attempt to take advantage of the Agency's exception. OSS Group were unable to do so because their recycled fuel oil derived from waste lubricating oil, and not a fuel. OSS Group appealed the decision. The question was simply whether lubricating oil, not originally used as fuel, that became waste, could thereafter be burnt as anything other than waste.

At first instance, the High Court referred to *ARCO* as authority for the proposition that a waste material is not exempt from control under the European waste regime merely because it has the same or a similar specification to an equivalent natural product.[88] The true guide as to whether a material constitutes waste was said to hinge on the requirement that the holder discards it or intends or is required to discard it.[89] As in *ARCO*, this leaves open the possibility that after certain types of recovery operation, a material may nevertheless be deemed to be waste if it is discarded. Burton J rejected Lord Reed's broad interpretation of 'recovery' in *Scottish Power Generation Ltd.* v. *Scottish Environment Protection Agency*.[90] In that case Lord Reed, pointing to AG Alber's Opinion in *ARCO*,[91] had suggested a test of recovery based upon whether the material could be used in the same manner as a non-waste material without any increased risk to human health or the environment. The WID, Burton J explained, aimed to provide an overarching control until the point of incineration to ensure the absence of any harmful effects. There were far too many uncertainties in the operation of 'the Alber tests' based on the dangers posed by typical materials for them to be workable either as a replacement for, or as any exemption from, the controls imposed by the waste regime.[92]

[88] N. 52 above, para. 63.
[89] Ibid., para. C1.
[90] (2005) *Environmental Law Reports* 38.
[91] N. 6 above, para. 109.
[92] Joined Cases *Solvent Resource Management* v. *Environment Agency*; *OSS Group* v. *Environment Agency*, n. 52 above, para. 71.

Instead, the High Court drew support for its stance from the ECJ's decisions in *Palin Granit*[93] and *Niselli*[94] in which it was held that the issue of whether a material posed any real risk to human health or the environment was not a determinative factor in assessing its 'waste' status. Although Burton J admitted to being attracted to the prospect of accepting as products (i.e. not as waste) fuels having no more of a polluting effect than natural gas oil,[95] he held that Article 3(2)(b) of the WID stood in the way of this interpretation. Article 3(2)(b) implies that waste fuels should still be classified as hazardous waste and incinerated in accordance with the WID *notwithstanding* the possibility that its emissions when incinerated would be equivalent to those of gas oil. Burton J concluded that, in light of the limited exemptions under the WID, recovered oils were subject to its controls even though the equivalent natural product would not be so covered.

On appeal, the Secretary of State for the Department of Environment, Food and Rural Affairs (DEFRA) appeared as an intervener proposing a less stringent line than the Environment Agency. The proceedings illustrate perfectly the implications of lacking consensus over the core definitions contained in the Waste Framework Directive—not only between different Member States but also between national authorities within the same Member State.[96] In response to the question posed on appeal (i.e. whether the waste lubricating oil could be burnt other than as waste) DEFRA and the Environment Agency adopted different positions. Unsurprisingly, OSS Group argued that the lubricating oil could be burnt other than as waste. DEFRA agreed providing that the oil was processed to a standard making it 'analogous to' or 'hardly distinguishable' from virgin oil. The Agency maintained its position in the hearing at first instance, submitting that the waste lubricating oil destined for combustion continued to be waste until it is burnt, *regardless* of the standard of any prior processing.

In giving judgment in the Court of Appeal, Lord Justice Carnwath was in equal measures puzzled by and critical of the jurisprudence emanating from the ECJ, stating that 'a search for logical coherence in the Luxembourg case law is probably doomed to failure'.[97] The crux of the problem, according to his Lordship, was the pivotal role assigned to the intention of the holder of waste and strict adherence to the requirement that the holder discards it.[98] In particular, Carnwath LJ was of the opinion that EC case law upheld the 'discard' test even where it could be 'of no practical relevance'.[99] Reliance on the concept of 'discarding' stemming from cases such as *ARCO* made little sense when the original producer (of lubricating oil, in this instance) had long ago discarded it, and it was now in the hands

[93] *Palin Granit*, n. 6 above.
[94] Case C-457/02 *Criminal Proceedings against Antonio Niselli* [2004] ECR I-10853.
[95] N. 52 above, para. 72.
[96] For another instance in relation to packaging waste see *The Queen* v. *Environment Agency, ex parte Mayer Parry (No 2)* (2001) 2 *Environmental Law Reports* 45.
[97] *OSS Group* v. *Environment Agency*, n. 5 above, para. 55.
[98] Ibid.
[99] Ibid.

of someone (OSS Group) who buys it to put it to some other valuable use.[100] Whilst the 'intention to discard' test might be useful in determining the status of a material in the hands of the original producer, it was difficult to apply in situations where waste materials had been sold to a third party for recycling or reprocessing, or put to another valuable use.[101] Moreover, Carnwath LJ held that, in such circumstances, the search for an 'intention to discard' led to an illogical outcome. In his Lordship's words: '[i]n no ordinary sense was such a person [OSS Group] discarding or getting rid of the material. His intention was precisely the opposite.'[102] Accordingly, picking up from Lord Reed in *Scottish Power*:

> It should be enough that the holder has converted the waste material into a distinct, marketable product which can be used in exactly the same way as an ordinary fuel, and with no worse environmental effects.[103]

In his Lordship's view, the subjective test of establishing an intention to discard was of little use in these latter stages of waste determination. Carnwath LJ explained that the ECJ's excessive reliance on the concept of 'discarding' in *ARCO* was unwarranted. The ECJ in *ARCO* held that a complete recovery operation 'does not necessarily deprive an object of it classification as waste'.[104] This is recognized as one of the key principles to emerge from the *ARCO* judgment. The ECJ, therefore, concedes that a complete recovery operation under Article IIB is at least possible. However, the ECJ went on to specify that the holder of a recovered material under Article IIB might still *subsequently* develop an intention to discard it. According to Carnwath LJ, the focus of the ECJ on post-recovery intention was misguided. Recourse to this extraneous test was meaningless. In *ARCO*, Epon wanted to *re-use* the wood chips to generate electricity, not discard them. Commenting on the circumstances of Epon's business, Carnwath LJ observed that the issue was not whether the original users of the wood chips possessed an intention to discard them.[105] No doubt the original users did indeed have such an intention. The issue was whether Epon intended to discard. Yet as Carnwath LJ pointed out, the question was not whether the wood chips were waste when they were transferred to Epon, but whether they had ceased to be waste.[106] The same, then, could be said of OSS Group's re-use of lubricating oil. OSS Group had no intention to discard. On the contrary, OSS Group displayed a clear intention to re-use the waste oil for different purpose.

In light of the shortcomings of the notion of 'discarding', Carnwath LJ was unyielding in his conclusion that a practical common-sense approach was

[100] Ibid., para. 40.
[101] Ibid., para. 55.
[102] Ibid.
[103] Ibid., para. 63.
[104] N. 6 above, para. 96.
[105] *OSS Group* v. *Environment Agency*, n. 5 above, para. 55.
[106] Ibid., para. 56.

required.[107] Although the Court continued to pay lip-service to a test based on 'discarding',[108] his Lordship was of the view that it had been replaced by a number of objective indicators which were more consistent with the Waste Framework Directive's goals. In particular, dispensing with the 'intention to discard' constraint was in keeping with the objective of encouraging the recovery of waste materials for uses which replace raw materials.[109] It was held that it could not be said that OSS Group 'discarded' the lubricating oil in any ordinary sense of the term, and furthermore, that there was 'nothing in the objectives of the Directive which requires any fictitious assumption to that effect'.[110] The simple fact that OSS Group had converted the oil into a distinct, marketable product that could be used in the same way as ordinary fuel without bringing about any worse environmental impact led the Court of Appeal to find in favour of OSS Group, and to conclude that the oil *could* be burnt otherwise than as waste.

Interestingly, the Court of Appeal declined to make a reference to the ECJ, and one is almost able to detect the frustration of Carnwath LJ when he says:

> I would have doubts about the appropriateness of a further reference in this area of the law. I would hesitate to describe the matter as *'acte clair'*, in the traditional sense. But that is not because of lack of opportunity for the Court to provide clarification if it had wished to do so. *ARCO* itself, in which the Court had the assistance not only of the Advocate-General and the Commission, but of five intervening states, would have been an ideal opportunity. One must assume that the decision not to do so was deliberate. Any lack of clarity is inherent in the imprecision of the test which the court has declared.[111]

V. Concluding Remarks—Creating Markets in Secondary Materials

The impact of the Court of Appeal's decision in *OSS Group* v. *Environment Agency* is far-reaching. It effectively rejects the excessively broad approach of the ECJ in favour of a more commonsensical treatment of notions of 'waste' and 'discarding', and in so doing exhibits greater coherence with aims of re-using and recycling waste materials for other purposes. By highlighting the implications of the ECJ's habitual focus on inferring from the holder an intention to discard, Carnwath LJ illustrates how widening the definition of waste to give effect to the protective aims of the Directive can at the same time undermine the Directive's capacity to motivate the re-incorporation of waste into the economic cycle. The failure of the definition of waste to set clear boundaries for when waste has been adequately treated and should be considered as a product has led to undue emphasis in ECJ case law on the notion of an 'intention to discard'.[112]

107 Ibid., para. 63.
108 Ibid., para. 59.
109 Ibid., para. 63.
110 Ibid.
111 Ibid., para. 69.
112 COM(2005)666, n. 17 above, 13.

Yet, this emphasis does not always promote best environmental practice.[113] *OSS Group* v. *Environment Agency* shifts this focus somewhat, and in so doing underlines the resounding capacity of the definition of waste to create markets in the re-use of waste materials—a capacity which has been largely untapped by ECJ jurisprudence. Contrary to patterns emerging from EC case law, the UK Court of Appeal in *OSS Group* v. *Environment Agency* has demonstrated a willingness to adopt a more flexible approach in accord with a wider waste strategy.

Three conclusions might be drawn from this case. Firstly, the Court of Appeal's decision represents an attempt to construe waste in a manner which upholds the aim of EC waste policy to encourage the re-use and recycling of waste materials. Secondly, it strongly indicates that, if the Waste Framework Directive is to promote this goal (which is explicitly contained in Article 3), the ECJ needs to strive harder to overcome definitional weakness. This concern has been picked up by the Commission, and proposed revisions to the Directive seek to set out clearer and simplified definitions.[114] The Commission makes a clear case for a refinement of the Directive in an attempt to resolve legal uncertainties, particularly in end-of-waste scenarios where the distinction between recovery and disposal has proven to be so difficult to ascertain.[115] Though the definition of waste contained in the Waste Framework is retained, the Commission proposes to introduce procedures to clarify when waste ceases to be waste for certain waste streams.[116] Most notably, the proposed Directive inserts Chapter III on 'End of Waste' focusing specifically on secondary products. Accordingly, in determining whether it is appropriate to reclassify waste as secondary products, materials, or substances, the Commission is to assess whether the following conditions are met, namely: (i) reclassification would not lead to overall negative environmental impacts; and (ii) a market exists for such a secondary product, material, or substance.[117] If nothing else, this shifts focus from the notion of 'discard', and represents something of a concession that the 'discarding' test has its limitations.

Arguably, the more the definitional problem is attacked in this way, the more likely it is that the Directive will be used as a vehicle for invigorating markets in the re-use of waste materials. This leads to the final conclusion that there is now unequivocally a need for greater guidance. At the end of his judgment Carnwath LJ expresses the hope for the UK that 'it may be possible for DEFRA and the Agency to join forces in providing practical guidance for those affected'.[118] Given that in spite of the abundance of case law the 1994 Circular has never

[113] Ibid., 14.

[114] Commission Proposal for a Directive on Waste COM(2005)667, 21 Dec. 2005; also see EP Doc. No. A6–0466/2006, Amendment 5, Recital 11: 'A definition of re-use should be added in order to clarify the ambit of this operation in general waste treatment and the role of the re-use of materials or products that are within the scope of the definition of waste.'

[115] COM(2005)667, ibid., 2.

[116] Ibid., 7, and Recital 14.

[117] Ibid., Art. 11.

[118] *OSS Group* v. *Environment Agency*, n. 5 above, para. 68.

been re-issued, one can sympathize with this statement, but while *OSS Group* v. *Environment Agency* provides an answer in relation to a particular waste stream and leads us in the broad direction of greater flexibility to recover materials, the appointed task is an onerous one indeed. This is particularly so because any such guidance would need to reflect EC law as enunciated by the ECJ and could not rest upon the aspirations of the UK Court of Appeal.

Ultimately it is to the EC that we must turn for a lead in this definitional jungle. Recognizing the ongoing difficulties with waste definitions, the Commission in 2007 issued an *Interpretative Communication on Waste and By-Products*,[119] to clarify the distinction between waste and non-waste. Although a substantial portion of the Communication is spent simply recapping principles to be derived from EC case law, its Annex sets out examples of wastes and non-wastes designed to illustrate the classification process. These include, for example, slag and dusts from iron and steel production, by-products from the food and drink industry, and offcuts from primary production processes. This type of approach might suggest a way ahead. The European Waste Catalogue[120] codifies and offers descriptions of standard waste streams from industry sectors. Although with the help of materials science we are seeking to divert as many of these waste streams as possible to fruitful end use, as yet there are not endless applications for such substances. They are in their nature problematic to re-use, recycle, or recover. If this were not the case there would be ready markets for them and they would not be classed as waste. Might it not be possible to produce reference notes on acceptable practice in treating the major waste streams to include when recovery can be regarded as complete? This is no small task, but more broad brush attempts at addressing this question appear to have failed. The *OSS Group* judgment is a clear indication that the UK courts feel this to be so. It may have done a great service if it directs attention to how wastes might be deployed to generate secondary material resources rather than placing regulatory obstacles along this path.

[119] COM(2007)59, n. 15 above.

[120] Commission Decision Replacing Decision 94/3/EC Establishing a List of Wastes pursuant to Article 1(a) of Council Directive 75/442/EEC on Waste and Council Decision 94/904/EC Establishing a List of Hazardous Waste pursuant to Article 1(4) of Council Directive 91/689/EEC on Hazardous Waste [2000] OJ L226/3.

The Resurrection of the EURATOM Treaty: Contributing to the Legal and Constitutional Framework for Secure, Competitive, and Sustainable Energy in the European Union

*Pamela M. Barnes**

I. Introduction

Among the most difficult challenges facing the Member States of the European Union (EU) are the interrelated challenges of increasing energy security and combating climate change. As nuclear generated electricity provides 30 per cent of the electricity used in the EU and is regarded as a virtually carbon free energy resource, one highly controversial solution to these challenges would be to increase the amount of electricity produced by nuclear technology. Nuclear generation of electricity is not a new solution to the search for secure and accessible energy in Europe. The first European reactors began to produce nuclear electricity in the 1950s. Cooperation among European states in nuclear energy production also began at the same time. The view was that not only would the speedy establishment and growth of the industry assist the re-invigoration of the European economies but that cooperation in its development would contribute to peace.

Accordingly in 1957 the governments of France, the Federal Republic of Germany, Italy, Belgium, the Netherlands, and Luxembourg signed the EURATOM Treaty which established the European Atomic Energy Community (EAEC). The objectives of the EAEC were to provide the legal and institutional structures to govern the generation and peaceful use of the nuclear technologies among the signatory states. At that time the underlying paradigm upon which the regulatory environment for electrical power generation was based was one in which public bodies were responsible for developments, supported by long-term state investment and subsidies. The EURATOM Treaty consequently provided

* Principal Lecturer, Jean Monnet *ad personam* Chair in European Political Integration, School of Law, Faculty of Business and Law, University of Lincoln, Brayford Pool, Lincoln (UK). The chapter is based on P. M. Barnes *Going forward into the past—the Resurrection of the EURATOM Treaty*, paper presented at European Union Studies Association (EUSA), Tenth Biennial International Conference, Le Centre Sheraton, Montreal, Canada, 17–19 May 2007.

a framework which included support for a high level of state intervention in the electronuclear industry.

The political and economic environments in which the contemporary electronuclear industry is operating are very different from that of the 1950s. As a result of changes in the energy sector there has been a move to a different paradigm—that of liberalized power markets in which all modes of generating electricity should be competitive without state support. But the EURATOM Treaty has not been subject to any substantive changes since its adoption in 1957. The terms of the Treaty therefore do not appear to be able to meet the new realities of the industry. There are deep divisions between the EU's Member States about the use of nuclear electricity. For some nuclear electricity is the most cost effective (Slovakia), widely used (France), and a provider of 50 per cent of electricity needs (Belgium, Sweden). For others, particularly Austria, nuclear electricity is not an option. As a result, differing and highly divergent national nuclear energy policies have evolved, which would suggest that there is a strong rationale for repeal of the Treaty and to return its competences to Member States. To do so would require a vote by unanimity among the national governments of the Member States of the EU but there is little evidence to suggest that there is support for such action.[1] Instead in recent debates about Treaty changes in the EU the concept of a *separate legal personality* for the EAEC has been retained. The only proposals with regard to the EURATOM Treaty in the Reform Treaty are to include an annexed Protocol to enable technical amendments agreed during the 2004 Intergovernmental Conference to be made.[2] Thus the *status quo* of the EURATOM Treaty, unchanged throughout the history of the EU, will be maintained.[3]

This chapter questions why the national governments of the EU appear so reluctant to repeal, or even significantly change this Treaty. Is the Treaty as some assert 'undemocratic, out-dated and biased towards the electro-nuclear industry',[4] carrying 'the stigma of an undemocratic, outdated alien in the world of the liberalized market'[5] or is it 'a remarkable document that expresses the essential

[1] Following the Inter-governmental Conference of 2004 it was concluded that 'while Ireland and some other Member States proposed a more extensive debate on EURATOM it was clear that there was no consensus in support of this', cited in Irish Government, *The European Constitution—White Paper,* (London: Department of Foreign Affairs, 2005), at 92.

[2] Protocol no. 11 of the proposed Reform Treaty amending the protocols annexed to the TEU, the TEC, and EURATOM to adapt them to the new rules laid down by the Treaty (i.e. predominantly procedural issues).

[3] The Merger Treaty in 1967 merged the institutional structures of the ECSC, the EEC, and the EURATOM Treaties but did not change the provisions of the Treaties. However the ECSC Treaty has now expired, the EEC Treaty was amended in the Single European Act in 1987, included in the TEU in 1993 and subject to further amendments in the Treaties of Amsterdam (1999), and Nice (2003).

[4] *The EP and the EURATOM Treaty: past, present and future,* Energy and Research Paper ENER 114 (Luxembourg: European Parliament, 2002), at 2.

[5] D. Fouquet, 'The Legal Perspective: the EURATOM Treaty and the new Constitution', presentation to Energy Intelligence for Europe conference', Copenhagen 23 Sept. 2003, published on the Internet at: http://www.energyintelligenceforEurope.dk.

commitments of the parties in a flexible and forward looking language'.[6] Firstly, the origins and history of the EURATOM Treaty are investigated in order to establish if the answer to this question may be found in the 1950s. The changes in the political and socio-economic environments for the European energy sector are evaluated to establish why there is a current resurgence of interest in the electronuclear industry, following a period of uncertainty in the 1980s and early 1990s. In the final section of the chapter the *value added* of the continued existence of the EURATOM Treaty to the European Union in the search for mechanisms to establish a legal and constitutional framework for secure, competitive, and sustainable energy is discussed.

It is argued that, in view of the reluctance of the national governments of the EU to repeal the Treaty and develop a comprehensive climate change/energy chapter in the Reform Treaty, the EURATOM Treaty does retain its relevance as the basis for a legal framework of action for the nuclear sector. The use of nuclear technology to generate electricity is highly controversial within the EU, but in the absence of an alternative the EURATOM Treaty has and continues to offer opportunities to address issues relating to safety and security in particular.[7] In short as Nina Commeau-Yannoussis asserts, 'I believe that you can be against nuclear and love the existence of EURATOM'.[8]

II. The Origins of the EURATOM Treaty

Does the explanation of the reluctance of the national governments to repeal this Treaty lie in the negotiations of 1956 and 1957? In this section the socio-economic and political environments of the 1950s are discussed in order to determine if the continued existence of the Treaty owes anything to the way in which it was negotiated in 1957. Certainly the negotiations to create the EAEC were more difficult than initially anticipated by those proposing the project. However, this did not render the Treaty immortal. If the national governments of the EU 27 decided to do so the Treaty could be changed. The EURATOM Treaty, however, continues as part of the energy *acquis* to which EU Member States have to agree as they accede to the EU. This includes States such as Austria which has a

[6] *High Level Expert Group Review of the EURATOM Safeguards Office* (Brussels: High Level Expert Group, 2002), at 7.

[7] The *acquis* on nuclear energy includes 86 legal acts of which 6 are Council Regulations.

[8] N. Commeau-Yannoussis, cited at 34 in EIE Conference report *The EURATOM Treaty and Future Energy Options*, organized by NOAH, 23 Sept. 2005, Danish Parliament Building, Christiansborg, published on the Internet at: http://www.energyintelligenceforEurope.dk. Commeau-Yannoussis is Head of Unit of Energy Policy and Security of Supply, European Commission, Directorate-General for Energy and Transport. Her comments during this conference were made in a personal capacity and so did not necessarily reflect the views of the European Commission. However see nn. 50–2 for comments by Commission President Barroso, Commissioner for Energy, Piebalgs and Commissioner for Competition, Kroes in autumn 2007 which appear to support developments in nuclear electricity.

clearly focused anti-nuclear policy and France, Finland, Lithuania where there is support for the construction of new reactors and high dependency on nuclear electricity.

The EAEC was established on the basis of a Treaty negotiated between the signatory states which had established the ECSC in 1951 (France, Germany, Italy, Belgium, the Netherlands, and Luxembourg). As with the ECSC the EAEC had a limited focus on energy cooperation, but unlike the Coal and Steel Community Treaty the EURATOM Treaty was not time dated when it was adopted. The EAEC was established to provide the conditions for the development of nuclear energy in Europe by sharing the resources required (financial, materials, technical, and expertise), to provide protection of the workers in the industry and the general public and to enable agreements to be developed with third parties and international organizations on issues relating to supply and peaceful use of the technology. This concentration on one sector differed from the more extensive European integration project to establish the European Economic Community (EEC) which the signatory states were engaged in at the same time.[9]

Exclusive Community competence for action focused on eight main areas which were outlined in Article 2 EURATOM, with prominence being given to safety of the workers in the industry and the public in the areas surrounding the nuclear power plants.

In order to perform its task, the Community shall, as provided in this Treaty:

(a) promote research and ensure the dissemination of technical information;
(b) establish uniform safety standards to protect the health of workers and of the general public and ensure that they are applied;
(c) facilitate investment and ensure, particularly by encouraging ventures on the part of undertakings, the establishment of the basic installations necessary for the development of nuclear energy in the Community;
(d) ensure that all users in the Community receive a regular and equitable supply of ores and nuclear fuels;
(e) make certain, by appropriate supervision, that nuclear materials are not diverted to purposes other than those for which they are intended;
(f) exercise the right of ownership conferred upon it with respect to special fissile materials;
(g) ensure wide commercial outlets and access to the best technical facilities by the creation of a common market in specialised materials and equipment, by the free

[9] The electronuclear industry is also subject to regulation on the basis of the EC Treaty. Electricity is a product which may be moved within the integrated market, irrespective of how it is generated. During the 1990s and early 2000s legislation has been adopted to liberalize national markets in electricity and thus reduce prices for domestic, commercial, and industrial users by enabling increased competition to take place. Although trade in electricity within the EU remains relatively limited, these developments have added to the pressures for interoperability of national transmission networks to become an important element in future EU energy strategies.

movement of capital for investment in the field of nuclear energy and by freedom of employment for specialists within the Community;

(h) establish with other countries and international organizations such relations as will foster progress in the peaceful uses of nuclear energy.

The EURATOM Treaty also provided the basis for the free movement of the staff, capital, and services required in the nuclear sector. But the safety of the nuclear installations themselves was to remain within the competences of the national government—an arrangement which continues to attract much criticism, which is further discussed below in Section B.

Cooperation on the peaceful civilian use of nuclear energy had been proposed as an alternative integration project when attempts to achieve political integration among the six signatory states of the ECSC had failed in 1954. In the resolution following the Messina Conference held in 1955 the Ministers of Foreign Affairs of the ECSC Member States had declared that more and cheaper energy policy was fundamental to the economic progress of the European economies. Further adding that: 'Before long, the development of nuclear energy for peaceful purposes will open up prospects of a new industrial revolution far beyond anything achieved during the past one hundred years.'[10] The civilian use of the nuclear technologies appeared to be an exciting new development offering an opportunity to re-energize the enthusiasm and impetus for further policy integration and stimulate economic growth.

The view held by Jean Monnet,[11] drafting the plan for a Treaty incorporating these ideas, was that the nuclear energy sector was de-politicized. As such it would be open to political integration and the possibilities of supranational action. The vision of Monnet, and the other proponents of this view, was however flawed. Support for the nuclear sector and the EURATOM Treaty in 1957 was not born from a rational plan for a supranational Treaty to develop nuclear energy (action which Monnet envisaged would be under the guidance of a '*benevolent technocracy*', i.e. the Commission, working on behalf of the Community).[12] Rather the

[10] Res. adopted by the Ministers of Foreign Affairs of the ECSC Member States at their meeting at Messina on 1–2 June 1955, para. 3.

[11] Jean Monnet was responsible for the French Plan for Economic Development following the ending of World War II. He proposed that by pooling basic production and resources of coal, iron, and steel under the management of a supranational authority whose decisions would be binding on the governments of France and Germany a framework for peaceful cooperation between the States would be established. His proposal was supported by Robert Schuman, the French Foreign Minster, and led to the establishment of the ECSC between France, Germany, Italy, Belgium, the Netherlands, and Luxembourg. Monnet was appointed as the first President of the High Authority (Commission) of the ECSC serving from 1952 until 1955. When the signatory states of the ECSC were seeking another European integration project, following the failure of the French Assembly to ratify the European Defence Community in 1954, Monnet proposed that the ECSC model should be used in another energy sector , i.e. in the development of the peaceful use of nuclear technology to provide electricity. See also F. Duchene, *Jean Monnet—the first statesman of interdependence* (New York: Norton & Company, 1994).

[12] Report to the Committee established under the chairmanship of Paul-Henri Spaak to 'relaunch' the European Project following the failure of the European Defence Community.

Treaty emerged from political compromises brokered during the negotiations of the following year which left the national interests in the ascendancy. Whilst the Commission was given a great deal of power to act on behalf of the EAEC the areas over which this competence was transferred from the national to the supranational level was limited.

The limitations on the competences given to the EAEC were the result of the emergent national nuclear policies of the 1950s. They were admittedly haphazard, but they were being developed in response to strong national interests and commercial pressures and thus supranational action was constrained. The French government supported the growing electronuclear industry in which French industry and business had important interests. A Commission for Nuclear Energy (the *Commissariat a l'energie atomique* (CEA)) had been created in France as early as 1945 to develop both military and civilian applications of nuclear technology. The state owned *Electricité de France* (EDF) had begun to build reactors in Marcoule in 1952[13] and Chinon in 1957.[14] In Belgium too strong preferences for national developments were expressed. The German and Italian governments on the other hand were looking to forge agreements with the United States (US) to obtain cheap supplies of enriched uranium and US built reactors. It was evident that the EAEC's signatory states were not prepared to open their national industry to the possibility of *interference*.

Overall the negotiations for the EURATOM Treaty led to an outcome which was based on a traditional model of intergovernmental agreement. It was much narrower in focus than the EEC Treaty, also signed at the same time. The terms of the EURATOM Treaty were to facilitate investment in the nuclear industry. As the electricity utilities were predominantly state owned in the 1950s this was in effect to agree to a considerable degree of state aid to the developing industry and conformed to the prevailing energy paradigm of the period. The paradigm upon which the EEC was based was that of market functionality which included ensuring that liberalization of the market was supported, a much more controversial view. Indeed, Andrew Moravscik has concluded that the EURATOM Treaty had been nothing more than a 'smokescreen' to cover the adoption of proposals for the more controversial customs union proposed for the EEC.[15]

The Preamble to the Treaty did indeed point to wider objectives and a possible contribution to European integration by '[r]ecognising that nuclear energy represents an essential resource for the development and invigoration of industry and will permit the advancement of the cause of peace', but the specific objective

[13] The reactors at Marcole began commercial operation—reactor 1 in Sept. 1957, reactor 2 in Apr. 1959 and reactor 3 in Apr. 1960. (In the UK the development of the Calder Hall nuclear power plant had begun in 1953. Its primary purpose was to manufacture weapons grade plutonium. However in Oct. 1957 it began to operate commercially as the world's first industrial scale production of electricity.)

[14] The Chinon reactor took longer to begin commercial operations which did not begin at the site until Feb. 1964.

[15] A. Moravscik, *The Choice for Europe* (Ithaca: Cornell University Press, 1998), at 120.

of the EAEC was to raise the standards of living in its Member States 'by creating the conditions for speedy establishment and growth of nuclear industries'. (Preamble, EURATOM) The rationale for the commitments made by the EAEC signatory states was that, as new technology, nuclear technology would be very costly and would need a great deal of investment. Underpinning this was a view that all the Member States of the EAEC would gain from cooperation as the investment needed was not something which they were in a position to make on their own. But if all the states worked together to integrate their nuclear energy policies and shared the costs, Article 1 EURATOM envisaged that all would benefit from the 'prospect of achievements commensurate with the creative capacities of their countries'. Further development of the electronuclear industry would be achieved through the promotion of research by funding from an agreed budget for the EAEC and dissemination of the information gained among the signatory states.

Such a commitment seemed to be contradictory when compared with the objective of promotion of use of coal supported in the ECSC. But coal was dependent on old established technology which did not need high levels of capital investment and sharing of the cost burden of future developments. Nuclear was the newer technology. It was considered that in the post-experimental research phase other benefits, including lower prices and cleaner energy technology, would result. This in turn would ensure that the long-term benefits of the technology would outweigh the costs involved.

Neither the EEC Treaty nor the EURATOM Treaty however contained explicit references to environmental protection. The first explicit statement of commitment to environmental protection was included in the Single European Act in 1987, which amended the EEC Treaty (although the European Commission had introduced the First Environmental Action Programme, adopted in 1972). But Article 35 EURATOM did require Member States to establish facilities to carry out the continuous monitoring of the level of radioactivity in the air, water, and soil and to ensure compliance with basic standards. In addition Article 37 EURATOM required national governments to transfer information to the Commission so that an impact assessment of disposal of radioactive waste could be made:

> Each Member State shall provide the Commission with such general data relating to any plan for the disposal of radioactive waste in whatever form as will make it possible to determine whether the implementation of such plan is liable to result in the radioactive contamination of the water, soil or airspace of another Member State.

As the US had a monopoly in the procurement of uranium in the 1950s, the EURATOM Treaty supported the creation of a common market for trade in nuclear ores and materials within the EU so that sufficient supplies would be available for EAEC users. This comprised two elements. One was Chapter IV EURATOM which provided for the competence to be conferred on the EAEC for the sole rights of option and ownership of all fissile material being used for civilian purposes.[16] The role of the Euratom Supply Agency (ESA) was undermined as a result of the early development of a global uranium market. (The EU is however highly dependent on imported uranium supplies and the ESA, as a procurement agency arguably has a role to play in the future in monitoring imports.) In addition it was considered essential that the provisions of the Treaty brought international agreements and cooperation to the Commission's competence as a crucial element of the common supply of the raw materials for the industry. Article 2h EURATOM conferred competence on the EAEC 'to establish with other countries and international organisations such relations as will foster progress in the peaceful uses of nuclear energy'.[17]

The creation of the EAEC was not a commitment by the national governments of the six signatory states to any form of cooperation on the military use of nuclear technology. The underlying political philosophy for the creation of the EAEC was a search for peaceful cooperation, not collaboration so that weapons of war could be developed. The EURATOM Treaty therefore contained measures to ensure that the fissile materials being used in the nuclear reactors of the EAEC were only being used for peaceful purposes. The EURATOM Safeguards Office (ESO) was established pursuant to Chapter VII EURATOM to deal with measures to ensure all EU Member States did not divert or acquire materials away from their intended and declared uses. (The ESO is now based under the supervision of the Commission (DG TREN)[18] with more robust mechanisms in place and a much clearer current role and mandate than the ESA.[19])

A range of safeguards have since been developed within the framework of the EURATOM Treaty and monitored by the ESO. They include measures which are applied to power stations, fuel fabrication, and re-processing plants. The type of safeguard measures applied will vary, depending on the nature of the nuclear

[16] The EURATOM Supplies Agency (ESA) was established on 1 June 1960 to ensure the equitable and regular supplies of nuclear ores and fuels for the EU's nuclear utilities (Ch. IV EURATOM Treaty). The Agency is a common supply agency for ores, source materials, and special fissile materials and under the supervision of the European Commission. Currently this is within DG TREN. However 'The Supplies Agency exists, but is a mere shadow of what was intended', *The EP and the EURATOM Treaty: past, present and future*, Energy and Research Paper ENER 114 (Luxembourg: European Parliament, 2002), at xiii. In 2006 the ESA had only ten employees.

[17] This proviso of the Treaty has enabled agreements to be signed with the main suppliers in the field—the US, Canada, Australia, Argentina, Uzbekistan, Ukraine, Japan, Kazakhstan.

[18] DG TREN was formed in 1999 by a merger of the former DG VII (Transport) with DG XVII (Energy) and the unit for Nuclear Safety of DG XI (Environment, Nuclear Safety and Civil Protection). In the European Commission 2004–2009 the portfolio for Transport was held by Jacques Barrot, and that of Energy by Andris Piebalgs. (The two directorates responsible for nuclear policy, nuclear safeguards and radiation protection within DG TREN are not based in Brussels but in Luxembourg).

[19] In 2002, a High Level Expert Group was established to report on the effectiveness of the ESO as the terms of the EURATOM Treaty had not been revised since 1957. The findings of the Group were that the ESO should remain the focus of EU wide controls for both practical and legal reasons. N. 6 above.

facility but they include audits of material use, analysis of the use of materials, surveillance, and on-site inspections. For example, a power station where there is on-site spent fuel storage will be subject to audits of materials, containment, and surveillance measures, including CCTV monitoring, and random re-verification procedures to ensure that the identified stocks of materials are still present on site. By 2006 the number of Community inspectors involved in this work had risen to 180.[20] They have 24/7 access to data and personnel who deal with materials, equipment, or installations subject to the safeguards.

The political realities of the 1950s were dominated by the reluctance of the national governments of the EU to proceed with strategic and military integration in a context other than the North Atlantic Treaty Organization (NATO). For some of the Member States this was combined with ongoing military actions involving national forces outside the European region. The question of military action by either German or Italian forces was still regarded with some suspicion. Not all the EU's Member States had nuclear weapons capability. However, as a result of the mandate to establish international agreements in the EURATOM Treaty the EAEC acceded to developments within the framework of the Nuclear Non-Proliferation Treaty (NPT) signed on 1 July 1968.[21] It has also been possible for a number of tripartite verification agreements to be reached between the two states (France and the UK) possessing nuclear weapons, EURATOM and the International Atomic Energy Agency (IAEA), and also between those states of the EU which are not nuclear weapons states, EURATOM and the IAEA.[22] These agreements enable coordination of EURATOM's role with that of the IAEA in the monitoring of the terms of the NPT. For some of the supporters of the EURATOM Treaty this may be seen as the main success of the Treaty through time—i.e. that the Treaty created a 'firewall against proliferation of nuclear weapons (through the elements of ownership of fissile material and nuclear safeguards). This was and is its main success.'[23]

[20] *Fifty Years of the EURATOM Treaty*, COM(2007)124, 20 Mar. 2007, at 6.

[21] In 2007 the NPT had 188 signatory states, although Israel, India, and Pakistan, where nuclear weapons have been developed since the 1970s, have not signed.

[22] The International Atomic Energy Agency (IAEA) is an independent international organization reporting to the General Assembly and the Security Council of the United Nations on issues surrounding the compliance of states with their obligations with regard to nuclear safeguards. It was established in 1957. Verification agreements between the parties include INF CIRC/193 Euratom/IAEA and non-nuclear weapon states (1973), INF CIRC/263 Euratom/IAEA and UK (1976), INF CIRC/290 Euratom/IAEA and France (1978). These agreements have been updated and additional Protocols added to ensure that there is no duplication of the procedures of the IAEA and EURATOM. An additional Protocol to these agreements was added in Apr. 2004 to take account of enlargement of the EU. Currently for most of the 2004–2007 entrants to the EU a transition phase to these agreements is still in operation.

[23] R. Linkohr, *Assessing EURATOM—50 years of European nuclear policy*, Presentation given at Public Hearing, European Parliament Committee on Industry, Research and Energy, European Parliament, Brussels, 1 Feb. 2007.

III. Fifty Years of the EURATOM Treaty

On 25 March 2007 the EU commemorated the 50th anniversary of the signing of the Rome Treaties which created the EEC and the EAEC. Throughout the history of the EU the use of nuclear power has caused controversy at national level which has given rise to the development of highly divergent national nuclear policies. In view of these developments and differences it would appear that the EURATOM Treaty should have been repealed. But the EURATOM Treaty has shown remarkable resilience to remain substantively unchanged throughout the history of the EU.[24] This is despite radical changes to the other Treaties founding the EEC and the ECSC. It is a Treaty which is based on a different paradigm to that of the EU's Energy Policy as it has developed in response to events such as the global oil crisis of the 1970s and the completion of the European integrated market in the 1980s. High levels of state support for a specific energy sector as supported by the EURATOM Treaty appeared to be no longer relevant in a scenario based on market liberalization. Environmental and energy security concerns have dominated energy policy debates in the 1990s and 2000s. But no significant amendments have been made to the Treaty since 1957.

As a result of the legal framework for action provided in the EURATOM Treaty the Western European states developed a significant body of regulation on health protection of the workers in the nuclear industry and surveillance to ensure the separation of the civil from the military use of the technology. Despite nuclear events occurring as early in the history of the development of the technology as 1957, when the Windscale military reactor was damaged by fire and there was an off-site release of radioactive materials, a spirit of complacency about the safe operation of Western Europe's reactors had developed by the 1980s.[25] This complacency was shattered in 1986 by the Chernobyl disaster.

Admittedly the reactors in Western Europe had been built to different designs from those of the Soviet designed technology used at Chernobyl. But the widespread nature of the devastation which followed the explosion and fire undermined overall levels of support and confidence in the nuclear industry. Chernobyl was the catalyst for a number of developments in Western Europe. It caused a re-think in some Member States of the EU, for example in Italy where reactor developments had been pioneered in the early 1960s. In November 1987 the outcome of a referendum held in Italy was to halt all new reactor construction programmes and initiate a programme of de-commissioning of existing reactors from 1990. For the EU Chernobyl was the catalyst for the Commission to be given a mandate, based on its EURATOM Treaty competences, to undertake careful monitoring and review of the Russian technology nuclear reactors of the

[24] N. 3 above.

[25] For further discussion of nuclear events see Annex 2 The International nuclear event scale and Annex 3 Examples of events rated as INES 3 and above in Europe.

former Eastern European Soviet states as they became potential applicants for EU membership in the early 1990s.

Although some discussion of the continued usefulness of the Treaty did take place during the 1980s and early 1990s no moves were made to abolish or amend the EURATOM Treaty. As a Treaty supporting a declining industry it appeared to be of little consequence for most Member States, apart from France. Responding to public concerns, licensing of the construction of reactors declined and closures of some units had been initiated by national governments during the 1990s. The electronuclear industry did not appear viable because of the heavy investment costs required in the construction of the nuclear power plants. For some opposing the nuclear sector it appeared that the market was operating and would ensure the death of the industry and thus end the need for the EAEC and the legal framework of the EURATOM Treaty.

On the other hand, the mechanisms for sharing the competence regarding the electronuclear industry in the EU appears to have created a structure that did not intrude on the national interests. As such it did not pose a threat to national nuclear policies which had to be addressed. In addition the existence of the EURATOM Treaty had supported the development of regulation and voluntary harmonization of national measures to reach a high level of safety standards for the workers in the industry.[26] For the policy-makers of the EU to engage in negotiations for its repeal at a time when the negotiations for the Maastricht Treaty were taking place and there were challenges to meet from the ending of the cold war and the demise of the Soviet Empire would have taken too much political effort for little gain.

At the same time, however, despite reactor closures in the 1990s, newer technology developments and increased operating licences in those which remained improved the efficiency levels of the operating reactors. The capacity of the nuclear power plants to provide for volume base-load demand improved by ten points on average globally during the decade, with most dramatic improvements coming in the US (growth from 66 to 90 per cent). Plants in Europe were able to achieve levels of over 90 per cent.[27] The result was that by the early 2000s the electronuclear industry was able to provide one-third of the electricity being used within the EU 15. By 2005, the EU 25 was the world's largest nuclear electricity generating region.[28] In 2007, following the accession of Bulgaria and Romania, 15 of the EU's states produced nuclear electricity from 152 nuclear reactors. Levels of dependency on the technology varied from 4 per cent of electricity generated in the Netherlands to 72 per cent in Lithuania and 78 per cent in France (further details are provided in Annex 1).

[26] P. M. Barnes, 'Nuclear safety for nuclear electricity—the search for a solid legal basis for nuclear safety in an enlarged European Union' (2003) 45 *Managerial Law* 5/6, 115–43.

[27] World Nuclear Association (WNA), *The New Economics of Nuclear Power,* (London: WNA, 2005), at 10.

[28] *Nuclear Illustrative Programme*, COM(2006)844, at 3.

In 2002, the European Parliament (EP) had concluded that the Treaty was outdated, undemocratic, and biased towards the electronuclear industry and proposed that the Treaty should be phased out at the same time as the ECSC Treaty was due to expire. The criticisms of lack of democracy come from a number of aspects of the Treaty provisions. The institutional framework of the EURATOM Treaty was established in the Treaty in 1957. It was the same as that outlined for the EEC but the role for the General Assembly of the EAEC at the time was minimal.[29] As no substantial changes had been made to the Treaty since 1957, despite the introduction of direct elections to the EP in 1979 and subsequent changes to the TEC, the EP continued to have a minimal role in EAEC decision-making.[30] As a consequence of this there is no requirement for the Council of Ministers to do anything more than formally consult the EP on substantive issues. Under the provisions of the EURATOM Treaty the unelected European Economic and Social Committee (ESC) and the Scientific and Technical Committee (STC) (with memberships nominated by national governments) have similar formal rights of consultation as the EP. In addition Article 101 EURATOM excludes the EP from involvement in international agreements based on its terms. Yet the EP is co-budgetary authority for expenditure which is based on the Treaty.

EURATOM legislation is also subject to vote by qualified majority (QMV) in the Council of Ministers, but not to the co-legislation and co-decision procedures. In other areas of action covered by the provisions of the TEC there have been substantial changes made to the role of the EP which now has the power to act as co-legislator with the Council on a considerable number of market related issues which have an impact on the electro-nuclear industry. In addition there are a number of safety related issues considered of importance to the public and the EP view is that 'it can be plausibly argued that it is precisely in these areas . . . relating to safety that the public most feels the need for rigorous democratic scrutiny, control and accountability'.[31] Further that 'there is probably no area of human endeavour which should remain outside the scrutiny remit of the EP, either implicitly or explicitly'.[32]

The view of the Parliamentarians was supported by the Commission during the debates in the Convention on the Future of Europe in 2003.[33] The Penelope

[29] As a result of the Merger Treaty in 1967 the institutions of the three 1950s communities were merged, including the General Assembly of the EAEC, with those of the ECSC and the EEC, becoming the European Parliament (EP).

[30] The EURATOM Treaty is now part of the *first pillar* of the TEU, but the changes for this have been technical and procedural. The substantive terms of the EURATOM Treaty have not been altered.

[31] *The EP and the EURATOM Treaty; past, present and future*, Energy and Research Paper ENER 114, (Luxembourg: European Parliament, 2002), at 2.

[32] Ibid at 147.

[33] A task force, convened by Francois Lamoureux, the Director General of DG TREN, presented a proposal to the Convention for an Additional Act to be added to the Constitution on the Peaceful Use of Atomic Energy (this proposal was known as the 'Penelope Paper'). The objective of the Penelope Paper was to make the Treaty more compatible with the EU's electricity market. The

Paper proposals of the European Commission sought to address the inconsistency of the role of the EP between the EURATOM Treaty and the TEC and supported the extension of QMV and co-decision to nuclear energy policy proposing that 'Parliament is restored to the institutional system, as it is given the power to adopt with the Council, "Laws" for basic standards (for the nuclear industry) whereas at present it is very much outside the decision-making process'.[34] The argument being that if the powers of the EP are increasing as co-legislators on other matters associated with the development of a secure, competitive, and sustainable energy sector, it appears illogical for the EP to continue to be excluded from this right in the EAEC.

More recently in 2005 the objectives of EURATOM Treaty were castigated as it 'carries the stigma of an undemocratic, outdated alien in the world of the liberalized market'.[35] This criticism focused on the role of government subsidies for nuclear technology developments and their apparent support in the terms of the EURATOM Treaty. Although many of the energy utilities in Europe are no longer state owned enterprises there is still nevertheless a considerable element of state involvement in the energy industry. As a result any subsidies given to energy developments may be seen in terms of unfair advantage for the electronuclear industry over other aspects of the energy sector. But the economics of the sector has altered and from the viewpoint of the electronuclear industry representatives has 'demonstrated that nuclear power does not, over the long term, require subsidy'.[36]

IV. Reluctance to Repeal the EURATOM Treaty

With the growth of criticisms from politicians and industry alike and changes to the economics of the nuclear sector it would appear that the EURATOM Treaty is no longer needed and should be repealed. As one of the founding Treaties of the EU the EURATOM Treaty was included in the list of treaties to be reviewed outlined in the Laeken Declaration. In this Declaration calling for a Convention to be established on the Future of Europe the Heads of Government were responding to pressures building within the EU. In particular, pressure had been growing for a debate about how to make the EU more relevant to its citizens, particularly the younger citizens.[37] Among the issues which the Convention sought to

main thrust was to simplify the Treaty by identifying and removing those provisions which duplicated those in the TEC.

[34] Ibid.

[35] N. 5 above.

[36] N. 27 above, at 2.

[37] European Council Presidency Conclusions, 14–15 Dec. 2001, Annex 1 *Laeken Declaration on the future of Europe* 'The Union needs to become more democratic, more transparent and efficient. It has to resolve three basic challenges: how to bring citizens, and primarily the young, closer to the European design and the European institutions, how to organise politics and the European political

address was how to simplify the founding treaties in such a way that the drafting of a Constitution for the European Union might result.

Discussion of the EURATOM Treaty was limited within the context of the Convention's debates. The Praesidium of the Convention regarded the Treaty as a distinct, complex, and technical subject which it was not appropriate for the Convention to consider.[38] The EURATOM Treaty was retained instead as a Protocol annexed to the Draft Constitutional Treaty. Some minor changes were outlined in this Protocol but they related mainly to the adaptation of the Treaty to the new rules for institutional and financial arrangements within the EU. However a declaration was appended to the Constitutional Treaty, signed by Germany, Ireland, Hungary, Austria, and Sweden noting that the Treaty had been unchanged since its adoption in 1957 and supporting an Intergovernmental Conference to review its terms as soon as possible.[39]

Failure by all the Member States of the EU to ratify the Constitutional Treaty created a difficult period of reflection and then negotiation on alternatives among the national governments which concluded with the introduction of a draft Reform Treaty by the German presidency in 2007. At the same time the EU has been engaged in a search for an Energy Strategy which would ensure that secure, competitive, and sustainable energy policy for the EU. This commitment is included in a more explicit manner in the Reform Treaty proposals than it has been to date in the Treaties. Yet the Reform Treaty proposals leave the EURATOM Treaty with a separate legal personality as one of the founding Treaties of the EU. Given that the national governments of the EU appear reluctant to repeal the Treaty (or indeed make substantial changes to it) this chapter now addresses the question of what 'value added' the Treaty may bring to the EU to enable the Member States to meet the challenges of climate change and energy solidarity which the Reform Treaty proposals target.

The commitment to energy solidarity may be more a response to the concerns of the Polish government and the governments of the Baltic States which are heavily reliant on Russian cooperation on energy resource transfer.[40] The Reform Treaty proposals confirm that the supranational competences with regard to the energy sector are still to be limited. It is proposed that measures in the field of energy should be taken by ordinary legislative procedures with qualified majority voting and co-decision in the EP. But this should not affect the rights of Member States

area in an enlarged Union and how to develop the Union into a stabilising factor and model in the new, multi-polar world.'

[38] Secretariat of the European Convention, *Suggested Approach for the EURATOM Treaty*, CONV 621/03 Brussels, 14 March 2003.

[39] Declaration 44 annexed to the Constitutional Treaty. For further discussion of the debate about the EURATOM Treaty during the Convention see P. M. Barnes, 'The Future of Euratom' in N. Neuwhal and S. Haack S (eds.), *Unresolved Issues of the Constitution for Europe* (Montreal: Les Editions Themis, 2007).

[40] S. Taylor, 'Securing EU energy and tackling climate change—what the Reform Treaty will do to help', *European Voice*, 2–29 Aug. 2007, at 6.

to decide on the choice of energy resources and the structure of their national energy industries. Furthermore decisions which significantly affect a Member State's energy choices and the general structure of energy supply remain subject to unanimity vote. It would thus appear that the Reform Treaty is proposing little change to the decision-making process which underpins the development of energy policy and measures in the EU.

The nuclear energy option is one without which the countries of the EU cannot balance their growing energy demands in a manner which would be both competitive and sustainable. This assumption is discussed in the section that follows. It is a pragmatic recognition that some states of the EU are more heavily dependent on the sector than others, that some states are in the process of developing new reactors, that others which have 'no-nuclear' policies nevertheless import electricity from states which are nuclear electricity producers. It is also recognition that the EURATOM Treaty continues to exist because it still retains value. It does provide a legal framework for action which might not be provided if the Treaty was subject to re-negotiation. The manner in which the national governments of the EU have decided to continue to 'guard' their rights to choose their national energy resources demonstrates how little room there is for bargaining and consensus building between the national governments. As such, agreement would be difficult to achieve on regulation of an energy resource and technology which is regarded as unsafe by many among the electorates of the EU's Member States. From a practical perspective the impact of failures to ensure safe operation of the industry in the geographical area of the EU could result in major environmental consequences including damage to human health and life. Politically it is unacceptable for the decisions made about one state's energy policy to carry with it the potential to significantly affect its fellow EU Member States.

V. The Changing Economic and Political Environments for Nuclear Energy

This section turns to a discussion of recent changes in the economic and political environments which underlie the evolution of the EU's new Energy Policy for Europe and the role of the nuclear sector in this policy.[41] The energy system of the EU is reliant on fossil fuels which because of the intensity of their usage have had major detrimental impacts on the environment. The EU is heavily dependent on imported supplies of the fossil fuels needed to meet its growing energy demand. An increasing element of this demand is being met by the use of renewable sources of energy which have the advantages of being indigenous and less damaging to the environment. However, the evidence would suggest that the

[41] *An Energy Policy for Europe* COM(2007)1, 10 Jan. 2007.

renewable technologies are not able to match the growing demand for energy in the foreseeable future.[42]

Nuclear electricity does require high levels of capital investment to be made at the construction phase but has low marginal operating costs and an ability to run most economically at very high load factors thus meeting the demand for volume base-load electricity. Increased global demand for energy will impact on the energy resources which the EU and the developing world are increasingly competing for. It is in this context that governments and the EU in recent years have looked with more interest at the benefits of the nuclear option.

Inability to meet demand with alternative sources was a major factor in the decision of French and Finnish governments in the period 2005–2007 to commission new reactors. It has been the driving force behind the decision of the Lithuanian, Latvian, Estonian, and Polish governments to enter into discussion for a joint project to build a new reactor at the Ignalina site in Lithuania. Bulgaria and Romania, acceding to the EU in January 2007, have a high level of dependency on the electronuclear industry and so support its continuance. Italy, which phased out its nuclear power plants following the referendum in 1987, is in a somewhat ambivalent position with regard to the electronuclear industry. The country is the world's largest importer of electricity from a variety of sources, including from nuclear generation. A new Energy Law, passed in 2004 reflected a change in the public's view of the nuclear sector with more support for the industry coming from younger Italians. The 2004 legislation opened up the possibility for joint ventures between the Italian energy companies and foreign companies producing nuclear electricity. The Italian state-owned utility ENEL now has a 12.5 per cent stake in a new reactor being constructed in France including in the design, construction phases as well as operation of the reactor. This is seen as a way of re-building Italy's nuclear technology skills and competences. In addition ENEL's subsidiary Slovenske Elektrame operates nuclear reactors in Slovakia. The debate about nuclear electricity has also been re-opened in other EU States such as Germany and the UK.

In March 2006, the European Commission launched a debate about how the EU was to achieve the competitive, sustainable, and secure energy policy which

[42] The contribution which renewable energy (RES) makes to the energy supply within the EU has risen by more than 50 per cent in absolute terms since the publication of the White Paper *Energy for the future—renewable sources of energy* COM(97)599, which set a target of 12 per cent of energy consumption to be met by renewable resources by 2010. Subsequent to this White Paper, Dir. 2001/77/EC on the Promotion of Electricity Produced from Renewable Energy Resources in the Internal Electricity Market set a target of 21 per cent of electricity generated to come from RES by 2010. Indicative targets were specified for the Member States in the Directive with a requirement to report on progress to the European Commission on an annual basis. As part of the Strategic European Energy Review which was undertaken by the European Commission in 2006 in preparation for the Energy Policy for Europe (n. 44 below), a strategy was also prepared for the RES. However, in the *Renewable Energy Road Map,* the somewhat disappointing conclusion was reached that: 'In spite of this progress... the EU looks unlikely to reach a contribution from energy resources exceeding 10% by 2010', COM(2006)848, 10 Jan 2007, at 4.

is required for the future. During the deliberations which ensued between March 2006 and March 2007 it was evident that the national governments of the EU continue to jealously guard their competence to choose their national energy policies, particularly their rights to choose the mix of energy resources which they use.[43] At the Brussels European Council of 8 and 9 March 2007, the European Commission presented an Action Plan for an Energy Policy for Europe which would achieve the aims of security of energy supply, ensuring the competitiveness of European economies and at the same time promoting environmental sustainability and combating climate change. This Action Plan was accepted by the European Council and accompanied by some ambitious targets to achieve curbs in greenhouse gas emissions. Furthermore, the European Council 'emphasize(d) that the EU is committed to transforming Europe into a highly energy-efficient and low greenhouse gas emitting economy'.[44]

It was acknowledged in the Energy Policy for Europe Action Plan (EPE) that no single element of policy provided all the answers and that energy policy must be addressed by many different policy areas including nuclear energy.[45] As a consequence of the changing acceptance of the nuclear sector, its increased economic viability, continued safety concerns, and developments of the EU's technological lead in this field certain conclusions about an increased use of nuclear electricity were highlighted in the EPE:

> Recalling that the EPE will fully respect Member States' choice of energy mix the European Council notes the Commission's assessment of the contribution of nuclear energy in meeting the growing concerns about safety of energy supply and CO2 emissions reductions while ensuring that nuclear safety and security are paramount in the decision-making process, confirms that it is for each and every Member State to decide whether to rely on nuclear energy and stresses that this has to be done while further improving nuclear safety and the management of radioactive waste...[46]

The role for the EU is thus identified 'to develop further, in conformity with Community law, the most advanced framework for nuclear energy in those Member States that choose nuclear power, meeting the highest standards of safety, security and non-proliferation as required by the EURATOM Treaty'.[47]

These views were endorsed by the EP which 'considers it vital that the European energy strategy should be based on maximum subsidiarity and that decisions concerning the energy mix should remain the prerogative of the EU member

[43] *Green Paper—A European Strategy for Sustainable, Competitive and Secure Energy*, COM(2006)105, 8 Mar. 2006.

[44] Council of the European Union Presidency Conclusions, Brussels European Council, 8–9 March 2007, at para. 32.

[45] N. 43 above, at para. 18.

[46] N. 44 above, at para. 11.

[47] Ibid.

states'.[48] But 'urges the Commission to investigate the development of nuclear energy in Member States, taking account of both the benefits of that technology (low volatility of production costs and no CO_2 emissions) and the risks linked to the existence of nuclear power stations (failures and waste disposal)'.[49]

In the two areas of liberalization in the development of the single energy market and safety and security in the nuclear sector a considerable degree of control has been passed to the Commission as the supranational authority with the competence to deal with the issues. The terms of the EURATOM Treaty gave the Commission a role as a de-politicized and benevolent technocracy based on a model outlined and supported by Monnet. As the Treaty has remained substantially unaltered since its ratification 50 years ago this is the approach and model which continues to define the role of the Commission in the area of nuclear safety and security. It is not the intention of this chapter to investigate the role of the Commission in exercising this autonomy in the area of nuclear energy. However, as a result of the transfer of competences to the Commission, its officials have developed a considerable expertise in dealing with nuclear safeguard controls in EU nuclear installations and the monitoring of levels of radioactive materials in the environment including radioactive waste. The outcome has been to develop a high level safety regime which is based on regulation supported by the terms of the EURATOM Treaty and voluntary harmonization of action by the national nuclear regulatory authorities.

Although the European Commission has the competence for a great deal of autonomy in dealing with nuclear issues on behalf of the EAEC, it has been traditionally seen as agnostic in the debates about the use of the nuclear technologies. This has been to respect and acknowledge the right of the national governments to choose the energy mix they considered appropriate for their national energy policies. But following some high profile comments made by Commission President Barroso,[50] Commissioner for Energy Andris Piebalgs,[51] and Commissioner for Competition Neelie Kroes[52] in autumn 2007 it would appear that there is support for an increased use of the technology within the Commission. This change

[48] *Report on a European strategy for sustainable, competitive and secure energy—Green Paper*, Committee ITRE raporteur, Eluned Morgan, EP(2006) A6–0426/2006, para. 31.

[49] N. 43 above, at para. 50.

[50] 'I believe that we are now standing on the brink of a Third Industrial Revolution—the Low Carbon Age... this will be driven by technology and new forms of energy... I believe that the Member States cannot avoid the question of nuclear power there has to be a full and frank debate about the issue', Speech 07/580, Commission President Barroso, *Europe's energy policy and the third industrial revolution,* at Loyola de Palacio Energy Conference, Madrid, 1 Oct. 2007.

[51] 'Europe has so far always enjoyed leadership in the area of nuclear technology. We have mastered all aspects of the nuclear fuel cycle and we market equipment and services throughout the world. This is a non negligible part of the EU competitiveness and surely a valid input to our Lisbon strategy on growth and job creation', Speech 07/564, Commissioner Andris Piebalgs, *The Energy Challenges in the EU—security of supply, sustainability and competitiveness—focus on nuclear,* at Sustainable Nuclear Energy Technology Platform, Brussels, 21 Sep. 2007.

[52] 'On Monday, 1st October 2007 Commissioner Neelie Kroes stated at a high level energy conference in Madrid that she was completely in favour of nuclear power', Statement in letter from the

of stance by the Members of the Commission was further confirmed in another speech by Commissioner Piebalgs:

The European Commission is well aware of the renewed interest for nuclear energy we witness today... The Commission is therefore particularly attentive to the benefits... Nuclear energy increases our energy independence and our security of supplies and contributes to the reduction of carbon dioxide emissions, but it is also still confronted by a number of outstanding issues that need to be tackled...[53]

As these statements were also coupled with proposals to establish an EU High Level Group on Nuclear Safety and Security and enhanced cooperation with the International Atomic Energy Agency (IAEA)[54] on issues such as non-proliferation and nuclear safety and security it appeared that support was continuing for the nuclear industry and the EURATOM Treaty within the EU. Other developments included the launch of the Sustainable Nuclear Energy Technology Platform in September 2007 to contribute to research into the development of carbon-free sources of energy and the agreement to *co-host* the European nuclear energy forum in Bratislava and Prague. The first meeting of this forum took place on 26–27 November 2007 in Bratislava with subsequent meetings alternating between the two capitals.

VI. The *Value Added* of the Treaty

Why has the EURATOM Treaty, despite much criticism, proved to be so durable? Is it because the EU's national governments lack the political willingness to repeal the Treaty? Yes undoubtedly, but this reluctance of the national governments is founded on a number of difficult and conflicting political pressures which surround the issue of the electronuclear industry and its supporting legal framework. It includes the motivations of a number of other actors in the political process, in particular the European Commission which has 'as part of its responsibilities... played a leading role by proposing an evolving application of the Treaty, taking into account the wider needs of the EU, of its countries, of its industry and of its civil society'.[55] It is based on significant controversies within the national nuclear energy policies of the EU's Member States. These highly divergent national interests would be as difficult to accommodate in a Treaty on supranational action in 2008 as the divergent national interests of 1957. The controversies of 1957 produced a limited Treaty. There does not appear to be any

Greens/European Free Alliance in the European Parliament to Commission President Barroso, 4 Oct. 2007.

[53] Speech 07/599, Commissioner Andris Piebalgs, *The Euratom Treaty and development of the nuclear industry*, at the International Law Association Congress, Brussels, 3 Oct. 2007.

[54] 12 Oct. 2007 launch of the High Level Group on Nuclear Safety and Waste Management.

[55] Ibid.

guarantee that an Intergovernmental Conference convened to prepare a Treaty to support nuclear technology developments would achieve a significantly different outcome in 2008.

The urgency in 2008 is to address the challenge of developing a secure, competitive, and sustainable energy policy for the EU 27. This urgency is greater in 2008 than it was for the EU 6 in 1957, as the EU 27 is operating in a very different geo-political and geo-economic world. Solidarity amongst the Member States on energy measures appears to offer the most effective way forward to meet the challenges the EU 27 faces but the rhetoric of the national governments does not match their action and protection of national interests continues as a constraint to proposed strategies. On the other hand the EURATOM Treaty makes the preambular commitment to 'joint effort undertaken without delay...' and thus confirms a commitment (which has not been repealed) to solidarity on aspects of developments relating to the nuclear sector.

The EURATOM Treaty forms part of the energy *acquis* of the EU which all States accept on their accession. It would be legally possible for a Member State to withdraw from the EAEC as it continues to have a separate legal personality from that of the EU. However this may prove to be difficult. From a legal perspective there is no provision made in the EURATOM Treaty for the withdrawal of a Member State from the EAEC. If a Member State wished to do so this could only be achieved through re-negotiation and ratification of the Treaty by all its signatories. From a practical perspective the Merger Treaty in 1967 brought together into a single set of institutions the work of the three Communities and thus gave the Commission a considerable element of autonomy of action in the area of nuclear safety and protection of health. This has been developed into what is considered by the IAEA to represent a high level of safety which does not require duplication of effort in order to monitor what is done within the EU's Member States. In order to meet their international obligations, in the absence of the mechanisms of the EURATOM Treaty, the EU Member States would be required to initiate alternative national mechanisms.

The work of the EAEC began in the 1950s when the new technology was regarded as an important way to meet growing energy demand. The requirements of the 1950s were for investment in the state owned utilities to encourage energy developments and stimulate economic growth. Whilst aspects of safety and disposal of the waste from the electronuclear industry were included in EURATOM Treaty their significance was not as apparent as it has become after 50 years of operation of the industry. The underlying paradigm of state support has been increasingly replaced by one of market functionality and liberalization in the electricity market. A number of categories of risk have been identified in association with the nuclear sector. It is for these issues that the EURATOM Treaty retains its importance as a legal framework for cooperative and collaborative action. They include the cost of the technology and in particular decommissioning of the large number of now-ageing European reactors, safety (including safe operation of reactors, prevention of accidents, safety in the context of terrorism attack at nuclear power plants), waste disposal, in particular long-term management of waste, and the possibilities of nuclear weapons proliferation if the use of nuclear technology is increased.

A. The Economics of Nuclear Developments

It is evident that none of the most commonly used technologies is the cheapest form of electricity production in all situations—there is both room and need for coal, gas, and nuclear to be utilized.[56] The economics of the electro-nuclear industry, long considered to be the major obstacle to its development, appear more favourable in 2007 in comparison with the increasing costs of other energy sources.[57] The cost of generation of electricity depends on a number of factors including the location of the plant, the price of the fuel used (apart from that for some renewables), the costs of labour in the industry, and the costs of borrowing to pay for the construction of the required power plant. Unlike other major producers of electricity, coal, and natural gas, nuclear prices are not determined by fluctuations in price of the basic raw materials. The price of nuclear electricity is mainly from the capital costs needed for the nuclear power plants. An advantage of the electronuclear electricity for the consumer is the stability of price and availability which may be assured. In combination these factors have led to a significant growth in support for the nuclear sector which is further enhanced by concerns about the rising price of oil and natural gas.

The EURATOM Treaty is based on the paradigm of a high level of state support for the development of the new technologies because of the high costs entailed. As such the Treaty supports what is an out-dated concept in EU energy policy where the paradigm of market functionality appears to have replaced it. The argument of this chapter is not that it is desirable to maintain this support for the electronuclear industry. Rather, the argument is that in the light of a number of practical issues with regard to the provision of alternative sources of energy a pragmatic decision has to be taken about the use of the technology. The costs of the renewable and other alternative sources of low carbon energy remain high. The nuclear option is therefore one considered by many national governments as the way forward to meet their national energy demands.

While there is strong support for the completion of the internal markets for gas and electricity through the adoption of market opening directives and regulations the accompanying measures needed to ensure that this happens appear to require high levels of state funding also. This is particularly the case with regard to measures to increase interconnectivity of the infrastructures needed

[56] *Projected costs of generating electricity—2005 update,* Joint report NEA/IEA (Paris: OECD, 2005), at 81.

[57] Annex 4 Comparison of costs of selected sources of electricity production.

to transfer energy within the integrated European energy market. There is also strong support for what is considered to be an ambitious programme of energy efficiency measures at local, regional, national, and EU levels[58] as outlined in the Commission Action Plan of 19 October 2006.[59] A great deal of state aid is required in order to advance the renewable technology and energy efficiency developments. It appears somewhat contradictory to castigate, in the interests of the market, support to the electro-nuclear industry and not to these other aspects of energy policy developments.

Both the EURATOM Treaty and the TEC may be used in dealing with questions relating to state aid to the electronuclear industry and as a brief review of the following rulings would suggest there are opportunities to deal with issues of state aid without a requirement to change the Treaty. In 2002, state aid was agreed for British Energy (BE). British Energy (the UK's privately owned nuclear generator), had been experiencing financial difficulties during 2002, and an approach was made to the UK government for aid to continue operating. The UK government provided BE with a credit facility of £410 million and produced a re-structuring plan for the company. The re-structuring plan transferred BE's nuclear waste liabilities to the UK government, a series of measures approaching £6 billion of, in effect, state aid. Following an investigation of the re-structuring proposals the measure was approved by the European Commission. It was agreed by the Commission as an appropriate measure to address the stated objectives. It was also consistent with the EURATOM Treaty articles relevant to worker safety and public protection.[60]

It is however possible to bring actions against national governments which offer high levels of support to the electricity industry using the terms of the TEC. The TEC rather than the EURATOM Treaty was the basis of the 2006 ruling of the Court of First Instance (CFI) in the case of a German tax exemption scheme as applied to nuclear power plants.[61] Provisions in German law require nuclear power plants to set up reserves to cover the costs of disposing of irradiated fuel and radioactive waste and closure of plants. These reserves may be counted among the liabilities of the undertakings and are subject to a reduction in the tax burden. In 1999 three German utilities requested that the European Commission should investigate the tax exemption scheme which was being applied to those reserves. In presenting its findings the CFI found that there was an advantage from lower taxes to the nuclear power plants but that it did not grant the specific advantage inherent to the idea of state aid.

[58] *Action Plan for Energy Efficiency, Realising the Potential*, COM(2006)545.

[59] Ibid.

[60] Dec. on State Aid which the UK government is planning to implement for BE Plc., COM(2004)3474.

[61] Case T-92/02 *Stadtwerke Schwabisch Hall GmbH et al* v. *the European Commission* [2006] ECR II-11.

In February 2005, the Finnish government issued a licence for the construction of an advanced Generation III European Pressurized Water Reactor (EPR) based on Pressurized Water Reactor (PWR) technology at the Olkiluoto site in Finland. The impression given of the project was that it was being built and developed without state aid. Subsequently two complaints were filed with DG Competition of the European Commission calling for an investigation of the new reactor development. One by Greenpeace concerned an export credit guarantee given by the French credit agency COFACE to the French nuclear company AREVA. The European Renewable Energies Federation (EREF) filed a broader action on the grounds of infractions of EU state aid requirements, export credits, public procurement legislation, and safety. The EREF complaint listed organizations not just in Finland and France but also in Sweden and Germany and the governments of those countries as being in probable violation of EU legislation. The complaints were lodged with DG Competition in 2004 but no resolution had been reached when the Commission launched an investigation of competition in the electricity sector as a whole in 2006. The overall objective of the sector enquiry was to address a number of matters impeding the development of a functioning, open, and competitive EU-wide energy market by 1 July 2007.

In September 2007, the Commission found that the financing of the Olkiluoto reactor did not constitute state aid nor did the export credit guarantee from COFACE to AREVA. The importance of the challenges by Greenpeace and the EREF were that they could potentially establish the principle that the electronuclear industry should be subsidized as it requires considerable input of capital. But the agreement of the Commission for state investment, loans at special rates, and support for the export of materials was not based on the difficulty of the nuclear sector operating in the market without state support. The findings of the Commission were based on the overall impact on the European energy market of the production of electricity from the new reactor development. In reviewing the findings both Greenpeace[62] and the EREF[63] however expressed a view that the Commission had not acted impartially but had acted in contradiction of early decisions about the use of export guarantees in intra-Community trade. In addition, for Greenpeace the ruling raised concerns that the result would be to discourage investment in alternative renewable energy technologies.[64]

B. Nuclear Safety and Security

Safety issues surrounding the nuclear sector became particularly prominent on the EU's policy agenda in the early 1990s as the prospect of enlargement to states of the former Soviet Union in Central and Eastern Europe became more realistic.

62 Greenpeace, Press release, 26 Sept. 2007.
63 EREF, Press release, 26 Sept. 2007.
64 N. 62 above.

Many of the reactors at the nuclear power plants in the candidate states were based on similar, graphite moderated light water reactors (RBMK) to those of the nuclear power plant in Chernobyl. The Chernobyl explosion in 1986 had been the result of a combination of seven examples of human error. However, other problems were evident in the Chernobyl type reactors as the safety standards appeared to have been sacrificed to the needs of building reactors which would serve dual purposes and have the potential to meet both military and civilian needs. In addition to this the political structures in the former Soviet Union left many concerns about the failure of staff in the nuclear power plants to have developed an overall safety culture.

Once the formal application and accession process was begun, the prospective new Member States were the subject of intensive review by the EU's institutions of all areas of their economic and political development to determine if they fulfilled the core requirements and conditions of membership. Among these was the overall objective of bringing the nuclear reactors operating in the candidate states to the same standards of safe operation as those operating in the existing member states. A mandate was given to the Commission, and in particular the personnel of DG TREN, which enabled them to play a unique lead role in the investigation, analysis, and monitoring of the various reactors in the candidate states.

The mandate for the Commission was possible because of the powers given in the terms of the EURATOM Treaty. Working with the International Atomic Energy Agency and supported by the acceptance in the candidate states of the legal *acquis* of the EURATOM Treaty, the Commission was involved in making recommendations which have led to closure of some reactors or the introduction of radical measures to improve safety in others. These closures have been the subject of much heated controversy among and between all the EU's Member States, old and new, those in which there is support for the industry and those where there is opposition to its use. However, closure programmes have been carried out, supported by EU funding.

There is a high dependency on nuclear electricity in the new Member States with little prospect of quickly and easily finding alternatives and commitment to further developments.[65] Whilst it was generally acknowledged that the EU has a comprehensive nuclear safety regime based on international standards there was nevertheless significant concern that as a result of the accession of the new states the measures might become less stringent. Indeed in the view of the Commission 'it is no longer desirable to consider nuclear safety in a purely national perspective. Only a common approach can guarantee the maintenance of a high level of nuclear safety in an enlarged EU.'[66] In 2002, the Commission introduced a Nuclear Safety Strategy including a series of legislative measures targeting safety

[65] For example, in 2006 the governments of Latvia, Estonia, Lithuania, and Poland signed an agreement for the construction of a new reactor at the Ignalina power plant.

[66] *Nuclear Safety in the EU*, COM(2002)605, at 11.

at nuclear installations and also national arrangements for funding to decommission reactors. The Commission officials recommended that this legislation should be in place before the new Member States acceded in 2004.[67]

The objective of the proposed legislation was to change aspects of the *non-binding acquis* of voluntary harmonization of national safety practices.[68] The national regulatory authorities were to retain responsibility for safety at the national installations but with increased competence for the EU in the monitoring of the national provisions. An important element of the proposed legislation was a definition of nuclear installations to be any civilian facility and its associated land, buildings, or equipment used throughout the nuclear fuel cycle until the facility was cleared of any radiological restrictions placed on its use. This includes the processing, use, handling, storage, and disposal (temporarily or permanently) of radioactive materials and would bring into the competence of the EU aspects of the safe management of high level radioactive waste which is a major problem for the industry.

The legal basis for these proposals came from several articles of the EURATOM Treaty. Article 2b EURATOM stipulates that the Community should establish uniform safety standards to protect the health of workers and the general public and have the competence to ensure that they are applied. Article 30 EURATOM gives greater clarity and definition of what the expression 'standards' means. Article 31 EURATOM provides for the scrutiny of the legislation by a group of scientific experts appointed by the Member States and consultation of the EP. Article 32 EURATOM provides for revision of the basis of the safety standards. Although these articles do not include the safety of the installations, a ruling by the European Court of Justice (ECJ) in December 2002 had confirmed that the technical competence of national authorities to deal with the safety of nuclear installations did not preclude the EU from legislating on the issue.[69] In the opinion of the ECJ, it was not appropriate for the safety of the workers and the public to be seen in some way as separate to the issue of safety of the installations themselves.

Under the terms of the EURATOM Treaty there is no requirement for the Council of Ministers to do anything more than formally consult the EP on proposed measures. In practice the Commission does take the concerns of the EP

[67] The nuclear 'package', proposed by the Commission on 6 Nov. 2003 comprised:
—Framework Dir. on Safety of Nuclear Installations (not adopted at time of writing);
—Dir. on radioactive waste (not adopted);
—Dec. authorizing the Commission to negotiate an agreement with Russia on trade in nuclear materials (adopted by the European Council on 6 Nov. 2002).

[68] This so-called non-binding *acquis* is based on a Council Res. of 22 July 1975 (77/C 181/1), which referred to the desirability of aligning safety requirements in the context of a harmonized approach which would draw on collaboration between the national governments.

[69] Case C-29/99 *Commission* v. *Council* [2002] ECR I-11221.

into account and there is much cooperation between the two institutions.[70] This cooperation was evident during the discussions about these legislative proposals. More than one hundred amendments to the proposed legislation were identified by the EP during 2003. Many of these proposals were focused on the provisions dealing with the national financing arrangements for decommissioning. The Commission's view was that the EP's expectations on financing were too high and would not be acceptable to the Council of Ministers. EP amendments which were adopted were those relating to public information dissemination and research and technology development.

In November 2003 there was deadlock in the Council of Ministers as the Swedish, Finnish, and British governments proposed a non-legally binding alternative to the proposed Directives. On the other hand the commitment of the Commission for the proposals has remained unaltered:

> A Community intervention is indispensable to guarantee the maintenance of a high level of nuclear safety within the enlarged European Union...The absence of Community legislation would be prejudicial to Community citizens and to the interest of the enlarged EU.[71]

However amendments were introduced by the Commission in 2004, but the proposals were still unadopted in autumn 2007 as a result of the strength of the opposition from the national governments.

Of all the concerns which are currently affecting the electronuclear industry safety related issues are the most difficult to address. They encompass a number of areas amongst which are safe disposal of the radioactive waste, safe decommissioning of nuclear plants at the end of their operational lives in addition to concerns about the possible use by terrorists of attack of nuclear installations or the use of materials intended for civilian purposes for weapons manufacture. Lack of accurate information often plays a factor in public disquiet about forms of technology developments. The media plays an important role in the safety debate. The Chernobyl accident received a great deal of media attention and it was the publicity of horrific injuries to those who were among the first to tackle the fires in the reactor which have become associated by many people with the whole industry.

With the passage of time people's concerns about Chernobyl have been quietened particularly as the plant is now closed and assurances about the nature

[70] This relationship between the EP and the European Commission is more than informal willingness to cooperate, it is supported also by the Framework Agreement on relations between the two institutions which was signed in 2000 and renewed in 2005. This agreement covers areas of dialogue and political cooperation between the two institutions, political responsibility, the flow of information, and organization of parliamentary proceedings. These points are expanded in annexes to the agreements pointing to the involvement of the EP in international relations and the transmission of confidential information.

[71] Amended proposal for Council Directive (EURATOM) laying down basic obligations and general principles on the safety of nuclear installations and amended proposal for Council Directive (EURATOM) on the safe management of spent nuclear fuels and radioactive waste, COM(2004)526, 23 Sept. 2004, at 4.

of similar technology used elsewhere have been made. However 'public opinion surveys conducted by the Commission show that while they know little about radioactive waste... (they are) concerned about it and have very little trust in the nuclear industry' and 'ninety percent of respondents thought that the lack of a decision on how to dispose of high level waste had a negative effect on the image of nuclear energy'.[72] Other public opinion surveys show that 53 per cent of the Europeans perceive nuclear power as more of a risk than an advantage with lack of confidence in the safe disposal of radioactive waste, the protection of radioactive materials against misuse, and fear of terrorist attacks on nuclear facilities featuring among a high proportion of respondents concerns.[73] It would therefore appear that for many people the safe disposal of the radioactive waste is the major concern and if that was resolved then there would be more popular support for the nuclear option.

Setting aside new nuclear plant construction which may come from the pressure of the pro-nuclear environmental lobby, about one-third of the EU's electricity demand is currently met by nuclear generation. It is unlikely that this will alter to any major extent in the foreseeable future. Waste has been generated already and it will continue to be produced. As EU Member States decommission older reactors or respond to the concerns of their populations for phase out of the nuclear capacity, appropriate management of spent nuclear fuels and other forms of radioactive waste has become of vital importance. Low level waste is disposed of in shallow burial sites, some waste is stored in ponds in order to reduce its temperature before storage. How to deal with the long-term management of the most dangerous, albeit relatively small, amounts of high level and long lived intermediate waste have still to be addressed. After 50 years of operation of the nuclear industry there is a considerable amount of these materials in intermediate storage facilities still to be dealt with.

Despite media speculation early in 2004 that the UK government was considering shooting high level waste at the sun, the scientific evidence favours the more earthbound concept of deep geological disposal.[74] Discussion of the development of regional facilities which may be used by more than one Member State has begun. While there appear to be no technical difficulties to geological disposal the identification of appropriate sites has not yet been made. The 2002 proposals for legislation had included objectives to promote the development of common standards and good practice with regard to spent nuclear fuel and radioactive waste management, requirements for the EU Member States to establish clearly defined programmes for waste management, to encourage more coordination of

[72] D. M. Taylor, 'The Management of Radioactive waste in the EU—opinions, situation and proposals for changes' (2005) 9 *Practice Periodical of Hazardous, Toxic and Radioactive Waste Management* 1, 13–19.

[73] CEC *Europeans and Nuclear Safety*, Special Eurobarometer Report 271, Feb. 2007.

[74] P. Brown, 'Shoot it at the sun', *The Guardian*, 14 Apr. 2004, at 3.

the research into waste disposal across the EU, and to encourage greater public involvement and transparency within the sector.

Whilst the measures remain unadopted, the proposals were based on the EURATOM Treaty and have demonstrated how the Treaty may be used to raise the issues for debate amongst the EU's 27 Member States. The UK has remained one of the EU States which did not support the legislative proposals. But in 2006 the UK House of Lords Select Committee on the EU concluded that an important role did exist for the EU to take a lead in safe management and disposal of radioactive waste because of 'grave concerns that Member States are failing to educate citizens about the use of nuclear power, how the safety of nuclear installations is maintained and of the action taken and options available to Member States to manage the radioactive waste produced'.[75] The EURATOM Treaty thus gives an opportunity to establish a legal framework to support this exhortation to ensure that the general public in all Member States is encouraged to become involved in these decisions through open and transparent public debates.

C. Nuclear Non-proliferation and the EURATOM Treaty

This chapter has focused on the peaceful use of nuclear technology to generate electricity but a number of security matters are of major concern and have the potential to be exacerbated as a result of the growth of interest in nuclear generated electricity. They include global disquiet about the access to weapons of mass destruction in some politically unstable states and the possibility of terrorist groups gaining access to nuclear materials. Despite the commitment of the EU's Member States to the peaceful use of the technology similar types of advanced technologies are involved in both civilian and military use of the nuclear materials. This has led to the description of Siamese twins of nuclear power being applied to the technology—the military atom and the civilian atom.[76] Indeed the UK and France, as holders of nuclear weapons in the EU, had developed their military capabilities before they began to use nuclear technology to generate electricity in the 1950s. It was a reality recognized in the EU's 2000 Green Paper on security of energy supply where nuclear energy was described as 'a less than perfect energy option...(one of the) undesirables...a source of energy in doubt...tainted by the original sin of dual usage—civil and military'.[77]

Pressure on the availability of high grade ore for both types of developments will lead to more emphasis on recovery and reprocessing in turn leading to expansion

[75] House of Lords, *Managing nuclear safety and waste: the role of the EU*, EU Committee 37th Report 2005–2006, 6 July 2006 (London: Stationery Office, 2006), at 110.

[76] Hannes Alven, Swedish Noble Prize-winning nuclear physicist cited in F. Barnaby and J. Kemp, *Secure energy civil nuclear power, security and global warming*, Briefing Paper, March 2007, at 10. Published on the Internet by the Oxford Research Group: http://www.oxfordresearchgroup.org.uk.

[77] *Towards a European Strategy for the security of energy supply—Green Paper*, COM(2000)769, at 31–2.

of capabilities in developments in the technologies in those states globally which are users of nuclear electricity.[78] As a result levels of concern about security and nuclear weapons proliferation are increasing with these global developments in the civilian use of the technology. Nuclear non-proliferation represents a major plank of the EU's Security and Defence Policy (ESDP). But the variations which exist among the EU's Member States on questions relating to nuclear weapons strategy add to the difficulties of adopting a coherent approach to the ESDP. Furthermore it is difficult to envisage a situation where the governments of either the UK or France (the only states of the EU with nuclear weapons) would accept any European action which might impinge on their national nuclear weapons policies.

The EURATOM Treaty is one of two treaties which have an impact on the approach to nuclear non-proliferation which the EU may adopt—the Nuclear Non-Proliferation Treaty of 1968) (NPT) being the other.[79] Both contain measures and statutes on safeguards of materials. India, Pakistan, and Israel are known to have nuclear weapons and have not signed the NPT and North Korea is now withdrawn. France and the UK of the 188 signatory states of the NPT are declared Nuclear Weapons States (the others being the US, Russia, and China). Some NATO countries, the EU Member States of Germany, the Netherlands, Belgium, Italy, Greece, and the applicant state of Turkey, have forces which are trained to use US nuclear weapons. All the NPT signatory states (those which are nuclear weapons states and those which have agreed to exclusively peaceful uses of the technology) have voluntary agreements and protocols with the IAEA for inspection to ensure that nuclear materials are not being diverted to military use.

There is overlap in the work of the IAEA and the European Commission on nuclear safeguards. The safety regime which has been adopted within the EU is based on the 25 safety principles of the IAEA which are also the basis of the International Convention on Nuclear Safety. In instances of duplication of effort the IAEA procedures are invoked to verify that those of the EURATOM Treaty have been adhered to. Through the European Safeguards Agency the EU states have in place a more comprehensive and effectively monitored system. As the EURATOM Treaty is part of the *acquis* for all EU Member States, the measures which are in place have the support of the rulings of the ECJ and a range of implementation mechanisms. For the IAEA and its monitoring through inspection of what is happening in nuclear power plants issues of non-compliance with the terms of the NPT are harder to determine.

[78] The price of uranium ore tripled in 2007 as a result of increased demand.

[79] The Nuclear Non-Proliferation Treaty has 188 signatory states and is the major international Treaty dealing with the use of nuclear weapons.

D. Support for New Developments—Something for Everyone?

The primary objective of the EURATOM Treaty is to support the development of the nuclear industry and provision for funding for research and technology developments was included in Article 7 of the EURATOM Treaty in 1957. The TEC on the other hand had no such provision for research and technology funding in its original provisions. However, since the 1980s, the EU has developed a successive series of Research and Technology Development (RTD) programmes, which now include the EURATOM programmes. In the Seventh Framework RTD programme (FP7) proposed by the European Commission (2007–2013) the proposals for funding of the EURATOM Research Programme were also identified. But FP7 is a multi-annual programme to run for seven years, and the EURATOM regulations are for a multi-annual programme for five years. The possibility of an extension of the EURATOM funding is included for 2011–2013 to bring the funding for both areas into line and enable more effective management of the transfer of the funds to the national level. The EURATOM budget was not forwarded for scrutiny to the EP with the other elements of the FP7 Budget, as this is not a requirement under the terms of the Treaty.

Agreement on the budget for the EURATOM Research Programme 2007–2011 was difficult to achieve because of the divergent views of the national governments about further developments in nuclear fission technology. The Austrian government exercised its prerogative of veto with regard to funding for nuclear fission technology, other than that associated with decommissioning reactors and safe disposal of radioactive waste.[80] Agreement was eventually reached in the Council of Ministers on 24 July 2006 with the bulk of available funding being directed to new fusion technology developments.[81] The resolution of the controversy on this funding showed the flexibility of the EURATOM Treaty to respond to the concerns of those who are not in favour of the continued use of nuclear technology as well as those Member States which are.

Of the total budget for EURATOM research of €2.7 billion, €2.1 billion are to be allocated to fusion research and in particular the development of the International Thermonuclear Experimental Reactor (ITER) which is under the auspices of the International Atomic Energy Agency (IAEA). The agreement for the ITER development in Cadarache, France, was signed in June 2006 and will include input from partners in Japan, China, India, Russia, South Korea, and the US. Fusion technology is regarded by many as having the potential to make a major contribution to sustainable and secure energy supplies in Europe but is unlikely to be at the stage of commercial production before 2050 because of the

[80] Nuclear fission is the process of splitting molecules of uranium-235 in order to produce energy and is the basis of the nuclear technology currently used.

[81] Nuclear fusion is the process of fusing two hydrogen atoms to form a single atom of helium. One gram of the fuel produced can develop the same energy as 45 barrels of oil. However, the process requires extremely high temperatures which it is not yet possible to achieve and sustain in a reactor.

difficulties of achieving and maintaining the high temperatures needed for the reaction to take place.

VII. Conclusions

There are many problems to be overcome by the EU in the search for a legal and constitutional framework to meet the challenges of climate change and energy security. Although considered to be one of the founding Communities of the EU the EAEC, established by the EURATOM Treaty, was focused solely on joint action on limited aspects of nuclear energy policy development. As it has remained substantively unchanged throughout the history of the EU and retains a separate legal personality to the TEU, the EURATOM Treaty contributes to the complexities involved in the development of a more coherent and holistic EU energy strategy. The purpose of this chapter has been to investigate the reasons why the national governments of the EU are reluctant to take what appears to be a logical step and repeal this Treaty.

In reviewing the history of the negotiations for the EAEC established by the EURATOM Treaty the evidence pointed to a crowded policy space which constrained supranational action. Fifty years later, despite significant changes in the political and economic environments for the nuclear sector, national differences and lack of consensus about supranational action remain deeply entrenched. National governments in the EU 27 jealously guard their competence to choose their national energy policies. As a result, although there is a revival of interest in the use of nuclear technology, it appears that there is no opportunity or willingness for policy bargaining amongst the national governments to produce an alternative legal framework.

The underlying paradigm of the EURATOM Treaty was that of an energy sector which was heavily regulated and in which public bodies were supported by high levels of state support. This was a characteristic feature of the European energy sector in the 1950s but has been increasingly replaced within the EU by the paradigm of market functionality. The change of dominant paradigm has brought radical changes to the European energy sector. It has moved from heavily regulated structures dominated by monopolistic (often state-owned companies) to more openness, deregulation, and liberalization. Support for which has been confirmed in the 2007 Reform Treaty proposals which highlight the importance of the liberalized energy market and energy solidarity in order to meet the challenges of climate change and energy security.

As the market mechanisms of liberalization and deregulation have come to dominate the operating environment of the electricity industry issues such as the safety of operation of the industry have gained added prominence. Firstly because of fears that privatized utilities may not address them as assiduously as the state-owned enterprises (the French state-owned enterprises had developed a reputation for very high levels of safety for example). Secondly, as energy demands in the EU have grown, governments have extended the operating licences of existing reactors in addition to the commissioning of new developments. The EU 27 has 152 reactors, 25 per cent of the global total of 442 reactors, operating within its geographical region. The *value added* of the EURATOM Treaty for the EU is that a significant body of safety related legislation has been developed to protect the workers in the industry and the general public living in the vicinity of nuclear power plants based on its articles.[82]

The EURATOM Treaty also provides the legal framework for the European Commission to engage in intensive monitoring of the safety practices at nuclear power plants. The Safeguards Office and the regime which has been established as a result to ensure that the nuclear technology and materials are not diverted to military purposes provides an effective guarantee of control of nuclear materials, particularly as this is also supported by the rulings and case law of the ECJ. In addition a substantial and complementary range of actions have been established on the basis of the accession of the EAEC to the conventions of the IAEA on safety of nuclear materials. Although the Treaty may bring complexity to the process of decision-making, through it the EU does have the capacity to provide the framework for action on these issues throughout the whole geographical region of the EU's 27 Member States.

The provision of state aid to the modern electronuclear industry is more difficult to address through the terms of the EURATOM Treaty. Although the promotional aspect of the Treaty is less important than it was, funding for nuclear technology developments remains available. The budget for nuclear research continues as a separate budgetary line, and as such might be considered to be a continued support for the industry. However, in the 2006 debate about the allocation of the EURATOM funds evidence was provided that this budget may be used in the development of what is considered to be the safer nuclear fusion technology. Also, while not all would agree (for example the environmental NGOs, Greenpeace, and the EREF), issues of inappropriate state aid to the electronuclear industry have been resolved using the terms of the TEC.

Major questions remain about how to ensure that future developments in nuclear technology take place in an open, transparent, and accountable way. The EP is regarded as an important contributor to increasing openness and transparency of action for the citizens of the EU. For the objectives of the Treaty to be achieved a considerable degree of autonomy of competence for action was given to the European Commission. But the decision-making process remained based on inter-governmental action between the national governments of the signatory states of the European Atomic Energy Community with only a minimal role accorded to the EP. It is in this aspect of the Treaty that the ineffectiveness

[82] The focus of attention in this chapter has been on the electronuclear industry but other safety standards, e.g. for radiological protection in the use of medical procedures, protection of aircrews in civil aviation, fixing permissible levels or radioactive contamination for foodstuffs, arrangements for exchanging information and radiological emergency plans, have also been introduced using the terms of the Treaty.

of measures based on its articles is most clearly demonstrated. An environment of cooperation between the EP and the European Commission has developed in the discussion of proposals for nuclear energy policy and legislation. However, this is not within the Treaty framework and the EP is not given the same powers of co-decision and co-legislature as it has in other areas of EU energy legislation. Without significant Treaty changes the potential role for the EP to ensure that the decision-making processes of the EAEC reflect greater openness and accountability will remain constrained.

In the introduction to this chapter criticisms that the EURATOM Treaty was out of date and biased towards the electronuclear industry were highlighted. The evidence suggests that some aspects of the Treaty do indeed render it out-dated and biased. On the other hand the flexibility of the Treaty is demonstrated in its effectiveness as a basis for a legal and constitutional framework to respond to concerns about safety and security. The Treaty may not be a perfect instrument, but until such time as it is repealed or radically reformed it does retain the potential to make a positive contribution to the EU's search for a framework to deal with the problems of energy security and climate change.

Annex 1 Number of reactors by Member and Candidate State (to Summer 2007)

	% of national electricity produced by the nuclear sector	Number of operable reactors	Reactors under construction	Reactors planned and proposed
Belgium	55	7		
UK	19	23		
Finland	26	4	1	
France	78	59		2
Netherlands	4	1		
Spain	23	9		
Sweden	52	10		
Germany	32	17		
Czech Rep	41	6		2
Hungary	34	4		
Lithuania (1)	72	1		1*
Slovakia	55	6		2
Slovenia (2)	39	1		
Bulgaria	44	4		2
Romania	8	1	1	3
Croatia		(with Slovenia)		
Turkey (3)		0		3/5
EU 27 + candidates		152	2	11
World (4)		442	28	204

Source: various European Commission and IAEA.

Notes

1. Lithuania—planned new nuclear power plant with Latvia, Estonia, and Poland
2. Croatia—no nuclear power plant of its own but Croatian national electricity company has co-ownership of plant at Krsko in Slovenia
3. Turkey—accession to the EU estimated by 2020
4. 68 of the global total of planned reactors are in China

Annex 2 The international nuclear event scale (INES)

Event type	INES level	Description
Deviation	0	Event with no safety significance
	1	*Anomaly* On- and off-site impact: nil Defence-in-depth degradation: beyond the authorised operating regime
Incident	2	*Incident* Off-site impact: nil On-site impact: significant spread of contamination, *or* over-exposure of worker Defence-in-depth degradation: significant failures in safety provisions
	3	*Serious incident* Off-site impact: very small release—public exposure at a fraction of prescribed limits On-site impact: Major contamination, *or* acute health effects to a worker Defence-in-depth degradation: near-accident—no safety layers remaining
	4	*Accident without significant off-site risk* Off-site impact: minor release—public exposure of the order of prescribed limits On-site impact: significant damage to the reactor core or radiological barriers, *or* worker fatality
Accident	5	*Accident with off-site risk* Off-site impact: limited release—partial implementation of local emergency plans On-site impact: severe damage to the reactor core or radiological barriers
	6	*Serious accident* Off-site impact: significant release—full implementation of local emergency plans
	7	*Major accident* Off site impact: major release, widespread health and environmental effects

Source: Sustainable Development Commission, *The role of nuclear power in a low carbon economy, Paper 6: Safety and Security* (Sustainable Development Commission, UK, 2006), at 37.

Annex 3 Examples of events rated INES 3 and above in Europe

Level	Date	Place	Characteristics
7	1986	Chernobyl, USSR (power station)	Widespread environmental and human health consequences
6	1957	Kyshtym, USSR (reprocessing plant)	Large off-site release and evacuation of local population
5[1]	1957	Windscale, UK (military reactor)	Off-site release and restrictions on consuming food produced locally
4	1973	Windscale, UK (reprocessing plant)	Release of radioactive material into a plant operating area
4	1977	Bohunice A1, Czechoslovakia (power station)	Accident during fuel loading resulted in corrosion damage to fuel and activity release into plant area. Reactor shut down and decommissioned
4	1980	Saint-Laurent, France (power station)	Partial damage to reactor core: no off-site release (reactor repaired and operated until 1992)
3	1989	Vandellos, Spain (power station)	Turbine fire degraded plant's safety systems. No core damage or off-site release. [Violation of safety procedures, lax safety management]
3	2005	Sellafield, UK (reprocessing plant)	Leakage of highly active liquid into secondary containment: undetected for several months

Source: Adapted from Sustainable Development Commission, *The role of nuclear power in a low carbon economy, Paper 6: Safety and Security* (Sustainable Development Commission, UK, 2006), at 38.

[1] Although classified as INES 5 the Windscale fire of 1957 was considered in a study by J. Garland and R. Wakeford, published in the journal *Atmospheric Environment*, autumn 2007, to be more severe than reported at the time and as such should be re-classified as INES 7.

Annex 4 Comparison of costs of selected sources of electricity production

	Coal	Gas	Nuclear	Wind	Hydro	Solar
Construction times in years	4	2–3	4–5	1–2	Na (3)	Na
Lifetime of use in years	45	25	30–60	Na	Na	Na
Cost (2005) in euros/ MWh (1)	30–50	35–75	40–45	35–175	25–95	140–430
Projected cost (2030) euros/ MWh with 20–30 euros/t(CO2)	45–70	40–85	40–45	28–170	25–90	55–260
Investment costs as % of total costs	30	15	50	Na	Na	Na
GHG emissions (kg CO2 eq/ MWh)	750–800	400–440	15	10–30	5–20	100
EU 27 Import dependency 2005	39%	57%	Almost 100% for uranium ores (2)	Nil	Nil	Nil
2030	59%	82%				
Proven reserves/ Annual Production	155 years	64 years	85 years of reasonable reserves	Renewable	Renewable	Renewable
Operation and maintenance costs as % of total costs	20	10	30	13	Na	Na
Efficiency	40–48%	40–50%	33%	95–98%	95–98%	Na
Fuel costs % of total costs	45	80–90	20	Na	Na	Na
Fuel price sensitivity	Medium	Very high	Low	Nil	Nil	Nil

Source: various IEA and Commission

Notes

1. Dependent on the technology used.
2. Uranium is however available from a wide range of sources including reprocessing. Also in the opinion of the Nuclear Industry Association 'it would be possible to purchase the entire lifetime supply for a reactor and stockpile it next to the reactor if it was considered that there was any danger to supplies' House of Lords, *Managing nuclear safety and waste: the role of the EU*, EU Committee 37th Report 2005–2006, 6 July 2006, 83.
3. Na: Comparable figures not available.

Biodiversity Loss and the Prospects for International Cooperation: EU Law and the Conservation of Migratory Species of Wild Animals

*Richard Caddell**

I. Introduction

One of the primary components of the Sixth and current Environmental Action Programme (EAP)[1] of the European Union (EU) is the need to halt biodiversity decline within the Community as a matter of priority, an obligation augmented by the commitments prescribed under the Convention on Biological Diversity (CBD) to meet this ambitious target by 2010. As is well known, nature conservation law under the purview of the EU is focused primarily through two key legislative provisions, Directive 79/409/EEC on the Conservation of Wild Birds (Wild Birds Directive)[2] and Directive 92/43/EEC on the Conservation of Natural Habitats and of Wild Fauna and Flora (Habitats Directive),[3] augmented in recent years by the elaboration of a distinct European Community Biodiversity Strategy which seeks to direct efforts towards attaining the 2010 objectives prescribed by the CBD and the Sixth EAP.

This article focuses on efforts to address the conservation needs and, in many cases, the parlous conservation status of a particular type of wild fauna under EU law, namely migratory species. Migratory species of wild animals are especially susceptible to anthropogenic pressures; yet, conversely, the development of effective conservation and management measures in relation to such species has proved

* Lecturer in Law, Swansea University, Wales (UK). I am greatly indebted to the two anonymous reviewers and the *Yearbook* editor, Thijs Etty, for their assistance and highly constructive comments on previous drafts of the paper; to Professor Robin Churchill (University of Dundee) for helping to shape my knowledge and understanding of many of the issues raised in this paper; and to Mr Konstantin Kreiser (Birdlife International) and Dr Mark Simmonds (Whale and Dolphin Conservation Society) for sharing their insights into NGO participation within the CMS umbrella. Any subsequent errors or misconceptions of law, fact, or science are solely the responsibility of the author.

1 [2002] OJ L242/1.

2 [1979] OJ L103/1.

3 [1992] OJ L206/7.

to be highly problematic in practice. The sheer diversity of migratory behaviour and the transnational nature of migration necessitate broad-based cooperation in respect of such animals, while remaining cognisant of the limitations inherent in an overly generalized approach, with a series of species- and region-specific solutions required in order to develop effective conservation measures. Given the demands that the development of these policies will inevitably entail in terms of resources and expertise, it is perhaps unsurprising that such initiatives have often developed in a disjointed and ad hoc manner and that, correspondingly, the protection of migratory species has been chronically understudied from a legal perspective.

The primary international instrument in this respect is the Convention on the Conservation of Migratory Species of Wild Animals 1979 (Bonn Convention),[4] which mandates national action to protect endangered species and facilitates the development of subsidiary agreements to elaborate pragmatic and effective solutions in the context of individual species deemed to have an unfavourable conservation status. The Bonn Convention has proved rather inadequate in the past; however it is currently considered to be evolving as an increasingly well-supported regime with the potential to generate a substantial body of conservation initiatives.[5] Some of the individual subsidiary agreements to the Bonn Convention are also in the process of becoming sophisticated regimes themselves, with the ability to develop viable policies that may advance progress towards the conservation of migratory species. Nevertheless, considerable problems remain within the structure of the Bonn Convention, not least its lack of enforcement powers, endemic under-funding, and its inherent Eurocentricity,[6] with the overwhelming majority of its major subsidiary agreements based in and around Europe, and many parties and eligible Range States also constituting Member States of the EU.

Thus far, the capability of the key EU nature conservation policies to effectively address the array of migratory species that constitute a sizeable proportion of European biodiversity has been virtually unexplored.[7] The EU has not to date elaborated a general policy on migratory species, a position born presumably out of reasons of pragmatism. Instead, migrants are currently afforded protection primarily under the two cornerstone nature conservation directives. Both instruments have strongly assisted in the protection of migratory species from anthropogenic threats—especially those related to habitats—and sectoral polices, such as those in the fields of fisheries and agriculture, also continue to

[4] Germany, 19 November 1979 (entered into force 1 Nov. 1983), (1979) 19 *International Legal Materials* 11. Ratified by 99 countries (status as of 4 Feb. 2007).

[5] On the problems associated with the Bonn Convention see R. Caddell, 'International Law and the Protection of Migratory Wildlife: An Appraisal of Twenty-Five Years of the Bonn Convention' (2005) 16 *Colorado Journal of International Environmental Law and Policy*, 113.

[6] Ibid., at 152.

[7] For a concise exception see N. Matz, 'Chaos or Coherence? Implementing and Enforcing the Conservation of Migratory Species through Various Legal Instruments' (2005) 65 *Zeitschrift für ausländisches öffentliches Recht und Völkerrecht* 197–216, at 208–10.

play a key role in the conservation of such species. However, despite the strong European element present in the current operation of the Bonn Convention, the relevant international and EC initiatives on migratory species operate almost exclusively in parallel to each other with little deliberate synergy between the two systems, notwithstanding the great potential that exists for complementary activity between the international and EU regimes in this respect.

Accordingly, this article seeks to offer a critical appraisal of the ability of the EC nature conservation directives to deliver effective solutions in respect of the conservation needs of migratory species. In so doing, there will also be a concise examination of the Bonn Convention structure and its inherent deficiencies, which accordingly mandate a strong EU-wide tier of regulation as far as threatened species of European migrants are concerned. There then follows an evaluation of the scope for interaction between the two systems, observing that the establishment of a pragmatic working relationship between the Bonn Convention and EU may have the potential to enhance conservation measures under both regimes, and advocating that these possibilities are explored further by both actors as a means of working towards achieving current commitments in respect of halting biodiversity loss.

II. Migration and the Limits of the Law

Migration remains one of the more mysterious events of the natural world. A vast array of species may be termed 'migratory' in nature, ranging from birds, land mammals, fresh and saltwater species, and even insects, all of which will undertake some form of regular movement. As observed by de Klemm, '[m]igration may be defined as a cyclical, and therefore predictable, phenomenon whereby certain animals perform periodic movements between two separate geographic areas, one area usually being where they breed'.[8] Despite the utility of this general definition, however, the phenomenon of migration corresponds to few generic principles and migratory behaviour varies substantially between species.

Scientists predominantly view migration as a series of synchronized movements whereby populations of a particular species will relocate between their 'two worlds', namely their breeding ground and wintering area.[9] The primary motivation for such movement, often involving arduous and perilous journeys, is considered to be related to the quality of habitat available to the individual species in question.[10] Migrants are generally required to traverse a particular geographical

[8] C. de Klemm, 'Migratory Species in International Law' (1989) 29 *Natural Resources Journal* 935–78, at 935.

[9] H. Dingle, *Migration: The Biology of Life on the Move* (New York: Oxford University Press, 1996).

[10] H. Dingle and V. A. Drake, 'What is Migration?' (2007) 57 *BioScience* 2, 113–21, at 117. The authors note that '[m]igration can be viewed as an adaptation specific to arenas in which changes in

area due to the highly changeable nature of their habitat, with distinct locations able to provide an optimal source of food and sanctuary at varying times of the year; hence the demands of survival and propagation of the species mandates a regular cycle of movement. In this way migratory species are distinguished from 'dormant' species, non-migrants that are blessed with a consistent abundance of favourable living conditions and are not therefore obliged to abandon and return to such sites on a cyclical basis.

Migratory species vary enormously in terms of how and when they migrate, and even in their motivation for undertaking migration. Insects, for instance, tend to pursue 'one-way' migration, moving only once in their lives to reproduce and then die. In many bird species 'partial migration' may occur, where a proportion of the population will stay behind in one of the 'worlds', while the remainder will migrate. Additionally, while migration carries connotations of extraordinary feats of endurance and movement over great distances, many species in fact have extremely short migratory patterns: some fish, for instance, will simply move to a higher or lower point in the water column, while other land-based species will move to higher or lower ground. A broad distinction is also drawn between migrants that may be considered 'faculative'—meaning that the urge towards migration is ingrained as a biological reflex—and those termed 'obligate' species, which are not natural migrants but are essentially forced to move due to their habitat having been compromised through natural or anthropogenic processes. Further species, ostentatiously termed 'migratory', are in fact nomadic in nature, and will spend the entire course of their lives moving from a series of temporary habitats, rather than undertaking the more orthodox 'round-trip' approach.[11]

This extraordinary range and variety of migratory behaviour creates significant practical difficulties in terms of legislating for such species. Firstly, and rather self-evidently in view of their constant movement throughout areas of national jurisdiction, any regulatory initiatives adopted in relation to migratory species must necessarily be multilateral in nature. Isolated domestic responses—while undoubtedly welcome from a conservation perspective—offer solutions of limited practical value in the wider context of the regulation of migratory wildlife, since they may be heavily undermined by a lack of complementary action in neighbouring territories. The most effective solution is therefore to develop a series of pragmatic international or regional standards that engage the cooperation and support of the maximum number of parties possible.

habitat quality in different regions occur asynchronously so that movement allows a succession of temporary resources to be exploited as they arise', ibid.

[11] The issue of determining which species are 'true' migrants and should therefore be granted priority in terms of the development of conservation and management measures has in recent years been addressed by the establishment of the Global Register of Migratory Species (GROMS) programme initiated under the auspices of the Bonn Convention in 2004. The database, while still a work in progress, seeks to list migrant species that merit attention by the Bonn Convention, while excluding exclusively nomadic species.

Likewise, and assuming that the requisite political and legislative will is in fact present, migrants cannot be treated as a generic bloc—as outlined above, the many thousands of species considered 'migratory' all correspond to their own distinct patterns of behaviour, follow differing migration routes and, accordingly, have very different conservation needs. Therefore, the elaboration and development of meaningful conservation and management initiatives in relation to migratory species is both an expensive and an expansive undertaking, involving a substantial and sustained investment of expertise and resources. Furthermore, these difficulties are compounded by a general lack of scientific knowledge about many migratory species, since their extended ranges create additional practical and financial complications in conducting an effective body of research on such animals.

III. The International Regulation of Migratory Species: The Bonn Convention

While a number of international and regional instruments have an important role to play in the protection of migratory species—either by addressing a specific type of habitat,[12] by dealing with particular species that also happen to be migratory in nature,[13] by dealing solely with a particular type of migratory species,[14] or by prescribing conservation and management measures for a host of wild animals, which include migrants among their ranks[15]—the Bonn Convention is the only international treaty that operates specifically to improve the conservation status of migratory species as its sole objective. However, given the difficulties inherent in legislating for such species, the Bonn Convention has largely been forced to operate in the face of adversity since its inception as the 'broadly based conven-

[12] See, for instance, the Convention on Wetlands of International Importance Especially as Waterfowl Habitat (better known as the 'Ramsar Convention'); Ramsar, Iran, 2 Feb. 1971 (entered into force 21 Dec. 1975), (1972) 11 *International Legal Materials* 969. Ratified by 154 countries (status as of 7 Feb. 2007).

[13] See, for instance, the International Convention for the Regulation of Whaling; Washington, US, 4 December 1946 (entered into force on 10 Nov. 1948), reproduced at 161 UNTS 72. Ratified by 78 countries (status as of 16 Jan. 2008).

[14] See, for instance, the UN Agreement for the Implementation of the Provisions of the United Nations Convention on the Law of the Sea of 10 Dec. 1982 Relating to the Conservation and Management of Straddling Fish Stocks and Highly Migratory Species (better known as the 'UN Fish Stocks Agreement'); New York, US, 4 December 1996 (entered into force 11 Dec. 2001), (1995) 34 *International Legal Materials* 1542. Ratified by 63 countries (status as of 4 Feb. 2007).

[15] See, for instance, the Convention on Biological Diversity; Rio de Janeiro, Brazil, 5 June 1992 (entered into force 29 Dec. 1993), (1992) 31 *International Legal Materials* 822. Ratified by 190 countries (status as of 4 Feb. 2007); the Convention on International Trade in Endangered Species (better known as 'CITES'); Washington DC, US, 3 March 1973 (entered into force 1 July 1975); (1973) 12 *International Legal Materials* 1085. Ratified by 169 countries (status as of 4 Feb. 2007).

tion' envisaged by the UN Conference on the Human Environment in 1972 to develop the global conservation agenda in respect of migratory wildlife.[16]

Indeed, for much of its existence the Bonn Convention has been subject to sustained criticism, not least given that it experienced a somewhat languid start to the early years of its existence, earning the sobriquet of a 'sleeping treaty' lacking the concerted impetus to effectively address the problems facing the vast range of migratory species subject to its regulatory purview.[17] Furthermore, the Bonn Convention has been (justifiably) accused of lacking both teeth and participants,[18] which has led some well-placed commentators to question its utility and the viability of its continued existence.[19] Although the Bonn Convention regime remains far from a perfect instrument, retaining a limited ability to recruit members and to develop initiatives from outside its traditional Eurasian support base, as well as a propensity to be adversely affected by a host of regulatory competitors,[20] over the past five years it has experienced something of a surge in membership and must now undoubtedly be considered better placed than at any point in its previous existence to address the conservation needs of a host of migratory species.[21]

A. Fundamental Principles and Objectives

The Bonn Convention recognizes that 'wild animals in their innumerable forms are an irreplaceable part of the earth's natural system which must be conserved for the good of mankind' and that 'each generation of man holds the resources of the earth for future generations and has an obligation to ensure that this legacy is conserved and, where utilized, is used wisely'.[22] Consequently, in the light of the constant movement of such species and the practical implications of this cross-boundary travel, the parties note that successful conservation and management measures in relation to migratory animals will therefore require 'the concerted action of all States within the national jurisdictional boundaries of which such species spend any part of their life cycle'.[23]

[16] Rec. 32 of the Stockholm Action Plan, Stockholm, Sweden, 16 June 1972, (1972) 11 *International Legal Materials* 1416. The Bonn Convention opened for signature in Bonn, in the then Federal Republic of Germany, and entered into force on 1 Nov. 1983 following ratification by the requisite 15 parties.

[17] S. Lyster, *International Wildlife Law: An Analysis of International Treaties Concerned with the Conservation of Wildlife* (Cambridge: Grotius, 1985), at 301.

[18] Matz, n. 7 above, at 202.

[19] Bonn, Switzerland, 19 Nov. 1979 (entered into force 1 Nov. 1983), (1979) 19 *International Legal Materials* 11. Ratified by 99 countries (status as of 4 Feb. 2007).

[20] Caddell, n. 5 above at 152–5.

[21] There are currently 104 parties to the Bonn Convention, as well as a further two signatories—Central African Republic and Jamaica—that have yet to ratify the Convention (as of 1 Oct. 2007).

[22] Preamble to the Bonn Convention.

[23] Ibid.

In pursuing such aspirations, the parties expressly acknowledge 'the importance of migratory species being conserved and of Range States agreeing to take action to this end whenever possible and appropriate'.[24] 'Migratory species' are defined within the CMS as being 'the entire population or any geographically separate part of the population of any species or lower taxon of wild animals, a significant proportion of whose members cyclically and predictably cross one or more national jurisdictional boundaries'.[25] Lyster notes that the extension of this definition to geographically separate populations is significant in that, following a trend set by the Convention on International Trade in Endangered Species (CITES), such a principle allows the parties to exploit non-endangered populations of a particular species, while providing an opportunity to address the individual conservation needs of a distinct species that is endangered only in certain locations, yet present in abundant numbers elsewhere and would not therefore ordinarily qualify for general protection measures.[26]

Accordingly, the parties to the Bonn Convention agree to take action to avoid any migratory species becoming endangered,[27] and to promote, cooperate in and support research relating to migratory species.[28] In addressing the conservation needs of migratory wildlife, the Bonn Convention adopts a two-tier approach, with the parties drawing a distinction between species identified as 'endangered' and those considered to have an 'unfavourable conservation status', with differing obligations and policies prescribed in relation to each category. To this end, like the majority of international biodiversity treaties, species falling into these categories are placed on designated lists, annexed to the text of the Convention, with 'endangered' species assigned to Appendix I and those species with an 'unfavourable conservation status' to Appendix II. Broadly speaking, in relation to Appendix I species, the parties are to 'endeavour to provide immediate protection for these animals',[29] while for those species listed in Appendix II, the parties are to endeavour to conclude a series of subsidiary instruments to address the long-term conservation and management needs of these animals.[30]

B. Appendix I Species

The first category of migratory fauna recognized by the Bonn Convention is 'endangered species', defined within the Convention as a species 'in danger of

[24] Art. II(1). 'Range States' are defined as any State 'that exercises jurisdiction over any part of the range of that migratory species, or a State, flag vessels of which are engaged outside national jurisdictional limits in taking that migratory species', Art. I(1)(h).

[25] Art. I(1)(a).

[26] N. 19 above, at 982–3.

[27] Art. II(2).

[28] Art. II(3)(a).

[29] Art. II(3)(b).

[30] Art. II(3)(c).

extinction throughout all or a significant part of its range'.[31] To date, well over a hundred species have been so designated.[32] Species may be listed in Appendix I 'provided that reliable evidence, including the best scientific evidence available, indicates that the species is endangered'.[33]

Three broad objectives are prescribed for Range States of species listed in Appendix I, namely to conserve and, where feasible and appropriate, restore those habitats of the species which are of importance in removing the species from danger of extinction; to prevent, remove, compensate for, or minimize, as appropriate, the adverse effects of activities or obstacles that seriously impede or prevent the migration of the species; and 'to the extent feasible and appropriate', to prevent, reduce or control factors that are endangering or are likely to further endanger the species, including strictly controlling and regulating the presence of exotic species.[34] Range States of Appendix I species are also required to prohibit the taking of such animals.[35] In addition to these requirements, the Conference of the Parties (COP) may recommend 'further measures considered appropriate to benefit the species' which are to be taken by the relevant Range States in relation to such animals.[36]

C. Appendix II Species

The second category of migratory wildlife recognized by the Bonn Convention as requiring specific attention are species classed as having an 'unfavourable conservation status'. The conservation status of a migratory species is defined under the Bonn Convention as being 'favourable' where:

(i) 'population dynamics data indicate that the migratory species is maintaining itself on a long-term basis as a viable component of its ecosystems;

(ii) the range of the migratory species is neither currently being reduced, nor is likely to be reduced, on a long-term basis;

[31] Art. I(1)(e).

[32] Caddell, n. 5 above, at 117.

[33] Art. III(2). Under Art. III(3), migratory species may be removed from Appendix I by a vote at the Conference of the Parties stating that reliable evidence—including the 'best scientific evidence available'—indicates that the species is no longer endangered and the species is not likely to become endangered again because of a loss of protection due to its removal from Appendix I.

[34] Art. III(4).

[35] Art. III(5). 'Taking' is defined in Art. I(1)(i) as: 'Taking, hunting, fishing, capturing, harassing, deliberate killing, or attempting to engage in such conduct.' Limited exceptions are permitted to this general rule, and taking Appendix I species is permitted if this is for scientific purposes, to enhance the propagation or survival of the species in question, to accommodate the needs of traditional subsistence users of these species or if 'extraordinary circumstances so require', in which case such exceptions must be 'precise as to content and limited in space and time' and should not operate to the disadvantage of the species—Art. III(5). Where taking is permitted pursuant to this provision, under Art. III(7) the party in question must inform the Secretariat of the CMS 'as soon as possible'.

[36] Art. III(6).

(iii) there is, and will be in the foreseeable future, sufficient habitat to maintain the population of the migratory species on a long-term basis; and

(iv) the distribution and abundance of the migratory species approach historic coverage and levels to the extent that potentially suitable ecosystems exist and to the extent consistent with wise wildlife management'.[37]

The conservation status of a particular species is therefore taken to be 'unfavourable' where any of these four criteria are not met.[38]

As far as Appendix II species are concerned, the approach taken by the Bonn Convention is substantially different to that advanced in relation to 'endangered' species. Instead of requiring parties to adopt national measures to address the various threats to such species, 'Appendix II shall list migratory species which have an unfavourable conservation status and which require international agreements for their conservation and management, as well as those which have a conservation status which would significantly benefit from the international cooperation that could be achieved by an international agreement'.[39]

In this respect, two types of instrument are envisaged for species listed in Appendix II, namely an AGREEMENT established under the aegis of Article IV(3) of the Convention, or an agreement concluded pursuant to Article IV(4).[40] In addition, the conservation needs of migratory species may also be addressed in the form of less formal arrangements, such as the adoption of Memoranda of Understanding or individual initiatives or action plans between Range States acting under the auspices of the Bonn Convention.

i. AGREEMENTS

Under Article IV(3), '[p]arties that are Range States of migratory species listed in Appendix II shall endeavour to conclude AGREEMENTS where these would benefit the species and should give priority to those species in an unfavourable conservation status'. Guidelines for the conclusion of such AGREEMENTS are advanced under Article V of the CMS. The main objective of Article IV(3) AGREEMENTS is established in Article V(1), and is stated as being 'to restore the migratory species concerned to a favourable conservation status or to maintain it in such a status. Each AGREEMENT should deal with those aspects of

[37] Art. I(1)(c).

[38] Art. I(1)(d). The 'conservation status' of a migratory species is defined as 'the sum of the influences acting on the migratory species that may affect its long-term distribution and abundance', Art. I(1)(b).

[39] Art. IV(1). Art. IV(2) permits migratory species to be listed in both Appendix I and Appendix II, 'if the circumstances so warrant'. Unlike Appendix I species, once a particular species has been listed on Appendix II there is no procedure under the Bonn Convention to reverse this designation: Caddell n. 5 above, at 118. Lyster suggests that the reason for this is 'the capacity of a species to benefit from international cooperation is unlikely to change even if its conservation status improves': n. 17 above, at 278.

[40] The term AGREEMENT is emphasized in capital letters in order to distinguish this type of instrument from the kind provided for under Art. IV(4)—see Caddell, n. 5 above, at 119.

the conservation and management of the migratory species concerned which serve to achieve that object.' In this regard, the conclusion of such instruments allows the parties to address the specific conservation needs of the species in question and to elaborate the necessary strategies to pursue these aims. Where such AGREEMENTS are concluded, they should 'cover the whole of the range of the migratory species concerned and should be open to accession by all Range States of that species, whether or not they are parties to this Convention'.[41] Additionally, AGREEMENTS should also 'wherever possible' deal with more than one migratory species.[42]

Article V(4) specifies five fundamental features that should be common to each AGREEMENT, namely that they should identify the migratory species concerned; describe the range and migration route of the species in question; make provision for each party to designate a national authority concerned with the implementation of the AGREEMENT; establish appropriate machinery to assist in implementing the AGREEMENT, monitor its effectiveness and prepare reports for the Conference of the Parties; and to provide for procedures for the resolution of disputes.[43]

Under Article V(5), a non-exhaustive list of features is specified for each AGREEMENT, which should be incorporated 'where appropriate and feasible'. These issues include making provision for the periodic review of the conservation status of the species in question and the identification of potential threats; developing coordinated conservation and management plans; conducting research into the ecology and population dynamics of the species concerned; facilitating the exchange of information and research; ensuring the conservation and, 'where required and feasible', the restoration of important areas of habitat, and the protection of these areas from disturbance and the control of exotic species; maintaining a network of suitable habitats appropriate to migratory routes; providing 'where it appears desirable' new habitats or reintroducing migratory species into favourable habitats; eliminating or compensating for impediments to migration; preventing, reducing or controlling the release of harmful substances into the habitat of such species; introducing measures 'based on sound

[41] Art. V(2).

[42] Art. V(3).

[43] A sixth requirement is prescribed in relation to migratory cetaceans, requiring any such AGREEMENT to prohibit at a minimum 'any taking that is not permitted for that migratory species under any other multilateral agreement and provide for accession to the AGREEMENT by States that are not Range States of that migratory species': Art. V(4)(f). This position is prescribed due to the existence of the International Whaling Commission (IWC) and its remit to regulate directed hunting activities in relation to a number of species of large cetaceans, of which many such animals are migratory in nature. In this way, the Bonn Convention appears to support fully the relevant IWC policy in relation to migratory cetaceans, and it may be suggested that the Bonn Convention should take its lead from the IWC in this respect. Nonetheless, this point is largely moot at present: no AGREEMENTS pertaining to cetaceans have yet been elaborated under the auspices of Art. IV(3), with the Agreements discussed below having been developed under Art. IV(4), which is silent on cetaceans.

ecological principles' to control and manage the taking of the migratory species; coordinating action to suppress illegal takings; exchanging information on 'substantial threats' to migratory species; developing emergency procedures to strengthen conservation action if the conservation status of the species is seriously affected; and making the general public aware of the aims and provisions of the AGREEMENT.

To date, three such AGREEMENTS have been concluded under the umbrella of the Bonn Convention, relating to European species of bats, waterbirds in the African-Eurasian region and albatrosses and petrels in the Southern Hemisphere.

ii. Agreements

The second type of subsidiary instrument provided for under the Bonn Convention umbrella is an agreement concluded under Article IV(4). Article IV(4) states that '[p]arties are encouraged to take action with a view to concluding agreements for any population or any geographically separate part of the population of any species or lower taxon of wild animals, members of which periodically cross one or more national jurisdictional boundaries'. Unlike Article IV(3) AGREEMENTS, the Bonn Convention does not specify any guidelines for the elaboration of such instruments, with the parties free to structure Article IV(4) agreements in the manner that they deem appropriate. To date, the overwhelming majority of the subsidiary instruments concluded under the auspices of the Bonn Convention have been founded on the basis of Article IV(4)[44] and, as noted by Lyster, the purpose of this provision 'is to encourage parties to conclude agreements to protect species which would benefit from international cooperation in situations where for some reason the species has not yet been listed in appendix II or does not technically qualify for appendix II'.[45] Thus far, the agreements concluded under Article IV(4) have tended to fall into one of two categories, namely formal instruments following a similar structure to Article IV(3) AGREEMENTS, and less formal memoranda of understanding. The more formal agreements relate to seal populations in the Wadden Sea, small cetaceans in the Baltic and North Seas and cetaceans of the Mediterranean and Black Seas and contiguous Atlantic region.

iii. Memoranda of Understanding

In addition to the subsidiary Agreements adopted to date, the Bonn Convention also provides for the elaboration of less formal instruments, in the form of Memoranda of Understanding (MOU).[46] In this regard, ten such instruments

[44] Art. IV(4) has been used as a basis for conservatory action in the form of both Agreements and, more frequently, in the case of the less formal arrangements advanced under the Bonn Convention.

[45] N. 19 above, at 992.

[46] On the role of such instruments within the umbrella of the Bonn Convention see C. Shine, 'Selected Agreements Concluded Pursuant to the Convention on the Conservation of Migratory Species of Wild Animals' in D. Shelton (ed.), *Commitment and Compliance: The Role of Non-Binding*

have been established to date, addressing the conservation needs of great bustards, Siberian cranes, slender-billed curlews, African and Asian populations of marine turtles, Bukhara deer, aquatic warblers, Saiga antelopes, West African elephants, and South Pacific populations of cetaceans.[47] The expanding range of less formal instruments, primarily concluded over the course of the past five years, may indicate that the Bonn Convention is at least moving to acknowledge the conservation needs of an extended range of species.[48] That said, it may also be indicative of a trend within the Bonn Convention away from the conclusion of more binding agreements capable of generating tangible protection measures, towards a policy of developing rather more aspirational objectives that, while attracting media attention and Range State interest, do not necessarily commit participants to any meaningful conservation obligations.

D. Challenges and Shortcomings

Notwithstanding the practical utility of the CMS regime in generating initiatives to further the conservation status of threatened migrants, Bonn Convention has experienced substantial difficulties throughout its existence, which have tended to negate its value in the eyes of many commentators.[49] Indeed, four key challenges to the umbrella of the Bonn Convention can be identified, which may be summarized as follows. Firstly, commitments engaged under the Bonn Convention—which were already largely aspirational and deliberately vague in definition[50]—are currently receding further in overall strength, towards a MOU-dominant approach which, as outlined above, offers little in terms of binding commitments. Secondly, the Bonn Convention has long been chronically under funded which, given the expense involved in assessing and developing meaningful conservation initiatives for migratory species, has long undermined the ability of the convention and its subsidiaries to operate effectively.[51] Thirdly, the Bonn Convention has few formal enforcement powers or compliance incentives, providing a highly limited opportunity to pursue recalcitrant parties for failing to adhere to their commitments. Finally, the umbrella of the Bonn Convention itself has proven largely incapable of developing strong subsidiary regimes outside its traditional support base within Europe, with five of the six key Agreements

Norms in the International Legal System (Oxford: Oxford University Press, 2003), 196. In addition to the use of MOUs, other less formal instruments have been concluded under the auspices of the Bonn Convention including an Action Plan for antelopes, as well as 'Initiatives' in respect of dugongs, gorillas, raptors, sharks, and Western African aquatic mammals.

[47] For a concise discussion of these developments see Caddell, n. 5 above, at 137–9.

[48] Matz, n. 7 above, at 202.

[49] See Caddell, n. 5 above; Matz, n. 7 above and Lyster, nn. 17 and 19 above.

[50] As Matz notes, habitat conservation in particular 'is not elaborated on in terms of obligation': ibid., at 202.

[51] Caddell, n. 5 above, at 140–1.

adopted to date applying wholly or in part to European territories, leading to a sense that the Convention is largely preaching to the converted.[52]

IV. EU Law and the Conservation of Migratory Species

Given the inherent difficulties in prescribing legislative solutions for migratory species, and the proven shortcomings in adopting a generalized approach to the wide variety of migrant fauna, it is perhaps rather unsurprising that no single unified policy document or legislative instrument addressing migratory species has to date been developed under European law. That is not to suggest, however, that migrants have been ignored by the EU institutions—especially since the EU has formally ratified the Bonn Convention[53] and plays a full part in the COPs to the Convention—and a number of key nature protection provisions may indeed be seen to have a substantial application in respect of the conservation needs of such species.

As noted above, the conservation status of migratory species has been addressed predominantly through the prism of the Wild Birds Directive and the Habitats Directive, both of which—as will be detailed below—offer a strong degree of protection to migratory wildlife. In this respect, it can be seen that the Wild Birds Directive in particular has developed a highly effective regulatory system to promote the conservation of migratory birds, with both the Directive itself —complemented by key judgments of the European Court of Justice (ECJ) in interpreting its legislative provisions—establishing strident protection for such species, with Member States expected to play a proactive role in protecting vulnerable migrants. Likewise the Habitats Directive, although less explicitly applicable to migratory species in general, nevertheless prescribes and extends valuable conservation measures for a range of non-avian migratory fauna listed in its annexes.

Given the inherent limitations of the system of the Bonn Convention in promoting the conservation status of migrant fauna, there is a pressing need for a strong EU-tier of conservation measures vis-à-vis such species. Indeed, it is clear that the EU nature Directives, with their clear and unequivocal obligations, are immediately better placed to offer tangible conservation benefits to a host of migratory species under their regulatory purview in comparison with the Bonn Convention and its subsidiaries, which are drafted primarily in hortatory, aspirational, and highly permissive terms. Likewise, the Wild Birds Directive and the Habitats Directive are two of the most commonly litigated provisions of EU environmental law, with the Commission (supported by a host of vigilant and well-funded NGOs) proving keen to enforce these measures where damaging defects in compliance are detected. Furthermore, the EU system also has

[52] Ibid., at 152–5. [53] Council Dec. 82/72/EEC, [1982] OJ L210/10.

recourse to substantial financial resources to promote the establishment of the requisite conservation areas and policies, in marked distinction, as noted above, to the structure of the Bonn Convention.

A. The Wild Birds Directive

The Wild Birds Directive is one of the most long-standing and entrenched provisions of EU environmental law currently in existence, and must also be considered to be one of the leading and most effective regional instruments to regulate anthropogenic activities affecting avian fauna. Since its adoption in 1979, the Wild Birds Directive has played a key role in the conservation of birds—migratory and otherwise—and, while it is in general very difficult to assess objectively the 'effectiveness' of nature conservation laws,[54] recent scientific research has demonstrated that the Directive itself has proven capable of delivering tangible benefits to the conservation status of the majority of species addressed under its auspices.[55]

Migratory species are central to the scope of the Wild Birds Directive and, indeed, to a considerable extent constitute the inspiration behind the establishment of the Directive itself, as concerns over the wholesale slaughter of birds migrating through southern Europe and north Africa led to a series of questions being raised in the European Parliament, which ultimately resulted in the development of distinct legislation by the European Commission in 1976.[56] Consequently, the conservation of migratory species permeates the legislative sentiment of the Directive, which prescribes a series of measures to protect vulnerable species of birds across the various Member States of the EU.

Migratory species are explicitly referred to throughout the Directive and a series of distinct conservation measures are formally prescribed under its auspices. The Wild Birds Directive specifically observes in its preamble that the species of birds naturally occurring in the territories of the Member States are mainly migratory in nature—a statement that is as applicable to an enlarged EU of 27 Member States as it was to the more modest membership of the EEC at the time of the conclusion of the Directive—and that 'such species constitute a common heritage and whereas effective bird protection is typically a trans-frontier environment problem entailing common responsibilities'. Furthermore, and despite its

[54] On the issue of the effectiveness of transnational environmental law see P. Sand, *The Effectiveness of International Environmental Agreements: A Survey of Existing Legal Instruments* (Cambridge: Grotius, 1992); for a discussion of this issue in the EU/US biodiversity context see J. Verschuuren, 'Effectiveness of Nature Protection Legislation in the EU and the US: The Birds and Habitats Directives and the Endangered Species Act' (2003) 3 *Yearbook of European Environmental Law*, at 305.

[55] P. Donald et al., 'International Conservation Policy Delivers Benefits for Birds in Europe' (2007) 317 *Science* 810–13.

[56] P. Davies, *European Union Environmental Law: An Introduction to Key Selected Issues* (Aldershot: Ashgate Publishing, 2004), at 120–1.

legislative origins, while migratory species are not the primary focus of the Wild Birds Directive and its conservation measures, it is nevertheless recognized that 'such measures must also take account of migratory species and be coordinated with a view to setting up a coherent whole'.[57]

Migratory species have occupied a prominent position in a substantial proportion of the relatively voluminous case law generated to date under the Wild Birds Directive,[58] with a considerable number of decisions rendered by the ECJ relating in whole or in part to the conservation needs of migrating birds. Indeed, the ECJ has reiterated the tone of the Directive in relation to migratory birds in strident fashion, explicitly ruling in *Commission* v. *France*,[59] the first action brought by the Commission for an alleged infringement of the Wild Birds Directive, that:

> [t]he protection of migratory species is typically a transfrontier environment problem entailing common responsibilities for the Member States. The importance of complete and effective protection of wild birds throughout the Community, irrespective of the areas they stray in or pass through, causes any national legislation which delimits the protection of wild birds by reference to the concept of national heritage to be incompatible with the Directive.[60]

Accordingly, it is incumbent upon individual Member States to promote a full and coherent regime of protection for all wild birds that may enter the Community by virtue of residence or migration, and any attempts to dilute this approach through the operation of national legislation will be annulled by the ECJ.[61] Indeed, the rationale for protection measures to be applied to migratory species—that they constitute a common heritage of the Community—has also been repeatedly stressed by the ECJ.[62] Furthermore, the concept of migration has

[57] Preamble to the Directive. It is also noted at this juncture that 'the conservation of birds and, in particular, migratory birds still presents problems which call for scientific research; whereas such research will also make it possible to assess the effectiveness of the measures taken', ibid. Indeed, the shortcomings of scientific research and monitoring in this respect are highlighted as an inhibiting factor in determining the continued effectiveness of the Directive as a whole: Donald et al., n. 55 above, at 812.

[58] On the case law of the Wild Birds Directive see W. Wils, 'The Birds Directive 15 Years Later: A Survey of the Case Law and a Comparison with the Habitats Directive' (1994) 6 *Journal of Environmental Law* 218–42; also D. Freestone, 'The Enforcement of the Wild Birds Directive: A Case Study' in H. Somsen (ed.), *Protecting the European Environment: Enforcing EC Environmental Law* (London: Blackstone Publishing, 1996), at 229. Additionally, the leading NGO Birdlife International has compiled a comprehensive report of the Directive's jurisprudence: *Report on Birds Directive European Court of Justice Cases with Case Summaries* (Birdlife International, 2004), published on the Internet at: http://www.birdlife.org/eu/birds_directive.html (accessed 1 Oct. 2007).

[59] Case C-252/86 [1988] ECR 2243.

[60] Para. 15.

[61] In this case the French authorities were deemed to have taken an overly restrictive approach to the protection of migratory birds by enacting legislation that limited protection to 'national biological heritage', a concept that did not extend to protecting birds that had migrated to or through France from other Member States or beyond the (then) EEC.

[62] See, for instance, Case C-169/89 *Criminal proceedings against Gourmetterie Van den Burg* [1990] ECR I-2143 (at para. 11); Case C-44/95 *R* v. *Secretary of State for the Environment, ex parte Royal Society for the Protection of Birds* [1996] ECR I-3805 (para. 23).

been interpreted generously to include accidental migrants that would not ordinarily enter the Community.[63]

As far as the operative mechanisms of the Wild Birds Directive are concerned, the conservation status of migratory species may be considered to be addressed in three key ways. Firstly, the Directive prescribes a series of measures to be taken by the Member States to protect areas of importance to migratory species and, by virtue of key decisions of the ECJ (detailed below), the relevant provision of the Directive enshrining this commitment—Article 4(2)—has been formally recognized as a strident obligation incumbent upon the national authorities. Secondly, and of considerable practical significance, Member States are required to regulate hunting activities, especially those that impact upon migratory species. Thirdly, and of over-arching application, these two obligations are robustly policed by vociferous and well-resourced NGOs acting as a regulatory spur to the European Commission, with infringement proceedings having been invoked regularly against Member States for violations of these measures.[64]

With regard to the conservation of migratory species, the Wild Birds Directive requires Member States to establish a general system of protection for avian species addressed by the Directive.[65] In particular, this commitment involves taking the requisite measures to maintain the population of such species,[66] with an emphasis upon preserving, maintaining, or re-establishing areas of habitat primarily through the creation of protected areas.[67] This may in practice entail wide-ranging commitments, and for instance involves a duty not to destroy empty nests, with the ECJ having ruled that these are of particular value to migratory species, with a failure to adhere to this requirement considered to fall short of the 'uninterrupted protection' of habitats demanded by the Directive.[68]

[63] Case C-202/94 *Criminal Proceedings against Godefridus van der Feesten* [1996] ECR I-355; see Verschuuren, n. 54 above, at 318–19.

[64] For instance, as noted by Somsen, the Royal Society for the Protection of Birds, the leading NGO acting in the interests of wild birds in the UK, has proved to be more effective in securing compliance with the Wild Birds Directive 'than the Commission could ever hope to be': H. Somsen, 'The Private Enforcement of Member State Compliance with EC Environmental Law: An Unfulfilled Promise?' (2000) 1 *Yearbook of European Environmental Law* 311, 312. On the role of NGOs generally, see P. Newell and W. Grant, 'Environmental NGOs and EU Environmental Law' (2000) 1 *Yearbook of European Environmental Law*, 225–52.

[65] Art. 5. Under Art. 1, the Dir. applies to 'all species of naturally occurring birds in the wild state in the European territory of the Member States to which the treaty applies' and is concerned with birds, eggs, nests and habitats, although by virtue of the decision in *van der Feesten*, which clarified the concept of a 'species', non-European sub-species are excluded from the application of the Wild Birds Directive unless it can be proven that they belong to a species of bird that does occur naturally in the wild in the Community—a decision that has implications rather more for the trade in wild birds than for migrant species.

[66] Art. 2.

[67] Art. 3.

[68] Case C-252/86 *Commission* v. *France*, n. 59 above. Here the French authorities failed, inter alia, to protect such nests during the hunting period, a problematic omission in the view of Advocate General Da Cruz Vilaça since '[t]here are in fact birds (in particular among the migratory species)

To a significant extent, the main operative provision of the Wild Birds Directive in relation to habitats may be considered to be Article 4, which has given rise to a substantial volume of case law since the inception of the Directive. Article 4(1) mandates that the species listed in Annex I of the Directive are to be subject to 'special conservation measures' in respect of habitats so as to ensure the survival and reproduction of the species in their areas of distribution.[69] To this end, it is incumbent upon the Member States to classify the 'most suitable territories in number and size as special protection areas (SPAs), taking into account the marine[70] and land areas subject to the directive'. Article 4(1) has a direct application to a significant number of migratory species, since a considerable proportion of the species listed in Annex I are migratory in nature, including several species of goose, pigeon, seabird, curlew, and warbler, as well as the great bustard, an individual species subject to a distinct subsidiary instrument of the Bonn Convention itself.

Notwithstanding the listing of individual species of migrants in Annex I, the Wild Birds Directive also explicitly addresses migratory species as a general class of avian fauna in the context of Article 4(2), which states:

> Member States shall take similar measures for regularly occurring migratory species not listed in Annex I, bearing in mind their need for protection in the geographical sea and land area where this Directive applies, as regards their breeding, moulting and wintering areas and staging posts along their migration routes. To this end, Member States shall pay particular attention to the protection of wetlands and particularly to wetlands of international importance.

The combined effect of Article 4(1) and (2) was articulated in the *Seine Estuary* case[71] as requiring the various Member States 'to provide SPAs with a legal protection regime that is capable, in particular, of ensuring both the survival and reproduction of the bird species listed in Annex I of the Directive and the breeding, moulting and wintering of migratory species not listed in Annex I which are, nevertheless, regular visitors'.[72] That the ECJ seemingly read the provisions of Article 4(1) and (2) as an amalgamation of these measures stems largely from a series of earlier judgments in which the dual application of Article 4 to both

which re-use nests built in previous years' (para. 16), an observation that was upheld by the ECJ in finding a violation of the Directive (para. 9 of the judgment).

[69] In particular, Art. 4(1) stresses that due account should be taken of whether the species in question is in danger of extinction, vulnerable to changes in its habitat, considered to be rare due to its small population or restricted local distribution or is vulnerable due to the specific nature of its habitat.

[70] On the maritime application of the Directive see D. Owen, 'The Application of the Wild Birds Directive beyond the Territorial Sea of European Community Member States' (2001) 13 *Journal of Environmental Law*, 39–78.

[71] Case C-166/97 *Commission* v. *France* [1999] ECR I-1719.

[72] Para. 21. In this particular case, the proposed construction of a titanogypsum plant and the storage of gypsum up to a maximum of 25 metres so as not to disturb migrating corncrakes were held not to have infringed Art. 4(1) and (2) in substance.

Annex I species and migratory species in general had caused some interpretative consternation. In another key decision on the Wild Birds Directive, the *Leybucht Dykes* case,[73] the interrelationship between the two provisions was explored in some detail by Advocate General Van Gerven, who declared that Article 4(2) 'is poorly drafted and difficult to understand'.[74] In outlining the synergies between the two provisions, he further stated that:

> [t]he question arises *inter alia* whether the 'similar measures' referred to in that provision include the obligation to designate special protection areas in accordance with the fourth subparagraph of Article 4(1). If paragraph 2 is read in conjunction with paragraphs 3 and 4 (which speak of the protection areas referred to in paragraph 2) it must be considered that the obligation laid down in the fourth subparagraph of Article 4(1) applies *mutatis mutandis* to the habitat areas of migratory birds referred to in paragraph 2.[75]

Accordingly, in the opinion of Advocate General Van Gerven, Article 4(2) engenders a positive obligation for Member States to identify and to designate areas of importance to migratory birds as SPAs in a manner analogous to those species listed in Annex I. This interpretation of Article 4(2) has been seemingly recognized by both the European Commission and the Member States: tellingly, there was no dissent to this position by either the Commission or the government of Spain in the *Santoña Marshes* case,[76] where the interrelationship between Article 4(1) and (2) and (4) was again in issue, shortly after judgment was rendered in *Leybucht Dykes*. On this basis, given the high proportion of migratory species that regularly visited the Santoña Marshes,[77] as well as its particular value as a staging post for endangered spoonbills migrating from the Netherlands, Spain was adjudged to have acted in breach of the Wild Birds Directive by failing to formally classify the marshes as an SPA.[78] Insofar as general migratory species are concerned, as well as all species listed in Annex I of the Directive, the obligations in Article 4(1) and (2) trigger a further set of commitments in Article 4(4) to take 'appropriate steps' to avoid pollution to or deterioration of habitats, as well as disturbances affecting such birds.[79]

Likewise, concerns over the conservation needs of migrants also constitute an important component of the duty incumbent upon Member States to establish SPAs under the Wild Birds Directive. As established in *Commission* v.

[73] Case C-57/89 *Commission* v. *Germany* [1991] ECR I-883.

[74] Para. 27 of the Opinion of the Advocate General.

[75] Ibid.

[76] Case C-355/90 *Commission* v. *Spain* [1993] ECR I-4221. The mutual acceptance of this assertion is noted by AG Van Gerven, who also acted in this case, at para. 7 of his Opinion to the ECJ.

[77] Some 14 different migratory species were identified as regular visitors, along with a further 19 Annex I species.

[78] Para. 32. The importance of the area to migratory birds was considered to have constituted an especially pressing reason for such a designation in the view of the ECJ: para. 27.

[79] Additionally, under Art. 4(4) Member States are to 'strive towards' the avoidance of pollution or deterioration of habitats lying outside designated SPAs.

Netherlands,[80] the margin of appreciation afforded to Member States to establish an SPA is restricted and, where having applied the requisite ornithological criteria, if the site appears to be most suitable for the conservation of endangered or migratory species under Article 4, there is a legal obligation to so designate it as an SPA. Furthermore, in assessing the 'ornithological criteria' to be taken into consideration by the national authorities in assessing SPAs, an EC-wide approach must be taken[81] which, in line with the early decision in *Commission* v. *France*,[82] requires the Member States to abandon narrow national considerations where migratory species are concerned and instead remain cognisant of the transnational application of the Directive and the corresponding need to promote the protection of certain species throughout the extension of their natural range.

Nonetheless, the practical application of Article 4(2) has been correctly tempered by the demands of realism and does not entail spiralling obligations upon Member States to prescribe blanket SPA protection across every conceivable permutation of the migratory route of particular species. Indeed, as noted by Advocate General Alber in the *Basses Corbières* case,[83] 'the simple fact that the area lies in a flying corridor used by migratory birds cannot be sufficient to unleash duties incumbent on a Member State under Article 4(2) of the birds directive',[84] with the designation threshold for an SPA in relation to migratory species seemingly reached only where the location in question can be demonstrated as being either a breeding, moulting, wintering, or staging post for migrant birds, with no discretion for an insistence upon a more broad-ranging application of this provision in areas that such species merely frequent.[85]

A strident set of obligations are also prescribed in relation to migratory species in the context of hunting activities, which is perhaps the most obvious threat to migrating birds: strong protection measures in one area of the Community count for nought if vulnerable birds are enthusiastically hunted in another.[86] The hunting of wild birds is permitted under the terms of the Wild Birds Directive—a list of species is maintained that may be hunted in accordance with specific national legislation, so designated under Annex II[87]—although these activities are restricted in the case of migratory species, with Member States obliged to

[80] Case C-3/96 *Commission* v. *Netherlands* [1998] ECR I-3031.

[81] N. de Sadeleer, 'Habitats Conservation in EC Law—From Nature Sanctuaries to Ecological Networks' (2005) 5 *Yearbook of European Environmental Law* 215–52, at 224.

[82] Case C-252/86, n. 59 above.

[83] Case C-374/98 *Commission* v. *France* [2000] ECR I-10799.

[84] Para. 70 of the Opinion of AG Alber to the ECJ.

[85] Ibid. at para. 68. The ECJ upheld that the French authorities were under no obligation to have established an SPA acting under Art. 4(2) in this particular instance at para. 16 of its judgment.

[86] Indeed, in Oct. 2007 Malta was issued with a Reasoned Opinion by the Commission in respect of the hunting of a host of migratory birds, including a substantial volume of turtle doves and common quails while proceedings against Cyprus with regard to the spring hunting of turtle doves were formally discontinued on the same day due to a withdrawal of a derogation by the national authorities: Press release IP/07/1509 of 17 Oct. 2007.

[87] Art. 7(1).

ensure that hunting does not occur during sensitive periods for migrants, such as during rearing or reproduction. The ECJ has taken a robust approach to the conservation needs of migratory birds in this respect. Indeed, in the first decided case addressing the Wild Birds Directive, *Commission* v. *Italy*,[88] the Court ruled that broad powers under Italian law to permit regional authorities to allow for the capture and sale of migratory birds breached the Directive, as did the use of mutilated migrants as live decoys in hunting activities.

Moreover, the Member States are obliged to consider migratory patterns of behaviour in establishing rules on the setting of hunting seasons pursuant to Article 7(4), as established in the strident decision in *L'Association pour la Protection des Animaux Sauvages et Préfet de Maine-et-Loire et Préfet de la Loire-Atlantique*[89] where, in a strong application of the precautionary principle,[90] the ECJ ruled that Member States should set 'one single date for all the species concerned for the closing of hunting, which is equivalent to that fixed for the species which is the earliest to migrate'.[91] Furthermore, the ECJ considered that the staggering of these dates should only be permitted if the national authorities can adduce evidence based on scientific and technical data pertaining to each individual case that such a move would not affect 'the complete protection' of the species in question.[92] Indeed, the ECJ has found a number of violations of Article 7(4) where hunting activities have been sanctioned by the national authorities close to the return of migrating birds to their rearing grounds.[93] Additionally, attempts to enter derogations to the provisions of Article 7(4) under Article 9(1)[94] have been interpreted narrowly by the ECJ, especially so where the introduction of such measures is motivated in whole or in part to extend the hunting season in relation to migratory species.[95]

It is therefore clear that, by virtue of the operation of the obligations incumbent in Article 4(2) and the corresponding need to take account of the conservation

[88] Case C-262/85 *Commission* v. *Italy* [1987] ECR 3073.

[89] Case C-435/92 *L'Association pour la Protection des Animaux Sauvages et Préfet de Maine-et-Loire et Préfet de la Loire-Atlantique* [1994] ECR I-67.

[90] For a fuller discussion of this case in the context of precaution see N. de Sadeleer, *Environmental Principles: From Political Slogans to Legal Rules* (Oxford: Oxford University Press, 2005), at 122.

[91] Para. 21.

[92] Ibid.

[93] See in particular Case C-38/99 *Commission* v. *France* [2000] ECR I-10941, and the recent decision addressing the *caza a contrapasa* technique of hunting migratory woodpigeons in Case C-135/04 *Commission* v. *Spain* [2005] ECR I-5261.

[94] Art. 9 permits derogations to the hunting restrictions established under Art. 7, Case C-247/85 *Commission* v. *Belgium* [1987] ECR 3029; Case C-118/94 *Associazione Italiana per il WWF and Others* [1996] ECR I-1223, especially if there is 'no other satisfactory solution' as prescribed under Art. 9(1)(c).

[95] Case C-182/02 *Ligue pour la protection des oiseaux and Others* v. *Premier Ministre, Ministre de l'Aménagement du Terretoire et de l'Environnement* [2003] ECR I-12105; Case C-135/04 *Commission* v. *Spain*, ibid. See also the recent case of Case C-79/03 *Commission* v. *Spain* [2004] ECR I-11619, where the use of the *parany*, a particularly indiscriminate method of capture using lime-coated twigs to immobilize migrating thrushes, was not held to have been justified on the basis of protecting agricultural interests as was claimed by the Spanish authorities.

needs of migratory birds in establishing SPAs, supported by the proactive policing of the conduct of Member States in designating and creating such areas and controlling hunting activities, that the Wild Birds Directive is of substantial value to migratory species. Accordingly, it must be considered to be one of the most effective and pragmatic transnational instruments to regulate activities affecting migratory avian fauna, and to fulfil its stated remit of inter alia promoting common responsibilities towards such species.

B. The Habitats Directive

Unlike the Wild Birds Directive, the Habitats Directive is not as overtly concerned about the conservation status of migratory species as a distinct class of fauna. Indeed, as noted by Matz, 'apart from the conservation of migratory birds under the Birds Directive, other migrants are not specifically addressed by European Community Law but referred to only more or less implicitly'.[96] This is indeed the approach taken by the Habitats Directive in practice, although it does contain a number of key provisions that recognize, in general terms, the problems faced by migratory species and accordingly are of practical value in addressing such animals in the context of the protected areas established under the auspices of the Directive. In essence, the Habitats Directive provides for the establishment of an ecological network of Special Areas of Conservation (SACs), dubbed Natura 2000, with such areas comprising a distinct set of habitat types, listed in Annex I to the Directive, as well as areas of habitat for a wide array of species, listed in Annex II,[97] the latter of which has seen a considerable body of migratory species so designated.

In contrast to the Wild Birds Directive, the Habitats Directive affords no special status to migratory fauna not specifically listed as eligible for protection under the Natura 2000 scheme. Nevertheless, migrants are not divorced from the general ambit of the Directive and it appears that migratory behaviour may be taken into consideration in determining the scope of the SACs designated under the Habitats Directive. In particular, for 'animal species ranging over wide areas', SACs are to 'correspond to the places within the natural range of such species which present the physical or biological factors essential to their life and reproduction',[98] which could potentially require the designation of substantial areas of land with regard to migrants listed in Annex II. However, there appears to be a lesser degree of protection afforded to aquatic species with a similarly extended range, as Member States are required to only to designate such sites 'where there is a clearly identifiable area representing the physical and biological factors essential to their life and reproduction'.[99]

[96] N. 7 above, at 209. [97] Art. 3. [98] Art. 4(1). [99] Ibid.

Furthermore, the importance of migratory routes is acknowledged within the provisions of Article 10, requiring Member States to 'encourage the management of features of the landscape which are of major importance for wild fauna and flora' when implementing national land-use and development policies. Such features include those which 'are essential for the migration, dispersal and genetic exchange of wild species'. Additionally, the susceptibility of migratory wildlife to anthropogenic disturbance is noted in Article 12, whereby strict protection is prescribed for certain species listed in Annex IV(a)—of which a number of migratory species are so designated—with Member States to take 'all requisite measures' to prohibit inter alia the 'deliberate disturbance of these species, particularly during the period of breeding, rearing, hibernation and migration'.[100] Moreover, this requirement applies to such species 'in their natural range', again raising the possibility of prescribing extensive participation for migratory wildlife with an extended range.

One particularly instructive example of the application of the Habitats Directive to address the conservation needs of migratory species on this basis is the case of *Commission* v. *Greece*.[101] These infringement proceedings concerned the failure of the national authorities to adequately protect loggerhead sea turtles *caretta caretta*, a species listed in Annex IV(a) and one that has also been subject to much anxiety within the structure of the Bonn Convention itself.[102] In this case, the Commission had been concerned that the nesting sites of sea turtles in the Bay of Laganas, situated in the popular resort of Zakinthos and considered to be the most important breeding area within the Mediterranean region for this highly migratory species, had been compromised by the nuisance and noise created through tourist activities, illegal construction and the use of beach vehicles during sensitive stages of the reproduction, incubation, and hatching processes. In finding a host of violations of Article 12 of the Habitats Directive, the ECJ ruled inter alia that the migration of baby turtles, undertaken at a time at which they are most vulnerable to natural and anthropogenic pressures, had been consistently impeded, which could pose serious implications for the survival of individual animals already subject to a high natural infant mortality rate.[103]

[100] Art. 12(1)(b). Such species are considered to be 'of Community interest' and are either listed as endangered, vulnerable, rare, or endemic but in need of particular attention due to their habitat needs: Art. 1(g).

[101] Case C-103/00 *Commission* v. *Greece* [2002] ECR I-1147.

[102] The conservation status of marine turtles has constituted a major cause for concern amongst the parties to the Bonn Convention, with two distinct subsidiary agreements having been concluded in respect of these animals, namely the Memorandum of Understanding Concerning Conservation Measures for Marine Turtles of the Atlantic Coast of Africa, which was concluded in May 1999 and entered into force on 1 July 1999, and the Memorandum of Understanding on the Conservation and Management of Marine Turtles and their Habitats of the Indian Ocean and South-East Asia, which was concluded in June 2001 and entered into force on 1 Sept. 2001. The text of both MoUs is available in full on the institutional website of the Bonn Convention at : http://www.cms.int/ (accessed 1 Oct. 2007).

[103] Para. 34.

Notwithstanding these clear advantages for the conservation of individual migratory species subject to key provisions of the Directive, there are however shortcomings in the application of this over-arching regime. Firstly, the Habitats Directive itself is subject to a delicate balancing act whereby ecological considerations are weighed against the economic demands of the Member States, with a series of exemptions to the Natura 2000 scheme prescribed where there are 'imperative reasons of overriding public interest'.[104] As Matz observes, the balance of interests derogation has the potential to affect linkages between Natura 2000 sites,[105] which are especially important for land-based migrants and serves to undermine the effectiveness of the Habitats Directive as regards migratory species. Indeed, as Verschuuren notes, '[s]o far, many of the SPAs and SACs are small islands where large-scale economic activities are dominant'[106]. Secondly, and rather more generally, the Directive itself has been undermined by a lack of Member State designations,[107] and the late development of marine SACs, for which the Commission has only recently issued guidelines for the designation of such sites, with a view towards extending the Natura 2000 network seawards, which has very real implications for the conservation of sea-based migrants (as well as aquatic species generally) under the current EU system.

C. The EC Biodiversity Strategy

Despite the unquestioned utility of both of the keystone nature conservation Directives in relation to biodiversity protection in general, and their application to migratory species in particular, considerable problems remain in addressing biodiversity loss within the EC. Indeed, notwithstanding the enforcement will of the Commission—as well as the key role played by private actors—biodiversity loss continues apace and, as noted ruefully by one leading commentator, 'despite our best efforts, nature slowly withdraws from Western Europe'.[108] This is especially true in the context of the nature conservation Directives, which have experienced substantial delays in the establishment of protected areas, seemingly irrespective of welcome judicial processes to catalyse Member State activities and, as de Sadeleer observes, even if these provisions 'were to be correctly and quickly applied, they would probably still not be able to halt the diminution of biological diversity in Europe'.[109]

[104] Art. 6(4). On this issue generally see A. Nollkaemper, 'Habitat Protection in European Community Law: Evolving Conceptions of a Balance of Interests' (1997) 9 *Journal of Environmental Law* 271–86. By virtue of Art. 7 of the Habitats Directive, this provision also applies *mutatis mutandis* to the Wild Birds Directive.

[105] N. 7 above, at 210.

[106] N. 54 above, at 328.

[107] De Sadeleer, n. 81 above, at 251.

[108] L. Krämer, 'Thirty Years of EC Environmental Law: Perspectives and Prospectives' (2002) 2 *Yearbook of European Environmental Law* 155–82, at 179.

[109] N. 81 above, at 251.

In the context of such a gloomy prognosis for European wildlife the EU institutions have moved to evolve regional biodiversity policies further, from what may be termed a sanctuary-based approach, which is predominantly reliant upon the effective establishment and operation of protected areas for threatened species, towards a more proactive approach that seeks to develop action plans and other policies to rehabilitate threatened biodiversity. The primary instrument in this respect at present within the EU is the EC Biodiversity Strategy[110] which seeks to 'anticipate, prevent and attack the causes of significant reduction or loss of biodiversity at the source'.[111] The Biodiversity Strategy in turn has led to the development of four distinct sectoral Biodiversity Action Plans (BAPs), which were duly established in 2001,[112] addressing the conservation of natural resources, agriculture, fisheries, and economic and development cooperation respectively.

Of most immediate relevance to the protection of migratory species is the BAP on the conservation of natural resources. This particular BAP focuses explicitly on the need to fully implement the two leading nature conservation Directives, as well as providing adequate financial and technical support for the maintenance of protected areas.[113] As part of the broad objectives of the BAP, there is a particular emphasis upon the development of 'measures to promote a better coordination between different initiatives in international forums to optimise opportunities for synergy and coherence'.[114] In this respect, it may be suggested that the Bonn Convention will have a role to play in the achievement of such an objective.

Despite this, however, there is little overt mention of the Bonn Convention itself within this policy and the application of the BAP to migratory species and the Convention is instead rather more implicit as opposed to defining a clear mandate for the Bonn Convention and its subsidiaries.[115] The one clear reference to the Bonn Convention is to be found in a solitary action point within the BAP on natural resources, identifying the importance of 'collaborating with International Conventions (Bern, Bonn...) to prepare action plans for the most endangered species other than birds',[116] with the utility of such action plans

[110] COM(98)42.

[111] Ibid.

[112] Communication from the Commission to the Council and the European Parliament—Biodiversity Action Plans in the areas of Conservation of Natural Resources, Agriculture, Fisheries, and Development and Economic Co-operation, COM(2001)162.

[113] Para. 2 of the BAP on natural resources.

[114] Para. 8.

[115] Indeed, reference to the Bonn Convention is omitted entirely in the summary document outlining the aims of the BAP on natural resources in respect of developing synergies with relevant international agreements, although the summary cites a series of potential international partner institutions including 'in particular, the CITES, Climate Change, Desertification, Barcelona and OSPAR Conventions, the Cartagena and Montreal Protocols, WTO/TRIPS, FAO and the international process on forests'. It is noted furthermore that 'coherence in their development and implementation is needed to prevent potential threats to and maximise benefits for biodiversity', n. 112 above.

[116] Para. 31.

formally noted within the BAP.[117] Less explicit is the role envisaged for the Bonn Convention in the elaboration and development of conservation measures concerning wild birds, with the Commission pledging its support for the preparation of similar action plans for globally threatened avian species 'which aim to ensure appropriate conservation measures and their implementation by different actors', a task with which the Bonn Convention umbrella is clearly well equipped to assist. Elsewhere, however, the application of the BAP to the conservation needs of migratory species is rather more cryptic and, with no further reference to the Bonn Convention or indeed to migrants themselves, measures in respect of such species will be linked to general policies towards issues affecting all types of biodiversity, including the impact of invasive species and the release of genetically modified organisms (GMOs).

In addition, the BAP on economic and development cooperation, which largely addresses the possibilities for generating and supporting conservation initiatives in the developing world, also has some application to migratory species, especially in the context of rural development. In this respect, the BAP observes that the development of rural areas often occurs in a haphazard and poorly coordinated manner, which can result in the loss of vital habitats, noting that '[k]ey habitats that support populations of important species are being destroyed: breeding grounds, migratory routes, seasonal resting areas etc'.[118] Accordingly, the BAP states that EC support for rural development programmes is to focus on a diverse range of habitats and species, so as to mitigate the impacts of such activities upon biodiversity, which provides some scope at least for promoting conservation measures in areas of importance for migratory species. Attention within the BAP is also given to the need to extend the information base on a variety of habitats, especially wetlands, dry-lands and forestry, and to focus on 'the reversal of negative environmental trends in developing countries, especially through the implementation of obligations under multilateral environmental agreements and addressing regional environmental problems',[119] which again may have some relevance to migratory species.

Elsewhere, modest attention is paid towards the conservation needs of migratory species within the BAPs on fisheries and agriculture. Migratory species are only fleetingly noted in the BAP on agriculture,[120] although the fisheries BAP does observe that migrating fish, especially those species that migrate between fresh and salt water, will require management and conservation measures to be

[117] Ibid.

[118] Para. 31 of the BAP on economic and development cooperation.

[119] Para. 54.

[120] For instance, the correlation between responsible farming and flourishing rural biodiversity is observed, with the example of the Great Bustard— species subject to a distinct MoU under the auspices of the Bonn Convention—cited as a particular beneficiary of sustainable grassland policies: para. 17 of the BAP on agriculture.

applied under the auspices of the Common Fisheries Policy (CFP) of the EC.[121] The BAP also states explicitly, however, that it is bound by inter alia the Bonn Convention in respect of fisheries issues and notes the need to ensure effective cooperation with a host of international bodies in respect of species affected by fisheries policies,[122] although the relevant Bonn Convention subsidiaries are not referred to in a list of multilateral instruments adopted in respect of the marine environment in the seas governed by the EC.

Since the development of the various BAPs, however, the European Commission has conducted a series of reviews of the practical effectiveness of EU biodiversity policy and judged it to be inadequate for the purposes of meeting the 2010 target of halting the loss of biodiversity within the EU area. In May 2005, a conference on biodiversity in the EU was held in Malahide, Ireland, following which the European Commission issued a Communication[123] in an attempt to catalyse meaningful activity to address biodiversity loss in the EU, which has some potential application to the needs of migratory species—although again, such fauna are allocated a rather peripheral role in this initiative.

At this juncture, two main threats were specifically identified in relation to biodiversity, namely ill-considered land usage and development and global climate change. Indeed, both of these issues are highly pertinent to migratory species too, since poorly regulated development projects may impact upon important areas of habitat or impede migratory routes, while climate change may also constitute a strong adverse effect upon habitats and migratory behaviour. As part of the Commission's policy towards mitigating these twin threats to biodiversity, the need to fully implement the Habitats Directive and Wild Birds Directive, especially in marine areas, is considered to be especially important, as well as the need to 'focus on more effective implementation of the CBD and related agreements'.[124] This particular policy must be considered especially welcome from the point of view of the Bonn Convention umbrella and a new emphasis on cooperation with multilateral environmental agreements within EU biodiversity policy does suggest that increased opportunities may be forthcoming for the Bonn Convention to work more closely with the EU institutions, especially since the need to strengthen international governance and synergies has since been endorsed by the European Council[125] and the European Parliament (EP).[126]

[121] Para. 20 of the BAP on fisheries.

[122] Para. 37. Migratory fish stocks are addressed on a Community level primarily through EC participation in a substantial number of Regional Fisheries Management Organizations. The Commission has recently instituted legislative processes to update and amend the relevant provisions on highly migratory fish stocks in line with adjustments in the EC's international commitments: Proposal for a Council Regulation laying down Technical Measures for the Conservation of Certain Stocks of Highly Migratory Species COM(2006)100.

[123] Communication from the Commission: *Halting the Loss of Biodiversity by 2010—and Beyond. Sustaining Ecosystem Services for Human Well-Being*, COM(2006)216.

[124] Ibid., 12.

[125] Press release 16164/06 (presse 349) of 18 Dec. 2006, para. 21.

[126] EP Res. of 22 May 2007 on halting the loss of biodiversity by 2010 (A6–0089/2007).

V. EU Law and the Bonn Convention

Given that the EU institutions have seemingly identified the elaboration of closer synergies with key international conventions as an important component in seeking to halt biodiversity loss within the Community, it may be suggested that as far as migratory species are concerned it would be prudent to develop similar links with the regime of the Bonn Convention. The EU, as noted above, is a full party to the Bonn Convention itself; however it currently retains a somewhat curious relationship with a significant number of the subsidiary agreements. To date, although its status as a Regional Economic Integration Organization renders the EU eligible to accede to most of these agreements, it has opted to do so only in the case of the African-Eurasian Waterbird Agreement (AEWA) and has proved to be a rather ambivalent participant in the other such agreements; most notably in the case of the regional cetacean instruments, which the EC authorities have signed but procrastinated for a number of years over ratifying.

As discussed earlier, thus far the CMS structure has yielded a total of six key subsidiary Agreements, concluded under the auspices of Article IV(3) and (4) respectively, of which the overwhelming majority are operational in whole or in part within the EU. For the purposes of comparison, two of these agreements may be immediately discounted. Firstly, the Agreement on the Conservation of Seals in the Wadden Sea, established in 1990, constitutes a significant part of an ongoing project of trilateral cooperation between Germany, Denmark, and the Netherlands in respect of the environment of the Wadden Sea region and, while the EU is undoubtedly relevant to such activities, it is not currently eligible for formal membership of this initiative. Likewise, while the EU is technically able to join the Southern Hemisphere-based Agreement on the Conservation of Albatrosses and Petrels (ACAP),[127] it has neither signed nor ratified the Agreement to date.[128] Therefore, as far as EU/Bonn Convention synergies are concerned, the analysis will essentially focus upon the remaining subsidiary instruments of the Bonn Convention, namely the two Europe-based cetacean agreements, as well as AEWA and EUROBATS, the latter of which is charged with developing conservation and management measures in respect of migratory (and non-migratory) species of bats in Europe.

An analysis of the working relationship between the Bonn Convention subsidiaries and the EU reveals some striking results from a conservation perspective. As far as cetaceans are concerned, this has proved to be the area with the greatest scope for potential conflict, given that the majority of the Range States party (as well as a number of non-parties) to these instruments are also EU

[127] Art. I(3) of the Agreement on the Conservation of Albatrosses and Petrels, 2001.

[128] Three EU Member States—France, Spain, and the UK—have become parties to ACAP in their individual capacity, however, largely as a result of holding dependent territories within the Agreement Area.

Member States and, accordingly, have vested competence in fisheries issues exclusively to the European Community (EC).[129] This has created particular difficulties since cetacean conservation, notwithstanding the central role of the Habitats Directive and other relevant biodiversity provisions of EU law, has been advanced in recent years primarily as part of the ongoing reform of the Common Fisheries Policy (CFP) of the EC. Furthermore, there is evidence that the EC has paid limited attention to the possibilities of attaining assistance from the relevant Bonn Convention agreements in formulating a distinct cetacean policy in recent years which, despite the utility of the EC measures, may be considered flawed in certain key aspects, and it may be suggested that a closer working relationship with the Bonn Convention subsidiaries may have enhanced the current provisions substantially. On the other hand, as far as migratory waterbirds are concerned, the EU and AEWA are starting to develop a mutually satisfactory working relationship, which has helped to generate potentially effective conservation initiatives within both systems. Likewise, there is some scope for EUROBATS to play a supporting role in the development of the Habitats Directive agenda, especially in the new EU Member States drawn from Central and Eastern Europe, as well as candidate countries in the Balkan region.

A. The Bonn Convention Cetacean Agreements

An examination of the interrelationship between the Bonn Convention regime and the relevant EU legislation reveals that the fault-lines are perhaps most evident in respect of the Agreements established under the Bonn Convention to address the conservation needs of cetaceans in European and adjacent waters. To date, as noted above, two key subsidiary Agreements have been adopted in relation to such species, namely the Agreement on the Conservation of Small Cetaceans of the Baltic and North Seas (ASCOBANS) and the Agreement on the Conservation of Cetaceans of the Black Sea, Mediterranean Sea, and Contiguous Atlantic Area (ACCOBAMS).

The primary reason behind the current conflict between the Bonn Convention and EU law in this regard is due to the sudden development of a distinct conservation policy towards cetaceans recently adopted by the EC. Although these measures could potentially revolutionize the ability of the Bonn Convention Agreements to elaborate effective conservation policies to address the wide range of anthropogenic threats facing depleted European stocks of such species, the

[129] Legal competence over the development of fisheries legislation in the 27 Member States of the EU is vested exclusively in the EC. Acceptance of this position, as well as the Community *acquis* of existing fisheries legislation, policy and case law, is one of the pre-requisites for formal membership of the EU.

EC initiatives have been developed in relative isolation to these regional regimes which, in turn, may ultimately impact negatively upon the efficacy of the European provisions.

In recent years, cetaceans have attracted the regulatory attention of the EU institutions on an unprecedented scale, with particular reference to the growing threat to stocks posed by interactions with commercial fisheries and habitat degradation and disturbance.[130] This relatively uncharacteristic legislative interest in cetaceans is heavily linked to the recent reform of the CFP of the EC which, with its narrow focus upon the setting of catch quotas, was considered to be ecologically deficient and even a contributory factor to the parlous state of the marine environment in many EC fishing grounds. Cetaceans were not neglected by the EU up until this point: most notably, 'all species' of cetaceans are listed in Annex IV(a) of the Habitats Directive which, as noted above, offers a strong system of protection to listed migrant species, including in this particular case an emphasis upon addressing incidental mortality rates of such animals. However, the potential utility of the Habitats Directive aside, little in the way of a coordinated and coherent policy to address the conservation needs of cetaceans, migratory or otherwise, had emerged under the auspices of the EC until the CFP was fundamentally revised in 2002, with a view towards entrenching the integration principle into this previously neglected sector of Community policy.[131] Accordingly, Regulation (EC) No. 2371/2002 on the Conservation and Sustainable Development of Fisheries Resources Under the Common Fisheries Policy demanded that the CFP should exploit marine living resources in a manner that satisfies 'sustainable economic, environmental and social considerations', applying the precautionary approach to minimize the impact of Community fisheries upon marine ecosystems.[132] With this objective in mind, further measures to 'green' the Bonn Convention were further identified, including inter alia the elaboration of a distinct policy in respect of cetaceans, focusing explicitly on incidental catches.

As far as cetaceans are concerned, the current EC legislative position is primarily advanced under Regulation (EC) No. 812/2004 concerning Incidental Catches of Cetaceans in Fisheries and amending Regulation (EC) No. 88/98 (Incidental Catches Regulation),[133] which was intended specifically to address the wholesale by-catches of European populations of both large and small

[130] For an appraisal of this process see R. Caddell, 'By-Catch Mitigation and the Protection of Cetaceans: Recent Developments in EC Law' (2005) 8 *Journal of International Wildlife Law and Policy*, 241–60.

[131] [2002] OJ L358/59.

[132] Art. 2(1).

[133] [2004] OJ L150/12.

cetaceans[134] in Community waters.[135] To this end, the EC Regulation adopts a three-pronged approach to mitigating cetacean by-catches, namely by expanding and entrenching the general Community-wide prohibition on driftnet fishing to the Baltic Sea region, by instituting a programme of vessel-based monitoring of incidental cetacean mortality and by making the use of acoustic deterrent devices, known as 'pingers', mandatory across all EC fisheries.

In many respects, the elaboration of a coordinated policy to address cetacean mortality is a very welcome development from the point of view of ASCOBANS and ACCOBAMS, especially given the resources and legal processes available to the EU institutions to monitor and enforce these provisions, not least the operation of distinct non-compliance procedures under EU law that are absent from the international system. Indeed, the development of allied policies by the EC has a strong scope to advance and augment the conservation and management objectives of both of the Bonn Convention subsidiary agreements. Problems have arisen, however, largely due to the fact that the possibilities for ASCOBANS and ACCOBAMS to influence and assist in the EC agenda have proved to be rather limited in practice. This has led, in turn, to small but significant distinctions between the conservation measures advanced by the EC and those advocated by the regional cetacean agreements and, given the operation of Community fisheries law, EC Member States are obliged to follow the Brussels line in the case of a conflict between the two systems. Moreover, given the high proportion of EU Member States participating in both ASCOBANS and ACCOBAMS, there has also at times been a stagnation of conservation initiatives on the part of the CMS agreements, as these States are obliged to ascertain their legal standing to pursue such policies under the auspices of the regional agreements. These problems appear to have afflicted ASCOBANS and ACCOBAMS in subtly different ways, with ASCOBANS suffering more from stagnation, while ACCOBAMS has encountered conflicts with certain key policies, especially in the vital arena of by-catch mitigation.

i. ASCOBANS

One of the most sophisticated Agreements adopted under Article IV(4) of the Bonn Convention to date is the Agreement on the Conservation of Small Cetaceans of the Baltic and North Seas,[136] which was concluded in September

[134] The distinction between 'large' and 'small' cetaceans has caused significant problems in international law, and is presently a major bone of contention within the IWC. As a rule of thumb, large cetaceans are considered to be whales, while dolphins and porpoises are deemed small cetaceans, although in legal circles at least, the distinction is somewhat arbitrary and scientifically problematic.

[135] For a preliminary analysis of the prospects of Reg. (EC) No. 812/2004, n. 133 above, to promote successful conservation measures in respect of cetaceans, see Caddell, n. 130 above, at 248–57.

[136] Published on the Internet at: http://www.ascobans.org (accessed 1 Oct. 2007). For a full appraisal of ASCOBANS and its potential for developing coordinated conservation and management measures for small cetaceans see H. Nijkamp and A. Nollkaemper, 'The Protection of Small Cetaceans in the Face of Uncertainty: An Analysis of the ASCOBANS Agreement' (1997) 9 *Georgetown*

1991 and entered into force on 29 March 1994. The conclusion of an instrument in relation to migratory cetaceans was envisaged at an early stage in the development of the Bonn Convention, and a Resolution adopted at the first COP called for regional action to protect populations of dolphins and porpoises in the Baltic and North Seas.[137] ASCOBANS applies only to small cetaceans[138] in the Baltic and North Seas. There are currently ten parties to the Agreement, all of which are also Member States of the EU.[139]

The purpose of ASCOBANS is to facilitate cooperation between the Range States party to the Agreement to achieve and maintain a favourable conservation status for small cetaceans.[140] Appended to the Agreement text is a concise conservation and management plan, which should be applied by each party 'within the limits of its jurisdiction and in accordance with its international obligations'.[141] To this end, the conservation and management plan requires the parties to 'work towards' preventing the release of substances that may pose a potential threat to the health of small cetaceans, developing modifications to fishing gear to mitigate by-catches, regulating activities that may seriously affect food resources of small cetaceans and preventing other significant disturbances, 'especially of an acoustic nature'. The conservation and management plan also requires the coordination of research on small cetaceans, the prohibition of directed hunting under domestic law and facilitating the dissemination of information to the general public.

ASCOBANS is one of the most long-standing and highly-developed subsidiary instruments of the Bonn Convention and has adopted a series of initiatives to address the various threats to small cetaceans in the Agreement waters, which have been elaborated at the various Meetings of the Parties (MOPs), of which five have been held to date. In this regard, considerable progress has been made in relation to by-catch mitigation, which is believed to pose the most pressing threat to these animals. To this end, the parties introduced a comprehensive recovery plan for populations of harbour porpoises in the Baltic Sea,[142] and endorsed the

International Environmental Law Review, 281–302; see also R. Churchill, 'The Agreement on the Conservation of Small Cetaceans of the Baltic and North Seas' in W. Burns and A. Gillespie (eds.) *The Future of Cetaceans in a Changing World* (New York: Transnational Publishers, 2003), at 283.

[137] *Proceedings of the First Meeting of the Conference of the Parties* (UNEP, 1985), at 50.

[138] Small cetaceans are defined in Art. 1.2(a) as 'any species, subspecies or population of toothed whales Odontoceti, except the sperm whale *Physeter macrocephalus*'.

[139] Namely Belgium, Denmark, Finland, France, Germany, Lithuania, the Netherlands, Poland, Sweden, and the UK. In addition, Estonia has indicated that it intends to ratify the Agreement within the course of 2007. Latvia, another EU Member State is a Range State to the Agreement but has displayed little inclination to join ASCOBANS, choosing instead to concentrate on working through other CMS instruments in respect of its national policies towards migratory species. A further two Range States of ASCOBANS (which have not become parties) are also non-members of the European Union, namely Norway and the Russian Federation.

[140] Art. 2.1. Nevertheless, a 'favourable conservation status' is not defined within the ASCOBANS text and is presumed to carry the same meaning as that advanced under the Bonn Convention.

[141] Art. 2.2.

[142] *ASCOBANS Recovery Plan for Harbour Porpoises in the Baltic Sea* (ASCOBANS, 2002); reproduced in full on the ASCOBANS institutional website, n. 136 above (accessed 1 Oct. 2006).

conclusion of a similar initiative in relation to the North Sea in 2003, at the Fourth MOP.[143] However, the future role of ASCOBANS has been complicated somewhat by the recent accession of the Baltic States and Poland to the EU, which means that these Range States are now subject to a series of overriding—and potentially conflicting—measures in relation to cetaceans under EC law.

The EC has historically maintained a somewhat ambivalent relationship with ASCOBANS. The EC has signed the Agreement itself, but has not ratified it, despite a number of communications from ASCOBANS urging it to do so; hence the two organizations exist in a state of institutional cohabitation in relation to these waters. This leaves the EC outside the circle of ASCOBANS itself, yet endowed with the power to adopt measures that may differ to or, conversely, strongly support initiatives advanced by ASCOBANS. In the early years of the Agreement, relations between ASCOBANS and the EC were relatively poor, with the Advisory Committee (AC) of ASCOBANS having previously declared the attitude of the EC towards ASCOBANS to be 'disappointing and unsatisfactory'[144] and 'not helpful'.[145] In more recent years, however, there has been a marked improvement in this position, with the European Commission having noted the possibilities for ASCOBANS to play a valuable advisory role in the establishment of SACs for two species of small cetaceans under the Habitats Directive, namely the harbour porpoise and bottlenose dolphin.[146] A concerted programme of action to develop and improve links between the EC has been highlighted as an official policy of the ASCOBANS Advisory Committee over the coming triennium, with a Resolution adopted at the Fifth MOP in September 2006 calling for this body to 'explore ways in which ASCOBANS can better liaise and work with the EC on issues of mutual interest'.[147]

Despite this, however, there are signs that the ASCOBANS conservation measures may be beginning to stagnate, although this position cannot be attributed solely to the EC/Bonn Convention divide and is instead more pertinently the product of multiple causes, including funding issues and disagreement between the parties on the future direction of ASCOBANS. That said, part of this disagreement stems from the unusual position in which ASCOBANS finds itself, where States parties, wary of developing national policies that could potentially

[143] *Resolution 10: Recovery Plan for Harbour Porpoise in the North Sea* (2003). The North Sea initiative has since been renamed a 'Conservation Plan' and this project remains a work in progress after the Fifth MOP: *Resolution 1: Conservation Plan for Harbour Porpoises in the North Sea* (2006). On by-catch mitigation strategies introduced under the auspices of the Bonn Convention generally see S. Bache and S. Rajkumar, 'Marine Wildlife Bycatch under the CMS: Progress and Prospects' (2003) 18 *International Journal of Marine and Coastal Law*, 215–40.

[144] *Report of the Third Meeting of the Advisory Committee to ASCOBANS* (Chittagong, Bangladesh 7–10 Nov. 1978: ASCOBANS, 1996), 6.

[145] *Report of the Fourth Meeting of the Advisory Committee to ASCOBANS* (Stockholm, Sweden, 19–21 Apr. 1999: ASCOBANS, 1997), 15.

[146] *Report of the Fifth Meeting of the Advisory Committee to ASCOBANS* (Zagreb, Croatia, 21–23 Feb. 2000: ASCOBANS, 1998), 12–13.

[147] Res. No. 6; Activities of the ASCOBANS Advisory Committee 2007–2010 (2006).

deviate from the EC line, may prove hesitant in applying conservation measures that were created within the ASCOBANS forum. In particular, some governments have questioned their continuing involvement in an Agreement that is forced to operate under these conditions, and the withdrawal of individual States would be likely to have a domino effect upon other parties in a current climate of uncertainty within ASCOBANS.

Moreover, the practical difficulties faced by ASCOBANS were starkly illustrated at the recent MOP in the context of the developing recovery plan for North Sea stocks of harbour porpoises, for which the intention of the parties had been to formally adopt this instrument at this juncture. During the discussion of the recovery plan a series of objections were raised by the representative of the European Commission, on the basis that the conservation objectives of the proposed instrument conflicted with the Habitats Directive.[148] Eventually the ASCOBANS parties postponed the adoption of the North Sea plan until the next MOP due to a number of other concerns with the document in its present format; however this episode is indicative of some of the problems that ASCOBANS will face in attempting to prescribe meaningful conservation measures under these conditions.

ii. ACCOBAMS

The other Agreement adopted under the auspices of Article IV(4) of the Bonn Convention relating to cetaceans is the Agreement on the Conservation of Cetaceans of the Black Sea, Mediterranean Sea and Contiguous Atlantic Area,[149] which was concluded in November 1996 and entered into force on 1 June 2001. ACCOBAMS is more broadly based than its counterpart in the Baltic and North Seas, and applies to 'all cetaceans that have a range which lies entirely or partly within the Agreement area or that accidentally or occasionally frequent the Agreement area'.[150] There are currently 18 parties to the Agreement, of which ten are also Member States of the EU.[151]

[148] Ironically, the conservation objectives had been reproduced largely *verbatim* from the Bonn Convention itself.

[149] The text of the Agreement is reproduced in full on the ACCOBAMS institutional website published on the Internet at: http://www.accobams.org (accessed 1 Oct. 2007). For a full appraisal of ACCOBAMS see W. Burns, 'The Agreement on the Conservation of Cetaceans of the Black Sea, Mediterranean Sea and Contiguous Atlantic Area' (1998) 1 *Journal of International Wildlife Law and Policy*, 113–32. For an introductory analysis comparing the two regional instruments addressing cetaceans see R. Churchill, 'Sustaining Small Cetaceans: A Preliminary Evaluation of the ASCOBANS and ACCOBAMS Agreements' in A. Boyle and D. Freestone (eds.), *International Law and Sustainable Development: Past Achievements and Future Challenges* (Oxford: Oxford University Press, 2001), at 225.

[150] Art. I(2). Cetaceans are defined in Art. I(3)(a) as 'animals, including individuals, of those species, subspecies or populations of *Odontoceti* or *Mysticeti*'.

[151] Namely Bulgaria, Cyprus, France, Greece, Italy, Malta, Portugal, Romania, Slovenia, and Spain.

Like ASCOBANS, parties to ACCOBAMS undertake to take coordinated measures to achieve and maintain a favourable conservation status for cetaceans, and are to apply within the areas under their jurisdiction a series of conservation, research, and management plans prescribed in a substantive Conservation Plan, appended to the Agreement text. Unlike ASCOBANS, however, parties to ACCOBAMS must explicitly apply the precautionary principle in implementing such measures.[152] To this end, the Conservation Plan details a series of legislative, regulatory, and conservation measures that the parties 'shall' apply including, inter alia, mitigating by-catches and banning the use of large-scale pelagic driftnets, undertaking impact assessments in relation to future activities that may affect cetaceans or their habitats, regulating the discharge of harmful pollutants and creating or strengthening national institutions to implement the Agreement further. In addition, parties are to endeavour to establish and manage protected areas of habitat for cetaceans, undertake coordinated research and monitoring exercises, develop and implement appropriate emergency measures, and raise public awareness of the conservation needs of cetaceans in the Agreement area.

The implementation of these measures is supported by initiatives introduced at regular MOPs, of which two have been held to date. The First MOP was largely concerned with the establishment of the ACCOBAMS institutions. However, encouraging progress was made at the Second MOP, held in November 2004, at which a series of resolutions were adopted, advancing policies in relation to by-catch mitigation, acoustic disturbances and the establishment of protected areas.

As far as the synergies between ACCOBAMS and the EC are concerned, there has been little obvious duplication of the sustained friction that characterized the early working relationship between ASCOBANS and the European officials. This position may be explained primarily by the lesser influence exerted upon ACCOBAMS on the part of the EC, given that a substantial number of the Range States eligible for participation in ACCOBAMS is drawn from outside the EU, most notably from North Africa and the Middle East. Instead, conflict has been generated largely as a result of two key differences in relation to the Community cetacean provisions.

Firstly, as noted above, one of the primary aims of the EC in addressing the incidental mortality of cetaceans is the eradication of driftnet fishing in all Community waters. Driftnets are considered to be an especially destructive form of fishing equipment due to the inherent lack of selectivity involved in this technique, which has been widely blamed for decimating stocks of target and non-target species alike.[153] As a result of concerted pressure in the UN General Assembly the use of driftnets on the high seas was subject to a maximum limit of 2.5 km,[154]

152 Art. II(4).

153 See A. Richards, 'Problems of Drift-Net Fisheries in the South Pacific' (1994) 29 *Marine Pollution Bulletin*, 106–11.

154 On the evolution of UN policy see W. Burke, M. Freeburg, and E. Miles, 'United Nations Resolutions on Driftnet Fishing: An Unsustainable Precedent for High Seas and Coastal Fisheries Management' (1994) 25 *Ocean Development and International Law*, 127–86.

which has since been interpreted as a rule of customary international law.[155] The overwhelming majority of coastal states and regional fisheries management organizations have endorsed the 2.5 km limit—including ACCOBAMS—while the EC has instituted a 'zero tolerance' approach to such equipment, banning it in its entirety.[156] Although there have been substantial problems in ensuring compliance with these provisions,[157] Community fisheries officials are nonetheless deeply committed to the driftnet ban and there is little realistic prospect of the restrictions being modified to permit the limited use of such netting envisaged by bodies such as ACCOBAMS.

At present, the divergence of approaches is not a significant problem in practice as incidences of non-compliance with the EC driftnet legislation are 'not violations of the distinct technical measures adopted by the EC, in the sense that such netting fulfils the international criteria but breaches the narrower European rules; rather they entail the use of driftnets significantly in excess of permitted international standards'[158] and therefore contravene the stated policies of both organizations. Nonetheless, while both ACCOBAMS and the EC maintain a mutual interest in eradicating such fishing equipment in these waters, efforts in this regard may be complicated and undermined by a failure to agree upon the type of gear that merits regulatory opprobrium.

Secondly, and rather more significantly, a schism is developing between ACCOBAMS and the EC over the mandatory use of acoustic by-catch mitigation devices in Community fisheries, as prescribed under the Incidental Catches Regulation. The motivation behind this policy on the part of the EC stems from good intentions, with the use of pingers considered by fisheries scientists to potentially reduce by-catches of marine mammals significantly.[159] Nevertheless, substantial concerns remain over the widespread use of this equipment, with studies demonstrating that the performance of pingers in reducing incidental cetacean mortality is highly variable in practice.[160] In particular, concerns have been raised that cetaceans may either habituate to such devices, in which case they lose their inherent utility, or conversely that they may prove to be a disruptive influence and exclude populations from their traditional areas of habitat. Despite these concerns, however, and the fact that pingers have not been sanctioned on an extended basis to date by other fisheries management authorities, the Incidental

[155] G. Hewison, 'The Legally Binding Nature of the Moratorium on Large-Scale High Seas Driftnet Fishing' (1994) 25 *Journal of Maritime Law and Commerce*, 557–80.

[156] On the elaboration and enforcement of the EC position see R. Caddell, 'The Prohibition on Driftnet Fishing in European Community Waters: Problems, Progress and Prospects' (2007) 13 *Journal of International Maritime Law*, 265–88.

[157] Ibid., at 279–87.

[158] Ibid., at 266.

[159] S. Kraus et al., 'Acoustic Alarms Reduce Incidental Mortality of Porpoises in Gill Nets' (2002) 388 *Nature*, at 525.

[160] S. Dawson, A. Reid, and E. Slooten, 'Pingers, Porpoises and Power: Uncertainties with using Pingers to Reduce Bycatch of Small Cetaceans' (1998) 84 *Biological Conservation*, 141–6.

Catches Regulation requires the deployment of these appliances on all fishing vessels over 12m in length in Community waters. This policy has drawn sustained and strident criticism from the ACCOBAMS institutions, concerned that the impact of pingers on the cetaceans is not yet well understood, nor has the sustained use of pingers been demonstrated to be an effective conservation tool in the short to medium term and, indeed, may ultimately prove to be an adverse presence in the marine environment.[161] Accordingly ACCOBAMS has recently adopted a distinct Resolution on the use of pingers,[162] in which it 'urges the parties to strictly regulate the use of AHDs to alleviate conflicts between cetaceans and fisheries or mariculture operations in the Agreement area', bringing it directly into conflict with the EC on this issue, which could create an uncomfortable state of affairs for those countries that are members of both organizations. The (albeit unspoken) suggestion that the EC may be in breach of its own legislation mandating a precautionary approach to fisheries management remains a live issue, and one that is likely to receive further attention within ACCOBAMS at its next MOP, scheduled to be held in October 2007.

Despite these practical difficulties in attaining synergies between the EC and the cetacean agreements of the Bonn Convention experienced to date, there remains scope for these agreements to play a useful supporting role within the EC cetacean agenda, while practical cooperation between these entities continues to develop. ASCOBANS, for instance, has formally acknowledged the need to explore the possibilities of forming closer ties, possibly through the establishment of a designated EC liaison officer, and progress in this respect will undoubtedly prove instructive for the other Europe-based Bonn Convention subsidiaries. ASCOBANS is also currently in the process of conducting a review of relevant EC cetacean policies and legislation, with a view towards clarifying its own role within the Agreement Area as well as presenting constructive advice to the EC as to the deficiencies affecting its current policy. For its part, EC representatives have agreed to make the national reports on cetacean by-catches returned under the Incidental Catches Regulation available to ASCOBANS, which will be of practical value to the AC in reviewing policies advanced under the Agreement.[163]

Although the primary regulatory authority in respect of cetaceans in European waters will unquestionably continue to be the EC, acting under the Habitats Directive and relevant specific legislation advanced under the CFP, ASCOBANS and ACCOBAMS do present valuable avenues to the EC through which cetacean policies may be further elaborated and advanced. In particular, both Agreements

[161] Guidelines for Technical Measures to Minimise Cetacean-Fishery Conflicts in the Mediterranean and Black Seas, annexed to Resolution 2.12 on pingers, adopted at the Second Meeting of the Parties to ACCOBAMS.

[162] Ibid.

[163] *Proceedings of the 5th Meeting of the Parties to ASCOBANS* (The Netherlands, 18–20 Sept. and 12 Dec. 2006: ASCOBANS, 2007), 6. A further motivation behind this move is that it could help meet EC commitments under the Aarhus Convention.

maintain considerable technical and scientific expertise that could be drawn upon in identifying potential SACs in respect of cetaceans, which are likely to develop in the coming years. Furthermore, both ASCOBANS and ACCOBANS have a considerable education and publicity remit that is largely absent from the Habitats Directive, yet is vital in engaging the general public and other stakeholders in the conservation of cetaceans,[164] while the distinct conservation and management plans adopted under the auspices of these Agreements could also provide Member States with an opportunity of fulfilling EC nature conservation commitments through a coordinated, coherent, and unified programme of action.

iii. AEWA

The African-Eurasian Waterbird Agreement (AEWA),[165] which opened for signature in June 1995 and entered into force on 1 November 1999, is an AGREEMENT adopted under the aegis of Article IV(3) of the CMS. Despite having only been in force for a relatively brief period of time, AEWA 'is quickly becoming the most significant Agreement concluded under the auspices of the Bonn Convention so far'.[166] AEWA is currently the largest and most broad-ranging subsidiary instrument of the Bonn Convention, encompassing some 117 Range States,[167] and exercising responsibility for some 235 species of waterbirds,[168] listed in Annex 2 of the Agreement.[169] There are currently 59 parties to AEWA, of which 22 are EU Member States[170] and, rather more significantly, the EU itself has also become a full party to the agreement.[171]

The fundamental objectives of AEWA are stated as being to take coordinated measures to maintain species of migratory waterbirds in a favourable conservation status or to restore them to such a status, taking into account the precautionary

[164] A primary example of this is the current Year of the Dolphin programme for 2007 operated under the auspices of the Bonn Convention, which seeks to raise awareness of the conservation needs of cetaceans, as well as the various regulatory initiatives advanced to date.

[165] The text of the Agreement is reproduced in full on the AEWA institutional website published on the Internet at: http://www.unep-aewa.org (accessed 1 Oct. 2007).

[166] Caddell, n. 5 above, at 132.

[167] 'Range States' are not defined within the Agreement text, and presumably carry the same definition as that advanced in the Bonn Convention itself.

[168] 'Waterbirds' are defined as 'those species of birds that are ecologically dependent on wetlands for at least part of their annual cycle, have a range which lies entirely or partly within the Agreement Area and are listed in Annex 2 to this Agreement', Art. I(c).

[169] Additionally, AEWA specifically notes that actions taken in pursuit of the protection of migratory waterbirds will also have vicarious benefits for the ecosystem as a whole. Indeed, the Agreement was established with the parties '[c]onvinced that the conclusion of a multilateral Agreement and its implementation through coordinated or concerted action will contribute significantly to the conservation of migratory waterbirds and their habitats in the most efficient manner, and will have ancillary benefits for many other species of animals and plants': preamble to the Agreement.

[170] Namely Belgium, Bulgaria, Czech Republic, Denmark, Finland, France, Germany, Greece, Hungary, Italy, Ireland, Latvia, Lithuania, Luxembourg, Netherlands, Portugal, Romania, Slovakia, Slovenia, Spain, Sweden, and the UK.

[171] Council Dec. 2006/871/EC, [2006] OJ L345/25.

principle.[172] To this end, the Agreement prescribes a series of general conservatory measures to be taken by the parties including, inter alia, identifying sites and habitats for migratory waterbirds within their territories and encouraging the protection, management, rehabilitation, and restoration of these sites; coordinating efforts to ensure that a network of suitable habitats is maintained, especially in transboundary areas; investigating potential problems posed to migratory waterbirds by human activities and endeavouring to mitigate these issues; cooperating in emergency situations; prohibiting the introduction of exotic species; developing programmes to raise awareness of migratory waterbird conservation issues; and exchanging information and research.[173]

These activities are to be guided by a designated Action Plan,[174] which is to be reviewed at each MOP.[175] The Action Plan provides for the parties to take legal measures to protect migratory waterbirds, as well as developing a series of single-species action plans for certain species[176] and introducing measures to conserve habitats. The Action Plan also provides for the management of human activities, such as directed hunting, and the elaboration of 'cooperative programmes between all concerned to develop sensitive and appropriate eco-tourism at wetlands holding concentrations of populations listed in Table 1'.[177] In addition, the parties are to endeavour to undertake research and monitoring activities to improve the state of knowledge of migratory waterbirds and develop programmes of education to promote awareness of the conservation needs of these species. In addition to this, an innovative feature of the Agreement is its express acknowledgement of the need to ensure that the AEWA Secretariat maintains mutually harmonious relations between itself and other supranational bodies charged with wetlands issues, so as to minimize the risks of duplication or conflict of work.[178] To this end, the Secretariat is to consult with other competent secretariats and organizations 'on a regular basis' on matters of a common interest, with a view towards implementing and developing the Action Plan appropriately.[179] Although designed primarily in the spirit of inter-agency cooperation between the five biodiversity-related international conventions, this provision may also be interpreted as providing a remit to develop a close working relationship with the EU authorities, especially in the context of the Wild Birds Directive.

[172] Art. II.

[173] Art. III.

[174] Appended as Annex 3 to the Agreement.

[175] Art. IV. The procedures for the MOP are detailed under Art. VI of the Agreement.

[176] The species identified as being subject to such initiatives are listed in a table within the Action Plan. This table 'forms an integral part of this Annex. Any reference to this Action Plan includes a reference to Table 1', para. 1.2 of the AEWA Action Plan.

[177] Para. 4.2.1 of the AEWA Action Plan.

[178] Art. IX of the Agreement; see Caddell, n. 5 above, at 150–1. For a comprehensive overview of the various international instruments addressing wild birds see M. Bowman, 'International Treaties and the Global Protection of Birds' (1999) 11 *Journal of Environmental Law*, 87 and 281.

[179] Art. IX, ibid.

To date, three MOPs have been held under the auspices of AEWA, the first of which was predominantly concerned with establishing the institutional structure of the Agreement. The Second MOP (held in Bonn, Germany, in September 2002) and Third MOP (held in Dakar, Senegal, in October 2005) advanced a series of initiatives to protect migratory waterbirds, including the elaboration of a small conservation grants fund and the development of a series of coordinated single-species action plans.

The participation of the EC in AEWA affords an insight into the interrelationship between the Wild Birds Directive and international law addressing bird species. For the most part, the two systems have existed in splendid isolation to each other, apart from one rather obscure occasion where the Bonn Convention was used explicitly in legal proceedings as an interpretive guide to the Wild Birds Directive which, notwithstanding its value to avian conservation, has proven susceptible to drafting weakness in past disputes. In the *Leybucht Dykes* case[180] Advocate General Van Gerven considered the text of the Bonn Convention to be highly instructive, especially given the close proximity in time between the conclusion of the two instruments, with relevant provisions of the Bonn Convention used to define the concepts of 'habitat' and 'area of distribution' that had been left undefined within the Directive.[181] This, however, appears to have been the only time that the Court has utilized the Bonn Convention so overtly in deciding on a biodiversity-related dispute.

Despite the interpretive value of the Bonn Convention to the European provisions, it is nonetheless clear that the EC views AEWA as subordinate to the Wild Birds Directive as far as its application towards the species and geographical locations covered by the application of the Directive. Tellingly, the Council Decision approving EC membership of AEWA categorically states that such an authorization is 'limited to those amendments that are consistent with, and do not entail modification of, Community legislation on the conservation of wild birds and their natural habitats'.[182] Furthermore, the influence of AEWA over the agenda of the Wild Birds Directive is controlled through a strongly worded provision requiring any amendments to the Agreement to be subject to full implementation in the 'relevant Community legislation within ninety days of the date of its adoption', with the Commission required to enter a formal reservation to the amendment in question in the absence of an explicit acceptance of such a development under the relevant legislative processes.[183]

In addition to this, the EC guards a strong negotiating stance within the institutional meetings both of AEWA and other the subsidiary instruments, as well as the Bonn Convention itself, with the practical requirement of an 'EU Coordination Meeting' at the start of each day throughout the duration of each

[180] Case C-57/89 *Commission* v. *Germany*, n. 73 above.
[181] Footnoted at paras 4 and 7 of the Opinion of AG Van Gerven: ibid.
[182] Art. 3 of Council Dec. 2006/871/EC, n. 171 above.
[183] Ibid., Art. 4.

MOP and COP. This rather mysterious and secretive event, during which the Heads of Delegation liaise for up to an hour with the official EC representative, presents valid concerns for NGO observers and non-Member State officials who are precluded from attending; indeed, one long-standing observer notes with resignation that 'positions are taken on behalf of a large and powerful aggregation of states, which are not then negotiable in the open sessions of the Conference or Meeting... there is a genuine reduction in the freedom of debate'.[184] However, with an apparently limited scope to address questions of transparency demonstrated by most of the Bonn Convention agreements to date,[185] it appears that the EU Coordination Meeting is likely to remain a curious daily ritual at the various institutional meetings convened under the Bonn Convention umbrella, to the consternation of observers and non-Member States of the EU.

With the rules of engagement clearly specified, and notwithstanding that AEWA is currently at a relatively early stage in its existence, a series of productive synergies have started to form between the agreement and the EU in two key respects. Firstly, as a formal party to AEWA, the EU is required to implement the general policies advanced under the agreement, which are then to be incorporated into the relevant EU provisions addressing migratory birds. In particular, one such policy that has started to be implemented by the European Commission is the proposed establishment of a ban on the use of lead shot in wetland areas. At this juncture, however, it is still somewhat premature to judge the effectiveness of this measure on a Community level; at the time of writing very little tangible progress had been made in terms of developing a distinct EU-wide policy on this issue. Secondly, a number of Species Action Plans advanced under AEWA in respect of migratory waterfowl were drafted jointly with the European Commission,[186] with the possibility that further initiatives of this nature may be developed to the considerable benefit of individual species.

iv. EUROBATS

The first AGREEMENT to be concluded under Article IV(3) of the Bonn Convention was the Agreement on the Conservation of Bats in Europe,[187] which opened for signature in December 1991 and entered into force on 16

[184] Personal correspondence with Mr Konstantin Kreiser, EU Policy Manager. Birdlife International (on file with the author).

[185] Transparency issues have also been raised by another leading NGO negotiating lobby, the Whale and Dolphin Conservation Society, in respect of practices within ASCOBANS: *Proceedings of the 5th Meeting of the Parties to ASCOBANS* (The Netherlands, 18–20 Sept. and 12 Dec. 2006: ASCOBANS, 2007), 8.

[186] In particular the Species Action Plans advanced in respect of the Corncrake, White-Headed Duck and Great Snape.

[187] In July 2000, this instrument was formally renamed the 'Agreement on the Conservation of Populations of European Bats', Res. 3.7, adopted at the Third Session of the Meeting of the Parties. The text of the Agreement is reproduced in full (as amended) on the EUROBATS institutional website, published at the Internet at: http://www.eurobats.org (accessed 1 Oct. 2007).

January 1994. EUROBATS, as the Agreement is popularly known, was established shortly after the first Conference of Parties to the CMS and applies only in Europe,[188] encompassing some 48 Range States.[189] The EUROBATS Agreement is responsible for the elaboration of conservation measures in relation to 45 species of bats commonly found in Europe, and relates to both migratory and non-migratory species, since different species of bats have a tendency to share roosts and face a series of common threats, regardless of whether such species migrate or not.[190] There are currently 31 parties to EUROBATS, including virtually all of the Member States of the EU, although the EC has neither signed nor ratified the Agreement.[191]

EUROBATS prescribes a series of 'fundamental obligations' in relation to bat conservation, which are incumbent on the parties to the Agreement. These include, inter alia, prohibiting the deliberate capture, keeping, or killing of bats, unless under permit; identifying sites within areas under national jurisdiction that are important for the conservation status of bats and preventing damage or disturbance to such areas; taking 'appropriate measures' to promote conservation of bats and improve public awareness of these issues; assigning internal responsibility for bat protection to an appropriate body; and promoting research programmes.[192] The parties are responsible for adopting and enforcing 'such legislative and administrative measures as may be necessary for the purpose of giving effect to this Agreement'.[193] Key decisions are made at a 'periodic' Meeting of the Parties (MOP),[194] of which five have been held to date. The primary function of the MOP is to evaluate national implementation reports presented by each of the parties[195] and to consider proposed amendments to the AGREEMENT.[196]

[188] 'Europe' is defined in the EUROBATS Agreement simply as 'the continent of Europe', Art. I(f). However, bats are defined as 'European populations of MICROCHIROPTERA (Molossidae, Rhinolophidae and Vespertilionidae) occurring in Europe and non-European Range States', Art. I(b) (as amended).

[189] A Range State is defined as 'any State (whether or not it is a Party to the Convention) that exercises jurisdiction over any part of the range of a species covered by this Agreement', Art. I(c). Thus far, 31 of the 48 Range States have become parties to the Agreement.

[190] Preamble to the Agreement. The species currently subject to EUROBATS are listed in Annex 1 of the Agreement.

[191] 23 of the EU Member States are parties to EUROBATS, the four exceptions being Austria, Cyprus, Greece, and Spain.

[192] Art. III.

[193] Art. IV(1). Under Art. IV(2), parties may adopt stricter national measures to protect bats than are provided for under this instrument.

[194] Provision for the holding of MOPs is made under Art. V of EUROBATS. Meetings are held on an approximately triennial basis.

[195] Each party is responsible for presenting an up-to-date report on its implementation of the Agreement at the MOP, which must be forwarded to the Secretariat at least 90 days prior to the Meeting—Art. VI.

[196] Under Art. VIII(4) any amendment to the Agreement requires the support of a two-thirds majority of the parties present and voting at an MOP. To date, the EUROBATS text has been amended twice, in 1995 and 2000.

Notwithstanding the longevity of EUROBATS and the various conservation initiatives advanced to date under its auspices, it is clear that the primary mechanism for the protection of species of bats in Europe is the Habitats Directive. Bat species are well-represented within the Habitats Directive and, like cetaceans, 'all species' of *microchiroptera*[197] are listed in Annex IV(a) to the directive, ensuring that such species will qualify for the strict protection measures provided for under Article 12. To date it appears that bats have been particular beneficiaries of the Natura 2000 project, with the Directive having fostered a growing network of protected areas for such species. Indeed, the National Implementation Reports of the various parties to EUROBATS reveals that the Habitats Directive has had a substantial influence upon the practice of the parties that are also EU Member States—long-standing EU members have identified and, more importantly, put into operation a significant number of SACs in relation to bat habitats, while more recent accession countries, such as the Czech Republic for instance, have explicitly noted that the requirements of the Directive have catalysed national legislation to protect these species.[198]

In view of the comparative strength and efficiency of the Habitats Directive as a legal instrument, any future role that EUROBATS may have to play in the conservation framework concerning migratory bats is likely to be largely consultative in nature, as the institutional auspices of this Bonn Convention subsidiary provide a forum for leading experts on bat conservation issues to develop conservation and management guidelines and research activities, which may in turn assist in the identification of future Natura 2000 sites, as opposed to establishing strident and enforceable obligations upon the parties. Nonetheless, there remains some considerable merit in this approach, since in many respects the Habitats Directive is a somewhat blunt—if effective—instrument with which to secure conservation measures in respect of bats. Indeed, bat conservation in practice raises issues that transcend the sanctuary approach, such as population monitoring, which is of particular significance in assessing the effectiveness of the conservatory measures adopted, as well as educational initiatives such as the popular European Bat Night, which engages the interest of the general public and helps to dispel the fears and superstitions traditionally attached to these misunderstood mammals that bear considerable responsibility for the decline in populations in the first place.

[197] Bat species are grouped into the order *chiroptera*, and classified further into two sub-orders, *megachiroptera* and *microchiroptera*. *Microchiroptera* are by far the most numerous and common species of bats; *megachiroptera* consist solely of species of fruit bat, of which only the Egyptian fruit bat *rousettus aegyptiacus* (which is also listed both in Annex IV of the Habitats Dir. and in Annex I of EUROBATS) commonly visits Europe along its migratory path.

[198] See the EUROBATS National Implementation Reports presented to the Fifth MOP in Sept. 2006, published on the Internet at: http://www.eurobats.org/documents/List_of_documents_MoP5.htm (accessed 1 Oct. 2007).

B. EU Law and The CMS Umbrella: Some Potential Benefits of Enhanced Synergies

An analysis of both the international and EU systems addressing migratory species reveals a series of strengths and deficiencies within the two tiers, with an increased level of synergy between the EU institutions and the Bonn Convention offering a potential scope to enhance the conservation agenda and address some of the potential weaknesses within these respective approaches.

As far as the EU is concerned, an impressive array of nature conservation legislation has been in operation across the Member States for a considerable period of time, capable of advancing policies with the ability to prescribe effective conservation policies for biodiversity generally, which also has a clear application to migratory species. These are supported by robust infringement proceedings and underpinned by substantial financial resources to pursue the conservation agenda of the EU institutions. Nevertheless, the EU does face problems in this respect, not least in that successive rounds of enlargement have redrawn the boundaries and ecosystems of the EU and advanced the application of these provisions to an unprecedented scale. Moreover, there are current deficiencies in the practical operation of these nature conservation laws, with biodiversity strategies explicitly judged by the EU itself to be in real danger of failing to fulfil their primary objectives.

Regarding the Bonn Convention, experience in recent years has demonstrated that it is capable of generating subsidiary agreements with the scope and personnel to advance bold conservation and management measures. However, the regime of the Bonn Convention itself faces significant challenges in that the sheer practical difficulties inherent in legislating for the range of migratory species under its regulatory purview render the pursuit of its goals to be, at best, highly ambitious. The Bonn Convention has also suffered from a distinct lack of enforcement possibilities and faces a constant struggle to generate sufficient funding to maintain its activities, with a by-product of this relative impecuniosity being a marked dilution in the scope of the conservatory measures currently advanced under its auspices.

Both systems, therefore, have the potential to offer the other practical benefits. In the case of the EU, it has been seen that the Commission has recently sought to improve its synergies with key multilateral environmental agreements, albeit centred predominantly on the Convention on Biodiversity (CBD) and CITES at present. A closer working relationship with the regime of the Bonn Convention has the potential to deliver tangible benefits to biodiversity policies in a number of respects. Firstly, biodiversity policies have identified a deficient knowledge base as an inhibiting factor towards the development of effective conservation policies, an issue that could to an extent be addressed in tandem with a number of Bonn Convention agreements, especially in relation to marine species which are notoriously difficult (and expensive) to study in the wild. The elaboration of joint research programmes and agendas could help to fill lacunae in the existing levels of scientific understanding, a shortcoming that has already been identified as problematic in assessing the extent of the success, or otherwise, of conservation measures adopted under the Wild Birds Directive.[199]

Secondly, public participation in biodiversity conservation, also identified in the Biodiversity Strategy, can be augmented through the Bonn Convention subsidiaries, with the success of events such as European Bat Night or the Year of the Dolphin presenting a useful model to follow. Thirdly, as called for in the BAP on nature conservation, the Bonn Convention could assist in the development of individual action plans for certain species. For instance, there is a burgeoning interrelationship between the EU and AEWA to develop such plans, and possibilities exist in respect of other animals, especially marine species given the range of expertise under ASCOBANS and ACCOBAMS. Fourthly, and linked to the opportunities for the development of action plans, the Bonn Convention agreements can offer assistance in the development of individual conservation policies. Indeed, as demonstrated by EC cetacean policy, a closer working relationship with the expert subsidiaries of the Bonn Convention could enhance the initiatives advanced by the EU substantially in certain instances. Fifthly, the Bonn Convention umbrella could also form a useful avenue through which to implement key aspects of the Habitats Directive that are currently in their infancy. For instance, the Habitats Directive has only recently advanced guidelines on the elaboration of marine SACs, for which ASCOBANS and ACCOBAMS could potentially assist identifying and establishing suitable candidate areas within the waters under their jurisdiction. Likewise, the Bonn Convention could assist in the development of conservation initiatives outside the demarcated areas of wildlife conservation—another key failing of the Habitats Directive at present—with the formation of linkages between SACs constituting a challenge to the effectiveness of the EU measures.

Likewise, the EU has much to offer the Bonn Convention umbrella. Firstly, the EU offers substantial opportunities for funding and sponsorship, which are vital to the activities both of the subsidiary agreements and for the Bonn Convention itself to generate conservation initiatives in developing countries. To date, the EU LIFE project has made an invaluable contribution to a number of the subsidiaries. For instance, much of the funding for the SCANS project initiated under the auspices of ASCOBANS to ascertain the population status of small cetaceans—and thereby the key threats facing such species, for which conservation measures could be prioritized—was donated by the European Commission. Likewise, and in conformity with the expressed policy within the BAP on economic and development cooperation, the European Commission recently underwrote the costs of a series of projects to address the conservation needs of threatened addax (cheetahs and gazelles) in Niger and Chad through the donation of a grant of

[199] Donald et al., n. 55 above.

almost €2 million.[200] Secondly, the EU has a range of compliance mechanisms that could be used to enforce the operation of allied conservation measures adopted by the Bonn Convention in Europe, especially in relation to activities that engage the various protection measures advanced under the Wild Birds Directive and the Habitats Directive, thereby providing the Bonn Convention itself with a long-awaited (if ultimately borrowed) set of regulatory teeth. Accordingly, as far as the Bonn Convention umbrella is concerned, the EU could prove to be an invaluable ally and, given that much of its primary activities have been confined to European locations to date, a mutually supportive working relationship must therefore be considered essential to its continued operation.

VI. Concluding Remarks

Substantial challenges are posed to regulatory actors seeking to address the conservation status and needs of migratory species of wild animals. Insofar as a coherent and effective system at the international level is concerned, the Bonn Convention must be considered to be subject to serious constraints in respect of its ability to deliver meaningful conservation measures for migratory species, with a lack of enforcement powers, a relative paucity of resources and an increasing dilution of commitments experienced under the Bonn Convention umbrella. Faced with these limitations it is clear that if biodiversity loss is indeed to be halted within the Member States of the EU by 2010, in the context of migratory species European law offers a markedly more robust and effective regulatory system, by virtue of the operation of the Habitats Directive and the Wild Birds Directive, than the Bonn Convention regime. Indeed, the Wild Birds Directive in particular has proved to be of great value as far as the protection of migratory birds is concerned, with other key migratory species such as marine mammals also potentially well served by the Habitats Directive.

Nevertheless, there are limitations inherent in the approach adopted by these Directives, with the traditional emphasis on the establishment of protected areas having proven insufficient to address the continuing decline in biodiversity within the EU. With this in mind, the Commission has sought to elaborate a new generation of conservation policies vis-à-vis threatened fauna and flora through the development of the EC Biodiversity Strategy. The Biodiversity Strategy has a particular focus on the development of sectoral policies and action plans to promote biodiversity conservation, with the onus upon the Commission and the Member States to develop proactive approaches to halting biodiversity loss within the Community. At present, such an approach is largely in its infancy, but it may

200 'CMS and EC Determined to Help Niger and Chad Conserve the Last Population of Addax', CMS Press Release 6 Jan. 2007, published on the Internet at: http://www.cms.int/news/news_archive_2007.htm (accessed 1 Oct. 2007).

be considered that this will become increasingly important in future years as the EU seeks to attain the highly ambitious 2010 targets set under its own guiding policy documents and its international commitments.

One advantage of the Bonn Convention structure is that such an approach is already well advanced under the parent convention, as well as the key subsidiary instruments established under its auspices. In this respect these subsidiaries, the majority of which are Europe-based, offer substantial opportunities to assist the EU in developing biodiversity strategies that are species- and region-specific with the potential to promote tangible benefits to European fauna.

It is advocated that the EU should further explore the possibility of availing itself of these opportunities. Indeed, a concise examination of the interrelationship the two systems, through the prism of the Bonn Convention agreements on migratory species of European cetaceans, birds and bats, reveals some inherent advantages in establishing an effective working relationship. The cetacean agreements may be considered to be something of a cautionary tale, where the EC has shown a limited (if improving) interest in the activities of ASCOBANS and ACCOBAMS, with the result that a conservation policy for cetaceans has been developed that could potentially improve the conservation status of such animals in Community waters, yet it is also undermined by key deficiencies—consistently highlighted within the CMS agreements—that may serve to adversely effect the efficacy and merit of the EC initiative. In contrast, AEWA and the EU, while not acting in direct synergy, have nonetheless formulated a mutually supportive working relationship, which has led to the development of promising policies on both sides. Likewise, EUROBATS has the potential to play a supporting role in relation to the Habitats Directive, particularly in the context of elaborating the range of Natura 2000 sites—especially among many of the more recent entrants to the EU, whose experiences in EUROBATS substantially pre-date their involvement with EU nature conservation law.

Nevertheless, if current practice is a reliable barometer, there appears to be little prospect that the EU will embrace the Bonn Convention regime to a greater extent in the near future by becoming a full party to a number of key subsidiary agreements, notwithstanding the significance of biodiversity conservation to the formulation of current environmental policy and the professed importance placed by the EU upon its synergies with key provisions of international environmental law. Instead it appears that if a closer relationship is to be developed, the Bonn Convention will have to take the lead and seek to forge enhanced links with the EU institutions. In this regard, those occupying key positions within both the Bonn Convention and the institutional structure of the various subsidiary agreements will have to maintain a consistent course of dialogue with the EU. This approach, perhaps also supported by an informal agreement between the two entities such as a memorandum of understanding, could help to foster a closer degree of cooperation between the two systems. Furthermore, the Bonn

Convention agreements could consider adopting distinct Resolutions on EU/EC cooperation at their various MOPs which, if combined with a viable programme of activity, could also facilitate closer ties. Ultimately, however, and perhaps rather more ambitiously given the challenges that face the Convention umbrella, the most effective policy will be to secure a tangible improvement in the conservation record of the Bonn Convention itself, so as to render a closer working relationship a rather more attractive proposition to the EU than the rather patchy record of the Bonn Convention has suggested in the past.

Overall, the great difficulties inherent in addressing the conservation needs of migratory species require the formulation of species- and region-specific measures that engage the support of the maximum number of Range States and international and regional actors possible. Given that the main thrust of the Bonn Convention is likely to remain Eurocentric for the foreseeable future, the importance of an effective and mutually supportive working relationship with the EU is arguably more pressing than ever.

The Disclosure of Origin Requirement: Europe Moving Towards Pro-CBD Implementation

*Fleur Claessens**

I. Introduction

Developing countries hold the majority of the world's genetic resources and traditional knowledge and are concerned about contemporary practices to appropriate biological diversity and associated knowledge. In order to put a halt to the misappropriation of their resources and to minimize the granting of bad or erroneous patents, incorporating naturally occurring genetic resources without due recognition or compensation, several countries and regions have applied disclosure of origin measures in relation to patent applications for inventions derived from genetic resources. Such certification of origin essentially functions as a tracing mechanism.

The disclosure of origin requirement refers to an obligation for patent applicants to provide certain information when an invention involves, or is based on, either genetic resources and/or traditional knowledge. The requirement is intended to help realize fair and equitable benefit-sharing as required by the Convention on Biological Diversity (CBD).[1] It is designed to verify that the resources, and possibly associated traditional knowledge, were acquired in accordance with biodiversity access and benefit-sharing regulations, including prior informed consent (PIC) in the provider countries, and other provisions of the CBD relating to national sovereignty, technology transfer, and the knowledge and practices of indigenous and local communities embodying traditional lifestyles.[2]

Disclosure of origin was originally demanded by civil society organizations and has been accepted mostly by developing countries. Interestingly, more and

* The author is a programme officer on Intellectual Property at the International Centre for Trade and Sustainable Development (ICTSD) and a PhD candidate at the University of Maastricht.

[1] Rio de Janeiro (Brazil), 5 June 1992 (entered into force 29 Dec. 1993), (1992) 31 *International Legal Materials* 818. The overall objective of the CBD is to guarantee sustainable use of genetic resources.

[2] Report on the Disclosure of Origin in Patent Applications, prepared by Queen Mary IP Research Institute, for the European Commission DG-Trade, Oct. 2004

more developed countries are introducing some form of a disclosure regime in their policy and legislative framework—albeit differing in approach as to the justification, scope, concepts, and terminology used, and the legal effect of the requirement and consequences of non-compliance.[3] It has been argued that for a disclosure of origin requirement to be effective, it needs to be embraced at the international level to ensure uniform compliance. Therefore, analogous with the development of domestic policy and legal frameworks, a number of countries have also made proposals for introducing some sort of disclosure of origin requirement internationally.[4]

It has been suggested by a group of developing countries and Norway to amend the Agreement on Trade Related Aspects of Intellectual Property Rights (TRIPS Agreement) to include a disclosure of origin requirement.[5] Others, in particular Switzerland, have identified the World Intellectual Property Organization (WIPO) as the appropriate body to deal with these issues, and submitted proposals to amend the Patent Co-operation Treaty (PCT) and the Substantive Patent Law Treaty (SPLT), both administered by the WIPO International Bureau. This paper focuses on the issue of the mandatory disclosure requirement within the World Trade Organization (WTO) TRIPS Council, and seeks to identify the main issues regarding these discussions, focusing on the position of key actors with a special emphasis on the European proposals submitted by Norway, Switzerland, and the European Commission.[6] After analysing the different proposals of European countries within the TRIPS Council, it concludes that Europe is gradually moving to embrace a disclosure requirement at the international level. Nonetheless, countries differ on how this requirement should be implemented and what legal effects it should have. Many implementation challenges remain, because of different options for a disclosure of origin requirement. For instance, questions arise as to the feasibility of introducing a new system and its associated costs and benefits. These deliberations are not addressed in detail in this paper. Rather, the aim is to give an overview of the disclosure measures

[3] As explained in later parts of the article.

[4] Introducing some sort of Certificate of Origin is not a new phenomenon, as early as 1923 the Geneva Convention relating to the Simplification of Customs Formalities was established referring to a document (Art. 11) that is used in the international trade to prove that goods in a particular export shipment are wholly obtained, produced, manufactured, or processed in a particular country (the country of origin). In fact it is normal practice that countries (custom borders authorities) consider the origin of imported goods when determining what duty will be imposed on the goods or, in some cases, whether the goods may be legally imported at all. In most cases, it is the local chamber of commerce that issues the certificate. The International Chamber of Commerce cautions that it is best to avoid confusion with existing systems like this one. See 'Issues for Consideration by the Group of Technical Experts Concerning a Certificate Relating to Genetic Resources' by the International Chamber of Commerce, published on the Internet at: http://www.iccwbo.org.

[5] Argentina, Canada, Korea, Japan, and New Zealand said that calls for an amendment of the TRIPS Agreement are premature and argue that changing WTO intellectual property rules was not necessary to pursue the objective. See (2007) 11 *Bridges* (Weekly Trade News Digest) at 5. Published on the Internet at: http://www.ictsd.org/weekly/07–02-14/BRIDGESWeekly11–05.pdf.

[6] This paper is based on written positions.

which have been proposed at the international level by European countries, and to compare these with other proposals.

II. The CBD *versus* IPR Agreements

A. CBD *versus* TRIPS

In the 1990s, the relationship between intellectual property rights (IPRs)[7] and sustainable development gained prominence in international environmental law and policy-making, especially in the CBD and the TRIPS Agreement. At the centre of these discussions was the question of developing an in-built mechanism as part of the patent filing system to prevent misappropriation of genetic resources and associated traditional knowledge. While many WTO Members recognized the need to reconcile and ensure mutual supportiveness between both international instruments, no consensus has yet been achieved on how to realize this in practice. What should be the role of the patent system in dealing with the implementation of CBD objectives[8] and misappropriation issues remains highly controversial.[9] At the heart of the debate is the question of how a mechanism

[7] IPRs and commercial marketing of products are relevant in providing incentives to bioprospecting and related sampling, research, and product development processes for pharmaceuticals, neutraceuticals (nutritional supplements), and cosmetics. IPRs are increasingly seen as a useful instrument in facilitating benefit-sharing that should be covered by agreements on access to genetic resources. Moreover IPRs, and in particular the process for granting patents, might form a support mechanism for tracking the flow of genetic resources and providing the opportunity to assure that genetic resources are not misappropriated and have been obtained in accordance with domestic laws on ABS and prior informed consent. As a result, IPRs are intrinsically linked to access to genetic resources, and requirements of equitable benefit-sharing.

[8] The CBD envisages three principal obligations for Contracting Parties under its Art. 1: (1) conservation of biological diversity; (2) sustainable use of biological diversity; and (3) fair and equitable sharing of benefits arising out of the utilization of genetic resources (including appropriate access to genetic resources and transfer of relevant technologies). In order to fulfil these obligations, countries are entitled to sovereign rights over biological resources occurring within their territories—Art. 15 CBD.

[9] Two closely related subsidiary bodies of the CBD negotiating key elements of facilitating the implementation of the CBD are the Ad Hoc Open-ended Working Group on Access and Benefit-Sharing and the Ad Hoc Open-ended Working Group on Art. 8(j), Traditional Knowledge and Related Provisions. The Working group on Access and Benefit-Sharing is exploring possibilities to realize in practice an internationally recognized 'certificate of origin' to comply with CBD requirements on access and benefit-sharing and the promotion of wider use of indigenous knowledge and equitable benefit-sharing. Amongst proposals discussed was a codification system (comparable to a patent registration coding system) linking a code to the certificate enabling easier recognition. The code would be used to track the provider, the source, the use of the genetic resource, transfer to third parties, the limitations etc. The Working Group got the mandate to establish a group of experts 'Group of Technical Experts on an Internationally Recognized Certificate of Origin/Source/Legal Provenance' at COP-8 VIII/4 C. Discussions within the CBD focus on establishing a 'certificate of origin' and not on a 'disclosure of origin requirement'. A certificate of origin requires that ABS and PIC rules are complied with. Two different checkpoints were identified as likely to be most effective to verify if the certificate's of origin conditions are complied with: (i) at the patent office simultaneously when patent registration takes place; (ii) at the point of marketing approval assessment. The latter

should be developed to diminish the misappropriation of genetic resources and associated traditional knowledge. The viewpoints range from the incorporation of a requirement to disclose the origin of genetic resources and traditional knowledge used in an invention, and evidence of PIC and benefit-sharing in patent applications, to developing a *sui generis* system to cover these issues outside of the patent system. Some WTO Members think the rights of indigenous communities are adequately protected within the existing legal IPR rules. If the patent system does need to be altered, on the other hand, the question becomes whether amendments should be made within the framework of the TRIPS Agreement, or rather within the WIPO context.

There is intense debate over whether the CBD conflicts with the TRIPS Agreement and, if so, how any such conflict can best be resolved. The debate is obstructed by the reality that if one side decides that there is no conflict it does not examine the matter any further. The debate therefore has become polarized; the two constituencies are unwilling to, or incapable of, communicating. The reality, however, is that neither of the treaties is likely to disappear in the near future, and that a way needs to be found to stop the misappropriation of unauthorized access to genetic resources and traditional knowledge.

TRIPS was negotiated within the Uruguay Round of trade negotiations over eight years and meetings took place in various countries making it cumbersome for developing countries to be properly informed negotiation partners. Developing countries hindered by logistical, financial, and capacity constraints were not fully aware of the consequences. Moreover, TRIPS was part of a much larger multilateral framework of trade negotiations and developing countries committed to adhere to harmonized IPR rules in exchange for trade-offs in other areas such as market access for tropical products and cotton.

At the heart of conflicts between the two regimes lies the nature of the formation of the agreements. During the treaties negotiations there was a tendency to prioritize short-term benefits of trade above long-term environmental benefits, including the conservation of biodiversity. TRIPS, being part of the GATT-WTO system, was regarded mainly as a trade issue of obvious interest for intellectual property offices and multinational companies.[10] The CBD was perceived as an environmental issue. This categorization determined the participation of officials involved, i.e. the TRIPS Agreement negotiations were attended predominantly

option would be suitable to indicate the commercial benefits the genetic resource might generate, and to cover genetic resources which are not patented. Participants in the working group agreed that transaction costs and bureaucracy should be minimal. For this reason, it was felt that it was important to find one single competent authority. Participants also addressed the practicality and feasibility of the different options, in particular for developing countries lacking technology and in need of financial support and capacity building. See (2007) 7 *BioRes* 2, 2 Feb. 2007, published on the Internet at: http://www.iprsonline.org or http://www.ictsd.org/biores.

[10] R. Lettington, 'The Biodiversity Convention and TRIPS' (1999) Discussion paper seminar International Centre for Trade and Sustainable Development (ICTSD) Regional Trade and Environmental Seminar for Governments and Civil Society, Harare, Zimbabwe, 10–12 Feb. 1999, 3.

by trade ministry officials and IPR experts; the CBD by environment ministry officials and environmental activists. At the time of the negotiations most parties therefore failed to recognize the connections between the two fora. Civil society organizations only became active at the international level after the adoption of the WTO Agreement. Hence, there is a lot of catching up to do. Both intergovernmental organizations (IGOs) and non-governmental organizations (NGOs) have an important role to play in adequately addressing the relationship between IPR and environmental agreements, and in ensuring that the WTO, the CBD, and relevant UN agencies improve communication on this matter, thus moving the debate forward.

According to Article 16.5 of the CBD, the CBD and IPR agreements need to be mutually supportive. Nonetheless, often IPRs are granted without respecting CBD obligations pertaining to legal access, and currently TRIPS does not contain safeguards against misappropriation of genetic resources. In part, this is because the treaties have different objectives and associated structures. Thus, TRIPS first and foremost protects inventions, creations, and signs (trademarks). It grants exclusive and private rights to the right holders including a right to remuneration. It also endeavours to promote innovation and technology transfer.[11] The CBD protects genetic resources and traditional knowledge, safeguarding national sovereign rights. It provides for public good and collective rights. It sets out detailed rules on access and benefits-sharing and the conservation and sustainable use of genetic resources.

IPRs in the context of access to genetic resources have been high on the international agenda ever since the adoption of TRIPS and the CBD. A multitude of IGOs and NGOs[12] have addressed the interconnection between IPRs and access to genetic resources, associated traditional knowledge, benefit-sharing, and explored innovative disclosure options in this context.[13]

The WTO has addressed these issues within the TRIPS Council in the context of the review of Article 27.3(b) of TRIPS and the Doha Round negotiations. The relationship between TRIPS and the CBD is an outstanding implementation issue following the WTO Doha Declaration,[14] and a prominent agenda item of TRIPS Council meetings.[15] Although the review of Article 27(3) TRIPS

[11] Arts. 7, 8 and 66.2 TRIPS.

[12] For instance, the International Union for the Conservation of Nature and Natural Resources (IUCN) has carried out a number of projects on IPRs and ABS. Further information is published on the Internet at: http://www.iucn.org.

[13] For an overview of the compatibility of TRIPS and the CBD see Lettington, n. 10 above.

[14] The fourth WTO Ministerial Conference in Doha, Qatar addressed the problems of developing countries implementing TRIPS. Deliberations of the highest level body of the WTO resulted in the Doha Declaration, which provides a mandate for further deliberations on a number of issues including intellectual property and the relationship with the CBD. See WTO Doha Declaration, 14 Nov. 2001, WT/MIN(01)/DEC/1.

[15] Following para. 19 of the WTO Doha Declaration, which reads: 'We instruct the Council for TRIPS, in pursuing its work programme including under the review of Art. 27.3(b), the review of the implementation of the TRIPS Agreement under Art. 71.1 and the work foreseen pursuant to para.

comprised several issues, the current discussion focuses on the introduction of a mandatory disclosure requirement of the source and origin of biological resources and traditional knowledge.

B. The CBD *versus* WIPO

The Intergovernmental Committee on Intellectual Property and Genetic Resources, Traditional Knowledge and Folklore (IGC) has also discussed the relationship between IPRs and biodiversity, traditional knowledge, and access to genetic resources: The IGC was set up in 2000 by the WIPO General Assembly to work towards a shared international understanding of how best to protect traditional knowledge and traditional cultural expressions against misappropriation and misuse. The Committee was based on two premises: that the existing IPR framework offers poor protection for traditional knowledge, and that this has contributed to misappropriation of traditional knowledge. A key aspiration of the IGC was to find ways for holders and custodians of traditional knowledge and traditional cultural expressions to exercise greater authority over how these central elements of their cultural identity are used, and to strengthen the legal aspects of respect, sovereignty, and recognition. Views on how to facilitate the protection of traditional knowledge differ greatly: from incorporating the protection of traditional knowledge within the existing framework of IPRs, to establishing new binding *sui generis* legislation to protect against the misappropriation of genetic material, including associated traditional knowledge.[16]

Despite six years of discussions, and although the IGC is one of the very few platforms where issues concerning indigenous and local communities are discussed, WIPO remains divided as to whether to create a new binding international treaty to protect genetic resources, traditional knowledge, and folklore against misappropriation. The 2007 WIPO General Assembly has agreed to expand the mandate of the IGC for two years and has invited the working group 'to accelerate its work and to present a progress report to the [2008] General Assembly'. The renewed mandate also underlines that 'no outcome of its work is excluded, including the possible development of an international instrument or instruments'.[17]

12 of this declaration, to examine, inter alia, the relationship between the TRIPS Agreement and the Convention on Biological Diversity, the protection of traditional knowledge and folklore, and other relevant new developments raised by members pursuant to Art. 71.1. In undertaking this work, the TRIPS Council shall be guided by the objectives and principles set out in Art. 7 and 8 of the TRIPS Agreement and shall take fully into account the development dimension.'

[16] 'The Gap between Indigenous Peoples' Demands and WIPO's Framework on Traditional Knowledge' (Autumn 2007), Center for International Environmental Law (CIEL) paper. Published on the Internet at: http://www.ciel.org/Publications/WIPO_Gap_Sept07.pdf.

[17] The WIPO General assembly gathered from 24 Sept. to 3 Oct. 2007 at the Geneva headquarters.

Complicating the debate on traditional knowledge is the fact that it involves no less than 11 UN bodies. The UN Permanent Forum on Indigenous Issues has therefore called for improved cooperation and information sharing, particularly between the UN Educational, Scientific, and Cultural Organization (UNESCO), the CBD, and the Food and Agriculture Organization (FAO).[18]

WIPO is also discussing a disclosure requirement in the context of reforming the Patent Cooperation Treaty (PCT),[19] where it has been proposed that such a disclosure in international patent applications is allowed. The PCT facilitates the international filing of patents (application process). Introducing the disclosure of origin (source) into this instrument would imply adding an administrative requirement to filing patents, as opposed to a substantive requirement, as the grant of the patent is left to the national or regional patent offices. Non-compliance with the disclosure requirement will be regarded as not fulfilling the administrative requirements and the applicant will be asked to file the required correction. A disclosure requirement is also being discussed in the context of further international harmonization of the patent system under the draft SPLT.[20] It is likely that, with the adoption of the WIPO Development Agenda, the debate on a disclosure requirement will increase in momentum. For instance, the WIPO Development Agenda[21] makes note of promoting 'work on any initiative intended to facilitate the implementation of technology-related provisions of multilateral environmental agreements (MEAs), so as to ensure that countries where biological, traditional or other environmental resources originate from, participate in the process of research and development'.[22] The recently adopted WIPO

[18] 'WIPO Committee Extends, Adjusts Mandate on Traditional Knowledge, Folklore' (2007), Intellectual Property Watch. Published on the Internet at: http://www.ip-watch.org.

[19] The PCT makes it possible to seek patent protection for an invention simultaneously in each of a large number of countries by filing a single 'international' patent application instead of filing several separate national or regional patent applications. The granting of patents remains under the control of the national or regional patent Offices in what is called the 'national phase'. It carries out an international search as to prior art and can do the preliminary examination as to the patentability of the invention. The PCT is administered by WIPO, enacted in 1970, amended in 1979, and subsequently modified in 1984 and 2001.

[20] The proposed SPLT aims at going far beyond formalities as set out in the Patent Law Treaty (2001) to harmonize substantive requirements such as novelty, inventive step and non-obviousness, industrial applicability and utility, as well as sufficient disclosure or claim drafting and interpretation.

[21] The Development Agenda negotiations started in Sept. 2004, and have been pushed by the 'friends of development' (FoD), a group of 15 developing countries (led by Brazil and Argentina) calling for considerations about the impact of intellectual property on developing economies to be incorporated into every aspect of WIPO's activities. The FoD questioned whether or not the organization is fulfilling its 'development mandate' as a specialized agency of the UN. Firstly, the FoD called for a review of the mandate and governance of WIPO; secondly, it seeks the promotion of pro-development norm-setting in WIPO; thirdly, it proposes principles and guidelines for the provision and evaluation of WIPO's technical assistance; and finally, it suggests guidelines for future work on the transfer and dissemination of technology and related competition policies. The Development Agenda was adopted during the 2007 WIPO General Assembly consisting of a series of recommendations to enhance the development dimension of the organization's activities.

[22] WIPO Provisional Committee for the Development Agenda (PCDA), Annex B proposal 44.

Development Agenda[23] also contains references to the protection of traditional knowledge and genetic resources: it urges 'the IGC to accelerate the process on the protection of genetic resources, traditional knowledge and folklore without prejudice to any outcome, including the possible development of an international instrument or instruments'.[24]

C. The CBD

The contracting parties to the CBD are looking for ways to respond to the call from the World Summit on Sustainable Development to negotiate an international regime to promote and safeguard fair and equitable sharing of benefits arising from the utilization of genetic resources. Article 16 of the CBD calls for IPRs to support the objectives of the CBD, but there is controversy on how to bring this about. The starting point of the discussion lies in the two key provisions of the CBD: Articles 15 and 8(j). Article 15 creates a regime for access to genetic resources and benefit-sharing, based on the principles of national sovereignty over genetic resources, prior informed consent over access to genetic resources, and the need for mutually agreed terms in any access agreements. In addition, Article 8(j) calls for indigenous and local knowledge to be respected, preserved, and maintained.

Deliberations within the CBD have proposed the development of a certificate of origin. This would serve as a type of passport or permit which would accompany the genetic resource along the whole chain of the access and benefit-sharing (ABS) process and could be verified at various points, particularly once the genetic resource has left the provider country. It would therefore accompany the genetic resource from the collection phase until the marketing of a resultant product. The main objective of an internationally recognized system of certificate of origin would be to ensure the traceability of genetic resources from the moment they have been accessed, thereby increasing transparency. Developing countries hope the certificate would aid in combating bio-piracy.[25]

The discussions within the CBD resulted in the adoption of the Bonn guidelines which brought disclosure requirements into the patent application process.[26]

[23] The Development Agenda was adopted during the 2007 WIPO General Assembly consisting of a series of recommendations to enhance the development dimension of the organization's activities. The recommendations include a set of 45 agreed proposals covering six clusters of activities including Technical Assistance and Capacity Building; Norm-setting, Flexibilities, Public Policy, and Public Domain; Technology Transfer, Information and Communication Technology (ICT), and Access to Knowledge; Assessments, Evaluation, and Impact Studies; Institutional Matters including Mandate and Governance; and other issues.

[24] WIPO Provisional Committee for the Development Agenda (PCDA), Annex B proposal.

[25] Bio-piracy refers to the missappropriation, generally by means of patents, of indigenous/traditional (biomedical) knowledge by foreign entities (including corporations, universities, and governments) without compensatory payment.

[26] The Bonn Guidelines are an attempt to implement the CBD provisions on access to genetic resources and benefit-sharing. The Bonn Guidelines on Access to Genetic Resources and Fair

The Bonn Guidelines advocate the adoption of 'a legally recognized certification of origin system as evidence of prior informed consent and mutually agreed terms'. This soft law instrument endeavours to harmonize the various proposals and to make the disclosure requirement operate effectively. For instance, it proposes to develop a standardized international certificate of origin which could be used and recognized by the patent offices around the world. In this context, the recent adoption of the UN Declaration on the Rights of Indigenous Peoples by the UN General Assembly last September might contribute to strengthening developing countries' appeal to pursue their sovereign rights over access to their genetic resources.[27] The UN Declaration boosts the demands of the indigenous groups in the ABS negotiations.

III. The Disclosure of Origin Requirement

A. Rationale Behind a Disclosure of Origin Requirement

If one supports the effective implementation of rules established under the CBD, it follows that it is necessary to facilitate the effective implementation of fair and equitable benefit-sharing from the exploitation of genetic resources—one of the key objectives of the CBD. It has been proposed that this could be done by reviewing patent applications to ensure that any genetic resources and traditional knowledge used in an invention have been obtained in compliance with biodiversity access and ABS regulations, including rules on prior informed consent in the provider countries' domestic legislation. A disclosure obligation would smooth the process of verifying whether genetic resources have been collected in accordance with national rules requiring consent, and whether the conditions for such consent have been met. The disclosure obligation would also make patent applicants aware of the importance of complying with the CBD, as adopted by 190 parties. The same would also apply where states have rules requiring consent for the exploitation of traditional knowledge independently of the CBD.

One can argue that a disclosure of origin requirement would also facilitate determining whether the patentability requirements in the TRIPS Agreement have been met and, for example, help prevent patenting where the novelty or inventive step requirements have not been met. For example, a disclosure of origin obligation would contribute in simplifying database searches on traditional

and Equitable Sharing of the Benefits Arising out of their Utilization were adopted at the 6th CBD Conference of the Parties (COP). See COP 6 Decision, The Hague, 7–19 April 2002. Published on the Internet at http://www.cbd.int/decisions/?m=cop-06&d=24.

[27] The Declaration sets out the individual and collective rights of indigenous peoples, recognizes their rights to land and other resources, calls for the maintenance and strengthening of their cultural identities, and emphasizes their right to pursue development in keeping with their own needs and aspirations. It also prohibits discrimination against indigenous peoples and promotes their full and effective participation in all matters that concern them.

knowledge by providing an additional basis for such an attack on validity of patent.[28] A disclosure obligation would, therefore, also be useful in ensuring that patents are not granted contrary to the fundamental principles of patent law.

B. What Type of Disclosure Requirement?

The disclosure requirement raises a number of questions that have not been answered. For instance, there is no agreement as to what the ideal disclosure of origin requirement should look like, the necessity of having such a regime, in what form, with what objective, legal consequences, and so forth. Therefore, proposals submitted to the international organizations differ in scope and use of terminology.

For instance, the information required may be:

(a) evidence of prior informed consent for access and utilization of genetic resources;

(b) evidence of fair and equitable benefit-sharing agreements;

(c) references to geographical origin, provenance, or source of the genetic resources and/or traditional knowledge.[29]

As to the legal effect and practical consequences, the disclosure could be mandatory or voluntary; and the materialization of the requirement could lead to the adding of a fourth requirement to the patent system[30] (as in the Belgian domestic legislation) or the requirement could be part of the grant procedure (as in the Swiss proposal). Proposals included various options as for the consequences of non-compliance, e.g. revocation of the patent or punishment outside the patent system. As mentioned above, the use of specific terms have different legal and practical consequences. For instance, the terminology used to define the role of the genetic resource in an invention relates to the extent to which a genetic resource, or traditional knowledge, is involved in an invention. And the need for a disclosure of origin or PIC could also depend on the extent to which a genetic

[28] See G. Utkarsh, 'Documentation of traditional knowledge: People's Biodiversity registers' in C. Bellman, G. Dutfield, and R. Melendez-Ortiz (eds.) *Trading in Knowledge*. (London: Earthscan, 2003).

[29] For instance, current legislation and proposals refer to: (a) Country of origin; providing country; geographical origin; source; (b) Genetic resources, genetic material, biological material of plant or animal origin; components of biodiversity; (c) Traditional knowledge of indigenous and/or local communities; collective knowledge; and (d) Inventions that are: 'obtained from...'; 'obtained or developed on the basis of...'; 'use samples or components of...'; 'concern or use...'; 'whose subject matter is...'; or are 'directly based on...'; e.g. genetic resources. See A. L. Hoare, 'Disclosure Requirements in Patent Applications: the State of the Art of National and Regional Measures', Background Paper for the Chatham House Workshop: *Disclosure Requirements in Patent Applications—Options and Perspectives of Users and Providers of Genetic Resources*, London, 9–10 Feb. 2006. Published on the Internet at: http://www.chathamhouse.org.uk.

[30] The three patent criteria set out in the TRIPS Agreement are: novelty, inventive step, and industrial applicability.

resource, or traditional knowledge, is involved in an invention. The use and definition of terms is the subject of ongoing debate.

Dispute remains as to whether or not incorporating a disclosure requirement is compatible with the TRIPS Agreement, as it may add a new condition for patentability (the position of the US). For advocates of a disclosure of origin obligation, the TRIPS Agreement is commonly understood to permit Members to introduce such a requirement in their national legislation. That reasoning comes from the fact that TRIPS provide minimum standards allowing members flexible implementation, and thus incorporating additional requirements into their domestic legislation. Nonetheless, in order to oblige Members to introduce a mandatory disclosure obligation, the TRIPS Agreement would need to be amended.

Enforcement is another issue of contention: there are countries that suggest using civil penalties or criminal sanctions outside the patent system to punish non-compliance (e.g. Norway), whilst others propose revoking the patent if it becomes apparent that the applicant has given incorrect or incomplete information (e.g. Brazil and the group of developing countries proposing Article 29*bis*).

One can broadly identify three forms of disclosure with differing legal consequences for non-compliance:

1. voluntary measure—disclosure would be encouraged and recommended but failure to do so would not affect the patent;
2. mandatory regime—failure to comply would have consequences within the patent system or lead to civil or administrative sanctions outside the patent system;
3. going beyond a disclosure requirement in patent applications in requiring adherence to domestic or regional legislation on access and benefit-sharing and prior informed consent.[31]

The legal basis of disclosure requirements may lie within the patent system, adding another substantive requirement or introducing disclosure into the grant of patent phase. The legal basis may also be found outside patent law mechanisms, for instance in environment/conservation laws relating to access and benefit-sharing.

C. Country Proposals to the WTO

i. Norway

Norway has been one of the first advocates of a disclosure requirement at both the domestic and the international level.[32] The Norwegian Patent Act[33] stipulates:

[31] See n. 2 above.

[32] An amended Norwegian Patent Act was adopted by Parliament in Dec. 2003. It came into force for patent applications submitted from 1 Feb. 2004.

[33] Para. 8(b) of the Norwegian Patent Act. This is an unofficial translation taken from the Queen Mary IP Research Institute Study, published on the Internet at: http://trade.ec.europa.eu/doclib/docs/2005/june/tradoc_123533.pdf.

> If an invention concerns or uses biological material, the inventor shall disclose in the patent application the country providing such material. If national legislation in the providing country requires prior informed consent before providing such material, the application shall include information on whether such consent has been sought.
>
> In cases where the providing country is different from the country of origin of the biological material, the country of origin shall also be disclosed. Country of origin is defined as the country from where the material is accessed in *in situ* conditions. In cases where national legislation in the country of origin requires prior informed consent before providing such material, the application shall include information on whether such consent has been sought. If the applicant does not know the country of origin or whether prior informed consent is required, the applicant shall state this fact in the application.
>
> These obligations are applicable even if the inventor has changed the structure of the material. They do not concern human material. Violations of the requirement to disclose information is punishable under paragraph 166 of the Penal Code. The requirement to disclose information does not affect that handling of a patent application or the validity of a patent.

The Norwegian Patents Act sets out that these measures are not applicable to international applications received through the PCT, as this would be contrary to the obligations under the PCT.[34] Notably, penalties for non-compliance could be the imposition of a fine or up to two years in prison.[35]

The rationale

Norway argues that a disclosure requirement is necessary to enhance the interaction between the CBD and the TRIPS Agreement, because an obligation under the TRIPS Agreement to disclose the origin of genetic resources when applying for patent protection would ensure transparency with regards to the origin of biological materials that are to be patented.[36] In Norway's view, this would facilitate the effectiveness of the CBD, as a disclosure obligation would make it easier to verify whether genetic resources have been collected in accordance with national rules requiring PIC, and whether the conditions for such consent have been met. In addition, it would allow parties to enforce their rights to their own genetic resources when they form part of a patent application. In particular it would support the CBD in securing an equitable sharing of the benefits of exploiting genetic resources. Norway argues that a disclosure obligation would contribute towards giving effect to Article 16(5) of the CBD, which sets out that the Contracting Parties should cooperate to ensure that intellectual property rights are supportive of and do not run counter to the objectives of the CBD. In addition to facilitating the implementation of the CBD, Norway believes that a disclosure requirement

[34] Para. 33 of the amended Norwegian Patent Act.

[35] Para. 166 of the Norwegian General Civil Penal Code.

[36] See Norway's WTO communication dated 14 June 2006 'The Relationship between the TRIPS Agreement, the Convention on Biological Diversity and the Protection of Traditional Knowledge—Amending the TRIPS Agreement to Introduce an Obligation to Disclose the Origin of Genetic Resources and Traditional Knowledge in Patent Applications', IP/C/W473.

serves the IPR system, as in its view 'it would ensure that novelty criteria are met, which accords with the basic intentions and principles of the patent system and increases its credibility'.[37] In Norway's view a general obligation to disclose any traditional knowledge upon which an invention is based would help to prevent patents being erroneously granted.

Disclosure requirements hence would allow original knowledge holders to become aware of patents for inventions based on their knowledge and resources and to take appropriate action. Hence, Norway argues that a disclosure requirement should apply to all patent applications; the PCT, and Patent Law Treaty (PLT) should be amended, as well as the TRIPS Agreement.[38]

Scope and legal effect at international level

Norway favours the incorporation of a disclosure requirement in the TRIPS Agreement. It suggests amending the TRIPS Agreement to incorporate a mandatory obligation to disclose the origin of genetic resources and traditional knowledge in patent applications. In Norway's view, the disclosure obligation should be introduced in a new Article 29*bis* and should provide that patent applications should not be processed unless the required information has been submitted. However, with regards to enforcement it proposes that non-compliance with the disclosure obligation, discovered post-grant, should not affect the validity of the patent.

Norway favours a disclosure obligation based on the following elements:

1. a binding international obligation should be introduced to include information on the supplier country and the country of origin, if known and different, of genetic resources and traditional knowledge in patent applications. It should obey national rules (in the supplier country or country of origin) for access to genetic resources or traditional knowledge and the disclosure obligation must also encompass a duty to make reference to whether such consent has been given. It should specify if the country of origin is unknown;
2. the disclosure obligation should apply to all patent applications whether they are international, regional, and/or national;
3. it should set out that the provisions of the disclosure obligation are compatible with the International Treaty on Plant Genetic Resources for Food and Agriculture (International Treaty);
4. if the patent applicant is unable to provide information or refuses to do so, the application should not be allowed to proceed;

[37] Ibid.

[38] See document IP/C/W/491 in which Norway replies to questions posed by Switzerland in TRIPS Council IP/C/M/52.

5. a breach of the disclosure obligation should be treated as a formal error, i.e. the application should not be processed until the required information has been submitted. Where appropriate, the application could eventually be rejected;
6. if it is discovered that incorrect or incomplete information has been given after the grant of patent, this should not affect the validity of the granted patent, but there should be a penalty in an effective and proportionate way outside the patent system, e.g. by criminal or administrative sanctions. Upholding post-grant patent protection, despite non-compliance with the disclosure obligation, is important to avoid creating unnecessary uncertainty in the patent system. If the applicant has acted in good faith, the fact that incorrect or incomplete information has been given may have no consequence at all;
7. a notification system should be introduced, under which patent offices send all declarations of origin they receive to the CBD Clearing House Mechanism.[39]

Norway argues that revoking a patent as a consequence of non-compliance with the disclosure obligation would not be in the interest of those who consider themselves entitled to a share of the benefits of the invention. This means that, once patent protection is revoked, there are no exclusive rights from which benefits could be derived. However, Norway provides an exception to this rule—when a patent does not differ from traditional knowledge to the degree required to constitute a patentable invention, in this particular case the patent can be revoked. In such a case the substantive patentability criteria have not been met, but it is the lack of novelty or an inventive step that constitutes the reason for invalidity, and not the breach of the disclosure obligation.

In Norway's view the TRIPS Agreement is commonly understood to permit members to introduce disclosure of origin obligations in their national legislation. Nonetheless, in order to oblige members to introduce a mandatory disclosure obligation, the TRIPS Agreement would need to be amended. The obligation to disclose origin is linked to the patent application, but does not constitute a substantive patent criterion. In Norway's view, it would therefore be most appropriate to introduce a new provision in the TRIPS Agreement immediately following Article 29, which contains provisions on the disclosure of information related to the invention.

In summary: Norway supports the amendment of the TRIPS Agreement to introduce a disclosure of origin requirement.

[39] An international clearing house mechanism refers to an international database capable of functioning as a referral point to enable genetic resource holders to track their resources. It would function as a measure of transparency. Thus, the moment the certificate is issued its record will go into an international database.

ii Switzerland

Switzerland has taken a leading position in the field of bridging the relationship between IPR agreements and the CBD, and has been active in the relevant international deliberations on these issues. It has submitted proposals on the disclosure of the source of genetic resources and traditional knowledge in patent applications to the WIPO Working Group of the PCT.[40] It has also pursued the same line in the WIPO Intergovernmental Committee on Intellectual Property and Genetic Resources, Traditional Knowledge and Folklore, in the TRIPS Council and to the Ad Hoc Open-Ended Working Group on Access and Benefit-sharing of the CBD.[41]

Rationale

It is the view of Switzerland that including the disclosure of source of genetic resources enhances transparency, traceability, technical prior art, and mutual trust.[42] In addition, it would also support the determination of prior art with regard to traditional knowledge, as it would simplify searching the traditional knowledge databases that are increasingly being established at the local and national levels.

It has presented various communications to the TRIPS Council and within the WIPO Working Group on PCT Reform on its proposals for the declaration of the source. Switzerland proposes to amend the regulations under the PCT explicitly to enable the national patent legislation to require the declaration of the source of genetic resources and traditional knowledge in patent applications if the invention is directly based on such resources or knowledge.[43] Based on the reference to the PCT contained in Article 6.1 of the WIPO administered PLT, the proposed amendment to the PCT would also apply to the PLT. If made effective, these proposals would enable the national patent legislation to require patent applicants to declare the source of genetic resources and traditional knowledge in patent applications, if an invention is *directly* based on these resources or this knowledge. The proposals would also grant applicants the possibility of satisfying this requirement at the time of filing an international patent application, or later during the international phase. This declaration of source would be included in the publication of the international patent application in order to render it

[40] Communication from Switzerland to the WIPO PCT: PCT/R/WG/4/13.

[41] Communication from Switzerland to the WTO TRIPS Council, IP/C/W/400, IP/C/W/423, IP/C/W/433, IP/C/W466, 30 May 2006, WIPO GRTKF/IC/11/10.

[42] F. Addor, 'Switzerland's Proposals Regarding the Declaration of the Source of Genetic Resources and Traditional Knowledge in Patent Applications and Switzerland's View on the Declaration of Evidence of Prior Informed Consent and Benefit-sharing in Patent Applications' (2005), *ICTSD, CIEL, IDDRI, IUCN, QUNO Dialogue on Disclosure Requirements: Incorporating the CBD Principles in the TRIPS Agreement, On the Road to Hong Kong, WTO Public Symposium* (Geneva, Switzerland, 2005). See IP/C/W/400, IP/C/W/423, IP/C/W/433, IP/C/W466, 30 May 2006, WIPO GRTKF/IC/11/10.

[43] Proposed Rule 51*bis*.1(g) PCT.

accessible to the public at the earliest possible stage.[44] In contrast, according to the Swiss, any amendment of the TRIPS Agreement would not apply to international patent applications, and would thus not bring the same results as an amendment to the PCT. Moreover, Switzerland believes that the relevant TRIPS Agreement provisions (e.g. Articles 27.1, 29.1, and 62.1) provide for adequate flexibility regarding source disclosure requirements, so there is no need to amend the TRIPS Agreement. In addition it believes that it will take considerably more time to alter the TRIPS Agreement then amending the PCT regulations.[45]

Switzerland has opted to 'explicitly enable' the national legislator to introduce a disclosure requirement but which does not make this mandatory. In Switzerland's view a mandatory regime would not be in the interest of the developing countries, and it would be difficult to achieve consensus at international level. In addition, it would allow national governments time to get used to the disclosure concept without prejudicing further international efforts.[46]

According to Switzerland, the proposed disclosure of the source achieves four policy objectives, namely transparency, traceability, technical prior art, and mutual trust:

1. Transparency: with a requirement in national and international patent applications to disclose the source, the patent system would increase transparency in access and benefit-sharing with regard to genetic resources and traditional knowledge.
2. Traceability: disclosing the source in patent applications would allow the providers of genetic resources and traditional knowledge to keep track of the use of their resources or knowledge in research and development resulting in patentable inventions.
3. Technical prior art: disclosing the source of genetic resources and traditional knowledge in patent applications would assist patent examiners and judges in the establishment of prior art with regard to inventions that somehow relate to these resources or this knowledge. In particular, it may facilitate the establishment of prior public use as well as the finding of lack of novelty or inventive step, as was the case with regard to the so-called 'neem tree oil' patent (European Patent 0 436 257). This applies in particular to prior art regarding traditional knowledge, as disclosing the source would simplify searching the databases on traditional knowledge that are increasingly being established at the local, regional and national level.
4. Mutual trust: the disclosure of the source would increase mutual trust among the various stakeholders involved in access and benefit-sharing, including among developing and developed countries, indigenous and local communities, private companies and research institutions. All of these stakeholders may be providers and/or users of genetic resources and traditional knowledge. Accordingly,

44 F. Addor and M. Girsberger, 'How to address the Disclosure Requirement at the International Level' (2005) 9 *Bridges* (Weekly Trade News Digest) 9. Published on the Internet at: http://www.iprsonline.org/ictsd/docs/BridgesMonthly9–9Disclosure.pdf.

45 Ibid.

46 Ibid.

disclosing the source would build mutual trust in the North-South-relationship. Moreover, it would strengthen the mutual supportiveness between the access and benefit-sharing system and the patent system.[47]

Scope and legal effect at international level

Article 49a of the Draft Swiss Federal Patent Law states that:

> For inventions based on genetic resources or traditional knowledge the patent application must contain information concerning the source: a) of the genetic resource to which the inventor or the applicant had access, when the invention is based directly on that resource; b) of the traditional knowledge of indigenous or local communities related to the genetic resources to which the inventor or applicant had access, when the invention is based directly on that knowledge.
>
> If the source is not known to either the inventor or the applicant, the applicant must confirm this in writing.

Applicants have the possibility of satisfying this requirement at the time of filing an international patent application or later during the international phase. In case an international patent application does not contain the required declaration, national law may see that in the national phase the application is not processed any further until the patent applicant has furnished the required declaration.

In relation to the terminology used, Switzerland has chosen to refer to disclosure of 'source' instead of 'origin'. The reason behind this terminology is that in Switzerland's view 'origin' is too limited as most of the genetic resources are derived from *ex situ* sources, such as botanical gardens, gene banks, or databases. In the view of Switzerland 'source' goes beyond 'origin' as it comprises not only country of origin but in addition communities or regions within the country. The reference to 'source' as opposed to 'origin' enhances the interests of particular indigenous communities or regions within a particular country or region. The Swiss proposals deliberately use the terms 'genetic resources' and 'traditional knowledge related to genetic resources' to ensure consistency with the CBD, the Bonn Guidelines, and the International Treaty. It explains that source should be understood in its broadest sense referring to genetic resources and associated traditional knowledge. The Swiss amendment does not deal with the issues of access and benefit-sharing or prior informed consent which in its view are important questions currently under discussion within the CBD. Switzerland believes the disclosure of source requirement would function as a gate-keeper in order for PIC/ABS to work. Switzerland believes that benefit-sharing is an element that should be addressed later in the process—after the grant of patent. Moreover as most countries do not have domestic ABS systems in place yet, it would be unfeasible and of no added value at this point to ask for adherence to ABS rules

[47] See Addor, n. 42 above.

in the country of origin/source as part of patent applications.[48] According to Switzerland patent authorities are not in a position to determine whether the sharing of benefits is 'fair and equitable'. Moreover, at the time of filing patent applications, no monetary benefits have yet arisen, and the commercial success of the invention is generally unknown—hence making it very difficult for patent applicants to provide the required evidence of 'fair and equitable' benefit-sharing when filing a patent application.[49] However, Switzerland emphasizes that its proposal on disclosure of source would allow parties to contract on access and benefit-sharing and to verify whether the other contracting party is complying with its obligations.

Under Swiss proposals, it would be mandatory for patent applicants to disclose the source at the national level (e.g. in Switzerland itself) and non-compliance would lead to sanctions currently allowed under the PCT and the PLT, as well as sanctions outside of the patent system. Notably, through reference, the proposals would also apply to the PLT and thus to national and regional patent applications.

In comparison, Directive 98/44/EC on the Legal Protection of Biotechnological Inventions (Biotech Directive)[50] refers to disclosure of origin which does not necessarily refer to the pre-existing rights that holders of traditional knowledge might have over the genetic resources.[51] The Swiss draft amendment is more comprehensive than the Biotech Directive. Firstly, it requires disclosure not only of resources related to plant and animals but also to micro-organisms, but also disclosure of traditional knowledge of indigenous and local communities associated with the inventions. Secondly, it states that lack of declaration of source can result in the non-granting of the patent. Thirdly, an intentionally erroneous declaration, known to the inventor or patent applicant, is subject to criminal sanctions.

In its PCT submissions, Switzerland has proposed to establish some sort of notification system to facilitate transparency of the patent system and to trace genetic resources (this is not part of the draft revised Swiss patent law). This would imply that the IP institute (authority receiving the patent applications) would inform/notify the competent authority in the country of source about the

[48] Examples of countries that have detailed domestic or regional rules on ABS in place are the Andean Community and India. See, for instance, R. Sagar, 'Intellectual Property, Benefit-Sharing and Traditional Knowledge—How Effective is the Indian Biological Diversity Act, 2002?' (2005) 8 *The Journal of World Intellectual Property* 3, 383–400. Sagar points out that the Indian Act makes substantial differentiation between people and organizations of Indian origin and foreign nationals and organizations as the duties and procedures for foreigners are more onerous as compared to those applied to Indians. This differentiation is most notable in obtaining in the following aspects: access to biological resources, research activities, and benefit-sharing.

[49] See Addor and Girsberger, n. 44 above.

[50] [1998] OJ L213/13.

[51] (2007) 7 *Bridges* (Weekly Trade News Digest) at 7. Published on the Internet at: http://www.ictsd.org/biores/07–04-13/story3.htm.

received patent application and its specificities. In order for this process to work efficiently, countries of source would need to identify focal points in their territories to deal with these matters.

Switzerland has repeatedly expressed that it is not a '*demandeur*'[52] of a disclosure of origin requirement in patent applications, but that it has submitted supportive proposals because it is interested both in a balanced patent protection (for biotechnological inventions) in the interest of all involved and in finding solutions that take account of the various other interests at stake.[53] The Draft Swiss Federal Patent Act has received its approval from Parliament, and it is now up to the Swiss Federal Council (the executive body) to determine when the revised law will come into force. This is expected to be in the Summer of 2008. Once the new patent act comes into force, the disclosure of source requirement will become part of the formal administrative obligations that need to be complied with before a patent application can be processed. Article 81a of the Draft Swiss Federal Patent Act provides that an applicant can state it does not know where the genetic material originates from. If, however, later it becomes clear that the applicant has lied about this lack of knowledge, the patent will not be invalidated. But fines are foreseen under criminal law (*ex officio* offence) that can be quiet severe, 100,000 Swiss Francs for intentionally withholding essential information. A further sanction is the publication of the court ruling, accusing the patent applicant of an intentionally false declaration as to the source of biological material.

iii. The European Proposal

Some form of 'weak' disclosure was adopted by the European Union (EU) through the Biotech Directive.[54] Recital 27 states:

> Whereas if an invention is based on biological material of plant or animal origin or if it uses such material, the patent application should, where appropriate, include information on the geographical origin of such material, if known; whereas this is without prejudice to the processing of patent applications or the validity of rights arising from granted patents.

Hence, under the Biotech Directive, disclosure of geographical origin is encouraged, but not mandatory, and failure to comply does not affect the granting of patents.[55] In particular, the Biotech Directive does not refer to the term disclosure of origin.

52 Switzerland is not part of the group of mega diverse countries (CBD working group) also referred to as the 'demandeurs' of a disclosure requirement. The 'demandeurs' propose a mandatory requirement, whereas Switzerland would explicitly enable the national legislator to introduce the disclosure requirement at the national level.

53 Addor, n. 46 above.

54 N. 50 above.

55 Legal opinion differs as to the legal effect of recitals of EU directives. In any event, one can argue that the use of the word 'should' rather than 'shall' implies absence of an absolute legal requirement. In addition, recital 27 resulted from a compromise between Denmark, which had originally proposed

The European Community (EC) has expressed its willingness to discuss and examine the introduction of 'a system' that would allow states to keep track, at a global level, of all patent applications with regard to genetic resources within a proposal to the WIPO IGC and to the TRIPS Council.[56] According to the EC, such a requirement should be applied to all patent applications and 'be implemented in a legally binding and universal manner'.[57] In its view '[a] global and compulsory system creates a level playing field for industry and the commercial exploitation of patents, and also facilitates the possibilities under Article 15(7) of the CBD for the sharing of the benefits arising from the use of genetic resources'. The EC believes that such a system should be related to the existing international legal framework for patents. In order to achieve such a binding disclosure requirement, amendment of the PLT, the PCT, and regional agreements such as the European Patent Convention will be necessary. Only then will the disclosure requirement apply to all international, regional, and national patent applications at the earliest stage possible.

The applicant should be required to declare the country of origin of genetic resources, but only 'if he is aware of it' and '[no] additional research on his part would be required'.[58]

If applicants are not capable of indicating the country of origin, they may refer to a broader notion of 'source'. Hence, if the country of origin is unknown, the applicant should declare the source of the specific genetic resource to which the inventor has had physical access, and which is still known to him. According to the European Commission, the term 'source' refers to any source from which the applicant has acquired the genetic resource, other than the country of origin, such as a research centre, gene bank, or botanical garden. The EC links its proposal with the multilateral system as established under the FAO International Treaty indicating that the source can include the 'Multilateral System' as a source of genetic resources belonging to crops included in Annex 1 of the FAO International Treaty.[59]

As regards the relationship between genetic material and inventions, the EC sets out that the applicant must have used the genetic resources in the claimed

that such an 'information disclosure' become part of the Directive, and other Member States that considered that this would add another substantive condition for patentability, and would therefore violate the TRIPS Agreement. See n. 2 above.

[56] Communication submitted by the European Communities and its Member States to the TRIPS Council, IP/C/W/383 and WIPO Document, WIPO/GRTKF/IC/6/13.

[57] Proposal of the European Community and its Member States to WIPO, entitled 'Disclosure of origin or source of genetic resources and associated traditional knowledge in patent applications', received 16 Dec. 2004, Proposal made by the European Community and its Member States in response to an invitation by WIPO to submit comments and proposals, see DOC WO/GA/31/8 to advance collaboration between WIPO and the CBD. Published on the Internet at: http://www.wipo.int/tk/en/genetic/proposals.

[58] Ibid.

[59] According to Art. 12.3(b) of the International Treaty, 'access shall be accorded expeditiously, without the need to track individual accessions'. The Multilateral System is in fact the source of the genetic resources, as well as the beneficiary of the sharing of profits from their commercialization.

invention. More particularly, the EC proposes that the invention must be *directly* based on the specific genetic resources in that the invention must make immediate use of the genetic resource and be dependent on the specific properties of this resource. The EC takes the position that there is good reason for an obligation to disclose that an invention is directly based on traditional knowledge associated with the use of genetic resources. This is because it would facilitate implementation of Article 8(j) of the CBD, which sets out that there is a commitment to respect, preserve, and maintain traditional knowledge. The EC proposes that the introduction of a disclosure system should be 'organized in a non-bureaucratic and cost-efficient manner'.[60] It points out that '[a]n overwhelming majority of patent applicants do not base their inventions on genetic resources and/or associated traditional knowledge and for them the burden should be limited to an absolute minimum'.[61] Hence, the patent authorities should not make an assessment of the contents of the submitted information, nor should they be obliged to keep track of whether the patent applicant has obtained the relevant material in a way compatible with benefit-sharing and PIC provisions. On the contrary, their role should be limited to checking whether the formal requirements have been complied with. The EC argue that, for reasons of legal certainty, the submission of incorrect or incomplete information should not have any effect on the validity of the granted patent or on its enforceability against patent infringers. However, the EC leaves it to the national sovereignty to determine 'the character and the level of these sanctions, in accordance with domestic legal practices and respecting general principles of law'.

The EC does favour the introduction of a simple notification procedure to be followed by the patent offices every time they receive a declaration. It identifies the Clearing House Mechanism of the CBD as the central body that all patent offices should notify about granted patents.

The EC also supports a system that would ensure transparency, and allow the authorities of countries granting access to their resources to keep track of patent applications linked to the use of these resources. Under such a system, the information to be provided by patent applicants should be limited to information on the geographic origin of genetic resources or traditional knowledge used in the invention, but such a disclosure requirement should not act, de facto or *de jure*, as an additional formal or substantial patentability criterion. The legal consequences of non-compliance should lie outside the realm of patent law, e.g. in civil law (through a claim for compensation), or in administrative law (with a fee for refusal to submit information or for submitting the wrong information). The EC proposes that problems arising from genetic resources originating from more than one country should be dealt with through arrangements between the source countries, and/or in the context of the CBD.[62]

[60] N. 57 above.
[61] Ibid.
[62] Report on the Disclosure of Origin in Patent Applications, prepared by Queen Mary IP Research Institute, for the European Commission DG-Trade, Oct. 2004.

The EC sets out that in cases where traditional knowledge is used as a basis for further innovations, then it can be patented. In such cases, applicants should disclose the source of this information, but as with genetic resources, this should not determine the patentability of the invention. In this regard, the EC supports further work on the development of an international *sui generis* system for the protection of traditional knowledge within the IGC.

Similarly, the EU is of the opinion that Article 29 of the TRIPS Agreement does not prevent members from requiring the patent applicant to disclose the source of origin or to provide evidence that ABS rules had been respected, as long as such requirements do not constitute a patentability criterion or invoke the validity of the patent. Hence the introduction of such a system on the national level is permitted.

The EC decided that the IGC should be the body to respond to an invitation from COP-7 of CBD to address the interrelation of access to genetic resources and disclosure requirements in IP applications, as in its view it is 'the only body with a legitimate mandate to discuss these issues'. The EC was content with Switzerland's proposal to amend the PCT to allow enhanced disclosure.[63]

iv. Draft Article 29bis Proposal by a group of developing countries led by Brazil

In May 2006, Brazil, India, Pakistan, Peru, Thailand, and Tanzania submitted a draft text[64] to the WTO meeting to speed up negotiations on the disclosure of origin. This proposal is now also co-sponsored by China, Colombia, Cuba, Ecuador, Paraguay, South Africa, Venezuela, the WTO African Group, and the WTO Least Developed Country Group. This potential addition to multilateral trade rules has been championed by Peru,[65] one of the most vocal critics of the misappropriation of biological resources and traditional knowledge through patents without adequate recompense (bio-piracy). The Peruvian delegation presented to the TRIPS Council a document on the country's experience of 'bad' patents—those that failed to involve proof of consent or benefit-sharing. The delegation reiterated that a formal TRIPS amendment was necessary to combat bio-piracy. It stated that 'the patent system works only if the rights of those who made the invention possible are acknowledged (…) there is an urgent need to rethink the patent system and to consider how to make it more balanced'.[66]

The session of the WTO Council for TRIPS, on 23–24 October 2007, also saw the group of 32 WTO least-developed countries support a proposal to amend TRIPS rules so as to require patent applicants to disclose the origin of genetic

[63] (2004) 4 *Bridges* (Weekly Trade News Digest) 10. Published on the Internet at: http://www.ictsd.org/biores/04–05-28/story1.htm.

[64] WT/GC/W/564, TN/C/W/41, 31 May 2006.

[65] Communication from Peru, IP/C/W/458.

[66] (2007) 11 *Bridges* (Weekly Trade News Digest) at 37. Published on the Internet at: http://www.ictsd.org/weekly/07–10-31/story2.htm.

resources or traditional knowledge used in their inventions. The African Group had already done this earlier in the year. The addition of both of these groups creates a supermajority of countries supporting the proposal. The issue of disclosure is of crucial interest to least-developed countries (LDCs), as they want cross-border misappropriation of biological resources to end, and in their view an international disclosure of origin requirement is the only way to ensure transparent and fair tracking of the use and misuse of LDC biological resources and associated traditional knowledge. In addition, an international disclosure of origin is necessary to enable the proper functioning and enforcement of national ABS systems. The LDC group seeks not only to prevent misappropriation, but wishes to reclaim the resources so that the rightful owners of biological resources and associated traditional knowledge can exercise their rights—introducing a CBD plus measure.[67] The LDC group indicated that they might want to discuss a possible trade-off between disclosure and GI extension/register. This is something that has been proposed informally also by Brazil.

The proposed Article 29*bis* entitled 'Disclosure of Origin of Biological Resources and/or Associated Traditional Knowledge' sets out that:

> [w]here the subject matter of a patent application concerns, is derived from or developed with biological resources and/or associated traditional knowledge, Members shall require applicants to disclose the country providing the resources and/or associated traditional knowledge, from whom in the providing country they were obtained, and, as known after reasonable inquiry, the country of origin. Members shall also require that applicants provide information including evidence of compliance with the applicable legal requirements in the providing country for prior informed consent for access and fair and equitable benefit-sharing arising from the commercial or other utilization of such resources and/or associated traditional knowledge.

The article proposes that this information should be published jointly with the application or grant of the patent.

The proposed text requires that countries provide the legal and administrative means to stop the application or the grant of a patent and to revoke the patent if the disclosure requirement has not been complied with.[68] This implies that developing countries have chosen a mandatory disclosure of origin. However, it provides some flexibility as to the legal effect of non-compliance, as it leaves it up to the scrutiny of the country how to act in case of non-compliance. The legal and administrative means to act should be available, but it does not set out that a country must act.

67 Other countries, including Switzerland, think that the law should not be retroactive.

68 Members need to put in place enforcement mechanisms to ensure compliance. In particular, Members 'shall ensure that administrative and/or judicial authorities have the authority to prevent the further processing of an application or the grant of a patent and to revoke, subject to the provisions of Art. 32 of this Agreement, or render unenforceable a patent when the applicant has, knowingly or with reasonable grounds to know, failed to comply with the obligations in paragraphs 2 and 3 of this Article or provided false or fraudulent information'. See proposed Art. 29*bis*(3).

v. Japan

Japan believes that the CBD and the patent system are not in conflict.[69] In Japan's view the treaties have different objectives—protection of IPRs and conservation of biological diversity—therefore the objects, content, and subject matter for the CBD differ from the treaties relating to IP. In its view, the patent system may complement the CBD in facilitating the benefit-sharing or technological transfer specified in the CBD. Japan does not support the addition of new obligations into the TRIPS Agreement, such as disclosure requirements, as proposed by Brazil and others. Japan leaves it to countries' discretion to decide about disclosure of origin requirements.

Japan submitted a proposal for the creation of (worldwide accessible) restricted-access databases that would enable patent examiners to determine whether inventions used traditional knowledge or genetic resources, and could thus could avoid erroneously granting patents.[70] The paper, which was identical to the one Japan had already submitted to the WIPO, urged WTO Members to consider the work being done on this at WIPO. Japan does not accept that 'the risk of erroneously granted patents is reduced by disclosing the country of origin/providing country/source, evidence of prior informed consent, and evidence of benefit-sharing in patent applications, because such disclosure provides additional information which patent examiners can use when they conduct prior art search'. This rejection is because Japan believes that country of origin evidence of PIC and benefit-sharing are irrelevant to the judgement of novelty and inventive steps. In its view 'even if a genetic resource collected in a specific place has its own specific characteristics, this does not sufficiently explain the necessity of imposing the new obligations of disclosure'. Japan, along with the US, wants discussions of these issues to take place within WIPO, specifically the IGC, rather than the TRIPS Council.[71]

vi. The US

The US does not see any conflict between the CBD and TRIPS.[72] The US notes that the CBD does not require or discuss patent disclosure requirements, and points out that it is not a contracting party to the CBD. In the view of the US:

[69] Communication to the TRIPS Council by Japan, IP/C/W/472, dated 13 June 2006. This document is an annex from a document at the 9th session of IGC in Apr. 2006. Japan bases that decision on Art. 22.1 CBD that reads 'The provisions of this Convention shall not affect the rights and obligations of any Contracting Party deriving from any existing international agreement, except where the exercise of those rights and obligations would cause a serious damage or threat to biological diversity.'

[70] Communication from Japan, IP/C/W/504.

[71] (2004) 4 *Bridges* (Weekly Trade New Digest) at 5, Published on the Internet at http://www.ictsd.org/biores/04–03-19/story2.htm.

[72] Communication by the US to the TRIPS Council IP/C/W/434, IP/C/W/449 and IP/C/W/469.

[i]t is not the lack of safeguards in TRIPS, but lack of clearly defined national systems directly regulating the use of genetic resources that creates 'erroneous' treatment of relevant sources. The national ABS systems are directed to the goals of providing appropriate access and equitable benefit-sharing. And a searchable database with disclosed information and a post-grant opposition/re-examination procedure will handle bad patents. The most appropriate solution for any kind of misappropriation is to strengthen national regimes. Patenting in and of itself does not amount to misappropriation.[73]

Hence the US does not believe that a disclosure requirement would establish certainty in the patent system. It does not regard the patent system to be in crisis: although overloaded, the system works well. According to the US, a national ABS system must be established in a majority of the member states before supplementary requirements can be developed. In its view, any attempt to single out applications involving genetic material or based on traditional knowledge and then deal with them through a new patent disclosure requirement may negatively affect technological development. According to the US, it would be more appropriate to strengthen a comprehensive and holistic national regime outside the patent system to address the effect of commercialization on traditional knowledge. Further, the US holds that additional disclosure requirements would violate the principle within TRIPS of non-discrimination between fields of technology.[74] The US believes the IGC to be the most appropriate forum to discuss these matters.

The US argues that although the TRIPS Agreement does not include provisions to protect genetic resources from misappropriation and theft, such an absence does not indicate a conflict between the CBD and the TRIPS Agreement.[75] The US believes those acts fall outside of the purview of the TRIPS Agreement, and it argues that countries should focus on establishing their own ABS regimes, including provisions on PIC. It argues that bio-piracy should be prevented with the help of a 'searchable, organized database, disclosure of information material to patentability and the use of post-grant opposition and/or re-examination systems as an alternative to litigation'. Other countries also opposing an amendment to the TRIPS Agreement on this issue are Korea and Canada. Some countries (including New Zealand and Canada) responded that it was too early to discuss these issues or they were of the opinion that the TRIPS Council was not the appropriate place to discuss issues like bio-piracy and disclosure of origin requirements, and found WIPO a more suitable place to pursue discussions.

Other countries counter the US arguments and refer to Article 16.5 CBD, which obliges countries to cooperate to ensure IPRs do not counter the objectives of the CBD, and refer to Article 16.5 CBD to support their claims.[76]

[73] Communication by the US to the TRIPS Council, IP/C/W/469, 13 Mar. 2006.

[74] Communication by the US to the TRIPS Council, IP/C/W/403, 28 May 2003, paras. 10–11.

[75] Communication by the US to the TRIPS Council, IP/C/W/469.

[76] Art. 16.5 CBD reads: 'The Contracting Parties, recognizing that patents and other intellectual property rights may have an influence on the implementation of this Convention, shall cooperate in

IV. Is a Disclosure of Origin the Solution?

Some countries have high expectations about the introduction of a disclosure of origin requirement. But can the introduction of a disclosure requirement realize its potential in putting a halt to the misappropriation of genetic resources and associated traditional knowledge? To be sure, introducing a disclosure of origin requirement brings about many practical problems. For instance, even an operational disclosure requirement will not change the fact that so many resources and traditional knowledge, relevant to an invention being patented, can be acquired or learned about without visiting any of the countries of origin or source. Thus the measure will only be applicable to a small number of patents. It is therefore questionable if a disclosure requirement will improve patent quality, and put a halt to the misappropriation of genetic resources (biodiversity). In addition the question remains as to what extent the genetic resources and/or associated traditional knowledge contributes to the patent. In many cases, knowledge, information, and material relevant to an invention are manifold. Hence, various sources and material may have contributed to the ultimate invention. In that case, is it feasible to ask whether all sources of knowledge and material should be remunerated, no matter how far-flung and peripheral? This brings with it the additional difficulty of tracing all countries of origin. Indeed, how would one deal with several countries that could all legitimately claim to be countries of origin of the same resource?[77] A solution to this problem can be found in the establishment of community funds.[78]

It is estimated that the annual market for products derived from genetic resources is between US$500 billion and US$800 billion. This figure is based on statistics from the following industrial sectors which depend in varying degrees on biogenetic resources: pharmaceuticals, botanical medicines, agricultural produce (including agricultural seed), ornamental horticultural products, crop protection products, biotechnologies in fields other than health care and agriculture,

this regard subject to national legislation and international law in order to ensure that such rights are supportive of and do not run counter to its objectives.'

[77] Legal ownership of genetic resources can be in different hands because of wide diffusion in the course of history. Most of the genetic resources used in breeding currently commercialized varieties were almost all obtained before the CBD came into force, when free exchange of such resources was customary. Increase in trade and globalization has made the world a smaller place and genetic resources that used to be found only in a particular geographical area may now be widely available from many countries through common trade channels. See G. Dutfield, 'Thinking Aloud on Disclosure of Origin' (2005) QUNO Occasional Paper 18, QUNO Geneva, published on the Internet at: http://www.iprsonline.org/unctadictsd/docs/Disclosure_Dutfield.pdf.

[78] For example, under Peruvian law in order to access genetic material for the purposes of commercial or industrial application a licence agreement ought to be signed ensuring that due reward for the access and the equitable distribution of the benefits deriving therefrom is guaranteed. A percentage of the revenue resulting from the commercialization and marketing of goods developed on the basis of collective knowledge goes to the Fund of the Development of Indigenous Peoples.

and personal care and cosmetics products.[79] Of these, the pharmaceutical and agricultural seed sectors are the most dependent on biogenetic resources.

But one caveat applies: although it is clear that industry depends heavily on biogenetic resources and traditional knowledge in the past, this does not necessarily mean that in the future they will equally depend on resources and knowledge that are currently undiscovered.

The failure of Shaman Pharmaceuticals, which sought to develop new drugs from ethnobotanical information provided by indigenous communities, is sometimes cited to demonstrate that traditional knowledge provides no short-cuts for the industry in its costly search for profitable new cures.[80]

Ten Kate and Laird argue that 'natural products are likely to remain an important, although minor, component of drug discovery' but that the 'techniques of molecular biology and genetic engineering are likely to become the dominating factor in drug, discovery, design and development'.[81] However, traditional knowledge is widely used, especially in the botanical medicine industry, as the basis for determining safety and efficacy, to develop agronomic practices for the cultivation of materials, and to guide the development of new products.[82]

The International Chamber of Commerce (ICC) believes that it is premature to consider amending the TRIPS Agreement to provide for special disclosure requirements in patent applications. The ICC is of the opinion 'that patent disclosure proposals should take into account the broader context of access and benefit-sharing and the specific implications of such proposals for the patent system and innovation'.[83]

With certainty, one can deduce that the disclosure requirement provides only part of the solution to ensure that patents are granted in such a way that they further key objectives of conservation of biological diversity, sustainable use of its components, and the achievement of social equity.

V. Conclusion

In the past decade, the misappropriation of genetic resources and traditional knowledge has emerged as an important issue of global concern, and has been addressed in a number of international fora such as the CBD, the WTO, and WIPO. National proposals, academic literature, as well as civil society

[79] See K. ten Kate and S. A. Laird, *The Commercial Use of Biodiversity: Access to Genetic Resources and Benefit Sharing* (London: Earthscan, 1999).

[80] N. 2 above.

[81] N. 79, above at 57.

[82] Ibid.

[83] International Chamber of Commerce, 'TRIPS Should Not be Re-opened to Mandate Special Disclosure Requirements in Patent Applications', Document No 450/1006, published on the Internet at: http://www.iccwbo.org.

organizations, provide for the building blocks of an effective disclosure mechanism, i.e. which addresses concerns over misappropriation and potential burdens on the patent system.

Whether special patent disclosure requirements are a desirable objective is contentious, however, and key terms are still to be defined. While some countries strongly support these requirements, others vigorously contest them in all multilateral fora addressing the issue, arguing that a disclosure of origin requirement will not advance the aims of ABS. However, recent TRIPS Council meetings have shown a tendency to start fact-based dialogues, and a willingness to continue technical discussions.[84]

The US and Japan are sceptical of claims that a mandatory disclosure requirement in the TRIPS Agreement is necessary. They argue that bio-piracy should be addressed by other means.[85] Both countries favour government databases (documenting traditional knowledge, to help avoid bio-piracy), as opposed to patent applicants taking responsibility for the disclosure of the use of biological resources and traditional knowledge.

The EU and Switzerland support the introduction of some form of a disclosure requirement, but have expressed concerns over the introduction of a mandatory requirement and the legal consequences of non-compliance. Both countries prefer WIPO to be the appropriate platform to deal with these issues. There are some developing countries (including Chile) that have not yet joined the Article 29*bis* proposal for fear of parallel developments on geographical indications. Norway agrees with the mandatory nature of the requirement, but does not support the revocation of patent as a sanction for non-compliance.

Possibly, because the developing countries and the US are so divided on the topic, the EC might act as a bridge-maker between the two in resolving the question whether a requirement should be introduced into the TRIPS Agreement. Meanwhile Brazil and the LDCs believe that governments should consider potential trade-offs between geographical indications (multilateral register for wines and spirits) and disclosure requirements.

A number of suggestions and recommendations can be proposed to point everyone in the right direction.

First, countries should be allowed ample time to develop their own policies, and enact domestic legislation that is supportive of intellectual property protection and CBD objectives, including a detailed disclosure mechanism. It is important that the issues are well considered before renegotiation of TRIPS. This includes the development of national systems of disclosure and access, and benefit-sharing agreements. An established domestic administrative and legal regime, supportive of ABS of genetic resources, will strengthen international claims and proposals

[84] (2007) 11 *Bridges* (Weekly Trade News Digest) 5. Published on the Internet at: http://www.ictsd.org/weekly/07–02-14/wtoinbrief.htm.

[85] Ibid.

for such a regime, including the disclosure of origin. It is important that countries that have not done so already, in particular most developing countries, set in motion processes to create ABS rules including a disclosure of origin requirement implemented in their domestic legislation.

Second, it is best that countries actively participate in FAO, WHO, CBD, and other fora aimed at establishing an ABS regime for national and international application.

Third, the impact of special patent disclosure requirements, already introduced in national laws on the rate of bio-prospecting and ABS, is worth studying, as is the extent to which patent applicants already provide source information in their applications when it is materially relevant to the application.

Fourth, more solid consensus should be achieved in international fora on what the disclosure requirement should look like, and how it should work in practice, e.g. scope, nature, key elements, objectives. This requires the commissioning of more technical work to facilitate this process.

The majority of developing countries and LDCs favour an amendment of the WTO TRIPS Agreement to introduce a disclosure requirement in their laws. However, most developed WTO members either oppose such a requirement, or favour WIPO to be the competent forum to address this issue. Nonetheless, a movement towards some form of a disclosure of origin/source requirement is discernable amongst European countries. As discussed, Norway, Switzerland, and the European Commission have expressed support for such a requirement both at the national, regional, and international level, and have suggested various proposals to realize this in practice.

Export Credits for Sustainable Development?

Markus W. Gehring and Kristin Price***

I. Introduction

A growing debate has emerged in recent years regarding the relationship between Export Credit Agencies (ECAs) and the global promotion of sustainable development principles and practices.[1] As central components of the global finance architecture, ECAs provide a significant source of public finance and support for private investors conducting business abroad.[2] Through the granting of export credits, guaranteed loans, and various forms of risk insurance, ECAs promote the export of capital, goods, and services, notably to developing countries. In this

* Lecturer in International and European Law, University of Cambridge, Centre of International Studies and Lead Counsel for Trade, Investment and Competition Law, Centre for International Sustainable Development Law (CISDL).

** Associate Fellow with the CISDL. The authors wish to thank the participants of the 2006 Amsterdam Seminar in Honour of Konrad von Moltke on Investment and Sustainable Development (organized by Dr Kyla Tienhaara at the Institute for Environmental Studies of the Vrije Universiteit Amsterdam) for the stimulating discussion of an earlier draft of the paper as well as Dr Doerte Fouquet for her guidance and support in the research. The authors also wish to thank CISDL colleagues Marie-Claire Cordonier Segger, Ashfaq Khalfan, Roman Picherack, David Hornsby, and Michael Kerr for their helpful comments.

[1] See W. Zwier, 'Export Credit Agencies and the Environment: Implications of the Aarhus Convention for Export Credit Agency Accountability' (2006) 6 *Yearbook of European Environmental Law* 204.

[2] More countries are becoming active in this area, see on the Chinese ECA, E. Suzuk, 'Bi-Lateral Policy Orientation in the Multilateral Development Policy: A Challenge for the China Exim Bank and Its Accountability' (2007) 6 *Chinese Journal of International Law* 127. Statistics provided by the OECD indicate that the net operating cash flow (all maturities) for the ECAs of both EC and non-EC OECD members was 22,547.4 million SDR in 2006 and 65,002.7 million SDR from 1996–2006. The recent rate of increase in net operating cash flow for this same group of ECAs is noteworthy: 4,972.9 (2004), 13,081.3 (2005), and 22,547.4 (2006) million SDR. See 2006 Cash flow results for officially supported export credits. Published on the Internet at: http://www.oecd.org/dataoecd/13/59/39787191.pdf (accessed 18 Dec. 2007). D. Gianturco reports that that one out of every eight dollars of world trade is now financed by ECAs in *Export Credit Agencies: The Unsung Giants of International Trade and Finance* (Westport/London: Quorum, 2001). He also notes that 'ECA activity far exceeds that of all multilateral development banks (MDBs), such as the World Bank and the Asian Development Bank. ECA loans, guarantees, and insurance are also far greater than the activity of all overseas development agencies (ODAs), such as the U.S. Agency for International Development', at 1.

fashion, ECAs provide considerable support for the development of markets and the undertaking of large infrastructure projects in often volatile, emerging economies. Many of the activities and projects that ECAs finance and insure have substantial environmental and social implications. Thus, the chapter's point of departure is an assessment of to what extent ECAs are required—either through national or multilateral rules, regulations, and conventions—to take sustainable development objectives into consideration when extending export financing and insurance.

ECAs are unique in that they are often *quasi*-public, *quasi*-private entities. Most industrialized nations have at least one ECA, which is usually under official or *quasi*-official (i.e. arm's length) control of their government, and often publicly funded. Because ECAs are relying on public funds and sometimes may even follow a government controlled and determined mandate, there is an argument to be made that they should operate in a socially and environmentally responsible manner when deliberating about which projects and activities will receive credit. A possible response would be for individual States to apply stronger regulations and criteria according to which export credits are granted by the relevant national agencies. Domestic and international non-governmental organizations (NGOs), for example, are actively promoting stronger control and conditionality (including the use of *ex ante* sustainable impact assessments (SIAs)) to grant export credits to their domestic industries especially where such credits involve government-supported funds.

On the other hand, industry associations and developing countries may view this argument with scepticism and reject the notion that ECAs should condition their support with 'sustainability' criteria defined by the host state of a specific ECA. The development and application of additional 'sustainability' criteria, the argument goes, risks imposing a particular view of development needs and objectives on importing countries. The upshot of this conditionality is the potential curtailment of capital and guarantees needed for infrastructure improvement and the constriction of policy space for devising economic development strategies. As a consequence, a careful balance needs to be embodied within the ECA legal framework that does not unduly restrain the flow of funds to initiatives that are geared towards sustainable development objectives yet, mitigates the danger of imposing unilateral and unreasonable demands on developing country project partners.

However, construing this debate to be polarized along North versus South lines is perhaps an oversimplification. The transnational advocacy network campaigning on this topic has made a strategic choice not to be proactive in terms of demanding policy revisions; rather, these groups are primarily concerned that ECAs do no harm to affected communities by complying with their existing international legal obligations.

A multilateral regime for the regulation of ECAs increasingly provides for the inclusion of environmental considerations into the scope of the operations and undertakings of ECAs. Principal instruments in this multilateral regime include the 2005 OECD Arrangement on Officially Supported Export Credits (the Arrangement) and the OECD Common Approaches on Officially Supported Export Credits and the Environment.[3] However, it must be stressed that the inclusion of environmental considerations remains largely non-binding, and thus such instruments ought to be considered as 'soft law' in this regard.[4] Moreover, the OECD Arrangement's main purpose remains to create fair conditions for competing ECAs and ultimately the exporters who rely on them. Thus, the addition of environmental considerations currently remains ancillary at best to the current process.

Several questions about the multilateral regime regulating export credits and its future progression with regards to sustainable development can be raised. Should ECAs be closely regulated according to social and environmental criteria or should they base their decision-making solely on economic criteria? Should they be used as a tool to promote environmental protection goals or should they continue to remain deregulated in this regard so as to allow the greatest access to export credit and risk insurance? Could collaboration with the various secretariats of the multilateral environmental accords (MEAs) or the ILO be a fruitful endeavour in enhancing environmental and social safeguards in this domain without imposing or second guessing sovereign decisions in importing countries? Collectively, the questions raised in this emerging conversation reveal a more systemic and fundamental question regarding ECAs and sustainable development: is the current legal framework governing ECAs adequate to ensure that they support and contribute to sustainable development by granting export credits according to relevant sustainable development criteria?

This chapter seeks to illuminate and assess options and avenues available for furthering a multilateral framework regulating export credits that incorporates and promotes sustainable development principles, practices, and objectives. The first part will introduce and describe the emerging regime governing ECAs and export credits at both the global and domestic levels. It will outline the laws governing export credit activity by various OECD Member States and will describe the legal frameworks promulgated by various relevant organizations that comprise the current regulatory structure at the international level. Within this description, the recent efforts to address environmental concerns regarding export credits, largely by encouraging the use of procedural tools such as environmental impact assessments (EIAs) will be discussed. The remainder of the

[3] Published on the Internet at: http://webdomino1.oecd.org/olis/2005doc.nsf/Linkto/td-pg(2005)38-final and http://webdomino1.oecd.org/olis/2007doc.nsf/Linkto/tad-ecg(2007)9 respectively.

[4] The concept of soft law encompasses rules and norms that are not attributable to an official author of statutory rules or formal sources of law: J. J. Kirton and M. J. Trebilcock (eds.), *Hard Choices, Soft Law: Voluntary Standards in Global Trade, Environment and Social Governance* (Burlington, VT: Ashgate Publishing Company, 2004), at 9.

chapter will then analyse methods by which integrative decision-making, that is, the inclusion of environmental, economic, and development priorities, can be realized within the emerging regime regulating export credits, so as to promote, rather than frustrate, the objectives of sustainable development.

II. The Sustainable Development Implications of Export Credits Within the International Financial System

A. Export Credits

The contemporary global economy has an intensely competitive dynamic that supersedes political boundaries. Firms bid on projects and perform services abroad; increasingly, the viability of enterprises in certain areas is predicated on extensive international operations. Transactions are instantaneous, frequently international and involve sectors (i.e. massive infrastructure projects) that used to be the remit of the State. Importers can almost always find a supplier willing to extend credit for their endeavours; an exporter's failure to come up with financing effectively rules them out of the bidding process. An export credit instrument solves this problem for the exporter by passing the risk of importer non-payment to a third party—such as a bank (letters of credit); an insurance provider (export credit insurance); or an official export credit agency (official export credit guarantees). This financial intermediation assists exporters in offering competitive credit options while maintaining a viable risk portfolio and sufficient liquidity to increase business and the overall volume of trade.[5] These instruments inevitably cover exporters from one country, importers from another, and a financial intermediary possibly from a third.[6] Thus, the international quality of these transactions prevents adequate regulation if the legal frameworks are enshrined solely at the domestic level.

ECAs play a significant role in expanding national export. Through ECA financing, corporations are able to open up new markets and accrue alliances with other States and companies overseas.[7] In addition, through the same export facility that allows the domestic supplier to enter into a sales agreement, credit is made available to buyers in developing countries that would not otherwise have taken part in transborder sales.[8]

Export credits describe a whole range of usually long-term financial services provided to exporters, often supported through governmental funds. The *OECD*

[5] J. K. Levit, 'A Bottom-Up Approach to International Law Making: The Tale of Three Trade Finance Instruments' (2005) 30 *Yale Journal of International Law*, at 125.

[6] Ibid.

[7] Zwier, n. 1 above.

[8] Ibid.

Arrangement on officially supported Export Credits (the Arrangement) for example, defines its scope of applications as including export credit guarantee or insurance (pure cover), direct credit/financing and refinancing, or interest rate support granted on a term longer than two years.

B. Sustainable Development

The World Commission on Environment and Development (WCED)[9] defined the concept of sustainable development in 1987 as 'development that meets the needs of the present without compromising the ability of future generations to meet their own needs'. Following this definition, the concept of sustainable development was further galvanized and substantiated within the field of international law through soft law instruments such as the 1992 *Rio Declaration* and *Agenda 21*, and the 2002 *Johannesburg Plan of Implementation* that resulted from the 2002 World Summit on Sustainable Development.[10] These soft law instruments highlighted the need to integrate social development and environmental protection objectives into the economic development framework in order to achieve sustainable development. For example, Principle 4 of the 1992 Rio Declaration states that in 'order to achieve sustainable development, environmental protection shall constitute an integral part of the development process and cannot be considered in isolation from it'.[11] As such, international law pertaining to sustainable development, or, international sustainable development law,[12] can be properly understood as the intersection and integration of economic, environmental, and social (including human rights) law at the global level.

The International Law Association *Committee on the Legal Aspects of Sustainable Development* provided further substance and content to the concepts of sustainable development and international sustainable development law through its '2002 New Delhi Declaration on Principles of International Law for Sustainable Development'.[13] These principles include elements of a substantive

[9] World Commission on Environment and Development, *Our Common Future* (Oxford: Oxford University Press, 1987), 8. See A. Kiss and D. Shelton, *International Environmental Law (2nd edn.)* (New York: Transnational Publishers, 1994), at 248–9.

[10] Published on the Internet at: http://www.un.org/events/wssd/.

[11] *Rio Declaration on Environment and Development*, United Nations Conference on Environment and Development, UN Doc. A/CONF.151/6/Rev.1 (1992), (1992) 31 *International Legal Materials* 874 at Principle 4. See also the Stockholm Declaration on the Human Environment (1972) at Principle 13. Stockholm, 5–16 June 1972 (entered into force in 1994) (1972) 11 *International Legal Materials* 1.

[12] See with many further references M.-C. Cordonier Segger and A Khalfan, *Sustainable Development Law: Principles, Practices and Prospects* (Oxford: Oxford University Press, 2004).

[13] International Law Association, *New Delhi Declaration of Principles of International Law Relating to Sustainable Development*, ILA Resolution 2.2002, 70th Conference, UN Doc. A/57/329 (2002) *Report of the Expert Group on Identification of Principles of International Law for Sustainable Development* (London: ILA, 1995). See also International Law Association (ILA), *Report of the Sixty-Second Conference* (Seoul: ILA, 1987) at 1–11, 409–87.

nature (sovereignty over natural resources and the duty of sustainable use of natural resources, the principle of observance of human rights, inter- and intragenerational equity, common but differentiated obligations and the recognition of the special needs and interests of economies in transition and least-developed countries and peoples, common heritage and common concern of humankind, and the precautionary principle) as well as procedural ones (the duty to cooperate for global development and protection of the environment, public participation and access to information and justice, and good governance).

The principles of international law relating to sustainable development can help to provide guidance on ways in which sustainable development considerations may be introduced into the operations and decision-making processes of ECAs. The principles of international law relating to sustainable development go considerably further than the mere inclusion of environmental considerations through such procedures as EIAs. Procedural requirements such as duties to engage local communities in consultations on social implications of individual projects, obligations to adopt a precautionary approach where immediate or long-term social or environmental risks may be particularly acute, and obligations of continuing transparency and disclosure with regards to ECA supported activities may further the legitimacy of ECAs as well as increase the integrity of particular projects they finance and insure. Application of the principles is likely to be especially pertinent where ECAs are engaged in financing and insuring large infrastructure projects where environmental and social concerns within and beyond the local community are prevalent.

III. The International Regime Regulating Export Credits and Environmental Protection

In contrast to government procurement (governed by a multilateral WTO covenant),[14] there is no singular international binding agreement that regulates export credits and other guarantees. The precursor to the current regime centred on the OECD Arrangement was the infamous Multilateral Agreement on Investment (MAI). The MAI was largely abandoned due to a vigorous campaign by civil society groups that construed the Agreement as a compact that protected the rights of foreign investors while limiting any substantial obligations on their part. Against this backdrop, the OECD chose instead to promote cooperation on international investment through its Declaration on International Investment

[14] The WTO Agreement on Government Procurement, Annex 4(b) of the 1994 Agreement Establishing the WTO, published on the Internet at: http://www.wto.org/english/docs_e/legal_e/gpr-94_e.pdf (accessed 6 Mar. 2006).

and Multinational Enterprises (the Declaration).[15] The Declaration, adopted on 27 June 2000, outlines non-binding principles and standards addressed to both governments and enterprises.[16] This Declaration was followed in 2005 by OECD Arrangement on Officially Supported Export Credits (the Arrangement), which is central to the legal regime regulating the operations of ECAs.[17]

A. OECD Arrangement on Officially Supported Export Credits

Among OECD Member States, the Arrangement constitutes a soft law agreement—not an OECD Act—that sets forth the most generous export credit terms and conditions that are supported by consensus. In tandem, the OECD Arrangement and the WTO limit the array of services that ECAs can offer, but it is argued that competition ensures that innovations in one agency will permeate to others and consequently expand the scope of activities and benefits offered.[18] The codes contained within the Arrangement for the most part 'do not generally constitute a de facto standard of commitments in the areas they cover';[19] the main purpose is to foment a level playing field for official support, 'in order to encourage competition among exporters based on quality and price of goods and services exported rather than on the most favourable officially supported financial terms and conditions'.[20]

Signatories of the Arrangement have obligations to non-Participants; the scope of the application dictates that 'Participants shall, on the basis of reciprocity, reply to a request from a non-Participant in a competitive situation on the financial terms and conditions offered for its official support, as it would reply to a request from a Participant'.[21] The definition of 'official support' contained within the Arrangement includes 'all official support provided by or on behalf of a govern-

[15] OECD Directorate for Fin., Fiscal & Enter. Affairs, The OECD Declaration and Decisions on International Investment and Multinational Enterprises: Basic Texts at 5–23, OECD Doc. DAFFE/IME(2000)20 (2000), available on the Internet at: http://www.olis.oecd.org/olis/2000doc.nsf.

[16] Ibid.

[17] The OECD Arrangement has been in existence since 1978 and sets out the financial framework under which ECAs are exempted from the WTO Agreement on Subsidies and Countervailing Measures. The OECD Arrangement on Officially Supported Export Credits, published on the Internet at: http://webdomino1.oecd.org/olis/2005doc.nsf/43bb6130e5e86e5fc12569fa005d004c/23013c0293535d25c12570cf003e35ed/$FILE/JT00195558.PDF (accessed 6 Mar. 2006). The Participants to the Arrangement currently are: Australia, Canada, the European Community, Japan, Korea, New Zealand, Norway, Switzerland, and the US. Other OECD Members and non-Members may be invited to become Participants by the current Participants.

[18] R. Short, 'Export Credit Agencies, Project Finance and Commercial Risk: Whose Risk is it, Anyway?' (2001) 24 *Fordham International Law Journal*, 1371–81.

[19] K. Gordon, 'Enabling Conditions for Environmental Sustainability: Private and Public Roles', OECD Global Forum on Sustainable Development: Conference on Financing Environmental Dimension of Sustainable Development (2002), at 7, published on the Internet at: http://www.oecd.org/dataoecd/19/0/2080741.pdf.

[20] Ibid., at General Provisions: Purpose (b).

[21] Ibid., at General Provisions: Information Available to Non-Participants 4(b).

ment for export of goods and/or services, including financial leases, which have a repayment term of two years or more'.[22] Although agricultural commodities and military equipment exports are exempted, export credit guarantees or insurance (pure cover), official financing support (direct credit/financing and refinancing, or interest rate support), tied aid,[23] and trade-related un-tied aid is all within the Arrangement's remit.[24]

The financial terms and conditions for the OECD Arrangement have clearly articulated limitations:

> the Participants recognise that more restrictive financial terms and conditions than those provided for by the Arrangement traditionally apply to certain trade or industrial sectors. The Participants shall continue to respect such customary financial terms and conditions, in particular the principle by which repayment terms do not exceed the useful life of the goods.[25]

Provisions facilitating the sharing of information abound in the Arrangement; transparency is compulsory through notifications, dissemination of information on official support, and procedures for matching.[26] The OECD intends for Member governments to 'determine the basic framework in this field and to be responsible for periodically consulting stakeholders on the most appropriate way forward'.[27] Consultation processes and reviews specific to certain sectors are meticulously laid out in the text, as are classification schemes related to risk assessment, repayment terms, and eligibility for different types of aid.[28]

[22] Ibid., at General Provisions: Scope of the Application 5(a).

[23] The definition of tied aid is contained in Annex XI: 'aid which is in effect (in law or in fact) tied to the procurement of goods and/or services from the donor country and/or a restricted number of countries; it includes loans, grants or associated financing packages with a concessionality level greater than zero per cent'.

The Agreement, at Chapter III: Provisions for Tied Aid, notes that 'aid policies should provide needed external resources to countries, sectors or projects with little or no access to market financing. Tied aid policies should ensure best value for money, minimize trade distortion, and contribute to developmentally effective use of these resources'. The tied aid provisions of the Arrangement do not apply to the aid programmes of multilateral or regional institutions.

[24] Ibid., at General Provisions: Scope of the Application 5(b) and (c).

[25] Ibid., at Chapter II: Financial Terms and Conditions for Export Credits.

[26] Ibid., at Chapter IV: Procedures.

[27] See OECD, The OECD Guidelines for Multinational Enterprises: Revision 2000 (2000), at 5–6, available on the Internet at: http://www.oecd.org/document/28/0,3343,fr_2649_34889_2397532_1_1_1_1,00.html.

[28] Ibid., Members are expected (after giving due regard to the competitive context in which they operate and the constraints of business confidentiality) to:

(1) Publish national ECA environmental policy statements/principles and procedural guidance;

(2) When appropriate, exchange views with stakeholders;

(3) Share information with a view to seeking, where appropriate, common positions on the environmental review of projects, and reply in a timely manner to requests from other Members in a co-financing or a competitive situation on the environmental standards accepted by the Member;

(4) Encourage project sponsors to make environmental impact information publicly available; and

(5) Make available to the public at least annually, subject to legal provisions on public disclosure in Members' countries, information on projects classified in Categories A and B.

Each OECD member country has agreed to recommend these Guidelines to their enterprises, and has established a National Contact Point (NCP) in its administration to deal with inquiries. The *raison d'être* of NCPs is to 'further the effectiveness of the Guidelines',[29] thus, they undertake promotional activities, handle inquiries, and mediate discussions between Parties that concern matters covered by the compact.[30] Procedurally, OECD member countries are given a great deal of flexibility to organize their NCPs as they see fit and often seek the active support of partners which may include representatives from the business community, employee organizations, and other interested parties such as NGOs.[31] However, the small amount of oversight wielded by NCPs was diluted in the 2000 Amendments 'to good offices and facilitating access to non-adversarial means'.[32] Thus, although the NCP may issue a statement and make recommendations as appropriate on the implementation of the Guidelines, scenarios have shown that recalcitrant multinational enterprises may resist changing their corporate behaviour. Consequently, the content and effectiveness of the final NCP report is limited.

In a positive development for promoting investments directed at sustainable development, the latest amendment to the Agreement eased rules for renewable energy and clean water projects.[33] However, the Guidelines do not provide for monitoring schemes or accounting methods integrating social or environmental dimensions of corporate performance. As an informal agreement, the Arrangement does not have the attributes of hard law: it is concretized without the need for formal signature, ratification, and amendment processes. Although the Arrangement benefits from OECD administrative support, it is not an official act. Rather than being within the domain of soft law, Levit argues that the Arrangement closely approximates a social norm among ECAs and maybe even a codification of customary practice among ECAs.[34] The terms of entry, exit, and amendment procedures as well as the text's insistence on its non-binding status

[29] OECD, Decision of the Council on the OECD Guidelines for Multinational Enterprises at 4, OECD Doc. C(2000)96/FINAL (2000), published on the Internet at: http://www.olis.oecd.org/olis/2000doc.nsf.

[30] OECD Directorate for Fin., Fiscal & Enter. Affairs, Survey of OECD Work on International Investment (1998), at 6 published on the Internet at: http://www.oecd.org/dataoecd/0/59/2111393.pdf.

[31] See Organization for Economic Co-operation and Development (OECD), OECD Statistics Portal, published on the Internet at: http://www.oecd.org/statsportal/0,3352,en_2825_293564_1_1_1_1_1,00.html.

[32] OECD, Decision of the Council on the OECD Guidelines for Multinational Enterprises at 4, OECD Doc. C(2000)96/FINAL (2000), published on the Internet at: http://www.olis.oecd.org/olis/2000doc.nsf.

[33] Ibid., Annex IV: Sector Understanding on Export Credits, Renewable Energies and Water Projects, in force for a trial period until 30 June 2007. Eligible sectors include wind energy; geothermal energy; tidal and tidal stream power; wave power; solar and photovoltaic power; solar thermal energy; ocean thermal energy, and bio-energy. Also included are projects related to the supply of water for human use and wastewater treatment facilities: infrastructure providing drinking water to households; waste water collection and treatment facilities; and hydropower.

[34] Levit, n. 5 above.

definitely give credence to the soft law stance. The Arrangement serves as a safe harbour for the WTO's Agreement on Subsidies and Countervailing Measures (Agreement on Subsidies); it prohibits export subsidies that are conditioned on export performance (i.e. ECAs to promote exports) but condones ECA support of domestic exports under certain conditions. In addition, some Participant countries have incorporated the Arrangement into domestic law.

B. From Common Approaches to the Recommendation of Common Approaches under the OECD Arrangement

In 2001, due to a veto of two Member States, the OECD countries were not able to reach a legally binding agreement on common approaches on environment and officially supported export credits. During this time, environmental reviews of projects benefiting from officially supported export credits were conducted by OECD members on a voluntary basis and largely followed the 2001 Common Approaches. Following two years of practice and an extensive review by OECD Member States, the OECD Council adopted the 2003 Recommendation of Common Approaches. The Recommendation is not a legally binding document, but according to the OECD's own assessment, it carries an enhanced 'moral' weight that should compel Member States to implement the principles in full.

The 2003 Recommendation slightly strengthened the Common Approaches in the following ways:

- Projects should, in all cases, comply with the environmental standards of the host country. When the relevant international standards against which the project has been benchmarked are more stringent, these standards should be applied.
- The relevant international standards are those of the World Bank Group and, where applicable from a geographical viewpoint, those of Regional Development Banks. Members may also benchmark against any higher internationally recognised environmental standards, such as those of the European Community.
- With regard to the most sensitive projects, the environmental standards to be applied will be reported and monitored by the ECG and exceptional deviations below international standards will have to be justified.
- For the most sensitive projects, ECG members will seek to make environmental information, particularly Environmental Impact Assessment Reports, publicly available 30 calendar days before final commitment.[35]

According to these provisions, it is incumbent on OECD members to request from exporters, financial institutions, and project sponsors information not only on a project's potential environmental impacts, but also 'the environmental

[35] OECD, 'OECD Adopts Stronger Environmental Common Approaches for Export Credits' published on the Internet at: http://www.oecd.org/document/56/0,3343,en_2649_34181_21688824_1_1_1_1,00.html.

standards, practices and processes' to be applied to the project; 'the results of any public consultations on the project with relevant stakeholders'; and where appropriate, whether the project indicates the need for an EIA.[36]

The OECD later updated the Recommendation in 2005 to clarify the size of power plants regulated and finally revised the entire document in 2007.[37] The 2007 Common Approaches tightens the language and contains several clarifications including a modified Annex III outlining new *ex post* reporting obligations. Moreover, the Preamble states that risks emanating from existing operations should also be evaluated in the environmental reviews undertaken by ECAs. While existing projects do not require a full-fledged environmental review by the ECA, the environmental risk should be evaluated if the contribution to an existing project is above the 10 million SDR threshold ('Screening': para. 4).

It is clear from the amended objectives of the updated instrument that further strengthening of the international dimension of this policy is of pre-eminent importance (a modification likely stemming from awareness that several non-OECD countries were becoming increasingly active in the export credit domain). Members agreed that their goal is to: 'Promote a level playing field for officially supported export credits and increase awareness and understanding, including among Non-Member Economies, of the benefits of applying this Recommendation' (Objectives, para. 2). The 2007 Recommendation also details the international benchmarks against which the projects should be evaluated. International environmental standards (conforming to those of the EC in the case of the OECD) should be used if they are stricter than domestic standards that would normally take precedence. In the event that an ECA eschews a stricter set of standards, the rationales behind the decision must be provided in the annual report. The benchmarks now expressly include all ten World Bank safeguard policies:[38] safeguard policies relating to Environmental Assessment (OP 4.01); Natural Habitats (OP 4.04); Pest Management (OP 4.09); Indigenous Peoples (OP 4.10); Physical Cultural Resources (OP 4.11); Involuntary Resettlement (OP 4.12); Forests (OP 4.36); Safety of Dams (OP 4.37); International Waterways (OP 7.50); and Disputed Areas (OP 7.60).[39] For projects limited to the private sector or non-recourse project finance cases, the standards are provided by the relevant aspects of all eight World Bank International Finance Corporation

[36] Ibid.

[37] OECD, 'Revised Council Recommendation on Common Approaches on the Environment and officially supported Export Credits' OECD Doc. TAD/ECG(2007)9 of 12 June 2007, published on the Internet at: http://webdomino1.oecd.org/olis/2007doc.nsf/43bb6130e5e86e5fc12569fa005d004c/d4572f5ee6bc6d72c12572f800561d56/$FILE/JT03228987.PDF.

[38] For details on World Bank safeguard policies, see M. Gehring, *Nachhaltigkeit durch Verfahren im Welthandelsrecht—Umwelt—und Nachhaltigkeitsprüfungen und die WTO* (Berlin: Dunker & Humblot, 2007), at 52.

[39] See footnote 4 of the 2007 OECD Recommendation of Common Approaches on Environment and Officially Export Credits, published on the Internet at: http://www.exim.gov/news/21684464.pdf.

Performance Standard including the Social and Environmental Assessment and Management System; Labour and Working Conditions and Pollution Prevention and Abatement.[40] The 2007 Recommendation also strengthened the publication requirements: ECAs are now obliged to publish their environmental policies and procedures, make large projects public and allow EIAs to be accessible where possible (para. 19). ECAs are also encouraged to consult with civil society organizations and share their experience with non-OECD member agencies (para. 20) and to build up a body of knowledge surrounding the application of the Recommendation for *ex post* reporting purposes.

From a broader perspective, it appears that the modest intensification of obligations and outreach to non-OECD states active in export credit activities (such as Russia and China) strikes a fair balance between ECA responsibilities and developing country sovereignty. Advancements aside, the 2007 Recommendation is simply one of many existing voluntary universal codes of conduct, or 'soft law' recommendations and guidelines that address corporate social responsibility (CSR). Other instruments in this category include the Business Charter for Sustainable Development of the International Chamber of Commerce (the ICC Charter), the CERES Principles, the Global Reporting Initiative, the Global Sullivan Principles, the Principles for Global Corporate Responsibility: Benchmarks, and the United Nations Global Compact.[41]

C. International Union of Credit and Investment Insurers (Berne Union)

The International Union of Credit and Investment Insurers (Berne Union) is a non-governmental institution composed of both private and public export credit insurers that regulates the way its members conduct business. On the basis of industry practice, the Berne Union has codified technical rules that circumscribe the nature and scope of members export credit insurance policies. Over time, international law-making institutions have appropriated some of these rules and effectively transformed them into hard law. The Berne Union has a three-fold mandate:

1. promote 'sound principles of export credit insurance' at the international level;
2. act as a conduit for the exchange of information to assist Berne Union members in their formulation of sound insurance practices; and
3. oversee and discipline the terms of credit extended for international trade.[42]

[40] Ibid., at footnote 5.

[41] For details and a legal discussion on these initiatives see M. Kerr and M.-C. Cordonier Segger, 'Corporate Social Responsibility: International Strategies and Regimes' in M.-C. Cordonier Segger and C. G. Weeramantry (eds.) *Sustainable Justice: Reconciling Economic, Social and Environmental Law*, (The Hague: Martinus Nijhoff, 2004), at 135.

[42] International Union of Credit and Investment Insurers, The Berne Union Agreements, Understandings and Obligations in the Export Credit Insurance Field: General Understanding art I(i) (2001).

Overall, the Berne Union rules promote information exchange and transactional transparency. The Berne Union compiles and disseminates information obtained from members regarding claims on public sector and private sector buyers, payment problems in transactions financed by international institutions, and instances of fraud. The Berne Union is an example of a 'small, niche lawmaking group bound by a type of stubborn, constitutional secrecy that clashes with prevailing international norms of accountability and transparency'.[43] Although the Berne Union's General Understanding is classified as soft international law, it is possible that Members view the rules as more compelling than mere guidelines or suggested best practices. This perception is exemplified by steadfast adherence and the fact that behaviour that breaches the Understanding requires notification. Through appropriation by the Arrangement, many Berne Union rules have hardened into law—international and domestic—applicable to both credit insurance and the provision of other types of export credit.

In sum, the Arrangement is explicitly a soft law agreement; its terms and the nature of mutual understandings of the participants preclude characterization as formal international law. The Berne Union's General Understanding is merely a set of 'understandings and agreements' that members have 'summarized and consolidated' for their convenience and is devoid of a firm legal commitment. The Uniform Customs and Practices 500 is a set of guidelines that describe bank practice and are drafted by private parties that happen to be members of the International Chamber of Commerce; it cannot be classified as binding international law as it evades technical international law categories.

To date, the Berne Union has only acknowledged a minimal responsibility to ensure that sustainable development objectives are buttressed—not contravened—by its membership. In its 2006 Guiding Principles, the organizations 'confirm[ed] [their] commitment to operate in a professional manner that is financially responsible, respectful of the environment and which demonstrates high ethical values'.[44] To that end, 'various members' of the Berne Union have inter alia worked on environmental, social, and ethical assessment of projects and towards combating bribery. Unfortunately, this tentative endorsement is much weaker than the OECD Recommendation on Common Approaches or other affiliated CSR business principles.

IV. Sustainable Development Challenges

The following section discusses sustainable development challenges—both systematic and practical—that confront modifications to the legal regime regulating ECAs.

[43] Levit, n. 5 above.

[44] Berne Union, 'Berne Union Guiding Principles', published on the Internet at: http://www.berneunion.org.uk/Berne%20Union%20Guiding%20Principles.pdf.

One of the most obvious manners in which ECA activity can impact on sustainable development is the fact a large proportion of the financing is directed towards large infrastructure projects in developing countries. Indeed, while the international community pressures developing countries to ensure that their poverty alleviation strategies do not have huge negative environmental externalities—like contributing to greenhouse gas emissions—ECAs are financing activities that often result in severe ecosystem deterioration. Indeed, as it is inherently complicated to fruitfully balance the positive developmental aspects of providing reliable energy (in the case of dams, for instance) or other societal benefits and the negative implications of environmental deterioration and population dislocation, ECAs together with exporters and importers operate in a highly controversial space. There is no doubt that ECAs profit handsomely from undertaking projects that may degrade the quality of live and viability of ecosystem services provided to local communities.

As mentioned previously, one of the systematic challenges for the OECD regime is its soft law status whereby member States are free to adopt stricter or more lenient rules. This flexibility creates a degree of uncertainty which might be useful for exporters in certain instances but has the potential to make decisions in developing countries by buyers and their governments a complex, ambiguous undertaking. Thus, the lack of a binding international legal regime that comprehensively regulates the transactions involving export credits and other similar instruments and services offered by export credit agencies can be seen as a gap in legal certainty on all sides. A firm legal framework on the other hand, could stipulate that socio-economic development is balanced with environmental protection in a manner that fits the imperatives of the particular context. However, in no way should export credits be a vehicle for imposing views on what constitutes sustainable development on recipient groups.

One other systematic challenge is the right degree of supervision. ECAs should not be forced to second guess sustainable development considerations in a third country. Northern NGOs might argue that until recently, ECAs evaded monitoring by civil society.[45] However, some high profile projects—both underway and in the preliminary design process—have precipitated fervent backlash about the ambiguous status of these agencies and dearth of stakeholder consultation.[46]

[45] ECA Watch: International NGO Campaign on Export Credit Agencies is an example of a network of civil society groups seeking to rectify the information deficit on ECA activity and advocating the derivation of more stringent social and environmental rules in this realm. ECA Watch indicts ECAs as 'one of the biggest sources of financing for harmful projects; undercutting progress and violating laws; fueling a "race to the bottom" almost completely lacking transparency; contemptuous of affected communities; promoting corrupt practices; adding to a crushing debt for developing nations; facilitating arms transfers and human rights abuses; increasing the very risks they were created to protect companies against; assuming no responsibility'. Published on the Internet at: http://www.eca-watch.org/problems/energy/index.html.

[46] Some examples, highlighted by the NGO network and verified by independent expert assessments include the proposed Ilisu Dam (Turkey), Maheshwar Dam (India), and San Roque Hydropower and Irrigation Project (Philippines), ibid.

Advocacy groups also complain about a lack of transparency surrounding ECA operations and accuse ECAs of impeding sustainable development and causing irreparable environmental damage and social dislocation.

On the other hand, it is a fair question if countries (even where ECAs are now privatized, but where States retain at least nominal public ownership) could incur a degree of international responsibility arising from the operations of their ECAs. It has long been recognized that sanctioning financing activities can result in international state responsibility.[47] Depending on the degree of control over ECA activities wielded by the sponsoring State, there is the possibility that it could be liable for violations of international law (such as international environmental or human rights norms) resulting from its supported projects. Even though this debate is in its incipient stages, it has arguably had the effect of compelling States to seek to exercise a high degree of control over the assessment of ECA sponsored projects. These criticisms led in part to the development of the OECD Recommendation that seems to strike a fair balance because it mainly relies on procedural promotion and documentation such as EIAs. Moving forward, the debate about State responsibility could have the effect of further multilateralizing the process whereby the review of documentation is not confined to the relevant ECA but is delegated to international environmental institutions that could provide expert advice and guidance.

On a more practical level, there is potential for the OECD Arrangement and Recommendation to be conceived of as a foundation upon which Member States may actively and unilaterally use procedural tools geared towards sustainable development. New instruments such as sustainability impact assessment could be employed to expand the scope of the impact assessments to encompass social and perhaps even human rights provisions.

A. Sustainability Impact Assessment

The European Union (EU) has developed and applied an integrated Sustainability Impact Assessment (SIA) to its trade policy proposals but the methodology could be used for a much broader range of assessments.[48] One of the first examples was the Sustainability Impact Assessment Study of the proposed *Millennium Round* negotiations in the World Trade Organization (WTO), which was commissioned by the European Commission. The first phase of the SIA included a review of

[47] J Crawford, *The International Law Commission's Articles on State Responsibility Introduction, Text and Commentaries* (Cambridge: Cambridge University Press, 2002).

[48] See for a description of the EU Trade SIA, M. C. Cordonier Segger and M. W. Gehring, 'Sustainable Development Through Process in World Trade Law' in M. C. Cordonier Segger and M. W. Gehring (eds.), *Sustainable Development and World Trade Law* (The Hague: Kluwer Law International, 2005) and for project SIAs, R. B. Gibson, *Sustainability Assessment—Criteria and Processes* (London: Earthscan, 2005).

literature on trade-related assessments (covering economic, social, and environmental impacts relevant to sustainable development), an examination of relevant cases where these assessment methodologies have been applied with an evaluation of their effectiveness, and a proposal for a fully defined SIA methodology.[49]

The second phase was quite comprehensive, involving an examination of the potential sustainability impact of each measure that might have been covered within the WTO negotiations. Impacts, positive and negative, were assessed for four groups of countries—the EU, developing countries, least-developed countries, and the world as a whole. The findings distinguished those areas where negotiations were likely to have a relatively limited impact and those where the impact might have been greater. Additionally, proposals were formulated for mitigation and enhancing measures. In particular, the study examined 'core sustainability indicators' (including economic factors such as average real income, net fixed capital information and employment; social factors such as equity and poverty; health and education, and gender inequalities; and environmental factors such as ecological quality (covering air, water, and land), biological diversity; and other natural resource stocks. This was done in the context of 'significance criteria' (including the extent of existing economic, social, and environmental stress, in affected areas; direction of changes to baseline conditions; nature, order of magnitude, geographic extent and duration of changes; and regulatory and institutional capacity to implement mitigation measures). The SIA then consisted of four main phases:

1. *screening*: to determine which measures require SIA because they are likely to have significant impacts;
2. *scoping*: to establish the appropriate coverage of each SIA;
3. *preliminary sustainability assessment*: to identify potentially significant effects, positive and negative, on sustainable development; and
4. *mitigation and enhancement analysis*: to suggest types of improvements which may enhance the overall impact on sustainable development of New Round Agenda measures.

There were also extensive procedures for public participation and consultation with civil society organizations. Numerous workshops and consultations were held at each phase of reports, and a website was designated with reports, timely publications and informal mechanisms for involvement during the process.[50]

[49] See recent overview by C. George and C. Kirkpatrick, 'Trade and Development: Assessing the impact of Trade Liberalisation on Sustainable Development' (2004) 38 *Journal of World Trade* 3, at 441 and earlier C. Kirkpatrick, N. Lee, and O. Morrissey, *WTO New Round: Sustainability Impact Assessment Study (Phase One Report)* (Manchester: IDPM University of Manchester, 1999).

[50] C. Kirkpatrick and N. Lee, *WTO New Round: Sustainability Impact Assessment Study (Phase Two Report)*, Published on the Internet at: http://trade.ec.europa.eu/doclib/docs/2005/february/tradoc_111191.pdf. The Study examined changes to agreement on agriculture, changes to the

The SIA shows evidence of being a fully integrated instrument, which takes into consideration economic, social, and environmental concerns at the level of methodology and indicators. While the original mechanism, EIA, developed out of a rapidly evolving aspect of international environmental law, the more it was used, the more pressure was generated to include social criteria in this instrument designed to evaluate economic development initiatives. This appears to be a successful way to address sustainable development concerns in a more holistic manner.

Another type of assessment tool might be applicable: human rights assessment work has been undertaken by the International Center for Human Rights and Democratic Development, an independent Canadian institution created by an Act of Parliament.[51] The international mandate of the organization is to cooperate with the Canadian government, governments abroad, and civil society in order to defend the democratic and human rights specified in the International Bill of Human Rights. The overarching principles that inform this sort of impact assessment framework are transparency (important in both process and content, stakeholders have the right to seek and receive information); accountability (duty bearers include government and corporate actors: access to an adequate remedy is crucial); participation (both at the individual and community level, the applicable rights include right to information, freedom of expression and opinion, security of the person, and the right to privacy); non-discrimination (encompasses the right to equality and protection before the law: vulnerable groups are identified and empowered); and indivisibility (social, economic, cultural, civil, and political human rights are interconnected). The methodology developed included ten steps. The preparation of the case study includes scoping which is an overview of the human rights situation at the national level including ratified international human rights instruments; reports published by NGOs, UN agencies, and experts; national policies and legislation and other related data.

General Agreement on Trade in Services (GATS), development of a multilateral framework of rules relating to international investment, development of a multilateral framework of rules relating to competition, measures relating to trade facilitation, further measures relating to tariffs on non-agricultural products, clarification of the relationship between WTO rules and trade measures taken pursuant to multilateral environmental agreements and other environmental policy initiatives, changes to the agreement to strengthen the global protection of intellectual property rights (TRIPS), measures to improve market access in government procurement policies and practices, measures relating to technical barriers to trade (TBT), measures relating to the protection of human health, measures relating to the use of trade defence instruments (anti-dumping, subsidies, agreement on safeguards), horizontal measures to promote development, various trade and core labour standard issues, various other issues relating to treatment of products of least-developed countries, transparency, coherence of policies between WTO and other international organizations, the dispute settlement mechanism, and electronic commerce.

[51] For more information, see also S. Walker, 'Human Rights Impact Assessments of Trade-Related Policies', in Gehring and Cordonier Segger (eds.), n. 48 above.

The scoping process includes input from affected stakeholders; NGOs; company representatives; governments; and other experts. The second phase entails specific research on the investment project including collecting available data about the company and the prospective investment; records of interaction with both home and host states; existing social and environmental impact assessments related to the project; and information about financing from ECAs, banks, or other multilateral agencies. Based on the two preliminary steps, the impact assessment is adapted to the project by pinpointing the relevant questions and indicators. Next, the application of the research guide necessitates seeking expert opinion on key human rights issues; interviewing representatives of the community, workers, company and government; and verifying information and reconciling factual disputes. The report preparation involves creating a draft report, developing conclusions and recommendations for corrective action, and issuing a final report. After the report is completed, provisions are made for ongoing monitoring and evaluation as necessary. It is important to note that there are different methodologies for human rights impact assessment that may have substantive variations from the one outlined above.[52]

In practical terms, and to harness the potential for export credit activities to further sustainable development goals, it should be ensured that projects conform to sustainable development precepts such as public participation, transparency, and an integrated impact assessment process conducted during the preliminary design stages. Further, true adherence to the essence of sustainable development could mandate the availability of judicial remedies. Simply raising design and implementation standards is hardly a panacea as ECAs exist within a highly competitive realm. Further, invoking policies that suffocate the extension of credit would effectively impede funds that are no longer provided through Official Development Assistance (ODA) avenues. Cognizant of the fact that that Agenda 21, adopted at the 1992 Earth Summit, estimated that more than $600 billion would be needed each year between 1993 and 2000 to assist developing countries in achieving sustainable development,[53] and that ODA levels have been steadily declining since 1993, the increase in foreign direct investment (FDI) is considered by many to be imperative.

[52] A report on the experiences of the Philippines, Tibet, the Democratic Republic of Congo, Argentina, and Peru has been published on the Internet at: http://www.dd-rd.ca/site/_PDF/publications/globalization/hria/full%20report_may_2007.pdf (accessed 7 Oct. 2007).

[53] UN Conference on Environment and Development, Agenda 21: Programme of Action for Sustainable Development, UN Sales No. E.93.I.11 (1992), at 3, 251, published on the Internet at: http://www.un.org/esa/sustdev/documents/docs.htm.

V. Case Studies: Export Credits Practice, Related Adjudication and Sustainable Development Implications in the European Union, Germany, France, Canada, and the US

A. Export Credits and Sustainable Development in the EU

OECD Arrangement has been integrated into EU law via Council Decision 2001/76/EC on the Application of Certain Guidelines in the Field of Officially Supported Export Credits,[54] Directive 98/29/EC on Export Credit Insurance for Transactions with Medium and Long-term Cover (Credit Insurance Directive) based on Articles 132 and 133 EC,[55] and a Communication on Short-Term Coverage based on Articles 87 and 89 EC.[56] Export financing is partially governed by the Treaty's provisions on external trade: Article 132 and 133 EC provide for the harmonization of export aid. Article 132 EC determines that:

> [...] Member States shall progressively harmonize the systems by which they grant aid for exports to third countries, to the extent necessary to ensure that competition between undertakings of the Community is not distorted.

However, the Credit Insurance Directive fails to specify the terms of and procedural steps under which environmental impact assessments need to be conducted prior to insuring or financing a particular project or what levels of environmental sustainability must be attained. The Credit Insurance Directive also neglects to provide avenues for public participation—especially for those affected by the project—or minimum requirements for project transparency.

Export guarantees in intra-European and especially intra-EU trade are very rare and highly contentious. Short-term export guarantees and loans are generally forbidden unless granted under market conditions because they directly compete with commercial banks; even long-term guarantees in the inner-European context typically compete with commercial loan facilities. Thus, it is in this space that the true purpose of export guarantees (i.e. to cover export risks resulting from unstable economic relations) is actualized. A recent case study taking place within the EC illustrated the dissention that the European regime has failed to mitigate entirely. Among other points of contention, the altercation had environmental elements at its core.

Finland is in the process of constructing Europe's first new, allegedly subsidy-free (a private consortium is providing the funds) nuclear power plant.[57] The

[54] [2001] OJ L32/1.

[55] [1998] OJ L148/22.

[56] Communication of the Commission to Member States amending the communication pursuant to Art. 93(1) of the EC Treaty applying Arts. 92 and 93 of the Treaty to short-term export credit insurance, [1998] OJ C217/2.

[57] See Commission Dec. in Case NN 62/B/2006 and CFI, Case T-94/07 *EREF* v. *Commission*, Application published in [2007] OJ C117/31.

French and Swedish export credit agencies are heavily supporting the reactor: the Swedish export credit agency granted a loan worth €100 million and the French Export Guarantee Agency (Coface) provided a non-notified amount of €610 million. The magnitude of the finances involved prompted a legal challenge under EU subsidy rules whereby an export credit provided to one company in one Member State can be deemed a prohibited subsidy that is actionable by competitors. The main question to be resolved is whether in fact the French guarantee and Swedish loan can be classified as subsidies. Under the OECD Arrangement, any export credit compliant with the precepts should be exempt from subsidy scrutiny. However, export credits directed towards the financing of nuclear projects have a special set of conditions attached.[58] Moreover, even though environmental impact assessments compulsory under Finnish law were carried out, the findings from this process failed to diffuse environmental questions emanating from the special regime levied on renewable energy producers. In other words, it begs the question whether inherently risky and some say dangerous technologies do not require an extra regime for granting export credits. While there is little doubt in this case that international standards will be complied with, further deference to international organizations such as the International Atomic Energy Agency (IAEA), could have become involved to help the French authorities to assess the applied standards.[59]

In sustainable development terms it is interesting that Sweden has noted in the EC CSR register that it 'believes that export credits are an important instrument in promoting CSR'.[60] The Swedish Export Credits Guarantee Board provides all its customers with information on the Swedish Partnership for Global Responsibility, existing regulations on bribery, and the OECD Guidelines for Multinational Enterprises.[61]

[58] The 2005 OECD Arrangement on Export Credits contains regulations pertaining to the financing of nuclear power plants in Annex II, published on the Internet at: http://webdomino1.oecd.org/olis/2005doc.nsf/43bb6130e5e86e5fc12569fa005d004c/23013c0293535d25c12570cf003e35ed/$FILE/JT00195558.PDF.

[59] A second issue involved the incongruent environmental priorities among Member States bound within a common electricity market. In 1969 the European Court of Justice (ECJ) decided that export credits and insurance subsidies are generally deemed illegal for intra-Community commerce: 'export aid in intra-Community trade cannot qualify for derogation whatever their intensity, form, grounds or purpose' and that Arts. 92 and 93 EC apply. Subsequently, a Commission Communication in 1977 reiterated this legal assessment. Among other insights, this particular example illustrates that the requirement of an EIA might not always be sufficient for environmental concerns to be defused: in some cases, a subsidy challenge by competitors is the only way to reinforce sustainable development priorities shared by several countries. The Commission's decision to open a formal subsidy investigation, however, did not result in a tightening of legal scrutiny for the flow of export credits that remain within the Community. The Commission decided that the record export credit granted could have been obtained on the financial markets and thus did not constitute state aid. See EU Press release 'State aid: Commission concludes that French state guarantee for Finnish nuclear power plant operator TVO does not constitute aid' IP/07/1400 of 26 Sept. 2007.

[60] EC DG Employment & Social, published on the Internet at: http://ec.europa.eu/employment_social/emplweb/csr-matrix/csr_topic_allcountries_en.cfm?field=15.

[61] Ibid.

B. Export Credits and Sustainable Development in Germany

In 1949, the Federal Government of Germany issued a mandate entrusting the management of the export guarantee scheme to two private companies: Euler Hermes Kreditversicherungs-AG and PwC AG.[62] Since Euler Hermes is lead partner in this consortium, export guarantees provided from this group became known among German companies as 'Hermes cover'. The consortium functions as a consultancy service that offers advice to exporters and banks; prepares cover applications to be submitted to the Federal government; and in the event that submission is successful, Euler Hermes supplies the insured companies with ongoing advice as the project proceeds.[63] In instances where receivables are lost, the consortium is tasked with processing claims. The Federal Ministry for Economics and Labour, the pre-eminent ministry where export credits are concerned, deliberates on the merits of an application for cover in the Inter-ministerial Committee (IMC).[64] Analogous to the policies enacted by other OECD Member States, the Federal German Government supports direct investments by German companies in developing and emerging countries by covering political risks and by offering investors long-term protection.[65]

The environmental procedure applied by the Federal Government for all applications for officially supported export credits is based on two bodies of guiding principles. The relevant text at the national level is 'Guiding Principles Environment: Consideration of Ecological, Social and Developmental Aspects' adopted by the IMC on 26 April 2001, and at OECD level, Germany adheres to the 'Recommendation on Common Approaches on Environment and Officially Supported Export Credits' discussed above. The legal framework of the national 'Guiding Principles' is the Foreign Trade and Payments law—in particular the export control regulations.[66] However, the document also suggests that 'general laws and legal provisions of inter-governmental institutions and relevant international arrangements with direct binding effects in the Federal Republic of Germany' are legally relevant (i.e. regulations to safeguard against hazardous chemicals).[67] The primary criteria for receipt of cover are the eligibility of support and the justifiability of risk.[68]

[62] More information is available on the Internet at: http://www.eulerhermes.com/ger/ger/ (accessed 6 Mar. 2006).

[63] Ibid.

[64] Ibid. The IMC is composed of the Federal Ministry of Economics and Labour—lead function—the Federal Ministry of Finance, the Federal Foreign Office, and the Federal Ministry for Economic Co-operation and Development.

[65] Ibid.

[66] The Official Export Guarantee Scheme of the Federal Republic of Germany Guiding Principles Environment: Consideration of Ecological, Social and Developmental Aspects is published on the Internet at: http://www.agaportal.de/pdf/eng/guiding_principles_e.pdf (accessed 6 Mar. 2006).

[67] Ibid.

[68] Ibid.

As reinforcing sustainable development in developing and transitioning countries is a chief goal of its foreign policy, the Federal Government shows itself eager to support projects that are ecologically and socially sustainable (in particular, renewable energies) through export guarantees.[69] Thus, ecological, social, and developmental impacts are encompassed under the environmental reviews undertaken for every prospective project beyond a certain monetary threshold. Transparency and public disclosure are reiterated at various points throughout the screening process as well as during subsequent environmental assessments and project monitoring phases.[70] As a signatory of the OECD Recommendation, Germany's typology scheme for projects and the description concerning compliance with benchmarking standards are consistent with those contained in the international agreement.

Despite their adherence to the OECD Recommendation, Euler Hermes has recently come under the scrutiny of environmental groups. In particular, the German ECA has been accused of supporting projects that contravene sustainable development goals by emitting high quantities of greenhouse gases (GHG). In a mutual settlement before the Administrative Court of Berlin, the German Federal Government agreed to provide the litigants with the GHG emission information for energy projects supported by Euler Hermes.[71] Germany's ECA has also funded coal plants: the Paiton 2 coal energy plant in Indonesia has received criticism because of alleged corruption and Indonesia's great potential for sustainable alternatives, such as geothermal or solar power.[72] Another contention case, involving Euler Hermes' support of a dam in India's Uttaranchal region in partnership with the Tehri Hydro Development Corporation (THDC), began in 1972 and has been plagued with environmental concerns such as its ill-advised location in the Central Himalayan Seismic Zone, making it vulnerable to direct damage from earthquakes or indirect destruction from landslides. Germany's ECA, alongside the ECAs of the UK, France, Italy, the US, and Japan has supported the financing of the Baku-T'bilisi-Ceyhan pipeline which is intended to carry oil from the Caspian to the Mediterranean Sea for shipment to the West. NGO lead investigations have shown that the pipeline does not adhere to any formal environmental standards and has been a source of social and political conflicts across Azerbaijan, Georgia, and Turkey.[73] Financiers have been criticized

[69] Ibid.

[70] Ibid. Should special environmental covenants be the basis for granting cover, the exporter can be bound to inform about their fulfillment by means of regular monitoring reports.

[71] See T. Schomerus and S. Clausen, 'Informationspflicht Privater nach dem neuen Umweltinformationsgesetz am Beispiel der Exportkreditversicherung' (2005) 12 *Zeitschrift für Umweltrecht*, 575.

[72] Project details can be found at ECA Watch, published on the Internet at: http://www.eca-watch.org/problems/eu_russ/germany/index.html#Hermes (accessed 5 Oct. 2007).

[73] Ibid.

for their lack of dependability in monitoring the construction of the project.[74] Again these examples can show that a multilateral approach could probably have dampened some of the NGO criticisms. If the assessment of the environmental and social impacts is carried out by a third party and not in the trilateral relationship between ECA, exporter, and host country, a larger degree of objectivity would be possible.

C. Export Credits and Sustainable Development in France

Compagnie Française d'Assurance pour le Commerce Extérieur (Coface) is France's ECA; it specializes in the provision of medium and long-term credit insurance; marketing services; information about prospective markets and financing of various sorts.[75] Coface employs two environmental specialists in the medium and long term insurance department that collaborate with underwriters. All applications for credit insurance must be accompanied by an 'environment appendix' completed by the exporter. In order to comply with the OECD Directive, Coface has created a list of sector-based environmental guidelines and publishes information on major contracts on a quarterly basis. From an environmental perspective, this list includes a description of the project as well as an elucidation of the likely environmental impacts emanating from the endeavour and Coface's response to the anticipated results. Since March 2004, France's ECA has ensured that environmental information for particularly sensitive projects is available to the public 30 days prior to a final decision on the matter.

Environmental screening of a project is non-negotiable if the total amount of the contract is greater than or equal to €10 million or if the project is located in an environmentally sensitive area.[76] However, Coface may determine on a case-by-case basis whether a full EIA is obligatory for the exporter. Similar to the taxonomy used by other ECAs, there are three classifications of projects with varying degrees of environmental interaction. For Classes A and B, there must be an identification of the potential impacts (i.e. atmospheric emission; consumption of natural resources; management of waste and hazardous material); an exploration of the impacts on the ecosystem (including the human element of indigenous peoples and cultural heritage); an assessment of the necessary mitigation techniques to be employed; a final expert opinion and eventual follow up if necessary.[77] According to its documentation, Coface aspires to apply the strictest standards—whether international or local—in the analysis process.

[74] Ibid. See 'Casualties of the Oil Stampede Along the BTC' *The Guardian*, 15 June 2005; 'Now That Oil Flow Has Begun: the BTC Explained', *The Guardian*, 26 May 2005.

[75] Coface's website is published on the Internet at: http://www.coface.fr/CofacePortal/redirection.jsp?pageID=pages/home&site=FR_fr_FR (accessed 24 Sept. 2007).

[76] For the complete policy framework see the Coface website at : http://www.coface.fr/dmt/en/_docs/environmentGB.pdf (accessed 24 Sept. 2007).

[77] Ibid.

The French government has submitted to the EC that French companies are systematically informed about the OECD guidelines in a process whereby a letter issued by Coface is sent to companies which subsequently return a signed statement attesting to the fact that they are aware of the expectations.[78]

D. Export Credits and Sustainable Development in Canada

Canada's ECA—'Export Development Canada' (EDC)—provides services such as financing, insurance, and bonding in 200 markets worldwide including 130 emerging markets.[79] As a publicly owned corporation, EDC reports to Parliament through the Minister for International Trade and is regulated primarily through the *Financial Administration Act*. EDC's annual report and corporate plan summary are tabled yearly in Parliament and the Auditor General of Canada is the auditor of the corporation. The Minister for International Trade and Treasury Board must approve EDC's corporate plan and the Minister of Finance must approve EDC's borrowing plan each year.

The purported focus of the Agency is to assist small and medium-sized enterprises with flexible coverage of losses up to 90 per cent; short-term coverage for one customer,[80] and insurance for online transactions of up to US$250 000. In terms of contract insurance for capital goods, service contracts and projects, the EDC provides protection against wrongful bond draws; coverage against losses and 'Political Risk Insurance' (PRI) which guards against instability in emerging markets.[81] The PRI service provides asset protection of up to 90 per cent regardless of the size of investment. Contract Frustration Insurance protects Canadian companies against losses related to specific export contracts for services, capital goods, or projects and covers up to 90 per cent of the costs incurred or receivables lost. Contract Frustration Insurance insures Canadian companies against a range of commercial and political risks, including: buyer insolvency; cancellation of export or import licences and permits; host government's moratorium on debt; non-conversion of currency or inability to transfer funds; non-payment or default by the customer; termination or cancellation of the contract by the customer; and war, revolution, insurrection, or other political disturbances.

[78] EC DG Employment & Social, 'CSR: National Public Policies in the European Union' published on the Internet at: http://ec.europa.eu/employment_social/emplweb/csr-matrix/csr_topic_allcountries_en.cfm?field=15.

[79] For information about Export Development Canada, see their website published on the Internet: at http://www.edc.ca/english/index.htm (accessed 24 Sept. 2007).

[80] The policy insures up to 90 per cent of a Canadian company's losses against non-payment after its customer has accepted the goods that may occur for a number of reasons, including: failure to pay; bankruptcy or insolvency; currency conversion and transfer; war, revolution, or insurrection.

[81] Political risks covered by PRI include: breach of contract risk; conversion risk; expropriation risk (including gradual or creeping expropriation); non-payment by a sovereign obligor; political violence risk; repossession risk; and transfer risk.

'Canada Account' is used to support export transactions which EDC is unable to support, but which the Minister for International Trade considers to be in Canada's national interest. EDC's inability to support is usually due to a combination of risks, which can include the size of the transaction, market risks, EDC's country capacity, borrower risks, and/or the financing conditions. National interest considerations include: economic benefits and costs to Canada; importance of the export market to Canada; and foreign policy implications. Canada Account transactions are negotiated, executed, and administered by EDC on the same basis as Corporate Account activities but the risks under Canada Account are assumed by the Federal government. Before EDC enters into a Canada Account transaction, it requires the authorization of the Minister for International Trade, with the concurrence of the Minister of Finance.

In 2001, the ECD published its first formal Disclosure Policy,[82] subsequently amended to conform to the OECD Arrangement in 2005. In order to ensure transparency in cases of financing, the provision of political risk insurance to lenders or equity, the EDC will seek consent to inform the public via its website that it is considering support to such project. In addition to the 'Environmental and Social Reporting' there is both individual transaction and aggregate quarterly reporting. However, it is crucial to note that Canada's ECA is not bound by Canada's Access to Information Act.

The Environmental Review Directive sets out the process by which the EDC will, prior to entering a project-related transaction; determine whether the endeavour is likely to have negative environmental implications.[83] Akin to the OECD Arrangement, Projects are categorized according to their likelihood of environmental degradation and more or less comprehensive investigatory and reporting criteria corresponding to the nature of the activity.[84] The threshold for the Directive to become binding is a minimum two years repayment or coverage term and a value of more the SDR 10 million.[85] The environment review information requirements vary from the least comprehensive entailing no EIA for 'Category C' projects to a full EIA for projects classified as 'Category A'.[86]

[82] The text of the policy is published on the Internet at: https://www.edc.ca/english/docs/disclosure_policy_e.pdf (accessed 24 Sept. 2007).

[83] EDC, Environmental Review Dir., published on the Internet at: https://www.edc.ca/english/docs/Environmental_Review_Directive_e.pdf (accessed 24 Sept. 2007). EDC is developing its own environmental assessment framework in consultation with Canadian exporters, environmental organizations, and other stakeholders.

[84] Ibid., at para. 6.

[85] Ibid., at para. 5.

[86] Level 'A' projects include crude oil refineries and gasification installations; thermal power and combustion installations; nuclear power stations; installations designed for the production and enrichment of nuclear fuels; smelting of cast iron and steel; installations for the extraction, processing, and transformation of asbestos; integrated chemical installations; construction of motorways and large airports; pipelines; sea ports; waste processing and disposal installations; ground water abstraction and large scale logging. The full list is found in Annex 2. Category 'B' projects include agri-industry and aquaculture; housing and real estate; irrigation, rural water supply and sanitation

The EIA must conform to both the host country's national laws and the pertinent international standards invoked by multilateral financial institutions and an assortment of mitigation measures may be required depending on the outcome of the exploration process.[87]

The Canadian version of the inclusion of the OECD MNE guidelines is quite outspoken about their voluntary nature.

> The Guidelines provide principles and standards of good practice that countries recommend for the activities of MNEs operating in or from their territories. Observance of the Guidelines is voluntary, and not legally enforceable. Nevertheless, for those countries who have signed the Guidelines (including Canada), they represent concrete expectations for MNEs' behaviour ... The Guidelines are not a substitute for national laws; they represent supplementary standards of behaviour of a non-legal character. Companies operating abroad are expected to observe the national laws of the country where business operations take place.[88]

The two most prominent projects with EDC backing are the Three Gorges Dam in China and the Cernavoda 2 nuclear reactor in Romania. In the former case, the EDC lent the Chinese government CDN $189 million to finance the dam, specifically; it is supporting Canadian companies which provide the Chinese government with generators and a supercomputer to organize the dam's construction. Some parts of civil society have complained about detrimental sustainable development implications of this project, including the displacement of over a million people.[89] In the latter example, the nuclear energy plant has been a magnet for controversy not the least because CANDU reactors have a checkered past that includes malfunctions in similar plants in Argentina and Mexico. The EDC also provided USD $163 million for the Omai Gold Mine in Guyana which filled the Guyanese Amazon with cyanide and heavy metals in 1995 after a dam blocking a waste pond burst. All the local industries that depended on the river could no longer sell their products after exposure to the chemicals.[90]

projects; general manufacturing; textiles; electrical transmission and distribution; tourism and thermal power stations. The full list can be found in Annex 5.

[87] According to the Directive, an EIA should contain the following items: executive summary; policy, legal and administrative framework within which the EIA is carried out; project description (including geographic, ecological, social, and temporal context); baseline data; environmental impacts (quantified where possible, identifies residual negative impacts and mitigation measures; explores opportunities for environmental enhancement; clarification of uncertainties); analysis of alternatives; environmental management plan (describes mitigation, monitoring and institutional measures to be taken during construction and operation to eliminate adverse impacts, offset them or reduce them to acceptable levels); consultation (included affected populations, NGOs and other agencies). Other environmental assessment instruments are listed including an environmental audit; environmental management plan; hazard assessment; environmental risk assessment; corrective action plan; and resettlement action plan. See Annex 4 for details.

[88] EDC, published on the Internet at: http://www.edc.ca/english/social_9582.htm.

[89] See information on the ECA Watch published on the Internet at: http://www.eca-watch.org/problems/americas/canada/index.html (accessed 4 Oct. 2007).

[90] Ibid.

E. Export Credits and Sustainable Development in the US

The Office of International Affairs, and specifically the Office of Trade Finance (ITF), has lead responsibility within the US government for the development, implementation, and enforcement of international trade and aid finance policy.[91] The US government offers US companies insurance for both export transactions (Export-Import Bank) and for overseas investments (OPIC). Coverage includes losses for non-payment, currency inconvertibility, asset expropriation, and political violence.[92] Domestically, ITF oversees US export financing and aid programmes to ensure their compliance with the OECD rules. US government agencies such as the Agency for International Development, Department of Agriculture, Export-Import Bank, Maritime Administration, Overseas Private Investment Corporation, and Trade & Development Agency operate export financing and/or aid programmes.[93] The US advocates strong rules restraining the use of aid subsidies in commercial export competitions, the application of a minimum interest rate and risk-fee rules for officially supported export credits.[94]

In 2005, the actions of Export-Import Bank and the OPIC were challenged when Friends of the Earth, Greenpeace, and four cities joined together to denounce export credit support for large-scale projects involving fossil fuels, such as pipelines, oil fields, and power generation.[95] The plaintiffs tried to force the agencies to apply National Environmental Policy Act (NEPA) to their decision-making process (another reason why the OECD Recommendation only contains text about environmental review not environmental impact assessment when discussing the ECAs' review process) and alleged that both agencies had violated NEPA by failing to consider the GHG emissions of the project they financed. The US District Court for the Northern District of California denied summary judgments for the alleged lack of standing and thus granted an interim victory to the plaintiffs by allowing them to pursue their case further.[96] The final decision delivered mixed results for all adversaries. The overall motion was denied because the agencies were not incumbent to implement federal programmes as required by NEPA. There were also factual issues that could not be resolved in their entirety, preventing a decision in favour of the plaintiffs from being handed down. However, the judge confirmed his earlier standing decision and denied that the

[91] Information provided by the US Department of Treasury is published on the Internet at: http://www.treas.gov/offices/international-affairs/trade_invest_finance/trade_finance.shtml (accessed 6 Mar. 2006).

[92] Ibid.

[93] Ibid.

[94] Ibid.

[95] S. C. Aminzadeh, 'A Moral Imperative: The Human Rights Implications of Climate Change' (2007) 30 *Hastings International and Comparative Law Review* 231, at 236.

[96] United States District Court, N.D. California, *Friends of the Earth, Inc.; Greenpeace, Inc.; City of Boulder, Colorado; City of Arcata, California; and City of Oakland, California* v. *Peter Watson and Phillip Merrill*, decision of 23 Aug. 2005, 35 (2005) *Environmental Law Reports* 20, at 179.

plaintiffs where seeking to make an argument for the extraterritorial application of NEPA. The judge approved of the plaintiffs' arguments:

> Plaintiffs, however, make clear that they seek to apply NEPA because the projects that Defendants support purportedly significantly affect the *domestic environment* [. . .] Finally, notwithstanding Defendants' arguments regarding foreign policy relations, there is evidence to suggest that the Defendants may have control over the manner in which these projects operate.[97]

The judgment contains two interesting observations. Firstly, climate change is depicted as a truly global phenomenon and, as such, might require an enhanced review on the part of ECAs and one might add perhaps a multilateral approach. The second observation relates to the general responsibility argument because the judge interpreted that the provision of funding and guarantees gave the agencies increased leverage to influence the overall project operation. In this manner, the case for adding *ex post* monitoring to OECD Guidelines is compelling.

F. Comparison

This comparative analysis shows that while the degree to which various OECD Members adhere to and implement the voluntary guidelines varies, the Arrangement and its environmental Recommendation serve as a reference point and have a definite normative presence. Practice has indicated that Recommendations are taken seriously at the national level when regulating the functioning of official export credit agencies and conferral of subsidies. This interim conclusion might be relatively surprising; the argument could be made that countries are letting economically important opportunities slip through their hands by requiring a minimal degree of environmental compliance for large export projects. Practice shows, however, that even ECAs within the EU interpret their environmental obligations and requirements in an incongruent manner. An example of these disparities is evident in the refusal of Germany's ECA to support the new Finnish TVO nuclear reactor whilst French Coface granted a record high level of export insurance. The details of this particular case and the review of the OECD notified projects reveals a somewhat more mixed picture in the type and size of projects supported by ECAs across the OECD. This assessment also indicates that the OECD Arrangement leaves enough room for different levels of scrutiny and supervision.

In all of the cases mentioned above, environmental impact assessments are required for prospective endeavours beyond a certain monetary threshold for projects that are situated in environmentally fragile areas and/or are classified to be particularly environmentally invasive. Statistics indicate a growing proportion

[97] United States District Court, N.D. California, *Friends of the Earth, Inc., et al.* v. *Robert Mosbacher, Jr., et al.*, decision of 30 March 2007, 488 F.Supp.2d 889, at 908.

of projects have undergone varying degrees of pre-emptive environmental assessment in recent years.

However, due in part to the competitive terrain within which ECAs operate, provisions for transparency and channels for public participation remain somewhat constricted and subject to confidentiality rationales. Moreover, there have been recent advancements in the area of impact assessments resulting in the promulgation of more flexible, yet holistic tools to achieve the similar goals of ensuring that plans, policies, and projects conform to the objectives of sustainable development—not just environmental protection.[98] Indeed, using mechanisms explicitly oriented to accomplishing sustainable development imperatives corresponds to export credit activity as the concept of sustainable development is based upon the need to reconcile environmental protection with socio-economic development—the latter being the ostensible rationale for many of the large infrastructure projects financed by ECAs.

VI. Conclusion

The current OECD legal regime for export credits, especially the 2007 Recommendation, should be viewed as a step towards further multilateralization rather than an ideal endpoint. Requiring EIAs by the project partners provides the impetus towards mainstreaming sustainable development precepts, but the soft law nature of the Recommendation and the propensity for governments to distance themselves from ECA operations makes a legally binding instrument preferable. In combination with the MNE guidelines, the OECD regime makes useful proposals to address the sustainable development challenges on both the credit granting and receiving end. It is the voluntary nature and lack of obligation to underwrite CSR provisions in these compacts that is of particular concern.

Although the OECD Recommendation seems to enjoy a high threshold of voluntary compliance, additional sustainable development elements (particularly within the social domain) should factor into the decision-making process. Specifically, the social pillar of sustainable development should be better represented and expanded to encompass human rights impact assessments and participation from diverse stakeholders in civil society beyond the annual review process currently recommended by the OECD. In order to facilitate public participation, disclosure polices that facilitate the provision of information on loans and guarantees *before* approval should be adopted. At minimum, this information should include the type of project, the amount and nature of support requested, the companies involved, the country involved, and the likely human rights, environmental, and development impacts of the project.

[98] Gehring and Cordonier Segger, n. 51 above.

A possible middle road could be advocating the multilateralization of ECA decision-making through collaboration with MEA and International Labour Organization (ILO) secretariats. By making these procedural changes, the scrutiny by the ECAs would then centre exclusively on adherence to internationally agreed or common standards and not solely on World Bank or EU metrics. In this way, a clearer connection between ECA activities, existing international MEAs and human rights accords is possible. This institutional change may also undercut avenues for corruption that have traditionally accompanied large infrastructure projects in developing States. The inauguration of independent investigation and accountability mechanisms that can serve as autonomous fact-finding organs and means of redress to which local communities and other stakeholders can appeal in the case of problems with an ECA supported project.[99]

Another viable alternative would be the development of a multilateral and jointly undertaken SIA embedded into a hard law framework. The SIA methodology would encompass inter alia social, economic, and environmental scoping; pinpointing of pertinent questions and issues that require resolution; multi-stakeholder consultation; plans for ameliorating impacts from the venture that require mitigation and the derivation of an *ex post* monitoring scheme to ensure compliance. SIAs are an important tool to precipitate dialogue between the financers and the recipient government and civil society as well as to recognize the different views on the trade-sustainability reconciliation process.

Insofar as the funds disbursed by ECAs come from public sources, some form of international responsibility can be linked to decision-making. Thus, regarding issues such as arms deals (not covered by the OECD regime), evaluation of the risk posed to the funding government should be carefully contemplated.

In conclusion, it might be advisable in the long-term to decouple development finance from exports and relocate it within the mandate of regional development banks and their multilateral governance structure to ensure that increased specification of the regime does not unduly constrain funding for sustainable development initiatives. This paper has suggested that the emerging export credit regime is starting to take the competing variables that States face when implementing sustainable development norms into account. By addressing some of the systemic challenges, through an international legal regime and multilateralization and some of the practical challenges, through implementation of SIA as a standard assessment method, it can be ensured that more export credits support rather than frustrate sustainable development.

[99] See Center for International Environmental Law, 'Export Credit Agencies and Sustainable Development: An Issue Brief for the World Summit on Sustainable Development 26 August–4 September 2002', published on the Internet at: http://www.ciel.org/Publications/ECAs.pdf (accessed 7 Oct. 2007).

CURRENT SURVEY

Substantive European Community Environmental Law

I. Atmospheric Pollution

*Alexandra González-Calatayud**

A. Introduction

2006 started with not one, but two new reports by the European Environment Agency (EEA) on Europe's unsustainable transport trends.[1] Both of them highlight the urgent need to tackle vehicle pollution, firstly, through the draft Euro 5, which was published by the European Commission (Commission) in 2005 and, secondly, through the decision on how to continue the voluntary agreement with car manufacturers on CO_2 emissions from new cars, which will expire in 2008. The other focal point should be the Thematic Strategy on Air Pollution and its accompanying Proposal for a new Air Quality Directive in the European Union (EU),[2] this Strategy and its lack of ambition being one of the major disappointments in 2005.

B. Legislation Adopted

i. Ozone-depleting Substances

A cap on the EU's consumption of methyl bromide was officially adopted in May 2006.[3] The Commission Decision limits the use of this ozone-depleting substance at 1,607 tonnes for 2006. The new EU quota represents a reduction of 42 per cent compared with 2005, fulfilling a commitment made at the 2005 meeting of parties of the Montreal Protocol for the Protection of the Ozone Layer.[4] Less than half of the Member States still use methyl bromide, which the Montreal Protocol banned for developing countries as of 2005, except for critical uses.

* Policy Officer of the Royal Society for the Protection of Birds, London (United Kingdom). The views expressed are personal to the author.

[1] EEA, *Transport and Environment 2005: Facing a Dilemma* (Mar. 2006); and EEA, *Air Pollution at Street Level in European Cities* (Mar. 2006).

[2] NN. 5 and 6 below.

[3] Dec. 2006/350/EC determining the Quantities of Methyl Bromide permitted to be used for Critical Uses in the Community from 1 January to 31 December 2006 pursuant to Regulation (EC) No. 2037/2000 of the European Parliament and of the Council on Substances that Deplete the Ozone Layer (2006/350/EC) [2006] OJ L130/29.

[4] Montreal (Canada), 16 Sept. 1987 (entered into force 1 Jan. 1989), published on the Internet at: http://www.unep.org/ozone/pdfs/Montreal-Protocol2000.pdf.

C. Legislation in Progress

i. Air Quality

In September 2005, the Commission presented a Thematic Strategy on Air Pollution[5] and a Proposal for a new Air Quality Directive in the EU.[6] The draft Directive aims to revise the current ambient air quality legislation by merging the existing five Air Quality Directives into one single Directive, and by introducing new air quality standards for fine particulate matter (PM2.5) in the air. Following a debate at the Environment Council in December 2005 and Council conclusions cautiously welcoming the Strategy in March 2006, Environment Ministers reached a provisional agreement on the proposed legislation at their meeting of 27 June 2006.[7] The agreed text slightly weakened the limits proposed by the Commission, although they were still stronger than the ones proposed by the European Parliament's (EP) Environment Committee, which had voted on the draft only the day before.[8] The main amendments of the Council included a delay by five years (from 2010 to 2015) of a deadline to meet new limits of 25 micrograms per cubic metre on PM2.5 and a delay by two years (from 2005 to 2007) of the deadline to cut ambient concentrations of coarse particulate mater (PM10). For already existing limit values the possibility for postponement would be limited to PM10 until three years after entry into force of the Directive.

In September, the EP's plenary voted on the Proposal in its first reading, following the recommendations of the Committee and thus weakening the Commission's draft.[9] The Parliament's amendments included the following.

For PM2.5 the EP stated that, as the available data for PM2.5 are not yet sufficient in order to introduce a limit value, a target value should apply initially until such time as a concentration cap can enter into force. The target value is lower than that proposed by the Commission: 20 micrograms per cubic metre (µg/m3) from 2010 instead of 25µg/m3.

For PM10, MEPs want to reduce maximum concentration levels to 33 µg/m3 on average per year from 2010, as compared to the Commission's proposal to keep the limit at 40µg/m3. The figure applies unless this cannot be achieved because of site-specific dispersion characteristics, adverse meteorological or geographical conditions, or significant transboundary contributions. Member States must lay down the exact number of days the limit value can be exceeded, up to a maximum of 55 days (rather than 35), and forthwith communicate to the Commission the text of that provision.

[5] Commission Communication to the Council and the European Parliament on a Thematic Strategy on Air Pollution COM(2005)446, 21 Sept. 2005.

[6] Commission Proposal for a Directive of the European Parliament and of the Council on Ambient Air Quality and Cleaner Air for Europe COM(2005)447, 21 Sept. 2005.

[7] 10876/1/06 REV 1 (Presse 192), 2740th Council Meeting, 27 June 2006.

[8] A6–0234/2006, 26 June 2006, *Rapporteur* Holger Krähmer.

[9] P6_TA(2006)0362, 26 Sept. 2006, published on the Internet at: http://www.europarl.europa.eu/sides/getDoc.do?pubRef=-//EP//TEXT+TA+P6-TA-2006–0362+0+DOC+XML+V0//EN.

The agreed text called for more flexibility over allowing extensions to the deadline in areas or cities which fail to meet the criteria. Accordingly, where in a given zone or agglomeration conformity with the limit values for nitrogen dioxide, benzene, PM10, or the target value for PM2.5 cannot be achieved by the deadline specified, a Member State may postpone by a maximum of four years from the entry into force of the Directive for that particular zone or agglomeration. The Member State must show that all appropriate measures have been taken at national, regional, and local level to meet the deadlines referred to above. A plan or a programme must be drawn up for the zone demonstrating what measures will be taken in order to meet the limit or target values by the new deadline.

Following the finalization of the EP's first reading, the Council voted in October to make its provisional agreement definitive.[10]

ii. Euro 5 Emission Limits

In December 2005, the Commission published a draft package for the so-called Euro 5 emission limits for cars.[11] The objective of the Euro 5 standards is to lay down harmonized rules on the construction of motor vehicles with regard to their atmospheric emissions. The priorities are to reduce emissions of both particulates and nitrogen oxides, particularly from diesel cars. The new limits should lead to the introduction of particulate filters on all new diesel cars and vans.

The Council discussed the proposed package in March 2006, with several governments expressing a willingness to toughen the plan by adding a further stage (Euro 6) of tighter limits on nitrogen oxides. At the meeting, the German government presented a note, in which it proposed that the Euro 5 limit for diesel cars should be further reduced to 180 milligrams per kilometre (mg/km), and that the EU should agree now on an ambitious 80 mg/km standard for 2013.[12] Officials argued that deciding this now would give greater planning certainty to manufacturers.

Germany also called for nitrogen oxides limits for petrol cars to be left at their current level of 80 mg/km, rather than being reduced to 60 mg/km as proposed by the Commission for Euro 5, with the aim of harmonizing petrol and diesel nitrogen oxides limits at 80 mg/km.

Germany's proposals were widely accepted by other EU Member States and also by the EP's Environment Committee, which voted on the draft package on 13 September 2006.[13] It has demanded the introduction of tougher limits on

[10] 13989/06 (Presse 287), 2757th Council Meeting, 23 Oct. 2006.

[11] Commission Proposal for a Regulation of the European Parliament and of the Council on type approval of motor vehicles with respect to emissions and on access to vehicle repair information, amending Directive 72/306/EEC COM(2005)683, 21 Dec. 2005.

[12] Note published on the Internet at: http://register.consilium.eu.int/pdf/en/06/st07/st07158.en06.pdf.

[13] EP ENV Committee Report on the Proposal for a Regulation of the European Parliament and of the Council on Type Approval of Motor Vehicles with respect to Emissions and on Access to Vehicle Repair Information, amending Directive 72/306/EEC and Directive ../../EC (COM(2005)

passenger car pollution from 2014, in addition to interim standards due before the end of this decade.

In light of the Council's and Parliament's position, the Commission decided to carry out a new impact assessment for a Euro 6 limit of 80 mg/km for nitrogen oxides from diesel cars by 2014, which convinced it to endorse the new approach.[14] The new assessment concluded that the Euro 6 standard would deliver an additional 24 per cent reduction in nitrogen oxides emissions in 2020 compared with Euro 5, at an additional cost of €213 per vehicle. It also showed that the tougher limits would increase health benefits by 60–90 per cent relative to Euro 5.

Subsequently, representatives of the EP and Council provisionally agreed a common position, with the Council accepting the Parliament's proposed timetable in return for the Council's preferred nitrogen oxides standards. The draft Directive will set new Euro 5 standards for fine particles, hydrocarbons, and nitrogen oxides from 2009, and tougher Euro 6 standards for nitrogen oxides only from 2014.

The provisional common position includes an agreement on a Euro 5 nitrogen oxide limit of 60 mg/km for petrol cars—10g lower than demanded by the EP's environment committee—and 180 mg/km for diesel cars. MEPs also dropped demands for a 'technology neutral' Euro 6 nitrogen oxides limit of 70 mg/km for all passenger cars in favour of Council's preferred values of 60 and 80 mg/km respectively for petrol and diesel vehicles.

All Euro 5 standards will enter into force in 2009, one year later than proposed by the Commission. Euro 6 nitrogen oxides limits will apply from 2014, which is also a year later than demanded by some EU governments.

Regarding a timetable for including sport utility vehicles over 2.5 tonnes subject to car emission standards rather than those for heavy goods vehicles, the two sides agreed on 2012.

Finally, Member States will be able to offer financial incentives for the purchase of vehicles meeting the Euro 5 and 6 standards before the standards actually come into force.

The EP plenary approved the compromise deal on 13 December 2006.[15] It is expected that the Council will give its approval early in 2007.

0683 – C6–0007/2006 – 2005/0282(COD)), A6–0301/2006, 13 Sept. 2006, published on the Internet at: http://www.europarl.europa.eu/registre.

[14] See Commission press release MEMO/06/409, 7 Nov. 2006, published on the Internet at: http://europa.eu/rapid/pressReleasesAction.do?reference=MEMO/06/409.

[15] EP legislative resolution on the proposal for a Regulation of the European Parliament and of the Council on Type Approval of Motor Vehicles with respect to Emissions and on Access to Vehicle Repair Information, amending Directive 72/306/EEC and Directive ../../EC (COM(2005)0683 – C6–0007/2006 – 2005/0282(COD)), P6_TA(2006)0561, 13 Dec. 2006, published on the Internet at: http://www.europarl.europa.eu/registre.

iii. Clean Vehicles for Public Authorities

Attached to the draft Euro 5 standards was a draft Directive on clean vehicles for public authorities.[16] The Proposal intended to kick-start a market in currently non-economic technologies, through public procurement rules. Instead, it started a wave of rejections ranging from hauliers to the MEPs. In June 2006, the EP's Environment Committee rejected the Proposal under the first reading of the co-decision procedure.[17] The Committee argued that the Proposal had been put forward too late and therefore, in its current form, would not have the desired impact on the environment and human health. It therefore called on the Commission to withdraw the Proposal and to focus its efforts instead on coming forward with a Proposal on environmentally ambitious, technology-driving and stringent Euro 6 standards as soon as possible. The Commission paid heed to these recommendations and announced it would redraft plans for the Directive on public procurement of clean vehicles in 2007.[18]

D. Case Law

Early in 2006, the European Court of Justice (ECJ) condemned Italy for breaching two Directives on air quality assessment and EU limit values for air pollutants.[19] On 15 March 2004, the Commission had brought proceedings to the Court for considering that Italy had failed to comply with its information obligations relating to limit values for sulphur dioxide, nitrogen dioxide, and oxides of nitrogen, particulate matter, and lead in ambient air, as required under Article 11 of Directive 96/62/EC concerning Ambient Air Quality and Management (Air Quality Framework Directive)[20] in conjunction with Article 4(1) of that Directive, and with Directive 1999/30 relating to Limit Values for Sulphur Dioxide, Nitrogen Dioxide and Oxides of Nitrogen, Particulate Matter, and Lead in Ambient Air (First Air Quality Daughter Directive)[21] and Article 1 of Decision 2001/839/EC laying down a Questionnaire to be used for Annual Reporting on Ambient Air Quality Assessment under Council Directives 96/62/EC and 1999/30/EC.[22]

Article 1 of Decision 2001/839 states that:

> Member States shall use the questionnaire set out in the Annex as a basis for forwarding the information to be provided on an annual basis under Article 11 of Directive

[16] Commission Proposal for a Directive of the European Parliament and of the Council on the Promotion of Clean Road Transport Vehicles COM(2005)634, 21 Dec. 2001.

[17] EP ENV Committee Report on the Proposal for a Directive of the European Parliament and of the Council on the Promotion of Clean Road Transport Vehicles, A6–0232/2006, 21 June 2006, published on the Internet at: http://www.europarl.europa.eu/registre.

[18] 'EU To Rethink Clean Vehicle Quotas Plan', *ENDS Europe Daily*, 23 Nov. 2006.

[19] Case C-139/04 *Commission* v. *Italy* [2006] ECR I-5.

[20] [1996] OJ L296/55.

[21] [1999] OJ L182/1.

[22] [2001] OJ L319/45.

96/62/EC, in conjunction with Annexes I, II, III, IV and V, and Articles 3, 5 and 9(6) of Directive 1999/30/EC.

Moreover, according to Article 11 of Directive 96/62/EC, after adoption by the Council of the first proposal referred to in the first indent of Article 4(1), Member States should notify to the Commission the competent authorities, laboratories, and bodies referred to in Article 3.

Italy admitted that it had not provided the required information within the timeframes stipulated in the Directive, but claimed that it had corrected this since. However, the ECJ maintained that whether a Member State has failed to fulfil its obligations must be determined by reference to the situation obtaining in the Member State at the end of the period laid down in the reasoned opinion and the Court cannot take account of any subsequent changes, as confirmed in earlier rulings.[23] It therefore declared that Italy had failed to comply with the provisions cited by the Commission and condemned the Italian Republic to pay the costs.

December 2006 saw three rulings by the ECJ over failures to implement Community legislation relating to air pollution. The three cases involved the United Kingdom (UK) over a failure to transpose a 2002 law on environmental noise assessment; Greece for failing to set minimum qualifications for workers handling ozone-depleting substances; and Luxembourg for failing to report on the implementation of EU legislation requiring CO_2 emission labels on new cars.

In the first case, the Commission considered that the UK, by failing to adopt the laws, regulations, and administrative provisions necessary to comply with Directive 2002/49/EC relating to the Assessment and Management of Environmental Noise,[24] or, in any event, by not informing the Commission of those provisions, had failed to fulfil its obligations under that Directive.[25] A letter of formal notice was sent to the UK in December 2004 and following that, the Commission, on 13 July 2005, issued a reasoned opinion.

Article 14(1) of the Directive requires Member States to bring into force the laws, regulations, and administrative provisions necessary to comply therewith no later than 18 July 2004 and to inform the Commission thereof.

The UK admitted that the Directive had not been transposed within the prescribed period, but stated that the laws and regulations intended to effect such transposition should have been adopted, at the latest, during November 2006. As with the above-described case involving Greece, the ECJ concluded that a Member State's failure to fulfil its obligations must be determined by reference to the situation pertaining in the Member State at the end of the period laid down in the reasoned opinion. The period of time laid down in the reasoned opinion in this case was of two months, but the UK had not taken the necessary measures

[23] Cf. Case C-207/00 *Commission* v. *Italy* [2001] ECR I-4571, para. 27.

[24] [2002] OJ L189/12.

[25] Case C-138/06 *Commission* v. *UK* [2006] ECR I-136.

to effect the Directive's transposition into law. Therefore, the Court deemed the Commission's action well founded and condemned the UK.

The second case concerned Greece,[26] which was condemned for failing to fulfil its obligations under Articles 16(5), (6), and 17(1) of Regulation (EC) No. 2037/2000 on Substances that Deplete the Ozone Layer (Ozone Regulation).[27] The ECJ agreed with the arguments of the Commission and ruled that Greece:

- had not taken the measures necessary for determining minimum qualification requirements for the personnel charged with the recovery, recycling, reclamation, and destruction of controlled substances that deplete the ozone layer;
- had infringed its obligations under Article 16(6) of the Ozone Regulation given that it had not submitted a report to the Commission in accordance with the requirements of that provision, concerning the facilities available and the quantities of used controlled substances recovered, recycled, reclaimed, or destroyed;
- had infringed Article 17(1) of the abovementioned Regulation because it did not adopt, as provided for thereunder, all practicable measures to arrange for annual checks of leakages from fixed equipment with a refrigerating fluid charge of more than 3 kg.

A third case involved Luxembourg,[28] which faced the ECJ over the alleged failure to transmit the report required under Article 9 of Directive 1999/94/EC relating to the Availability of Consumer Information on Fuel Economy and CO_2 Emissions in respect of the Marketing of New Passenger Cars.[29] Luxembourg always admitted that it was in fault, though it claimed that legislation to remedy the shortfall was in the process of being implemented. As in the previous cases the Court did not deem this to be sufficient, as the period to be considered was the timeframe given in the reasoned opinion, which had already lapsed. Luxembourg lost the case and was condemned to pay the costs.

E. Policy Documents

i. Shipping

In May 2006, the Commission issued a Recommendation encouraging Member States to make it possible for ships berthed in port to plug into the electricity grid instead of burning fuel for their power needs while docked.[30] Shore-side

26 Case C-390/05 *Commission* v. *Greece* [2005] ECR I-135.
27 [2000] OJ L244/1.
28 Case C-198/06 *Commission* v. *Luxembourg* [2006] ECR I-137.
29 [2000] OJ L12/16.
30 Rec. 2006/339/EC on the Promotion of Shore-side Electricity for Use by Ships at Berth in Community Ports [2006] OJ L125/38.

electricity reduces ship emissions of particulate matter, volatile organic compounds (VOCs), oxides of nitrogen (NO_x), and sulphur dioxide (SO_2). In some port areas, ship emissions may jeopardize cities' ability to comply with EU air quality standards. The 2005 Thematic Strategy on Air Pollution had identified ships as a major and increasingly important source of air pollution affecting human health and the environment in Europe, particularly due to polluting emissions from ships at berth.[31] Promoting shore-side electricity was one of the specific actions foreseen in the Strategy and is also in line with the Commission's 2002 Strategy for Reducing Emissions from Seagoing Ships.[32] In this sense, the Recommendation will also complement Directive 2005/33/EC on Sulphur in Marine Fuels.[33] The Recommendation promotes shore-side electricity by providing information on its practicalities, benefits, and costs, by encouraging the development of harmonized international standards, and by highlighting the possibility for Member States to grant electricity tax reductions as an incentive to ship operators to connect to the grid. One of the obstacles to greater availability of shore-side electricity is that it requires action by port authorities, shipowners, and in some cases also local authorities. The Recommendation aims to help raise awareness of the benefits of shore-side electricity among these key actors. It also asks Member States to work within the International Maritime Organization (IMO) to promote the development of international standards for shore-side electricity, and to consider offering economic incentives to operators to encourage its use.

ii. Integrated Pollution Prevention and Control

On 18 September 2006, the Commission published the first consolidated European inventory of pollution from small or non-industrial sources.[34] The inventory of EU-wide data on 'diffuse' pollution brings together for the first time information currently held in a range of different inventories. It represents an important step towards the development of a future European Pollutant Release and Transfer Register (European PRTR), which will allow more effective policy-making.

The inventory shows that emissions of heavy metals from diffuse sources tend to be higher than those from major installations. Of all sectors, road transport, domestic heating, and agriculture are the largest emitters of pollutants and greenhouse gases. For most of the 25 pollutants covered, these sectors account for more than 90 per cent of all emissions. Almost all emissions of ammonia and other

[31] Commission Communication to the Council and the European Parliament on a Thematic Strategy on Air Pollution COM(2005)446, 21 Sept. 2005.

[32] Communication from the Commission to the European Parliament and the Council on A European Union Strategy to Reduce Atmospheric Emissions from Seagoing Ships COM(2002)595, 20 Nov. 2002.

[33] [2005] OJ L191/59.

[34] The inventory can be found on the Internet at: http://www.bipro.de/__prtr/index.htm.

chemicals like hexachlorobenzene (HCB) come from agriculture. The road transport sector is responsible for half of all CO_2 emissions and two-thirds of NO_x emissions. A significant proportion of CO_2 is emitted by domestic heating. This sector is also largely responsible for emissions of mercury, and dioxins and furans. The other sectors covered are shipping, aviation, railways, military activities, gas distribution, roofing and road paving with asphalt, and solvent use.

The data show that Germany produces most CO_2 and methane from diffuse sources, followed by France, the UK, and Italy. The UK has by far the largest diffuse emissions of SO_2, followed by Poland and the Netherlands. Diffuse emissions of heavy metals such as lead are mainly concentrated in Poland, Cyprus, France, and Spain.

iii. Particulate Emissions

In 2006, the Commission also rejected a Dutch proposal to ban diesel cars and light vans with fine particle emissions above five milligrams per kilometre (mg/km) from 1 January 2007.[35] The Dutch authorities had notified the Commission of the adoption of a measure that would have constituted an amendment to Community legislation concerning the requirements that must be complied with by vehicles and their components parts throughout their useful life. According to the Dutch authorities, the measure would not have concerned the type-approval procedure, as vehicles type-approved in another Member State would not have been refused registration in the Netherlands, and vehicles complying with the requirements of Directive 70/220/EEC on the approximation of the laws of the Member States relating to measures to be taken against Air Pollution by Gases from Positive-ignition Engines of Motor Vehicles,[36] would have continued to have been granted type-approval by the Dutch authorities. However, the first time these vehicles would have gone through technical inspection (or whenever they would have been checked by the police), they would have been found not to be compliant with the notified measure. The Commission therefore considered that the measure imposed a ban on the use of new vehicles of category N1, Class I, and M1 emitting than 5 mg/km of particulate matter.

The Commission decided to veto the Dutch plans under Article 95 EC. It considered that the Netherlands had failed to prove it had a nationally specific problem with motor vehicle emissions. Even if it had proven this, the proposed ban would have constituted 'a disproportionate obstacle' to the internal market. The Commission also quoted a Dutch recent study showing that PM10 levels were 10 to 15 per cent lower than previously assumed as part of its argument.

[35] Dec. 2006/372/EC concerning draft national provisions notified by the Kingdom of the Netherlands under Article 95(5) of the EC Treaty laying down limits on the emissions of particulate matter by diesel powered vehicles [2006] OJ L142/16.

[36] [1970] OJ L76/1.

iv. Transport

Article 8 of Directive 98/70/EC relating to the Quality of Petrol and Diesel Fuels and amending Council Directive 93/12/EEC requires the Commission annually to publish a report on the fuel quality in the different Member States.[37] In May, the Commission published the third of these Reports, which analyses the data submitted by Member States for the year 2004.[38] The monitoring of fuel quality in 2004 shows that the specifications for petrol and diesel laid down in Directive 98/70/EC are in general met and few violations were identified. However, the declines in sulphur in European petrol and diesel stalled in 2004. The EU 15 States would in fact have recorded an increase but for an upward revision of 2003 data. Average petrol sulphur levels in the enlarged EU 25 rose slightly because of higher levels in the new Member States.

Excluding France, which has failed to report for two years running, average EU 15 sulphur levels were 35 parts per million (ppm) in petrol and 109 ppm in diesel in 2004, down from 37 ppm and 125 ppm respectively in 2003. For the first time, the new Report includes data on the ten Member States that joined the EU in 2004. In this group, sulphur levels averaged 64 ppm in petrol and 149 ppm in diesel in 2004. The aggregate EU 25 average sulphur level in 2004 was 38 ppm in petrol and 113 ppm in diesel. Eleven countries reported petrol sulphur and/or diesel sulphur levels above the 50 ppm limit in 2004, seven of them new Member States. At the other end of the scale, Austria and Germany have already achieved virtually complete penetration of sulphur-free fuels, followed by Slovakia and Ireland for petrol and Sweden for diesel.

v. Mercury Strategy

At the beginning of 2005, the Commission had presented a widely expected Strategy on Mercury Pollution.[39] A key objective of the Strategy was to reduce mercury levels in the environment and human exposure, especially mercury in fish. The EP passed a Resolution on the Communication in March 2006.[40] The Resolution was based on the own-initiative report drafted by MEP Marios Matsakis and called on the Commission to strengthen its efforts, either through binding legislation or by bringing forward proposed actions.

The Parliament underlined the importance of applying the polluter pays principle, in particular as far as storage of surplus mercury is concerned. The industry sectors responsible for the production of mercury should contribute to the financing of the safe storage of surplus mercury. Among the specific measures

[37] [1998] OJ L350/58.

[38] Report from the Commission on Quality of petrol and diesel fuel used for road transport in the European Union: Third Annual Report (Reporting year 2004) COM(2006)186, 28 Apr. 2006.

[39] Communication from the Commission to the European Parliament and to the Council: Community Strategy Concerning Mercury COM(2005)20, 28 Jan. 2005.

[40] P6_TA(2006)0078, 14 Mar. 2006, published on the Internet at: http://www.europarl.europa.eu/registre.

proposed, the EP states that the Commission should introduce legislation curbing mercury emissions from large and small-scale combustion processes. It also demands restrictions on mercury use in gold mining and for the EU to introduce a labelling scheme for gold produced in third countries. The Commission should evaluate the use of mercury in vaccines 'with a view to a total ban'.

A centrepiece of the Commission's Proposal was for a ban on mercury exports from the EU to enter into force in 2011. The EP wants this prohibition to be brought forward to 2010. It calls for the Commission to begin tracking trade in mercury from 2008. On mercury use in the chlor-alkali industry the EP has gone much further, calling for a phase-out deadline of 2010 rather than 2020 as proposed by the Commission. The Resolution also demands legal controls to ensure safe storage of surplus mercury and a requirement for the sector to co-finance safe storage.

F. International Cooperation

i. North Sea Conference

At a meeting in May 2006, the eight ministers of the countries belonging to the North Sea Conference, reached an agreement on tough new reduction targets for maritime air emissions of nitrogen oxides (NO_x) and sulphur dioxide (SO_2).[41] The Conference, which last gathered in Norway in 2002, met in 2006 in the Swedish city of Gothenburg.

Ministers called for a 40 per cent cut in NO_x emissions in the long term and a reduction in the permitted sulphur content of fuel from the current limit of 1.5 to 1 per cent. They also agreed on the launch of the 'clean ship approach', defined as 'criteria for evaluating environmental performance of ships [. . .] as an incentive to encourage sustainable shipping', and on tax incentives to encourage the use of shore-side electricity for ships in ports as a clean-air measure. Furthermore, a series of initiatives aimed at the fisheries industry include the introduction of environmental impact assessments of new fishing methods and gear. The Gothenburg event is expected to be the last conference in the series.

ii. Montreal Protocol

The twenty-sixth meeting of the Open-ended Working Group (OEWG-26) of the parties to the Montreal Protocol on Substances that Deplete the Ozone Layer convened in Montreal, Canada, from 3 to 6 July 2006.[42] Delegates agreed to forward seven draft decisions to the eighteenth Meeting of the Parties (MOP-18), to

[41] Declaration, North Sea Ministerial Meeting on the Environmental Impact of Shipping and Fisheries, Göteborg (Sweden), 4–5 May 2006, published on the Internet at: http://www.sweden.gov.se/content/1/c6/05/78/43/a479808a.pdf.

[42] Montreal (Canada), 16 Sept. 1987 (entered into force 1 Jan. 1989). Protocol and all meeting documents published on the Internet at: http://www.unep.org/ozone/.

be held in New Delhi, India, in October. While methyl bromide-related matters, such as nominations for critical-use exemptions and quarantine and pre-shipment were a central part of delegates' deliberations, a variety of other issues, such as the difficulties arising from the transition to CFC-free metered-dose inhalers in developing country parties (Article 5), compliance issues associated with this transition as well as with stockpiles of ozone-depleting substances (ODS), and launching a discussion on the future of the Montreal Protocol, were not.

MOP-18 opened with one of the heaviest agendas in years. The main issues were methyl bromide critical use nominations and CFC-free metered-dose inhalers (MDIs).

On methyl bromide, industrialized countries worldwide will be able to use up to about 9,000 tonnes of methyl bromide in 2007. The EU has agreed to cut its consumption of the ozone-depleting pesticide methyl bromide to a maximum 690 tonnes in 2007. The United States' (US) 2008 cap on methyl bromide use was set at 5,355 tonnes. Much lower caps were also agreed for Australia, Japan, and Canada.

Delegates also discussed the difficulties faced by some Article 5 parties manufacturing MDIs using CFCs. In the talks, many participants highlighted problems such as lack of affordable alternatives in phasing out CFCs in MDIs and the burden implied if non-CFC-based MDIs are imported. A number of governments also requested financial and technical assistance for the phase-out, and highlighted the need for closer cooperation and partnerships for technology transfer.

The final Decision recognizes the potential uncertainties of availability of pharmaceutical-grade CFCs in the near future and requests the Executive Committee urgently to consider funding projects to facilitate transition from CFC-based MDIs for Article 5 parties.

Parties did not agree to a draft or final decision on Canada's proposal to adjust the Montreal Protocol to meet the basic domestic needs of Article 5 parties. Items deferred for consideration until OEWG-27 included multi-year exemptions for Critical Use Exemptions (CUEs) and options that parties may consider for preventing harmful trade in methyl bromide stocks.

iii. POPs Treaty

The second Conference of the Parties (COP-2) to the Stockholm Convention on Persistent Organic Pollutants (POPs) was held from 1 to 5 May 2006, in Geneva, Switzerland.[43] COP-2 considered several reports on activities within the Convention's mandate and adopted 18 Decisions on, inter alia, Dichloro-Diphenyl-Trichloroethane (DDT), exemptions, financial resources

[43] Stockholm (Sweden), 22 May 2001 (entered into force 17 May 2004). Convention and meeting documents published on the Internet at: http://www.pops.int.

and mechanisms, implementation plans, technical assistance, synergies, and effectiveness evaluation.

While the mandate for COP-2 centred on decisions on financial resources and effectiveness evaluation, various parties pushed hard on other issues, particularly on synergies and technical assistance. The question of synergies between the Stockholm Convention and the Rotterdam and Basel Conventions occupied a significant portion of the time available at COP-2.[44] The strongest push for immediate progress on this issue came from Switzerland and Norway, which sought to capitalize on the COPs of all three relevant Chemicals Conventions in 2006, as lack of decisive action at this time could delay meaningful coordination for several years.

However, many parties sought to delay a decision that would result in action, fearing that a decision at COP-2 could have left secretariats, rather than parties, in a position to drive decisions on what form such cooperation may take. Moreover, some were concerned that the full implications of taking immediate action on synergies were unclear, and that deciding on near-term administrative cooperation could stifle debate on the substantive implications of such administrative cooperation. The final decision delayed a decision on action in the short term, in favour of initiating an inclusive consultative process to analyse the appropriate degree of integration within the chemicals and waste cluster.

The other dominant issue on the COP-2 agenda was technical assistance. The close links between technical assistance, synergies, and effectiveness evaluation complicated discussions on all three issues. It appeared that many developing countries viewed the subject to be their opportunity to ensure that the implementation of their National Implementation Plans (NIPs) had adequate financial backing. Developed countries, however, indicated that they saw the issue from a very different viewpoint, noting repeatedly their preference to provide technical assistance in a way that capitalizes on existing institutions and mechanisms, thereby ensuring that the available funds stretch as far as possible.

G. Conclusion

2006 was a year of relatively low activity on the atmospheric pollution front. Little progress was made in important dossiers, such as the one concerning the Thematic Strategy on Air Pollution[45] or CO_2 emissions from cars, and no new initiatives were undertaken. Almost all movement concentrated around policy documents, where some important subjects were tackled, particularly the

[44] Rotterdam Convention on the Prior Informed Consent Procedure for Certain Hazardous Chemicals and Pesticides in International Trade, Rotterdam (the Netherlands), 10 Sept. 1998 (entered into force 24 Feb. 2004) (1999) 38 *International Legal Materials* 1; and Basel Convention on the Control of Transboundary Movements of Hazardous Waste and their Disposal, Basel (Switzerland), 22 Mar. 1989 (entered into force 5 May 1992), (1989) 28 *International Legal Materials* 3, 657.

[45] N. 5 above.

Community Strategy concerning Mercury.[46] The Strategy should lead to some stringent new legislation, if the EP and environmental groups have their way.

All of the above means that some important issues remain to be tackled in 2008. In August 2006, the Commission launched a public consultation on the potential EU initiatives to reduce unintentional releases of POPs. The consultation was accompanied by a draft EU implementation plan required under the Stockholm Convention,[47] which should be launched in January 2007. Early in 2007, the Commission should also bring out the proposals on how to continue reducing carbon emissions from new cars after 2008/2009, when an existing voluntary agreement with manufacturers expires. The proposals should have been published in December 2006, but were delayed amongst conflicting views within the Commission on how to deal with carmakers.

II. Energy

Michael Rodi and Michael Mehling***

A. Introduction

After previous years had seen a number of landmark breakthroughs in climate and energy policy, optimism and elation gave way to a more sober assessment of actual developments in 2006. In January, for instance, climatologists at the National Aeronautics and Space Agency (NASA) reported that the previous year had seen the highest global annual average surface temperature on record, affirming that 'rapid warming gives urgency to discussions about how to slow greenhouse gas emissions'.[1] A study released in early 2006 by the Tyndall Centre for Climate Change Research even concluded that greenhouse gas emissions must 'end completely' by the end of the next century if global warming is to be kept within a safe range.[2] But different emissions projections released in 2006 showed no sign of slowing. Data submitted by parties to the Secretariat of the United Nations Framework Convention on Climate Change (UNFCCC),[3] for instance, suggested that emissions from industrialized countries had reached their highest

[46] N. 39 above.
[47] N. 43 above.

* Professor of Law, University of Greifswald, Greifswald (Germany).
** Research Associate, University of Greifswald, Greifswald (Germany).
[1] 'World Temperatures Reach New High in 2005', *ENDS Europe Daily*, 25 Jan. 2006.
[2] T. Lenton et al., *Climate Change on the Millennial Timescale* (Norwich: Tyndall Centre, 2006), 15.
[3] Rio de Janeiro (Brazil), 4 June 1992 (entered into force 21 Mar. 1994), (1992) 31 *International Legal Materials* 849.

levels since the early 1990s.[4] Likewise, the International Energy Agency (IEA) warned that global carbon dioxide (CO_2) emissions would more than double by 2050 unless further mitigation efforts were taken.[5] In its influential World Energy Outlook, moreover, the IEA specified that global energy-related CO_2 emissions would increase by 55 per cent between 2004 and 2030 if no further action is taken, with fossil fuels remaining the dominant source of energy and coal consolidating its position as the leading contributor to global energy-related CO_2 emissions, thereby increasing the average carbon content of primary energy consumption.[6]

And even in the European Union (EU), which laboriously established a reputation for leadership in climate and energy policy, the factual outlook was everything but favourable. In a report published late in 2005, the statistical agency Eurostat reported that 'both greenhouse gas emissions and energy consumption have increased since 2000'[7] and several Member States 'are moving away from their agreed targets',[8] a trend confirmed by the European Environment Agency (EEA) in a later study released in 2006.[9] Responding to these worrisome projections, the European Commission (Commission) submitted a progress report urging Member States to 'accelerate their efforts in implementing policies and measures'[10] for compliance with the mandatory commitments entered under the Kyoto Protocol.[11] Clearly, European climate policy has reached a critical stage in its development, with ambitious rhetoric on climate leadership threatening to diverge from actual emissions trends, potentially undermining the credibility Europe fought so hard to earn in global negotiations.

Despite their momentous implications, however, these surveys largely met with tepid attention, and it was not until a report by Nicholas Stern outlined the

[4] *National Greenhouse Gas Inventory Data for the Period 1990–2004 and Status of Reporting—Note by the Secretariat*, UN Doc. FCCC/SBI/2006/26, 19 Oct. 2006, published on the Internet at: http://unfccc.int/resource/docs/2006/sbi/eng/26.pdf.

[5] IEA, *Energy Technology Perspectives—Scenarios & Strategies to 2050* (Paris: OECD, 2006).

[6] IEA, *World Energy Outlook 2006* (Paris: OECD, 2006), 53–84.

[7] Eurostat, *Measuring Progress towards a More Sustainable Europe: Sustainable Development Indicators for the European Union* (Luxembourg: Office for Official Publications of the European Communities, 2005), 80.

[8] Ibid., 84

[9] EEA, *Greenhouse Gas Emission Trends and Projections in Europe 2006* (Copenhagen: EEA, 2006), 5. According to the EEA, existing domestic policies and measures in the 15 original Member States, which are obliged to reduce emissions by 8.0 per cent relative to 1990 levels, will only achieve a reduction of 0.6 per cent.

[10] Commission Report on Progress towards Achieving the Kyoto Targets COM(2006)658, 27 Oct. 2006, 3.

[11] Kyoto (Japan), 10 Dec. 1997 (entered into force 16 Feb. 2005) (1998) 37 *International Legal Materials* 22. Under the Kyoto Protocol, the EU has bound itself to an average reduction of greenhouse gases by 8 per cent by 2012, distributed among its Member States through an elaborate burden sharing agreement. See Dec. 2002/358/EC concerning the Approval, on Behalf of the European Community, of the Kyoto Protocol to the United Nations Framework Convention on Climate Change and the Joint Fulfilment of Commitments Thereunder [2002] OJ L130/1.

potential consequences of inaction for economic progress[12] that decision-makers around the world were truly mobilized, marking what has been described as a 'tipping point' in the debate on climate change.[13] Partly, this can be ascribed to the long list of policy recommendations contained in the report promising stabilization of greenhouse gas levels at a far lower cost than the costs global warming would incur in the absence of stronger efforts, establishing that ambitious climate policies can be implemented without compromising global economic growth.[14] A second major catalyst arguably emanated from the highly successful documentary *An Inconvenient Truth*, which reached a global audience and propelled climate issues into the media on an almost daily basis.[15] After years of debate on global warming and its existence, attention shifted to the urgency of adequate responses, launching mitigation and adaptation strategies onto the political agenda of nearly every nation on the planet.

In hindsight, thus, 2006 might best be described as a year in which earlier scepticism about climate change gave way to largely universal recognition. At the political level, however, the earlier proliferation of new policies ironically decelerated, giving way to critical reflection on their performance, with several existing measures under revision for future amendments. Emerging carbon markets entered a more mature phase,[16] accompanied by the consolidation and professionalism of a growing services sector. And on the diplomatic stage, decision-makers set forth on the thorny path towards a future climate regime, but refrained from discussing substantive commitments by taking what commentators described as a 'deep breath' before negotiations begin in earnest.[17] Progress had indeed been achieved in preceding years, but the greater challenges still lie ahead, challenges that would be largely political in nature and arise from deep divisions across geographical and economic lines.

Only the role of technological innovation continued to generate optimism, with various reports and surveys suggesting that existing technologies could abate

[12] N. Stern, *The Economics of Climate Change: The Stern Review* (Cambridge: Cambridge University Press, 2006).

[13] 'Rampant Climate Change "Will Cost the Earth"', *ENDS Europe Daily*, 30 Oct. 2006, citing an environmental interest group.

[14] The 'Stern Review', as it has become known, advocates stabilizing greenhouse gas concentrations in the atmosphere at a level of 450–550 parts per million (ppm), and concludes that the worst impacts of climate change can be avoided at a cost of 1 per cent of global GDP per year by 2050, as opposed to annual costs of 5–20 per cent per year if greenhouse gas emissions continue increasing at their present rate, see Stern, n. 12 above, 285.

[15] *An Inconvenient Truth* (US, 2006), a documentary directed by D. Guggenheim and presented by the former Vice President of the US, Al Gore.

[16] According to a survey by the World Bank, the carbon market grew in value to an estimated €23 billion in 2006, three times greater than the previous year, see World Bank, *State and Trends of the Carbon Market 2007* (Washington, DC: World Bank, 2007), 3.

[17] W. Sterk et al., 'The Nairobi Climate Change Summit (COP 12/MOP 2): Taking a Deep Breath before Negotiating Post-2012 Targets?' (2007) 4 *Journal for European Environmental and Planning Law* 140.

global warming without compromising economic growth.[18] In a study published in October 2006, for instance, the consultancy PricewaterhouseCoopers estimated that emissions could decline by 15 per cent between 2004 and 2050 with a strategy based on energy efficiency, a switch to lower carbon energy sources, and the use of carbon capture and storage technologies for fossil fuel combustion.[19] Likewise, the IEA report cited earlier highlighted the importance of green technology promotion, arguing that further energy efficiency measures in the building, industry, and transport sectors could reduce electricity demand by more than a third compared with current levels.[20] In a separate report on renewable energy, the IEA recommended elevating global research and development budgets for renewable energy to the record levels reached after the oil shocks of the 1970s.[21] And already, new breakthroughs and the deployment of alternative technologies began to show results. In April 2006, for instance, a renewable energy consortium announced that photovoltaic solar power had grown by 64 per cent in the EU in 2005, setting a new annual record.[22]

Judging by the foregoing wealth of studies, sufficient technological and policy options exist to counter the rising threat of global warming. And after years of adopting new measures on climate change and energy sustainability, including two climate change programmes and the largest trading scheme for greenhouse gas emission allowances in the world, Europe has seen no shortage of legislative action. Altogether, an information brochure published by the Commission in early 2006 listed 36 individual policies adopted by the EU to counter the challenge of global warming.[23] And yet, despite this overt activism, several Member States are far from achieving compliance with their national targets, raising doubts as to the ability of the EU to meet its reduction commitments under the Kyoto Protocol.[24]

Faced with this stark contradiction, casual observers are likely to ask where the Community strategy has gone wrong. But it has not, is how this question should probably be answered: while substantial tensions and room for improvement remain, understandable for any strategy espousing a high level of ambition and

[18] Such studies frequently expand on the suggestions contained in the seminal article by S. Pacala and R. Socolow, 'Stabilization Wedges: Solving the Climate Problem for the Next 50 Years with Current Technologies' (2004) 305 *Science* 968.

[19] J. Hawksworth, *The World in 2050: Implications of Global Growth for Carbon Emissions and Climate Change Policy* (London: PricewaterhouseCoopers, 2006), 44–5.

[20] IEA, *Energy Technology Perspectives*, n. 5 above, 253 *et seq.*

[21] IEA, *Renewable Energy: RD&D Priorities* (Paris: OECD, 2006), 185–6.

[22] EurObserv'ER, *Photovoltaic Energy Barometer*, 20 Apr. 2006, published on the Internet at: http://www.systemes-solaires.com/observ-er/stat_baro/observ/baro172.pdf.

[23] Commission, *EU Action against Climate Change: The European Climate Change Programme* (Luxembourg: European Communities, 2006), 10–21.

[24] See EEA, *Greenhouse Gas Emission Trends and Projections in Europe 2006* (Luxembourg: European Communities, 2006), 17: 'Greenhouse gases emissions in the EU-15 have risen since 1999 and emission levels in 2004 were the highest since 1996 . . . seven Member States (Belgium, Denmark, Ireland, Spain, Austria, Italy and Portugal) project that they will miss their targets despite the implementation of additional measures or the use of Kyoto mechanisms or carbon sinks.'

remarkable willingness to embrace new policy approaches, the European Climate Change Programme is not so much impeded by design flaws as by the reluctance of various Member States to adopt adequate implementation measures. No case study could illustrate this better and more soberly than the development of emission allowance prices in the first half of 2006, when information was leaked on the generous allocation decisions of most Member States, causing the market price to collapse from more than €30 to less than €1 a year later.[25] Accordingly, it is the stringency of domestic implementation measures and the coordination between Member States, both legal as well as highly political issues, which require the greatest attention in the future. For Europe and its Member States, that translates into a recognition that, in the area of energy and the environment, much has been achieved, yet even more remains to be done.

B. Legislation Adopted

As stated in the Introduction, less new legislation was adopted relative to previous years. With a substantial number of measures already in force, the focus in 2006 rested on implementation, review, and further development of existing legislation. The European emission allowances trading scheme and the overall climate strategy were particularly affected, both of which will be described in further detail below. As for new legislation, the most noteworthy event was the final adoption of the Energy Services Directive,[26] which represents an important addition to the body of measures on improved energy efficiency and demand management, as well as a European Commission decision on the avoidance of double counting within the emissions trading scheme.

i. Energy Services

On 5 April 2006, the EP and Council signed a Directive on Energy End-use Efficiency and Energy Services (Energy Efficiency and Energy Services Directive),[27] nearly three years after the Commission had submitted its initial Proposal.[28] During the legislative process, the EP had suggested a substantial number of amendments, and it was only with the approval by the Council at its second reading on 14 March 2006 that the Directive could finally be adopted.[29]

[25] For further discussion, see, for instance, A. D. Ellerman and B. K. Buchner, 'The European Union Emissions Trading Scheme: Origins, Allocation, and Early Results' (2007) 1 *Review of Environmental Economics and Policy*, 66–87.

[26] N. 27 below.

[27] Dir. 2006/32/EC on Energy End-use Efficiency and Energy Services and Repealing Council Directive 93/76/EEC [2006] OJ L114/64.

[28] Commission's Proposal for a Parliament and Council Directive on Energy End-use Efficiency and Energy Services COM(2003)739, 10 Dec. 2003.

[29] Draft Minutes of the 2717th meeting of the Council (Transport, Telecommunications and Energy), 14 Mar. 2006, Doc. No. 7424/06, 24 Mar. 2006, 3, published on the Internet at: http://register.consilium.europa.eu.

As a central element of the Community strategy on energy efficiency, it aims to enhance the cost-effective improvement of energy end-use efficiency in the Member States by providing the necessary indicative targets as well as mechanisms, incentives and institutional, financial, and legal frameworks to remove existing market barriers and imperfections that impede the efficient end-use of energy, as well as creating the conditions for the development and promotion of a market for energy services and for the delivery of other energy efficiency improvement measures to final consumers.[30]

To achieve this dual purpose, the Directive first requires Member States to adopt a general indicative energy-savings target of 9 per cent for the ninth year of its application,[31] and to create the conditions for the development and promotion of a market for energy services[32] and for the delivery of other energy efficiency improvement measures to retail consumers.[33] Additionally, Member States will have to prepare three national energy efficiency action plans to ensure that the public sector fulfils an exemplary role regarding investments, maintenance, and other expenditures on energy-using equipment and energy services.[34] To enable final consumers to make more informed decisions on their individual energy consumption, the Energy Efficiency and Energy Services Directive also requires Member States to provide a reasonable amount of information, for instance on available energy efficiency improvement measures, comparative final consumer profiles, or objective technical specifications for energy-using equipment.[35] It also requires a better metering and billing of energy consumption.[36] Six annexes contain detailed information on methodological aspects and the measurement and verification of energy savings, the energy content of selected fuels, examples of energy efficiency improvement measures, and eligible energy efficient public procurement measures.

At its second reading on 13 December 2005, the EP again proposed several amendments aimed at improving the environmental performance of the Directive by including an intermediate energy savings target, rigorous reporting obligations for Member States, and separate savings targets for the public sector.[37] All amendments were accepted in full by the Commission in its Opinion of 7 February 2006 for being 'in line with the objectives of the Commission's

[30] Energy Efficiency and Energy Services Dir., n. 27 above, Art. 1.

[31] Ibid., Art. 4(1).

[32] For the purposes of this Directive, 'energy services' are defined as: 'the physical benefit, utility or good derived from a combination of energy with energy efficient technology and/or with action, which may include the operations, maintenance and control necessary to deliver the service, which is delivered on the basis of a contract and in normal circumstances has proven to lead to verifiable and measurable or estimable energy efficiency improvement and/or primary energy savings', ibid., Art. 3(e).

[33] Ibid., Art. 6.

[34] Ibid., Art. 5.

[35] Ibid., Art. 7.

[36] Ibid., Art. 13.

[37] EP Doc. No. A6–0343/2005.

proposal'.[38] Since the proposed amendments had been part of a compromise agreed between the Parliament and the Council, the latter was able to endorse the revised Proposal with all amendments at its own second reading. From an environmental perspective, a regrettable aspect of this compromise was the omission of mandatory energy savings targets, which have now been replaced with indicative targets to accommodate the objections of various Member States. Still, with the approval of both institutions, the Energy Efficiency and Energy Services Directive finally entered into force on 17 May 2006,[39] and despite the inclusion of mere indicative targets, it provides a number of important incentives to improve energy demand management both with final customers and the public sector. Also, it establishes a framework to secure the environmental performance of the 'energy services' sector, thereby introducing a concept which was not previously subject to comprehensive regulation at this level. From its entry into force, Member States have two years in which to comply with its provisions, with the exception of the first energy efficiency action plan, which must be submitted no later than 30 June 2007.[40]

ii. Emissions Trading

On 13 November 2006, the Commission adopted a Decision on the avoidance of 'double counting' of greenhouse gas emission reductions under the Community emissions trading scheme for project activities under the Kyoto Protocol.[41] Member States need to ensure that, when hosting project activities under the flexible mechanisms of the Kyoto Protocol to the United Nations Framework Convention on Climate Change (UNFCCC),[42] no emission reduction units (ERUs) or certified emission reductions (CERs) are issued for reductions or limitations of greenhouse gas emissions that take place in installations that participate in the Community emissions trading scheme, as this would result in a double counting of emission reductions or limitations and could thereby undermine the environmental integrity of the emissions trading scheme.[43] To this end, the Decision lays down provisions for the implementation of relevant provisions of the Directive 2003/87/EC establishing a Scheme for Greenhouse Gas Emission Allowance Trading within the Community and Amending Council Directive

[38] Commission Opinion pursuant to Article 251(2), third subparagraph, point (c) of the EC Treaty, on the European Parliament's Amendments to the Council's Common Position regarding the Proposal for a Parliament and Council Directive on Energy End-use Efficiency and Energy Services (and repealing Council Dir. 93/76/EEC) COM(2003)739 final, C6–0298/2005–2003/0300 (COD), amending the Proposal of the Commission pursuant to Article 250(2) of the EC Treaty Brussels COM(2006)53, 7 Feb. 2006, 3.

[39] Energy Efficiency and Energy Services Dir., n. 27 above, Art. 19.

[40] Ibid., Art. 18.

[41] Dec. 2006/780/EC on Avoiding Double Counting of Greenhouse Gas Emission Reductions under the Community Emissions Trading Scheme for Project Activities under the Kyoto Protocol pursuant to Directive 2003/87/EC [2006] OJ L 316/12.

[42] Kyoto Protocol, n. 11 above.

[43] Dec. 2006/780/EC, n. 41 above, Preamble, Rec. 1.

96/61 (Emissions Trading Directive).[44] In particular, it specifies a provision which recognizes that Member States might have committed themselves to the issuance of ERUs or CERs prior to the adoption of the ban on double counting, and therefore allows for issuance of such units until 31 December 2012 if an equal number of allowances is cancelled.[45] Under the Decision, Member States are required to include a set-aside of allowances for each such project activity in their national allocation plan for the period 2008 to 2012.[46] Two Annexes set out the format for Member States wishing to set aside allowances for this purpose.

C. Legislation in Progress

Among legislation adopted in the recent past by the Community, the most significant developments could be observed in the area of emissions trading, where practical implementation gave rise to numerous challenges as the European market for greenhouse gas allowances entered its second year, and preparations for a review of the scheme and its operation in the trading period from 2008 to 2012 were in full swing. Altogether, market activity in 2006 was high, with 1 billion tonnes of CO_2 transacted, worth €18.1 billion, representing a growth in volume of nearly 250 per cent compared to the previous year, and rendering the European market the most 'dominant emissions trading scheme in the world'.[47] By the compliance deadline of 30 April 2006, 8,980 installations had fulfilled their reporting obligations under the Emissions Trading Directive, accounting for more than 99 per cent of allowances allocated to installations in the 21 Member States with functioning electronic registries on that date.[48]

Still, a dramatic decline in the price of allowances in May 2005 from over €30 to a figure in the single digits dominated the public perception of this scheme and was commonly described as a 'market crash'.[49] A first set of independently verified emissions reports for the year 2005 had been released by the Member States, indicating that aggregate emissions in that year, at just over 2 billion tonnes, were significantly below the annual average allocation for the first period of close to 2.2 billion tonnes.[50] Although at least partly suggesting that covered installations had reduced emissions through improved technologies and procedures, the

[44] [2003] OJ L275/32, Art. 11b (3) and (4).

[45] Ibid., Art. 11b (3) and (4).

[46] Dec. 2006/780/EC, n. 41 above, Art. 3.

[47] K. Røine and H. Hasselknippe (eds.), *Carbon 2007—A New Climate for Carbon Trading* (Oslo: Point Carbon, 2007), 8.

[48] Communication from the Commission to the Council, the European Parliament, the European Economic and Social Committee and the Committee of the Regions on Building a Global Carbon Market—Report pursuant to Article 30 of Directive 2003/87/EC COM(2006)676, 13 Nov. 2006, 3.

[49] 'Price Crash Leaves EU Carbon Market Jittery', *ENDS Europe Daily*, 5 May 2006.

[50] 'EU Emissions Trading Scheme Delivers First Verified Emissions Data for Installations', Commission's Press Release IP/06/612, 15 May 2006, published on the Internet at: http://www.europa.eu.int (RAPID database).

resulting surplus of allowances was clearly also a result of overly generous allocation decisions of the Member States, and naturally exerted a strong downward pressure on allowance prices. Such volatility is generally considered a symptom of market immaturity, and is spurned by market participants. But an overly generous allocation scenario does not merely impact the market, and interest groups soon began voicing alarm about the environmental effectiveness of the emissions trading scheme.

Indeed, the Commission itself expressed concern about the ability of the emissions trading scheme to achieve its environmental objective. 'Hence, if more allowances were to be issued by Member States than the likely quantity of actual emissions in 2008 to 2012 from the installations covered, meeting the Kyoto commitments would be severely compromised and little or no environmental benefit would be provided', the Commission stated at one point, adding that the 'development and deployment of existing and new clean technologies would stall, and the evolution of a dynamic and liquid global market would be seriously undermined'.[51] With the allocation decisions for the first trading period already largely approved, attention therefore shifted to the National Allocation Plans for the second period, and the need for sufficient scarcity of allowances in the market. Coincidentally, the very day the Polish Allocation Plan for the first trading period was belatedly endorsed by the Commission,[52] 30 June 2006, also marked the deadline for submission of the Allocation Plans for the second trading period from 2008 to 2012.[53] As with the first period however, less than a third of Member States had finalized their National Allocation Plans in time,[54] prompting the Commission to launch infringement proceedings on 12 October 2006 on all outstanding Plans.

By 29 November 2006, 19 Member States had notified a National Allocation Plan to the Commission, representing about half of the overall quantity of allowances allocated in the previous trading period. Of these, ten plans were sufficiently complete to allow the Commission to take a decision on their compatibility with the Directive.[55] In the forefront, an independent analysis of several draft plans had suggested that the second trading period would again suffer from the same shortcomings as the first, compromising the ability of the trading scheme 'to

[51] See Communication from the Commission to the Council and to the European Parliament on the Assessment of National Allocation Plans for the Allocation of Greenhouse Gas Emission Allowances in the second period of the EU Emissions Trading Scheme accompanying Commission Decisions of 29 November 2006 on the National Allocation Plans of Germany, Greece, Ireland, Latvia, Lithuania, Luxembourg, Malta, Slovakia, Sweden and the United Kingdom in accordance with Directive 2003/87/EC COM(2006)725, 29 Nov. 2006, 2.

[52] See 'Poland Enters CO_2 Emissions Trading Scheme', *ENDS Europe Daily*, 30 June 2006.

[53] Emissions Trading Dir. 2003/87/EC, n. 44 above, Art. 9(1). For each trading period, every Member State is obliged to notify a National Allocation Plan to the Commission, which assesses each plan according to the same criteria set out in Annex III to and Art. 10 of the Directive.

[54] 'Commission Unperturbed by Phase-two Nap Delays', *ENDS Europe Daily*, 6 Sept. 2006.

[55] See Commission Communication COM(2006)725, n. 51 above.

deliver any net domestic emission reductions at all in its second phase' because of 'very weak' national emission caps and 'extremely generous' provisions on project credits acquired abroad under the Kyoto Protocol.[56] Surprising some observers, perhaps, the Commission responded in the allocation decisions by 'making good' on its 'promise to be tough'[57] and demanding that several Member States set much stricter caps on greenhouse gas emissions in the second period.

In the ten decisions published on 29 November 2006, affecting the National Allocation Plans of Germany, Greece, Ireland, Latvia, Lithuania, Luxembourg, Malta, Slovakia, Sweden, and the UK, it called for an average cut in emissions of 7 per cent compared to draft Plans submitted by the Member States.[58] Several Member States were required to reduce the number of allocated allowances by over 25 per cent, in one case by even more than half.[59] Additionally, the Commission called for substantive changes in each National Allocation Plan, notably with a view to transfer rules guaranteeing a certain allocation methodology from one trading period to the next, *ex post* adjustments changing the amount allocated to individual operators following adoption of the Plan, and the ability of Member States to purchase carbon credits from project mechanisms under the Kyoto Protocol. According to the Commission, the main considerations guiding these decisions were: consistency with the path towards achievement of the Kyoto commitments entered by each Member State; consistency with emissions growth expectations and reduction potential; and supplementarity of credits acquired under the Kyoto Protocol vis-à-vis domestic action.[60]

As forward prices for the second trading period soon implied, the strict position assumed by the Commission successfully created the scarcity required to elevate demand and restore confidence in the market for allowances. While the price for first phase allowances reached new lows, allowance prices for the second trading period steadily rose throughout November to reach a price of over €18 per tonne by the end of 2006.[61] Clearly, the Commission drew a number of lessons from the first trading period, which, at any rate, had always been intended as a 'learning phase'.[62] But it remains to be seen whether these lessons will also be fully implemented in the review of the emissions trading scheme, a process which involves an assessment of its functioning and its scope, in particular as regards its future expansion to other sectors and gases beyond the second trading period from 2008

56 'EU ETS "Risks Failing to Cut Emissions', *ENDS Europe Daily*, 5 Oct. 2006.

57 'Dimas Makes Good on Naps', *ENDS Europe Daily*, 29 Nov. 2006.

58 Commission Communication COM(2006)725, n. 51 above.

59 Large reductions were required from, inter alia, Latvia (57 per cent), Lithuania (47 per cent), and Luxembourg (32 per cent).

60 See 'Emissions Trading: Commission Decides on First Set of National Allocation Plans for the 2008–2012 Trading Period', Commission's Press Release IP/06/1650, 29 Nov. 2006, published on the Internet at: http://www.europa.eu.int (RAPID database).

61 'EU Carbon Prices take High and Low Roads', *ENDS Europe Daily*, 6 Dec. 2006.

62 COM(2006)725, n. 51 above, 2.

to 2012.[63] Priorities for this review will be the scope of the scheme, opportunities for further harmonization and increased predictability, more robust compliance and enforcement, and linking to emission trading schemes in third countries.[64]

D. Case Law

i. Emissions Trading

On 12 January 2006, the Fifth Chamber of the European Court of Justice (ECJ) declared that, by failing to adopt the laws, regulations, and administrative provisions necessary to comply with the Emissions Trading Directive in the province of Åland, the Finnish Republic had failed to fulfil its obligations under that Directive.[65] Åland is an archipelago in the Gulf of Bothnia forming an autonomous administrative province of Finland, and frequently gives rise to difficulties when it comes to the implementation of European Community legislation. For the environmental performance of the emissions trading scheme, however, its significance—with a very limited number of installations—is minor.

On 18 May 2006, the Fifth Chamber also condemned Italy for failure to adopt the legislation necessary to comply with the Emissions Trading Directive.[66] On 7 July 2004, the Commission had issued a letter of formal notice, or first written warning, against Italy for not fully transposing the Directive into national law by 31 December 2003,[67] followed by a reasoned opinion, or final written warning. While the Italian government was able to document adoption of pertinent legislation by the time of the oral hearing, the Court followed established case law by basing its judgment on the situation prevailing at the end of the period laid down in the reasoned opinion.[68] Italy is commonly perceived as a laggard in the implementation of European climate policies and did not contest the case, making it the first Member State to have been condemned for failure to transpose the Emissions Trading Directive.[69]

[63] For further details on the review process, see Section D.*iii.* below.

[64] Communication from the Commission to the Council, the European Parliament, the European Economic and Social Committee and the Committee of the Regions on Building a Global Carbon Market—Report pursuant to Article 30 of Directive 2003/87/EC COM(2006)676, 13 Nov. 2006.

[65] Case C-107/05 *Commission* v. *Finland* [2006] ECR I-10.

[66] Case C-122/05 *Commission* v. *Italy* [2006] OJ C 115/1; published (in Italian) on the Internet at: http://curia.europa.eu/jurisp/cgi-bin/gettext.pl?lang=it&num=79939481C19050122&doc=T&ouvert=T&seance=ARRET.

[67] 'Emissions trading: Commission Takes Legal Action to Speed up Member States' Preparations', Commission's Press Release IP/04/861, 7 July 2004, published on the Internet at: http://www.europa.eu.int (RAPID database).

[68] Case C-122/05, n. 66 above, pt. 5. The ECJ referred, in particular, to Case C-323/01 *Commission* v. *Italy* [2002] ECR I-4711, pt. 8; and Case C-140/03 *Commission* v. *Greece* [2005] ECR I-3177, pt. 21.

[69] 'Italy Condemned over Emission Trading Delay', *ENDS Europe Daily*, 19 May 2006.

Later during the year, on 12 December 2006, the Commission initiated proceedings against several Member States over delayed National Allocation Plans and incomplete emission reports.[70] Under the Emissions Trading Directive, Member States were obliged to submit their National Allocation Plans for the second trading period to the Commission by 30 June 2006.[71] Following a first written warning issued on 12 October 2006,[72] the Commission sent final written warnings to Austria, Denmark, Hungary, and Italy for failure to meet the deadline. At the same time, it issued first written warnings to France, Germany, Poland, and Slovenia, and final written warnings to Estonia, Luxembourg, and Spain for failure to provide complete reports on their progress in limiting or cutting greenhouse gas emissions as required by a Decision on monitoring emissions and implementing the Kyoto Protocol.[73] The deadline for Member States to submit these reports had elapsed on 15 January 2006. If the affected Member States fail to respond to the final written warning, or if the Commission is not satisfied with their response, the Commission can take the Member States before the ECJ under Article 226 of the EC Treaty (EC).

ii. Renewable Energy

On 4 April 2006, the Commission sent a letter of formal notice to Italy, Poland, the Czech Republic, and the UK for failure to report their progress on the use of electricity from renewable energy sources, and to Italy, Latvia, Cyprus, Greece, and Ireland for adopting insufficient measures to enable an adequate promotion of renewable energies.[74] According to the Commission, these Member States had thereby failed to comply with Directive 2001/77/EC on the Promotion of Electricity Produced from Renewable Energy Sources in the Internal Electricity Market,[75] which requires Member States to implement legislation, administrative provisions and measures—including fair grid access and a guarantee of origin—to enhance the use of renewable electricity in the Community. It sets an indicative target of 21.1 per cent for the share of electricity from renewable energy sources in total European electricity consumption by 2010, and requires Member States to set national indicative targets and implement the appropriate measures

[70] 'Climate Change: Commission Takes Legal Action Over Missing National Allocation Plans, Incomplete Emission Reports', Commission's Press Release IP/06/1763, 12 Dec. 2006, published on the Internet at: http://www.europa.eu.int (RAPID database).

[71] See Emissions Trading Dir, n. 44 above, Art. 9(1).

[72] 'Commission Asks Member States to Provide Important Information in the Fight Against Climate Change', Commission's Press Release IP/06/1364, 12 Oct. 2006, published on the Internet at: http://www.europa.eu.int (RAPID database).

[73] Dec. 280/2004/EC concerning a Mechanism for Monitoring Community Greenhouse Gas Emissions and for Implementing the Kyoto Protocol [2004] OJ L49/1.

[74] 'Eight Member States Still Not in Compliance with Community Legislation Promoting Renewable Electricity', Commission's Press Release IP/06/429, 4 Apr. 2006, published on the Internet at: http://www.europa.eu.int (RAPID database).

[75] [2001] OJ L283/33.

to achieve the global target.[76] The deadline for implementation had elapsed on 27 October 2003.[77]

On the same day, the Commission sent a reasoned opinion to Finland and a letter of formal notice to Denmark,[78] claiming that both Member States had failed to give adequate reasons for having set targets considerably lower than the 2 per cent reference value laid down by Directive 2003/30/EC on the Promotion of the Use of Biofuels and other Renewable Fuels for Transport (Biofuels Directive) for 2005.[79] A letter of formal notice was also sent to Luxembourg due to an incomplete biofuel report for 2005, and a reasoned opinion to Italy due to its failure to submit such a report. The Biofuels Directive sets out reference values for the share of biofuels in a 2 per cent share in 2005 and a 5.75 per cent share in 2010.[80] Member States may set their own indicative targets, but need to provide a motivation for deviations from the reference value in their reports to the Commission.[81]

E. Policy Documents

i. Common Energy Policy

Following years of substantive division, with traditional energy concerns such as energy security and market liberalization assigned to different institutional bodies than the environmental impacts of energy production, distribution, and consumption,[82] the Commission published a Green Paper on 8 March 2006 with a view to developing a common and coherent European energy policy.[83] According to the Green Paper, a common energy policy should meet three core objectives: sustainable development; competitiveness; and security of supply. With a view to improved environmental protection, the Green Paper calls for 'major steps forward in developing competitive renewable sources of energy and other low carbon sources', seeks to 'curb energy demand' and prompts the Community to 'lead global efforts to halt climate change and improve local

[76] Ibid., Art. 3(4).

[77] Ibid., Art. 10.

[78] 'European Commission Urges Member States to Implement the Biofuels Directive', Commission's Press Release IP/06/431, 4 Apr. 2006, published on the Internet at: http://www.europa.eu.int (RAPID database).

[79] [2003] OJ L123/1.

[80] Ibid., Art. 3(1).

[81] Ibid., Art. 4(1).

[82] Of major importance in this regard is the division of responsibilities between the Directorate-General (DG) for Transport and Energy and DG Environment at the Commission, but also between different formations of the Council of Ministers. For an ample critique, see L. van Schaik and C. Egenhofer, *Reform of the EU Institutions: Implications for the EU's Performance in Climate Negotiations* (Brussels: CEPS, 2003).

[83] Green Paper—A European Strategy for Sustainable, Competitive and Secure Energy COM(2006)105, 8 Mar. 2006.

air quality'.[84] It invites comments on six specific priority areas 'where action is necessary to address the challenges' currently faced,[85] and contains a number of suggestions for possible new action in each area.

A first priority area identified in the Green Paper is the completion of the internal market for electricity and gas, and to this end the Commission proposes, inter alia, adopting an energy grid code and a priority interconnection plan, a European energy regulator, and new initiatives to ensure fair competition, particularly with regard to the unbundling of networks from competitive activities.[86] Security of supply in the internal energy market constitutes the second priority area, with suggested measures including the establishment of a European Energy Supply Observatory and a revision of existing Community legislation on oil and gas stocks to avoid potential supply disruptions.[87] A more sustainable, efficient and diverse energy mix is identified as the third priority area, and while the Commission argues in favour of subsidiarity of Community action in this matter, it proposes a Strategic Energy Review—covering all aspects of energy policy—to analyse the advantages and drawbacks of different energy sources. Eventually, the Commission adds, such a review could result in the adoption of an 'overall strategic objective' for the energy mix at the Community level, balancing the freedom of Member States to choose between different energy sources and the need for an energy mix that, overall, meets the European energy objectives of sustainable energy use, competitiveness, and security of supply.[88]

For the fourth priority area, designated an 'integrated approach to tackling climate change' and thus the most interesting priority area in the context of this survey, the Commission suggests a series of measures to decouple economic growth from increased energy consumption, with an emphasis on an Action Plan on Energy Efficiency aimed at reducing energy consumption in the EU by 20 per cent by 2020.[89] The Commission envisions the following measures on energy efficiency: efficiency campaigns, including on buildings; use of financial instruments and mechanisms to stimulate investment; a renewed effort for greater energy efficiency in the transport sector; a Europe-wide 'white certificates' trading system and better information on the energy performance of some appliances, vehicles, and industrial equipment, possibly coupled with minimum performance standards. In the area of renewable energy, moreover, the Green Paper proposes a long-term Renewable Energy Road Map with possible targets for 2020 and beyond in order to provide a stable investment climate to generate more competitive renewable energy in Europe.[90] According to the Commission, concrete measures in this road map could include a renewed effort to meet existing targets, consideration of necessary targets or objectives beyond 2010, a new Community Directive on heating and cooling, a detailed plan to stabilize and gradually reduce European dependence on imported oil, and initiatives to bring

[84] Ibid., 17. [85] Ibid., 4. [86] Ibid., 5–7. [87] Ibid., 8–9.
[88] Ibid., 9–10. [89] Ibid., 10–11. [90] Ibid., 12–13.

clean and renewable energy sources closer to markets. Carbon capture and geological storage is also mentioned as a viable instrument, with further incentives for its research and deployment recommended.

A strategic energy technology plan, proposed as the fifth priority area, should help ensure that European industry can compete on global markets for new energy technologies and processes.[91] And finally, the Green Paper stresses the need for a common external energy policy to react better to the global challenges of growing demand, high and volatile energy prices, increasing import dependency and climate change.[92] Among other measures, the Green Paper urges the Community to propose and promote an international agreement on energy efficiency to expand the energy star eco-labelling scheme. On the basis of replies and comments to this Green Paper as well as the conclusions of the European Council and Parliament, the Commission announced it would elaborate a series of proposals on concrete measures. Following its publication, however, the Green Paper met with mixed responses, with interest groups representing European business largely welcoming the strong cooperation on energy policy it envisions, while environmentalists mostly censured it for an absence of binding targets and timelines on energy efficiency and renewable energy sources.[93] Still, the concept of a common European energy policy secured an endorsement by the Council of Energy Ministers later that month, as ministers backed the 'shared general orientations' on energy in the medium and long term to ensure policy coherence at the European level.[94]

ii. Emissions Trading

With the deadline for submission of National Allocation Plans (NAPs) for the second trading period rapidly approaching, the Commission announced a new guidance document on 9 January 2006.[95] Like the earlier guidance document for the first trading period,[96] it provides Member States with information on the design of their NAPs. Drawing on the lessons learnt during the first allocation round, the new guidance document aims for greater transparency and ease of implementation by proposing a set of standardized 'Common Format Tables' for the presentation of important information, such as projected emissions,

[91] Ibid., 13–14.

[92] Ibid., 14–17.

[93] 'EU Energy Paper Draws Praise and Criticism', *ENDS Europe Daily*, 8 Mar. 2006.

[94] 'Ministers Endorse Common EU Energy Policy', *ENDS Europe Daily*, 15 Mar. 2006.

[95] Communication from the Commission on Further Guidance on Allocation Plans for the 2008 to 2012 Trading Period of the EU Emission Trading Scheme COM(2005)703, 22 Dec. 2005. The guidance document was sent to Member States in Dec. 2005, but not published until 9 Jan. 2006, see 'Starting Gun Fired for EU Carbon Trade Part Two', *ENDS Europe Daily*, 6 Nov. 2006.

[96] Communication from the Commission on Guidance to Assist Member States in the Implementation of the Criteria listed in Annex III to Directive 2003/87/EC establishing a Scheme for Greenhouse Gas Emission Allowance Trading within the Community and amending Council Directive 96/61/EC, and on the Circumstances under which Force Majeure is demonstrated COM(2003)830, 7 Jan. 2004.

assumptions regarding fuel prices, and the reductions expected from other policies and measures.[97] Because the second trading period coincides with the first commitment period under the Kyoto Protocol, the Commission has particularly stressed the need for Member States to ensure their climate strategies, including NAPs, contribute towards achievement of their respective greenhouse gas mitigation obligations.[98]

Specifically, Member States are requested to substantiate the effects of other climate policies and measures, thereby allowing the Commission to assess whether the cap imposed on the sectors covered by the emissions trading scheme is sufficiently stringent.[99] In the same vein, Member States are obliged to provide information on the intended government purchase of Kyoto Protocol units, for instance by demonstrating the existence of relevant national legislation and budget allocations.[100] Following calls from Member States and stakeholders for increased harmonization of allocation rules, the new guidance document also offers a consistent methodology for Member States to set caps for their emissions. Finally, with a view to more uniform interpretation of central definitions, the Commission outlines the categories of combustion installations which should be covered by specifying a minimum size threshold, and also addresses the situation of 'small' installations.[101] According to the guidance document, these common definitions will bring in many 'large installations with significant emissions' and resolve the 'highly unsatisfactory' and distorting situation which had prevailed during the first trading period.[102]

Another important policy document adopted in this context concerned the review of the emissions trading scheme with a view to its improvement as an instrument of climate policy and an expansion to new sectors and gases. Article 30 of the Emissions Trading Directive provides for the Commission to draw up a report to the EP and the Council by 30 June 2006 on the application of the Directive, accompanied by proposals as appropriate. Declaring that 'more experience and evaluation [are] needed' for addressing the key strategic issues, and that it 'would therefore be premature for the Commission to make legislative proposals at this stage', the Commission 'took additional time' to finally submit a report on 13 November 2006 setting out its agenda for the review process.[103] In the Communication, evocatively titled 'Building a Global Carbon Market', the Commission sets out four broad categories of issues on which the review will focus. For reasons of 'regulatory stability and predictability', however,

[97] COM(2005)703, n. 95 above, 2 and Annex 10.

[98] 'Emissions Trading: Commission Sets Out Guidance on National Allocations for 2008–2012', Commission's Press Release IP/06/09, 9 Jan. 2006, published on the Internet at: http://www.europa.eu.int (RAPID database).

[99] COM(2005)703, n. 95 above, Annex 6.

[100] Ibid., Annex 5.

[101] Ibid., Annexes 8 and 9.

[102] Ibid., 9.

[103] COM(2006)676, n. 48 above, 2.

any amendments to the Directive prompted by this review should not take effect before the third trading period in 2013 and follow a broad stakeholder consultation process involving contributions from a Working Group on the Review of the EU ETS within the framework of the European Climate Change Programme (ECCP).[104]

Under the first category, concerning the scope of the scheme, the Commission announced it will consider an expansion of the trading scheme to other sectors and other greenhouse gases besides carbon dioxide, for instance nitrous oxide from ammonia production and methane from coal mines. Likewise, the review will assess options to improve participation by small installations and promote clarity on which types of combustion installations should be covered.[105] A second priority identified in the report is further harmonization and increased predictability of the trading scheme, two areas where the European Environment Agency (EEA) had pointed out several shortcomings earlier during the year.[106] Clearly, the most important cause of diversity between Member States is the allocation process, giving rise to very different levels of environmental stringency and thus to competitive distortions. According to the Commission, therefore, greater harmonization is needed in relation to how Member States set their overall cap and distribute allowances, in particular with regard to new entrants and installations closures. As a means of increasing predictability and harmonization, moreover, the Commission plans to explore options for the setting of a single European cap after 2012.[107]

A third focus area for the review process will be improved compliance and enforcement of the trading scheme, with attention devoted to the elaboration of guidelines for monitoring and reporting emissions to be potentially adopted by way of a regulation, and to rules for third-party verification of emissions reports.[108] Finally, returning to the title of its report for the fourth category, the Commission report opens a discussion on how the EU trading scheme might be linked to existing or future schemes in third countries. Moreover, the report expresses a commitment to maintaining the recognition of credits from emission-saving projects carried out in developing countries and elsewhere.[109] A concluding section of the report addresses procedural and institutional issues as well as the relationship of emissions trading to other market-based regulatory instruments.[110] According to the Commission, legislative proposals can be expected for the second half of 2007. A likely implication of many foregoing suggestions

[104] Ibid., 5–6.

[105] Ibid., 7.

[106] EEA, *Application of the Emissions Trading Directive by EU Member States* (EEA: Copenhagen, 2006), 41.

[107] COM(2006)676, n. 48 above, 8.

[108] Ibid.

[109] Ibid.

[110] COM(2006)676, n. 48 above, 9.

will be a stronger role of the Community in the management of the trading scheme.[111]

With a view to an expansion of the trading scheme to a new sector, albeit not as a part of the foregoing review, the Commission released a Proposal on 20 December 2006 to bring air transport into the scope of emissions trading.[112] Responding to the rapid growth of emissions from international air transport,[113] the Proposal—which follows up on an earlier Communication of 27 September 2005[114]—aims at extending the trading scheme to all domestic and international flights between EU airports from 2011, and to all international flights arriving at or departing from EU airports from 2012. According to the Commission, estimates suggest that inclusion in the trading scheme will allow annual CO_2 savings of as much as 46 per cent by 2020, or 183 million tonnes.[115] Overall, allocation of allowances will be harmonized across the Community, with the number of available allowances capped at the average emissions level in 2004 to 2006.[116] A fixed percentage of the total quantity of allowances will be allocated free of charge on the basis of an efficiency benchmark reflecting the historical share of each operator in air traffic, and the remainder auctioned subject to the provisions of a Commission Regulation.[117] Auctioning proceeds should be used to mitigate and adapt to the impacts of climate change and to cover administrative costs. Also, to reduce administrative costs, very light aircraft will not be covered, and each operator will be administered by only one Member State.[118]

iii. Energy Efficiency

After a high-level stakeholder advisory group set up to advise the EU on competitiveness, energy, and the environment recommended addressing energy efficiency with a 'new sense of urgency'[119] and the EP called for a 'market transformation' in

[111] 'Starting Gun Fired for EU ETS Review', *ENDS Europe Daily*, 13 Nov. 2006.

[112] Commission's Proposal for a Directive of the European Parliament and of the Council amending Directive 2003/87/EC so as to Include Aviation Activities in the Scheme for Greenhouse Gas Emission Allowance Trading within the Community COM(2006)818, 20 Dec. 2006.

[113] Greenhouse gas emissions from aviation are expected to rise threefold between 1992 and 2025, rendering aviation the fastest-growing source of greenhouse gases worldwide; as a result, the proportion of anthropogenic climate change attributable to aviation is projected to increase from its present level of 3.5 per cent to 15 per cent by the year 2050, see generally Intergovernmental Panel on Climate Change, *Special Report on Aviation and the Global Atmosphere* (Cambridge: Cambridge University Press, 1999).

[114] Communication from the Commission to the Council, the European Parliament, the European Economic and Social Committee and the Committee of the Regions on Reducing the Climate Change Impact of Aviation COM(2005)459, 27 Sep. 2005.

[115] 'Climate Change: Commission Proposes Bringing Air Transport into EU Emissions Trading Scheme', Commission's Press Release IP/06/1862, 20 Dec. 2006, published on the Internet at: http://www.europa.eu.int (RAPID database).

[116] COM(2006)818, n. 112 above, 15, Art. 3b.

[117] Ibid., 16, Arts. 3c and 3d.

[118] Ibid., 24 (Annex).

[119] 'High-level Industry Group Issues First Report', *ENDS Europe Daily*, 7 June 2006.

energy-using products and an 'energy efficiency revolution',[120] the Commission followed up on its Green Paper on energy efficiency of 22 June 2005[121] with a detailed Action Plan on Energy Efficiency to lower energy consumption by 20 per cent by 2020.[122] It contains a set of over 75 measures in ten priority areas to be implemented over the course of the next six years. Proposed actions cover a wide range of energy efficiency initiatives, including minimum energy performance standards for energy appliances and buildings, stronger promotion of energy services, as well as specific financing mechanisms to support more energy efficient products.[123] Such standards will be implemented as voluntary industry agreements or binding legislative targets, and the Commission also announced a 'substantial expansion' of Directive 2002/91/EC on the Energy Performance of Buildings[124] to include minimum energy requirements for new and renovated buildings.[125] Accompanying these measures will be strengthened energy labelling schemes.

In the area of electricity generation, transmission, and distribution, the Action Plan proposes targeted instruments to improve the efficiency of both new and existing generation capacity and to reduce transmission and distribution losses, including minimum binding efficiency requirements for new electricity, heating, and cooling installations lower than 20 megawatts.[126] For the challenging transport sector, moreover, it aims to increase the fuel efficiency of cars, develop markets for cleaner vehicles, ensure proper tyre pressure and improve the efficiency of urban, rail, maritime, and aviation transport systems. If necessary, the Commission will propose legislation to ensure achievement of the objective of 120 grams per kilometre by 2012 for average new vehicle emissions.[127] Appropriate and predictable price signals and a number of additional measures to raise energy efficiency awareness, such as education and training, are also prioritized by the Commission, as are initiatives to further elaborate energy taxation and address energy efficiency on a global level through international partnerships, including cooperation between large municipalities and an international framework agreement on energy efficiency.[128] While most initiatives proposed in the final version are based on the implementation or revision of existing legislation,[129] if the Action Plan is fully implemented, the Commission anticipates it will reduce the direct cost of energy consumption in the EU by more than €100 billion annually

[120] 'EU Parliament Urges Energy Efficiency Revolution', *ENDS Europe Daily*, 2 June 2006.

[121] Green Paper on Energy Efficiency, or Doing More With Less COM(2005)265, 22 June 2005.

[122] Communication from the Commission on an Action Plan for Energy Efficiency—Realising the Potential COM(2006)545, 19 Oct. 2006.

[123] Ibid., 9–12.

[124] [2003] OJ L1/65.

[125] COM(2006)545, n. 122 above, 12.

[126] Ibid., 13–14.

[127] Ibid., 15.

[128] Ibid., 18–19 and 24.

[129] 'EU Energy Efficiency Action Plan in Detail', *ENDS Europe Daily*, 19 Oct. 2006.

by 2020, and also avoid emissions of approximately 780 millions tonnes of CO_2 every year.[130] Overall, the Action Plan was welcomed by representatives from both trade and industry and by legislators.[131]

Also in the area of energy efficiency, the Commission launched the procedure to negotiate a new agreement on the Energy Star labelling programme for office equipment with the United States.[132] This programme was originally developed by the US Environmental Protection Agency (EPA) and adopted by the EU through an agreement concluded in 2000 for an initial period of five years.[133] It encourages and supports procurers and consumers in purchasing efficient products through the provision of a label for equipment complying with specified energy efficiency criteria. As such, the Energy Star programme forms part of the Commission strategy to improve the efficiency of energy use and to implement a sustainable energy policy in the EU. In a Communication on the implementation of the Energy Star programme, the Commission conceded that it was unable to quantify the extent to which the programme had contributed to an improvement of the energy efficiency of office equipment, but nonetheless considered it 'the most adequate policy instrument for the Community to capture the potential energy savings',[134] especially compared to compulsory energy labelling under existing legislation such as Directive 92/75/EEC on the Indication by Labelling and Standard Product Information of the Consumption of Energy and other Resources by Household Appliances.[135] A new agreement should therefore include more ambitious energy efficiency standards for office equipment to respond to technological progress, increased office equipment stocks and more powerful equipment.[136] While this would mean that roughly three quarters of currently certified equipment will be unable to carry the Energy Star label, the initiative met with a 'cautious welcome' from industry representatives.[137]

iv. Biomass

Biofuels have been attracting much attention in recent years as a means to achieve simultaneous economic, social, and environmental benefits as well as a strategy

[130] 'Saving 20% by 2020: European Commission Unveils its Action Plan on Energy Efficiency', Commission's Press Release IP/06/1434, 19 Oct. 2006, published on the Internet at: http://www.europa.eu.int (RAPID database).

[131] 'Commission Sets out EU Energy Efficiency Vision', *ENDS Europe Daily*, 19 Oct. 2006.

[132] 'Energy Savings: Further Development of International Cooperation on Energy Efficiency of Office Equipment', Commission's Press Release IP/06/393, 28 Mar. 2006, published on the Internet at: http://www.europa.eu.int (RAPID database).

[133] Agreement between the United States of America and the European Community on the Coordination of Energy Efficient Labeling Programs for Office Equipment [2001] OJ L172/3.

[134] Communication from the Commission to the Council and the European Parliament on the Implementation of the ENERGY STAR Programme in the European Community in the Period 2001–2005 COM(2006)140, 27 Mar. 2006, 8.

[135] [1992]OJ L297/16.

[136] COM(2006)140, n. 134 above, *passim*.

[137] 'EU Bids to Revolutionise Energy Star Label', *ENDS Europe Daily*, 31 Mar. 2006.

to improve energy security and independence from politically risky fossil fuels. Nonetheless, because of perceived environmental and development risks, biofuels have also prompted highly critical responses from various interest groups. Still, according to the EEA, the Community could derive up to 16 per cent of its primary energy demand from domestically produced biomass by 2030 without putting additional pressure on the environment.[138] Seeking to harness this potential, the Commission adopted a comprehensive strategy for biofuels on 8 February 2006, with a range of market-based, legislative and research proposals to boost production of fuels from agricultural raw materials.[139] Building on an earlier biomass action plan adopted on 7 December 2005,[140] it sets out three main aims: to promote biofuels both in Europe and in developing countries; to prepare for large-scale use of biofuels by improving their cost-competitiveness and increasing research into 'second generation' fuels; and to support developing countries where biofuel production could stimulate sustainable economic growth. According to the Commission, increased use of biofuels will bring numerous benefits by reducing European dependence on fossil fuel imports, reducing greenhouse gas emissions, providing new outlets for farmers, and opening up new economic possibilities in several developing countries.[141] The Strategy identifies six 'policy axes', drawing together measures the Commission will adopt to promote the production and use of biofuels.

In the order listed in the strategy document, these 'policy axes' are: improved stimulation of the demand for biofuels, notably through a revision of Directive 2003/30/EC on the Promotion of the Use of Biofuels or other Renewable Fuels for Transport (Biofuels Directive);[142] harnessing the environmental benefits of biofuels by ensuring sustainability of biofuel feedstock cultivation and possible limits on biofuel content in petrol and diesel; enhanced opportunities for the production and distribution of biofuels through rural development programmes and stricter monitoring to prevent discrimination against biofuels; extended supplies of feedstock and better trade opportunities; support for developing countries, notably through a coherent Biofuels Assistance Package; and expanded research and development, with the Commission envisaging a 'Biofuel Technology Platform'.[143] Although promoted as a balanced approach to achieve political, social, economic, and environmental benefits, the Strategy faced immediate criticism from environmental groups, which called for mandatory eco-certification

[138] EEA, 'How Much Bioenergy can Europe Produce without Harming the Environment?' (Luxembourg: Office for Official Publications of the European Communities, 2006), 51.

[139] Communication from the Commission on an EU Strategy for Biofuels COM(2006)34, 8 Feb. 2006.

[140] Communication from the Commission on a Biomass Action Plan COM(2005)628, 7 Dec. 2005.

[141] 'Commission Urges New Drive to Boost Production of Biofuels', Commission's Press Release IP/06/135, 8 Feb. 2006, published on the Internet at: http://www.europa.eu.int (RAPID database).

[142] [2003] OJ L123/42.

[143] COM(2006)34, n. 139 above, 7–17.

for both domestic and imported biofuels.[144] In particular, environmental groups opposed the proposal of counting biofuel use towards CO_2 emission targets for car fleets, describing it as an 'outrageous idea'.[145] Despite the mixed responses, the Council of Energy Ministers adopted a Resolution on 8 June 2006 endorsing the Commission Strategy on Transport Biofuels.[146]

F. International Cooperation

i. United Nations

Convening in Nairobi, Kenya, from 6 to 17 November 2006, the 12th Session of the Conference of the Parties (COP) to the United Nations Framework Convention on Climate Change (UNFCCC) and the 2nd Session of the Meeting of the Parties (MOP) to the Kyoto Protocol aspired to the adoption of a wide range of decisions designed to mitigate climate change and assist developing countries with adaptation to the effects of global warming.[147] Attended by around 6,000 participants, the discussions largely focused on long-term action and commitments for the period after the first commitment period of the Kyoto Protocol, which expires in 2012, as well as adaptation action and improved assessment of vulnerability and adaptation to climate change in developing countries. With a view to the latter, a Nairobi Work Programme on Impacts, Vulnerability and Adaptation was adopted, as were an agreement on the management of the Adaptation Fund under the Kyoto Protocol and rules for the Special Climate Change Fund, both of which are aimed at providing financial resources for the poorest and most vulnerable regions. While the Nairobi Conference did not result in any major breakthrough in negotiations, it did mark a staging post as negotiators seek to pave the way for a future post-2012 agreement.[148]

ii. Bilateral Cooperation

After already finding common ground on transport biofuels during informal talks in April 2006,[149] the EU and the US agreed on a High-Level Dialogue

[144] 'EU Drive for Biofuels Sparks Green Concerns', *ENDS Europe Daily*, 8 Feb. 2006.

[145] 'Biofuels no Panacea: EEB Urges Commission to Keep Close Watch on Wider Environmental and Social Impacts', European Environmental Bureau (EEB) Press Release of 8 Feb. 2006, published on the Internet at: http://www.eeb.org/press/pr_biofuels_no_panacea_080206.htm.

[146] 'EU Governments Take Position on Biomass Energy', *ENDS Europe Daily*, 8 June 2006.

[147] '"Spirit of Nairobi" Prevails as United Nations Climate Change Conference Successfully Concludes with Decisions to Support Developing Countries', UNFCCC Press Release, 17 Nov. 2006, published on the Internet at: http://unfccc.int/files/press/news_room/press_releases_and_advisories/application/pdf/20061117_cop_12_closing-english.pdf.

[148] See generally IISD, 'Summary of the Twelfth Conference of the Parties to the UN Framework Convention on Climate Change and Second Meeting of the Parties to the Kyoto Protocol: 6–17 November 2006' (2006) 12 *Earth Negotiations Bulletin* 318, published on the Internet at: http://www.iisd.ca/climate/cop12.

[149] 'EU and US Find Common Ground on Biofuels', *ENDS Europe Daily*, 26 Apr. 2006.

on Climate Change, Clean Energy and Sustainable Development during their annual summit in Vienna on 21 June 2006.[150] In a joint declaration highlighting the priorities of transatlantic cooperation, both sides agreed to 'act with resolve and urgency to reduce greenhouse gas emissions'.[151] Announcing a reinforced strategic energy cooperation, the declaration calls for accelerated investment in and development of low pollution and low carbon technologies, more and better use of renewable energy sources, and more responsible use of energy, in particular by cooperation to improve the efficiency of worldwide traded products. Future discussion should also address the use of market-based mechanisms to achieve greenhouse gas emission cuts. Later in the year, on 24 to 25 October, the EU and the US held the inaugural meeting of the High Level Dialogue on Climate Change, Clean Energy and Sustainable Development in Helsinki, Finland.[152] According to officials from the Commission, the event was the 'most significant bilateral meeting between the two [nations] since the US decided to abandon the Kyoto Protocol in 2001',[153] and revealed changing attitudes on both sides. Still, quantified commitments on emission targets, arguably the most divisive issue between the both regions, were not on the agenda, with a focus instead on practical actions, such as tax and labelling schemes, and opportunities for technological collaboration on carbon sequestration, the recovery of methane emissions, and second generation biofuels.

Improved cooperation on climate issues was also an issue discussed at the sixth Asia-Europe Meeting (ASEM), which took place in Helsinki on 10 and 11 September 2006. Involving 39 countries from both regions, the meeting resulted in the adoption of a Declaration on Climate Change with the aim of adding momentum to efforts to reach agreement in international climate negotiations.[154] It supports the objectives of the UNFCCC and other measures to reduce greenhouse gas concentrations in the atmosphere, but gives no indication as to whether large Asian emitters such as China will adopt commitments when the Kyoto Protocol expires in 2012.[155] Meanwhile, on 8 December 2006, senior representatives of the EU and the Russian Federation convening at the second meeting of the Permanent Partnership Council on Energy agreed to strengthen their energy efficiency cooperation, approving a series of expert recommendations on sharing

[150] 'EU and USA Agree Climate Change Dialogue', *ENDS Europe Daily*, 21 June 2006.

[151] Vienna Summit Declaration, 21 June 2006, published on the Internet at: http://www.ue2006.at/includes/Download_Dokumente/2106EUUSDeclaration.pdf, 10.

[152] 'EU and U.S. Will Continue Dialogue on Climate Change, Clean Energy and Sustainable Development', EU–US Joint Press Release, 25 Oct. 2006, published on the Internet at: http://www.eu2006.fi/news_and_documents/press_releases/vko43/en_GB/172262.

[153] 'EU and USA Find Common Ground on Climate Change', *ENDS Europe Daily*, 26 Oct. 2006.

[154] 'A Decision on the Enlargement of ASEM in the Helsinki Summit', ASEM Press Release, 11 Sep. 2006, published on the Internet at: http://www.asem6.fi/news_and_documents/en_GB/1157984048115/.

[155] 'Europe and Asia Plot Climate Futures', *ENDS Europe Daily*, 11 Sept. 2006.

information and enhancing mutual trust and confidence.[156] The Permanent Partnership Council consists of Ministers from Russia, the EU Presidency, the incoming EU Presidency, and a European Commissioner.

G. Conclusion

More than ever before, it might be argued that climate and energy policies have arrived at a crossroads. At the interface of these two issue areas, a certain maturity has clearly been achieved. Legislative measures have proliferated, actors become increasingly professionalized, and rapid advances in the scientific understanding of global warming and its causes as well as the development of technological responses offer improved solutions. But with proliferation has come a worrisome degree of fragmentation, as innovative and frequently untested policy approaches are adopted at an unprecedented pace and give rise to concerns about their effectiveness and mutual compatibility. At the same time, with any issue area attracting as much attention as climate change, the likelihood of symbolic legislation adopted purely for political reasons is particularly high. Despite recent statements that might have casual observers believe otherwise, international cooperation on global warming still faces the same diplomatic barriers it has suffered from for more than a decade. Consolidation and reform of existing policies and renewed efforts on the international stage are therefore urgent priorities as the EC strategy on climate change and energy sustainability enters a new phase. Clearly, the Community is cognizant of these challenges, launching a fundamental initiative to integrate climate and energy policies at the European level and review its instrumental centrepiece: the EU emissions trading scheme.

Already, the Commission has indicated that climate change will remain at the top of its agenda in 2007. As the Commissioner for the Environment, Stavros Dimas, stated during a meeting with EP representatives: '[c]limate change remains the most urgent priority and is—thankfully—on the top of the international political agenda... Mandatory reductions, an international price on carbon and a global cap and trade scheme are necessary.'[157] In November 2006, Commission President José Manuel Barroso further announced that energy and climate issues would feature strongly in the strategic initiatives planned for 2007, with great weight placed on the elaboration of 'the first ever Strategic Energy Review for Europe' and an energy efficiency action plan.[158] But there are also

[156] 'Russia and the EU Agree to Join Efforts to Promote Energy Efficiency', Commission's Press Release IP/06/1715, 8 Dec. 2006, published on the Internet at: http://www.europa.eu.int (RAPID database).

[157] Stavros Dimas, Political Priorities in Environment Policy 2007: Speech for the Environment Committee at the European Parliament, SPEECH/06/393, Brussels, 20 June 2006, published on the Internet at: http://europa.eu/rapid/pressReleasesAction.do?reference=SPEECH/06/393. See also Annual Policy Strategy for 2007: Boosting Trust through Action COM(2006)122, 9.

[158] José Manuel Barroso, Presentation of the European Commission's 2007 Work Programme, SPEECH/06/683, Strasbourg, 14 Nov. 2006, published on the Internet at: http://europa.eu/rapid/pressReleasesAction.do?reference=SPEECH/06/683.

more tempering forces operating in the Commission, as a document circulated barely a week later by Vice President Günter Verheugen demonstrated. Outlining ten actions to reconcile the objectives of environmental sustainability, competitiveness, and energy security, this document warns against moving too fast on climate change lest the European economy suffer harm, and firms be encouraged to relocate in other regions of the world.[159] Ultimately, it would seem that the necessary policy options and technologies are available—what may still be absent is the political resolve of Member States and parts of the Commission to implement and enforce such policies without major concessions to opposing interests. And as we move forward, the quest to muster such resolve is likely to become one of the most challenging trials of our time.

III. Biotechnology

*Thijs Etty**

A. Introduction

The survey year 2006 was one of mixed accomplishments in the policy area of 'green' biotechnology and genetically modified organisms (GMOs). On the European Union (EU) front, last year's trend of a slow but steady pace was continued, with mainly small amendments and implementing measures being adopted, following what has been an exceptionally dynamic few years in terms of European biotechnology decision-making. While the de facto moratorium on GMO authorizations has formally moved to the annals of history, its shadow is proving to be long and looming. The deep divide between the Member States is still far from bridged, and the Commission's unilateral approval of (few) new GMOs that may subsequently be barred through Member State precautionary safeguard bans has done little to resolve the contested European hostility towards GM crops. In fact, those safeguard bans have proven to be the only type of biotech-related policy issues for which the Member States are able to unite in qualified majority decision-making at all, illustrating the highly politicized issue that GMO comitology decision-making remains.

In March 2006, two months into its EU presidency term, Austria initiated a 'Policy Orientation Debate' on the framework of EU biotechnology laws and

[159] See 'EU "Must Get Real on Energy-Climate Policies" ', *ENDS Europe Daily*, 24 Nov. 2006.

* Researcher/Lecturer at the Vrije Universiteit Amsterdam (the Netherlands), Institute for Environmental Studies (IVM), Department of Environmental Policy Analysis; and the Faculty of Law, Department of International and Comparative Law.

policies, and the approach to the future use of GM crops and foods. The discussion was a follow-up to the ideas floated at the last Environment Council meeting by one of the other GMO-critical Member States—Luxembourg, at the very end of its presidency in December 2005.[1] Backed by the like-minded Member States Greece and Italy, Austria and Luxembourg proposed, inter alia, to reduce the required majority for comitology decision-making on GMO authorizations from a qualified majority to a simple majority. This effective scrapping of the comitology procedures would almost certainly break the current consistent deadlock. Other items of discussion involved, inter alia, the risk assessment and management process, and the role played therein by the European Food Safety Authority (EFSA), as well a reassessment of the current approach to coexistence, GMO-free zoning issues, and seed labelling and purity thresholds.[2] However, unsurprisingly, the Member States failed to reach consensus on any substantive changes to the regulatory regime.

Shortly thereafter, in April 2006, the Commission made an attempt of its own to address this impasse by presenting specific recommendations for 'practical improvements to the way [the regime] is implemented'.[3] Following persistent criticism from Member States, other EU institutions and advisory bodies, and civil society groups, Commissioners Dimas (Environment, who has been rather critical of EFSA himself) and Kyprianou (SANCO) presented amendments to the role and focus of the scientific work of EFSA, to 'improve the scientific consistency and transparency for decisions on GMOs and... developing consensus between all interested parties'.[4] For example, that it should pay more attention to the potential long-term effects and biodiversity issues of GMOs, cooperate more fully with national competent authorities and scientific bodies, and provide detailed justifications if it overrules scientific objections raised by the Member States.

Although the alleged 'GMO-bias' of EFSA has indeed been an often heard criticism, the Commission's assertion that these changes were necessary to 'reassure Member States, stakeholders, and the general public that Community decisions are based on high quality scientific assessments which deliver a high level of protection of human health and environment' appears to ignore the overarching reality that it is politics, not science, that is most prominently ruling GMO decision-making in the EU at this point. Similarly, the disclaimer that '[t]hese improvements will be made within the existing legal framework, in compliance with [European Community (EC)] and [World Trade Organization (WTO)] law,

[1] See Minutes of the 2 Dec. 2005 Environment Council meeting.

[2] See Minutes of the 9 Mar. 2006 Environment Council meeting. Also, 'EU Reconsiders Biotech Position, Process', *BRIDGES Trade BioRes*, 17 Mar. 2006; 'Cracks Start to Show in EU GMO Policy', *EurActiv*, 6 Apr. 2006.

[3] See Commission Press Release IP/06/498, 12 Apr. 2006; and 'Shake-up Proposed for EU GMO Approvals', *ENDS Report*, May 2006, 50.

[4] Ibid., and Minutes of the 27 June 2006 Environment Council meeting.

and avoiding any undue delays in authorization procedures' appears to underestimate the political reality that it is precisely this 'existing legal system' (most notably the role of comitology in that system) that causes the alleged 'undue delays in authorization' in WTO terms, as it allows Member States to divest their responsibility in GMO decision-making to the Commission.[5] It appears, therefore, that the Commission's 'practical improvements for implementation' failed to tackle the deep-rooted political stalemate that the foregoing Orientation Debate in the Council had (unsuccessfully) sought to address.

All of these problems and political sensitivities were further exacerbated by yet another major illegal GMO contamination incident, this time affecting the world's most important staple food, rice, following last year's *Bt*10/*Bt*11 maize mix-up the effects of which were still resounding during 2006. Besides the GM rice escape, a number of smaller-scale accidental releases involving unauthorized GMO products also stirred European and global controversy during 2006. The vast majority of these illegal releases to the EU market originated from the United States of America (US). It is somewhat ironic, then, that during the same year the US claimed a certain victory over the EU's precautionary stance in the long-awaited and much-delayed WTO Dispute Settlement Panel ruling in the *EU–Biotech Products* case.

Further noteworthy developments in the international realm took place predominantly in the context of the Cartagena Protocol on Biosafety (BSP),[6] and its parent Convention on Biological Diversity (CBD).[7] The highly controversial international labelling and documentation requirements for GMOs were finally concluded under the BSP, or at least provisionally, while the CBD Parties agreed on a continuation of the moratorium on Genetic Use Restriction Technologies (GURTs), and on the need for a precautionary approach to GM applications to forestry.

B. Legislation Adopted

i. Commission Regulation on the Community Reference Laboratory for GMOs

On 22 December 2006, the Commission adopted Regulation (EC) No. 1981/2006 on Detailed Rules for the Implementation of Article 32 of Regulation

[5] See similarly M. Papic, 'Dynamics of Strategic Institutional Decay: EC Comitology and GMO Approvals' (Paper presented at the SWPSA Annual Conference, Albuquerque, NM (US), Mar. 2007), published on the Internet at: http://www.markopapic.com/PublicationsPresentations/SWPSA%20Marko%20Papic.pdf.

[6] Montréal, QC (Canada), 29 Jan. 2000 (entered into force 11 Sept. 2003), (2000) 39 *International Legal Materials* 5, 1027. All official BSP documents mentioned below are published on the Internet at: http://www.biodiv.org/biosafety.

[7] Rio de Janeiro (Brazil), 5 June 1992 (entered into force 29 Dec. 1993), (1992) 31 *International Legal Materials* 818.

(EC) No. 1829/2003 as Regards the Community Reference Laboratory for Genetically Modified Organisms (CRL Regulation).[8] In 2003, the Community Reference Laboratory (CRL) for GMOs was set up within the Commission's Joint Research Centre (JRC), with a view to the coordination of the technical evaluation and validation of quantitative sampling, detection, and identification methods for GMOs in the context of the revised EC regulatory regime for GMOs, by Article 32 of Regulation (EC) No. 1829/2003 on Genetically Modified Food and Feed (GM Food and Feed Regulation).[9] The ability to sample, detect, and identify GMO traces in products is imperative for the operation and enforcement of this regime. Although Regulation (EC) No. 1830/2003 concerning the Traceability and Labelling of Genetically Modified Organisms and the Traceability of Food and Feed Products Produced from Genetically Modified Organisms and Amending Directive 2001/18/EC (GM Traceability and Labelling Regulation)[10] requires operators to retain and transmit information on GMOs and GM content of their products at all stages of the market placement, they are under no obligation to sample and test products for GM content at each stage. Sample checks and qualitative and quantitative testing are thus crucial elements of the inspections and control measures that Member States are to undertake to ensure compliance.

With the assistance of a consortium of national reference laboratories, jointly referred to as the European Network of GMO Laboratories (ENGL),[11] the CRL is responsible for the testing and validation of the methods for sampling, detection, and identification; for the reception, preparation, storage, maintenance, and distribution of control samples; for the evaluation of detection and sampling data provided in applications for authorizations by operators, and for advising Member States and the European Food Safety Authority (EFSA).[12] Previously, in October 2004, the Commission had adopted Recommendation 2004/787/EC on Technical Guidance for Sampling and Detection of Genetically Modified Organisms and Material Produced from Genetically Modified Organisms as or in Products in the Context of Regulation (EC) No. 1830/2003,[13] with a view to ensuring the consistency and reliability of the sampling and detection methods used by reference laboratories throughout the Community.

The new CRL Regulation provides further detailed rules for the implementation of Article 32 of the GM Food and Feed Regulation by laying down the financial contributions to be paid by applicants towards the costs incurred by the CRL and ENGL in executing sampling and detection procedures (Articles 3–5), and by stipulating the criteria for, and the formal rules for the establishment and

8 [2006] OJ L368/99.
9 [2003] OJ L268/1.
10 [2003] OJ L268/24.
11 Details published on the Internet at: http://engl.jrc.it.
12 Annex and Art. 32 of the GM Food and Feed Reg.
13 [2004] OJ L348/18.

appointment of, national reference laboratories to assist the CRL in such procedures (Article 6 and Annexes I and II). Annex II details the lists of currently formally recognized national reference laboratories as part of ENGL. Finally, Annex III updates the Annex to the GM Food and Feed Regulation to reflect these amendments.

ii. EC Conclusion of the GMOs Amendment to the Aarhus Convention

By adopting Decision 2006/957/EC,[14] on 18 December 2006, the EC and its Member States committed to 'endeavour to deposit as soon as possible, and not later than 1 February 2008', their instruments of ratification, acceptance, or approval of the so-called 'Almaty GMO Amendment' to the Convention on Access to Information, Public Participation in Decision-Making and Access to Justice in Environmental Matters (Aarhus Convention).[15] Following a protracted debate of several years on the application of Aarhus rights to matters involving GMOs,[16] this compromise amendment was adopted in May 2005, at the second meeting of the Parties (MOP-2) to the Aarhus Convention, with the objective of strengthening the rights of the public to participate in decision-making on GMOs.[17] The ratification status of the amendment is further discussed in Section F.*ii* below.

iii. Unauthorized Liberty Link 601 Rice Contamination Emergency Measures

On 23 August 2006, the Commission adopted Decision 2006/578/EC on Emergency Measures Regarding the Non-Authorised Genetically Modified Organism LL RICE 601 in Rice Products (Provisional LL 601 Rice Emergency Measure Decision),[18] as a provisional emergency measure for extra-Community food and feed imports to protect human and animal health or the environment, on the basis of Article 53 of Regulation (EC) No. 178/2002 laying down the General Principles and Requirements of Food Law, establishing the European Food Safety Authority and laying down Procedures in Matters of Food Safety

[14] Dec. 2006/957/EC on the Conclusion, on Behalf of the European Community, of an Amendment to the Convention on Access to Information, Public Participation in Decision-making and Access to Justice in Environmental Matters [2006] OJ L386/46.

[15] Aarhus (Denmark), 25 June 1998 (entered into force 30 Oct. 2001), (1999) 38 *International Legal Materials* 3, 517. All official Aarhus documents published on the Internet at: http://www.unece.org/env/pp/.

[16] See T. F. M. Etty , 'Biotechnology' (2007) 7 *Yearbook of European Environmental Law*, 287–332, at 209–11; and T. F. M. Etty, 'Biotechnology' (2006) 6 *Yearbook of European Environmental Law*, 245–86, at 270–3; and T. F. M. Etty, 'Biotechnology' (2005) 5 *Yearbook of European Environmental Law*, 287–326, at 314–15.

[17] Dec. II/1 on Genetically Modified Organisms, Report ECE/MP.PP/2005/2, 12 July 2005.

[18] [2006] OJ L230/8.

(General Food Law Regulation).[19] The Decision was adopted within a week of the announcement, on 18 August, by the US authorities that the GM herbicide tolerant (HT) rice variety Liberty Link 601 (LL 601 Rice) had been detected in US samples of the 2005 long-grain rice crop grown in at least half a dozen US states. The US authorities, in turn, had been informed by the GMO's producer, Bayer Crop Science, 18 days earlier, on 31 July 2006. Apparently, embarrassing experiences with the initial handling and communication in last year's *Bt*10/*Bt*11 mix-up scandal had spurred US and European authorities to act more swiftly and ensure that the news was made public by regulatory authorities, rather than the popular media.[20] Still, the US authorities were criticized for having waited almost three weeks to alert international trade partners and, what is more, the producer Bayer (allegedly) had already been aware of the contamination since January 2006.[21]

The EU is a major export destination for US long grain rice, with average monthly imports of approximately 20,000 tonnes, valued at some $86.5 million per year.[22] None of this includes (or at least should include) any GM varieties, as none have been approved in the EU to date. Similar to the *Bt*10/*Bt*11 scenario, LL 601 Rice was an experimental variety which had been abandoned for commercialization following extensive field trials between 1998 and 2001.[23] Thus, it was neither authorized for market placement in the EU, nor registered for commercial use in the US or in any other jurisdiction. Its two successor varieties, LL 62 Rice and LL 06 Rice, which are also genetically modified for tolerance to the *Liberty* herbicide, are deregulated in the US, meaning they can legally be grown and sold there, and an application for food and feed use is currently pending for LL 62 Rice.[24] Also highly reminiscent of the *Bt*10 scandal, in contrast with the EU emergency measures, the US regulatory response consisted of a fast-track deregulation (i.e. post hoc approval) of LL 601 Rice, leading to fierce criticism of the US regulatory oversight of biotechnology, both from within and outside the

19 [2002] OJ L31/1.

20 See Etty (2007), n. 16 above, 319–24.

21 Riceland, the largest US producer and exporter of rice, allegedly discovered the contamination in rice destined for export, in January 2006. It alerted Bayer, and conducted further testing in several US states, many of which returned positive results. However, Bayer claimed that it became aware of the incident only in May. See also A. Pollack, 'Unapproved Rice Strain Found in Wide Area'. *New York Times,* 22 Aug. 2006; and Greenpeace International and GeneWatch, *GM Contamination Register Report: Annual Review of Cases of Contamination, Illegal Planting and Negative Side Effects of Genetically Modified Organisms* (Amsterdam: Greenpeace International, 2007), 15–16, also published on the Internet at: http://www.gmcontaminationregister.org.

22 Statistics of the United States Department of Agriculture (USDA) Foreign Agricultural Service, published on the Internet at: http://www.useu.be/agri.

23 The GMO was developed by Aventis, and was abandoned for commercialization by Bayer after it purchased Aventis in 2002.

24 See Commission MEMO/06/310, 'Q&A on the Finding of Unauthorised GM Rice on the US Market', 23 Aug. 2006. See also Pollack, n. 21 above.

US.[25] Meanwhile, the source of the contamination could not yet be pinpointed, while it seemed unlikely that such a widespread admixture could have been the result of the 1999–2001 field trials only.

As is required by the General Food Law Regulation, the Commission's unilateral provisional emergency decision was subsequently confirmed and replaced by a proper comitology Decision in collaboration with the Standing Committee on the Food Chain and Animal Health (SCFCAH) within a fortnight, on 5 September 2006. Almost too coincidental to be true, the Decision on emergency measures for LL 601 Rice bears the numeric indicator 601; Decision 2006/601/EC on Emergency Measures Regarding the Non-Authorised Genetically Modified Organism LL RICE 601 in Rice Products (LL 601 Rice Emergency Measure Decision).[26] The measures will be reviewed by the SCFCAH by 28 February 2007 at the latest. Until then, all export consignments of rice originating from the US that are deemed likely to be contaminated must be certified as having tested negative for the presence of the illegal GM rice before entering the EU. In addition, Member States are to verify the absence of LL 601 Rice in food and feed products already marketed prior to the adoption of the emergency measures through random sampling and analysis, and communicate any irregularities through the Rapid Alert System for Food and Feed (RASFF). Whereas the *Bt*10 Emergency Measures Decision had received much criticism for exempting food imports from the purity certification, the measures for LL 601 Rice apply equally to food and feed products. However, the fact that they apply only to products that are 'likely to be contaminated'[27] raised much criticism in turn for being too narrow in scope, also given that the US authorities had still not been able to determine to what extent the supply chain had been contaminated. These critiques soon proved founded when in the ensuing months Member States reported LL 601 Rice contamination in previously unsuspected rice products. What is more, checks carried out in the Member States also revealed the presence of the illegal rice in some large consignments despite being accompanied by an original analytical report and US purity certificate, as required by the Decision. However, around the same time in mid-September, EFSA had adopted a scientific opinion concluding that the consumption of trace levels of LL 601 Rice is 'not likely to pose an imminent safety concern to humans or animals', while acknowledging that the insufficient available data did not allow for a full risk assessment.

In view of these findings, the emergency measures were beefed up by widening the scope of the products to be tested, and by replacing the random checks

[25] See USDA, Animal and Plant Health Inspection Service (APHIS), Docket No. APHIS–2006–0140, 8 Sept. 2006, (2006) 71(174) *Federal Register*, 53076–7; and C. Lee, 'Genetically Engineered Rice Wins USDA Approval: Grain Tainted U.S. Supply This Summer'. *Washington Post*, 25 Nov. 2006; R. Weiss, 'Biotech Rice Saga Yields Bushel of Questions for Feds: USDA Approval Shortcut Emerges as Issue'. *Washington Post*, 6 Nov. 2006.

[26] [2006] OJ L244/27.

[27] Ibid., Art. 1.

with systematic, official sampling and analysis of each import consignment at the EU port of entry, by Commission Decision 2006/754/EC Amending Decision 2006/601/EC on Emergency Measures Regarding the Non-Authorised Genetically Modified Organism 'LL RICE 601' in Rice Products.[28]

Many of the US' other trading partners took even more drastic emergency measures than the EU in response to the news of the contamination of rice, the world's most important staple food. For example, Japan enacted a complete import ban against all US rice imports on 20 August 2006.[29] According to a variety of NGO and public media sources, by the end of 2006, LL 601 Rice contamination had become widespread across the globe, with reported cases in, inter alia, the vast majority of EU Member States,[30] the US, Canada, Norway, Switzerland, Japan, South Korea, the United Arab Emirates (UAE), Dubai, Kuwait, the Philippines, Ghana, Sierra Leone, and Russia.[31] In view of the effective embargo in the EU and other countries, as well as the financial risk of likely product rejection in foreign ports, the export of US long-grain rice 'all but stopped' during 2006.[32]

Two other contamination incidents involving GMO rice occurred during 2006. In October 2006, the abovementioned LL 62 Rice was detected in France, in rice consignments imported from the US.[33] Although LL 62 Rice is deregulated in the US, and an application for its use in Europe is currently pending, according to the EU biotechnology laws as long as it has not received authorization, it is illegal there even in trace amounts. In April and September 2006, Friends of the Earth and Greenpeace announced that unauthorized GM *Bt*63 rice had been detected in processed rice products (e.g. rice noodles) imported from China.[34] During 2005, the same NGOs had uncovered the sale and cultivation of the illegal GMO in China, following which the Chinese authorities had vowed to take appropriate action. Nonetheless, since then the contaminated products had turned up on French, Austrian, German, and UK supermarket shelves, and those governments issued official alerts through the RASFF following the initial disclosure by NGOs.[35] The *Bt*63 rice is an experimental GMO

[28] [2006] OJ L306/17.

[29] See 'Japan Suspends US Long-grain Rice Imports'. *Dow Jones*, 20 Aug. 2006; and *GM Contamination Register Report*, n. 21 above, 16.

[30] Including Austria, Belgium, Cyprus, Denmark, Finland, France, Germany, Greece, Ireland, Italy, Luxembourg, the Netherlands, Poland, Slovenia, Sweden, and the UK.

[31] See, e.g., *GM Contamination Register Report*, n. 21 above, 15–19, with various external sources at 21.

[32] See n. 22 above.

[33] See, e.g., *GM Contamination Register Report*, n. 21 above, 19.

[34] See S. Jackson, 'Illegal GE Experimental Rice from China: Now Entering Europe's Food Chain', Report for Greenpeace International, of 5 Sept. 2006, published on the Internet at: http://www.greenpeace.org/raw/content/international/press/reports/IllegalChinaGErice.pdf. See also J. Smith, 'Gene-Altered Rice from China Found in EU—Greens', *Reuters*, 5 Sept. 2006; and ibid.

[35] See RASFF alerts of on 21, 27, 28, and 29 Sept., and 6 Oct. 2006, published on the Internet at: http://ec.europa.eu/food/food/rapidalert/index_en.htm.

which is being field tested in China, but has not been authorized for commercialization anywhere in the world. By the end of 2006, the Commission was still in the process of obtaining further information from the Chinese authorities, and a method of detection had not yet been provided by China. However, despite discussions in the SCFCAH in September and October 2006, and January 2007, neither of these additional contamination incidents led to EU-level regulatory emergency measures.

iv. GMO Authorizations

As regards the authorization of GMOs for market placement, the survey year 2006 confirmed the trend of last year, both in terms of their quantity as well as the contentiousness and length of the procedures. In effect, all four of the dossiers had been decided last year already, as by the very end of 2005 the familiar blockage of qualified majority voting (QMV) in both the Regulatory Committee on GMOs and in the Council had cleared the last remaining hurdles for the Commission's unilateral authorization. All that was left in the first months of 2006 was for the Commission to rubber stamp these authorizations by legal default in the controversial comitology procedure.

First, on 13 January 2006, the Commission extended the permitted applications of Monsanto's MON 863 maize to food uses with the adoption of Decision 2006/68/EC Authorising the Placing on the Market of Foods and Food Ingredients Derived from Genetically Modified Maize Line MON 863 as Novel Foods or Novel Food Ingredients under Regulation (EC) No. 258/97.[36] On the same date and under the same 'old' Regulation, it approved another of Monsanto's GM maize lines for human consumption, by Decision 2006/69/EC Authorising the Placing on the Market of Foods and Food Ingredients Produced from Genetically Modified Roundup Ready Maize Line GA21 as Novel Foods or Novel Food Ingredients under Regulation (EC) No. 258/97.[37] The initial application for this authorization dates back to 1998, when Monsanto notified it to the competent authority in the Netherlands.

On 16 January, the Commission approved Monsanto's maize hybrid MON 863 × MON 810 for market placement but not for food or feed purposes or cultivation, with Decision 2006/47/EC concerning the Placing on the Market, in Accordance with Directive 2001/18/EC, of a Maize Product (Zea Mays L., Hybrid MON 863 × MON 810) Genetically Modified for Resistance to Corn Rootworm and Certain Lepidopteran Pests of Maize.[38] The two constituent maize varieties had previously received individual regulatory clearance; MON

[36] [2006] OJ L34/26. Application of 15 July 2002.
[37] [2006] OJ L34/29.
[38] [2006] OJ L26/17.

810 already in 1998,[39] and MON 863 in August 2005.[40] The hybrid application had initially also sought to permit feed applications, until a separate application was filed, on 5 July 2005, for all food and feed uses combined, under the GM Food and Feed Regulation. Hence, the current authorization covers only import and processing, for non-food or feed purposes.

Finally, on 3 March 2006, yet another GM maize, this time produced by Pioneer and Dow Agrosciences was cleared for food use, under the 'new' regulatory procedures, by Decision 2006/197/EC Authorising the Placing on the Market of Food containing, consisting of, or produced from Genetically Modified Maize Line 1507 (DAS-Ø15Ø7–1) pursuant to Regulation (EC) No. 1829/2003.[41]

C. Legislation in Progress

i. Pending GMO Authorization Dossiers

In addition to the authorization Decisions described in the foregoing B.*iv*, several other GMO authorization dossiers also advanced during 2006. Two draft Council Decisions were presented by the Commission for voting in the Regulatory Committee and subsequently the Council; one in July for a herbicide tolerant (HT) GM oilseed rape variety,[42] and another in December for a carnation flower genetically modified for its colour.[43]

Given the predictable and consistent deadlock in the comitology procedure with respect to these controversial regulatory decisions, it is close to certain that authorizations in the form of Commission Decisions will follow in both of these dossiers during 2007. A slight increase in draft authorization decisions may also be expected during the next survey year, with a view to the progress made towards scientific opinions by the EFSA GMO Panel for several pending dossiers,[44] as well as the Commission's commitment to clearing the backlog of applications.[45]

[39] Dec. 98/294/EC concerning the Placing on the Market of Genetically Modified Maize (Zea Mays L. Line MON 810), Pursuant to Council Directive 90/220/EEC [1998] OJ L131/32.

[40] Dec. 2005/608/EC concerning the Placing on the Market, in Accordance with Directive 2001/18/EC, of a Maize Product (Zea Mays L., Line MON 863) Genetically Modified for Resistance to Corn Rootworm [2005] OJ L207/17.

[41] [2006] OJ L70/82.

[42] Commission Proposal for a Council Decision concerning the Placing on the Market, in Accordance with Directive 2001/18/EC, of Oilseed Rape Products (Brassica Napus L., Lines Ms8, Rf3 and Ms8×Rf3) Genetically Modified for Tolerance to the Herbicide Glufosinate-Ammonium COM(2006)78, 11 July 2006.

[43] Commission Proposal for a Council Decision concerning the Placing on the Market, in Accordance with Directive 2001/18/EC, of a Carnation (Dianthus Caryophyllus L., Line 123.2.38) Genetically Modified for Flower Colour COM(2006)758, 4 Dec. 2006.

[44] Published on the Internet at: http://www.efsa.europa.eu/en/science/gmo/gmo_opinions.html.

[45] Published on the Internet at: http://www.efsa.europa.eu/en/science/gmo/gm_ff_applications.html.

ii. *New Comitology Procedure—Amendments to GM Food and Feed Regulation and Deliberate Release Directive*

Both the GM Food and Feed Regulation and the Deliberate Release Directive were among the legislative acts pinpointed for urgent amendment to incorporate the recently revised comitology procedure.[46] In fact, some commentators have suggested that these biotechnology laws played a key role in the adoption of the new comitology rules, which afford the European Parliament (EP) increased control in this controversial regulatory committee decision-making process.[47] However, as will be discussed below, the practical impact in this regard is likely to be minimal, and a breakthrough in the GMO authorization legitimacy impasse is certainly not be expected as a result of the new rules.

Decision 2006/512/EC Amending Decision 1999/468/EC laying down the Procedures for the Exercise of Implementing Powers Conferred on the Commission (New Comitology Decision),[48] adopted by the Commission in July 2006, introduced a new 'regulatory procedure with scrutiny', which provides that:

> [the EP], acting by a majority of its component members, or the Council, acting by a qualified majority, may oppose the adoption of [a Commission draft Decision], justifying their opposition by indicating that the draft measures proposed by the Commission exceed the implementing powers provided for in the basic instrument or that the draft is not compatible with the aim or the content of the basic instrument or does not respect the principles of subsidiarity or proportionality.[49]

Three conditions are to be fulfilled for this 'regulatory scrutiny' procedure to apply: (i) the basic instrument must have been adopted through *co-decision* with the EP; (ii) the basic instrument must provide for the adoption of measures of *general scope*; and (iii) those measures are designed to amend *non-essential elements* of the basic instrument, e.g. by deleting (some of) them or by supplementing them with new non-essential elements. In view of the latter two requirements, the most contentious and frequent application of comitology decision-making in biotech matters will continue to be exempt from parliamentary control. As before, the EP will not be able to vote down individual draft GMO authorization Decisions. It will, however, be able to intervene (with a simple majority, in contrast with the QMV requirement for the regulatory committees and the Council) in decision-making relating to, inter alia, whether a particular type of product fits within the scope of the existing EC biotech legislation; the threshold levels for labelling

[46] See Joint Statement of the EP, the Council, and the Commission on Dec. 2006/512/EC, [2006] OJ C255/1.

[47] Cf. Papic, n. 5 above.

[48] [2006] OJ L200/11.

[49] Ibid., Art. 1(7), inserting a new Art. 5a into Dec. 1999/468/EC laying down the Procedures for the Exercise of Implementing Powers conferred on the Commission [1999] OJ L184/23.

and/or adventitious presence of GM content; criteria for notification; and the adaptation of certain Annexes.

On 22 December 2006, the Commission adopted two legislative proposals to amend the Directive[50] and the Regulation[51] to incorporate the new regulatory procedure with scrutiny.

iii. Proposed Codification of Contained Use Directive

On 14 June 2006, the Commission adopted a Proposal for a Directive on the Contained Use of Genetically Modified Microorganisms (Codified Version).[52] The aim of this proposed Directive is to codify the various scattered ad hoc amendments that have been made throughout the past two decades to the original framework Directive 90/219/EEC on the Contained Use of Genetically Modified Micro-Organisms (Contained Use Directive).[53] As part of the Commission's general strategy of 'a people's Europe' to simplify and clarify Community legislation in order to enhance the clarity and accessibility of EC law for ordinary citizens, the new Directive will incorporate and supersede all existing legation in this field. The aim is to provide a single, consolidated legislative framework, without making any substantive changes to the provisions being codified. The proposed Directive is therefore uncharacteristically uncontroversial for a legislative act on biotechnology, and will most likely be adopted without substantial amendments by the EP and Council during 2007.

D. Case Law and Enforcement Activity

i. Implementation of the Deliberate Release and Contained Use Directives

Following the bonanza of infringement proceedings regarding the implementation of the 2001 Deliberate Release Directive in the previous two years, there was a relative calm during 2006. By end of the year, the Commission was gearing up to bring an action for an order of periodic penalty payments against France for its failure to comply with the July 2004 ruling[54] by the European Court of Justice (ECJ) condemning France's persisting failure to implement the Directive.[55]

In February 2006, similar infringement proceedings seeking penalty payments were brought against France over its continued failure sufficiently to transpose

[50] Commission Proposal for a Directive Amending Directive 2001/18/EC, as Regards the Implementing Powers Conferred on the Commission COM(2006)920, 22 Dec. 2006.

[51] Commission Proposal for Regulation Amending Regulation (EC) No. 1829/2003, as Regards the Implementing Powers Conferred on the Commission COM(2006)912, 22 Dec. 2006.

[52] COM(2006)286, 14 June 2006.

[53] [1990] OJ L117/1.

[54] Case C-419/03 *Commission* v. *France* [2004] OJ C228/15.

[55] The action was eventually brought on 28 February 2007, and was assigned case number C-121/07, [2007] OJ C95/31.

the 1990 Contained Use Directive,[56] despite the ECJ's infringement judgment of 27 November 2003.[57] However, by the very end of the survey year, on 20 December 2006, the Commission had requested the Court to remove the case from the register, in view of France's efforts towards compliance in the interim.[58]

E. Policy Documents

i. Report on the Implementation of National Coexistence Measures and European Council Conclusions

On 9 March 2006, the Commission adopted its first Report on the implementation of Member States' coexistence measures,[59] to assess progress made in the three years since the adoption of its non-binding Recommendation 2003/556/EC on Guidelines for the Development of National Strategies and Best Practices to Ensure the Coexistence of Genetically Modified Crops with Conventional and Organic Farming (Coexistence Guidelines Recommendation).[60] In that Recommendation, the Commission had committed itself to a deadline of July 2005 for the first review,[61] but as with the other reports discussed in this section, it was considerably delayed, and appears to cover developments up to the end of 2005. In the relatively brief report the Commission reiterated its (arguably) narrow definition of coexistence as relating only to the *economic* aspects of GMO cultivation, and confirmed its justifications for the subsidiarity-based approach it had taken to regulate coexistence. Given that this biotechnology chapter in previous volumes of this *Yearbook* has devoted considerable attention to the developments covered by this Commission Report, the present analysis will not go into the details of coexistence legislation previously discussed.[62]

The review is based on a questionnaire among national competent authorities, their communications in the Coexistence Coordination and Exchange Network (COEX-NET), and on the notifications of draft national coexistence legislation in the context of the Technical Regulations Information System (TRIS) procedure, under Directive 98/34/EC laying down a Procedure for the Provision of Information in the Field of Technical Standards and Regulations.[63]

Although coexistence has been thrust to the fore in recent years as the 'final frontier' of the EU regulation of biotechnology, now that the authorization and

[56] N. 53 above.

[57] Case C-429/01 *Commission* v. *France* [2004] OJ C21/4.

[58] Ultimately, the case was removed from the ECJ register on 7 Feb. 2007, [2007] OJ C82/27.

[59] Commission Communication: Report on the Implementation of National Measures on the Coexistence of Genetically Modified Crops with Conventional and Organic Farming COM(2006)104, 9 Mar. 2006; supported by Annex: Commission Staff Working Document SEC(2006)313, 27 Feb 2006.

[60] [2003] OJ L189/36.

[61] Ibid., recital 10.

[62] See n. 16 above.

[63] [1998] OJ L204/37.

marketing regulations have been completely revamped, practical experience with the growing of GMOs on European soil continues to be very limited. The report notes that commercial cultivation of GM crops had been limited to two events of GM maize (*Bt*176 and MON810), and took place predominantly in Spain (58,000 hectares (ha) in 2004, or 12 per cent of the total Spanish maize area). The national experience with the adoption of coexistence legislation has also been rather limited. The Report notes that by the end of 2005 only four Member States had adopted specific coexistence laws (Austria (regionally), Denmark, Germany, and Poland). The legislative progress in the remaining Member States is highly varied. In total, 20 draft national laws had been notified to the Commission in the context of the TRIS, ten of which had met with Commission objections for being potential obstacles to intra-Community trade, four were approved, another four were still pending at the end of 2005, and the final two had been withdrawn. The Annex provides detailed information on all of these national provisions. The Report also makes note of other types of national coexistence measures, such as Upper Austria and Salzburg's recourse to Article 95(5) EC for a derogation from the harmonized EC regulations to enact an effective ban on GM crop cultivation, Denmark's state aid notification for its GMO compensation scheme, and the Czech Republic and Slovenia's coexistence provisions in the context of their rural development programmes. It also points to the growing GMO free regions network, while stressing that most of these regions do not have legislative competence in this area.

The crux of all discussions between Member States and the Commission on coexistence is the proportionality of proposed measures. The Commission's narrow definition of the concept of coexistence, and in particular its interpretation of the adventitious presence exemptions of the EU GMOs regime, play a decisive, and in the view of this author problematic, role. In scrutinizing Member States' approaches to coexistence, the Commission applies the 0.9 per cent GMO content figure of the recently adopted labelling rules as a *minimum regulatory target* below which Member States cannot legislate. It is here submitted that this interpretation is not compatible with the intended nature of this purity rule as a *maximum tolerable impurity threshold*, which furthermore is conditional on being adventitious or technically unavoidable, and hence seems inherently incapable of serving as a (mandatory) *target impurity*.[64] However, this is precisely the interpretation which the Commission has consistently employed, and which it reiterates in the review report, warning of the presumed disproportionality of stricter national purity targets. In the view of the Commission, then, the concept of coexistence is not to be understood as a system of measures to ensure that GMO-free

[64] For similar criticism, see K. P. E. Lasok QC and R. Haynes, 'Advice—In the Matter of Co-existence, Traceability and Labelling of GMOs', 21 Jan. 2005, an independent legal advice commissioned by a group of NGOs including FoE, published on the Internet at: http://www.gmofree-europe.org/Summary_Lasok_Advice.pdf.

agriculture can continue to exist in the EU, but as a policy to ensure that 0.9 per cent GMO impurity becomes the standard for conventional and organic produce.

The fact that the Report notes that many of the elements of the Coexistence Guidelines Recommendation have been taken into account by the Member States is hardly surprising given that the Commission uses this (otherwise) *non-binding* document as the decisive benchmark for national draft legislation scrutinized in the TRIS-procedure. Despite this obvious eagerness on the part of the Commission to create some level of uniformity in the approach to coexistence, and despite repeatedly voiced calls by the EP, the EESC, the CoR, several Member States, and civil society organizations, the Report once again reiterates the Commission's position that a (formal) harmonized approach to coexistence is neither necessary nor viable. However, the keynote addresses made by Commissioners Fischer Boel (Agriculture) and Dimas (Environment) at the April 2006 Vienna Stakeholder Conference 'Coexistence of Genetically Modified, Conventional and Organic Crops—Freedom of Choice', organized by the Austrian presidency in cooperation with the Commission's DG Agriculture, clearly illustrated the variation in perspectives on this issue within the Commission. Having said that, the Commission's official position remains that a continued subsidiarity-based approach is justified by the 'need to conclude the process of implementing national coexistence measures' in view of the limited experiences to date. This argument is peculiar in that it appears evident that as the number and the diversity of national coexistence regimes expands, it will become ever more difficult to revert to a harmonized EU-wide policy. One could also argue that the Commission's reasoning that a re-evaluation of the need for harmonization should be put off until further practical experiences have been gained appears rather forced, given that such experiences are not likely to be gained any time soon since a significant surge in the uptake of GM crops for cultivation is highly unlikely in most Member States, at least for the foreseeable future. What is more, a timely re-evaluation of the EU coexistence policy might also be advised in view of the imminent new challenges posed by next-generation GM crops with novel applications aimed at, for example, bio-pharming, biofuels, and industrials.

Besides the 'harmonization vs. subsidiarity debate', the Report concluded with several concrete proposals for the improvement of the EU coexistence strategy. Firstly, the Commission urged a strengthening of the cooperation and communication between Member States and the Commission, e.g. in the context of COEX-NET. Secondly, a review should be undertaken of the latest scientific and economic information relating to segregation measures in crop and seed production. Thirdly, the Commission and the Member States should jointly develop 'best practices' for technical segregation measures, leading to crop-specific recommendations. Fourthly, an evaluation should be made of the various civil liability systems existing in the Member States, and the extent to which these apply to GMO-related liabilities. Finally, the Commission has committed itself to reviewing progress again in 2008.

ii. Report on the Implementation of the GM Food and Feed Regulation

According to Article 48 of the GM Food and Feed Regulation, the Commission had until 7 November 2005 to report to the EP and the Council, as well as the public, on the experiences gained with the implementation of this Regulation during the first 18 months of its application. Just two weeks shy of a full-year delay, the Report was finally published on 25 October 2006.[65] The Report is based on the results of a questionnaire circulated by the Commission among all the Member States' competent authorities and 'relevant stakeholders from all involved sectors', in conjunction with various discussions in the SCFCAH and in the Council, and finally the inspection reports by the Food and Veterinary Office of DG SANCO (FVO).

Needless to say, experiences gained with the new authorization regime have been very limited to date. In fact, there would not have been a single authorization to report on, had the Report been completed within the formal deadline. It was only owing to the extensive delay of the Report that the first and, to date, only 'new style' GMO authorization Decision could be incorporated, having been adopted in March 2006.[66] The Commission does note, however, that ten authorizations have been granted under the 'old' regime in accordance with the transitional measures provided for in Article 46 of the Regulation,[67] that 26 previously approved ('existing') GMO products have been validated under the 'new' regime,[68] and that EFSA had completed six complete scientific opinions on applications for GM food and feed uses under the Regulation.

Somewhat ironically perhaps, the number of *unauthorized* GMO products entering the EU market accounted for by the Report exceed by at least a fivefold figure the single *lawful* market placement.[69] Each of the 'accidental releases' discussed in the Report originated from the US: GM papaya (from Hawaii), *Bt*10 maize, and LL601 Rice. The Report makes no mention of other similar incidents, including the illegal Chinese *Bt*63 rice, and the LL62 Rice variety from the US, discussed in Section B.*iii* above.

While acknowledging that evidently such incidents cannot be avoided, the Commission praised the contingency plan responses for each of these incidents, in particular the effective role of the Rapid Alert System for Food and Feed (RASFF). The Report does stress the need for enhanced cooperation and

[65] Commission Report on the Implementation of Regulation (EC) No. 1829/2003 on Genetically Modified Food and Feed COM(2006)626, 25 Oct. 2006.

[66] Dec. 2006/197/EC, n. 41 above.

[67] See also Section B.*iv* above.

[68] On the basis of Reg. (EC) No. 641/2004 on Detailed Rules for the Implementation of Regulation (EC) No. 1829/2003 as Regards the Application for the Authorization of New Genetically Modified Food and Feed, the Notification of Existing Products and Adventitious or Technically Unavoidable Presence of Genetically Modified Material which has Benefited from a Favourable Risk Evaluation [2004] OJ L102/14.

[69] See in further detail Section B.*iii*, and Etty (2006), n. 16 above, at 319–24.

communication at the international level. It also acknowledges that although EFSA and the CRL were able to provide scientific safety assessments and validate the required detection methods in these cases, it is unlikely that similar success will be attainable in the event of accidental releases of GMOs which have not already been authorized in other jurisdictions, or are not intended to be commercialized at all.

As regards labelling, the Report notes that both compliance and enforcement of the new rules is considerably more diligent in respect of food than in the animal feed sector. Although the statistics vary between, and even within, the Member States, the average non-compliance is estimated at below 2 per cent for food products, and at 6 per cent for feed. Problems in this regard in the feed sector are not only a result of the predominance of GM soy in the global supply chain and in the EU feed market, paired with the considerable price premium for non-GM soy, but importantly also stem from idiosyncratic labelling policies that are incompatible with the Regulation, including systematic labelling as 'contains GMO' irrespective of the actual content, or systematic ambiguous labelling as 'may contain GMOs'. Overall, the Commission concludes that few GM labelled food products have been marketed, and that the new labelling requirements have not, as such, had an impact on the sale of such products.

The FVO inspections have also shown that problems exist in respect of sampling and detection operations. In nearly half of the Member States visited, sampling controls were not performed at the point of entry for food and feed, whereas a quarter did not have sampling controls to check consignments of seed, food, or feed, for adventitious presence of GMOs, and hence were unable to enforce the 0.9 per cent *de minimis* labelling threshold.[70] Furthermore, the Commission's recommended technical guidance on sampling and detection methods were not routinely complied with by the Member States' competent authorities.[71]

In sum, the Report concludes that experience in terms of the implementation of the Regulation is 'extremely limited', that it would hence be premature to propose any amendments at this early stage, and finally, that a second report should be prepared only after a sufficient period of time allowing more substantive insights.[72]

iii. Report on the Implementation of the Traceability and Labelling Regulation

Closely related to the former implementation review, the report on the Traceability and Labelling Regulation was also delayed for considerable time,

[70] Art. 12 of the GM Food and Feed Reg.

[71] Commission Rec. 2004/787/EC, n. 13 above.

[72] Although no specific deadline is set for this second report, unlike for the second implementation review of the Traceability and Labelling Reg., which is due by May 2008.

missing its formal deadline of 18 October 2005 by nearly seven months.[73] The Report,[74] eventually adopted on 10 May 2006, accounts in some detail the criticism, praise, and comments received by the Commission in a questionnaire distributed among all competent authorities, relevant stakeholders from the food, feed, and seed industry, trading partners, NGOs, and Member States' government officials. Similar to the situation of its sibling Regulation, there has been little practical experience gained with the implementation of the Traceability and Labelling Regulation. In addition to the short operational period of the regime to date, this lack of experience is due to the continued negative market climate for GM products in the EU, at least for food and seed. These factors notwithstanding, the Report's overall conclusion is that the provisions of the Regulation are being correctly applied, following some initial 'teething problems'. Moreover, it notes that a large majority of Member States describe the Regulation as having had a positive effect on the provision of relevant information, consumer choice, as well as the necessary safety guarantees.

However, problems are, once again, reported in respect of sampling and testing, with particular reference to the complexity of the techniques involved for the detection of adventitious presence. Member States complain about the excessive demand on time and finances and, once again, the Commission's technical guidance on sampling and detection methods are criticized, ironically both for being too detailed as well as too vague.[75] Some suggestions are made for a harmonized legislative approach to this subject, rather than non-binding guidance, or alternatively a 'practical operating manual' for the uniform implementation of the Regulation. Enhanced communication and cooperation are also stressed towards this end.

The Commission will draw up a second, hopefully more substantive, report on the implementation of the Regulation in 24 months, i.e. by May 2008.

F. International Cooperation

i. Cartagena Biosafety Protocol

In March 2006, tensions were high at the start of the third Conference of the Parties to the Convention on Biological Diversity Serving as the Meeting of the Parties to the Cartagena Protocol on Biosafety (COP/MOP-3), in Brazil.[76] It was clearly recognized that important progress would have to be made towards fleshing out some of the key elements of the Cartagena Protocol on Biosafety

[73] According to Art. 12 of the Traceability and Labelling Reg.

[74] Commission Report on the Implementation of Regulation (EC) No. 1830/2003 concerning the Traceability and Labelling of Genetically Modified Organisms and the Traceability of Food and Feed Products Produced from Genetically Modified Organisms and Amending Directive 2001/18/EC COM(2006)197, 10 May 2006.

[75] N. 13 above.

[76] Report UNEP/CBD/BS/COP-MOP/3/15, 8 May 2006.

(BSP)[77] which have been fiercely debated in the years leading up to, as well as in the six years since, its adoption in January 2000.[78] These implementation issues have become particularly pressing now that the BSP has been in force for some time, since September 2003, and the formally agreed deadline for elaborating these provisions lapsed at COP/MOP-2. Predictions were widespread that another failure to agree on these key provisions would put the BSP at serious risk of becoming redundant.

The agenda at COP/MOP-3 was almost exclusively dominated by the contentious issue of handling, transport, packaging and identification (HTPI) requirements for bulk shipments of living modified organisms (LMOs—as GMOs are referred to under the BSP), most importantly LMOs intended for direct use as food or feed (LMO-FFPs). Other issues were either agreed relatively expediently or, in most cases, postponed for future deliberations at COP/MOP-4 or even further down.

Handling, Transport, Packaging, and Identification (HTPI): Documentation Requirements for LMO-FFPs (Article 18(2)(a) BSP)

The HTPI requirements for bulk shipments of LMOs, of Article 18(2)(a) BSP, have been among the most divisive elements of the BSP since its inception, owing to their substantial potential impact on trade. For obvious reasons, the main GMO exporters (notably the US, Canada, Argentina, and Australia) are eager to minimize the documentation requirements, whereas the importing nations (including the EC and African developing nations) are pushing for stringent and comprehensive identification requirements for goods entering their domestic markets. The HTPI debate essentially boils down to a trade-off between the usefulness of detailed documentation for the facilitation of safe global handling of GMOs against the costs implied by such information requirements. This question of proportionality hinges on the conflicting perceptions of agricultural biotechnology as such: the GMO-exporting States do not consider GMOs as per se hazardous and therefore argue that the costly and complex segregation and traceability schemes necessitated by detailed HTPI documentation requirements are disproportionate. In contrast, importing States at the very least wish to err on the side of (pre)caution, but evidently would prefer to have the onus and cost of sampling, detection, and identification transferred onto the exporters. This is particularly important for developing nations, which are concerned that with their limited resources and capacity it will be all but impossible to detect unidentified GM traces in bulk shipments.

As before, the main bone of contention is the level of detail required of export documentation and the possible inclusion of *de minimis* labelling thresholds for adventitious or technically unavoidable presence of LMO traces in non-LMO

[77] N. 6 above.

[78] For background discussion, see Etty, n. 16 above, (2007), 287–332, and (2006), 267–70.

shipments. The level of detail required for labelling varies between allowing exporters to indicate simply that their shipment 'may contain' LMOs (as currently required by Article 18(2)(a) BSP), or requiring a less ambiguous and more precise documentation, possibly including unique identification of each LMO that is, or could be, present in the shipment.

Given that Brazil had played a leading role (along with New Zealand) in blocking the (fragile) consensus on HTPI requirements at COP/MOP-2, it was rather ironic that the decisive negotiations on this issue were to take place in Curitiba, Brazil, of all places. However, some hopes were also held that this coincidence might in fact facilitate a positive outcome, given the responsibility and special interest inherent to the role of host Party, which might serve to soften Brazil's rigid stance. Ultimately, these hopes proved founded, and in fact the progress that was ultimately made was attributed by many to the commitment and proactive leadership role played by Brazil and its President Lula da Silva and Environment Minister Marina Silva. Some commentators have also suggested that Brazil's renewed stance may have been inspired by its potential competitive trade advantage compared to other Latin American countries in terms of its ability to enact GMO segregation systems, combined with the observation that the Paraná region, where the meeting was held, has GMO-free status. New Zealand largely kept to the background during negotiations at COP/MOP-3. However, ironically, the previously strict positions held by Brazil and New Zealand were now taken up by other Parties, notably Mexico, as well as Paraguay and Peru, who in some cases even attempted to reverse progress made in previous years on these issues. Explanations provided by commentators to explain this shift in negotiating positions and dynamics included the pressure of the major GMO-exporters (and *non*-Parties) US and Canada on their Latin American counterparts, in the context of (pre-existing and new) bilateral trade agreements, as well as the rapid evolution of biosafety regimes, and the increasing number of countries authorizing GMO production, and as a result being confronted with the trade implications of exporting restrictions, and finally pointing also to the increased participation of trade and finance representatives in delegations, sometimes replacing the environment and agriculture representatives.[79] Mexico's position is also likely to have been influenced by its own rapidly developing biotechnology capacity and its trilateral trade agreement on these specific documentation issues. This was also reflected in Mexico's insistence—almost making this a last-minute 'deal-breaker'—that the final Decision should acknowledge that the BSP's HTPI documentation requirements do not apply to transboundary shipments of LMOs between Parties and *non*-Parties. This was paired with an 'encouragement' for non-Parties to adhere to the BSP. Although these provisions simply reaffirm what was already evident, it provides further evidence of

[79] 'Summary of the Third Meeting of the Parties to the Cartagena Protocol on Biosafety'(2006) 9(351) *Earth Negotiations Bulletin* 11.

the limited practical consequences of the BSP's rules, if they fail to cover the vast majority of all global LMO shipments (i.e. those from non-Party exporters). This political reality has always cast an influential shadow over the BSP's negotiations, in which Parties are effectively forced to accommodate (to a certain extent) the demands and concerns of non-Parties, since sidestepping the trade interests and concerns of major LMO-exporting non-Parties would threaten to reduce the BSP to little more than a paper tiger.

Following prolonged and fierce discussions throughout the week, delegations eventually returned to, and by and large confirmed, a draft compromise text which Brazil had presented at the very start of the negotiations. Following this draft, the so-called 'Curitiba rules', ultimately adopted in Decision BS-III/8, differentiate between shipments of LMO-FFPs whose identity and GM-traits are known through, e.g. identity preservation (IP) production systems (these must be labelled as 'contains' LMOs), and those which have not been identified and segregated through such an IP scheme (for these shipments a 'may contain' LMOs label suffices).[80] Specifically, the Decision 'requests' Parties and 'urges' other governments to ensure that each shipment of LMO-FFPs is accompanied by documentation in compliance with the requirements of the country of import and clearly stating that it 'contains' LMOs in the event that its identity is known through, e.g. IP systems, or that it 'may contain' LMOs where such identification is not possible, as well as the indication that the LMOs are not intended for intentional introduction into the environment but rather for direct use as food or feed, or for processing. In addition, all the other documentation requirements of the previous Decision BS-I/6-A will continue to apply, such as the need to state the transformation event or unique identifier code, etc.[81]

The ultimate outcome of the protracted documentation debate is, as always, a political compromise with sufficient vagueness to appease all sides, and essentially provides little more than an interim solution. For example, given that it is the existence of (undefined) IP-production systems that will trigger the more stringent 'contains' language, the choice continues to fall entirely to the exporting States, as before. Examples of other ambiguities include the meaning of the specific acknowledgment that a 'may contain' LMOs label does not require the listing of LMOs of species other than those that 'constitute the shipment', which has been subject to widely diverging interpretations. Whether or not, and if so to what extent, this provision covers the issue of adventitious presence in LMO-FFP shipments, essentially depends on what is understood to 'constitute a shipment'. In particular the African developing countries had preferred to shift the burden of sampling and testing for adventitious presence to exporters, through a requirement to list all potentially contained LMOs. As a compromise, a specific provision was incorporated on capacity-building, to assist developing nations in the development of sampling and detection techniques. Another ambiguity in the

[80] Dec. BS-III/8. [81] Dec. BS-I/6-A.

Decision includes the question of whether the mention of 'authorised in accordance with domestic regulatory frameworks' should be interpreted to refer to the framework in the exporting or in the importing State, and how this might reflect on States which have not (yet) adopted such a domestic regulatory framework.

The new differentiated documentation rules will apply for the next six years. The initial Brazilian proposal to make the 'contains' labels mandatory for all shipments from 2010 onwards was watered down in the final Decision to a review of experiences at COP/MOP-5, with a view to (rather weakly stated) 'considering' at COP/MOP-6 a decision on requiring the more specific 'contains' language for all LMO-FFP shipments. As the Parties agreed at the 2005 meeting to hold COP/MOPs every two years from now on, the contentious and divisive 'may contain' labels will continue to be allowed at least until 2012.

Liability and Redress (Article 27 BSP)

Nearly as contentious, but still at a much more preliminary stage, are the preparations for negotiations on liability and redress provisions under the BSP. Under the mandate of Article 27 BSP—inserted as a compromise by the deadlocked Signatories in 2000—Parties are mandated to elaborate such rules within four years of the Protocol's entry into force. To this end, COP/MOP-1 Decision BS-I/8 established an Open-Ended Ad Hoc Working Group of Legal and Technical Experts on Liability and Redress in the Context of the Protocol (WGLR), to make recommendations for a Decision at COP/MOP-4, in 2007.[82] In February 2006, the WGLR at its second meeting discussed options, scenarios, and approaches to such a liability and redress regime, covering: the definition and nature of damage, including scope; valuation of damage to biodiversity and human health; threshold of damage; causation; channelling of liability; roles of Parties of import and export; standard of liability; mechanisms of financial security; standing or right to bring claims; scientific analysis and risk assessment; determination of damage to the conservation and sustainable use of biodiversity (including, perhaps, baselines) and determination of socio-economic damage; the availability of financial security to cover liability, including insurability; and other international regimes and initiatives for liability and redress. One of the most fundamental and divisive issues is the choice of instrument, with positions varying from a non-legally binding instrument or simply dependence on national regulations, to an internationally legally binding instrument, along with variations and combinations between both options, or even a 'zero-option'. Despite its crucial importance, this element was not discussed in detail at the second WGLR meeting, as members felt other issues required priority clarification and elaboration.

In the COP/MOP-1 Decision BS-I/8, an interim review of this preparatory work was planned for COP/MOP-3. Although the WGLR did make certain progress at its second meeting by formulating operational texts on some of the most

[82] Dec. BS-I/8, see COP/MOP-1 Report, UNEP/CBD/BS/COP-MOP/1/15.

crucial issues (scope, definition, valuation of damage to biodiversity, and causation), their reports have essentially entailed still rather preliminary exploration and refinement of the key issues for future negotiations. Therefore, much like last year, the Parties at COP/MOP-3 had little more to do than to welcome the progress made and to encourage further preparatory work for negotiations at COP/MOP-4. It was agreed that, in light of the vast number of issues still needing to be fleshed out before actual negotiations can begin, the WGLR should reconvene three more times in the next two years to try to meet its 2008 deadline.[83]

Compliance and Enforcement Mechanisms (Article 34 BSP)

Although at COP/MOP-2 most of the rules of procedure drafted by the BSP Compliance Committee at its first meeting had been adopted without significant amendments, one element in particular had met with resistance among Parties. Despite efforts to reach a compromise, the bracketed text for this draft Rule 18 remained unresolved. It would allow for two-thirds majority decision-making as a last resort in the event that consensus in the Compliance Committee should be unattainable. Some delegations argued that this would be contrary to the Committee's facilitative role. The recommendation to Parties at COP/MOP-3, from the Compliance Committee's second meeting, in February 2006, was to remove the brackets around the draft Rule 18 text, and to formally adopt the qualified majority voting procedure, also pointing to the existence of majority or qualified majority voting under such circumstances in various other multilateral environmental agreements (MEAs). The most important decision on compliance at COP/MOP-3 was to follow this recommendation, and indeed to confirm the previously bracketed text, which means that the full set of rules of procedure have now been adopted.

ii. Aarhus Convention and Public Participation in GMO Decision-making

Public participation in GMO decision-making has been an issue of debate under the Convention on Access to Information, Public Participation in Decision-Making and Access to Justice in Environmental Matters (Aarhus Convention)[84] since its inception. This debate came to a (provisional) conclusion in May 2005, when the second meeting of the Parties (MOP-2) adopted the so-called 'Almaty GMO Amendment' to the Aarhus Convention with the objective of strengthening the rights of the public to participate in decision-making on GMOs.[85] However, the practical consequences of the political breakthrough in this protracted debate are not likely to materialize any time soon. The amendment will

[83] Dec. BS-III/12.

[84] N. 15 above.

[85] Dec. II/1, Report ECE/MP.PP/2005/2, 12 July 2005. For background discussion see Etty, n. 16 above, (2007), 309–11; (2006), 270–3.

enter into force only after it has been ratified by three-quarters of the Parties, and will be binding only upon those Parties. In the interim, as before, the previously adopted non-binding GMO Guidelines will continue to apply as a voluntary instrument. The Parties have agreed to review the progress of the ratification, acceptance and approval of the amendment at MOP-3, in 2008, as well as to review the implementation of the GMO Guidelines, which for now have more practical relevance.

During the present survey year (2006), only a single Party ratified the Almaty GMO Amendment. As the proverbial 'godfather' of the Aarhus Convention, Denmark was the first to approve the amendment Decision, on 18 October 2006, with a territorial exclusion with regard to the Faroe Islands and Greenland. A second Party may be added if the reporting year is stretched by a week, as Luxembourg joined on 4 January 2007. As for the other EU Member States, they have together with the EC committed themselves to 'endeavour to deposit as soon as possible, and not later than 1 February 2008', their instruments of ratification, acceptance or approval, with the adoption of Decision 2006/957/EC of 18 December 2006, discussed in Section B.*iii* above.[86]

iii. Codex Alimentarius

GM Food Labelling

One of the most contentious issues regarding agricultural biotechnology in the work of the Codex Alimentarius concerns the labelling provisions for GM foods and derived foodstuffs. Labelling standards have been at the top of the agenda of the Codex Committee on Food Labelling (CCFL) for well over a decade, without much substantive progress to date.

Two documents currently under discussion are, first, the Proposed Draft Guidelines for the Labelling of Foods and Food Ingredients Obtained Through Certain Techniques of Genetic Modification/Genetic Engineering: Labelling Provisions;[87] and second, the Draft Recommendations for the Labelling of Foods Obtained Through Certain Techniques of Genetic Modification/Genetic Engineering (Draft Amendment to the General Standard for the Labelling of Prepackaged Foods): Definitions.[88] The first of these documents, referred to as the Draft Guidelines, contains the actual draft labelling provisions for GM foods, and as such is more controversial than the second document, known as the Draft Amendment, which merely provides definitions related to these labelling provisions. Although the draft Amendment is *less* contentious, the fact that it has been 'stuck' for some time now at the penultimate step in the Codex standard-setting procedure (step 7 of 8) provides ample evidence of the political difficulty

[86] N. 14 above.

[87] ALINORM 04/27/22, Appendix VI. All Codex Alimentarius documents referred to in this survey are published on the Internet at: http://www.codexalimentarius.net.

[88] ALINORM 04/27/22, Appendix VI.

surrounding the labelling issue. Just as in 2005, the CCFL failed to advance the draft Amendment to the final step during 2006, and retained it at step 7, in fact this time even without raising any discussion on it whatsoever.[89] Discussions were held on the Draft Guidelines, but without any substantive results. The political deadlock on this issue has always been rigid, with the opposing camps disagreeing on whether the GM labelling provisions should convey only information relating to human health and safety concerns (triggered by changes in nutrient content, product composition and/or final use), or also information reflecting the production method per se, so as to (principally) identify the application of biotechnology in the production process even if the final product bears little or no sign of this. Each camp has reiterated its arguments and mutual objections time and again, with the US-led coalition opposing method of production labelling, on the one end, and the EC-led group pushing such labelling standards, on the other side.

2005's CCFL session did bring some hope for new impetus to this rather stale debate, when the CCFL agreed to a Canadian and EC joint proposal to reconstruct the Draft Guidelines, to enable a differentiation between mandatory labelling provisions based on health and food safety concerns, and voluntary provisions for method of production labelling. In May 2006, the CCFL discussed at step 4 the revised Draft Guidelines in which this new differentiation had been incorporated. However, just as the working group chaired by Canada had not been able to reach consensus on the revised draft, the delegations in the CCFL continued to disagree on the appropriateness of separated mandatory and voluntary provisions. Given this longstanding and persisting stalemate, and the lack of any reasonable prospect of consensus in the near future, the chairperson raised the suggestion of discontinuing or suspending work on these Draft Labelling Guidelines for the moment. It was instead decided to make a final effort to break the impasse by establishing a physical Working Group with a modest mandate essentially to assess the feasibility of future deliberations. Hence, the progress made on this labelling issue during this survey year was restricted to preserving its place on the CCFL's agenda at all, despite the US-led efforts to abandon the issue. For the time being, the Draft Guidelines will be held at the rather preliminary step 4 at least until the CCFL will reconvene for its 35th session, in May 2007.

Detection and Identification of GM Foods

The operationalization of GM food labelling provisions—whatever form, if any, they may take in future Codex standards—obviously hinges on the ability to detect and identify GM traces in food products and ingredients. For this reason, the Codex Committee on Methods of Analysis and Sampling (CCMAS) has been preparing Criteria for the Detection and Identification of Foods Derived

[89] ALINORM 06/29/22, paras. 82–101.

From Biotechnology.[90] Just as last year, consensus could not be reached on the second revised draft version of the Criteria, and a third draft was commissioned for the next CCMAS session, in March 2007.

Ad Hoc GM Foods Task Force

At the sixth meeting of the Ad Hoc Intergovernmental Task Force on Foods Derived from Biotechnology (GM Food Task Force), the main items on the agenda were the Draft Guideline for the Conduct of Food Safety Assessment of Foods Derived from Recombinant-DNA Animals (Draft r-DNA Animal Guideline); and the Draft Annex to the Codex Guideline for the Conduct of Food Safety Assessment of Foods Derived from Recombinant-DNA Plants (CAC/GL 45–2003) Regarding Food Safety Assessment of Foods Derived from Recombinant-DNA Plants Modified for Nutritional or Health Benefits (Draft Nutritional or Health Benefits r-DNA Plants Annex).[91]

The Draft r-DNA Animal Guideline largely followed the template of the existing Plant Guideline, deviating from that text only in the event of scientifically justified biological differences between plants and animals. Detailed discussions were held on the draft text, with a view to confirming or removing all the remaining bracketed text, including debates on whether or not foods derived from r-DNA animals intended for non-food use should be covered by the food safety assessment guidelines—which was ultimately left to each members' discretion. Ironically, once the Task Force members had succeeded to agree on a text without any square brackets left, lengthy discussions followed on the extent to which the document should be advanced in the Codex standard-setting process, with some delegations suggesting an expedited procedure by advancing to step 5 out of 8 with a recommendation to omit steps 6 and 7. Ultimately, the majority of the Draft Guideline was retained at step 4, while the contentious section on the use of antibiotic resistance marker genes was separately returned to step 3 for comments, and it was agreed to hold an FAO/WHO expert consultation in early 2007 to advise on the Task Force's next session.

There was a principal agreement on the Draft Nutritional or Health Benefits r-DNA Plants Annex initiated at the 2005 session, which covers so-called 'second generation' GM foods. A number of amendments were discussed, and it was agreed to return the Draft Annex to step 2 for redrafting by a physical working group co-chaired by Canada, Argentina, and New Zealand, and subsequently to circulate it for comments at step 3 with a view to it being considered at step 4 at the next Task Force session.

In 2005, three discussion papers had been invited by the Task Force: one by Kenya on safety issues related to food derived from animals exposed to gene therapy or GM vaccines; another from India on comparative food composition

[90] CX/MAS 05/26/9.

[91] ALINORM 07/30/34, 27 Nov. to 1 Dec. 2006.

analysis of staple foods (e.g. GM rice); and finally one from Mexico on post-market sanitary surveillance. Having evaluated these papers, the Task Force decided against initiating new work in these areas, with reference to similar ongoing work within the Codex or within other international organizations. For example, initiatives in the Organization for Animal Health (OIE) were considered to overlap with the Kenyan paper on safety issues related to food derived from animals exposed to gene therapy or GM vaccines.[92] Despite Kenya's insistence that the OIE's work approached these issues from the perspective of animal health and welfare rather than human health and food safety aspects, and that the latter should therefore be addressed in the Codex, the GM Foods Task Force declined to initiate work at present, but did agree to monitor progress in the OIE activities with respect to food safety aspects, and to request the Codex Secretariat to liaise with the OIE, and to discuss its report in the next Task Force session.

Another discussion paper was presented by the US delegation, entitled 'Food Safety Assessment of the Low-Level Presence of Recombinant-DNA Plant Material in Food Resulting from Asynchronous Authorizations'. It proposed, as an Annex to the Plant Guideline, guidance on food safety assessments in situations in which GM crops have already been authorized in one or more countries for marketing in or as food, according to the Codex Plant Guidelines, but are then found to be unintentionally present in low levels in food in countries which have not (yet) provided regulatory clearance, as a result of what the US proposal terms 'asynchronous' authorizations worldwide. Although the term 'low-level' is preferred in US regulatory circles, in the EU and several other jurisdictions, the concept is known as 'adventitious' or 'unintentional' presence. In 2005, when the US had proposed similar new work, but then focusing on low-level presence of r-DNA plant material arising from field testing or from older, discontinued GM crop varieties being taken off the market, the Task Force had not agreed to initiate such new work, but encouraged the US to further study the issue and to submit a discussion paper at a future session.

In its revised form, the proposal gained broad support in the GM Task Force, and following some relatively minor amendments (including the replacement of 'asymmetric' for 'asynchronous' authorizations, since the latter was felt by some delegations to imply that the unapproved GM crops would in all cases eventually be authorized by both the importing and exporting States), the Task Force agreed to establish a physical working group to elaborate the low-level presence guidance. The working group, to be co-chaired by the US, Germany, and Thailand, will first meet in March 2007.

The members of the Ad Hoc GM Foods Task Force will reconvene for their 7th session in September 2007.

[92] See also Section F.*vi* below.

iv. GM Forestry

The recent growth in the political momentum for the issue of GM forestry continued also in the 2006 survey year. GM trees are gaining particular attention in the context of the climate change debate, being cited as important potential components in adaptation and mitigation strategies. This has been catalyzed by the Decision[93] at COP-9 of the United Nations Framework Convention on Climate Change (UNFCCC)[94] to allow the use of GM trees for forestation projects to offset global warming under the Kyoto Protocol.[95] Counteracting initiatives, including calls for a worldwide moratorium on GM trees, have been under discussion in the context of the CBD and its BSP. Although just before the summer of 2005, the Parties at the BSP's COP/MOP-2 did not substantively address the issue, the CBD Subsidiary Body on Scientific, Technical and Technological Advice (SBSTTA) did, at the very end of the foregoing reporting year, make an important reference to it in the final paragraph of its Recommendation XI/11 on Forest Biodiversity, by recommending that the CBD Parties at COP-8 should: 'Take note of the potential impacts of genetically modified trees on forest biological diversity and suggest a process on how to address this issue.'[96]

On the basis of this Recommendation, compounded by the concerted efforts of civil society delegations to reiterate their plea for a moratorium on GM trees, substantive discussions were in fact held at COP-8 in March 2006, in Brazil, on this most controversial agenda item under Forest Biological Diversity. A number of Party delegations[97] as well as civil society organizations delegations voiced the call for a strict, precautionary approach on the introduction of GM trees, if not a mandatory moratorium. Although the ultimate decision of the Parties reflects a political compromise, proposed by the EC delegation, its message is undeniably stronger than most would have expected, formally recommending countries to exercise caution. The text of COP-8 Decision VIII/19 on Forest Biological Diversity: Implementation of the Programme of Work reads:

> The [COP], recognizing the uncertainties related to the potential environmental and socio-economic impacts, including long-term and trans-boundary impacts, of [GM] trees on global forest biological diversity, as well as on the livelihoods of indigenous and local communities, and given the absence of reliable data and of capacity in some countries to undertake risk assessments and to evaluate those potential impacts... *recommends parties to take a precautionary approach when addressing the issue of genetically modified trees.*[98]

[93] Dec. 19/CP.9 on Modalities and Procedures for Afforestation and Reforestation Projects under the Clean Development Mechanism in the First Commitment Period of the Kyoto Protocol.

[94] New York, NY (US), 9 May 1992 (entered into force 21 Mar. 1994), (1992) 31 *International Legal Materials*, 849.

[95] Kyoto (Japan), 10 Dec. 1997 (entered into force 16 Feb. 2005), (1998) 37 *International Legal Materials* 1, 22.

[96] Rec. XI/11, Report UNEP/CBD/COP/8/3.

[97] Including Liberia, Iran, Ghana, Malawi, Ecuador, the Philippines, Senegal, Madagascar, Egypt, Rwanda, Norway, and the EC.

[98] Report UNEP/CBD/COP/8/31, 15 June 2006, emphasis added.

The Parties also requested the Executive Secretary to compile further information on the issue, as well as inviting Parties, other governments, and relevant organizations and stakeholders to contribute their views, to enable the SBSTTA to assess the potential environmental, cultural, and socio-economic impacts of GM trees on the conservation and sustainable use of forest biological diversity, for consideration at COP-9.

Similar caution was advised by the Forestry Department of the FAO, at the end of 2006, building on its 2005 global study of biotechnology in forestry.[99] In a working paper entitled 'Responsible Management of Planted Forests: Voluntary Guidelines', the FAO Forestry Department advised that 'caution should be observed in using [GM] trees, as their long-term impacts may not be known'.[100] Having explained that GM technology is still a relatively new tool in planted forest management that has potential benefits and drawbacks which should be assessed on a case-by-case basis under stringent national regulatory conditions, it stressed that GM forestry has become more than a technical issue, and that socio-cultural values and public acceptance also need to be taken into account in future decisions on the introduction of GM trees.[101]

v. Genetic Use Restriction Technologies (GURTs)—Terminator Seeds

So-called Genetic Use Restriction Technologies (GURTs), a term referring to plants that have been genetically modified to produce sterile seeds at harvest by switching off their ability to germinate more than once, are one of the most controversial applications of modern biotechnology in agriculture today. This controversy stems largely from the large potential for socio-economic impacts, in particular a threat to smallholder, subsistence, and indigenous farmers, who are prevented by GURTs from saving and evolving their best seeds each season, and instead are forced to purchase high-tech seeds at high prices annually from the globally concentrated GMO seed industry. Hence the technology's nicknames of 'terminator technology', 'traitor technology', or 'suicide seeds', in contrast to its official rather tame name of 'Technology Protection System' (TPS).

Since 2000, the CBD has had a de facto moratorium on GURTs, based on COP-5 Decision V/5-III, which advised that:

> products incorporating such technologies should not be approved by Parties for field testing until appropriate scientific data can justify such testing, and for commercial use until appropriate, authorized and strictly controlled scientific assessments with regard to, *inter alia*, their ecological and socio-economic impacts and any adverse effects for biological

[99] Food and Agriculture Organization (FAO) Forest Resources Division, *Preliminary Review of Biotechnology in Forestry, Including Genetic Modification* (Rome: FAO, 2005), also published on the Internet at: http://www.fao.org/docrep/008/ae574e/ae574e00.htm.

[100] Published on the Internet at: http://www.fao.org/docrep/009/j9256e/j9256e00.htm, at 28. However, note that these working papers do not necessarily reflect an official FAO position.

[101] Ibid., at 28 and 32.

diversity, food security and human health have been carried out in a transparent manner and the conditions for their safe and beneficial use validated.[102]

However, although most developing countries and civil society groups are pushing for a firm and lasting prohibition on GURTs, with the EC taking a somewhat more ambiguous position, countries like Canada (despite having supported the Decision in 2000), Australia, and New Zealand, as well as the non-party US and evidently the biotech seed industry, are now actively pushing for a more lenient approach, in particular to allow field trials with GURTs on a case-by-case basis.

The ultimate outcome of the controversial SBSTTA meeting of February 2005 had been a recommendation for the Parties at COP-8 to reaffirm their previous Decision V/5-III on GURTs, and encouraged them to respect traditional knowledge and farmer's rights to save seeds, and to undertake and disseminate further research on the impacts of GURTs, including their ecological, social, economic, and cultural impacts, particularly on indigenous and local communities.[103] In addition, the Ad Hoc Open-Ended Inter-Sessional Working Group on Article 8(j) and Related Provisions of the CBD addressed the issue at the end of January 2006, also with a view to making a recommendation to COP-8 for a decision on GURTs, this time focusing in particular on the socio-economic impacts of GURTs on indigenous and local communities given the group's mandate. Although initial drafts of the recommendation largely resembled that of the SBSTTA, also urging a reaffirmation of Decision V/5-III of 2000, the GURTs proponents camp, including the Australian, Canadian, New Zealand, and Swiss delegations, with the non-party US and industry directing behind the scenes, successfully negotiated the introduction of a controversial reference to 'case-by-case risk assessment' which despite being subject to the 'precautionary approach' did open the possibility of an end to the longstanding de facto moratorium on GURTs, to be decided at COP-8.[104]

With its 'hot potato' status only compounded by these diplomatic controversies surrounding the preparatory negotiations in the SBSTTA and the Ad Hoc Article 8(j) Working Group, the issue of GURTs featured among the most contentious and divisive points on the COP-8 agenda, and caused major mobilizations surrounding the summit by the public and civil society organizations. Much to the relief of those groups, the Parties at COP-8 ultimately decided to follow the SBSTTA recommendation instead of that of the Article 8(j) Working Group. Hence, the final COP-8 decision reaffirmed the previous Decision V/5-III while rejecting the inclusion of the contested new reference to 'case-by-case risk assessments' of field trials. What is more, it also urges that the agricultural biodiversity mandate of Decision V/5 should be respected with regard to future research on

[102] UNEP/CBD/COP/5/23, 22 June 2000.
[103] Rec. X/11, Report UNEP/CBD/COP/8/2, 18 Apr. 2005.
[104] Rec. 4/7, Report UNEP/CBD/COP/8/7, 30 Jan. 2006.

the impacts of GURTs. As a result, the de facto moratorium on GURTs has been upheld under the CBD.[105]

vi. World Organization for Animal Health—OIE

In 2005, the World Organization for Animal Health (OIE) established an Ad Hoc Group on Biotechnology, with a view to providing increased scientific support to develop harmonized technical standards for GM applications in livestock and animal products. This group, which operates under the auspices of the OIE Biological Standards Commission (BSC), had its first two meetings during 2006.

At the first meeting, in April 2006,[106] it identified three main priority issues to be addressed in its future work, in the perspective of the worldwide improvement of animal health and welfare as the OIE's principal mandate. First and foremost was the role of biotechnology towards this overall OIE goal, for example through the use of GM techniques for the development of veterinary vaccines, drugs, etc. Second was the safety of cloned and transgenic animals, which had been the subject of the 2005 OIE Resolution No. XXVIII.[107] It was emphasized that this Resolution should be considered in the context of animal and public health, but not in the context of food safety to the extent that this would impinge on the work of the Codex Alimentarius, or other OIE working groups. A third priority was the need to develop guidelines for research priorities in biotechnology in relation to animal health and welfare. In addition to these three main priorities, several further considerations for the group were mentioned: the need for a definition of nanoscience/nanotechnology in the context of animal health; animal conservation and ecological issues, including consideration of the use of biotechnology in the biological control of invasive species and conservation of animal genetic resources; animal feed safety, including GM feeds; validation of diagnostic tests; GM insects; and the emerging issue of GM pet animals, to date including predominantly fish. The issue of xenotransplantation, which had also been discussed, was left aside for the time being, as it was not seen as an immediate priority for action given its current stage of scientific advancement. It was agreed to establish three subgroups within the Ad Hoc Group on Biotechnology, to address the following specific issues: reproductive animal biotechnologies (cloned and transgenic animals); vaccines; and nanotechnology and animal health.

At its second meeting, in October 2006,[108] the group discussed the amendments made by the BSC to its work objectives/'mission', which now read: to develop guidelines for new vaccine technologies (e.g. DNA vaccines, plant-expressed antigens); to develop guidelines on the animal health risks arising from somatic cell nuclear transfer cloning of production animals, including criteria

[105] Dec. VIII/23(C), Report UNEP/CBD/COP/8/31, 15 June 2006.

[106] Report 75-SG/12/CS2-A, Appendix IV, Sept. 2006. All OIE documents referred to in this survey are published on the Internet at: http://www.oie.int.

[107] Ibid.

[108] Report 75-SG/12/CS2-B, Appendix VI, Jan. 2007.

for assessing the health of embryos and animals derived from such cloning; to monitor developments in the applications of nanotechnology related to animal health and to inform OIE; and to advise OIE on suitable procedures for the identification and tracing of animals and animal products that have resulted from biotechnological interventions. The specific mandates for the three subgroups were updated, including that subgroup 1 on Reproductive Animal Biotechnology will develop a discussion white paper on identification and tracing of animals and animal products that have resulted from biotechnological interventions. Lastly, the Ad Hoc Group discussed the need for a specific definition and scope of biotechnology in relation to the OIE mandate of improving animal health and welfare, pointing to the various somewhat diverging definitions and scopes applied by the various international organizations (e.g. the OIE, Codex Alimentarius, IPPC, FAO etc.). The third meeting of the Ad Hoc Group is scheduled for June 2007.

vii. World Trade Organization: EC–Biotech Products Case

The most noteworthy development in the field of international biotechnology and biosafety law and policy was the much-delayed WTO dispute panel ruling in the case *EC–Measures Affecting the Approval and Marketing of Biotech Products* (*EC–Biotech Products*).[109] Although originally launched in the summer of 2003, the dispute did not come to a conclusion until February 2006, when the WTO dispute panel issued its (classified) preliminary ruling, almost two years later than anticipated. Although the final ruling was only passed down in May, the preliminary verdict (which was largely identical to the final one) had already been made public by NGOs and was publicly discussed both in the popular media as well as in academic and diplomatic circles.[110]

In fact, even prior to but certainly following its publication, this most voluminous ruling in world trade dispute settlement history, spanning some 2,000 pages in total, has been the subject of a tidal wave of scholarly attention. Since the level of detailed scrutiny and commentary in those publications obviously cannot be matched in the limited scope and nature of this overview, the reader is directed to those other sources for in-depth information about the case. Examples of such intricacies as cannot be discussed here include very interesting aspects of the case with relevance for future WTO disputes, both in terms of procedural questions (e.g. the use and role of expert panels, the relevance and role of amicus curiae briefs, and the appropriate timeframe for scientifically or technically complicated cases), as well as substantive issues (e.g. the definition of the concept of 'undue delay', the role of scientific evidence, and the relevance, scope, and definition of 'precaution' in risk related disputes, as well as the interaction between WTO rules

[109] WT/DS291 (US), WT/DS292 (Canada), and WT/DS291 (Argentina). All official WTO documents are in the WTO's dispute settlement documents database published on the Internet at: http://www.wto.org/english/tratop_e/dispu_e/dispu_e.htm.

[110] Published on the Internet at: http://www.foeeurope.org/biteback/WTO_decision.htm.

and other provisions of international law concerned with, in particular, the protection of the environment or human health). Instead, the following will provide only a brief overview of the main elements of the ruling, and its potential implications.

The complainants had contested three separate but interrelated categories of EC measures on biotech products: first, the EC's (alleged) *general* moratorium on approvals of any new GMOs; second, the EC's *product-specific* moratorium, blocking the consideration (without 'undue delay') for approval of a list of a number of specific GMO products, which were pending during the enactment of the general moratorium; and, third, the national measures of several EC Member States (Austria, France, Germany, Greece, Italy, and Luxembourg), prohibiting import or market-placement of GMO products, in spite of their EC-wide approval.

For present purposes, the dispute panel's extensive ruling can be boiled down to the following findings. Firstly, it held that the EC did, as had been alleged by the complainants, have a de facto general moratorium in place which prevented the authorization of new GMO import applications between June 1999 and August 2003 (i.e. the formal start of the dispute, not the end of the moratorium, which followed almost a year later, in May 2004). The panel held that the moratorium did not constitute a 'measure' in the sense of the WTO's Agreement on Sanitary and Phytosanitary Measures (SPS), but that it was nonetheless SPS-inconsistent as a collective procedural decision to avoid completing the authorization procedures, thereby causing an 'undue delay'. Secondly, the panel made a similar finding in respect of the product-specific moratorium, or measures, ruling that for all but 3 of the 27 pending applications the authorization procedures had been 'unduly delayed', in violation of Article 8 and Annex C of the SPS Agreement. Thirdly, it deemed the nine contested national bans, or safeguard measures, to be in violation of Article 5.1 SPS since they were not sufficiently supported by risk assessments, and that they failed to fulfil the requirements of Article 5.7 SPS for provisional measures in the absence of 'sufficient scientific evidence', referring specifically to the EC's own positive risk assessments for the affected GMO products.

In the conclusions of the final report of unprecedented length, the dispute panel made an explicit point of emphasizing what it had specifically *not* assessed, such as the safety of biotech products per se and the various safety assessments of specific biotech products by the EC scientific bodies; the 'likeness', in WTO rule terms, of biotech products with their 'conventional' counterparts; and the legitimacy, appropriateness, or WTO-consistency of the EC's regulatory regime and pre-marketing authorization procedures per se, rather than their application in practice.

One of the most interesting elements of the ruling concerns the relevance of multilateral environmental agreement (MEA) provisions, and their interaction with WTO trade rules. Specifically, in risk-related cases, this concerns the problem of the precautionary principle being recognized in various international law provisions and MEAs (*in casu* most importantly the BSP), but not by international trade law. Despite its growing recognition in international law, in the absence of convincing evidence that the precautionary principle has become a *general principle* of *customary* international law, the principle is not, or at least not per se, relevant or binding for countries that have not signed or ratified those MEAs containing the principle. *In casu*, the panel questioned the status of the precautionary principle as a *general principle* of customary law, with reference to the Appellate Body (AB) ruling in the *EC–Hormones*.[111] But just as that AB ruling, its conclusions in the *EC–Biotech Products* case fails to provide conclusive guidance on this issue. Moreover, the panel took to a restrictive reading of Article 31 of the Vienna Convention on the Law of Treaties (VCLT),[112] in holding that the application of the precautionary principle as enshrined in the BSP was restricted to relations between *Parties* to that MEA, and since none of the complainants were Parties, the BSP was deemed inapplicable. This outcome is somewhat ironic given the obvious role played by the BSP not only in the defence of the EC, but also in the very launching of complaints by the disputants. After all, the starting date of the dispute, in the summer months of 2003, did not accidentally coincide with the entry into force of the BSP. Rather, it may be presumed to have constituted, to a significant extent, a direct attempt to mitigate the implications of the BSP for the increase of national (precautionary) biosafety regulations, in an effort to send a proactive signal to (developing) countries which might otherwise be inclined to follow the relatively (pre)cautious approach adopted by the EU.

Given the ambiguities left by the panel ruling, in particular as regards the role and relevance of MEAs in world trade law, and the tremendous potential impacts of these and other aspects of this case, it is regrettable that the EC has announced that it will not appeal the decision.[113] An AB ruling in this case had been readily assumed by most commentators and observers, and it is submitted that such a second scrutiny might have been of paramount importance to the development of international biosafety law and related areas of environmental regulation.

G. MISCELLANEOUS

i. European Ombudsman Decision on Complaint against the European Commission: Maladministration of GMO Access to Information Request

In July 2006, the European Ombudsman, Nikiforos Diamandouros, issued his Decision on a complaint made in February 2005 by Friends of the Earth Europe

[111] *EC–Measures concerning Meat and Meat Products (Hormones)*, WT/DS26, WT/DS48.

[112] Vienna (Austria), 23 May 1969 (entered into force 27 Jan. 1980), (1969) 8 *International Legal Materials* 4, 679.

[113] At the DSB meeting on 19 Dec. 2006, the EC announced its intention to 'implement the recommendations and rulings of the DSB in a manner consistent with its WTO obligations', within a 'reasonable period of time for implementation', owing to the 'complexity and sensitivity of the issues involved'. This 'reasonable period' was subsequently agreed at 12 months from the adoption of the final panel reports, i.e. expiring on 21 Nov. 2007. See documents WT/DS291/35, and WT/DS291/34, WT/DS292/28, and WT/DS293/28, n. 108 above.

against the Commission over access to information relating to GMOs.[114] In August 2004, the Commission had refused the NGO access to its *second submission* to the WTO dispute panel in the *EC–Measures Affecting the Approval and Marketing of Biotech Products* case (*EC–Biotech Products*),[115] contending that the trade dispute proceedings could be equated to[116] court proceedings and should hence be afforded the same level of confidentiality. The requested document contained the Commission's defence strategy in the WTO panel proceedings, which was evidently of such a 'particularly sensitive'[117] nature that it relied on Article 4(2)(2) of Regulation (EC) No. 1049/2001 regarding Public Access to European Parliament, Council, and Commission Documents (Access to EU Documents Regulation),[118] according to which access shall be refused 'where disclosure would undermine the protection of: ... court proceedings and legal advice'. Despite Friends of the Earth's insistence on the document's release, this refusal was confirmed in October by the Commission's Secretary-General, on the same legal basis, denying the NGO's claim that there was an 'overriding public interest' in disclosure.

The Ombudsman ultimately rejected the Commission's contention that the WTO dispute panel adjudication could be 'assimilated to' a court proceeding, describing it as a disproportionate and ill-founded extension of the Community legislator's intended interpretation of Article 4(2) of the Access to EU Documents Regulation. This conclusion followed the argument made by Friends of the Earth, that the legislative history of the Regulation showed that the wider exception for 'legal proceedings' had explicitly been rejected in favour of the more narrow 'court proceedings', and that according to settled EC case law 'exceptions to public access must be construed and applied strictly'.[119] However, although the Ombudsman deemed this particular denial of public access to constitute 'maladministration' by the Commission in violation of the Access to EU Documents Regulation, it withheld support for the NGO's claim that all future WTO submissions should be made public by the Commission at the time of filing with the WTO panel.

This otherwise rather procedural matter gained public interest in the Spring of 2005, when the Commission released its contested *second submission* following the second hearing with the WTO panel in February, as it had previously agreed to do. The content and nature of the document spurred criticism that the

[114] European Ombudsman Decision of 11 July 2006 on Complaint 582/2005/PB of 16 February 2005, by Adrian Bebb for Friends of the Earth Europe (FOEE), against the European Commission; published on the Internet at: http://www.ombudsman.europa.eu/decision/en/050582.htm.

[115] See n. 109 above.

[116] Or, in the words of the Commission's Secretary-General: 'assimilated to'.

[117] According to the Commission's own comments on the complaint before the Ombudsman, ibid.

[118] [2001] OJ L145/43.

[119] See, e.g., Joined Cases T-110/03, T-150/03, and T-405/03 *Jose Maria Sison* v. *Council* [2005] ECR II-1429, para. 45.

Commission's GMOs policy was janus-faced. Commentators argued that the Commission's stance on GMOs for external purposes, e.g. in its WTO defence strategy, by emphasizing the risks and uncertainties of GMOs and advocating a precautionary approach, contradicts its policy position for internal EU purposes, e.g. its efforts to lift the de facto moratorium and the national safeguard bans.[120]

ii. Member State Safeguard Bans on GMOs and GM Seeds

Competing with GMO authorizations for the top spot at the Commission's political agenda for biotech matters are the persisting Member State safeguard bans on specific GMOs and GM seeds. Some of these precautionary provisions have been in place for nearly a decade, and they have been heavily battled ever since. The recent WTO dispute panel ruling exacerbated the pressure on the Commission to lift the bans and ensure the free circulation of GMO products throughout the EC internal market. However, the Commission's efforts to this end during 2005 backfired; rather than being suspended, the national bans actually grew in number. Hungary invoked the safeguard clause of Article 23 of the Deliberate Release Directive in order to prohibit all uses (cultivation, food, feed, and industrial processing) of MON810 maize on its territory,[121] while Poland and Greece relied on the safeguard clauses of Articles 16 and 18 of Directive 2002/53/EC on the Common Catalogue of Varieties of Agricultural Plant Species (Common Catalogue Directive)[122] in order to prohibit the planting of MON810 GM maize seeds. Moreover, the Commission's draft Decisions to suspend the national bans yielded a surprisingly historic event in European GMO decision-making when, for the first time ever, the Member States in the Council united for a qualified majority vote *against* a Commission proposal on GMOs, thereby robbing the Commission of its by now commonplace unilateral power in the comitology process.[123]

[120] See, e.g., a critical NGO report outlining the alleged conflicts between the Commission's WTO submissions and its policy statements and regulatory decision-making within the EU: Friends of the Earth Europe (FOEE) and Greenpeace, *Hidden Uncertainties: What the European Commission Doesn't Want Us to Know about the Risks of GMOs* (Apr. 2006), published on the Internet at: http://www.foeeurope.org/publications/2006/hidden_uncertainties.pdf. See also, e.g., FOEE and Greenpeace joint press release of 18 Apr. 2006, 'EU Approves Genetically Modified Foods Despite Serious Concerns: New Documents Reveal EU Commission's Double Standards', published on the Internet at: http://www.foeeurope.org/press/2006/joint_18_April_GMOs.htm. Also R. Wootliff, 'EU Guilty of Withholding Genetically-Modified Food Data', *Dow Jones Newswires*, 18 July 2006; and 'European Ombudsman Overrules Commission on Release of Biotech Submission', *Bridges Trade BioRes*, 28 July 2006.

[121] Hungarian invocation of Art. 23 of Dir. 2001/18/EC in respect of MON810 maize, on 20 Jan. 2005.

[122] [2002] OJ L193/1.

[123] See Minutes of the 24 June 2005 Environment Council meeting; and an NGO-leaked breakdown of confidential voting results at: http://www.foeeurope.org/ban_risky_gm_food/index.php.

In October 2006, the Commission re-submitted the draft Council Decisions to have the Austrian bans suspended,[124] having used the intermediate year to strengthen its case with an updated EFSA Scientific Opinion largely confirming its 2004 evaluation which had dismissed the science supporting the national safeguard bans.[125] However, at the December 2006 Environment Council meeting, a resounding qualified majority of the Member States once again rejected the Commission's proposals. Only the UK, the Netherlands, Sweden, and the Czech Republic supported suspension of the bans.[126] Given the obvious apprehensions of several Member States that normally tend to abstain in GMO-related voting, in view of political repercussions or retaliatory voting, the same fate appears to be likely for the Commission's draft Council Decision to have the Hungarian safeguard ban suspended. This proposal was presented by the Commission on 23 November 2006, and will be up for voting at the Environment Council in February 2007.[127]

As regards the national bans on MON 810 GM maize seeds, the results were mixed. The Polish application for a prohibition was formally granted on 8 May 2006 by Commission Decision 2006/335/EC Authorising the Republic of Poland to Prohibit on Its Territory the Use of 16 Genetically Modified Varieties of Maize with the Genetic Modification MON 810 Listed in the Common Catalogue of Varieties of Agricultural Plant Species, Pursuant to Council Directive 2002/53/EC.[128] However, the Greek two-year provisional ban of April 2005 based on Article 18 of the Common Catalogue Directive was less successful. In effect, its fate had already been sealed by the end of last year, as neither the Standing Committee on Seeds and Propagating Material for Agriculture, Horticulture, and Forestry (SCSP) nor the Council of Ministers had managed to reach a QMV for or against the Commission's proposal.[129] Hence, all that was left was for the Commission to 'rubber stamp' its own rejection decision, which it did on 10 January 2006.[130] The fact that no QMV could be mustered up in either regulatory body to condemn a safeguard ban which had not been supported by

[124] Proposal for a Council Decision concerning the Provisional Prohibition of the Use and Sale in Austria of Genetically Modified Maize (Zea Mays L. Line T25) Pursuant to Directive 2001/18/EC COM(2006)510; and Proposal for a Council Decision concerning the Provisional Prohibition of the Use and Sale in Austria of Genetically Modified Maize (Zea Mays L. Line MON 810) Pursuant to Directive 2001/18/EC COM(2006)509.

[125] EFSA Scientific Opinion of 29 Mar. 2006 reiterating that 'there is no reason to believe that the continued placing on the market of these products is likely to cause any adverse effects for human and animal health or the environment'.

[126] See Minutes of the 18 Dec. 2006 Environment Council meeting.

[127] Commission Proposal for a Council Decision concerning the Provisional Prohibition of the Use and Sale in Hungary of Genetically Modified Maize (Zea Mays L. Line MON810) Expressing the Bt CryIA(b) Gene, Pursuant to Directive 2001/18/EC COM(2006)713, 23 Nov. 2006.

[128] [2006] OJ L124/26.

[129] For a background discussion see Etty (2006), n. 16 above, 329–30.

[130] Dec. 2006/10/EC concerning the Provisional Prohibition in Greece of the Marketing of Seeds of Maize Hybrids with the Genetic Modification MON 810 Inscribed in the Common Catalogue of Varieties of Agricultural Plant Species, Pursuant to Directive 2002/53/EC [2006] OJ L7/27.

any scientific justifications and was in fact, as the Greek government itself had acknowledged, not founded on environmental or health risks but economic concerns, provides ample evidence of the highly politicized nature that the GMO comitology decision-making has assumed. In defiance of the Commission's Decision, which had allowed Greece a 20-day compliance period to suspend the ban, on 31 January 2006, Greece in fact announced an 18-month extension of the safeguard measure, as well as a widening of its scope to include 31 types of MON 810 derived GM maize varieties, instead of the 17 initially banned.[131]

iii. Commission Rejects Separate Shelving of GM Foods in Cypriot Supermarkets

On 14 March 2006, the Commission rejected a notification by Cyprus that required GM food products to be displayed separately from non-GM foods in supermarkets on the island.[132] When the draft legislation had first been notified in September 2005, it had met with angered responses from the US, which had warned for harm to bilateral ties, stressing Cyprus' WTO obligations also in the context of the *EU–Biotech Products* case. In fact, the US response had also predicted a possible contradiction of EC law.[133]

By the end of the standard six-month consultation and evaluation period, the Commission declared that Cyprus' notification was inadmissible under Article 95(5) EC as it did not make any reference to either of the objectives listed in this provision, as it was aimed at enabling consumers to distinguish GM foods more easily so as to allow for informed consumer choice, rather than the protection of the environment or human health. Hence, there was no standing basis for a substantive verification of the draft legislation under Article 95(6) EC, and the Commission explicitly reserved judgment on whether the notification concerns an area of EC harmonized law, and on its WTO law consistency.

Notwithstanding this formalistic set-back, the Cypriot parliament led by the Green Party appears eager to have the draft law enacted in defiance of pressures from the US and Brussels. In fact, there is also a strong move towards having Cyprus declared entirely GMO-free, on the basis that the island would be too small to allow for effective coexistence measures to be implemented.[134] More news will undoubtedly follow on these developments during the 2007 survey year.

131 See, e.g., 'Greece Firm on GM Corn', *Reuters*, 31 Jan. 2006.

132 Dec. 2006/255/EC concerning National Provisions Imposing on Supermarkets an Obligation to Place Genetically Modified Foods on Separate Shelves from Non-Genetically Modified Foods, Notified by Cyprus Pursuant to Article 95(5) of the EC Treaty [2006] OJ L92/12.

133 See 'US Says Cyprus Ties Could Suffer over GMO Plan', *Reuters*, 6 July 2005.

134 See, e.g., 'Greens Urge Battle against GM Foods', *Cyprus Mail*, 12 Jan. 2007; and 'EU Slaps Down Cyprus on Draft GMO Supermarket Law', *Reuters*, 16 Mar. 2006.

iv. Review of the Bt10 Contamination Emergency Measure Decision

The emergency measures which had been put into place in April 2005 in response to the accidental commingling incident involving the GM maize varieties *Bt*10 and *Bt*11 were up for review in March 2006. At the first scheduled review, in October 2005, the period of application of Decision 2005/317/EC on Emergency Measures Regarding the Non-Authorised Genetically Modified Organism *Bt*10 in Maize Products (*Bt*10 Emergency Measure Decision)[135] had been extended by the SCFCAH's section on GM Food and Feed and Environmental Risk.[136] Despite the fact that in the intermediate period, since November 2005, no further *Bt*10 contaminations were reported, the committee was not yet convinced that sufficient guarantees had been provided that the risk of *Bt*10 had been entirely eradicated. Several Member States requested further assurances by US authorities, and possibly even an *in situ* inspection at Syngenta's facilities in the US by an FVO delegation, to ensure that the *Bt*10 transformation event is no longer propagated.[137] For their part, on 21 December 2006, the US Environmental Protection Agency (EPA) announced that it had reached agreement with *Bt*10's producer Syngenta, on a $1.5 million penalty payment for the *Bt*10 incident.[138]

The third review of the *Bt*10 Emergency Measure Decision was scheduled for January 2007, and its application is extended until then. Since the absence of positive testing for *Bt*10 continued throughout 2006, that Decision was repealed in the Spring of 2007.[139]

H. Conclusion

At the close of the survey year 2006, the overall conclusion must be that this was, once again, a very interesting and important period in the contemporary history of the regulation of 'green' biotechnology. The impact of many of this year's legal and political developments is as yet difficult to predict, and will only take shape during the course of 2007. It will be particularly interesting to see how the EU (led in this regard by the Commission) will juggle the building pressures from within its own ranks (Member States) and from the international community (international trade partners). Caught between these two highly critical masters, and with the inconsistencies between it internal policies and its external representation becoming increasingly apparent, the EU will face a daunting balancing act in the years to come.

135 [2005] OJ L101/14.

136 See Summary Report of the 8th SCFCAH meeting, of 27 Oct. 2005, published on the Internet at: http://ec.europa.eu/food/committees/regulatory/scfcah/modif_genet/summary07_en.pdf.

137 See Summary Report of the 9th SCFCAH meeting, of 27 Oct. 2005, published on the Internet at: http://ec.europa.eu/food/committees/regulatory/scfcah/modif_genet/summary08_en.pdf.

138 The EPA dossier is published on the Internet at: http://www.epa.gov/compliance/resources/cases/civil/fifra/syngenta.html.

139 Dec. 2007/157/EC repealing Decision 2005/317/EC on Emergency Measures regarding the Non-authorised Genetically Modified Organism Bt10 in Maize Products [2007] OJ L68/8.

IV. Chemicals

*Candido Garcia Molyneux**

In the middle of an icy chemicals labyrinth, a new European Chemicals Agency has been left with the mission of subduing the REACH Minotaur, but will this Agency even be able to survive?

A. Introduction

After more than seven years of discussions, 2006 was the year the European Parliament (EP) and the Council finally adopted Regulation (EC) No. 1907/2006 on the Registration, Evaluation, Authorisation and Restriction of Chemicals (REACH) and establishing a European Chemicals Agency (REACH Regulation).[1] Its adoption was accompanied by the highest expectations as a measure that 'may prove to be one of the most significant measures that [the European Union] has ever taken' and that will become 'some of the most advanced legislation in the world'.[2]

Indeed, the REACH Regulation's entry into force and the establishment of a European Chemicals Agency (ECHA) in Helsinki in June 2007 may just be the beginning of a new era in European chemicals law and policy. While industry is currently busy figuring out how to meet all the new REACH requirements and counting its costs,[3] the main importance of REACH is that it establishes a radically new regulatory environment that goes far beyond its individual requirements. This new environment is characterized by the following features.

Firstly, REACH's main characteristic is the shifting of the burden of proof from regulators to producers. REACH requires producers to know what substances are contained in their products and their characteristics, and to prove that they are safe. Although not always successful, REACH sends the message of 'no data, no market'.

Secondly, REACH establishes fast-track procedures for the phasing-out of particular dangerous substances on the basis of the precautionary principle. The so-called authorization procedure is, in effect, nothing else than a phase-out mechanism of substances identified as being of very high concern whereby producers are given temporary authorizations with the expectation that they will progressively withdraw their products. The new restrictions procedure allows the

* Special Counsel at the law firm Covington & Burling in Brussels (Belgium) and external professor of Environmental Law and Policy and International Trade Law at the College of Europe, Natolin (Poland). The author would like to thank Marisa Kakoulas for her invaluable assistance in revising and editing this survey. The views expressed in this survey are personal to the author and are not intended as legal advice.

1 [2007] OJ L136/3; 'EU Reach Regulation Becomes Reality', *ENDS Europe Daily*, 3 Jan. 2007.

2 'MEPs Take Stock of Reach Agreement', *ENDS Europe Daily*, 12 Dec. 2006.

3 M. Jacob, 'Curbs on Chemicals Loom' *Wall Street Journal Europe*, 13 Dec. 2006, 1.

European Commission (Commission) to ban substances posing an 'unacceptable risk' to human health or the environment without requiring the approval of the Council and the EP through the EC co-decision procedure. These phase-out procedures are accompanied by the regulatory discretion that the wording of the REACH Regulation provides—and the European Court of Justice (ECJ) tends to confirm—to the Commission.

Thirdly, REACH applies virtually to all goods that are manufactured and imported. Thus, the chemical rules no longer concern solely chemical manufacturers and importers, but now the new rules (including those on the disclosure of information) apply to practically all manufacturers or importers of goods. An impressive example of this is the potential regulatory impact of REACH on tobacco products.

Fourthly, REACH requires and assumes (sometimes wrongly) the existence of an information chain starting with the substance manufacturer and ending with the final supplier of goods. REACH requires every actor in the chain to gather and share information on the substances contained in their products. For example, consumers are entitled to ask retailers about the presence of substances of very high concern in the articles they purchase.

Yet, even without challenging the theoretical correctness of this regulatory regime, one cannot but question whether it will, in practice, be credible. In the author's view, this can only be achieved if the new system is perceived as being fair, and this will require a second European regulatory revolution: the rules must be strictly enforced, and all parties concerned must be given sufficient procedural rights.

REACH will have failed if European policy-makers, and most importantly Member States, continue the practice of adopting high environmental standards that they rarely enforce. While producers may submit thousands of pre-registrations and registration dossiers within the next years, REACH will be discredited if measures are not taken to ensure against free riders among all EU manufacturers and importers. Particularly, this must be done in a strict and harmonized way throughout Europe.

On the other hand, given the large discretion that regulatory authorities will enjoy, the implementation of the REACH requirements should guarantee that all parties have ample opportunities to participate. While the Regulation is also revolutionary in laying down specific procedural rights, the Community institutions must make certain that the rules are applied to ensure this participation of all parties concerned. Procedural rights should be applied, not only for the benefit of industry, but also to provide public interest groups ample opportunity to be involved and secure the fairness of the system. Thus, both EU institutions and NGOs themselves should make sure that they participate in the REACH decision procedures by, for example, making full use of the rights provided by Regulation (EC) No. 1367/2006 on the application of the provisions of the Aarhus Convention on Access to Information, Public Participation in Decision-making, and Access to Justice in Environmental Matters to Community Institutions and Bodies.[4]

The following survey is largely devoted to reviewing the requirements that the new REACH Regulation will impose on chemical manufacturers and importers and, in effect, virtually all manufacturers and importers of goods. The survey, however, also reports on significant developments on chemical classification, biocides, pesticides, and mercury, among others.

B. Legislation Adopted

i. The REACH Regulation

The new Regulation imposes on chemical manufacturers, importers, and downstream users new requirements on registration, data sharing, evaluation, downstream use reporting, authorization, restrictions, and the provision of information through the supply chain and to consumers. The Regulation also imposes specific rules for substances contained in articles.

Scope

REACH applies to virtually all substances and goods. A substance is defined in very broad terms as 'a chemical element and its compounds in the natural state or obtained by any manufacturing process, including any additive necessary to preserve its stability and any impurity deriving from the process used, but excluding any solvent which may be separated without affecting the stability of the substance or changing its composition'.[5] Virtually all goods are made of such substances.

The Regulation, however, excludes from its scope radioactive substances, substances under special customs procedures provided there is no treatment or processing, non-isolated intermediates, and the carriage of dangerous substances or substances in dangerous preparations.

Waste is also excluded because the Regulation provides that waste, as defined in Directive 2006/12/EC on Waste (Waste Directive),[6] 'is not a substance, preparation or article'.[7] Recycled substances and substances contained in recycled materials, however, will be subject to at least some of the REACH requirements. Furthermore, a strict and rather legalist interpretation of the Regulation would lead to the conclusion that all substances contained in recycled materials, and not only those 'new' substances produced during the recycling process, would be subject to all of the REACH requirements, including registration. From this definition of waste, it could be inferred that the recycling process always results in the manufacture of substances because the input of the process is waste, which is not a substance, and its output is a substance on its own, in a preparation, or

[4] [2006] OJ L264/13. [5] REACH Reg., Art. 3(1). [6] [2006] OJ L114/9.
[7] REACH Reg., Art. 2(2).

an article. The legalistic interpretation would also arguably be supported by the Regulation's broad definition of 'manufacturing' as 'production or extraction of substances in the natural state'.[8] If this unfortunate legalistic interpretation is confirmed, recyclers would, in practice, be required to test each and every batch of recycled materials to establish the substances that are contained therein.

While Article 2(6)(d) of the Regulation provides an exception for recycled materials, it is unfortunately not likely to benefit most recyclers. It provides that substances on their own, in preparations, or in articles that have been registered and recovered in the Community are exempted from registration (but not authorization) if they meet the following two stringent requirements: (i) the substances resulting from the recovery process are the same as those that have already been registered; and (ii) the recycler has available the information on the substances provided in a safety data sheet or the information required by Article 32 for substances where a safety data sheet is not required. This exemption will be useless for most recyclers as it wrongly assumes that recyclers are part of an information chain and therefore have received a safety data sheet or the Article 32 information. In the real world, however, that information chain is always broken when the material is discarded and becomes waste. Furthermore, the first condition of this unfortunate exception could, in effect, be interpreted as confirming that the general rule is that all recycled materials are, in principle, subject to registration.

The Regulation also provides broad exemptions for substances 'used in' medicinal products, and food and feedingstuffs. Exemptions from the Regulation's requirements on registration, downstream users, evaluation, and authorization[9] apply to substances used in medicinal products falling within the scope of Regulation (EC) No. 726/2004 laying down Community Procedures for the Authorization and Supervision of Medicinal Products for Human and Veterinary Use and establishing the European Medicines Agency (Pharmaceuticals Regulation),[10] Directive 2001/82/EC on the Community Code relating to Veterinary Products,[11] or Directive 2001/83/EC on the Community Code relating to Medicinal Products for Human Use.[12] However, at least in principle, these substances will not be exempted from the REACH restrictions procedure. The Regulation's exemptions could also be interpreted as not applying to magistral formulae nor to medicines used in clinical trials. Yet, the Regulation does provide for the possibility for manufacturers to obtain an exemption for product and process oriented research and development purposes. Processing aids that are used in the manufacture of medicines but that do not remain in the final product are also not likely to benefit from the exemption.

Furthermore, under a strict interpretation, substances manufactured or imported to be used in medicinal products, but not yet contained in the final product, would not benefit from the exemption for medicinal products as they

[8] Ibid. Art. 3(8). [9] Ibid., Art. 2(5)(a). [10] [2004] OJ L136/1.
[11] [2001] OJ L311/1. [12] [2001] OJ L311/67.

are not 'used in' in medicinal products. Even if this strict interpretation is not followed, medicine manufacturers are likely to see the market withdraw as well as face higher costs for substances they use because these are also imported and manufactured for other purposes that will be subject in full to the REACH requirements.[13] Substances contained in the packaging of medicinal products are also not likely to benefit from the exemptions.

Substances used in food or feedingstuffs, as defined under Regulation (EC) No. 178/2002 laying down the General Principles and Requirements of Food Law (General Food Law Regulation),[14] will benefit from the same exemptions as those for medicinal products. The main difference, however, is that most substances used in the manufacture of food and feeding stuffs are food and feeding stuffs themselves; therefore, they are also likely to be exempted from most of the REACH requirements even before they are part of the final food or feeding stuff product. Nevertheless, REACH may significantly affect processing aids and, to some limited extent, chemical intermediates that are not themselves part of the final product. Substances in food packaging will not benefit from the exemptions, but substances released from intelligent packaging are likely to be considered as food additives and thus benefiting from the REACH exemptions.

The Regulation also provides limited exemptions for specific categories of products. For example, with respect to substances used in cosmetic products, the Regulation makes sure that their environmental impact will be assessed while, as a general principle, it leaves their health assessment to be regulated under the specific cosmetic legislation. Thus, the Regulation provides that the chemical safety report that may have to be included in the registration dossier of the substance's manufacturer or importer, or may have to be prepared by the cosmetic manufacturer, need not include the substance's risks to human health during use in cosmetic products.[15] The use of substances in cosmetics products will also not be subject to the authorization requirement if the substances are Category 1 and 2 carcinogens, mutagens or toxic to reproduction substances (CMRs), or substances raising an 'equivalent level of concern' for health reasons.[16] Similarly, the REACH restrictions procedure may not be used to address the health risks resulting from the use of a substance in cosmetic products.[17]

The REACH Regulation also provides specific provisions with respect to the testing of cosmetic products in vertebrate animals, which may be interpreted as limiting the animal testing ban of the Cosmetics Directive. Article 2(4)(b) provides that the 'Regulation shall apply without prejudice' to Directive 76/768/

[13] C. O'Driscoll, 'Medicines Threatened: REACH Could Leave Drug Companies Without Intermediates' *The Society of Chemical Industry* (Dec. 2006), 'La Directive REACH Inquiète Plusieurs Laboratories Pharmaceutiques' *Le Monde*, 14 Dec. 2006.

[14] [2002] OJ L31/1.

[15] REACH Reg., Art. 14(5)(b).

[16] Ibid., Art. 56(5)(a).

[17] Ibid., Art. 67(2).

EEC on Cosmetic Products (Cosmetics Directive)[18] 'as regards testing involving vertebrate animals within the scope of this Directive'. This provision is complemented by the thirteenth recital of the Regulation, which provides that 'this Regulation should apply without prejudice to the prohibitions and restrictions laid down in Council Directive 76/768/EEC [...] in so far as substances are used and marketed as cosmetic ingredients and are within the scope of this Regulation'. The provisions' wording and their legislative history suggest that the animal testing ban on cosmetics products should not be interpreted as applying to a substance used in cosmetics where that substance has been tested on vertebrate animals to meet requirements outside the Cosmetics Directive.[19]

The Regulation also allows Member States to grant, on a case-by-case basis, exemptions for substances on their own, in preparations, or articles 'where necessary in the interest of defence'.[20]

Registration

As of June 2008, manufacturers and importers of substances will be required to register those substances that they manufacture or import in quantities of one tonne or more. The requirement of registration applies to 'substances on their own or in preparations',[21] and therefore, importers of preparations (e.g. cosmetic products, paints, detergents) are required to register each and every substance contained in the imported products should they import one tonne or more per year in the same or other preparations or in bulk. In the case of corporations, the quantities must be calculated on the basis of each different legal entity rather than the corporate group as a whole.

Only EU manufacturers and importers, but not foreign manufacturers, must comply with the different REACH requirements, including registration. However, foreign manufacturers may register and comply with the other REACH requirements by appointing an 'only representative' in the Community. The representative must have, among other things, sufficient background in the practical handling of substances and the information related to them.[22] In this case, the representative, and not the foreign manufacturer, is likely to be liable under REACH.

The Regulation exempts polymers from registration, but it requires the Commission to review this exemption and present the necessary legislative proposals 'as soon as a practicable and cost-efficient way of selecting polymers for

[18] [1976] OJ L262/169, as amended.

[19] Letter from the Council to Karl-Heinz Florenz, Chair of the EP Committee on Environment, Public Health and Food Safety on the Proposal for a Regulation of the European Parliament and the Council concerning the Registration, Evaluation, Authorization, and Restriction of Chemicals (REACH), establishing the European Chemicals Agency and amending Directive 1999/45/EC and Regulation (EC) (on persistent organic pollutants) (5 Dec. 2006).

[20] REACH Reg., Art. 2(3).

[21] Ibid., Art. 5.

[22] Ibid., Art. 8(2).

registration on the basis of sound technical and valid scientific criteria can be established'.[23] The monomers or other substances contained in the polymers, however, may be subject to registration if: (i) they have not already been registered by an actor up the supply chain; (ii) the polymer consists of 2 per cent or more of such monomer or other substance in the form of monomeric units and chemically bound substances; and (iii) the total quantity of such monomer or substance makes up one tonne or more per year. An actor up the supply chain is an EU manufacturer, importer, or downstream user. Therefore, all foreign suppliers of polymers meet the first threshold, triggering the registration of monomers or other substances contained in their polymers unless they or their suppliers have registered them through an only representative in the Community.

On-site and transported isolated intermediates are also subject to limited registration requirements if their manufacturer can confirm that the substance is rigorously contained by technical means during its whole life cycle.[24] Intermediates are defined as substances that are 'manufactured for and consumed in or used for' chemical processing in order to be transformed into another substance.[25] On-site isolated intermediates are intermediates that, during synthesis, are intentionally removed from the equipment in which the synthesis takes place but where the manufacture of the intermediate and the synthesis substance take place on the same site. Transported isolated intermediates are those where the manufacture of the intermediate and the synthesis substance take place at different sites. Monomers that are used as on-site isolated intermediates or transported isolated intermediates to manufacture polymers may not benefit from the limited registration requirements that apply to intermediates.[26]

The Regulation also exempts from registration (but not from other REACH requirements, such as authorization) substances listed in Annex IV or falling within the categories listed in Annex V. Annex IV lists substances that were equally excluded from reporting requirements under Regulation (EEC) No. 793/93 on the Evaluation and Control of the Risks of Existing Substances (Existing Substances Regulation)[27] and pulp. Annex V includes several categories that are considered to be harmless, such as substances that do not meet the criteria for classification as dangerous under Council Directive 67/548 on the Classification, Packaging and Labelling of Dangerous Substances (Dangerous Substances Packaging Directive)[28] and that are not chemically modified. This Annex also includes several categories of substances that seem intended to be exempt from registration, among others, substances that are created as the result of a non-intended chemical reaction of other substances during the use of a formulation (e.g. cosmetics). The Commission, however, is required to review and amend Annexes IV and V by June 2008.[29]

[23] Ibid., Art. 138(2).
[24] Ibid., Arts. 17 and 18.
[25] Ibid., Art. 3(15).
[26] Ibid., Art. 6(2).
[27] [1993] OJ L84/1.
[28] [1967] OJ L196/1, as amended.
[29] REACH Reg., Art. 138(4).

As stated above, generally, manufacturers and importers are required to register their substances as of June 2008. The Regulation, however, provides for a transitional period for so-called 'phase-in' substances if they are pre-registered between 1 June and 1 December 2008. Phase-in substances include three general groups: (i) substances listed in the European Inventory of Existing Commercial Chemical Substances (EINECS), which are substances that were put on the European market between 1 January 1971 and 18 September 1981; (ii) substances meeting the definition of 'no-longer polymers', which are substances that were originally considered as polymers under the Dangerous Substances Packaging Directive, but that no longer meet the definition of polymers introduced by Directive 92/32/EEC amending for the seventh time Directive 67/548/EEC;[30] and (iii) substances manufactured in the Community or Member States that acceded on January 1995 or May 2004 but were not placed on the market between June 1992 and June 2007.[31] Notifiers of new substances under the Dangerous Substances Packaging Directive will be considered to have registered their notified substances provided they stay within their notified volume ranges.[32]

Pre-registered phase-in substances must be registered within the following deadlines: (i) 1 December 2010 for Category 1 and 2 CMRs, substances that are classified as toxic to aquatic organisms that may cause long-term adverse effects in the aquatic environment (R50/53) if they are manufactured or imported in quantities reaching 100 tonnes, and substances manufactured or imported in quantities of 1,000 tonnes or more; (ii) 1 June 2013 for substances manufactured or imported in quantities of 100 tonnes or more; and (iii) 1 June 2018, for substances manufactured or imported in quantities of one tonne or more.[33]

Phase-in substances that are not pre-registered must arguably be registered by 1 December 2008. Persons manufacturing or importing phase-in substances in volumes above one tonne for the first time after 1 December 2008 may pre-register them as of that date if they do so within the following deadlines: (i) six months from the first manufacturing or importing in quantities above one tonne; and (ii) at least 12 months prior to their applicable registration deadline.[34] In principle, only EU manufacturers and importers of substances would be able to pre-register, but arguably downstream users may also import substances in quantities above one tonne to be able to pre-register, and therefore, ensure that their substances benefit from the registration phase-in period.

Registration will require the submission of a technical dossier and may also require the submission of a chemical safety report where the registrant manufactures or imports the substance in quantities above ten tonnes per year. A chemical safety report, however, need not be submitted where the substance is present in concentrations below specified thresholds.[35]

[30] [1992] OJ L154/1.
[31] REACH Reg., Art. 3(20).
[32] Ibid., Art. 24.
[33] Ibid., Art. 23.
[34] Ibid., Art. 28(6).
[35] Ibid., Art. 14(2).

The technical dossier must include all physico-chemical, toxicological, and ecotoxicological information that 'is relevant and available' to the registrant.[36] In addition, the Regulation requires the submission of data sets on the basis of the volumes of the substance, which are defined in Annex VII to XI to the Regulation. Annex VII lists physico-chemical and basic toxicity and eco-toxicity information requirements; Annex VIII lists short-term toxicity and ecotoxicity information requirements; while Annexes IX and X require long-term chronic toxicity and ecotoxicity information. These Annexes establish the general rule that, before carrying out new tests, manufacturers should assess all available *in vitro* data, historical human data, data valid from (Q)SARs, and data from structurally related substances. Annex IX and X also specify that the registrant must first include a testing proposal in its registration in order to obtain the information required in such Annexes. Annex XI provides additional guidance on gathering and submission of required data. The Commission is required to adopt a Regulation on test methods, which it must amend regularly with a view to reducing testing on vertebrate animals.[37]

In a compromise that was strongly opposed by environmental NGOs, the Regulation requires particularly low data requirements for phase-in substances in quantities below ten tonnes.[38] These limited information requirements, however, will not benefit substances predicted to be Category 1 and 2 CMRs, and substances predicted to be classified as dangerous under the Dangerous Substances Packaging Directive with 'disperse or diffuse uses particularly where such substances are used in consumer preparations or are incorporated into consumer articles'.[39] Thus, in practice, substances predicted to be classified as dangerous and used in consumer goods, such as cosmetics, detergents, and paper, will not benefit from the limited information requirements even if they are manufactured or imported in quantities below ten tonnes.

Where the registrant must submit a chemical safety report, it must include at least an assessment of human health hazards, physicochemical hazards, environmental hazards, and whether the substance is persistent, bioaccumulative, and toxic (PBT) or very persistent and very bioaccumulative (vPvB). If the assessment concludes that the substance should be classified as dangerous under the Dangerous Substances Packaging Directive or is a PBT or a vPvB,

[36] Ibid., Art. 12(1).

[37] Ibid., Art. 13.

[38] Friends of the Earth Europe, *Five years of legislation process in the EU to ban toxic chemicals: Verheugen's competitiveness agenda fatally poisons REACH*, Press Release, 13 Feb. 2006, published on the Internet at: http://www.foeeurope.org/press/2006/AK_13_Feb_REACH.htm; WWF, *REACH after five years. Will the EU defend what little is left?*, 13 Feb. 2006, published on the Internet at: http://www.panda.org/news_facts/newsroom/index.cfm?uNewsID=59460; 'NGOs Grumble About "Fatally Poisoned" Reach', *ENDS Europe Daily*, 13 Feb. 2006; A. Bounds and R. Minder, 'Chemicals Companies "Watered Down Law"' *Financial Times*, 4 Mar. 2006 (also reporting on NGO allegations of close relations between the Commission and CEFIC and the hiring by the Commission and the EP of former employees of CEFIC and chemical companies).

[39] REACH Reg., Ann. III.

the chemical safety report must also include: (i) an exposure assessment including the generation of exposure scenarios and exposure estimation; and (ii) a risk characterization.

The Commission expects that around 30,000 substances will be registered, and 80,000 registration dossiers will be submitted between June 2008 and June 2018.[40] In order to save costs, Article 11 requires the joint submission of data by multiple registrants of a same substance (the so-called 'one substance, one registration rule'—OSOR).

Data Sharing

All pre-registrants of a same phase-in substance will be required to join a substance information exchange forum (SIEF) where participants will be required to share data on the substance.[41] Manufacturers and importers of the substance in quantities below one tonne (who therefore need not register), downstream users, and any third party holding information on the substance may also join the SIEF of a substance. Parties that are not required to register may still decide to join a SIEF in order to influence the data that is submitted to ECHA.

All participants of a SIEF will be required to share the data they own where requested by another SIEF member even if they are not yet required to register themselves. Before carrying out any testing for the purposes of registration, a SIEF member must request the data from other SIEF members if it involves testing on vertebrate animals; where the data does not involve testing on vertebrate animals, the member may decide not to request it from other SIEF members.

Where the holder of data involving animal testing is requested to share it, it will not be able to continue with its registration and will be fined if it does not share the data or it does not provide proof of its costs. In that case, the other member may also proceed with the registration without the data. In contrast, where the data holder agrees to share the data and provides proof of its costs, the Regulation indicates that the costs must be shared in a 'fair, transparent and non-discriminatory way'. However, where no agreement is reached, the costs must be 'shared equally'.[42] Still, in cases where the costs are shared equally, it is unclear whether the recipient of the data may only refer to it for the purposes of registration or may also have full access to the study.

In contrast, if a registration containing the data has already been submitted by a third party, the Agency must give the new registrant permission to refer to the data in that registration. The data owner will then have a claim for an equal share of the costs 'provided that he makes the full study report available to the other participant'.[43]

[40] 'Questions and Answers on REACH', Feb. 2007, published on the Internet at: http://ec.europa.eu/environment/chemicals/pdf/qa.pdf.

[41] The data sharing requirements are in addition to the OSOR rule.

[42] REACH Reg., Art. 30(1).

[43] Ibid., Art. 30(3).

If a study involving testing on vertebrate animals is not available in the SIEF, the study must be conducted by only one SIEF participant acting on behalf of all others. All participants of the SIEF requiring the study must contribute to the costs of the study with a share corresponding to the number of participating potential registrants. The Regulation also specifies that all those participants will have the right to receive the full study report.[44]

The Regulation provides for similar data sharing rules for the registration of non-phase-in substances and phase-in substances that have not been pre-registered.[45]

Information Through the Supply Chain and Downstream User Requirements

The obligations on downstream users will largely depend on the obligations of their suppliers and the information that they supply to each other. Generally, downstream users will only have obligations where the registration dossiers of their suppliers do not cover the substance usage of the downstream users. Only those using substances in the Community (or the EEA countries) and purchasing substances from EU suppliers or foreign suppliers with an only representative in the EU/EEA may be considered downstream users.[46] Importers of chemicals in downstream uses (e.g. preparations in different forms, such as detergents or cosmetics) are not considered downstream users but importers of substances (and therefore, are subject to the registration requirements), unless their foreign suppliers register the substances through an only representative in the Community.[47]

The requirements for downstream users are linked to the obligation of their suppliers to pass information down the supply chain. The Regulation requires suppliers of substances on their own or in preparations to provide their customers with a safety data sheet (SDS) if the substance or preparation is dangerous under the criteria of the Dangerous Substances Packaging Directive and Directive 1999/45/EC on the Classification, Packaging, and Labelling of Dangerous Preparations (Dangerous Preparations Directive),[48] or where the substance is a PBT, vPvB, or a substance raising an equivalent level of concern.[49] The Regulation also requires suppliers of preparations, upon the request of their customers, to provide them with a SDS if the preparation contains, above specified concentration levels, substances that are classified as dangerous, PBTs or vPvBs, substances identified as raising an equivalent level of concern, or substances for which there are Community workplace exposure limits. Where the supplier must include a chemical safety report in its registration dossier, it must include the report's exposure scenarios covering the identified uses in an annex to the SDS.

Downstream users (i.e. customers) are entitled to identify their uses of the substance to the supplier, who must include them in the exposure scenarios unless

[44] Ibid., Art. 30(2).
[45] Ibid., Arts. 26 and 27.
[46] REACH Reg., Art. 3(13).
[47] REACH Reg., Art. 8(3).
[48] [1999] OJ L200/1.
[49] REACH Reg., Art. 31.

unable to do so for reasons of protection of human health or the environment. Upon receipt of the SDS, the downstream users must check whether the exposure scenarios cover their uses. If their use is not included in the SDS (because they have not identified the use to the supplier or the supplier has refused to include it), downstream users must prepare a chemical safety report and/or notify ECHA.

Downstream users, however, are not required to draft a chemical safety report and/or notify the Agency if their supplier is not required to supply a SDS, their supplier was not required to prepare a chemical safety report, or they use the substance in quantities below one tonne per year, among others. Thus, in practice, downstream users will not be required to prepare chemical safety reports and/or notify ECHA where, among others, they are supplied with substances that are not classified as dangerous or where their suppliers manufacture or import the substance in quantities below ten tonnes.

The Regulation, however, is unclear as to what would happen when a downstream user procures its substance from two different suppliers. For example, what would happen where only one of two current suppliers covers the use of the downstream user? Could the downstream user consider that its use of the substance (including the volumes supplied by the supplier who did not register its use) is covered by the supplier who did register its use? Or as the timing of the downstream user's obligations effectively depend on the registration deadlines of their suppliers, what would happen where one supplier must register by 2010 while another must only register by 2018? Should the downstream user shift procurement to the later supplier in order to delay the obligation to draft a chemical safety report or notify the Agency? Or if the downstream user procures a substance from an EU supplier but also imports between one and ten tonnes of the same substance (therefore, it can pre-register and benefit from a delayed registration of June 2018), could the downstream user benefit from this delay even for those volumes of the same substance that it procured from an EU supplier? These 'hypothetical' issues may become particularly important where the downstream user considers that it is essential to protect the secrecy of its substance use. In any case, it is clear that a downstream user can always shift its procurement among suppliers in order to get the best 'REACH deal'.

Evaluation

The rules on evaluation, in effect, lay down three evaluation procedures. Firstly, the Agency must decide on testing proposals included in registration dossiers or downstream user reports to provide the information specified in Annexes IX and X. The Agency must give priority to substances that have, or may have, PBT, vPvB, sensitizing, or CMR properties, or substances that are classified as dangerous under the Dangerous Substances Packaging Directive and manufactured or imported in quantities above 100 tonnes per manufacturer or importer per year.

Before deciding, ECHA must publish all information relating to testing proposals involving tests on vertebrate animals and invite third parties to comment.[50]

Secondly, the Agency must check the compliance of at least 5 per cent of all registration dossiers submitted.[51] Within 12 months of the evaluation of the dossier, the Agency must draft a decision requiring the registrant to submit additional information in order to comply with the registration requirements and specifying the time limits for doing so.

Decisions on testing proposals and compliance checks must be adopted in the following way: ECHA must notify its draft decision to the registrant, take the registrant's comments into account and, if necessary, amend the draft decision. This draft must then be notified to the Member States, which may propose amendments. If no amendments are proposed, ECHA may adopt the decision. If amendments are proposed, the Agency must notify them to the registrant. ECHA must refer the draft, the proposed amendments, and any comments from the registrant to the Member State Committee. If the Committee reaches a unanimous agreement, ECHA must adopt the decision. If no unanimity can be reached, the Commission must adopt the decision in accordance with the regulatory comitology procedure of Decision 1999/468/EC laying down the Procedures for the Exercise of the Implementing Powers conferred on the Commission.[52] Where the Agency adopts the decision, the registrant may appeal it before ECHA's Board of Appeal.

Thirdly, Member States are to evaluate substances on the basis of all relevant information submitted. By December 2011, and thereafter, ECHA is to draft a Community rolling action plan covering the substances that should be evaluated within the following three years. This plan must prioritize substances on a risk-based approach by taking into account the substance's hazard information, exposure information, and tonnage.

The competent authorities of Member States may choose substances from the rolling action plan in order to become the competent authority for the evaluation of such substances. They may draft decisions, which must be adopted by ECHA or, where no agreement can be reached, the Commission, and require the registrant to submit additional information, including information not required in Annexes VII to X. The competent authorities must review the information submitted and draft a decision.

This draft decision must be notified to the registrant, which must be allowed to comment. The competent authority must then circulate the draft decision and any comments of the registrant among ECHA and other Member States. If other Member States do not propose amendments, the decision must be adopted. If Member States propose amendments, the draft must be discussed by the Member

[50] Ibid., Art. 40.
[51] Ibid., Art. 41.
[52] [1999] OJ L184/23, as amended by Dec. 2006/512/EC [2006] OJ L200/11.

State Committee. If this Committee agrees by unanimity on the draft decision, ECHA must adopt it. Where no agreement can be reached, the Commission must adopt a decision through the comitology regulatory procedure.[53] As with the prior evaluation procedures, registrants may appeal the decision to ECHA's Board of Appeals only if the Agency (and not the Commission) adopts the decision (i.e. there is unanimity within the Member State Committee).

Authorization

Under the authorization procedure, manufacturers are required to apply for the prior authorization of the marketing and use of certain substances, on their own or in preparations. This procedure is designed to ensure that producers progressively phase out substances that are considered to be of particular concern.

The authorization procedure applies to substances on their own or in preparations but not to substances in articles. This is because Article 56 provides that prior authorization is required for 'the use(s) of that substance on its own or in preparation on the incorporation of the substance into an article',[54] but not the use of the substance 'in an article'. This interpretation is also confirmed by Article 69(2), which provides that, after a substance is listed as subject to authorization, 'the Agency must consider whether the use of that substance in articles poses a risk to human health or the environment that is not adequately controlled' and make proposals under the restrictions procedure.[55] The exemption arguably would even apply to substances that are intended to be released from articles.

The authorization procedure may apply to substances that: (i) meet the criteria for classification as Category 1 or 2 CMRs; (ii) are PBTs; (iii) are vPvBs; or that do not meet the criteria of (i), (ii), or (iii) but for which 'there is scientific evidence of probable serious effects to human health or the environment which give rise to an equivalent level of concern [...] and which are identified on a case-by-case basis'.[56] These four categories of substances are generally referred to as substances of very high concern. The identification of PBTs and vPvBs must be done on the basis of the criteria of Annex XIII to the Regulation, which the Commission must amend.

[53] Ibid.

[54] REACH Reg., Art. 56(1).

[55] The Council's Statement of Reasons on its Common Position also provides the following: 'In order to close a potential loophole, the Agency will consider the need for EU-wide restrictions on the use of a substance in articles at the time of inclusion of that substance in Annex XIV'. See EU Council, Statement of Reasons on the Common position adopted by the Council on [.........] with a view to adopting a Regulation of the European Parliament and of the Council concerning the Registration, Evaluation, Authorisation and Restriction of Chemicals (REACH), establishing a European Chemicals Agency and amending Directive 1999/45/EC and Regulation (EC) (on Persistent Organic Pollutants) and a Directive of the European Parliament and of the Council amending Council Directive 67/548/EEC in order to adapt it to Regulation (EC) of the European Parliament and of the Council concerning the registration, evaluation, authorisation and restriction of chemicals (7524/06) Brussels, 28 Apr. 2006.

[56] REACH Reg., Art. 57.

Yet, the procedure is not likely to apply to all substances meeting the criteria described above. ECHA, upon request of the Commission or on the basis of a Member State proposal, must first identify the substances of very high concern that will become candidates for inclusion within the list of substances subject to authorization of Annex XIV to the Regulation. The identification of substances must be done on the basis of a dossier following criteria contained in Annex XV and must allow all interested parties to comment. Decisions identifying substances are adopted by ECHA if the Member States Committee can reach a unanimous agreement; where no unanimity can be reached, the Commission must adopt the decision through the regulatory comitology procedure.[57]

The Commission must thereafter decide to include substances identified as candidates within the list of substances subject to authorization of Annex XIV. It must do so on the basis of a proposal from ECHA, which must prioritize substances with PBT or vPvB properties, wide dispersive use, or high volumes. Before sending its recommendation to the Commission, the Agency must publish the draft on its website and allow all interested parties to comment. ECHA must put forward its first recommendation by June 2009.[58]

The Commission decision listing substances in Annex XIV must be adopted through the regulatory comitology procedure with scrutiny, and therefore, is subject to the blocking power of the EP.[59] For each substance, the decision must provide any applicable exceptions, the date after which the substance may not be marketed or used unless an authorization is granted or an application for authorization has been submitted (so-called 'sunset date'), and the date within which all applications must be submitted, among others.[60]

Applications may be submitted by importers, manufacturers, or downstream users.[61] Where manufacturers or importers obtain an authorization, this can also cover the uses of their downstream users. There are, however, at least two reasons why downstream users should consider applying themselves for authorization. First, after the application deadline, no more applications may be submitted; thus, where the supplier fails to obtain the authorization, the downstream will have to find a supplier with authorization or stop using the substance. Second, where a downstream user obtains an authorization for its use, it will be free to choose any supplier even if it the latter does not have an authorization of its own.

All applications for authorization must include, among others, an analysis of alternatives considering their risks and technical economic feasibility of substitution, and, where alternatives are available, a substitution plan including a timetable. The applications must be submitted to ECHA, whose Committees on Risk Assessment and Socio-Economic Analysis must draft opinions within ten months of receipt of the application. ECHA must also publish all information available on its website and allow interested parties to comment on alternative

[57] Ibid., Art. 59.
[58] Ibid., Art. 58(4).
[59] See n. 52 above.
[60] REACH Reg., Art. 58.
[61] Ibid., Art. 62(1).

substances or technologies available; this information must be taken into account by the two committees. Once the committees conclude their draft decisions, the Agency must forward them to the applicant, who must be allowed to comment within one month. The committees must take into account the applicant's comments. Then ECHA must submit the draft decisions with the applicant's comments to the Commission.[62]

The Commission *must* grant authorizations for uses of substances if the risk to human health or the environment of the use of a substance 'is adequately controlled'. However, authorization may be granted only if it is shown that socio-economic benefits outweigh the risk to human health or the environment arising from the use of the substance and if there are no suitable alternative substances or technologies in the following four cases: (i) where it cannot be shown that the risks are adequately controlled; (ii) the substances are Category 1 or 2 CMRs and it is not possible to establish an exposure threshold; (iii) the substances are PBTs or vPvBs; or (iv) the substance is identified as raising an equivalent level of concern to PBTs or vPvBs. The Commission must adopt its decision through the regulatory comitology procedure.[63]

All authorizations are time limited and subject to review. Authorization holders wishing to extend the authorization must submit a review report at least 18 months prior to the deadline specified in the authorization. The review report must include an update of alternative substances or technologies and a substitution plan if alternatives are available. Only authorization holders, and not latecomers, are likely to be able to request the extension.[64]

The Commission may also decide to review an authorization at any time if: (i) the circumstances of the original authorization have changed so as to affect the risk to human health or the environment or the socio-economic concerns; or (ii) new information on possible substitutes becomes available.[65]

Restrictions

The REACH Regulation also provides for a restrictions procedure through which the Commission may restrict the manufacture, marketing, or use of substances that pose 'an unacceptable risk to human health or the environment'.[66] Thus, under this procedure, the adoption of new chemical restrictions will no longer require its legislative adoption by the EP and the Council through the EC Treaty co-decision procedure.

The restrictions must be adopted on the basis of opinions of ECHA's Committees for Risk Assessment and Socio-Economic Analysis and after allowing interested parties to comment. The procedure can be initiated by a dossier prepared by ECHA, upon the Commission's request, or a Member State. As indicated above, where a substance is listed as subject to authorization, ECHA

[62] Ibid., Art. 64. [63] Ibid., Art. 60. [64] Ibid., Art. 61(1).
[65] Ibid., Art. 61(2). [66] Ibid., Title VIII.

must consider whether the use of that substance in articles must be restricted. The restrictions must be listed in Annex XVII to the Regulation.

Annex XVIII already includes the restrictions listed in the Annex to Directive 76/769/EEC on Restrictions on the Marketing and Use of Dangerous Substances and Preparations (Marketing and Use Restrictions Directive),[67] and its restrictions will enter into force on 1 June 2009 when Directive 76/769/EEC will be repealed.[68]

While the Regulation includes a free movement clause for substances meeting the requirements of the REACH Regulation,[69] it allows Member States to keep their own restrictions in place until 1 June 2013 provided those restrictions have been notified to the Commission in accordance with the EC Treaty.[70]

Articles

The Regulation imposes less stringent requirements on substances contained in articles than on substances on their own or in preparations. In practice, the real impact of this will be on imported articles because, for the purposes of REACH, EU/EEA manufacturers of articles are downstream users of the substances they use in their manufacturing processes and may even be substance importers as well.

An article is defined as 'an object which during production is given a special shape, surface or design which determines its function to a greater degree than does its chemical composition'. Thus, an article must meet two conditions: (i) it must be an object with a special shape, surface or design; and (ii) the shape, surface or design must determine the article's function to a greater degree than its chemical composition.[71]

While in most cases it will be relatively easy to identify an article (e.g. a chair, a wheel, a teething ring), there are likely to be many borderline cases where it will be difficult to make a distinction between an article and a container of a preparation. This distinction will have important regulatory implications because, as stated above, the REACH Regulation imposes less stringent requirements on articles than on preparations in containers. For example, substances in imported articles are not subject to the prior authorization requirement even if they are intended to be released from the article. Another important regulatory difference results from the different method for calculating volumes for substances/preparations in containers than for substances/preparations in articles. For example, the volume of a substance imported in bulk must be added to the volumes

67 [1976] OJ L262/201, as amended.
68 REACH Reg., Art. 139.
69 Ibid., Art. 128.
70 Ibid., Art. 67(3).
71 DHI Water & Environment, Danish Toxicology Center, Ökopol, GmbH, et al, *Draft Technical Guidance Document on requirements for substances in articles: Reach Implementation Project 3.8 Final Report* (26 May 2006).

of the same substance that is part of a preparation in an imported container. In contrast, the volumes of the substance imported in bulk, or even as part of a preparation in a container, must not be added to the volume of a substance contained in an imported article. This different method of calculating the volumes may have important regulatory implications because, among others, the amount of data to be submitted in the registration of the substance and its timing depend on the volumes of the substance per manufacturer or importer per year. Another important regulatory difference is that while in the case of substances on their own or in preparations all their manufacturers and importers must register the substance if they meet the volume thresholds, producers and importers of articles are not required to register or notify the substances in their articles if the use of the substance in the article has already been registered by any other third party.

The evolution of the discussions on guidance for borderline cases between articles and containers of preparations in the REACH Implementation Project (RIP) 3.8 on substances in articles reflects a u-turn in the approach of stakeholders and the Commission towards a much stricter interpretation of the definition of articles. This change is likely to be the result of an attempt by the agencies of some Member States to re-open the negotiations on the REACH requirements on substances in articles by restricting the concept of article.[72] The latest discussions indicate that most Member States and the Commission view as containers of preparations rather than articles spray cans, ink cartridges, carbon papers, printed ribbons, fire crackers, car batteries, and wet tissues if the main purpose of the tissue is to release a substance or preparation. In contrast, thermometers with liquid in them, scented erasers and adhesive tapes tend to be perceived as articles.[73] These discussions also suggest that for borderline cases useful criteria could be: (i) the primary and an ancillary function of the product (i.e. is the object merely acting as a container or carrier to deliver the substance?); and (ii) whether the preparation is an integral part of the article, and therefore, they are used and, where relevant, discarded concurrently.

The Regulation requires producers and importers of articles to register the substances contained in them if the following three conditions are met: (i) the substance is present in 'those articles' in quantities over one tonne per producer or importer per year; (ii) the substance is intended to be released under normal reasonably foreseeable conditions of use;[74] and (iii) the substance has not already

[72] See Federal Institute for Occupational Safety and Health, *German Comments on the Draft Technical Guidance Document on Requirements for Substances in Articles Reach Implementation Project 3.8 Final Report, May 26th 2005* (20 Sept. 2006); Federal Institute for Occupational Safety and Health, *9th CWG—Agenda Item 3—RIP 3.8 Requirements for Articles: Example Cases for Substances—Article Interpretations by the German Institute* (11 Jan. 2007).

[73] Commission, *Draft Summary of Meeting of the Sub-Group Commission Working Group on Substances in Articles of 9 February 2007* (Brussels, 19 Feb. 2007); Commission, *Borderline Cases Discussed at the Commission Working Group Sub-Group on Substances in Articles* (Brussels, 4 May 2007).

[74] REACH Reg., Art. 7(1).

been registered 'for that use' by a third party.[75] The use of the term of 'those articles' when referring to the volumes per producer or importer per year suggests that the threshold should apply to the entire article output of a producer or importer rather than to individual article types. For example, it is likely that the volumes of the substance in different models of the same article should be added. Furthermore, an interpretation of the three different thresholds for registration as a whole would suggest that the volumes of substances in articles imported or produced by the same person should be added provided that the substances in the articles have the same use. Thus, the volumes of a substance in diapers and tissue paper should be added provided that the substance has the same use in those articles. Not surprisingly, the concept of use of a substance is subject to much debate within the RIP discussions.[76]

The data to be submitted during the registration of substances in articles and their timing is the same as that applicable to the registration of substances on their own or in preparations. Registrants of substances in articles are also subject to the REACH Regulation's requirements on data sharing.

Producers and importers of articles are also required to notify the substances contained in their articles if the following five conditions are met: (i) the substance has already been identified as a substance of very high concern and as a candidate to be subject to the prior authorization requirement; (ii) the substance is present in those articles in quantities over one tonne per producer or importer per year; (iii) the substance is present in those articles above a concentration of 0.1 per cent weight by weight;[77] (iv) the substance has not already been registered for that use by a third party;[78] and (v) the producer or importer cannot exclude human or environmental exposure during normal or reasonable conditions of use, including disposal.[79]

Not surprisingly, the RIP 3.8 discussions indicate that there is a debate on how to measure the concentration limit of 0.1 per cent in order to decide whether a substance in an article should be notified. For example, where a substance is contained in the wheel of an imported car, should the concentration be calculated on the basis of the wheel or of the whole car? While the original interpretation of the Commission was that the concentration threshold should be measured on the basis of the article as a whole,[80] as a result of concerns raised by NGOs and Scandinavian countries the Commission has asked its legal services to review this question.

75 Ibid., Art. 7(6).

76 CEFIC, DHI, BfR, et al., *RIP 3.2–2 (Task IV) Work Package 2—Task A5 (Task Group 1) Proposal for a Common Descriptor System with Regard to Uses* (23 Jan. 2007).

77 REACH Reg., Art. 7(2).

78 Ibid., Art. 7(6).

79 Ibid., Art. 7(3).

80 Commission, *Draft Summary of Meeting of the Sub-Group of Commission Working Group on Substances in Articles of 9 February 2007* (19 Feb. 2007).

Notifications of substances in articles require the submission of limited information, such as the contact details of the producer or importer, the substance's identity, classification, and tonnage, and a brief description of its uses.[81] Notifications will be due within six months from the moment that the substance is identified as a substance of very high concern and a candidate for the authorization procedure, as of June 2011.[82]

In addition, ECHA may require producers and importers of articles to submit a registration if the following three conditions are met: (i) the substance is present in the articles in quantities over one tonne per producer or importer per year; (ii) the Agency has grounds for suspecting that the substance is released from the articles; (iii) the Agency has grounds for suspecting that the release of the substance from the articles presents a risk to human health or the environment;[83] and (iv) the substance has not already been registered for that use by a third party.[84] Arguably, ECHA should be allowed to require the registration of these substances not earlier than the registration deadline for the particular substances on their own or in preparations.

The Regulation also requires ECHA to consider whether the use of a substance that has been subject to authorization poses risks to human health and the environment that are not adequately controlled and that merit a restriction under the Regulation's restrictions procedure once the authorization sunset deadline for those substances has passed.[85] Thus, the Regulation envisions that the Agency will use the information obtained during the notification and registration of substances in articles to restrict the use in articles of those substances that have been subject to the authorization requirement. The adoption of restrictions for the use of substances in articles, however, would still be limited to those cases where there are 'unacceptable risks' to humans or the environment.[86]

Finally, an important innovation of the REACH Regulation is that it requires all persons engaged in the trade of articles to inform their customers of the presence in their articles of substances identified as being of very high concern. All suppliers—and not only producers or importers—of articles containing substances that have been identified as being of very high concern and candidates for the authorization procedure in concentrations above 0.1 per cent weight per weight must provide their professional customers, including distributors, wholesalers and professional end users, with sufficient information to allow the safe use of the article.[87] Suppliers are also required to provide the same information to consumers within 45 days of the receipt of their request.[88] In both cases, the information to be supplied must include at a minimum the name of the substance that has been identified as being of very high concern and a candidate for authorization and that is present in the article.

[81] REACH Reg., Art. 7(4).
[82] Ibid., Art. 7(7).
[83] Ibid., Art. 7(5).
[84] Ibid., Art. 7(6).
[85] Ibid., Art. 69(2).
[86] Ibid., Art. 68(1).
[87] Ibid., Art. 33(1).
[88] Ibid., Art. 33(2).

ii. Marketing and Use Restrictions

The Commission adopted Directive 2006/139/EC amending Council Directive 76/769/EEC as regards Restrictions on the Marketing and Use of Arsenic Compounds for the purpose of adapting its Annex I to Technical Progress.[89]

The Directive amends the existing restrictions on arsenic in the Marketing and Use Restrictions Directive to align them with the requirements of Directive 98/8/EC on the placing of Biocidal Products on the Market (Biocides Directive),[90] and Regulation (EC) No. 2032/2003 on the Second Phase of the Ten-year Work Programme referred to in Article 16(2) of Directive 98/8,[91] as amended. According to the Commission, these rules on biocides required prohibiting the use of biocidal products containing arsenic and arsenic compounds for wood preservation purposes as of 1 September 2006 unless such substances are authorized as new active biocidal substances under the Biocides Directive. Thus, the main amendment of the Directive is to condition the application of the Marketing and Use Restrictions Directive to limited exceptions on the use of arsenic compounds as solutions of inorganic compounds of copper, chromium, arsenic (CCA) type C upon obtaining an authorization to use such substances as new active biocidal substances under the Biocides Directive.

The new requirements will apply as of 30 September 2007. Note that the Directive also clarifies the distinction between the placing on the market and reuse of treated wood and, in particular, clarifies the rules on the placing of treated wood on the second-hand market. Specifically, the Directive provides that wood treated with arsenic compounds that was in use in the Community before 30 September 2007, or that was placed on the market in accordance with the new requirements, may continue to be used until it reaches the end of its service life; and wood treated with CCA type C that was in use in the Community before 30 September 2007 or that was placed on the market in accordance with the Directive may be reused and may be placed on the second-hand market, subject to the Directive's conditions of use. The Directive also allows Member States to permit wood treated with other types of CCA solutions in use in the Community before 30 September 2007 to be used or reused or to be placed on the second-hand market, subject to compliance with the conditions of use of the Directive.

iii. Biocides

The Commission adopted Regulation (EC) No. 1849/2006 amending Regulation (EC) No. 2032/2003 (Second Review Regulation)[92] for the following purposes: (i) introducing legal certainty on the phase-out period of substances that were notified for evaluation during the review programme but for which it was decided not to include one or all of their notified product types; (ii) introducing transparency requirements for the assessment report of substances, on which the Standing

[89] [2006] OJ L384/94. [90] [1998] OJ L123/1. [91] [2003] OJ L307/1.
[92] [2006] OJ L355/63.

Committee on Biocidal Products must base its decision on a substance's status; and (iii) introducing several substances in the review programme and deleting others.

Firstly, Regulation (EC) No. 1849/2006 introduces a new Article 4(2) into the Second Review Regulation. For substances notified for review but for which a decision is taken not to include in the review certain or all of the substances' notified product types, the new Article requires Member States to prohibit the placing on the market of such product types within 12 months from the entry into force of the decision.

Secondly, Regulation (EC) No. 1849/2006 introduces a new Article 11(4) into the Second Review Regulation. It requires Member States to draft an assessment report based on the Member State competent authority report, any other evaluation documents of the Member State, comments from other Member States, advice from advisory scientific committees, comments from the applicant, and any other information. The Standing Committee on Biocidal Products must review the assessment report and base its decision on the substance on this assessment. Regulation (EC) No. 1849/2006 also requires the Commission to publish on the Internet both the Member State competent authority report and the assessment report.

Finally, the Regulation introduces on the basis of Article 4(b) applications for several substances in the review programme,[93] and deletes others for which applicants have withdrawn or have failed to comply with the reporting obligations.[94] Deleted substances will have to be withdrawn from the market by January 2008.

The Commission also adopted Directive 2006/50/EC amending Annexes IVA and IVB to Directive 98/8/EC on the Placing on the Market of Biocidal Products.[95] Annex IVA specifies the data set for micro-organisms, including viruses and fungi, that applicants must submit in support of the inclusion of micro-organisms as authorized active biocidal substances in Annexes I or IA of the Biocides Directive. Annex IVB specifies the data set that must be submitted for those micro-organisms in support of the authorization of biocidal products based on such micro-organisms.

The Commission's Directive is intended to adapt the requirements for micro-organisms of Annexes IVA and IVB to similar amendments under Directive 91/414/EEC on the Placing of Plant Protection Products on the Market (Pesticides Directive),[96] and Directive 2001/18/EC on the Deliberate Release into the Environment of Genetically Modified Organisms ((Revised) Deliberate Release Directive).[97] According to the Commission, aligning the data requirements under the Biocides Directive with those of the Pesticides Directive will

[93] The introduced substances include hydrogen cyanide, ammonium sulphate, lauric acid, and cetalkonomium.

[94] The deleted substances include sodium hydrogencarbonate, phathaladehyde, and pirimphos-methyl.

[95] [2006] OJ L142/6.

[96] [1991] OJ L230/1.

[97] [2001] OJ L106/1.

facilitate the work of applicants submitting dossiers under both legal frameworks and the work of the Member State competent authorities. The amendments are also justified on grounds of scientific and technical developments in the field of microbiology and biotechnology.

The new data set requirements of Annexes IVA and IVB will be applicable as of 1 January 2008.

The Commission adopted Directive 2006/140/EC amending Directive 98/8/EC to include sulfuryl fluoride as an active substance in Annex I.[98] The Directive lists, for the first time, an active substance (i.e. sulfuryl fluoride) as an authorized substance in Annex I to the Biocides Directive on the basis of the review programme of existing active substances provided for in Article 16 of said Directive. Sulfuryl fluoride was reviewed as an active biocidal substance for use in product types 8—wood preservatives, with Sweden acting as the Member State Rapporteur. Sweden's assessment was reviewed by the Commission and other Member States, and the findings of the review were incorporated in an assessment report of the Standing Committee on Biocidal Products. No questions or concerns were addressed to the Commission's Scientific Committee on Health and Environmental Risks.

The 2006 Directive provides an illustration of how Annex I with the list of authorized active biocidal substances will look like. It lists sulfuryl fluoride with the following entries: (i) its listing number (1); (ii) its name; (iii) its IUPAC name and identification numbers; (iv) the minimum purity of the active substance in the biocidal product as placed on the market (i.e. more than 994 grams per kilogram); (v) the effective date of inclusion of the substance in Annex I (1 January 2009); (vi) the date as of which Member States must ensure that authorizations or registrations of biocidal products containing this substance (unless they also contain other active substances) are granted, modified, or cancelled (31 December 2010); (vii) the date of expiry of the inclusion of the substance in Annex I (31 December 2018); (viii) the product type (8—wood preservatives); and (ix) the specific conditions of the authorization.

On the basis of the review of sulfuryl fluoride, Annex I specifies conditions of authorization for this substance. In particular, the substance can only be used in biocidal products if the following three conditions are met: (i) the product may only be sold to, and used by, professionals trained to use it; (ii) appropriate risk mitigation measures are included for operators and bystanders; and (iii) concentrations of sulfuryl fluoride in remote tropospheric air are monitored. Authorization holders must submit these monitoring reports to the Commission every five years as of 1 January 2009.

[98] [2006] OJ L414/78.

iv. Pesticides

The Commission adopted Directive 2006/39/EC amending Council Directive 91/414/EEC to include clodainfop, pirimicarb, risufuron, tolclofos-methyl and triticonazole as active substances.[99] These substances are therefore authorized as active substances in pesticide products subject to the conditions of use and limitations specified in Annex I to the Pesticides Directive, and subject to a further assessment by Member States. The Commission also adopted six controversial Directives authorizing the use of six active substances in plant protection products after concluding their review under the Pesticides Directive and Regulation (EEC) No. 3600/92 on detailed rules for the Implementation of the First Stage of the Programme of Work of Council Directive 91/414/EEC.[100] The six substances are methamidophos,[101] procymidone,[102] flusilazole,[103] fenarimol,[104] carbendazim,[105] and dinocap.[106]

The six Directives were adopted by the Commission against the will of a majority of Member States only because Member States were unable to reach a position by qualified majority.[107] As a result, the decisions authorize the substances for unusually short periods (only until June 2008 or December 2010 rather than the usual ten years), limit the use of the substance to a small number of crops, and impose strict conditions.

In contrast, the Commission decided not to authorize the use and order the withdrawal of dimethenamid[108] and phosalone.[109] The Commission justified the rejection of dimethenamid on grounds that its assessment report showed that the substance could result in groundwater contamination due to the formation of soil degradation unidentified compounds with possible annual average leachate concentrations higher than 0.1 micrograms per litre (μg/l), and the consumer risk

[99] [2006] OJ L104/30.

[100] [1992] OJ L366/10.

[101] Dir. 2006/131/EC amending Council Directive 91/414/EEC to include Methamidophos as an Active Substance [2006] OJ L349/17.

[102] Dir. 2006/132/EC amending Council Directive 91/414/EEC to include Procymidone as an Active Substance [2006] OJ L349/22.

[103] Dir. 2006/133/EC amending Council Directive 91/414/EEC to include Flusilazole as an Active Substance [2006] OJ L349/27.

[104] Dir. 2006/134/EEC amending Council Directive 91/414/EEC to include Fenarimol as an Active Substance [2006] OJ L349/32.

[105] Dir. 2006/135/EC amending Council Directive 91/414/EEC to include Carbendazim as an Active Substance [2006] OJ L149/37.

[106] Dir. 2006/136/EC amending Council Directive 91/414/EEC to include Dinocap as an Active Substance [2006] OJ L149/42.

[107] 'EU confirms controversial pesticide controls', *ENDS Europe Daily*, 15 Dec. 2006.

[108] Dec. 2006/1009/EC concerning the Non-inclusion of Dimethanamid in Annex I to Council Directive 91/414/ECC and the Withdrawal of the Authorizations for Plant Protection Products containing that Substance [2006] OJ L379/125.

[109] Dec. 2006/1010 concerning the Non-inclusion of Phosalone in Annex I to Council Directive 91/414/EEC and the Withdrawal of Authorizations for Plant Protection Products containing that Substance [2006] OJ L379/127.

assessment could not be finalized due to the lack of data on the breakdown products. The rejection of phosalone was based on an assessment report that showed that for particular vulnerable groups of consumers the estimated exposures to phosalone were not demonstrated to be acceptable, and some of the metabolites and impurities of the substance required further toxicological characterization and additional concerns had been identified concerning the risk for birds, mammals, aquatic organisms, bees, and non-target anthropods.

v. Detergents

The Commission adopted Regulation (EC) No. 907/2006 amending Regulation (EC) No. 648/2004 on Detergents,[110] and in particular its Annexes III and VII. The Regulation amends Annex III by introducing test method ISO 1078:1997 ('Water quality—Evaluation in aqueous medium of the ultimate aerobic biodegradability of organic compounds') as an additional method to measure the biodegradability of surfactants in detergents. The new method is intended for use with surfactants that are poorly soluble in water.

Regulation (EC) No. 907/2006 also amends Annex VII of Regulation (EC) No. 648/2004 in the following ways: (i) requiring manufacturers of detergents to label the packaging of their products with the address of a website containing the list of ingredients of the detergent; (ii) requiring manufacturers to declare the presence of allergic fragrances independently of whether they are added as pure substances or as constituents of complex ingredients, such as essential oils and perfumes; (iii) requiring that the ingredient information for the general public utilize the INCI nomenclature; and (iv) providing the same labelling requirements for industrial and institutional detergents independently of whether they contain surfactants.

The new test method was applicable as of July 2006, while the amendments to Annex VII entered into force in January 2007.

vi. Dangerous Preparations Directive

The Commission adopted Directive 2006/8/EC amending, for the purposes of their adaptation to technical progress, Annex II, III and VI to Directive 1999/45/EC on the Classification, Packaging and Labelling of Dangerous Preparations (Dangerous Preparations Directive).[111] The 2006 Directive amends Annexes II, III, and VI to the Dangerous Preparations Directive[112] with four main purposes in mind. Firstly, the Commission Directive requires that where a preparation contains more than one Category 1 or 2 and 3 CMR (in concentrations above specified thresholds), the preparation be classified and labelled with the risk phrases of the higher Category.

[110] [2006] OJ L168/5. [111] [2006] OJ L19/12. [112] [1999] OJ L200/1, as amended.

Secondly, the Directive requires that the specified concentration limits indicated for substances classified as N (i.e. dangerous to the environment) and with risk phrases R50 or R50/53 in Annex I to the Dangerous Substances Packaging Directive also apply to substances that chemical manufacturers and importers self-classify with the same classification. Thirdly, in line with the amendments to the Dangerous Substances Packaging Directive,[113] the Commission Directive amends Annex III to the Dangerous Preparations Directive in order to include the symbol N and R-phrase R59 for preparations containing ozone-depleting substances. Finally, the Commission Directive amends the terminology used to describe the packaging and labelling requirements in Annex V on special provisions concerning the labelling of certain preparations.

Member States must implement the amendments introduced by Directive 2006/8/EC by 1 March 2007.

C. Legislation in Progress

i. Global Harmonized System

On 21 August 2006, the Commission launched a public consultation on its draft Proposal for a Regulation on Classification and Labelling of Substances and Mixtures based on the Globally Harmonised System.[114] The draft Regulation is intended to implement the rules on the chemical classification, packaging, and labelling of dangerous substances and mixtures of the Globally Harmonized System of Classification and Labelling of Chemicals (GHS), which was adopted by the United Nations Economic and Social Council in 2003, and to amend the chemical classification reporting obligations of the REACH Regulation. The Commission intends to implement the transport rules of the GHS by proposing specific Community transport legislation.

The draft Regulation would replace the Dangerous Substances Packaging Directive and the Dangerous Preparations Directive. It would, among others, introduce new rules on: (i) criteria for the classification of dangerous substances and preparations (now so-called mixtures); (ii) labelling; (iii) packaging; (iv) reporting of classification of substances and preparations to ECHA; and (v) advertising.

The draft introduces the hazard classes and categories of the GHS and those from Community legislation that are not yet covered by the GHS (e.g. environmental hazards classifications).[115] The Commission's explanatory memorandum

[113] Dir. 2001/59/EC adapting to technical progress for the 28th time Council Directive 67/548/EEC on the Classification, Packaging and Labelling of Dangerous Substances [2001] OJ L225/1.

[114] The draft is available on the Internet at: http://ec.europa.eu/enterprise/reach/ghs_consultation_en.htm.

[115] The draft lays down the following 29 hazard classes: (1) explosives, (2) flammable gases, (3) flammable aerosols, (4) oxidizing gases, (5) gases under pressure, (6) flammable liquids, (7) flammable solids, (8) self-reactive substances and mixtures, (9) pyrophoric liquids, (10) pyrophoric solids,

of the draft indicates that, while it expects the number of dangerous substances to remain the same overall (although some will be reclassified), the new classification criteria are likely to increase the number of mixtures that are classified as dangerous. This, in turn, is likely to increase the obligations of downstream users under the REACH Regulation as some of their obligations (e.g. drafting a chemical safety report and notifying ECHA) are dependent upon receiving a safety data sheet, which is only supplied for dangerous substances and preparations.

The draft Regulation would require suppliers of substances and mixtures to classify their substances by identifying the information on the hazards of the substances and mixtures that is available and comparing it with the classification criteria of Annex I to the draft Regulation. Suppliers are also required to re-evaluate the classification of their substances and preparations if they become aware of new scientific or technical information.

The draft Regulation does not require suppliers to carry out new testing, but provides testing requirements where the supplier decides to do so. Among others, the draft imposes limits on animal testing and prohibits any testing on humans.

However, the draft prevents suppliers from classifying their substances if they are already listed in Annex VI to the Regulation as subject to a harmonized classification. In accordance with the REACH Regulation, the draft Regulation requires the Commission to adopt the harmonized classification of substances that are carcinogens, mutagens, toxic to reproduction, respiratory sensitizers, and any other substance that merits a harmonized classification on a case-by-case basis. Substances for which a harmonized classification is agreed would be listed in Annex VI. Arguably, Annex VI would also list all substances with a harmonized classification that are currently listed in Annex I to the Dangerous Substances Packaging Directive, although this is not clear.

Where a substance is listed in Annex VI with a harmonized classification, the supplier must classify it in accordance with the agreed class. If the supplier has different information on the classification of the substance, it may submit a proposal for classification to ECHA. In effect, these provisions should complement those of the REACH Regulation, which requires both chemical suppliers and downstream users to disclose and/or report new information on the hazardous properties of their substances.

The draft Regulation also establishes specific rules for the classification of mixtures. In particular, it establishes the general rule that mixtures should be classified on generally available test data on the mixtures. However, where the mixture

(11) self-heating substances and mixtures, (12) substances and mixtures that in contact with water emit flammable gases, (13) oxidizing liquids, (14) oxidizing solids, (15) organic peroxides, (16) substances and mixtures corrosive to metals, (17) acute toxicity, (18) skin corrosion/irritation, (19) serious eye damage/eye irritation, (20) respiratory skin sensitization, (21) germ cell mutagenicity, (22) carcinogenicity, (23) reproductive toxicity, (24) specific target organ systemic toxicity from single exposure, (25) specific target organ systematic toxicity from repeated exposure, (26) aspiration hazards, (27) acute aquatic hazard, (28) chronic aquatic hazard, and (29) ozone depletion.

contains substances with specific properties (e.g. CMRs), its classification must be based on information on those substances. Annex I also provides a series of 'bridging principles' to allow suppliers to classify the mixtures where no test data are available on them.

The GHS labelling rules on pictograms, signal words, hazard statements, product identifiers, and precautionary statements are also introduced by the draft Regulation. However, it also keeps the current Community labelling elements for specific substances and mixtures and risk phrases. The draft Regulation prohibits including in the label any indications, such as 'non-toxic', 'non-harmful', 'non-polluting', 'ecological', or any statements 'that are inconsistent with the classification' of the substance or mixture.

Moreover, under the draft Regulation a transition period is provided for the introduction of new classification and labelling. During the first phase (i.e. until June 2010), the current system based on the Dangerous Substances Packaging Directive and the Dangerous Preparations Directive would apply for both substances and preparations. However, chemical manufacturers and importers would be able to apply the rules of the GHS Regulation on a voluntary basis. In that case, safety data sheets would have to be based on the current system and on the new rules of the GHS Regulation, while the labelling must be done in accordance with the GHS Regulation.

During the second phase (i.e. until June 2014 or 2015), substances would have to be labelled in accordance with the new GHS Regulation while their safety data sheets would have to be based on both the current system and the new GHS Regulation. The current system would continue to apply to the labelling and safety data sheets of preparations. However, manufacturers and importers would be able to apply GHS Regulation to preparations on a voluntary basis. In that case, safety data sheets would have to be based on the current system and the new rules of the GHS Regulation, while the labelling would have to be based on the GHS Regulation.

After June 2014–2015, the classification and labelling rules of the GHS Regulation would apply to both substances and preparations.

The draft Regulation would significantly reduce the classification reporting requirements of the REACH Regulation. It would require manufacturers and importers placing a substance classified as dangerous on the market to notify the identity and classification of the substance to ECHA. This requirement contrasts with that of the current Article 113 of the REACH Regulation, which requires 'any manufacturer, producer of articles or importer, or group of manufacturers or importers, or producers of articles, who place on the market a substance (classified as dangerous or subject to registration)' to notify the classification of such substance. Firstly, Article 113 requires the notification of substances that are either dangerous or subject to registration, and in principle, the classification reporting obligation could take place before the registration requirement. Secondly, the current language of Article 113 suggests that the classification reporting requirement applies to suppliers of single substances and to suppliers of substances in mixtures and articles. Thirdly, if the wording of Article 113 is interpreted as also requiring reporting the classification of substances contained in marketed mixtures, then this requirement could apply to substances contained in medicines, foods, and cosmetics. The draft Regulation, in contrast, explicitly exempts from its scope medicines, cosmetics, medical devices, and foods in the finished state and intended for the final user.

On the basis of the classification reports received, ECHA would be required to publish an inventory of substances and their classifications on the Internet. Where the classification reports result in different entries for the same substance, suppliers would be required to 'make every effort' to agree on a single classification.

Finally, the draft Regulation would prohibit any advertisement of a substance or mixture that is dangerous if no mention is made of the concerned hazard class and/or category.

ii. Pesticides

In line with its Thematic Strategy on the Sustainable Use of Pesticides,[116] the Commission presented two significant Proposals on the regulation of pesticides. First the Commission presented a Proposal for a Directive establishing a framework for a Community action to achieve a Sustainable Use of Pesticides.[117] The proposed Directive aims at achieving a more sustainable use of pesticides by requiring Member States to: (i) adopt national action plans to reduce risks and dependence on pesticides; (ii) ensure that professionals engaged in the trade of pesticides have appropriate training; (iii) ensure that pesticide application equipment is subject to regular inspections; (iv) prohibit aerial spraying of pesticides; (v) impose specific protection measures on the use of pesticides in the vicinity of water bodies; (vi) prohibit or reduce significantly the use of pesticides in certain protected sensitive areas; (vii) adopt measures to ensure the safe handling and storage of pesticides and their packaging; (viii) support the adoption of integrated pest management measures; and (ix) report to the Commission.

Specifically, the Proposal would require Member States to adopt national action plans setting up targets, measures, and timetables to reduce risks and dependence on pesticides. The plans would have to take into account the social, economic, and environmental impact of the envisaged measures. Moreover, they must be adopted and modified in consultation with the public in accordance with Directive 2003/35/EC on Public Participation in respect of the Drawing Up of Certain Plans and Programmes Relating to the Environment (Public

[116] Commission Communication to the Council, the European Parliament, the European Economic and Social Committee and the Committee of the Regions on a Thematic Strategy on the Sustainable Use of Pesticides COM(2006)372, 12 July 2006.

[117] Commission Proposal for a Directive establishing a framework for Community action to achieve a Sustainable Use of Pesticides COM(2006)373, 12 July 2006.

Participation in Plans and Programmes Directive).[118] The Proposal, however, does not require that the plans cover a minimum of points or that they set national quantitative targets for the recovery of packaging and obsolete pesticides, which reportedly were included in earlier drafts of the proposal.[119]

To ensure that all professional users, distributors, and advisers on pesticides have appropriate training, Member States would be required to establish certificate systems providing evidence of attendance at training sessions covering the programme specified in Annex I. Distributors selling pesticides classified as toxic or very toxic would be required to have at least one employee with this certificate responsible for providing information on the use of pesticides to customers. Only professionals holding such certificates would be allowed to sell pesticides that are not authorized for non-professional use. Such requirements must be effected within four years from the Directive's entry into force.

Member States would also be required to ensure that pesticide application equipment is regularly inspected to verify that it complies with the essential health and safety and environmental requirements listed in Annex II to the Directive. Equipment and accessories complying with harmonized standards published by the Commission shall be presumed to comply with those requirements.

The Proposal would also prohibit aerial spraying of pesticides except on those crops and areas defined by Member States where derogations would be possible. In such areas, derogations would be allowed only if all of the following conditions are met: (i) no viable alternatives are available or there are advantages in terms of reduced impact on health and the environment in comparison to land-based application of pesticides; (ii) the pesticides used are authorized for aerial spraying; and (iii) the operator carrying out the spraying holds an adequate certificate.

To protect the aquatic environment, Member States would be required to adopt specific measures, such as giving preference to products that are not dangerous to the aquatic environment and to the most efficient application techniques. Member States would also have to establish appropriate buffer zones where pesticides would not be applied or stored. Such buffer zones must be established on fields adjacent to water courses on the basis of the risks of pollution and the agricultural characteristics of the area concerned.

In addition, the use of pesticides would have to be prohibited or reduced to a minimum in sensitive areas, which include those used by the general public or sensitive populations, such as parks, public gardens, sports grounds and playgrounds, as well as areas protected by EC legislation on the conservation of wild birds and natural habitats, and wild fauna and flora.

Secondly, as announced in its Thematic Strategy on the Sustainable Use of Pesticides, the Commission proposed a Regulation concerning the placing of plant

[118] [2003] OJ L156/17.

[119] 'Commission Tables Dilute Pesticides Use Law', *ENDS Europe Daily,* 12 July 2006.

protection products on the market.[120] The Proposal would establish rules on the authorization of active substances and other substances used in plant protection products and on the authorization of plant protection products themselves. Plant protection products are defined as products consisting of or containing active substances, safeners or synergists and intended for: (i) protecting plants or plant products against harmful organisms or preventing the action of such organisms, unless their main purpose is for hygiene reasons rather than the protection of plants or plant products; (ii) influencing the life process of plants; (iii) preserving plant products, (iv) destroying undesired plants or parts of plants, except algae; and (v) checking or preventing undesired growth of plants, except algae.

The proposed Regulation would replace the Pesticides Directive. It would maintain the Directive's two-tier approach to EC authorization of active substances and Member State authorization of plant protection products, and many of the principles of the Directive. However, the Proposal would, among other things: (i) introduce and clarify the criteria for the authorization of substances, and in particular introduce a hazard assessment; (ii) introduce rules for the identification of substances 'candidates for substitution', and a comparative assessment and substitution of plant protection products containing them; (iii) require only one renewal of the authorization of active substances, after which no renewals would be required; (iv) require the mutual recognition of nationally approved plant protection products among Member States included in the same geographical zone; (v) remove the possibility of provisional national authorizations of plant protection products of non-authorized active substances; (vi) maintain the current ten-year data protection period for studies submitted to obtain an authorization, but exclude from protection data submitted under reviews or authorization renewals; (vii) require the sharing of tests and studies involving vertebrate animals; and (viii) require the publication of information on the substance and plant protection products unless it undermines commercial interests.

The Commission, under the proposed Regulation, would be required to identify substances that are 'candidates for substitution' during the assessment of applications for authorization of active substances. Candidates for substitution would be identified among substances: (i) with an acceptable daily intake (ADI), acute reference dose (ARfD) or acceptable operator exposure level (AOLE) that is significantly lower than those of the majority of the approved active substances; (ii) meeting two of the three criteria of persistent, bioaccumulative, and toxic substances (PBTs); (iii) for which there are reasons for concern linked to the nature of critical effects, which, in combination with the use/exposure patterns, amount to situations of use that could still cause concern, even with very restrictive risk management measures; or (iv) containing a significant proportion of non-active isomers.

[120] Commission Proposal for a Regulation concerning the Placing of Plant Protection Products on the Market COM(2006)388, 12 July 2006.

Substances identified as candidates for substitution would only be authorized as active substances for seven years. In addition, at the time of authorizing plant protection products containing such substances, Member States would be required to perform a comparative assessment with other plant protection products. Member States would be prohibited from granting an authorization to a plant protection product containing candidates for substitution if the assessment shows that: (i) for the specified uses, an authorized product or a non-chemical control or prevention method already exists and is significantly safer for human or animal health or the environment; (ii) the use of the substitution product or method does not present significant economic or practical disadvantages; and (iii) the chemical diversity of the active substances is adequate to minimize the occurrence of resistance in the target organism. In addition, any authorization for plant protection products containing candidates for substitution would be subject to review every four years at the latest.

However, Member States would be allowed to authorize, for three years, plant protection products containing candidates for substitution without a comparative assessment if it is necessary to acquire experience first through using that product in practice.

The Proposal would continue to grant a ten-year protection for the tests and study reports submitted during the application for an authorization if the applicant: (i) requested such protection at the time of submitting its dossier; (ii) justified that the test and study reports submitted are necessary for the first authorization or for the amendment of the authorization of plant protection product; and (iii) provided confirmation that any period of data protection granted for the test or study report has not expired.

The protection would cover only those tests and reports submitted that are in compliance with the principles of Good Laboratory Practice or Good Experimental Practice. Studies that were only necessary for the renewal or review of an authorization would not be protected.

Where a report is protected, it may not be used for the benefit of other applicants. However, the Proposal encourages the sharing of data and requires such sharing in the case of tests and studies involving vertebrate animals. Owners of data involving vertebrate animals and prospective applicants are required to 'make every effort' to share the tests and studies as well as their costs. If they fail to reach an agreement, the competent authorities may use the studies for the prospective applicant without prejudice to the data owner's right to claim an equal share of the costs from the applicant in court.

iii. Exports of Mercury

As announced in the Commission's Communication for a Community Strategy Concerning Mercury,[121] the Commission proposed a Regulation on the Banning

[121] Communication from the Commission to the Council and the European Parliament on a Community Strategy Concerning Mercury COM(2005)20, 28 Jan. 2005.

of Exports and Safe Storage of Metallic Mercury.[122] The Proposal aims at banning the export of metallic mercury from the Community and at ensuring that this mercury does not re-enter the market and is safely stored.

The Proposal would ban, as of 1 July 2011, the export of metallic mercury from the Community. According to the Commission, metallic mercury is the most relevant substance in terms of quantity of all the mercury compounds and products containing mercury. The ban would not apply, however, to preparations or articles containing mercury.

The proposed ban follows the UNEP Mercury Programme Council's decision asking governments to take immediate action to reduce the risks to human health and the environment posed by mercury in products and production processes, such as limiting the trade of mercury.[123] Furthermore, in its Proposal, the Commission also commits to further develop global action on mercury. In particular, by 2010 the Commission must report to the Council and the EP on progress in multilateral activities and negotiations on mercury, assessing the consistency of the proposed Regulation with international developments.

The proposed ban would be adopted as a separate legal instrument rather than an amendment to Regulation (EC) No. 304/2003 on the Export and Import of Dangerous Chemicals[124] because, while the Regulation requires that any export ban be accompanied by a prohibition to use the chemical in the Community, the use of mercury would continue to be allowed in the Community although subject to strict restrictions.

The Proposal would also require that metallic mercury 'no longer used in the chlor-alkali industry', mercury gained from the cleaning of natural gas, and mercury gained as a by-product from non-ferrous mining and smelting operations be 'stored' in a way that is safe for human health and the environment. The Commission's explanatory memorandum of the Proposal indicates that the use of the wording 'no longer used in the chlor-alkali industry' implies that transfers from one chlor-alkali installation to another within the Community would remain allowed, subject to the voluntary commitment of the chlor-alkali industry.

The Proposal's storage obligation applies to mercury independently of whether it is classified as waste. Therefore, the Proposal also introduces several amendments to Community waste legislation in order to allow the storage of waste metallic mercury in underground salt mines adapted for waste facility or in facilities exclusively dedicated to and equipped for the temporary storage of metallic mercury prior to its final disposal; and to facilitate the shipments of waste metallic mercury within the Community.

[122] Commission Proposal for a Regulation on the Banning of Exports and Safe Storage of Metallic Mercury COM(2006)636, 26 Oct. 2006.

[123] UNEP Governing Council 23/99, 25 Feb. 2005.

[124] [2003] OJ L63/1.

The Proposal would also require the Commission to organize an exchange of information between Member States and industries concerned. The exchange of information must examine the potential need for extending the export ban to mercury compounds and products containing mercury, extending the storage obligation to metallic mercury from other sources, and time limits concerning storage in a facility specifically dedicated to the temporary storage of metallic mercury.

D. Case Law

In two cases, the European Court of Justice (ECJ) was asked to interpret the transitional provisions of the Pesticides Directive and of the Biocides Directive. The two cases responded to references for a preliminary ruling from Dutch courts in the context of proceedings between nature foundations and the Dutch government, and followed a previous case on a similar reference decided in 2005.[125]

Firstly, in Case C-174/05,[126] the Court was asked to assess the compatibility of Decision 2003/199/EC on the non-inclusion of aldicard in Annex I to Council Directive 91/414[127] with the transitional provisions of Article 8(2) of the Pesticides Directive. Decision 2003/199 was adopted after the assessment of aldicard showed that the substance did not meet the safety requirements of the Pesticides Directive. However, while the Decision rejected the inclusion of aldicard in Annex I to Council Directive 91/414/EEC and required Member States to withdraw their marketing authorizations of the substance, the Decision did allow specific Member States to postpone the withdrawal of marketing authorizations for specific 'essential uses'. According to the recitals of the Decision, this transitional relief was necessary due to the absence of efficient alternatives for specific uses.

Article 8(2) of the Pesticides Directive, in turn, requires Member States to ensure that the relevant market authorizations are 'withdrawn or varied [...] within a prescribed period'. The Stichting Zuid-Hollandse Milieufederatie maintained that this provision did not allow the granting of transitional periods for specific uses of substances that are not included in Annex I of the Pesticides Directive and that the different time limit for specific uses violated the principle of proportionality.

The ECJ, however, took a different approach. Firstly, it considered that, despite the different wording of the Dutch version of Decision 2003/199, the Decision should be interpreted as allowing Member States to maintain their market authorizations of the substance until January 2007 for specific uses but not

[125] Case C-316/04 *Stichting Zuid-Hollandse Milieufederatie* v. *College voor de toelating van bestrijdingsmiddelen* [2005] ECR I-9579.

[126] Case C-174/05 *Stichting Zuid-Hollandse Milieufederatie and Stichting Natuur en Milieu* v. *College voor de toelating van bestrijdingsmiddelen* [2006] ECR I-2443.

[127] [2003] OJ L76/21.

to grant new authorizations for such uses. Secondly, the ECJ held that Article 8(2) of the Pesticides Directive allows for this transitional period. While Article 8(2) requires Member States to withdraw their marketing authorizations for a substance that has been decided not to be included in Annex I, it refers to a 'prescribed period'. According to the Court, this prescribed period must be established by implementing measures, such as Decision 2003/199. Furthermore, the Court considered that there is nothing in the Pesticides Directive that prevents the approach of Decision 2003/199.

Finally, the ECJ held that the Decision's transitional period for specific essential uses of aldicard under strict conditions of use to minimize any risks was not disproportionate. This was because the transitional period was based on an assessment that took into account that aldicard did not meet the safety requirements of the Directive and no efficient alternatives were available for specific essential uses. The Court held that this assessment was not manifestly inappropriate because: (i) the adopted system established different time limits for the withdrawal of authorizations depending on the uses made of aldicard; (ii) the list of essential uses was restricted; and (iii) the exceptions were granted only to some Member States and subject to a stringent follow-up and monitoring programme.

In Case C-138/2005,[128] the Court was asked to decide on Member States' discretion under the transitional provisions of Article 8(2) of the Pesticides Directive. Article 8(2) provides that Member States may, during a period of 12 years following the notification of the Directive, authorize the placing on the market of plant protection products containing active substances not listed in Annex I to the Directive but that were already on the market two years after the date of notification of the Directive. The ECJ first confirmed that Article 16(1) of the Biocides Directive (providing a transitional period for biocidal products) has the same meaning as Article 8(2) of the Pesticides Directive, as it had already stated in Case C-316/04 one year before.[129] Moreover, while Article 8(2) does not impose a standstill on Member States, the ECJ held that it does impose safety limits on Member State discretion, particularly the following: (i) Member States may not authorize a plant protection product without taking due account of the effects of that product on human and animal health and on the environment; (ii) when granting any authorization decision, Member States must consider those effects on the basis of a dossier containing the information necessary to enable a genuine assessment; and (iii) Member States may not exempt any person applying for authorization from the obligation to submit a dossier.

The ECJ justified these limits on Member State discretion on two grounds. Firstly, the Pesticides Directive is aimed at protecting human and animal health and the environment. Secondly, the duty of cooperation of Article 10 EC and

[128] Case C-138/05 *Stichting Zuid-Hollandse Milieufederatie* v. *Minister van Landbouw, Natuur en Voedselkwaliteit* [2006] ECR I-8339.

[129] C-316/04, n. 125 above.

Article 249 EC's prescription that Directives are binding as to the result to be achieved of Article 249 EC requires Member States to refrain from taking any measures liable seriously to compromise the Directive's objective.

Finally, the ECJ confirmed that, during the transitional period, the authorization of plant protection products of active substances not listed in Annex I of the Pesticides Directive but that were already on the market two years after the notification of the Directive is subject to the Member State's own rules and is not subject to Articles 4 and 8(3) of the Directive. It also held that the review of Article 8(3) entails that the plant protection product has already been authorized and its authorization is still valid at the time of the review; in addition, the review refers to the plant protection product and not to its active substance.

E. Policy Documents

The Commission presented a Communication on a Thematic Strategy on the Sustainable Use of Pesticides,[130] as promised in the Sixth Community Environment Action Programme.[131] The Communication argues that current legislation on pesticides fails to address the use phase of pesticides. Such legislation includes the Pesticides Directive and Regulation (EC) No. 396/2005 on Maximum Residue Levels of Pesticides in Food and Feed.[132] In particular, the Commission argues that, despite current legislation, the actual consumption of pesticides has not decreased in the EU in recent years; at least 5 per cent of food and feed samples exceed the maximum regulatory limits, and a high proportion in lowland rivers is contaminated beyond the 0.1 μg/l limit.

Thus, the Communication proposes adopting a coherent and consistent overall policy framework to address the actual use phase of pesticides. The particular objectives of this Strategy are: (i) minimizing the hazards and risks to health and environment from the use of pesticides; (ii) improving controls on the use and distribution of pesticides; (iii) reducing the levels of harmful active substances through substituting the most dangerous with safer alternatives; (iv) encouraging low-input or pesticide-free cultivation by raising users' awareness, promoting the use of good practices and consideration of the possible application of financial instruments; and (v) establishing a transparent system for reporting and monitoring progress made in the fulfilling of the objectives of the strategy.

The Communication, however, limits the Strategy to plant protection products and suggests postponing any action on biocides until it has finalized the preliminary evaluations of biocidal active substances under the Biocides Directive.

[130] N. 116 above.

[131] Dec. 1600/2002/EC laying down the Sixth Community Environment Action Programme [2002] OJ L242/1.

[132] [2005] OJ L70/1.

In order to achieve the Strategy's goals, the Communication announces the Commission's intent to present five legislative proposals. Firstly, the Commission presented a Proposal for a Directive on a framework for Community action to achieve a Sustainable Use of Pesticides.[133] Secondly, the Commission presented a Proposal for a Regulation amending the Pesticides Directive.[134] Thirdly, the Commission will present water quality objectives for several pesticides under Directive 2000/60/EC on a Framework for Community Action in the Field of Water Policy (Water Framework Directive).[135] Fourthly, the Commission expects to present a Proposal for a Regulation on statistics on the use of plant protection products. Finally, by 2008, the Commission should also present a Proposal for a Directive on essential environmental protection requirements of new pesticide application equipment and accessories.

The Communication, however, also announces the Commission's intention not to present proposals defining quantitative-use reduction targets and setting up a system of taxes to influence qualitative pesticide use. The Communication argues that there is no systematic and direct link between the overall reduction of the quantities of pesticides used and the risks involved, and that there is no adequate information on the baseline consumption that could be used as a reference to establish the targets. On taxes on pesticide use, the Communication argues that, currently, it is virtually impossible to devise an effective and manageable system of taxes that would reflect the adverse effects of individual pesticides.

F. Miscellaneous

i. Derogations

The Commission assessed four requests for derogations under Article 95(4) EC for Austrian,[136] Finnish,[137] Swedish,[138] and Czech[139] restrictions on fertilizers containing cadmium. As Regulation (EC) No. 2003/2003 on Fertilizers[140] does not impose restrictions on the use of cadmium in fertilizers, Member States are

[133] See Section C.*ii.* above.

[134] Ibid.

[135] [2000] OJ L372/1.

[136] Dec. 2006/349/EC on the national provisions notified by the Republic of Austria under Article 95(4) of the EC Treaty concerning the maximum content of cadmium in fertilizers [2006] OJ L129/31.

[137] Dec. 2006/348/EC on the national provisions notified by the Republic of Finland under Article 95(4) of the EC Treaty concerning maximum admissible content of cadmium in fertilizers [2006] OJ L129/25.

[138] Dec. 2006/374/EC on the national provisions notified by the Kingdom of Sweden under Article 95(4) of the EC Treaty concerning the maximum admissible content of cadmium in fertilizers [2006] OJ L129/19.

[139] Dec. 2006/39/EC on the national provisions notified by the Czech Republic under Article 95(4) of the EC Treaty concerning the maximum admissible content of cadmium in fertilizers [2006] OJ L150/15,

[140] [2003] OJ L304/1.

required to allow the marketing of EC fertilizers independently of their cadmium content unless they have obtained a derogation. Austria, Finland, and Sweden were allowed to maintain the restrictions on cadmium containing fertilizers until the Community adopts harmonized measures on cadmium in fertilizers. However, the Czech Republic was only allowed to maintain its measures until December 2006, by which time the Commission Scientific Committee on Health and Environmental Risks (SCHER) was to evaluate the risk assessment submitted by that Member State.

The Commission decisions on the Austrian, Finnish, and Swedish measures are hardly surprising taking into account the following factors: (i) the Accession Treaties of these Member States provided a derogation for measures restricting the use of cadmium in fertilizers; (ii) the three countries had obtained a derogation under Article 95(4) EC to maintain their measures; (iii) the three countries already submitted a risk assessment on the use of cadmium in fertilizers at the time of applying for their first Article 95(4) derogation; (iv) the Commission Scientific Committee on Toxicity, Ecotoxicity and the Environment (now renamed SCHER) had rendered an opinion stating that the content of cadmium in fertilizers needs to be limited; (v) a Community draft risk assessment on cadmium concludes that caution is needed as the risk to human health or the environment from cadmium cannot be excluded; and (vi) the Commission is currently preparing a proposal to restrict the content of cadmium in fertilizers.

It is worth noting, however, the Commission's interpretation of two of the criteria of Article 95(4) in its three decisions. With respect to the 'absence of a disguised restriction on trade', the Commission held that this criterion is intended to prevent national provisions from being applied for inappropriate reasons and, in reality, constituting economic measures intended to impede the import of products from other Member States in order indirectly to protect national restrictions. The Commission also indicated that there is no 'disguised restriction of trade' where it has been shown that the measure is necessary to protect the environment and human health.

The Commission also interpreted the criterion of 'absence of obstacle to the functioning of the internal market' as not prohibiting any measure that derogates from Community harmonization, but requiring, instead, an assessment of the proportionality between the objectives of the measure and the obstacles to Community trade that the measure imposes.

G. Conclusions

2006 and the adoption of the REACH Regulation will mark a milestone in the development of EU chemical legislation and policy. REACH's future interpretation and application, however, will pose at least two main categories of questions to those interested in EU chemical regulatory issues.

Firstly, during the next years, observers will be following closely REACH developments to assess whether the system is workable, and most importantly whether it can become a world standard as hoped when originally proposed.[141] This, among other things, will depend on whether the REACH requirements prove to ensure a sufficient level of environmental and health safety, and whether both industry and regulatory authorities can meet such requirements. Related to this is, of course, the interpretation that regulatory authorities and EU courts will make of the Regulation's clear statement that its provisions are underpinned by the precautionary principle.[142] And certainly the legal services of the Commission and the new European Chemicals Agency are likely to keep themselves busy by, among other things, analysing the relationship and balance of power between these two bodies.

Yet, as explained at the beginning of this survey, REACH can only succeed if its requirements and their application are perceived as fair, and this will require both a strict enforcement throughout Europe to ensure against free riding and sufficient opportunities for all interested parties to participate in the REACH decision-making process.

Secondly, observers are also likely to monitor closely how regulatory authorities and courts interpret the interrelation between the REACH Regulation and other vertical legislation. While it is clear that current regimes on specific categories of substances, such as pesticides and biocides, and rules complementary to those of REACH, such as rules on classification, will continue to apply in parallel to those of the REACH Regulation, the fate of other specific product category legislation (also called 'vertical legislation') is questionable. For example, regulatory authorities could be tempted to override the chemical restrictions of Directive 2002/95/EC on the Restriction of the Use of Certain Hazardous Substances in Electrical and Electronic Equipment (RoHS Directive)[143] by simply using the fast-track restrictions procedure of the REACH Regulation. Restrictions under other product category legislation, such as that for batteries, packaging, or vehicles may suffer the same fate. While this would reflect a more holistic approach to product regulation, it may, however, fail to take into account the particularities of such product categories. In any case, it is clear that the vast information that regulatory authorities should obtain under REACH will be used to assess the environmental and health safety of these specific product categories, and that undoubtedly there will be continuous spill-over effects between REACH and other pieces of EU legislation.

Developments relating to these issues, and many other matters, will surely be reviewed in the chemicals surveys of the years to come.

[141] Communication by Mr Liikanen and Ms Wallström—Chemicals Orientation Paper, 1 Apr. 2003.

[142] REACH Reg., Art. 1(3).

[143] [2003] OJ L37/19, as amended.

V. Nature Conservation

*Agustín García-Ureta**

A. Introduction

The year 2006 brought several interesting developments in the field of nature protection. Firstly, the European Commission (Commission) adopted a Decision on the completion of the biogeographical regions in which the Natura 2000 network is divided, even though this should have been done by 2004 at the latest.[1] Secondly, it delivered a Communication on halting the loss of biodiversity by 2010.[2] Despite the number of initiatives enshrined in the Communication, it is doubtful whether that objective will be attained bearing in mind the progressive loss of species and of habitats confirmed by successive reports delivered by almost all Community institutions. The discussion regarding the adoption of the Financial Instrument for the Environment (LIFE+) also led to contentious debates in the European Parliament (EP). MEPs expressed their opposition to rules granting the Member States the management of the majority of the funds. Arguably, the most important developments took place on the judicial front. The European Court of Justice (ECJ) put into question the approach adopted by Germany in its nature protection legislation following the strict criteria set out in previous cases concerning the requirements for the assessment of activities, i.e. plans and programmes, affecting Natura 2000 areas. Further cases addressed the protection of sites designated by the Member States with a view to their recognition as sites of Community importance, but whose inclusion on the corresponding Commission's list awaited a decision by this institution, and the use of hunting methods.

B. Legislation Adopted

i. Birds Directive and Habitats Directive

As in previous years Directive 79/409/EEC on the Conservation of Wild Birds (Birds Directive)[3] was not subject to amendments. However, the Council adopted Decision 2006/871/EC on the conclusion on behalf of the European Community of the Agreement on the Conservation of African-Eurasian Migratory Waterbirds.[4] This Agreement is based on Article IV of the Bonn Guidelines which provide for the conclusion of regional agreements for species

* Professor of Law, University of the Basque Country, Bilbao (Spain).

[1] N. 6 below.

[2] N. 147 below.

[3] [1979] OJ L103/1.

[4] [2006] OJ L345/24.

with an unfavourable conservation status (Appendix II species). The Agreement was finally adopted at the negotiation meeting that took place from 12 to 16 June 1995 in The Hague, and it came into effect on 1 November 1999. The Annexes to the Agreement were subsequently amended by Resolutions at the first Meeting of the Parties, held in Cape Town, South Africa, in November 1999, and at the second Meeting of the Parties, held in Bonn, Germany, in September 2002. As regards matters falling within Community competence, the Council Decision authorizes the Commission to approve, on behalf of the Community, amendments to the Annexes to the Agreement adopted in accordance with Article X(5) of the Agreement. However, that authorization is limited to those amendments that are consistent with, and do not entail any modification of, Community legislation on the conservation of wild birds and their natural habitats.

Directive 92/43/EEC on the Conservation of Natural Habitats and of Wild Fauna (Habitats Directive)[5] also remained unaltered. For the completion of the Natura 2000 network the Commission approved Decision 2006/613/EC adopting, pursuant to Directive 92/43/EEC, the List of Sites of Community Importance for the Mediterranean biogeographical region.[6] This region comprises the territory of Greece, Malta and Cyprus, and parts of the territory of France, Italy, Portugal, Spain, and the United Kingdom (UK). The lists of sites proposed as sites of Community importance had been transmitted to the Commission between January 2003 and March 2006. However, the Decision does not cover the territories of the Member States that joined the European Community (EC) on May 2004 since the Commission was not in a position to integrate the information from those Member States into the initial list of sites of Community importance. Those data were to be included in a future Commission Decision. As in previous cases, the preamble to Decision 2006/613/EC also acknowledges that some (unnamed) Member States have not proposed sufficient sites to meet the requirements of the Habitats Directive for certain (unnamed) habitat types and species.[7]

ii. CITES

As in previous years no changes were made to Regulation (EC) No. 338/97 on the Protection of Species of Wild Fauna and Flora by Regulating Trade therein (CITES Regulation).[8] The Commission adopted Regulation (EC) No. 605/2006 amending Regulation (EC) No. 349/2003 suspending the introduction into the Community of specimens of certain species of wild fauna and flora.[9] According to the Regulation, the Scientific Review Group had concluded that the conservation status of certain species listed in Annexes A and B to the CITES Regulation would

[5] [1992] OJ L206/7.
[6] [2006] OJ L259/1.
[7] Dec. 2006/613/EC, tenth recital of the preamble.
[8] [1997] OJ L61/1.
[9] [2006] OJ L107/3; [2005] OJ L43/3.

be seriously jeopardized if their introduction into the Community from certain countries of origin was not suspended. The introduction of the following species should therefore be suspended: *Ursus thibetanus* from the Russian Federation; *Cryptoprocta ferox*, *Scaphiophryne gottlebei*, *Euphorbia banae* and *E. kondoi* from Madagascar; *Panthera leo* from Ethiopia; *Balaeniceps rex*, *Grus carunculatus* and *Chamaeleo fuelleborni* from the United Republic of Tanzania; *Poicephalus gulielmi* from Congo; *Accipiter melanoleucus*, *A. ovampensis*, *Aviceda cuculoides*, *Hieraaetus ayresii*, *H. spilogaster*, *Macheiramphus alcinus*, *Spizaetus africanus*, *Urotriorchis macrourus*, *Falco chicquera*, *Asio capensis*, *Bubo lacteus*, *B. poensis*, *Glaucidium perlatum*, *Scotopelia peli* and *Python regius* from Guinea; *Sagittarius serpentarius* and *Varanus exanthematicus* from Togo; *Agapornis pullarius* from the Democratic Republic of the Congo; *Cuora galbinifrons* from China; *Heosemys spinosa*, *Leucocephalon yuwonoi*, *Siebenrockiella crassicollis*, *Liasis fuscus*, *Euphyllia cristata*, *E. divisa*, *E. fimbriata*, *Hydnophora microconos* and *Scolymia vitiensis* from Indonesia; *Geochelone pardalis* from Uganda and Zambia; *Uromastyx geyri* from Mali and Niger; *Cordylus mossambicus*, *C. vittifer*, *Tridacna maxima* and *T. squamosa* from Mozambique; *Dendrobates pumilio* from Nicaragua; *Hippopus hippopus* from Vanuatu; *Hippopus hippopus*, *Tridacna gigas* and *T. maxima* from Tonga and Vietnam; *Tridacna crocea*, *T. derasa*, *T. maxima* and *T. squamosa* from Fiji and Vanuatu; *Tridacna crocea* from Tonga; *Tridacna maxima* from the Federated States of Micronesia and the Marshall Islands; *Tridacna tevoroa* from Tonga and *Catalaphyllia jardinei* from the Solomon Islands.

The Scientific Review Group had also concluded that, on the basis of the most recent available information, the suspension of the introduction into the Community of the following species should no longer be required: *Galago senegalensis* from Djibouti; *Galagoides demidoff* from Kenya and Senegal; *Callithrix argentata* from Paraguay; *Saguinus labiatus* from Colombia; *Callicebus torquatus* from Ecuador; *Cebus albifrons* from Guyana; *Cebus capucinus and Aratinga solstitialis* from Venezuela; *Cebus olivaceus* from Peru; *Allenopithecus nigroviridis* from all range States; *Colobus guereza* from Equatorial Guinea; *Lophocebus albigena* from Kenya; *Papio hamadryas* and *Hippopotamus amphibius* from Liberia; *Cynogale bennettii* from Singapore; *Ara ararauna* from Trinidad and Tobago; *Neophema splendida* from Australia; *Poicephalus gulielmi* from Democratic Republic of the Congo; *Geochelone chilensis*, *Homopus areolatus*, *H. boulengeri*, *H. femoralis*, *H. signatus*, *Kinixys natalensis* and *Psammobates spp.* from all range States; *Geochelone denticulata* from all range States except for Bolivia and Ecuador; *Geochelone elegans* from all range States except for Pakistan; *Kinixys belliana* from all range States except for Mozambique and Benin; *Kinixys erosa* from all range States except for Togo; *Kinixys homeana* from all range States except for Benin; *Manouria emys* from all range States except for Bangladesh, India, Indonesia, Myanmar, and Thailand; *Testudo horsfieldii* from all range States except for China, Pakistan, and Kazakhstan; *Manouria impressa* from all range States except for Vietnam; *Phelsuma cepediana* and *P. trilineata* from

Madagascar; *Phelsuma edwardnewtonii* from Mauritius; *Varanus albigularis* from Lesotho; *Varanus rudicollis* from the Philippines; *Ptyas mucosus* from Indonesia and *Dactylorhiza incarnata* from Norway. Since the CITES Regulation, as last amended by Regulation (EC) No. 1332/2005,[10] provided inter alia for the transfer of *Cacatua sulphurea* and *Pyxis arachnoides* from Annex B to Annex A and the deletion from the Annexes of *Agapornis roseicollis*, import suspensions in respect of those species were no longer required.

The Commission also adopted Regulation (EC) No. 865/2006 laying down Detailed Rules concerning the Implementation of the CITES Regulation.[11] This Regulation sets out: (i) conditions and criteria for the consideration of permit and certificate applications and for the issue, validity, and use of such documents; (ii) provisions relating to the conditions and criteria for the treatment of specimens of animal species born and bred in captivity and of specimens of plant species artificially propagated in order to ensure the common implementation of the derogations applicable to such specimens. It also specifies provisions to: (i) ensure compliance with Article VII (paragraph 3) of the Convention on International Trade in Endangered Species of Wild Fauna and Flora (CITES Convention)[12] regarding the derogations for specimens that are personal and household effects; and (ii) ensure that general derogations from the internal trade prohibitions contained in Article 8(1) of the CITES Regulation are uniformly applied. Regulation 865/2006 sets out procedures for the marking of certain specimens of species in order to facilitate their identification and ensure enforcement of the provisions of the CITES Regulation. Those amendments justified the repeal of Regulation (EC) No. 1808/2001.[13]

iii. Conservation of Migratory Wild Animals

On 21 February 2006, the Council authorized the Commission to enter a reservation on behalf of the EC with respect to the addition of *Cetorhinus maximus* species to Annex I of the Bonn Convention on the Conservation of Migratory Wild Animals (Bonn Convention).[14]

iv. Avian Influenza and Wild Birds

The Commission adopted Decision 2006/86/EC concerning Certain Interim Protection Measures in relation to Suspected Cases of Highly Pathogenic Avian

[10] [2005] OJ L215/1.

[11] [2006] OJ L166/1.

[12] Washington DC (USA), 3 Mar. 1973 (entered into force 1 July 1975), amended at Bonn (Germany) 22 June 1979, and at Gabarone (Botswana) 30 Apr. 1983. Published on the Internet at: http://www.cites.org.

[13] [2001] OJ L250/1.

[14] Bonn (Germany), 23 June 1979 (entered into force 1983), published on the Internet at: http://www.cms.int. Bull. EU 1/2–2006, point 1.20.9.

Influenza in Wild Birds in Greece.[15] The Commission also adopted Decision 2006/115/EC concerning Certain Protection Measures in relation to Highly Pathogenic Avian Influenza in Wild Birds in the Community and repealing Decisions 2006/86/EC, 2006/90/EC, 2006/91/EC, 2006/94/EC, 2006/104/EC, and 2006/105/EC.[16] The specific measures provided for in this Decision should apply without prejudice to the measures to be taken by Member States in the framework of Directive 92/40/EEC introducing Community Measures for the Control of Avian Influenza.[17]

v. Protection of the Alpine Region

On 19 June 2006, the Council adopted Decision 2006/655/EC on the approval, on behalf of the European Community, of the Protocol on the Implementation of the 1991 Alpine Convention in the Field of Mountain Farming.[18] The Alpine Convention[19] was concluded on behalf of the Community by Decision 96/191/EC.[20]

vi. Forests

The Commission enacted Regulation (EC) No. 1737/2006 laying down detailed rules for the implementation of Regulation (EC) No. 2152/2003 of the European Parliament and of the Council concerning Monitoring of Forests and Environmental Interactions in the Community.[21] This Regulation governs the implementation of several rules of Regulation 2152/2003, namely: (i) network of observation points and plots; (ii) European forest fire information system; (iii) studies, experiments, and demonstration projects; (iv) competent bodies; (v) national programmes and adaptations; (vi) financial management and monitoring; (vii) payments; (viii) amounts lost through irregularities or negligence; (ix) checks, audits, and technical visits; (x) scientific advisory group; and (xi) access to data.

C. Legislation in Progress

i. Financial Instrument for the Environment (LIFE+)

In June 2006, the Council adopted its Common Position (EC) No. 10/2006 with a view to adopting a Regulation concerning the Financial Instrument for the

[15] [2006] OJ L40/26.
[16] [2006] OJ L48/28.
[17] [1992] OJ L167/1.
[18] [2006] OJ L271/61.
[19] Salzburg (Austria) 7 Nov. 1991 (entered into force 6 Mar. 1995), published on the Internet at: http://www.alpenkonvention.org.
[20] [1996] OJ L61/31.
[21] [2006] OJ L334/1; [2003] OJ L324/1.

Environment (LIFE+).[22] The general objective of LIFE+ is to contribute to the implementation, updating, and development of Community policy, in particular to support the implementation of the Sixth Environmental Action Programme.[23] It is expected that the future Regulation will apply for a period of seven years beginning on 1 January 2007 and ending on 31 December 2013. According to Article 11 of the Common Position, the financial envelope for the implementation of LIFE+ shall be set at €1,854,372,000 for the said period. LIFE+ shall consist of three components, namely, LIFE+ Nature and Biodiversity, LIFE+ Environment Policy and Governance, and LIFE+ Information and Communication. As regards LIFE+ Nature and Biodiversity, the main objectives stated in the Common Position are as follows: (a) to contribute to the implementation of Community policy and legislation on nature and biodiversity, in particular the Birds and Habitats Directives, and to support the further development and implementation of the Natura 2000 network, including coastal and marine habitats and species; (b) to contribute to the consolidation of the knowledge base for development, assessment, monitoring, and evaluation of Community nature and biodiversity policy and legislation; (c) to support the design and implementation of policy approaches and instruments for the monitoring and assessment of nature and biodiversity and the factors, pressures and responses that impact on them, in particular in relation to the achievement of the target of halting biodiversity loss within the Community by 2010; and (d) to provide support for better environmental governance by broadening stakeholder involvement, including that of NGOs, in consultation on, and in the implementation of, nature and biodiversity policy and legislation. As regards the programmes implementing the Regulation, Article 6 provides that the Commission shall draw up a first multi-annual strategic programme for 2007 to 2010 and a second multi-annual strategic programme for 2011 to 2013. Those programmes are to include allocations between Member States and indicate those parts of the budget subject to central direct management and those subject to delegated management. This second type of management is enshrined in Article 7(2), according to which the Commission 'may entrust' part of the implementation of the budget to national agencies designated in agreement with the Member States. Article 6(1) (second paragraph) sets out a controversial provision indicating that 'at least' 80 per cent of the budget shall be subject to delegated management.

In its Communication to the EP concerning the Common Position of the Council on the adoption of a Regulation concerning LIFE+,[24] the Commission indicated that the changes that had been introduced by the Council had helped

[22] [2006] OJ C238E/1. See also the 2740th environment Council meeting, Luxembourg, 27 June 2006, available on the Internet at: http://www.consilium.europa.eu/ueDocs/cms_Data/docs/pressdata/en/envir/90281.pdf.

[23] Dec. 1600/2002/EC laying down the Sixth Community Environment Action Programme [2002] OJ L242/1.

[24] COM(2006)355, 28 June 2006.

to clarify the Commission's proposal especially as regards defining more clearly European added value, and clarifying the role of the Member States, national agencies, and the Commission in the programme planning and delivery mechanisms. However, on 24 October 2006, the MEPs adopted a report on LIFE+ rejecting by an overwhelming majority (65 in favour, 525 against, and 25 abstentions) the Council's Common Position intending to allocate at least 80 per cent of the LIFE+ budget for 2007 to 2013 to delegated management to the Member States.[25] The MEPs also adopted an amendment urging the Commission, in the absence of an agreement between the co-legislators on LIFE+ at second reading, to present a solution permitting the financing of activities falling under the institutional prerogatives that from 2007 onwards were due to fall under the LIFE+ programme.

ii. Alien Species in Aquaculture

In April 2006, the Commission submitted a Proposal for a Regulation concerning Use of Alien and Locally Absent Species in Aquaculture.[26] According to the explanatory memorandum, in the past aquaculture has benefited economically from the introduction of alien species (e.g. rainbow trout, Pacific oyster) and from the farming of species which do not occur in an area owing to biogeographical barriers. It is therefore likely that the aquaculture industry will continue to use new species in order to satisfy the needs of the market. According to the Proposal, it would thus be prudent to decouple this economic growth from the potential threats to ecosystems posed by alien species by anticipating and preventing negative biological interaction with indigenous populations, including genetic change, and by restricting the spread of non-target species and other detrimental impacts. Although there are provisions in the Habitats Directive concerning the deliberate introduction into the wild of any species which is not native to the territory, the Proposal indicates that it is unclear whether both accidental, non-deliberate introductions, and introductions into non-wild environments are covered by this legislation. Even though it is acknowledged that there is a possibility of some duplication or overlap between the administrative measures already taken in compliance with the Habitats Directive and the new Proposal, in the Commission's opinion this is not necessarily a problem, as it is hoped that the experience gained with the former process will enhance the setting up and functioning of the new permit system required by the Proposal. Although other Community legislation, such as the Directive establishing a Framework for Community Action in the Field of Water Policy (Water Framework Directive),[27] do cover the harmful effects of alien species, the Proposal affirms that they are not specific to aquaculture and leave room for risks of spreading of alien species

[25] P6_TA-PROV(2006)0431.

[26] COM(2006)154, 4 Apr. 2006.

[27] [2000] OJ L327/1.

and consequent environmental damage. Hence, the Proposal concludes that the existing provisions are 'not entirely adequate' to govern the use of alien species in aquaculture at the present time.

iii. Sharks

The Commission submitted on 28 September 2006 a Proposal for a Regulation fixing for 2007 and 2008 the Fishing Opportunities for Community Fishing Vessels for Certain Deep-sea Fish Stocks.[28] Deep-sea stocks are fish stocks caught in waters beyond the main fishing grounds of continental shelves. They are distributed on the continental slopes or associated with seamounts. These species, including sharks, are slow-growing and particularly vulnerable to overexploitation. The Proposal takes into account a report of the International Council for the Exploration of the Sea (ICES)[29] delivered in June 2006 that indicated that most exploited deepwater species were harvested unsustainably. The report recommended immediate reductions in established deep-sea fisheries unless they could be shown to be sustainable. However, as the Proposal indicates, no deep-sea fisheries currently meet this criterion. Even though ICES advised that the most appropriate conservation measures for those species would be based on effort limitation and reduction, the Proposal indicates that restricting catches by means of quota management of fisheries is considered 'a useful additional step' in applying conservation measures. The scope of the Proposal is therefore limited to the setting of Total Allowance Catches (TACs).

D. Case Law

i. Birds Directive

Case C-209/04 concerned the application of the Birds and Habitats Directive in Austria.[30] The Commission alleged that Austria had failed to include in the area of a nature reserve (Lauteracher Ried), classified as a special protection area (SPA), two sites (Soren and Gleggen-Köblern) which according to scientific criteria were, together with that SPA, among the most suitable territories in number and size for the purposes of Article 4(1) and (2) of the Birds Directive. The Commission also alleged that Austria had failed, when authorizing a federal dual carriageway, to comply properly with the requirements laid down in Article 6(4) of the Habitats Directive. It should also be noted that both Directives were fully applicable in Austria from the date of its accession to the EU (1 January 1995).

The first complaint related to the failure to comply with Article 4(1) and (2) of the Birds Directive. The Commission argued that the classification and definition of the boundaries of the SPA did not comply with the requirements of

28 COM(2006)554, 28 Sept. 2006.

29 Information is published on the Internet at: http://www.ices.dk.

30 Case C-209/04 *Commission* v. *Austria* [2006] ECR I-2755.

protection and sustainable conservation of the bird species present in that area, particularly the corncrake (*Crex crex*) and other migratory grassland-nesting species. Accordingly, the surface area of that SPA had to be expanded to the other two sites (Soren and Gleggen-Köblern). In the light of scientific information and the results of monitoring carried out between 2000 and 2002, those two sites were not only habitats but also formed part of the principal breeding ground for the corncrake and other migratory grassland-nesting species. Significantly, the Commission furthermore claimed that the obligation to designate as SPAs all areas which seemed most suitable on the basis of ornithological criteria did not come to an end with the first declaration made. In its opinion, the objective of conservation of endangered species requires re-examination of a declaration in the light of more recent scientific knowledge and a possible re-definition of the boundaries of an existing SPA. Finally, the Commission argued that the fact that Austria had classified as SPAs two sites (Bangs and Matschels), which were also situated in the same province as the Lauteracher Ried SPA, as part of a conservation effort for the corncrake, in no way affected that Member State's obligation to do likewise for the Soren and Gleggen-Köblern sites, which were adjacent to the declared SPA.

In the light of the foregoing considerations, the ECJ first recalled the wording of Article 4(1) of the Birds Directive and its settled case law, according to which Member States must provide SPAs with a legal status protecting them and capable, in particular, of ensuring both the survival and reproduction of the bird species listed in Annex I and the breeding, moulting, and wintering of regularly occurring migratory species not listed in Annex I.[31] The ECJ also recalled its judgment in Case C-3/96,[32] whereby the Member States' margin of discretion in choosing the most suitable territories for classification as SPAs concerned *not the appropriateness* of classifying as SPAs the territories which appeared the most suitable according to ornithological criteria, but *only the application* of those criteria for identifying the most suitable territories for conservation of the species listed in Annex I.[33] The ECJ noted that according to the results of scientific studies and a monitoring exercise which were submitted by the Commission during the infringement procedure, not contested by the Austrian government, in the years 2000 to 2002, respectively four or five, four, and three singing male corncrakes were observed within the 580 hectare SPA. The sightings concerning the Soren and Gleggen-Köblern sites, covering 64 and 352 hectares, were only 'slightly lower'; the birds observed numbering four, two, and three respectively. In addition, the Commission had affirmed, without being contradicted on that point either, that in 2001 there were likewise large numbers of migratory common snipe (*Gallinago gallinago*), Northern lapwings (*Vanellus vanellus*), and Eurasian

31 Ibid., para. 32.

32 Case C-3/96 *Commission* v. *The Netherlands* [1998] ECR I-3031.

33 Ibid., para. 61.

curlews (*Numenius arquata*) breeding in the two sites not designated as SPAs by the Austrian authorities. Within the already designated SPA there were three to five pairs of common snipe nesting, 11 or 12 pairs of Northern lapwings, and three pairs of Eurasian curlews. In the Soren and Gleggen-Köblern sites, there were three and three or four pairs of common snipe, six and nine pairs of Northern lapwings, and one (probably) and eight pairs of Eurasian curlews.[34] In the light of the aforementioned data the conclusion was apparent, i.e. the Soren and Gleggen-Köblern sites were of 'at least comparable importance' to the Lauteracher Ried SPA for both the corncrake and migratory bird species not listed in Annex I, such as the common snipe, Northern lapwing, and Eurasian curlew. Moreover, the figures provided by the Austrian government in the Commission's standard data form[35] relating to those last three species were reached only if account was taken also of the land situated outside that SPA.[36]

The Austrian government, in turn, argued that, firstly, the Soren and Gleggen-Köblern sites were not the most suitable ones for protecting the abovementioned bird species due to existing pollution and constraints, as well as the condition and quality of those sites. That argument was not upheld by the ECJ since those two sites hosted, in a smaller area than the Lauteracher Ried SPA, a similar number of nesting birds to that observed in the SPA.[37] The second allegation brought forward by the Austrian government was that it was appropriate to take account, if only indirectly, of economic and social criteria in the necessary assessment of the characteristics of the area to be classified as a SPA. However, this second allegation had been systematically rejected by the ECJ in its case law.[38] This position, also sustained in the case of the Habitats Directive,[39] is fully consistent with the purpose and structure of both Community rules. The ECJ also rejected the Austrian government's argument that the results of the on-site monitoring did not lead to the conclusion that the Soren and Gleggen-Köblern sites were suitable for the conservation of the bird species to be protected. According to the ECJ, that argument was not such as to provide scientific justification for excluding those sites from the SPA. On the contrary, the classification of those sites as SPAs should safeguard the conservation status of the corncrake, a species listed in Annex I, and other regularly occurring migratory bird species, in accordance with the objectives of the Birds Directive.[40]

Arguably, the most important matter dealt with by the ECJ in this case was whether there was an open-ended obligation to amend and adapt existing SPAs

[34] Case C-209/04, n. 30 above, para. 35.

[35] See Dec. 97/266/EC concerning a Site Information Format for Proposed Natura 2000 Sites [1997] OJ L107/1.

[36] Case C-209/04, n. 30 above, para. 36.

[37] Ibid., para. 37.

[38] Case C-44/95 *Royal Society for the Protection of Birds* [1996] ECR I-3805, paras. 31–2.

[39] Case C-371/98 *The Queen* v. *Secretary of State for the Environment, Transport and the Regions, ex parte First Corporate Shipping Ltd.* [2000] ECR I-9235, paras. 23–4.

[40] Case C-209/04 *Commission* v. *Austria* [2006] ECR I-2755, para. 41.

according to the requirements of the Birds Directive. The ECJ held that although it was common ground that the obligation to classify the most suitable territories for establishing an SPA entered fully into force with respect to Austria on 1 January 1995, it did not end on that date. Neither the Birds Directive nor the wording of its Article 4 contained 'the slightest indication' that the effects of the obligation to transpose the Directive were exhausted on that date. Moreover, it was incompatible with the objective of effective protection of birds if outstanding areas for the conservation of the species to be protected were not brought under protection merely because the outstanding nature of a site came to light only after transposition of the Birds Directive.[41]

The ECJ held that the scientific information on which the Austrian government had relied to support its decisions was not sufficient. In fact, the defendant government had followed what it called the 'only reliable inventory' and scientific assessment existing at the time, a study carried out in 1995 by the Federal Environment Agency in collaboration with BirdLife. However, the ECJ held that the obligation to classify SPAs was not limited by the state of scientific knowledge 'at any given time'.[42] By contrast, other scientific ornithological studies and expert reports, as well as the results of monitoring more recent than that on which the classification of the Lauteracher Ried SPA had been based, were available. As the ECJ put it, it was on the basis of that more recent evidence, the accuracy of which was not disputed by the defendant government, that the classification of the SPA had to be reconsidered. Further arguments brought forward by the Austrian government were also rejected by the ECJ. The first one was that having classified two other sites as SPAs, where the corncrake was also present, there was no need to classify the Soren and Gleggen-Köblern sites as SPAs. The second claim was that the Soren and Gleggen-Köblern sites were not left entirely unprotected. By reference to Case C-3/96,[43] the ECJ highlighted the lack of consistency of this claim by indicating that Member States were obliged to classify as SPAs 'all the sites' which, applying ornithological criteria, appeared the most suitable for conservation of the species in question.

The Commission's second complaint concerned the alleged failure to comply with the requirements of Article 6(4) of the Habitats Directive. The ECJ first considered the temporal applicability of the Habitats Directive. The procedure for the authorization of the carriageway had begun in 1992. The procedure was suspended and then resumed on 8 March 1994, the date on which it was formally presented and made subject to an assessment procedure pursuant to a Law on federal roads of 1971. The ECJ then recalled its settled case law, according to which projects likely to have significant effects on the environment were not subject to an environmental assessment if the application for authorization for a project had been formally lodged before the expiry of the time limit for

41 Ibid., para. 43.
42 Ibid., para. 44.
43 Case C-3/96, n. 32 above.

transposition of a Directive,[44] in particular, Directive 85/337/EEC on the Assessment of the Effects of Certain Public and Private Projects on the Environment (EIA Directive).[45] Relying on the principle of legal certainty, the ECJ explained that a directive such as the Habitats Directive was primarily designed to cover large-scale projects which would most often require a long time to complete. It would therefore not be appropriate for the relevant procedures, which were already complex at the national level and which were formally initiated prior to the date of the expiry of the period for transposing the Directive, to be made more cumbersome and time-consuming by the specific requirements imposed by the Directive and for situations already established to be affected by it.[46] Drawing a parallel between the EIA Directive and the Habitats Directive, the ECJ held that in both cases the assessment procedure had to take place before the project was finally decided upon. The results of that assessment had to be considered when the decision on the project was made, and the decision could be amended depending on the results. The various phases of examination of a project were so closely connected that they represented 'a complex operation'.[47] The fact that the content of some requirements differed, did not affect that assessment. The ECJ then concluded that the Commission's complaint had to be considered as at the date on which the project was formally presented, namely 8 March 1994. However, it followed from the Act of Accession that the obligations under the Birds Directive and the Habitats Directive had entered into force with respect to Austria on 1 January 1995 and that no derogation or transitional period was granted to it. Accordingly, the procedure for authorization of the project for the construction of the carriageway was formally initiated prior to the date of Austria's accession. Therefore, the obligations under the Habitats Directive were not binding on Austria.[48]

Case C-60/05, *WWF Italia and Others* v. *Regione Lombardia*[49] addressed the application of the exceptions set out in Article 9 of the Birds Directive. According to Article 9(1)(c), Member States may derogate from the prohibitions of Articles 5, 6, 7, and 8 where there is no other satisfactory solution, for a number of justifications, inter alia, to permit, under strictly supervised conditions and on a selective basis, the capture, keeping, or other judicious use of certain birds in small numbers. An Italian court submitted several questions before the ECJ in proceedings between WWF Italia and three other associations in the Regione Lombardia (Region of Lombardy) concerning the hunting of the finch (*Fringilla coelebs*) and brambling (*Fringilla montifringilla*) species for the 2003/2004 hunting season.

[44] Case C-209/04, n. 30 above, para. 56.

[45] [1985] OJ L175/40. See Case C-431/92 *Commission* v. *Germany* [1995] ECR I-2189; Case C-81/96 *Gedeputeerde Staten van Noord-Holland* [1998] ECR I-3923.

[46] Case C-209/04, n. 30 above, para. 57.

[47] Ibid., para. 58.

[48] Ibid., paras. 60–1.

[49] [2006] ECR I-5083.

The first question concerned whether the national provisions transposing the Birds Directive governed all the situations subject to the system of protection laid down by that Directive, in particular the condition in Article 9(1)(c) that any hunting derogations had to be restricted to 'small numbers' of birds. The ECJ recalled three basic matters already held in previous cases: (i) that the criteria on the basis of which the Member States were entitled to derogate from the prohibitions laid down by the Directive had to be set out in national provisions sufficiently clearly and precisely, given that a faithful transposition was particularly important in a case in which the management of the common heritage was entrusted to the Member States in respect of their respective territories;[50] (ii) that in exercising their powers concerning the grant of derogations, the authorities of the Member States had to take account of various criteria relating to geographic, climatic, environmental, and biological factors and, in particular, to the situation regarding the species' reproduction and total annual mortality rate owing to natural causes; and (iii) that according to a document entitled 'Second report of the Commission on the application of Directive 79/409/EEC on the conservation of wild birds' of 24 November 1993,[51] 'small numbers' were any sample of less than 1 per cent of the total annual mortality rate of the population in question (average value) for those species which were not to be hunted, and a sample in the order of 1 per cent for those species which could be hunted, those quantities being based on the work of the ORNIS Committee for the Adaptation to Technical and Scientific Progress under the Directive, instituted under Article 16 of the latter, and consisting of representatives of the Member States.[52] According to the ECJ, it was also clear from consistent case law that although the percentages referred to above were not legally binding, they could nonetheless constitute, by reason of the scientific value of the work of the ORNIS Committee and the absence before the ECJ of any element of scientific proof to the contrary, 'a basis of reference' for assessing whether a derogation granted under Article 9(1)(c) of the Directive complied with that provision.[53] The ECJ concluded that irrespective of the internal allocation of powers prescribed by the national legal system, the Member States were required to provide for a legislative and regulatory framework ensuring that the hunting of birds was carried out only in compliance with the condition relating to 'small numbers' laid down in Article 9(1)(c) of the Directive, and on the basis of strict scientific data, irrespective of the species concerned.[54]

The second question concerned the level of precision which had to characterize national implementing provisions in respect of the technical criteria on

[50] Case 247/85 *Commission* v. *Belgium* [1987] ECR 3029, para. 9; Case 252/85 *Commission* v. *France* [1988] ECR 2243, para. 5.

[51] COM(93)572, 24 Nov. 1993.

[52] Case C-79/03 *Commission* v. *Spain* [2004] ECR I-11619, para. 36; Case C-344/03 *Commission* v. *Finland* [2005] ECR I-0000, para. 53.

[53] Case C-60/05 *WWF Italia and Others* v. *Regione Lombardia* [2006] ECR I-5083, para. 27.

[54] Ibid., para. 28.

the basis of which a quota corresponding to 'small numbers' of birds could be fixed under Article 9(1)(c) of the Directive. The ECJ first noted that the 11th recital in the preamble to the Directive stated that the condition relating to 'small numbers', to which authorized hunting derogations had to be restricted, could not be determined by reference to an absolute criterion but had to be related to the population level of the species concerned and its annual reproduction and mortality rates. By reference to previous case law, the ECJ held that derogations under Article 9 of the Directive were to be granted only if it was ensured that the population of the species concerned was maintained at a satisfactory level. If that condition was not fulfilled, hunting of birds could not, in any event, be considered judicious and, accordingly, acceptable for the purposes of the 11th recital in the preamble to the Directive.[55] In order to permit the competent authorities to resort to the derogations laid down in Article 9 of the Directive in a manner complying with Community law, the national legislative and regulatory framework had to be designed in such a way that the application of the derogating provisions set out there was consonant with the principle of legal certainty. The relevant national legislation applicable had to specify the criteria for the derogation in a clear and precise manner and require the authorities responsible for applying them to take account of those criteria. In respect of exceptional arrangements, the Member States were required to ensure that all action affecting the protected species was authorized only on the basis of decisions containing a clear and sufficient statement of reasons referring to the reasons, conditions, and requirements laid down in Article 9(1) and (2) of the Directive.[56] The ECJ added that any decision derogating from the system of protection required by the Directive had to take account of the situation of the species at issue.

The third question asked how the competent authorities of the Member States were to ensure that, upon application of Article 9(1), the maximum number of birds of a given species subject to hunting was not to be exceeded in the entire national territory. The ECJ held three basic obligations already enshrined in previous case law: (i) the criteria to be met by the Member States in order to derogate from the prohibitions laid down in the Directive had to be reproduced in specific national provisions;[57] (ii) a situation in which national provisions implementing the Directive did not ensure that the authorities within a State which were responsible for applying them were required to take account of those criteria would be contrary to the principle of legal certainty;[58] and (iii) where the application of Article 9(1)(c) of the Directive was delegated to entities within a State, the applicable legislative and regulatory framework had to ensure that the amount of hunting of birds which could be authorized by those entities remained, 'for

[55] Case C-182/02 *Ligue pour la protection des oiseaux and Others* [2003] ECR I-12105, para. 17; Case C-60/05, n. 49 above, para. 32.

[56] Ibid., para. 34.

[57] Case C-339/87 *Commission* v. *Netherlands* [1990] ECR I-851, para. 28.

[58] Case C-157/89 *Commission* v. *Italy* [1991] ECR I-57, paras. 16–17.

the entire national territory', within the limit of 'small numbers' imposed by that provision.[59]

The fourth and last question addressed the possible requirement of maximum time periods within which administrative decisions related to the control of hunting derogations and compliance with their conditions should be taken. The ECJ first held that national implementing legislation had to guarantee that the hunting of birds was carried out on a strictly controlled and selective basis. Therefore, effective controls were to be carried out during the periods referred to by the decisions derogating from the system of protection laid down by the Directive, and the relevant national procedural framework applicable had to guarantee not only that the lawfulness of decisions granting authorizations derogating from the system of protection laid down by the Directive could be verified in a timely manner but also that the conditions attached to those decisions were complied with. However, a control mechanism under which annulment of a decision authorizing a hunting derogation adopted in breach of Article 9 of the Directive would take effect only on expiry of the period laid down for carrying out that hunting would render ineffective the system of protection established by the Directive.[60] The power to intervene in a timely and effective manner in situations in which decisions of the competent authorities could lead or threaten to lead to a result inconsistent with the protection requirements of the Directive could be deduced from the guarantee concerning compliance with the maximum numbers of birds which could be hunted under the system of derogation established by Article 9(1)(c) of the Directive.[61]

Case C-191/05 concerned the alteration of the territorial demarcation of an SPA in Portugal, excluding certain areas which provided a habitat for species of wild birds.[62] The Portuguese authorities had previously declared the SPA by a Decree-Law of 1999 since it fulfilled the requirements of Article 4 of the Directive. However, by another Decree-Law of 2002 the national authorities subsequently decided to reduce the extension of the SPA by almost 3,000 hectares. The Commission challenged such reduction claiming that the Portuguese authorities excluded from protection several species of wild birds listed on the Natura 2000 standard data form, which was used as a basis for creating that SPA, although those species were to be protected under the Birds Directive. The ECJ first recalled consistent case law according to which Article 4 of the Directive had laid down a protection regime which was specifically targeted and reinforced both for the species listed in Annex I and for migratory species, an approach justified by the fact that they were, respectively, the most endangered species and the

[59] Case C-60/05, n. 49 above, para. 40.
[60] Ibid., para. 45.
[61] Ibid., para. 46.
[62] Case C-191/05 *Commission* v. *Portugal* [2006] ECR I-6853.

species constituting a common heritage of the Community.[63] The ECJ also held that only scientific criteria could be taken into account when designating and, in particular, defining the boundaries of SPAs.[64] The ECJ observed that the Portuguese Decree-Law of 2002 had altered the boundaries of the SPA on the ground that the area included zones which were not important habitats for steppe-land birds. While it was true that the areas excluded from the SPA concerned by that Decree-Law did not provide a habitat for steppe-land birds, the ECJ continued, 'they did provide a habitat for other species of wild birds listed in Annex I to the Directive for whose protection that SPA had been designated'.[65] In those circumstances a Member State was not entitled to reduce the surface area of an SPA or alter its boundaries unless the areas excluded from the SPA were no longer the most suitable territories for the conservation of species of wild birds within the meaning of Article 4(1) of the Directive.[66] Since the Portuguese authorities had not been able to prove this, the ECJ held that the Commission's action was well founded.[67]

In Case C-503/06 R,[68] the Commission brought an action for the suspension of an Italian law adopted for the application of the derogations set out in Article 9 of the Birds Directive and allowing the hunting of a species (*sturnus vulgaris*) included in Annex II, part 2 to the Directive. According to the Commission, the law put in force the provisions of a previous law that contradicted the provisions of the Directive; the finding of alternative solutions, as required by Article 9, had not been verified; and the derogation allowed by the Italian law was not exceptional; on the contrary, it authorized the maintenance of regular hunting practices of species protected by the Directive. The President of the ECJ accepted the allegations submitted by the Commission and ordered the suspension of the law.

ii. Habitats Directive

Case 98/03, *Commission* v. *Germany*, put into question several provisions of German nature protection legislation implementing the Habitats Directive.[69] In April 2000, the Commission sent to the German authorities a letter of formal notice requesting observations on the implementation of Article 6(3) and (4), and Articles 12, 13, and 16 of the Habitats Directive. A reasoned opinion was delivered in July 2001, requesting Germany to adopt measures to comply with the opinion within two months of the date of its notification.[70] However, the Commission did not bring forward its action before the ECJ until February 2003. Meanwhile, the Federal Nature Protection Law of 2002 entered into force. The German

[63] Ibid., para. 9. see *R.* v. *Secretary of State for the Environment, ex parte Royal Society for the Protection of Birds* [1996] ECR I-3805, paras. 23 and 26.
[64] Case C-191/05, n. 62 above, para. 10.
[65] Ibid., para. 12.
[66] Ibid., para. 13.
[67] Ibid., para. 14–15.
[68] Case C-503/06 R *Commission* v. *Italy* [2006] ECR I-141.
[69] [2006] ECR I-53.
[70] 25 July 2001.

government put into question the admissibility of the Commission's action since, in its opinion, it had failed to take into account the new provisions introduced by the abovementioned Law of 2002 and other specific rules. However, the ECJ dismissed that claim. The ECJ first held that the issue of whether the Commission had taken account of certain legislative changes in the assessment of the compatibility of German law with the Directive related 'to the substance of the proceedings and, therefore, to the merits of the case and not to its admissibility'.[71] The fact that in its original application the Commission had based its pleas on certain provisions of the Federal Nature Protection Law of 2002, mentioning the earlier provisions of the Law of 1998 between brackets, while the reasoned opinion had only referred to those earlier provisions, was not capable of rendering the action inadmissible. Recalling consistent case law, the ECJ acknowledged that the subject matter of an action brought under Article 226 EC was delimited by the pre-litigation procedure and that, accordingly, the original application could not be based on provisions other than those stated in that procedure. Nevertheless, that requirement could not go so far as to make it necessary for the national provisions mentioned in the reasoned opinion and those in the application 'to be completely identical'.[72] Where a change in the legislation had taken place between those two procedural stages, it was sufficient that the system established by the legislation contested in the pre-litigation procedure had, 'on the whole', been maintained by the new measures which had been adopted by the Member State after the issue of the reasoned opinion and had been challenged in the application. In the case before the ECJ the provisions of the Federal Nature Protection Law of 2002, to which the Commission had referred in its original application, were 'almost identical' to the provisions in the Federal Law of 1998 that it had criticized in its reasoned opinion.[73]

The Commission's first complaint concerned the scope of German legislation in the light of Article 6(3) and (4) of the Habitats Directive. The Commission alleged that Germany had failed to transpose that provision into its national law since the definition of 'project' in the Federal Law on Nature protection was too restrictive and excluded the duty to carry out an assessment of the implications of certain acts and other activities which were potentially harmful to protected sites.[74] As regards projects within the meaning of Paragraph 10(1)(11)(b) of the

[71] Case C-98/03, n. 69 above, para. 25.
[72] Ibid., para. 27.
[73] Ibid., para. 27.
[74] Para. 10(1)(11) of the Federal Nature Protection Law of 2002 defined the concept of projects within the meaning of the law as follows: 'a) projects and measures planned within a site of Community importance or a European site for the protection of birds, in so far as they are subject to a decision by an authority or to notification to an authority or that they are carried out by an authority, and b) acts affecting nature and the countryside, within the meaning of Paragraph 18, in so far as they are subject to a decision by an authority or to notification to an authority or are carried out by an authority, and c) installations subject to an authorization under the Federal law on protection against pollution and the use of water, which are subject to an authorization or to approval under the Law on

Federal Law of 2002, the Commission submitted that since they only included acts affecting nature and the countryside, within the meaning of Paragraph 18 of the German Law, certain projects likely to have a significant effect on protected sites were not subject to a prior assessment of the implications for the site in accordance with Article 6(3) and (4) of the Habitats Directive. In its opinion, Paragraph 18(1) of the Federal Law covered only changes of form or use of surface areas, but failed to take account of any other activities or measures which did not concern the surface area of a protected site or those which did not result in any change, even where they were likely to have a significant effect on such a site. The Commission pointed out that the term 'project', within the meaning of Paragraph 10(1)(11)(b) of the Federal Law, which referred to acts carried out *outside* the special areas of conservation (SACs), was narrower than that in Paragraph 10(1)(11)(a), which concerned projects carried out *within* a SAC. However, the Directive had not drawn up a distinction between measures taken outside or inside a protected site. The Commission also highlighted several other breaches of the Directive in the German Federal Law. In particular, it claimed that Paragraph 18(2) excluded from the term 'project', within the meaning of Paragraph 10(1)(11)(b), the use of soil for the purposes of agriculture, forestry, and fishing, where that project had taken account of the objectives and principles of nature protection and countryside conservation. As regards Paragraph 10(1)(11)(c), the Commission also criticized the fact that the definition of 'project' was limited, on the one hand, to installations subject to authorization under the Federal Law on Protection against Pollution and, on the other hand, to the use of water which was subject to authorization or approval under the Law on Water Use. In the light of the foregoing considerations, the Commission concluded that the installations and uses of water not subject to authorization or approval were excluded from the duty to carry out an assessment of the implications for the site laid down in Article 6(3) of the Habitats Directive, regardless of whether they could have a significant impact on the protected sites.

The German government argued that the Commission had interpreted the term 'project' too widely, since it did not permit any limit on the duty to carry out an assessment of the implications that the activities referred to by German law could have on the sites. In its opinion, the definition of that term was to be

water use, in so far as, separately or in conjunction with other projects or plans, they are likely to have a significant effect on a site of importance to the Community or a European site for the protection of birds (…).' In addition, Para. 18 of the same Law indicated that: '1. Acts affecting nature and the countryside, within the meaning of this Law, are changes of form or use of surface areas or changes to the level of the water table connected to the surface soil stratum which may alter to a considerable extent the capacity and functioning of the ecosystem or the countryside. 2. The use of soil for the purpose of agriculture, forestry and fishing shall not constitute an intervention where it takes account of the objectives and the principles of nature protection and countryside conservation. The use of soil for the purposes of agriculture, forestry and fishing does not, in principle, undermine the objectives and principles set out above, provided that it complies with the conditions in Paragraph 5(4) to (6) and the rules of professional practice under the Law on agriculture forestry and fishing and Paragraph 17(2) of the Federal Law on soil protection.'

done in the light of that set out in the EIA Directive, which defines a 'project' as: '(i) the execution of construction works or of other installations or schemes; and (ii) other interventions in the natural surroundings and landscape including those involving the extraction of mineral resources.'[75] The German government also indicated that the term 'act', within the meaning of Paragraph 18(1) of the Federal Law of 2002, required a case-by-case assessment in the light of the objectives of the Directive. Therefore, in practice, that provision did not represent a limitation of the term 'project'. In its opinion, Paragraph 18(1) of the Federal Law did not require a change of form or use of the surface area, but that there be an act where an activity had an effect on the surface area with impacts on the protected site. As regards the derogation laid down in Paragraph 18(2) of the Federal Law, the German government submitted that it was mandatory to take into account the objectives and principles of nature protection and countryside conservation, so that the use of soil for the purposes of agriculture, forestry, and fishing did not constitute a project which had to be subject to an assessment of its implications. Regarding Paragraph 10(1)(11)(c) of the Federal Law, the German government also argued that the installations which were not subject to authorization or approval under the Federal Law on protection against pollution had to comply with requirements taking account of the Directive. That Law required, inter alia, verification that serious environmental damage, which was preventable by the state of current technology, was in fact prevented, and that the damage that could not be avoided by current technology was reduced to the minimum. As regards the use of water which did not require an authorization under the Law on water use, the German government contended, in particular, that such use concerned 'very small quantities of water', a criterion compatible with the Water Framework Directive. In the light of the foregoing, it concluded that if uses which did not have any significant impact on the status of a body of water were not taken into consideration under the Water Framework Directive, they could not have any significant impact on neighbouring SACs.

The ECJ first recalled its previous case law and indicated that the requirement for an appropriate assessment of the implications of a plan or project was conditional on its likely significant effect on the site. Referring to the precautionary principle, it held that such a risk existed if it could not be excluded, on the basis of objective information, that the plan or project was likely to have a significant effect on the site concerned.[76] It also indicated that the condition to which the assessment of the implications of a plan or a project on a particular site was subject, which required such an assessment to be carried out where there were doubts as to the existence of significant effects, did not permit that assessment to be avoided, as did Paragraph 10(1)(11)(b) of the Federal Law, read in conjunction with Paragraphs 18 and 10(1)(11)(c) of the same Law.[77] In particular, Paragraph 10(1)(11)(b) and (c) of the Federal Law excluded from the assessment obligation:

[75] EIA Dir., Art. 1. [76] Case C-98/03, n. 69 above, para. 40. [77] Ibid., para. 41.

(i) projects consisting of acts affecting nature and the countryside other than changes of form or use of surface areas, or changes to the level of the water table connected to the surface soil stratum; and (ii) projects relating to installations or to use of water, on account of the fact that they were not subject to authorization. In the ECJ's opinion, it did not appear that those criteria excluding the duty to carry out an assessment were capable of ensuring that those projects were never likely to have a significant effect on the protected sites.[78]

The other two pieces of German legislation, i.e. the Law on Protection Against Pollution and the Law on Water Use, were also the subject of further criticism on the part of the ECJ. As regards installations not subject to authorization under the former law, the ECJ observed that the fact that it required verification that serious environmental damage which could be prevented by current technology was in fact prevented, and that damage which could not be prevented by current technology was reduced to the minimum, did not suffice to ensure compliance with the duty laid down in Article 6(3) of the Habitats Directive. The duty of verification laid down by the Law on Protection Against Pollution was not, 'in any event', capable of ensuring that a project relating to such an installation did not adversely affect the integrity of the protected site.[79] Similarly, the use of water not requiring an authorization under the Law on Water Use, even if it concerned the exploitation of small quantities, did not preclude the possibility that some of those uses were likely to have a significant effect on a protected site. Moreover, even assuming that such uses of water were not likely to have a significant effect on the status of a body of water, it did not follow that they were not likely to have a significant effect on neighbouring protected sites.[80]

However, it should be noted that, unlike the Commission, the ECJ did not expressly refer to the wording of Paragraph 10(1)(11)(a) of the Federal Nature Protection Law, which only took into account projects and measures planned *within* SACs or SPAs, thus openly contradicting Article 6(3). This matter was mainly tackled by the ECJ when considering the second complaint (below) regarding activities causing emissions.

The second complaint concerned the refusal to grant an authorization for installations causing emissions only where it was foreseeable that they directly affected a SAC situated in an area where those installations were operating. Accordingly, as the Commission rightly put it, material nuisances caused outside such an area were not taken into account, contrary to the provisions of the Directive. The German government unsuccessfully countered that monitoring of material nuisance caused by air pollutants or noise from the area affected by the installation had to be carried out on an individual basis taking account of local data and the various pollutants emitted by the installation. Further, in practice, an authorization for a project involving material nuisance could only be issued if it did not have any harmful effects on the areas protected by the Directive.

78 Ibid., para. 42. 79 Ibid., para. 43. 80 Ibid., para. 44.

The contradiction between EC and German Federal Law was apparent. As the ECJ held, the system established by German law, so far as it covered emissions within an area of impact, 'as defined in technical circulars in accordance with general criteria on installations', did not appear capable of ensuring compliance with Article 6(3) and (4) of the Habitats Directive. In the absence of established scientific criteria not mentioned by the German government, which could a priori rule out emissions affecting a protected site situated outside the area of impact of the installation concerned having a significant effect on that site, the system put in place by German law was not compliant.[81] In fact, as the ECJ rightly observed, the German authorities had tried to justify the legality of the Federal Law on nature protection relying on technical rules and administrative practices. However, the case law had a long time ago made it clear that such practices were not sufficient to transpose the requirements set out in environmental directives.[82]

The third complaint concerned the alleged failure to transpose Article 12(1)(d) of the Habitats Directive. The key question was whether the Directive required Member States to prohibit both deliberate and non-deliberate acts. The Commission alleged that the Federal Law authorized a number of derogations from the rules protecting the sites provided that animals, including their nesting or incubation sites, habitat or resting places were not intentionally affected. The German government argued that an interpretation also prohibiting non-deliberate acts was, in any event, contrary to the principle of proportionality. Recalling the Community legislature's intention to give breeding grounds or resting places increased protection against acts causing their deterioration or destruction, and bearing in mind the importance of the objectives of protecting biodiversity, the ECJ held that it was by no means disproportionate that the prohibition laid down in Article 12(1)(d) was not limited to deliberate acts.[83]

In its fourth complaint the Commission argued that Germany had inserted two derogations which did not sufficiently take account of the conditions to which the derogations authorized by Article 16 of the Directive were subject. The Federal Law read as follows:

> the prohibitions laid down in Paragraph 42(1) and (2) shall not apply to acts intending to use land for the purposes of agriculture, forestry or fishing and carried out in accordance with good professional practice and the requirements laid down in Paragraph 5(4) to (6); acts intending to process the products obtained in the course of those activities; acts designed to implement an act authorized under Paragraph 19, or an assessment of the effect on the environment within the framework of the Law on the assessment of environmental impact; acts to implement a measure authorized under Paragraph 30; provided

[81] Ibid., paras. 50–1.

[82] See Case C-131/88 *Commission* v. *Germany* [1991] ECR 825, para. 61.

[83] Case C-98/03, n. 69 above, para. 55.

that animals and their nesting and incubation sites, habitats and resting places, and plant species which are specifically protected, are not intentionally damaged as a result.

The German government indicated that the acts and measures which were the subject of the derogations required administrative decisions and that in order to adopt such decisions the competent authorities were, in any event, bound to observe the conditions laid down in Article 16 of the Directive. As expected, the ECJ did not accept this line of reasoning. Recalling the wording of the 4th and 11th recitals in the preamble to the Habitats Directive, which indicate that the threatened habitats and species form part of the European Community's natural heritage and that the threats to them are often of a transboundary nature, so that the adoption of conservation measures is a common responsibility of all Member States, the ECJ concluded that faithful transposition was particularly important in an instance where management of the common heritage was entrusted to the Member States in their respective territories.[84] Accordingly, the Member States were under a particular duty to ensure that their legislation intended to transpose that Directive was 'clear and precise'. The fact that German legislation required the grant of administrative decisions was not sufficient to guarantee the correct application of the Directive because German Law did not provide a legal framework consistent with the derogatory regime established by Article 16. In addition, the ECJ observed that the German provisions did not submit the grant of the two derogations in question to all of the conditions laid down in Article 16 of the Directive. It merely provided as the sole condition for authorization for those derogations that animals, including their nesting or incubation sites, habitat or resting places and plant species which were particularly protected could not be subject to deliberate harm.[85]

The subject matter of the fifth complaint was Paragraph 6(1) of the 1998 Law on Plant Protection, which prohibits the use of pesticides if it is foreseeable that it will produce harmful effects on humans or animals or the water table, or other serious harmful effects, in particular, on the balance of nature. The competent authority must order the measures necessary in order to satisfy these requirements. The Commission alleged that this provision did not correctly transpose Articles 12, 13, and 16 of the Directive. As in previous complaints, the German government mainly relied on the fact that the Law demanded good professional practice when handling pesticides and also that the competent authority was entitled to order the measures necessary to fulfil the requirements also mentioned in that provision. However, in the light of the general principles that pervade the Directive, i.e. that Member States are under a particular duty to ensure that their legislation intended to transpose the Directive is clear and precise, it was apparent that those two conditions set out in the applicable Law were not sufficient. The

[84] Ibid., para. 59. This is consistent case law, see, for instance, Case C-38/99 *Commission* v. *France* [2000] ECR I-10941.

[85] Case C-98/03, n. 69 above, para. 61.

ECJ made it clear that the system of prohibitions and derogations were inextricably intertwined. In that particular case the wording employed by the German law, which referred to the overall balance of nature, was not as clear, precise, and strict as the prohibition on the deterioration of breeding sites or resting places of protected animals laid down in Article 12(1)(d) of the Directive, or the prohibition of the deliberate destruction in the wild of protected plants laid down in Article 13(1)(a) of the Directive.[86] In fact, the German legislation, by stating the cases in which the use of pesticides was prohibited, not only did not refer to the Habitats Directive but above all did not clearly and specifically include the prohibitions on causing damage to protected species laid down in Articles 12 and 13.

The final complaint brought forward by the Commission concerned the failure to notify the fishery catch legislation or provisions containing adequate bans on fishing. The Commission indicated that the legislation in three Länder was not in accordance with the Directive. In Bavaria, the fish known by the scientific name *coregonus oxyrhynchus* did not feature among the species protected all year round. In Brandenberg, that species and the mollusc *unio crassus* were not protected. In Bremen, the legislation did not include in the list of fishing bans the three species which had to be protected in that Land, namely, the two species previously mentioned and the fish *acipenser sturio*. Furthermore, that legislation expressly authorized fishing of specimens of *acipenser sturio* which were at least 100 centimetres (cm) long, and specimens of the species *coregonus oxyrhynchus* which were at least 30 cm long. Moreover, no information was available on any fishing bans in the Länder of Berlin, Hamburg, Mecklenburg-West Pomerania, Lower Saxony, North Rhine-Westphalia, Saarland, Saxony, and Saxe-Anhalt. The ECJ first observed that *coregonus oxyrhynchus*, *unio crassus*, and *acipenser sturio*, mentioned in Annex IV(a) to the Directive, were species found in Germany.[87] Therefore, they were subject to a system of strict protection prohibiting all forms of deliberate capture or killing of members of those species in the wild. When the period set down in the reasoned opinion had expired, Bremen's legislation authorized, inter alia, the capture of fish all year round so long as no fishing bans were issued. *Coregonus oxyrhynchus* was not the subject of a fishing ban. In Brandenburg neither that species nor *unio crassus* was the subject of a fishing ban. As to Bremen's legislation, the German government had already acknowledged that it was not in accordance with the Directive. The ECJ noted that although it was true that the Federal Law on Nature Protection prohibited, inter alia, the capture and killing of the animal species covered by a system of strict protection, the fact remained that that Law did not affect the laws on the protection of animals, hunting, and fishing.[88] It is against this background that the ECJ held

86 Ibid., para. 68.

87 Ibid., para. 74.

88 Ibid., para. 77. The first sentence of Para. 39(2) of the Federal Law on Nature Protection of 2002, entitled 'Relationship with other legislative provisions', provided: 'The laws on the protection of plants, the protection of animals, protection against epizootic diseases and the laws on

that the legislative framework existing in Germany, in which regional provisions infringing Community law coexisted with a Federal law complying with it, did not ensure effectively, and in a clear and precise manner, the strict protection required by Article 12(1)(a) of the Directive, with respect to the prohibition of all forms of deliberate capture and killing of specimens of those species in the wild.[89] However, as regards the rules on fishing in the other Länder, which had not been communicated to the Commission, it could not be held that they did not satisfy the provisions of Articles 12 and 16 of the Directive, since no information was available on any fishing bans in those Länder, and the Federal Law on Nature Protection prohibited the capture and killing of specimens of the species *coregonus oxyrhynchus*, *unio crassus* and *acipenser sturio*. Finally, the ECJ observed that the Commission had not based its action on Article 23(3) of the Directive requiring the Member States to communicate to the Commission the main provisions of national law adopted in the field covered by this Directive.[90]

In Case C-221/04, *Commission* v. *Spain*,[91] the Commission put into question the authorization by the Spanish authorities of the setting of stopped snares in several private hunting areas, since it was of the opinion that it breached Article 12(1) and Annex VI of the Habitats Directive. The action related to three permits for the use of stopped snares for fox hunting issued by the authorities of an Autonomous Community between 2000 and 2003. As a preliminary matter, the ECJ had to consider two pleas of inadmissibility put forward by the Spanish government. The first one concerned the alleged alteration of the subject matter of the application and, in the alternative, its lack of precision. The second one related to the insufficient statement of grounds in the Commission's application. However, the ECJ rejected those allegations. As was clear from the documents in the file, the debate regarding the incorrect transposition of the Directive had its origin in the position taken by the Spanish government in its defence which consisted of justifying the contested permits with regard to the derogations provided for in the Directive. The subject matter of the action was not the possible incorrect transposition into Spanish law of that Directive, but the alleged infringement by the grant of the contested permits. In the light of consistent case law, the ECJ also held that the permit of 24 May 2001 was granted for a limited period ending on 15 June 2001, that is well before the reasoned opinion was sent, and that it had not been shown that that permit continued to produce legal effects after the expiry of the period laid down in the reasoned opinion. The conclusion was apparent: the action was inadmissible insofar as it related to the permit issued on 24 May 2001. As regards the permit of 13 December 2002, the ECJ noted that it was granted as an extension to the permit of 10 January 2000. According to settled case law,

forests, hunting and fishing shall not be affected either by the provisions of this section or by the laws adopted pursuant thereto.'

[89] Case C-98/03, n. 69 above, para. 78.

[90] Ibid., para. 81.

[91] [2006] ECR I-4515.

the subject matter of a dispute could be extended to events taking place after the deliverance of the reasoned opinion insofar as they were 'of the same kind' and constituted 'the same conduct' as the events to which the opinion referred.[92] The ECJ observed that the permit of 13 December 2002 was of the same kind as the permit of 10 January 2000 and that the grant of those two permits constituted the same conduct. Consequently, the fact that the permit of 13 December 2002 had been cited as an example by the Commission in the reasoned opinion and was referred to again in that application had not deprived Spain of the rights conferred by Article 226 EC. Therefore, that permit had lawfully been incorporated into the subject matter of the Commission's action.[93]

The ECJ added that it was 'absolutely clear' from the Commission's application that it had alleged that Spain had failed to fulfil specific obligations stemming from Article 12(1)(a) of and Annex VI to the Habitats Directive, namely the obligation to establish a system of strict protection for the animal species listed in Annex IV(a) to the Directive (among which the otter was included) prohibiting all forms of deliberate capture or killing, and the obligation to prohibit means of capture and killing which were non-selective according to their principle or their conditions of use.

As regards the permit of 13 December 2002, which related to a hunting area situated in a municipality, the Commission argued that the authorization to use stopped snares infringed Annex VI(a) to the Directive since it involved a means of hunting which was non-selective according to its principle and its conditions of use. The ECJ observed that under the Directive the methods and means of capture and killing listed in Annex VI(a) were prohibited only as regards the cases referred to in Article 15 of the Directive, the only Article referring to that Annex. According to that provision, it was prohibited to use non-selective means, in particular those listed in Annex VI(a) to the Directive, to capture or to kill species of wild fauna listed in Annex V(a) to the Directive and where, in accordance with Article 16, derogations were applied, to take, capture, or kill species listed in Annex IV(a) to the Directive. However, the contested permit was issued for fox hunting and the fox was an animal species not referred to in either Annex IV(a) or Annex V(a) to the Directive. Therefore, the prohibition with regard to non-selective means of hunting was not binding on the Spanish authorities in the case. Hence, the complaint concerning infringement of Annex VI(a) to the Directive was rejected. As regards the complaint concerning the infringement of Article 12(1)(a) of the Directive, the ECJ indicated that in order to assess the validity of the complaint put forward by the Commission, the presence of the otter in the area concerned had to be ascertained, and the circumstances under which the capture or killing of that species was deliberate had also to be established.[94]

[92] Case 42/82 *Commission* v. *France* [1983] ECR 1013, para. 20; Case 113/86 *Commission* v. *Italy* [1988] ECR 607, para. 11.

[93] Case C-221/04, n. 91 above, para. 29.

[94] Ibid., para. 49.

Concerning the scientific information sheets 'Natura 2000', the ECJ observed that they covered the Quilamas site, with a surface area of over 10,000 hectares. Admittedly, the area concerned was situated in the immediate vicinity of that site, to the north-west. However, it was common ground that the largest waterways on that site flew to the south-east and were separated from the area concerned by a range of hills with a height of several hundred metres. Therefore, according to the ECJ, it was unlikely that otters from the populations living in the network of waterways on the Quilamas site would move into the area concerned.[95] The ECJ added that the Spanish government had stated, without being contradicted by the Commission, that although waterways were a necessary component of the habitat of otters, those which crossed the area concerned or flew near it were of 'a seasonal nature'.[96] The ECJ also noted that the monographs produced by the Commission contained contradictory information so that no certainty regarding the presence of the otter in the area concerned was apparent from them.

The final matter was whether the capture of the otter was deliberate. As regards the condition in Article 12(1)(a) of deliberate action, the ECJ held that it was 'clear' from a reading of the different language versions that 'deliberate' referred to both the capture and the killing of protected animal species.[97] Previous case law had already categorized as deliberate disturbance matters such as the use of mopeds on a beach notwithstanding warnings as to the presence of protected sea turtles' nests and the presence of pedalos and small boats in the sea area of the beaches concerned.[98] The case law had also held that a Member State failed to fulfil its obligations under Article 12(1)(b) and (d) of the Directive where it did not take all the requisite specific measures to prevent the deliberate disturbance of the animal species concerned during its breeding period or the deterioration or destruction of its breeding sites. Therefore, for the condition as to 'deliberate' action in Article 12(1)(a) of the Directive to be met, it had to be proven that the author of the act intended the capture or killing of a specimen belonging to a protected animal species or, at the very least, accepted the possibility of such capture or killing.[99] However, in the case before the ECJ it was common ground that the contested permit related to fox hunting and thus it was not intended to allow the capture of otters. In addition, the ECJ held that the presence of otters in the area concerned had not been formally proven, so that it had also not been established that by issuing the contested permit for fox hunting the Spanish authorities knew that they risked endangering otters.[100]

Case C-239/04, *Commission* v. *Portugal*,[101] concerned the construction of a motorway in Portugal, whose route crossed a SPA, notwithstanding the negative

[95] Ibid., para. 60.
[96] Ibid., para. 61.
[97] Ibid., para. 69.
[98] See Case C-103/00 *Commission* v. *Greece* [2002] ECR I-1147, paras. 36 and 39.
[99] Case C-221/04, n. 91 above, para. 71.
[100] Ibid., 74.
[101] [2006] ECR I-10183.

environmental impact assessment and the existence of alternative solutions for the route concerned. The Commission argued that Portugal had failed to fulfil its obligations under Article 6(4) of the Habitats Directive. The ECJ first recalled the wording of Article 6(3) of the Habitats Directive and held, in the light of Case C-127/02,[102] that this provision established a procedure intended to ensure, by means of a prior examination, that a plan or project not directly connected with or necessary to the management of the site concerned but likely to have a significant effect on it was authorized only to the extent that it would not adversely affect the integrity of that site. It added that a plan or project such as the one in question could be granted authorization only on the condition that the competent national authorities were certain that it would not have adverse effects on the integrity of the site concerned, and where no reasonable scientific doubt remained as to the absence of such effects. In Case C-239/04, the environmental impact study mentioned the presence, in the SPA, of 17 species of birds listed in Annex I to the Birds Directive and the high sensitivity of certain of them to the disturbance and/or the fragmentation of their habitat resulting from the planned route of the section of the motorway. Consequently, the ECJ held that it was apparent from that study that the project in question had a 'significantly high' overall impact and a 'high negative impact' on the avifauna present in the SPA.[103] Accordingly, the 'inevitable conclusion' was that, when authorizing the planned route of the motorway, the Portuguese authorities were not entitled to take the view that it would have no adverse effects on the SPA's integrity.[104] The fact that, after its completion, the project could not have produced such effects was 'immaterial' to that assessment. It was at the time of adoption of the decision authorizing implementation of the project that there had to be no reasonable scientific doubt remaining as to the absence of adverse effects on the integrity of the site in question.[105] In those circumstances, the Portuguese authorities had the choice of either refusing authorization for the project or of authorizing it under Article 6(4) of the Habitats Directive, provided that the conditions laid down in that provision were satisfied. In this context, the Commission submitted that the Portuguese government had not complied with that provision since the Portuguese authorities had failed to study certain alternative routes with no adverse effects on the SPA or on the population of that area. Recalling the wording of Article 6(4) of the Habitats Directive, the ECJ held that the implementation of a plan or project under that provision was, inter alia, subject to the condition that the absence of alternative solutions be demonstrated. The ECJ acknowledged that the Portuguese authorities had examined and rejected a number of solutions whose routes bypassed

[102] Case C-127/02 *Landelijke Vereniging tot Behoud van de Waddenzee en Nederlandse Vereniging tot Bescherming van Vogels* v. *Staatssecretaris van Landbouw, Natuurbeheer en Visserij* [2004] ECR I-7405, para. 34.

[103] Case C-239/04, n. 101 above, para. 22.

[104] Ibid., para. 23.

[105] Ibid., para. 24.

certain settlements but crossed the western side of the SPA.[106] However, it was not apparent that those authorities had examined solutions falling outside that SPA and to the west of those settlements, although, on the basis of information supplied by the Commission, it could not be ruled out immediately that such solutions were capable of amounting to alternative solutions within the meaning of Article 6(4) of the Habitats Directive, even if they were, as asserted by the Portuguese government, liable to present certain difficulties.[107] By failing to examine that type of solution, the Portuguese authorities had not demonstrated the absence of alternative solutions within the meaning of that provision.[108]

Case C-518/04, *Commission* v. *Greece*,[109] concerned the failure by the Greek authorities to adopt and implement measures for the protection of the snake *Vipera schweizeri* in the island of Milos in order to avoid any intentional disturbance, particularly during the period of breeding, rearing, and hibernation, and the deterioration or destruction of breeding sites or resting places, as required by Article 12(1)(b) and (d) of the Habitats Directive. The Commission argued that Greece had failed to comply with that provision since national laws merely introduced general principles without setting up a precise and binding legal regime. The Greek government indicated that several measures under discussion at that time, including a draft decree, could sufficiently guarantee the protection afforded by the Directive. The ECJ did not consider it necessary to examine the draft decree. It first recalled the wording of Article 12 of the Directive according to which the Member States were required to take the requisite measures to establish a system of strict protection for the animal species listed in Annex IV(a) in their natural range. It then noted that the island of Milos was an essential region for the reproduction and survival of *Vipera schweizeri*, a species included in that Annex. In fact, the western side of the island comprised half of the population of the species in the whole world. In addition, one of the three sites proposed by the Greek authorities for its inclusion in the Natura 2000 network was in the island of Milos.[110] After holding that a strict protection system demanded the adoption of coherent and coordinated precautionary measures, the ECJ ruled that the existing Greek framework did not meet this standard. The ECJ further noted that the Greek authorities had not mentioned any specific measure in force at the time of the expiry of the Commission's reasoned opinion likely to fulfil the conditions set out in Article 12(1)(b) and (d) of the Habitats Directive.[111] The ECJ also held that certain circumstances, such as the good environmental quality existing on the island or the stable number of specimens of *Vipera schweizeri* did not put into question the aforementioned findings.[112]

Case C-244/05, *Bund Naturschutz in Bayern eV, Johann Märkl and Others, Angelika Graubner-Riedelsheimer and Others, Friederike Nischwitz and Others,*

[106] Ibid., para. 37.
[107] Ibid., para. 38.
[108] Ibid., para. 39.
[109] [2006] ECR I-42.
[110] Ibid., para. 15.
[111] Ibid., para. 19.
[112] Ibid., para. 21.

v. *Freistaat Bayern*,[113] concerned the interpretation of Article 3 of the Habitats Directive and the protection mechanisms applicable to the sites submitted to the Commission for the inclusion in the corresponding lists of biogeographical regions. A German court referred some questions to the ECJ in the course of proceedings regarding a decision to approve a motorway project. By its first and second questions, the referring court raised the issue of the protection scheme applicable to sites designated by the national competent authorities with a view to their recognition as sites of Community importance, but whose inclusion on the list awaited a decision by the Commission. The ECJ indicated that it was clear from Article 3(2) of the Directive that the decision of the national competent authorities relating to the designation of a site eligible to be considered as the element forming the European ecological network of SACs constituted 'the first step of a process leading to the creation of the "Natura 2000" network'.[114] Following that process, it was the Commission's duty, on the basis of the selection criteria established in Annex III of the Directive, to establish, in agreement with each of the Member States, a draft list of the sites of Community importance, showing in particular the sites hosting one or more priority natural habitat types or one or more priority species.[115] More specifically, as regards the level of protection applicable to the sites appearing on the national list transmitted to the Commission, the ECJ indicated that, in accordance with Article 4(5) of the Directive, the protection scheme for SACs laid down in Article 6(2), (3), and (4) was applicable to a site once the latter was placed on the list of sites selected as sites of Community importance, adopted by the Commission. Recalling the ruling in Case C-117/03,[116] the ECJ held that the protective measures prescribed in Article 6(2) to (4) of the Directive were required only as regards sites which were placed on the list of sites selected as sites of Community importance. However, that did not mean that the Member States were not to protect sites as soon as they proposed them, under Article 4(1) of the Directive, as sites eligible for identification as sites of Community importance on the national list transmitted to the Commission. In that case, the Member States were, by virtue of the Directive, required to take protective measures 'appropriate' for the purpose of safeguarding that ecological interest.[117]

Now, the question raised by the German court was the meaning to be given to the word 'appropriate' because the ECJ had not addressed this matter in Case C-117/03. The ECJ recalled a previous judgment in *First Corporate Shipping*,[118] in

[113] [2006] ECR I-8445.

[114] Ibid., para. 32.

[115] Ibid., para. 34.

[116] Case C-117/03 *Società Italiana Dragaggi SpA and Others* v. *Ministero delle Infrastrutture e dei Trasporti and Regione Autonoma Friuli Venezia Giulia* [2005] ECR I-167, para. 25.

[117] Ibid., para. 26.

[118] Case C-371/98 *The Queen* v. *Secretary of State for the Environment, Transport and the Regions, ex parte First Corporate Shipping Ltd, interveners: World Wide Fund for Nature UK (WWF) and Avon Wildlife Trust* [2000] ECR I-9235, paras. 22–3.

which it had held that to produce a draft list of sites of Community importance, capable of leading to the creation of a coherent European ecological network of SACs, the Commission had to have available an exhaustive list of the sites which, at national level, had an ecological interest relevant from the point of view of the Directive's objective of conservation of natural habitats and wild fauna and flora. Only in that way was it possible to realize the objective, in Article 3(1) of the Directive, of maintaining or restoring the natural habitat types and the species' habitats concerned at a favourable conservation status in their natural range, in the entire European territory of the Member States. When a Member State was drawing up the national list of sites, it was not in a position to have precise detailed knowledge of the situation of habitats in the other Member States, and therefore it could not exclude sites which at national level had an ecological interest relevant from the point of view of the objective of conservation without jeopardizing the realization of that objective at Community level. Consequently, the Commission had to be sure of having available an exhaustive list of sites eligible as SACs. Furthermore, at the time of the decision which the Commission was called upon to take under Article 4 of the Habitats Directive, the sites identified by the Member States had to reflect the situation on the basis of which the scientific evaluations of potential sites of Community importance had been carried out.[119] If that were not the case, the Community decision-making process, which is not only based on the integrity of the sites as notified by the Member States, but was also characterized by the ecological comparisons between the different sites proposed by the Member States, would run the risk of being distorted and the Commission would no longer be in a position to fulfil its duties.[120] The ECJ added that, in accordance with Annex III, Stage 2, paragraph 1 of the Directive, all the sites identified by the Member States in Stage 1 containing priority natural habitat types and/or species had to be considered as sites of Community importance. Accordingly, those sites had to appear on the Commission's list, and the Member States could not authorize interventions which could pose the risk of seriously compromising the ecological characteristics of a site, as defined by the criteria set out in Annex III to the Directive. According to the ECJ, that was particularly the case when an intervention posed the risk of either significantly reducing the area of a site, or leading to the disappearance of priority species present on the site, or, finally, of having as an outcome the destruction of the site or the destruction of its representative characteristics.[121]

The third question submitted by the German court concerned the methods of implementation of the abovementioned protection scheme. Here, the ECJ refrained itself from providing a clear-cut response. It held that it was for the

[119] Case C-244/05, *Bund Naturschutz in Bayern eV, Johann Märkl and Others, Angelika Graubner-Riedelsheimer and Others, Friederike Nischwitz and Others*, v. *Freistaat Bayern* [2006] ECR I-0000, para. 41.

[120] Ibid., para. 42.

[121] Ibid., para. 46.

Member States to take all the measures necessary. The detailed procedural rules applicable fell within the ambit of the domestic legal order of each Member State, provided that such rules were not less favourable than those governing similar domestic situations of an internal nature and did not render impossible in practice or excessively difficult the exercise of rights conferred by Community law.[122]

In 2006, the Court of First Instance (CFI) dealt with a range of private applications for annulment of Commission Decisions adopting lists of sites of Community importance. Confirming that the Court's restrictive view on standing for private applicants in judicial review cases is alive and well, all of these were deemed inadmissible and, hence, dismissed.[123]

E. Policy Documents and Resolutions

i. Enforcement of Community Environmental Law and Commission Monitoring of the Application of Community Law

In September 2006, the Commission released its seventh annual Report on the implementation and enforcement of Community environmental law 2005.[124] As regards nature protection, the Report indicates that guidelines are being developed on compensatory measures required under Article 6(4) of the Habitats Directive, species protection (Articles 12 and 16 of the same Directive), and marine issues 'in order to clarify implementation problems'. The Report also summarizes the main judgments adopted by the ECJ concerning the Birds and Habitats Directives in 2005.

During 2006 the Commission began proceedings against several Member States on issues concerning nature protection. Basic binding rules were not complied with by the Member States despite the existence of a developed body of case law clarifying the scope of the Birds and Habitats Directives. As in previous years, many infringements concerned development projects. Italy and Germany received reasoned opinions for alleged breaches of the Birds Directive.[125] The Commission initiated legal proceedings in the ECJ against Spain for failure to fulfil its obligations under Articles 2, 3, and 4(1) of the Birds Directive in respect

[122] Ibid., para. 50.

[123] Case T-80/05 *Bavendam and Others* v. *Commission* [2005] OJ C143/36 (relating to sites of Community importance in the Continental and Atlantic biogeographical region); Case T-136/04 *Freiherr von Cramer-Klett and Rechtlerverband Pfronten* v. *Commission* [2004] OJ C190/17 (Alpine biogeographical region); Case T-100/05 *Compagnie d'enterprises CFE SA (Brussels, Belgium)* v. *Commission* [2005] OJ C106 (Atlantic biogeographical region); Case T-117/05 R *Andreas Rodenbröker* v. *Commission* [2005] ECR II-2593 (Atlantic biogeographical region); and Case T-122/05 *Benkö and Others* v. *Commission* [2006] OJ C249/49 (Continental biogeographical region).

[124] SEC(2006) 1143, 8 Sept. 2006, available on the Internet at: http://ec.europa.eu/environment/law/pdf/7th_en.pdf.

[125] Commission Press Releases IP/06/478, 4 Apr. 2006, published in the RAPID database on the Internet at: http://europa.eu/rapid/searchAction.do (RAPID).

of an irrigation plan affecting a SPA,[126] and also against Austria and Italy in respect of their hunting regulations.[127] Furthermore, a number of pending investigations concern alleged failures by Member States to comply with earlier ECJ rulings on nature conservation, which could ultimately result in the ECJ imposing a fine on the non-compliant Member State. Such are the prospects for Greece, Finland, and Spain (for breaches regarding two earlier judgments).[128]

The Commission advised that it had received the first Maltese Government Report on the transition measure related to bird trapping on 29 March 2006. According to the Report, while there was some initial delay in implementing elements of the transition programme, in 2005, the Maltese authorities had put in place significant elements of the programme: (i) drafting of a legal notice for registration of trapping sites (registration foreseen by third quarter of 2006); (ii) carrying out a study on the mortality of captive birds for the different species held in captivity; (iii) carrying out a survey of captive breeding by trappers for the different species and the success rates; and (iv) establishing the first of two planned captive breeding centres and appointing a coordinator for the programme. The Commission considered that, albeit with some delay, the Report represented 'real progress' with the programme and demonstrated the commitment of the Maltese authorities to respect their engagement. On the issue of the commercial sale of trapped birds, the Commission declared that it was prohibited by the Birds Directive, and was therefore an enforcement responsibility of the Maltese authorities. At the time of the Report, the Commission had not received any complaints.[129]

A similarly high level of enforcement activity characterizes the implementation of the Habitats Directive. Spain was the subject of extensive Commission scrutiny, as the latter commenced two proceedings against the Member State for failure to undertake an environmental impact assessment before authorizing urban development projects.[130] Furthermore, in October 2006 the Commission sent a reasoned opinion to Spain requesting the adoption of sufficient and effective measures to protect species threatened by the upgrading of a former rural track passing through the Doñana area, an area designated as a SCA. According to the Commission, the protection measures already implemented by the Spanish authorities were not sufficient to safeguard the wildlife in the area, in particular the Iberian lynx (*Lynx pardinus*). The Commission also began proceedings for the widening and upgrading of the M-501 road in the Madrid Region. It considered that Spain had split the works of the M-501 road into five separate subprojects.

[126] Case C-186/06 *Commission* v. *Spain* [2006] OJ C154/10.

[127] Commission Press Release IP/06/1766, 12 Dec. 2006 (RAPID).

[128] Commission Press Release IP/06/1395, 13 Oct. 2006 (RAPID); Commission Press Release IP/06/1396, 13 Oct. 2006 (RAPID); Commission Press Release IP/06/479, 4 Apr. 2006 (RAPID).

[129] B. Staes, M. Auken, M. I Béguin, S. Kusstatscher, D. Hammerstein Mintz, P. Casaca, R. Evans, W. Kreissl-Dörfler, K. Scheele, C. Jackson, P. Olajos, N. Parish, J. Bowis, and J. Sjöstedt, written question E-2870/06.

[130] Commission Press Release IP/06/445, 4 Apr. 2006 (RAPID).

However, no assessment of the combined effects of the subprojects had taken place and for one of the subprojects no assessment had been carried out at all, which, in the Commission's view, risks to 'seriously compromise' the ecological characteristics of the sites.[131] Regarding a project to harness and commercially exploit some of the waters of a river in Spain, affecting an SPA and a proposed site of community importance (pSCI), the Commission indicated that the competent authorities had analysed the implication of the project on the sites after the work had already been started. However, that analysis had led to the adoption of measures to prevent significant effects thereon, including the suppression of three drawing-off points and the restoration of the damaged habitats. The Commission also indicated that further action against Spain would not have any added value.[132]

Italy too is embroiled in infringement proceedings for carrying out environmentally significant alterations to a development without performing an impact assessment.[133] In September 2006, the Commission furthermore informed that it had opened infringement procedures under Article 226 EC against several Member States (Belgium, France, Greece, Italy, The Netherlands, Portugal, Spain, and the UK) for insufficient implementation of certain provisions concerning cetacean protection under the Habitats Directive. In December 2006, the Commission initiated legal proceedings against Poland for allowing the carrying out of eight projects linked to the Via Baltica, the Helsinki-Warsaw road corridor, those projects encroaching upon SACs and pSCIs. The Commission also began a different procedure against this Member State for failure to designate a sufficient number of Natura 2000 sites and areas.[134] Ireland faces proceedings for non-compliance with earlier Court rulings concerning the implementation of the Habitats Directive.[135] Germany received better news, as the Commission decided to close an infringement procedure brought against Germany for failing to comply fully with an ECJ judgment in Case C-71/99[136] requiring it to propose sufficient nature sites for the Natura 2000 network, under the Habitats Directive. The ECJ had ruled that Germany had not submitted an exhaustive list of pSCIs as it should have done by 5 June 1995. However, Germany finally proposed further designations and the Commission considered that this initiative allowed it to close the infringement procedure.[137]

In January and May 2006, the Commission provided information regarding the situation in the Zakynthos national Marine Park in Greece. In its judgment

[131] Commission Press Release IP/06/1395, 13 Oct. 2006 (RAPID); see also C. Carnero González, written question P-4626/06.
[132] Cf. Case C-362/90 *Commission* v. *Italy* [1992] ECR I-2353.
[133] Case C-179/06 *Commission* v. *Italy* [2006] OJ C143/26.
[134] Commission Press Release IP/06/1757, 12 Dec. 2006 (RAPID).
[135] Commission Press Release IP/06/1394, 13 Oct. 2006 (RAPID).
[136] Case C-71/93 *Commission* v. *Germany* [2001] ECR I-5811.
[137] Commission Press Release IP/06/1396, 13 Oct. 2006 (RAPID).

delivered on 30 January 2002,[138] the ECJ had declared that Greece had failed to take measures to establish and implement an effective system of strict protection for the sea turtle (*caretta caretta*) on Zakynthos. The Commission indicated that by adopting a presidential decree establishing the Marine Park and laying down provisions aimed at the strict protection of the turtle, Greece had already 'partially complied' with the ECJ judgment.[139]

Finally, the Commission considered the legality, from the point of view of the Habitats Directive, of the killing of 'Bruno' the bear in July 2006 in Germany. It indicated that the decision of the Bavarian authorities for classifying it as a 'risk' and removing it from the wild had been taken on assessment criteria established by the World Wild Federation Austria during a previous LIFE-funded project 'Bear protection program for Austria'. The Commission did not consider that the removal of an individual bear identified as a risk bear caused any damage to the long-term objective of re-establishing a viable brown bear population in the Alps, nor to the 'LIFE ursus' project in particular.[140]

In February 2006, the Commission decided to investigate the application of Directive 1999/22/EC relating to the Keeping of Wild Animals in Zoos.[141] By virtue of the Italian Minister of the Environment's decree of 18 January 2006, the Italian government had deleted the date 17 November 2005 as the deadline by which the legal representative of zoos existing on the date of the entry into force of the Italian law implementing the Directive should have submitted an application for the issue of a licence. This contradicted Article 4(2) of the Directive which states that every zoo must have a licence granted by the competent authority by 9 April 2003.[142]

ii. Implementation of the Birds Directive: Overall Progress Update 1999 to 2001

In April 2006, the Commission released a Report on the implementation of the Birds Directive.[143] The Report was drawn up on the basis of the information provided in the national three-year reports by the Member States pursuant to Article 12 of the Directive and covered implementation efforts over the reporting period 1999 to 2001. The Report was confined to significant changes as compared with the previous situation, and was divided into two parts: Part I providing for the EU-15 a summary of progress achieved, particularly in relation to the main aims and provisions of the Directive, which were briefly outlined; and Part II

[138] Case C-103/00 *Commission* v. *Greece* [2002] ECR I-1147.

[139] D. Papadimoulis, written question E-0033/06.

[140] See C. Muscardini, written question E-3075/06; H. Breyer, written question P-3178/06; I. Braghetto, written question E-3187/06.

[141] [1999] OJ L94/24.

[142] P. Napoletano, written question E-0676/06; see also M. Ebner, written question E-1764/06.

[143] COM(2006)164, 12 Apr. 2006.

containing a summary of national reports of Member States' implementation efforts over the period 1999 to 2001, as required under Article 12 of the Directive.

As regards new legislation pursuant to the Directive, the Report indicated that no major overhauls of legislation were undertaken during the period, although most Member States had reported some changes. In many cases, they related to secondary legislation concerning specific conditions for hunting, impact assessment, and the keeping of birds. In particular, the report highlighted that changes to UK legislation had strengthened powers of enforcement and penalties for illegal activities. Most Member States had added new SPAs to their national lists, and/or extended the area of existing SPAs. In some cases, 'significant additions' had been made to the SPA suite (e.g. Italy, Netherlands, Portugal, Spain, and Sweden). Only Belgium had reported the removal of an area, which had been subsequently compensated in other regions. However, Finland had reduced a number of SPAs in size. The UK had carried out a detailed review of SPAs, but the results of that review were not detailed. Regarding measures taken in and outside the SPAs, the Report stated that LIFE projects had played a role in some Member States, most obviously Finland. Measures had included agro-environment and management schemes (particularly in Germany, Spain, Finland, the Netherlands, and the UK) and land acquisition (Portugal). Management plans were in place in many Member States (Italy, Portugal), although not comprehensively (the Netherlands). Most countries referred to the use of contractual and agro-environment measures.

The Report also considered the main prohibitions enshrined in Article 5 of the Directive. Even though in Austria, Finland, Italy, the Netherlands, Spain, Sweden, and the UK species management plans or strategies had been put in place, the Commission indicated that they were in most cases for a very limited number of species. In several countries (Belgium, Denmark, France, Germany, Ireland, and Sweden), legislation had been reinforced, in order to extend the level of protection offered against intentional capture, disturbance, destruction, and collection of eggs, etc. In Ireland, licences were required for additional activities to limit the risk of disturbance. LIFE projects were only mentioned in the case of the UK and Portugal.

As regards the prohibition to sell, transport for sale, and keep for sale live or dead birds, or any parts of birds, the UK report provided details on the level of inspections and of successful prosecutions for illegally keeping birds. However, apart from this, only Ireland, Italy, Belgium, and Austria had reported on the issue of sales and keeping of birds. The Member States had also introduced certain changes regarding hunting legislation (Denmark, France, Finland, Greece, Portugal, Spain, Sweden, the UK—Scotland). In several cases (Belgium—Flemish Region, Italy, Ireland, Greece), hunting was regulated on an annual basis, although it was not self-evident on what basis permits were issued and whether they fully respected the Directive. In a similar fashion, most Member States had reported on the legal situation as regards permitted methods of capture or killing (Article 8 of the Directive), whilst some had simply referred to the legal text without specifying its content. None of the countries had indicated whether problems existed with practical implementation of the legislation.

The application of the derogation clause set out in Article 9 of the Directive was also considered. In Finland, 121 derogations have been given, mainly for research and teaching. The cormorant was mentioned in some national reports (Austria, France, and Ireland). The most immediately notable derogations concerned seven species in Italy, affecting 80,000 birds. Only Sweden had referred to the need for derogations to be compatible with favourable conservation status. The Member States had submitted under Article 10 a long and varied list of research projects. Most frequently listed were breeding bird censuses, waterbird counts, bird ringing schemes, research considering habitat requirements/choice, bird distribution and inventories, and research considering monitoring and management programmes. Finally, no new introductions of non-native species had been reported. In Spain, control measures appeared to have been effective with no hybrids sighted for over a year; in Sweden and Ireland hunting was a means of controlling numbers. A number of species were causing some concern, notably geese in the UK and Ireland. Monitoring schemes were in place for non-native species in Italy (110 non-native species) and the UK (introduced species with small breeding populations; non-native, non-breeding waterfowl and hybrids).

The Report concluded that over 3,000 SPAs had been classified, covering nearly 8 per cent of EU terrestrial territory as well as an additional significant marine area of over 2.7 million hectare, although only four countries (Belgium, Denmark, Luxembourg, and the Netherlands) had largely completed their contribution to the SPA network. Also, the percentage of national territory designated as SPAs varied widely from less than 2 per cent in France to over 15 per cent in Spain. The protection and conservation management of those sites, especially wetlands, combined with the development of species action plans, had resulted in that the populations of some (unnamed) severely threatened species were recovering. But action varied from country to country, and some (unnamed) important sites were still unprotected. The Report also acknowledged that there was still some controversy over the compatibility of some Member States' hunting regimes and practices with the Directive. Notably in France, Spain, and Italy, conflicts were longstanding, and this situation had been accompanied by extensive litigation on the subject.

iii. Environmental Policy Review

In February 2006, the Commission published a Communication to the Council and the EP entitled '2005 Environmental Policy Review'.[144] Regarding biodiversity and ecosystems, the Commission indicated that it had integrated biodiver-

[144] COM(2006)70, 16 Feb. 2005.

sity into the thematic strategies (TS), in particular: (i) the Marine Environment TS which aims to protect the resource base upon which economic and social activities depend; and (ii) the Air Pollution TS, in order to reduce two of the main pressures on biodiversity, acidification, and eutrophication. Without providing factual data, the Commission added that the completion of the Natura 2000 network progressed 'substantially' and that biodiversity protection was further integrated into the Common Agricultural Policy, notably through the Community strategic guidelines for rural development,[145] and the adoption of a Rural Development Regulation[146] providing financing opportunities for beneficial agricultural and forestry activities. However, the Commission indicated: (i) that many European species remained threatened, e.g. 42 per cent of native mammals, 15 per cent of birds, and 52 per cent of freshwater fish; (ii) the lack of attention to the linkages between biodiversity and economic development might jeopardize the achievement of the Millennium Development Goals; and (iii) the great majority of ecosystem services had been degraded in the last 15 years, such as marine fisheries, timber production, or water purification.

iv. Halting the Loss of Biodiversity by 2010

In May 2006, the Commission issued a Communication entitled 'Halting the Loss of Biodiversity by 2010—and Beyond'.[147] The Communication showed contradictory views regarding this matter, which is a constant feature of biodiversity protection policy. According to the Commission, while important progress was made and there were first signs of slowing rates of loss, the pace and extent of implementation was 'insufficient'. Much of the biodiversity remained 'greatly impoverished' and continued to decline. Achievement of the 2010 target was still possible but required accelerated implementation at both Community and Member State levels. This seemed to be rather optimistic bearing in mind the data put forward by the Commission, according to which only 1 to 3 per cent of western Europe's forests could be classed as 'undisturbed by humans'. Since the 1950s, Europe has lost more than half of its wetlands and most high-nature-value farmland; and many of the EU's marine ecosystems are degraded. At the species level, 42 per cent of Europe's native mammals, 43 per cent of birds, 45 per cent of butterflies, 30 per cent of amphibians, 45 per cent of reptiles, and 52 per cent of freshwater fish are threatened with extinction; most major marine fish stocks are below safe biological limits; some 800 plant species in Europe are at risk of global extinction; and unknown but potentially significant changes occur in lower life forms, including invertebrate and microbial diversity. The main pressures are habitat fragmentation, degradation and destruction due to land use change arising, inter alia, from conversion, intensification of production systems, aban-

[145] COM(2005)304, 5 July 2005.
[146] [2005] OJ L277/1.
[147] COM(2006)216, 22 May 2006.

donment of traditional (often biodiversity-friendly) practices, construction, and catastrophic events including fire. Other key pressures are over-exploitation, the spread of invasive alien species, and pollution. In addition, climate change may cause a temperature rise between 2 and 6.3 degrees Celcius above 1990 temperatures by the year 2100, having 'profound effects' on biodiversity.

The Communication also provided information on the internal and external policy of the EU regarding biodiversity. It acknowledged that remaining problems included the absence, as yet, of the Natura 2000 network within the marine environment, the damaging impacts of developmental activities on Natura 2000 sites, and the limited funds available for effective site management and supporting actions. In addition, in recent decades, intensification and specialization, and at the same time marginalization and under-utilization of land, had resulted in significant biodiversity loss. The same was said concerning EU fisheries and aquaculture. According to the Commission, while recent years had seen progress in integrating biodiversity into fisheries policy, it was too soon to judge effectiveness. It also indicated, perhaps rather optimistically, that the reformed Common Fisheries Policy (CFP), when fully implemented, would reduce fishing pressure, improve the status of harvested stocks, and better protect non-target species and habitats. As to the external policy, the Communication emphasized that Member States were important donors to the Global Environment Facility (GEF) which supports biodiversity projects.[148] However, those funds amounted to less than one-hundredth of Community and Member States' total annual development aid budgets.

The Communication faced the key question of what more needed to be done. In response, it provided four key policy areas and ten priority objectives. Policy area 1, entitled 'Biodiversity in the EU', comprised the following objectives. Firstly, to safeguard the EU's most important habitats and species, which would require 'greater commitment' from Member States to propose, designate, protect, and effectively manage Natura 2000 sites. Secondly, to conserve and restore biodiversity and ecosystem services in the wider EU. Thirdly, to conserve and restore biodiversity and ecosystem services in the wider EU marine environment, arguably one of the most underdeveloped aspects within EU nature protection policy. The Communication referred to general measures such as the restoration of fish stocks and the reduction of impacts on non-target species or of diffuse pollutant pressures (e.g. airborne acidifying and eutrophicating substances, nitrates from farm sources, pesticides). Fourthly, to reinforce compatibility of regional and territorial development with biodiversity in the EU, which required taking account of biodiversity needs 'further upstream' in the decision-making process. Fifthly, substantially to reduce the impact on EU biodiversity of invasive alien species and alien genotypes.

[148] See: http://www.gefweb.org.

Policy area 2 concerned global biodiversity and included the following objectives. Firstly, substantially to strengthen effectiveness of international governance for biodiversity and ecosystem services. Secondly, to strengthen support for biodiversity and ecosystem services in EU external assistance; and, thirdly, substantially to reduce the impact of international trade on global biodiversity.

Policy area 3 referred to biodiversity and climate change. It is interesting that the first objective within this area was to support 'biodiversity adaptation to climate change', which seemed to acknowledge that the effects of climate change on biodiversity were unavoidable, no matter how many efforts could be devoted to combat temperature increases. Adaptation policies required, in particular, securing the coherence of the Natura 2000 network. However, the Communication did not explain the meaning and implications of 'coherence'.

Finally, policy area 4 concerned the knowledge base, comprising a single objective, namely substantially to strengthen the knowledge base for conservation and sustainable use of biodiversity, in the EU and globally. This objective was also explained in rather broad terms referring to the strengthening of the European Research Area, its international dimension, research infrastructures, the science-policy interface and data interoperability for biodiversity.

The four key supporting measures included in the Communication, supplemented by others set out in an Annex, were as follows. The first one was entitled 'Ensuring adequate financing'. Whilst declaring that adequate financing, both for Natura 2000 and for biodiversity outside Natura 2000, was essential, the Communication plainly acknowledged that the budget reduction foreseen by the December European Council would certainly influence funding options for biodiversity under those instruments. The second supporting measure was 'Strengthening EU decision-making'. That involved rather broad measures such as improving coordination and complementarity between Community and Member States; ensuring existing and new policies and budgets (including those developed under Lisbon Strategy National Reform Programmes); taking due account of biodiversity needs; taking account of environmental costs (including loss of natural capital and ecosystem services) in decision-making; improving coherence at national level between various plans and programmes affecting biodiversity; and ensuring consistency between regional and local decision-making and high-level commitments for biodiversity. The third supporting measure, 'Building partnerships', included building progressive partnerships between government, academia, conservation practitioners, landowners and users, private sector, finance sector, educational sector, and the media to frame solutions. The last measure, 'Building public education, awareness and participation', seemed to be a catch-all clause since it involved development and implementation of a communications strategy in support of the Action Plan, working closely with the Countdown 2010 initiative, and implementation of the Convention on Access to

Information, Public Participation in Decision-Making and Access to Justice in Environmental Matters (Aarhus Convention),[149] and related Directives.

The Communication summarized in Section 4 what progress had been made in terms of the development and implementation of policy up to May 2006, and presented a schedule for reporting on future progress providing for annual reports to the Council and Parliament. The second Report (to the end of 2008) would include a concise mid-term evaluation of progress towards the 2010 targets. The fourth Report (to the end of 2010) would include an evaluation of the extent to which the EU had met its 2010 commitments. To address the problem of limited availability of quantifiable data and to support the evaluation and reporting needs, the Communication proposed a set of biodiversity indicators to be developed and implemented. Overall, despite the need for a coherent number of objectives and supporting measures, the Communication reflected a sense of dejà vu since most of the objectives were already enshrined in existing reports and more importantly in binding Community laws. The Communication was nonethteless welcomed by the Council in its conclusions concerning its 2773rd Meeting of 18 December 2006.[150] The Council supported the Communication's ten priority objectives and endorsed the general approach of strengthening integration of biodiversity and ecosystem services into relevant horizontal and sectoral policies. It also emphasized the importance of strengthened cooperation and coordination between the Commission and the Member States. It urged the Commission and the Member States to strengthen efforts to finalize the Natura 2000 network both on land and at sea, and to ensure effective management and adequate financing of the network, and called upon the Commission and the Member States to assess and strengthen, where necessary, the coherence, connectivity, and resilience of the Natura 2000 network as well as the resilience of the ecosystems. It also called upon the Commission to initiate a scientific review of species, and of habitats as a second step, listed in the annexes of the Habitats Directive, building, inter alia, on the analysis of the Member States' reports under the Habitats Directive and in the light of progress made by 2010. Regarding the need to strengthen efforts to protect marine biodiversity, the Council called upon the Member States further to reduce pollution and nutrient load from agricultural and other diffuse sources as well as from urban, industrial, and other point sources. The Council also urged the Commission and the Member States to pursue efforts to implement the EU Forest Action Plan.

In September 2006, the Commission informed that within the framework of its work programme 'Environment in Developing Countries', it was going to

[149] Aarhus (Denmark), 25 June 1998 (entered into force 30 Oct. 2001), (1999) 38 *International Legal Materials* 3, 517. All official Aarhus documents published on the Internet at: http://www.unece.org/env/pp/.

[150] Available on the Internet at: http://www.consilium.europa.eu/ueDocs/cms_Data/docs/pressData/en/envir/92249.pdf.

commit more than €35 million to a range of projects contributing to achieving the global 2010 target.[151]

v. Forestry Strategy

In February 2006, the EP issued a Resolution on the Implementation of a European Union Forestry Strategy.[152] The Parliament emphasized the importance of intact forest ecosystems for the preservation of biodiversity in accordance with commitments under international agreements. It welcomed the Commission's FLEGT (Forest Law Enforcement, Governance and Trade) action plan,[153] set up to combat the problems associated with illegal logging. However, the Parliament indicated that it was of 'crucial importance' that the factors underlying the problem, such as lack of clarity about ownership, corruption, and poverty, were eliminated and furthermore that serious sanctions and punishments should be imposed on people and businesses dealing in illegally logged timber. The Resolution endorsed the Commission's view that the European Forestry Strategy should be more integrated into European policies as a whole and that Member States should cooperate in this field. In view of the many effects of the Community's sectoral policies on forests, and in view of the Lisbon and Göteborg Strategies, the Resolution indicated that the Commission and Council should have an objective report drawn up to examine the scope for creating a separate legal basis for forests in the EC Treaty or in a future draft Constitution. It also called on the Commission to draw up the necessary studies on the fiscal measures to be taken by the individual Member States with a view to applying positive differentiation with regard to taxation for producers who had fewer negative impacts on the environment. The Resolution took the view that the implementation of measures aimed at the prevention of fires and desertification, afforestation with native species, the promotion of biodiversity, the sustainable management of natural forests, and the fostering of environmental benefits such as protection for water systems and the combating of erosion, represented positive externalities which such producers provided to society and for which they should be 'duly compensated'.

In February, the European Economic and Social Committee (EESC) published an Opinion on the 'Communication from the Commission to the Council and the European Parliament—Reporting on the Implementation of the EU Forestry Strategy',[154] which it subsequently adopted on 26 October 2005. The EESC considered the prevention of illegal logging and illegal selling of timber to be of 'utmost importance'. As far as preventing illegal logging was concerned,

[151] R. Corbett, written question E-3654/06.

[152] P6_TA(2006) 0068, available on the Internet at: http://www.europarl.europa.eu. See Council Resolution of 15 Dec. 1998 on a Forestry Strategy for the European Union [1999] OJ C56/1.

[153] See COM(2003)25, 21 May 2003; Reg. (EC) No. 2173/2005 on the Establishment of a FLEGT Licensing Scheme for Imports of Timber into the European Community [2005] OJ L347/1.

[154] [2006] OJ C28/57.

the EESC indicated that the emphasis should be on measures that could be taken in collaboration with timber-producing countries to tighten up administrative processes and improve law enforcement. The EESC criticized the fact that although a significant portion of funding was used for afforestation measures, no clear operational objectives had been set regarding how afforestation measures could be deployed under the forestry strategy, in particular taking environmental objectives into account. In its opinion, the complexity of decision-making had limited the extent to which rural development policy was used in implementing the EU forestry strategy. It had to be clarified whether it would be more efficient to concentrate EU resources not on subsidizing afforestation but on timber market promotion, on reward mechanisms for environmental services, on research, training and information, and on rural development measures to secure long-term improvements in conditions and employment in the forestry sector and in environmental services provided by forests. As regards forest certification, the EESC indicated that it should remain a 'voluntary instrument'.

In May 2006, it was the Committee of the Regions' (CoR) turn to publish its Opinion on the abovementioned Commission Communication.[155] Regarding the global development of the European forestry strategy, the CoR expressed satisfaction with the exhaustive list of existing documents and agreements, but noted that the subsidiarity principle was also applicable in that field and that it required either the ratification of international agreements by the Member States or the development of coordination arrangements between the Community bodies. It supported the development of forestry certification. However, the CoR declared that the certification systems should remain voluntary and procedures should be framed by the various organizations requesting them. Member States should not interfere by imposing regulations, with the exception of those necessary for ensuring transparency and preventing the dissemination of fraudulent information.

In June 2006, the Council adopted its conclusions on forest law enforcement, governance and trade (FLEGT).[156] The Council reiterated the EU's firm commitment to contribute to the sustainable management of the world's forests and noted the need for action-oriented cooperation among countries, as well as effective participation of stakeholders in order to achieve sustainable forest management including the need for collaborative action to combat illegal logging, associated trade, and corruption. The Council also acknowledged the great value of regional forest law enforcement and governance (FLEG) processes co-organized by the World Bank to address the complex and urgent issue of illegal logging, associated trade, and corruption. Finally, it welcomed the outcome of the Europe and north Asia (ENA) FLEG ministerial conference which took place

[155] [2006] OJ C115/84.

[156] Bull. EU 6–2006, point 1.29.6. See Reg. (EC) No. 2173/2005, n. 153 above.

in St. Petersburg from 22 to 25 November 2005,[157] bringing together nearly 300 participants from 48 countries representing governments, the private sector, civil society, and international organizations.

vi. Marine Strategy

In April 2006, the CoR issued its Opinion on the Directive of the European Parliament and of the Council establishing a Framework for Community Action in the field of Marine Environmental Policy (Marine Strategy Directive) and on the Communication from the Commission to the Council and the European Parliament—Thematic Strategy on the Protection and Conservation of the Marine Environment.[158] The Committee noted that the Strategy was a positive step forward in terms of recognizing the value of protecting and conserving the marine environment and the diversity of its ecosystems. However, it indicated that the existing monitoring and assessment programmes within the European area were neither integrated nor complete, and that there were significant information gaps on the state of Europe's marine environment. Whilst noting that goals and objectives should be defined at supranational level, the Committee welcomed the intention—in line with the subsidiarity principle—to ensure that the actual planning and implementation of measures would remain the responsibility of marine regions, thereby taking account of their individual conditions, problems, and needs. However, the CoR was concerned that in certain instances, particularly where a marine region was bordered by a sizeable number of non-Member States, actual implementation could be hindered through lack of coordination and commitment on the part of the parties involved. The Committee recommended that the target date for achieving good environmental status of Europe's marine environment should be 2018 at the latest, and that the deadlines for the development and implementation of the programme of measures envisaged in the Proposal should be 2013 and 2015 respectively.

The EESC also released its Opinion on the issue in April 2006.[159] The EESC believed that while the Proposal was necessary, it did not go far enough. The status of seas and oceans had deteriorated so badly that more coercive measures were needed to implement and monitor compliance with existing measures. Moreover, the Proposal only partially covered the status of the marine environment. The EESC therefore believed that a Framework Directive would be more effective when subsequently integrating and developing the aspects that were not covered in depth here. According to the EESC, it was necessary to clarify and strengthen the Commission's monitoring and coordinating role vis-à-vis the regional authorities that were required to assess and plan the targets and the measures for

[157] Information concerning this Conference is available on the Internet at: http://web.worldbank.org.

[158] [2006] OJ C206/5; See COM(2005)505, 24 Oct. 2005; and COM(2005)504, 24 Oct. 2005.

[159] [2006] C185/20.

applying these to the marine environment under their control. The aim should be to harmonize and balance actions throughout coastal areas, bearing in mind that seas and oceans stretched across borders. However, the EESC criticized the facts: (i) that while the Commission's Communication pointed out the inefficiency of individual policies and the Community framework, this model of action was maintained in the Proposal for a Directive; and (ii) that the Communication gave an exhaustive definition of criteria, targets, and actions, which corresponded only in part to those in the Proposal for a Directive.

vii. Financial Instrument for the Environment (LIFE Nature)

The Commission approved funding for 61 nature conservation projects, situated in 20 Member States under the LIFE-Nature programme 2006.[160] The projects are devoted to restoring protected nature areas and their fauna and flora, establishing sustainable management structures, and strengthening public awareness and cooperation with stakeholders. They represent a total investment of €141.6 million, of which the EU covers €70.1 million.

F. International Cooperation

i. Convention on Biological Diversity

In March 2006, the EP adopted a Resolution on the preparations for the COP-MOP meetings on biological diversity and biosafety in Curitiba, Brazil.[161] The Parliament urged the Commission and the Member States: (i) to set specific, measurable, realistic, and time-bound global targets for the review of the 2010 halt of biodiversity loss target; (ii) to allocate additional resources and develop new international financing mechanisms to establish a global network of protected areas by 2010 on land, and by 2012 at sea, with special emphasis on large intact ecosystems; (iii) to protect marine biodiversity from destructive practices affecting vulnerable marine ecosystems; (iv) to reject any proposal on the field-testing and marketing of so-called terminator technologies through a case-by-case assessment or approval of genetic use restriction technologies; (v) to ensure the development of biodiversity indicators, due to the lack of coherent information on the effectiveness of measures already taken; and (vi) to reach an agreement on a robust regime of requirements for the documentation accompanying shipments of living modified organisms.

Also in March 2006, the Council adopted its conclusions regarding the third meeting of the Conference of the Parties (COP/MOP 3) serving as the meeting of the Parties to the Cartagena Protocol on Biosafety (CBD) (Curitiba, Brazil, 13

[160] Commission Press Release IP/06/1428, 19 Oct. 2006 (RAPID).

[161] P6_TA(2006)0098, available on the Internet at: http://www.europarl.europa.eu/; see also Bulletin EU 3–2006, point 1.21.6. Convention on Biological Diversity (CBD), Rio de Janeiro (Brazil), 5 June 1992 (entered into force 29 Dec. 1993), (1992) 31 *International Legal Materials* 818.

to 17 March 2006).[162] The Council called for the adoption of a decision on documentation requirements for shipments of living modified organisms (LMOs) intended for direct use as food or feed or for processing. It also called for COP/MOP 3 to take necessary steps further to implement and to arrive at an effective international biosafety framework: (i) by improving effective information exchange through the Biosafety Clearing House, in particular by urging parties to provide relevant information, enhancing interoperability, facilitating information access, and strengthening capacity-building efforts; (ii) by strengthening efforts on risk assessment through the exchange of knowledge and practical experiences, where cooperation and training activities could be modelled on EU capacity-building projects, and by deciding to convene national, regional, or sub-regional workshops, the outcome of which should be reviewed at COP/MOP 4; (iii) by ensuring user-friendly and easy-to-handle monitoring and reporting requirements, having regard to Parties' capacity, and establishing an adequate system for the effective implementation of the Protocol; (iv) by initiating a simple and efficient assessment and review process for the evaluation of effectiveness of the Protocol with the overall goal of furthering its effective implementation; and (v) by agreeing a realistic budget consistent with the agreed priorities and programme of work for the Protocol.

The Council also issued in March 2006 its conclusions regarding the eighth ordinary meeting of the Conference of the Parties (COP 8) to the CBD.[163] The Council expressed its 'deep concern' over the continuing and unprecendented rate of overall loss of biodiversity, as starkly highlighted by the findings of the Millennium Ecosystem Assessment[164] and the Global Biodiversity Outlook.[165] While underlining that the effective protection of marine biodiversity could only be achieved if measures taken in areas beyond and within national jurisdiction were coherent, compatible, and without prejudice to the rights and obligations of coastal states under international law, the Council stressed the importance of the international community working towards integrated governance of marine biodiversity in areas beyond national jurisdiction, inter alia, by: (i) developing an implementation agreement under the United Nations Convention on the Law of the Sea (UNCLOS)[166] on the conservation and sustainable use of marine biodiversity, so as to adopt an integrated management approach to these marine areas, including to facilitate and formalize the identification, establishment and management by 2012 of representative networks of marine protected areas;

[162] 2713th environment Council meeting, Brussels 9 Mar. 2006, available on the Internet at: http://www.consilium.europa.eu/ueDocs/cms_Data/docs/pressdata/en/envir/88721.pdf. Cartagena Protocol on Biosafety (BSP), Montréal, QC (Canada), 29 Jan. 2000 (entered into force 11 Sept. 2003), (2000) 39 *International Legal Materials* 5, 1027.

[163] Bull. EU 3–2006, point 1.21.5.

[164] See: http://www.maweb.org.

[165] See: http://www.biodiv.org/gbo.

[166] Montego Bay (Jamaica), 10 Dec. 1982 (entered into force 16 Nov. 1994), published on the Internet at: http://www.un.org/Depts/los/index.htm.

and (ii) considering/analysing options and approaches as necessary for the further conservation of biodiversity, including in relation to genetic resources. The Council also called for urgent action to halt destructive practices affecting vulnerable marine ecosystems and for the consideration on a case-by-case basis and on a scientific basis, including the application of the precautionary approach, of the interim prohibition of destructive fishing practices, including bottom trawling.

The Council welcomed the outcome of the eighth meeting of the Conference of the Parties to the CBD (COP 8), urged the Commission and the Member States to play an active and constructive role in those, and called upon them to ensure the implementation of the CBD Bonn Guidelines and other Access and Benefit Sharing (ABS) related agreements.[167] The Council emphasized the importance of the full implementation of the Cartagena Protocol on Biosafety[168] and of the MOP 3 decision on documentation requirements for transboundary movements of GMOs. It reiterated the support for a process of elaborating an implementation agreement on the protection of marine biodiversity in areas beyond national jurisdiction under UNCLOS and considered this as an important contribution to achieving, inter alia, the objective agreed in the Johannesburg Plan of Implementation of establishing representative networks of marine protected areas by the year 2012. The Council also addressed trade and environment matters. It called upon the Commission to continue efforts to promote integration of biodiversity in the WTO Doha negotiations, and to enhance mutual support between multilateral trade agreements and biodiversity-related Multilateral Environmental Agreements (MEAs), as well as bilateral and regional agreements. It urged the Commission to explore options for further ensuring that imports of wild fauna and flora, including wild birds, to the EU were fully supportive of biodiversity objectives and did not pose a risk for their survival in the wild.

ii. International Agreement on Tropical Timber

In August 2006, the Commission submitted a Proposal for a Council Decision regarding the position to be taken by the Community within the International Tropical Timber Council on the extension of the International Agreement on Tropical Timber, 1994.[169] This International Agreement had entered into force on 1 January 1996 and was due to expire on 31 December 2006, after two periods of extension. A successor Agreement to the International Tropical Timber Agreement of 1994 was negotiated and concluded within the United Nations

[167] Council conclusions concerning its 2773rd Meeting of 18 Dec. 2006, published on the Internet at: http://www.consilium.europa.eu/ueDocs/cms_Data/docs/pressData/en/envir/92249.pdf.

[168] N. 162 above.

[169] COM(2006)469, 29 Aug. 2006.

Conference on Trade and Development (UNCTAD) in January 2006.[170] Under the provisions of Article 46 of the International Tropical Timber Agreement of 1994, a proposal was made at the 40th session of the International Tropical Timber Council held from 29 May to 3 June 2006 in Mérida (Mexico) to extend the Agreement until the entry into force of the successor Agreement of 2006. The purpose of the proposal was to authorize the EC to vote in favour of extending the Agreement. On 7 November 2006, the Council adopted a Decision regarding the position to be taken by the Community.[171] According to the Decision, the EC's position was to vote in favour of extending of the International Agreement on Tropical Timber, 1994, until the provisional or definitive entry into force of the successor Agreement of 2006.[172] In addition, the EC was to seek for an International Tropical Timber Council Decision aiming at limiting the duration of the extension of the International Tropical Timber Agreement, 1994, or establishing a review clause.[173]

iii. International Whaling Commission

The Commission regretted that the Member States did not present a united position at the International Whaling Commission (IWC) meeting in St Kitts and Nevis from 16 to 20 June 2006, in which a motion that a ban on hunting whales was no longer necessary was adopted.[174] The Commission acknowledged that the increasing strength of pro-whaling nations in the IWC was a reminder of the urgency of joining EU forces around a common position on that important issue. The Commission also recalled that the Community was not a party to the IWC. As long as that situation prevailed, the Community had only observer status at the IWC meeting. The Commission was determined to use the Community's observer status in the IWC 'to the fullest extent' in order to increase EU coordination and support all initiatives aiming at ensuring an appropriate level of protection of whales worldwide, already achieved at Community level under the Habitats Directive and also under the CITES Regulation.

G. Conclusion

It is undeniable that the EU institutions are concerned about the progressive deterioration of biodiversity in Europe and worldwide. However, the variety of instruments and, particularly, policy instruments submitted by the Commission

[170] Information available on the Internet at: http://www.unctad.org/Templates/Meeting.asp?m=11153&intItemID=1942&lang=1.

[171] [2006] OJ C298/1.

[172] Ibid., Art. 1.

[173] Ibid., Art. 2.

[174] Information on this meeting is available on the Internet at: http://www.iwcoffice.org/meetings/meeting2006.htm. See also A. Smith, written question E-3145/06; C. Stihler, written question E-31885/06.

seem to repeat previous aims and actions, albeit in a different format and order. In addition, the continuous release of further instruments trying to outline, in a comprehensive manner, the main actions to be adopted at different levels may paradoxically hinder the reach of the two basic pillar of EU biodiversity strategy, namely, the Birds and Habitats Directives. What really matters is, as usual, the correct enforcement of those obligations for the proper completion of the Natura 2000 network. As questions submitted by MEPs reflect, the Commission cannot cope with the amount of projects that are currently being developed in the EU breaching the basic tenets in Article 6(3) and (4) of the Habitats Directive. The ECJ has adopted a rather strict standpoint regarding the application of that provision. Nevertheless, national authorities are either slow to integrate that body of case law in their national legislation and/or practices, as reflected by Commission's actions demanding compliance with previous ECJ rulings, or unwilling fully to apply it to projects and plans, particularly those encouraged by the authorities themselves. This attitude may be favoured by the Commission since this institution has refrained itself from publishing its opinions delivered under Article 6(4) of the Habitats Directive. This contradicts the basic tenets of the transparency principle and hinders public knowledge of activities that are currently affecting a variety of Natura 2000 zones.

VI. Waste

Geert van Calster and Wim Vandenberghe***

A. Legislation Adopted

i. Codification of EC Waste Rules

The Waste Framework Directive (WFD) was originally adopted in 1975 as Directive 75/442/EEC.[1] Because of the extent to which it had been amended since its original adoption in 1975, most substantially in 1991 through Directive 91/156/EEC amending Directive 75/442/EEC,[2] a decision was made by the European Commission (Commission) to clarify the WFD by consolidating legislation. The outcome is that Directive 75/442/EEC (as amended) was repealed with effect from 17 May 2006 and the WFD's provisions are now contained in Directive 2006/12/EC on Waste (2006 Waste Framework Directive or

* Institute for Environmental and Energy Law (IMER); Collegium Falconis, K.U.Leuven (Belgium); visiting lecturer, Oxford University; Member of the Brussels Bar, of counsel, DLA Piper, Brussels (Belgium).

** Member of the Brussels Bar, DLA Piper, Brussels (Belgium).

[1] [1975] OJ L194/38.

[2] [1991] OJ L78/32.

2006 WFD).[3] The 2006 WFD is nothing more than a codification of Directives 75/442/EEC and 91/156/EEC and is *not* connected to the proposed revision of the WFD—which is still being discussed in the European Parliament (EP).[4] The question arises why the Commission deemed it necessary to draw up a codification when at the same time a substantial revision of the WFD is planned (see below).

ii. Waste Shipments Regulation

On 14 June 2006, the EP and Council agreed on Regulation (EC) No. 1013/2006 on Shipments of Waste (2006 Waste Shipments Regulation).[5] This Regulation will replace Regulation (EEC) No. 259/93 on the Supervision and Control of Shipments of Waste within, into and out of the European Community (Waste Shipments Regulation)[6] with effect from 12 July 2007. Its aim is to reinforce, simplify, and specify the existing procedures for controlling waste shipments in order to reduce the risk of waste shipments not being controlled.

Key changes include: (i) provision for a simplified control procedure; (ii) more generic waste codes and one waste code per notification; (iii) introduction of a concept of 'interim' recovery or disposal; (iv) inclusion of shipments of non-notifiable waste within the scope of the Regulation; and (v) a requirement to ensure any waste shipped is dealt with and managed in an environmentally sound manner throughout the shipment and during recovery/disposal.

Article 2 first of all introduces a series of new definitions: hazardous waste, mixtures of waste, interim disposal, interim recovery, environmentally sound management, producer, holder, collector, dealer, broker, area under the national jurisdiction of a country, overseas countries and territories, customs office of export from the Community, customs office of exit from the Community, customs office of entry into the Community, import, export, transit, transport, shipment, illegal shipment.

The new Regulation further reduces the three existing waste shipment control procedures which apply to waste shipments down to two:

1. the procedure for prior written notification and consent: applicable to all shipments of waste intended for disposal and hazardous and semi-hazardous waste intended for recovery;
2. the procedure in which shipments are accompanied by certain information: applicable to non-hazardous waste intended for recovery.

Which one of the above two procedures applies depends on: (i) the purpose for which the shipment is made (disposal or recovery); (ii) the classification of the

3 [2006] OJ L114/1.
4 Commission Proposal for a Directive on Waste COM(2005)667, 21 Dec. 2005.
5 [2006] OJ L190/1.
6 [1993] OJ L30/1.

waste; and (iii) the route which the waste takes. The control procedures have been simplified so that the same procedure of prior notification and written consent generally applies to all regulated (i.e. notifiable) shipments of waste, regardless of whether the shipment is for disposal or recovery and where it is destined. Title II of the Regulation sets out the detail of the control procedure, subject to some minor modifications in respect of particular types of movements.

The Regulation further reduces the number of lists of waste authorized for shipment from three to two, corresponding to the two control procedures described above: waste subject to notification and consent features in the 'orange list' (Annex IV), while waste referred to for information purposes only features in the 'green list' (Annex III). On the other hand, waste that is prohibited for shipment features in separate lists (Annex V). The new Regulation no longer contains a separate 'Red List'. Waste that was previously classified under the Red List is now found under various sections of Annex V (on waste subject to various prohibitions) of the new Regulation. The waste lists of the revised Waste Shipments Regulation have been changed to bring them into line with the lists annexed to the Convention on the Control of Transboundary Movements of Wastes and their Disposal (Basel Convention)[7] and the revised Organization for Economic Cooperation and Development (OECD) Decision. The new waste codes are much more generic than the ones in the existing Waste Shipments Regulation.

Waste shipments must be the subject of a contract between the person responsible for shipping the waste (the notifier), or having it shipped, and the consignee of such waste. With respect to the mandatory contract between the consignee and the notifier, the old Regulation listed information that could be included in the contract. It also required three conditions: (i) the notifier had to take back waste if the shipment had not been completed as planned or was effected in violation of the Regulation; (ii) the consignee was required to provide a certificate to the notifier stating that the waste had been disposed of/recovered in an environmentally sound manner; and (iii) if the waste was being transported for recovery and re-transferred to another Member State or third country, the consignee had to notify the initial country of dispatch.

As a new element, Article 5 provides that the contract between the notifier and the consignee must be concluded and effective at the time of notification. The new Regulation provides for the following contractual obligations:

- the notifier must take back the waste if the shipment, recovery, or disposal has not been completed as intended or has been effected as an illegal shipment and is the responsibility of the notifier;
- the consignee must recover/dispose of the waste if it has been effected as an illegal shipment and is the responsibility of the consignee;

[7] Basel (Switzerland) 22 Mar. 1989 (entered into force 5 May 1992), (1989) 28 *International Legal Materials* 3, 657.

- the facility of (non-interim) recovery or disposal must send a certificate of completion to the notifier and authorities concerned no later than 30 days after completion of the recovery/disposal, and no later than one calendar year or shorter if required by authorities, following receipt of the waste. Additional provisions must be included in the contract if the waste is shipped for interim recovery/disposal so as to enhance the traceability of the waste throughout the treatment chain.

Under the revised Waste Shipments Regulation, where shipments are made initially for storage or other 'interim' recovery or disposal operations, as defined by the Community Regulation, controls will continue until the notified waste is subjected to a substantive recovery or disposal operation. Notifiers will be required to provide information on the proposed substantive operations at the time of notification. Reference should be made to Article 15, which contains additional provisions regarding interim recovery and disposal operations. This Article establishes additional information and documentation requirements that connect the initial interim operation with all the subsequent treatment operations to which the waste will be submitted in order to improve the traceability of the waste and to reduce the possibilities of carrying out sham recovery.

In the old Regulation (in instances of certain wastes being shipped, for disposal or recovery, from one Member State to another and/or passing in transit through one or more additional Member States), the notifier was required to apply for authorization to the authorities of *destination*. The notifier was also required to send a copy of the application to the authorities of the States of dispatch, transit, and of the consignee (unless national legislation permitted otherwise). In the new Regulation, all applications for authorization must now be submitted to and through the competent authorities of dispatch which, in turn, will be responsible for passing it on to the competent authorities of destination and transit. The competent authorities must give their consent (with or without conditions) or express their objections within 30 days. Any changes involving the main aspects of the shipment (quantity, itinerary, etc.) must be the subject of a new notification, save in cases where all the competent authorities grant the notifier an exemption from this obligation. A new obligation is now placed on the competent authority to provide the notifier upon his/her request with a reasoned explanation if the notification has not been transmitted to the relevant authorities (Article 7).

An important simplification is provided for in Article 13. This provision allows for a general notification to cover several shipments insofar as they concern waste with essentially similar physical and chemical characteristics, which goes to the same consignee or facility and follows the same route. It is also worth noticing that such a general notification can only be valid for one calendar year, unless the receiving facility benefits from a pre-consent (see Article 14). In such a case the validity of the general notification may be extended up to three years.

The possible objections to shipments of waste destined for disposal are listed in Article 11. The grounds for objecting to a shipment for disposal still refer to the principles of proximity, priority for recovery, and self-sufficiency. These grounds have been extended when compared to Article 4(3) of the old Regulation with the following elements:

- reference is made to Article 4(1) of the Basel Convention that allows Member States to prohibit the import of inter alia hazardous waste (paragraph 1(e));
- if a facility is covered by Directive 96/61/EC concerning Integrated Pollution Prevention and Control (IPPC Directive)[8] and does not apply Best Available Techniques (BAT) (paragraph 1(h));
- if the waste is mixed municipal waste collected from households (paragraph 1(i));
- if the waste will not be treated in accordance with legally binding environmental protection standards established in Community legislation (paragraph 1(j)).

Article 12 provides for the possible objections to shipments of waste destined for recovery and has been extended when compared to Article 7(4) of the old Regulation with the following elements:

- the reference made to the WFD now includes not only Article 7 but also Articles 3, 4, and 10 (paragraph 1(a));
- standard dumping (paragraph 1(b));
- that the planned shipment or recovery would not be in accordance with national legislation in the country of dispatch relating to the recovery of waste, including where the planned shipment would concern waste destined for recovery in a facility which has lower treatment standards for the particular waste than those of the country of dispatch, respecting the need to ensure the proper functioning of the internal market (paragraph 1(c));
- environmental considerations alone may now be invoked to document that the recovery cannot be justified (paragraph 1(g)).[9] The Commission may draft guidelines for the application of the provision on this so-called 'sham recovery';
- if the waste is destined for disposal and not for recovery (paragraph 1(h));
- if a facility is covered by the IPPC Directive and does not apply BAT (paragraph 1(i));

[8] [1996] OJ L257/26.

[9] In Reg. 1993/25, n. 6 above, Art. 7(4)(a), fifth indent, economic and environmental factors had to be considered simultaneously.

- if the waste will not be treated in accordance with legally binding environmental protection standards or legally binding recovery or recycling obligations established in Community legislation (paragraph 1(j));
- if the waste will not be treated in accordance with waste management plans drawn up to ensure the implementation of legally binding recovery or recycling obligations established in Community legislation (paragraph 1(k)).

The objections foreseen in paragraph 1(c) in particular are contested. The previous Regulation already provided for the possibility for Member States to block shipments on the basis of their national 'waste management plans'. Common understanding of this exception was that it ought to be read in conjunction with the Treaty's Articles on the free movement of goods, an understanding which the ECJ however threw into doubt firstly with its *Daimler Chrysler* judgment (reported in earlier overviews) and subsequently in its *EU Wood Trading* and *Pedersen* judgments (reported below). In the two latter judgments, the Court also allowed Member States to block shipments on the basis that environment, health and safety regulations in the country of destination are less strict than in the country of dispatch. The Council of Ministers wanted to increase Member States' room for manoeuvre under this proviso, a move which was blocked by the Commission, arguing it would be incompatible with the Treaty to give Member States a blank cheque in relation to their waste management plans. The result is a rather complicated compromise (not quoted in its totality above) which inevitably will lead to further judicial review with the European Court of Justice (ECJ).

There is a further obligation on the producer, notifier, and other undertakings involved in a shipment of waste, and/or its recovery or disposal, to take the necessary steps to ensure that any waste they ship is managed in an environmentally sound manner and without endangering human health throughout the shipment and during its recovery and disposal (Article 49). This applies to both notifiable and non-notifiable shipments. For now, Article 49 refers to Annex VIII which lists briefly the guidelines which were adopted under the Basel Convention by the OECD and the International Maritime Organization. However, consideration 33 states that the European Union (EU) should establish a list of non-binding guidelines in which guidance is given on environmentally sound management of waste.

Articles 22 to 25 give a detailed description of the conditions under which the so-called take-back obligation applies and of who shall be charged for the costs arising. Different rules apply when the shipment cannot be completed and when the shipment is illegal.

Finally, the Regulation includes other general provisions, such as a ban on the mixing of waste during shipment, an obligation to make available to the general public the appropriate information, and the obligation on the part of the notifier, the competent authority, the consignee, and the facilities concerned to archive documents and information.

iii. Radioactive Waste Shipment Rules

Directive 92/3/Euratom on the Supervision and Control of Shipments of Radioactive Waste between Member States and into and out of the Community[10] was adopted to establish a system of strict control and prior authorization for shipments of radioactive waste in order to avoid illicit traffic of such materials. The Directive applies both to the shipments between the Member States and to import into and export from the Community.

The revision process of Directive 92/3/Euratom was initiated in 2004 and resulted in Directive 2006/117/Euratom on the Supervision and Control of Shipments of Radioactive Waste and Spent Fuel.[11] The Directive fulfils a fourfold goal: (i) consistency with latest Euratom Directives;[12] (ii) consistency with international Conventions, in particular in view of the International Atomic Energy Agency (IAEA) Joint Convention on the Safety of Spent Fuel Management and on the Safety of Radioactive Waste Management;[13] (iii) clarification of the procedure in practice and improvement of the Directive's structure; and (iv) extension of the scope to spent fuel.

The new Directive extends first of all its rules so as to cover shipments of spent nuclear fuel—including those for reprocessing—rather than just radioactive waste.[14] Under Directive 92/3/Euratom, spent fuel for which no use is foreseen is considered as 'radioactive waste' and shipments of such materials are subject to the uniform control procedure laid down in the Directive. However, shipments of spent fuel for reprocessing were not subject to such a procedure. This led to the inconsistency that the same material is or is not subject to this procedure depending on its intended use. Shipments of spent fuel not considered as waste are now also subject to the procedures laid down in the new Directive. Taking into account the tensions between pro- and anti-nuclear Member States, a new Article 3 stresses that the Directive shall not affect the right of governments to export spent fuel for reprocessing.

Article 5 provides for a bunch of new or amended definitions: spent fuel; shipment; reprocessing; intra-community shipment; extra-community shipment; disposal; storage; country or Member State of transit; disused source; recognized installation; duly completed application.

10 [1992] OJ L35/24.

11 [2006] OJ L337/28.

12 Dir. 96/29/Euratom laying down Basic Safety Standards for the Protection of the Health of Workers and the General Public against the Dangers arising from Ionising Radiation [1996] OJ L314/20; and Dir. 2003/122/Euratom on the Control of High-activity Sealed Radioactive Sources and Orphan Sources [2003] OJ L346/57, in particular relating to the wording of the provisions on reshipment of radioactive sealed sources.

13 Vienna (Austria), 5 Sept. 1997 (entered into force 18 June 2001), published on the Internet at: http://www.iaea.org/Publications/Documents/Conventions/jointconv.html.

14 Art. 5(1) defines spent fuel as: 'nuclear fuel that has been irradiated in and permanently removed from a reactor core; spent fuel may either be considered as usable resource that can be reprocessed or be destined for final disposal with no further use foreseen and treated as radioactive waste'.

Article 6 contains the rules on the application for a shipment authorization—which is done through the competent authorities of the Member State of origin.[15] Article 6(1) now uses the less ambiguous wording—'who plans to carry out a shipment'—instead of 'intends to carry out a shipment' as mentioned in the old Directive. This new expression will avoid in practice difficulties deriving from considerations as to the 'intentional' character of a shipment, while ensuring the timeliness of applications (so that they are not lodged too far in advance).

Contrary to the provision in Article 6(4) of the old Directive 92/3/Euratom, the automatic consent procedure is no longer optional, but shall apply to any shipment (see Article 9).[16] A country of transit or of destination that does not give any reply as regards an intended shipment is deemed to have approved such shipment (Article 9(2) provides for this tacit approval). Now, acknowledgement of receipt is requested within one month, and the period for notifying acceptance/refusal is extended to maximum three months (two months reply + one month extension on request).[17] This new timetable for consent or refusal should lessen the administrative burden and generate more legal certainty.

Like its predecessor, the Directive imposes a system of mandatory prior consent from authorities in countries of destination or transit before a radioactive shipment transport can proceed. For the first time, it extends this requirement to non-EU countries of destination (see Chapter 3 of the Directive).

Article 12 deals with shipment failure. This provision corresponds to Article 15 of Directive 92/3/Euratom, but the following points have been clarified: (i) the right of the Member State of origin, transit, or destination to abort a shipment, in the conditions laid down in the same provision; and (ii) the obligation of the Member State of origin in connection with take-back responsibility of the holder. In line with article 27 of the Joint Convention, the possibility to make an alternative safe arrangement is given, for such cases where the taking-back is not justified from the radiological point of view. Article 12(3) further holds the requirement that the holder is liable for the costs arising in case of shipment failure. This requirement should not prevent mechanisms established by the Member States at the national level or any contractual arrangement between the holder and any other person involved in the shipment, from applying.

Member States are required to transpose the Directive into national law by 25 December 2008, at which time the 1992 Directive will be repealed. The Commission is required to issue a new standard document for consent procedures by the same time (Article 17). The Member States should also report on the Directive's implementation by 25 December 2011 and every three years afterwards (Article 20).

[15] Shipment authorizations do not replace any specific national requirements for the shipments such as transport licences.

[16] Under the old Directive, Member States (of destination or of transit) had the possibility of refusing the automatic procedure for granting consent to shipments.

[17] Arts. 8 and 9.

iv. EU Mining Waste Directive

The new Directive 2006/21/EC on the Management of Waste from Extractive Industries and amending Directive 2004/35/EC entered into force on 1 May 2006.[18] Member States must transpose the Directive into national law by 1 May 2008. They must subject mine waste facilities to the new provisions by 2012.[19]

The Directive aims at preventing accidents and consequent damage to the environment and human health arising from the treatment and disposal of mining waste, by setting minimum requirements intended to improve mining waste management. Waste is understood as waste arising from the prospecting, extraction (including the pre-production development stage), treatment and storage of mineral resources and from the working of quarries.[20] The Directive exempts mining waste from the provisions of Directive 1999/31/EC on the Landfill of Waste (Landfill Directive)[21] and of the Waste Framework Directive (except for aspects which are not specifically covered by the provisions of the new Directive).

In order to obtain the above objective, the following are the main elements of the Directive: conditions for operating permits; general obligations concerning waste management; the duty to characterize waste before disposing of it or treating it; measures to ensure the safety of waste management facilities; a requirement to draw up closure plans; a duty to provide for an appropriate level of financial security.

The Directive requires in Article 7 that all operators must apply for a permit, which demands a waste management plan, to be allowed to operate. The Directive lists conditions to be attached to operating permits in order to ensure that sufficient environmental and safety measures are in place before waste facilities receive authorization. In addition, Member States should take the necessary measures to ensure that the competent authorities periodically reconsider and, where necessary, update the permit conditions.

The competent authority shall require a financial guarantee from the operator before the latter begins to operate the facility (Article 14).[22] The financial guarantee should ensure that all obligations flowing from the permit will be fulfilled,

[18] [2006] OJ L102/15. See also G. Van Calster and W. Vandenberghe, 'Substantive European Community Environmental Law: Waste' (2006) 6 *Yearbook of European Environmental Law*, 341–2.

[19] Dir. 2006/21/EC, n. 18 above, Arts. 22, 24, 25, and 26 (implementing, transitional and transposition provisions).

[20] Thus not those waste streams which, albeit generated in the course of mineral extraction or treatment operations, are not directly linked to the extraction or treatment process, e.g. food waste, waste oil, end-of-life vehicles, spent batteries, and accumulators. See also Art. 2(2), which exempts certain waste streams from the Directive's range of application and which further gives Member States the freedom to exempt other non-hazardous waste types. Significant is also that (extractive) waste is defined by reference to the broad definition of 'waste' contained in the Waste Framework Directive, as interpreted by the ECJ (in particularly the *Palin Granit* case, Case C-9/00 *Palin Granit Oy* [2002] ECR I-2357).

[21] [1999] OJ L182/1.

[22] Dir, 2006/21/EC, n. 18 above. Art. 14(1) gives as examples: a financial deposit, including industry-sponsored mutual guarantee funds.

including those relating to the closure and after-closure of the waste facility. The guarantee should also ensure that funds should be readily available at any given time for the rehabilitation of all land affected by the waste facility. However, this more stringent environmental safeguard, which could result in substantial potential financial liabilities of the industry, is tempered by the linkage of the financial guarantee to the operator's mining permit, thus effectively limiting the liability to a specific limited geographical scope (a demand of the Council of Ministers). The size of the guarantee shall be periodically adjusted in accordance with any rehabilitation work needed to be carried out on the land affected by the waste facility.

All operators will have to report on their facilities at least once a year. Waste management plans for the prevention or minimization, treatment, recovery, and disposal of extractive waste need to be drawn up (Article 5). Such plans should be structured in such a way as to ensure appropriate planning of waste management options with a view to minimizing waste generation and its harmfulness, and encouraging waste recovery. The plans will be reviewed every five years. Consideration 13 further obliges the operator to characterize waste before disposing of it or treating it with respect to its composition in order to ensure that, as far as possible, such waste reacts only in predictable ways. Annex II provides to this end a list of aspects which should be included in the waste characterization.

Member States are now also required to ensure that operators, when placing extractive waste back into excavation voids for rehabilitation and construction purposes, monitor not only the extractive waste but also the excavation void itself (Article 10). Excavation voids are large holes remaining after mineral extraction, which very often contain waste rock etc. and which can give rise to water pollution.

The Directive also lays out specific duties on prevention of air, soil, and water pollution (Article 13). With regard to water pollution prevention, the Directive provides that the disposal of extractive waste into any receiving body of water (groundwater, surface waters etc.) should comply with Directive 2000/60/EC establishing a Framework for Community Action in the Field of Water Policy (Water Framework Directive)[23] as a mine waste site is regarded as a point source under this Directive.

The obligation to draw up closure plans for waste management facilities is a key provision to ensure that closure operations form an integral part of the overall exploitation plan of the operator.

Article 6 obliges Member States to ensure that major-accident hazards with regard to so-called category A waste facilities are identified and that the necessary features are incorporated into the design, construction, operation and maintenance, closure and after-closure of the waste facility in order to prevent such accidents and to limit their adverse consequences for human health and/or the

[23] [2000] OJ L327/1.

environment, including any transboundary impacts.[24] Apart from these major-accident policy obligations, operators are obliged to draw up emergency plans and appoint a safety manager.

Finally, the Directive covers not only the operational phase but also closure and after-care, and imposes an obligation for proper monitoring (Article 12). Once a waste facility is closed, operators will still be bound by provisions on major accident hazards, cyanide pollution, and water status deterioration, but will be exempt from requirements for waste management plans, permits, and financial guarantees.

v. More Stringent EU Battery Rules

The Commission argued that the existing Directive 91/157/EEC on Batteries and Accumulators containing Certain Dangerous Substances (Batteries Directive)[25] has failed adequately to control the risks posed by batteries in the waste stream and to create a homogeneous framework for battery collection and recycling. The Batteries Directive indeed has a limited scope since it only applies to batteries with a certain mercury, cadmium, and lead content. Those batteries are classified as 'hazardous waste' on the basis of the European Waste List. This Directive only covers 7 per cent of all portable batteries placed on the EU market annually. This has hindered the setting up of efficient national collection and recycling schemes. It also confused consumers about what to collect and not to collect, leading to little participation in the national collection schemes. The Directive also did not set a collection target in order to monitor the efficiency of the national collection schemes.

The Batteries Directive further needed to be revised to be aligned with the Sixth Environment Action Programme[26] and Directive 2002/96/EC on Waste Electrical and Electronic Equipment (WEEE Directive).[27]

The Commission subsequently proposed to revise the Batteries Directive and this, eventually, after protracted negotiations indeed, led to the adoption of Directive 2006/66/EC on Batteries and Accumulators and Waste Batteries and Accumulators and repealing Directive 91/157/EEC (New Batteries Directive).[28] The New Batteries Directive must be implemented in all EU Member States by 26 September 2008. The goal of the Directive is to (further) harmonize Member States' legislation to minimize the negative impact of batteries and accumulators on the environment.

The main requirements of the new Directive are summarized below.

[24] 'Category A' facilities are the most high-risk extractive waste facilities.

[25] [1991] OJ L78/38.

[26] Dec. 1600/2002/EC laying down the Sixth Community Environment Action Programme [2002] OJ L242/13.

[27] [2003] OJ L37/24. As will be seen below, the producer registration, take-back, and financial responsibilities closely parallel those outlined in the WEEE Dir.

[28] [2006] OJ L266/1.

The New Batteries Directive applies to all types of batteries and accumulators, regardless of their shape, volume, weight, material composition, or use. This means that the Directive applies to batteries and accumulators that are sold separately and also batteries and accumulators within electronic devices (e.g. mp3 players, laptops, PDAs).[29] However, the new Directive will not apply to equipment specifically intended for military purposes or equipment designed to be sent into space (Article 2).

In line with the former Batteries Directive, the new Directive restricts the use of certain substances in batteries. However, the New Batteries Directive holds greater substance restrictions (Article 4). It bans first of all the sale of all batteries and accumulators containing more than 0.0005 per cent of mercury (Hg) per weight, except for button cells with less than 2 per cent mercury by weight. For portable batteries and accumulators, it is prohibited to use more than 0.002 per cent of cadmium (Cd) per weight.[30] There is an exemption for emergency lighting and alarm systems, cordless powertools (hotly contested), and medical equipment.[31] Though the Directive imposes strict limits on the content of cadmium and mercury in batteries, the new law is less stringent than earlier drafts that proposed a total ban on cadmium batteries. Member States are required to promote research and the marketing of batteries with less polluting substances (in particular mercury, cadmium, and lead).

Further, collection schemes must be in place for certain types of batteries and accumulators (Article 8). For portable batteries, Member States will be required to set up national collection systems to allow consumers to return spent portable batteries free of charge. Some Member States already have such systems in place, like BEBAT in Belgium, but by September 2008, every EU country will have to have a collection scheme for spent batteries, with easily accessible collection points made available to consumers. The 2008 deadline for setting up collection schemes will apply to the collection of industrial and automotive batteries and accumulators. Producers of industrial batteries will have to take back industrial batteries from end-users.[32] Producers of automotive batteries will also have to set up collection schemes for the batteries not collected according to the requirements of Directive 2000/53/EC on End-of-Life Vehicles (ELV Directive).[33] According

[29] This equipment is already covered by the WEEE Dir. and Dir. 2002/95/EC on the Restriction of the Use of Certain Hazardous Substances in Electrical and Electronic Equipment (RoHS Dir.) [2003] OJ L37/19.

[30] New Batteries Dir., n. 28 above, Art. 3(3) defines portable batteries as: 'sealed batteries, capable of being carried by hand by a single person without effort, and are neither industrial nor automotive batteries'. This includes single-cell batteries, batteries and accumulators used by consumers in mobile phones, toys, household appliances (electric toothbrushes, razors, etc.), and other consumer products.

[31] The exemption for cordless power tools will be reviewed by 2010.

[32] These collection schemes also lead to an obligatory role for distributors to take back portable batteries.

[33] [2000] OJ L269/43. Note that if a battery is incorporated in an end-of-life vehicle, it will be collected on the basis of the ELV Dir. Collection will be paid by the car producers. Battery

to Article 10, Member States will have to achieve a minimum collection rate of 25 per cent by 2012 (to be increased to 45 per cent by 2016).

Treatment and recycling schemes must be established by 26 September 2009 at the latest (Article 12). Member States will still be able to landfill portable batteries containing cadmium, mercury, or lead, instead of recycling them, if no viable end-market is available, or as part of a strategy to phase out heavy metals showing, on the basis of an impact assessment, that disposal is a better option than recycling.[34] Minimum treatment requirements are detailed in Annex III to the Directive and foresee for example that treatment must include, as a minimum, removal of all fluids and acids. Member States must meet a target to recycle 50 per cent of general consumer batteries by 2010. By the same date, countries must achieve stricter recycling targets for lead-acid and nickel-cadmium batteries of 65 and 75 per cent respectively (Annex III). The Directive includes provisions requiring Member States to encourage the development of new recycling and treatment technologies for batteries and accumulators (Article 13). It also allows Member States to use economic instruments, such as taxes, to promote the collection of waste batteries and accumulators or to promote the use of batteries and accumulators containing less polluting substances (Article 9).

To meet the above collection and recycling targets (stated respectively in Articles 10 and 12), Member States must ensure that, in line with the producer responsibility principle, battery producers finance the collection, treatment, and recycling of waste batteries and accumulators collected (Article 16). In addition to collection, treatment, and recycling, producers will have to finance public information campaigns to encourage the separate collection of used portable batteries.[35] 'Producers' include producers of batteries and accumulators and products incorporating a battery or accumulator. They are thus financially responsible for the waste management of batteries and accumulators they place on the EU market.

'Battery producer' is every producer who places a battery on the national market.[36] This means that if a battery is incorporated in electrical or electronic equipment or a car, the equipment producers/car producers are also regarded as 'battery producers' under the new Batteries Directive.[37] In the case of electrical and

producers become responsible for further treatment once the car battery is removed from the end-of-life vehicle.

34 This is an exemption to the 100 per cent ban on the landfilling and incineration of automotive and industrial batteries as stated in Art. 14.

35 See also New Batteries Dir., n. 28 above, Art. 20.

36 Ibid., Art. 3(12).

37 In the Commission Proposal, producers of electrical and electronic equipment as well as car producers were not covered by the 'battery producer' definition. In its Common Position, the Council changed this producer definition in two ways. Firstly, producers of electrical and electronic equipment as well as car producers were covered by this definition if their products would also contain a battery the moment the product was placed on the market. This broader definition of the term 'battery producer' was considered necessary in order to avoid any gaps in the financing system for the waste management of batteries. Secondly, on the basis of experience with the implementation of the

electronic products containing batteries, however, Member States must ensure that producers are not double-charged under both the New Battery Directive and the WEEE Directive.[38]

Producers must now register with the Member States where they export batteries and accumulators (Article 17). It is not clear at this stage whether an EU address or a bank account will be required, as it is currently the case in some Member States for electrical and electronic waste. However, the Battery Directive specifies that the same registration procedures should be used in all Member States.

Regarding compliance, the Battery Directive does provide some flexibility for exempting producers who place very small quantities of batteries and accumulators on their national market from the obligation to finance costs arising from collection, treatment, and recycling, on the condition that this exemption does not impede the functioning of the collection and recycling schemes (Article 18).

Article 11 imposes a new design obligation on the manufacturers of all appliances containing batteries: they have to design products to allow batteries to be removed easily at the end of their life. This requirement continues the Eco-design life cycle thinking goal of the WEEE Directive for improving product design to both 'prevent WEEE' and to increase product recoverability, reusability, and recyclability. Appliances must be accompanied by instructions showing how batteries can be removed safely. These provisions do not apply where for 'safety, performance, medical or data integrity reasons' continuity of power supply is necessary. This vague exception may be interpreted differently (i.e. restrictively or not) by Member States.

In order to tackle the free rider problem, Member States must keep a national register of all battery producers and importers who market their product in the national territories (Article 17). The procedural requirements will be harmonized on the basis of a comitology procedure.

The Directive also sets out a range of information that must be provided to product end-users, and minimum labelling obligations.[39] Battery producers must label batteries and accumulators with the crossed-out wheeled bin symbol to indicate separate collection. In addition, batteries containing more than

WEEE Dir., the Council was of the opinion that battery producers should be defined referring to the national market, not to the Community market as initially proposed by the Commission. Member States claim that it is only possible to implement the producer responsibility requirements if a responsible producer can be found on the national territory. See Commission Proposal for a Directive of the European Parliament and of the Council on Batteries and Accumulators and Spent Batteries and Accumulators 2003(COM)723, 24 Nov. 2003, and Common Position (EC) No. 30/2005 of 18 July 2005 adopted by the Council, acting in accordance with the procedure referred to in Article 251 of the Treaty establishing the European Community, with a view to adopting a Directive of the European Parliament and of the Council on Batteries and Accumulators and Waste Batteries and Accumulators and repealing Directive 91/157/EEC [2005] OJ C264E/1.

[38] New Batteries Dir., n. 28 above, Art. 16(2).

[39] Ibid., Arts. 20 and 21.

0.0005 per cent mercury, more than 0.002 per cent cadmium, or more than 0.004 per cent lead must be marked with the appropriate chemical symbol (Hg, Cd, Pb). As of 26 September 2009, portable and automotive batteries will have to carry labels showing their capacity, to be defined in terms of hours of use. The requirement to provide this end-user visibility of battery/accumulator capacity is aimed at encouraging the use of longer-lasting batteries. The detailed rules for implementing this requirement including the harmonized method for determining capacity and appropriate use will be determined no later than 26 March 2009. Producers will then have six months (i.e. until 26 September 2009) to implement this capacity labelling requirement.

The Directive encourages Member States to conclude environmental agreements on the obligations relating to waste stream monitoring, collection and recycling, and consumer information, provided that such agreements are enforceable (Article 27).

vi. Exemptions in the RoHS Directive

The RoHS Directive restricts the use of certain substances, such as lead, mercury, cadmium, hexavalent chromium, and certain brominated flame retardants in electrical and electronic equipment.[40] It lays down provisions to ensure that from 1 July 2006 new electrical and electronic equipment put on the market does not contain any of these substances. Certain exemptions apply, inter alia, to the use of mercury in compact and straight fluorescent lamps, as well as to the use of lead in different types of solders and as an alloying element. The RoHS Directive requires the Commission to evaluate certain hazardous substances prohibited pursuant to Article 4(1). Pursuant to Article 5(1)(c), each exemption listed in the Annex must be subject to a review at least every four years or four years after an item has been added to the list.

Following a review by technical experts, the Commission adopted four Decisions in October 2006 which exempt certain materials and components which contain lead, cadmium, and/or hexavalent chromium.[41] The exemptions are justified since the use of these hazardous substances in those specific materials and components is still unavoidable or technically or scientifically impracticable,

[40] N. 29 above.

[41] Dec. 2006/310/EC amending, for the purposes of adapting to the technical progress, the Annex to Directive 2002/95/EC of the European Parliament and of the Council as regards Exemptions for Applications of Lead (notified under document number C(2006)1622) [2006] OJ L115/38; Dec. 2006/690/EC amending, for the purposes of adapting to technical progress, the Annex to Directive 2002/95/EC of the European Parliament and of the Council as regards Exemptions for Applications of Lead in Crystal Glass (notified under document number C(2006)4789) [2006] OJ L283/47; Dec. 2006/691/EC amending, for the purposes of adapting to technical progress, the Annex to Directive 2002/95/EC of the European Parliament and of the Council as regards Exemptions for Applications of Lead and Cadmium (notified under document number C(2006)4790) [2006] OJ L283/48; Dec. 2006/692/EC amending, for the purposes of adapting to technical progress, the Annex to Directive 2002/95/EC of the European Parliament and of the Council as regards Exemptions for Applications of Hexavalent Chromium (notified under document number C(2006)4791) [2006] OJ L283/50.

or because the negative environmental, health, or consumer safety impacts caused by substitution are likely to outweigh the environmental, health, or consumer safety benefits thereof.

vii. Special Provisions for the Shipment of Waste to New Member States

Five acceding countries (Hungary, Latvia, Malta, Poland, and Slovakia) benefit in their respective Accession Treaties from transition periods for the implementation of legislative requirements applying to facilities which treat waste.[42] This has given rise to the need, for a limited time, to complement the Waste Shipments Regulation (now revised) by additional provisions guaranteeing that waste is not shipped from other Member States to facilities in these five new Member States. These restrictions have two main objectives: (i) to prevent such shipments from damaging the environment of the new Member State; (ii) to allow the new Member State to carry out a harmonious development of its waste management infrastructure and be fully capable of managing its own waste before facing imports of waste for recovery.

B. Legislation in Progress

i. Revision of the Waste Framework Directive

Slow progress is being made with the revision of the Waste Framework Directive. The approach taken is that it is better to get it right than to rush to an early adoption. The most important discussion in 2006 took place during the EP's Environmental Committee meeting of 28 November.[43] The Committee remarked during this first reading of the co-decision procedure on the Commission's Proposal[44] that the new approach suggested by the Commission, based on the life cycle of a product, was too theoretical and that it preferred to stick 'as a general rule' to the current policy of waste hierarchy. The latter ranks treatments in five categories, from the most to the least environmentally sound.[45] The Committee said that Member States should be allowed to depart from this hierarchy 'when life-cycle assessments and cost-benefit analyses indicate clearly that an alternative treatment option shows a better record' (Article 1). Other amendments by the Committee focused on the following areas (evidently not all of these proposed amendments carry the approval of Council):

[42] The transitional arrangements are contained in the Annexes to the Treaty of Accession 2003. The full text of this Treaty is published on the Internet at: http://eurlex.europa.eu/JOHtml.do?uri=OJ:L:2003:236:SOM:EN:HTML.

[43] A summary of this meeting is published on the Internet at: http://www.europarl.europa.eu/oeil/FindByProcnum.do?lang=2&procnum=COD/2005/0281.

[44] N. 4 above.

[45] I.e. prevention, reuse, recycling, recovery, and disposal.

- There should be a better distinction between waste and by-products which can still be used industrially, such as glass, metal, or compost. The Commission should issue 'interpretative guidelines on the basis of existing jurisprudence' and propose, if appropriate, 'criteria for determining case by case' when such materials or substances cannot be regarded as waste. Where necessary the Commission should also propose environmental criteria to be met by each category of waste which could be used as a secondary product, material or substance, two years after entry into force of the Directive. Five years after entry into force it should also, if appropriate, state what specifications should apply to compost, aggregates, paper, glass, metal, end-of-life tyres, and second-hand clothing.
- Regarding binding targets, Member States should stabilize their total waste production by 2012 'as compared to their overall annual waste production in 2008' (Article 29). The Commission should submit by 2008 a list of indicators to enable Member States to monitor, assess, and report their progress, and should formulate by 2010 a product eco-design policy and an action plan seeking to change consumption patterns. The Committee also called on the Commission to set, by 2010, 'further qualitative and quantitative waste reduction objectives for 2020, based on best available practice'.
- If energy efficiency criteria are met by a particular energy from a waste plant, then that plant would be categorized as a recovery rather than a disposal operation.[46] Such a designation has of course environmental, commercial, and public relations advantages. The criteria for designation as a recovery operation need to be high enough to be something of a 'gold standard'. It should mean, if adopted, that anyone thinking of building a new incinerator aims for such a standard. The Committee adopted an amendment that accepted the principle that energy from waste could qualify as recovery and moved the definition from the annex into the main body of the Directive in Article 19.
- Concerning Member States' obligations, the Committee wanted to simplify the requirements for national waste management programmes so as to make them less bureaucratic and more compatible with the subsidiarity principle. The requirement for Member States to ensure that 'all waste undergoes recovery operations' should apply 'where practicable'. A new Article laid down provisions on the traceability and control of hazardous waste,

[46] On the Commission's proposal to include energy efficiency thresholds for classification of municipal incinerators, see Commission Non-paper on the Background of the Development of the Commission Proposal on the Distinction between Energy Recovery and Disposal of Waste in Municipal Incinerators, published on the Internet at: http://ec.europa.eu/environment/waste/pdf/background.pdf. By letter of 28 Aug. 2006, Commissioner Stavros Dimas further informed the EP of the impacts of the proposed classification of municipal waste incinerators as recovery installations using an energy efficiency threshold, published on the Internet at: http://ec.europa.eu/environment/waste/pdf/energy_recovery.pdf.

stipulating that national authorities should do whatever is needed to ensure that the collection, production, and transportation of such waste, as well as its storage and treatment, are carried out in conditions providing optimum protection for the environment, including measures to ensure traceability and control 'from production to final destination'. Member States should also ensure that mineral waste oils are collected separately and that all hazardous waste treatment installations have a permit.

- A new Article introduced the principle of producer responsibility, with suggestions for implementing it: take-back obligations, information for consumers saying to what extent the product is recyclable, requests to producers concerning materials and design, and separate collection of the products at the end of their lives.
- The Committee proposed new clauses containing clear definitions of 'prevention', 'recovery', 'disposal', and 'energy recovery'.

This proposed substantive revision is not affected by the above-discussed codification of the Waste Framework Directive.[47] Codification is a process by which legal texts that have been revised several times are codified into one new text that replaces all the previous versions. No legal or political changes are made to the text during the codification process.

C. Case Law and Enforcement Actions

i. ECJ Rules on the Notification of Waste Shipments

The ECJ clarified in its *Pedersen* judgment of 16 February 2006 the application of the notification procedure for cross-border waste shipments under the Waste Shipments Regulation.[48] The preliminary ruling dealt with the notification of a local Danish undertaking which collects electronic scrap and which asked the Environment Agency of Denmark for authorization to transport 2,000 tonnes of electronic scrap to its partner undertaking established in Germany, for the purposes of recovery. The Agency, however, refused to authorize the transport on the ground that the undertaking had failed to supply it with the information necessary for it to consider the request for authorization, particularly proof that the installation established in Germany would treat the waste in a manner giving a level of environmental protection corresponding to that required under the Danish rules.

The local waste collector challenged the Danish Environment Agency's refusal to authorize the shipment. One of the questions referred to the ECJ by the regional court was whether the Waste Shipments Regulation provides a possibility for the competent authorities of the country of dispatch to raise an objection against a

[47] See Section A.*i.* above.

[48] Case C-215/04 *Marius Pedersen A/S* v. *Miljostyrelsen* [2006] ECR I-1465.

specific request for authorization to export waste for the purpose of recycling if there is no information from the notifier that the recipient plant's treatment of the waste in question will, from an environmental point of view, be of the same standard as is required under national rules in the country of dispatch.

The cases in which Member States may object to a shipment of waste between Member States are, for shipments of waste for recovery, those exhaustively listed in Article 7(4) of that Regulation, as provided by Article 7(2) thereof.[49] Application of Article 7(4), which defines the cases in which the competent authorities of dispatch, transit, and destination may raise objections to transports of waste for recovery, assumes that the competent authority has the information necessary in order to check whether or not a shipment falls within one of those cases. In that regard, Article 6(5) of the Waste Shipments Regulation provides that the notifier must supply certain information. Furthermore, it is clear from Article 6(4) of the Regulation that the competent authorities may request additional information and documentation from the notifier.

In *Pedersen* the Court first of all reiterated its *EU-Wood-Trading* case law which interpreted Article 7(4)(a) of the Waste Shipments Regulation as authorizing the competent authorities of dispatch to raise objections to a shipment of waste for recovery on the ground that the planned recovery disregards the requirements arising from Article 4 of the Waste Framework Directive.[50] In *EU-Wood-Trading*, the ECJ held that the provisions of the first indent of Article 7(4)(a) of the Waste Shipments Regulation imply that the competent authorities, in assessing the risks which recovery of waste carried out in the State of destination would entail for human health and the environment, may take account of all relevant criteria in that regard, including those which are in force in the State of dispatch, even if they are stricter than those of the State of destination, and provided they are intended to avoid those risks. The competent authorities of dispatch cannot, however, be bound by the criteria of their State if such criteria are no more apt to avoid those risks than those of the State of destination. Moreover, opposition by the competent authority of dispatch on the basis of its national waste recovery standards to a shipment can only be lawful insofar as those standards, in compliance with the principle of proportionality, are apt to attain the objectives pursued which are intended to prevent risks for human health and the environment, and do not go beyond what is necessary to attain them.

In line with *EU-Wood-Trading*, the Court stated in *Pedersen* that, in the context of the prior notification put into place by Article 6 of the Waste Shipments Regulation, the notifier must, in accordance with Article 6(5) thereof, supply on the consignment note supplementing the notification information concerning not only the composition and quantity of waste for recovery and the method

[49] See Case C-6/00 *Abfall Service AG (ASA)* v. *Bundesminster für Umwelt, Jugend und Familie* [2002] ECR I-1961.

[50] Case C-277/02 *EU-Wood-Trading GmbH* [2004] ECR I-11957.

of transport but also the conditions under which the waste will be recovered. However, the notifier cannot be required to prove that the recovery in the State of destination will be equivalent to that required by the rules in the State of dispatch. On the contrary, if the competent authority of dispatch wishes, pursuant to the first indent of Article 7(4)(a), to object to a shipment on the basis of its national standards for recovery, it is for the authority to demonstrate the risks to human health and the environment which recovery in the State of destination would entail.

The ECJ concluded that the competent authority of dispatch is entitled, pursuant to the first indent of Article 7(4)(a) of the Waste Shipments Regulation, to object to a shipment of waste in the absence of information on the conditions of recovery of that waste in the State of destination. However, the notifier cannot be required to prove that the recovery in the State of destination will be equivalent to that required by the rules in the State of dispatch.

ii. State Aid Probe Clears Dutch Waste Collector

A year-long investigation by the Commission into two loans granted to a Dutch recyclable waste collection association has found no evidence of illegal State aid.[51]

VAOP is an association created by several Dutch municipalities to organize the collection and sale of different types of recyclable waste.[52] In May 2005, the Commission initiated, on the basis of a complaint, a formal investigation procedure to verify whether a loan from the BNG bank and a loan from several municipalities had been granted on market terms and did not include State aid elements.

The Commission concluded with regard to the loan granted by the public sector BNG bank in 1998 that this loan was made against market conditions and did not constitute State aid as BNG had requested adequate securities from VAOP. In addition, at that time a privately owned bank was ready to provide similar financing to VAOP, which was considered to be a growing company offering good prospects. Finally, the interest rate charged by BNG is close to the one proposed by the private bank.

The second loan was granted in 2001 by the municipalities which were members of VAOP. They had certain financial claims against VAOP and transformed a part of these claims into a subordinated loan. The Commission found that this partial transformation constituted the best alternative available to the municipalities. Indeed, were VAOP to have gone bankrupt, they could have expected to recover only a very limited part of their claims, as BNG had rights to nearly all of

[51] Commission Press Release IP/06/1037, 20 July 2006, published in the RAPID database on the Internet at: http://europa.eu/rapid/searchAction.do (RAPID).

[52] 'Vereniging van Aanbieders van Oud Papier' (Association of Suppliers of Waste Paper).

VAOP's assets to cover the company's debts towards BNG. Therefore, the second loan did not include State aid elements either.

Given that all parties had acted as 'normal economic operators', no State aid elements were present in either loan.

D. Miscellaneous

i. Reports and Studies

The Commission issued a Report on the environmental, economic, social, and internal market aspects of Directive 94/62/EC on Packaging and Packaging Waste (Packaging and Packaging Waste Directive).[53] The Report also provides for an evaluation of the need for complementary measures for the prevention and recycling of packaging waste and the free circulation of packaging in the internal market.

The Commission further published a Report on the implementation of EU waste legislation for the period 2001 to 2003.[54] The Report deals with the six waste Directives, namely the Waste Framework Directive; Directive 91/689/EEC on Hazardous Waste (Hazardous Waste Directive);[55] Directive 75/439/EEC on the Disposal of Waste Oils (Waste Oils Directive);[56] Directive 86/278/EEC on the Protection of the Environment, and in particular of the Soil, when Sewage Sludge is Used in Agriculture (Sewage Sludge Directive);[57] the Packaging and Packaging Waste Directive; and the Landfill Directive. The Commission concludes that whilst overall progress has been made, the implementation of the waste legislation still cannot be considered satisfactory, as demonstrated by the large number of infringement procedures concerning waste. Significant efforts therefore need to be made towards full implementation, especially in the form of promoting waste prevention and recycling.

The Commission also published a Report on the implementation of the Waste Electric and Electronic Equipment Directive in the EU 25.[58] The Report states that several countries have been late with the transposition of the WEEE Directive and many of the countries that did create a timely transposition did so by simply translating the EU Directive, without specifying how the

[53] Report from the Commission to the Council and the European Parliament on the Targets on the Implementation of Directive 94/62/EC on Packaging and Packaging Waste and its Impact on the Environment, as well as on the Functioning of the Internal Market COM(2006)767, 6 Dec. 2006. Packaging and Packaging Waste Dir. [1994] OJ L365/10.

[54] Report from the Commission to the Council and the European Parliament on Implementation of the Community Waste Legislation for the Period 2001–2003 COM(2006)406, 19 July 2006.

[55] [1991] OJ L377/20.

[56] [1975] OJ L194/23.

[57] [1986] OJ L181/6.

[58] Implementation of Waste Electric and Electronic Equipment Dir. in EU 25, EUR 22231 EN, published on the Internet at: http://ec.europa.eu/environment/waste/weee/index_en.htm.

legislation would be applied in practice. The Report concludes by stating that further secondary regulations and clarifications are needed.

VII. Water

*Mark Stallworthy**

A. Introduction

i. Unfolding Policy Trends

The year 2006 saw further progress in updating legislative coverage in the aquatic policy field, particularly in support of the gradual, staged progress towards full implementation of Directive 2000/60/EC establishing a Framework for Community Action in the Field of Water Policy (Water Framework Directive).[1] The range of protection strategies pursued reflects the need for synergies to be accorded with the Framework Directive. These legislative themes have included in particular a newly updated and extended Bathing Water Directive,[2] as well as considerable progress towards finalizing the shape and content of proposed Directives to establish further dangerous substance controls for both groundwaters and surface waters.

As will be seen in ensuing sections, there have also been policy developments in the areas of floods and coastal protection, as well as maritime policy-making more generally. Here again, linkages with Framework Directive objectives and related approaches to delivery have been recognized. Perhaps also, these themes—especially in the face of continued pressures on ecosystems and also the ballooning threats concerned with climate change—constitute harbingers of a new generation of water policy and law-making at Community level.

B. Legislation Adopted

i. Fresh Water Quality and Support of Fish Life

Directive 2006/44/EC on the Quality of Fresh Waters Needing Protection or Improvement in order to Support Fish Life introduces a consolidation, ecosystem related, measure in respect of the protection of water quality in support of fish life.[3] The new Directive retains key features concerning Member State

* Professor of Environmental Law, School of Law, Swansea University, Wales (UK).

[1] [2000] OJ L327/1.

[2] Dir. 2006/7/EC concerning the Management of Bathing Water Quality and repealing Directive 76/160/EEC [2006] OJ L64/37 (New Bathing Water Directive).

[3] [2006] OJ L264/20.

responsibility for designation of relevant fresh waters. Achievement of compliance with limit values, that must correspond with both minimum and guide parameters, is to be required within five years of designation.[4] To this end, Article 5 mandates the establishment by Member States of necessary programmes in order to ensure conformity.

ii. Bathing Water

The New Bathing Water Directive, so long in gestation, has finally been adopted.[5] The reforming measure seeks to secure a tightening of requisite health standards in light of developments in scientific and technical understandings. Improved operational measures are additionally to apply in respect of site management, monitoring arrangements, and public information. The measure duly forms part of a wider Community strategy for both protecting quality and increasing efficiency of use of water resources, sitting alongside the Water Framework Directive, and sister sectoral measures, Directive 91/271/EEC concerning Urban Waste-water Treatment (Urban Waste-water Directive),[6] and Directive 91/676/EEC concerning the Protection of Waters against Pollution Caused by Nitrates from Agricultural Sources (Nitrates Directive).[7] Member States have been set a 24 March 2008 transposition deadline.

C. Legislation in Progress

i. Groundwater

Chronic problems of groundwater pollution have remained stubbornly persistent throughout the Community. The challenges faced reflect the multiple nature of polluting sources, from both industrial and agricultural practices as well as transport and land use patterns. Following agreement reached in conciliation by the European Parliament (EP) and the Council, a new Directive, replacing its main (1980) precursor,[8] is anticipated to come into force in 2007,[9] with a likely transposition deadline in 2009. In light of the aim of securing further groundwater pollution reductions, and assuring good chemical status under the Framework Directive, this measure will provide an explicit setting out of common indicators for the assessment of chemical status. It will further require the establishment of comprehensive monitoring systems. Mandatory targets are to apply in respect of

[4] Ibid., Art. 3; parameters are set out in Annex I.
[5] N. 2 above.
[6] [1991] OJ L135/40.
[7] [1991] OJ L375/1.
[8] Dir. 80/68/EEC on the Protection of Groundwater against Pollution caused by Certain Dangerous Substances [1980] OJ L20/43, as amended by 90/656/EEC and 91/692/EEC (Groundwater Directive).
[9] Proposal for a Directive on the Protection of Groundwater against Pollution COM(2003)550, 19 Sept. 2003.

hazardous substances (including cyanide, arsenic, biocides, and phytopharmaceutical substances) as designated under the Water Framework Directive, with a view to securing quality objectives. Experience of operation of the new Directive is to be reviewed six years following entry into force.

ii. Dangerous Substances

Integration of Community policy for dangerous substance control, in accord with the Water Framework Directive, has taken a further step forward in 2006. The Water Framework Directive requires that all EU waters achieve the broad objective of securing good ecological status by 2015. In order to facilitate this goal, the Commission has established a new regime for the control and prevention of chemical pollution of water.[10] The newly proposed Directive discussed below is to apply to surface waters,[11] just as protection of groundwaters is to be furthered under the proposed Groundwater Directive, referred to in the previous section.[12]

A key Water Framework Directive objective is to further secure the progressive reduction of emissions of priority substances harmful to surface waters.[13] A related aim is for a full phasing out of emissions of priority hazardous substances (such as mercury and cadmium compounds) to be achieved.[14] The Proposal amounts to a strategy for securing a phased reduction in releases of priority substances, alongside a prohibition of releases of hazardous substances. In this way the Commission is seeking directly to address aspects of an endemic problem, as multiple sources of chemical pollution pose particular threats to aquatic biodiversity and ecosystems, including plant and animal life, the accumulation of which (especially in the food chain) threatens the health of humans as well as other vulnerable species.

The motivation underlying the current Proposal is to secure the necessary reductions in identified water pollutants in surface waters through compliance with set environmental quality standards. Member States would be required to specify measures for achieving the agreed standards in their River Basin Management Plans, preparation of which is a requirement under the Water Framework Directive by 2009. The Commission rejected the imposition of harmonized measures, leaving operational discretion to Member States as to how to secure the necessary reductions. The Commission's reliance on quality standards inclines to longstanding UK arguments in favour of approaches based upon

[10] Commission Communication on Integrated Prevention and Control of Chemical Pollution in Surface Waters in the EU COM(2006)398, 17 July 2006.

[11] Commission Proposal for a Directive on Environmental Quality Standards in the Field of Water Policy and Amending Dir. 2000/60/EC COM(2006)397, 17 July 2006.

[12] N. 8 above.

[13] Water Framework Dir., n. 1 above, preamble para. 22; also, Art. 16.

[14] Ibid., preamble, paras. 27, 43–5.

quality standards, here preferred to reliance upon emission limits as originally intended.

The scheme relies on the setting of maximum concentrations and annual average values, and will fix strict concentration values for 41 substances (including pesticides, biocides, heavy metals, and certain flame retardants). Of these, 33 are identified as a significant risk to surface waters, and designated priority substances for the purposes of the Framework Directive,[15] whilst the remainder have been identified as chemical pollutants in previous legislation.[16] Of 13 priority substances identified as 'hazardous', strict limit values are to apply pending the required elimination in due course, on grounds of toxicity, persistence in the environment without breaking down, and bioaccumulation in the food chain.

Transparency should be enhanced by measures requiring the preparation and communication of emissions inventories, in accord with Article 4. Remedial actions will be mandated through Member State designation of 'transitional areas of exceedance' (*sic*) under Article 3, leading to reviews of industrial permits, in order to bring about progressive reductions. It appears that there has been some slippage in timing, as in respect of priority hazardous substances a 2025 deadline has replaced an earlier target date of 2020. The earlier deadline for priority substance reduction and control is 2015.

iii. Flood Protection

The Commission has produced a Community response in the wake of a series of major flood events in recent years (including the disastrous consequences of the Danube and Elbe flooding during 2002). These have cumulatively resulted in 700 fatalities, alongside displacement of around 500,000 people, as well as insured losses exceeding €25 billion. Indeed, in the light of settlement patterns and the impacts of climate change, higher flood risks are anticipated for the future. A proposed Directive on the Assessment and Management of Floods[17] aims to bring about the reduction and management of consequent risks to human health, the environment, infrastructure and property. Member States would be required to carry out preliminary assessments, and thereafter to produce flood risk maps and flood risk management plans focused on prevention, protection, and preparedness in respect of those areas where a significant flooding risk exists.

[15] Dec. No. 2455/2001/EC establishing the List of Priority Substances in the Field of Water Policy and amending Directive 2000/60/EC [2001] OJ L331/1.

[16] Dir. 82/176/EEC on Limit Values and Quality Objectives for Mercury Discharges from the Chlor-alkali Electrolysis Industry [1982] OJ L81/29; Dir. 83/513/EEC on Limit Values and Quality Objectives for Cadmium Discharges [1983] OJ L291/1; Dir. 84/156/EEC on Limit Values and Quality Objectives for Mercury Discharges by Sectors other than the Chlor-alkali Electrolysis Industry [1984] OJ L74/49; Dir. 84/491/EEC on Limit Values and Quality Objectives for Discharges of Hexachlorocyclohexane [1984] OJ L274/11; and Dir. 86/280/EEC on Limit Values and Quality Objectives for Discharges of Certain Dangerous Substances included in List 1 of the Annex to Dir. 76/464/EEC, n. 44 below [1986] OJ L221/51.

[17] COM(2006)15, 18 Jan. 2006.

The aim of preliminary flood risk assessments would be to evaluate significant flood risks within particular river basins, sub-basins, or coastal areas. Flood risk maps would be required for such areas (where not already in place), enabling prioritizing and the development of sustainable policies and strategies (to include flood risk management, spatial planning, and emergency plans), as well as fuller public awareness. The flood risk management plans would also be applied at river basin (and sub-basin) level, and aim to fulfil the purposes of flood risk analysis and assessment, the setting of protection levels, and identification and implementation of sustainable measures.

The Proposal contains specific reference to the principle of solidarity, which in this context appears to mean that problems should not be transferred to regions upstream or downstream, and that measures should preferably contribute to risk reduction elsewhere. This could mark a significant departure from the standpoint at least of English law, where the prevailing common enemy rule adopts a markedly indulgent view towards self protection on the part of threatened riparian owners irrespective of consequences elsewhere.[18]

Mirroring approaches elsewhere in modern Community environmental protection legislation, the Commission is seeking to avoid prescriptive approaches as to choice of management methods towards delivering improvements. This pertains here, as regards the setting of detailed protection objectives, and even deadlines. Thus Member States will determine appropriate protection levels for each river basin or coastal area. Generally there is considerable synergy with requirements under the Framework Directive with regard to the approach to securing water quality objectives. To that end, the Commission proposes an equivalence of competent authorities as well as administrative units (based upon river basin districts). There would likewise be equivalent implementation cycles and public participation mechanisms.

D. Case Law and Enforcement Actions

i. European Court Rulings

Article 226 of the EC Treaty (EC) proceedings in respect of failures in meeting the December 2003 deadline for national implementing legislation under the Water Framework Directive have resulted in rulings by the European Court of Justice (ECJ) that Belgium and Germany had failed to adopt the necessary legislation in due time.[19] The Court has further ruled that France was in breach of a requirement to communicate information collected by responsible authorities concerning monitoring of discharges from treatment plants, alongside

[18] *Arscott* v. *The Coal Authority* [2005] Env Law Rep 6.

[19] Cases C-33/05 *Commission* v. *Belgium* [2006] OJ C48/9; and C-67/05, *Commission* v. *Germany* [2006] OJ C36/17.

composition details, to the Commission.[20] By contrast, in a ruling in favour of Luxembourg the ECJ has emphasized that the Water Framework Directive does not require complete harmonization, citing the mostly generalized expression of objectives, and the according of broad levels of discretion to Member States as to the precise nature of measures to secure compliance. Furthermore, the stated purpose of establishing a framework for protection of the stated types of water, under Article 1, did not itself require transposition.[21]

Enforcement proceedings before the ECJ have also been successful in respect of breach by Belgium of the Nitrates Directive. This related to national failures in the identification of waters that suffer from or are at risk from nitrate pollution, in satisfactory designation of vulnerable zones requiring further action, and in compliance with requirements for establishing action programmes.[22]

ii. Commission Enforcement

The Commission's most recent annual survey suggests a general improvement in levels of Member State compliance with environmental legislation.[23] Environmental breaches accounted for about one-quarter of Commission enforcement cases during the year (compared with one-third in the previous year). The specific area of water protection showed a continuing, if somewhat slender, improvement, contributing around 14.7 per cent of open infringements by sector (compared to 15.1 per cent in 2004). This ranked ahead of the worse performing sectors: conservation protection, waste control, and environmental impact control. Most water infringements now relate to failures in application (19.7 per cent, previously 19.4 per cent of the total) and non-conformity (14 per cent, previously 18.4 per cent of the total). It is perhaps scarcely surprising that, with comparatively few relevant deadlines at issue, non-communication proceedings represented only 4 per cent of the total.

Slack compliance levels by Member States with the Urban Waste-water Directive continue to be a prevalent feature in enforcement activity. The Commission has issued a formal notice to France under Article 228 EC, asserting non-compliance with a 2004 judgment under the same Directive, concerning failures to identify sufficient sensitive areas, and also to meet standards for discharge into sensitive areas (agglomerations of 10,000 population), respectively in due time.[24] The original litigation had been notable in that France had challenged the Commission on the technical validity of its position on nutrients in relation to algae formation. In finding against France, the Court had adopted a precautionary approach, ruling that the degree of probability of a causal link

[20] Case C-191/04 *Commission* v. *France* [2005] OJ C193/7.

[21] Case C-32/05 *Commission* v. *Luxembourg* [2006] ECR I-11323.

[22] Case C-221/03 *Commission* v. *Belgium* [2005] ECR I-8307.

[23] Commission, *Seventh Annual Survey on the Implementation and Enforcement of Community Environmental Law 2005* SEC(2006)1143, 8 Sept. 2006.

[24] Case C-280/02 *Commission* v. *France* [2004] ECR I-8573.

was sufficient to require what amounted to the mandatory compliance under the Directive as demanded by the Commission. Furthermore, the Commission is seeking to institute proceedings against Portugal,[25] on grounds of failure to comply with a previous Commission Decision,[26] which exceptionally had approved a lesser level of treatment for discharges of waste-water into the sea (from an area of over 700,000 people at Estoril), resulting in breaches of a requirement only for primary treatment and disinfection during the summer bathing season.

The UK continues to attract enforcement action under the same Directive. The Commission announced a follow up to initial procedures, by sending a second written warning concerning continuing breaches in respect of collection and secondary treatment systems affecting London and three other urban areas.[27] The Commission alleges that in each case overflow systems operating where facilities became overloaded allowed the regular discharge of untreated water to rivers or sea, resulting in substantial fish kills and prevention of bathing and other recreational uses. Similarly, the Commission intends to bring Finland and Sweden before the Court for respective failures to comply with the Directive in respect of requirements for numerous inland urban areas,[28] and discharges into sensitive areas.[29] The Commission cites especial concerns at increased eutrophication in the Baltic Sea on account of excessive nutrient inputs, alleging failures to remove nitrogen from such urban waste-water discharges.[30] The respondent Member States may raise counter-arguments to the effect that, on account of processes of natural retention, removal is unnecessary on the basis that lakes and rivers slow relevant nutrient transfers.

Once again under the same Directive, the Commission alleges non-compliance by Greece with a 2004 judgment of the ECJ.[31] This concerned failures to take measures to build a collecting system (at Thriassou Pedio) and to provide tertiary treatment (for the removal of nutrients, such as organic matter, nitrogen, and phosphorus) before discharge into a sensitive area (the Gulf of Elefsina). Whilst compliance measures had been instigated, the Commission's particular concern was prompted by an apparent failure to keep collection and treatment projects (which were to be subject to Commission co-financing) to schedule. A first written warning was accordingly served under Article 228 EC.[32] Similarly,

[25] Commission Press Release IP/06/1769, 12 Dec. 2006, published in the RAPID database on the Internet at: http://europa.eu/rapid/searchAction.do (RAPID).

[26] Dec. 2001/720/EC granting Portugal a derogation regarding urban waste water treatment for the agglomeration of the Estoril coast [2001] OJ L269/14.

[27] Namely, Kilbarchan, Torbay, Whitburn. See Commission Press Release IP/06/444, 4 Apr. 2006 (RAPID).

[28] Around 60 and 76 in Sweden and Finland respectively.

[29] IP/06/1769, n. 25 above.

[30] See the earlier Case C-396/00 *Commission* v. *Italy* [2002] ECR I-3949.

[31] Case C-119/02 *Commission* v. *Greece* [2004] OJ C201/4.

[32] Commission Press Release IP/06/479, 7 Apr. 2006 (RAPID); also, for a final written warning in respect of alleged breaches, Commission Press Release IP/06/1760, 12 Dec. 2006 (RAPID).

a first written warning has been issued, affecting the same region, over alleged failure to comply with an earlier ECJ ruling concerning the pollution of groundwater and the introduction of hazardous material.[33] Despite partial compliance (through preparation of a hazardous waste inventory, alongside evaluations followed by closure of certain sites), the Commission alleges failure to produce an adequate regional hazardous waste management plan.[34]

The Commission's annual survey also reported further proceedings against Spain under the Shellfish Waters Directive, for failure to adopt a pollution reduction programme for certain shellfish waters (Ria da Vigo),[35] despite an earlier ruling of the ECJ,[36] and a first written warning followed.[37] Further action against Spain relates to non-compliance with the Nitrates Directive in areas of intensive pig farming (Rambla de Mojacar in Almeira), with the Commission asserting a failure to comply fully with a ruling that the area should have been designated a nitrate vulnerable zone.[38] Proceedings are also pending in connection with further alleged failures: firstly, properly to transpose in due time Directive 98/83/EC on the Quality of Water Intended for Human Consumption (Drinking Water Directive),[39] which action reinforces the Commission's insistence on time limit compliance (here, December 2000, despite subsequent adoption); and, secondly, to comply fully with an earlier ruling,[40] concerning a breach of Directive 76/464/EEC on Pollution caused by Certain Dangerous Substances Discharged into the Aquatic Environment of the Community (Dangerous Substances Discharge Directive),[41] because reduction programmes failed satisfactorily to address pollution of coastal waters.

E. Policy Developments

i. Towards an EU Maritime Policy

The proposed EU Environmental Marine Protection Strategy is planned as the environmental pillar of a future EU maritime policy.[42] It aims at the difficult balancing of the needs of environmental protection alongside the securing of economic use benefits. The reconciliation of conflicts is problematic, given on the one hand marine economic utility value to humankind and on the other ecological

[33] Case C-163/03 *Commission* v. *Greece* [2005] OJ C143/8.

[34] IP/06/1760, n. 32 above.

[35] Dir. 79/923/EEC on Shellfish Water Quality [1979] OJ L281/47.

[36] Case C-26/04 *Commission* v. *Spain* [2005] ECR I-11059.

[37] Commission Press Release IP/06/1761, 12 Dec. 2006 (RAPID).

[38] Cases C-416/02 *Commission* v. *Spain* [2005] ECR I-7487; C-121/03 *Commission* v. *Spain* [2005] ECR I-7569.

[39] [1998] OJ L330/32.

[40] Case C-214/96 *Commission* v. *Spain* [1998] ECR I-7661.

[41] [1976] OJ L129/23.

[42] Proposal for a Directive Establishing a Framework for Community Action in the Field of Marine Environmental Policy COM(2005)505, 24 Oct. 2005.

imperatives that understand the sea as not only a food supplier but also a provider of essential functions, such as climate regulation and distribution of solar energy alongside a vast richness of biodiversity.

It is notable that climate change impacts are becoming increasingly important factors for the development of necessary strategies. Whilst the proposed strategy has now received broad support from the EP,[43] stress has been laid on the vulnerability of the Arctic region, calling for fuller protection of 'an extremely fragile ecosystem under constant and emerging threats'.[44] The Parliament's Resolution calls upon the Commission to investigate the question of establishing a protected area designated as 'a natural reserve devoted to peace and science'. At the same time, in the closely related area of energy, the question of environmental impact (and its relation to co-financing) is likely to become contentious in related climate and energy debates. Here, Parliament has voiced criticism at what it terms a lack of 'environmental guarantee' in connection with the construction of the North European gas pipeline in the face of potential environmental disaster in the Baltic Sea region.

The Commission has in the meantime produced a Green Paper on Maritime Policy,[45] which appears to steer Community policy in a new direction. Particular marine pressures follow from high levels of development at the coastlines, as well as over-fishing, and climate change is threatening both sea level rises and deleterious impacts upon ecosystems as a consequence of carbon-induced ocean acidification. In consequence, the Commission has concluded that it is no longer sustainable to exclude the marine environment from regulatory purview, whereby marine issues, where dealt with at all, appear to be ancillary to other policies.

In particular, the Green Paper has an objective of encouraging sustainable marine development through more holistic approaches. Indeed, a recent independent study by marine biologists has highlighted the urgent need for an holistic ecosystem-based approach to future management, to assure sustainability of both fish stocks and marine ecosystems more generally.[46] As well as the risks associated with habitat loss and pollution damage, both ecosystem stability and global food security (for instance projecting a collapse of fish stocks within 50 years should current trends continue) are under threat.

The difficulties of ensuring progress will however be considerable, for as seen above marine activities offer a prime illustration of the kinds of pressures that impact upon environmental limbs of sustainability commitments, given the pressures of key economic and social interests. The aim of the proposed strategy is

[43] EP Resolution on a Thematic Strategy on the Protection and Conservation of the Marine Environment (2006/2174), 14 Nov. 2006, published on the Internet at: http://www.europarl.europa.eu/.

[44] Ibid., Arts. 29–30.

[45] Commission Green Paper—Towards a Future Maritime Policy for the Union—a European Vision for the Oceans and Seas COM(2006)275, 7 June 2006.

[46] Worm, et al., 'Impacts of Biodiversity Loss on Ocean Ecosystem Services' (2006) *Science* 314.

to protect Europe's seas and promote sustainable use and conservation of marine ecosystems, in the face of marine activities such as shipping, hazardous substance deposition, waste dumping, commercial fishing, energy exploitation, dredging, and aggregate extraction. A range of threats is accordingly targeted, including dangerous substance and nutrient contamination, biodiversity damage, and habitat loss.

It is anticipated that the new strategic measures would seek a framework for achieving good environmental status in the marine environment by a latest date of 2021, with protection and preservation obligations to apply thereafter. Such obligations would be aimed at protecting the resource base underlying social and economic marine activities. In order to achieve this, by 2016 Member States would accordingly be required to have developed marine strategies, alongside specific programmes for delivery, applying target setting and monitoring.[47] Detailed assessments would be required of Member States as to the state of their marine environments, leading to the preparation of strategies to take account of available scientific evidence, with details of measures proposed for the achievement of good environmental status, analysed for potential economic, social, and environmental impacts. In a fashion that mirrors River Basin Management Plans under the Water Framework Directive, it appears to be recognized that ecological realities pay no heed to human boundaries. Thus it is likely that European Marine Regions will be identified on the basis of geographical and environmental criteria. Cooperative arrangements across Member States (and third countries) will then be required so that appropriate strategies can be developed.

The possible timeframes for developing the necessary strategies outlined above would likely reflect a degree of convergence with the staging of implementation under the Water Framework Directive, for both the achievement of good ecological status generally (2015) and thence review of River Basin Management Plans (2021). The EP is seeking an accelerated deadline of 2017, which would appear to be more in line with the ongoing timetable under the Water Framework Directive. Parliament has also called for a fast tracking of a pilot project for the Baltic region, in light of the generally receptive stances of concerned Member States.[48] A generally welcoming tone is mitigated by the EP's concern at the continued definitional hiatus (also under the Water Framework Directive) as to the notion of good ecological status. It would accordingly prefer the adoption of an EU definition, to reflect the management of marine ecosystems 'in ways which allow them to function in a balanced and self-sustaining way in the face of environmental change, supporting both biodiversity and human activities'.[49] It may be that the anticipated setting out by the Commission in due course of generic qualitative descriptors, with criteria and standards for recognition, will go some way to satisfying such a goal. It will nevertheless be important to assess the impact

[47] N. 45 above, Arts. 4, 7. [48] N. 43 above, Arts. 25, 28. [49] Ibid., Art. 4.

of protective measures in view of the Green Paper's espousing of a detailed cost-benefit analysis prior to introducing any new measures.

More generally, a wider maritime strategy would seek to incorporate the principle of 'ecosystem-based management', implemented at regional levels, to enable activities to be managed in an integrated manner. Integration would be pursued through improved coordination between sectoral policy areas, taking account of such impacts as coastal development, nutrient enrichment, and impacts of climate change. An emerging strategy would incorporate commitments to build upon the knowledge base, on the basis of detailed assessments and measurements of activities and impacts, in order to inform future action. This would include a European Marine Observation and Data Network, with comprehensive mapping of coastal waters, the location of marine fauna and flora, and water and seabed activities.

F. International Cooperation

i. Water Stress

Environmental justice issues affecting the developing world, concerning the devastating impacts of acute clean water shortage, remain widespread, life-threatening, and persistent. These regions are also amongst the most vulnerable to desertification and drought, as well as rising sea levels, in consequence of climate change. Whilst of a different order, in terms of both vulnerability and capacities to mitigate and adapt, the developed world also faces a deteriorating situation of its own, as water systems have a decreasing capacity to sustain current social and economic life patterns.

A new World Wide Fund for Nature (WWF) report cites an increasing incidence of water crises now posing threats to both wealthy and fast emerging economies.[50] Indeed, economic interaction between developed and developing countries, such as through support for dams and other infrastructure projects, can result in severe 'positive feedback' consequences for the natural replenishment of water sources. Fast developing economies, such as China, are proving prone to water crises over critically short time frames.[51] Of the richer countries considered by WWF, within Europe, explicit reference is made to Spain and the United Kingdom (UK), the WWF pointing variously to climate change impacts, drought, loss of the storage potential on account of loss of wetlands, and poor resource management. The report calls for greater international cooperation in order to find solutions to the benefit of both rich and poor states, focusing especially upon infrastructure repair, water pollutant reduction, and reformed irrigation practices.

[50] WWF, *Rich Countries, Poor Water* (Zeist, Netherlands), Aug. 2006.

[51] J. Watts, 'The Dry Facts—China is Running Out of Water, While Industrial Pollution is an Increasing Problem in the Dwindling Supplies that it has', *Guardian*, 4 Oct. 2006.

ii. Mediterranean Protection Strategy

Following 'Horizon 2020', an initiative to tackle major sources of Mediterranean pollution by the year 2020 endorsed by leaders of Euro-Mediterranean (Euro-Med) countries at the 2005 Summit in Barcelona, the Commission is seeking to implement related commitments. During 2006 it proposed a long-term environmental strategy to protect the Mediterranean Sea, in the face of intense environmental pressures, from industrial, shipping, and household pollution, and from development, as well as specific events such as marine oil spills.[52] Environmental pressures include the loss of open areas and the destruction of coastal ecosystems to make way for development (with 50 per cent of the Mediterranean coastline on current projections expected to be built up by 2025).

The Commission cites problems such as ineffective international action due to lack of finance, low political priorities, weak institutional cooperation, and limited public awareness. Key aims for the developing strategy are: the reduction of pollution levels across the region; promotion of sustainable use of both sea and coastline; encouragement of international cooperation on environmental issues; and the development of effective institutions and environmental protection policies, involving NGOs and the wider public. Four methods for achieving these objectives are suggested: financial assistance from existing EU aid programmes; strengthened dialogue with the region's representatives; improved coordination with other organizations and partners; and sharing of EU experience in dealing with the problems of the Mediterranean and other regions.

G. Miscellaneous

i. Bathing Water

The Commission has reported on levels of compliance with the Bathing Water Directive for 2005.[53] The 1976 Directive is due to be repealed as its replacement legislation progressively comes into force. In respect of mandatory values, the figures were as follows: for coastal sites, 96.1 per cent (96.7 per cent for 1994), and for freshwater sites 85.6 per cent (89.4 per cent for 2004). As for the more aspirational guide values, returns were for coastal waters 89.1 per cent (88.5 per cent for 1994), and for freshwaters, 63.1 per cent (66.4 per cent for 2004). The figures on their face suggest a continuing slight general deterioration, as witnessed over the previous two years. However, sampling defaults are counted as non-compliance for the purposes of compilation. Pre-accession states broadly maintained performance in respect of mandatory values, at 96.7 per cent and 91.4 per cent for coastal and freshwater areas respectively.

[52] Commission Press Release IP06/1155, 6 Sept. 2006 (RAPID).

[53] Commission, Bathing Water Report 2005, published on the Internet at: http://www.ec.europa.eu/environment/water/water-bathing/index_en.html.

It is perhaps inevitable that it will take some time before many accession states will achieve the sought after improvements, and the six accession states (Cyprus, Czech Republic, Estonia, Lithuania, Slovakia, Slovenia) compiling returns for a second year generally achieved improvements. The Report suggests that compliance with mandatory and guide values in Hungary (the first year in which data was provided) stood respectively at 39.4 per cent and 26.3 per cent. In contrast, compliance in respect of freshwater sites in Latvia (also in its first return year) stood at 89 per cent and 53 per cent for mandatory and guide values respectively. There, coastal compliance rates for mandatory values and guide values were respectively 88.1 per cent and 50 per cent.

Moreover, a further 103 coastal sites and 223 freshwater sites were delisted (contrast subsisting site numbers Community-wide of 14,230 coastal areas and 6,684 freshwater areas respectively). The Commission has expressed concern at delisting in some cases masking pollution problems, and has opened infringement cases against 11 Member States.[54] Overall, declassification of sites (since a base year of 1990) now stands at respectively 17.2 per cent and 39.3 per cent of the total number of coastal and freshwater sites ever listed. Very high levels of performance by certain Member States by reference in particular to mandatory values, such as the Netherlands, contrast with cumulated rates of withdrawal, there affecting 38.8 per cent of coastal and 44.9 per cent of freshwater sites respectively. Similarly, compliance with mandatory values by Spain is generally impressive, although a total of 69.2 per cent of freshwater sites (though only 15.3 per cent of coastal sites) has been withdrawn over the whole period.

ii. Water Scarcity in Europe

In recognition of the acuteness of European water scarcity and related drought challenges, and following the June 2006 Council Meeting, the Commission has undertaken an in-depth assessment focused upon situations of scarcity, drought events, key causative factors, affected populations, and economic, social, and environmental impacts, as well as upon Member State uses of EU funds and water pricing, taking account also of potential Water Framework Directive impacts.[55] A drafting group (from representatives of water directors across Member States) has already during 2006 produced a technical paper on drought events and questions of imbalance in the long term.[56] Participatory processes are to apply, as have been seen in the current maritime strategy discussions, and an integral part of this is the setting up of a stakeholder forum. The Commission intends to produce a Communication during 2007.

[54] Commission Press Release, IP/06/470, 6 Apr. 2006 (RAPID).

[55] Commission, Water Scarcity and Drought: First Interim Report (Nov. 2006).

[56] Water Scarcity Drafting Group, Water Scarcity Management in the Context of the Waste Framework Directive (June 2006).

iii. Protection of the Coastal Zone

A Report has been produced for the Commission, evaluating Integrated Coastal Zone Management (ICZM) in Europe,[57] in light of delivery of Member States' reports concerning development of national strategies. A Communication is to be prepared for 2007 by the Commission, setting out policy orientations for ICZM across the Community.

H. Conclusions

A Future Strategic Approach to the Marine Environment?

Potentially the most far reaching current development is the prospect of an integrated EU maritime policy. The commitment to delivering an EU strategy focused upon sustainable use of maritime resources appears a most positive and exciting approach to an issue of crucial importance across the Community, though it also remains highly problematic both in political and technical terms. Commitment to integrated and cross-cutting approaches, especially when we consider such core questions as biodiversity protection and ecosystem services, would be a profoundly significant step in the search for more sustainable relationships between human activities and maritime ecological realities.

In the face of mounting sustainability challenges, the introduction of a more strategic marine policy concept as a basis for future regulatory frameworks and decisions could fill important gaps in current, especially nationally based, approaches. It must be remembered that strategic planning has traditionally been bound by national jurisdictions—as well as progressing along terrestrial lines. Thus activities affecting the marine environment have remained broadly unregulated, save for sector-based schemes (such as energy exploitation licensing). Nevertheless Community competence has intensified in the planning field generally (for instance, through environmental impact assessment, and now strategic environmental assessment), a trend that can also be seen in the present development under the Water Framework Directive of River Basin Management Plans, as well as the recent embracing of Integrated Coastal Zone Management.

Particularly as marine impacts can be immune to boundary limits—irrespective of such legal 'rights' as territorial waters, exclusive economic zones, and renewable energy zones—a new strategic approach could provide three notable opportunities. Foremost would be the promise of a harmonized approach across Member States, towards shared principles and rules in the delivery of defined environmental, social, and economic objectives. Secondly, there could be fuller coordination across activities, offering integrated responses to conflicting demands, and greater focus upon tensions between terrestrial activities and the

[57] Rupprecht Consult—Forschung & Beratung GmbH, Evaluation of Integrated Coastal Zone Management (ICZM) in Europe—Final Report (Cologne, Germany), Aug. 2006.

marine environment. Indeed, the Community is becoming increasingly active in related sectors, such as the management of floods and coastal erosion, integrated coastal management generally, and sustainable energy supply. Finally, this opens an opportunity towards a commitment to biodiversity protection, which could be aligned with support for progress through UNCLOS mechanisms towards establishing Marine Protected Areas. The eventual goal is significant, namely, the achievement of an ecosystem-orientated approach to the impacts of marine resource use, with an emphasis on the need to secure the sustainability of marine ecosystem services.

VIII. Horizontal Instruments and Miscellaneous Issues

*Diane Ryland**

A. Introduction

The Aarhus Convention on Access to Information, Public Participation in Decision-making and Access to Justice in Environmental Matters (Aarhus Convention)[1] featured prominently in the survey year 2006. The Aarhus Convention recognizes, inter alia, that increased public access to environmental information and its dissemination lead to a greater awareness of environmental matters, more effective participation by the public in environmental decision-making and, ultimately, to a better environment. Accordingly, legislation in 2006 set up a European pollutant release and transfer register as a tool for encouraging improvements in environmental performance, for providing public access to information on releases of pollutants and off-site transfers of pollutants and waste.[2] A very significant development towards the objectives of the Aarhus Convention is the application of its requirements to Community institutions and bodies. The Council and the European Parliament (EP), meeting on 2 May 2006 in the Conciliation Committee, reached an agreement on a Regulation on the application of the Aarhus Convention to European Community (EC) institutions and bodies. The main changes to the common position resulting from the conciliation agreement are: Community institutions and bodies would take into account the outcome of the public participation in taking a decision on a plan or programme relating to the environment and inform the public; encouragement for databases or registers to include information on steps taken in proceedings

* Senior Lecturer in Law, University of Lincoln (UK).

[1] Aarhus (Denmark), 25 June 1998 (entered into force 30 Oct. 2001), (1999) 38 *International Legal Materials* 3, 517. Approved by the EC in Dec. 2005/370/EC [2005] OJ L124/1.

[2] See Section B.*i* below.

for infringement of Community law; the establishment of a delay of 15 working days for an answer from the Community institutions or bodies for a request for access to information; Community institutions and bodies would have to interpret any grounds for refusing access to information in a restrictive way, taking into account the public interest served by disclosure and whether the information relates to emissions into the environment.[3] Eventually, a Regulation applying the provisions of the Aarhus Convention to Community institutions and bodies was adopted in this current survey year.[4]

2006 saw the establishment of a revised working plan comprised of objectives and actions to further develop the eco-label scheme, while the environmental management systems of the eco-management and audit scheme were amended in order to achieve consistency pursuant to modifications made to the European standard.[5]

Moreover, in 2006 the Commission maintained its vigour in adopting, and also furthering with legislative proposals, thematic strategies for the cross protection of the environment.[6]

An improvement in the implementation of environmental legislation is evident from the Commission's Annual Survey on the Implementation and Enforcement of Community Environmental Law in 2005.[7] The Commission also published its first Report, in 2006, on the implementation of Directive 96/61/EC concerning Integrated Pollution Prevention and Control (IPPC Directive).[8]

Furthermore, it became evident in this current survey year that the Strategic Environment Assessment Directive newly encompasses the Community Fund Regulations in the programming period 2007 to 2013.[9]

B. Legislation Adopted

i. Pollutant Release and Transfer Register

In 2006, Regulation (EC) No. 166/2006 established an integrated European Pollutant Release and Transfer Register[10] (the European PRTR) and amends

[3] Council of the European Union, 8966/06 (Presse 123) Brussels, 3 May 2006. Minutes published on the Internet at: http://www.consilium.europa.eu/cms3_applications/applications/search/newsSearch.asp?lang=EN&cmsid=377.

[4] Reg. (EC) No. 1367/2006 applying the provisions of the Aarhus Convention on Access to Information, Public Participation in Decision-Making, and Access to Justice in Environmental Matters to Community Institutions and Bodies [2006] OJ L264/13. See Section B.*ii* below.

[5] See Sections B.*iii* and B.*iv* below.

[6] See Sections D.*vii* and C.*iv* below.

[7] See Section E.*iii* below.

[8] [1996] OJ L257/26. See Section F.*iii* below.

[9] See Section F.*iv* below.

[10] [2006] OJ L33/1. The UN/ECE Protocol on Pollutant Release and Transfer Registers (PRTR Protocol) is approved on behalf of the EC in Dec. 2006/61/EC [2006] OJ L32/54. PRTR Protocol, Kiev (Ukraine), 21 May 2003, published on the Internet at: http://www.unece.org/env/pp/prtr.htm.

Directives 91/689/EEC on Hazardous Waste (Hazardous Waste Directive)[11] and the IPPC Directive.[12] The European PRTR is in the form of a publicly accessible electronic database and the Regulation lays down rules for its functioning, in order to implement the PRTR Protocol[13] and facilitate public participation in environmental decision-making, as well as to contribute to the prevention and reduction of pollution of the environment.[14] The European PRTR will include information on:

(i) releases[15] to air, water, and land of any pollutant[16] referred to in Annex II of the Regulation for which the applicable threshold value specified is exceeded, which must be reported by the operators[17] of facilities[18] carrying out the activities listed in Annex I of the Regulation, in accordance with Article 5 of the Regulation;

(ii) off-site transfers[19] of waste referred to in the Regulation[20] and of pollutants in waste water, also in accordance with the Regulation,[21]

[11] [1991] OJ L377/20, amended by Dir. 94/31/EC [1994] OJ L168/28. Art. 8(3) of Dir. 91/689/EEC is deleted.

[12] Art. 15(3) of the IPPC Dir. is deleted.

[13] N. 10 above. A European Pollutant Emission Register (EPER) was established by Dec. 2000/479/EC [2000] OJ L192/36. The Protocol, going beyond the EPER, includes reporting on more pollutants, more activities, releases to land, releases from diffuse sources, and off-site transfers. Recital 6 to Reg. (EC) No. 166/2006, n. 10 above.

[14] Ibid., Art. 1.

[15] Release is defined as: 'any introduction of pollutants into the environment as a result of any human activity, whether deliberate or accidental, routine or non-routine, including spilling, emitting, discharging, injecting, disposing or dumping, or through sewer systems without final waste-water treatment'. Ibid., Art. 2(10).

[16] The definition of pollutant is: 'a substance or a group of substances that may be harmful to the environment or to human health on account of its properties and of its introduction into the environment'. Ibid., Art. 2(9).

[17] Operator means: 'any natural or legal person who operates or controls the facility or, where this is provided for in national legislation, to whom decisive economic power over the technical functioning of the facility has been delegated'. Ibid., Art. 2(6).

[18] Facility is defined as: 'one or more installations on the same site that are operated by the same natural or legal person'. Ibid., Art. 2(4). Moreover, installation means: 'a stationary technical unit where one or more activities listed in Annex I of this Regulation are carried out, and any other directly associated activities which have a technical connection with the activities carried out on that site and which could have an effect on emissions and pollution'. Ibid., Art. 2(3).

[19] Off-site transfer means: 'the movement beyond the boundaries of a facility of waste destined for recovery or disposal and of pollutants in waste water destined for waste-water treatment'. Ibid., Art. 2(11).

[20] Off-site transfers of hazardous waste exceeding 2 tonnes per year or of non-hazardous waste exceeding 2,000 tonnes per year, for any operations of recovery or disposal with the exception of the disposal operations of land treatment and deep injection referred to in Art. 6, indicating with 'R' or 'D' respectively whether the waste is destined for recovery or disposal and, for transboundary movements of hazardous waste, the name and address of the recoverer or the disposer of the waste and the actual recovery or disposal site. Ibid., Art. 5(1)(b). Waste which is subject to 'land treatment' or 'deep injection' disposal operations, as specified in Annex IIA to Dir. 75/442/EEC on Waste (Waste Framework Dir.) [1975] OJ L194/39, as last amended by Reg. (EC) No. 1882/2003 [2003] OJ L284/1, is required to be reported as a release to land only by the operator of the facility originating the waste. Ibid., Art. 6.

[21] Off-site transfers of any pollutant specified in Annex II in waste water destined for waste-water treatment for which the threshold value specified in Annex II, column 1b is exceeded. Ibid., Art. 5(1)(c).

which again must be reported by the operators of the facilities carrying out the activities listed in Annex I of the Regulation, in accordance with Article 5 of the Regulation; and

(iii) releases of pollutants from diffuse sources,[22] where available.[23]

The Commission is mandated to publish the European PRTR, presenting the data in both aggregated and non-aggregated forms, so that releases and transfers can be searched for and identified by: (i) facility, including the facility's parent company where applicable, and its geographical location, including the river basin; (ii) activity; (iii) occurrence at Member State or Community level; (iv) pollutant or waste, as appropriate; (v) each environmental medium (air, water, land) into which the pollutant is released; (vi) off-site transfers of waste and their destination, as appropriate; (vii) off-site transfers of pollutants in waste water; (viii) diffuse sources; (ix) facility owner or operator.[24] The European PRTR will be designed for maximum ease of public access to allow the information, under normal operating conditions, to be continuously and readily accessible on the Internet and by other electronic means. Furthermore, its design will take into account the possibility of its future expansion and will include all data reported for at least the last ten previous reporting years.[25] The European PRTR will include links to: (i) the national PRTRs of Member States; (ii) other relevant existing, publicly accessible databases on subject matters related to PRTRs, including national PRTRs of other Parties to the PRTR Protocol and, where feasible, those of other countries; (iii) facilities' websites if they exist and links are volunteered by the facilities.[26]

Under the Regulation, Member States will determine a date by which operators must provide the requisite data and information to its competent authority. Thereafter, Member States are required to provide the data specified in the Regulation to the Commission by electronic transfer in accordance with Annex III of the Regulation and within the time limits laid down. The first reporting year will be in 2007 when the Commission, assisted by the European Environment Agency (EEA) will incorporate the information reported by the Member States into the European PRTR within the time limits stipulated in the Regulation.[27]

The Regulation further provides that the Commission, assisted by the EEA, must include in the European PRTR information on releases from diffuse

[22] Diffuse sources means: 'the many smaller or scattered sources from which pollutants may be released to land, air or water, whose combined impact on those media may be significant and for which it is impractical to collect reports from each individual source'. Ibid., Art. 2(12).

[23] Ibid., Arts. 3(a)–(c) and 5(1)(a)–(c). See further Art. 5(1), second, third, and fourth indents, 5(2), (3), (4), and (5). The Commission, assisted by the European Environment Agency (EEA), is required to include in the European PRTR information on releases from diffuse sources where such information exists and has already been reported by the Member States. Ibid., Art. 8.

[24] Ibid., Art. 4(1)(a)–(i).

[25] Ibid., Art. (4)(2).

[26] Ibid., Art. 4(3)(a)–(c).

[27] Ibid., Art. 7(1)(2)(a)–(b), second indent, and (3)(a)–(b).

sources where such information exists and has already been reported by the Member States. This information is required to be organized so as to allow users to search for and identify releases of pollutants from diffuse sources according to an adequate geographical disaggregation and must include information on the type of methodology used to derive the information. Should the Commission determine that data on releases from diffuse sources do not exist, the Regulation obligates the Commission to take measures to initiate reporting on releases of relevant pollutants from one or more diffuse sources in accordance with the procedure laid down in the Regulation, using internationally approved methodologies where appropriate.[28] Quality assurance and assessment provisions, respectively, entail the operator of each facility assuring the quality of the information they report and the competent authorities assessing the quality of the data provided by the operators of the facilities, in particular as to their completeness, consistency, and credibility. Work on quality assurance and assessment will be coordinated by the Commission assisted by, and in consultation with, a Committee.[29]

In order to facilitate access to information, the Regulation requires the Commission, assisted by the EEA, to make the European PRTR publicly accessible by dissemination free of charge, within a timeframe, on the Internet. Where the information contained in the European PRTR is not easily accessible to the public by direct electronic means, the Member State concerned and the Commission must facilitate electronic access to the European PRTR in publicly accessible locations.[30]

With regard to confidentiality, whenever information is kept confidential by a Member State in accordance with Article 4 of Directive 2003/4/EC on Public Access to Environmental Information ((New) Environmental Information Directive),[31] the Member State, in its report under this Regulation for the reporting year concerned, is required to indicate separately for each facility claiming confidentiality the type of information that has been withheld and the reason for which it has been withheld.[32]

As for public participation, the Regulation requires the Commission to provide the public[33] with early and effective opportunities to participate in the further development of the European PRTR, including capacity-building and the preparation of amendments to this Regulation. The public will have the opportunity to submit any relevant comments, information, analyses, or opinions within a reasonable timeframe. The Commission is obligated to take due account

[28] Ibid., Art. 8(1)–(3).
[29] Ibid., Art. 9(1)–(3).
[30] Ibid., Art. 10(1) and (2).
[31] [2003] OJ L41/26.
[32] Reg. (EC) No. 166/2006, n. 10 above, Art. 11.
[33] The public means: 'one or more natural or legal persons, and, in accordance with national legislation and practice, their associations, organisations or groups'. Ibid., Art. 2(1).

of such input and must inform the public about the outcome of the public participation.[34]

Access to justice in matters relating to public access to environmental information must be ensured in accordance with Article 6 of the New Environmental Information Directive and, where the institutions of the Community are involved, in accordance with Articles 6, 7, and 8 of Regulation (EC) No. 1049/2001 regarding Public Access to European Parliament, Council and Commission Documents (Public Access to Documents Regulation).[35]

The Commission is mandated to draw up a guidance document, in consultation with the aforementioned Committee, supporting the implementation of the European PRTR as soon as possible but no later than four months before the first reporting year (in 2007). This guidance document will address in particular details on the following: (i) reporting procedures; (ii) the data to be reported; (iii) quality assurance and assessment; (iv) indication of type of withheld data and reasons why they were withheld in the case of confidential data; (v) reference to internationally approved release determination and analytical methods, sampling, and methodologies; (vi) indication of parent companies; and (vii) coding of activities according to Annex I to this Regulation and to the IPPC Directive.[36]

The Commission and the Member States are instructed to promote the awareness of the public of the European PRTR and to ensure that assistance is provided in accessing the European PRTR and in understanding and using the information contained in it.[37] Additionally, Member States are required to inform the Commission on practice and measures regarding: (i) reporting by operators of releases of pollutants; (ii) quality assurance and assessment; (iii) access to information; (iv) awareness raising activities; (v) confidentiality of information; and (vi) penalties provided for infringements of the provisions of the Regulation and experience with their application. Under the Regulation Member States must take all measures necessary to ensure that penalties are implemented and that penalties provided for are effective, proportionate, and dissuasive.[38]

ii. Access to Information, Public Participation in Decision-Making, and Access to Justice

Of great significance and at long last in 2006, the provisions of the Aarhus Convention[39] were applied to Community Institutions and Bodies by Regulation (EC) No. 1367/2006 on the application of the provisions of the Aarhus Convention on Access to Information, Public Participation in Decision-making and Access to Justice in Environmental Matters to Community Institutions and

[34] Ibid., Art. 12(1)–(3).
[35] [2001] OJ L145/43. Reg. (EC) No. 166/2006, n. 10 above, Art. 13.
[36] Ibid., Art. 14(1) and (2)(a)–(g).
[37] Ibid., Art. 15.
[38] Ibid., Arts. 16(1)(a)–(f) and 20.
[39] N. 1 above.

Bodies (the Community Institutions and Bodies Regulation).[40] The objective of this Regulation is to contribute to the implementation of the obligations arising under the Aarhus Convention by laying down rules to apply the provisions of the Convention to Community institutions and bodies, in particular by:

(i) guaranteeing the right of public access to environmental information received or produced by Community institutions or bodies and held by them, and by setting out the basic terms and conditions of, and practical arrangements for, the exercise of that right;

(ii) ensuring that environmental information is progressively made available and disseminated to the public in order to achieve its widest possible systematic availability and dissemination. To that end, the use, in particular, of computer telecommunication and/or electronic technology, where available, will be promoted;

(iii) providing for public participation concerning plans and programmes relating to the environment; and

(iv) granting access to justice in environmental matters at Community level under the conditions laid down by the Community Institutions and Bodies Regulation.[41]

In applying the provisions of the Regulation, the Community institutions and bodies must endeavour to assist and provide guidance to the public with regard to access to information, participation in decision-making, and access to justice in environmental matters.[42]

In Title II on Access to Environmental Information, provision is made for the Public Access to Documents Regulation[43] to apply to any request by an applicant (defined under the Community Institutions and Bodies Regulation as 'any natural or legal person requesting environmental information'[44]) for access to environmental information held by Community institutions and bodies without discrimination as to citizenship, nationality, or domicile and, in the case of a legal person, without discrimination as to where it has its registered seat or an effective centre of its activities. For the purposes of the Community Institutions and Bodies Regulation, Community institution or body means: 'any public institution, body, office or agency established by, or on the basis of, the Treaty except when acting in a judicial or legislative capacity'.[45] It is to be noted that

[40] [2006] OJ L264/13.

[41] Ibid., Art. 1(a)–(d).

[42] Ibid., Art. 1(2).

[43] N. 35 above.

[44] Community Institutions and Bodies Reg., Art. 2(1)(a).

[45] Ibid., Art. 2(1)(c). Contrary to the Aarhus Convention under which Community institutions and bodies can be excluded from the scope of the application of the Convention when acting in a judicial or legislative capacity. Ibid., recital 7.

Article 9(3) of the Aarhus Convention provides for access to judicial or other review procedures for challenging acts and omissions by *private* and public authorities which contravene provisions of law relating to the environment.[46] Recital 8 to the Community Institutions and Bodies Regulation continues by saying that provisions on access to justice should be consistent with the Treaty and that it is appropriate in this context that this Regulation addresses *only acts and omissions by public authorities*. However, the provisions under Title II will apply to Community institutions or bodies acting in a legislative capacity.[47] It has been necessary to extend the application of the Public Access to Documents Regulation to all Community institutions and bodies for the purposes of Title II of the Community Institutions and Bodies Regulation in order to comply with the Aarhus Convention.[48] Environmental information is defined under the latter Regulation as any information in written, visual, aural, electronic, or any other material form on:

(i) the state of the elements of the environment, such as air and atmosphere, water, soil, land, landscape and natural sites including wetlands, coastal and marine areas, biological diversity and its components, and the interaction among these elements;

(ii) factors, such as substances, energy, noise, radiation or waste, including radioactive waste, emissions, discharges and other releases into the environment, affecting or likely to affect the aforementioned elements of the environment;

(iii) measures (including administrative measures), such as policies, legislation, plans, programmes, environmental agreements, and activities affecting or likely to affect the aforementioned elements and factors as well as measures or activities designed to protect those elements;

(iv) reports on the implementation of environmental legislation;

(v) cost-benefit and other economic analyses and assumptions used within the framework of the measures and activities referred to in point (iii); and

(vi) the state of human health and safety, including the contamination of the food chain, where relevant, conditions of human life, cultural sites and built structures in as much as they are or may be affected by the state of the elements of the environment referred to in point (i) or, through those elements, by any of the matters referred to in points (ii) and (iii).[49]

[46] Ibid., recital 8.

[47] For reasons of consistency with the Public Access to Documents Reg., the provisions on access to environmental information will apply to Community institutions and bodies acting in a legislative capacity. Community Institutions and Bodies Reg., recital 7.

[48] Ibid., recital 12.

[49] Ibid., Art. 2(1)(d)(i)–(vi).

With regard to the collection and dissemination of environmental information, Community institutions and bodies are instructed by the 2006 Regulation to organize the environmental information which is relevant to their functions and which is held by them, with a view to its active and systematic dissemination to the public, in particular by means of computer telecommunications and/or electronic technology in accordance with Articles 11(1) and (2), and 12 of the Public Access to Documents Regulation. They are instructed further to make this environmental information progressively available in electronic databases that are easily accessible to the public through public telecommunication networks. To that end, they must place the environmental information that they hold on databases and equip these with search aids and other forms of software designed to assist the public in locating the information they require.[50] Nevertheless, the information made available by means of computer telecommunication and/or electronic technology need not include information collected before the entry into force of this Regulation unless it is already available in electronic form. Community institutions and bodies, however, are required, as far as possible, to indicate where information collected before entry into force of this Regulation, which is not available in electronic form, is located.[51] Also, Community institutions and bodies are required to make all reasonable efforts to maintain environmental information held by them in forms or formats that are readily reproducible and accessible by computer telecommunications or by other electronic means.[52] Furthermore, the environmental information to be made available and disseminated must be updated as appropriate. In addition to the documents listed in Article 12(2) and (3) and in Article 13(1) and (2) of the Public Access to Documents Regulation, the Community Institutions and Bodies Regulation makes it obligatory for the databases or registers to include the following:

(i) texts of international treaties, conventions or agreements, and of Community legislation on the environment or relating to it, and of policies, plans and programmes relating to the environment;

(ii) progress reports on the implementation of the items referred to under (i) where prepared or held in electronic form by the Community institutions or bodies;

(iii) steps taken in proceedings for infringements of Community law from the stage of the reasoned opinion pursuant to Article 226(1) EC;

(iv) reports on the state of the environment (as referred to below);

(v) data or summaries of data derived from the monitoring of activities affecting, or likely to affect, the environment;

[50] Ibid., Art. 4(1), first indent.

[51] Ibid., Art. 4(1), second indent.

[52] Ibid., Art. 4(1), third indent.

(vi) authorizations with a significant impact on the environment, and environmental agreements, or a reference to the place where such information can be requested or accessed; and

(vii) environmental impact studies and risk assessments concerning environmental elements, or a reference to the place where such information can be requested or accessed.[53]

It is possible, in appropriate cases, for Community institutions and bodies to satisfy this Regulation's requirements concerning the collection and dissemination of environmental information by creating links to Internet sites where the information can be found.[54] Additionally, the Commission is charged with ensuring that, at regular intervals not exceeding four years, a report on the state of the environment, including information on the quality of, and pressures on, the environment is published and disseminated.[55]

As far as quality is concerned, this Regulation instructs Community institutions and bodies, insofar as is within their power, to ensure that any information that is compiled by them, or on their behalf, is up to date, accurate, and comparable. Moreover, Community institutions and bodies must, upon request, inform the applicant of the place where information on the measurement procedures, including methods of analysis, sampling and pre-treatment of samples, used in compiling the information can be found, if it is available. Alternatively they may refer them to the standardized procedure that was used.[56]

As a general rule, the Community Institutions and Bodies Regulation applies the exceptions to disclosure of environmental information laid down in the Public Access to Documents Regulation, subject to the more specific provisions in the 2006 Regulation concerning requests for environmental information.[57] Accordingly, as regards Article 4(2), first and third indents of the Public Access to Documents Regulation, with the exception of investigations in particular those concerning possible infringements of Community law, an overriding public interest in disclosure will be deemed to exist where the information relates to emissions into the environment. Furthermore, as regards the other exceptions set out in Article 4 of the Public Access to Documents Regulation, under the Community Institutions and Bodies Regulation the grounds for refusal will be interpreted in a restrictive way, taking into account the public interest served by disclosure and whether the information relates to emissions into the environment. Nevertheless, in addition to the exceptions set out in Article 4 of the Public Access to Documents Regulation, Community institutions and bodies under the 2006 Regulation may refuse access to environmental information where disclosure of the information would adversely affect the protection of the environment to which the information relates, such as the breeding sites of rare species.[58]

[53] Ibid., Art. 2(a)–(g).
[54] Ibid., Art. 2(3).
[55] Ibid, Art. 2(4).
[56] Ibid., Art. 5(1)(2).
[57] Ibid., recital 15.
[58] Ibid., Art. 6(1)(2).

Acting in accordance with this Regulation, where a Community institution or body receives a request for access to environmental information and where this information is not held by that Community institution or body, it is required to act as promptly as possible, but is given 15 working days at the latest to inform the applicant of the Community institution or body or the public authority, within the meaning of the New Access to Environmental Information Directive, to which it believes it is possible to apply for the information requested or to transfer the request to the relevant Community institution or body or the public authority and to inform the applicant accordingly.[59]

In the event of an imminent threat to human health, life, or the environment, whether caused by human activities or due to natural causes, this Regulation further instructs Community institutions and bodies, upon the request of public authorities within the meaning of the New Access to Environmental Information Directive, to collaborate with and assist those public authorities in order to enable the latter to disseminate immediately and without delay to the public that might be affected all environmental information which could enable it to take measures to prevent or mitigate harm arising from the threat, to the extent that this information is held by or on behalf of Community institutions and/or those public authorities.[60]

Title III of the Community Institutions and Bodies Regulation addresses the second pillar of the Aarhus Convention, namely, public participation concerning plans and programmes relating to the environment. Plans and programmes relating to the environment are defined as plans and programmes:

(i) which are subject to preparation and, as appropriate, adoption by a Community institution or body;

(ii) which are required under legislative, regulatory, or administrative provisions; and

(iii) which contribute to, or are likely to have significant effects on, the achievement of the objectives of Community environmental policy, such as laid down in the Sixth Community Environment Action Programme,[61] or in any subsequent general environmental action programme.[62]

General environmental action programmes will also be considered as plans and programmes relating to the environment. This definition, however, explicitly

[59] Ibid., Art. 7.

[60] Ibid., Art. 8, first indent. This requirement of cooperation is stated to apply without prejudice to any specific obligation laid down by Community legislation, in particular by Dec. No. 2119/98/EC setting up a Network for the Epidemiological Surveillance and Control of Communicable Diseases in the Community [1998] OJ L268/1, and by Dec. No. 1786/2002/EC adopting a Programme of Community Action in the Field of Public Health [2002] OJ L271/1.

[61] Dec. 1600/2002/EC laying down the Sixth Community Environment Action Programme [2002] OJ L242/1.

[62] Community Institutions and Bodies Reg., Art. 2(1)(e), first indent, (i)–(iii).

excludes financial or budget plans and programmes, namely those laying down how particular projects or activities should be financed or those related to the proposed annual budgets, internal work programmes of a Community institution or body, or emergency plans and programmes designed for the sole purpose of civil protection.[63]

Community institutions and bodies are placed under an obligation to provide, through appropriate practical and/or other provisions, early and effective opportunities for the public to participate during the preparation, modification, or review of plans or programmes relating to the environment when all options are still open. In particular, where the Commission prepares a proposal for such a plan or programme which is submitted to other Community institutions or bodies for decision, it is required to provide for public participation at that preparatory stage.[64] 'The public' means one or more natural or legal persons, and associations, organizations or groups of such persons.[65] Community institutions and bodies are instructed to identify the public affected or likely to be affected by, or having an interest in, a plan or programme of the type referred to in this Regulation, taking into account its objectives.[66] Furthermore, Community institutions and bodies must ensure that the aforementioned public is informed, whether by public notices or other appropriate means, such as electronic media where available, of the draft proposal, where available; of the environmental information or assessment relevant to the plan or programme under preparation, where available; and of practical arrangements for participation. Information on practical arrangements should cover: (i) the administrative entity from which the relevant information may be obtained; (ii) the administrative entity to which comments, opinions, or questions may be submitted; and (iii) reasonable time-frames allowing sufficient time for the public to be informed and to prepare and participate effectively in the environmental decision-making process.[67]

It is mandatory for a time limit of at least eight weeks to be set for receiving comments, and where meetings or hearings are organized, prior notice of at least four weeks must be given. Provision is made under this Community Institutions and Bodies Regulation for time limits to be shortened in urgent cases or where the public has already had the opportunity to comment on the plan or programme in question.[68] Finally, in taking a decision on a plan or programme relating to the environment, Community institutions and bodies are required to take due account of the outcome of the public participation. Community institutions and bodies are also required to inform the public of that plan or programme,

[63] Ibid. Art. 2(1)(e), second and third indents.
[64] Ibid., Art. 9(1).
[65] Ibid., Art. 2(1)(b).
[66] Ibid., Art. 9(2).
[67] Ibid., Art. 9(3)(a)–(c)(iii).
[68] Ibid., Art. 9(4).

including its text, and of the reasons and consideration upon which the decision is based, including information on public participation.[69]

Internal Review and Access to Justice are treated in Title IV of the Community Institutions and Bodies Regulation. Thereunder, any non-governmental organization (NGO) which meets the criteria set out in this Regulation is entitled to make a request for internal review to the Community institution or body that has adopted an administrative act under environmental law,[70] or, in case of an alleged administrative omission, should have adopted such an act.[71] Under this Regulation, 'administrative act' means any measure of individual scope under environmental law, taken by a Community institution or body, and having legally binding effects;[72] and 'administrative omission' means any failure of a Community institution or body to adopt an administrative act so defined.[73] It is provided further that administrative acts and omissions will not include measures taken or omissions by a Community institution or body in its capacity as an administrative review body, such as under Articles 81, 82, 86, and 87 EC (competition rules); Articles 226 and 228 EC (infringement proceedings); Article 195 EC (Ombudsman proceedings); and Article 280 EC (anti-fraud investigations).[74]

Such a request for the internal review of an administrative act must be made in writing and within a time limit not exceeding six weeks after the administrative act was adopted, notified, or published, whichever is the latest, or, in the case of an alleged omission, six weeks after the date when the administrative act was required. It is further provided that the request must state the grounds for the review.[75] The responsible Community institution or body is placed under an obligation to consider any such request, unless it is clearly unsubstantiated. It is also obligated to state its reasons in a written reply as soon as possible, but no later than 12 weeks after receipt of the request.[76] The Community Institutions and Bodies Regulation goes on to provide that where the Community institution or body is unable, despite exercising due diligence, to act in accordance with the aforementioned two obligations, it is required to inform the NGO which made the request as soon as possible and at the latest within the period mentioned in the Regulation, of the reasons for its failure to act and when it intends to do so.

[69] Ibid., Art. 9(5).

[70] Ibid., Art. 2(i) defines environmental law as: 'Community legislation which, irrespective of its legal basis, contributes to the pursuit of the objectives of the Community policy on the environment as set out in the Treaty: preserving, protecting and improving the quality of the environment, protecting human health, the prudent and rational utilization of natural resources, and promoting measures at international level to deal with regional or worldwide environmental problems'.

[71] Ibid., Art. 10(1), first indent.

[72] Ibid., Art. 2(1)(g).

[73] Ibid., Art. 2(1)(h).

[74] Ibid., Art. 2(2)(a)–(d).

[75] Ibid., Art. 10(1), second indent.

[76] Ibid., Art. 10(2).

In any event, the Community institution or body must act within 18 weeks from receipt of the request.[77]

An NGO will be entitled to make a request for internal review in accordance with this Community Institutions and Bodies Regulation, provided that, firstly, it is an independent non-profit-making legal person according to a Member State's national law or practice; secondly, it has the primary stated objective of promoting environmental protection in the context of environmental law; and, thirdly, it has existed for more than two years and is actively pursuing the aforementioned objective. Additionally, the subject matter in respect of which the request for internal review is made must be covered by its objective and activities.[78] The Commission is charged with the task of adopting the necessary provisions in order to ensure the transparent and consistent application of the criteria for entitlement as an NGO.[79]

It is provided further that the NGO, which made the request for internal review pursuant to this Regulation, may institute proceedings before the European Court of Justice (ECJ) in accordance with the relevant provisions of the Treaty.[80] Furthermore, where the Community institution or body fails to consider a request that is not clearly unsubstantiated, fails to state its reasons in writing within the stipulated time limit, or is unable to do so despite exercising due diligence, and fails to inform the NGO in accordance with this Regulation, the latter may institute proceedings before the ECJ in accordance with the relevant provisions of the Treaty.[81]

In conclusion, where necessary the Community is required to adapt its rules of procedure to the provisions of the Community Institutions and Bodies Regulation in order to take effect from 28 June 2007.[82]

iii. Eco-Label

Decision 2006/402/EC established in 2006 a revised Community Eco-label Working Plan for the period 1 January 2005 to 31 December 2007, and also called for a review of the Working Plan before 31 December 2007.[83] A priority objective is for the European Union Eco-labeling Board (EUEB), Member States, and the Commission to develop and adapt the long-term policy and strategy of the Eco-label Scheme in the light of the revision of Regulation (EC) No. 1980/2000 on a Revised Community Eco-label Award Scheme (Eco-label Regulation).[84] This strategy seeks the contribution of the aforementioned parties to the integration

77 Ibid., Art. 10(3), first and second indents.
78 Ibid., Art. 11(1)(a)–(d).
79 Ibid., Art. 11(2).
80 Ibid., Art. 12(1).
81 Ibid., Art. 12(2).
82 Ibid., Art. 13.
83 [2006] OJ L162/78. Arts. 1 and 2.
84 [2000] OJ L237/1.

of the eco-label in the various policy developments taking place in relation to sustainable consumption such as, for example, integrated product policy, green public procurement, wider labelling, reduced taxation for green products, etc. Accordingly, the Working Plan calls for action in the form of dedicated meetings, investigations, and the mobilization of expertise. Further objectives for environmental improvement and market penetration feature in the Working Plan. These aim, in particular:

(i) to widen the number of markets potentially open to eco-labelled products by progressively expanding the range of eco-label product groups (currently 23) and making the eco-label more attractive to manufacturers;

(ii) within each of these markets/product groups, to increase significantly the visibility of the eco-label, i.e. the number of eco-labelled products on the market;

(iii) to consider the overall environmental benefits of the scheme and its contribution in making consumption more sustainable; and

(iv) to build further on the potential interrelationship between the Community eco-label and eco-management and audit scheme.

The Working Plan identifies, inter alia, the objective of increasing the number of established product groups to between 30 and 35 within five years. Scheduled actions would include updating the priority product group list regularly, following consultation with, and reassessment by, the EUEB and, also, revising, updating, and weighting the prioritization criteria.

As far as market penetration, visibility, and consumer awareness are concerned, it is documented that Community eco-labelled products still account for less than one per cent of the total market for the different product groups. Accordingly, an objective would be to target an annual increase of at least 50 per cent of the value and/or number of eco-labelled articles. A further objective is to achieve before the end of this Working Plan a minimum level of visibility in all the Member States, new and old, including a methodology on how to measure visibility in a cost-effective way. A stated long-term aim would be for more than half of European consumers to recognize the Community eco-label as a label of environmental excellence. Towards these ends, the EUEB are urged to improve the reporting mechanisms already in place to establish annual statistics for tracking market penetration for the different product groups. The EUEB, Member States, and the Commission further are encouraged to promote the Community eco-label in order to reach the agreed targets, in particular of retailers and public procurement officers. Additional actions would involve each Member State developing a marketing strategy which includes the relevant activities in order of priority; and would also involve the EUEB, Member States, and the Commission in promoting the sharing of experiences in the implementation of the eco-label between the 'old' and 'new' Member States, for example, in the form of organized tutoring sessions. Furthermore, the Working Plan foresees the necessity of building up alliances with all interested parties (including NGOs, producers, consumer organizations, and retailers) in order to increase the knowledge of the scheme in these organizations and to encourage marketing of the Flower (the symbol of the European Eco-Label) through their contact networks.

According to the Working Plan, whereas the direct environmental benefits of the eco-label relate mainly to the environmental savings that could be gained if the market share of eco-labelled products were to increase, indirect benefits include other positive effects the eco-label has had, and could potentially have in the future. Moreover, a recently completed study shows that with a 20 per cent increase of its market uptake the Community eco-label could achieve significant savings through its indirect benefits, potentially working as one of the more cost-effective instruments for reducing emissions of carbon dioxide. The EUEB is, thus, urged to continue to work to estimate the direct and indirect environmental benefits of the eco-label as a whole, and systematically to estimate the potential benefits for all new or revised product group criteria. The EUEB, Member States, and the Commission are encouraged to act to inform public and private procurement officers of the opportunities for using Community eco-label criteria in their calls for tenders.

The Working Plan underlines the necessity of analysing and upgrading to a real partnership the complementary and mutually supportive roles of the Community eco-label and environmental management and audit scheme; and concludes that close cooperation and a clear understanding of how they will work together is essential to assure the success of both schemes. A further objective highlighted in the Working Plan is that of progressively and systematically stepping up the cooperation, coordination, and linkages between the Community eco-label and other eco-labels in all Member States (new and old), specifically with a view to the revision of the eco-label scheme. The Working Plan calls upon the cooperation and coordination management group to prepare and implement a strategy on how to encourage national Type 1 eco-labels to further cooperate and link with the Community eco-label. Additionally, a stated objective of the Working Plan is progressively to enhance the coordination of product group development in the different labelling schemes in the European Union (EU), again specifically in light of the revision of the eco-label scheme. Towards this end actions would include, inter alia, the EUEB encouraging cooperation with the national labels in Member States in order to review and catalogue all product groups covered by eco-labels in the EU and continuing the work on establishing and updating a central register of these product groups and their criteria. It is proposed that this work should be used to consider how the revision of the Community Eco-label Regulation could contribute to better coordination with national and international labels. Moreover, the systematic exchange of information is aimed for. The Working Plan calls for joint actions to promote the Community eco-label scheme and other eco-labels in Member States, and their eco-labelled products, in order to raise consumer awareness and understanding of the common and complementary (as opposed to competitive) roles of the schemes, and for promotional activities to be aimed at improving stakeholder awareness and also public and private purchaser awareness. A strategy and actions for setting up eco-label support networks for small and medium-sized businesses is advocated, as is the development of strategic partnerships between the EUEB and retailers. Finally, the Working Plan identifies the long-term objective of achieving self-financing of the eco-label scheme and the need for action on the part of the EUEB in establishing a strategy in order to achieve this goal.

iv. Eco-Management and Audit System

Regulation (EC) No. 196/2006[85] amends Annex 1 to Regulation (EC) No. 761/2001 Allowing Voluntary Participation by Organisations in a Community Eco-Management and Audit Scheme ((Revised) EMAS Regulation)[86] to take account of the European Standard EN ISO 14001:2004, and repeals Decision 97/265/EC on the recognition of the International Standard ISO 14001:1996 and the European Standard EN ISO 14001:1996.[87] The International Standard ISO 14001:1996 was modified in 2004 following the work of the International Organization for Standardization (ISO) Committee TC207/SC1 Environment Management System, in order to improve compatibility of ISO 14001 with ISO 9001 and to clarify the existing text of ISO 14001 without adding any new additional requirements.[88] The ISO has subsequently released a new revised version of the International Standard ISO 14001:2004 and of the European Standard EN ISO 14001:2004.[89] Accordingly, Part A 'Environment Management System Requirements' of Annex I to the EMAS Regulation 761/2001 has been amended to take account of the European Standard EN ISO 14001:2004, and organizations participating in the eco-management and audit scheme are required to implement the requirements of EN ISO 14001:2004.[90] Part A of Annex I to the EMAS Regulation is replaced by the Annex to Regulation (EC) No. 196/2006.[91] Transitional arrangements exist, however, for organizations already registered under EMAS.[92] Provision is made for organizations registered in the EMAS register at the time of entry into force of this Regulation to remain on the EMAS register, subject to the verification referred to in the 2006 Regulation.[93] Compliance with the requirements of the EMAS Regulation as amended by this Regulation must be checked at the time of the next verification of the organ-

85 [2006] OJ L32/4.
86 [2001] OJ L114/1, as amended by the 2003 Act of Accession.
87 [1997] OJ L104/37.
88 Reg. (EC) No. 196/2006, n. 85 above, recital 2.
89 Ibid., recital 3.
90 Ibid., recitals 4 and 5 and Annex I.
91 Ibid., Art. 1.
92 Ibid., recital 6.
93 Ibid., Art. 2(1).

ization.[94] Nevertheless, it is further provided that if the next verification is to be carried out sooner than six months after entry into force of this Regulation, the date of the next verification may be extended by six months in agreement with the environmental verifier and the competent body.[95]

Decision 2006/193/EC lays down rules, under the EMAS Regulation, on the use of the EMAS logo in the exceptional cases of transport packaging and tertiary packaging.[96]

v. European Environment Agency

Decision 2006/235/EC approves, on behalf of the EC, the Agreement between the Community and Switzerland concerning the latter's participation in the EEA and the European Environment Information and Observation Network.[97]

vi. Integrated Pollution Prevention and Control

A questionnaire relating to the IPPC Directive,[98] repealing Decision 1999/391/EC, is set out in the Annex to Decision 2006/194/EC.[99] Member States are required to use that questionnaire as a basis for drawing up the report to be submitted to the Commission pursuant to Article 16(3) of the IPPC Directive covering the period from 1 January 2006 to 31 December 2008.[100]

C. Legislation in Progress

i. Aarhus Convention

In 2006, the Commission proposed that the Community should approve the amendment to the Aarhus Convention[101] concerning public participation in decision-making on genetically modified organisms (GMO), by means of a Council Decision.[102] The Second Meeting of the Parties, meeting in May 2005, agreed on an amendment to the Aarhus Convention making more specific the obligations placed on parties with regard to public participation in GMO decision-making processes. According to the proposed Decision, relevant Community law governing GMOs, and in particular Directive 2001/18/EC on the Deliberate Release of Genetically Modified Organisms into the Environment and Repealing

[94] Ibid., Art. 2(2), first indent.
[95] Ibid., Art. 2(2), second indent.
[96] [2006] OJ L70/63.
[97] [2006] OJ L90/36.
[98] N. 8 above.
[99] [2006] OJ L70/65.
[100] See also Section F.*iii* below.
[101] N. 1 above.
[102] Proposal for a Council Decision on the conclusion, on behalf of the European Community, of an amendment to the Convention on Access to Information, Public Participation in Decision Making and Access to Justice in Environmental Matters COM(2006)338, 26 June 2006.

Directive 90/220/EEC (Deliberate Release Directive),[103] and Regulation (EC) No. 1829/2003 on Genetically Modified Food and Feed (GM Food and Feed Regulation),[104] incorporates provisions for public participation in decision-making on GMOs, consistent with the amendment to the Aarhus Convention.

ii. Civil Protection

The Commission also recast and presented a Proposal for a Council Decision establishing a Community Civil Protection Mechanism,[105] the main objectives of which are to strengthen the mechanism based upon the lessons learned in past emergencies, and to provide a legal basis for additional Community actions that are necessary. The present Proposal relates to Decision 2001/792/EC, Euratom establishing a Community mechanism to Facilitate Reinforced Cooperation in Civil Protection Assistance Interventions,[106] amending this Decision to allow improved cooperation and coordination.

iii. Cohesion Fund

At the beginning of 2006, the Commission presented an Amended Proposal for a Council Regulation establishing a Cohesion Fund,[107] which provides, inter alia, that from the date of accession until 31 December 2006 the ten new EU Member States will also be eligible for assistance from the Fund.

iv. Sustainable Use of Pesticides

A Commission Proposal for a Directive establishing a framework for Community action to Achieve a Sustainable Use of Pesticides[108] focuses on plant production products. Based on Article 175(1) EC, the proposed Directive aims to implement those provisions of the Thematic Strategy on the Sustainable Use of Pesticides[109] that cannot be included in existing instruments or policies, with the exception of the collection of statistical information regarding the placing on the market and use of plant protection products. The draft Directive is comprised of provisions on:

(i) establishment of National Action Plans (NAPs) to set objectives to reduce hazards, risks, and dependence on chemical control for plant protection, which will allow for the necessary flexibility to adapt the measures to the specific situations in the Member States;

(ii) involvement of stakeholders in the setting up, implementation, and adaptation of the NAPs;

(iii) creation of a system of training and awareness-raising for distributors and professional users of pesticides in order to ensure that they are fully aware

[103] [2001] OJ L106/1. [104] [2003] OJ L268/1. [105] COM(2006)29, 26 Jan. 2006.
[106] [2001] OJ L297/7. [107] COM(2006)5, 16 Jan. 2006.
[108] COM(2006)373, 12 July 2006. [109] See Section D.*v* below.

of the risks involved. Better information for the general public through awareness-raising campaigns, information passed on through retailers, and other appropriate measures;

(iv) regular inspection of application equipment in order to reduce adverse impacts of pesticides on human health (in particular as regards operator exposure) and the environment during application;

(v) prohibition of aerial spraying with derogation possible, to limit the risks of significant adverse impacts on human health and the environment, in particular from spray drift;

(vi) specific measures to protect the aquatic environment from pollution by pesticides;

(vii) defining areas of significantly reduced or zero pesticide use in line with measures taken under other legislation or to protect sensitive groups;

(viii) handling and storage of pesticides and their packaging and remnants;

(ix) development of Community-wide standards on Integrated Pest Management (IPM), and establishment of necessary conditions for implementation of IPM;

(x) measuring progress in risk reduction through appropriate harmonized indicators; and

(xi) establishment of a system of information exchange for continuous development and improvement of appropriate guidance, best practices, and recommendations.

It is interesting to note that the proposed Directive would create the legal framework under which Member States would retain a significant amount of flexibility to determine the necessary implementing measures appropriate to their specific geographic, agricultural and climatic situations, national legislation, and programmes. Where deemed feasible (e.g. for the collection of empty packaging), the Directive leaves the possibility of self-regulation.

v. Soil

Also of significance in 2006 was the Commission Proposal for a Directive establishing a Framework for the Protection of Soil and amending Directive 2004/35/EC.[110] The Soil Strategy was the last of the seven Thematic Strategies

[110] COM(2006)232, 22 Sept. 2006. See also, Commission Press Release IP/06/1241, 22 September 2006, available on the Internet at http://europa.eu/rapid/ (RAPID). Dir. 2004/35/EC on Environmental Liability with regard to the Prevention and Remedying of Environmental Damage [2004] OJ L143/56, establishes that, for orphan sites, remedial action may be taken by the competent authority as a last resort. It should therefore be amended in order to align it with the remediation obligations laid down in the Proposal.

that the Commission presented pursuant to the Sixth Environmental Action Programme.[111] The proposed Directive describes soil as essentially a non-renewable resource in that the degradation rates can be rapid whereas the formation and regeneration processes are extremely slow. Moreover, it is a very dynamic system which performs many functions and delivers services vital to human activities and to the survival of ecosystems. These functions are biomass production, storing, filtering and transforming nutrients and water, hosting the biodiversity pool, acting as a platform for most human activities, providing raw materials, acting as a carbon pool, and storing the geological and archeological heritage.[112] Furthermore, soil degradation or soil improvements have a major impact on other areas of Community interest, such as surface water and groundwater protection, human health, climate change, protection of nature and biodiversity, and food safety.[113] The objective of this Proposal is to establish a common strategy for the protection and sustainable use of soil based on the principles of integration of soil concerns into other policies, preservation of soil functions within the context of sustainable use, prevention of threats to soil and mitigation of their effects, as well as restoration of degraded soils to a level of functionality consistent with current and approved future use. The Commission has identified the main threats confronting soils in the EU, namely: erosion; organic matter decline; contamination; salinization; compaction; soil biodiversity loss; sealing; and landslides and flooding.[114] The proposed Directive is the result of a consultation of interested parties, in response to which a majority of citizens as well as soil experts and organizations favours action taken under the form of a framework adopted at Community level and concrete measures adopted at national or local level. It is important to note that abundant calls for mandatory restrictions on urban and tourist developments have not been endorsed in this Proposal since the Community has limited competences on restricting land use. According to the Commission, there was unanimous consensus that soil should be guaranteed the same level of protection as that provided to other environmental media, such as air or water, because soil functions are crucial for human and ecosystem survival. It was always projected that because of the enormous variability of soil across Europe, a 'one-fits-all' approach could not be adopted as the basis for Community soil policy. In the event, most expressed opinions advocating a flexible system which would allow local specificities of soil and land use to be taken into account. Accordingly, there was a broad consensus for a European framework to be adopted which would establish common objectives and principles leaving to Member States the adoption of detailed measures at the appropriate administrative and geographical level. The reports drafted by the Working Groups have been published and

[111] N. 61 above.
[112] COM(2006)232, n. 110 above, recital 1.
[113] Ibid., recital 2.
[114] Commission Communication, 'Towards a Thematic Strategy on Soil Protection' COM(2002)179, 16 Apr. 2002.

are available on the Internet; the website also displays the replies to the public questionnaire from experts and organizations.[115] In arriving at the Proposal for a framework Directive for the Protection of Soil, based on Article 175(1) EC, the following options were considered:

(i) the encouragement of Member States to take action under a general non-binding community soil strategy;
(ii) a flexible legal instrument which would take the form of a Soil Framework Directive, ambitious in its scope but not overly prescriptive in its content;[116] or
(iii) legislative proposals for the different soil threats, setting also all targets and means at Community level.

In summary, the proposed Directive includes the following provisions.

(i) The establishment of a common framework to protect soil on the basis of the principles of preservation of soil functions, prevention of soil degradation, mitigation of its effects, restoration of degraded soils, and integration in other sectoral policies.
(ii) The requirement to identify, describe, and assess the impact of some sectoral policies on soil degradation processes with a view to protect soil functions.
(iii) The requirement for land users to take precautionary measures when their use of the soil can be expected to hamper significantly soil functions.
(iv) An approach to soil sealing to ensure a more rational use of land in accordance with Article 174 EC and to maintain as many soil functions as possible.
(v) Identification of areas at risk of erosion, organic matter decline, salinization, compaction and landslides, and establishment of national programmes of measures. According to the Commission, the extent of the areas at risk of these threats need to be identified, and to ensure a coherent and comparable approach, the identification of risk must be carried out on the basis of common elements. These elements include parameters which are known to be driving forces for the different threats. Risk reduction targets and programmes of measures to reach those targets will have to be adopted. Programmes can build on standards and measures already identified and implemented in national and Community contexts.

[115] See: http://ec.europa.eu/comm/environment/soil/index.htm.

[116] The Commission carried out an Impact Assessment, which is available at: http://ec.europa.eu/comm/environment/soil/index.htm.

(vi) Measures to limit the introduction of dangerous substances into the soil, to avoid accumulation in soil that would hamper soil functions and create a risk to human health and the environment.

(vii) Setting up an inventory of contaminated sites, a mechanism for funding the remediation of orphan sites, a soil status report, and establishing a national strategy for remediation of the contaminated sites identified. The definition of contaminated sites and a list of potentially soil polluting activities are established, which serve as the basis for locating the sites which potentially can be contaminated, as a preliminary step to the establishment of an inventory of effectively contaminated sites. This would be complemented by the obligation for the seller or the prospective buyer to provide a soil status report for any transaction of land where a potentially contaminating activity has taken or is taking place.

D. Policy Documents

i. Biomass

The Biomass Action Plan, adopted in a Communication from the Commission,[117] sets out measures to increase the development of biomass energy from wood, wastes, and agricultural crops by creating market-based incentives to its use and removing barriers to the development of the market. This Action Plan establishes measures to promote biomass in heating, electricity, and transport, followed by cross-cutting measures affecting biomass supply, finance, and research.

ii. Global Monitoring for Environment and Security

The objective of Global Monitoring for Environment and Security (GMES) is to provide, on a sustained basis, reliable and timely services related to environmental and security issues in support of public policy-makers' needs. A Communication from the Commission on 'Global Monitoring for Environment and Security (GMES): From Concept to Reality' sets out a strategy for delivering GMES, beginning with the pilot phase of the first three operational GMES services by 2008.[118]

iii. Sustainable Development Strategy

The objective of the 'Communication from the Commission On the Review of the Sustainable Development Strategy—a Platform for Action'[119] is to further

[117] COM(2005)628, 7 Dec. 2005. It is accompanied by an Impact Assessment SEC(2005)1573, 7 Dec. 2005.

[118] COM(2005)565, 10 Nov. 2005.

[119] COM(2005)658, 13 Dec. 2005.

develop the EU Sustainable Development Strategy. The review identifies key issues where a stronger impetus is needed in coming years, suggests that the external dimension of sustainable development (e.g. global resource use, international development concerns) be factored into internal policy-making and that the impact of European policy choices on global sustainable development be more consistently assessed, and proposes ways to measure progress and regularly review priorities, with a view to facilitating greater coherence between Member State and EU strategies. It recommends a continuous dialogue with the people and organizations—business leaders, regional and local authorities, NGOs, academia, and citizens organizations—who are engaged and committed to making change happen.

Key issues identified are: climate change and clean energy; public health; social exclusion, demography and migration; management of natural resources; sustainable transport; and global poverty and development challenges. Key actions are advocated in respect of each of these issues. For example, as far as climate change is concerned, the EU intends, inter alia, to develop future climate policy through the second phase of the European Climate Change Programme, working with stakeholders to develop new actions systematically to exploit cost-effective options, covering for example cars, aviation, technology development and adaptation. The EU and Member States will review the EU Emissions Trading Scheme and consider its extension to other greenhouse gases and sectors, such as aviation. Key actions in public health include the EU and its Member States upgrading their action plans on handling health threats (in preparation for a possible pandemic); and coordinating research into the links between environmental pollutants, exposure, and health impacts to improve understanding of what environmental factors cause health problems and how best to prevent them. In order to manage natural resources, Member States are encouraged, together with the Commission, to exchange experiences and best practice on shifting taxation from labour to consumption and/or pollution in a revenue-neutral way, to contribute to the EU goals of increasing employment and of protecting the environment. Also, the Commission undertakes to draw up an action plan to promote sustainable production and consumption, building on ongoing initiatives and instruments such as resource and waste policies, integrated product policy and standards, environmental management schemes and innovation and technology policies, to reinforce their impact, address any gaps and ensure their contribution to global initiatives. The Review continues to state that the EU and its Member States should focus on making alternatives to road transport a more attractive option for freight and passengers, including by developing Trans-European Networks and intermodal links for freight logistics, to allow goods to shift easily between road, rail, and water transport. Towards the eradication of global poverty, the Review urges the EU and its Member States to increase both their volume of development aid and the effectiveness, coherence, and quality of their aid policies in the period 2005 to 2010.

Overall, the Review of the EU Sustainable Development Strategy advocates the need for more effective monitoring, better policy-making, and use of the most effective mix of instruments.

iv. Sustainable Development: Employment and Environment

The Commission, in a Staff Working Document, sets out the most recent evidence on the Links between Employment and Environmental Policies.[120] Having considered environmental policy and the number of working people, the Commission delivers the following messages.

- (i) Environmental policy has a neutral or even mildly positive impact on the overall number of jobs.
- (ii) The ongoing shift in environmental policy away from prescriptive approaches and towards flexibility should be strengthened so as to minimize the risk for negative employment implications. Market-based instruments should play their part in this shift.
- (iii) Promotion of environmental technologies should contribute to more and better jobs as the global demand for sustainable solutions grows.
- (iv) Long-term trends point in the direction of shifting resources from polluting to environmentally friendly sectors, which for certain sectors or regions may create difficulties over the short term, and a need, therefore, for measures to manage that transition.

With regard to the links between environmental policy and labour market restructuring, the Working Document identifies the fact that as environmental policy shifts resources from polluting products and processes towards environmentally friendly ones, it affects the composition of employment. In addition, however, there is a structural shift in the economy that is in any case ongoing towards the service sector. The message to be gleaned from this shift, which is especially pronounced in the new Member States, relates to the environmental consequences which will need to be anticipated. According to the Commission, the ten new Member States provide a high potential to improve the efficiency of energy use and linked to these improvements could be the creation of a considerable number of jobs.

Furthermore, a clear positive link is found to exist between environmental policies and the quality of jobs. Nevertheless, the Commission is of the opinion that substantial investment in learning and training is required to ensure that the potential for environmentally related innovations is exploited overall and that emerging eco-job opportunities in all skill ranges can be met. The Commission advocates that policy should support the shift towards integrated environmental technologies and away from end-of-pipe solutions. Moreover, efforts at integrated

[120] SEC(2005)1530, 17 Nov. 2005.

policy development embracing simultaneously health and safety, environmental, and public health aspects should be strengthened.

Social inclusion is also considered in this Working Document because of its strong correlation with labour market inclusion and potential relationship with environmental policies. The conclusion is reached that the link between social inclusion and environmental quality needs to be better understood so that policies can take advantage of positive interactions and avoid negative interactions. In particular, distributive impacts should be analysed, not only as regards impact on sectors or regions but also in terms of, for example, households with different incomes, gender differences etc., as this may lead to increased efficiency and legitimacy. The Commission concludes that the poor generally suffer most from environmental degradation and so may benefit most from environmental policy, but at the same time some environmental policies may cost them a higher percentage of their income than other groups unless potentially regressive impacts are identified and tackled from the outset.

v. Thematic Strategies

Prevention and Recycling of Waste

The Commission, in its Communication entitled 'Taking Sustainable Use of Resources Forward: A Thematic Strategy on the Prevention and Recycling of Waste',[121] identifies the problems of waste. Accordingly, waste volumes continue to grow; legislation is, in some cases, poorly implemented with significant differences between national approaches; the potential for waste prevention and recycling is not yet fully tapped; and the emerging knowledge about the environmental impact of resource use is not yet fully reflected in waste policy.

Sustainable Use of Natural Resources

The overall objective of the Thematic Strategy on the Sustainable Use of Natural Resources, set out in a Communication from the Commission,[122] is to reduce the negative environmental impacts generated by the use of natural resources in a growing economy.

External Action: Environment and Sustainable Management of Natural Resources including Energy

A Thematic Programme for the Environment and Sustainable Management of Natural Resources, including Energy, concerned with External Action, is proposed in a further Communication from the Commission to address the environmental dimension of development and other external policies, as well as to help promote the EU's environmental and energy policies abroad.[123]

[121] COM(2005)666, 21 Dec. 2005.

[122] COM(2005)670, 21 Dec. 2005.

[123] COM(2006)20, 25 Jan. 2006.

Sustainable Use of Pesticides

Mainly comprised of plant protection products and biocidal products, pesticides, beyond their target organisms and perceived economic benefits, continue to pose threats to human health and the environment. The sustainable use of pesticides is the overall objective of the Thematic Strategy adopted by the Commission[124] in order to address these concerns. Pursuant to the two-track approach outlined in the Sixth Environment Action Programme,[125] this Thematic Strategy on the Sustainable Use of Pesticides complements existing legislation controlling which pesticides can be placed on the market.[126] The Commission underlines the fact that the actual use phase, which is a key element for determining the overall risks that pesticides pose, is barely addressed in the existing legislation. The Thematic Strategy, therefore, proposes measures aimed at correcting this deficiency, in order to create an overall policy framework for the sustainable use of pesticides.[127] One of the overall objectives of the Strategy, namely to increase awareness of consumers and society about the possible risks from the use of pesticides, has, according to the Commission, recently triggered actions by certain retailers and governments as well as the Community, to support forms of agriculture and pest management methods that restrict or better target the use of plant protection products, such as organic farming, integrated pest management, or the use of less susceptible varieties. The importance of encouraging a rational and precise pesticide use, as well as appropriate crop and soil management practices, is highlighted, as is the importance of improving the behaviour of pesticide users, and in particular of professional users, who are responsible for a number of misuses including overuses, by ensuring better training and education. Improvement of the quality and efficacy of pesticide application equipment is also deemed necessary to enable pesticide users to optimize the effectiveness of the treatments whilst minimizing any adverse impact on human health and the environment. Specific objectives of the Thematic Strategy designed to contribute to achieving these overall objectives include:

(i) to minimize the hazards and risks to health and the environment from the use of pesticides;

(ii) to improve controls on the use and distribution of pesticides;

[124] COM(2006)372, 12 July 2006.

[125] N. 61 above.

[126] Dir. 91/414/EEC on the Placing of Plant Protection Products on the Market (Pesticides Dir.) [1991] OJ L230/1; Reg. (EC) No. 396/2005 on the Maximum Residue Levels of Pesticides in Food and Feed of Plant and Animal Origin [2005] OJ L70/1. Dir. 98/8/EC on the Placing on the Market of Biocidal Products (Biocides Dir.) [1998] OJ L123/1.

[127] For the time being, the Strategy only treats the largest group of pesticides, namely plant protection products. At a second stage its scope may be extended to biocides once the impacts of the Biocides Dir. have been evaluated. See further, Commission Press Release IP/06/981, 12 July 2006 (RAPID).

(iii) to reduce the levels of harmful active substances including through substituting the most dangerous with safer (including non-chemical) alternatives;
(iv) to encourage low-input or pesticide-free cultivation, inter alia, through raising users' awareness, promoting the use of codes of good practice and promoting consideration of the possible application of financial instruments;
(v) to establish a transparent system for reporting and monitoring progress made in the fulfilment of the objectives of the strategy, including the development of suitable indicators.

In addition to this Strategy, the Commission intends to incorporate into two separate legislative proposals scheduled to be adopted at the latest by 2008, the following measures:

(i) improved systems for the collection of information on distribution and use of plant protection products, at the level of active substances, and regular reporting to tackle the lack of reliable data in particular with a view to the calculation of risk indicators; and
(ii) essential requirements for the protection of the environment to be satisfied by new pesticide application equipment to be placed on the market.

Urban Environment

In accordance with the Sixth Environmental Action Programme,[128] the Commission set out its initial analysis of the challenges facing urban areas in an interim Communication,[129] and suggested actions in four priority themes: urban management; sustainable transport; construction; and urban design. Possible actions included the mainstreaming of good practice and possible Community obligations to adopt plans at the local level. Extensive consultations of stakeholders and thorough analysis of possible ways forward have taken place, the results of which are the bases for the present Thematic Strategy on the Urban Environment, as set out in a Communication from the Commission.[130] Therein, the environmental problems facing urban areas are underlined, namely: poor air quality; high levels of traffic and congestion; high levels of ambient noise; poor quality built environment; derelict land; greenhouse gas emissions; urban sprawl; and the generation of waste and waste-water. It is recognized that these problems are complex, since their causes are interrelated, and an integrated approach to manage the urban environment is suggested as the solution. Based on the principle of subsidiarity, this Strategy foresees a decisive role for local authorities and

[128] N. 61 above.
[129] Commission Communication 'Towards a Thematic Strategy on the Urban Environment' COM(2004)60, 11 Feb. 2004.
[130] COM(2005)718, 11 Jan. 2006.

locally developed, tailor-made solutions for the urban environment, but as part of a broader initiative in which coordination takes place between national and regional authorities and the EU. Given the diversity of urban areas and existing national, regional, and local obligations, and the difficulties in establishing common standards on urban environmental issues, guidelines, and coordination of best practice are advocated measures, rather than legislation, in order to contribute to the improvement of the quality of the urban environment and also to reduce the adverse environmental impact of cities on, inter alia, climate change.

The Commission strongly recommends local authorities to take the necessary steps to achieve greater use of integrated management at the local level and encourages regional and local authorities to support this process. On the part of the EU, the Strategy proposes, inter alia:

(i) technical guidance on integrated environmental management, based on good practice and experience, for the integration of environmental issues into urban policies;

(ii) technical guidance on sustainable urban transport plans based on expert advice;

(iii) the use of the future LIFE+ Regulation[131] and other instruments to support training and capacity building for local and regional authorities on urban management issues;

(iv) in support of EU-wide exchanges of best practices, the evaluation of a pilot network of national focal points (the European Knowledge Platform) providing structured and evaluated information on social, economic, and environmental issues in urban areas in response to enquiries from local authorities;[132] and

(v) assessment of the feasibility of establishing a thematic Internet portal for local authorities.

E. Case Law and Enforcement Action

i. Access to Justice, Standing, and Non-Governmental Organizations

Case T-94/04 *European Environmental Bureau (EEB), Pesticides Action Network Europe, International Union of Food, Agricultural, Hotel, Restaurant, Catering,*

[131] Commission Proposal for a Regulation of the European Parliament and of the Council Concerning the Financial Instrument for the Environment (LIFE +) COM(2004)621, 29 Sept. 2004.

[132] The Commission proposes to consider whether this pilot can be used as a building block for a 'European framework programme for the exchange of experience on urban development' under the proposed Cohesion Policy 2007–2013. See Commission Proposal for a Regulation of the European Parliament and of the Council on the European Regional Development Fund COM(2004)495, 14 July 2004.

Tobacco and Allied Worker's Associations (IUF), European Federation of Trade Unions in the Food, Agricultural and Tourism sectors and allied branches (EFFAT), Stichting Natuur en Milieu and Sevenska Naturskyddföreningen v. *Commission*[133] concerned the issue of standing to bring proceedings for the annulment of a Commission Directive.[134] The applicants claimed that they had standing because, firstly, the Commission, in the statement of reasons of the Proposal for a Regulation on the application of the provisions of the Aarhus Convention on Access to Information, Public Participation in Decision-making and Access to Justice in Environmental Matters to EC institutions and bodies (The Aarhus Regulation Proposal),[135] stated that European environmental protection organizations which meet certain objective criteria have standing for the purposes of the fourth paragraph of Article 230 EC and, secondly, in the present case the applicants meet those objective criteria.[136] The Court noted, firstly, that the principles governing the hierarchy of norms[137] preclude secondary legislation from conferring standing on individuals who do not meet the requirements of the fourth paragraph of Article 230 EC. A fortiori the same holds true for the statement of reasons of a Proposal for secondary legislation.[138] Accordingly, declared the Court, the statement of reasons relied on by the applicants does not release them from having to show that they are individually concerned by the contested act.[139] Moreover, even if the applicants were acknowledged as qualified entities for the purposes of the Aarhus Regulation Proposal, it was clear to the Court that they had not put forward any reason why that status would lead to the conclusion that they were individually concerned by that act.

ii. Environmental Impact Assessment

On a reference for a preliminary ruling under Article 234 EC, from the House of Lords in the UK, in the Case of *The Queen, on the application of Diane Barker* v. *London Borough of Bromley*,[140] the ECJ ruled that classification of a decision as a 'development consent' within the meaning of Article 1(2) of Directive 85/337/EEC on the Assessment of the Effects of Certain Public and Private Projects on the Environment (Environmental Impact Assessment or EIA Directive)[141] must be carried out pursuant to national law in a manner consistent with Community

[133] [2005] ECR II-4919. See also Joined Cases T-236/04 and T-241/04 *European Environmental Bureau (EEB) and Stichting Natuur en Milieu* v. *Commission* [2005] ECR II-4945.

[134] Dir. 2003/112/EC amending Dir. 91/414/EEC to include Paraquat as an Active Substance [2003] OJ L321/32.

[135] COM(2003)622, 24 Oct. 2003. The provisions of the Proposal are now enshrined in the Community Institutions and Bodies Regulation, see Section B.*ii* above.

[136] Case T-94/04, n. 133 above, paras. 42 and 66.

[137] See, inter alia, Case C-240/90 *Germany* v. *Commission* [1992] ECR I-5383, para. 42.

[138] Case T-94/04, n. 133 above, para. 67.

[139] Cf. Community Institutions and Bodies Reg., Art. 12(1) and (2).

[140] [2006] ECR I-3949.

[141] [1985] OJ L175/40, as amended by Dir. 97/11/EC, [1997] OJ L73/5.

law. The Court further ruled that Articles 2(1) and 4(2) of the EIA Directive are to be interpreted as requiring an environmental impact assessment to be carried out if, in the case of grant of consent comprising more than one stage, it becomes apparent, in the course of the second stage, that the project is likely to have significant effects on the environment by virtue of its nature, size, or location.[142]

This case should be read in conjunction with Case C-508/03 *Commission* v. *United Kingdom*,[143] in which the Court held that the UK had failed to fulfil its obligations under Community law by incorrectly transposing into domestic law Articles 2(1) and 4(2) of the EIA Directive, as amended, as a result of the national rules under which, in the case of outline planning permission with a requirement of subsequent approval of the reserved matters, an assessment may be carried out only at the initial stage of granting such permission, and not at the later reserved matters stage.

iii. Implementation and Enforcement Actions

The Environment Directorate-General (DG) has maintained its efforts to improve the effective handling of open infringement cases, according to the Commission's Seventh Annual Survey on the implementation and enforcement of Community environmental law in 2005.[144] In 2005, the Commission closed 266 environment infringement cases, resulting in a total number of 489 open infringements at the end of 2005.[145] This reduction in the number of open cases purportedly is because the Commission has adopted a more rationalized way of handling complaints and infringements. Structural problems in Member States are confronted through the grouping together of cases concerning the same subject matter and through launching horizontal cases to address systemic problems of poor implementation. Furthermore, open cases have been settled as a result of proactive follow-up action on the part of the Commission by way of package meetings and bilateral contacts with Member States. In 89 per cent of the cases closed, closure was the result of remedial action taken by Member States following the identification of a violation of Community environmental law by the Commission. In 2005, the Commission issued 141 reasoned opinions on the basis of Article 226 EC and brought 42 environmental infringement cases against Member States before the ECJ. Directive 2003/35/EC providing for Public Participation in respect of the Drawing Up of Certain Plans and Programmes relating to the Environment (Public Participation in Plans and Programmes Directive)[146] was required to be transposed into national law by 25 June 2005. Reasoned opinions

[142] Case C-290/03, n. 140 above, paras. 41 and 49.
[143] [2006] ECR I-3969.
[144] SEC(2006)1143, 8 Sept. 2006.
[145] This still accounts for 22.4 per cent of the total number of open cases concerning non-compliance with Community law under investigation by the Commission. See further, Commission Press Release, IP/06/1232, 21 Sept. 2006, available on the Internet at: http://europa.eu/rapid/.
[146] [2003] OJ L156/17.

were sent to Cyprus, the Czech Republic, Germany, Spain, Finland, Hungary, Ireland, Italy, Luxembourg, Malta, and Slovakia in 2005 for failing to meet this deadline. In addition, the New Environmental Information Directive[147] was due to be transposed into national law by 14 February 2005. The Commission sent reasoned opinions to Austria, France, Hungary, Ireland, and Portugal and decided to refer Belgium, Greece, Spain, and Luxembourg to the ECJ for failure to do so. Furthermore during 2005, because of non-conformity of national legislation with the IPPC Directive,[148] the Commission sent reasoned opinions to Luxembourg and the Czech Republic and decided to refer France to the Court of Justice.

The Commission also issued 21 letters of formal notice and 11 reasoned opinions under Article 228 EC to Member States. In 2005, the Commission sent the UK a letter of formal notice under Article 228 EC for not complying with a 2004 Court judgment for incomplete transposition of the EIA Directive in Scotland and Northern Ireland.[149]

Implementation task forces were set up in the Environment DG in 2005. In the Commission's opinion, the work of the implementation task forces has resulted in the identification of a comprehensive set of proactive measures to foster the implementation of nature, air, waste, water, and impact assessment legislation. These five sectors have the highest number of open cases and jointly account for about 90 per cent of the total number of complaints and infringements in the field of the environment. The task forces have been working primarily on the drafting or updating of implementation action plans, the identification and development of proactive measures to improve implementation, and the definition of priority-setting criteria for the handling of infringement cases.

Moreover, in 2005, the Commission continued to work closely with Member States through the production of interpretation and guidance documents for many pieces of legislation in order to ensure better implementation of Community environmental law.

F. Miscellaneous

i. Cohesion Fund

The Commission has issued its Annual Report of the Cohesion Fund (2004).[150]

The main points of Decisions to grant financial assistance under Regulation (EC) No. 1164/94 establishing a Cohesion Fund, as amended by Regulations (EC) No. 1264/1999 and (EC) No. 1265/1999, have also been published.[151]

[147] N. 31 above.
[148] N. 8 above.
[149] Case C-421/02 *Commission* v. *UK* [2004] OJ C201/5.
[150] COM(2005)544, 7 Nov. 2005.
[151] [2006] OJ C118/23.

ii. European Environment Agency

The third State and Outlook Report on the European Environment was produced by the EEA in 2006.[152] This Report provides timely input to the mid-term review of the Sixth Environment Action Programme. It is divided into four parts.

Part A provides a European integrated assessment across the main challenges that Europe faces. It is structured in five main sections, each containing two chapters. The first section, 'setting the scene', addresses the environment's contribution to our quality of life and how, lately, European landscape patterns have changed. The first chapter looks at how citizens perceive the role of the environment alongside social and economic aspects in improving their overall welfare. The chapter on landscape assesses the potential of Europe's land area to continue providing ecological goods and services in the face of changing pressures, and explains the main policy instruments influencing change. An atmospheric environment section treats climate change and the impact on health of air pollution. The focus of attention in both chapters is on the challenges posed by pollution from households, energy supply, and transport, and the sensitivities in dealing with these through policy responses aimed at behavioural change. Future challenges, uncertainty and the costs of action or inaction receive attention. In the section on the aquatic environment, the freshwater chapter looks at the main pollution sources and trends (with less focus on ecological and ecosystem aspects because of lack of data), and at how the management of freshwaters in Europe will continue to be a long-term and costly endeavour. The marine and coastal chapter has an ecosystem focus with an emphasis on climate change. The soil chapter in the terrestrial environment section, in view of the lack of data and analysis, provides insight and a basis for understanding the challenges for Europe in soil monitoring and modelling. In this section, the chapter on biodiversity contains a broad analysis of terrestrial ecosystems and species and of how Europe influences the use of natural resources globally. The final integration section assesses the environmental impacts of the main economic sectors of agriculture, transport, energy, and households, in the improvement of eco-efficiency. Improved policy design, governance structures, and eco-innovation investments, together, are foreseen as having the potential to deliver cost-effective improvements to Europe's environment, economy, and quality of life.

Part B of the Report presents the first detailed European assessment using the EEA and European Environment Information and Observation Network (EEA/Eionet) core set of 37 indicators. This core set includes selected indicators relevant to the main environmental problems—air pollution and ozone depletion, climate change, biodiversity, waste, terrestrial environment, and water—as well as the main economic sectors—agriculture, transport, energy, and fisheries. Because of a lack of data, inter alia, other relevant priority areas—chemicals, noise, material

[152] 29 Nov. 2005, ISBN 92–9167-776–0. Available on the Internet at: http://reports.eea.eu.int/state_of_environment_report_2005_1/en.

flows, industry, and household sectors—have not yet been included. The assessments for each indicator are written in a more technical language than the more accessible style of Part A of the Report.

Part C is comprised of a country analysis of progress in performance on environmental issues, using a scorecard based on nine indicators from the core set of 37. The nine indicators are relevant to main policy priorities in the environment and in the economic sectors that have the most impact. They are: greenhouse gas emissions and removals; total energy consumption (energy intensity); share of renewables in electricity; emissions of ozone precursors; freight transport demand; share of organic farming; municipal waste generation; and use of freshwater resources. For the first time in an EEA Report, Part C also includes more detailed information on the situation in each country across the nine indicators, including the different types of actions and challenges each country faces. This is a unique feature of the Report.

Part D of the Report provides an overview of the Reports published by the EEA since the previous five-year Report entitled 'Environment in the European Union at the Turn of the Century'.

iii. Integrated Pollution Prevention and Control

The first Report on the Implementation (by the 15 EU Member States) of the IPPC Directive[153] was published by the Commission in 2006.[154] The Report concentrates on the years 2000 to 2002 and therefore concerns the 15 old Member States. The Commission recalls the fact that the IPPC Directive has applied to new installations since 30 October 1999, the date for final transposition. For existing installations, the deadline by which to achieve full compliance with the Directive is 30 October 2007, unless an installation is subject to a 'substantial change' before that date. Generally, the Commission reports that the IPPC Directive has been transposed with considerable delays. At the end of 2004, all 15 Member States had transposed the Directive, but with some remaining gaps in the legislation of some Member States, with the result that infringement cases are ongoing against Belgium, Denmark, France, Germany, Greece, the Netherlands, Luxembourg, and Spain. The ECJ ruled in 2004 for the first time on incomplete transposition of the IPPC Directive.[155] According to the Commission, there is a considerable diversity in the exact approaches used by the various Member States in order to transpose the IPPC Directive. Only a limited number of IPPC permits were issued in the reporting period,

[153] IPPC Dir., n. 8 above. Art. 16(3).

[154] COM (2005)540, 3 Nov. 2005. On 16 Aug. 2006, the Commission adopted the complete texts of five reference documents for the purpose of the IPPC Dir., namely: best available techniques (BAT) for waste incineration; BAT for waste treatment industries; BAT for the surface treatment of metals and plants; BAT for organic fine chemicals; BAT for food, drink, and milk industries. These documents are available on the Internet at: http://eippcb.jrc.es.

[155] Case C-78/04 *Commission* v. *Austria* [2005] OJ C2005/18.

representing approximately 13 per cent of all installations. The Report goes on to state that these numbers do not, however, reflect the total numbers of IPPC permits issued, since the reporting questionnaire did not require figures on new, updated or reconsidered permits for existing installations to be reported. As a result, therefore, only a partial picture of the implementation situation is possible at this stage. Nevertheless, the Commission is of the opinion that the limited data available still point to significant variations between Member States concerning the number of permits issued. The Report emphasizes the need to accelerate progress in order to ensure full implementation of the Directive by October 2007. A number of Member States appear to have made only limited progress in the Directive's practical implementation and there is a concern, therefore, that a disproportionate number of permit applications will be filed immediately prior to the deadline of October 2007. It is perceived that this may result in a disproportionate load falling on the competent authorities, which may not be able to cope, and that the end result could be failure to meet the deadline for the issue or updating of permits, or reduced regulatory attention, thus not meeting the full requirements of the Directive. In addition, the Report notes that it is not sufficient to simply issue a permit by 30 October 2007. Installations should be given sufficient time to comply fully with the requirements of the Directive by this date. In particular, as laid down in Article 9(4) of the Directive, all installations should operate according to conditions fixed in a permit based on best available technology (BAT), taking into account the technical characteristics of the installation concerned, its geographical location, and the local environmental conditions. The Commission, therefore, continues to urge Member States to take a planned and proactive approach towards meeting the Directive's full requirements by 30 October 2007.

The Report then details specific transposition and implementation issues under the following subheadings: (i) general obligations of operators and permit applications; (ii) coordination between authorities during the permitting procedure; (iii) determination of permit conditions based on BAT; (iv) permit conditions and changes to installations; (v) reconsideration and review of permits; (vi) environmental quality standards; (vii) compliance with permit conditions; (viii) information and public participation; (ix) transboundary effects; and (x) reporting of emission limit values.

Furthermore, the Commission reports that, although a number of Member States stressed their limited practical experience in the implementation of the IPPC Directive over the reporting period, the general view among Member States is that this Directive is an effective tool in combating pollution from industrial installations, bringing a number of benefits, in particular as regards the integrated and preventive approach, the implementation of permit conditions based on BAT, the updating of permits, improved monitoring, access to information, and public participation in the permit procedure.

The Report concludes that the Commission has decided to intensify its actions, in order to best ensure that full compliance will be achieved smoothly and in good time, as follows.

(i) The Commission will pursue the infringement cases diligently in order to ensure full transposition on the part of those Member States that still have not transposed the IPPC Directive.

(ii) The Commission is setting up indicators to monitor regularly the progress made by Member States towards the full implementation of the IPPC Directive by 30 October 2007. These indicators will, in particular, include information on the number of installations identified and the number of permits issued or updated by Member States. The Commission will also visit the authorities of the Member States where significant additional efforts are required to implement fully the Directive.

(iii) In view of the possible abuse of the inherent flexibility of the IPPC Directive, the Commission has launched several actions in order to check compliance with the Directive.

(iv) Finalization of the first round of BAT Reference Documents (BREFs) and the start of their review.

(v) Clarification of certain legal issues and technical review of the IPPC Directive.

(vi) Assessment of ways to streamline existing legislation on industrial emissions in the context of Better Regulation.

(vii) Assessment of the use of possible market-based instruments and other incentives.

The Commission foresees that the IPPC review will be concluded in 2007 by a Commission Communication, accompanied by a legislative proposal if deemed appropriate.

iv. Relationship Between the SEA Directive and Community Funds

Article 12(4) of Directive 2001/42/EC on the Assessment of the Effects of Certain Plans and Programmes on the Environment (Strategic Environmental Assessment or SEA Directive)[156] requires the Commission to report on the relationship between this Directive and Regulations (EC) No. 1260/1999 laying down general provisions on the Structural Funds (Structural Funds Regulation)[157] and Regulation (EC) No. 1257/1999 on Support for Rural Development from the European Agricultural Guidance and Guarantee Fund

[156] [2001] OJ L197/30. [157] [1999] OJ L161/1.

(EAGGF) and amending and repealing certain Regulations,[158] well ahead of the expiry of the programming periods provided for in those Regulations, with a view to ensuring a coherent approach with regard to the SEA Directive and subsequent Community Regulations. That obligation is met by the Commission's Report on the Relationship between the SEA Directive and Community Funds.[159] Therein, the Commission reports that the SEA Directive requires a range of plans and programmes to undergo an environmental assessment prior to their adoption, and that similar, although not the same, requirements for an *ex ante* environmental evaluation have applied, during the current programming period (2000 to 2006), to Structural Fund development plans, assistance, and programme complements in accordance with the Structural Fund Regulation.[160] These Structural Fund (SF) plans and programmes, the Commission continues, were specifically exempted from the application of the SEA Directive for the current programming period,[161] for the reason that SF plans and programmes would almost certainly have been adopted before the date the SEA Directive was to be transposed in the Member States, i.e. 21 July 2004, and would have undergone *ex ante* environmental evaluation. According to the Commission, this exemption avoided any risk of duplicate or conflicting requirements for assessment arising from the application of the two legal instruments and any potential uncertainty. It is important to note that this exemption does not apply to future programming periods—from 2007 onwards—under the new Community Fund Regulations.[162]

This Report, inter alia, explains how the scope of application of the SEA Directive should be identified and how that relates to the 2007 to 2013 programming period, compares *ex ante* environmental evaluation for 2000 to 2006 with Strategic Environmental Assessment under the SEA Directive, and draws some conclusions about the SEA-SF relationship based on past experience.

In particular, the SEA Directive applies to any plan or programme which comes within its scope of application as defined in Articles 2 and 3. The exemption for Structural Fund plans and programmes will not apply in the 2007 to 2013 programming period, and both Regulations (EC) No. 1083/2006[163] and

[158] [1999] OJ L160/80.

[159] COM(2006)639, 27 Oct. 2006.

[160] The Structural Fund Reg. defines Structural Funds as meaning: the European Regional Development Fund (ERDF), European Social Fund (ESF), European Agricultural Guidance and Guarantee Fund (EAGGF) under Reg. (EC) No. 1257/1999, and the Financial Instrument for Fisheries Guidance (FIFG). See Reg. (EC) No. 1260/1999, n. 157 above, Art. 2; Reg. (EC) No. 1257/1999, n. 158 above, Art. 49; FIFG Reg. (EC) No. 1263/1999 [1999] OJ L161/54, Art. 1.

[161] SEA Dir., Art. 3(9).

[162] Reg. (EC) No. 1083/2006 laying down general provisions on the European Regional Development Fund, the European Social Fund and the Cohesion Fund and repealing Reg. (EC) No. 1260/1999 [2006] OJ L239/248; Reg. (EC) No. 1698/2005 on Support for Rural Development by the European Agricultural Fund for Rural Development (EAFRD) [2005] OJ L277/1; Reg. (EC) No. 1198/2006 on the European Fisheries Fund (EFF) [2006] OJ L223/1.

[163] See Reg. (EC) No. 1083/2006, n. 162 above, Art. 47.

(EC) No. 1698/2005[164] refer explicitly to the need to take EIA and SEA legislation into account in the evaluations which are to be carried out under the Funds. It follows, reports the Commission, that any post-2006 plan or programme under the new Regulations which come within the scope of application of the SEA Directive will require an assessment as provided for in that Directive.

In comparing *ex ante* evaluation in the 2000 to 2006 period under the Structural Fund Regulations with the SEA Directive's provisions, the Report concludes that although there are marked differences in the way the requirements of the respective legal instruments are expressed, in practice the move from *ex ante* environmental evaluation to Strategic Environment Assessment in accordance with the SEA Directive should be a development from previous best practice which should not present Member States with insuperable difficulties. Moreover, it should be noted that the SEA Directive is specific in its requirements, that it introduces some additional elements, and that it is legally enforceable, unlike the previous guidance.

The concluding comments of the Report are, inter alia, that the relationship between the SEA Directive and the Regulations governing the 2007 to 2013 programming period appears legally coherent and complementary, and observance of the Strategic Environment Assessment requirements should achieve some worthwhile improvements in comparison with the current procedure. The absence of any requirement for an *ex ante* environmental evaluation, together with the provisions of Article 11(2) of the SEA Directive which allows coordinated or joint procedures to be established to avoid duplication means that there is no legal obstacle to establishing a single assessment procedure at the programming level. Nevertheless, in order to ensure that programming and assessment both proceed smoothly, and to derive maximum benefit from the Strategic Environment Assessment in developing the programme, the Report warns that authorities will need to plan the activities carefully and that it will be in the authorities' interest to consider the application of the SEA Directive and involve environmental authorities at the earliest moment so as to avoid delays.

v. State Aid

The Report on the State Aid Scoreboard—Autumn 2005 update—presented by the Commission,[165] briefly summarizes the Community Guidelines on State Aid for Environmental Protection[166] (valid until the end of 2007), and provides, inter alia, case studies on environmental and energy measures qualifying as compatible State aid. The Commission concludes that the underlying trend in expenditure on environmental and energy saving aid is clearly upward.

164 See Reg. (EC) No. 1698/2005, n. 162 above, Art. 84.
165 COM(2005)624, 9 Dec. 205.
166 [2001] OJ C37/3.

IX. Case Law of the European Court of Justice

*Nicola Notaro**

A. Introduction

Surprisingly, the two most interesting decisions of the European Court of Justice (ECJ) in 2006 did not concern questions of substantive European Community (EC) environmental law but rather institutional questions. These concerned the choice of the appropriate legal base for the ratification of a Multilateral Environmental Treaty (MEA) by the Community and the extent of the jurisdiction of the Court over controversies among Member States that regard, at the same time, mixed agreements and EC environmental law. These decisions, on balance, clarify and reinforce the basis of EC external competence on environmental matters and, if appropriately followed up, may help to ensure that the EC acts as a single coherent actor in the multilateral environmental fora. These Court decisions are not without some nuances and ambiguities but can be inscribed in a jurisprudential trend that tries to protect and expand the Community's external powers in order to achieve the EC Treaty's objectives and that the Member States try to counter at each revision of that Treaty by seeking modifications that curtail the external role of the Community.[1]

Apart from institutional questions, in 2006 the ECJ was also called upon to interpret EC secondary law on nature conservation, impact assessment, water, and waste. Several of these decisions are strongly coloured by the principle of subsidiarity conceding wide flexibility in the implementation of EC Directives.

The decisions referred to above and other interesting cases decided in 2006 are commented on in the following sections. This survey does not give a full account of all cases decided in 2006 but focuses only on those that, in the author's view, are the most significant. Other cases decided in 2006 are, when relevant, referred to in the footnotes at the beginning of each section.

B. Institutional Issues

The two most interesting cases decided by the ECJ in 2006 in the environmental field concern fundamental institutional issues with implications well beyond environment policy: the extent of the Court's jurisdiction to adjudicate a dispute

* Civil Servant in the Environment Directorate General, European Commission, Brussels (Belgium). The views expressed here are the author's only.

[1] See on this the excellent piece by I. Govaere, 'External Competence: What's in a Name? The Difficult Conciliation between Dynamism of the ECJ and Dynamics of European Integration' in P. Demaret, I. Govaere , and D. Hanf (eds.) '30 Years of European Legal Studies at the College of Europe', College of Europe Studies 2, P. I. E. Lang (2005).

concerning both international and European environmental law, and the interaction between the trade and environment legal bases for the ratification and implementation of a MEA.

In Case C-459/03 *Commission* v. *Ireland*,[2] the Commission brought Ireland to the Court because it had instituted dispute settlement proceedings against the United Kingdom (UK) under the United Nations Convention on the Law of the Sea (UNCLOS)[3] concerning the MOX plant located at Sellafield (UK), thereby failing to fulfil its obligations under the EC Treaty with regard to the exclusive jurisdiction of the ECJ and the duty of loyal cooperation with the Community institutions.[4] The Commission also claimed that Ireland had unlawfully asked the UNCLOS Arbitral Tribunal to interpret and apply EC law and had failed to inform the Community institutions before bringing the case to UNCLOS.

The background to the case is the existence at Sellafield, on the coast of the Irish Sea, of a number of nuclear facilities including the MOX and THORP plants. The MOX plant is designed to recycle plutonium from spent nuclear fuel, mixing it with uranium and converting it into a new fuel known as MOX. Some of the material used in the MOX plant originates in the thermal oxide reprocessing plant, or THORP, in which spent nuclear fuel from nuclear reactors in the UK and other countries is reprocessed in order to extract from it the plutonium dioxide and uranium dioxide.

Between 1994 and June 2001 Ireland repeatedly questioned the soundness of MOX's environmental statement and of the UK decision concerning the economic justification for the plant. Eventually, in October 2001 Ireland lodged a complaint before the Arbitral Tribunal provided for in Annex VII of UNCLOS, centring its claims on the failure by the UK to carry out a proper assessment of the impact the MOX plant would have on the environment.

The Court analysed first the Commission complaint that, by instituting the dispute settlement proceedings provided for under UNCLOS, Ireland had failed to respect the exclusive jurisdiction of the Court in regard to disputes concerning the interpretation and application of Community law as per Article 292 EC. Ireland had argued that since Community rules related to the implementation of UNCLOS are only minimum rules in the areas of shared competence, the provisions of UNCLOS do not affect them. Therefore, the areas they cover still belong to the Member States and have not been transferred to the Community. The ECJ took a different view. It first recalled that UNCLOS has been ratified by the EC and is an integral part of the Community legal order. In ensuring respect for mixed agreements such as UNCLOS, the Member States fulfil an obligation in relation to the Community that has assumed responsibility for the

[2] [2006] ECR I-4635.

[3] Montego Bay (Jamaica), 10 Dec. 1992 (entered into force 16 Nov. 1994), published on the Internet at: http://www.un.org/Depts/los/convention_agreements/convention_overview_convention.htm.

[4] Respectively, Arts. 292 and 10 EC and Arts. 192 and 193 EA.

due performance of those agreements. Then, the Court analysed whether the provisions of UNCLOS relied upon by Ireland before the Arbitral Tribunal come within the scope of Community competence. The ECJ recognized that the external competence of the Community in the environmental field is, in principle, a shared one, but, it stated:

> the question as to whether a provision of a mixed agreement comes within the competence of the Community is one which relates to the attribution and, thus, the very existence of that competence, and not to its exclusive or shared nature.[5]

This statement sweeps away the argument advanced by Ireland that in areas of shared competence there is no transfer of competence to the Community when only minimum rules are adopted: either there is competence or not; once the existence of the competence is established, its legal character can be assessed. Moreover, the fact that the Court recognizes that EC competence in the environmental field is shared 'in principle' also clarifies that there are cases where this competence may become exclusive, for instance where exhaustive secondary legislation is adopted. This confirms that the existence of Article 176 EC cannot be used to argue that EC competence on environment can never be exclusive.

In order to clarify that the Community external competence in marine environment matters exists, the Court went on affirming:

> that the existence of the Community's external competence in regard to protection of the marine environment is not, in principle, contingent on the adoption of measures of secondary law covering the area in question and liable to be affected if Member States were to take part in the procedure for concluding the agreement in question, within the terms of the principle formulated by the Court in paragraph 17 of the *AETR* judgment. The Community can enter into agreements in the area of environmental protection even if the specific matters covered by those agreements are not yet, or are only very partially, the subject of rules at Community level, which, by reason of that fact, are not likely to be affected (paragraphs 94 and 95).[6]

In these seminal paragraphs the Court reaffirms something that may seem obvious but that has been continuously questioned by some Member States: EC competence on external environmental matters stems from the EC Treaty itself and is based on the adoption of EC legislation. This is logical, as Article 174(4) EC explicitly gives the Community the power to negotiate international agreements in the field of the environment. Moreover, if the competence did not exist in the first place it could not be exercised by promulgating secondary law. The different view held by certain Member States,[7] namely that EC external competence on

[5] Case C-459/03, n. 2 above, para. 93.

[6] Ibid., paras. 94–6. Opinion 2/00 [2001] ECR I-9713, paras. 44–7; and Case C-239/03 *Commission* v. *France* [2004] ECR I-9325, para. 30.

[7] Paradoxically, the UK argued, against its own interest in seeing Ireland losing the case, that EC external competence in environmental matters is based on secondary legislation and not on the EC Treaty (Case C-459/03, n. 2 above, paras. 77–8).

environment only exists when secondary legislation exists, is to be seen as an attempt to limit Community powers by misinterpreting the *AETR* judgment.[8] The latter ruled that the Community's authority to enter into international agreements may not only derive from an express conferment by a specific Treaty provision, but also from other provisions of the Treaty and secondary legislation ('implied powers'). Furthermore, according to *AETR*, Member States cannot assume obligations which might affect Community rules or alter their scope to the extent that the latter rules have been promulgated. Some Member States like to interpret the *AETR* case as meaning that, as long as there is no EC secondary legislation or the latter only lays down minimum standards, there is no external Community competence in environment matters. This is, of course, a conscious misinterpretation of the implied powers doctrine due more to political objectives than to ignorance. The implied powers were conceptualized in a field—transport policy—in which the Treaty did not explicitly provide for the EC's power to conclude international agreements. However, such an explicit conferment does exist for environment policy under Article 174(4) EC and, intrinsically, it covers any area of environmental policy falling within the objectives set out in Article 174 EC. One hopes that the present judgment would clear the ground from the abovementioned misrepresentations of this area of Community shared competence.

Having established that the Community had exercised its competence in external environmental matters by ratifying UNCLOS, the Court went on to address the somewhat confusing Declaration of Community competence added to the EC Decision on the ratification of UNCLOS.[9] This Declaration confirms that a transfer of competence to the Community in areas of shared competence has taken place without any Community rules being affected but it also makes the transfer of areas of shared competence subject to the existence of Community rules. This latter aspect is clearly in contradiction with the principle established by the ECJ in paragraphs 94 and 95 analysed above. However, the validity of the Declaration was not, as such, the subject matter of the case and the Court accepted that, 'within the specific context of the Convention', a finding that there has been a transfer to the Community of areas of shared competence is contingent on the existence of Community rules within the areas covered by the Convention provisions in issue, irrespective of what may otherwise be the scope and nature of those rules.[10] It is regrettable that the ECJ accepts this undermining of the clear principle it had just clarified. However, one can understand the unwillingness of the ECJ to go beyond the claim of the Commission and *ex officio* invalidate the Declaration of competence decided upon by the Member State in the Council

[8] Case C-22/70 *Commission* v. *Council* [1971] ECR 263.

[9] Dec. 98/414/EC on the ratification by the European Community of the Agreement for the implementing of the provisions of the United Nations Convention on the Law of the Sea of 10 December 1982 relating to the Conservation and Management of Straddling Stocks and Highly Migratory Fish Stocks [1998] OJ L189/14.

[10] Case C-459/03, n. 2 above, para. 108.

due to the political sensitivity of such a decision. Instead, the Court looked into existing secondary legislation and found that the matters covered by UNCLOS and relied upon by Ireland before the Arbitral Tribunal are very largely regulated by Community measures which form part of the Community legal order and on which the Court has exclusive jurisdiction on the basis of Articles 220 and 292 EC. The ECJ also rejected a number of alternative arguments put forward by Ireland such as that the UNCLOS dispute settlement system has become, through the EC ratification, an integral part of Community law and constitutes a method of dispute settlement within the terms of Article 292 EC: UNCLOS itself contains clauses preserving the jurisdiction of the ECJ. Therefore, the ECJ upheld the Commission's claims that Ireland, by taking the UK before the UNCLOS Arbitral Tribunal, failed to respect the exclusive jurisdiction vested in the ECJ by Article 292 EC to rule on any dispute concerning Community law and that it also breached Articles 292 EC and 193 EA by referring to the Arbitral Tribunal a dispute which requires for its resolution the interpretation and application of measures of Community law. The Court considered that it was not necessary for it to ascertain if the same behaviour by Ireland also constituted a violation of Article 10 EC and 192 EA. Article 292 being an expression of the general duty of loyalty in Article 10 EC, there was no need to find a separate violation of Article 10.

The Commission had also criticized Ireland for having breached Articles 10 EC and 192 EA on another ground, i.e. by bringing the proceedings before the Arbitral Tribunal without having first informed and consulted the competent Community institutions. Article 10 EC requires Member States to facilitate the achievement of the Community's tasks and to abstain from any measure which could jeopardize the attainment of the objectives of the Treaty. This duty is particularly important for areas of joint competence such as mixed agreements. Considering the risk of violating the exclusive jurisdiction of the Court, Ireland should have informed the Commission, therefore the ECJ found that Ireland had failed to respect the Treaty also on this ground.

No doubt some of the implications of the present judgment call for further clarification. While it is clear that Member States cannot refer each other to a dispute settlement mechanism under an MEA on matters falling within Community competence, be it exclusive or shared,[11] it is less clear if such ruling applies also to compliance mechanisms under MEAs. These mechanisms generally have, at least in a first phase, a facilitative purpose that is to help a Party going back to compliance. In this respect, they do not adjudicate and there should be no legal obstacle to a Member State using a Party-to-Party trigger under a MEA compliance mechanism vis-à-vis another Member State. One could even argue that this would be an application of the principle of loyal cooperation under Article

[11] At least when a significant part of the dispute comes within the scope of Community law. Ibid., para. 135.

10 EC. On the other hand, some compliance mechanisms have stronger powers than others and may apply sanctions in case of persistent non-compliance so they are not merely facilitative. Moreover, the use of a Party-to-Party trigger by a Member State vis-à-vis another Member State would create confusion in non-member countries with regard to the external representation and the internal cohesion of the Community as a Party and would be damaging to the effectiveness and coherence of the Community's external action. In any event, resorting to a Party-to-Party trigger by a Member State vis-à-vis another is unthinkable when it requires the compliance mechanism to interpret EC law.

The second important decision taken by the ECJ on institutional issues is reflected in two cases, decided by the ECJ on very closely related matters. In Case C-94/03 *Commission* v. *Council*,[12] the Commission sought the annulment of the Council Decision concerning the approval, on behalf of the EC, of the Rotterdam Convention on the Prior Informed Consent Procedure for Certain Hazardous Chemicals and Pesticides in International Trade[13] since it was based on the environment (Article 175(1) EC) rather than on the trade (Article 133 EC) legal base. The original Proposal from the Commission for such a Council Decision was indeed based on Article 133 EC but the Council changed the legal base and the Commission, considering the Decision illegal, brought the Council before the ECJ. Similarly, in Case C-178/03 *Commission* v. *Parliament and Council*,[14] the Commission sought the annulment of Regulation (EC) No. 304/2003 concerning the Export and Import of Dangerous Chemicals[15] insofar as it was based on Article 175(1) EC rather than on Article 133 EC. Also in this case, the original Commission Proposal had chosen the trade legal base. This Regulation is aimed at implementing in the EC the Rotterdam Convention; it was therefore clear that a decision of the ECJ in the first case would most likely be followed by a similar ruling in the second case.

The ECJ's analysis recalled its traditional dicta that the choice of the legal base for a Community measure 'must be based on objective factors which are amenable to judicial review and include in particular the aim and content of the measure'.[16] When a measure pursues a double purpose or has a double component, the act will be based on the legal base required by the main or predominant purpose or component. Exceptionally, if an act simultaneously pursues objectives or has components that are indissociably linked, without one being secondary and indirect with respect to the other, such an act will be founded on cumulative legal bases.

[12] [2006] ECR I-1.

[13] [2003] OJ L63/27. Rotterdam Convention, Rotterdam (the Netherlands), 10 Sept. 1998 (entered into force 24 Feb. 2004), 1999 *International Legal Materials*, 1.

[14] [2006] ECR I-107.

[15] [2003] OJ L63/1.

[16] C-94/03, n. 12 above, para. 34.

Then, the Court reverted to the analysis of the text of the Rotterdam Convention. It recognized that the protection of health and the environment was the most important concern in the mind of the signatories as it appears from the preamble and from the actual text in several provisions. This is also apparent from the international fora in which the Convention was discussed or negotiated.[17] However, the Court also took the view that the commercial component of the Convention is not purely incidental. The objective of health and environmental protection is pursued through commercial measures. The Rotterdam Convention specifically applies to products that are traded internationally and this is also the precondition for those products being subject to the prior informed consent procedure it sets up. Such an explicit link, the Court says, was not present in the Cartagena Protocol on Biosafety (BSP),[18] examined by the Court in Opinion 2/00.[19] In the latter, the transboundary movement of living modified organisms was only one of the aspects governed by the BSP. The Rotterdam Convention contains several measures governing or regulating trade and this cannot be called into question by the fact that the Convention tends more to restrict trade than to promote it. Therefore, the Court concluded that the trade and environment aims and components are indissociably linked and the decision on the ratification should have been based on Articles 133 and 175(1) EC in conjunction with the relevant provisions of Article 300 EC. The Court also ruled that the procedures laid down by the two legal bases are compatible as they both provide for qualified majority voting. Similarly, recourse to Article 133 EC in addition to the original legal base is not going to undermine the prerogatives of the European Parliament (EP) because, even though Article 133 EC, in conjunction with Article 300(3) EC, first subparagraph, does not provide for consultation of the EP, Article 175(1) leads to such a result. In view of the convergence between the Council Decision at stake in this case and the Regulation contested in Case C-178/03, the Court reached the same conclusion in the latter case.[20] There, however, the Court decided to maintain the effects of that Regulation until the adoption, within a reasonable period, of a new Regulation founded on the appropriate legal bases.

The above rulings are not likely to simplify the choice of the legal base for Community measures in the future. While the basic criteria applied by the Court

[17] Respectively, the Rio Conference on Environment and Development and the Johannesburg World Summit on Sustainable Development; and the FAO and UNEP.

[18] Montreal, QC (Canada), 29 Jan. 2000 (entered into force 11 Sept. 2003), (2000) 39 *International Legal Materials* 5, 1027. All official BSP documents mentioned below are published on the Internet at: http://www.biodiv.org/biosafety.

[19] [2001] ECR I-9713. In that Opinion, the Court rejected the Commission's claim that the ratification of the BSP by the EC should have been based on Art. 133 EC.

[20] C-178/03, n. 14 above, para. 46, in which the ECJ recognized that: 'It is true that the fact that one or more provisions of the Treaty have been chosen as legal bases for the approval of an international agreement is not sufficient to show that those same provisions must also be used as legal bases for the adoption of measures intended to implement that agreement at Community level', but considering the parallelism between the Convention and the Regulation the same legal base needs to be applied for both.

are relatively clear, what is not clear is their interaction and on which basis one determines the 'centre of gravity' of agreements that pursue multiple objectives and have various components. The ECJ is right in highlighting the fact that the Rotterdam Convention is more focused on trade than the BSP as the latter, for which trade is certainly a central component, also addressed wider issues. Moreover, it is also true that the PIC procedure, which is central to both Treaties, applies to trade in chemicals under Rotterdam but not to trade in GMOs commodities under Cartagena. This said, one cannot help feeling that there is a wide discretion in the Court's choice for a double legal base in this case but not for the BSP. It would perhaps be useful for the ECJ to rank the criteria it resorts to (aim, content etc.) in order to decide in a more predictable way which one prevails.

On a different issue, it is also noticeable that the ECJ 'forgot' to address the consequences of its annulment of the Council Decision on ratification while it addressed those of the annulment of the Regulation. In any event, it is clear from the application of the Vienna Convention on the Law of the Treaties (VCLT)[21] that the EC remains bound to the Rotterdam Convention even until a new ratification decision is adopted.[22]

With regard to the annulment of the Regulation, one can raise questions as to the full compatibility of the two legal bases. For instance, can a Member State resort to Article 176 EC—which applies to measures adopted on the basis of Article 175 EC—and adopt stricter measures as those prescribed by the Regulation which is now based also on Article 133 EC? This seems to remain an open question but the need to preserve the integrity of EC common commercial policy would plead against this possibility. In any event, the question may be only theoretical as resorting to Article 176 would require the fulfilment of the conditions provided thereunder and Member States may not be ready to take this risk.

A final remark provoked by this case concerns the ECJ's dictum in paragraph 53 that the two legal bases at issue are compatible as they provide for the same voting procedures. One could deduce from this, a contrario, that legal bases with different procedures are incompatible. This would be quite new as, so far, EC legislation has resorted often to legal bases with different voting procedures on the idea that the 'stronger procedure'—e.g. unanimity versus qualified majority—would apply. In our view, the Court is not seeking here a reformulation of previous decisions, but rather continuity with the case law quoted in paragraph 52 of

[21] Vienna (Austria), 23 May 1969 (entered into force 27 Jan. 1980), (1969) 8 *International Legal Materials*, 4.

[22] Ibid., Art. 46: '1.A State may not invoke the fact that its consent to be bound by a treaty has been expressed in violation of a provision of its internal law regarding competence to conclude treaties as invalidating its consent unless that violation was manifest and concerned a rule of its internal law of fundamental importance. 2.A violation is manifest if it would be objectively evident to any State conducting itself in the matter in accordance with normal practice and in good faith.' In the present case, it appears that the violation was not manifest. Upon a proposal by the Commission the Council has adopted a new ratification Decision on 25 Sept. 2006: Dec. 2006/730/EC [2006] OJ L299/9.

the judgment.[23] Therefore, one should read the Court's decision as implying that when two legal bases provide for different voting procedures they are incompatible only if the choice of one voting procedure would undermine the prerogatives of the EP.

C. Nature Conservation

In this field, a number of cases addressed 'usual infringements' by Member States of the EC nature conservation rules.[24] More interestingly, two preliminary rulings were also decided.

In Case C-244/05 *Bund Naturschutz in Bayern and Others* v. *Freistaat Bayern*,[25] the referring German court raised the question of the protection applicable to sites which have been designated by the national competent authorities with a view to their inclusion in the list of sites of Community importance under the Habitats Directive,[26] but whose inclusion awaits a decision by the Commission. The ECJ reiterated that, according to its previous case law, the protection deriving from the Habitats Directive only applies when the sites in question are actually listed as sites of Community importance but also stated that this does not mean that the Member States should not protect sites as soon as they propose them for the national list transmitted to the Commission. The Member States are, by virtue of the Habitats Directive, required to take protective measures 'appropriate' for the purpose of safeguarding their eligibility.

Upon the request of the national court, the ECJ clarified what taking 'appropriate protective measures' entails. It pointed to the first part of Annex III to the Directive, where the ecological characteristics of a site identified by the competent national authorities are defined by a number of listed assessment criteria. On this basis, the Court ruled that a Member State cannot:

> authorise interventions which may pose the risk of seriously compromising the ecological characteristics of a site, as defined by those criteria. This is particularly the case when an intervention poses the risk either of significantly reducing the area of a site, or of leading to the disappearance of priority species present on the site, or, finally, of having as an outcome the destruction of the site or the destruction of its representative characteristics.[27]

[23] Joined Cases C-164/97 and C-165/97 *Parliament* v. *Council* [1999] ECR I-1139, para. 14; and Case C-338/01 *Commission* v. *Council* [2004] ECR I-4829, para. 57.

[24] See, e.g., Case C-98/03 *Commission* v. *Germany*, [2006] ECR I-53, where Germany was found to have failed to respect the Habitats Directive ([1992] OJ L206/7) on six different grounds and Case C-239/04 *Commission* v. *Portugal*, [2006] ECR I-10183; in which Portugal was found to have violated the same Directive having built a motorway through a special protection area despite a negative environmental assessment and without having demonstrated the absence of alternative solutions.

[25] [2006] ECR I-8445.

[26] N. 24 above.

[27] C-244/05, n. 25 above, para. 46.

Finally, the Court restated the principle of procedural autonomy of the Member State according to which it is for them to take all the measures which are necessary for the implementation of the protection scheme applicable to the site concerned, provided that these detailed procedural rules are not less favourable than those governing similar domestic situations and do not render impossible in practice or excessively difficult the exercise of the rights conferred by Community law.[28]

The present case is a welcome clarification of the ECJ's approach to the protection of sites pending their designation as sites of Community importance. It extends to them a considerable part of the protection obligations deriving from Directive 79/409/EEC on the Conservation of Wild Birds (Birds Directive).[29] This is logical as the likelihood of those sites being listed as sites of Community importance is high. A possible loophole in the system is therefore closed.

The questions from the referring court focused quite precisely on what protection regime Member States should implement and also on the sufficiency of the Bavarian law in question in relation to the Directive. The ECJ was therefore obliged to broaden the questions as, in accordance with the principle of subsidiarity, the Directive fixes the objectives to be achieved but leaves Member States with a certain margin of manoeuvre with regard to the concrete measures they are expected to take. Moreover, the ECJ cannot, in a preliminary reference, rule on the compatibility of national legislation with Community law but can only provide the national Court with an interpretation of EC law that should help it to decide by itself. This approach is hardly surprising. More unexpected however is the ECJ's reference to the principle of procedural autonomy as mentioned above. The protection scheme to be implemented by the Member States is of a substantive rather than procedural nature. Therefore, recalling the principle of subsidiarity, it is submitted, would have been more appropriate in that context.

In another preliminary ruling, Case C-60/05 *WWF Italia and Others* v. *Regione Lombardia*,[30] the national court raised a number of questions related to the national provisions transposing the Birds Directive, in particular in relation to the condition in Article 9(1)(c) thereof that any hunting derogations must be restricted to 'small numbers' of birds.

The ECJ clarified that Article 9(1)(c) of the Directive requires the Member States, irrespective of the internal allocation of powers, to ensure that, in all cases and for all protected species, authorized hunting does not exceed a ceiling limited to 'small numbers'. That ceiling must be determined on the basis of strict scientific data. The Court did not go as far as fixing a figure itself but, in keeping with its previous jurisprudence, it pointed to the work of the ORNIS Committee, constituted under the Birds Directive, as a reference in this field.

The ECJ also stressed that national implementing provisions concerning the 'small numbers' ceiling must enable the authorities responsible for authorizing hunting derogations to rely on criteria which are sufficiently precise as to the

[28] Ibid., para. 50. [29] [1979] OJ L103/1. [30] [2006] ECR I-5083.

quantitative ceilings to be complied with. The Member States are required to ensure that, irrespective of the number and identity of the authorities within their territory responsible for applying that provision, the amount of authorized hunting derogations in respect of each protected species by each of those authorities does not exceed the ceiling fixed for that species for the entire national territory.

According to the Court, the Member States have to ensure that their administrative procedures are such that both the decisions of the competent authorities authorizing hunting derogations and their application are subject to effective control exercised in a timely manner. A control mechanism under which the annulment of a decision authorizing a derogation would take place only after the expiry of the authorized hunting period would render the protection system under the Directive useless and is therefore not allowed.

Also in this case, the ECJ walks a fine line striking a balance between the need to respect the flexibility granted by the legislator to the Member State in implementing the Birds Directive and the necessity of ensuring that the application of derogations therein do not undermine the overall objective of the Directive. The result appears balanced as, in particular, the need for Member States to identify ceilings for the hunting derogations is quite narrowly framed, especially through the reference to the work of the ORNIS Committee. Equally important is the Court's insistence on the fact that the delegation of powers from the central government to the regions must not endanger the correct application of the Directive and that monitoring and enforcement procedures must be speedy in order to be effective.

D. Waste

In a reference for a preliminary ruling[31] several questions arose concerning the interpretation of Articles 2(g), 6(5) and 7(1), (2), and (4)(a) of Regulation 259/93/EEC on the Supervision and Control of Shipments of Waste within, into and out of the European Community (Waste Shipments Regulation).[32] By its first question, the national court asked whether Article 2(g)(ii) of the Waste Shipments Regulation is to be interpreted as meaning that a licensed waste collector is not automatically authorized to give notification of the transport thereof for recovery.[33]

[31] Case C-215/04 *Pedersen* v. *Miljostyrelsen* [2006] ECR I-1465.

[32] [1993] OJ L30/1.

[33] Waste Shipments Reg., Art. 2(g), defines notifier as follows: 'any natural person or corporate body to whom or to which the duty to notify is assigned, that is to say the person referred to hereinafter who proposes to ship waste or have waste shipped: (i) the person whose activities produced the waste (original producer); or (ii) where this is not possible, a collector licensed to this effect by a Member State or a registered or licensed dealer or broker who arranges for the disposal or the recovery of waste'.

The ECJ focused on the phrase 'where this is not possible' in Article 2(g)(ii) of the Regulation, which must be interpreted as meaning that the simple fact that a person is a licensed collector does not confer on him the status of notifier of a shipment of waste for recovery. However, when the producer of the waste is unknown or the number of waste producers is so great that it would be unreasonable for each to be required to notify the transport of the waste, it may be justified for the licensed collector to be the notifier of a shipment of waste for recovery. The Court's answer is inspired by pragmatic considerations aimed at facilitating rather than hindering the free movement of waste which is after all a 'good' and has a solid base in the flexibility enshrined in the Regulation itself.

In its second question, the national court asked whether the State of dispatch is entitled to raise an objection against a request for authorization to export waste for the purpose of recovery for the sole reason that the information supplied by the notifier does not indicate that the legislation of the State of destination requires the same level of environmental protection as that of the State of dispatch.

In accordance with Article 6(5)of the Regulation, the notifier must supply, on the consignment note supplementing the notification, information concerning not only the composition and quantity of waste for recovery and the method of transport but also the conditions under which the waste will be recovered. However, the Court stated, the notifier cannot be required to prove that the recovery in the State of destination will be equivalent to that required by the rules in the State of dispatch. On the contrary, if the competent authority of dispatch wishes, pursuant to the first indent of Article 7(4)(a) of the Regulation, to object to a shipment on the basis of its national standards for recovery, it is its responsibility to show the risks to human health and the environment which recovery in the State of destination would entail. Again, the ECJ's approach is inspired by considerations balancing the need for the internal market to function and environmental protection. In a market based on the principle of mutual recognition among the various standards applied by the Member State, the Court places the burden of proving the existence of environmental and health risks on the State of dispatch. This is a logical application of general rules in relation to the burden of proof (*onus probandi incumbit ei qui dicit*)[34] but is also an expression of the logic of the EC Treaty provisions on free movement of goods and the exceptions thereof (Articles 28 to 30 EC). Moreover, objections from States of dispatch are often not based on real environmental concerns but rather on the economic objective of keeping national waste recovery facilities profitable by disallowing waste exports.[35]

With its third question, the national court asked whether the mention, in the context of the notification of a shipment, of a category of waste such as

[34] From Roman law, 'the burden of proof lies upon the one who affirms'.

[35] See more in N. Notaro, 'European Community Waste Movements: The Copenhagen Waste Case', (2000) *European Environmental Law Review* 9, 304–12.

'electronic scrap' satisfies the obligation to supply information concerning the composition of waste under the first indent of Article 6(5) of the Regulation. Without hesitation, the ECJ declared that mentioning 'electronic scrap' does not meet the conditions of the Waste Shipments Regulation, given the abstract and imprecise nature of this expression and because of the lack of details on the specific characteristics of the waste in question.

In its last question, the national court wanted to know whether the fact that the competent authority of dispatch considers that it does not have all the information necessary concerning the shipment of waste for recovery affects the date from which the period of 30 days to object to the shipment, as laid down in Article 7(2) of the Waste Shipments Regulation, starts to run. In addition, that court asked whether the expiry of that period precludes the competent authorities' objecting to the shipment or requesting additional information from the notifier. The ECJ concluded that the period in Article 7(2) begins to run when the competent authorities of the State of destination have sent the acknowledgement of receipt of the notification, irrespective of the fact that the competent authorities of the State of dispatch do not consider that they have received all of the information set out in Article 6(5) of that Regulation. The effect of the expiry of that time limit is that the competent authorities can no longer raise objections to the shipment or request additional information from the notifier. In other words, the 30-day period is for the Court an absolute limit. Objections to waste exports cannot be raised after that and the State of dispatch must object, if it so wishes, within that period on the basis of the information which has been made available to it. Apart from the fact that the letter of the Waste Shipments Regulation is quite clear, the ECJ's answer is certainly also inspired by the considerations we have recalled in relation to the second question above: the respect of time limits and a speedy procedure is essential for internal market operators.

E. Water

Among a number of rather uninteresting infringement cases decided in this area in the period of reference, it is worth mentioning briefly Case C-32/05 *Commission* v. *Luxembourg*.[36] Here Luxembourg was condemned because it failed fully to transpose Directive 2000/60/EC establishing a Framework for Community Action in the Field of Water Policy (Water Framework Directive)[37] and to fulfil reporting obligations thereunder. More importantly, the ECJ accepted that the adoption of framework legislation to transpose at national level the Directive is not as such a necessity. The Court recognized that adopting framework legislation may be an appropriate method of implementing the Directive, since it may provide the competent authorities with clear legal bases, in a single document, for drawing up the various measures laid down by the Water Framework Directive as regards water

[36] [2006] ECR I-11323. [37] [2000] OJ L327/1.

and whose implementation is to be spread over a period of time. The adoption of such framework legislation may also facilitate the work of the Commission, which has to ensure that the obligations imposed on Member States by the Directive are complied with. However, since the Commission had not, in the present case, indicated either the provisions of the Directive requiring Member States to adopt framework legislation or established that such a measure is necessary in order to ensure the result which the Water Framework Directive seeks to achieve, the Court rejected its claim that resorting to framework legislation to implement the Directive is necessary. The Court's decision is very much tainted by the subsidiarity principle and the fact that Member States are generally left with wide discretion in the choice of the most appropriate means to implement directives in their legal orders. However, the result in terms of environmental protection is disappointing: implementing the very complex Water Framework Directive properly would certainly require that Member States review exhaustively the national bodies of water law and rearrange it in a coherent framework. In other words, they should mirror at national level what the EC has done at Community level. Instead, relying on piecemeal adjustments and integrations of existing national laws is bound to bring about inconsistencies and lack of legal clarity.

F. Horizontal Instruments

As usual, Directive 85/337/EEC on the Assessment of the Effects of Certain Public and Private Projects on the Environment (Environmental Impact Assessment or EIA Directive)[38] has been the subject of a number of the ECJ's decisions in 2006.[39] In Case C-508/03 *Commission* v. *United Kingdom*,[40] the Commission claimed that the UK had misapplied the Directive on a number of grounds including by not subjecting to EIA assessment some urban development projects in the London area. The ECJ rejected the UK claim that the Commission action was inadmissible because it offended against the principle of legal certainty as a long time had elapsed after the granting of the planning permissions at stake and national developers had acquired rights that deserved protection. The Court recognized that legal certainty requires that unlawful measures must be withdrawn within a reasonable time and that regard must be had to the situation of the persons concerned but such a withdrawal is, in principle, permitted and cannot be, as such, a reason to bar the Commission from seeking an objective finding that

[38] [1985] OJ L175/40.

[39] For additional decisions of the ECJ not commented here see, inter alia, Case C-332/04 *Commission* v. *Spain* [2006] ECR I-40, where Spain was condemned for incomplete transposition and misapplication of the EIA Directive, particularly in relation to requirements related to information to the public and application of the Directive to developments in urban areas. See also Case C-37/05 *Commission* v. *United Kingdom* [2006] ECR I-6, where the UK was condemned for incorrect transposition of the EIA Directive.

[40] [2006] ECR I-3969.

a Member State failed to fulfil its obligations under EC law. Nor could the existence of remedies before national courts prejudice the bringing of an action under Article 226 EC since the two procedures have different objectives and effects. Even if the planning permission at stake had expired without being implemented, it was in force at the expiry of the period laid down in the Commission's reasoned opinion; therefore the Commission's action was admissible. The Court's dictum on the principle of legal certainty is important. Considering the duration of pre-litigation procedures and then of the litigation itself before the ECJ, it is presumably often the case that acquired rights of individuals may be affected by the Court's judgments. While it is clear that Member States have to take a reasonable approach to deal with such rights when implementing the ECJ's decisions, this principle cannot preclude the Commission's infringement actions if the latter is to be able to fulfil its role of warden in the respect of EC law much to the displeasure of the Member States.

The Commission's action proved less successful on the merit of the case. The ECJ recalled that, as it is clear from settled case law, all projects falling within Annex II of the EIA Directive that are likely to have significant effects on the environment are to be made subject to an assessment in accordance with Article 2(1) of the Directive. However, proof that the latter has been infringed requires the Commission to demonstrate that a Member State has failed to adopt all measures necessary to ensure that, before consent is given, projects likely to have significant effects on the environment by virtue inter alia of their nature, size, or location, are made subject to an assessment with regard to their effects. That proof may effectively be furnished by demonstrating that a Member State did not take the measures necessary to ascertain whether a project which does not reach the thresholds envisaged in Article 4(2) of the EIA Directive is nevertheless likely to have significant effects on the environment by virtue inter alia of its nature, size, or location. The Commission might also establish that a project likely to have significant effects on the environment was not the subject of an impact assessment although it should have been. In the present case, the Commission did not back up its own assertions and refute those of the defendant Member State by providing tangible and specific evidence which might have enabled the Court to assess whether the competent authorities did in fact exceed the limits of their discretion. Therefore, the Court dismissed this part of the action.

In its second complaint, the Commission contended that the national rules at issue, under which an EIA may be carried out only at the initial 'outline planning permission' stage, and not at the later 'reserved matters' stage, incorrectly transposed into domestic law Articles 2(1), 4(2), 5(3), and 8 of the EIA Directive as amended. The Commission argued that, where national law provides for a consent procedure comprising more than one stage, the Directive requires that an assessment may in principle be carried out at each stage in that procedure if it appears that the project in question is likely to have significant effects on the environment. This time, the Court followed the Commission. It was clear that, under UK law, in the present case a developer could not commence works in implementation of his project until he obtained reserved matters approval. Until such approval, the development was still not (entirely) authorized. Therefore, the outline planning permission and the decision approving reserved matters in the present case, must be considered to constitute, as a whole, a (multi-stage) 'development consent' within the meaning of Article 1(2) of the EIA Directive. In those circumstances, it is clear that projects likely to have significant effects on the environment must be made subject to an assessment with regard to their effects before (multi-stage) development consent is given. The UK had therefore not correctly transposed the Directive.

This case provides yet another demonstration of Member States' 'creativity' in order to reduce the scope of the application of EC directives in their national transposition. Fortunately, the decision of the ECJ maintains the unity of the notion of development consent and reduces the risks of Member States circumventing it via flawed national procedures. In a preliminary ruling decided on the same day regarding the same development projects,[41] the ECJ first clarified that while the term 'development consent' is modelled on certain elements of national law, it remains a Community concept which falls exclusively within Community law. Therefore, the classification of a decision as 'development consent' within the meaning of Article 1(2) of the EIA Directive must be carried out pursuant to national law in a manner consistent with Community law. Then, the Court went on stating that it is the task of the national court to verify whether the outline planning permission and the decision approving reserved matters constitute, as a whole, a 'development consent' for the purposes of the EIA Directive. The Court cross-referred to its decision in Case C-508/03 *Commission* v. *United Kingdom* above,[42] but left, in this case, some theoretical margins of manoeuvre to the national Court as, in a preliminary ruling, the Court is not supposed to rule on the compatibility of national law with EC law.[43] The Court concluded that the EIA Directive requires an environmental impact assessment to be carried out if, in the case of grant of consent comprising more than one stage, it becomes apparent, in the course of the second stage, that the project is likely to have significant effects on the environment by virtue inter alia of its nature, size, or location.

In a different case brought by the Commission against Ireland,[44] the Commission alleged that, by making the participation of the public in certain environmental impact assessments subject to prior payment of participation fees, the Irish legislation infringed Article 6 of the EIA Directive and, consequently,

[41] Case C-290/03 *Barker* v. *London Borough of Bromley* [2006] ECR I-3949.

[42] N. 40 above.

[43] Considering the above ruling in Case C-508/03, ibid., the national court will be bound to find that the outline planning permission and the decision approving reserved matters constitute, as a whole, a 'development consent' for the purposes of the EIA Directive since the two cases concern the same circumstances.

[44] Case C-216/05 *Commission* v. *Ireland* [2006] ECR I-10787.

Article 8 thereof. The Commission claimed that the Directive did not expressly authorize the charging of such fees and that they may dissuade members of the public from participating in the decision-making process. It also argued that the imposition of fees went beyond the 'detailed arrangements' for public consultation left to the Member State according to Article 6 of the Directive and that charging those fees created an obstacle for persons of low income for the exercise of the rights conferred upon them by the Directive. The ECJ rejected all the Commission's arguments and accepted the legitimacy of the Irish fees. The fact that, under the Environmental Information Directive,[45] the levying of fees is expressly permitted, cannot found a general presumption that fees are not allowed when not expressly provided for. The ECJ also interpreted the notion of 'detailed arrangements' as encompassing the levying of fees, provided that they do not constitute an obstacle to the exercise of the rights of participation conferred under Article 6 of the EIA Directive. The Court referred to the Environmental Information Directive recalling that thereunder the limit to the imposition of fees is that they be reasonable. Therefore, fees are also compatible with the EIA Directive, provided that their level does not prevent the Directive from being fully effective in accordance with its objective. The amount of the fees at issue, namely €20 in procedures before local authorities and €45 at the Board level, could not be regarded as constituting such an obstacle. The Commission had not succeeded in refuting Ireland's argument that the level of the fees is justified in the light of the administrative costs involved in processing the observations received from the persons concerned.

The right of participation in the EIA procedure is an essential one for the functioning of the Directive and it concerns specific projects and a specific public. Therefore, it seems unlikely that under the EIA Directive national administrative authorities may be flooded with requests—and consequent costs—as it is certainly possible for the much wider Environmental Information Directive. Despite this fact, one has to recognize that the wording of the EIA Directive does not prevent Member States from resorting to fees and the ECJ certainly always has in mind the principle of subsidiarity when deciding a case. Therefore, the ECJ's approach seems reasonable: rather than focusing on the principle 'fees yes or no', it emphasized that some minimal fee can be charged but the level should be reasonable. The level of the fees set by Ireland is however quite high and it is regrettable that it may be taken as a reference by other national administrations.

[45] Dir. 90/313/EEC on the Freedom of Access to Information on the Environment [1990] OJ L158/56, now replaced by Dir. 2003/4/EC on Public Access to Environmental Information ((New) Environmental Information Directive) [2003] OJ L41/26.

Reviews of Books

I. Introduction

Thijs Etty

This Reviews of Books chapter explores recent environmental law scholarship in three distinct subsections.

Firstly, in Section II, two review articles explore the state of the art literature in the policy areas of the law of the sea (analysed through the lens of positive political theory), by *Katrina Wyman*, and sustainable development law, by *Marie-Claire Cordonnier Segger* and *Ravi Shankar Kuar Singh*).

Secondly, in Section III, a further selection of noteworthy recent publications on topical issues in European and international environmental law and policy is critically discussed by a panel of established European and North-American scholars, in their respective areas of expertise.

Thirdly and finally, Section IV provides an overview of 'Highlights of Recent Publications' on the environment and the law, in the European, international, and domestic regulatory contexts. The categorization of these recent titles in broad policy areas will follow the basic topical structure adopted in the Current Survey chapters of this *Yearbook*.

II. Review Articles

A. A Positive Agenda for Public International Law of the Sea Scholarship

*Katrina M. Wyman**

The Law of the Sea: Progress and Prospects, edited by David Freestone, Richard Barnes, and David Ong. Oxford: Oxford University Press, 2006, 480 pp., £84 hb. ISBN 9780199299614;

* Associate Professor, New York University School of Law, New York, NY (US). This review essay benefited considerably from comments from Benedict Kingsbury.

Unresolved Issues and New Challenges to the Law of the Sea: Time Before and Time After, edited by Anastasia Strati, Maria Gavouneli, and Nikolaos Skourtos. Leiden: Brill Academic Publishers, 2006, 350 pp., €115 hb. ISBN 9789004151918.

i. Introduction

The recent volumes *The Law of the Sea: Progress and Prospects* and *Unresolved Issues and New Challenges to the Law of the Sea: Time Before and Time After*, underscore the maturation of the United Nations Convention on the Law of the Sea (UNCLOS)[1] into a well-established regime for governing the oceans. Collections of essays from two recent conferences on the law of the sea, these books paint a picture of the law as a dynamic instrument that is evolving through the handiwork of many actors. In turn, this picture suggests that there are now many questions related to the law of the sea that could be analysed through the lens of positive political theory.

This essay begins by discussing the range of subjects covered in the essays in both volumes, which will be referred to as *TLS* and *UI*, respectively. I will then briefly introduce positive political theory and emphasize its potential to shed light on questions concerning the law of the sea touched on in these essays. To illustrate the potential value of positive analysis of the law of the sea, I also examine through a positive lens a question raised in essays in both volumes. Specifically, I consider why marine fisheries and ecosystems in general have deteriorated under the UNCLOS's watch, notwithstanding the Convention's establishment of a property rights regime that was intended to internalize the externalities associated with overfishing. My overall purpose in this essay is to suggest that both volumes here discussed helpfully highlight many important questions that should be the subject of additional positive research. Such research could yield useful insights into the functioning of the law of the sea and potentially different normative prescriptions than those that are the mainstay of standard public international law of the sea scholarship.

ii. Overview of TLS and UI

Both volumes emphasize that 25 years after the UNCLOS was concluded, and 13 years after it came into force, the world's oceans are now regulated by a governance regime similar to more familiar ones covering natural resources such as land. Most of the essays in these books originally were presented at conferences about the current state of the law of the sea, the papers in *TLS* at one in London (UK) in 2005, and the papers in *UI* at a 2003 conference in Rhodes (Greece). *TLS* is a longer book with 22 chapters (including an overview chapter). *UI* has 10 chapters, two comments, an introductory overview, and a conclusion. The essays

[1] Montego Bay (Jamaica), 10 Dec. 1982 (entered into force 16 Nov. 1994), (1982) 21 *International Legal Materials*, 1261.

in the former volume also generally are of higher quality than those in the latter, although both books feature several outstanding essays.

Since there is considerable overlap in the subjects covered in the essays in the two books, it would be tedious to summarize the volumes essay-by-essay. Consider instead the three general categories of subjects addressed in these essays.

One category of essays concerns the evolution of law of the sea since 1982. For instance, various essays discuss changes in prominent law of the sea doctrines, such as the rules governing the delimitation of maritime boundaries (Evans in *TLS*, pp. 137–60), the rules concerning navigation on the high seas (Anderson in *TLS*, pp. 327–46), and the broadening of port stage jurisdiction (Molenaar in *TLS*, pp. 192–209). There also are essays about the process and the instruments by which the law of the sea has evolved since 1982, given the difficulty of formally amending the UNCLOS (Boyle in *TLS*, pp. 40–62; and Gavouneli in *UI*, pp. 205–34). Furthermore, there are essays describing the roles of organizations involved in implementing the law of the sea, such as International Tribunal on the Law of the Sea (ITLOS) (Churchil in *TLS*, pp. 388–416; and Dipla in *UI*, pp. 235–50), the International Court of Justice (ICJ) (in *TLS*: Evans, pp. 137–60, and Kwiatkowska pp. 433–58; and in *UI:* Dipla, pp. 235–50), the International Seabed Authority (ISA) (Nandan in *TLS*, pp. 75–92), the Commission on the Limits of the Continental Shelf (CLCS) (Johnson and Oude Elferink in *TLS*, pp. 161–79), the World Bank and the Global Environment Facility (GEF) (Freestone in *TLS*, pp. 308–26), and the United Nations (UN) (de La Fayette in *TLS*, pp. 63–74).

A second category of essays highlight emerging issues in the law of the sea. As I discuss further below, both books include essays highlighting the increased environmental threats to marine fisheries and ecosystems in general since 1982 (in *UI*: Oral, pp. 85–108, and Scovazzi, pp. 109–20; and in *TLS*: Franckx, pp., 210–32, Barnes, pp. 233–60, and Gjerde, pp. 281–307). Other issues flagged include the protection of culturally significant underwater objects and sites (in *TLS*: Scovazzi, pp. 120–36; and in *UI*: Strati, pp. 21–62, and Sioussiouras, pp. 63–70), and claims by nations such as the US of rights to act on the oceans in the name of national security (in *UI*: Liacouras, pp. 123–48, and Syrigos, pp. 149–202; and in *TLS*: Kaye, pp. 347–64).

Thirdly, these two books include a few discussions of issues in the law of the sea in specific areas of the world. *TLS* includes a fascinating account of the difficulties encountered in implementing the UNCLOS in East Asia because of its complicated maritime geography (Bateman, pp. 365–87). Reflecting its origins for a conference in Rhodes, *UI* includes chapters discussing the law of the sea in the Mediterranean (Scovazzi, pp. 109–20, Vukas, pp. 251–8, and Alexopoulos, pp. 259–70).

Most of the essays in *TLS* and *UI* are primarily descriptive or prescriptive, or a combination of both. When they are descriptive, they tend to elaborate the workings of an organization or a doctrine. When they are prescriptive, the essays tend to advocate stricter international legal obligations or improved compliance with existing obligations. However, lurking within these essays there are many fascinating questions about why the law of the sea has evolved in the ways that it has since 1982, and why the organizations elaborating it function the way that they do and generate the outcomes described in *TLS* and *UI*. It is a tribute to the richness of the essays in these books that they provide starting points for research entirely different from the kind that they pursue.

iii. The Potential Contribution of Positive Political Theory

Recently, public international law scholars increasingly have drawn on positive political theory.[2] However, as the absence of such theory from *TLS* and *UI* indicates, public international law of the sea scholarship, for the most part, traditionally has not included much positive analysis. The evolution documented in *TLS* and *UI* of the UNCLOS into an intricate governance regime with legal rules, adjudicatory institutions, and identifiable interests suggests that the time is ripe to expand the range of questions investigated about the law of the sea beyond the standard descriptive and normative topics.

A Very Brief Introduction to Positive Political Theory

Given the range of positive political theory, and the many existing overviews and applications of the theory, I do not propose to offer a thorough survey here.[3] But a brief description is in order by way of background to my argument that the law of the sea could benefit from positive analysis.

Positive political theory's distinct concern is explaining the evolution, the content, or the form of institutions. For these purposes, institutions should be defined broadly as including but not restricted to positive law (such as contracts, treaties, legislation, and constitutions), legal rules (in positive and customary law), and organizations (such as bureaucracies, courts, and legislatures). Positive political theorists offer a number of different kinds of explanations for the phenomena that they seek to understand.

One set are demand-side explanations.[4] These tend to assume that an institution is the product of demand by interest groups. Interest groups usually are assumed to seek institutions that will benefit their group members' preferences, or the preferences of group leaders if they have considerable autonomy from the group because of agency costs. The ability of interest groups to obtain the

[2] See, e.g., O. Hathaway and A. N. Lavinbuk, 'Rationalism and Revisionism in International Law' (2006) 119 *Harvard Law Review*, 1404–43, at 1303–7 (reviewing J. L. Goldsmith and E. A. Posner, *The Limits of International Law* (New York: Oxford University Press, 2005)).

[3] Helpful overviews of positive theories of environmental regulation include N. O. Keohane, R. L. Revesz, and R. N. Stavins, 'The Choice of Regulatory Instruments in Environmental Policy' (1998) 22 *Harvard Environmental Law Review* 2, 313–67; J. B. Wiener, 'On the Political Economy of Global Environmental Regulation' (1999) 87 *Georgetown Law Journal*, 749–94. This overview draws heavily on Keohane et al., above.

[4] Keohane et al., ibid., 319–21.

institutions they seek is assumed to vary with groups' costs of collective action. The conventional wisdom is that small groups with high stakes in a particular outcome are more likely to obtain the outcome they seek than large diffuse groups. But there are also countervailing hypotheses that large groups may be able to succeed in the political process, for instance because they include small groups with low costs of collective action.[5]

A second set of positive explanations are supply-side.[6] They attribute the existence, the content, or the shape of an institution to the suppliers of that institution, who could be legislators, civil servants, judges, or others. Supply-side explanations suggest that institutions are the product of the suppliers' preferences, and they therefore require some conception of these preferences. One important strand of supply-side explanations examine the significance of decision-making structures for outcomes. For example, this type of a supply-side explanation of the existence of a law enacted by a legislature might draw attention to the voting rules in that legislature.[7] Finally, there is a third category of positive equilibrium analyses that combine demand- and supply-side factors.[8]

What Positive Analysis Might Add to Public International Law of the Sea Scholarship

Positive political theory could make at least three contributions to public international law of the sea scholarship.

Firstly, approaching the law of the sea through the lens of positive theory could expand the range of questions asked in law of the sea scholarship. Consider, for example, the legal rules governing intelligence gathering on the high seas described in the essay by Petros Liacouras in *UI* (pp. 123–48). A positive theorist might seek to explain why these rules have their current content and form. In answering that question, the positive theorist likely would focus on several of the factors mentioned above, such as the groups whose interests might be served by the rules, and the process by which the rules have been developed.

Secondly, positive analysis could offer different kinds of answers to questions already considered in international public law of the sea scholarship. For example, in the course of trenchantly analysing the legal rules governing the delimitation of maritime boundaries, Malcolm Evans briefly considers whether the options that States increasingly have of adjudicating boundary disputes before the International Court of Justice (ICJ) or arbitral tribunals under LSOC will 'have any impact on the outcome of the cases submitted' (Evans in *TLS,* pp. 137–60, at 142). He tentatively suggests that the choice of forum will not have an impact,

[5] N. K. Komesar, *Imperfect Alternatives: Choosing Institutions in Law, Economics, and Public Policy* (Chicago: University of Chicago Press, 1994), 53–122; E. R. Elhauge, 'Does Interest Group Theory Justify More Intrusive Judicial Review?' (1991) 101 *Yale Law Journal*, 31–110, at 35–44, and 64–5.

[6] Keohane et al., n. 3 above, 321–2.

[7] Ibid., 322.

[8] Ibid., 322–46.

given the number of former ICJ judges who subsequently serve as arbitrators in arbitrations of boundary disputes (p. 142). His analysis already treads in a positive direction, since it focuses on the identity of the suppliers of the outcomes in boundary disputes. A more comprehensive positive analysis of the implications of the choice of forum for outcomes also might consider the implications of differences in the procedures used in arbitrations and before the ICJ, and demand-side related differences, such as effects that the choice of forum might have on the way that disputants present their cases.

Thirdly, positive analysis could suggest new lines of thought for prescriptively-inclined scholars. Important themes in existing prescriptive scholarship about the law of the sea are the desirability of imposing new or different international legal obligations on States, and additional mechanisms to promote compliance with existing or proposed obligations. Armed with a better understanding of the political dynamics that produce weak international legal obligations and non-compliance, a prescriptively inclined scholar might recommend changes to the underlying interest group interactions or decision-making structures that generate the weak obligations and non-compliance in the first place. In turn, changing the players or the procedures through which decisions are made might alter the outcomes produced.

An Example: a Positive Analysis of the Imperiled State of Marine Fisheries

To illustrate the potential contributions of positive analysis, I now examine through a positive lens a question raised in essays in both *TLS* and *UI*: why marine fisheries are imperiled, 25 years after the UNCLOS was concluded.

The depressed state of marine fisheries and ecosystems in general presents a theoretical puzzle. In theory, the UNCLOS should have improved the environmental conditions of the oceans according to the standard economic view that property rights internalize externalities provided the benefits of internalization exceed the costs.[9] The UNCLOS had two significant effects on property rights concerning marine fisheries. Firstly, it recognized that countries have property rights in fisheries in 200-mile Exclusive Economic Zones (EEZs) off national coasts. This change gave nation States considerable control over fisheries, since over 90 per cent of commercial fisheries are within EEZs (Barnes in *TLS*, pp. 233–60, at 242). Secondly, the UNCLOS relegated high seas fisheries beyond national EEZs to a global commons, where nation States have equal access to the fish.

Under the standard economic theory of property rights, the recognition of EEZs should have induced countries to take better care of fish within these zones, since every country stands to reap the benefits and the costs of its management measures. In addition, the recognition of EEZs should have promoted better care

[9] H. Demsetz, 'Toward A Theory of Property Rights' (1967) 57 *American Economic Review Papers & Proceedings*, 347–72.

of high seas fisheries. By recognizing EEZs, the UNCLOS created an identifiable constituency of countries that should have been motivated to negotiate to manage stocks left in the global commons outside their EEZs.[10]

But neither expectation has been realized. Twenty-five years after the signature of the UNCLOS, many fisheries within national EEZs and on the high seas are in poor shape. As Richard Barnes notes in his essay in *TLS* (pp. 233–60), the Food and Agriculture Organization (FAO) estimates that:

> 52 per cent of fish stocks [around the world] are fully exploited and producing catches at the maximum sustainable limit... [and]... 25 per cent of stocks are over-exploited, depleted, or recovering from depletion. (p. 233)

Nilufer Oral's essay in *UI* (pp. 85–108) emphasizes the ill-health of marine ecosystems in general, not just fisheries, noting 'the dangers... facing vulnerable marine ecosystems... such as coral reefs' and others (p. 87). Reaching beyond the two books, a recent study by Boris Worm and other researchers, covered prominently in the popular press, predicted 'the global collapse of all taxa currently fished by the mid-21st century' if present trends continue.[11]

Essays in both *TLS* and *UI* suggest a similar explanation for the current depressed state of marine fisheries and ecosystems in general: the limited obligations that international law imposes on nation States in relation to marine fisheries in EEZs and on the high seas, and the lack of compliance with the few existing obligations (in *TLS*: Barnes, pp. 233–60, and Gjerde, pp. 281–307; and in *UI*: Oral, pp. 85–108). The natural normative corollary to this explanation is a prescription for more binding international legal obligations in relation to marine fisheries, and mechanisms to promote greater compliance (see, e.g., Barnes in *TLS*, at pp. 242 and 258–9).

However, positive political theory suggests a different explanation of the poor state of marine fisheries and ecosystems that in turn counsels other policy prescriptions. This hypothesis treats the weakness of existing international legal standards and compliance as symptoms rather than underlying causes. According to this demand-side hypothesis, the depressed state of fisheries and marine ecosystems around the world is due to the influence that producer groups such as fishers historically have exerted domestically and internationally in the two-level game through which marine fisheries policy is formulated.[12]

[10] Ibid., 356.

[11] B. Worm et al., 'Impacts of Biodiversity Loss on Ocean Ecosystem Services' (2006) 314 *Science* 5800, 787–90.

[12] Other discussions of the regulation of the oceans as a two-level game include R. D. Putnam, 'Diplomacy and Domestic Politics: The Logic of Two-Level Games' (1988) 42 *International Organization* 3, 427–60, at 446 (describing negotiation of the UNCLOS as a two-level game); R. J. Schmidt, 'International Negotiations Paralyzed by Domestic Politics: Two-Level Game Theory and the Problem of the Pacific Salmon Commission' (1996) 26 *Environmental Law* 1, 95–140 (modelling a Canada-US dispute about allocation of Pacific Northwest salmon stocks as a two-level game, drawing on Putnam's article, above). See also E. Benvenisti, 'Exit and Voice In the Age of Globalization'

The starting point for the positive hypothesis is that marine fisheries policy is developed and implemented in both the domestic and international arenas. At the international level, states interact to develop and implement governance regimes for high seas fisheries. But these states are not unitary actors. Behind the States meeting at the international level there is a second domestic level. It is comprised of interest groups that influence domestic policy over national EEZs, and international policy about high seas fisheries through the interest groups' influence in domestic politics. Standard public choice theory would predict that producer groups such as fishers would be the dominant interest group at this second domestic level, because they have significant economic stakes in fisheries policy, and relatively low costs of collective action because of their geographic concentration in coastal communities.[13]

As evidence of producer dominance of the regulation of EEZs, consider the US experience. Since the US established its 200-mile fishery conservation zone in 1976, the principal initiators of fisheries regulation in this zone have been eight regional fishery management councils, each of which is assigned responsibility for a particular geographic region of the EEZ. Importantly, producers such as commercial fishers, processors, and recreational fishers have tended to dominate the voting membership of these councils.[14] Indeed, in 2003, only one of the eight councils included a single representative of a national environmental group.[15]

As evidence of producer influence in international policy-making, consider the access that producer groups have to the international policy process. In the US and other countries, fishers participate in developing national policy on international fisheries issues, including policy positions for meetings of regional fishery management organizations (RFMOs) that manage high seas fisheries. Sometimes fishers also are members of national delegations to international meetings, and represent their home countries as commissioners on RFMOs.[16]

Assuming that producers have dominated fisheries policy domestically and internationally, why might producers have supported the lax regulatory

(1999) 98 *Michigan Law Review* 1, 167–213, which attributes many global collective action failures to small groups such as producers dominating domestic politics, and therefore also international politics.

While the politics of marine fisheries regulation is not their central focus, the essays in *TLS* and *UI* about marine fisheries do suggest that politics and a lack of political will are contributors to the current state of fisheries. See, e.g., in *UI*: Oral, pp. 85–108, at pp. 107–8; and in *TLS*: Barnes, pp. 233–60, at pp. 249, 251, and 254; and Gjerde, pp. 281–307, at p. 304.

[13] See generally D. A. Dana, 'Overcoming the Political Tragedy of the Commons: Lessons Learned from the Reauthorization of the Magnuson Act' (1997) 24 *Ecology Law Quarterly* 4, 833–46.

[14] J. Eagle, S. Newkirk, and B. H. Thompson, *Taking Stock of the Regional Fishery Management Councils* (Washington, DC: Island Press, 2003), 24–6.

[15] Ibid., 24.

[16] C. J. Carr and H. N. Scheiber, 'Dealing with a Resource Crisis: Regulatory Regimes for Managing the World's Marine Fisheries' (2002) 21 *Stanford Environmental Law Journal* 1, 45–79, at 58.

standards and enforcement that historically have characterized fisheries policy?[17] Indeed, at first glance, we might expect that producers would prefer strict regulatory standards that curtail catches given that producers presumably have an economic interest in sustaining the fish populations that are key to producer livelihoods. But there are at least two possible explanations for producer support for the policies that have contributed to the current state of fisheries around the world. Firstly, producers might support lax standards that do not limit harvest levels as a rational response to the fact that producers generally have no, or only weak, individual property rights in fish before harvesting them. Without property rights in fish in the wild, producers have little incentive to favour conservation measures that will benefit other producers.[18] Alternatively, producer support for lax standards that allow over-exploitation could be irrational. For example, it could be due to the difficulties many people have giving up existing entitlements, deciding in the face of uncertainties such as those that plague fisheries science, and 'sacrific[ing] today in order to preserve resources for the future'.[19]

It is important to recognize, though, that there have been changes recently in the players in the two-level game through which marine fisheries policy is crafted, and accompanying shifts in policy outcomes. Some domestic producers have recognized the benefits of curtailing catches to sustain fish populations in the long term, sometimes in response to drastic declines in fish populations.[20] Also, domestic producers no longer have the virtually unchallenged influence over fisheries policy that they once did. As fish stocks have plummeted since the early 1990s, environmental groups in the US and other countries increasingly have taken an interest in the depletion of marine fisheries and not just charismatic species such as whales and dolphins.[21] In the US, the growing influence of environmental groups has been evident in the tightening of fisheries regulations since the 1990s.[22] It also has been reflected in US positions on international fisheries matters. While not recently considered a proponent of international

[17] B. H. Thompson, 'Tragically Difficult: The Obstacles to Governing the Commons' (2000) 30 *Environmental Law* 2, 241–78, at 248–9. Of course there are exceptions, where commercial fishers have supported conservation measures; see Dana, n. 13 above, 839.

[18] This would be the familiar tragedy of the commons, replayed within a regulated framework within national EEZs: G. Hardin, 'The Tragedy of the Commons' 1968) 162 *Science* 3859, 1243–8; H. S. Gordon, 'The Economic Theory of a Common-Property Resource: The Fishery' (1954) 62 *The Journal of Political Economy* 2, 124–42.

[19] Thompson, n. 17 above, 256.

[20] B. Daley and G. Cook, 'Sea Change: The New England Fisheries Crisis: Some Look For Hope Beyond Courtroom', *Boston Globe*, 28 Oct. 2003, A1.

[21] M. L. Weber, *From Abundance to Scarcity: A History of U.S. Marine Fisheries Policy* (Washington, DC: Island Press, 2002), 173–95; Daley and Cook, n. 20 above, 'From 1992 to 2000, the major philanthropies that fund environmental causes increased spending on fisheries issues from $3.6 million to more than $26 million', at A16.

[22] On the significance of the Sustainable Fisheries Act of 1996, see, e.g., Weber, ibid., 190–2. On the Magnuson-Stevens Fishery Conservation and Management Reauthorization Act of 2006, see, e.g., 'Editorial: Ocean Rescue', *New York Times*, 24 Dec. 2006; J. Eilperin, 'Fishing Industry Legislation Passes', *Washington Post*, 9 Dec. 2006.

environmental law, since the 1990s the US has taken a leading role in developing and enforcing international fisheries conservation standards.[23]

In emphasizing the benefits that positive political theory might yield for public international law of the sea scholarship I suggested above that positive analyses might generate new kinds of prescriptive recommendations. If it is correct, the positive hypothesis sketched above for the depressed state of marine fisheries and the recent initiatives to address suggest a different focus for reform initiatives than the additional international legal obligations and oversight mechanisms touted by Barnes and Gjerde in *TLS* (pp. 242, 258–9, and 298). In particular, this hypothesis counsels a new focus on opening up policy-making processes within nation States to interests other than producers, such as environmentalists. If domestic and international fisheries policy truly is the product of domestic demand-side influences, then developing more inclusive national decision-making processes that incorporate a broader range of interests than those of producers might lead to different policy outcomes. On the negative side, though, the benefits of more inclusive processes would have to be weighed against the difficulties that more open processes might create, such as the increased costs of reaching decisions.

A second policy suggestion that flows from my positive hypothesis about the causes of the current state of marine fisheries concerns the incentives of domestic producer groups. Assuming that producer groups will continue to play an important role in formulating fisheries policy because of factors such as their significant economic stakes in the policy arena, then we should take seriously proposals that might induce producers to support stricter regulatory standards that lower catch levels. Individual transferable quotas (ITQs) are a proposal in this vein. They often are touted by economists as individual property right-like mechanisms that should instill a conservationist ethic in commercial fishers by giving them a stake in wild fish before they are harvested.[24] Assuming that we accept the assumptions underlying economic analysis, altering the incentives of fishers by giving them property-like rights eventually should lead to different policy outcomes benefiting the fish in the sea. However, for some of the same reasons that fishers historically have supported lax regulatory standards, we should expect it to be difficult to implement ITQs.[25]

iv. Conclusion

A quarter of a century after the UNCLOS was concluded, it is time for public international law of the sea scholarship to add positive analysis to its mix of

[23] Carr and Scheiber, n. 16 above, at 62, 65–6, 71, and 73.

[24] Committee to Review Individual Fishing Quotas, National Research Council, *Sharing the Fish: Toward A National Policy on Individual Fishing Quotas* (Washington, DC: National Academy of Sciences, 1999), 35–6.

[25] On the US experience implementing ITQs, see, e.g., K. M. Wyman, 'From Fur to Fish: Reconsidering the Evolution of Private Property' (2005) 80 *New York University Law Review* 1, 117–240.

methodologies for examining the governance regime that the law of the sea represents. The essays in *TLS* and *UI* provide a useful starting point for such a research project. By succinctly discussing the evolution of the law of the sea since 1982, and identifying key issues in the law at the moment, the essays in these books offer a fruitful basis for expanding the range of questions asked and policy prescriptions offered concerning the law of the sea. As I have attempted to demonstrate through a positive analysis of the question of why marine fisheries are imperiled, such analysis has much add to law of the sea scholarship.

B. Taking Sustainable Development Seriously: Compliance Synergies in International Environmental and Economic Law

Marie-Claire Cordonier Segger and Ravi Shankar Kuar Singh***

Environmental Law for Sustainability, edited by Benjamin Richardson and Stepan Wood. Oxford: Hart Publishing, 2006, 450 pp., £25 pb. ISBN 1841135445;

Making Law Work: Environmental Compliance & Sustainable Development (Volumes I and II), edited by Durwood Zaelke, Donald Kaniaru, and Eva Kruzikova. London: Cameron May, 2005, 1150 pp., £100 pb. ISBN 190501709X;

Sustainability, Civil Society and International Governance: Local, North American and Global Contributions, edited by John Kirton and Peter Hajnal. Aldershot, Ashgate, 2006, 380 pp., £60 hb. ISBN 0754638847;

The WTO and Sustainable Development, by Gary Sampson. Tokyo: United Nations University Press, 2005, 310 pp., $45 pb. ISBN 9280811150.

Sustainable development is an objective of many economic, social, and environmental laws and treaties. The 2002 Johannesburg Plan of Implementation charges decision-makers, through the UN Commission on Sustainable Development, to 'take into account significant legal developments in the field of sustainable development'.[1] What are these significant legal developments, and how are they

* Director of International Affairs in the Strategic Policy Sector at the Canadian Ministry of Natural Resources, Ottowa (Canada); Director of the Centre for International Sustainable Development Law (CISDL), in Montreal (Canada); and a Fellow of the Lauterpacht Centre for International Law at the University of Cambridge (UK).

** Policy Analyst in the Sustainable Development and International Affairs Division of the Strategic Policy Sector at the Canadian Ministry of Natural Resources, Ottowa (Canada).

[1] Published on the Internet at: http://www.johannesburgsummit.org/html/documents/summit_docs/0409_plan_final.pdf.

evolving? Those entrusted with shaping the policies to implement national and international environmental laws often bear responsibility to promote the sustainable development of natural resources as well as environmental protection. However, as Joseph Stiglitz, in his recent foreword to *Economic Development and Environmental Sustainability: New Policy Options* notes:

> [t]oo often, those entrusted with shaping economic policy have put too little attention on the consequences of the policies for natural resources and the environment, and devoted even less attention to shaping policies that might actually improve the quality of the environment and resource management.[2]

Recent scholarship shows that as the actors responsible for sustainable development evolve, new generations of policy and law are developed, and innovative instruments emerge, are tested, and can be analysed. Quite a spectrum of actors and instruments is relevant today, and can be taken into consideration in the analysis of law and policy-making in this field.

This review article looks at four recent books which canvass recent legal developments in the field of sustainable development. Two explore themes related to the implementation of environmental law for sustainable development, and two address the contribution of economic law to sustainable development directly. We will consider how these talented editors and authors address the new roles of State and non-state actors in these debates, and how they link—but only just begin to integrate—their analysis of economic and environmental law and policy regimes for sustainable development. In particular, we will focus on how these volumes view the emerging roles of civil society organizations in making and implementing laws for sustainable development; innovative economic, social, and environmental compliance mechanisms; and transnational networks of State and non-state actors.

Development means expanding people's choices, enabling improvements in collective and individual quality of life, and the exercise of full freedoms and rights. Amartya Sen, in *Development as Freedom*, describes development as a process of expanding the real personal freedoms that people might enjoy.[3] Gro Harlem Brundtland, in *Our Common Future*,[4] called for a different, more sustainable type of development which could meet the needs of the present without compromising the ability of future generations to meet their own needs. Such development is intended to integrate and achieve environmental protection, social justice, and economic progress objectives in a balanced way. This is not a simple task—but nonetheless, it is a very valuable one. Indeed, it is a task worthy of serious international law and policy scholarship that focuses on the needs and views of the majority of our global economy: the developing world.

[2] J. E. Stiglitz, 'Foreword' in R. López and M. A. Toman (eds.), *Economic Development and Environmental Sustainability: New Policy Options* (New York: Oxford University Press, 2006), xv–xix, at xv.

[3] A. K. Sen, *Development as Freedom* (Oxford: Oxford University Press, 1999), 3.

[4] G. H. Brundtland, *Our Common Future* (Oxford: Oxford University Press, 1988).

In *Making Law Work: Environmental Compliance and Sustainable Development*, editors Durwood Zaelke, Donald Kaniaru, and Eva Kruzikova provide an insightful examination of relevant theoretical work and case studies in an attempt to bridge the worlds of academics and practitioners. These two volumes provide a compilation of dense, occasionally fragmented yet ultimately cutting-edge and insightful literature excerpted from a variety of sources and disciplines in developed and developing countries. The collections outline the initial foundations of a framework to address existing challenges in environmental governance and compliance with national and international environmental law toward sustainable development. Rather than exhaustively covering one particular topic, they bring together many of the best papers on these issues, and raise useful questions for further exploration by scholars, students, and practitioners. They serve as an introduction and valuable sourcebook for the relevant literature, addressing different elements of current debates on compliance, implementation, and enforcement of environmental law. The plethora of topics discussed relate broadly and narrowly to the question of how to ensure implementation of these laws, especially in developing countries. The compilation highlights, among other things, three innovative mechanisms that are worth further attention: the involvement of civil society organizations, the use of innovative compliance mechanisms, and the value of transnational networks.

The involvement of civil society is not a new concept. However, this collection of essays provides practical law and policy examples. Contributions focus on the means of empowerment for these non-state actors, and how to expand their roles in uncovering, highlighting, and ultimately deterring violations on environmental law and environmental norms. For instance, John Knox (excerpted in ch. 6.4)[5] discusses the strategies developed by the non-governmental organizations (NGOs) that use inter-governmental institutions as a means to promote environmental compliance. The volumes go beyond typical debates to discuss the value of public/private information transfers, and the disclosure of capital markets. Peter Sand (ch. 3.1)[6] discusses environmental information disclosure by government and industry, while Annette Killmer (ch. 7.2)[7] argues for mandatory disclosure as a means to promote synergies between public and private enforcement. Inter alia, Susmita Dasgupta (ch. 4.3),[8] and Benoit Laplante and David Wheeler (ch. 7.3)[9]

[5] J. Knox, 'Citizen Suits in International Environmental Law: The North American Experience' in J. Gerardu, D. Zaelke, K. Markowitz, T. Higdon, and C. Spangler (eds.), *6th INECE Conference Proceedings, Vol. 2* (Washington, DC: INECE Secretariat, 2002), 615–20.

[6] P. H. Sand, 'Institution-building to Assist Compliance with International Environmental Law: Perspectives' (1996) 56 *Heidelberg Journal of International Law* 3, 774–95.

[7] A. B. Killmer, 'Designing Mandatory Disclosure to Promote Synergies between Public and Private Enforcement' in J. Gerardu, D. Jones, K. Markowitz, and D. Zaelke (eds.), *7th INECE Conference Proceedings, Vol. 2* (Washington, DC: INECE Secretariat, 2005), 235–44.

[8] N. Dasgupta, 'Environmental Enforcement and Small Industries in India: Reworking the Problem in the Poverty Context' (2000) 28 *World Development* 5, 945–67.

[9] S. Afsah, B. Laplante, and D. Wheeler, 'Regulation in the Information Age: Indonesian Public Information Program for Environmental Management' (1997) World Bank 'New Ideas in Pollution

further the discussion by examining how developing country State and non-state actors, including firms, share information about environmental records. The volumes examine the role of 'information regulation' as a potential supplement to command and control regulation, as a means for civil society actors to secure compliance through non-governmental and non-judicial sanctions.

Ensuring compliance with international environmental law can be a significant challenge. However, as these volumes point out, a great deal of non-compliance—especially in developing countries—is caused by a lack of knowledge or a lack of capacity to comply. This would be unlikely to improve even if rigorous monitoring or increased sanctions could be imposed. In its treatment of these key questions, these companion volumes are invaluable. They focus on solutions, best practices, and innovative new instruments for compliance. Chapter 9, in particular, provides examples of compliance assistance from the State and the private sector. The essays examine efforts beyond compliance that seek to encourage those that have the capacity to comply to voluntarily meet a higher level of environmental performance. For instance, Tim Bartley (ch. 9.3)[10] discusses the role of the private sector in encouraging increased compliance in developing country industries. He provides a cogent comparison of case studies to examine why a remarkably similar approach to private regulation emerged and was implemented effectively in the two unrelated fields of apparel and forest products, each with their own set of institutional arrangements for regulating corporate activity. Chapter 10 complements this discussion by offering a view on the issues of compliance from a regulators perspective. For example, Peter Krahn (ch. 10.1)[11] discusses three pertinent case studies detailing how a public agency such as Environment Canada makes the decision on balancing and choosing appropriate environmental instruments to address specific challenges in their policy implementation.

An increasing awareness and analysis of the emergence and role of transgovernmental networks has presented a new idea of global environmental governance. Such networks are an essential tool and increasingly, even play their own roles in the development and implementation of international environmental law. In Chapter 12, the editors provide several leading contributions to examine the complex global webs of transgovernmental networks which include the State regulators, legislators, judges, and enforcement and compliance officers who interact directly with their peers globally. For instance, in *A New World*

Regulation' Working Paper Series.

[10] T. Bartley, 'Certifying Forests and Factories: States, Social Movements, and the Rise of Private Regulation in the Apparel and Forest Products Fields' (2003) 31 *Politics & Society* 3, 433–64.

[11] P. K. Krahn, 'Enforcement Versus Voluntary Compliance: An Examination of the Strategic Enforcement Initiatives Implemented by the Pacific and Yukon Regional Office of Environment Canada—1983 to 1998' in J. Gerardu and C. Wasserman (eds.), *5th INECE Conference Proceedings, Vol. 2* (Washington, DC: INECE Secretariat, 1998), 25–45.

Order, Anne-Marie Slaughter (excerpted in ch. 12.1)[12] provides a brief discussion of the drivers of terrorism and globalization, and a clear analysis of the reality of increased interaction of all government actors in environmental as well as economic fields such as finance securities and regulation. In this cornerstone essay, Slaughter argues that to understand and correctly analyse the networks which currently exist, scholars and others are required to make a conceptual shift. There is a need to move from a view of States as a unitary entity, to one that better describes today's reality of disaggregated polities, in which various institutions participate across national borders, between national and supranational institutions, to develop and implement laws and policies. In his engaging essay Kal Raustiala (ch. 12.2)[13] complements this analysis, arguing that transgovernmental cooperation, while significant, will likely only further support pre-existing liberal internationalism; while also suggesting that networks can provide a gap-filling role, providing an alternative mechanism for cooperation. This debate, an essential part of international scholarship on these issues, gives a necessarily forward-looking nuance to the sometimes disjointed but intellectually stimulating survey of current debates provided in these two volumes.

In comparison, in *Environment Law for Sustainability*, editors Ben Richardson and Stepan Wood provide a series of focused critical essays aimed at examining the environmental laws and policies which support sustainable development, though mainly viewed from a developed country mindset. The book is divided into four sections. It begins by examining current environmental regulation and administration as well as new directions in risk management and regulation. In a leading chapter, 'Institutions and Policy Change for Sustainability', Stephan Dovers and Robin Connor lay out their thoughts on the conditions that are necessary for policy and institutional change to adequately address sustainability (pp. 21–60). These conditions, in their view, include the need to understand that the causes for sustainability problems are systemic, and that the response of institutions and of policy-makers need to involve horizontal multi-layered strategies that have the potential to systemically address these causes. Dovers and Connor describe the goal of sustainability as a policy and institutional challenge. They consider why current policy instruments and processes are not able to effectively solve sustainability problems, providing examples and developing principles to inform policy and institutional change. The authors also broadly comment on the role of law and the need for adaptive approaches that are able to address policy and institutional change in the face of uncertainty. Carolyn Abbot continues this discussion in the next chapter, 'Environmental Command Regulation' (pp. 61–96), by detailing the reconsideration and reconfiguration of the role of the State in the regulation of business decisions that impact on the environment.

[12] A. M. Slaughter, *A New World Order* (Princeton, N.J.: Princeton University Press, 2004), 1–35 (Introduction).

[13] K. Raustiala, 'The Architecture of International Cooperation: Transgovernmental Networks and the Future of International Law' (2002) 43 *Virginia Journal of International Law* 1, 1–92.

As such, she focuses on a key issue in the next generation of environmental regulation, echoing the debates that are canvassed in *Making Law Work: Environmental Compliance and Sustainable Development*. In her view, it appears that a more effective method of attaining environmental goals by changing the conduct of firms is found by utilizing a carefully calibrated mix of instruments. However, Abbot highlights the options (and responsibilities) of regulators to introduce innovative ways of improving command and control regulations.

Part Two of *Environment Law for Sustainability* focuses on the social and human rights aspects of environmental law and sustainable development. This is a key pillar of the sustainable development debate, and one often regrettably forgotten or ignored by environmental law scholarship. However, the chapters canvass mainly traditional 'environmental law' issues, with less depth than the similar discussions in *Making Law Work*. The authors discuss perspectives of ecological justice and ethical change, as well as increased public participation in reforming environmental law, without necessarily confronting the deeper issues of human needs, economic, social and cultural rights, and capacity that are central to a serious treatment of sustainable development objectives. This recognized, in Chapter 7 entitled 'Indigenous Peoples, Law and the Environment' (pp. 195–226), Benjamin Richardson and Donna Craig do provide a helpful survey of the worldwide resurgence of indigenous groups and their pursuit for self-governance, with a focus on environmental management. However, though many experiences are highlighted, the legal conclusions do still appear to draw mainly on experiences from Canada, Australia, and the US. While interesting and well argued, these approaches may find shortcomings in their relevance to the 'majority world'. Discussions could benefit from a more serious consideration of development concerns which might appear to constrain environmental law and policy, but might also inspire creativity and improve compliance records.

The third part of *Environment Law for Sustainability* is quite creative, focusing on the growing reliance on economic mechanisms and tools in environmental law, including market incentives for improved environmental performance, the role of the financial services sector, and the emergence of self-regulation and voluntary measures for environmental governance. For instance, in Chapter 8, 'Voluntary Environmental Codes and Sustainability' (pp. 229–76), Stepan Wood provides an in-depth analysis of what these codes entail; their origins; the various forms that they can take; the drivers of their development and implementation; and how well they can be determined to perform. He examines the role and contribution of such instruments, suggesting that they should ultimately be evaluated with regard to their potential to advance ecological integrity and social emancipation. He argues that voluntary measures have historically only made a modest contribution to the improvement of existing systems, and suggests that there needs to be continuous improvement in their design and implementation which involves different kinds of collaboration, and knowledge to develop codes that meet present challenges. In this, the book complements essays on similar issues in *Making Law Work*, which find economic instruments useful tools to advance compliance, particularly if other incentives are hard to provide and even more difficult to realize.

The final part of *Environment Law for Sustainability* provides a survey of the current state of international law-making on the environment and the interaction between global economic law, environmental policy, and the experiences of developing countries in building environmental law regimes. Chapter 11 gives a succinct survey of international principles and instruments in the field of environmental protection and sustainable development (pp. 343–80). The next summarizes current debates that oppose trade and environmental law and policy-making (pp. 381–412). In the final Chapter 13, entitled 'Environmental Law in Post-colonial Societies: Aspirations, Achievements and Limitations' (pp. 413–44), Benjamin Richardson, Ikechi Mgbeoji, and Francis Botchway discuss the difficulties of creating effective systems of environmental management in post-colonial societies, mentioning environmental challenges of rapid industrialization, the role of transnational corporations, and the environmental effects of transnational investment. Good governance, strong legal frameworks, and international institutional cooperation are proposed, echoing the call for transnational networks in *Making Law Work*. In the recent Johannesburg Summit, developing countries were united in their clear demands for practical solutions to realize sustainable development promises from the Rio Earth Summit. However, these authors avoid detailed solutions or conclusions. They simply note that a diversity of possible approaches is possible, describing sustainability as a 'fluid concept', where rules and standards are still contested. In this, *Environment Law for Sustainability* lives up to its task, presenting legal scholarship that is critical and analytical rather than pragmatic.

These two pieces of scholarly work, taken together, are quite complementary and provide a useful addition to the library of any serious scholar in this field, as well as for any practitioner working on these issues. The first collection, *Making Law Work*, provides theoretical foundations, discussions of specific types of instruments, and a rich survey of case studies, as well as a helpful and comprehensive discussion of many innovative directions for compliances. It is a sourcebook, and also a toolkit which presents many ideas that could be useful in resolving theoretical and practical challenges for compliance with environmental law for sustainable development, especially in developing countries. *Environmental Law for Sustainability* then provides analytical critique, mainly from a developed country perspective. They canvass and question some of the instruments being used, without prescribing what is needed to ensure that environmental law can support sustainability. While some sections could be strengthened to better address the concerns of developing countries—where environmental law faces, perhaps, its greatest challenge—overall this book provides a solid contribution to legal scholarship in this area. Both sets of essays do recognize a growing practice of actively engaging civil society organizations in making and implementing environmental laws, with some authors arguing that unless this continues, compliance with the laws themselves is threatened. They both advocate, though not without caveats, the use of innovative economic and rights-based compliance mechanisms. Finally, the essays underscore the value of strengthening transnational networks of State and non-state actors in the implementation of international environmental law, focusing on this particular development as one of the institutional arrangements that has emerged to achieve compliance in this field.

There is, indeed, a need to implement environmental law and policy. However, a serious consideration of the governance questions related to international law in the field of sustainable development must also address ways to integrate environmental and social concerns into related economic law and policy. In particular, non-state actors appear to be assuming increasingly important roles that assist international economic regimes in taking their sustainable development objectives seriously. These issues are well canvassed in two additional books, which represent essential scholarship for lawyers and others in the field of international economic law, but also provide a helpful supplement to the first two collections, addressing recent legal developments in the field of sustainable development.

In *Sustainability, Civil Society and International Governance: Local, North American, and Global Perspectives*, John Kirton and Peter Hajnal present an analysis of how civil society has integrated into global governance structures, particularly in institutions with great influence in economic, ecological, and social sustainability today. The volume is divided into three sections in an effort to be descriptive, explanatory, and prescriptive. It begins by describing and critically evaluating current activities of civil society engagement at local, regional, and global levels. The essays assess why new processes have developed and what has been done to strengthen the partnerships between civil society and governments. In doing so, they highlight what has worked well in the local, regional, and multilateral spheres as well as community based alternatives. The essays also identify initiatives and provide a critical assessment of how mechanisms for civil society participation have positively or negatively affected specific economic, environmental, or political outcomes.

Non-state actors play different roles in the structures of international regimes, affecting their impact and reach. The first section contains interesting chapters discussing local and regional innovations which engage civil society in treaty negotiation, compliance, and dispute settlement on different levels. In Chapter 6, 'Local nongovernmental Organizations, Global Governance and the Challenges of a Global Movement for Sustainable Food Agriculture' (pp. 95–104), Debbie Field presents an interesting examination of how social movements have engaged civil society and built alliances that contest the global neo-liberal agenda in the post-NAFTA period. Her discussion touches on the success of some social movements at the grassroots and regional level, the relevant developments in agriculture and food movements, and the organization of effective resistance movements in agriculture in the future. The volume examines the role of multinational corporations as an important non-state actor. In the second section, Chapter 8 entitled 'Regional Multinational Corporations and Triad Strategy' (pp. 123–36), Alan Rugman and Alain Verbeke focus on certain flagship firms. They argue that these firms form part of clusters that are regionally based, in North America, the EU, and Asia, and debate recent engagements in various sectors, taking into account the regional location of business networks and global corporate strategies. The authors have developed an interesting framework, which they call a 'triad-centred regional' structure, which they find assists in describing the transnational governance of these firms. In Chapters 9 (pp. 137–76) and 10 (pp. 177–90), Julie Soloway and Chris Tollefson continue a debate from an earlier publication, considering whether NAFTA's Chapter 11 can adequately address social and environmental issues, and how investors and non-state actors have become engaged in its dispute settlement processes in this vein.

The last section focuses on the engagement of civil society in financial institutions and impacts on global governance. In Chapter 13, 'Civil Society and the Roots of Structural Conditionality in the World Bank and the International Monetary Fund' (pp. 231–60), Louis Pauly discusses the engagement of civil society in World Bank debates, and the evolving impact of the Bank on developing country domestic policy-making on a broad range of social and environmental issues. The chapter gives a brief overview of the practice of structural conditionality and the financial instruments within which it is embedded, highlighting the role of US ideologies, their reflections in financial governance, and resulting effects.

Other global economic institutions have a significant role to play. In *Environmental Law for Sustainability*, the environmental dimension of the World Trade Organization (WTO) was surveyed. A further essay from *Sustainability, Civil Society and International Governance* complements that chapter. In an insightful and analytically sound essay on 'World Trade Organization Gridlock and Alternative Regimes to Pursue an International Social Clause' (pp. 261–78), Scott Vaughan examines the major social justice issues that arise from the expanding mandate, universal membership, and internal governance structures of the WTO. He explores the governance of the organization, key linkages between trade and non-trade policies (notably labour and environment), and the lessons that the WTO debate could draw from other institutions. He argues that the WTO has been internally confused with regard to its mandate to address the relationship of the trade regime to labour and the environment. The mixed messages sent by the WTO to other legal regimes seeking the most effective enforcement mechanisms to pursue their objectives make it timely to examine these relationships, particularly in the context of the coherence issues raised in *Making Law Work*.

The institutional critiques, questions, and case studies debated in the texts in *Sustainability, Civil Society and International Governance* provide an important theoretical underpinning and many contextual examples to an examination of the evolving role of non-state actors in international law and policy-making on sustainable development. The book highlights the larger evolution of international economic and political relations and the increased importance continually given to trade and sustainable development. Many options are explored, and experiences analysed.

The leading views in international law on this fundamental challenge to economic law and policy are well represented in *The WTO and Sustainable Development* by Gary Sampson. In this pragmatic legal text, Sampson discusses the attention now being paid to policies that address sustainable development and the increasing overlap between polices specific to trade and those relating to sustainable development. He canvasses these issues in a text that is accessible, practical, and focused on the substance of the relationship in key areas of trade law and policy. This book takes the sustainable development objective of the WTO very seriously indeed. It is essential reading in this field. For international economic law, the 'devil is in the details' and while Sampson's review of the issues is necessarily broad, he addresses those details in a way that is focused, well-argued, and extremely pertinent to ongoing debates in global trade circles. While the discussions in Sampson's book are specific to the WTO and its role in sustainable development, he provides a poignant section dealing with the manner in which developing country concerns are being addressed—albeit imperfectly to date—in the multilateral trading system. Chapter 9 entitled 'Special and Differential Treatment and Sustainable Economic Development: Substance and Process' (pp. 192–244), discusses the need of developing countries to secure legal flexibility which would enable them to further implement the most appropriate development strategy. Sampson admits that there are many concepts of what an 'appropriate development strategy' may be. However, it is emphasized that successful implementation is very much dependent upon how legally flexible these strategies are in capturing the unique and diverse nature of the developing countries economies, resource endowments, institutions, and national characteristics.

Sampson also argues strongly—and in our view, correctly—for the need for greater consistency in international policy-making in regard to trade and sustainable development. He shows that by reforming the WTO agenda to support sustainable development and cohesive environmental law implementation, many barriers to implementation for developing countries can be removed. More importantly, this reform of the WTO, which he describes as already taking place, is occurring because of the involvement of civil society, the use of compliance mechanisms, and increased transgovernmental networks, as is well discussed in the previous volumes.

Taken together, these four works provide considerable illumination on recent developments in international governance, focusing on the emergence of new actors and instruments to make international law and policy in the field of sustainable development more effective. The implementation of international and domestic environmental law has been challenging. Some laws have even been critiqued as holding only theoretical, as opposed to practical, value. Similarly, many new trade, investment, and other economic laws and institutions are still evolving and seeking to accommodate with other objectives. As this happens, their implementation can have unanticipated outcomes, affecting the potential for social and environmental sustainability. These challenges are especially poignant in developing countries where sustainable development is a serious priority. International and domestic law in the field of sustainable development is only just beginning to emerge. Countries have just begun to recognize the necessary principles, processes, and practices to 'reconcile conflicting environmental, social and economic development norms ... in the interest of present and future generations'.[14] Global scholarly debate can offer a great deal to further our understanding, assisting with the sound evolution of these instruments. The four books reviewed in this essay are valuable contributions to these conversations.

III. Book Reviews

Enforcement of European Union Environmental Law: Legal Issues and Challenges, by Martin Hedemann-Robinson. London: Routledge-Cavendish, 2006, 570 pp., £35 hb. ISBN 1859419178.

The stated aim of the author in writing this book is to 'consider the various legal means by which EU law on environmental protection may be enforced effectively at the level of the Member State as well as by EU institutions' (p. 5). The work eminently succeeds in fulfilling this task and the author, a lecturer in law at Brunel University (UK) who has spent two years working in the European Commission's DG Environment, is to be applauded for producing a scholarly and highly readable addition to the literature.

Following a useful introduction in which the reader is, inter alia, given a useful overview of the development of European Community (EC) environmental law since the 1970s, Part 1 concentrates on the role of the Commission in the enforcement of EC environmental law. In meticulous detail the author describes the nature of the Article 226 EC procedure and the significant role played within it by the Commission in upholding the rule of law in this field. Attention is, however, also lucidly drawn to those aspects of the procedure which make it a less than ideal vehicle for ensuring compliance with environmental law: the length of time from start to finish of typical Article 226 EC proceedings; the lack of investigative powers vested in the Commission; the evident understaffing of the Commission's Environment Directorate-General's Legal Unit; and the inability of the Commission effectively to ensure practical compliance on the ground in

[14] M.-C. Cordonier Segger and A. Khalfan, *Sustainable Development Law: Principles, Practices, and Prospects* (New York: Oxford University Press, 2004), 365.

Member States. Nevertheless, since the entry into force of the Maastricht Treaty,[1] Article 228(2) EC proceedings—albeit also lengthy—can of course now be brought against a Member State for failure to remedy a breach of environmental law, and a chapter is devoted to this 'second round' of proceedings. Relevant case law is analysed and a helpful summary of criteria provided in relation to the finding of liability, as well as the imposition of financial penalties.

Part 1 concludes with the author's reflections on the role of the Commission and in doing so he clearly draws on his experience gained whilst working within this EC institution. For example, particular attention is drawn to the potential conflicts of interest faced by the Commission when exercising discretion whether or not to bring proceedings under Article 226 EC. The author pointedly shares his experience as an official in the Legal Unit of the DG Environment in relation to the *Prestige* oil tanker incident when it would seem that a clear legal case could have been made against Spanish and Portuguese authorities for their failure to act appropriately in dealing with the incident, but instead the actual legal advice provided by the Legal Unit 'overtly pointed to the strong political sensitivity surrounding the case' in recommending no action against the Member States concerned (pp. 183–4). Of course, this is not the first time that it has been suggested that political considerations have clouded the Commission's deliberations, but it is this sort of example which makes the work so readable. Indeed, a feature of the book is the giving of examples, mainly from the case law, to back up the author's submissions and analysis.

Having vividly underlined the Commission's limitations as 'Guardian of the Treaty', Part 2 reflects on the role of the private person in enforcement. The tools designed by the European Court of Justice (ECJ) to assist in the upholding of EC law by the individual (direct effect, indirect effect, and imposition of liability on the State under the *Francovich* ruling)[2] are analysed in detail in an environmental law context. Discussion then concentrates on the proposed Directive on Access to Justice in Environmental Matters,[3] designed to facilitate access to national courts and to Directive 2003/4/EC on Public Access to Environmental Information and Repealing Directive 90/313/EEC (Access to Information Directive).[4] The author goes on to assess the opportunity for individuals to gain access to the ECJ (particularly under Article 230 EC) before looking into the prospects for change in this regard under the then still *proposed* Regulation on the application of the Aarhus Convention;[5] which subsequently was adopted as Regulation

[1] Treaty on the European Union (Maastricht, the Netherlands, 7 Feb. 1992) [1992] OJ C191/1.

[2] Joined Cases C-6/90 and C-9/90 *Andrea Francovich and Danila Bonifaci and Others* v. *Italy* [1991] ECR I-5357 (*Francovich*).

[3] Commission Proposal for a Directive on Access to Justice in Environmental Matters COM(2003)624, 24 Oct. 2003.

[4] [2003] OJ L41/26.

[5] Commission Proposal for a Regulation on the Application of the Provisions of the Aarhus Convention on Access to Information, Public Participation in Decision-making and Access to Justice in Environmental Matters to EC Institutions and Bodies COM(2003)622, 24 Oct. 2003.

(EC) No. 1367/2006/EC on the Application of the Provisions of the Aarhus Convention on Access to Information, Public Participation in Decision-Making and Access to Justice in Environmental Matters to Community Institutions and Bodies.[6] The state of play in respect of access to information held by EC institutions is also addressed. Throughout this section of the book, the importance of the Convention on Access to Information, Public Participation in Decision-Making and Access to Justice in Environmental Matters (Aarhus Convention)[7] is acknowledged although perhaps the influence of the EU itself in the drafting of that international treaty could have been stressed to a greater extent. Part 2 of the work concludes with an assessment of the usefulness of the complaints procedures overseen by the European Ombudsman and European Parliament (EP). It is particularly refreshing to note the attention paid to the work of the former, a role which has arguably not attracted sufficient academic attention to date.

Part 3 is the final section of the work. Having assessed in Parts 1 and 2 the role of the Commission and of the individual in enforcement, Part 3 discusses the role of Member States in enforcing EC environmental law. Member States' obligations under Article 10 EC form a focus for discussion before an appraisal of the work of the EU Network for the Implementation and Enforcement of Environmental Law (IMPEL) is provided. Also addressed is the limited impact of the EP and Council Recommendation 2001/331/EC providing for minimum criteria for environmental inspections in the Member States.[8]

A chapter is then devoted to an analysis of Directive 2004/35/EC on Environmental Liability with regard to the Prevention and Remedying of Environmental Damage (Environmental Liability Directive),[9] before the EU's attempt to introduce a Framework Decision on combating serious environmental crime under the Third Pillar of the EU Treaty is analysed.[10] Of course, this Framework Decision was subsequently annulled by the ECJ in Case C-176/03 *Commission* v. *Council*,[11] and the author adds his own pithy comment on this controversial decision.

The book is well presented and also reasonably priced in view of its length. However, a criticism—perhaps to be aimed at the publisher rather than the author—is the manner in which case law is cited. Although the case number and title of ECJ cases is provided, there is no reference to the law report where the case can be read. Those familiar with EU law will be aware of the usefulness of CELEX and now EUR-Lex in allowing access to judgments, but those

[6] [2006] OJ L264/13.

[7] Aarhus (Denmark), 25 June 1998 (entered into force on 30 Oct. 2001), (1999) 38 *International Legal Materials* 3, 517; also published on the Internet at: http://www.unece.org/env/pp.

[8] [2001] OJ L118/41.

[9] [2004] OJ L143/56.

[10] Council Framework Dec. 2003/80/JHA on the Protection of the Environment through Criminal Law [2003] OJ L29/55 (Annulled).

[11] [2005] ECR I-7879.

unfamiliar with such electronic resources would have found a full citation of case law in the Table of Cases particularly useful.

It is always good to finish on an optimistic note and the author concludes his work by indicating that:

> the recent wave of EC legislative initiatives according civil society and national authorities far more opportunities and responsibilities [in relation to law enforcement] seem set to improve matters significantly (p. 558).

There is perhaps little doubt that this is true, but the pessimist would point to the delay in adopting the proposed Access to Justice in Environmental Matters Directive[12] as an indicator that not all are comfortable with the promotion of access to justice before national courts.

Anyone interested in this essential area of EC environmental law will find this work an invaluable source of information. It is certainly to be welcomed as an important addition to the literature and the author is to be highly commended for the clear, considered, and meticulous manner in which he has undertaken his task.

PETER DAVIES
Associate Professor, Director of the
Centre for Environmental Law
University of Nottingham (UK)

Implementing the Precautionary Principle: Perspectives and Prospects, edited by Elizabeth Fisher, Judith Jones, and René von Schomberg. Cheltenham: Edward Elgar Publishing, 2006, 350 pp., £79.95 hb. ISBN 1845427025.

The precautionary principle may well be—as the editors of this volume affirm in their concise introductory overview (pp. 1–18)—'one of the most significant principles of the contemporary era' (p. 11). Its authoritative international codification (as Principle 15 of the 1992 Rio Declaration on Environment and Development)[1] has certainly generated a very considerable amount of implementing action at the levels of both policy-making and law-making, as well as in judicial and academic interpretation. It also triggered a fair amount of controversy, and an ongoing worldwide debate of which this book is bound to become an important part.

[12] N. 3 above.

[1] Rio de Janeiro (Brazil), 3–14 June 1992, (1992) 31 *International Legal Materials*, 874.

The original occasion for this collection of essays was a conference held in 2003, at the Australian National University (ANU) in Canberra (Australia). The range of the dialogue subsequently expanded to include a number of European and American scholars involved in the assessment of contemporary environmental, public health, and technological risks. Given the prominent role of the principle in European Union (EU) policies in particular, the project thus turned into a broad interdisciplinary and comparative stock-taking endeavour.

There are obvious pitfalls in any comparative analysis at this level of generality. What may or may not have started from the German *Vorsorge-Prinzip*[2] (as presented here by Joel Tickner and David Kriebel, in Chapter 3 (pp. 42–62) adapted from their 2003 United States (US) congressional testimony, at p. 43) has taken on very diverse meanings in different legal systems today. In Australia—where the precautionary principle was first read into an existing statutory regime by Justice Paul Stein's landmark 1993 judgment in *Leatch* v. *National Parks & Wildlife Service*[3]—it seems perfectly plausible and sensible to interpret the principle by reference to existing standards of proof familiar from criminal law and general administrative law, as outlined in Chapter 7 by Judith Jones and Simon Bronitt (pp. 137–59); or to convert the principle's triggering definition ('when there are threats of serious or irreversible environmental damage') into a 'threshold test' for judicial review, in the light of recent Australian and New Zealand court decisions as summarized and distinguished in Chapter 9 by Warwick Gullett (pp. 182–201). The authors may have been surprised, though, to learn from Olivier Godard's Chapter 4 (pp. 63–87) that French courts use an entirely different threshold test—because the 1995 *Loi Barnier* purporting to translate the precautionary principle into French law changed the formula to read 'serious and irreversible environmental damage', with the result of shifting the legal debate in France towards proof of irreversibility alone.[4]

Similar discrepancies turn up in other textual elements of the principle—starting with the rider 'cost-effective', which the US delegation managed to slip into the definition of preventive measures in Rio Principle 15 (over the

[2] Some even trace its cultural roots to the mystical figure of *Sorge* (care, *cura*) in Goethe's *Faust* of 1832 (Part II, Act V, Scene IV); see B. Rich, *Mortgaging the Earth: the World Bank, Environmental Impoverishment, and the Crisis of Development* (Boston, MA: Beacon Press, 1994), 318; and K. Burdach, 'Faust und die Sorge' (1923) 1 *Deutsche Vierteljahresschrift für Literaturwissenschaft und Geistesgeschichte*, 1. Others point out that the principle was first laid down as a legal rule in the 1969 Swedish Environment Protection Act; i.e. years before the concept surfaced in modern German legislation; see S. Westerlund, 'Legal Antipollution Standards in Sweden' (1981) 25 *Scandinavian Studies in Law*, 223–44, at 231; and P. H. Sand, 'The Precautionary Principle: A European Perspective' (2000) 6 *Human and Ecological Risk Assessment* 3, 445–58, at 448.

[3] Land and Environment Court of New South Wales, No. 10376 of 1993, 23 Nov. 1993.

[4] See, e.g., M. Fritz-Legendre, 'Biodiversité et irreversibilité' (1998) 23 *Revue Juridique de l'Environnement—special issue*, 79–100. Art. 5 of the 2004 *Charte de l'Environnement* uses the same formula; see Godard, at p. 74.

objections of the EU and Japan),[5] and which is conspicuously absent from the relevant Australian text, the 1992 Intergovernmental Agreement on the Environment (IGAE) between the Commonwealth and the Australian States and Territories.[6] Even more significant perhaps is the other rider, 'proportionate', which now qualifies preventive measures not only in French law but also in the EU's own interpretative guidelines of 2000.[7] The so-called 'proportionality test'—which appears nowhere in Rio Principle 15, nor for that matter in its Australian IGAE equivalent—also remains prominent among the 'balancing disciplines' used in the context of the World Trade Organization (WTO), such as Article 2.4 of the Agreement on Technical Barriers to Trade (TBT), as listed in Chapter 8 by Jan McDonald (pp. 160–81, at p. 165).[8] Godard considers it so essential for the French variant of the precautionary principle that he labels it 'the proportionate precautionary principle' (p. 84), and claims that following its incorporation into French constitutional law since 2005, it would now have precedence over any different interpretations 'in case of conflict between French law and EU law or international agreements' (p. 80). Under those circumstances, René von Schomberg's valiant plea, in Chapter 2 (pp. 19–41), for a common rational 'policy definition of the precautionary principle' in the EU (at pp. 37–8) seems all the more commendable if somewhat Sisyphean.

The difficulty of defining a 'common' precautionary policy in substantive terms becomes readily apparent when moving to specific risk categories. Prima facie the least controversial case would seem to be biodiversity conservation, outlined in Chapter 11 by Rosie Cooney (pp. 223–44). Yet, the author shows that even in this field where there is a broad basis of universally shared values, some of the costs of precaution may end up being borne inequitably by disadvantaged groups or countries. It is perhaps unfortunate that the editors did not include a separate chapter on marine living resources, and on the whaling issue in particular, where precautionary restrictions in the face of scientific uncertainty (moratorium versus 'scientific' catch) continue to fuel international disputes.

[5] Curiously, the equally authentic French text of Rio Principle 15 had omitted the 'cost' prefix; but the 1995 *Loi Barnier* then more than made up for the omission by adding the new terms 'at economically acceptable cost'; see Sand (n. 2 above), 447 and 450.

[6] 1 May 1992, published on the Internet at: http://www.environment.gov.au/esd/national/igae/index.html.

[7] Commission Communication on the Precautionary Principle COM(2000)1, 2 Feb. 2000; see W. M. Kühn, 'Die Entwicklung des Vorsorge-Prinzips im Europarecht' (2006) 9 *Zeitschrift für Europarechtliche Studien* 4, 487–520.

[8] McDonald also identifies (on p. 178) what is probably the most perverse opposite of the precautionary approach by any international risk assessment body: The Procedural Manual of the Codex Alimentarius Commission (13th edn., Rome: FAO/WHO, 2001, at 43), provides that 'when there is evidence that a risk to human health exists but scientific data are insufficient or incomplete, the Commission should not proceed to elaborate a standard but should consider elaborating a related text, such as a code of practice, provided that such a text would be supported by the available scientific evidence'.

It is gratifying to note that this book, for one, does not seek to perpetuate the myth of an 'Atlantic divide' over precautionary regulation—a stereotype sufficiently disproved by recent comparative studies.[9] Not even in the politically charged field of climate change, discussed by Jeroen van der Sluijs and Wim Turkenburg in Chapter 12 (pp. 245–69), is there tangible evidence of any 'cultural' divergence between US and EU attitudes. Whether or not there are two distinct regulatory camps in the modern industrialized world, as claimed in a 1991 study commissioned by the German Federal Environmental Agency (so-called 'precaution countries' including Germany, the Netherlands, Sweden, and Switzerland, along with the US; and so-called 'protection countries' including France and the UK, and Japan),[10] remains a matter of opinion. It would certainly have been interesting in this regard to compare national approaches to nuclear energy risks, a classical legal battleground for the precautionary principle from the 1978 *Kalkar* judgment of the German Federal Constitutional Court to the 1997 *Superphénix* decision of the French Conseil d'État, and regrettably absent from the case studies here presented.

Yet the major contribution of this collection—well beyond its reflections on the normative legitimacy of the precautionary principle as empirically implemented in various fields—is the recognition that precautionary regulation is essentially a process of good governance. In what is arguably the most stimulating and innovative section of the book (Chapter 6, pp. 113–36), Elizabeth Fisher and Ronnie Harding set forth two basic frameworks of administrative decision-making within which precaution operates, and which in turn are said to be inspired by distinct theories of 'administrative constitutionalism':[11] on the one hand, the European Commission's 'rational-instrumental' approach (as formulated in its 2000 Communication on the Precautionary Principle,[12] intended at least in part to legitimize EU policies vis-à-vis the WTO); and on the other hand, the 'deliberative-constitutive' approach developed in 1997 for Australia's public administration to deal with indeterminate future environmental and public health risks.[13] The ensuing focus on process rather than outcome is also reflected in another Australian contribution, by Stephen Dovers (Chapter 5, pp. 88–112, emphasizing institutional design to ensure strategic environmental assessment); and in another Dutch contribution, by Arie Rip (Chapter 13, pp. 270–83, on the—as yet—fictional risks of nanotechnology).

[9] J. B. Wiener and M. D. Rogers, 'Comparing Precaution in the United States and Europe' (2002) 5 *Journal of Risk Research* 4, 317–49; see also J. B. Wiener, M. D. Rogers, P. H. Sand, and J. K. Hammitt (eds.), *The Reality of Precaution: Comparing Risk Regulation in the United States and Europe* (Cambridge: Cambridge University Press, 2007).

[10] E. Rehbinder, *Das Vorsorge-Prinzip im internationalen Vergleich* (Düsseldorf: Werner, 1991).

[11] See also E. Fisher, *Risk Regulation and Administrative Constitutionalism* (Oxford: Hart Publishing, 2007).

[12] N. 7 above.

[13] A. Deville and R. Harding, *Applying the Precautionary Principle* (Sydney: Federation Press, 1997).

Central to this governance-oriented perspective, of course, is the role accorded to experts in administrative decisions coping with environmental risks under conditions of uncertainty. Taking Australian regulation of genetically modified organisms (GMOs) as an example in point, Jacqueline Peel's Chapter 10 (pp. 202–22) demonstrates how a system relying solely on so-called 'authoritative' scientific evaluation of health and safety risks—to the virtual exclusion of other socio-economic and ethical concerns—may end up losing public 'trust', and hence democratic legitimacy.[14] A similar argument is presented in Chapter 14 by Andy Stirling, Ortwin Renn, and Patrick van Zwanenberg (pp. 284–315) analysing food safety regulation by the European Commission, and calling for more 'discursive' and participatory procedures. It would indeed have been useful to place this argument in the wider context of the Convention on Access to Information, Public Participation in Decision-Making and Access to Justice in Environmental Matters (Aarhus Convention)[15]—to which the EU is a party—especially after its GMO amendment of 2005.[16] There also are striking parallels here with current discourses in North America, where—under overwhelming pressure from industry—all attempts at introducing 'right-to-know' legislation for GMO food were narrowly defeated,[17] and where the very principle of public disclosure of risk information (be it government-held or industry-held), once hailed by European observers as 'the new Magna Carta of ecological democracy',[18] now seems to give way to a kind of 'soft paternalism',[19] with a benevolent avuncular State determining what citizens and consumers do or do not *need* to know.[20]

[14] See R. E. Löfstedt, *Risk Management in Post-Trust Society* (Basingstoke: Palgrave MacMillan, 2005).

[15] Aarhus (Denmark), 25 June 1998 (entered into force on 30 Oct. 2001), (1999) 38 *International Legal Materials* 3, 517; also published on the Internet at: http://www.unece.org/env/pp.

[16] Dec. II/1 on Genetically Modified Organisms, of 27 May 2005, replacing Art. 6(11) and inserting a new Art. *6bis*; UN Doc. No. ECE/MP.PP/2005/2/Add.2/Annex. See further T. F. M. Etty, 'Substantive European Community Law: Biotechnology' (2007) 7 *Yearbook of European Environmental Law*, 307–9.

[17] See, e.g., the Genetically Engineered Food Right-to-Know Acts introduced by Senator Barbara Boxer (D-California) on 22 Feb. 2000/S. 2080, and by Representative Dennis Kucinich (D-Ohio) on 21 May 2002/H.R. 4814, reintroduced on 2 May 2006/H.R. 5269; see D. M. Strauss, 'Genetically Modified Organisms in Food: A Model of Labelling and Monitoring with Positive Implications for International Trade' (2006) 40 *International Lawyer* 1, 95–119, at 100. The Consumers' Right to Know (Food Information) Bill introduced in the New Zealand Parliament by MP Sue Kedgley (Green Party), on 30 Mar. 2006, also failed.

[18] J. Fischer, *Der Umbau der Industriegesellschaft: Plädoyer wider die herrschende Umweltlüge* (Frankfurt: Eichborn, 1989), 152; English translation in: U. Beck (ed.), *Ecological Enlightenment: Essays on the Politics of Risk Society* (Atlantic Highlands, NJ: Humanity Press, 1995).

[19] See R. H. Thaler and C. R. Sunstein, 'Libertarian Paternalism' (2003) 93 *American Economic Review* 2, 175–9; C. R. Sunstein and R. H. Thaler, 'Libertarian Paternalism is not an Oxymoron' (2003) 70 *University of Chicago Law Review*, 1159–99, at 1166; and E. L. Glaeser, 'Paternalism and Psychology' (2006) 73 *University of Chicago Law* Review, 133–56, at 149.

[20] See 'The New Paternalism: The Avuncular State', *The Economist*, 8 Apr. 2006, 75. Considering, though, that the *avunculus* in Roman law was the maternal rather than the paternal uncle (i.e. *patruus*; I owe this clarification to Anne Petitpierre), it would perhaps be more accurate for 'soft paternalism' to be re-labelled maternalism, or Big Mother Syndrome.

As the editors of this timely book state in their preface, the global debate on implementation of the precautionary principle has only just begun. The principle itself may be a prime example of what autopoietic legal theory defines as a 'legal irritant':[21]

> Legal irritants cannot be domesticated; they are not transferred from something alien into something familiar, not adapted to a new cultural context, rather they will unleash an evolutionary dynamic in which the external rule's meaning will be reconstructed and the internal context will undergo fundamental change.[22]

PETER H. SAND
Lecturer, Institute of International Law
University of Munich (Germany)

Precautionary Rights and Duties of States, by Arie Trouwborst. Leiden: Brill Academic Publishers, 2006, 350 pp., €85 hb. ISBN 9004152121.

Having completed a monograph on the precautionary principle as a rule of customary public international law,[1] Arie Trouwborst now sets himself a different task: to identify the implications for States of the legal obligations flowing from the principle. He organizes his arguments around the metaphor of a tripod whose three legs are threat of harm, uncertainty, and action.

With respect to the first leg of the tripod, harm, Trouwborst argues that there is a sliding scale of obligation depending on the gravity of the risk of harm. 'Significant' harm, he argues, gives States a *right* to take precautionary action, while serious or irreversible harm places upon them an *obligation* to do so. Trouwborst's conclusion that this right/obligation dichotomy is reflected in current law requires further elucidation; it does not seem to be supported by the evidence that he presents. Furthermore, although the reader can imagine contexts in which a *right* to take precautionary action might be relevant, Trouwborst provides no discussion on this point. Such a right would be most relevant in cases where another set of obligations, such as international trade obligations, are in tension with precaution. If Trouwborst is correct, this would mean that

21 G. Teubner, 'Legal Irritants: Good Faith in British Law or How Unifying Law Ends Up in New Divergences' (1998) 61 *Modern Law Review* 1, 11–32.

22 D. Nelken, 'Beyond the Metaphor of Legal Transplants? Consequences of Autopoietic Theory for the Study of Cross-Cultural Legal Adaptation', in J. Přibań and D. Nelken (eds.), *Law's New Boundaries: The Consequences of Legal Autopoiesis* (Aldershot: Ashgate/Dartmouth, 2001), 265–302, at 270.

1 A. Trouwborst, *Evolution and Status of the Precautionary Principle in International Law* (The Hague/New York: Kluwer Law International, 2002).

paragraph 5(7) of the World Trade Organization (WTO) Agreement on Sanitary and Phytosanitary Measures (SPS) creates a *right* to precautionary action. This is a plausible reading of this provision, but it may be difficult to square, for example, with the recent WTO dispute panel decision on biotechnological resources.[2]

The second leg of Trouwborst's precautionary tripod is uncertainty. This requires a preliminary exposition of the nature of scientific knowledge and the differences among knowledge, risk, and uncertainty, which Trouwborst handles very well: the discussion covers the salient points and is both informative and accessible to an audience of jurists, whose scientific literacy may be low. Regarding the level of scientific uncertainty required to trigger precaution, Trouwborst points out that a duty to take precautionary action cannot arise every time it is impossible to rule out risk—that is, all the time. He concludes, rather, that an obligation to take precautionary action only arises 'when there are at least some indications, some (reasonable) grounds for concern that environmental harm, of whatever nature, may be brought about' (p. 109). In the absence of such reasonable grounds for concern, he argues, States have neither a right nor a duty to take precautionary action. Once again, this notion of a *right* to precautionary action requires further elaboration. It is only in cases where precautionary action may interfere with the fulfilment of other obligations that a right to precautionary action becomes relevant. Absent such potentially conflicting international obligations, however, States need not demonstrate a right to take precautionary action: if they wish to refuse permission for the building of a road or dam despite good scientific evidence that risks, both known and uncertain, of environmental harm are insignificant, they need not justify that decision to the international community.

The third leg of Trouwborst's tripod is action: what is it that the precautionary principle obliges States to do? This is by far and away the most fraught question in discussions about the precautionary principle. Trouwborst comes down firmly in favour of a substantive rather than a procedural approach: precaution, he concludes, implies 'an *obligation* to take action' (p. 121). This is a surprising proposition, and requires some fancy interpretive footwork. Principle 15 of the 1992 Rio Declaration on Environment and Development,[3] the most well-known and well-accepted version of the precautionary principle, tells States not to use scientific uncertainty to *postpone* environmental protection measures. Trouwborst reads the word 'postpone' as a prohibition on *not* taking measures. In fact, what is prohibited is the invocation of scientific uncertainty as a reason for postponing environmental measures; States may still invoke other reasons, such as, for example,

[2] *EC–Measures Affecting the Approval and Marketing of Biotech Products* (*EC–Biotech Products*), WT/DS291 (US), WT/DS292 (Canada), and WT/DS291 (Argentina), Panel Report of 29 Sept. 2006.

[3] Rio de Janeiro (Brazil), 3–14 June 1992, (1992) 31 *International Legal Materials*, 874.

a determination that precautionary measures are not necessary or would in turn impose various kinds of risks and costs that would outweigh their benefit.

The nub of the issue, however, is elsewhere, namely in a determination of what is meant by 'action'. Importantly, Trouwborst's definition of precautionary action is very broad: 'any measure can be a precautionary measure' (p. 179). He makes specific reference to some obvious candidates, namely bans, the introduction of margins of safety into regulatory standards, and research. Ultimately, it seems, precaution informs decision-making procedures, but it does not tell decision-makers what to do. That is, we could treat precaution as an essentially procedural rather than substantive obligation. Trouwborst comes close to acknowledging this in Chapter 7, where he states:

> [I]n the practical implementation of the precautionary principle states have tended to simply select the effective and proportional measure, or combination of measures, that suits the circumstances of the case best. Thinking it over this could hardly be different, bearing in mind the huge variety of natural conditions and human actions, i.e., the huge variety of environmental risks to which the precautionary principle is potentially applicable... It can thus be concluded that the precautionary principle does not as a rule dictate any regulatory measures in particular. (pp. 180–1)

The assertion that States currently hold a duty at customary law to take precautionary action when thresholds for the application of precaution are triggered seems somewhat less bold when we realize that 'precautionary action' is defined in this broad manner.

In Trouwborst's discussion of tradeoffs among different types of risk, this point about the potential breadth of precautionary action seems to be lost. Trouwborst seems to wish to avoid concluding that precaution is really as open-ended as it sometimes seems in his argument, and therefore continues to assert that the implications of precaution are real: when various thresholds are reached, States will be obligated to do something concrete. For similar reasons, he seems to wish to hold at bay suggestions that factors other than environmental protection could be relevant in precautionary decision-making.

Trouwborst is quite willing to accept that tradeoffs among different environmental risks will often be necessary. In this context, he uses the metaphor of a jury in a criminal trial: the various legal principles at play do not point out the answer; rather, we must 'weigh up the evidence... and come to a decision' (p. 187).[4] But there will also be occasions on which environmental risks need to be compared to other types of risks. Trouwborst does not go so far as to argue that socio-economic factors are irrelevant to precautionary decision-making, but he seems unsure how they should be handled. Trouwborst seems determined, in particular, to keep traditional cost-benefit analysis at bay, but in the process he often forgets that socio-economic costs include injury or sickness in human

[4] Citing M. Wan Ho and P. Saunders, *The Precautionary Principle is Coherent* (2000), published on the Internet at: http://www.i-sis.org.uk/precautionary-pr.php.

populations, loss of livelihood, disruption of communities dependent on fishing or forestry, and so on. Critics of precaution are more likely to point out precaution's apparent insensitivity to these kinds of costs than economic costs of a more commercial nature, and Trouwborst, by failing to address head-on potential conflicts between, say, environmental protection and human health and safety, leaves himself vulnerable to criticism that his approach to precaution is excessively rigid.

The problem with traditional cost-benefit analysis is precisely that it is unlike the process that juries engage in. Cost-benefit analysis involves consideration of only those costs and benefits susceptible of calculation in monetary terms. Attempts to attenuate the most egregious blind spots inherent in such an approach through the establishment of monetary proxies for environmental or human health impacts are arbitrary and unsatisfactory. Jurors, on the other hand, are not expected to reduce all considerations to a single metric prior to beginning the process of weighing evidence, nor are they obliged to justify their decisions to one another based on a ratio of costs and benefits expressed in numeric terms. What is required in environmental decision-making is a process in which costs and benefits, broadly defined and including uncertainty, are considered on their own terms and in a holistic fashion.

This seems to be the direction in which Trouwborst is heading. For example, he refers to arguments in the literature that:

> costs and benefits of precautionary action, whether economic, social or environmental, should be considered, but in a truly comprehensive way, meaning that effects on *all* values of the environment, including the long term, are accorded their genuine weight and any uncertainties are accounted for. (p. 253).

He also refers to an alternative to mainstream cost-benefit analysis, namely trade-off analysis, in which monetary values are not assigned to non-monetary impacts (p. 253). However, in seeking to answer the question whether State practice contains evidence of 'weighing environmental, social and economic interests when determining what precautionary action to take' (p. 266), he seems to reach a very different conclusion. He states that, on the one hand, the precautionary principle as it exists in international law today does not set out a separate requirement of cost-effectiveness: 'rather... precautionary measures to deal with significant harm are *assumed* to be so' (p. 280). He then states that 'traditional cost-benefit analysis has no role to play in the implementation of the principle' (p. 280). He goes on to say that 'there *is* room for states to balance environmental, social and economic interests' (p. 280), but he has very little to say about how this balancing process might be carried out. This would have been an excellent opportunity for Trouwborst to explore the approaches to weighing and balancing he alludes to earlier on.

Some comments on Trouwborst's methodology are in order. Trouwborst's discussion is organized around two different goals: an account of the current state of the law, and a broader discussion in which an argument about a particular approach to precaution is presented. This approach is entirely appropriate; indeed, it is probably necessary in order to permit the reader to understand what conclusions may be drawn from the vast collection of evidence concerning precaution's role in international law. However, there does appear to be some tension between the two objectives. For example, Trouwborst takes a rather catholic approach to sources in his discussion of the current state of the law. On one hand, this is the hallmark of a careful and thorough researcher, which Trouwborst most certainly is. However, once this evidence has been gathered, some sifting is required. Trouwborst has a tendency to prevent conventions appearing alongside declarations as if they were to be given the same weight, despite his acknowledgement on p. 10 of the importance of giving careful consideration to the manner in which various pieces of evidence may be used in building a customary law argument. Furthermore, for the most part he is satisfied to look for State practice in international conventions, without canvassing domestic legislation and bureaucratic decision-making procedures. Clearly, Trouwborst is obliged to make some choices about the type of evidence he looks at, since it would be an overwhelming task to canvas all potential sources of evidence of State practice and *opinio iuris*. Nevertheless, he would have done well to explain to the reader his process of selection and analysis of evidence.

On the whole, this is an ambitious and informative work which presents, perhaps without meaning to, a novel interpretation of precaution that will no doubt be welcomed by proponents of this principle.

JAYE ELLIS
Assistant Professor,
Faculty of Law and School of Environment,
McGill University, Montreal, Quebec (Canada)

EU Climate Change Policy: The Challenge of New Regulatory Initiatives, edited by Marjan Peeters and Kurt Deketelaere. Cheltenham: Edward Elgar, 2006, 330 pp., £75 hb. ISBN 1845426053.

This book comes at a time when, thanks to the preview of the newest IPCC reports, the world seems finally to have taken notice of how severely human induced climate change threatens people and nature alike. Its aim is an important one: to explore how the European Union (EU) responds to this threat in practice and law, i.e. to scrutinize policies and measures taken by the EU on behalf of its Member States who are, after all, some of the major emitters of greenhouse gases. It also comes at a time where the EU—most recently in March 2007—takes important climate-related decisions, which are relevant both for EU legislation and for the international climate negotiations. This is also to some extent unfortunate, as the analysis has—in some, but not all cases—been overhauled by political events (such as the adoption of the binding renewable energy target of 20 per cent by 2020)[5] or legal decisions (such as the European Commission's decisions on the second National Allocation Plans (NAPs)).[6]

The book is divided into four parts—an introduction, the main thrust of the volume on 'greenhouse gas emissions trading within the EU' with eight distinct chapters, the rather slim part on 'energy and climate change measures' comprised of three chapters, and the last part on 'good governance for climate change' with two contributions. As the title suggests—and reinforced by the introductory remarks by the editors—it is a volume about the regulatory approaches taken by the EU to respond to the challenge of climate change. The expectation is, therefore, a discussion of 'policies and measures', their legal framework and difficulties, and their efficacy. Given the EU's approach to the climate issue from the very start of the international negotiations of the United Nations Framework Convention on Climate Change (UNFCCC),[7] as rightly explained by Pallemaarts and Williams (pp. 22–50) in their chapter on the international framework, one would expect a comprehensive review of the EU's attempts to tackle the issue—in all possible sectors, including industry, energy, households, and transport.

Yet, the book falls somehow short of the expectations it sets. This is mainly because it focuses very much on one particular tool—Emissions Trading—and fails to discuss other important sources of greenhouse gases entirely, such as the transport sector and households. Moreover, the reader is presented with a mix of chapters, some of which do not seem to belong to the volume altogether, as interesting and well thought through they might be. This is the case for the chapter by Douma (pp. 51–68) on EU policies towards Russia, but also for the—albeit very interesting—chapter by MacDonald and Makuch (pp. 125–52), exploring the extent to which the emissions trading regime corresponds to the Convention on Access to Information, Public Participation in Decision-Making and Access to Justice in Environmental Matters (Aarhus Convention).[8] Still, the various contributions have value for practitioners and researchers alike.

The chapter by Pallemaarts and Williams (pp. 22–50), exploring the international context for EU climate policy and law, is a good summary of the rules enshrined in the UNFCCC and its Kyoto Protocol.[9] Pallemaarts, as someone

[5] European Council, 8–9 Mar. 2007, Conclusions, Council Doc. 7224/07, para. 36 and Annex I (European Council Energy Action Plan 2007–2009), para. 5.

[6] All the country-specific decisions are published on the Internet at: http://ec.europa.eu/environment/climat/2nd_phase_ep.htm.

[7] New York, NY (US), 9 May 1992 (entered into force 21 Mar. 1994), (1992) 31 *International Legal Materials* 4, 849.

[8] Aarhus (Denmark), 25 June 1998 (entered into force on 30 Oct. 2001), (1999) 38 *International Legal Materials* 3, 517; also published on the Internet at: http://www.unece.org/env/pp.

[9] Kyoto (Japan), 10 Dec. 1997 (entered into force 16 Feb. 2005), (1998) 37 *International Legal Materials* 1, 22.

having participated in the negotiations himself for many years, easily describes the main features of the international treaties as well as of EU climate policy. On the latter, he provides the reader with a useful and comprehensive summary—which is unfortunately reiterated by other authors (for example by Bruggeman and Delvaux in Chapter 12 on EU Energy policy, pp. 223–39).

After this general introduction, it would have been useful to set the context for EU policy and law-making first, which necessitates a discussion of the legislative competences. It would thus have been useful to set Krämer's chapter (pp. 279–96) up front, as it presents a review of the existing competences and shortfalls in the EU and EC Treaties. As it is, the reader is somewhat plunged into a detailed analysis of the EU Emissions Trading Scheme. This begins with the analysis of Member State liability (by Eritja, pp. 69–82), which is based on the assumption that in many Member States, the administrative and political framework has not been set for the implementation of the Emissions Trading scheme. The author asks himself if and under what circumstances: (i) Member States might be held liable for failure to implement by and before EU institutions; (ii) EU citizens might sue a Member State, using the landmark *Francovich* formula[10] developed by the European Court of Justice (ECJ); and (iii) Kyoto Parties could have any right to commence proceedings. The issue of enforcement at EU level is well discussed and does not differ from the implementation and transposition of other EU law. With respect to individual claims on Member State level, the author falls short of outlining what damage an individual, a company, or a non-governmental organization (NGO) might incur due to a failure of implementation of Directive 2003/87/EC establishing a Scheme for Greenhouse Gas Emission Allowance Trading within the Community and Amending Directive 96/61/EC (Emissions Trading Directive)[11] and, therefore, the legal analysis remains hazy. To explore whether other Kyoto Parties or individual EU Member States could claim implementation of a piece of EU legislation, in fact, seems to be entirely useless, as it is—of course—impossible.

Next, Schmitt-Rady (pp. 83–97) explores the details of the Emissions Trading Directive with respect to 'a level playing field' for companies. This chapter is clearly written from the practitioner's perspective and is therefore a useful piece in the wealth of (legal and economic) scientific discussion that exists about the Directive. She highlights some of the issues that have become virulent with the Commission's NAPs decisions. Her conclusion, that the Emissions Trading Directive and its Annexes are too vague to provide a level playing field for participating companies, is not surprising—but she disregards the ongoing discussion about subsidiarity and the fact that other legal writers have found the Directive to leave too little discretion to Member States.

[10] Joined Cases C-6/90 and C-9/90 *Andrea Francovich and Danila Bonifaci and Others* v. *Italy* [1991] ECR I-5357 (*Francovich*).

[11] [2003] OJ L275/32.

The following chapter, by de Larragan (pp. 98–124), on linking the Kyoto Protocol's project-based mechanisms into the Emissions Trading Directive, is generally useful and a good summary of Directive 2004/101/EC amending Directive 2003/87/EC establishing a Scheme for Greenhouse Gas Emission Allowance Trading within the Community, in respect of the Kyoto Protocol's Project Mechanisms (Linking Directive).[12] Yet, it is to some extent overhauled by the way Member States have by now in fact incorporated the Linking Directive into their national setting. Sadly, de Larragan's analysis does not include any discussion of such national laws.

Chapter 8, by Egelund Olsen (pp. 153–68), discusses the pre-existing permit system for the new greenhouse gas permit: the Integrated Pollution Prevention and Control (IPPC) scheme.[13] It is a useful contribution, although it again lacks examples from Member States practice. The way the Emissions Trading Scheme permit would be incorporated into the existing national schemes was a major issue of debate and some exemplary remarks of this would have benefited Olsen's analysis.

Peeters (pp. 169–87) then proceeds to look at enforcement issues of the EU Emissions Trading Scheme. He rightly highlights the importance of enforcement of the scheme's settings and conditions and discusses the Commission's guidelines pursuant to Article 14 of the Emissions Trading Directive in-depth. He concludes that monitoring and reporting provisions lead to a large degree of harmonization, while leaving some room for Member States discretion. He is critical of the naming-and-shaming provision in Article 16 of the Directive, but states at the same time that the foreseen sanction for breaching the obligation to surrender sufficient allowances of €100 per ton of carbon equivalent seems low. His contribution is exemplary of how reporting and verification provisions of legislation should be analysed, given their role in practice.

Pring's discussion of the United States' (US) sulphur dioxide (SO_2) emissions trading scheme (Chapter 10, pp. 188–204) brings nothing new, but might serve as a summary of the extensive research undertaken as part of the European Climate Change Programme (ECCP) to highlight lessons learnt and crucial issues to consider for the EU Emissions Trading Scheme.

The following chapter by van Calster (pp. 205–22) is, in fact, not a contribution to the emissions trading discussion, but rather an analysis of climate taxes and the feasibility of the specific World Trade Organization (WTO) compatibility of border tax adjustments (BTA). Van Calster concludes that BTA introduction might be unworkable and, legally, feasible only on the export side—which

[12] [2004] OJ L338/18.

[13] Dir. 96/61/EC concerning Integrated Pollution Prevention and Control (IPPC Dir.) [1996] OJ L257/26.

is not environmentally desirable. He also rightly points out that it is not the Kyoto Protocol that might raise WTO concerns, but rather unilateral measures. He concludes that it is unlikely that the EU Emissions Trading Scheme, be it under the WTO's General Agreement on Tariffs and Trade (GATT), the General Agreement on Trade in Services (GATS), or the Agreement on Trade-Related Investment Measures (TRIMS), should encounter legal difficulties. It is a well-written and well-researched piece in the wealth of WTO literature and the never ceasing debate on the compatibility of multilateral environmental agreements (MEAs). In the context of the volume in which it appears, however, it might have been desirable to explore the necessity of BTAs by the EU and the relationship between the (extensive) external trade competences as opposed to the (limited) tax competences.

Bruggemann and Delvaux (pp. 223–39) present a useful summary of the existing energy-related legislation, but unfortunately fail to analyse their effectiveness. Often, the analysis seems to be a reiteration of the Commission's writings, and their conclusion, that the EU has 'created a comprehensive EU regulatory framework' does not follow from their description of non-binding targets, framework legislation, and voluntary measures. The contributions by Rosenstock (Chapter 13, pp. 240–55) and Dias Soares (Chapter 14, pp. 256–78) provide a good analysis of the options and challenges in introducing EU-wide energy taxes. They present and discuss the (watered-down) directive on energy products taxation which *could* have paved the way towards taxing energy/electricity according to the carbon content—had it not been for the continuous opposition of many major Member States. Both come to the conclusion that the existing framework does not correspond to the polluter pays principle. As Dias Soares shows, this is partially due to the lack of clear competences in the field of energy.

Finally, the EU environmental law veteran Krämer (pp. 279–96) presents a review of EU competences, structures, and activities to combat climate change with an overview of tools which, as was said before, should actually be read first, before any of the other detailed contribution of the book. He calls for an EU climate change policy which, at least to some extent, seems to have started to grow on the basis of the March 2007 Council Conclusions.[14] And then, in the final chapter (pp. 297–316), Gupta's piece on good governance and climate change from a North-South perspective leads the reader back to the international level but also highlights how certain choices on the EU or domestic level might influence development in countries in the south. She argues, essentially, that climate change, being a global issue, can only be solved through a global, comprehensive regime. This shows that any EU climate change policy and tool is only good

[14] N. 1 above.

enough if it leads the way towards sincere and global action to reduce greenhouse gas emissions, in order to prevent dangerous climate change from happening to all of us.

RODA VERHEYEN
Attorney at Günther, *Heidel, Wollenteit, Hack*, Hamburg (Germany)
Freelance member of the Research Unit for Environmental
Law, Co-Director of the Climate Justice Programme
(http://www.climatelaw.org),
University of Hamburg (Germany)

Institutional Interaction in Global Environmental Governance: Synergy and Conflict among International and EU Policies, edited by Sebastian Oberthür and Thomas Gehring. Cambridge, MA: MIT Press, 2006, 425 pp., £18.95 pb, £43.95 hb. ISBN 0262651106 pb, and 026205115X hb.

This edited volume is the latest excellent addition to the MIT Press Global Environmental Accord series, examining institutional aspects of international environmental governance. It tackles the relatively novel subject of institutional interaction by investigating the interaction among international and European Union (EU) institutions. Through the presentation of a theoretical framework, which is then applied to ten detailed case studies and followed by a systematic analysis of results, the book offers the first broad overview of this field of research showing ways in which international and European policies can either reinforce or undermine one another. This book will be of interest to all readers interested in international environmental governance.

The book follows a reductionist approach. Oberthür and Gehring argue that analysis of institutional interaction requires disaggregation of a complex situation into a number of cases of interaction. Therefore, they break down interaction into a single source institution and a single target institution and a unidirectional causal pathway. Once we understand interplay in its simplest form, they suggest that we can then recombine cases to gain a more complex picture. While others might argue that this could mean we miss some of the more complex dynamics, from a readers' point of view, this approach makes for a good starting place to explore this new research area. It also offers the opportunity to see the sheer volume of potential interactions in global environmental governance. The case studies unearth a list of 163 interactions from a sample of just 11 source or target institutions. Since we are informed that there are at least 200 international environmental agreements and at least the same number of equivalent EU environmental institutions the number of interactions is likely to be colossal!

The book offers a clear conceptual framework which centres around causal mechanisms. Using the familiar classification of outputs, outcomes, and impacts, three causal mechanisms are identified by which institutional interaction can affect environmental governance. Cognitive interaction highlights inter-institutional learning; interaction through commitment features the effects of commitment on the part of members of the source institution on the preferences of those associated with the target institution; and behavioural interaction centres on ways that behaviour taking place within the source institution affects the operation of the target institution. These mechanisms are explained in detail before the empirical chapters allowing them to guide the exploration of the ten case studies to follow.

The first six cases use an international institution as their starting point and the last four begin with an EU legal instrument, which the authors explain, are a 'suitable functional equivalent of specific international institutions' for the purpose of the study. Each case study introduces the 'core' institution, sets out the main interactions with other institutions, and picks a number of these interactions to examine in detail focusing on investigating the causal mechanism driving the case of interaction in question and examining its momentum and effects. Cases for in-depth analysis were selected so as to ensure that horizontal interaction at the international level, horizontal interaction between EU legal instruments, and vertical interaction between international institutions and EU instruments were roughly equally represented.

The international regimes examined include the Convention on International Trade in Endangered Species of Wild Flora and Fauna (CITES),[1] the Convention on Biological Diversity (CBD),[2] and the World Trade Organization (WTO) and the United Nations Framework Convention on Climate Change (UNFCCC).[3] The EU instruments analysed include directives on the protection of habitats, the deliberate release of genetically modified organisms into the environment, and air quality.

The final chapter contains a comprehensive comparative analysis of institutional interaction based on a database (included in an appendix) covering all 163 cases of interaction found in the empirical cases. These had been codified according to a number of criteria including: whether the effect within the target institution could be classed as a synergy, disruption or the effect was neutral; whether the interaction was intentional or unintentional; if the interaction happened within the same policy field or across different policy fields; whether there has been policy responses; and what if any the key differences between the institutions were. The database enabled the aggregation of data on individual cases and the identification of dominant patterns of institutional interaction. From these

[1] Washington, DC (US), 3 Mar. 1973; (1973) 12 *International Legal Materials* 5, 1085.

[2] Rio de Janeiro (Brazil), 5 June 1992 (entered into force 29 Dec. 1993), (1992) 31 *International Legal Materials*, 818.

[3] New York, NY (US), 9 May 1992 (entered into force 21 Mar. 1994), (1992) 31 *International Legal Materials* 4, 849.

patterns, ideal types of institutional interaction were elaborated perhaps providing the basis for future testing research.

The findings of the volume demonstrate that interaction between international and EU environmental institutions matter for the development and performance of these institutions. While this may have been remarked on before, this study makes its considerable added value by providing the first systematic examination of this phenomenon. Cases were identified independently of their political salience, from the degree of intentionality of interested actors, and from their effects on the target, i.e. they were not the subject of study because actors had noticed a particular problem. Thus, this sample provides the first broad picture of the extent and nature of institutional interactions. This leads to the interesting finding that, contrary to the conventional wisdom, the clear majority of the interactions were positive while only a quarter resulted in interference. The book, therefore, concludes that institutional interaction may not be a bad thing that ought to be diminished as far as possible. This is a well-written and important contribution to understanding international environmental governance and sets the stage for fruitful future research in the area.

CAMILLA ADELLE
Researcher
University of East Anglia (UK)

Analyzing International Environmental Regimes: From Case Study to Database, by Helmut Breitmeier, Oran Young, and Michael Zürn. Cambridge, MA: MIT Press, 2006, 320 pp., £17.95 pb, £43.95 hb. ISBN 0262524619 pb, and 0262026023 hb.

The study of international regimes has developed into one of the most fruitful and robust fields of inquiry in International Relations (IR), in particular in the area of international political economy and international environmental politics. The question of effectiveness of institutions is one of the most important, yet also most complex fields in political science, and more so probably in the field of IR, which has to struggle with additional layers of complexity that range from global to local. Most research on international regimes employs qualitative methods, often using case studies to develop larger theoretical arguments; but a lack of standardization makes comparative analysis difficult. As an alternative to qualitative case study approaches, multivariate or regression analyses are essentially dependent on collecting a rich data set on which the analysis is performed.

Analyzing International Environmental Regimes introduces the International Regimes Database (IRD) as an important methodological innovation that allows scholars to adopt a quantitative approach to the study of international regimes.

The significance of this volume is twofold: firstly, it presents an unique attempt to provide scholars with a an easy-to-use tool for the analysis of regimes, thereby reflecting and facilitating further analysis of major theoretical and conceptual issues dominating the study of international institutions for the last decades. Secondly, and possibly even more important, the book reminds us that achieving such a project is only possible through a collaborative effort and the ingenuity and stubbornness of a number of people throughout the years. Originated in 1991, the project came to a successful close in 2006 only because the authors firmly believed in the importance of a database-building project.

The book is organized into six chapters. The first chapter gives a concise overview of the state of the art in regime theory and subsequently argues that to overcome some of the existing shortcomings of the predominant qualitative case study approach, a database that allows for comparative inquiries across a large number of cases is the methodology of choice. The second chapter provides a short and non-technical summary of the basic database architecture, the case structure, and the coding procedures applied in the course of the project. Chapters 3 to 5 exemplify the usefulness of the IRD by discussing three prominent questions: sources of compliance with international regimes; decision rules and their relation to effectiveness; and the role of information in environmental problem solving. Finally, Chapter 6 summarizes the findings and points to potential weaknesses of the database approach and ways ahead.

The IRD is a relational database that makes it possible to compare records on specific aspects of a number of international environmental regimes that are coded using a common set of concepts and definitions. The high quality of the volume derives from linking the process of data gathering to broadly defined areas of theoretical interest. In this way, the IRD is not only a descriptive tool but allows for a wide variety of theory-driven inquiries into the nature and consequences of international environmental regimes. In more detail, the project team has decided to code data in four categories: regime formation, regime attributes, regime consequences, and regime dynamics. This focus on four debates that have featured prominently on the agenda of scholars when the IRD was first conceived imposes certain constraints. For example, whereas at the time of conceptualizing the initial data protocol questions of regime emergence and persistence featured high on the scholarly agenda, current debates focus to a large extent on the question of regime effectiveness and the explanatory factors of varying regime performance. However, through carefully crafting new variables and linking them to indicators coded within the IRD it is possible to accommodate new theoretical developments that have not been anticipated by the IRD team before. The IRD protocol asks coders to supply data in 135 forms containing more than 200 variables. To increase the number of cases, the project team has decided to disaggregate regimes into smaller components (the units of analysis) that reflect distinct regime components (such as a protocol or amendment to an existing treaty) and watershed events (changes in the nature of the regime). From this perspective, for example, the long-range transboundary air pollution regime of 1979 consists of several distinct regime components that address different pollutants through specific protocols (e.g. sulphur dioxide, nitrogen oxide, and persistent organic pollutants).[1] The IRD contains 23 regimes with 172 regime elements or cases, 1998 marking the end point of data entry.

In order to illustrate the usefulness of the database approach, the book offers three concrete applications of the IRD. In a nutshell, the authors argue that it is high time to leave behind debates about the role and relevance of international environmental regimes (that have been questioned ever since the regime debate emerged) and instead focus more on the extent to which regimes matter, the ways in which they matter and finally the causal factors that account for variance in the performance of international regimes. This is a well-founded argument, and the three analytical chapters provide much new insight into highly relevant theoretical questions such as the role of compliance mechanisms in increasing regime effectiveness and the role of cognitive factors in problem solving. However, the real value of the book is not limited to these three illustrations, but goes far beyond. Researchers have at their disposal a highly relevant and well-crafted tool for advancing the frontier of regime theory beyond qualitative reasoning (a CD-ROM that accompanies the book contains the complete protocol and the database that is accessible via Microsoft Access). Hopefully, the research community will embrace this opportunity to the fullest extent.

A project as ambitious as the IRD naturally does not go unchallenged. A number of criticisms can be raised against the methodology applied and the concrete decisions taken in the course of the data gathering process. Firstly, the use of the IRD is limited by the relative small number of institutions covered, and by the more distant timeframe, which makes it less usable to study more recent institutions or their more recent developments. Secondly, the decision to disaggregate regimes into smaller regime components may lead to analytical problems, as the discrete components might well interact with each other and thereby distort the reasoning based on a relational analysis. However, the authors have remained cautious with regard to generalizations and predictions. It is now in the hands of the scholarly community to critically engage with the IRD and thereby to consolidate and advance the findings of more than two decades of international regime analysis.

PHILIPP PATTBERG
Senior Researcher
Institute for Environmental Studies (IVM),
Department of Environmental Policy Analysis
Vrije Universiteit Amsterdam (The Netherlands)

[1] UN/ECE Convention on Long-Range Transboundary Air Pollution (LRTAP Convention), Geneva (Switzerland) 13 Nov. 1979 (entered into force 16 Mar. 1983). The Convention and all its Protocols are published on the Internet at: http://www.unece.org/env/lrtap.

Derecho ambiental de la Union Europea, by Carmen Plaza Martín. Valencia: Tirant Lo Blanch, 2006, 1240 pp., €99 hb. ISBN 9788484564737.

An opus magnum of a Spanish author, the volume of which becomes even more impressive, when one realizes that Plaza only examined primary European law, but left aside all secondary environmental legislation which the European Community (EC) adopted during the last 30 years. The book was essentially written before the enlargements of the European Union (EU) in 2004 and 2007, and thus reflects the Community of 15 Member States which still was expecting that the Constitution of the European Union[1] would, sooner or later, become the basis of the Union's activities.

Plaza writes from a Spanish perspective and certainly for Spanish readers, though she extensively quotes—relatively rare in Spanish environmental legal literature—English and less frequently French writers.

The book is divided in four sections: general questions of European environmental law (1), principles, procedures and instruments of adopting secondary environmental legislation (2), the implementation of European environmental law by Member States (3), and the monitoring of the application of European environmental law by the European institutions and by national courts (4).

In the first section, a short history of the origin of EC environmental policy and law is given. The author leaves the following question, which she herself puts, unanswered: is EC policy of environmental law a success story or a failure (p. 56)? She only underlines the importance of an effective application of the European provisions in and by Member States. The section also deals with the repartition of competencies between the EU and its Member States as well as the general (subsidiarity and proportionality), and environmental-oriented principles (precaution, prevention etc.) of the EC Treaty.

In section two (330 pages), Plaza successively deals with the choice of the legal basis, the decision-making process, information and participation in this process, the sources of secondary environmental law, and the conditions of Article 174 (3) EC to reach the objective of a high level of environmental protection. On the choice of the legal basis, Plaza describes in great detail the different judgments of the European Court of Justice (ECJ) since the mid-1980s which oriented the discussion in the environmental sector. She is less explicit on the question of a double legal basis (Articles 95 and 175 EC; Articles 133 and 175 EC), where different ECJ judgments increased the difficulties rather than solving them. Also on the question of Member State competencies under Article 28 to 30 EC on the one hand, and under Articles 95(4) and (5) EC and 176 EC on the other, I would have loved to read more.

[1] Treaty establishing a Constitution for Europe, Rome (Italy), 29 Oct. 2004 (not yet in force), [2004] OJ C310/1.

Section three, more than 400 pages long, deals with the implementation of Community measures by Member States. An introductory chapter describes the general frame of implementation obligations of Member States, again with strong emphasis of the different ECJ judgments and Member States' arguments before the ECJ. This is followed by a chapter on the implementation of EC environmental law in decentralized Member States, where a specific emphasis is placed on the Spanish situation. Also the next chapter is dedicated to Spain; here, the author discusses all the different cases that were decided by the ECJ against Spain. Unfortunately, she largely limits herself to these court cases and does not mention cases which did not reach the ECJ (*Itoiz*, *Sabinanigo*, and *Portman* spring to my mind); cases which were discussed before Spanish courts and cases which just remained without judicial control. Of all three categories, there are numerous examples which could have been quoted. The reader does not either learn about the different practice of the Spanish *Comunidades Autónomas*, and it would have been of great interest to learn, whether, for example, Catalunya has another practice of implementing EC environmental law other than Extremadura, Asturias, or Navarra. Two chapters deal with the correct transposition of EC environmental law and the discretionary powers of Member States in this regard. The final part of this section addresses environmental agreements, plans, and programmes.

The last section analyses in detail the control which is exercised on the implementation of EC environmental law, on the one hand by the European Commission, and on the other hand by the national courts, in particular with regard to the direct-effect doctrine of the ECJ. With regard to the Commission's control, the author is rather succinct. The problem of practical application of environmental law is mentioned, but only briefly discussed. The citizens' possibility to participate in the protection of the environment by contributing to the monitoring system via the complaint system is not really raised. The author looks at the whole problem of the efficiency of environmental law and its application from a descriptive perspective, referring mainly to Commission documents, but not lending her ear to the legal publications of environmental organizations. She does not offer solutions, of how a better application of environmental law could be achieved, or how the environment could, generally, be better protected.

And there is, after these many pages and the 3,351 footnotes, no conclusive chapter: Plaza does not tell us what she thinks of all this EC environmental law, where and how reforms could or should be made in order reach an adequate protection of the environment—which is, after all, the objective of all these political and legal efforts. In view of such a wealth of knowledge that she deploys in her book, I would like to have seen her own opinion, be it pro or contra, her own assessment of 30 years of EC efforts, her advice to Spanish and European administrations, citizens and economic operators, where things went wrong, where they went well and where one could do better. In her introduction, Plaza rightly underlines how important the efficiency of environmental legislation is. However, she hardly addresses questions of tensions between vested interests and legislators, between national administrations and EC institutions, between citizens who look for a protection of 'their' environment and the technocrats, who all too often pursue other objectives. It is these tensions which mainly contribute to explaining the state of EC environmental law and its limited efficiency. And at the Community level, such tensions are normally even stronger than within the Member States, though seldom described and analysed.

I would thus have liked to have seen more accents placed on the legal policy in the environmental sector, the analysis, why this or that solution had been taken or this and that attempt of legislative regulation failed. Certainly, had Plaza also analysed the numerous environmental regulations and directives, this topic would inevitably have come to the forefront. However, also in primary law are there ample opportunities for discussing this issue: the choice of the 'internal market' or 'environmental' legal basis—in the waste sector, in the area of biotechnology—the choice of a regulation or a directive, the Commission's strategy in monitoring the application of EC environmental law in and by Member States or the drafting, implementation, and efficiency of the environmental action programmes are examples.

In his prologue to the book, Professor Tomás-Ramón Fernández underlines that 'nothing, absolutely nothing' of environmental law has escaped the attention of the author. Of course, such a statement looks for objections. Indeed, I do miss something in this treatise. The omission to comment on secondary law and the omission of any conclusion was already mentioned. Furthermore, almost nothing is said about the external EC environmental law competencies as well as the existence of numerous international environmental law conventions and their effects—including direct effects—within the EC and its Member States. And Plaza neither discusses the relevance of 'sustainable development' for environmental law, nor Article 6 EC, a central provision of the EC Treaty which requires the day-by-day integration of environmental requirements into the elaboration and implementation of the other EC policies. If this provision were taken in its legal meaning, EC policy in many areas—energy, transport, agriculture, fisheries, development, and regional policy, to name but a few—would look rather different.

On a more formal point, a book of such length would have profited from a keyword index. Also a numerical or alphabetical list of Court cases that were quoted, a list of regulations, directives, and decisions would have been useful. In contrast, the bibliography is very comprehensive (30 pages), and Spanish and English sources very largely dominate.

In Spain and probably also in Spanish-speaking countries in other parts of the world, the protection of the environment is not part of mainstream policy. In this sense, Plaza's book is a very thorough and useful introduction into EC (environmental) law, explaining in great detail the different terms and procedures, all the more useful as environmental law does not play a very important role in Spain. The book may explain to many a student and other persons what the difference between a (environmental) directive and a regulation is, what the direct effect of a provision means, and how far Member States' discretion and powers under EC environmental law reach. The clear and transparent style in which the book was written, will make it comprehensible even to beginners of EC law and is likely to be used as a reference book for many years. The book will hopefully promote the understanding of the intricacies of EC environmental law and be a valuable manual for use in libraries, research centres, and in offices which have to deal with EC environmental law. Perhaps it will also show South American readers looking for inspiration for their Mercosur integration project, what can be done to promote environmental cooperation and integration with the means of law.

LUDWIG KRÄMER
Honorary Professor of European Environmental Law
at the University of Bremen (Germany), and at the
College of Europe, Brussels (Belgium)

IV. Highlights of Recent Publications in Environmental Law and Policy

A. Atmospheric Pollution, Climate Change, and Energy

B. Barton, C. Redgwell, A. Rønne, and D. N. Zillman (eds.), *Energy Security: Managing Risk in a Dynamic Legal and Regulatory Environment* (Oxford: Oxford University Press, 2005), 500 pp., £95 hb. ISBN 9780199271610

F. Bosselman, J. B. Eisen, J. Rossi, D. B. Spence, and J. Weaver, *Energy, Economics and the Environment (2nd Edn.)* (New York, NY: Foundation Press, 2006), 1350 pp., $95 hb. ISBN 1587789248

J. Deutch, A. Lauvergeon, and W. Prawiraatmadja, *Energy Security and Climate Change* (Washington, DC: Brookings Institution Press, 2007), 100 pp., $15 pb. ISBN 9780930503901

J. F. C. DiMento and P. M. Doughman (eds.), *Climate Change: What It Means for Us, Our Children, and Our Grandchildren* (Cambridge, MA: MIT Press, 2007), 220 pp., $19.95 pb, $60 hb. ISBN 9780262541939 pb, and 9780262042413 hb

M. Doelle, *From Hot Air to Action? Climate Change, Compliance and the Future of International Environmental Law* (Toronto: Thomson Carswell, 2005), 420 pp., CDN $85 pb. ISBN 0459242776

W. Th. Douma, L. Massai, and M. Montini (eds.), *The Kyoto Protocol and Beyond—Legal and Policy Challenges of Climate Change* (The Hague: TMC Asser Press, 2007), 250 pp., £45 hb. ISBN 9789067042284

C. Egenhofer, J. C. Jansen, and S. J. A. Bakker, *Revisiting EU Policy Options for Tackling Climate Change: A Review of the Literature on Social Cost-Benefit Analysis of GHG Emissions Reduction Strategies* (Washington, DC: Brookings Institution Press, 2006), 150 pp., $19.95 pb. ISBN 9789290796312

S. S. Haghighi, *Energy Security: The External Legal Relations of the European Union with Major Oil and Gas Supplying Countries* (Oxford: Hart Publishing, 2007), 510 pp., £65 hb. ISBN 9781841137285

D. Helm (ed.), *The New Energy Paradigm* (Oxford: Oxford University Press, 2007), 544 pp., £35 hb. ISBN 0199229708

B. Hillebrand, A. Smajgl, W. Ströbele, J.-M. Behringer, B. Heins, E.-C. Meyer (eds.), *CO_2 Emissions Trading Put to Test: Design Problems of the EU Proposal for an Emissions Trading System in Europe* (Münster: LIT Verlag, 2003), 165 pp., €20.90 pb. ISBN 3825866548

M. S. Ho and C. P. Nielsen (eds.), *Clearing the Air: The Health and Economic Damages of Air Pollution in China* (Cambridge, MA: MIT Press, 2007), 392 pp. + CD, $50 hb. ISBN 9780262083584

M. Humphreys, J. D. Sachs, and J. E. Stiglitz (eds.), *Escaping the Resource Curse* (New York, NY: Columbia University Press, 2007), 420 pp., $29.95 hb. ISBN 9780231141963

V. Lauber (ed.), *Switching to Renewable Power: A Framework for the 21st Century* (London: Earthscan, 2005), 275 pp., £50 hb. ISBN 1902916654

T. E. Lovejoy and L. Hannah (eds.), *Climate Change and Biodiversity* (New Haven, CT/London: Yale University Press, 2006), 440 pp., $35 pb, $65 hb. ISBN 9780300119800 pb, and 9780300104257 hb

C. Mitchell, *The Political Economy of Sustainable Energy* (Basingtoke/New York, NY: Palgrave MacMillan, 2008), 245 pp., £50 hb. ISBN 9780230537118

P. Newell, *Climate for Change: Non-State Actors and the Global Politics of the Greenhouse* (Cambridge: Cambridge University Press, 2006), 232 pp., £22.99 pb, £70 hb. ISBN 9780521021234 pb, and 9780521632508 hb

H. T. Odum, *Environment, Power, and Society for the Twenty-first Century: The Hierarchy of Energy* (New York, NY: Columbia University Press, 2007), 435 pp., $39.50 pb, $74.50 hb. ISBN 9780231128872 pb, and 9780231128865 hb

M. Peeters and K. Deketelaere (eds.), *EU Climate Change Policy: The Challenge of New Regulatory Initiatives* (Cheltenham: Edward Elgar, 2006), 330 pp., £75 hb. ISBN 1845426053

M. E. Pettenger (eds.), *The Social Construction of Climate Change: Power, Knowledge, Norms, Discourses* (Aldershot: Ashgate, 2007), 265 pp., £55 hb. ISBN 9780754648024

A. Rappaport and S. H. Creighton, *Degrees That Matter: Climate Change and the University* (Cambridge, MA: MIT Press, 2007), 376 pp., $24.95 pb, $62 hb. ISBN 9780262681667 pb, and 9780262182584 hb

J. T. Roberts and B.C. Parks, *Climate of Injustice: Global Inequality, North-South Politics, and Climate Policy* (Cambridge, MA: MIT Press, 2007), 400 pp., £16.95 pb, £41.95 hb. ISBN 0262681617 pb, and 0262182564 hb

M. Roggenkamp, C. Redgwell, A. Rønne, and I. del Guayo (eds.), *Energy Law in Europe: National, EU and International Law and Institutions (2nd Edn.)* (Oxford: Oxford University Press, 2007), 1456 pp., £225 hb. ISBN 019921719X

S. Shackley and C. Gough (eds.), *Carbon Capture and Its Storage: An Integrated Assessment* (Aldershot: Ashgate, 2006), 336 pp., £65 hb. ISBN 9780754644996

T. H. Tietenberg, *Emissions Trading Principles and Practice (2nd Edn.)* (Washington, DC: RFF Press, 2006), 235 pp., $38.95 pb, $80 hb. ISBN 1933115319 pb, and 1933115300 hb

M. Winkler, *Klimaschutzrecht: Völker-, europa- und verfassungsrechtliche Grundlagen sowie instrumentelle Umsetzung der deutschen Klimaschutzpolitik unter besonderer*

Berücksichtigung des Emissionshandels (Münster: LIT Verlag, 2006), 370 pp., €34.90 pb. ISBN 3825889238

B. Biotechnology and Food Safety

J. S. Ach and L. Siep (eds.), *Nano-Bio-Ethics: Ethical Dimensions of Nanobiotechnology* (Münster: LIT Verlag, 2006), 88 pp., €19.90 pb. ISBN 3825890589

M. A. Altieri, *Genetic Engineering in Agriculture: The Myths, Environmental Risks, and Alternatives (2nd Edn.)* (Oakland, CA: Food First Books, 2004), 115 pp., $11.95 pb. ISBN 0935028935

P. Andrée, *Genetically Modified Diplomacy: The Global Politics of Agricultural Biotechnology and the Environment* (Vancouver, BC: University of British Columbia Press, 2007/8), 330 pp., $29.95 hb (2008), $85 hb (2007). ISBN 9780774812696 pb, and 9780774812689 hb

C. Ansell and D. Vogel (eds.), *What's the Beef? The Contested Governance of European Food Safety* (Cambridge, MA: MIT Press, 2006), 400 pp., £17.95 pb, £43.95 hb. ISBN 0262511924 pb, and 0262012251 hb

R. C. Beier, S. D. Pillai, T. D. Phillips, and R. L. Ziprin (eds.), *Preharvest and Postharvest Food Safety: Contemporary Issues and Future Directions* (Ames, IA: Blackwell Publishing, 2004), 465 pp., $169.99 hb. ISBN 0813808847

S. Biber-Klemm and T. Cottier (eds.), *Rights to Plant Genetic Resources and Traditional Knowledge: Basic Issues and Perspectives* (Wallingford/Cambridge, MA: CABI Publishing, 2006), 400 pp., £85 hb. ISBN 0851990339

D. Brossard, J. Shanahan, and T. C. Nesbitt (eds.), *The Public, the Media and Agricultural Biotechnology* (Wallingford/Cambridge, MA: CABI Publishing, 2007), 405 pp., £75 hb. ISBN 1845932048

R. Burdon, *The Suffering Gene: Environmental Threats to Our Health* (London: Zed Books, 2003), 255 pp., £15.95 pb, £50 hb. ISBN 1842772856 pb, and 1842772848 hb

B. Cain, *Legal Aspects of Gene Technology* (London: Sweet & Maxwell, 2003), 260 pp., £205 hb. ISBN 0421783303

R. A. Carruth (ed.), *Global Governance of Food and Agriculture Industries: Transatlantic Regulatory Harmonization and Multilateral Policy Cooperation for Food Safety* (Cheltenham: Edward Elgar, 2006), 500 pp., £120 hb. ISBN 1843761963

D. Castle, C. Cline, A. S. Daar, P. A. Singer, and C. Tsamis, *Science, Society and the Supermarket: The Opportunities and Challenges of Nutrigenomics* (Hoboken, NJ: Wiley, 2007), 160 pp., £35.50 hb. ISBN 0471770000

C. B. Cohen, *Renewing the Stuff of Life: Stem Cells, Ethics, and Public Policy* (Oxford: Oxford University Press, 2007), 320 pp., £19.99 hb. ISBN 100195305248

G. Cook, *Genetically Modified Language: The Discourse of Arguments for GM Crops and Food* (London/New York, NY: Routledge, 2004/5), 170 pp., £15.99 pb (2005), £55 hb (2004). ISBN 0415314682 pb, and 0415314674 hb

T. R. DeGregori, *Origins of the Organic Agriculture Debate* (Ames, IA: Blackwell Publishing, 2004), 220 pp., $62.99 hb. ISBN 0813805139

J. Entine (ed.), *Let Them Eat Precaution: How Politics Is Undermining the Genetic Revolution in Agriculture* (Washington, DC: AEI Press, 2006), 205 pp., $25 hb. ISBN 0844742007

L. E. Foster (ed.), *Nanotechnology: Science, Innovation, and Opportunity* (Upper Saddle River: Pearson Prentice Hall, 2006), 300 pp., £21.99 hb. ISBN 0131927566

F. Francioni (ed.), *Biotechnologies and International Human Rights* (Oxford: Hart Publishing, 2007), 420 pp., £60 hb. ISBN 97818411370302

G. Gaskell and M. Bauer (eds.), *Genomics and Society: Legal, Ethical and Social Dimensions* (London: Earthscan, 2006), 256 pp., £55 hb. ISBN 1844071138

C. Gavaghan, *Defending the Genetic Supermarket: The Law and Ethics of Selecting the Next Generation* (London: Routledge-Cavendish, 2007), 250 pp., £25.99 pb, £65 hb. ISBN 1844720586 pb, and 1844720594 hb

E. S. Grace, *Biotechnology Unzipped: Promises and Realities (2nd Edn.)* (Washington, DC: Joseph Henry Press, 2006), 233 pp., $19.95 pb. ISBN 0309096219

R. M. Green, *Babies by Design: The Ethics of Genetic Choice* (New Haven, CT: Yale University Press, 2008), 280 pp., $26 hb. ISBN 9780300125467

K. F. Greif and J. F. Merz, *Current Controversies in the Biological Sciences: Case Studies of Policy Challenges from New Technologies* (Cambridge, MA: MIT Press, 2007), 395 pp., $25 pb, $62 hb. ISBN 9780262572392 pb, and 9780262072803 hb

D. Holland and H. Pope, *EU Food Law and Policy* (The Hague: Kluwer Law International, 2005), 230 pp., €95 hb. ISBN 9041121242

G. Hunt and M. Mehta (eds.), *Nanotechnology: Risk, Ethics and Law* (London: Earthscan, 2006), 300 pp., £24.95 hb. ISBN 1844073580

R. E. Just, J. M. Alston, and D. Zilberman (eds.), *Regulating Agricultural Biotechnology: Economics and Policy* (New York, NY: Springer, 2006), 730 pp., €119.95 hb. ISBN 038736952X

J. P. Kesan, *Agricultural Biotechnology and Intellectual Property Protection: Seeds of Change* (Wallingford/Cambridge, MA: CABI Publishing, 2007), 410 pp., £75 hb. ISBN 1845932013

U. Kjaernes, M. Harvey, and A. Warde, *Trust in Food: A Comparative and Institutional Analysis* (Basingstoke/New York, NY: Palgrave MacMillan, 2007), 230 pp., £45 hb. ISBN 1403998914

N. Knoepffler, D. Schipanski, and S. L. Sorgner (eds.), *Human Biotechnology as Social Challenge: An Interdisciplinary Introduction to Bioethics* (Aldershot: Ashgate, 2007), 180 pp., £55 hb. ISBN 9780754657552

C. MacMaoláin, *EU Food Law: Protecting Consumers and Health in a Common Market* (Oxford: Hart Publishing, 2007), 300 pp., £35 pb. ISBN 9781841134987

M. T. Mariani, *The Intersection of International Law, Agricultural Biotechnology, and Infectious Disease* (Leiden: Brill Academic Publishers, 2007), 230 pp., €85 hb. ISBN 9781571053732

M. D. Masson-Matthee, *The Codex Alimentarius Commission and Its Standards* (The Hague: TMC Asser Press, 2007), 345 pp., £60 hb. ISBN 9789067042567

S. P. McGiffen, *Biotechnology: Corporate Power Versus the Public Interest* (London: Pluto Press, 2005), 250 pp., £15.99 pb, £50 hb. ISBN 0745319742 pb, and 0745319750 hb

M. McKelvey and L. Orsenigo (eds.), *The Economics of Biotechnology (Two Volume Set)* (Cheltenham: Edward Elgar, 2006), 880 pp., £230 hb. ISBN 1843767767

E. Meins, *Politics and Public Outrage: Explaining Transatlantic and Intra-European Diversity of Regulations on Food Irradiation and Genetically Modified Food* (Münster: LIT Verlag, 2003), 210 pp., €20.90 pb. ISBN 3825867676

I. Mgbeoji, *Global Biopiracy: Patents, Plants, and Indigenous Knowledge* (Ithaca, NY: Cornell University Press, 2006), 336 pp., $22.95 pb. ISBN 9780801473111

E. Montpetit, C. Rothmayr, and F. Varone (eds.), *The Politics of Biotechnology in North America and Europe: Policy Networks, Institutions and Internationalization* (Lanham, MD: Lexington Books, 2007), 300 pp., $32.95 pb, $90 hb. ISBN 0739112481 pb, and 0739112473 hb

D. J. Murphy, *People, Plants and Genes: The Story of Crops and Humanity* (Oxford: Oxford University Press, 2007), 432 pp., £70 hb, £32.50 pb. ISBN 9780199207138 hb, ISBN 978019920714 pb

S. Parthasarathy, *Building Genetic Medicine: Breast Cancer, Technology, and the Comparative Politics of Health Care* (Cambridge, MA: MIT Press, 2007), 280 pp., $35 hb. ISBN 9780262162425

P. Pechan and G. de Vries (eds.), *Genes on the Menu: Facts for Knowledge-Based Decisions* (Heidelberg/New York, NY: Springer, 2005), 220 pp., €29.95 hb. ISBN 3540201785

G. E. Pence, *Cloning After Dolly: Who's Still Afraid?* (Lanham, MD: Rowman & Littlefield, 2005), 215 pp., $22.95 hb. ISBN 9780742534087

K. S. Rajan, *Biocapital: The Constitution of Postgenomic Life* (Durham, NC: Duke University Press, 2006), 350 pp., $23.95 pb, $84.95 hb. ISBN 0822337207 pb, and 0822337088 hb

B. Rappert, *Biotechnology, Security and the Search for Limits: An Inquiry into Research and Methods* (Basingstoke/New York, NY: Palgrave MacMillan, 2007), 205 pp., £45 hb. ISBN 9780230002487

N. E. Redman, *Food Safety: A Reference Handbook (2nd Edn.)* (Santa Barbara, CA: ABC-CLIO, 2007), 330 pp., $55 hb. ISBN 1598840487

A. Rees, Genetically Modified Food: A Short Guide for the Confused (London: Pluto Press, 2006), 250 pp., £12.99 pb, £40 hb. ISBN 0745324398, and 0745324401 hb

A. Sasson, *Medical Biotechnology: Achievements, Prospects and Perceptions* (Tokyo: United Nations University Press, 2005), 152 pp., $28 pb. ISBN 9280811142

S. Striffler, *Chicken: The Dangerous Transformation of America's Favorite Food* (New Haven, CT: Yale University Press, 2005/7), 210 pp., $16 pb (2007), $25 hb (2005). ISBN 9780300123678 pb, and 9780300095296 hb

E. Thacker, *The Global Genome: Biotechnology, Politics, and Culture* (Cambridge, MA: MIT Press, 2005/6), 464 pp., £12.95 pb (2006), £25.95 hb (2005). ISBN 0262701162 pb, and 0262201550 hb

S. Vellema and D. Boselie (eds.), *Cooperation and Competence in Global Food Chains: Perspectives on Food Quality and Safety* (Maastricht: Shaker Publishing, 2003), 200 pp., €36 pb. ISBN 9042302321

R. Wilk (ed.), *Fast Food/Slow Food: The Cultural Economy of the Global Food System* (Lanham, MD: AltaMira Press, 2006), 272 pp., $29.95 pb, $72 hb. ISBN 075910915X pb, and 0759109141

C. Chemicals

P. Brown, *Toxic Exposures: Contested Illnesses and the Environmental Health Movement* (New York, NY: Columbia University Press, 2007), 395 pp., $29.50 hb. ISBN 9780231129480

A. Petryna, A. Lakoff, and A. Kleinman (eds.), *Global Pharmaceuticals: Ethics, Markets, Practices* (Durham, NC: Duke University Press, 2006), 310 pp., $22.95 pb, $79.95 hb. ISBN 082233741 pb, and 0822337290 hb

D. Nature Conservation

R. Boardman, *The International Politics of Bird Conservation: Biodiversity, Regionalism and Global Governance* (Cheltenham: Edward Elgar, 2006), 288 pp., £65 hb. ISBN 1845424034

T. J. Farnham, *Saving Nature's Legacy: Origins of the Idea of Biological Diversity* (New Haven, CT: Yale University Press, 2007), 288 pp., $45 hb. ISBN 0300120052

E. T. Freyfogle, *Why Conservation Is Failing and How It Can Regain Ground* (New Haven, CT/London: Yale University Press, 2006), 320 pp., $35 hb. ISBN 0300110405

P. M. Johnson, K. Mayrand, and M. Paquin (eds.), *Governing Global Desertification: Linking Environmental Degradation, Poverty and Participation* (Aldershot: Ashgate, 2006), 300 pp., £55 hb. ISBN 9780754643593

H. Kaufman, *The Forest Ranger: A Study in Administrative Behavior (Special Reprint Edn.)* (Washington, DC: RFF Press, 2006), 270 pp., $21.95 pb, $55 hb. ISBN 1933115270 pb, and 1933115262 hb

N. Koch, *Die FFH-Richtlinie im Spannungsfeld ökologischer und nicht-ökologischer Belange: Schutzregime und Vorhabenszulassung* (Münster: LIT Verlag, 2005), 170 pp., €24.90 pb. ISBN 3825882217

K. M. Murchison, *The Snail Darter Case: TVA versus the Endangered Species Act* (Lawrence, KS: University Press of Kansas, 2007), 240 pp., $15.95 pb, $35 hb. ISBN 9780700615056 pb, and 9780700615049 hb

J. C. Nagle and J. B. Ruhl, *The Law of Biodiversity and Ecosystem Management (2nd Edn.)* (New York, NY: Foundation Press, 2006), 1150 pp., $100 hb. ISBN 159941158X

E. Waste

S. Almeria, V. A. Dean, and B. A. Zarlengo (eds.), *RCRA Regulations and Keyword Index: 2006 Edition* (New York, NY: Aspen Publishers, 2006), 2000 pp., $289 pb. ISBN 0735559643

G. van Calster, *Handbook of EU Waste Law* (Oxford: Oxford University Press, 2006), 181 pp., £95 hb. ISBN 1904501621

J. G. Miller and C. N. Johnston, *Miller and Johnston's The Law of Hazardous Waste Disposal and Remediation: Cases-Legislation-Regulations-Policies (2nd Edn.)* (St. Paul, MN: Thomson/West, 2005), 900 pp., $82 hb. ISBN 031424929X

F. Water and Fisheries

K. Bakker (ed.), *Eau Canada: The Future of Canada's Water* (Vancouver, BC: University of British Columbia Press, 2006), 440 pp., $29.95 pb, $85 hb. ISBN 9780774813402 pb, and 9780774813396 hb

A. Chircop, S. Coffen-Smout, and M. McConnell (eds.), Ocean Yearbook (Vol. 20) (New York, NY: Transnational Publishers, 2006), 800 pp., $130 hb. ISBN 1571053514

K. Conca, *Governing Water: Contentious Transnational Politics and Global Institution Building* (Cambridge, MA: MIT Press, 2005), 456 pp., £18.95 pb, £45.95 hb. ISBN 0262532735 pb, and 0262033399 hb

K. W. Easter and N. Zeitouni (eds.), *The Economics of Water Quality* (Aldershot: Ashgate, 2006), 600 pp., £450 hb. ISBN 0754623718

M. G. Faure and J. Hu, *Prevention and Compensation of Marine Pollution Damage: Recent Developments in Europe, China and the US* (Boston: Kluwer Academic Publishers, 2006), 350 pp., €90 hb. ISBN 9041123385

M. Finger, L. Tamiotti, and J. Allouche (eds.), *The Multi-Governance of Water: Four Case Studies* (Albany, NY: SUNY Press, 2005/6), 200 pp., $21.95 pb (2006), $60 hb (2005). ISBN 079146606X pb, and 0791466051 hb

V. Frank, *The European Community and Marine Environmental Protection in the International Law of the Sea: Implementing Global Obligations at the Regional Level* (Leiden: Brill Academic Publishers, 2007), 500 pp., €160 hb. ISBN 9789004156951

M. J. Haddadin (ed.), *Water Resources in Jordan: Evolving Polices for Development, the Environment, and Conflict Resolution* (Washington, DC: RFF Press, 2006), 310 pp., $65 hb. ISBN 1933115327

R. Hannesson, *The Privatization of the Oceans* (Cambridge, MA: MIT Press, 2004), 224 pp., £12.95 pb, £22.95 hb. ISBN 0262582651 pb, and 0262083345 hb

T. Henriksen, G. Hønneland, and A. K. Sydnes, *Law and Politics in Ocean Governance: The UN Fish Stocks Agreement and Regional Fisheries Management Regimes* (Leiden: Brill Academic Publishers, 2006), 220 pp., €75 hb. ISBN 9004149686

P. Jacques, *Globalization and the World Ocean* (Lanham, MD: AltaMira Press, 2006), 210 pp., $28.95 pb, $72 hb. ISBN 0759105855 pb, and 0759105855 hb

D. K. Leary, *International Law and the Genetic Resources of the Deep Sea* (Leiden: Brill Academic Publishers, 2006), 310 pp., €120 hb. ISBN 9004155007

H. Seckinelgin, *The Environment and International Politics: International Fisheries, Heidegger and Social Method* (London/New York, NY: Routledge, 2006), 215 pp., £70 hb. ISBN 0415356768

G. Horizontal Instruments and Aarhus Convention Rights

H. Ashiabor, K. Deketelaere, L. Kreiser, and J. Milne (eds.), *Critical Issues in Environmental Taxation—Volume IV: International and Comparative Perspective* (Oxford: Oxford University Press, 2007), 560 pp., £110 hb. ISBN 0199231265

E. Bohne, *The Quest for Environmental Regulatory Integration in the European Union: IPPC, EIA, and Major Accident Prevention* (Boston: Kluwer Academic Publishers, 2006), 640 pp., €110 hb. ISBN 9041120815

R. B. Gibson, with S. Hassan, S. Holtz, J. Tansey, and G. Whitelaw, *Sustainability Assessment: Criteria, Processes and Applications* (London: Earthscan, 2005), 255pp. £22.95 pb, £80 hb. ISBN 1844070514 pb, and 1844070506 hb

A. Hardin (ed.), *Access to Environmental Justice: A Comparative Study* (Leiden: Brill Academic Publishers, 2007), 400 pp., €120 hb. ISBN 9789004157835

J. Holder and D. McGillivray (eds.), *Taking Stock of Environmental Assessment: Law, Policy and Practice* (London: Routledge-Cavendish, 2007), 300 pp., £25.99 pb, £75 hb. ISBN 1844721000 pb, and 1844721019 hb

C. Jones, M. Baker, J. Carter, S. Jay, M. Short, and C. Wood (eds.), *Strategic Environmental Assessment and Land Use Planning: An International Evaluation* (London: Earthscan, 2005), 300 pp., £22.95 pb, £80 hb. ISBN 1844071103 pb, and 184407109X hb

R. D. Morgenstern and W. A. Pizer (eds.), *Reality Check: The Nature and Performance of Voluntary Environmental Programs in the United States, Europe, and Japan* (Washington,

DC: RFF Press, 2007), 195 pp., $38.95 pb, $80 hb. ISBN 9781933115375 pb, and 9781933115368 hb

T. Muller and A. Sterner (eds.), *Environmental Taxation in Practice* (Aldershot: Ashgate, 2006), 580 pp., £150 hb. ISBN 075462594X

C. Sheldon and M. Yoxon, *Environmental Management Systems: A Step-by-Step Guide to Implementation and Maintenance (3rd Edn.)* (London: Earthscan, 2006), 300 pp., £45 hb. ISBN 1844072576

G. Soloman and G. Messent, *Property Transactions: Planning and Environment* (London: Sweet & Maxwell, 2007), 500 pp., £79 pb. ISBN 9780421917606

J. Steffek, C. Kissling, and P. Nanz (eds.), *Civil Society Participation in European and Global Governance: A Cure for the Democratic Deficit?* (Basingstoke/New York, NY: Palgrave MacMillan, 2008), 260 pp., £50 hb. ISBN 9780230006393

H. Trade and Environment, World Trade Organization

S. Baughen, *International Trade and Protection of the Environment* (London: Routledge-Cavendish, 2007), 440 pp., £31.99 pb, £90 hb. ISBN 9780415448109 pb, and 9781845680091 hb

N. Bernasconi-Osterwalder, D. Magraw, M. J. Oliva, M. Orellana, and E. Tuerk, *Environment and Trade: A Guide to WTO Jurisprudence* (London: Earthscan, 2006), 390 pp., £79.95 hb. ISBN 1844072983

S. Bhuiyan, *National Law in WTO Law: Effectiveness and Good Governance in the World Trading System* (Cambridge: Cambridge University Press, 2007), 340 pp. £60 hb. ISBN 9780521875318

D. Blandford and B. Hill (eds.), *Policy Reform and Adjustment in the Agricultural Sectors of Developed Countries* (Wallingford/Cambridge, MA: CABI Publishing, 2006), 280 pp., £45 hb. ISBN 1845930339

E. K. Choi and J. C. Hartigan (eds.), *Handbook of International Trade, Volume II: Economic and Legal Analyses of Trade Policy and Institutions* (Oxford: Blackwell Publishing, 2005), 580 pp., £95 hb. ISBN 1405120622

B. J. Condon, *Environmental Sovereignty and the WTO: Trade Sanctions and International Law* (New York, NY: Transnational Publishers, 2006), 350 pp., $125 hb. ISBN 1571053666

E. Diaz-Bonilla, S. E. Frandsen, and S. Robinson (eds.), *WTO Negotiations and Agricultural Trade Liberalization: The Effect of Developed Countries' Policies on Developing Countries* (Wallingford/Cambridge, MA: CABI Publishing, 2006), 320 pp., £65 hb. ISBN 1845930509

F. Jawara and A. Kwa, *Behind the Scenes at the WTO: The Real World of International Trade Negotiations/Lessons of Cancun—Updated Edition* (London: Zed Books, 2004), 340 pp., £14.99 pb, £40 hb. ISBN 1842775332 pb, and 1842775324 hb

C. Joerges and E.-U. Petersmann (eds.), *Constitutionalism, Multilevel Trade Governance and Social Regulation* (Oxford: Hart Publishing, 2006), 550 pp., £75 hb. ISBN 19781841136653

H. Kalimo, *E-Cycling: Linking Trade and Environmental Law in the EC and the US* (New York, NY: Transnational Publishers, 2006), 760 pp., $165 hb. ISBN 1571053565

M. Llewelyn and M. Adcock, *European Plant Intellectual Property* (Oxford: Hart Publishing, 2006), 580 pp., £100 hb. ISBN 9781841133225

J. W. Maxwell and R. Reuveny (eds.), *Trade And Environment: Theory and Policy in the Context of EU Enlargement and Economic Transition* (Cheltenham: Edward Elgar, 2005), 346 pp., £75 hb. ISBN 1845421647

L. Nielsen, *The WTO, Animals and PPMs* (Leiden/Boston: Brill Academic Publishers, 2007), 365 pp., $115 hb. ISBN 9781571051868

E.-U. Petersmann (ed.), *Reforming the World Trading System: Legitimacy, Efficiency, and Democratic Governance* (Oxford: Oxford University Press, 2005), 590 pp., £35 pb, £100 hb. ISBN 0199282633 pb, and 0199282625 hb

J. Scott, *The WTO Agreement on Sanitary and Phytosanitary Measures: A Commentary* (Oxford: Oxford University Press, 2007), 356 pp., £75 hb. ISBN 0199271127

A. Thiedemann, *WTO und Umwelt: Die Auslegung des Art. XX GATT in der Praxis der GATT/WTO-Streitbeilegungsorgane* (Münster: LIT Verlag, 2005), 210 pp., €24.90 pb. ISBN 3825886220

R. Wolfrum, P.-T. Stoll, and A. Seibert-Fohr (eds.), *WTO—Technical Barriers and SPS Measures* (Leiden: Brill Academic Publishers, 2007), 400 pp., €120 hb. ISBN 9004145648

S. Woolcock (ed.), *Trade and Investment Rule-making: The Role of Regional and Bilateral Agreements* (Tokyo: United Nations University Press, 2006), 300 pp., $36 pb. ISBN 9280811320

I. Agriculture

J. Cooper (ed.), *Global Agriculture Policy Reform and Trade: Environmental Gains and Losses* (Cheltenham: Edward Elgar, 2005/6), 200 pp., £19.95 pb (2006), £55 hb (2005). ISBN 1847200583 pb, and 1843768879 hb

G. C. Holt and M. Reed (eds.), *Sociological Perspectives of Organic Agriculture: From Pioneer to Policy* (Wallingford/Cambridge, MA: CABI Publishing, 2006), 300 pp., £55 hb. ISBN 184593038X

R. D. Knutson, J. B. Penn, B. L. Flinchbaugh, and J. L. Outlaw, *Agricultural and Food Policy (6th Edn.)* (New York, NY/London: Pearson Longman, 2007), 200 pp., £49.99 pb. ISBN 0131718738

K. Lynggaard, *The Common Agricultural Policy and Organic Farming: An Institutional Perspective on Continuity and Change* (Wallingford/Cambridge, MA: CABI Publishing, 2006), 225 pp., £49.95 hb. ISBN 1845931149

J. Madeley, *Food for All: The Need for A New Agriculture* (London: Zed Books, 2003), 195 pp., £9.99 pb, £32.95 hb. ISBN 1842770195 pb, and 1842770187 hb

J. A. McMahon, *EU Agricultural Law* (Oxford: Oxford University Press, 2007), 448 pp., £115 hb. ISBN 1904501656

L. J. A. Mougeot (ed.), *Agropolis: The Social, Political and Environmental Dimensions of Urban Agriculture* (London: Earthscan, 2005), 295 pp., £22.95 pb, £80 hb. ISBN 1844072320 pb, and 1844072312 hb

J. Pretty (ed.), *The Earthscan Reader in Sustainable Agriculture* (London: Earthscan, 2005), 400 pp., £24.95 pb, £85 hb. ISBN 1844072363 pb, and 1844072355 hb

J. F. M. Swinnen (ed.), *Global Supply Chains, Standards and the Poor: How the Globalization of Food Systems and Standards Affects Rural Development and Poverty* (Wallingford/Cambridge, MA: CABI Publishing, 2007), 320 pp., £65 hb. ISBN 1845931858

R. Tripp, *Self-Sufficient Agriculture: Labour and Knowledge in Small-Scale Farming* (London: Earthscan, 2005), 242 pp., £17.99 pb, £70 hb. ISBN 1844072975 pb, and 1844072967 hb

J. Risk, Precaution, Science, and Technology in Law and Policy

R. Cooney and B. Dickson (eds.), *Biodiversity and the Precautionary Principle: Risk and Uncertainty in Conservation and Sustainable Use* (London: Earthscan, 2005), 315 pp., £22.95 pb, £80 hb. ISBN 1844072770 pb, and 1844072762 hb

J. Entine (ed.), *Let Them Eat Precaution: How Politics Is Undermining the Genetic Revolution in Agriculture* (Washington, DC: AEI Press, 2006), 205 pp., $25 hb. ISBN 0844742007

E. Fisher, *Risk Regulation and Administrative Constitutionalism* (Oxford: Hart Publishing, 2007), 300 pp., £45 hb. ISBN 1841130338

E. Fisher, J. Jones, and R. von Schomberg (eds.), *Implementing the Precautionary Principle: Perspectives and Prospects* (Cheltenham: Edward Elgar, 2006), 320 pp., £79.95 hb. ISBN 1845427025

R. Flynn and P. Bellaby (eds.), *Risk and the Public Acceptance of New Technologies* (Basingstoke/New York, NY: Palgrave MacMillan, 2007), 272 pp., £50 hb. ISBN 9780230517059

F. Fukuyama (ed.), *Blindside: How to Anticipate Forcing Events and Wild Cards in Global Politics* (Washington, DC: Brookings Institution Press, 2007), 200 pp., $27.95 hb. ISBN 9780815729907

L. O. Gostin, J. Areen, P. A. King, S. Goldberg, and P. D. Jacobson, *Law, Science, and Medicine (3rd Edn.)* (New York, NY: Foundation Press, 2005), 1400 pp., $105.50 hb. ISBN 158778517X

A. Guimarães Pereira, S. Guedes Vaz, and S. Tognetti (eds.), *Interfaces between Science and Society* (Sheffield: Greenleaf Publishing, 2006), 366 pp., £35 hb. ISBN 1874719977

M. Leach, I. Scoones, and B. Wynne (eds.), *Science and Citizens: Globalization and the Challenge of Engagement* (London: Zed Books, 2007), 295 pp., £18.99 pb, £55 hb. ISBN 1842775510 pb, and 1842775502 hb

C. Lenk, N. Hoppe, and R. Andorno (eds.), *Ethics and Law of Intellectual Property: Current Problems in Politics, Science and Technology* (Aldershot: Ashgate, 2007), 300 pp., £60 hb. ISBN 9780754626985

G. E. Marchant and K.L. Mossman, *Arbitrary and Capricious: The Precautionary Principle in the European Union Courts* (Washington, DC: AEI Press, 2004), 100 pp., $20 pb. ISBN 0844741892

M. D. Mehta, *Risky Business: Nuclear Power and Public Protest in Canada* (Lanham, MD: Lexington Books, 2005), 130 pp., $72 hb. ISBN 9780739109106

C. R. Sunstein, *Laws of Fear: Beyond the Precautionary Principle* (Cambridge: Cambridge University Press, 2005), 246 pp., £16.99 pb, £45 hb. ISBN 9780521615127 pb, and 9780521848237 hb

P. Taylor-Gooby and J. O. Zinn (eds.), *Risk in Social Science* (Oxford: Oxford University Press, 2006), 320 pp., £19.99 pb. ISBN 0199285950

W. Wagner and R. Steinzor (eds.), *Rescuing Science from Politics: Regulation and the Distortion of Scientific Research* (Cambridge: Cambridge University Press, 2006), 328 pp., £19.99 pb, £48 hb. ISBN 9780521540097 pb, and 9780521855209 hb

K. H. Whiteside, *Precautionary Politics: Principle and Practice in Confronting Environmental Risk* (Cambridge, MA: MIT Press, 2006), 200 pp., £12.95 pb, £32.95 hb. ISBN 0262731797 pb, and 0262232553 hb

K. Sustainable Development

G. Ayre and R. Callway (eds.), *Governance for Sustainable Development: Foundation for the Future* (London: Earthscan, 2005), 208 pp., £19.99 pb, £70 hb. ISBN 1844072088 pb, and 184407207X hb

J. Barry, B. Baxter, and R. Dunphy (eds.), *Europe, Globalization and Sustainable Development* (London/New York, NY: Routledge, 2005), 220 pp., £75 hb. ISBN 0415302765

V. A. Brown, J. Grootjans, J. Ritchie, M. Townsend, and G. Verrinder, *Sustainability and Health: Supporting Global Ecological Integrity in Public Health* (London: Earthscan, 2005), 330 pp., £24.95 pb, £70 hb. ISBN 1844071731 pb, and 184407174X hb

K. Bruno and J. Karliner, *Earthsummit.biz: The Corporate Takeover of Sustainable Development* (Oakland, CA: Food First Books, 2003), 173 pp., $12.95 pb. ISBN 0935028897

A. F. Cooper, J. J. Kirton, and T. Schrecker (eds.), *Governing Global Health: Challenge, Response, Innovation* (Aldershot: Ashgate, 2007), 310 pp., £55 hb. ISBN 9780754648734

J. F. Green and W. B. Chambers (eds.), *The Politics of Participation in Sustainable Development Governance* (Tokyo: United Nations University Press, 2006), 275 pp., $34 pb. ISBN 9280811339

B. Hettne (ed.), *Sustainable Development in a Globalized World: Studies in Development Security and Culture, Vol. 1* (Basingstoke/New York, NY: Palgrave MacMillan, 2008), 295 pp., £50 hb. ISBN 9780230551275

T. Jackson (ed.), *The Earthscan Reader on Sustainable Consumption* (London: Earthscan, 2006), 410 pp., £22.95 pb, £80 hb. ISBN 1844071642 pb, and 1844071650 hb

M. E. Kahn, *Green Cities: Urban Growth and the Environment* (Washington, DC: Brookings Institution Press, 2006), 160 pp., $18.95 pb, $44.95 hb. ISBN 0815748159 pb, and 0815748167 hb

J. Sayer (ed.), *The Earthscan Reader in Forestry and Development* (London: Earthscan, 2005), 440 pp., £24.95 pb, £85 hb. ISBN 1844071545 pb, and 1844071537 hb

D. J. Shaw, *World Food Security: A History Since 1945* (Basingstoke/New York, NY: Palgrave MacMillan, 2007), 520 pp., £80 hb. ISBN 9780230553552

P. Stricker, *Toward a Culture of Nature: Environmental Policy and Sustainable Development in Cuba* (Lanham, MD: Lexington Books, 2007), 160 pp., $65 hb. ISBN 9780739120231

S. Thoyer and B. Martimort-Asso (eds.), *Participation for Sustainability in Trade* (Aldershot: Ashgate, 2007), 308 pp., £55 hb. ISBN 9780754646792

P. Vandergeest, P. Idahosa, and P. S. Bose (eds.), *Development's Displacements: Economies, Ecologies, and Cultures at Risk* (Vancouver, BC: University of British Columbia Press, 2006/7), 290 pp., $34.95 pb (2007), $85 hb (2006). ISBN 9780774812061 pb, and 9780774812054 hb

J. Vandermeer and I. Perfecto, *Breakfast of Biodiversity: The Political Ecology of Rain Forest Destruction (2nd Edn.)* (Oakland, CA: Food First Books, 2005), 204 pp., $16.95. ISBN 093502896X

L. Environmental Economics, Management, and Accounting

A. Blackman (ed.), *Small Firms and the Environment in Developing Countries: Collective Impacts, Collective Action* (Washington, DC: RFF Press, 2006), 250 pp., $32.95 pb, $75 hb. ISBN 1933115297 pb, and 1933115289 hb

M. Boyer, Y. Hiriart and D. Martimort (eds.), *Frontiers in the Economics of Environmental Regulation and Liability* (Aldershot, Ashgate, 2006), 345 pp., £65 hb. ISBN 0754642089

D. Campbell and R. Lee (eds.), *Environmental Law and Economics: Volumes I and II (Vol. I: Private Law and Property Rights; Vol. II: Pollution, Property and Public Law)* (Aldershot: Ashgate, 2007), 1280 pp., £320 hb. ISBN 9780754623434

C. Coglianese and J. Nash (eds.), *Leveraging the Private Sector: Management-Based Strategies for Improving Environmental Performance* (Washington, DC: RFF Press, 2006), 275 pp., $34.95 pb, $70 hb. ISBN 193311505X pb, and 1933115041 hb

J. Cramer, *Corporate Social Responsibility and Globalisation: An Action Plan for Business* (Sheffield: Greenleaf Publishing, 2006), 160 pp., £21.95 hb. ISBN 9781874719311

A. Dobson and A. Valencia Sáiz (eds.), *Citizenship, Environment, Economy* (London/New York, NY: Routledge, 2006), 165 pp., £65 hb. ISBN 0415366720

D. C. Esty and A.S. Winston, *Green to Gold: How Smart Companies Use Environmental Strategy to Innovate, Create Value, and Build Competitive Advantage* (New Haven, CT: Yale University Press, 2006), 380 pp., $27.50 hb. ISBN 9780300119978

R. Q. Grafton, W. Adamowicz, D. Dupont, H. Nelson, R. J. Hill, and S. Renzetti, *The Economics of the Environment and Natural Resources* (Oxford: Blackwell Publishing, 2005), 510 pp., £26.99 pb, £75 hb. ISBN 0631215646 pb, and 0631215638 hb

P. E. Graves, *Environmental Economics: A Critique of Benefit-Cost Analysis* (Lanham, MD: Rowman & Littlefield, 2007), 190 pp., $24.95 pb, $65 hb. ISBN 9780742546998 pb, and 9780742546981 hb

J. Hamschmidt (ed.), *Case Studies in Sustainability Management and Strategy: The Oikos Collection* (Sheffield: Greenleaf Publishing, 2007), 330 pp., £25 hb. ISBN 9781906093013

C. T. Hendrickson, L. B. Lave, and H. S. Matthews, *Environmental Life Cycle Assessments of Goods and Services: An Input-Output Approach* (Washington, DC: RFF Press, 2006), 255 pp., $35 pb, $80 hb. ISBN 1933115246 pb, and 1933115238 hb

R. J. Johnston and S. K. Swallow (eds.), *Economics and Contemporary Land Use Policy: Development and Conservation at the Rural-Urban Fringe* (Washington, DC: RFF Press, 2006), 295 pp., $36.95 pb, $70 hb. ISBN 193311522X pb, and 1933115211 hb

M. E. Kraft and S. Kamieniecki (eds.), *Business and Environmental Policy: Corporate Interests in the American Political System* (Cambridge, MA: MIT Press, 2007), 370 pp., $25 pb, $62 hb. ISBN 9780262612180 pb, and 9780262113052 hb

G. Marshall, *Economics for Collaborative Environmental Management: Renegotiating the Commons* (London: Earthscan, 2005), 170 pp., £22.95 pb, £80 hb. ISBN 1844070956 pb, and 1844070948 hb

T. H. Moran, E.M. Graham, and M. Blomström, *Does Foreign Direct Investment Promote Development?* (Washington, DC: Institute for International Economics, 2005), 440 pp., $28.95 pb. ISBN 0881323810

S. Parto and B. Herbert-Copley (eds.), *Industrial Innovation and Environmental Regulation: Developing Workable Solutions* (Tokyo: United Nations University Press, 2007), 320 pp., $36 pb. ISBN 9789280811278

S. Schaltegger and M. Wagner (eds.), *Managing the Business Case for Sustainability: The Integration of Social, Environmental and Economic Performance* (Sheffield: Greenleaf Publishing, 2006), 635 pp., £55 hb. ISBN 9781874719953

R. Sroufe and J. Sarkis (eds.), *Strategic Sustainability: The State of the Art in Corporate Environmental Management Systems* (Sheffield: Greenleaf Publishing, 2007), 280 pp., £35 hb. ISBN 9781874719618

T. Tietenberg, *Environmental Economics and Policy (5th Edn.)* New York, NY/London: Pearson Longman, 2006), 550 pp., £44.99 pb. ISBN 0321348907

M. Environmental Sociology, Philosophy, Ethics, Environmental Justice, and Human Rights

J. Baron, *Against Bioethics* (Cambridge, MA: MIT Press, 2006), 240 pp., £18.95 hb. ISBN 0262025965

S. Barrientos and C. Dolan (eds.), *Ethical Sourcing in the Global Food System* (London: Earthscan, 2006), 192 pp., £22.95 pb, £80 hb. ISBN 1844071995 pb, and 1844071898

C. J. Bosso, *Environment, Inc.: From Grassroots to Beltway* (Lawrence, KS: University Press of Kansas, 2005), 200 pp., $15.95 pb, $35 hb. ISBN 0700613684 pb, and 0700613676 hb

R. L. Bryant, *Nongovernmental Organizations in Environmental Struggles: Politics and the Making of Moral Capital in the Philippines* (New Haven, CT/London: Yale University Press, 2005), 288 pp., $45 hb. ISBN 0300106599

R. D. Bullard (ed.), *Growing Smarter: Achieving Livable Communities, Environmental Justice, and Regional Equity* (Cambridge, MA: MIT Press, 2007), 425 pp., $27 pb, $67 hb. ISBN 9780262524704 pb, and 9780262026109 hb

A. Cooper, J. Kirton, and T. Schrecker (eds.), *Governing Global Health: Challenge, Response, Innovation* (Aldershot: Ashgate, 2007), 320 pp., £55 hb. ISBN 0754648737

S. L. Cutter, *Hazards, Vulnerability and Environmental Justice* (London: Earthscan, 2006), 425 pp., £24.95 pb, £85 hb. ISBN 1844073114 pb, and 1844073106 hb

T. Doyle, *Environmental Movements in Majority and Minority Worlds: A Global Perspective* (Piscataway, NJ: Rutgers University Press, 2005), 200 pp., $23.95 pb. ISBN 081353495X

M. Goldman, *Imperial Nature: The World Bank and Struggles for Social Justice in the Age of Globalization* (New Haven, CT: Yale University Press, 2006), 375 pp., $22 pb, $40 hb. ISBN 9780300119749 pb, and 9780300104080 hb

J. C. Gordon and J. K. Berry, *Environmental Leadership Equals Essential Leadership: Redefining Who Leads and How* (New Haven, CT/London: Yale University Press, 2006), 192 pp., $22 hb. ISBN 0300108915

G. Grendstad, P. Selle, O. Bortne, and K. Strømsnes, *Unique Environmentalism: A Comparative Perspective* (Dordrecht: Springer, 2006), 190 pp., €72.95 hb. ISBN 0387305246

C. L. Harper and B. F. le Beau, *Food, Society, and Environment* (Upper Saddle River, NJ: Prentice Hall, 2003), 240 pp., $43.95 pb. ISBN 0130305669

H. M. Haugen, *The Right to Food and the TRIPS Agreement: With a Particular Emphasis on Developing Countries' Measures for Food Production and Distribution* (Leiden: Brill Academic Publishers, 2007), 510 pp., €250 hb. ISBN 9789004161849

D. J. Hess, *Alternative Pathways in Science and Industry: Activism, Innovation, and the Environment in an Era of Globalization* (Cambridge, MA: MIT Press, 2007), 340 pp., $25 pb, $62 hb. ISBN 9780262582728 pb, and 9780262083591 hb

G. Ignatow, *Transnational Identity Politics and the Environment* (Lanham, MD: Lexington Books, 2007), 140 pp., $55 hb. ISBN 9780739120156

D. Jensen, *Endgame, Vol. 1: The Problem of Civilization* (New York, NY: Seven Stories Press, 2006), 500 pp., $18.95 pb. ISBN 158322730X

D. Jensen, *Endgame, Vol. 2: Resistance* (New York, NY: Seven Stories Press, 2006), 450 pp., $18.95 pb. ISBN 1583227245

G. Kent, *Freedom from Want: The Human Right to Adequate Food* (Washington, DC: Georgetown University Press, 2005), 290 pp., $26.95 pb, $49.95 hb. ISBN 1589010566 pb, and 1589010558 hb

C. Mauch, N. Stoltzfus, and D. R. Weiner (eds.), *Shades of Green: Environment Activism Around the Globe* (Lanham, MD: Rowman & Littlefield, 2006), 240 pp., $26.95 pb, $82.50 hb. ISBN 9780742546486 pb, and 9780742546479 hb

S. M. Meyer, *The End of the Wild* (Cambridge, MA: MIT Press/Boston Review, 2006), 100 pp., £9.95 hb. ISBN 026213473X

P. Newell and J. Wheeler (eds.), *Rights, Resources and the Politics of Accountability* (London: Zed Books, 2006), 275 pp., £18.99 pb, £59.99 hb. ISBN 1842775553 pb, and 1842775545

L. H. Newton, *Ethics and Sustainability: Sustainable Development and the Moral Life* (Upper Saddle River, NJ: Prentice Hall, 2003), 120 pp., $26.95 pb. ISBN 0130617962

D. Peterson del Mar, *Environmentalism* (New York, NY/London: Pearson Longman, 2007), 220 pp., £9.99 pb. ISBN 0582772974

D. N. Pellow, *Resisting Global Toxics: Transnational Movements for Environmental Justice* (Cambridge, MA: MIT Press, 2007), 350 pp., $25 pb, $62 hb. ISBN 9780262662017 pb, and 9780262162449 hb

A. Philippopoulos-Mihalopoulos, *Absent Environments, Theorising Environmental Law and the City* (London: Routledge-Cavendish, 2007), 275 pp., £50 hb. ISBN 184472154X

R. Picolotti and J. D. Taillant (eds.), *Linking Human Rights and the Environment* (Tuscon, AZ: University of Arizona Press, 2003), 264 pp., $45 hb. ISBN 0816522618

S. B. Pralle, *Branching out, Digging in: Environmental Advocacy and Agenda Setting* (Washington, DC: Georgetown University Press, 2006), 275 pp., $29.95 pb. ISBN 1589011236

R. L. Sandler, *Character and Environment: A Virtue-Oriented Approach to Environmental Ethics* (New York, NY: Columbia University Press, 2007), 200 pp., $45 hb. ISBN 9780231141062

R. Sandler and P. C. Pezzullo (eds.), *Environmental Justice and Environmentalism: The Social Justice Challenge to the Environmental Movement* (Cambridge, MA: MIT Press, 2007), 355 pp., £16.95 pb, £39.95 hb. ISBN 0262693402 pb, and 0262195526 hb

D. Schlosberg, *Defining Environmental Justice: Theories, Movements, and Nature* (Oxford: Oxford University Press, 2007), 252 pp., £45 hb. ISBN 0199286299

T. Shallcross and J. Robinson (eds.), *Global Citizenship and Environmental Justice* (Amsterdam/New York, NY: Rodopi, 2006), 200 pp., €42 pb. ISBN 904201668X

G. Smith, *Deliberative Democracy and the Environment* (London/New York, NY: Routledge, 2003), 165 pp., £20.99 pb. ISBN 0415309409

R. Stein (ed.), *New Perspectives on Environmental Justice: Gender, Sexuality, and Activism* (Piscataway, NJ: Rutgers University Press, 2004), 285 pp., $24.95 pb. ISBN 0813534275

J. V. Switzer, *Environmental Activism: A Reference Handbook* (Santa Barbara, CA: ABC-CLIO, 2003), 330 pp., $55 hb. ISBN 1576079015

J. G. Taylor and P. J. Scharlin, *Smart Alliance: How a Global Corporation and Environmental Activists Transformed a Tarnished Brand* (New Haven, CT/London: Yale University Press, 2004), 304 pp., $30 hb. ISBN 030010233X

J. Turner and J. D'Silva (eds.), *Animals, Ethics and Trade: The Challenge of Animal Sentience* (London: Earthscan, 2006), 300 pp., £16.99 pb, £65 hb. ISBN 184407255X pb, and 1844072541 hb

J. Vaughn, *Conflicts over Natural Resources: A Reference Handbook* (Santa Barbara, CA: ABC-CLIO, 2007), 300 pp., $55 hb. ISBN 1598840150

S. H. Washington, P. C. Rosier, and H. Goodall (eds.), *Echoes from the Poisoned Well: Global Memories of Environmental Injustice* (Lanham, MD: Lexington Books, 2006), 404 pp., $29.95 pb, $85 hb. ISBN 0739114328 pb, and 073910912X hb

M. Wissenburg and Y. Levy (eds.), *Liberal Democracy and Environmentalism: The End of Environmentalism?* (London/New York, NY: Routledge, 2004), 220 pp., £70 hb. ISBN 0415321956

J. D. Wulfhorst and A. K. Haugestad (eds.), *Building Sustainable Communities: Environmental Justice & Global Citizenship* (Amsterdam/New York, NY: Rodopi, 2006), 240 pp., €50 pb. ISBN 9042021233

N. General European (Environmental) Law, Policy, and Governance; and EU Member States' Environmental Law

I. Bache, *Europeanization and Multilevel Governance: Cohesion Policy in the European Union and Britain* (Lanham, MD: Rowman & Littlefield, 2007), 200 pp., $32.95 pb, $80 hb. ISBN 9780742541337 pb, and 9780742541320 hb

M. Büchs, *New Governance in European Social Policy: The Open Method of Coordination* (Basingstoke/New York, NY: Palgrave MacMillan, 2007), 224 pp., £45 hb. ISBN 9780230506510

N. Carter, *The Politics of the Environment: Ideas, Activism, Policy (2nd Edn.)* (Cambridge: Cambridge University Press, 2007), 425 pp., £17.99 pb, £45 hb. ISBN 9780521687454 pb, and 9780521868020 hb

D. Chalmers, C. Hadjiemmanuil, G. Monti, and A. Tomkins, *European Union Law: Text and Materials* (Cambridge: Cambridge University Press, 2006), 1362 pp., £35 pb, £75 hb. ISBN 9780521527414 pb, and 9780521820413 hb

D. Chalmers and A. Tomkins, *European Union Public Law: Text and Materials* (Cambridge: Cambridge University Press, 2007), 540 pp., £29.99 pb, £70 hb. ISBN 9780521709026 pb, and 9780521882378 hb

R. A. Cichowski, *The European Court and Civil Society: Litigation, Mobilization and Governance* (Cambridge: Cambridge University Press, 2007), 310 pp., £17.99 pb, £45 hb. ISBN 9780521671817 pb, and 9780521855853 hb

P. Craig and G. de Búrca, *EU Law: Text and Materials (4th Edn.)* (Oxford: Oxford University Press, 2007), 1300 pp., £36.99 pb. ISBN 9780199273898

J. Fairhurst, *Law of the European Union (6th Edn.)* (New York, NY/London: Pearson Longman, 2007), 872 pp., £30.99 pb. ISBN 1405846887

P. Foradori, P. Rosa, and R. Scartezzini (eds.), *Managing a Multilevel Foreign Policy: The EU in International Affairs* (Lanham, MD: Lexington Books, 2007), 250 pp., $34.95 pb, $80 hb. ISBN 9780739116432 pb, and 9780739116425 hb

J. Gillingham, *Design for A New Europe* (Cambridge: Cambridge University Press, 2006), 300 pp., £13.99 pb, £38 hb. ISBN 9780521686648 pb, and 9780521866941 hb

X. Groussot, *General Principles of Community Law* (Groningen: Europa Law Publishing, 2006), 480 pp., €92 hb. ISBN 9076871671

J. Holder and M. Lee (eds.), *Environmental Protection, Law and Policy: Text and Materials (2nd Edn.)* (Cambridge: Cambridge University Press, 2007), 818 pp., £40 pb. ISBN 9780521690263

J. H. Jans, R. de Lange, S. Prechal, and R. J. G. M. Widdershoven, *Europeanisation of Public Law* (Groningen: Europa Law Publishing, 2007), 425 pp., €49 pb, €95 hb. ISBN 9789076871585 pb, and 9789076871578 hb

A. Jordan, R. K. W. Wurzel, and A. R. Zito (eds.), *'New' Instruments of Environmental Governance?: National Experiences and Prospects* (London/Portland, OR: Frank Cass, 2003), 232 pp., £24.99 pb, £75 hb. ISBN 0714683000 pb, and 0714653667 hb

L. Krämer, *EC Environmental Law (6th Edn.)* (London: Sweet & Maxwell, 2007), 530 pp., £125 hb. ISBN 184703067X

K. Lenaerts, D. Arts, I. Maselis, and R. Bray, *Procedural Law of the European Union (2nd Edn.)* (London: Sweet & Maxwell, 2006), 850 pp., £34.95 pb. ISBN 0421947004

S. MacLeod (ed.), *Global Governance and the Quest for Justice—Vol. 2: Corporate Governance* (Oxford: Hart Publishing, 2006), 265 pp., £22.95 pb. ISBN 9781841134062

P. S. R. F. Mathijsen, *A Guide to European Union Law (7th Edn.)* (London: Sweet & Maxwell, 2007), 600 pp., £27.95 pb. ISBN 0421959703

A. McDonnell (ed.), *A Review Of Forty Years Of Community Law: Legal Developments in the European Communities and the European Union* (The Hague: Kluwer Law International, 2005), 375 pp., €90 pb. ISBN 9041123261

P. Nedergaard, *European Union Administration: Legitimacy and Efficiency* (Leiden: Brill Academic Publishers, 2006), 200 pp., €85 hb. ISBN 9004155732

C. J. Paraskevopoulos, P. Getimis, and N. Rees (eds.), *Adapting to EU Multi-Level Governance: Regional and Environmental Policies in Cohesion and CEE Countries* (Aldershot: Ashgate, 2006), 290 pp., £55 hb. ISBN 0754645339

T. J. Selck, *Preferences and Procedures: European Union Legislative Decision-Making* (Dordrecht: Springer, 2006), 100 pp., €69 hb. ISBN 038727555X

N. South and P. Beirne (eds.), *Green Criminology* (Aldershot: Ashgate, 2006), 614 pp., £145 hb. ISBN 0754625923

T. Tridimas, *The General Principles of EU Law (2nd Edn.)* (Oxford: Oxford University Press, 2006), 720 pp., £95 hb. ISBN 0199258066

S. A. de Vries, *Tensions within the Internal Market: The Functioning of the Internal Market and the Development of Horizontal and Flanking Policies* (Groningen: Europa Law Publishing, 2006), 465 pp., €89 hb. ISBN 9076871531

S. Weatherill (ed.), *Better Regulation* (Oxford: Hart Publishing, 2007), 450 pp., £50 hb. ISBN 9781841137155

P. Wenneras, *The Enforcement of EC Environmental Law* (Oxford: Oxford University Press, 2007), 370 pp., £50 hb. ISBN 0199229015

O. General International and Comparative (Environmental) Law, Policy, and Governance; and Non-EU National Environmental Law

R. N. L. Andrews, *Managing the Environment, Managing Ourselves: A History of American Environmental Policy (2nd Edn.)* (New Haven, CT: Yale University Press, 2006), 525 pp., $40 pb. ISBN 030011124X

J. S. Applegate and J. G. Laitos, *Environmental Law: RCRA, CERCLA, and the Management of Hazardous Waste* (New York, NY: Foundation Press, 2006), 320 pp., $16.50 pb. ISBN 1587787180

D. Armitage, F. Berkes, and N. Doubleday (eds.), *Adaptive Co-Management: Collaboration, Learning, and Multi-Level Governance* (Vancouver, BC: University of British Columbia Press, 2007/8), 350 pp., $34.95 pb (2008), $90 hb (2007). ISBN 9780774813907 pb, and 9780774813839 hb

S. A. Atapattu, *Emerging Principles of International Environmental Law* (New York, NY: Transnational Publishers, 2006), 530 pp., $125 hb. ISBN 1571051821

R. S. Axelrod, D. L. Downie, and N. J. Vig (eds.), *The Global Environment: Institutions, Law, and Policy (2nd Edn.)* (Washington, DC: CQ Press, 2005), 300 pp., $38.95 pb. ISBN 156802827X

M. M. Betsill and E. Corell (eds.), *NGO Diplomacy: The Influence of Nongovernmental Organizations in International Environmental Negotiations* (Cambridge, MA: MIT Press, 2007), 250 pp., $20 pb, $50 hb. ISBN 970262524766 pb, and 9780262026260 hb

H. Blatt, *America's Environmental Report Card: Are We Making the Grade?* (Cambridge, MA: MIT Press, 2005/6), 272 pp., £8.95 pb (2006), £18.95 hb (2005). ISBN 0262524678, and 0262025728 hb

R. M. Bratspies and R. A. Miller (eds.), *Transboundary Harm in International Law: Lessons from the Trail Smelter Arbitration* (Cambridge: Cambridge University Press, 2006), 370 pp., £53 hb. ISBN 9780521856434

H. Breitmeier, O.R. Young, and M. Zürn, *Analyzing International Environmental Regimes: From Case Study to Database (CD-ROM included)* (Cambridge, MA: MIT Press, 2006), 330 pp., £17.95 pb, £43.95 hb. ISBN 0262524619 pb, and 0262026023 hb

J. Brunnée, D. Bodansky, and E. Hey (eds.), *The Oxford Handbook of International Environmental Law* (Oxford: Oxford University Press, 2007), 850 pp., £85 hb. ISBN 019926970X

R. L. Bryant, *Nongovernmental Organizations in Environmental Struggles: Politics and the Making of Moral Capital in the Philippines* (New Haven, CT/London: Yale University Press, 2005), 275 pp., $45 hb. ISBN 0300106599

N. T. Carter and A. P. J. Mol (eds.), *Environmental Governance in China* (London/New York, NY: Routledge, 2007), 205 pp., £65 hb. ISBN 0415371694

R. K. Craig, *Environmental Law in Context: Cases and Materials* (St. Paul, MN: Thomson/West, 2005), 1100 pp., $89 hb. ISBN 031415163X

D. K. DeGarmo, *International Environmental Treaties and State Behavior: Factors Influencing Cooperation* (London/New York, NY: Routledge, 2005), 144pp., £60 hb. ISBN 0415971810

G. Desfor and R. Keil, *Nature and the City: Making Environmental Policy in Toronto and Los Angeles* (Tuscon, AZ: University of Arizona Press, 2004), 274 pp., $45 hb. ISBN 0816523738

C. Devereaux, R. Lawrence, and M. D. Watkins, *Case Studies in US Trade Negotiation: Two Volume Set* (Washington, DC: Institute for International Economics, 2005), 800 pp., $39.95 pb. ISBN 0881323640

R. F. Durant, *The Greening of the U.S. Military: Environmental Policy, National Security, and Organizational Change* (Washington, DC: Georgetown University Press, 2007), 300 pp., $29.95 pb. ISBN 1589011538

M. Egan, *Barry Commoner and the Science of Survival: The Remaking of American Environmentalism* (Cambridge, MA: MIT Press, 2007), 320 pp., $28 hb. ISBN 9780262050869

R. C. Ellickson and V. L. Been, *Land Use Controls: Cases and Materials (3rd Edn.)* (New York, NY: Aspen Publishers, 2005), 1020 pp., $108 hb. ISBN 0735539960

L. Elliott, *The Global Politics of the Environment (2nd Edn.)* (New York, NY: New York University Press, 2004), 300 pp., $22 pb, $65 hb. ISBN 0814722180 pb, and 0814722172 hb

D. A. Farber, J. L. Freeman, A. E. Carlson, and R. W. Findley, *Cases and Materials on Environmental Law (7th Edn.)* (St. Paul, MN: Thomson/West, 2006) 1050 pp., $98 hb. ISBN 0314162909

M. Faure and N. Niessen (eds.), *Environmental Law in Development: Lessons from the Indonesian Experience* (Cheltenham: Edward Elgar, 2006), 350 pp., £75 hb. ISBN 1845425197

S. Ferrey, *Environmental Law: Examples & Explanations (3rd Edn.)* (New York, NY: Aspen Publishers, 2004), 650 pp., $38.95 pb. ISBN 0735540136

D. J. Fiorino, *The New Environmental Regulation* (Cambridge, MA: MIT Press, 2006), 300 pp., £14.95 pb, £36.95 hb. ISBN 0262562189 pb, and 0262062569 hb

F. Funes, L. García, M. Bourque, N. Pérez, and P. Rosset (eds.), *Sustainable Agriculture and Resistance: Transforming Food Production in Cuba* (Oakland, CA: Food First Books, 2002), 315 pp., $18.95 pb. ISBN 0935028870

A. Gillespie, *Protected Areas and International Environmental Law* (Leiden: Brill Academic Publishers, 2007), 330 pp., €130 hb. ISBN 9789004161580

C. L. Harper, *Environment and Society: Human Perspectives on Environmental Issues (3rd Edn.)* (Upper Saddle River, NJ: Prentice Hall, 2004), 496 pp., $68.95 pb. ISBN 0131113410

D. Hunter, J. Salzman, and D. Zaelke, *International Environmental Law and Policy (2nd Edn.)* (New York, NY: Foundation Press, 2002), 1547 pp., $104 hb. ISBN 1587780844

D. Hunter, J. Salzman, and D. Zaelke, *Treaty Supplement to Accompany International Environmental Law and Policy (2nd Edn.)* (New York, NY: Foundation Press, 2002), 463 pp., $27 pb. ISBN 1587783797

T. L. Ilgen (ed.), *Hard Power, Soft Power and the Future of Transatlantic Relations* (Aldershot: Ashgate, 2006), 210 pp., £50 hb. ISBN 0754647536

C. N. Johnston, W. F. Funk, and V. B. Flatt, *Legal Protection of the Environment* (St. Paul, MN: Thomson/West, 2005), 800 pp., $92 hb. ISBN 0314152660

A. Jorgenson and E. Kick (eds.), *Globalization and the Environment* (Leiden: Brill Academic Publishers, 2006), 350 pp., €99 hb. ISBN 900415132X

R. B. Keiter, *Keeping Faith with Nature: Ecosystems, Democracy, and America's Public Lands* (New Haven, CT/London: Yale University Press, 2005), 448 pp., $45 hb. ISBN 0300092733

A. Kiss and D. Shelton, *Guide to International Environmental Law* (Leiden: Brill Academic Publishers, 2007), 310 pp., €50 hb. ISBN 9781571053442

M. E. Kraft, *Environmental Policy and Politics (4th Edn.)* (New York, NY/London: Pearson Longman, 2007), 310 pp., £25.99 pb. ISBN 0321243536

N. K. Kubasek and G. S. Silverman, *Environmental Law (5th Edn.)* (Upper Saddle River, NJ: Prentice Hall, 2004), 465 pp., $82.95 pb. ISBN 0131479210

E. Laferrière and P. J. Stoett (eds.), *International Ecopolitical Theory: Critical Approaches* (Vancouver, BC: University of British Columbia Press, 2006/7), 170 pp., $29.95 pb (2007), $85 hb (2006). ISBN 9780774813228 pb, and 9780774813211 hb

J.-E. Lane, *Globalization and Politics: Promises and Dangers* (Aldershot: Ashgate, 2006), 250 pp, £30 hb. ISBN 075464667X

J. A. Layzer, *The Environmental Case: Translating Values Into Policy (2nd Edn.)* (Washington, DC: CQ Press, 2006), 530 pp., $36.95 pb. ISBN 9781568028989

R. J. Lazarus and O. A. Houck (eds.), *Environmental Law Stories* (New York, NY: Foundation Press, 2005), 353 pp., $25 pb. ISBN 1587787288

K. Lee (ed.), *International Environmental Law Reports: Vol. 5, International Environmental Law in International Tribunals* (Cambridge: Cambridge University Press, 2007), 744 pp., £65 pb, £110 hb. ISBN 9780521659642 pb, and 9780521650380 hb

R. D. Lipschutz, *Global Environmental Politics: Power, Perspectives, and Practice* (Washington, DC: CQ Press, 2004), 290 pp., $35.95 pb. ISBN 1568027494

E. Louka, *International Environmental Law: Fairness, Effectiveness, and World Order* (Cambridge: Cambridge University Press, 2007), 535 pp., £32 pb, £59 hb. ISBN 9780521687594 pb, and 9780521868122 hb

V. Lowe, *International Law* (Oxford: Oxford University Press, 2007), 290 pp., £50 hb, £19.99 pb. ISBN 9780199230839 hb, 9780199268849 pb

M. S. Madden and G. W. Boston, *Law of Environmental and Toxic Torts: Cases, Materials and Problems (3rd Edn.)* (St. Paul, MN: Thomson/West, 2005), 1050 pp., $90 hb. ISBN 0314156070

J. McBeath, and J. Rosenberg, *Comparative Environmental Politics* (Dordrecht: Springer, 2006), 200 pp., €99.95 hb. ISBN 1402047622

P. C. Milazzo, *Unlikely Environmentalists: Congress and Clean Water, 1945–1972* (Lawrence, KS: University Press of Kansas, 2006), 340 pp., $29.95 hb. ISBN 9780700614752

R. B. Mitchell, W. C. Clark, D. W. Cash, and N. M. Dickson (eds.), *Global Environmental Assessments: Information and Influence* (Cambridge, MA: MIT Press, 2006), 350 pp., £17.95 pb, £39.95 hb. ISBN 0262633361 pb, and 0262134683 hb

B. Morgan and K. Yeung, *An Introduction to Law and Regulation: Text and Materials* (Cambridge: Cambridge University Press, 2007), 372 pp., £29.99 pb. ISBN 9780521685658

A. G. Nikolaev, *International Negotiations: Theory, Practice and the Connection with Domestic Politics* (Lanham, MD: Lexington Books, 2007), 350 pp., $85 hb. ISBN 9780739117583

S. Oberthür and T. Gehring (eds.), *Institutional Interaction in Global Environmental Governance: Synergy and Conflict among International and EU Policies* (Cambridge, MA: MIT Press, 2006), 424 pp., £18.95 pb, £43.95 hb. ISBN 0262651106 pb, and 026205115X hb

M. Orsini and M. Smith (eds.), *Critical Policy Studies* (Vancouver, BC: University of British Columbia Press, 2006/7), 400 pp., $29.95 pb (2007), $85 hb (2006). ISBN 9780774813181 pb, and 9780774813174 hb

R. V. Percival and C. H. Schroeder, *Environmental Law: Statutory and Case Supplement with Internet Guide, 2006–2007* (New York, NY: Aspen Publishers, 2006), 1110 pp., $41 pb. ISBN 0735557780

Z. J. B. Plater, R. H. Abrams, W. Goldfarb, R. L. Graham, L. Heinzerling, and D. A.Wirth, *Environmental Law and Policy: Nature, Law, and Society (3rd Edn.)* (New York, NY: Aspen Publishers, 2004), 1400 pp., $109 hb. ISBN 0735541434

P. Le Prestre and P. Stoett (eds.), *Bilateral Ecopolitics: Continuity and Change in Canadian-American Environmental Relations* (Aldershot: Ashgate, 2006), 290 pp., £55 hb. ISBN 0754641775

R. Repetto (ed.), *Punctuated Equilibrium and the Dynamics of U.S. Environmental Policy* (New Haven, CT: Yale University Press, 2006), 300 pp., $25 pb. ISBN 9780300110760

B. P. Resosudarmo (ed.), *The Politics and Economics of Indonesia's Natural Resources* (Washington, DC: RFF Press, 2006), 300 pp., $45 hb. ISBN 1933115254

R. L. Revesz, *Environmental Law Statutes: 2006–2007 Edn.* (New York, NY: Foundation Press, 2006), 1500 pp., $35 pb. ISBN 1599411148

W. A. Rosenbaum, *Environmental Politics and Policy (7th Edn.)* (Washington, DC: CQ Press, 2007), 400 pp., $47.95 pb. ISBN 9780872894402

J. Salzman and B. H. Thompson, *Environmental Law and Policy* (New York, NY: Foundation Press, 2003), 305 pp., $30 pb. ISBN 1566629845

D. Scheberle, *Federalism and Environmental Policy: Trust and the Politics of Implementations (2nd Edn.)* (Washington, DC: Georgetown University Press, 2004), 240 pp., $22.95 pb. ISBN 1589011007

R. A. Schnabel and F. X. Rocca, *The Next Superpower? The Rise of Europe and Its Challenge to the United States* (Lanham, MD: Rowman & Littlefield, 2005/7), 210 pp., $16.95 pb (2007), $22.95 hb (2005). ISBN 9780742545489 pb, and 9780742545472 hb

A. Schwabach, *International Environmental Disputes: A Reference Handbook* (Santa Barbara, CA: ABC-CLIO, 2005), 345 pp., $65 hb. ISBN 1851097732

P. de Senarclens and A. Kazancigil (eds.), *Regulating Globalization: Critical Approaches to Global Governance* (Tokyo: United Nations University Press, 2007), 310 pp., $38 pb. ISBN 9280811363

T. J. Schoenbaum, R. H. Rosenberg, and H. D. Doremus, *Environmental Policy Law, Problems, Cases, and Reasons (4th Edn.)* (New York, NY: Foundation Press, 2002), 1012 pp., $100.50 hb. ISBN 1566629373

J. R. Short, *Liquid City: Megalopolis and the Contemporary Northeast* (Washington, DC: RFF Press, 2007), 190 pp., $28.95 pb, $70 hb. ISBN 9781933115504 pb, and 9781933115498 hb

C. B. Simonsen, *Essentials of Environmental Law (3rd Edn.)* (Upper Saddle River: Pearson Prentice Hall, 2007), 320 pp., £33.99 pb. ISBN 0132280450

Z. A. Smith, *The Environmental Policy Paradox (4th Edn.)* (Upper Saddle River, NJ: Prentice Hall, 2004), 300 pp., $55.95 pb. ISBN 0130993085

C. L. Soskolne (ed.), *Sustaining Life on Earth: Environmental and Human Health through Global Governance* (Lanham, MD: Lexington Books, 2008), 470 pp., $44.95 pb, $95 hb. ISBN 9780739117309 pb, and 9780739117293 hb

J. G. Speth, *Red Sky at Morning: America and the Crisis of the Global Environment: A Citizen's Agenda for Action* (New Haven, CT/London: Yale University Press, 2005), 272 pp., $24 pb. ISBN 0300107765

G. Ulfstein, T. Marauhn, and A. Zimmerman (eds.), *Making Treaties Work: Human Rights, Environment and Arms Control* (Cambridge: Cambridge University Press, 2007), 440 pp., £55 hb. ISBN 9780521873178

A. Vedder (ed.), *NGO Involvement in International Governance and Policy: Sources of Legitimacy* (Leiden: Brill Academic Publishers, 2007), 240 pp., €80 hb. ISBN 9789004158467

G. Wahlers (ed.), *The United States of America and the European Union* (Washington, DC: Brookings Institution Press, 2007), 160 pp., $15 pb. ISBN 9780978882129

Z. Young, *A New Green Order? The World Bank and the Politics of the Global Environment Facility* (London: Pluto Press, 2002), 290 pp., £18.99 pb, £60 hb. ISBN 0745315488 pb, and 0745315534 hb

P. Yearbooks

Global Legal Group, *The International Comparative Legal Guide to: Environment Law 2005* (London: Global Legal Group, 2005), 360 pp, $295 pb. ISBN 190465410X

Global Legal Group, *The International Comparative Legal Guide to: Environment Law 2006* (London: Global Legal Group, 2006), 400 pp, $295 pb. ISBN 1904654177

Q. Journals

Global Environmental Politics, edited by P. Dauvergne, J. Clapp, and M. Paterson (Cambridge, MA: MIT Press), ISSN 15263800. Annual subscriptions (4 issues—print and electronic access), $54 (individual), $208 (institutional)

Journal of Environmental Law and Practice, edited by M.-A. Bowden and M. Phillipson (Toronto: Thomson Carswell), (2006) vol. 16. ISSN 11817534. Annual subscriptions (3 issues), bound volume service: CDN $239

Documents

*Paolo Galizzi**

I. Introduction

In the period under review,[1] the Commission has been extremely active in producing documents within, and relevant to, the field of environmental law. This chapter will examine some of the key communications in the following areas of crucial environmental concern for the European Community (EC): biodiversity and energy (both of which are stressed in the Sixth Environmental Action Programme),[2] as well as forests and soil.

The Commission's overall emphasis, in line with the mandate of the EC Treaty, is to coordinate its internal efforts with international strategies. Many of the problems tackled are, in fact, global in nature and require concerted efforts for their effective solution. Overall, the Commission's proposals reflect its leading role in dealing with the foremost environmental issues of our times. However, they are too often more about good intentions than concrete and specific actions. While this is largely the nature of such documents, greater specificity would better promote the achievement and implementation of their laudable objectives. Furthermore, in several instances, the documents under examination merely reiterate statements and 'commitments' previously made. In fairness, the reader should bear in mind that often it is the lack of political consensus among the Member States that so frequently frustrates the Commission's efforts to serve a more active and progressive role in calling for stronger Community action.

* Visiting Professor of Law and Director, Sustainable Development Legal Initiative (SDLI), Leitner Center for International Law and Justice, Fordham University School of Law, New York, NY (US).

[1] This survey covers documents published between 1 January 2006 and 31 October 2007.

[2] EP and Council Dec. 1600/2002/EC laying down the Sixth Community Environment Action Programme [2002] OJ L242/1.

II. Summaries of Communications, Green Papers, and White Papers

A. Commission Communication: Halting the Loss of Biodiversity by 2010—and Beyond—Sustaining Ecosystem Services For Human Well-Being[3]

This communication outlines an Action Plan for the conservation of biodiversity both in the European Union (EU) and worldwide. Two annexes set out specific actions for accomplishing the agreed upon objectives and supporting measures (I); and a set of headline biodiversity indicators for evaluating their implementation and achievement (II). In substance, it is largely concerned with clarifying responsibilities as to the implementation of the four prior action plans that have been adopted since 2001. Considering that only four years remain before the 2010 deadline, this is particularly worrisome. Rapid, concerted efforts will be required for this target to be met.

It begins with an overview of the importance of biodiversity and its current state, trends, and pressures. Europe's ecosystems have suffered the most human-induced habitat fragmentation in the world, and rates of biodiversity loss worldwide are still more alarming. The next part outlines the main drivers of the problem: habitat change, over-exploitation, invasive species, pollution, governance and valuation failures, globalization, and climate change. These factors attest to the Community's ongoing struggle to balance the constant demands placed on ecosystems and services with the environmental protection that will ensure their sustainability.

The Communication then examines the progress made in implementing the EC Biodiversity Strategy[4] and related Action Plans,[5] as well as its activities under the Convention on Biological Diversity (CBD)[6] and related international agreements. Its review of the implementation of EU internal biodiversity policies finds substantial progress under the Natura 2000 network, the Sustainable Development Strategy,[7] and the Lisbon partnership; promising regulations in the agricultural, fisheries, and regional and territorial development sectors; and the initiation of efforts to develop a comprehensive strategy on the control of alien species. The onus is now on the Member States and other stakeholders to

[3] COM(2006)216, 22 May 2006.

[4] Commission Communication on a European Community Biodiversity Strategy COM(98)42, 4 Feb. 1998.

[5] Commission Communication—Biodiversity Action Plan for Economic and Development Co-operation COM(2001)162, 27 Mar. 2001.

[6] Rio de Janeiro (Brazil), 5 June 1992 (entered into force 29 Dec. 1993), (1992) 31 *International Legal Materials* 818; published on the Internet at: http://www.biodiv.org.

[7] Commission's Proposal to the Gothenburg European Council on a Sustainable Europe for a Better World: A European Union Strategy for Sustainable Development COM(01)264, 15 May 2001.

deliver on the promise of this plan and begin to halt and reverse the decline of biodiversity on the continent.

In reviewing biodiversity in EU external policy, the Commission rightly concludes that implementation of the CBD needs to be substantially reinforced; that biodiversity needs to be better mainstreamed in EC and Member States' external assistance budgets; and that further efforts are required to address the impact of trade on tropical forests. The Commission also identifies important supporting measures in the areas of knowledge, public awareness raising, and monitoring and reporting.

The Communication then turns to activities to be pursued for the remainder of the decade, in accordance with the commitment undertaken at the World Summit for Sustainable Development (WSSD)[8] to significantly reduce biodiversity loss by 2010. In an apparent effort to revitalize and focus commitment and concerted efforts on biodiversity, it outlines four policy areas (Biodiversity in the EU; the EU and Global Biodiversity; Biodiversity and Climate Change; and finally the Knowledge Base) with ten priority objectives articulated thereunder (Safeguard the EU's most important habitats and species; Conserve and restore biodiversity and ecosystem services in wider EU countryside; Conserve and restore biodiversity and ecosystem services in wider EU marine environment; Reinforce compatibility of regional and territorial development with biodiversity in the EU; Substantially reduce the impact on EU biodiversity of invasive alien species and alien genotypes; Substantially strengthen effectiveness of international governance for biodiversity and ecosystem services; Substantially strengthen support for biodiversity and ecosystem services in EU external assistance; Substantially reduce the impact of international trade on global biodiversity and ecosystem services; Support biodiversity adaptation to climate change; and Substantially strengthen the knowledge base for conservation and sustainable use of biodiversity, in the EU and globally).

The policy areas and objectives are a welcome step beyond monitoring and documenting biodiversity loss. However, the Communication's fate is bound up with the species it aims to protect, wholly dependent on swift and successful implementation. In this context, the four key supporting measures, deemed essential to the achievement of the articulated targets and objectives, are promising as well: ensuring adequate funding; strengthening EU decision-making; building partnerships; and building public education, awareness, and participation.

Lastly, the Communication makes provision for monitoring, evaluation, and review of the progress in implementation of the Action Plan. The Commission commits to reporting to Council and European Parliament (EP) annually. The second report (late 2008) will serve as a mid-term review, the fourth (late 2010) will report whether the EU has met its 2010 commitments, and the seventh report (late 2013) will evaluate progress made towards the post-2010 targets included in

[8] Johannesburg (South Africa), 26 Aug.–4 Sept. 2002.

the plan. The Commission commits further to launch a debate on a longer-term vision for biodiversity in the EU. Thus far, biodiversity loss has been accelerating, rather than slowing down. Meaningful progress will require intensive efforts to overcome inertia and reverse these trends.

B. Commission Communication on an EU Forest Action Plan[9]

The Council adopted a forestry strategy resolution in 1998,[10] on which the Commission reported for five years, and proposed inter alia the launch of an EU Action Plan on sustainable forest management. The Council requested that the Commission present that action plan in 2006.[11] The answering Plan puts forward a framework for action and policy coordination at the Community and Member State levels. Its overall objective of supporting and enhancing sustainable forest management and the multifunctionality of forests reflects the primary challenges of forestry policy, namely balancing the many roles and services forests perform and the attendant overlaps to be negotiated across diverse policy areas. The Plan is built upon four basic principles: (i) national forest programmes as a suitable framework for implementing international forest-related commitments; (ii) the increasing importance of global and cross-sectoral issues in forest policy, calling for improved coherence and coordination; (iii) the need to enhance the competitiveness of the EU forest sector and good governance of EU forests; and (iv) respect for the principle of subsidiarity.

It is interesting to note the Communication's highlighting that the Plan's vision of forestry and the role of forests in modern society is one that is already shared between the Commission and the Member States. The Commission has chosen a concerted, agreed plan of action, under which long-term multifunctional forestry shall endeavour to meet present and future needs and support livelihoods. This common vision is to be implemented in accordance with four specific objectives: (i) improving long-term competitiveness; (ii) improving and protecting the environment; (iii) contributing to the quality of life; and (iv) fostering coordination and communication.

To ensure the implementation of the four mentioned objectives, the Plan translates them into a five-year Action Plan (2007 to 2011) requiring the Commission and the Members States to undertake the following specific *Key Actions*:

1. Study the effects of globalization on the economic viability and competitiveness of EU forestry, in order to identify the main factors influencing the sector and underpin discussions on further action for its enhancement;

[9] COM(2006)302, 15 June 2006.

[10] Council Resolution of 15 Dec. 1998 on a Forestry Strategy for the European Union [1999] OJ C56/26.

[11] Council Conclusions on an EU Forest Action Plan, 2662nd meeting of the Agriculture and Fisheries Council, 30–31 May 2005.

2. Encourage research and technological development to enhance the competitiveness of the forest sector;
3. Exchange and assess experiences on the valuation and marketing of non-wood forest goods and services, with the aim of quantifying the total value of forests and their functions, in order to introduce instruments to compensate for non-marketed goods and services;
4. Promote the use of forest biomass for energy generation, through support of existing efforts, exchange and evaluation of experiences and resource assessments, and ongoing technological research and design;
5. Foster cooperation between forest owners and enhance education and training in forestry, so as to contribute to new market-oriented approaches, dissemination of best practices, and forest-owners' skills in biodiversity enhancement and habitat restoration;
6. Facilitate EU compliance with obligations under the United Nations Framework Convention on Climate Change (UNFCCC)[12] and its Kyoto Protocol,[13] and encourage research on, and adaptation to, the effects of climate change;
7. Contribute to achieving the revised Community biodiversity objectives for 2010 and beyond, by supporting information exchange, pilot projects, monitoring and research;
8. Work towards a European Forest Monitoring System, to ensure a coherent data system that both draws and expands on existing information for environmental, economic, and social indicators;
9. Enhance the protection of EU forests from biotic and abiotic agents, through research and both voluntary and regulatory schemes;
10. Encourage environmental education and information, in order to ensure that the benefits of sustainable forest management are appreciated by society;
11. Maintain and enhance the protective functions of forests, through investment and awareness-raising activities;
12. Explore the potential of urban and peri-urban forests with the aim of establishing appropriate long-term indicators and frameworks for their maintenance and management;
13. Strengthen the role of the Standing Forestry Committee;
14. Strengthen coordination between policy areas in forest-related matters;

[12] New York, NY (US), 9 May 1992 (entered into force 21 Mar. 1994), (1992) 31 *International Legal Materials* 4, 849; published on the Internet at: http://unfccc.int.

[13] Kyoto (Japan), 10 Dec. 1997 (entered into force 16 Feb. 2005) (1998) 37 *International Legal Materials*, 22; published on the Internet at: http://unfccc.int.

15. Apply the open method of coordination to national forest programmes;
16. Strengthen the EU profile in international forest-related processes, through financial support and careful coordination at all levels within the EU, and ensuring that the role of forests is considered in economic and development cooperation resource allocation;
17. Encourage the use of wood and other forest products from sustainably managed forests, through innovation, research and development, education, training, and information activities; and
18. Improve information exchange and communication, in order to enhance public awareness and consideration of forestry in policy-making, including the development of a forestry site on the Europa website.[14]

The Communication also includes further actions that the Member States may implement according to their individual conditions and priorities. Because the Commission no longer has a financial instrument dedicated specifically to forests, the Communication lists alternative Community instruments that may provide financial support for forestry-related efforts, making note where they may provide support for additional efforts undertaken at the national level. The Plan calls for the Commission to carry out a mid-term evaluation of the Plan in 2009, and a final evaluation in 2012.

The Plan is disappointing, insofar as it tends to restate policy actions that have already been agreed upon in prior documents. Furthermore, many of the activities recommended are too vague and general to inform, let alone compel, meaningful action. With European forests struggling in the face of industry competition from the developing world, illegal logging, increased consumer demands, and ongoing environmental degradation, the Plan hardly seems sufficient. In addition, the Plan's promotion of forests as a source of bioenergy may have negative consequences for competing forestry industries and will require careful monitoring to protect and preserve these vital resources.

C. Commission Communication: Thematic Strategy for Soil Protection[15]

This Communication was produced in accordance with the call for the development of a Thematic Strategy on Soil Protection[16] under the Sixth Environmental Action Programme of 2002,[17] and is accompanied by a Proposal for a Directive Establishing a Framework for the Protection of Soil and Amending Directive

[14] See on the Internet at: http://europa.eu.int.

[15] COM(2006)231, 22 Sept. 2006.

[16] Commission Communication: Towards a Thematic Strategy for Soil Protection COM (2002)179, 6 Apr. 2002.

[17] N. 2 above.

2004/35/EC.[18] It begins with an accurate introduction to the definition and importance of soil, which provides food, biomass, raw materials; serves as a habitat and gene pool; and stores, filters and modifies water and nutrients, including carbon, of which it is the largest store on the planet. Soil is vital to human and ecosystem survival, and essentially non-renewable. Several degradation processes pose a serious threat to Europe's soil, spurred and exacerbated by human activity, with formidable environmental, economic, social, and cultural consequences.

The Communication then examines the current state of soil policy at the national, European, and international levels, rightly concluding that, while awareness of its importance is on the rise and several existing agricultural and environmental policies contribute to soil protection, the need for a comprehensive policy that addresses all soils and soil threats remains. The Communication proposes a strategy with an overall objective of protection and sustainable use, based on two principles:

1. Preventing further soil degradation and preserving its functions:
   - when soil is used and its functions are exploited, action has to be taken on soil use and management patterns; and
   - when soil acts as a sink/receptor of the effects of human activities or environmental phenomena, action has to be taken at source.
2. Restoring degraded soils to a level of functionality consistent at least with current and intended use, thus also considering the cost implications of the restoration of soil.

Action at the Community level is justified by reference to the impact soil degradation has on the EC's other environmental legislation and concerns; the need for consistency across the internal market; and concerns regarding transboundary impacts, protecting the health of European citizens, and international competitiveness and leadership. Unfortunately, the Strategy never moves beyond common principles, objectives and actions, leaving the most material aspects to the Member States and, ultimately, leaving much to be desired.

The strategy centres around four key pillars: (i) the adoption of framework legislation; (ii) the integration of soil protection in the formulation and implementation of national and Community policies; (iii) closing the current recognized knowledge gap in certain areas of soil protection through research supported by EC and national research programmes; and (iv) increasing public awareness on the need for soil protection. More specifically, with the first pillar of its strategy, the Commission proposes a Framework Directive requiring Member States to adopt specific measures for soil protection while providing for flexibility in tailoring their implementation to local needs. Member States would be required to identify areas threatened by erosion, organic matter decline, salinization,

[18] COM(2006)232, 22 Sept. 2006.

compaction, and landslides, and adopt objectives and programmes for their measurement and mitigation. The proposed Directive also calls for Member States to take appropriate measures to prevent, identify and remediate soil contamination, including reporting requirements for transactions involving potentially polluted sites. The Directive would also require Member States to take steps to limit sealing, including mitigation of impact where it cannot be avoided and brownfield rehabilitation. Lastly, the Directive calls for Member States to undertake efforts to raise awareness about the importance of soil, to promote knowledge and experience transfers, and to report to the Commission on their performance and implementation of these mandates. The proposed Directive seems to accord far too much discretion to the Member States. Stricter common Community criteria should be established to avoid too many national variations in the application of its provisions.

In addition to the four key pillars mentioned above, the Commission outlines several further steps to be undertaken in the immediate-term, including harmonizing soil protection with efforts underway in the fields of climate change, river basin and coastal waters management, product policies, and under the United Nations Convention to Combat Desertification (UNCCD),[19] the CBD,[20] the Kyoto Protocol,[21] and the Convention on the Protection of the Alps (Alpine Convention),[22] so as to ensure mutual support, consistency, and complementariness. Nonetheless, the absence of enforceable targets and uniform standards renders the strategy too weak to counter the ongoing degradation of Europe's soils.

D. Commission Communication: An EU Strategy for Biofuels[23]

Transport causes about 21 per cent of all greenhouse gases (GHGs) in the EU and its contribution to global warming is increasing. In order to meet its Kyoto commitments, the EU needs to find ways to reduce emissions from the transport sector. Oil is still the main source of energy for transport, a source which comes with environmental and several other challenges: security of supply, shortage and limited supply, increasing costs, and so on. This communication examines the role that biofuels can play in addressing energy needs in the transport sector. Biofuels are, in fact, a direct substitute for fossil fuels and are processed from biomass; a renewable, and therefore greener, resource. The Communication represents a

[19] Paris (France), 17 June 1994 (entered into force 26 Dec. 1996), (1994) 33 *International Legal Materials*, 1328; published on the Internet at: http://www.unccd.int.

[20] N. 6 above.

[21] N. 13 above.

[22] Salzburg (Austria), 7 Nov. 1991 (entered into force 6 Mar. 1995), (1991) 31 *International Legal* Materials, 767; published on the Internet at: http://www.conventionalpine.org.

[23] COM(2006)34, 18 Mar. 2006.

natural progression from the Biomass Action Plan.[24] It begins by setting out an EU Strategy for Biofuels that aims to: (i) promote biofuels in the EU and developing countries; (ii) prepare for the large-scale use of biofuels; and (iii) explore opportunities in the developing world to produce biofuel-feedstocks and biofuels. The Strategy itself is made up of the following seven policy axes, under which measures are introduced that will allow the Commission to promote the production and use of biofuels:

1. *Stimulating the demand for biofuels.* The Commission's Strategy will include new biofuel obligations in an effort to avoid the failed tax exemptions regime under Directive 2003/30/EC on the Promotion of the Use of Biofuels or Other Renewable Fuels for Transport (Biofuels Directive).[25] The Commission also suggests establishing a framework for incentives linked to the environmental performance of individual fuels;
2. *Capturing the environmental benefits of biofuels.* To capture these benefits, the Strategy rightly focuses on (i) optimizing GHG benefits; (ii) avoiding environmental damage linked to the production of biofuels and their feedstocks; and (iii) ensuring that the use of biofuels does not give rise to environmental or technical problems;
3. *Developing the production and distribution of biofuels.* The Communication recognizes a distinct comparative advantage in the production of biofuel feedstocks in Central and Eastern Europe (CEE), on account of the region's low labour costs and high resource availability. It therefore appropriately encourages CEE countries to take into account the benefits of biofuels when preparing their National Strategic Reference Frameworks and operational programmes;
4. *Expanding feedstock supplies.* An economic incentive to expand feedstock supplies already exists: The reform of the Common Agricultural Policy (CAP), which began in 1992, includes a set-aside obligation that prevents a certain amount of land from being used for any type of production; however, the cultivation of non-food crops is authorized, providing an incentive to utilize otherwise barren land. The Commission indicates that it is considering further incentives, as well;
5. *Enhancing trade opportunities.* Bio-ethanol currently enters the EU duty-free under a number of preferential trade arrangements. To continue this important preferential treatment, the Commission will pursue a balanced approach in ongoing bilateral and multilateral trade negotiations with ethanol producing countries, with the goal of maintaining its market access through favourable conditions;

[24] Commission Communication: Biomass Action Plan COM(2005)628, 7 Dec. 2005.
[25] [2003] OJ L123/42.

6. *Supporting developing countries.* The Commission's proposal for accompanying measures to the EU sugar reform is essential. These measures will provide the framework needed to support the ethanol sector in countries affected by the reform;
7. *Supporting research and development.* The Commission's Cooperation Specific Programme will address this issue by focusing on reducing the unit cost of fuels by improving conventional technologies and developing second-generation biofuels. The Commission is also rightly interested in applying life sciences and biotechnology to improve biomass production systems.

The Commission hopes these measures will help support biofuels in an effort to reduce GHG emissions, boost the decarbonization of transport fuels, diversify fuels supply sources, and develop long-term replacements for fossil oil. However, while the Strategy outlines a wide range of promising initiatives, the relative paucity of specific commitments largely leaves implementation up to a Union that, in many areas, has yet to prove capable of translating political rhetoric into action.

E. Commission Communication—Action Plan for Energy Efficiency: Realizing the Potential[26]

Europe wastes at least 20 per cent of its energy due to inefficiency. The cost of this inefficiency will amount to more than €100 billion annually by 2020. This Communication combats the trend by setting forth an Action Plan, outlining a framework of policies and measures for realizing the 20 per cent estimated savings potential in the EU's annual energy consumption. The specific measures the Commission plans to take are set out in an accompanying Annex. The Communication focuses on the four sectors with the greatest cost-effective savings potential: (i) commercial buildings; (ii) households; (iii) transport; and (iv) the manufacturing industry.

Ten priority actions covering all energy sectors are proposed for immediate initiation and implementation as soon as possible: (i) appliance and equipment labelling and minimum energy performance standards; (ii)building performance requirements and very low energy buildings ('passive houses'); (iii) making power generation and distribution more efficient; (iv) achieving fuel efficiency of cars; (v) facilitating appropriate financing of energy efficiency investments for small and medium enterprises and Energy Service Companies; (vi) spurring energy efficiency in the new Member States; (vii) a coherent use of taxation; (viii) raising energy efficiency awareness; (ix) energy efficiency in built-up areas; and (x) foster energy efficiency worldwide.

[26] COM(2006)545, 19 Oct. 2006.

The recommended actions and priority actions are all laudable. However, little details are given on how they are to be achieved in the near future. Furthermore, scepticism on the possibility of implementing some of these actions is justified by the Community's failure over the years to make significant progress, for example, in the use of taxation for environmental purposes or in its quest for achieving better fuel efficiency in cars. Probably, to limit these criticisms, these measures will be subject to thorough individual impact assessments, and a mid-term review in 2009 to assess the progress achieved in the framework of the regular Strategic European Energy Reviews. While the Plan presents an impressive range of initiatives for increasing energy efficiency, persistent concerns about rebound effects undermine the championing of energy efficiency as a solution to both climate change and energy dependency.

F. Commission Communication: An Energy Policy for Europe[27]

This Communication is the central document in the Commission's 'Energy Package', which includes a total of eight other proposals, accompanied by corresponding impact assessments:

1. Communication on Prospects for the Internal Gas and Electricity Market;[28]
2. Communication on Priority Interconnection Plan;[29]
3. Communication on Green Paper Follow-up Action, Report on Progress in Renewable Electricity;[30]
4. Communication on Renewable Energy Road Map, Renewable Energies in the 21st Century: Building a Sustainable Future;[31]
5. Communication on Biofuels Progress Report, Report on the Progress Made in the Use of Biofuels and Other Renewable Fuels in the Member States of the European Union;[32]
6. Communication on Towards a European Strategic Energy Technology Plan;[33]
7. Communication on Sustainable Power Generation from Fossil Fuels: Aiming at Near-Zero Emissions from Coal after 2020;[34] and

[27] COM(2007)1, 10 Jan. 2007.
[28] COM(2006)841, 10 Jan. 2007.
[29] COM(2006)846, 10 Jan. 2007.
[30] COM(2006)849, 10 Jan. 2007.
[31] COM(2006)848, 10 Jan. 2007.
[32] COM(2006)845, 10 Jan. 2007.
[33] COM(2006)847, 10 Jan. 2007.
[34] COM(2006)843, 10 Jan. 2007.

8. Communication on Nuclear Illustrative Programme Presented under Article 40 of the Euratom Treaty for the opinion of the European Economic and Social Committee.[35]

The Overview Communication orders the package's various elements and presents an overall vision for the future of energy in Europe. It begins by laying out the three primary challenges that the package is intended to address: (i) sustainability, specifically in the context of climate change; (ii) energy security and independence; and (iii) market competitiveness, in terms of affordability for consumers, growth, job creation, and innovation. The challenges identified, in turn, inform a three-fold strategic objective directed at their resolution, which emphasizes the centrality of addressing GHG emissions to the creation of a sustainable, competitive, and secure energy market.

In the section that follows, the Communication presents its Action Plan for achieving the target objective by swiftly:

> transforming Europe into a high energy efficient and low CO_2 energy economy, [and] catalyzing a new industrial revolution . . . in a way that maximizes the potential competitiveness gains for Europe, and limits the potential costs.[36]

The accompanying Internal Energy Market Communication[37] reveals that, in spite of the many energy market measures already in place, Europe's energy system is still failing to deliver real choice for EU consumers. Furthermore, it appears that the shortcomings at the EU-level are leading to distortionary caps in national gas and electricity markets that may potentially suppress market entry, function and signals and, thereby, investment and performance. The Overview Communication, therefore, correctly emphasizes the need for cohesion across the EU's many energy industries, policies, and dimensions. In addition, the Commission identifies several additional requirements for meeting its 'revolutionary' goals:

Firstly, the energy network must undergo ownership 'unbundling', in which network companies are wholly separated from the supply and generation companies. Secondly, there is a need for effective regulation. The Commission calls for uniform, effective regulatory standards and a network of powerful, independent regulators tasked with promoting both their national energy markets and the new internal EU energy market. Thirdly, as requisite components of the new energy plan, the Commission calls for transparency, network security, adequate generation and supply capacity, and the establishment of an Energy Customers' Charter to assist the vulnerable, to increase public information, to cut down on paperwork, and to protect customers. Finally, the Commission refers to the five

[35] COM(2006)844, 10 Jan. 2007.
[36] N. 26 above, 5.
[37] COM(2006)841, 10 Jan. 2007.

infrastructure priorities set forth in the accompanying Priority Interconnection Plan Communication:[38]

1. identifying gaps and ensuring political support for their closure;
2. appointing European coordinators for key projects;
3. limiting planning and approval procedures to a five-year maximum for projects 'of European interest';
4. examining the need for funding increases, particularly for renewable electricity; and
5. establishing a new arrangement for Transmission System Operators.

Next, the Communication emphasizes the need to reinforce the bonds between Member States to promote the security of the oil supply and ensure solidarity should there ever be an energy crisis. In particular, the Commission calls for measures to strengthen existing solidarity mechanisms; to assist Member States that are overwhelmingly dependent on a single gas supplier to diversify; and to improve electricity interconnections, and gas stocks, transport capacity and storage strategies.

The next four parts of the Communication address the future of technologies required to meet EU goals. Firstly, the Commission reviews the progress achieved to date in the field of renewable energy. In spite of a 55 per cent increase in production, the EU is still not on track to meet its 2010 target of doubling 1997 renewables levels to a 12 per cent share in its overall energy mix. The Commission blames this pending shortfall on the lack of a coherent, effective framework and long-term vision at the EU level, which has led to uneven performance among Member States and a failure to achieve economy of scale. The Commission's solution is its Renewable Energy Road Map,[39] which calls for a new binding target of increasing renewables' share to 20 per cent of the overall EU energy mix by 2020. In conjunction with the Biofuels Progress Report Communication,[40] the Road Map also proposes a binding sectoral target for biofuels in vehicle fuels of 10 per cent. The biofuels target is worrisome because its underlying impact assessment does not examine the impacts and relative desirability of competing land-uses, and generally fails to make a compelling case for how the proposed scheme will ensure pro-environment outcomes. At the same time, the lack of any specific targets in other sectors is quite disappointing. While the Roadmap proposes a strengthening and expansion of the current regulatory framework, aside from the biofuels target, the Member States retain flexibility in selecting and promoting the renewable energies and policies of their choice. By not specifying measures or commitments for electricity, heating or cooling, the Road Map disserves the

[38] COM(2006)846, 10 Jan. 2007.
[39] COM(2006)848, 10 Jan. 2007.
[40] COM(2006)845, 10 Jan. 2007.

diverse needs of these emerging industries and markets, and risks succumbing to the same sad fate as its 2010-target predecessor.

Next, the Commission reviews its proposal for a European Strategic Energy Technology (SET) Plan,[41] which focuses on the technology that will play a vital role in the EU's efforts to extricate economic growth from environmental degradation. The SET-Plan proposal communication argues that investment in new energy technologies should be made a strategic priority for the EU. While several research framework programmes have yielded progress in wind energy, photovoltaics, and clean coal, a 'business as usual' approach is declared to be unacceptable moving forward. Likewise, greater investment is needed, above and beyond the 50 per cent spending increase provided for under the Seventh Framework Research Programme (FP7).[42] The Commission calls on Member States to mobilize public and private resources more effectively in response to the challenge. In an effort to guide the mobilization process, the envisioned SET-Plan would include a variety of technology push, demand pull, and integrated innovation instruments, with the goal of developing a world-class portfolio of affordable, competitive, efficient, and low-carbon technologies. With low carbon technology research and development chronically underfunded and poorly coordinated at this time, this proposal should be welcomed as a key requisite for meeting the EU's twin goals of sustainability across all sectors, and world leadership in low carbon innovation.

Thirdly, the Overview Communication highlights the importance of coal and gas to the European energy supply, and the Commission's Sustainable Power Generation Communication,[43] which discusses options for retaining these resources as generating fuels. The latter Communication identifies clean coal technologies and carbon dioxide (CO_2) capture and storage (CCS) as the processes that will usher in sustainable fossil fuels. It introduces plans to increase research and development funding; to support large-scale technology demonstrations; to create a consistent CCS regulatory framework at the EU level; to achieve international acceptance of CCS; and to establish a clear EU framework for phasing-in sustainable fossil fuels. The Communication concludes that the research and development costs and environmental risks associated with its strategy are outweighed by the emissions reductions and market competitiveness to be gained. There are several reasons to be sceptical of this cost-benefit analysis. To begin with, the technologies on which the predicted emissions reductions depend are still at an experimental stage; heavy emphasis is not yet warranted and quite risky. Furthermore, even assuming that CCS may one day be a viable option, the decades of delay while it is tested and perfected should effectively disqualify it

[41] COM(2006)847, 10 Jan. 2007.

[42] EP and Council Dec. No. 1982/2006/EC concerning the Seventh Framework Programme of the European Community for Research, Technological Development and Demonstration Activities (2007–2013) [2006] OJ L412/1.

[43] COM(2006)843, 10 Jan. 2007.

from high prioritization, given the urgent need for emissions reductions today. One should also take note that the success of these initiatives would largely depend on the cooperation and initiative of the fossil fuels industries, a reliance that may very well be misplaced. Lastly, the Commission's failure to address the issue of coal sector subsidies, on which a report was due in late 2006, constitutes an omission as glaring as it is disappointing.

The last technology to be considered is nuclear power. The Commission recognizes nuclear energy as one of the cheapest and most stable sources of low carbon energy produced in the EU; however, it also acknowledges the risks involved. Rather than pronouncing a European position, the overview document leaves the fate of nuclear power to the Member States. The accompanying discussion paper, the Illustrative Nuclear Programme Communication[44] sets out a field of EU activities that is limited to ensuring that any reduction in nuclear electricity be made up by other low-carbon sources; supporting advances in waste management and decommissioning; developing an advanced framework for ensuring the highest standards of safety, security, and non-proliferation; and promoting compliance with such standards internationally. While the proposed Programme also includes the establishment of an EU High Level Group on Nuclear Safety and Security, charged with developing understanding and regulations in the nuclear field, the reality is that in fact this proposal contains nothing in the way of significant new initiatives. Ultimately, the Programme is arguably a plan for doing very little, which suggests that the Commission shares the environmental community's valid doubts and reservations about nuclear power, and preference for alternative low-carbon sources.

The Commission concludes the overview energy policy document by noting the importance of international cooperation. In light of its ever shrinking share of global energy emissions and consumption, neither the EU, nor its individual Member States, can achieve climate and energy security alone. It is, therefore, of the utmost importance that the Community agree on uniform policies with which to engage its international partners in mutual trust, cooperation, and interdependence. Trade is highlighted as an area in which the Commission encourages ongoing and future international agreement on legally binding commitments, particularly in the extension of reciprocal access and liberalization. The international climate regime, energy supply stream, financial structures, and nuclear safety are, likewise, identified as priority areas for the new external energy policy. In addition, the Commission calls for a comprehensive Africa-Europe energy partnership, and for a more general integration of Europe's energy and development policies, which it heralds as a win-win situation. Europe and its developing country partners share a vital interest in price stability, diversification, and energy efficiency. The Communication, therefore, suggests that the EU concentrate on delivering affordable, reliable, and sustainable energy services to

[44] COM(2006)844, 10 Jan. 2007.

the poor, thereby building a market for its energy innovations while assisting the South to develop its own clean energy future.

While inspiring and admirable in its aspirations, this closing section cannot redeem its predecessors, which overwhelmingly fall into one of two disappointing categories: benign pronouncements lacking any real commitments, as in the renewables and nuclear fields, or troublesome initiatives on less desirable sources, such as biofuels, coal, and gas. Overall, the Communication falls short of delivering on its promise of revolution, taking, instead, a path which too seldom breaks from the past, and too often in the wrong direction.

G. Commission Communication—Limiting Global Climate Change to 2 Degrees Celsius: The Way Ahead for 2020 and Beyond[45]

This Communication was adopted alongside the energy policy package reviewed above, and contributes a central element to the Commission's vision for a revolution in EU energy policy: a unilateral commitment to reduce EU GHG emissions to 20 per cent below the 1990 baseline by 2020; and a commitment to adopt a 30 per cent target if agreement can be reached on a post-2012 framework that includes comparable commitments from other industrialized nations, and contributions from advanced developing countries as well. The Communication presents a compelling case for immediate action to reduce emissions: failure to act on global climate change will have serious local and global security implications. It begins by weighing the costs and benefits associated with resource use efficiency. It cites the excellent Stern Review,[46] which claims that the failure to include the costs of climate change in market prices carries an enormous economic and social cost of 5 to 20 per cent of global GDP. The Commission also refers to its own Action Plan for Energy Efficiency to bolster the economic case for policies that increase resource efficiency. Based on these findings, the Commission concludes that the benefits of limiting climate change outweigh the costs. Where the Communication falters, however, is in proposing, as its solution, the unambitious 20 per cent target.

Present scientific consensus overwhelmingly suggests that a 20 per cent reduction will not be sufficient to achieve the EU's longstanding objective of limiting global average temperature increases to under two degrees Celsius above pre-industrialized levels. Furthermore, the unambitious unilateral commitment may well undermine European bargaining power and credibility in the international negotiations on the next Kyoto agreement, thereby effectively levelling aspirations for more vigorous reduction commitments at the global level.

[45] COM(2007)2, 10 Jan. 2007.

[46] N. Stern, *The Economics of Climate Change: The Stern Review* (Cambridge: Cambridge University Press, 2007); also published on the Internet at: http://www.sternreview.org.uk.

While the proposed 20 per cent unilateral commitment constitutes a major scientific and political disappointment, the Communication does offer some satisfactory recommendations, including strengthening the EU emission trading scheme; limiting transport emissions, and reducing emissions in other sectors; increasing research and technological development; and strengthening public awareness. The Communication also addresses the issue of Northern reductions being overwhelmed by the increasing emissions of the developing South with a number of suggestions including: (i) streamlining and expanding the Kyoto Protocol's CDM; (ii) improving access to finance for new electricity technology; (iii) introducing sector-wide emissions trading; and (iv) adjusting emissions limits in accordance with a nation's level of development.

Overall, however, there is nothing in this Communication that has not been heard before; no new ideas for tackling climate change. Instead, the Commission has disregarded the overwhelming scientific and political arguments for a far more rigorous and ambitious set of actions and objectives, ultimately settling for an approach that disappoints on all accounts.

H. Commission Communication—Mobilizing Public and Private Finance Towards Global Access to Climate-Friendly, Affordable and Secure Energy Services: The Global Energy Efficiency and Renewable Energy Fund[47]

This Communication, happily, introduces an exciting and innovative new public private partnership (PPP) for mobilizing investment in sustainable energy in the developing world. The document begins by reviewing the evidence of ever-increasing economic growth and energy consumption worldwide, followed by the observation that traditional energy sources are neither financially nor environmentally viable alternatives for meeting the ever-growing demand. In particular, the Commission highlights GHG emissions, air pollution, equality of access to energy resources, and energy security as primary obstacles to ongoing reliance on the existing energy infrastructure and investment scenario. In their place, the Communication advances investment in renewable energy and energy efficiency as the most promising approaches for addressing these concerns and realizing sustainable energy development worldwide. The challenge, which this Communication seeks to address, is enabling and incentivizing the private investment necessary to achieve a sustainable energy sector for the entire planet.

Part Two examines the current barriers to efficiency and renewables investment. Higher initial capital costs, private equity investor hesitancy to invest in many developing countries, and international financial institution (IFI) terms that are not suited to small-scale projects, are formidable obstacles that disadvantage

[47] COM(2006)583, 6 Oct. 2006.

these sustainable alternatives in the competitive equity sector. The Commission argues that the multitude of socio-economic and environmental benefits that renewables and efficiency have to offer, merit public support for dissolving the gridlock and dismantling the barriers to their financing and growth. Therefore, the Communication proposes a Global Energy Efficiency and Renewable Energy Fund (GEEREF), to create and finance regional sub-funds for global sustainable energy investment.

The GEEREF is the Commission's proposal for meeting the urgent need for innovative and flexible funding mechanisms to accelerate sustainable development, to enhance implementation of the Kyoto mechanisms, and to integrate energy solutions into development assistance. Enhancing private access to equity through public patient capital provides many benefits, including:

- lower returns are made more palatable, and eventually lifted towards commercial thresholds;
- longer investment and repayment periods balance high upfront investments and low operating and maintenance costs; and
- higher transaction costs become less of an obstacle, empowering smaller businesses and capital demands.

The envisioned global risk-capital fund, it is hoped, would mobilize private and public investment in sound energy technologies in the South.

The proposed GEEREF would be established under private law with a public sector mission of providing risk capital for sustainable energy projects, in close partnership with the European Investment Bank (EIB), and the European Bank for Reconstruction and Development (EBRD). The Fund would offer innovative risk sharing and co-funding options for investors through new and existing regional sub-funds that support small developers and enterprises of proven renewables and efficiency technologies. While renewable energy is expected to dominate, the Commission believes hydro, biomass, and on-shore wind also have great potential. The focus of the Fund would be on projects under €10 million, spanning from utility-based projects to manufacturing and assembly companies, as well as to consumer, small and medium-sized enterprises (SME), and microfinance intermediaries. In addition, 10 to 20 per cent of the Fund will be devoted to technical assistance, depending on actual capacity building needs, to make it a full-service entity and to reduce transaction costs and to improve its overall performance. While the GEEREF will place special emphasis on African, Caribbean and Pacific (ACP) countries, it will also support regional sub-funds in the European Neighborhood, Latin America, and Asia.

The minimum funding target for the proposed Fund is set at €100 million to ensure immediate effectiveness and long-term sustainability. In addition to the prospects of absorbing additional capital and reinvestment of the initial public funds, the Commission hopes the GEEREF could be replicated by other investors. With these benefits in mind, the Commission predicts that the fully invested and leveraged Fund could provide close to one Gigawatt of sustainable energy capacity to the developing country markets, serving one to three million people, and saving one to two million tonnes of CO_2 equivalents every year. Furthermore, the Fund would broaden the range of instruments for the transfer, development, and deployment of sustainable energy technologies, thereby accelerating their global reach and market.

The GEEREF Communication is a highly appealing proposal that brightens and comes close to redeeming the Commission's otherwise disappointing energy policy portfolio in the period under review. The expression of interest from the EIB is particularly welcome, in light of the many past critiques of its project selection, community relations, accountability, and project monitoring. The principles outlined in the GEEREF Communication have the potential to radically improve the social and environmental consequences of bank-lending. With its exciting promise of guiding and increasing investment in the technologies and countries that need and deserve it most, the GEEREF is a welcome initiative to watch.

I. Commission Communication—Establishing an Environment Strategy for the Mediterranean[48]

The Mediterranean is the largest sea in Europe, bordering seven Member States, two accession countries, and over a dozen third countries. This shared body of water creates clear ecosystem interdependence between its bordering nations and requires a coherent, region-wide system of environmental protection and cooperation. To this end, leaders of the nations under the Euro-Mediterranean Partnership (EMP) adopted a five-year work programme in 2005 for substantially reducing pollution of the Mediterranean Sea by 2020. The Commission prepared this Communication to outline this programme, which has come to be called the 'Horizon 2020' initiative, and to propose a depollution timetable. Additionally, the Communication suggests how the Commission may parallel national efforts through broader cooperation and coordination with third country partners.

As the Member States' are subject to existing EU environmental policies, legislation, and enforcement, this Communication focuses, instead, on a strategy for working with regional partners under the EMP. Its basic aims are as follows:

- to assist partner countries to develop environmental institutions, policy, and enforcement, and a legal framework for integrating environmental concerns into sectoral policies;
- to reduce pollution and uncontrolled activity across the region, leading to corresponding health benefits;

[48] COM(2006)475, 5 Sept. 2006.

- to promote preparedness of the environment administrations to address both emergency situations as well as punctual and long-term environment issues;
- to promote a more sustainable (economically efficient, socially appropriate and environmentally viable) use of the land and sea areas in the Mediterranean region;
- to promote a strengthened civil society, in which the public has access to environmental information, participates in environmental decision-making, and environmental awareness is enhanced; and
- to encourage regional cooperation amongst partner countries to support these aims.

The means to achieve these objectives are divided into four areas: (i) financial assistance; (ii) strengthening dialogue and ownership; (iii) coordination mechanisms; and (iv) sharing EU experience. While Community funding may be available through the European Neighbourhood and Partnership Instrument and other programmes, the Commission makes clear that primary assistance will continue to flow from international financial institutions, donors, and national resources.

The Communication details EU engagement in political dialogue with partner countries through formal regional and international structures (EMP, European Neighbourhood Policy, the New Partnership for Africa's Development (NEPAD), and the African Union (AU)), indicating that the Commission will ensure a heightened profile and integration of environmental considerations in all relevant policy sectors. The Commission will also support the development of regional networks of non-governmental organizations (NGOs), as well as national NGO platforms.

As far as concerns mechanisms to enhance coordination, the Commission pledges to continue its cooperation efforts under the 1976 Barcelona Convention,[49] the 2005 joint Mediterranean Action Plan/European Commission Work Programme, in particular the European Marine Strategy, the European Strategy for Integrated Coastal Zone Management, and pollution and biodiversity targets; and its relationships with the international financial institutions (World Bank, Global Environment Facility (GEF), and EIB). The Communication also promises the transfer, adaptation, and application of EU experience through the Tourism Sustainability Group (TSG) of the Technical Assistance and Information Exchange Instrument (TAIEX).

[49] Convention concerning Cooperation in Preventing Pollution from Ships and in Combating Pollution of the Mediterranean Sea by Oil and Hazardous and Noxious Substances in Cases of Emergency 1976, Barcelona (Spain), 16 Feb. 1976 (entered into force 12 Feb. 1978), revised on 10 June 1995, (1976) 15 *International Legal Materials*, 290; published on the Internet at: http://www.unep.ch/regionalseas/regions/med/t_barcel.htm.

With these means at its disposal, the Commission proposes the following four categories of Horizon 2020 activities, a timetable for which is provided in an Annex to the Communication:

1. Pollution reduction projects in the high priority sectors of municipal waste, urban waste-water, and industrial emissions;
2. Capacity building measures, including through development of legislation, institutions, and support for local authorities and civil society;
3. Research efforts will be continued to create, share, and communicate scientific knowledge supporting the aims of Horizon 2020; and
4. Monitoring, steering, and review of the programme, including the development of a scorecard for measuring progress and the formation of a consultative steering committee to oversee implementation.

Beyond the emphasis on pollution under Horizon 2020, the Commission proposes to engage the Mediterranean partners in several additional complimentary activities:

- Fully implementing the ENP Action Plans;
- Integrating environmental considerations into other sectors, including economics and trade;
- Addressing global and regional environmental threats, such as climate change, drought, flooding, biodiversity loss, soil degradation, forest fires, coastal zone management, and water scarcity;
- Promoting EIA and SEA throughout the region; and
- The production of relevant indicators through regional statistical cooperation mechanisms.

Through this promising strategy, the Commission seeks to assist its partners in meeting their environmental responsibilities in protecting and restoring this shared resource. In addition to contributing the knowledge gained in past European and regional efforts, the EU has an important role to play in raising the political profile of these issues, to encourage the greatest degree of interest and cooperation among the partners. As such, the success of the initiative, in many ways, depends on the EU's ability to lead its neighbours, while also encouraging them to bring their own experience and expertise to bear, so as to ensure coherence and synergy with existing initiatives and maximize local ownership and investment in the programme. To this end, the EU should focus intently on securing the involvement of all relevant actors, particularly local stakeholders and non-governmental and civil society organizations. By doing so, the EU would lay the foundation for the parallel political support and policy framework needed to ensure the long-term sustainability of the depollution infrastructure and its achievements.

III. Summaries of Reports

During the period under review, the Commission has produced several reports as required by various directives and regulations on their implementation, including the following:

- Commission Communication: Building a Global Carbon Market—Report pursuant to Article 30 of Directive 2003/87/EC;[50]
- Commission Communication: Report on the Operation of Regulation (EC) No. 304/2003 Concerning the Export and Import of Dangerous Chemicals;[51]
- Commission Communication: Report on the Implementation of Directive 94/62/EC on Packaging and Packaging Waste and its Impact on the Environment, as well as on the Functioning of the Internal Market;[52]
- Commission Communication: Report on the Implementation of Directive 79/409/EEC on the Conservation of Wild Birds;[53]
- Commission Communication: Second Report on the Experience of Member States with GMOs Placed on the Market under Directive 2001/18/EC on the Deliberate Release into the Environment of Genetically Modified Organisms;[54]
- Commission Communication: Report from the Commission to the Council and the European Parliament on the Implementation of Regulation (EC) No. 1830/2003 Concerning the Traceability and Labelling of Genetically Modified Organisms and the Traceability of Food and Feed Products Produced from Genetically Modified Organisms and Amending Directive 2001/18/EC;[55]
- Commission Communication: Towards Sustainable Water Management in the European Union—First Stage in the Implementation of the Water Framework Directive 2000/60/EC;[56]
- Commission Communication: Report on the Implementation of Community Waste Legislation;[57]
- Commission Communication: Report on the Implementation of Council Regulation (EEC) No. 259/93 on the Supervision and Control of Shipments of Waste within, into and out of the European Community—Generation,

[50] COM(2006)676, 13 Nov. 2006.
[51] COM(2006)747, 30 Nov. 2006.
[52] COM(2006)767, 6 Dec. 2006.
[53] COM(2006)164, 12 Apr. 2006.
[54] COM(2007)81, 5 Mar. 2007.
[55] COM(2006)197, 10 May 2006.
[56] COM(2007)128, 22 Mar. 2007.
[57] COM(2006)406, 19 July 2006.

Treatment and Transboundary Shipment of Hazardous Waste and Other Waste in the Member States of the European Union (1997–2000);[58]

- Commission Communication: Report on the Targets contained in Article 7(2)(b) of Directive 2000/53/EC on End-of-Life Vehicles.[59]

The following section will focus on one such document, that is of particular interest for readers of the *Yearbook*: the Commission's Progress Report on its Sustainable Development Strategy.

A. Commission Communication: Progress Report on the Sustainable Development Strategy 2007[60]

This progress report is the first evaluation of the EU Sustainable Development Strategy (SDS) since the adoption of the renewed Strategy in 2006,[61] which introduced seven core objectives, and is intended to serve as the baseline against which future progress shall be measured. It also provides the basis for discussions regarding the course and speed of activities in the context of adjusting longer-term targets and objectives.

Before reviewing progress under the seven key challenges set out in the 2006 SDS, the Communication notes that ensuring cohesion and partnership across all levels of governance and sectors is a key imperative and that developments under several of the core objectives demonstrate that engagement of all actors is possible. The Communication then examines the state of play in each of the seven challenge areas, as well as specific EU and Member State activities undertaken in their pursuit, observing their interlinkages and mutual support:

Climate change and clean energy: Europe is reducing greenhouse gases (GHGs) and is on track to achieve its Kyoto targets, pending Member State establishment and implementation of additional policies and measures as planned. In particular, the promotion of renewable energy sources will play an important role in meeting these commitments. Significant policy developments in furtherance of this objective include the EC's Integrated Climate Change and Energy policy, the Energy Efficiency Action Plan, and the Communications on an Energy Policy for Europe and on Limiting Global Climate Change, discussed above;[62] and Member States' national strategies, offices and scientific councils, and emissions trading (ET) allocation plans. Ongoing efforts are required in ensuring a successful ET scheme, increasing reliance on renewables, promoting sustainable biofuels use, and developing strategies and plans for adaptation.

[58] COM(2006)430, 1 Aug. 2006.

[59] COM(2007)5, 16 Jan. 2007.

[60] COM(2007)642, 22 Oct. 2007.

[61] Renewed EU Sustainable Development Strategy, adopted by the European Council on 15–16 June 2006, Council Doc. 10917/06, of 26 June 2006.

[62] See nn. 26 and 45 above, respectively.

Sustainable Transport: Further efforts are required to move the EU towards sustainable transport. While progress has been made on reducing pollutant emissions and accident fatalities, energy consumption in this sector is growing, with attendant increases in GHG emissions. Noteworthy policy developments include the Commission's mid-term review of the Transport White Paper,[63] and its proposals to amend the fuel quality and minimum road diesel excise rates directives, and include aviation in the ET scheme;[64] the Green Paper on Urban Mobility;[65] the revision of the legal framework for public transport services; and the adoption of the Euro 5 and 6 standards, and the railway liberalization package. At the national level, Member States' progress includes transport strategies, and the integration of sustainable transport into existing strategies; lorry tolls; tax and road infrastructure modernization; fiscal measures to encourage GHG emissions reductions; and public transport and road safety initiatives. Additional efforts are required to stimulate green technology; to tighten standards and GHG intensity; to map and reduce noise; to launch urban mobility and logistics action; and to devise methods for infrastructure charging.

Sustainable Consumption and Production: The Commission notes that consumption and production are difficult to measure; however, Resource Productivity indicators suggest that material consumption is being decoupled from economic growth. In addition, the number of businesses reporting on environmental performance is increasing, as is the marketing of sustainable products and services. Still, considerable potential remains. Efforts in this sector include eco-design under the Energy Using Products Directive;[66] the EU Environmental Technologies Plan;[67] an Environmental Technologies Verification System; and eco-labelling and environmental monitoring in cooperation with the Member States. The Member States are also making strides with publicity campaigns, corporate social responsibility, green public procurement, and business innovation and green technology. Additional opportunities are noted in strengthening these existing initiatives, fostering research, and implementing the Integrated Product Policy (IPP) approach.

[63] Commission Communication: Keep Europe Moving—Sustainable Mobility for Our Continent—Mid-term Review of the European Commission's 2001 Transport White Paper COM(2006)314, 22 June 2006.

[64] Commission Proposal for a Council Directive Amending Directive 2003/96/EC as regards the Adjustment of Special Tax Arrangements for Gas Oil Used as Motor Fuel for Commercial Purposes and the Coordination of Taxation of Unleaded Petrol and Gas Oil Used as Motor Fuel COM(2007)52, 13 Mar. 2007.

[65] Commission Green Paper: Towards a New Culture for Urban Mobility COM(2007)551, 25 Sept. 2007.

[66] Dir. 2005/32/EC Establishing a Framework for the Setting of Eco-design Requirements for Energy-using Products and Amending Directives 92/42/EEC, 96/57/EC and 2000/55/EC [2005] OJ L191/29.

[67] Commission Communication—Stimulating Technologies for Sustainable Development: An Environmental Technologies Action Plan for the European Union COM(2004)38, 28 Jan. 2004.

Conservation and Management of Natural Resources: Overall use of non-renewable natural resources has been decreasing since 2000, while resource productivity has increased. Nonetheless, while resource efficiency, forestry, bird populations, and waste generation have been stable, and groundwater abstraction and transport emissions have been reduced, the state of surface water resources is unclear, and soil quality continues to deteriorate, fish stocks are depleted, and many mammal species are threatened and undergoing population declines. Europe's efforts in pursuit of this objective include the Air Quality Framework,[68] Water Framework,[69] Birds,[70] and Habitats[71] Directives; the New European Fisheries Fund;[72] the Thematic Strategy on Soil Protection (discussed above);[73] and the EU's Forest Law Enforcement, Governance, and Trade (FLEGT) initiative.[74]

Most Member States are engaged in preserving natural resources, although the focus and performance vary and substantial additional efforts will be required, particularly at the national level, to reach the EU's 2010 targets. Future actions should further integrate biodiversity concerns into policies and programmes, implement existing directives, and strengthen international governance.

Public Health: Although Europeans are living longer, safer, healthier lives, obesity and mental illness present an increasing threat, while smoking remains a major concern. Health inequality is a persistent problem in many countries, and gaps have widened in several States. The EU has undertaken several public health initiatives, including a review of labelling options; a White Paper on Nutrition and Obesity;[75] an action plan for combating HIV/AIDS;[76] a proposal for a sustainable pesticide use framework directive;[77] and a New Animal and Health Strategy for 2007 to 2013.[78] While most policy action is taken at the national and local level, data and reporting has been limited. Member States report advances in addressing lifestyle related diseases, pandemic preparedness, and the handling of chemicals; however, further action is warranted on these fronts, as well as

[68] Dir. 96/62/EC On Ambient Air Quality and Management [1996] OJ L296/55 (Air Quality Framework Dir.).

[69] Dir. 2000/60/EC establishing a Framework for Community Action in the Field of Water Policy [2000] OJ L327/1 (Water Framework Dir.).

[70] Dir. 79/409/EEC on the Conservation of Wild Birds [1979] OJ L103/1 (Birds Dir.).

[71] Dir. 92/43/EEC on the Conservation of Natural Habitats and of Wild Fauna and Flora [1992] OJ L206/7 (Habitats Dir.).

[72] Reg. (EC) No. 1198/2006 on the European Fisheries Fund [2006] OJ L223/1.

[73] N. 16 above.

[74] See Reg. (EC) No. 2173/2005 on the Establishment of a FLEGT Licensing Scheme for Imports of Timber into the European Community [2005] OJ L347/1, and COM(2003)25, 21 May 2003.

[75] Commission White Paper on a Strategy for Europe on Nutrition, Overweight and Obesity-related Health Issues COM(2007)279.

[76] Commission Communication on Combating HIV/AIDS within the European Union and in the Neighbouring Countries, 2006–2009 COM(2005)654, 15 Dec. 2005.

[77] Commission Proposal for a Directive Establishing a Framework for Community Action to Achieve a Sustainable Use of Pesticides COM(2006)373, 12 July 2006.

[78] Commission Communication on a New Animal Health Strategy for the European Union (2007–2013) Where 'Prevention Is Better Than Cure' COM(2007)539, 19 Sept. 2007.

on health inequalities and environmental considerations, such as chemicals and airborne pollution.

Social Inclusion, Demography, and Migration: 16 per cent of the European population is at risk of poverty, the most vulnerable being children, single parents, and the elderly. Although unemployment has decreased overall, high rates among youth and non-native populations threaten integration and solidarity. Still, social protection, pension, and health care systems are undergoing reforms, women are participating more in the work force, and the retirement age is rising. The EU's main policy tool in this sector is the open method of coordination (OMC). Recent efforts include a new social protection and inclusion Council framework;[79] a new Gender Equality Roadmap for 2006 to 2010;[80] a Communication on Europe's future demographics;[81] and a legal migration policy plan which will be implemented in 2007 to 2009.[82] Member States have presented 2006 to 2008 strategies, which vary as to scale, phasing, and policy responses. Ongoing efforts are required in making existing initiatives stronger and more sustainable, and in developing flexicurity, comprehensive lifelong learning strategies, effective labour policies, and modern social security systems.

Global Poverty: The Communication reviews progress made towards achieving the Millennium Development Goals (MDGs), noting successes in the areas of global poverty, primary education, and aid quality, and effectiveness, and additional work to be done on environmental sustainability, extreme poverty, child health and mortality, and sanitation. The EU and the Member States are active in development policy and aid worldwide, and are working to ensure coherent, consistent, coordinated development assistance. Outstanding issues include increasing the volume of aid; addressing environmental migrants and the internally displaced; increasing commitment to water and forest initiatives; ensuring due attention to environmental considerations in aid allocation; and international environmental governance, particularly in trade policy.

In addition to these seven key objectives, the Communication also examines three crosscutting policies: (i) Education and training; (ii) Research and development; and (iii) Financing and economic instruments. Member States are integrating sustainable development challenges into their education activities under the Education and Training 2010 Work Programme.[83] While research and

[79] Commission Communication: Working Together, Working Better—A New Framework for the Open Coordination of Social Protection and Inclusion Policies in the European Union COM(2005)706, 22 Dec. 2005.

[80] Commission Communication: A Roadmap for Equality between Women and Men 2006–2010 COM(2006)92, 1 Mar. 2006.

[81] Commission Communication: The Demographic Future of Europe—From Challenge to Opportunity COM(2006)571, 12 Oct. 2006.

[82] Commission Communication: Policy Plan on Legal Migration COM(2005)669, 21 Dec. 2005.

[83] Commission Communication: 'Education & Training 2010'—The Success of the Lisbon Strategy Hinges on Urgent Reforms COM(2003)685, 11 Nov. 2003.

development stagnated between 2000 and 2005, mobilizing European research for sustainable development is a main objective of the FP7 Programme,[84] as well as for national research policies. Efforts are underway to explore market-based instruments for environmental and energy policies, the phasing-out of environmentally harmful subsidies, taxation of passenger cars and motor fuel, policy coherence, and public participation.

The final section of the Communication is entitled 'Delivering in Partnership', and begins by reviewing awareness across all levels of society, citizen input and stakeholder forums, and environmental and social performance of business. The Communication then discusses the new governance structure of the 2006 SDS; the development of progress indicators, peer reviews of national strategies, good practice sharing, and mutual learning; other reports on the EU's sustainable development progress; and Member States' efforts to conform their national strategies to the EU SDS. While progress on the ground has been modest, policy developments at the EU and national levels are encouraging and hold the promise of results in the years to come. Nonetheless, the failure to include concrete targets and timetables for improving performance under the Strategy is a missed opportunity to mandate and spur achievement of those objectives of which Europe is presently falling so very short.

[84] N. 42 above.

Index

Aarhus Convention (Convention on Access to Information, Public Participation in Decision-Making, and Access to Justice in Environmental Matters) xi, 158–9, 253, 368, 386–7, 404–5, 480–1, 524–5, 529–34, 541–2, 553, 600–1, 606, 612
  biotechnology 136, 151, 157–61, 368, 386–7, 397–9, 541–2
  genetically modified organisms (GMOs) 136, 151, 157–61, 368, 386–7, 397–9, 541–2
access to (environmental) information
  Aarhus Convention xi, 158–9, 253, 368, 386–7, 404–5, 480–1, 524–5, 529–34, 541–2, 553, 600–1, 606, 612
  biotechnology 136, 151, 157–61, 368, 386–7, 397–9, 541–2
  Canada 318
  Community institutions and bodies (Regulation (2006)) xi, 404–5, 524–5, 529–37, 553–4, 600–1
  Directive (1990) on xi, 578, 600
  Directive (2003) on xi, 158–9, 528–9, 534, 555, 578, 600
  genetically modified organisms (GMOs) 136, 151, 157–61, 368, 386–7, 397–9, 541–2
access to justice
  Aarhus Convention xi, 158–9, 253, 368, 386–7, 404–5, 480–1, 524–5, 529–34, 541–2, 553, 600–1, 606, 612
  case law 552–3
  Community institutions and bodies (Regulation (2006)) xi, 404–5, 524–5, 529–37, 553–4, 600–1
  standing for NGOs 552–3
action plans, programmes, and (thematic) strategies *see also* **financial instruments**
  atmospheric pollution
    Air Pollution/Quality, Thematic Strategy on 327–34, 339–40
    Mercury, Strategy on 336–7, 340, 434–6
  biodiversity
    Biodiversity Action Plan 359–61, 478–80, 546, 646–8
    Biodiversity Strategy 218, 239–43, 261–3, 359–61, 546, 646–8
  chemicals
    Mercury, Strategy on 336–7, 340, 434–6
    Pesticides, Thematic Strategy on the Sustainable Use of 431–4, 438–9, 542–3, 550–1
  energy
    Biofuels Strategy 359–61, 652–4
    Biomass Action Plan 359–61, 546, 652–4
    Energy Efficiency Action Plan 203, 343–5, 353, 357–9, 363, 654–5, 660, 667
    Energy Policy for Europe 198, 655–60
    Nuclear Safety Strategy 205–6
  environmental action programmes (EAP), EC
    First (EAP-1) 188
    Sixth (EAP-6) 173, 217, 438, 447, 499, 534, 556, 645
  forestry
    Forest Action Plan 481–3, 648–50
    Forestry Strategy 482–3, 648–9
  marine environment
    Marine Environment, Thematic Strategy on the Protection and Conservation of the 484–5, 517–20, 523–4, 664
    Mediterranean, Environment Strategy for the 663–5
  soil
    Thematic Strategy for Soil Protection 543–6, 650–2
  sustainable development
    Sustainable Development Strategy 2007 546–8, 646, 667–71
    Thematic Strategy on the Sustainable Use of Natural Resources 549
  urban environment
    Thematic Strategy on the Urban Environment 551–2
  waste
    Thematic Strategy on the Prevention and Recycling of Waste 164–5, 173, 549
air pollution *see* **atmospheric pollution**
air quality *see* **atmospheric pollution**
Argentina
  biotechnology 382
  Cartagena Protocol on Biosafety 382
  genetically modified organisms (GMOs) 382
  Intellectual Property, WTO Agreement on Trade Related Aspects of (TRIPS) 266

Trade Related Aspects of Intellectual Property, WTO Agreement on (TRIPS) 266
WTO genetically modified organisms (GMOs) dispute 133–6, 149, 153–6, 366, 395–401, 608
atmospheric pollution *see also* **climate change** *and* **Kyoto Protocol** 327–63
air quality (Directives) 328–32, 669
Austria 336
car emission limits (Euro 4/5/6) 329–31
case law 331–3
climate change *see* **climate change**
Cyprus 335
emission limits, car (Euro 4/5/6) 329–31, 335
emissions trading (Directive (2005)) 346–51, 354–7, 613–4, 666
France 335–6
Germany 329–31, 335–6
Greece 332–3
integrated pollution prevention and control (IPPC) Directive (1996) 334–5
international cooperation 337–9
Ireland 336
Italy 331–2, 335
Japan 338
legislation adopted 327
legislation in progress 328–31
Luxembourg 332–3
mercury, strategy on 336–7, 340, 434–6
motor vehicles 329–31, 335–6
Netherlands 335
North Sea Conference 337
Norway 337–9
ozone 241, 327, 332–3, 337–8, 428–9, 556–7
particulate emissions 335–6
persistent organic pollutants (POPs) Treaty 338–9
Poland 335
policy documents 333–7
PRTR Protocol (Pollutant Release and Transfer Registers) 334
shipping fuel 333–4
Slovakia 336
Spain 335
Sweden 336
Switzerland 338–9
taxation 334, 337, 668, 671
Thematic Strategy on Air Pollution/ Quality 327–34, 339–40
transport 336
United Kingdom 331–5
United States of America 338
Australia
biotechnology 382, 393
Cartagena Protocol on Biosafety 382
Convention on Biological Diversity (CBD) 393
genetically modified organisms (GMOs) 382, 393
Genetic Use Restriction Technologies (GURTs) 393
ozone (depleting substances) 338
precautionary principle 1, 603–6
Austria
atmospheric pollution 336
biotechnology 5, 14–5, 20, 56–64, 72–3, 77, 146, 150, 364–5, 370–1, 377–8, 396, 399–400
chemicals 54–68, 439–40
energy 183–5, 211
fuel 336
genetically modified organisms (GMOs) 5, 14–5, 20, 56–64, 72–3, 77, 146, 150, 364–5, 370–1, 377–8, 396, 399–400
nature conservation 449–53, 473, 475–7
Birds Directive 449–53, 476
Habitats Directive 452–3, 473
hunting 473
nuclear energy 183–5, 211
precautionary principle 5, 14–5, 20, 56–64, 72–3, 77, 146, 150, 364–5, 370–1, 377–8, 399–400

Basel Convention on the Control of Transboundary Movements of Hazardous Wastes and their Disposal 339, 487, 493–4
Belgium
biotechnology 371
disclosure of origin requirement 274
energy 183–7, 214
genetically modified organisms (GMOs) 371
integrated pollution prevention and control (IPPC) 557
intellectual property rights 274
nature conservation 474, 476–7
Birds Directive 476
Habitats Directive 474
hunting 476
nuclear energy 183–7, 214
patent law 274
waste 28, 41, 500
water 514–5
framework Directive (2000), water 514–5
nitrates (Directive (1991)) 515
biodiversity *see also* **Convention on Biological Diversity** *and* **nature conservation** *and* **Birds Directive** *and* **Habitats Directive** 80–132, 218–94, 365, 385–6, 393–4, 442, 447, 462, 477–89, 512, 518–9, 523–4, 544, 556, 604, 646–9, 664–5, 669

biodiversity strategy, EC 239–43, 646–8
biosafety *see* **Cartagena Protocol on Biosafety,** *see also* **biotechnology** *and* **genetically modified organisms (GMOs)**
biotechnology *see also* **genetically modified organisms (GMOs)** 133–161, 364–402
Aarhus Convention 368, 386–7, 397–9, 541–2
Argentina 382
Australia 393
Austria 5, 14–5, 20, 56–64, 72–3, 77, 146, 150, 364–5, 370–1, 377–8, 396, 399–400
authorizations of GMOs (2006) 364–5, 372–3
Belgium 371
Canada 155, 393
Cartagena Biosafety Protocol 1, 155, 241, 366, 381–6, 391, 396–7, 485–7, 568–9
case law 1–47, 133–6, 149, 153–8, 366, 395–401, 608
China 371–2
Codex Alimentarius 151, 387–90
coexistence (of GM and non-GM agriculture) 146–8, 376–8, 401
comitology 143–8, 364–6, 370–5, 399–401
Community Reference Laboratory for GMOs (CRL) 366–8
contamination emergency measures (Rice, Maize) 368–72, 402
Contained Use of GMMs (Directive (1990) 375–6
Cyprus 371, 400–1
Czech Republic 377, 400
Deliberate Release of GMOs (former Directive (1990)) 142, 375–6
Deliberate Release of GMOs (Directive (2001)) 1, 14–5, 20, 135, 142–7, 160–1, 371–6, 399–400, 424, 541–2, 666
Denmark 147, 371, 377, 387
emergency measures, unauthorized GMO contamination 368–72, 402
European Food Safety Authority (EFSA) 144–8, 364–73, 379–80, 400
Finland 371
Food and Feed Regulation (2003), GM 143–7, 366–8, 373–5, 379–80, 541–2
forestry, GM 391–2
France 371, 375–6, 396
genetically modified organisms (GMOs) *see* **genetically modified organisms**
Genetic Use Restriction Technologies (GURTs) 392–4
Germany 147, 371, 377, 390, 396
Greece 365, 371, 396–401
Hungary 399–400
international cooperation *see also* **Aarhus Convention** *and* **Cartagena Biosafety Protocol** *and* **Codex Alimentarius** *and* **WTO** 381–97
Ireland 371
Italy 14–9, 45, 365, 371, 396
Japan 140, 371
Kyoto Protocol 391–2
labelling 17–8, 135, 143–4, 366–7, 374–5, 380–8, 606
legislation adopted 366–73
legislation in progress 373–5
liability, environmental 147–8, 378, 385–6
Luxembourg 365, 371, 387, 396
national bans 399–400
Netherlands 371–2, 400
New Zealand 383, 389, 393, 606
Norway 371, 381
Poland 371, 377, 399–400
policy documents 376–81
precautionary principle 1–47, 72–5, 134–61, 364–6, 391–9
public participation, deliberative 136, 151, 157–61
safeguard bans, Member State 399–400
scientific paradigms 133–161
Slovenia 371, 377
Spain 377
Sweden 371, 400
Traceability and Labelling Regulation (2003) 144, 367, 380–1, 666
United Kingdom 147, 371, 400
United States of America 133–6, 149, 153–6, 366, 368–72, 379, 382–3, 388–402, 608
World Organization for Animal Health (OIE) 394–5
WTO (trade dispute over GMOs) x, 133–41, 148–58, 366, 395–401, 608
Birds Directive *see also* **nature conservation** viii, 92–4, 97, 109–10, 114–7, 127, 131, 218–9, 230–45, 255–6, 261–3, 442–3, 447–57, 468, 472–7, 489, 571–2, 666, 669
Austria 449–53, 476
Belgium 476
biodiversity *see* **biodiversity**
case law 449–57, 468
Cyprus 236
Denmark 476
Finland 476–7
France 236, 476

Birds Directive (*cont.*)
Germany 472, 476
implementation report 475–7
Ireland 476–7
Italy 237, 453–7, 472, 476, 571–2
Malta 236, 473
migratory species of wild animals 218–64
Netherlands 476
Portugal 456–7, 476
Spain 235–7, 472–3, 476–7
Sweden 476–7
United Kingdom 476
Bonn Convention *see* **Convention on the Conservation of Migratory Species of Wild Animals**
Bulgaria
energy 192, 197, 214
nature conservation 250, 254
nuclear energy 192, 197, 214

Canada
access to information (Act) 318
biotechnology 155, 371, 382–3, 393
Cartagena Protocol on Biosafety 382–3
Convention on Biological Diversity (CBD) 393
export credits and sustainable development 317–9, 321–2
genetically modified organisms 155, 382–3, 393
Genetic Use Restriction Technologies (GURTs) 393
Intellectual Property, WTO Agreement on Trade Related Aspects of (TRIPS) 266, 289
ozone 338
principles, environmental 1
Trade Related Aspects of Intellectual Property, WTO Agreement on (TRIPS) 266, 289
WTO genetically modified organisms (GMOs) dispute 133–6, 149, 153–6, 366, 395–401, 608
Cartagena Biosafety Protocol 1, 155, 241, 366, 381–6, 391, 396–7, 485–7, 568–9
Canada 382–3
compliance and enforcement mechanisms 386
handling, transport, packaging, and identification (HTPI) provisions 382–5
liability and redress 385–6
United States of America 382–3
chemicals 403–42
Austria 54–68, 439–40
authorization procedures 416–8
biocides (Directive (1998)) 423–5, 436–9, 550
case law 436–8
classification, packaging and labelling of dangerous substances (Directive (1967)) 70, 409–13, 428–31
comitology 415–8
Czech Republic 439–40
dangerous preparations (Directive (1999)) 408, 413–5, 427–31
detergents 427
derogations from harmonization 439–40
electrical and electronic equipment (WEEE), waste (Directive (2002)) 499–502, 509–10
electronic equipment (RoHS), restrictions on the use of certain hazardous substances in (Directive (2002)) 441, 500, 503–4
European Chemicals Agency (ECHA) 403, 412–22, 428–31
evaluation procedures 414–6
Finland 56, 68–70, 439–40
France 64–7
Globally Harmonized System of Classification and Labelling of Chemicals (GHS) 428–31
Germany 53–73
labelling 428–31
legislation adopted 405–28
legislation in progress 428–36
marketing and use restrictions (Directive (1976)) 70, 419–24
mercury 336–7, 339–40, 434–6, 499–503, 512–3
Netherlands, the 49–61, 436–8
pesticides 424–7, 431–9, 542–3, 550, 669
policy documents 438–9
precautionary principle 403, 430, 441
REACH (Registration, Evaluation, and Authorization of Chemicals), Regulation(2006) *see* **REACH**
safety data sheets (SDS) 406, 413–4, 429–30
substitution principle 72, 417–8, 433–4
Sweden 54–6, 68–70, 425, 439–40
taxation 439
China
biotechnology 371–2
energy 210–1, 215, 319, 362
export credit agencies (ECAs) 286, 294, 305, 319
genetically modified organisms (GMOs) 371–2
nature conservation 444
water 520

CITES (Convention on International Trade in Endangered Species) 222–4, 260, 443–5, 617
climate change *see also* **Kyoto Protocol** *and* **Convention on Climate Change (UNFCCC)** *ix*, 105–10, 182–4, 195–8, 212–4, 243, 320–1, 340–64, 391, 479–80, 510, 513, 518–20, 544, 547, 552, 556, 605, 611–7, 647–68
- biotechnology 391
- case law 350–2
- Convention on Climate Change (UNFCCC), United Nations Framework *see* **Convention on Climate Change (UNFCCC)**
- emissions trading (Directive (2003)) 346–51, 354–7, 613–4, 666
- energy 340–4
- Estonia 351
- Finland 350–2
- genetically modified organisms (GMOs) 391
- Germany 348–51
- Hungary 351
- international cooperation 361–3
- Ireland 343, 348–9
- Italy 350
- Kyoto Protocol *see* **Kyoto Protocol**
- Lithuania 348–9
- Luxembourg 348–52
- Malta 348–9
- Poland 348, 351
- policy documents 352–61
- Russia 362–3, 612
- Sweden 348–9
- United Kingdom 349
- United States of America 361–2
- water 510, 513, 518–20

CMS *see* **Convention on the Conservation of Migratory Species of Wild Animals**
Codex Alimentarius 85, 151, 387–90, 604
- Ad Hoc Intergovernmental Task Force on Food Derived From Biotechnology 389–90
- biotechnology 151, 387–90
- detection and identification of GM foods 388–9
- genetically modified organisms (GMOs)/ food 151, 387–90
- GM Food Task Force 389–90
- labelling standards, GM food 387–8
- precautionary principle 85, 604

comitology 143–8, 364–6, 370–5, 399–401, 415, 502
- biotechnology 143–8, 364–6, 370–5, 399–401
- chemicals 415–8
- Decision (1999), new comitology 143, 374–5, 415
- genetically modified organisms (GMOs) 374–5
- new comitology procedure (2006) 374–5
- waste 502

Convention on Access to Information, Public Participation in Decision–Making, and Access to Justice in Environmental Matters *see* **Aarhus Convention**
Convention on Biological Diversity (CBD) 83, 155, 218, 222, 243, 260, 265–94, 366–85, 391–4, 485–7, 617, 646–7, 652
- biosafety *see* **Cartagena Biosafety Protocol**
- biotechnology *see also* **Cartagena Biosafety Protocol** 392–4
- Genetic Use Restriction Technologies (GURTs) 392–4
- Cartagena Biosafety Protocol *see* **Cartagena Biosafety Protocol**
- disclosure of origin requirement 265–94
- implementation, EU 265–94
- genetically modified organisms (GMOs) *see also* **Cartagena Biosafety Protocol** 392–4
- Genetic Use Restriction Technologies (GURTs) 392–4
- intellectual property 265–94
- nature conservation 485–7
- Trade Related Aspects of Intellectual Property, WTO Agreement on (TRIPS) 241, 266–80, 286–93, 310
- World Intellectual Property Organization (WIPO) 266–72, 276–93

Convention on Climate Change (UNFCCC), Framework *see also* **climate change** *and* **Kyoto Protocol** 1, 340–1, 346–7, 361–2, 391, 612–3, 617, 649
- biotechnology 391–2
- forestry, GMO 391–2
- genetically modified organisms (GMOs) 391–2

Convention on the Conservation of Migratory Species of Wild Animals (Bonn Convention) 218–64, 443, 445
- Agreements 226–9
  - ACCOBAMS Agreement 245–53, 261–3
  - AEWA Agreement 244, 254–6, 442–3
  - ASCOBANS Agreement 245–63
  - Cetacean Agreements 245–63
  - EUROBATS Agreement 244–5, 257–9

Convention on the Conservation of Migratory Species of Wild Animals (Bonn Convention) (*cont.*)
- Appendix I species 224–5
- Appendix II species 225–6
- fundamental principles and objectives 223–4
- synergies with EU law (potential) 260–4

Convention on the Control of Transboundary Movements of Hazardous Wastes and their Disposal *see* **Basel Convention**

Convention on International Trade in Endangered Species *see* **CITES Convention**

Convention on the Law of the Sea (UNCLOS) 92, 222, 486–7, 563–7, 579–89

corporate social responsibility (CSR) 305–6, 313, 317, 322

Cyprus
- atmospheric pollution 335
- biotechnology 371, 400–1
- energy 351
- genetically modified organisms (GMOs) 371, 400–1
- integrated pollution prevention and control (IPPC) 335
- nature conservation 236, 250, 258, 443
- Birds Directive 236
- Habitats Directive 443
- hunting 236

Czech Republic
- biotechnology 377, 400
- chemicals 439–40
- energy 214–6, 351
- genetically modified organisms (GMOs) 377, 400
- nature conservation 254, 259
- nuclear energy 214–6

Denmark
- biotechnology 147, 371, 377, 387
- derogation from harmonization 14, 49–66, 73–7
- energy 351–2
- genetically modified organisms (GMOs) 147, 371, 377, 387
- integrated pollution prevention and control (IPPC) 557
- nature conservation 244, 248, 254, 476–7
  - Birds Directive 476
  - hunting 476
- precautionary principle 14, 41–3, 83
- waste, shipments 506–7

disclosure of origin requirement 265–94
- Convention on Biodiversity (CBD) 265–94
- implementation, EU 265–94
- Japan 288
- New Zealand 266, 289
- Norway 266, 275–8, 292–3
- Switzerland 266, 279–83, 286–7, 292–3
- Trade Related Aspects of Intellectual Property, WTO Agreement on (TRIPS) 241, 266–80, 286–93, 310
- United States of America 275, 288–9, 292
- World Intellectual Property Organization (WIPO) 266–72, 276–93

eco-audit *see* **Eco-Management and Audit Scheme (EMAS)**

eco-design 502, 505, 668

eco-labelling 135, 332, 337, 354, 358–9, 362, 365, 409, 413, 427–30, 502–3, 525, 537–40, 654, 668–9

Eco-Management and Audit Scheme (EMAS), Community 538–41
- Regulation (2001), EMAS 540–1

eco-tax *see* **taxation**

EFSA *see* **European Food Safety Authority**

EMAS *see* **Eco-Management and Audit Scheme**

emissions trading, greenhouse gas *see* **climate change** *and* **Kyoto Prococol**

energy 182–217, 340–63
- Austria 183–5, 211
- Belgium 183–7, 214
- biofuels 360–1, 652–4
- biomass/biofuels strategy/action plan 359–61, 546, 652–4
- Bulgaria 192, 197, 214
- case law 350–2
- China 210–1, 215, 319, 362
- climate change *see* **climate change**
- common energy policy 352–4
- Cyprus 351
- Czech Republic 214–6, 351
- Denmark 351–2
- emissions trading (Directive (2003)), greenhouse gas 346–51, 354–7, 613–4, 666
- Energy Efficiency Action Plan 203, 343–5, 353, 357–9, 363, 654–5, 660
- energy efficiency (Directive (2006)) 344–6, 357–9, 654–5, 661–3
- Energy Policy for Europe, Action Plan 198, 655–60, 667
- energy services and efficiency (Directive (2006)) 344–6
- Estonia 197, 205, 215, 351
- EURATOM Treaty 182–217
- Finland 184–5, 197, 204, 207, 214, 312–3, 321, 350–2
- France 182–7, 190–2, 197, 204, 209–16, 312–3, 317, 321–2, 351
- Germany 182, 185–7, 190, 195, 203–4, 210, 214, 348–51

Global Energy Efficiency and Renewable Energy Fund (GEEREF) 661–3
Greece 210, 348–51
Hungary 195, 214, 351
international cooperation *see also* **Kyoto Protocol** *and* **Convention on Climate Change (UNFCCC)** 361–3
Ireland 183, 195, 343, 348–9, 351
Italy 185–7, 190–1, 197, 210, 350–2
Japan 211
Kyoto Protocol 341–51, 355, 361–2
Latvia 197, 205, 215, 349–51
legislation adopted 344–7
legislation in progress 347–50
Lithuania 184–5, 192, 205, 214–5, 297, 348–9
Luxembourg 348–52
Malta 348–9
Netherlands 185–6, 192, 210, 214
nuclear energy 182–217
Poland 195–7, 205, 215, 348, 351
policy documents 352–61
renewable energy 351–2
Romania 192, 197, 214, 319
Russia 191, 195, 206, 210–1, 362–3, 612
Slovakia 183, 197, 214–6, 348–9
Slovenia 214–5, 351
Spain 351
Sweden 183, 195, 204, 207, 214, 313, 348–9
taxation 203, 334, 337, 358, 362, 614–5, 653–5
United Kingdom 187, 190, 197, 203, 208–10, 214–6, 349–51
United States of America 187–92, 210–1, 359, 361–2

environmental action programmes, EC *see* **action plans and programmes**

environmental impact assessment (EIA) *see also* **strategic environmental assessment (SEA)**
case law 552–3, 575–8
Directive (1985) 21, 453, 459–60, 553–5, 575–8
Directive (1997) 553–4
export credit agencies (ECAs) 296, 299, 304–22
Finland 313
Ireland 577–8
mining 123–8
Netherlands 123–8
United Kingdom 552–5, 575–7

Estonia
climate change 351
energy 197, 205, 215, 351
nature conservation 248
nuclear energy 197, 205, 215
water, bathing 522

EURATOM Treaty (Treaty Establishing the European Atomic Energy Community) ix, 182–217, 495–6
economic and political environments for nuclear energy 196–200, 202–4
energy, sustainable 182–76
fifty-year anniversary 191–4
new developments 211–2
nuclear energy 182–217
nuclear non-proliferation 209–10
nuclear safety and security 204–9
origins of the EURATOM Treaty 184–90
repeal (reluctance to) 194–6
value added of the Treaty 200-

European Chemicals Agency (ECHA) 403, 412–22, 428–31

European Food Safety Authority (EFSA) 144–8, 364–73, 379–80, 400

European Pollutant Release and Transfer Register (PRTR) 334, 525–9

export credit agencies(ECAs) 204, 294–323
Arrangement on Officially Supported Export Credits, OECD 294–323
Canada (export credits and sustainable development in) 317–9, 321–2
China 286, 294, 305, 319
environmental impact assessment (EIA) 296, 299, 304–22
EU (export credits and sustainable development in) 312–3, 321–2
Finland 313
France (export credits and sustainable development in) 204, 312–7, 317, 321–2
Germany (export credits and sustainable development in) 314–6, 321–2
International Union of Credit and Investment Insurers (Berne Union) 305–7
Japan 300, 315
New Zealand 300
Norway 300
Organisation for Economic Co-operation and Development (OECD) Arrangement on Officially Supported Export Credits 294–323
Russia 305
sustainable development 294–323
Sustainability Impact Assessment 308–11
Sweden 313
Switzerland 300
United Kingdom 315
United States of America 300, 320–2

financial instruments
Cohesion Fund 542, 555
Financial Instrument for the Environment (LIFE+) 261, 446–8, 475–6, 485, 552

financial instruments (*cont.*)
Fisheries Fund, New European 560, 669
Global Energy Efficiency and Renewable Energy Fund (GEEREF) 661–3
Structural Fund 559–61
Finland
biotechnology 371
chemicals 56, 68–70, 439–40
climate change 350–2
emissions trading 350–2
energy 184–5, 197, 204, 207, 214, 312–3, 350–2, 321
environmental impact assessment (EIA) 313
export credit agencies (ECAs) 313
genetically modified organisms (GMOs) 371
nature conservation 473, 476–7
Birds Directive 476–7
hunting 476
nuclear energy 184–5, 197, 204, 214, 312–3, 321
water 432, 516
waste-water, urban 516
fisheries 80–132, 222, 242–53, 448–9, 479, 488, 510–1, 560, 584–8, 669
forestry 241–2, 391–2, 446, 459–60, 478, 481–4, 592, 647–50, 669–70
France
atmospheric pollution 335–6
biotechnology 371, 375–6, 396
chemicals 64–7
energy 182–7, 190–2, 197, 204, 209–16, 312–3, 317, 321–2, 351
export credits agencies (ECAs) 204, 312–7, 317, 321–2
genetically modified organisms (GMOs) 371, 375–6, 396
integrated pollution prevention and control (IPPC) 555–7
nature conservation 232–7, 244, 247, 250, 254, 443, 454, 474–7
Birds Directive 236, 476
Habitats Directive 474
hunting 233, 476
nuclear energy 182–7, 190–2, 197, 204, 209–16, 312–3, 317, 321–2
precautionary principle 14, 21, 41–3, 144, 603–5
water 514–6
waste-water, urban 515–6

genetically modified organisms (GMOs) *see also* **biotechnology** 133–161, 364–402
Aarhus Convention 368, 386–7, 397–9, 541–2
Argentina 382
Australia 393
Austria 5, 14–5, 20, 56–64, 72–3, 77, 146, 150, 364–5, 370–1, 377–8, 396, 399–400
authorizations of GMOs (2006) 364–5, 372–3
Belgium 371
Canada 155, 393
Cartagena Biosafety Protocol 1, 155, 241, 366, 381–6, 391, 396–7, 485–7, 568–9
case law 1–47, 133–6, 149, 153–8, 366, 395–401, 608
China 371–2
Codex Alimentarius 151, 387–90
coexistence (of GM and non-GM agriculture) 146–8, 376–8, 401
comitology 143–8, 364–6, 370–5, 399–401
Community Reference Laboratory for GMOs (CRL) 366–8
contamination emergency measures (Rice, Maize) 368–72, 402
Contained Use of GMMs (Directive (1990) 375–6
Cyprus 371, 400–1
Czech Republic 377, 400
Deliberate Release of GMOs (former Directive (1990)) 142, 375–6
Deliberate Release of GMOs (Directive (2001)) 1, 14–5, 20, 135, 142–7, 160–1, 371–6, 399–400, 424, 541–2, 666
Denmark 147, 371, 377, 387
emergency measures, unauthorized GMO contamination 368–72, 402
European Food Safety Authority (EFSA) 144–8, 364–73, 379–80, 400
Finland 371
Food and Feed Regulation (2003), GM 143–7, 366–8, 373–5, 379–80, 541–2
forestry, GM 391–2
France 371, 375–6, 396
Genetic Use Restriction Technologies (GURTs) 392–4
Germany 147, 371, 377, 390, 396
Greece 365, 371, 396–401
Hungary 399–400
international cooperation *see also* **Aarhus Convention** *and* **Cartagena Biosafety Protocol** *and* **Codex Alimentarius** *and* **WTO** 381–97
Italy 14–9, 45, 365, 371, 396
Japan 140, 371
Kyoto Protocol 391–2

labelling 17–8, 135, 143–4, 366–7, 374–5, 380–8, 606
legislation adopted 366–73
legislation in progress 373–5
liability, environmental 147–8, 378, 385–6
Luxembourg 365, 371, 387, 396
national bans 399–400
Netherlands 371–2, 400
New Zealand 383, 389, 393, 606
Norway 371, 381
Poland 371, 377, 399–400
policy documents 376–81
precautionary principle 1–47, 72–5, 134–61, 364–6, 391–9
public participation, deliberative 136, 151, 157–61
safeguard bans, Member State 399–400
scientific paradigms 133–161
Slovenia 371, 377
Spain 377
Sweden 371, 400
Traceability and Labelling Regulation (2003) 144, 367, 380–1, 666
United Kingdom 147, 371, 400
United States of America 133–6, 149, 153–6, 366, 368–72, 279, 382–3, 388–401, 608
World Organization for Animal Health (OIE) 394–5
WTO (trade dispute over GMOs) x, 133–41, 148–58, 366, 395–402, 608

Genetic Use Restriction Technologies (GURTs) 392–4
Australia 393
Canada 393
Convention on Biological Diversity (CBD) 392–4
EU/EC 392–4
moratorium 392–4
New Zealand 393
Switzerland 393
United States of America392–4

Germany
atmospheric pollution 329–31, 335–6
biotechnology 147, 371, 377, 390, 396
chemicals 53–73
climate change 348–51
derogation from harmonization 53–73
emission limits, car (Euro 4/5/6) 329–31
emission trading, greenhouse gas 348–51
energy 182, 185–7, 190, 195, 203–4, 210, 214, 348–51
export credits and sustainable development 314–6, 321–2
fuel 336
genetically modified organisms (GMOs) 147, 371, 377, 390, 396
integrated pollution prevention and control (IPPC) 557
nature conservation 244, 248, 254–6, 442–3, 457–65, 469–76, 570–1
Birds Directive 472, 476, 570–1
Habitats Directive 457–65, 469–74
nuclear energy 182, 185–7, 190, 195, 203–4, 210, 214
precautionary principle 9, 603–5
taxation 203
waste 418, 478–80, 506–7
shipments of waste 506–7
water 514–5
Framework Directive (2000), water 514–5

Greece
atmospheric pollution 332–3
biotechnology 365, 371, 396–401
energy 210, 348–51
genetically modified organisms (GMO) 365, 371, 396–401
integrated pollution prevention and control (IPPC) 557
nature conservation 239, 250, 254, 258, 443–9, 469, 473–6
Habitats Directive 469, 474–5
hunting 476
nuclear energy 210
water 516–7
waste-water, urban 516–7

Habitats Directive *see also* **nature conservation** 21, 23, 92–5, 97, 109–10, 114–9, 123, 127, 131–2, 218–9, 230, 238–63, 442–3, 447–53, 457–75, 481, 488–9, 570–2, 669
Austria 452–3
Belgium 474
biodiversity *see* **biodiversity**
case law 447–65
Cyprus 443
France 474
Germany 457–65, 469–74
Greece 469, 474–5
Ireland 474
Italy 443, 474
Malta 443
migratory species of wild animals 218–64
Netherlands 474
Poland 474
Portugal 443, 456–7, 467–9, 474
Spain 465–7, 473–4
United Kingdom 443, 474

horizontal instruments *see* **access to information** *and* **access to justice** *and* **eco-labelling** *and* **eco-management and audit scheme (EMAS)** *and* **environmental impact assessment (EIA)** *and* **integrated pollution prevention and control (IPPC)** *and* **liability** *and* **strategic environmental assessment (SEA)** *and* **taxation** 524–62
Hungary
biotechnology 399–400
climate change 351
emissions trading, greenhouse 351
energy 195, 214, 351
genetically modified organisms (GMOs) 399–400
nature conservation 254
nuclear energy 195, 214
waste, shipments 504
water, bathing 522
hunting 225–7, 233, 236–8, 248, 255, 442, 453–7, 464–7, 472–3, 476–7, 488, 571–2

integrated pollution prevention and control (IPPC) 346–7, 493, 525–6, 529, 541, 555–9, 613–4
atmospheric pollution 334–5
Belgium 557
Cyprus 335
Denmark 557
Directive (1996) 346–7, 493, 525–6, 529, 541, 555–9, 613–4
France 555–7
Germany 557
Greece 557
implementation Report 557–9
Luxembourg 557
Netherlands 335, 557
Spain 335, 557
waste 493
integration principle 30, 60, 72, 84, 246, 623, 664
IPPC *see* **integrated pollution prevention and control**
Ireland
atmospheric pollution 336
biotechnology 371
climate change 343, 348–9
Convention on the Law of the Sea (UNCLOS) 563–7
emissions trading, greenhouse 343, 348–9
energy 183, 195, 343, 348–9, 351
environmental impact assessment (EIA) 577–8
fuel 336
genetically modified organisms (GMOs) 371
nature conservation 243, 254, 474, 476–7
Birds Directive 476
Habitats Directive 474
hunting 476–7
nuclear energy 183, 195
Italy
atmospheric pollution 331–2, 335
biotechnology 14–9, 45, 365, 371, 396
climate change 350
emissions trading, greenhouse gas 350–1
export credit agencies (ECAs) 315
energy 185–7, 190–1, 197, 210, 350–2
genetically modified organisms (GMOs) 14–9, 45, 365, 371, 396
nature conservation 237, 250, 254, 443, 453–7, 472–7, 571–2
Birds Directive 237, 453–7, 472, 476, 571–2
Habitats Directive 443, 474
hunting 473, 476
nuclear energy 185–7, 190–1, 197, 210
precautionary principle 14–9, 45
principles, environmental 14–9, 45
waste 15–6

Japan
atmospheric pollution 338
biotechnology 140, 371
disclosure of origin requirement 288
energy 211
export credit agencies (ECAs) 300, 315
genetically modified organisms (GMOs) 140, 371
intellectual property rights 288
Intellectual Property, WTO Agreement on Trade Related Aspects of (TRIPS) 266, 288, 292
nuclear energy 211
patent law 288, 292
precautionary principle 603–5
Trade Related Aspects of Intellectual Property, WTO Agreement on (TRIPS) 266, 288, 292
ozone (depleting substances) 338

Kyoto Protocol *see also* **climate change** *and* **Convention on Climate Change** 341–51, 355, 361–2, 391–2, 612–5, 649, 652–3, 660–2, 667
biotechnology 391–2
Clean Development Mechanism (CDM) 661
Emissions Trading Directive (2003) 346–51, 354–7, 613–4, 666
energy 341–51, 355, 361–2
genetically modified organisms (GMOs) 391–2

Linking Directive (2004), Kyoto mechanisms and EC emissions trading 614

labelling *see* **eco-labelling**
Latvia
energy 197, 205, 215, 349–51
nature conservation 248, 254
nuclear energy 197, 205, 215
waste, shipments 504
water, bathing 522
liability, environmental 4, 147–8, 378, 385–6, 498, 543, 600–1, 613
biotechnology 147–8, 378, 385–6
Cartagena Biosafety Protocol 385–6
Directive (2004) on 147, 497, 543–5, 601, 650–2
genetically modified organisms (GMOs) 147–8, 378, 385–6
waste 498
LIFE (Financial Instrument for the Environment) *see also* **financial instruments** 261, 446–8, 475–6, 485, 552
life sciences *see* **biotechnology**
Lithuania
climate change 348–9
energy 184–5, 192, 205, 214–5, 297, 348–9
nature conservation 248, 254
nuclear energy 184–5, 192, 205, 214–5, 297
water 522
Luxembourg
Aarhus Convention 387
atmospheric pollution 332–3
biotechnology 365, 371, 387, 396
climate change 348–52
energy 348–52
genetically modified organisms (GMOs) 365, 371, 387, 396
integrated pollution prevention and control (IPPC) 557
nature conservation 254, 477
water 515, 574–5
framework Directive (2000), water 515, 574–5

Malta
climate change 348–9
energy 348–9
nature conservation 236, 250, 443, 473
Birds Directive 236, 473
Habitats Directive 443
hunting 473
waste, shipments 504

Montreal Protocol on Substances that Deplete the Ozone Layer 241, 327, 337–8
Australia 338
Canada 338
Japan 338
United States of America 338

Natura 2000 Network *see also* **nature conservation** 91, 94, 115–6, 238–40, 259, 263, 442–3, 447, 451, 456, 466–70, 474, 478–81, 489, 646
nature conservation 218–64, 442–89
Alpine Convention 446, 652
avian influenza 445–6
aquaculture 318, 448–9, 479
Austria 449–53, 473, 475–7
Belgium 474, 476–7
biodiversity *see also* **Convention on Biodiversity (CBD)** 80–132, 218–94, 365, 385–6, 393–4, 442, 447, 462, 477–89, 512, 518–9, 523–4, 544, 556, 604, 646–9, 664–5, 669
birds (Directive (1979) *see* **Birds Directive**
Bulgaria 250, 254
case law 449–72, 460–1, 469, 570–2
China 444
CITES (Convention/Regulation (1997)) 222–4, 260, 443–5, 488, 617
climate change 479–80
Convention on Biological Diversity (CBD) *see* **Convention on Biological Diversity**
Cyprus 236, 250, 258, 443
Czech Republic 254, 259
Denmark 244, 248, 254, 476–7
enforcement and implementation, annual report 472–5
environmental policy review 477–8
Estonia 248
Financial Instrument for the Environment (LIFE+) 261, 446–8, 475–6, 485, 552
Finland 473, 476–7
fisheries 80–132, 222, 242–53, 448–9, 479, 510–1, 584–8, 669
forestry 241–2, 391–2, 446, 459–60, 478, 481–4, 592, 647–50, 669–70
France 232–7, 244, 247, 250, 254, 443, 454, 474–7
Germany 244, 248, 254–6, 442–3, 457–65, 469–76, 570–1
Greece 239, 250, 254, 258, 443–9, 469, 473–6
habitats (Directive 1992)) *see* **Habitats Directive**
Hungary 254
hunting 225–7, 233, 236–8, 248, 255, 442, 453–7, 464–7, 472–3, 476–7, 488, 571–2

nature conservation (*cont.*)
international cooperation *see also* **CITES Convention** *and* **Convention on Biological Diversity** 485–8
Ireland 243, 254, 474, 476–7
Italy 237, 250, 254, 443, 453–7, 472–7, 571–2
Latvia 248, 254
legislation adopted 442–6
legislation in progress 446–9
LIFE (Financial Instrument for the Environment) 261, 446–8, 475–6, 485, 552
Lithuania 248, 254
Luxembourg 254, 477
Malta 236, 250, 443, 473
marine environment policystrategy 484–5
migratory species of wild animals 218–64
Netherlands 80–132, 235–6, 244, 248, 254, 257, 450, 455, 474, 476–7
Natura 2000 Network 91, 94, 115–6, 238–40, 259, 263, 442–3, 447, 451, 456, 466–70, 474, 478–81, 489, 646
Norway 248
Poland 248–9, 474
policy documents and resolutions 472–85
Portugal 250, 254, 443, 456–7, 467–9, 474, 476, 570
precautionary principle 237–8, 251–4, 460–1, 469, 487
Romania 250, 254
Russia 248
Slovakia 254
Slovenia 250, 254
soil protection 119–29, 426, 459–61, 543–6, 556, 650–2, 669
Spain 235–7, 244, 250, 254, 258, 465–7, 472–4, 476–7
Sweden 248–9, 254, 476–7
taxation 483
timber, tropical 487–8
United Kingdom 244, 248, 254, 443, 474, 476–7
whaling, International Commission 488

Netherlands, The
atmospheric pollution 335
biotechnology 371–2, 400
chemicals 49–61, 436–8
biocides 437–8
pesticides 436–7
derogation from harmonization 49–62, 68, 76
energy 185–6, 192, 210, 214
environmental impact assessment (EIA) 123–8
fisheries 80–132
genetically modified organisms (GMOs) 371–2, 400
integrated pollution prevention and control (IPPC) 335, 557
mining 80–132
nature conservation 80–132, 235–6, 244, 248, 254, 257, 450, 455, 474, 476–7
Birds Directive 476
Habitats Directive 474
nuclear energy 185–6, 192, 210, 214
precautionary principle 43–4, 80–132, 605
Wadden Sea 80–132
waste 508–9
water 80–132, 522
bathing water 522
fisheries 80–132
Wadden Sea 80–132

New Zealand
biotechnology 383, 389, 393, 606
Convention on Biological Diversity (CBD) 383, 389, 393
disclosure of origin requirement 266, 289
export credit agencies (ECAs) 300
genetically modified organisms (GMOs) 383, 389, 393, 606
Genetic Use Restriction Technologies (GURTs) 393
Intellectual Property, WTO Agreement on Trade Related Aspects of (TRIPS) 266, 289
precautionary principle 603, 606
Trade Related Aspects of Intellectual Property, WTO Agreement on (TRIPS) 266, 289

Norway
atmospheric pollution 337–9
biotechnology 371, 381
disclosure of origin requirement 266, 275–8, 292–3
export credit agencies (ECAs) 300
genetically modified organisms (GMOs) 371, 381
intellectual property rights 266, 275–8, 292–3
nature conservation 248
patent law 275–8
Trade Related Aspects of Intellectual Property, WTO Agreement on (TRIPS) 266, 292–3

ozone (depleting substances) 241, 327, 332–3, 337–8, 428–9, 556–7
Australia 338
Canada 338
Japan 338
Montreal Protocol on Substances that Deplete the Ozone Layer 241, 327, 337–8
United States of America 338

Poland
atmospheric pollution 335
biotechnology 371, 377, 399–400
climate change 348, 351
energy 195–7, 205, 215, 348, 351
genetically modified organisms (GMOs) 371, 377, 399–400
nature conservation 248–9, 474
Habitats Directive 474
nuclear energy 195–7, 205, 215
waste, shipments 504
Pollutant Release and Transfer Register, European (PRTR) 334, 525–9
polluter-pays principle 1–4, 19, 25, 46, 336, 615
case law 1–4, 19, 25, 46
Portugal
nature conservation 250, 254, 443, 456–7, 467–9, 474, 476, 570
Birds Directive 456–7, 476
Habitats Directive 443, 456–7, 467–9, 474
hunting 476
water 516
waste-water, urban 516
precautionary principle 1–9, 13–48, 56, 72–5, 80–161, 237–8, 246, 251–4, 299, 364–6, 391–9, 403, 430, 441, 460–1, 469, 487, 515–6, 602–11
Australia 1, 603–6
Austria 5, 14–5, 20, 56–64, 72–3, 77, 146, 150, 364–5, 370–1, 377–8, 399–400
biotechnology 1–47, 72–5, 134–61, 364–6, 391–9
case law 1–47, 80–132, 153–8, 237–8, 460–1, 469, 515–6
chemicals 403, 430, 441
Denmark 14, 41–3, 83
France 14, 21, 41–3, 144, 603–5
genetically modified organisms (GMOs) 1–47, 72–5, 134–61, 364–6, 391–9
Germany 9, 603–5
Italy 14–9, 45
Japan 603–5
nature conservation 237–8, 251–4, 460–1, 469, 487
Netherlands 43–4, 80–132, 605
New Zealand 603, 606
REACH Regulation (2006) 403, 430, 441
Sweden 605
United States of America 603–5
water 515–6
prevention principle 1–7, 16, 22–3, 46, 84–5, 121, 131, 621
principles, environmental *see also* **integration principle** *and* **polluter-pays principle** *and* **precautionary principle** *and* **prevention principle** *and* **proximity principle** *and* **rectification at source principle** *and* **substitution principle** 1–132
case law 1–132
integration principle 30, 60, 72, 84, 246, 623, 664
polluter-pays principle 1–4, 19, 25, 46, 336, 615
precautionary principle
prevention principle 1–7, 16, 22–3, 46, 84–5, 121, 131, 621
proportionality principle 8, 13, 18, 26, 29–43, 50, 61, 65–70, 87–8, 129, 374–7, 436–7, 462, 507, 604
proximity principle 493
rectification at source principle 1–4, 19, 25, 28–9, 41, 46
substitution principle 72, 417–8, 433–4
proportionality principle 8, 13, 18, 26, 29–43, 50, 61, 65–70, 87–8, 129, 374–7, 436–7, 462, 507, 604
Protocol on Substances that Deplete the Ozone Layer *see* **ozone**
proximity principle 493
public participation (in decision-making)
Aarhus Convention xi, 158–9, 253, 368, 386–7, 404–5, 480–1, 524–5, 529–34, 541–2, 553, 600–1, 606, 612, 136, 151, 157–61, 368, 397–9
biotechnology 136, 151, 157–61, 368, 386–7, 397–9, 541–2
Community institutions and bodies (Regulation (2006)) xi, 404–5, 524–5, 529–37, 553–4, 600–1
Directive (2003), on 431–2, 554–5
genetically modified organisms (GMOs) 136, 151, 157–61, 368, 386–7, 397–9, 541–2
public procurement 189, 204, 299–301, 331, 345, 359, 414, 538–9, 668

REACH (Registration, Evaluation, and Authorization of Chemicals), Regulation (2006) *see also* **chemicals** 403–22, 428–31, 440–1
articles v. substances 419–22
authorization procedures 416–8
comitology 415–8
data sharing 412–3
European Chemicals Agency (ECHA) 403, 412–22
evaluation procedures 414–6
Globally Harmonized System of Classification and Labelling of Chemicals (GHS) 428–31
Implementation Project (RIP), REACH 420–1

REACH (*cont.*)
information trough supply chain and downstream user requirements 413–4
Pollutant Release and Transfer Register, (PRTR) 334, 525–9
precautionary principle 403, 430, 441
registration requirements 408–12
Regulation (2006) 403–22, 428–31, 440–1
restrictions procedure 418–9
safety data sheets (SDS) 406, 413–4, 429–30
scope 405–8
substance information exchange forum (SIEF) 412–3
rectification at source principle 1–4, 19, 25, 28–9, 41, 46
renewable energy *see* **energy**
Romania
energy 192, 197, 214, 319
export credit agencies (ECAs) 319
nature conservation 250, 254
nuclear energy 192, 197, 214, 319
Russia
biotechnology 371
climate change 362–3, 612
energy 191, 195, 206, 210–1, 362–3, 612
export credit agencies (ECAs) 305
genetically modified organisms (GMOs) 371
nature conservation 248
nuclear energy 191, 195, 206, 210–1

Slovakia
atmospheric pollution 336
energy 183, 197, 214–6, 348–9
fuel 336
nature conservation 254
nuclear energy 183, 197, 214–6
waste, shipments 504
water 522
Slovenia
biotechnology 371, 377
energy 214–5, 351
genetically modified organisms (GMOs) 371, 377
nature conservation 250, 254
nuclear energy 214–5
water 522
soil protection 119–29, 426, 459–61, 543–6, 556, 650–2, 669
South Korea
biotechnology 371
genetically modified organisms (GMOs) 371
Intellectual Property, WTO Agreement on Trade Related Aspects of (TRIPS) 266, 289
Trade Related Aspects of Intellectual Property, WTO Agreement on (TRIPS) 266, 289
Spain
atmospheric pollution 335
biotechnology 377
energy 351
genetically modified organisms (GMOs) 377
integrated pollution prevention and control (IPPC) 335, 557
nature conservation 235–7, 244, 250, 254, 258, 465–7, 472–4, 476–7
Birds Directive 235–7, 472–3, 476–7
Habitats Directive 465–7, 473–4
hunting 476
waste 174
water 517, 522
bathing water 522
shellfish waters 517
strategic environmental assessment (SEA) *see also* **environmental impact assessment (EIA)** 523–5, 559–61, 605
Community funds, relationship with 559–61
Directive on (2001) 525, 559–61
substitution principle 72, 417–8, 433–4
chemicals 417–8, 433–4
sustainable development 81, 246, 267, 272, 294–323, 352, 361–2, 546–9,589–99, 646, 667–71
compliance synergies in international environmental and economic law 589–99
employment and environment 548–9
energy 352, 361–2
export credits (agencies (ECAs)) 294–323
precautionary principle 299
Strategy, EU Sustainable Development 546–8, 646, 667–71
Sweden
atmospheric pollution 336
biotechnology 371, 400
chemicals 54–6, 68–70, 425, 439–40
climate change 348–9
energy 183, 195, 204, 207, 214, 313, 348–9
export credit agencies (ECAs) 313
fuel 336
genetically modified organisms (GMOs) 371, 400
nature conservation 248–9, 254, 476–7
Birds Directive 476–7
hunting 476
nuclear energy 183, 195, 204, 207, 214, 313

precautionary principle 605
water 516
waste-water, urban 516
Switzerland
atmospheric pollution 338–9
biotechnology 371, 393
Convention on Biological Diversity (CBD) 393
disclosure of origin requirement 266, 279–83, 286–7, 292–3
export credit agencies (ECAs) 300
genetically modified organisms (GMOs) 371, 393
Genetic Use Restriction Technologies (GURTs) 393
intellectual property rights 266, 279–83, 286–7, 292–3
Intellectual Property, WTO Agreement on Trade Related Aspects of (TRIPS) 266, 274, 277, 279–83, 286–7, 292–3
patent law 266, 279–83

taxation, environmental 165, 203, 334, 337, 358, 362, 439, 483, 501, 538, 547, 614–5, 653–5, 668, 671
atmospheric pollution 334, 337, 668, 671
chemicals 439
energy 203, 334, 337, 358, 362, 614–5, 653–5
Germany 203
nature conservation 483
nuclear energy 203
waste 165, 501
thematic strategies, EU environmental 164–5, 173, 299, 478, 549–52, 669
Air Pollution/Quality 478
prevention and recycling of waste 164–5, 173, 549
Marine Environment 478
sustainable use of natural resources 299, 549
sustainable use of pesticides 431–3, 438–9, 542–4, 550–1, 669
urban environment 551–2

UNCLOS *see* **Convention on the Law of the Sea**
UNFCCC *see* **Convention on Climate Change**
United Kingdom
atmospheric pollution 331–5
biotechnology 147, 371, 400
climate change 349
Convention on the Law of the Sea (UNCLOS) 563–7
energy 187, 190, 197, 203, 208–10, 214–6, 349–51
environmental impact assessment (EIA) 552–5, 575–7
export credit agencies (ECAs) 315
genetically modified organisms (GMOs) 147, 371, 400
nature conservation 244, 248, 254, 443, 474, 476–7
Birds Directive 476–7
Habitats Directive 443, 474
hunting 476–7
nuclear energy 187, 190, 197, 203, 208–10, 214–6, 605
waste 162–81
water 512–3, 516, 520
waste-water, urban 516
United States of America
atmospheric pollution 338
biotechnology 133–6, 149, 153–6, 366, 368–72, 379, 382–3, 388–402, 608
Cartagena Protocol on Biosafety 382–3
climate change 361–2
Codex Alimentarius 388–90
Convention on the Law of the Sea, (UNCLOS) 579–89
disclosure of origin requirement 275, 288–9, 292
energy 187–92, 210–1, 359, 361–2
export credit agencies (ECAs) 300, 320–2
genetically modified organisms (GMOs) 133–6, 149, 153–6, 366, 368–72, 279, 382–3, 388–402, 608
Genetic Use Restriction Technologies (GURTs) 392–4
intellectual property rights 266, 275, 288–9
Intellectual Property, WTO Agreement on Trade Related Aspects of (TRIPS) 266, 275, 288–9, 292
nuclear energy 187–92, 210–1
ozone (depleting substances) 338
precautionary principle 603–5
UNCLOS (Convention on the Law of the Sea) 579–89
WTO genetically modified organisms (GMOs) dispute 133–6, 149, 153–6, 366, 395–401, 608

waste 162–81, 489–510
Basel Convention *see* Convention on the Control of Transboundary Movements of
Hazardous Wastes and their Disposal
batteries and accumulators (Directives (2006/1991)) 499–503
Belgium 28, 41, 500
case law 162–81, 506–9, 572–4
comitology 502

waste (*cont.*)
Convention on the Control of Transboundary Movements of Hazardous Wastes and their Disposal (Basel Convention) 339, 487, 493–4
definition 162–81
Denmark 507–8
Directive (1975), Waste Framework 21–2, 25–6, 162–81, 489–90, 497, 504–9, 526
Directive (1991), Waste Framework 21–2, 25–6, 162–81, 489–90, 497, 504–9
Directive (2006), Waste Framework 162–81, 405, 489–90, 493, 497, 504–9
electrical and electronic equipment (WEEE), waste (Directive (2002)) 499–502, 509–10
electronic equipment (RoHS), restrictions on the use of certain hazardous substances in (Directive (2002)) 500, 503–4
end-of-life vehicles (ELVs), (Directive (2000)) 500–1, 666
Framework Directive (1975) 21–2, 25–6, 162–81, 489–90, 497, 504–9, 526
Framework Directive (1991) 21–2, 25–6, 162–81, 489–90, 497, 504–9
Framework Directive (2006) 162–81, 405, 489–90, 493, 497, 504–9
Germany 418, 478–80, 506–7
hazardous waste 509, 525–6
Hungary 504
integrated pollution prevention and control (IPPC) 493
international cooperation *see* **Basel Convention**
Italy 15–6
landfill of waste (Directive (1999)) 15, 497, 509
Latvia 504
legislation adopted 489–504
legislation in progress 504–6
liability, environmental 498
Malta 504
mining waste 497–9
Netherlands 508–9
packaging and packaging waste (Directive (1994)) 509, 666
Poland 504
policy documents 509–10
Pollutant Release and Transfer Register, (PRTR) 334, 525–9
proximity principle 493
radioactive waste 495–7
recycling and recovery 163–5, 169–81, 333, 405–6, 494, 499–509, 549, 563
secondary material resources 162–4, 171–81
shipments of waste, transboundary (Regulations (2006/1993)) 490–9, 504–8, 572–4, 666–7
Slovakia 504
Spain 174
taxation 165, 501
United Kingdom 162–81
WEEE(Directive (2002)), waste electrical and electronic equipment 499–502, 509–10
RoHS (Directive (2002)), restrictions on the use of certain hazardous substances in electronic equipment 500, 503–4

water 510–24
bathing water (Directives (2006/1976)) 510–1, 521–2
Belgium 514–5
case law 514–5, 574–5
China 520
climate change 510, 513, 518–20
coastal zone protection 523
dangerous substances discharges, (Directive (1976)) 512–3, 517
Directive (2000), Water Framework 70, 106, 439, 448–9, 460, 498, 510–23, 574–5, 666, 669
enforcement actions 515–7
Estonia 522
Finland 432, 516
flood risk management policy 513–4
Framework Directive (2000), Water 70, 106, 439, 448–9, 460, 498, 510–23, 574–5, 666, 669
France 514–6
fresh water quality and support of fish life (Directive (2006)) 510–1
Germany 514–5
Greece 516–7
groundwater 511–2
Hungary 522
international cooperation 520–1
Latvia 522
legislation adopted 510–1
legislation in progress 511–4
Lithuania 522
Luxembourg 515, 574–5
marine environment policy 517–20, 523–4
Mediterranean Protection Strategy 521
Netherlands 522
nitrates 19, 511, 515–7
policy documents 520–3
policy trends 510, 517–20

precautionary principle 515–6
Portugal 516
Slovakia 522
Slovenia 522
Spain 517, 522
stress/scarcity, water 520–2
Sweden 516
urban waste-water (Directive (1991)) 21, 511, 515–6
waste-water, urban 21, 511, 515–6
water stress/scarcity 520–2
United Kingdom 512–3, 516, 520

World Organization for Animal Health (OIE) 394–5
biotechnology 394–5
genetically modified organisms (GMOs) 394–5

World Trade Organization (WTO) x, 5–6, 36, 89, 133–41, 148–58, 241, 266–79, 286–93, 299–310, 365–6, 395–401, 487, 595–608, 614–7
biotechnology x, 133–41, 148–58, 366, 395–401, 608
Canada 155, 266, 289
case law x, 5–6, 36, 133–7, 149, 153–6, 366, 395–401, 608
genetically modified organisms (GMOs) disputex, 133–6, 149, 153–6, 366, 395–401, 608
Intellectual Property, Agreement on Trade Related Aspects of (TRIPS) 241, 266–80, 286–93, 310
Trade Related Aspects of Intellectual Property, Agreement on (TRIPS) 241, 266–80, 286–93, 310